The Scottish FIDDLE MUSIC INDEX

We'll gar them ring wi' mony a spring frae Fraser and Niel Gow,
Frae Marshall tae and mony mae brave champions o' the bow;
An' deep's the debt Auld Scotland owes to leal, true-hearted chiels,
Wha siccan legacy bequeath'd, "Oor Auld Strathspeys and Reels."

Robert Sanderson (Born West Linton, 1836)

© Charles Gore

Published in 1994 by
The Amaising Publishing House Ltd.
P.O. Box
Musselburgh EH21 7UJ
Scotland

Telephone 031 665 8237

ISBN 1 871512 99 9

Printed and bound by Scotprint Limited, Musselburgh

The Scottish FIDDLE MUSIC INDEX

CHARLES GORE *Editor*

MORAG ANNE ELDER, M. Phil. *Research*

LYNN MORRISON *Computer Input*

Tune Titles from the 18th & 19th Century
Printed Instrumental Music Collections

List of indexed and related collections
and where to find them

Index to numerical Musical Theme Codes

THE AMAISING PUBLISHING HOUSE LTD

1994

THE INDEX INCLUDES:

★ An A-Z listing by TUNE TITLE of the contributory collections published
in Scotland, London or Dublin from the 18th to the early 19th centuries.
*A "Not-Listed" label normally implies that a collection would merely
repeat information already listed, or that it was deemed to be outwith the
mainstream of the repertoire (eg: Mainly vocal, mainly English, etc.)*

★ A companion A-Z listing by TUNE TITLE of the 19th and early 20th
century published collections, concluding with the compositions of Peter
Milne (d.1908) and James Scott Skinner (d.1927). *Any publication
"Not-Listed" here is excluded for the reasons given above or because it
relates to material better treated elsewhere (eg: Pipe music, Gaelic,
Foreign and Dance Collections, mainly vocal, etc.)*

★ The BIBLIOGRAPHY, or Index to Sources, related to the A-Z listings
above, describing the nature of the publication, the publisher (composer,
editor, etc.) of each collection listed under the column "SOURCE CODE" in
the A-Z Index, adding a reference to a location where that collection may
be found (eg: AUL for Aberdeen University Library; DPL for Dundee Public
Library; NLS for National Library of Scotland, etc.) See: Abbreviations.

NOTE: Location information has been given on "Not-Listed" collections
wherever possible. Further information on collections, especially any
not so far included, is always welcome.

★ A THEME CODE Index, designed for cross-referencing and tune-finding.
It is ordered numerically, from the lowest starting note (first beat of
the bar) to the highest and includes every entry from the A-Z listings.
A code may be made for any known tune and a search will show if it is
listed. Its title & source can be discovered. The Theme Code Index will
also disclose: (1) If a tune has more than one title (2) If a tune has
been republished in A-Z(II) having originally appeared in A-Z(I)
(3) Where several tunes have the same starting sequence, whether the
melodies are related or divergent.

NOTE: Where a tune title has more than one distinct melody, or variations
in detail, this will appear in the A-Z Listings (which also include the
Theme Codes).

★ APPENDICES, listing various collections which, while not considered to
be fully related to the true tradition, are nevertheless useful reference
works. Listings include titles (A-Z) page numbers, etc. (For example:
J3 - Johnson's Musical Museum, 1771...vocal; (Mc3v2) - The Gesto
Collection, K.N. MacDonald, 1895 ...Gaelic, largely vocal)

EXCEPT as each occurs naturally in traditional Scottish music collections,
the Index does NOT include (1) The Pipe Music Repertoire (2) The Gaelic
vocal collections (3) Manuscript collections and random sheet music
(4) The music of Orkney & Shetland (quite separate until recent times)
(5) The traditional music of North America (6) The music of Ireland
(7) The music of the 20th Century after 1922 (The Index listings conclude
with Scott Skinner's "Cairngorm" Series, published in that year)

It is hoped that at least some of these other categories will find their
place in the Index in the not too distant future

Contents

Foreword

Scottish fiddle music is one of our country's great cultural glories. Yet it is so deeply rooted in our everyday life that we give very little thought to where it came from or how it developed. It can be thought of as part of "folk" culture, yet there is nothing about it to suggest that it was at any time reserved to any one social group, or that its popularity today has anything in common with the antiquarianism required to keep alive dance and fiddle traditions in other countries. Moreover, it has no archaic feel about it: the tunes of the 18th and of the 20th centuries can be played one after the other with no sense of incongruity. One may dance a country dance to an original tune already popular in the 1750s, a second tune composed around 1800, a third from the turn of the 20th century and a fourth from the last decade.

Because of the continuous popularity of the music and the need - perceived since the late 17th century - to bring it in accessible form to as wide a public as possible, the emphasis has always been on publishing it. Naturally, apart from the volumes of their own compositions produced by the fiddlers or their editors, the tendency was towards re-issue of the most popular material of the moment.

As a consequence, it has been the general belief that, while the fiddle tradition was rich and contained a great store of wonderful melody, it ran probably to between three and four thousand pieces in all. Even at that estimate, there remained a need for listing them, a guide to where they first appear and sources from which to obtain the music. It was this that Charles Gore set out to produce, following in the footsteps of John Murdoch Henderson and others who had seen the need, but had lacked the advancing technology of the computer to complete it.

(continued)

The treasure that Mr. Gore hoped to find at the end of this wide rainbow proved greater - and more elusive - than either he or anyone else would probably have expected. His index now contains 11,000 tunes from the period up to William Marshall's (posthumous) "Vol. 2nd. of a Collection of Scottish Melodies", published in 1845 and a further 3000 gathered from the later 19th century compilations.(*)

For this listing alone, Scotland owes Mr. Gore a great debt. While more tunes will no doubt come to light, any future work must now be based on this index and his list of sources is the fullest available bibliography of Scottish fiddle music.

But Mr. Gore has done something else. He has provided a system whereby the music itself is indexed, based on the original work of Breandan Breathnach in Ireland and of a pioneering research project by Morag Anne Elder of Dundee. The user requires to give a little time to study the workings of this system, but having mastered it, it is possible for the first time to go from a "scrap of a tune" in the head to the title and thence to the source without leaving the book.

No listing of this type can hope to be definitive and those who use Mr. Gore's index will no doubt find omissions (sheet music and the great manuscript collections, for example, are not included). But in all types of research a first step must be taken and all subsequent work advances from what one creative mind has begun. Mr. Gore has taken an enormous first stride and has provided us with what will be, for many years to come, the initial point of access to the treasures that lie in this area of Scotland's cultural life.

PATRICK CADELL
Keeper of the Records of Scotland

Edinburgh, September 1993

(These figures allow for deliberate duplication of titles originally published in the 18th Century but re-published in the 19th.)*

Some reasons for an index

THIS INDEX is not so much a work of original research as a design for the
retrieval of a great national resource - the traditional fiddle music of
Scotland. Though published in its time, from 1700 into the present
century, the larger proportion of the repertoire has never been
re-published, but lain dormant and much of it un-indexed in private hands
or on library shelves. One heroic attempt to right this state of affairs
was foiled only for want of the proper technology. John Murdoch Henderson
devoted all free time during his retirement from teaching to listing and
analysing the fiddle collections in his own and other hands and presented
his life's work as a gift to the national archive in what he described as
"seven precious books" (a series of hand-written notebooks). Of these, all
but Volume One appear to have been lost at the time of Henderson's death
in 1972, but his collection of printed books has survived and is held
jointly by Aberdeen Unversity Library and the National Library of
Scotland, Edinburgh. This, with the collections of Glen and Inglis, also
at the National Library, the Wighton Collection (Dundee Public Library),
the Athole Collection (Sandeman Library, Perth) and the Kidson Collection
(Mitchell Library, Glasgow) form the basis of the retrieval operation.
Possibly the largest holding of all resides - somewhat illogically - at
the British Library, London; there is also an interesting bequest lodged
at the Bodleian Library, Oxford - the Harding Collection.

To the collectors of the last years of the 19th century and the early
years of this century, we owe the survival of the source books which in
their day could be bought for a few pence in any secondhand bookshop. Most
of them are now exceedingly rare. The mighty collection of John Glen was
bought at auction by Lady Dorothea Ruggles-Brise and presented to the
National Library in memory of her brother, Lord George Stewart Murray,
killed in France in 1914. But the final dedication for the Index must go
to the late John Murdoch Henderson, whose labour of love went unrequited
for 20 years but which, thanks to the Computer Age and the incentive of
the fiddle revival of recent years, can now be brought to fulfilment.

(continued)

At the start of the project, the reasons for setting about it were:

(1) That there has never been a comprehensive fiddle music index

(2) That without it, musicians have no method of gauging the scale and scope of the Scottish traditional repertoire, so a large percentage of the music may never again see the light of day

(3) That fiddlers, particularly the young and those living at a distance from the main libraries, have little chance of access to any of the material unless it has been re-issued and is preferably still in print

There appeared to be no cause to alter these concepts as the project proceeded unless to add that the database used to produce this book is still intact and will be available for further research and expansion.

CHARLES GORE, Editor

Taynuilt, Argyll 1994

THE EDITORS ACKNOWLEDGE WITH GRATITUDE THE HELP OF:

Helena Bayler, William & Elizabeth Berry, Eibhlin Breathnach
Elizabeth Burchill, Patrick Cadell, Alastair Campbell of Airds
Nicholas Carolan, Dr. Peter Cooke, Ian Cunningham, John Drewry
Roger Duce, Anne Elder, Jean Gore, John Gore, Alastair J. Hardie
Donald Hardie, Alison Kinnaird, Magnus & Veronica Linklater
Tim Lawrence, Kirsteen McCue, Ann MacKay, Lynn Morrison
John Purser, Alastair Robertson, Archie Shaw Stewart
the late Alick Sherriff, Jan Tappan, Rosena Wood

...plus any who are not mentioned, as should have been, who have
offered a kindly deed or word of encouragement over five odd years

AND SPECIAL THANKS AND ACKNOWLEDGEMENT TO:

Elizabeth Cave; the late Hugh, Earl Cawdor; The Glenfiddich Living
Scotland Award (William Grant & Sons Ltd.); The Russell Trust (Founded
in memory of Captain J.P.O.Russell RA); Charles N. Watt and the
Directors of Scotprint Limited, Musselburgh

The print of "The Highland Dance" after the painting by David Allan,
1780 is from a private collection in Scotland and is reproduced by kind
permission of the owner

A number of the Title Pages in the Bibliography have been reproduced
by permission of the Trustees of the National Library of Scotland,
Edinburgh and acknowledgement is due for their use; also for generous
access to the Music Room and the magnificent collections of printed
music in the Library's care

Some further examples of Title Pages have been reproduced from original
copies in the MacCowan Collection, property of Oban & Lorne Strathspey
& Reel Society, by permission of the members

Abbreviations

Library Sources

```
AUL..............Aberdeen University Library
BL................British Library (British Museum), London
BOD.............Bodleian Library, Oxford (Harding Collection)
BUC.............British Union Catalogue (Pre-1800 music index)
CPM.............Catalogue of Printed Music (British Library)
DPL..............Dundee Public Library (Wighton Collection)
EUL..............Edinburgh University Library
GUL.............Glasgow University Library
Mitchell.........Mitchell Library, Glasgow (Kidson Collection)
NLI..............National Library of Ireland, Dublin
NLS..............National Library of Scotland, Edinburgh
Sandeman....Sandeman Library (Perth's Public Library, home of
                   "The Athole Collection" of fiddle music)
```

The Library of Congress, Washington D.C., the New York Public Library and many more of the world's principal libraries contain substantial holdings of fiddle music collections, but they have been discounted for the purpose of this index, though they can still be regarded as important sources for local research.

```
A..........Air
CD.......Country Dance
Coll......Collection
Comp...Composed (by)
Ded......Dedicated (to)
Fav.......Favourite (Favorite)
GF.......German Flute (also G/flt)
Hd.......Harpsichord
Hp.......Hornpipe
M.........March
Min......Minuet
n.d......"no date"(not dated)
N/L.......Not Listed
Pas......Pastoral
Pfte......Pianoforte
Pub......Published (by)
R..........Reel
SM.......Scots Measure
Sel.......Selection
Str.......Strathspey
Vc........Violoncello (also V/cello)
Vn........Violin
```

SOURCE CODE INDEX

[Bibliography]

This bibliography sets out to be *inclusive* as far as the printed fiddle collections are concerned; *selective* in the sector of London-published dance books & manuals; but *exclusive* of almost all the song books, both Gaelic and Scots, unless they contain a significant proportion of traditional song airs without words (eg: Oswald, or Gale's Pocket Companion)

Shortened titles of the Indexed Collections appear in **Bold Type**

Lists in the Appendix Section are shown in brackets ( )

A1   =   AIRD, JAMES
1-6   (No. of vols published)

The codes then appear in the A-Z Sections:

A1v1p1   =   AIRD / BOOK 1 / PAGE 1

(J3)   =   JOHNSON, JAMES in the APPENDIX SECTION

These listings have been added because the
publications include relevant music which
might otherwise have been excluded from the
index altogether

A1 AIRD, JAMES Publisher & Bookseller. Published:
1-6 **"A Selection of Scotch, English, Irish and Foreign Airs.
Adapted to the Fife, Violin, or German Flute, by James
Aird, Glasgow."** (1782-1801) in 6 vols.[AUL; NLS: Glen 16
a,b,c] Many copies available elsewhere.

ALBYN'S ANTHOLOGY. (See C10/Campbell, Alexander, below)

A4 ALEXANDER, JOHN. Composer: (1)" **Ten new tunes comp. and**
1-2 **dedicated to Miss Ogilvy of Clova by [J.A.], Forfar and
arr. for the pfte. by M. McDonald, Edin."**[Sandeman,
Athole Coll. Be53; DPL: Wighton H.7073] (2) **"Six new tunes
... ded. to Miss Laurenson of Invereighty"** [Sandeman]
[See also sheet music in NLS: Glen 348 (1-6)]

ALLAN, MOZART, Publisher, Glasgow. Among many other colls.
and publications, Pub: "Allan's Reels & Strathspeys, Quad-
rilles, Waltzes, &c." All trad. standards (Not listed).

ALTHAUS,B. Arranger. "100 Scotch Airs, arr. for V. by
[B.A.] with acco. for pfte. by W.H.Callcott ... Printed by
Moore, Smith & Co., Leipzig." n.d.(19th c) [NLS:MH.v.108]

A7 ANDERSON, JOHN. Prolific Composer/ Collector, published:
1-6 (1) **"A Coll. of New Highland Strathspey Reels. For the
V., G.F., with an Hd. or Vc. Bass. Comp. by [J.A.] .
Edinburgh,1790."** 16pp(2) **"A Selection of the most Approved
Highland Strathspeys, Country Dances, English & French
Dances, with a Hd. & Vc. Bass. Ded. to the Gentlemen of
the Musical Soc. of Greenock by [J.A.]"** Pub: Corri &
Sutherland, Edinburgh c. 1790 36pp (3) **" A Second
Selection ..."** (as above) Printed "for the author", Edin.
c.1791. 36pp (4) **"Anderson's Budget of S/spey Reels &
Country Dances, for the V. or G.F."** Pub: c.1810. 28pp (5)
"Anderson's Budget..."(as above) "Printed for and sold by
[J.A.], Edinburgh". C.1821. 40pp (6) **"Anderson's Pocket
Companion of the most approved Highland S/speys, C.D.s
&c., for the G.F., Fife, Hautboy & V. Printed and sold by
[J.A.], Music Seller, Perth."** 96pp Sources: AUL and NLS:
(2) MH.4; (2) & (3) Glen 355 (1-2); (4) MH.s.3; enquire.

ASTOR, G. "24 Dances for the Year 1800" [BL] Ref:(CDS)

B2 BAILLIE, PETER. Fiddler/Comp. (1774-1841)**"A Selection of
original tunes for the Pfte. and Violin. Comp. by [P.B.]"**
(Inc. sketch of his life) Pub: 1825 7pp. [NLS:MH.6(1)]

B4 BARIZEL, C. Comp: **"A Collection of Marches, Waltzes,
Quicksteps & Airs for the Pfte.. Comp. by [C.B.] Printed &
sold by Muir, Wood & Co., Leith."** 20pp. [DPL(Wighton)]

B5 BARSANTI, FRANCIS (Franceso) b. (Lucca) c.1690, d. London
1760. Composer/Collector. Pub: **"A Collection of Old Scots
Tunes. With a bass for Vc. or Hd. Set and most humbly ded.
to the Rt. Hon. the Lady Erskine by [F.B.]"** Pub: Edin.1742
15pp.[NLS: Glen 319;Sandeman (Athole) Be 13; DPL:(Wighton)
H.10458]

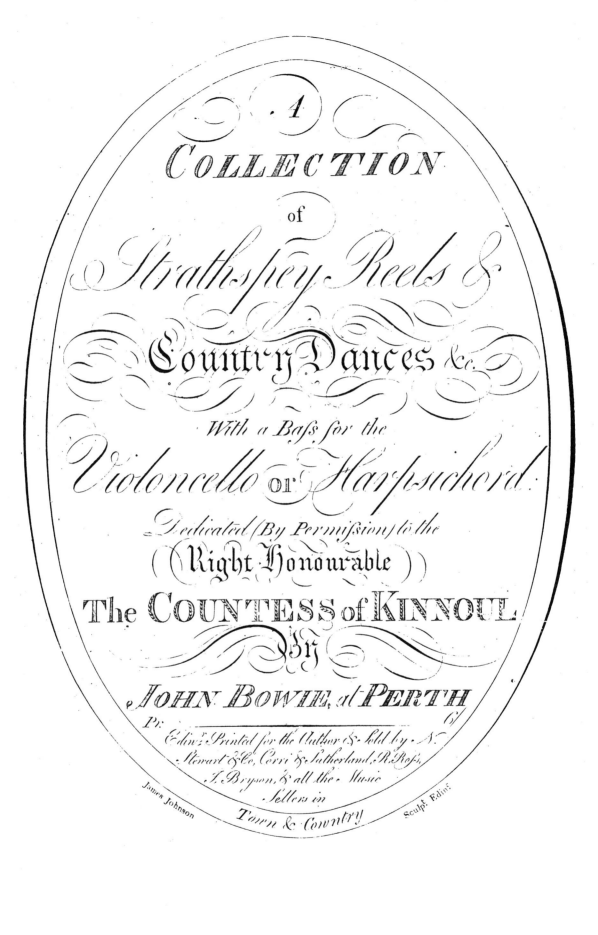

A

COLLECTION

of

Strathspey Reels &

Country Dances &c.

With a Bass for the

Violoncello or *Harpsichord.*

Dedicated (By Permission) to the

Right Honourable

The COUNTESS of KINNOUL

By

JOHN BOWIE, at PERTH

Pr: ——————— 6/

Edin.: Printed for the Author & Sold by N. Stewart & Co, Corri & Sutherland, R. Ross, J. Bryson, & all the Music Sellers in Town & Country

James Johnson   Sculp.t Edin.r

B6   BAYNE, CHARLES. Teacher of Dancing, Dundee. Composer; pub-
1-4 lications (sheet music): (1)**"The following tunes are most
     resp. ded. to Maj.-Gen. McDonald by [C.B]".**(1802) [MH.e.9]
     (2) **"Five new tunes composed by [C.B]"** [AUL/NLS:MH.e.10]
     (3) **"Five tunes composed by...[C.B.]"** (1815) [Glen 348(7)]
     (4) **"Six Fav. Scottish Dances..."**(1819) [MH.e.8]
     (The "MH" shelfmarks are all NLS)

B7   BEAUTIES OF MELODY, THE **"...Being a Collection of the most
     admired Airs, national & foreign, arr. for the G.F. by an
     Amateur. Many of the airs may suit the Flageolet or Violin
     Published by J. McFadyen ... Glasgow"** 48pp.[18th.C.] [DPL]

     BISHOP, H. Comp: "...Minuets, Country Dances for the year
     1788." 18pp [Sandeman (Athole) Bd43] Not Listed.

B9   BLAIR, WILLIAM. Fiddler/Comp:**"Original Reels & S/speys..."**
     Dundee c.1890. "The Queen's Fiddler" (Fiddler to Queen
     Victoria at Balmoral) 8pp. [NLS: MH.v.7]

     BLAND, A. "24 C.D.s for the Years 1792/94"[Ref:BUC/(CDS)]

     BLAND & WELLER "Annual Coll.s of CDs ..." 1800 etc. [BL]

B10 BOAG, W. **"A Coll. of fav. R. & Str. ... humbly ded. to the
     Public by... The Editor"** London, c.1797 [Sandeman,Athole]

B11 BOWIE, JOHN. Fiddler/Comp: **" A Collection of s/spey reels
     & Country Dances &c., with a bass for the Vc. or Hd., ded.
     (by permission) to the Rt. Hon. The Countess of Kinnoul by
     [J.B.] at Perth".** Pub: 1789 by N. Stewart. [NLS: Glen
     265; Sandeman (Athole) Be40, Bf29; DPL:(Wighton) H.10459
     (inc: "Four new tunes")

B12 BOWIE, PETER. Fiddler/Comp: **"A Collection of str., reels,
     marches, &c.; some with variations."** 1806 15pp
     [DPL(Wighton): H.31954] John's brother (1763-1846)

B15 BREMNER, ROBERT. (c. 1713-89) Music-seller & Publisher in
1-2 Edinburgh until 1760, thereafter in London. Pub: (As 14
     numbers of 8 pages each, c. 1751-61) (1) **" A Collection
     of Scots Reels or Country Dances, with a Bass for V/c ...
     Printed & Sold by [R.B.] at the Harp & Hautboy".** Followed
     by: **"A Second Collection ...(as above) Printed by
     [R.B.] in the Strand and sold at his music shop in
     Edinburgh ..."** (pp.97-112) Sources: see below.
     (2) **"A Curious Collection of Scots Tunes with variations
     for the violin, with a Bass for the Vc. or Hchd., Edin....
     Printed & Sold by [R.B.] at the Harp & Hautboy".** (c.1762)
     B15(1) from DPL (Wighton): H. 92496 (1st. & 2nd. Colls.)
     B15(2) from NLS: Inglis 295(3); DPL (Wighton) H. 31954;
     Sandeman (Athole) Bd19.

B16 BRIDE ...Collector. Pub: **"Bride's Favorite Collection of
1-4 two hundred select Country Dances, Cotillons and Allemands
     with the newest figures to each as they are now performed
     at Court, Bath, Almack's and all Polite Assemblies ..."**
     Vol.1(12pp)v2(12pp,1781)v3(96pp)v4-pp85-96(diff.vol.)[DPL]

BRODERIP & WILKINSON'S
HARP PIANOFORTE, VIOLIN, or TABOR & PIPE

Selection
— of the most Admired —
DANCES, REELS, WALTZ'S,
Strathspeys & Cotillons.
with their proper Figures as danced at
The COURT of S.t JAMES'S
BATH & other polite Assemblies
Adapted for the

Price 3.0

Price 3.0

London Printed for the Editors N.o 13 Hay-market

Ent.d at Stat.rs Hall

A
Collection
OF
STRATHSPEYS, REELS, JIGS, &c.
FOR THE
Piano Forte,
VIOLIN, AND VIOLONCELLO.
Composed
And Respectfully Dedicated to
The Right Hon.ble the
Countess of Dunmore.
BY
JOHN BURNS.

Ent. at Stat. Hall.

Price 5/.

EDINBURGH

Published for the Author, by ROB.T PURDIE at his Music & Musical Instrument Warehouse N.o 70 Princes Street.

B17 BRODERIP & WILKINSON. Publishers:"Selection of the most
     admircd Danccs, Rccls, Waltzcs, s/spcys & Cotillons,
     ...Adapted for the Harp, Pfte., Violin, or Tabor & Pipe."
     London (1800).Bk:8 only. 26pp [AUL] [NLS: Glen 152]

     BRYSON, JOHN (or BRYSSON) Publisher: "A Curious Selection
     of Favourite Scots Tunes..." Edin. (c.1791) Not listed.

     BURKHARDT, CARL. Pub: "Album of National Dances ..."
     (Popular country dances,etc) Late 19th.c.(?) Not listed.

B20 BURNS, JOHN. Fiddler/Comp. Pub: "A Collection of s/speys,
     reels, jigs &c., for the Pfte., Violin and Vc. Composed
     and respectfully dedicated to the Rt. Hon. the Countess of
     Dunmore by [J.B.]. Edinburgh." 21pp.(1822)[NLS:Glen289(1)]

[B21] BUTTON & WHITAKER, Pub: "Selection of Dances ..." No.6 of
     series [AUL] Also Nos: 1,4,5,6,9,10,12,& 14 [NLS:
     MH.e.22-29] See also BUTTON & PURDAY (or Purday & Button)
     [NLS: Mus.E.1.82(25)] Fragment, indicated in []

C1   CAHUSAC. Publisher: (1) "Twenty-four Country Dances for
     year 1795, with proper directions to each dance as they
     are perform'd at Court, Bath & all Public Assemblies.
     London. Printed by Cahusac". 12pp (2) "Cahusac's
     Collection of New Dances. London. Printed for the Editor."
     2pp(3) "Cahusac's Dances, 1813. London." 6pp(4) "Cahusac's
     Dances 1816 for Pfte. or Harp... London." 12pp (5) "Twelve
     Country Dances..." 1794 (Not listed) 12pp.[DPL,Wighton]

C4   CALEDONIAN MUSE, THE. "A Collection of Scarce & Favorite
     Scots Tunes both Highland and Lowland, viz. Songs,
     Luinigs, Laments, Reels, s/speys, Measures, Jiggs &c.,
     properly adapted for the V., G.F., Hd. & Pfte...to which
     is prefixed an Essay on Scots Music. London. Printed for
     the Editors." 72pp.(c.1800) [NLS: Glen 151(2); DPL]

C5   CALEDONIAN MUSEUM, THE. (Various): (1) " The Caledonian
1-3 Museum for the Flute, Edinburgh; published by Wood & Co."
     72pp.(2) "The [C.M] containing a favorite collection of
     Ancient and Modern Scots tunes adapted for the Flageolet,
     Flute or Violin. Edinburgh. Printed for & sold by
     Alexander Robertson at his music saloon..." 72pp (3) "The
     [C.M] containing a Favorite Collection of Ancient & Modern
     Scots Tunes, adapted to the G.F. or V. Edinburgh. Printed
     and sold by J. Hamilton..." Bk.3 only, pp52-75. Editions
     c.1810 /1830 (?) [NLS: Glen 153 & 94; DPL (Wighton)]

C6   CALLCOTT, W.H. Arranger: " Melodies of all nations,
     arranged for the Pfte. by William Hutchins C. Scotch Airs.
     London ..." 30pp. n.d. 19th C. [DPL (Wighton): H.7062]

C7   CALVERT, THOMAS. Composer: "A Collection of Marches, Quick
     Steps, s/speys & Reels by [T.C.]" [NLS: Glen 316; AUL]

C8   CAMERON, GEORGE. Pub: (1)"Cameron's selection of violin
1-2 music containing all the most popular airs, marches,
     s/peys, reels, hornpipes, jigs, country dances, q/steps,
     quadrilles, polkas, &c., Glasgow ..." (1854) 64pp.
     [NLS: Glen 63; DPL, Wighton H.92473]
     (2) "Cameron's selection of Flute Music (and as above)"...
     (1857) 64pp. [From NLS & DPL as above]

A

Collection

of

New Reels &: Highland

STRATHSPEYS

With a Bass for the

Violoncello or Harpsichord

By

JOSHUA CAMPBELL.

A number of which are his own Composition

GLASGOW,

Printed for the Author, and Sold at the Music Shops
—— in Edinburgh & Glasgow —— Price 5/6

J. Johnson Sculp. Edin.

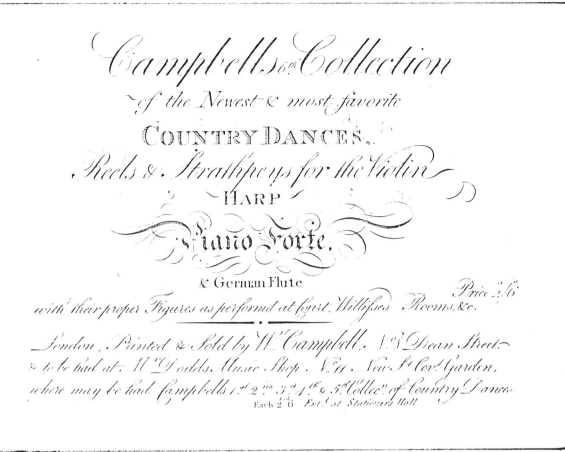

Campbell's 6th Collection

of the Newest & most favorite

COUNTRY DANCES,

Reels & Strathspeys for the Violin

HARP

Piano Forte,

& German Flute

Price 2/6

with their proper Figures as perform'd at Court, Williss's Rooms, &c.

London, Printed & Sold by W. Campbell, No. 8 Dean Street
& to be had at W. Dodds. Music Shop. No. 14 New St Covt Garden.
where may be had Campbells 1st 2nd 3rd 4th & 5th Collect. of Country Dances
Each 2/6. Ent.d at Stationers Hall

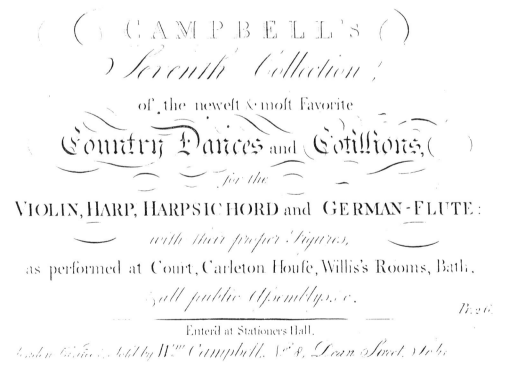

CAMPBELL's

Seventh Collection;

of the newest & most Favorite

Country Dances and *Cotillions,*

for the

VIOLIN, HARP, HARPSICHORD and GERMAN-FLUTE:

with their proper Figures,

as performed at Court, Carleton House, Willis's Rooms, Bath,

& all public Assemblys &c.

Pr 2/6

Enter'd at Stationers Hall.

London Printed & Sold by Wm. Campbell, No. 8, Dean Street Soho

A
COLLECTION
OF
STRATHSPEYS, REELS, HORNPIPES, WALTZES, &c.
ARRANGED AS MEDLEYS
FOR THE
Piano Forte Violin and Violoncello
BY
WILLIAM CHRISTIE,
Teacher of Dancing.

Ent. at Stat. Hall.   Price 3/

—— EDINBURGH ——
Printed for the Author, and to be had of him at Cuminestown by Turriff.
Also of Mr Purdie No 70 Princes Street, Mrs Penson & Robertson 47 Princes Street Edinr.
And Mr Morris Union Street Aberdeen.

Walker & Anderson Engr. Edinr.

C9   CAMERON, JOHN. Publisher: (1)"Cameron's violin music arr.d
1-2   as solos or duets for the violin, including the celebrated
Cuckoo Solo". Glasgow [J.C.] (2)" New collection of
Reels and Str. for the violin, containing the celebrated
Scotch Dance Tunes of Neil Gow &c., expressly arranged by
a professional violinist ..." Glasgow, pub: by [J.C] n.d.
[NLS: MH.s.45(2)

C10   CAMPBELL, ALEXANDER. Collector/Pub:(1)"A Coll. of Str..."
1   Edinburgh. [c.1800] 4pp. only. [NLS: Glen 348(15)]
2A,B   (2) "Albyn's Anthology or A Select Coll. of Melodies...
peculiar to Scotland & the Isles...arr. by [A.C.]" 2 vols.
(Edin.1816-18) [AUL; NLS: Glen 372,372a; Inglis 259,260]

CAMPBELL, DONALD Pub: "A Treatise of the Language, Poetry
and Music of the Highland Clans ... by [D.C.]" Edin. 1862
Mostly Gaelic vocal airs with a few dance tunes. [NLS]

C12   CAMPBELL, JAMES "A Collection of Marches, Quicksteps, &c.
&c..." (1798) 12pp [AUL]

C13   CAMPBELL, JOSHUA Composer. (C13-1) "A Coll. of New Reels
1-4   & Highland Str. with a bass for the V/cello or H/chd by
[J.C], A Number of which are his own..." (c.1786) 48pp.
Pub; Glasgow. [NLS: Glen 327; Inglis 170(2)]
(C13-2)"Coll. of Newest & Best Reels & Minuets..." Glasgow
1788. 80pp. [NLS: Glen 156(1)
(C13-3) "A Coll. of Favourite Tunes with new variations
adapted for the Vln. & G. Fl.witha bass for the V/cello &
thorough bass for the H/chd. by [J.C.] corrected by
P. Urbani..." Edinburgh, c. 1800; 80pp. [NLS: Glen 151(1)]
(C13-4) "A Coll. of New Reels & Highland STRATHSPEYS with
a bass for the v/cello or h/chd. by [J.C.] The Basses for
this Coll. are corrected by P. Urbani..." Edinburgh c.1800
36pp. "Book 1st." [NLS: MH.12]

C14   CAMPBELL, WILLIAM. Fiddler/Composer/Music-Seller: Pub-
1-27   lished 27 dance books of from 17-26 pp. (C14v1 to 27):
"Campbell's Book of New & Favorite Country Dances & Str.
Reels for the Harp, Pfte. & Violin, with their proper
figures as danced at Court, Bath, Willis's & Hanover
Square rooms, &c., printed and sold by R. Birchall."
London, 1790-1817. [NLS: Various; DPL; Brit.Lib.] It may
be wise to enquire at NLS or other source. The titles may
vary from the example shown above.

CHAPPELL & CO. Publishers: (1) " Chappell's one hundred
Hornpipes, Strathspeys, Reels, Jigs and C.D.s Arranged for
the Violin". London, c.1880 (2) Second Series (36pp)
reprinted material; not listed. [NLS: MH.s.89/90]

C18   CHRISTIE, WILLIAM (of Cuminestown, 1778-1849), Fiddler/
Composer: "A Coll. of Strathspeys, Reels, Hornpipes,
Waltzes, &c. arranged as medleys for the Harp., Pfte., Vn.
and V/cello. by [W.C.], Teacher of Dancing" Edinburgh,
1820. 44pp [NLS: Glen 343]

C19   CLAGGETT, WALTER (b. about 1760) English Composer, who
published (c.1794) "A New Medley Overture...of Scots tunes
and 36 Scots Airs" Edinburgh, 28pp. [NLS: Glen 263; AUL]
(Some medleys lack page no.s and are shown as [C19])

Flores Musicae,

or the

SCOTS MUSICIAN,

Being a general Collection *of the most celebrated*

Scots *Tunes,*

REELS, MINUETS *and MARCHES*

Adapted for the *Violin, Hautboy, or*

German *Flute;*

With a Bass for the *Violoncello or Harpsichord.*

Published the 1st June 1773 by

J. CLARK
Plate and Seal
Engraver.
PRINTER &c
First fore stair below the Head of
Forresters wynd
EDINBURGH

C20   CLARK, JOHN : "Flores Musicae, or the Scots Musician.
Being a general collection of the most celebrated Scots
tunes, reels, minuets & marches... published 1st. June,
1773 by [J.C]" Edinburgh 82pp [DPL(Wighton); NLS: MH.24]

C21   CLARK, JOHN. Fiddler/Composer. Pub: "A Coll. of New Str.
Reels, & C.D.s, with a bass for the v/cello or Hcd. ...
Dedicated to the Musical Society of Perth, comp. by [J.C.]
..." Perth,1795. 21pp [NLS: Glen 260]

C22   CLARKSON, JOHN. Violinist & D/Master. Pub: "A Complete
Coll. of much admired tunes, as danced at the Balls and
Public's of the late Mr. Strange....Respectfully ded. to
his scholars, by [J.C.], ... Edinburgh 1803" 50pp [AUL;
NLS: Glen 259]

C23   CLARKSON, John (Snr.) Father of the above. Pub (c.1796)
1   "Clarkson's Musical Entertainment, Being a Selection of
(2)   various tunes & Pieces of Music.." London. 20pp. [DPL]
"Book 2nd..." 12pp. Sep. listed. [NLS: MH.14 (2Bks in 1)]

COOKE, Bart(holomew, or Bartlett) "Selection of Present
Fav. CDs..." 1796/7, Dublin [BL]   Ref: (CDS)

C24   COOPER, ISAAC, of Banff (C.1755-1820) Fiddler/Comp. &
1-2   Teacher. Pub: (1) "Thirty New Str./R. for the Vn. or Hcd.,
comp. by [I.C.] ..." (1783) 10pp. [NLS: Glen 235]
(2) "A Coll. of Str., R. and Irish Jigs, for the Pfte., &
Vn., to which are added Scots,Irish & Welch Airs, comp.
and selected by [I.C.] at Banff, London, Edin., &c ..."
(c.1806) 25pp.[NLS: Glen 270, NLS: MH.6(2)]

[C25] CORRI, DOMENICO. Composer/Arranger (of songs) Pub: Dozens
of sheets & colls., inc: "A New & Complete Coll. of the
most fav. Scots Songs..." (2 vols) Edin., 1783 [AUL]

C26   CORRI DUSSEK & Co. (The pianist J.L. Dussek (1761-1812)
was married to Corri's daughter, Sophie). Pub: "For the
year 1797, Twenty-Four New C.D.s with their Proper Figures
...humbly ded. to the Nobility & Gentry..." London &
Edinburgh, 1797. 24pp. [DPL(Wighton) See also: CORRI]

COUNTRY DANCES "...Selected for Vn., G/Fl., or H/chd."
London (c.1760) pts.1-2 24pp. [NLS: Glen35(1)] Not listed.

COUNTRY DANCES (See Royal Scottish Country Dance Society
official publications, Books 1-37 and others. A valuable
source of traditional music still in print). NOTE: Some
of the Tune Titles given as the "original" tune for a
particular dance will not coincide with the tune title in
earlier printed collections. Change of title is often not
acknowledged, which can cause confusion.(See APPENDIX CDS)

C29   CRAIG, ADAM .Fiddler/Composer (b. about1667,d.1741) Pub:
"A Coll. of of the Choicest Scots Tunes adapted for the
Hchd.,or Spinnet and ...Voice, Vn., or G/Fl. by [A.C] ..."
Edinburgh (1730) 45pp [NLS: Glen 170; Glen 168(1)]

CRAIG, THOMAS . "Celebrated Scotch Reels ..." First Coll.
by T.C. Aberdeen/n.d. 7pp. Not listed [NLS: MH.v.9]

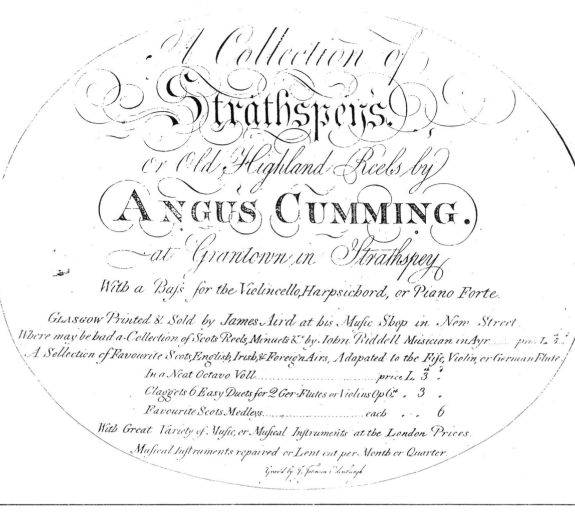

A Collection of

Strathspeys.

Or Old Highland Reels by

ANGUS CUMMING.

at Grantown in Strathspey

With a Bass for the Violincello, Harpsichord, or Piano Forte.

GLASGOW *Printed & Sold by James Aird at his Music Shop in New Street.*

Where may be had a Collection of Scots Reels, Minuets &c. by John Riddell Musician in Ayr ..... pr. L. 5

A Sellection of Favourite Scots, English, Irish, & Foreign Airs, Adapted to the Fife, Violin, or German Flute.

In a Neat Octavo Voll .... *price L. 3*

Claggets 6 Easy Duets for 2 Ger. Flutes or Violins Op 6th . 3 .

Favourite Scots Medleys .... *each* .. 6

With Great Variety of Music, or Musical Instruments at the London Prices.

Musical Instruments repaired or Lent out per Month or Quarter.

Grav'd by J. Johnson Edinburgh

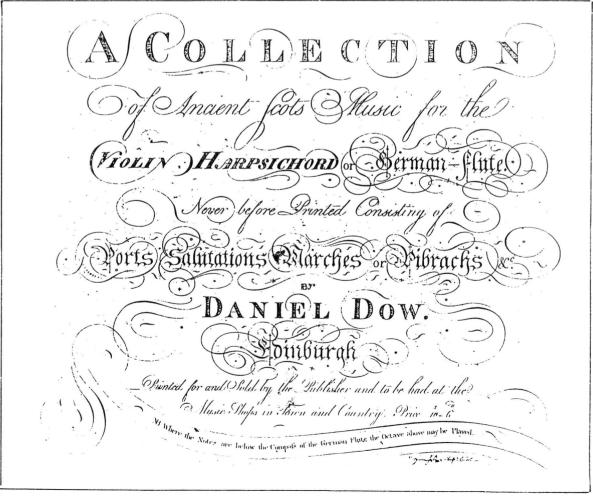

A COLLECTION

of Ancient Scots Music for the

VIOLIN HARPSICHORD *or* **German Flute**

Never before Printed Consisting of

Ports Salutations Marches *or* **Pibrachs** &c

BY

DANIEL DOW.

Edinburgh

Printed for and Sold by the Publisher and to be had at the

Music Shops in Town and Country. Price 10 . 6

N.B. Where the Notes are below the Compass of the German Flute the Octave above may be Played.

C33   CUMMING, ANGUS. Fiddler/Composer. Pub: " **A Coll. of Str.**
      or old Highland Reels by [A.C.] at Grantown in Strathspey
      with a bass for the v/cello, Hchd., or Pfte. Glasgow"
      (1782) 20pp [NLS: Glen 234]

D2   DALE, JOSEPH. Publisher/Composer (c.1760-1821). Pub:
      "Dales Coll. of of Reels & Dances..." (c.1802) Also pub.
      Dales Coll. of 60 Fav. Scotch Songs (3 vol.s of 60 each)
      London 1794 [AUL]

      DANCE MUSIC (Pub: WOOD & Co.) "Violin Edition, the Dance
      Music of Scotland. A Coll. of all the best R. & Str. both
      of the Highlands & Lowlands, in 3 books..."[NLS: MH.16]
      (Book1-14pp; Bk2-16pp; Bk3-12pp) Not Listed.

      DANCING MASTER, THE. (See P8/Playford, John and P7, his
      son, Henry, for reference to this work; not listed)

D6   DANIEL, JAMES. Fiddler/Composer (1810-89).Pub: **"A Coll. of**
      original music, consisting of Slow Airs, Str., R., Quad-
      rilles, Waltzes, H/pipes, &c ., adapted for the Pfte., Vn.
      and v/cello, by a Citizen..." Aberdeen, 1840. 39pp.
      [NLS: MH.13, listed under "Citizen]

      DAVIDSON, GEORGE. "Coll. of Scottish Melody for the Flute
      or Violin ..." London, c.1860 (80pp) 2 vols.[NLS:Glen 237]
      (Well-known tunes) Not listed.

      DAVIDSON, JOHN. "National Gems for the Vn., a Selection of
      original dance music, consisting of Strathspeys, Reels,
      Jigs, H/pipes, &c., by [J.D.], Aberdeen..." Pub: Glasgow
      19th.C. 46pp. Not listed. [NLS: MH.s.9]

      DAVIE, JAMES. Flautist/Composer/Teacher (c.1783-1857).
      (1): "Davie's Caledonian Repository of Favourite Scottish
      Slow Airs, Marches etc..." Edinburgh 1829 in 4 vols.
      D10-1A/1B; New Edn.1851 (160pp) [NLS:Glen 88]
      D10-2A/2B: "Davie's Cal. Repos..." (?1851-5) in 2 vols.
      [NLS: MH.s.88 (known as the 2nd. Series, 2 vols in one).
      Not listed. NOTE: Although James Davie's work and talent
      is widely known, much of what he published is standard
      material intended for study. His books are universally
      available and should be examined for the occasional unique
      item; he was publishing from c.1825, so linking the old
      world of the Gows and Marshall with Joseph Lowe (1840s),
      Scott Skinner (1860s on) and the later 19th c. compilers.

      DAVIE, James & MORRIS, Michael"Coll. of R., Dances, etc."
      Aberdeen (c.1815) 3pp. [NLS: MH.e.129]

      DEWAR, James "A Selection of 9 Scotch Airs..." Edinburgh
      11pp. n.d. [NLS: MH.125(7)] Not listed.

D13   DING, LAWRENCE. Music Publisher (c.1730-1800) **"A Curious**
      Coll of Scots Tunes with var. ..." Edin. (c.1800) [AUL]

D14   DOW, DANIEL. Fiddler/Composer(1732-83). From 1773, pub:
1-4   D14v1: **"20 Minuets and 16 Reels or C.D.s for the Vn.,**
      Hchd., or G.Fl. comp. by [D.D.], Edinburgh."[NLS: Glen 98]

      (Continued)

THE

Airs and Melodies

Peculiar to the

HIGHLANDS OF Scotland AND THE ISLES,

COMMUNICATED IN AN

ORIGINAL PLEASING & FAMILIAR STYLE,

Having

THE LIVELY AIRS INTRODUCED AS MEDLEYS

TO FORM A SEQUENCE TO EACH SLOWER MOVEMENT;

With

AN ADMIRED PLAIN HARMONY

for the

PIANO FORTE, HARP, ORGAN or VIOLONCELLO,

Intended rather to preserve Simplicity than load with Embellishment

EDITED

—by—

Captn S. Fraser.

And

Chiefly acquired during the Interesting Period from 1715 to 1745, through the Authentic Source narrated in the Accompanying Prospectus.

PUBLISHERS

LOGAN & COMPY. INVERNESS ABERDEEN & ELGIN.

(D14 Cont'd)

D14v2: "A Coll. of Ancient Scots Music for the Vn. Hchd.
or G.Fl. Never before printed Consisting of Ports, Salut-
ations, Marches, or Pibrochs, &c., by [D.D.] Edinburgh..."
[NLS: Glen 232; see also B. Lib./CPM, British Mus.]
D14v3: "37 New Reels and Str. for the Vn., Hchd., Pfte.,
or G.Fl., comp. by [D.D.]...Edinburgh..."[NLS: Glen 91(2)]
D14v4: "[14 New] Reels and Str..."(etc.) [NLS: MH.s.82]
D14v1(36pp);v2(46);v3(26);v4(14) Sources: (shown above).

D15   DUFF, ARCHIBALD. Musician/Dancing Master. Pub: (1)"A Coll.
1-2   of Str. Reels, &c. for the P/fte., Vn. and v/cello. Ded.
      by kind permission to Lady Carnegie of Southesk by [A.D.],
      D/Master Montrose..." Edinburgh, 1794. [NLS: Glen 269]30pp
      D15(2) "Part First of a Choice Selection of Minuets,
      Dances, etc.,[A.D.]..." Edinburgh, 1811/12(?) (Part 2nd.
      was never published) [NLS: Glen 305; MH.22] 50pp.

D16   DUFF, CHARLES. Musician/Music-seller (c.1760-1822),partner
      with Jas. Chalmers in booksellers in Dundee): Pub: "A
      Coll. of Str., Reels, Jiggs, &c..." Dundee 1792 (Glen)
      Some tunes attrib. to 'J.McD', John McDonald, D/M, Dundee.
      [NLS: Glen 229; Sandeman(Atholl): Be69]

      Note: D15v2..."Ded. to Lady Ramsay of Dalmain"; D16 ...to
      "The Duke of Athole".

E1   EDINBURGH REPOSITORY OF MUSIC: "Edin. Repos. of Mus. con-
1-2   taining the most select English, Scottish & Irish Airs,
      R., Str., &c., arr. for the G.Fl., or Vn., Edinburgh ..."
      (1818-25) 2 vols. in one Bk...E1-1: 120pp; E1-2:144pp.
      [NLS: Glen 31]

E2   EGLINTON, HUGH MONTGOMERIE, 12th Earl of (1739-1819).
      Fiddler/Composer. "New Str. R. for the Pfte., Vn. and
      v/cello, Comp. by a Gentleman and given with permission
      to be published by Nathl. Gow ...Edinburgh..." (1796) 24pp
      [NLS: Glen 272; listed under 'Gentleman']

F1   FORRESTER,GEORGE. Musician. Pub: "The Juvenile Flute
      Player, a Coll. of Nat. and Foreign Melodies with a number
      of original pieces never before published..." No.3 only;
      pp.27-35 [DPL] A fragment only.

CAPT. SIMON FRASER
(1773-1852)

F2   FRASER, CAPT. SIMON (of Ardachy, later of Knockie) Fidd/
1-2   Comp.(1773-1852) Pub. F2-1: " Thirty Highland Airs,
      Str., &c. With a bass for the v/cello or Hchd. Consisting
      chiefly of Tunes entirely New with a Few Old Tunes never
      before Published. Selected and Composed by Mr.S.F****r"
      1795 11pp. [NLS:Glen 360] F2-2: "The Airs & Melodies
      peculiar to the Highlands of Scotland and the Isles..."
      Mr. John Gow, Hanover St., Edin. & London, 1816, 120 pp.
      "New Edition ..." Revised Wm. Mackay & Angus Fraser, 1874
      (Inverness). The two edn.s differ in that the 1816 (1st)
      edition starts at p11; the 1874 at p1 (Index lists both).
      [NLS: 1816 Edn: Inglis 203; 1874 Edn: Mus.D.I.11; c.1876
      Edn (Pub: Logan & Co.): MH.174] (NOTE: The tune: "Oidhche
      Shamhna" (Hallowe'en) is listed as being in both 1816 and
      1874 edns. but is not printed in either, see F2v2p89/99).

THE GLEN COLLECTION

OF

SCOTTISH DANCE MUSIC

Strathspeys, Reels, and Jigs,

SELECTED from the EARLIEST PRINTED SOURCES,
or from the COMPOSER'S WORKS.

Arranged, with New Accompaniments for the

PIANOFORTE,

BY

JOHN GLEN.

Containing an Introduction on Scottish Dance Music, Sketches of Musicians and Musicsellers,
an Analytical Table to 1784, and a Chronological List of Works.

ENT. STA. HALL.

EDINBURGH : PUBLISHED AT 2 NORTH BANK STREET.

1891.

NOTE: Angus Fraser (see previous entry) was Simon's son
and planned to publish Vol. II of his late father's mss.
collections, but died before this could be accomplished.
The originals are housed in Edin. University Library (EUL
Manuscripts Dept) with his own ms. collection.

F3   FRENCH, JOHN (of Ayr) Fiddler/Composer. Pub: **"A Coll. of
New Str., R., etc., for Pfte., Vn. and v/cello. Ded. to
Mrs. Boswell of Auchinleck..."** Edinburgh, 1801. (Posth.
published "for behalf of Mr. F.'s widow and children")
199 pp. [NLS: Glen 262]

FULTON's Music for Violin and Cello (Source not yet found)

G1   GALE'S POCKET COMPANION, ...**"for the G.Fl., or Vn., con-
1-2   taining the most approved Scotch, English & Irish Airs,
Songs, Str., R., &c...Selected by the Author..."** c.1800 :
(Vol.1,pp1-48) [NLS: Mus.Box.s.19.14] (Vol.2, pp49-96)
[DPL/Wighton; G.92421] Continuously numbered.

GALLEY, JOHN. Musician, Newcastle. Pub:"12 Str. & 2 Hp.s
for Vn. or pfte...." (c. 1800) 14pp. [NLS: Mus.E.s.15]

G3   GIBB, ALEXANDER (Haddington), D/Master. Pub: **"A new Coll.
of Minuets, Medlies, High Dances, Marches, Str., & R..."**
Ded. to Miss C. Dalrymple...A. Gibb, Edinburgh, 1798.
[NLS: Glen 264]

GLEADHILL,THOMAS SWIFT(1827-1890) Musician/Composer. Pub:
(G5v1) "National Dance Album..." Glasgow (c.1870) 37pp.
(G5v2) "Gleadhills Selection of the Best R., Str., C.D.s,
H/Schottisches, etc..." London (In 2 Pts. of 24pp each)
[NLS: G5v1/MH.s.17; G5v2/MH.v.29] Standards, not listed.

G6   GLEN, JOHN Music Collector. Pub: **"The Glen Coll. of
1-2   Scottish Dance Music, Str., R. and Jigs ..."** Edinburgh
In two Bks. (1)1891 - 48pp (2) 1895 - 50pp   (Also pub.
"Early Scott. Melodies" - Edinr. 1900 - not listed)
[NLS: Glen 321/321A; Sandeman Bf2/3]

NOTE: Glen (1833-1904) amassed probably the most
comprehensive collection of printed editions and mss. from
the traditional repertoire ever assembled by one person.
At his death, this was put up for auction and acquired by
Lady Dorothea Stuart Murray (Lady D. Ruggles-Brise) who
gave it to the National Library in memory of her brother,
Lord George Stewart Murray (k. in France, 1914) in 1927.
NOTE: The collection was on loan to the British Library
until the National Library of Scotland (est. 1925) was
ready to receive it.

G7   GOW & MARSHALL. **"A Choice Selection of Reels and Str. from
the works of Gow & Marshall and the most popular Country
Dances, with portrait of Niel Gow..."** Edinburgh, Alexr.
Robertson & Coy., Music Sellers to the Queen ...
(Ran to many editions) [DPL: H 7072, 3rd.Edn.21pp]
[NLS: MH.42 (under "Gow") Copy thought to be 1st. Edn]

A
SECOND COLLECTION
of
Strathspey Reels &c.
With a Bass for the
Violoncello or *Harpsichord:*
Dedicated (By Permission) to the
Noblemen & Gentlemen
of the

CALEDONIAN HUNT.

By

NEIL GOW, *at* DUNKELD.

Pr: —————————————————— 6/

Edinburgh: Printed for Corri & Company Music Sellers to
Her Majesty, and Sold by Stewart & Co, R: Bremner,
R. Ross, — A: McGoun Glasgow, Messrs Longman
& Broadrip Music Sellers, & D. Corri
No 67 Dean Street London.

J. Johnson Sculpt

Entred in Stationers Hall

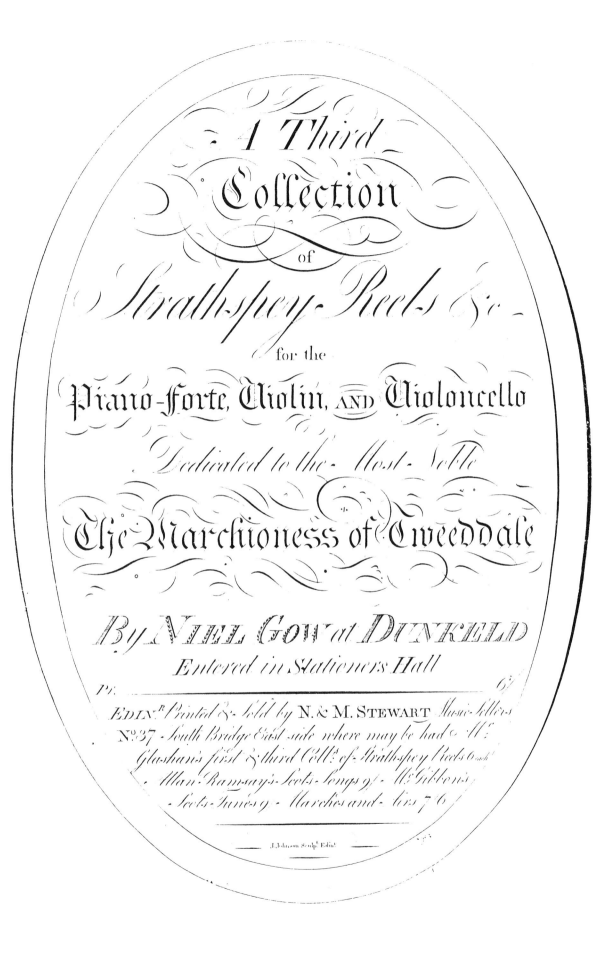

A Third
Collection
of
Strathspey Reels &c.
for the
Piano-Forte, Violin, and Violoncello
Dedicated to the Most Noble
The Marchioness of Tweeddale
By NIEL GOW at DUNKELD
Entered in Stationers Hall

Pr.   6/

EDIN.R Printed & Sold by N. & M. STEWART Music sellers
N.º 37 South Bridge East side where may be had McGlashan's first & third Coll.s of Strathspey Reels 6 each
Allan Ramsay's Scots Songs 9/ McGibbon's
Scots Tunes 9 Marches and airs 7 6

J. Johnson Sculp.t Edin.t

THIRD EDITION, CORRECTED & IMPROVED BY NATH: GOW.

FIFTH
Collection of Strathspeys, Reels &c.
For the
PIANO FORTE, HARP, VIOLIN & VIOLONCELLO
Dedicated to the Right Honorable the
Countess of Dalhousie
by
NIEL GOW & SONS

Entered at   Stationers Hall.

Price   8/.

Note

IN the Reliques of ROBERT BURNS, Published by R. H. Cromek in the 1808, Speaking of "Mac Pherson's Farewell," P. 235. 236. it is said 'GOW has published a Variation of this fine tune as his own Composition, which he calls The "Princess Augusta."

Again, in the same book "My Tocher's the Jewel" P. 291. it is said 'This tune is claimed by Nathaniel Gow. It is notoriously taken from the Muckin of Geordie's Byre — It is also to be found, long prior to Nathaniel Gow's æra, in Aird's Selection of Airs and Marches, the first edition, under the name of "The Highway to Edinburgh".

To the Public

NATH: GOW cannot for a moment suppose that Mr BURNS meant any thing injurious to him or any of his Father's family, the Bard evidently laboured under some mistake; which owing to his death cannot now be accounted for; suffice it to say, that both Assertions in the Reliques are false. Upon turning up Niel Gow's third Book, Page 32 and 33, it will be seen that the Tune named "Princess Augusta" is unclaimed by him or any of his family, And with respect to the other tune, my tocher's the jewel, by looking into Niel Gow and Son's 2d. book, Page 18, it will be seen that it is also unclaimed by Nath. Gow or any of his family. Nath. Gow found the Tune in Oswald's Caledonian Pocket Companion, book 3d. page 28th. as a quick Jigg it struck him that it would be pretty if slow, & it being without a name, he called it Lord Elcho's Favourite. Mr. Oswald's book was published as long prior to Aird's Æra, as Aird's was to that of Nath. Gow.

Edinburgh

Printed and Sold by Robt. Purdie, Music Seller, No. 70, Princes Street.

Where may be had all their Books.

PART FOURTH
Of The
Complete Repository,
Of Original Scots Slow
Strathspeys and Dances
(THE DANCES ARRANGED AS MEDLEYS,)
For The
Harp, Piano Forte, Violin and Violoncello &c.
Respectfully Dedicated to the
NOBILITY AND GENTRY
of
Scotland
by
NIEL GOW & SONS.

Entered at Stationers Hall.

Edinburgh

Published for the Proprietors, to be had of Nath. Gow 4 South Hanover Street & John Gow 31 Great Marlbro' Street.

LONDON.

NATHANIEL GOW
(1763-1831)

NIEL GOW
(1727-1807)

G8   GOW, JOHN & ANDREW, Fiddler/Composers (Sons of Niel Gow):
     "A Collection of Slow Airs, Str. & R..." W. Campbell,
     London, c.1795 - 36pp. One edit. entitled "A Fourth Coll"
     of which the contents is as the first. [NLS: MH.31 & .32]

G9   GOW, NATHANIEL, Fiddler/Composer (Eldest son of Niel) Pub:
1-5   (1) **"The Ancient Curious Coll...of Genuine Scotch Tunes.."**
      (1823) - 36pp. (2) **"A Coll. of Airs, R. & Str., being the
      posth. Comps. of Neil Gow Jnr. [his son] ..."** (1837) 22pp.
      (3) **"A Select Coll. of orig. Dances, Waltzes, Marches,
      Minuets & Airs..."**; (c.1815; 2/edit:c.1835) 36pp.
      (4) **"A Complete Coll. of Orig. German Waltz...with second
      violin accomp...."** (c.1796) 24pp. (5) **"A Coll. of Str. R.
      containing the most appr. Old and the most fashionable New
      Reels..."** (c.1797) 36pp. Some have two editions. [NLS:
      (1) Ancient Curious Coll.(1823) - Glen 403 (2) Neil Gow
      Jnr.'s Comps. (1837) - Glen 411 (3) Select Coll.(c.1815)
      - Glen 406 (4) Complete Coll. (c.1796) 24pp. - Mus.E.1.
      90.11 (5) Coll. of Str. R. (c.1797) 36pp. - Glen 402]
(G9) GOW, Nath: "Vocal Melodies of Scotland..." Pub: in 3 pts.
      (Edin. 1823; ded. to Sir Walter Scott) [NLS: Glen 405 1-3]

      NOTE (on G9v2): Neil Gow Jnr.'s collection ran to more
      than one edition, with pagination varying and with these
      two titles omitted (at least) from the NLS copy (Glen 411)
      "Cock of the North" (2/2 in A), p13 in other edn.
      "Miss Forbes's Reel" (a diff. tune from other in Index)

      GOW, NEIL, Jnr. (Nathaniel's son) See G9v2 (above)

G10   GOW, NIEL, Fiddler/Composer Pub: (1) **"A Coll. of Str. R.
1-6   with a bass etc...Printed for the Author: Edinburgh"** 1784
      -36pp. (2) **" A Second Coll..."** (3) **"A Third..."** (4) **" A
      Fourth ..."** Second & Subsequent edit.s published by Niel
      Gow & Sons. (5) **"A Fifth Coll..."** Pub: Niel Gow & Sons,
      Edinburgh (1809) (6) **"A Sixth Coll..."** Pub: Gow & Shep-
      herd and Nath. Gow, Edin., 1822. [NLS: Various editions,
      (1) A Coll. 1784 (ie: 1st. Edit)-36pp.......Glen 407(1)
         (Second Edit: 1801 &c.)
      (2) A Second Coll. 1788 - 36pp ....Glen 407(2)
      (3) A Third Coll. 1792 - 36pp ....Glen 407(3)
      (4) A Fourth Coll. 1800 - 36pp ....Glen 408(1)
      (5) A Fifth Coll. 1809 - 36pp ....Glen 408(2)
      (6) A Sixth Coll. 1822 - 36pp ....Glen 408(3)
      Library can supply list of later editions]

G11   GOW & SONS (Niel, Nathaniel, etc.) Published, largely as
1A-C re-issues but inc. some previously unpublished material:
2A-D (1) **" The Beauties of Niel Gow "**; 3 books ea. of 38 pp.,
      1819, "the most favourite tunes" from Niel Gow's 1st.,
      2nd. and 3rd. Colls. (2) **" The Complete Repository of
      Orig. S/Str. & Dances ..."**; 4 books ea. of 38 pp. which
      were pub. in var. edit.s 1799-1839; widely available.
      [NLS: (1) Beauties of Gow - MH.38, 3 Bks. in one, c.1826
      (2) Complete Repos. - Glen 410(1-4), the four pts. in one;
      Library has lists of all editions]

G13   GRAHAM, T.S. Arranger. Pub:**" The Portfolio, a coll. of
      Quadrilles, Waltzes, etc..."** 15pp [DPL/Wighton: H.10487]

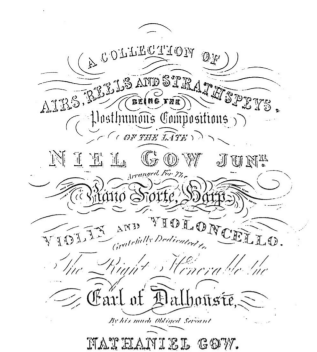

A COLLECTION OF
AIRS, REELS AND STRATHSPEYS,
BEING THE
Posthumous Compositions
OF THE LATE
NIEL GOW JUNᴿ
Arranged for the
Piano Forte, Harp,
VIOLIN AND VIOLONCELLO.
Gratefully Dedicated to
The Right Honorable the
Earl of Dalhousie,
By his much Obliged Servant
NATHANIEL GOW.

Ent. Stat. Hall.   Price 6/

EDINBURGH,
PUBLISHED & SOLD BY ALEXᴿ ROBERTSON & Cᵒ MUSIC SELLE
39 Princes Street.

[1837]

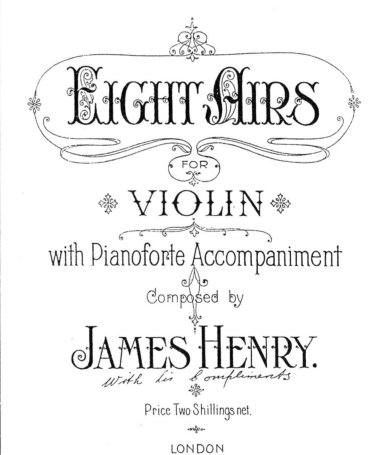

EIGHT AIRS

FOR

VIOLIN

with Pianoforte Accompaniment

Composed by

JAMES HENRY.

With his Compliments

Price Two Shillings net.

LONDON
BAYLEY & FERGUSON
2, Great Marlborough St. W.
Glasgow, 54 Queen Street.

G14 GRANT, CHARLES (1810-92). Fiddler/Composer & Schoolmaster,
     Aberlour. Pub:**"Str., R., Pibrochs & Marches"** (56 tunes in
     31pp) posth., for private circulation. [NLS: MH.s.20]

G15 GRANT, DONALD Fiddler/Composer, D/Master, Elgin (c.1760-
     1839). Pub: **"A Coll. of Airs, Str. etc..."** (1790 ? Re-pub.
     1820/21 as "Grant's 1st. Coll." ; a 2nd. coll. never seems
     to have materialised) 38pp. [NLS: Glen 291]

     GREY, A. OGILVIE, Musician/collector. Pub: "Scottish
     Music..." London, 1905. [NLS: MH.45] (Not listed)

G17 GUNN, JOHN , Musician, Edinburgh (c. 1765-1824) Pub:
     "40 Favorite Scotch Airs" (c.1791) [AUL/DPL: H.10489]

     GUNN, WILLIAM Bagpipe-maker, Glasgow Pub: "The Caledonian
     Repository of Music, adapted for the bagpipes" (1860; 7th.
     Edn: 1876) 110pp. Not listed. [NLS: MH.s.22/23]

H1   HALL, JOHN Fiddler/Composer, Ayr (c.1788-1862). Pub:
     "A Sel. of Str., R., Waltzes & Irish Jigs..." (1818) 34pp.
     [NLS: Glen 282]

H3   HAMILTON, JOHN Publisher, Edinburgh (1761-1814) Pub:
     "A Choice Coll. of Scots Reels, or C.D. & Str..." (n.d)
     40pp. [NLS: MH.s.52(3); DPL/Wighton: H.92465]
     For Hamilton's "Caledonian Repository" (3Bks.) see C5(1-3)

     HARBOUR, JACOB (Composer/Collector) Pub: "A Sel. of the
     most admired CDs, R., Str. &c ..." London, 1796 20pp
     Not listed, but worth a second look [NLS: MH.s.267]

     HARDING, WALTER N.H. English music collector; lived in USA
     (1883-1973). Of some 3-400,000 items, a small but signif-
     icant number are printed collections of fiddle music, both
     Irish & Scottish and these are housed with the rest in the
     Bodleian Library, Oxford. (BOD/Harding Collection)

(H4) HENDERSON, JOHN MURDOCH Collector/Composer, Schoolteacher,
     Aberdeen (d. Edinburgh, 1972) Pub: **"Flowers of Scottish
     Melody"** (1935) 56pp. Left his considerable collection
     of Printed Music Colls. & Mss to NLS and AUL.[NLS: MH.123]
     See sep. list. Also S8/J.Scott Skinner (Scott. Mus.Maker)

H5   HENRY, JAMES Fiddler/Comp., Shoemaker at Macduff & Portsoy
     (1860-1914) Pub: **"Eight Airs for Violin"** [NLS: MH.v.32]

H6   HIME & SON Publishers: **"Coll./Sel. of the Most Favorite
     Dances, Liverpool..."** Pub. in 3pp. numbers, No.s 1,2,5,
     10,22 and 23 are listed. [DPL Wighton] A brother had a
     publishing business in Dublin.

     HONEYMAN, Wm. C. Violinist (Born N. Zealand, 1845; d.1919)
     Author of var. tutors and "Scottish Violin Makers" (1894).
     Pub: "The Str., R. and Hp. Tutor ..." (Koehler, Edinburgh,
     Late 19th c.) Standards with 50 hornpipes. Not listed.

     INGLIS, ALEXANDER WOOD. Musician/Collector. (c.1844-1929)
     Became Sec. to the Board of Manufacturers in Scotland;
     at his death, left his valuable collection of trad. Scott.
     Music to the NLS, to enhance those of Glen, Henderson, the
     Lauriston Castle Coll., etc [NLS: under "Ing./Inglis"]

COLLECTION

of Original

Strathspey Reels, with Variations

WALTZES, MARCHES, IRISH AIRS, &c.

and

A New Sonata

for the

Piano Forte

VIOLIN or GERMAN FLUTE

Dedicated to the Right Honourable

Lady Madelina Sinclair

by a YOUNG LADY

Never before Published.

Entered at Stationers Hall. ———————————————— *Price 7/*

EDINBURGH

Printed by URBANI and LISTON

1804.

J. Johnson Sculp.

J1 JENKINS, GEORGE Fiddler/Composer, "Teacher of Scotch
    Dancing", London. Pub: **"New Scotch Music ...Slow Airs,
    Str., Quick Reels, C.D. ..."** (1793) in 3 Pts. 49pp.
    [NLS: Glen 381]

J2 JOHNSON, ABRAHAM Fiddler/Composer Pub: **A Coll. of New
    Reels..."** Edinburgh (c.1795) 16pp. [NLS: MH.138]

(J3) JOHNSON, JAMES Publisher. Pub: **"The Scots Musical Museum,
      ded. to The Catch Club, inst: 1771..."** 6 vols., dated
      1787, 88, 90, 92, 96 and 1803. One of the foundation
      source books of Scottish melody. Ref. is made to tunes in
      index (J3) but refer to sep. index. [NLS: Mus.41, etc]

K1 KEITH, MALCOLM Collector Pub: **"The Complete Repository
1-2 of Orig. Scots Slow Str. & Dances..."** in two vols. ea. of
    40pp. (1) c.1811 (2) c.1823 , Glasgow. [NLS: MH.56]

K2 KERR, JAMES S., Publisher, Glasgow (1841-93) Pub: from
1-4 1875 a number of compilations, the most important of which
    is **"Kerr's Coll. of Merry Melodies for the Violin"** (still
    pub: 1990s) In 4 books [K2v1-4] Listed excluding Irish,
    N. American and modern pages. [NLS: MH.s.27]

    (Also: Kerr's Caledonian Coll. (30 pp.) [NLS: MH.58(2)]
    Kerr's Coll. of R. & Str. (Pt.1 - 32pp; 2 - 33pp)[MH.s.29]
    Kerr's Modern Dance Album for Vn. [MH.s.29] Not listed)

    KIDSON, FRANK Musicologist/Collector. His collection is
    housed at the Mitchell Library (Glasgow) and contains a
    number of exceedingly rare items. [Ask for Kidson Coll.]

(K3) KOEHLER, ERNEST & SON Music Sellers & Publishers, Edin-
      burgh. Pub: " Violin Repository of Dance Music" (1881-85)
      3 books, 288pp. [NLS: Glen 224, 224a,b] See sep. index.
      NOTE: An excellent source book for later work, esp. Horn-
      pipes and N. American, with useful notes on authorship.

L1 LADIES **" A Coll. of entirely original Str. R...By Ladies
    resident in a remote part of the Highlands ... NB correct-
    by Nath. Gow "** Edin.(1798) [NLS: See GOW, Nath. Glen 412]
    (Thought to be the Misses White, or a Miss White and a
    Miss Brocky, possibly of Morayshire)

L2 LADY **" A Coll. of Orig. Str. R. with var.s, Waltzes,
    Marches, Irish Airs &c...by a young Lady ..."** Edinburgh
    (1804) 26pp. [NLS: MH.59(1); Glen 306]

L3 LADY **" A Coll. of much admired Marches..."**(c.1796) [AUL]

L4 LEBURN, ALEXANDER Fiddler/Composer (b.1750 ?) Auchter-
    muchty. Pub: **" A Coll. of New Str. R. &c..."** Edinburgh
    (1793) 12pp. [NLS: Inglis 183, Glen 373 (dated c.1800)]

    .LEES, JOHN KENYON Arranger Pub: "The Balmoral Reel Book
    ...A Coll. of the Most Admired R. Str., C.D, H/pipes &c"
    Glasgow. 37pp. [NLS: MH.s.31] Pop. Standards, not listed.

The Royal Collection

OF

REELS, STRATHSPEYS & JICS

AS PERFORMED AT

HER MAJESTY'S BALLS.

AT THE EDINBURGH &

GLASGOW ASSEMBLIES

HONI SOIT QUI MAL Y PENSE

DIEU ET MON DROIT

And at all Fashionable

BY

HOWARD'S BAND

Meetings in Scotland

DEDICATED BY SPECIAL PERMISSION TO HER MOST GRACIOUS MAJESTY

Queen Victoria

BY

JOSEPH LOWE

Price 5/. Nett

PUBLISHED BY J. LOWE, AT HIS DANCING ACADEMY 52 FREDERICK STREET, EDINBURGH.
AGENTS: PATERSON & SONS, EDINBURGH & GLASGOW. CHAPPELL & C.º 50 NEW BOND S.T LONDON.
AND TO BE HAD OF ALL MUSIC SELLERS.

(L6) LOGAN & CO. Music Sellers/Publishers, Inverness. Pub: (1)
"The Inverness Coll. of Highland Pibrochs, Laments, Q/S,
Marches..."(6 bks. in one) (2) "The Inverness Coll. of
R., Str. & C.D..." (2 bks. in one) (3) "Logan's Coll. of
Highland Music arr. for the Vn..." Glasgow (1924) 6 bks.
in one) [NLS: MH.s.33] See sep. index: APPENDIX (L6)

NOTE: Logan's "Coll. of Highland Music ...for the Violin"
(Glasgow, 1924) is listed as (L6) in the Appendix. It contains 600 tunes, predominantly pipe music, including some
"Bagpipe Imitations". The 6-vol. "Inverness Coll. of Highland Pibrochs ... for the pianoforte" is similar (in fact
about 80% of the contents is the same as the coll above).
This and the "Inverness Coll. of R. Str. & CDs" (2 vols.)
contain about 340 tunes. Not listed.

LONGMAN & BRODERIP Music Publishers, London. Pub: for
a number of years "Selections of the most fav. C.Ds ..."
for Years 1788 & (?) 1790 [Ref. BUC] See also Broderip
& Wilkinson, Longman, etc. in successive years.

L8   LOWE, JOSEPH Fiddler/Composer (1797-1866, son of John L.,
1-6   who composed the reels "Rachel Rae" and "Archie Menzies")
7   Pub: (L8v1-6) **"Lowe's Coll. of R., Str., Jigs.."** 6 bks.in
8A,B   one (1844) (L8v7) "Lowe's Sel. of Pop. C.Ds ..." (1853?)
       (Standards, not listed) (L8v8A & B) **"Lowe's Royal Coll.
       of R., Str. & Jigs..."** 2 bks. ea. 34pp. (c.1860)
       [NLS: (L8v1-6) Glen 341;(L8v7) Glen 323;(L8v8) MH.62]

L9   LINLEY,F Publisher, London Pub: **"The Shepherd's Delight
       containing twelve Scots Tunes, never before published..."**
       London (1781) 5pp.[DPL]

Mc1   MACDONALD, D. "A Coll. of the Ancient martial music ...
       Piobaireachd as performed on the Gt. Hd. B/pipe. Now also
       for the pfte., Vn, V., with a few old Hd. Lilts ..." N/L
       Edin. (c.1822/33) 5pp(Mc1A)/117pp(Mc1) [NLS: Glen 298]

       MACDONALD, JOHN (See D16, DUFF, Chas. who pub. his work)

Mc3   MACDONALD, KEITH NORMAN MD Collector/Composer, Skye. Pub:
1   (1) **"The Skye Collection of best Str. R..."** Edinburgh 1887
(2)   192pp. (Mc3v1) [NLS: Glen 384] also pub: (2) "The Gesto
       Coll. of Highland Music..." (Much is Gaelic Music, often
       with words), Leipsig, 1893, Edinburgh '95. Sep. listed.
       [NLS: 1897 (Leipsig) 2nd. Edn. - Mus.D.I.8]

Mc4   MACDONALD, MALCOLM Musician/Comp. b.Dunkeld (c.1750);
1-4   sometime 'cellist to Niel Gow. Pub: **"A Coll. of Str. R.
       ..."; "A Second... "; "A Third..."; "A Fourth ..."** thus:
       (Mc4v1) 1788, 24pp. [NLS: Glen 136]; (v2) 1789, 13pp.
       (v3) 1792, 12pp. (v4) 1797, 13pp. [NLS: Glen 293 (1-3)]

Mc5   MACDONALD, Rev. PATRICK, Minister at Kilmore, Argyll (1755
       -1824). Pub: **" A Coll. of Highland Vocal Airs...lively
       C.Ds or Reels..."** (1784) 42pp. Collected by his brother,
       Joseph (d. India,1762) and rescued by Sir John Murray
       MacGregor in Bengal. [NLS: Inglis 157, etc; DPL; AUL]

       MACEWAN, JAMES Composer. Pub:"A Musical Casket of Melodies
       for the Million" (London, c.1843) [NLS: MH.s.36/36a] N/L

A

Third Collection

of

Strathspey Reels &c.

With a Bass for the

Violoncello or *Harpsichord*

Dedicated by Permission to

MISS DRUMMOND of PERTH

BY

Malcolm McDonald

at Dunkeld

Price ——————————— 2/6

EDINBURGH

Printed for the Author and Sold by CORRI & Co.
JOHNSON & Co. R. BRYSON and all the
Music Sellers in Town and Country

J. Johnson Sculp.!

A

COLLECTION OF

New Strathspey Reels &c.

With a Bass for the

Violoncello OR *Harpsichord*

Composed By

ABR.M MACINTOSH.

with additions by the Publishers

Price ——————————— 6/

the Bass's Corrected by P. URBANI

Edinburgh

Printed for & Sold by URBANI & LISTON at their
Music Ware House N.º 10 Princes Street
and all the Music Sellers in Town and Country.

A 3.d Book of

Sixty eight

New Reels

AND STRATHSPEYS

Also above forty old famous Reels

FOR THE

Violin and Piano Forte.

With a Bass for the

VIOLONCELLO OR HARPSICHORD

Compiled & Composed by

ROBERT MACKINTOSH

& Dedicated by Permission to

M.rs OSWALD

of AUCHINCRUIVE

Ent.d in Stationers Hall

Price 7.sh.

may be had at the undermentioned places, the Authors 1.st & 2.d Book & Abr. Mimers Reels &c.

Printed & Sold by J. Hamilton N.º 24 North Bridge, Stewart & C.º South Bridge, & W.m White N.º 1 South S.t And.rs Street EDIN.r
A. Mac. Gowan. GLASGOW, & Longman & Clementi, LONDON.

WILLIAM MACGIBBON
(c1695-1756)

Mc7 MACFADYEN, JOSEPH " A Coll. of Highland Str. R. from the
Best Authors ..." Glasgow (c.1800) 36pp. [DPL] Also pub:
"The Repository of Scots & Irish Airs ...Part of the Slow
Tunes adapted for 2 Vn. & A Bass ..." (Glasgow 1802) 64pp.
(Airs), 64pp. (Str., etc) [NLS: Glen 134] (This is listed
under the name of A. McGOUN, Printer, Glasgow, Mc12)

Mc8 MACGIBBON, WILLIAM Musician/Collector (c.1695-1756) Pub:
1-3 (1) " A Coll. of Scots Tunes ..." Edinburgh (1742); then
Book II (1746) and Book III (1755), ea. of 36pp. [NLS;AUL]

4-7 "A Coll. of Scots Tunes ..." Edinburgh (1768) Pub: by
Robt. Bremner, Books 1-4, 120pp. [NLS (?Bk.4); AUL]

NOTE: The two collections are in essence the same; the
later edition has some 20 pp. added and varies in detail.

(McGIBBON, PETER (c.1800) published some sheet-music)

Mc9 MACGLASHAN, ALEXANDER (Known as "King") Fiddler/Collector
1-3 Edinburgh (1740-97) Pub: (1) "A Coll. of Str. R. ..."
Edinburgh (1778) 34pp. [NLS: Glen 236(1); Inglis 184(3)]
(2) "A Coll. of Scots Meas., Hps., Jigs, Allemands, etc."
Edinburgh (1781) 42pp. [NLS: Glen 236(3); Inglis 184(1)]
(3)"A Coll. of R., consisting chiefly of Str., Athole R."
Edinburgh (1786) 46pp. [NLS: Glen 236(2); Inglis 184(2)]
NOTE: The numbering of the volumes may vary from library
to library, but contemporary ms. numbering on a certain
set of copies appears to confirm this order.

Mc10 MACGLASHAN, JOHN (? Brother of Alex.) Fiddler/Composer
Pub: "A Coll. of Str. R. ..." Edinburgh (1798) 15pp.
(Appears as "Mr. MacG." on T/page) [NLS: Glen 363; MH68]

Mc11 MACGREGOR, JOHN Fiddler/Composer Pub: " A Set of Favorite Str. R. ..." London (1817) 11pp. [NLS: Glen 296 (2) -
Glen 296 (1) & (3) refer to pieces by the same composer]

Mc12 McGOUN, ARCHIBALD. Pub: "The Repository of Scots & Irish
1-2 Airs..." (?Edited/Published MacFadyen (Mc7) dated c.1807)
Pt.1 -"Str.R."-64pp; Pt.2-"Slow Tunes"-64pp.[NLS:Glen 134]

Mc13 MACINTOSH, ABRAHAM Fiddler/Composer (b.1769, son of "Red
1-2 Rob" Mackintosh or McIntosh) Pub: (1) " 30 New Str. R.
&c..." Edinburgh (c.1792) 11pp. [NLS: Glen 303] (2) " A
Coll. of Str., R., Jigs, &c " Newcastle, 1805. 36pp. [AUL]

MACINTOSH, JAMES "A Coll. of R., Str., M..." Perth (1930)
6pp. [NLS: MH.s.54(3); MH.s.1(3)] Not listed.

Mc15 MACINTYRE, DUNCAN Fiddler/ Comp/ Music Teacher, London
(c.1765-1807) Pub: "A Coll. of Slow Airs, R. & Str..."
London (1795) 40pp. [NLS: Glen 266]

Mc16 MACKAY, ALEXANDER Fiddler/Composer, Islay (b.1775) Pub:
"A Coll. of R., Str., and Slow Tunes ..." Glasgow (1802?)
36pp. [NLS: Glen 344]

Mc17 McINTOSH, ALEXANDER, Dancing Teacher, Dundee. Pub: "Eight
Cottillions and Four C.Ds..." [DPL/Wighton]

VOLUME 2ND

OF A COLLECTION OF

Scottish Melodies Reels Strathspeys
Jigs Slow Airs &c

FOR THE

Piano Forte,

VIOLIN AND VIOLONCELLO.

Being the Genuine &
Posthumous Works of

WILLIAM MARSHALL.

All the Airs in this collection are now published for the first time.

This Work is Copy-right   Price 6/

Edinburgh

Published by ALEXr ROBERTSON, Music Seller to
the Queen and Queen Dowager at the Royal Music Saloon
39, PRINCES STREET.
Where may be had Volume 1st by the same Composer
Price 10/

MARSHALL'S

Scottish AIRS, Melodies,

STRATHSPEYS, REELS, &c.

FOR THE

Piano Forte, Harp,

Violin & Violoncello,

WITH APPROPRIATE BASSES,

Dedicated

TO

THE MOST NOBLE, THE

Marchioness of Huntly.

Price 12/6
to non Subscribers 15/

Entered at
Stationers Hall.

TO THE PUBLIC

The Author of the following Sheets, now humbly submitted by him to the Public thinks it
necessary to mention that several of his Strathspeys & Reels have occasionally been Published by most
of the Collectors of Scottish Music without his Permission of this however he does not much Complain,
especially as he had not till now, any intention to Publish them himself. His only Complaint is their not
mentioning his Name along with those Reels of his Composition they Published, which for obvious reasons,
were by some neglected, but in particular their changing the original names given by him to other names,
according to their own fancy and this being not generally known the Author has thought it necessary to
apprize the Public of it, assuring them that this Work is entirely his own Composition & cannot be claimed
by any other Person Whatever.

EDINBURGH.

Published for the Author & Sold by Alexr Robertson at his Music Saloon 47 Prince Street & by the Music Sellers in
London, Dublin, Liverpool, Glasgow, Aberdeen, Inverness &c.

Walker & Andrew

MACKENZIE, ALEXANDER (also his son, Sir A.C. Mackenzie),
(Pub: (1) "100 Fav. Scotch Airs ..."(Edin. mid-19th c)
(2) "The Nat. Dance Music of Scotland..." (Lon. c.1856)
3 bks. in 1; re-published (3) As (2), London 1889, 146pp.
[NLS: (1) MH.125(6); (2) Glen 334; (3) Inglis 98] (His son
MACKENZIE, SIR A.C. "Dance Music"(Lon.1891) 20pp [NLS])

Mc19 MACKERCHER, DUNCAN Fiddler/Composer, Inver (1796-1873)
1-3 Pub: " **A Coll. of Str. R. ...**" (3 Bks. in one) Edinburgh
(c.1830) [NLS: Glen 365(1-3)] See: MENZIES, below.
(Also spelt "MacKerracher") NOTE: Older bibliographies
refer to "Two collections"; there are three, although Vol.
II borrows from Vol.I and Vol.III borrows from Vol.II.

Mc21 MACKINTOSH, ROBERT("Red Rob") Fiddler/Composer (c. 1745-
1-4 1807), Tullymet; moved to London. Pub: Four Collections:
(1) **"Airs, Minuets, Gavotts & Reels..."** Edinburgh (1783)
(2) **"68 New R., Str. & Q/steps ..."**   Edinburgh (1793)
(3) **"A 3rd. Bk. of 68 New R. & Str...."** Edinburgh (1796)
(4) **"A Fourth Bk. of New Str. R. ..."**   London (1803)
(Bk.1 - 40pp; Bks. 2 & 3 - 39pp; Bk.4 - 44pp. He uses the
spelling "Macintosh" in Book 1; otherwise as above)
[NLS: Bk.1 - Glen 357(1); Bk.2 - Glen 357(2)
     Bk.3 - Inglis 291(3); Bk.4 - Glen 258]
NOTE: Further works attrib. to R.M. occur in sheet music.

Mc22 McLAREN, DANIEL Fiddler/Composer, Taymouth, Perthshire
Pub: **"A Coll. of Str. R., &c..."** Edinburgh (1794) 22pp.
[NLS: Glen 288(1); Sandeman/Athole Coll. Be63]
(See also: Mc22A-C, extra tunes bound into NLS copy)

Mc23 McLEAN, CHARLES Musician (c.1700-73) Pub: (Posthumously)
"A Coll. of Favourite Scots Tunes with var.s for the Vn."
Edinburgh (c.1774) 37pp. [NLS: Glen 226]

M1   MANCOR, P. Musician, Dundee. Pub:**"...Tunes, resp. ded. to
Miss Carnegy of Lower"**(One tune by H. Johnstone) [AUL/DPL]
("Pub. by the Author[composer], sold by Muir Wood, Edin.")

M2   MARCHES **"A Select Coll. of Favourite Marches ..."** (1789)
["Selected by David Sime; pub: Stewart & Co.] 35pp [AUL]

MARR & CO. Music Publisher, Inverness & Glasgow Pub:
"Marr & Co.'s Royal Coll. of Highland Air, Q/steps, Str.,
R. and C.Ds ..." Inverness/Glasgow (n.d.) In print, 1990.
[NLS: MH.75/76] Not listed.
Also: Marr's (Late Camerons) Selection of Violin Music.

WILLIAM MARSHALL
(1748-1833)

M4   MARSHALL, WILLIAM Fiddler/Composer, House Steward to the
1-4 D. of Gordon, b. Fochabers (1748-1833) Pub: four colls.
(one posth.) containing approx. 287 of his own comp):
(1) **"A Coll. of Str. R. ..."** Edinburgh (1781) 12pp.
(2) **"A Second Book ..."** (as above ? Bound together, 4pp)
(3) **"Marshall's Scottish Airs, Melodies ..."** (1822) 60pp.
(4) **"Vol.2nd. of a Coll. of Scott. Melodies"** (1845) 35pp.
(posthumously); also "Kinrara" etc. (Edin. 1800) 2pp.
[NLS: M4v1 & 2 - Glen 386; M4v3 - Glen 284(1); M4v4 (the
posth. work) 284(2), also bound together]. Wm. Marshall or
his heirs re-titled some of his early works in later publications, so his music requires careful scrutiny.
NOTE: Marshall acquired the style "of Keithmore" in the
1790s when he moved to a large farm on the Gordon estate
and acted as the Duke's Factor until 1817.

HIGHLAND
AIRS & QUICKSTEPS,
ARRANGED FOR THE
PIANOFORTE,
BY
J. F. MORISON.

ENT. STA. HALL. ———— ✳ ———— PRICE 4/2

Inverness,
LOGAN & Cº (INVERNESS) Lᴰ
59 Church Street,
Also At Elgin, Nairn, & Dingwall.

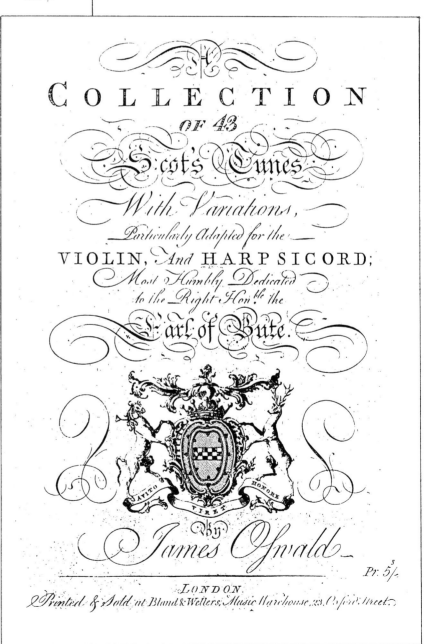

COLLECTION
OF 43
Scot's Tunes
With Variations,
Particularly Adapted for the
VIOLIN, And HARPSICORD;
Most Humbly Dedicated
to the Right Honᵇˡᵉ the
Earl of Bute.

By
James Oswald

Pr. 5/-

LONDON.
Printed & Sold at Bland & Wellers Music Warehouse, 23, Oxford Street.

M6 MAXWELL, ALEXANDER (Musician, Argyle Militia) Pub: **"R. &
Str., comp. by [A.M.]"** Edin. c.1809. [NLS: Glen 348(48)]

MENZIES, Capt. Daniel... Appears to have composed many of
the tunes in MacKercher's Coll. (Mc19v1) and a Mr. Duncan
Duff of Perth actually accused MacKercher of plagiarism.

M7 MIDDLETON, CHARLES Publisher, Keith & London Pub: var.
Dance Books (Album, Budget, Treasury, Cabinet) late 19th.
Cent., some of which were edited by Peter MILNE, see
below) [NLS: Have complete list] Not listed here.
"Middleton's Sel. of Str., R., etc..." Keith (1870) 38pp.
(Ran to 7 edns.) [NLS: Glen 78, 5th. edn.]

PETER MILNE
(1824-1908)

MILNE, PETER Fiddler/Composer ("The Tarland Minstrel")
(1824-1908) Said to have been one of Scott Skinner's many
teachers. At least some of his finest compositions have
survived, thanks to Chas. Middleton (above).

MOFFAT, ALFRED EDWARD Composer/Arranger (b.Edinburgh,
1866) Pub: several coll. of mainly pop. standards:
"The Braemar Coll. of Highland Music" London (1916) 85pp.
"30 Highland R. & Str. ..." (London, n.d./c.1900) 18pp.
"Dance Music of the North, 54 R., Str., M. &c." Glasgow
Not listed. [NLS: Braemar, MH.78; 30 Hd. R., MH.82; Dance
Music of the North, MH.80]

M10 MORISON, JANE FRASER Musician/Collector(Gaelic airs) Pub:
1-2 **"Highland Airs & Q/Steps..."**(2 books) Inverness (Bk2,1882)
Bk1 - 20pp; Bk2 - 29pp [NLS: Glen 336]

M11 MORISON, JOHN Fiddler/Composer, Peterhead (1772-1848) Pub:
1-2 **" A Coll. of New Str. R...."** Edinburgh (c.1797) 23pp.
[NLS: MH.85,MH.86] **"A Select Col. of Fav. Tunes"**
Peterhead (c.1815) 18pp. [NLS: MH.s.73(2)]

M12 MORRISON, WILLIAM Fiddler/Composer, (Inverness) Pub:
**"A Coll. of Highland Music, consisting of Str., R., M.,
W. & Slow Airs ..."** Inverness (1812) 36pp. [NLS: Glen 325]

MUELLER, ROBERT Publisher of: "200 select R. & Str. of
Scotland..." London (1852) 62pp. Not listed [NLS: MH.88]

MULHOLLAN, JOHN McPHERSON, Pub: "A Sel. of Ir. & Sc. Tunes
... Airs, Marches, Str., C.Ds, &c..." (Edinburgh, 1804)
51pp. Pr. for the Ed. by John Hamilton [NLS: Glen 300] N/L

M14 MUNRO, ALEXANDER Musician Pub: **" 12 Airs Ecossais..."**
(12 Scotch Airs) Paris (c.1730) [DPL/Wighton: H.21264]

MURDOCH, WM. MCKENZIE Musician & Publisher of innumerable
pieces for violin and piano, later 19th, early 20th. C.
Not listed. [NLS: Various, with the MH Shelfmark]

MUSICAL MISCELLANY, THE An anonymous publication:
"The Mus. Misc., a Select Coll. of Scots, English & Irish
Songs set to music..." Perth (1786) 347pp.[AUL] N/L.

N1 NAPIER, WILLIAM Musician/Music Seller, London Pub:
1-2 (1) **"Napier's Sel. of Dances & Str. ..."** London,1798.
37pp. [NLS: Glen 379] (2) **"A Sel. of the most Fav. Scots
Songs, chiefly pastoral..."** (3 vols., 1790, 92, 94) [AUL;
NLS: Glen 378 (1-3)]

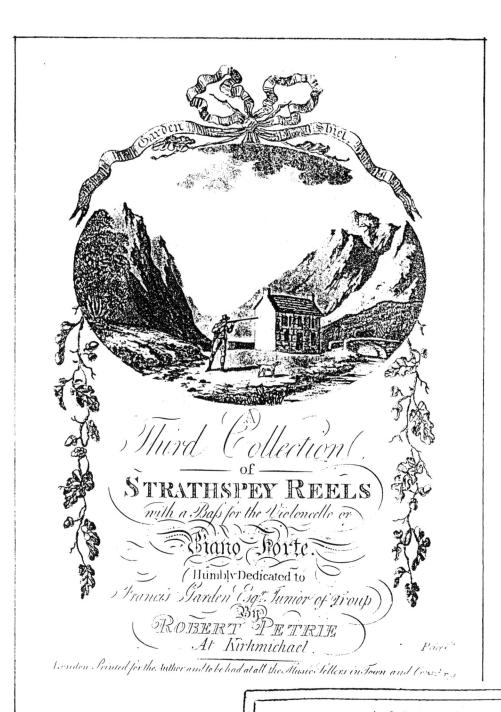

A

Third Collection

of

STRATHSPEY REELS

with a Bass for the Violoncello or

Piano Forte.

(Humbly Dedicated to

Francis Garden Esqr. Junior of Troup)

By

ROBERT PETRIE

At Kirhmichael .

Price

London Printed for the Author and to be had at all the Music Sellers in Town and Country

---

A COLLECTION of

Original Scotch-Tunes,

(Full of the *Highland Humours*) for the

VIOLIN:

Being the First of this Kind yet Printed :

Most of them being in the Compass of the *FLUTE*.

LONDON:

Printed by *William Pearson*, in *Red-Cross-Alley* in *Jewin-street*, for *Henry Playford*, at his
Shop in the *Temple-Change*, *Fleet-street*. 1700.

NEAL, JOHN & WILLIAM Publishers, Dublin. Pub: "A Coll.
of the Most Celebrated Scotch Tunes ..." (c.1724) 29pp.
Companion to a vol. of Irish Tunes, etc. and might be com-
pared to John Young's Coll. (1720), Y1, below. (Rare; a
copy at Queen's Univ., Belfast lacks p.29. Nat. Library of
Ireland has photostat - Add. Mus. 10,874) Not listed.

N2   NICOLSON, H. Dancing Master, Edinburgh Pub: " A Coll. of
     Fav. Dances, Comp., Arr. for the p/fte..." Edin. (c.1817)
     [NLS: Glen 331; DPL: H.10471]

O1   OSWALD, JAMES Musician, Dunfermline & Edinburgh (b.1710?)
1A-F Besides his "serious" works (eg: "Airs for the 4 seasons",
2-5 1747) and a fanciful inclination to ascribe old tunes to
     such as David Rizzio, Oswald published several tune books:
     (1)"The Caled. Pocket Companion" London, in 12 books, No:s
     1-9, 1743-48; 10-12, 1759) (2) "Curious Coll. of Scots
     Tunes..." Edin. (1740) 42pp. (3) "Coll. of Curious Scots
     Tunes..." London (1743) 47pp. (4) "A Second Coll..." (as
     in 3) London (1744) 46pp. (5) "A Coll. of 43 Scots Tunes"
     London (c.1795?) 37pp. [NLS: (1) Inglis 68.69, Bks. 1-8 &
     7-12; (2) Inglis 295(1), Glen 168(3) (3 & 4) Glen 310
     (5) Glen 397(1)]

P1   PARKER, MRS. Professional Dancer Pub: Two Collections:
1-2 (1) " A Sel. of Scots Tunes, Str. & R..." Dublin (1797)
     (2) " A 2nd. Sel..." (A "third" Sel. in Ms., at NLS). All
     published in Dublin (Hime/ Edmund Lee); NLI has "Mrs. P.'s
     Last Coll. of Fav. Dances for yr. 1795 ..." [NLI:(JM 5346)
     P1v1 (39 airs, 14pp) NLS: Mus. Box. 157.27; P1v2 (18 airs)
     Sandeman (Athole Coll.) Be45]

P3   PATERSON, JAMES Fiddler/Composer of questionable ability.
     Pub: "A Coll. of Orig. Music...Slow Airs, Str., R., M. .."
     Glasgow (1867 ?) 24pp. [NLS: Glen 189(2)]

P4   PEACOCK, FRANCIS Dancing-Master, Aberdeen (1723-1807)
     Pub: " 50 Favourite Scotch Airs for a Vn. ..." London
     (1767) 35pp. [NLS: Glen 307, Inglis 146]

P5   PETRIE, ROBERT Fiddler/Composer, Kirkmichael (1767-1830)
1-4 Pub: Four books: " A Coll. of Str. R. (,Jiggs & C.D.)..."
     followed by "A Second...", "A Third...", " A Fourth ..."
     All printed Edinburgh (1) 1790 - 22pp. (2) 1795/6 - 24pp.
     (3) 1800 - 26pp. (4) 1805 - 24pp. [NLS: 4 Bks. Glen 295]

P6   PLATTS, J. Music Seller, London Pub:("In single No.s 1s.
1-2 each") (1) "Eight cotillons & six C.D. for the year 1789"
     (2)"PLATTS'S Pop. & Orig. Dances for the Pfte or Vn."[AUL]

P7   PLAYFORD, HENRY Musician/Collector (Son of John, below)
     Continued the work begun by his father and Pub:
     "A Coll. of Scotch-Tunes (Full of the Highland Humours)
     for the Vn. ..." London (1700) 16pp. [NLS: Inglis 4]

P8   PLAYFORD, JOHN Music Publisher/Musician, London Pub:
     "The (English) Dancing Master...with the Tunes to each
     Dance etc." John P. pub: 1652-1686 (4 edns); Henry then
     pub: about 12 more edns. 1690-c.1728.("Scotch Tunes" did
     not appear in earliest edns.)

     (Continued)

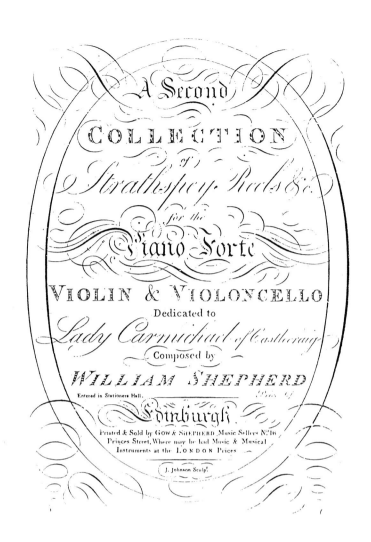

A Second
COLLECTION
of
Strathspey Reels &c.
for the
Piano Forte
VIOLIN & VIOLONCELLO
Dedicated to
Lady Carmichael of Castlecraig
Composed by
WILLIAM SHEPHERD
Entered in Stationers Hall.
Edinburgh
Printed & Sold by GOW & SHEPHERD Music Sellers N.º 16
Princes Street, Where may be had Music & Musical
Instruments at the LONDON Prices

J. Johnson Sculp.!

SKILLERN'S compleat Collection of
Two Hundred & four
REELS and COUNTRY DANCES,
Performed at Court, Almacks, the Pantheon,
and most Publick Assembly's,
with the newest and best directions for Dancing each Tune,
Set for the Violin, German Flute and Hoboy.
VOL. I.

London, Printed for T. SKILLERN N.º 17 S.t Martin's Lane, near Charing Cross,
Where may be had, A complete Vol: of Minuets for the Violin & Harp
(Circa 1780)

(P8, cont'd)

NOTE: For a studied analysis of the many editions of "The
Dancing Master", see BARLOW (Pub:1985) pp 132-6 + index.
[NLS: Mus.45] Orig. copies: Most libraries. Not Listed.
"Apollo's Banquet ...several New Scotch Tunes for the
Treble Vn." London, 1687 (First published 1663; 6th. 1690)
[NLS: 5th. Edn. (1687) Glen 66; DPL(Wighton)]

P9   PORTEOUS, JAMES Fiddler/Composer, Ecclefechan (1762-1847)
     Pub: " A Coll. of Str., R. & Jigs ..." Edin. (c.1820) 40pp
     [NLS: Glen 370, MH.97] (Shares with Jenkins and Paterson
     the wooden spoon for composition - Ed.)

P10 PRESTON Music Publishers, London **"Preston's Sel. of the
     Most Fav. C.D.s, R., &c. ..."** London (c.1791) 26pp. [AUL]
     (Also for years 1790, 1800, 1802 - Ref. BUC/Country Dance]

P11 PRINGLE, JOHN Fiddler/Composer (born c.1770, poss. in the
1-2 Borders) Pub: 2 books: (1) **" A Coll. of R., Str. & Jigs"**
     Edin. (1801) 19pp. (2) **" A Second Coll of Str., R., Jiggs,
     &c. ..."** Edin. (n.d.) 23pp. [NLS: 2Bks. Glen 281]

R4   REINAGLE, ALEXANDER Musician Pub: **" A Coll. of the Most
Fav. Scots Tunes ..."** Glasgow (1782) 26pp.[DPL: H.10400]
     His brother, JOSEPH, was also a composer at this period.

R5   RIDDELL, JOHN (or RIDDLE) Fiddler/Composer, Ayr (1718-95)
     Pub: **" A Coll. of Scots Reels or C.D.s and Minuets, with
     2 partic. Slow Tunes ..."** Edin. (c.1766) 45pp. and a 2nd.
     Edn. as above, but "Greatly Improved" Glasgow (1782) 60pp.
     [NLS: (1st. Edn.) F.s.f.33;(2nd. Edn.) Glen 97]

R6   RIDDELL, Capt. ROBERT, of Glenriddell Antiquarian/Composer
1-2 and friend of Robt. Burns (c.1745-94) Pub: (1) **"New Music
     for the p/fte or H/chd., comp. by a Gentleman...R., Min.,
     H/pipes, M. and 2 songs..."** Edin. (1787) 24pp. (2)**"A Coll.
     of Scotch Galwegian & Border Tunes for the Vn..."** Edin.
     (1794) 37pp. [NLS: (1)Inglis 296(1); (2) Glen 351]

R7   RITCHIE, MATTHEW Composer **"Five Fav. Tunes ...composed by
1-3 [M.R.]"** Vol. 1,2,3. [AUL]

     ROBERTSON, ALEXANDER Compiler of "Caled. Museum" (C5v2)
     (See also:"Sel. from the works...of Gow & Marshall"- G7)

R9   ROBERTSON, DANIEL Fiddler/Composer Pub: **"A Coll. of (New)
     R., Str., Jigs, Waltzes, &c..."** Edin. (c.1805) 26pp.
     [NLS: Glen 356]

R10 ROBERTSON, JAMES STEWART Collector/Fiddler Pub: one of the
     great compilations: **"The Athole Coll. of the Dance Music
     of Scotland"** Edin. (1884) In two vol. (conseq.) 302pp.
     Re-issued 1960 in two volumes. [NLS: Glen 385,385a]

R11 ROSS, ROBERT Music Seller & Publisher, Edin. Pub:
     " A Choice Coll. of Scots Reels or C.D.s & Str. ..." Edin.
     (1780) 40pp. [NLS: Glen 91(1), MH..s.52(3)] See also H3.

Respectfully Dedicated to the Numerous Subscribers

OF MY

MILLER O'HIRN COLLECTION.

Part 1.

The Elgin Collection

OF

Schottisches, Strathspeys, Reels, Hornpipes, &c.

FOR THE VIOLIN & PIANOFORTE,

BY

James Scott Skinner.

MAY BE HAD OF ALL MUSICSELLERS,
OR OF THE AUTHOR AT ELGIN.

ENT. STA. HALL. PRICE 2/6 NET.

The above Collection will be published in four parts. Price 2/each.
these will include the works of Gow, Marshall, Milne, Macintosh &c.

The Logie Collection

of

Original Music

for Voice, Violin and Pianoforte,

comprising

SONGS, SLOW AIRS, PASTORAL MELODIES, STRATHSPEYS,
REELS, QUICKSTEPS, SCHOTTISCHES, GAVOTTES
RONDOS, TARANTELLES Ec

composed by

J. Scott Skinner.

Ent⁴ Sta. Hall

Price 21 .. in Fine Clan Tartan Covers
15 in Cloth Covers
10 in Paper

1888

LONDON: J. B. CRAMER & C⁰, 201 Regent St.W.
EDINBURGH: WOOD & C⁰, 49 George Street.
KEITH: CHARLES MIDDLETON, Music-Publisher
(from whom all Scott Skinners Works may be obtained)

R12   RUTHERFORD, DAVID Music Publisher, London (Very early in
1-3   field of Dance Music) Pub: (1) **"Rutherford's compleat**
       Coll. of 200 of the most celebrated C.D.s both Old & New"
       London (1750) 100pp. [NLS:MH.s.60;DPL] (2) **"Twelve select-**
       ed C.D.s for the Year 1772, with the proper tunes etc..."
       London, 12pp [DPL(Wighton)] (3) **"The Gentleman's Pocket**
       Companion ..." [AUL] (4) "R.'s Choice Coll. of 60 ...CDs"
       - ? 2nd. vol. of (1) 60pp. [NLS: Mus.Box.s.70.16]

       SCHETKY, JOHANN Musician, Edinburgh. Was in Philadelphia
       in company with Alexander Reinagle (after 1786). They both
       published coll. of Scots tunes and other works there. N/L

S4   SHEPHERD, WILLIAM Fiddler/Composer/Music Publisher, Edin.
1-2   (c.1760-1812) (1) **" A Coll. of Str. R., &c..."** (1793) 26pp
       (2) **"A Second Coll. ..."** (c.1800) [NLS: 2 Bks. Glen 345]

S5   SHIRREFS, ANDREW Fiddler/Composer Pub: **"40 Pieces of**
       Orig. Music ..." Edin. (c.1788) 30pp. [Bodleian: F.142;
       NLS: Copy wanting pp2/3, Mus.E.I.67; Sandeman: Be39]

       SIME, D. Publisher, Edin. Pub: "The Edinburgh Musical
       Miscellany, A Coll. of the Most Appr. Scotch, English &
       Irish Songs; set to Music" Vol. (1) 1792; (2) 1793
       [AUL] Not listed.

S7   SKILLERN, THOMAS Publisher, London   Pub:
1-3   (1) **"[S's] Compleat Collection of Dances ..."** * (c.1780)
       [Mitchell (Kidson): M.9190; NLS have Xerox from Mitchell;
       both are wanting pp 101,102 (The titles: "The Maccarony" &
       "Hanoverian Dance"; "The Morning Post" & "Hamilton House")
       (2) **"24 New C.D.s for the year 1795..."** London(1795) 12pp.
       (3) **" 4 Minuets & 12 New & Most Fashionable Scotch &**
       English C.D.s ..." London (n.d.) 21pp. [DPL]
       NOTE: (3) "Composed by William Payne". (* Very rare)

JAMES SCOTT SKINNER
(1843-1927)

S8   SKINNER, JAMES SCOTT Violinist/Composer/Performer, from
3 &   Banchory (1843-1927) last of the so-called Fiddler/Com-
5-10   posers and a most prolific one. Pub:, with other works:
       (1) 12 New Str. & R... Edin. (1865) 6pp. } All re-pub: in
       (2) 30 New Str. & R... Edin. (1868) 16pp.} Logie (S8-6)
       (3) **"The Miller o' Hirn Coll."** Elgin (1881) 71pp.
       (4) "Beauties of the Ballroom" London (1883) 69pp. (Orig.
          pub. Keith, 1883) Not listed. [NLS: MH.s.63,64]
       (5) **"The Elgin Coll. of Schottisches"** Elgin (1883) 25pp.
       (6) **"The Logie Coll."** Keith (1888) 132pp. Some vocal scores
       (7) **"The Scottish Violinist"** London/Glasgow (20th.C) 49pp.
       (8) **"The Harp & Claymore"** London/Glasgow (1903/4) 182pp.
       (9) **"The Cairngorm Series"** London/Glasgow (1920s) Ser:1-9
       (10) **"The Scottish Music Maker"** (Unpublished works listed)
       Many further s/sheets make up JSS's complete output; see
       NLS: (3) Glen 394; (5) MH.110; (6) Glen 326; (7) Mus.Box.
       436.6; (8) Mus.D.1.41; (9) Ask for Fiddle Music List, NLS.
       ("Scottish Music Maker", pub: J. M. Henderson, 1957, has a
       further selection of later work. NLS: Mus.Box.188.22)

S9   STEPHANO, CH. **"100 R., Str., Jigs, H/pipes ..."** London
       (n.d./19th.c) 31pp. [NLS: MH.112(1)]

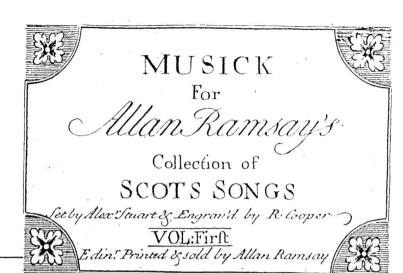

MUSICK
For
Allan Ramsay's
Collection of
SCOTS SONGS
Set by Alexr Stuart & Engrav'd by R. Cooper
VOL: First
Edinr Printed & sold by Allan Ramsay

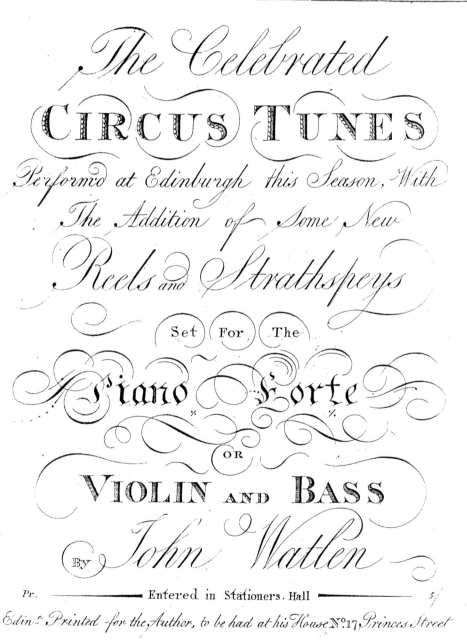

The Celebrated
CIRCUS TUNES
Perform'd at Edinburgh this Season, With
The Addition of Some New
Reels and Strathspeys
Set For The
Piano Forte
OR
VIOLIN AND BASS
By *John Watlen*

Pr. ——— Entered in Stationers. Hall ——— 5/
Edinr Printed for the Author, to be had at his House No 17 Princes Street

Whoever Reprints or Copy's any of the Original Tunes in this Book, Will be Prosicuted
According to Act of Parliment.

S11   STEWART, CHARLES Fiddler/Composer ("Musician to Mr.
1-2   Strange") Pub: (1) **" A Coll. of Str. R., Giggs &c ..."**
      Edin. (1799/1800) 25pp. [NLS: Glen 287(1)]
      (2) **"A Coll. of Minuets, Cotillons etc. ..."** [Sandeman:
      (Athole) Be51 - 2 Bks. bound in one]

S12   STEWART, NEIL Dancing-Master & Publisher, Edin. (c.1730-
      "before 1816") Pub: **"A Coll. of the Newest & Best R. or
      C.D.s for Vn. ..."** Edin. (1761) In 9 Nos.of 8pp. - 1,2
      (1761); 3-6 (1762); 7-9 (thereafter) (2) **"A Select Coll.
      of Scots, English, Irish & Foreign Airs, Jiggs & Marches
      with some of the newest & Most Fashionable Reels ..."**
      ("Vol. 1") Edinburgh 56pp. [AUL]   Neil Stewart also pub:
      "Sel. of Fav. Circus Tunes..." (Edinburgh) and "1st. Sel.
      Coll. of Fav. M., Airs ..." (c1756) Not Listed.

S13   STIRLING, Miss MAGDALINA (of Ardoch, Perthshire) musician,
      Pub: **" 12 Reels ..."** (her own Comp.s) (printed ? privately
      c.1812) [NLS: Mus.E.1.219(15); Sandeman/Athole:Be64]

S14   STRATHSPEYS **"Complete Repos. of Old & New Scotch Str...."**
      "Book 2", Edin. (n.d) 44pp. [NLS: Glen 126]

S15   STRATTON, ALEXANDER Teacher of Mus., Banff Pub: **"A New
      Coll. of Waltzes, Opera Dances, Str. & R. ..."** Banff (n.d)
      28pp. [NLS: MH.e.373]

S16   STUART, A **"Music for Allan Ramsay's Coll. ..."** (c.1728)
      [AUL; DPL; NLS: Inglis 38]

S17   SURENNES, JOHN THOMAS Musician/Collector (b. London 1814
      d. Edin. 1878) Pub: **"The Dance Music of Scotland"*** Edin.
      (1851) 164pp. Also "Songs of Scotland without words"
      (1852-54); "Songs of Ireland" (1855), etc. [NLS:*Glen 211]

T1   TAYLOR, JAMES Fiddler/Composer/Teacher of Mus., Fochabers
1-2   Pub: (1) **"A Coll. of Str. & R. + Set of Scotch Q/rilles"**
      Fochabers (c.1835) 6pp. (2) "A Coll. of Str. & R. ..."
      Edin. (c.1845) 16pp. [NLS: (1) MH.s.333; (2) Glen 278]

      THOMSON, ANDREW "Dance Music for the Vn. ..." Glasgow
      (c.1880) 48pp. [NLS: MH.s.92] Not listed.

      THOMPSON, C & S Publishers: "Thompson's 24 Dances for the
      year 1796..." London [DPL]   Not listed.

      THOMPSON, S,A & P,Publishers:"24 Country Dances ..."[DPL]

T6   THOMSON, WILLIAM Publisher, b. Edinburgh (c.1677) Pub:
1-2   **"Orpheus Caledonius...(Coll. of the best Scotch Songs)"**
      London 1725; in 2 vol.(2nd.Edn.) 1733.[NLS:Ing.242; AUL]

T7   THUMOTH, BURK J. Pub: **"12 Scotch & 12 Irish Airs with var.
      set for the G/fl., Vn etc...."** London (1745/6) in 2 bks.
      [NLS: Bks 1 & 2 - Glen 191; 2 Bks in one - Inglis 79]

T8   TURNBULL, JOHN Musician (1804-44) Pub: **"5 Fav. C.D.s
      Comp. and Arr. ...by Mr. Turnbull."** Edin. (n.d) 3pp.[NLS]

GENERAL NOTE ON SOURCES: There are innumerable references to "Country Dance" and "Dance" books, "pocket companions" and other fancy titles. Almost all of them contain a named tune (the "original") and instructions for dancing; almost all were published in London (or Dublin) between about 1710 and 1810. Many of them contain what may justly be called "Scotch" or Scottish (*) tunes which are interspersed with titles unequivocally English (Irish) in character. Dance enthusiasts have drawn widely from such sources and so have brought examples from them into the Scottish repertoire. In the Editors' view, these fascinating books are something of a specialist study, so such as are included in the Index must be regarded as a representative sample only.

(* A possible parallel to this may be found quoted in "The Songs of Scotland prior to Burns" (Ed: Robt. Chambers, 1890) where a song is described as "...composed by English wits in imitation of the Scots Manner" (See p.304). There is good reason to assume that, while the Scottish or Caledonian Country Dance was at its peak of popularity, it was "imitated" widely for the benefit of the English dancing public, who clearly expected the publishers to provide new amusements every season. Hence, "Dances for the Year ..." produced for decades up to the close of the 18th Century and well into the 19th.)

LATE ENTRY: Book 2nd of Clarkson's "Musical Entertainment" (C23v2) was locked out of the system due to lateness of discovery. (Listed at end of APPENDIX Section)

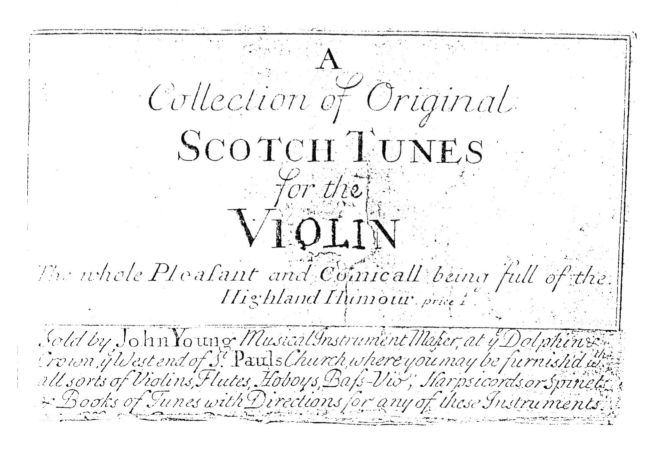

URBANI, PETER (or Pietro) Musician, b. Milan 1749; d.
Dublin 1816. Pub: "A Favourite Sel. of Scots Tunes, ...
arr. as duettos for G/flt. or Vn...." (Edin. 1794-99)
3 books in one. [NLS: Glen 180] Not listed

URQUHART, A. Musician, Edin. Pub: "Aria di Camera ...being
a choice Coll. of Scotch, Irish & Welsh Airs for the Vn."
London (c.1730) [NLS: F.7.g.10/11, Sth. Reading Rm.] N/L
NOTE: An excellent collection of great age and rarity, but
excluded from the Index because of contents (largely
standard titles which may however differ in detail).

W1 WALKER, ALEXANDER Fiddler/Composer (b. Forfar, 1837) and
a gardener to trade. Pub: **"A Coll. of orig. Scottish Str.
R., Marches &c. ..."** Aberdeen (1866) 67pp. [NLS: Glen 324]

W2 WALKER, JAMES Fiddler/Composer, Dysart (c.1760-1840) Pub:
1-2 **"A Coll. of New Scots R., Str., Jigs &c..."** Edin. (1797)
"A Second Coll..." Edin. (1800) - ea. of 14pp., sep. vol.s
[NLS: Glen 290(1) & (2)]

(W3) WALSH, JOHN Collector/Publisher, London. Pub: " Caled.
C.D.s ..." 4 Bks. in one or Vol.1 (c.1744); Vol.2 (c.1768)
(2) "The British Mus. Miscellany..." 6 vol. London (1734)
(3) " C.D.s Selected as Perform'd at Court..." (c.1760)
[NLS; AUL; BL/CPM] Not listed. NOTE: Walsh was clearly a
popular and successful publisher who, with Hare and others
continued a business over many years. His London-printed
collections, even those entitled "Caledonian" and "Scotch"
are, however, so intertwined with southern influences that
they would burden the index. (See "General Note" below).

W4 WATLEN, JOHN Publisher Edinburgh Pub: **"The Celebrated
1-2 Circus Tunes perform'd at Edin. this season ...some new R.
and Str. ..."** Edin. 2 Books (1) 1791, 30pp. (2) 1798, 36pp
[NLS: Glen 286, 2 Bks.]

WILSON, THOMAS, Publisher. "A Companion to the Ball Room"
London, 1816. [NLS, etc.) Contains much material of the
standard type, but may be interesting to connoisseurs of
the dance.

W6 WERNER, FRANCIS **"Book XV111 for the Year 1785, 8 Cotillions, 6 Fav. C.D.s and 2 Minuets"** London (1785) 19pp.[DPL]

WHITE, THE MISSES (See L1 LADIES)

WIGHTON, A.J. (1804-66) To quote Baptie: "Amateur musician
and collector, who proved himself a munificent patron of
art and benefactor to Dundee, by leaving it the noble library of music which bears his name - one of the conditions
being that it is only to be used as a reference library."
[DPL (Wighton) - an index of collections is available]

W7 WRIGHT, DANIEL. Pub:**"A Coll. of Scots, Irish & other airs"**
(No title p.) (c.1735) 26pp. [DPL]

Y1 YOUNG, JOHN Pub: **"A Coll. of orig. Scotch Tunes for the
Vn. The whole pleasant & comicall being full of the Highland Humour."** London (1720) 24pp. [NLS: Inglis 26]

Musical Theme Coding

A NOTE ON "NUMERICAL REPRESENTATION"

(MUSICAL THEME CODING)

The system used in this index for identifying musical themes is based on the work of the late Breandan Breathnach, the great Irish traditional music expert, editor of "Ceol Rince na hEireann", a collection of Irish dance music published in 1963 and of much else besides. The editors of The Scottish Fiddle Music Index acknowledge with gratitude the efficiency of the Numerical Representation system when applied to traditional music sharing the same ancestry.

HOW TO READ AND SET OUT MUSICAL THEME CODES

FIRST: establish the "Key Note"

SECOND: establish the Time Signature

THIRD: build the Theme Code, based upon Key and Time Signatures

Establishing the Key Note and setting out the Code

The Key Note is that to which the music returns naturally (as when finishing the phrase with a chord). In the majority of cases, this would normally be a simple matter of checking the key signature against the last note of the first eight bars of music*. For example:

3 Sharps (Key of A Major) Last Note: A Key Note: A
No Sharps (Key of A Minor or C Major)
                Last Note: A Key Note: A
                Last Note: C Key Note: C
1 Flat (Key of F Major)   Last Note: F Key Note: F etc., etc.

THE KEY NOTE IS REPRESENTED BY THE FIGURE "1"
This means that the CODE remains the same, no matter how many different keys the music may have been arranged in over the years.

* Where the first section of a melody does not return to the Key Note, thus producing doubt as to key, the best test is to try the "finishing chord". Among the older collections, there are examples of keys which can, literally, be "disputed"; however, these are rare.

Numbering the first note of the music

Now turn to the FIRST BEAT NOTE of the music. If it happens also to be the Key Note, it receives the coding "1". If it does not, it will receive the coding 2,3,4,5,6 or 7 ascending the scale.

Music set in the octave starting at Middle C (or ascending, to B Natural) are represented by the figures 1 to 7. For example:

Key of C Major: Key Note C = 1 (Note 7 = B Natural)
Key of D Major Key Note D = 1 (Note 7 = C Sharp) ... and so on

A note which falls in the octave BELOW this central octave (eg: in C Major, below Middle C), is followed by the letter "L" (1L to 7L); two octaves below, by the letter "F" (1F to 7F).

A note which falls in the octave ABOVE (eg: in C Major, the C above Middle C, ascending) is followed by the letter "H" (1H to 7H); two octaves above, by the letter "T" (1T to 7T).

In the MINOR MODE, the altered notes are indicated by a ♭ symbol.

If an accidental occurs on the beat of the music, interrupting the natural progression of the scale, it is indicated by a ♯ or a ♭

Grouping the codes according to Time Signature

The Musical Theme Code uses ONLY THE BEAT NOTES in the music. Though it may be decorated with quavers or many more notes of values less than a crotchet, the Code uses only the note which falls on the beat.

If a beat note is of LONGER DURATION than a crotchet, each beat within it is represented by the SAME FIGURE (eg: two beats to a minim, etc.)

If a beat falls on a rest in the music, it is indicated by "0" (Zero).

The number of BEATS used in the Musical Theme Code varies according to the Time Signature, but the code itself always fall into two groups

CODE A	&	CODE B

CODES GROUPED IN FOURS:
4/4 time has 4 beats to the bar and uses the first 2 bars of the melody
2/2 time (or ¢) may be regarded as the same as 4/4 for this purpose
2/4 time has 2 beats to the bar and uses the first 4 bars of the melody
6/8 time should be treated in the same way as 2/4 time (use 4 bars)
CODES GROUPED IN THREES:
3/4 time has 3 beats to the bar and uses the first 2 bars of the melody
9/8 time should be treated in the same way as 3/4 time (use 2 bars)
LESS FAMILIAR TIME SIGNATURES:
12/8 time with 4 beats to the bar uses the first two bars (Fours)
3/8 time with (in effect) one beat uses the first 6 bars (Threes)
6/4 time (in effect double 3/4 time) uses the first bar only (Threes)

Reading Theme Codes

Each melody in the Main Index has been given a Theme Code. Once having mastered the rules above, it should be possible to use the Theme Codes for cross- referencing. The various purposes to which these can be put are explained in the following section "Using the Theme Code Index".

Setting out Theme Codes

With a suitable photocopy of the music to hand, the numbers can be written under the beat notes directly. If the music is not in written form, it is as well to scribble down the first 8 bars of the music on manuscript and work from that. If the piece is in the Index, it can then be traced against the Theme Code Index (to give its title/s) and in the A-Z Index for its source.

USING THE THEME CODE INDEX

Once you have cracked the coding system, the THEME CODE INDEX can be brought fully into play. It has three purposes:

1. To facilitate a search for any tune of which the title is unknown or temporarily forgotten. Just the first two bars, a Key Note and Time Signature are all it is necessary to remember.

2. To create a cross-referencing system whereby tunes with a shared melody can be found listed together. Many of the older traditional tunes have been published under one or more titles, sometimes, it has been argued, for not entirely innocent reasons (For example, the Gows are alleged to have "borrowed" a number of tunes by Marshall and others and republished them under different titles). In the case of some of the most familiar vocal melodies, short titles and first lines are virtually interchangeable and this has led to confusion in the past.

3. To indicate, by means of the letter prefix (I) or (II), if a tune has been re-published in the later period (from about 1844 onwards). They are left in duplicate for a practical reason: When obtaining copies from library editions of books long out of print, the rule tends to be that pre-1800 volumes are stored on microfiche or film and are expensive to reproduce, whereas later collections may normally be photocopied for a fraction of the cost. It is always as well to ascertain how the material is stored.

THE PROGRESSION is numerical, beginning at the lowest CODE A coding (1L1L1L1L) and ending with the highest (1T1T3T1T) without any sub-division. Use the title and the letter prefix (I) or (II) to return to the appropriate A-Z section.

Examples of Theme Codes

Ossian's Hall (First four bars)   (Collection: John Anderson)

3 5 6 5   2 2 7♭2

The key is A Major; hum or play through the first two bars and this is confirmed. ₵ (or 2/2) is the same as 4/4 for the purpose of this exercise!

Sr. Adam Ferguson's Reel   (John Riddell of Ayr)

5L 1 1   2 4L 7♭L 7♭L 1

The key is E Minor; hum or play through the first two bars, then check the end of the phrase to verify the key signature

My Bonny Laddie has my Heart   (William Christie)

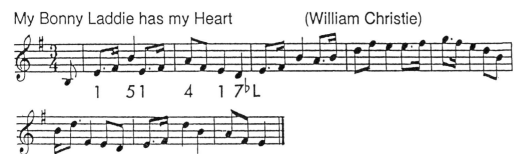

1 51   4 1 7♭L

The key is again E Minor; proceed as above to verify. 3/4 time gives a 6-digit numerical theme code, three beats to each bar.

Kiss me Fast   (James Aird)

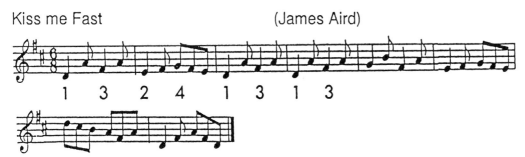

1 3 2 4   1 3 1 3

The key is D Major; verify as above. 6/8 time produces a dotted crotchet beat, so the 8-digit theme code occurs two to a bar and employs four bars of the music.

Examples of numbered scales

IN THE KEY OF

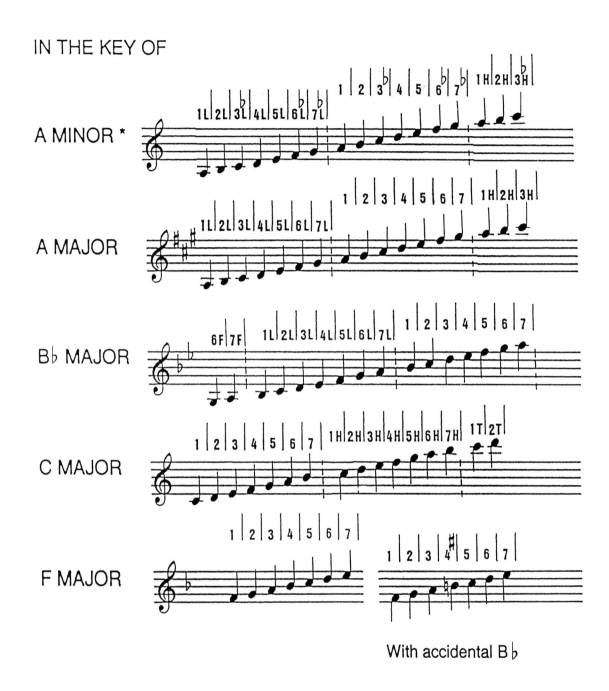

With accidental B♭

* Other MINOR KEYS which may occur in the Index are: E, B, F#, D & G
The altered notes fall on the **3rd, 6th & 7th** in each case, though the
actual notes on which they fall may vary according to key. Each note
altered is indicated by the ♭ symbol, as in the Am example.

4

TUNE TITLE INDEX (A-Z) (I)

The music of the period c.1700-1845, including William Marshall's "posthumous" collection

TITLE	CODE A	CODE B	KEY SIG	TIME SIG	SOURCE CODE/S

When a (II) is inserted under SOURCE CODE it indicates that the
piece was re-published in the 19th Century and can be referred
to in Section (II) also.

Title					
A BHANAIS IORTACH [A'BHANAIS IRTEACH]	1115	236L5L	A	2/2	F2v2p13(3)
A BHANARACH DHONN A' CHRUIDH	117b	511	A	3/4	Mc5p16
A BHEAN AN TAIGH NACH LEIG U STEACH	1111	516L6L	Bb	2/4	F2v2p58(48)
AM FEAR A THA AIR FOGAIRT					
A' BHLIADHNA GUS AN AIMSIR SO	5L5L15L	113b4L	A	6/8	Mc5p4
A' BODY LO'ES ME	1H1H62H	1H1H3H3H	D	2/2	S12v1p18 O1v1Fp16
A' BODY'S LIKE TO BE MARRI'D BUT ME	3131	1H2H65	G	6/8	C5v3p74
A 'CHEUD LUAN DO'N RAIDH	3b23b7bL	3b43b3b	E	4/4	Mc5p29
A CHRIODHALACHD [A' CHRIDHEALACHD]	3531H	357b2	F	2/2	F2v2p22(12) (II)
A DHONAIL RUAIDH GHAOLAICH	556	531	G	3/4	Mc5p17
A DO ADE A DO DH'FHALBH MI	51H5H6	5H3H3H1H	D	6/8	Mc5p11
A FAVOURITE COTILLON	3555	1H1H75	G	2/4	D15v2p37,38
A' FOR THE LOVE O' NANNY	3331H	5221	G	4/4	C5v3p66
A' GHLAS MHEUR	3333	2322	A G	4/4	Mc5p42 Mc1v1p7-12
A LEANNAIN MO RUIN	3b3b4#	552	A	3/4	Mc1v1p117
A. MARSHALL'S REEL	3561H	351H2H	C	2/2	C14v8p6
A MHIC IAIN MHIC SHEUMAIS	51H1H	61H5	D	3/4	Mc1v1p117
A PHIURAG GHAOLACH	1141	1154	A	6/8	C4p71 Mc5p5
A ROBAIDH, THA THU GORACH	426L1	5L5L11	A	4/4	Mc5p25
A ROCK AND A WEE PICKLE TOW	1262	3331	G	6/8	A1v1p67
A (SUPPOSED) CONFAB	1111	3311	G	4/4	G10v6p26
BETWEEN A QUAKER AND A SECEEDER					
A WAYS MY HEART THAT WE MUN SUNDER	3555	6665	C	2/2	P7p14
ABBOT'S STRATHSPEY, THE	3555	1H3H1H6	D	2/2	P9p13
ABERCAIRNEY HOUSE	53b53b	4242	G	4/4	G10v5p7
ABERCAIRNEY HOUSE [ABERCAIRNY HOUSE]	11H1H3bH	7b7b47bL	C	2/2	Mc4v3p4/5 (II)
ABERCARNEY'S REEL	13b53b	7bL27bL7bL	A	2/2	Mc9v1p25
ABERCORN WEDDING, THE	5326L	531H1H	A	2/2	T1v1p6
ABERCROMBIE PLACE	115L7bL	113b5	G	4/4	P9p24,25
ABERDEEN ASSEMBLY, THE	3135	317L2	Bb	6/8	A7v1p16
ABERDEEN BARRACKS, THE	1H1H2H5H	3H1H1H5	D	2/4	D6p18
ABERDEEN HOTEL	1H31H3	1H3H2H5L	D	6/8	D6p27
ABERDEEN HUNT	5L13b5	7b422	G	4/4	P5v1p3
ABERDEEN HUNT, THE	5351H	5562	F	6/8	A7v1p2
ABERDEEN RACES	15L5L5L	15L6L2L	Bb	6/8	Mc13v1p8 Mc13v2p8
ABERDEEN RACES, THE	5L13b2	7bL43b5	E	4/4	A7v3p18
(ABERDEEN) SCOTS MEASURE, (A/THE)	11H1H5H	3H3H1H1H	D	4/4*	O1v1Ep16 O1v4p12
ABERLOUR'S SQUEEZE	1H1H2H1H	51H2H4H	C	4/4	M4v3p44 (II)
ABOUT SHE GOES	151H5	4344	A	6/8	R12v2p1
ABOYNE CASTLE	5511	6L47L5L	E	2/4	Mc21v2p19 P5v1p21
ABOYNE CASTLE	315L5L	1L5L2L2L	A	4/4	T1v1p5
ABROAD AND AT HOME	3461	7L135L	Bb	6/8	C26v1p8
ACHARNAC'S REELL	5555	5562	D	4/4	C33p2
ACHORACHAN	5315L	1462	F	4/4	M4v3p53
ADESTE FIDELES	15L25L	3332	A	2/4	E1v1p100
ADIEU EDINA'S FRIENDLY TOW'RS	5H1H2H1H	1H2H3H4H	D	4/4	C5v2p27
ADIEU MY NATIVE LAND ADIEU	1H1H3H4H	3H1H1H1H	C	4/4	E1v2p107
ADIEU (TO FORTGEORGE)	4H3H2H5	44H3H2H	D	4/4*	A7v6p59 A7v5p10
ADIEW	4325L	4L432	Bb	2/4	A7v3p17
ADI. MITCHEL'S WALTZ	115L5L	5555	C	3/8	C14v15p3
ADMIRAL HOWE'S MARCH	1357	1H1H1H2H	D	4/4	A1v5p30 C5v1p30
ADMIRAL McBRIDE'S HORNPIPE	1754	36L16L	Eb	2/2	C14v10p3
ADMIRAL RODNEY'S TRIUMPH	1131	4325L	A	6/8	B16v3p56
ADMIRAL VERNON'S MARCH	1H1H1H3H	1H113	D	4/4	R12v3p23
ADVENTURE AT MARGATE, AN	5H5H6H5H	5H5H4H3H	C	6/8	S7v1p11
A.F. GRAY ESQr's HORNPIPE	111H1H	3H1H71H	D	4/4	D6p37
AFFRONT TAKEN, THE	1H531	44H1H6	F	2/2	B16v1p3
AFTON WATER	132	243	A F G	3/4	C6p21 (J3) C5v1p32
					C5v2p5 A1v5p32
AH! CA! IRA	1111	5531	G	4/4*	W4v1p25 A1v4p41 C5v1p41
AH! PERDONA	1H5H1H1H	61H3H3H	C	2/4	B7p18
AH SURE A PAIR	1351H	1H452	G	6/8	B7p4
AIKEN DRUM	3332	4443	G	4/4	E1v1p98 C5v2p71 G10v4p12
AIKEN DRUM	3H3H3H2H	661H1H	D	4/4	C8v2p52
AILEEN A ROON	5L6L1	221	G	3/4	O1v1Ep21 O1v5p12,13
AILEEN AROON	567	1H1H3H	D	3/4	C5v1p29 T7p26,27 K1v2p13
					A1v5p29 G11v2Bp11 Mc23p28
AIR	351H1	647L5L	E	2/4	Mc21v1p28,29
AIR	31H4H3H	2H5H3H2H	D	2/4	R12v3p17
AIR	1H53bH1H	2H51H1H	G	4/4	Mc21v1p21
AIR	3525	1443	A	4/4	Mc21v1p24,25
AIR	3L143	2532	Bb	2/4	H1p3
AIR	513	222	D	3/4	Mc21v1p26
AIR	111	23b1	G	3/2	Mc21v1p20
AIR BY DR BOYCE	3bH2H53bH	42H03b	E	2/2	P8v1p1
AIR BY FINGAL	5H3H2H6	1H1H3H3H	C	4/4	B11p32
AIR BY FINGAL	6H5H4H3H	2H2H6H6H	C	4/4	B11p32
AIR BY FINGAL	1H3H6	551H	C	3/4	B11p32
AIR BY MR ARNE	13b45	6b554	B	2/2	P8v1p7
AIR DE CHASSE	1152	3211	A	6/8	A1v3p225
AIR ESPAGNOL	1342	3210	Bb	6/8	B4p3,4
AIR FLAMAND	2311	2533	Bb	2/4	B4p18

Title					
AIR IN FORTUNATUS	3H1T5H5	33H2H2H	D	6/8	S12v2p22,23
AIR IN QUEEN MAB	5H3H3H6H	5H4H3H2H	D	6/8	S12v2p6,7
AIR IN STEIBELT'S STORM	3H4H5H3H	1H2H1H2H	D	6/8	B7p4
AIR M'ALLUIN BHEIRIN POG DHI	5313	51H62	Eb	2/2	F2v2p68,69(58/9)
[AIR M'FHALLUINN BHEIRINN...]					
AIR OF THE ISLE OF SKYE	1H1H1H7	5534	G	4/4	B7p20
AIRE DE L'OPERA FRANCOISE	1155	61H55	G	4/4	A1v2p62
AIRIAL FLIGHT, THE	5123	6523	F	6/8	G9v5p34
AIRNDALLY HOUSE	3135L	5132	F	2/2	A7v3p8,9
AIRS IN PYRAMUS AND THISBE	351H1H	2H543	G	2/2	P8v2p25-28
AIRSHIRE LASSES, THE	532H2H	3H3H1H6	C	4/4	C14v16p14
AIRTH CASTLE	1H135	41H22H	F	6/8	B20p7
AISLING	1H342	6555	D	4/4	Mc5p29
AITKEN'S REEL	1347L	6L5L4L2L	Bb	2/2	Mc13v1p8 Mc13v2p8
ALACK & A' WALL A DAY	751H3b	43b10	E	6/8	C20p73 O1v1Hp61
ALAMODE BEEF HOUSE, THE	5L5L15L	1232	Bb	6/8	C1v1p3
ALASTAIR M'ANSACHD	331H	216	F	3/4	F2v2p63(53) Mc5p30
[ALASTAIR M'ANNSACHD]					
ALASTAIR OG	3b21	27bL1	E	3/4	Mc5p30
ALBINA	1H3H2H1H	1H3H2H1H	D	6/8	A1v1p22
ALBINIA	1321	1321	Bb	6/8	S7v1p13
ALDAVALIGH	5L111	6L222	D	2/2	Mc9v1p24
ALDAVALOCH	5L111	6L242	D	4/4	G11v2Ap3 K1v1p3
ALDER-WOOD HOUSE	5H3H1H5	1H2H4H2H	C	6/8	L1p4
ALDRIDGE'S ALLEMAND	2H1H2H1H	661H1H	D	2/4	Mc9v2p37 A1v1p65
ALDRIDGE'S DANCE	3131	2427L	G Bb	6/8	A1v2p38 Mc9v2p16
ALDRIDGE'S HORNPIPE	1L5L35L	2L6L46L	Bb	2/2	Mc9v2p36
ALDRIDGE'S JIGG	5L3L1L1	322L2	Bb	6/8	D16p36
ALDRIGE FAVORITE HORNPIPE	113L1	27L5L2	Bb	2/4	A7v2p36
ALDRIGE HORNPIPE	1H1H31H	2H752H	C	2/4	A7v5p30 A7v6p39
ALE WIFE AND HER BARREL, THE	1122	1155	G	4/4*	A1v2p27 S12v1p52 R12v1p98
ALE WIFE AND HER BARREL, THE	1113	2121	G	2/2	O1v1Hp56,57
ALEE MARLEY	3111H	317bL7b	G	6/8	R12v1p68
ALEGRO [ALLEGRO]	136L2	7L5L15	F	6/8	D15v2p7
ALENBANK HOUSE	1L1L5L3b	4427bL	G	4/4	G8p28
ALEXANDER STEWART, ESQr	5651H	4542	D	2/2	Mc19v3p21
OF GLENCREPISD(A)LE'S STRATHSPEY					
ALEXANDER, THE	3543	1213	G	6/8	H6v22p3
ALEXr ARTHUR DUFF ESQr	3342	31H51H	G	2/2	M12p16
ALEXr BRODIE'S ESQR. STRATHSPEY	351H3H	5622H	C	4/4	A7v1p8
ALEXr. CHIVAS ESQr's HORNPIPE	1133	51H54	D	4/4	D6p36,37
ALEXr McGLASHAN'S FAREWELL	1555L	6L5L44	G	4/4	G9v5p26
ALL HAIL TO THEE THOU BALMY ROSE	3H3H2H	665	D	3/4	C5v2p36
ALL IN A BUSTLE	55L2L2	35L6L5L	G	6/8	P9p20
ALL IN THE DOWNS	51H2H	3bH2H1H	E D	3/4	A1v6p28
ALL THE WORLD'S A STAGE	311H1H	545L2	D	4/4	P9p31
ALLAMAND	1342	37L22	Bb	2/4	D15v2p20
ALLAN LOGANS CANT	117bL1	3b3b50	E	4/4	C5v3p61
ALLAN RAMSAY	5333	47bL7b7bL	A	6/8	K1v2p28 G11v2Bp26
ALLAN WATER	1133	6623	G	4/4	P4p12
ALLAN WATER	1131H	5221	D F G	4/4*	N1v2p37 Y1p18 P7p12 T6v2p65
					(J3) O1v1D25 Mc8v1Cp80
					Mc8v2Ap21 C20p49 P8v2p39
ALLEGRETTO	354H2H	6542	D	2/4	M2p27
ALLEGRETTO	1H4H5H4H	3H4H71H	C	2/4	M2p34,35
ALLEGRETTO	151H5	52H4H1H	D	2/4	M2p16,17
ALLEGRETTO	5562	3217L	G	6/8	M2p15
ALLEGRETTO	3H72H1H	51H3H2H	D	6/8	M2p9
ALLEGRETTO	3H3H2H2H	3H4H1H1H	D	6/8	M2p12,13
ALLEGRETTO	15L5L5L	4332	Bb	6/8	D15v2p32
ALLEGRETTO	5231	5266	D	6/8	M2p23
ALLEGRO	1122	3332	A	4/4	M2p24
ALLEGRO	5433	2253	G	2/4	D15v2p25,26
ALLEGRO	1231H	6413	D	2/4	M2p19
ALLEGRO	1355	661H1H	F	2/4	D15v2p34
ALLEGRO	551H7	6543	Bb	2/4	D15v2p41
ALLEGRO	1H1H77	1H1H5H5H	D	2/2	M2p13
ALLEGRO	1H1H2H2H	4H2H1H6	D	4/4	M2p17
ALLEGRO	1H1H5H5H	1T7H5H5H	D	2/4	M2p28
ALLEGRO	3334	5430	D	2/2	M2p20
ALLEGRO	1H553	4111	G	2/4	M2p25
ALLEGRO	3H1H53	5551H	D	2/2	M2p9
ALLEGRO	1021	3043	Bb	2/4	M2p33
ALLEGRO	115L5L	115L5L	G	2/2	M2p15
ALLEGRO	1H2H67	457L2	D	6/8	M2p18,19
ALLEGRO	1H2H1H1H	661H2H	D	6/8	M2p27
ALLEGRO	3H522H	3H561H	D	6/8	M2p29
ALLEGRO	5H1H2H5	6L242	C	6/8	M2p30,31
ALLEGRO	3H2H5H1H	2H1H55	Eb	6/8	M2p7
ALLEGRO	5322	4215L	G	6/8	M2p26
ALLEGRO	1H3H2H3H	51H3H2H	D	6/8	M2p5
ALLEGRO MODERATO	5H3H5H5H	6H5H5H6H	D	2/2	P8v1p13

ALLEMAND	3524	627L5L	Bb	2/4	C12p5
ALLEMAND DE GRACS	11H13H	5L2H11H	D	2/4	Mc9v2p19
ALLEMANDA	1H3H2H4H	1H3H2H5	D	2/4	A1v3p156
ALLEMANDA	1H3H5H5H	3H2H1H1H	C	2/4	A1v3p201
ALLEMANDA	1H5H1H6H	5H4H1H1H	D	6/8	A1v3p202
ALLEMANDE	1H1H3H3H	2H2H1H1H	D	2/4	A1v1p28
ALLOA HOUSE	5L12	3b3b2	G	3/4	Mc8v1Ap25 Mc8v2Ap12 G17p12
					P4p18,19 C20p21
ALLOA HOUSE	15L1	3b3b2	G E A B	3/4	C13v3p58,59 N1v2p54 (J3)
					O1v1Ap24 O1v2p21 C5v2p12
					G1v1p5
ALL'S RIGHT AT LAST	1H1H1H3H	4H2H63H	D	2/2	P9p31
ALL'S WELL	1111	3210	G	2/4	E1v2p52
ALLY CROAKER	1H1H1H1H	2H72H4H	D	2/4	E1v1p96,97
ALLY CROAKER	1111	27L24	G	2/4	C14v9p20
ALNWICK LODGE	5551H	5564	G	4/4	C14v22p7
ALPINE WALTZ	33H2H	1H55	G	3/4	G13p4
ALWAYS IN HUMOUR (/NEVER OUT OF HUMOUR)	1552	1555	D	2/2	Mc9v1p7 C13v1p11
ALWAYS PRETTY	1H1H65	13H75	D	2/4	A1v5p58 C5v1p58
AM BODACH A CHIANAMH	152	151	D	9/8	P5v1p18
AM BOTAL DUDH S'AN SLEIGA CHREACHUN	111H5	5642	F	2/2	F2v2p21(11)
[AM BOTAL DUBH...]					
AM BREACDHAN UR GU MEAL U E	3535	357b7bL	E	2/2	F2v2p104(94)
[AM BREACAN UR GUM MEAL THU E]					
AM FASAN AIG NO CAILLEAGAN	3b13b7bL	3b154	F	2/2	F2v2p100(90)
[AM FASAN AIG NA CAILEAGAN]					
AM MONADH LIADH [AM MONADH LIATH]	3bL1L15L	7bL4L2L7bF	B	4/4	F2v2p78,79(68/9)
AMAZON, THE	3H3H5H1H	2H1H1H1H	D	4/4	A1v3p227
AMBELREE [AMBULREE] [AMULREE]	3344	3327bL	G	2/2	G11v2Cp13 (II)
AMBIGNO	5H3H1H1H	4H2H77	D	6/8	R12v1p46
AMELIA	3142	3125L	A	2/2	C14v18p24
AMERICAN REEL	1H51H5	1H564	A	2/2	G9v5p28
AMOROUS GODDESS, (THE)	3H2H3H5H	3H1H1H5	D	4/4*	R12v1p81 A1v1p56
AMOROUS LOVER, THE	1434	5422	A	4/4	Mc1v1Ap7
AN AIR BY BARON KILMANSECK	1H1H2H2H	3bH555H	C	2/2	W7p25
AN COISIR [AN CHOISIR]	113L1	6L27L2	G	2/2	F2v2p80(70)
AN CRANN TAIRADH [AN CRANN-TARA]	3336	1H1H72H	Eb	6/8	F2v2p98(88)
AN CRONAN MUILEACH	1155	7bL6L7bL1	G	2/2	C10v2Bp61
AN CRONAN MUILLACH [AN CRONAN MUILEACH]	117L5L	3b3b42	A	4/4	F2v2p92,93(82/3)
AN CRUINEACHADH IOMLAN LUDHAIR	1H351H	2H1H52	D	6/8	F2v2p44(34)
[AN CRUINNEACHADH IOMLAN LUTHMHOR]					
AN CUALA SIBHS A'BHANAIS BHAN	2H1H65	6461H	C	4/4	Mc5p16
AN DILEACDHAN [AN DILLEACHDAN]	1H3bH1H5	3bH4H5H5	C	4/4	F2v2p15(5)
(A)N' EACAIG [AN EUCHDAG]	315	217L	Bb	3/4	F2v2p51(41) F2v1p9
AN FHIR' GHRUAIG [A'PHIORBHUIC]	1H1H2H7	1H653	G	2/2	F2v2p37(27)
AN GILLE DUBH CIAR DHUBH	1H754	4565	D	4/4	Mc5p22,23
AN GROATHA	1215	5555	G	2/4	Mc1v1p80-83
AN IRISH JIGG	5555	661H3H	D	6/8	A1v5p67
AN JORRAM	1H3H1H6	1H631	G	12/8	Mc5p28
(AN') O FOR ANE AND TWENTY TAM	5362	5266L	F G	6/8	(J3) C5v3p72 G1v1p35
AN OLD WELSH TUNE	113b	443b	G	3/4	P4p15
AN ORIGINAL SCOTCH HORNPIPE	31H51H	62H31H	D	2/4	G11v1Cp19
AN REIR BHRUADAIR MI M'CHADAL	3b13b	113b	A	3/4	Mc5p20
AN SEALLADH MO DHEIREADH DO	3b217bL	3b215	G	6/8	F2v2p94(84)
THUG TEARLACH					
AN SEANN STAOILEADH [AN SEANN STOILE]	5L13b1	3b7bL3b7bL	D	4/4	F2v2p86(76)
AN T' SEALG	5547L	5515	G	4/4	F2v2p80(70)
AN T'AISEADH DO DH'EIREANN	3b5L3bL5	24L2L4	F	12/8	F2v2p46(36)
AN TALL 'AM BU GNA DO MHACLEOID	533	15L5L	F	3/4	F2v2p23(13)
AN THE KIRK WAD LET ME BE	111	356	G	3/4	Mc8v1Ap18,19 C20p37
AN THOU WERE MINE AIN THING	5L5L13	326L3	A	4/4	G17p4
AN THOU WERE MY AIN THING	5572H	2H2H63H	D	4/4	C5v2p8
AN' THOU WERE MY AIN THING	5L5L13	226L6L	A	4/4	P4p22 O1v1Bp16 O1v4p29
AN THOU WERE MY AIN THING	5L5L13	226L3	A	4/4	C20p46
AN TOISEACHD	5L131	47L7bL4	D	4/4	F2v2p45(35)
AN TUR A BHITHINN URAD	117bL	7bL7bL55L	A	6/8	Mc5p5
AN YE HAD BEEN WHERE I HA'E BEEN	3H4H4H5H	3H4H3HO	D	2/4	A1v2p21
AN YE HAD BEEN WHERE I HAVE BEEN/	3H3H4H4H	3H4H3HO	D	2/2*	Mc8v1Bp43 Mc8v2Cp19 O1v1Ip80,81
YOU WOULD NOT BE(EN) SO CANTY					
AND I WONDER WHEN I'LL BE MARRIED	51H7b	6b53b	D	9/8	E1v2p138
AND THE KIRK WOULD LET ME BE	111	351H	G	3/4	O1v1Cp14
AND THE KIRK WOULD LET ME BE	111	356	D	6/4	S16p42,43 C29p41
(AND) THIS IS NO MINE AIN (HOUSE/THIN)	353H2H	1H57b2	D	2/2*	T6v2p72 C4p62 P8v2p16
AND THOU WERE MY AIN THING	5L5L13	226L3	A	4/4	C29p10 N1v2p34 S16p138,139
					(J3) Mc8v1Cp83 Mc8v2Ap6
AND WHEN SHE CAME BEN SHE BOBED	113b	3b3b3b	B	6/4	P7p17
AND WILL YOU BE	1H12H2	3H5H2H7	D	6/8	A1v2p54
AND YE SHALL WALK IN SILK ATTIRE	3H4H1T2T	5H6H3H2H	C	2/4	E1v2p80
ANDANTE	5364	531H1H	F	4/4	D15v2p15
ANDANTE	3350	2240	Eb	4/4	M2p6
ANDANTE	3355	1H1H5O	F	4/4	M2p10,11
ANDANTE	1H552	367L5L	Bb	2/4	M2p32,33

ANDANTE	5633	61H53	G	2/4	D15v2p43,44
ANDANTE	1531H	5622	G	2/4	M2p14,15
ANDANTE	1552	1555	Eb	6/8	M2p21
ANDANTE	16L6L1	5552	Bb	6/8	D15v2p11
ANDANTE GRASIOSO	5542	1232	E	2/4	D15v2p9
ANDANTINO	5532	4671H	G	2/4	P8v1p11
ANDANTINO	1122	3125L	Bb	6/8	D15v2p41
ANDERSON'S (FAREWELL/RANT)	13b55	7b7b27bL	E	2/2	H3p31 H1p20
ANDERSON'S FAVORITE	351H5	7b424	G	2/2	A7v1p15
ANDERSON'S MUSIC SHOP	1H1H5H5H	4H3H72H	C	2/2	C21p10,11
ANDERSON'S RANT	151H1H	5122	C	2/2	M4v1p7 (II)
ANDREW AND HIS CUTTIE GUN	5442	5441	G	4/4	G10v1p23,24 G11v1Cp12
ANDREW AND HIS CUTTY GUN	5142	5241	E A	2/4	A1v2p14
ANDREW CAREY	1H55	1H1H2H	D	9/8	A1v5p40
ANDREW CAREY	1H55	1H1H2H	D	9/8	C5v1p40
ANDREW CARR	355	467	D	9/8	K1v1p38 G11v2Ap36 (II)
ANDREW KERR	57b7b	51H2H	E	9/8	W7p6
ANDREW KERR	1H65	22H7	D	9/8	A7v3p14
ANDROMEDA, THE	1H655	553H4H	D	6/8	B11p28,29
ANDROMEDA, THE	16L5L5L	5L5L34	A	6/8	L1p19
ANGEL'S WHISPER, THE	117L5L	5L131	Bb	4/4	C8v1p40
ANN THOU WERE MY AIN THING	551H2H	4H2H66	C D	4/4	T6v1p47 P8v2p43
ANNA	1H1H3H3H	2H1H55	C	4/4	(C25)
ANNA HUME	3355	1H2H1H7	G	4/4	C5v2p58
ANNA THUG MI GRADH DHUIT	113L1	3216L	A	2/2	F2v2p20(10)
ANNEN POLKA [ANNAN POLKA]	5374	541H5	G	2/4	C8v2p52
ANNIE & COLIN	5212	4323	G	2/2	O1v1lp70
ANNIE LAURIE	11H70	5332	D	2/4	C8v2p46
ANNIE'S SCOTS MEASURE	5L117bL	5L3b3b3b	G	2/2	O1v1Fp8
ANNON SIDE	3bH2H51H	3bH5H3bH2H	E	4/4	O1v1Lp140
ANOTHER [St KILDA SONG AND DANCE]	3165	1H522	A	4/4	Mc5p31
ANTHIA (THE LOVELY)	3b254	6b422	G	4/4	O1v5p2 O1v1Dp8
ANTHONY MURRAY'S REEL	3L13L1	15L2L2L	A	2/2	Mc9v1p15
ANTIGUA BILLEY	133	133	G	9/8	R12v1p27
ANWICK LODGE [ALNWICK LODGE]	3355	6421	Bb	4/4	E2p9 G11v2Dp14
AP SHENKIN	4376	5532	F	6/8	C8v1p51
AP SHENKIN	5366	5542	D	6/8	C14v22p22
AP SHENKIN	3366	5532	G F	6/8	C8v2p21 P6v1p7 D15v2p38
APPIE McNABB	1H1H7b	1H7b5	D	3/4	O1v1Fp18,19
APPIN HOUSE	3133	26L22	A	2/2	G11v2Dp33 Mc9v1p21 (II)
ARABELLA	437L2	3356	G	4/4	C14v17p10
ARAIDH NAM BADAN	5153	3261H	G	6/8	A1v5p66 Mc5p32
ARBROATH ASSEMBLY	7551	7522	D	6/8	D16p10
ARCHd BUTTER, ESQr. OF PITLOCHRIE'S R.	331H5	6575	F	2/2*	Mc19v1p11 Mc19v2p14
ARDEMERSAY COTTAGE	5122	5151H	D	4/4	Mc16p25
ARDKINLASS'S DELIGHT	3561H	2H3H5H5H	D	2/2	A1v3p178
ARNDILLY'S REEL	3331	2227L	A	4/4*	A7v6p43 C33p8
ARDOCH HOUSE	5555	4H2H4H6	D	4/4	S13p3
ARDROSSAN CANAL, THE	1353	6L5L5L5L	F	4/4	G10v5p26
(ARE YOU) ALWAYS PLEASED	3152	3151	D	4/4*	M12p12 Mc9v1p2
ARGYLE IS MY NAME	51H3H2H	3H3H51H	C D	6/8	C6p14 C8v2p62 E1v2p55
ARGYLESHIRE DANCE	3bL1L1L5	553b5	D	4/4	C10v2Bp98
ARGYLL IS MY NAME	5L132	335L1	G Bb	6/8	(J3) G13p3
ARGYLL'S BOULING GREEN	11H1H3H	2H1H53	C	4/4	B15v1p70,71
ARGYLL('S) BOWLING GREEN, (THE)	11H1H3H	1H1H53	C	2/2	G11v2Dp31 N1v1p23 (II)
ARIA	5H55H5H	4H44H4H	E	4/4	R12v3p16
ARIDH NA M'BADAN	5155	3261H	F	6/8	F2v2p23(13)
ARMENIA	5523	5L142	G	6/8	G1v2p86
ARMSTRONG'S FAREWELL	554	3b17bL	G	3/4	O1v1lp75
ARNDILLY HOUSE	5L153	447L2	A	4/4	G15p19
ARNE'S GIGG	1333	7L222	G	2/2	S12v1p60
ARNISTON HOUSE	11H7b4	11H1H3bH	C	6/8	G10v4p6,7
ARRIVALS FROM INDIA	4253	427L5L	A	2/2	P9p31
ARROCAR HOUSE	3322	1155	D	4/4	D16p12
ARTHUR SEAT	5L353	5L332	A	2/2	P9p7
ARTHUR'S SEAT	153H1H	2H4H2H2H	E	2/2	M4v3p38 M4v1p1
ARTHUR'S SEAT	1563	436L2	G	4/4	O1v1lp83
ARTILLERY ROUT, THE	131H6	6427L	D	6/8	B16v3p89
ARTLESS ANNIE	5366	526L5L	Bb	4/4	O1v1lp79
AS A THOISEACH	7b57b5	7b527bL	E	2/2	F2v2p66,67(56/7) (II)
AS BLACK AS COAL	515L	514	D	9/8	B15v1p60
(AS I CAME O'ER) THE CAIRNEY MOUNT	3235	6422	D	4/4	C5v2p60 (J3) A1v3p164
AS NOW WE'RE MET	5H2H3H7	61H72H	D	6/8	A1v6p58
AS SYLVIA IN A FOREST LAY [PINKIE HOUSE]	3332	5551H	F	4/4	T6v2p52 P8v2p35
AS YOU LIKE IT	1154	1154	G	6/8	R12v1p41
ASCOT RACES	1H531	6L27L5L	G	6/8	C14v3p11
ASH GROVE, THE	1H3H5H	3H1H1H	D	3/4	B7p8
ASH WEDNESDAY	1112	1117L	G	6/8	R12v1p61
ASIOLTA FIGLIO	11H1	111	G	3/4	H1p13
ASLACHADH NA BAINTIGHEARNA	1H1H5	333	G	3/4	F2v2p90(80)
ASLEYS RIDE	1H1H2H2H	1H61H1H	D	2/4	A7v6p76 A7v3p33

4

ASSEMBLIES, THE	5L131	3342	A	6/8	D6p23
ASTLEY'S HORNPIPE	1364	2H755	G	4/4	C8v1p60 A7v6p75 C8v2p20
					A7v3p32
(AT) POLWART (ON THE) GREEN	3254	5501H	D C	4/4*	C19p13 C5v3p65 C4p13 (J3)
					N1v2p46
AT SETTING DAY	5415	671H1H	G	4/4	O1v1Gp17
ATHENAEUM, THE	51H65	3342	F	6/8	D6p24,25
ATHOL BRAYS	3236	3122	G	2/2	W7p10
ATHOL BROSE	315L1	3145	A D	4/4*	A7v6p58 C14v8p5 G10v3p22,23
					G11v1Bp32 A7v4p19 G7p14
ATHOL CUMMERS, THE	1115	1124	E (A)	4/4	A1v6p14 G11v2Ap16 K1v1p18
					Mc21v4p20 N1v1p7 B15v1p78
					(II)
ATHOL HIGHLANDERS MARCH, THE	1353	6553	A	4/4	M2p24 C8v1p47 C8v2p17 G9v3p29
ATHOLE CUMMERS, (THE)	1115	117bL4	E	4/4*	G1v2p95 Mc9v1p10
ATHOLE HOUSE	5356	537L2	F G	4/4*	K1v1p33 G9v5p35 G7p19 D14v1p21
					Mc9v3p27 G11v2Ap31 C13v2p52
					N1v1p20 P5v2p7 D14v4p1
					C14v19p5 Mc12v1p7 A1v4p8
					A1v3p203 E1v1p56 (II)
ATHOLE LADS, THE	3151	3152	A	2/2	Mc9v3p24/25
ATHOLE VOLUNTEER'S MARCH, THE	1155	1H2H75	F	4/4	G10v5p4
ATHOLE VOLUNTEER'S QUICK STEP, THE	5L3L5L1H	57L6L2	F	6/8	G10v5p5
ATHOLIAN HILLS	3L5L15L	3L5L22L	A	2/2	D14v3p12/13
ATHOLL REEL, THE	536L5L	4L3L22L	F	2/2	C14v5p14
AU CLAIR DE LA LUNE	1H1H3H2H	1H2H1H0	G	2/4	E1v2p78
AUBURN-HAIR'D BONNY DEY, THE	117b	552	G	3/4	C10v2Ap8
AUCHINCRUIVE	3L13L1	3122L	G	4/4	F3p10
AUCHTERTOOL VOLUNTEERS MARCH	1133	551H1H	D	4/4	W2v2p13
AUCHTERTOOL VOLUNTEERS QUICK STEP	1H5H75	6531	D	6/8	W2v2p13
AUCKRY	1H55	3H56	F	9/8	C18p1
AULD BESSY	5333	5322	G	6/8	A1v3p226
AULD EAGE AND YOUNG NEVER GREES THE GITHER	113b	3b54	G	6/4	P5v3p16
AULD GA'D AEVER, THE	3327L	3333	A	2/2	R6v2p21
AULD GOODMAN, THE	17L12	17L6L5L	G	6/8	T6v2p47 P8v2p23
AULD HILLIE'S RANT	5515	4562	E	2/2	B20p8
AULD LANG SYNE	1H1H1H3H	5321	Eb F	4/4	(J3) Mc8v1Ap14 Mc8v2Bp10
					N1v2p11 O1v1Cp21 C20p33
AULD LANG SYNE	1H1H1H3H	5342	F	2/2	T6v1p66
AULD LANGSYNE (SHOULD AULD ACQUAINTANCE BE FORGOT?)	1122	1366	G F A	4/4*	C5v2p19 E1v1p6 G1v1p11
					K1v2p11 C6p6 Mc19v1p17
AULD LANGSYNE	1H1H2H2H	1H3H6H6H	D	2/4	C8v2p35
AULD LUCKY OF THE GLEN	3H1H55	1H3H2H2H	C	4/4	L9p2
AULD MAID OF FIFE, THE	1152	5427bL	A	6/8	O1v1Gp21
AULD MAN'S MARE'S DEAD, THE	5L117b	417bL2	A	4/4	A1v2p58
AULD REEKIE	31H1H7	6562	D	6/8	A1v3p180
AULD ROB MORRIS, (THERE'S)	115L	6L11H	F G	3/4	N1v2p20 (J3) O1v5p15
					S16p116,117 T6v1p66 Mc8v1Ap4
					Mc8v2Cp4 O1v1Fp9 C4p27 P4p23
					E1v2p22 C20p10 C29p45 G1v1p38
AULD ROB THE LAIRD	5551	22H4H2H	G	4/4	A1v4p4
AULD ROBIN GRAY	3560	61H60	D G	4/4	C6p3 C8v2p31
AULD ROBIN GRAY	3356	5555	G	4/4	C5v2p59
AULD ROBIN GRAY	3555	61H55	F	4/4	E1v1p62
AULD ROBIN GRAY	3565	61H60	G	4/4	B7p11
AULD ROBIN GRAY	6652	5223	G	4/4	C5v2p59
AULD ROBIN GRAY	115L4L	7bL4L4L5L	D (?)	4/4	A1v3p222 N1v2p63 VC25 G17p3
AULD ROBIN GRAY	3550	61H60	G	4/4	G1v1p4,5
AULD ROBIN GRAY, (NEW SET OF)	3555	61H60	F D	4/4	C8v1p36 C4p66
AULD SIR SIMON THE KING	61H1H	61H4H	C	9/4	G9v1p14,15
AULD SPRINGS (TUNES) GEES NAE PRICE	11H65	11H22	G	4/4	G11v2Bp11
AULD STEWARD'S BACK AGAIN, THE	6535	6542	D	4/4	G1v2p60 (II)
AULD STEWARTS BACK AGAIN, THE	6535	6562	D	4/4*	G11v2Bp37 G7p8 K1v2p39 (II)
AULD STUART'S BACK AGAIN, THE	327L2	3236L	G	2/2	S12v1p23 O1v1Fp26
AULD TOON O' EDINBURGH, THE	1153	51H53	D	4/4	P9p8,9
AULD WIFE AYONT THE FIRE	327L2	3211H	G	4/4	G11v2Bp6
AULD WIFE AYONT THE FIRE, THE	427L2	4211H	G F	4/4*	R6v2p34 (II) (J3)
AULD WIFE (AYONT THE FIRE), THE	326L4	3211H	G	4/4*	G11v2Ap14 G7p13 K1v1p16
					S12v1p12 N1v1p11 Mc21v3p4,5
					O1v1Ep2 Mc7p23
AULD WIFE AYONT THE FIRE, THE	326L4	3311H	G	4/4	B15v1p90
AULD WIFE AYONT THE FIRE, THE	327L2	321H5	G	4/4	A7v6p61
AULD WIFE AYONT THE FIRE, THE	427L2	421H3	G	4/4	G9v5p22
AURETT'S DUCH SKIPPER	1324	37L11L	Bb	6/8	R12v1p77
AURETT'S MINUET	5H4H3H	2H2H1H	D	3/4	R12v3p12
AURORA WALTZ	1H72	444	G	3/4	C8v2p12 C8v1p38
AUSTRIAN REVEILE, THE	1357	1H1H77	G	4/4	Mc7p1
AUTHORS LAMENT FOR LORD MC.D-, THE	5L5L11	117L7L	G	4/4	W4v2p20
AWA WHIGS AWA	5555	5553	G	4/4*	(J3) A1v3p196 O1v1Fp19
AWA', WHIGS, AWA'	1H510	62H70	C	2/4	C6p30
AWAY WITH MELANCHOLY	3333	4404	G	4/4	C8v2p35

AY WAUKIN' O	1H1H6	533	D	3/2	C5v2p9 (J3)
AYR HARBOUR	13b15L	13b55	G	2/2	H1p21
AYR RACES	1135	1H642	F	4/4	F3p1
AYR RACES	1H515	1H526	D	6/8	G11v1Bp2
AYRSHIRE LASSES (STRATHSPEY), (THE)	532H2H	1H3H1H6	G C	2/2	A7v5p2 C8v1p21
AYRSHIRE LASSES, (THE)	532H2H	2H3H1H6	C G	4/4*	G7p15 G11v2Dp31 E2p14 (II)
					G1v1p39
BAB AT THE BOWSTER	4327L	1313	G	6/8	Mc7p33 C8v2p32 C8v1p52 A1v1p42
BABA MO LEANEABH [BABA MO LEANABH]	51H53b	53bH7b1H	D	6/8	F2v2p39(29)
BACHELERS MISERIES	11H31	11H44	F	2/2	P9p25
BACHELOR'S JIG, THE	5436L	237L5L	G	6/8	M12p16
BACH'S MARCH	5H5H5H6H	3H3H3H1H	C	4/4	A1v4p42
BACK OF THE CASTLE, THE	1313	1357	A	4/4	P9p16
BACK OF THE CHANGE HOUSE, (THE)	552H6	551H1H	D	4/4*	D15v1p30 G11v2Ap33 B15v1p93
					Mc21v3p21 A1v3p223 C14v8p7
					C8v2p34 A7v5p39 C8v1p55 G9v5p32
					A7v6p66 G7p9 K1v1p35 (II)
BACK OF THE SMITHIE, THE	6155	6542	A	2/2	P5v4p3
BADE MALT NE'ER MAKES GOOD ALE	3131	3562	C	4/4	E2p24
BAILLIE GRAY'S FAVOURITE STRATHSPEY	47bL11L	3bL5L7bL7bL	A	4/4	M11v2p15
BAINNAIS MARC HUNDFHUIN	536L5L	3L11H2H	A	4/4	F2v2p48(38)
[BANAIS MARCUS HUNNDFHUINN]					
BALANCE OF COMFORT, THE	1L3L5L5L	16L11	A	4/4	P9p16
BALDIE RUAPHORT'S REEL	1H51H5	22H2H6	G	2/2	Mc16p20
BALENDALLOCH'S DREAM	3151H	7b7b7bL4	A	4/4*	K1v2p29 G11v2Bp28 B15v1p33
[BALLINDALLOCH'S DREAM]					(II)
BALGAY HOUSE	3125L	3L6L37L	G	6/8	D16p16
BALL NA GRANDACH	5555	5562	D	4/4	G10v1p19,20
BALL ROOM, THE	115L1	1H12L2L	Bb	6/8	D6p25
BALL, THE	3215L	6L432	A	2/4	A7v2p36
BALL, THE	3215L	6L432	G	6/8	A7v6p18
BALLEMONNY RACES	136L3	136L7L	G	2/2	Mc16p14
BALLENDALLOCH CASTLE	1131	1132	Bb	4/4	M4v3p8
BALLENDALLOCH'S REELL	3366	5311	G	4/4	C33p7
BALLEST HEAVERS, THE	3531	1316L	Bb	4/4	B16v1p9
BALLNADALLACH	3366	3311	G	2/2	S12v1p55
BALLOON, THE	1122	5226L	A	2/2	C13v1p11 Mc9v3p32
BALOO MY BOY MY WEE BIT LADDIE	117b1	7bL7bL42	E	6/8	C10v2Bp93
BALOU MY BOY [BALOW MY BOY]	311	15L5L	G	3/4	O1v1Ap25
BALTHAYOCH HOUSE	5566	2H4H2H2H	D	4/4	C10v1p1
BALTIOURA	3353	3733	G	6/8	C5v1p34 A1v5p34
BALVENIE CASTLE	15L3L1L	4522	Bb	4/4	M4v3p10
BAN TIGHEARNA MHIC S'HIMI	51H63	51H62	D	4/4	F2v2p82(72)
[BAINTIGHEARNA MHIC SHIMI]					
BANDIT'S WALTZ	53H54H	561H1H	D	3/8	B7p41
BANFF CASTLE	135L3	2466	F	2/2	C24v1p2 G11v2Dp23
BANFF LASSES	1H3H53H	2H4H54H	F	2/2	C24v2p9
BANK O' CAYLE, THE	5145	7b61H1H	D	2/4	C10v2Ap36
BANK OF THE YARROW	31H37L	6L27L1H	G	3/8	C5v1p63 A1v5p63
[BANKS OF THE YARROW]					
BANK, THE	51H1H2H	3H4H3H1H	D	2/2	S7v1p93
BANK'S DANCE	5165	457L2	G	6/8	A1v3p213
BANKS O' TWEED, THE	1355	61H1H6	G	4/4	C5v3p72
BANKS OF ALLAN, THE	3335	6565	D	6/8	K1v2p40 C7p10 G11v2Bp38 W4v2p23
					(II)
BANKS OF ALLAN WATER	1H1H2H	1H55	D	3/4	C8v2p46
BANKS OF BANNA, (THE)	1H1H3H3H	2H1H55	D F	4/4	C19p18 E1v1p117
BANKS OF CLYDE, THE	3161H	5330	G	2/4	A1v4p31
BANKS OF EDEN	1H53H2H	2H2H55	D	4/4	L3p3
BANKS OF FORTH, (THE)	1351H	3H3H66	D C	4/4	Mc8v1Ap45 Mc8v2Bp10 O1v1Ap26
					C13v3p72 O1v2p26 N1v2p14
					(J3)
BANKS OF FORTH, THE	3b3b11	3b53b7bL	B	4/4	C5v2p71
BANKS OF GARY, THE	5551H	5522	D	4/4	Mc9v3p32 (II)
BANKS OF HELICON, THE	1554	3315	G	4/4	C5v3p71
BANKS OF NITH, THE	35L33	16L5L3	G	4/4	R6v1p23
BANKS OF NORTH ESK	5L121	7b47bL0	A	2/4	C5v1p20 A1v5p20
BANKS OF SEVERN, THE	351H1H	2H1H55	F	4/4	O1v1Ep29
BANKS OF SEVERN, THE	351H1H	1H1H2H2	F	4/4	O1v3p1
BANKS OF SLIGOE, THE	1H13	551H	D	3/4	O1v3p36 O1v1Bp8
BANKS OF SPEY, THE	1126L	1155	D	2/2	G15p9
BANKS OF SPEY, THE	1122	5226L	A	4/4	G11v2Dp27
BANKS OF SPEY, THE	351H1H	2H61H1H	D	4/4	C5v3p64 Mc8v1Cp74 Mc8v2Cp10
					O1v1Kp121
BANKS OF SPEY, THE	1113b	427bL7bL	B A	4/4	G1v2p49 Mc7p25/26 M4v3p48
					Mc9v3p3 Mc12v1p10 A1v5p15
BANKS OF TAY, (THE)	5L6L1	111	G	3/4	O1v3p37 P4p24 O1v1Bp5
BANKS OF THE DEE	51H4H4H	1H53H1H	D	6/8	G1v1p29
BANKS OF THE DEE, THE	5L144	35L31	G A	6/8	(J3) A7v3p23
BANKS OF THE DEVERON, THE	17bL3bL7bL	17bL3bL5	A	6/8	C18p11
BANKS OF THE SHANNON, THE	11H3	652	A	9/8	C1v4p11
BANKS OF TWEED	1H531	3322	A	2/4	S7v1p86

Title					
BANKS OF YARROW, THE	3352	11H1H1H	G	4/4	C19p17
BANNERS CROSS	1H2H62H	1H2H61H	D	6/8	S7v1p52
BANNOCKS O' BARLEY MEAL	51H3H2H	3H3H51H	C D	6/8	C8v1p34 G1v1p19
BANNOCKS O' BARLEY MEAL	113	223	F D Eb	3/4	(J3) Mc8v2Bp6 C6p27
					C5v1p60 Mc8v1Bp34,35 A1v5p60
					C20p75
BANOKS OF BEAR MEAL	113	226	G	3/4	O1v1Cp6
BANOSSE	5655	2322	G	6/8	C14v26p12,13
BANQUO'S GHOST	1H135	1H3H6H6H	D	4/4	O1v1Bp6
BANQUO'S GHOST	11L3L5L	1366	Bb	4/4	O1v3p38
BANTI, THE	1H11H1	1H355	D	6/8	S7v2p6
BANTRY BAY	5H3H1H2H	4H2H4H2H	D	2/4	C26v1p1
BARAIN CHULRABHAIG	5L3L5L3	3136L	Eb	4/4	F2v2p85(75
[BARAIN CHILL-REATHAIG]					
BARBARA ALLAN	1H1H3bH2H	7b2H4H3bH	D E	4/4	(J3) O1v1Bp27 Mc8v1Dp105
					O1v2p3 O1v3p33 C5v2p11
BARBARA NI' MHIC PHERSON	7L152	7bL13b1	F	4/4	F2v2p47(37)
[BARBARA NIC A' PHEARSAIN]					
BARBARA, THE	5L314	4512	G	6/8	C14v25p15
BARBERINI'S MINUET	11H1H3H	1H542	G	3/8	R12v3p16
BARCARO(L)LE FROM MASANIELLO	3333	6555	G	6/8	E1v2p142,143
BARD STRIKES HIS HARP, THE	3b111H	3bH7b43b	E	4/4	C5v3p73
BARGENNY BOWLING GREEN	1147bL	113bH2H	D	6/8	G11v2Bp33 K1v2p35
BARGENNY'S BOWLING GREEN	1147bL	112H2H	D	6/8*	B15v1p39 R5p46 (II)
BARLEY BROTH	151H3b	5424	E	6/8	F3p18,19
BARLEY (SUGAR) (CAKES)	3322	3351H	G	6/8	R12v1p35 B15v1p68 G11v2Cp17
					O1v1Jp88
BARNS OF CLYDE, THE	1H13b5	7b7b24	D	2/2*	C13v2p77 (II)
BARON DE STEINS COTILION	5422	4215	G	2/4	Mc15p22
BARRING OF THE DOOR, THE	1111	11H65	G	6/8	A1v2p3
BARSKEMMING BRIDGE	1343	5L6L4L2L	Bb	4/4	F3p14
BAS DHIARMID O DUINN	553	311	G	3/4	Mc5p9
BASKET OF OYSTERS, A	5353	5316L	E	6/8	A1v3p188
BASKET OF OYSTERS, THE	1H1H2H7	1H673	D	6/8	C5v1p5 A1v5p35
BASQUE ROADS	31H51	4542	Bb	2/4	P6v1p36
BASS REEL	3155	1H3H2H2	G	4/4	G11v2Bp16 K1v2p18
BATA BHARRA	311	316	A	9/8	Mc16p17
BATCHELOR'S HALL	1H3H72H	4H71H1H	D C	6/8	A1v5p6
BATCHELORS OF EVERY STATION	351H1H	61H53	G	2/4	A1v2p65
BATH MEDLEY, THE	1765	657L2	G	6/8	A1v1p11
BATH RACES	1H564	3437L	G	2/2	B16v3p55
BATH RACES	5L5L52	36L7L5L	Bb	6/8	C1v3p2
BATH WALTZ	1H1H3H3H	5H6H71H	C	3/8	B7p9
BATH WALTZ, THE	1565	1565	Bb	3/8	C14v20p24
BATTLE OF BOTHWELL BRIG	1565	51H3H2H	C	2/4	C6p23
BATTLE OF CULLEDEN, THE	6535	6562	D	2/2	R12v1p38
BATTLE OF FALKIRK, THE	111	333	G	3/4	O1v1lp64
BATTLE OF HARLAW, (THE)	1H1H66	1H155	D	4/4	(J3) D14v2p28-30
BATTLE OF LANGSIDE, THE	151H5	1566	C	4/4	G8p4
(BATTLE OF) PENTLAND HILL(S)	115	331H	G	3/4	P4p2 C20p53
BATTLE OF SALAMANCA, THE	1H1H4H4H	2H755	C	2/4	C1v3p1
BATTLE OF SHERIFF MOOR, THE	1H1H3H	1H55	F	3/4	B11p34
BATTLE OF THE BOYNE, THE	5547bL	5511	A	4/4	G11v1Cp22
BATTLE, THE	1326	1353H	D	2/4	A1v4p16 C5v1p16 W4v1p31
BAUK, THE	11L13b	27bL24	A	2/4	G10v6p34
BAY OF BISCAY, THE	51H1H6	2H2H55	D	2/4	C8v2p59
BAY OF BISCAY, THE	5L116L	225L5L	Bb	2/4	C8v1p13
BE CONSTANT STILL	35L6L	116	Bb	3/4	P4p5
BE CONSTANT STILL	35L6L	111H	Bb	3/4	O1v1Lp148
BE KIND TO THE YOUNG THING	3313	551H1H	C	2/2	Mc8v2Cp12
B'E SUD IORRAM NA TRUAIGH	124	452	A	9/8	Mc5p11
BEAM OF JOY, THE	1132	3232	G	2/2	O1v1Kp135
BEAN NA BAINNSE	1535	1527bL	D	2/2	F2v2p45(35)
BEARD OF THE THISTLE, THE	11H3H1H	5122	D	4/4*	A1v6p12 O1v1Lp156
[THISTLE'S BEARD, THE]					
BEAU NASH	5H4H3H3H	3H5H3H1H	D	2/4	R12v1p62
BEAUFORT CASTLE	153b5	1544	E	6/8	F2v1p5
BEAUTIFUL CHARMER, THE	3H5H6H3H	2H3H2H5	C	6/8	B16v3p89
BEAUTIFULL TOWN OF GLASGOW, THE	3b13b5	227b2	G	2/2	Mc13v2p20 C13v1p2
BEAUTY IN TEARS	1H3H5H	3H1H1H	G	3/4	E1v2p38
BEAUX STRATAGEM, THE	1122	1125	Bb	4/4	P9p36
BECAUSE HE WAS A BONNY LAD	3165	4642	G	4/4	A1v2p45
BECAUSE (HE/I) WAS A BONNY LAD	3165	4522	G A	4/4*	A1v6p28 E1v1p9 C8v2p31
					G9v5p17 C8v1p32 Mc7p25 C4p40
					R12v1p30 K1v2p25 G11v2Ap23
					B15v1p14 N1v1p13 S12v1p8
					C13v2p23 Mc9v3p44 A1v4p26
					O1v1Lp149 (II)
BECKFORD'S ELECTION	13L32	13L5L5L	Bb	4/4	B16v3p36
BECKY MURRAY	311H6	27bL7b2	D	2/2	Mc9v3p7
BEDDING OF THE BRIDE, THE	1524	1515	A	2/2	A1v4p23 Mc9v3p15
BEDFORD JIG, THE	115	642	A	9/8	P6v1p14

BEDS OF ROSES, (THE)	5564	2425L	G A	4/4*	A7v6p11 A7v2p35 Mc9v3p40
BEETHOVENS FAVORITE POLLACCA	4H3H03H	7602H	D	4/4	B7p9
BEGGAR GIRL, (THE)	5523	5521	G A	6/8	E1v1p61 D15v2p17
BEGGAR'S BENNISON	3H1H5H5H	3H1H55	D	2/2	C33p14
BEGGAR'S DANCE, THE	1H1H4H2H	72H55	D	4/4	O1v1Jp89
BEGGARS' MEAL POKES, THE	1351	11H66	G	4/4*	G10v5p29 O1v1lp78
BEGIN THE DANCE	311H5	4H3H72H	D	6/8	B16v4p90
BEGONE DULL CARE	1H2H3H0	5H4H3H0	D	6/8	E1v1p42
BEGONE DULL CARE	1H2H3H3H	5H4H3H3H	D	6/8	C5v1p68 A1v4p65
BEGONE DULL CARE	1H2H3H3H	5H5H3H2H	D	6/8	C8v2p29
BEHIND THE BUSH IN THE GARDEN	3322	3355	G	6/8	A1v2p1
BEHIND YON HILLS	5155	3b117bL	E	2/2	Mc16p6
BELFAST ALMANACK, THE	17L6L1	3434	G	6/8	G10v4p12 (II)
BELHELVIE HOUSE	11H1H3bH	2H7b4H7b	C	4/4	M4v3p28
BELIEVE MY	5555	23H1H7	D	4/4	P8v2p13
BELINDA	1L3bL5L1	2425	G	4/4	P9p15
BELL OF CRAIGFOODIE, THE	1554	2665	G	2/2	O1v1lp83
BELLADRUM('S STRATHSPEY)	113b5	7bL424	E	4/4	F2v1p8 (II)
BELLEISLE MARCH, (THE)	1122	31H55	G	4/4	A1v5p21 C5v1p21 C8v2p13
					C8v1p39
BELLEROPHON, THE	1H1H5H3H	4H675	C	6/8	C1v4p12
BELLES OF WALTHAMSTOW, THE	1H3H75	6231	E	2/4	P6v2p16,17
BELL'S WELL	1125L	1126L	E	2/2	J2p1
BELVEDIERE	1H1H76	1H3H5H2H	C	2/4	C14v11p23
BELVOIR CASTLE	1H51H1H	1H51H2	D	2/2	C14v15p8
BEN LOMOND	5555	662H2H	D	4/4	G11v2Cp33 (II)
BENNET'S HORNPIPE	31H1H4	22H2H5	D	4/4	H1p10
BENNEVIS	1155	1152	D	2/2	G11v2Cp33 (II)
BENNY SIDE	13b1H2H	7b443b	D E	4/4	P4p27 Mc8v1Dp98
BENNY SIDE	13b1H3bH	7b443b	E G	4/4	C5v3p74 O1v1Lp156
BERKES OF PLUNKETTY, THE	314	324	C	3/4	P7p4
BERKS OF ABERGELDE, THE	1135	1H1H76	F	2/2	P7p11 W7p6
BERKS OF ENDERMAY, THE	5H5H5H2H	2H2H66	D	4/4	O1v1Bp21 C4p67 T7p2,3
					O1v4p34,35 P8v2p9
BERKS OF ENDERMAY, THE	5H5H5H2H	2H4H66	D	4/4	R12v3p17
BERNARD'S WELL	3564	3127bL	G	2/2	S12v1p25
BERWICK ASSEMBLY	61H51	2216L	A	4/4	C7p12
BERWICK BEAUTY	1H1H2H2H	3H2H1H1H	G	6/8	S7v2p6
BERWICK BRIDGE	1142	6750	G	4/4	L9p5
BERWICKSHIRE MILITIA'S QUICK STEP, THE	1251	127L5L	A	6/8	Mc22Cp1
BERWICKSHIRE YEOMANRY'S MARCH, THE	3H2H75	3115	C	4/4	C7p2
BESS BELL	345	551H	D	6/4	P7p8
BESS THE GAWKIE	5553	5755	D	4/4	N1v2p68
BESSIE BELL (AND MARY GRAY)	3564	353H4H	D	6/8	A1v2p24 C4p61 C29p5 Mc8v1Cp73
					Mc8v2Bp4 O1v1Cp6,7 C20p17
					P8v2p16
BESSIE'S HAGGES	5335	6422	D	4/4	C29p4
BESSIE'S HAGGIES	1316	2422H	D	4/4	C19p27 O1v1Cp22 Mc8v1Bp32
					Mc8v2Bp3
BESSIES HAGGIES	1315	6422	D	4/4	Mc12v2p42,43
BESSY BELL (AND MARY GRAY)	3564	351H3H	C D	6/8	(J3) T6v1p3 G1v2p79 C5v2p2
					S16p106,107
BESSY BELL AND MARY GRAY	3564	351H4H	D	6/8	Mc9v2p5
BESSY HAGGICE	5L113	6422	D	2/2	W7p11
BESSY'S HAGGIES	1315	6420	D	4/4	T6v2p69 P8v2p40
BETSY HOWISON'S FAVORITE	15L15L	11H52	G	6/8	P11v2p17
BETTER LATE THAN NEVER	3322	4433	A G	2/4	W4v1p18 A1v4p45 C5v1p45
BEVERLY ASSEMBLY	3H5H5H5H	4H3H2H1H	D	6/8	R12v1p47
BEVERLY SCHOLL BOYS	1335	61H31	F	2/4	R12v1p84
BEVIS MOUNT	3554	1322	G	2/4	S7v1p16
BEWARE O' BONIE ANN	521H1H	5234	G F	4/4	C5v2p18 (J3)
BEWARE OF THE RIPPLES	7L257	5332	G	4/4	O1v1Kp138
BEYNONS DELIGHT	551H5	3465	G	6/8	B16v4p87
B'FHEARR LEAM FHIN NA LAIR IS OIGEACH	336L2	1515	G	6/8	Mc5p8
B'FHEARRLEAMSA NA BREACAN	7bL111	1417bL	B	4/4	Mc1v1p117
BHANARACH DHONN A CHRUIDH	157b2	1551	G	3/8	F2v2p29(19)
BHEIR MI SORAIDH (THUN A' BHAILE)	3331	3361H	C	4/4	Mc5p30 C4p10
BHLIADHNA DH'EIRICH AN IOMAIRT	5257bL	5L5L3bL5L	A	6/8	Mc5p14
BHLIAN UR ['BHLIADHNA' UR]	113b5	67b67b	G	4/4	F2v2p24(14)
BIDE YE YET	51H57b	51H51H	D	6/8	G13p2 E1v2p122
BIG BOAT OF ENWARE, THE	1H1H51	2222	A	2/2	N1v1p34
BIG BOW WOW, THE	3144	3122	G	6/8	Mc7p18 H3p32 A1v3p190
BIG BOW-WOW	3565	3565	G	6/8	A1v1p37
BILLET DOUX, THE	1H531	1230	G	2/4	C5v1p38 A1v5p38
BIODAG AIR MACTHOMAIS	3331	2427bL	A	4/4	Mc19v1p12 (II)
BIRD CATCHER, THE	1H2H2H2H	55H3H1H	G	2/4	E1v2p36
BIRKS OF ABERFELDY, (THE)	131H1H	1H1H71H	D F G	2/2	(J3) E1v1p7 (II) G1v1p37
BIRKS OF ABERGELDIE	131H1H	1H1H1H1H	G	2/2	A1v3p166
BIRKS OF ABERGELDIE	131H1H	1H1H2H2H	F G	4/4	A7v4p11 A7v5p13 A7v6p93 (II)
[BIRKS OF ABERFELDIE]					
BIRKS OF ABERGELDY	131H7	1H771H	F	2/4	G9v5p5 B15v1p35 O1v1Hp50
[BERKS OF ABERGELDE, THE]					

Title					References
BIRKS OF ABERGELDY, (THE)	131H1H	1H1H71H	F	4/4*	S12v1p3 G7p19 K1v1p28 N1v1p25
					G11v2Ap26 P5v2p18
BIRKS OF BALNABOATH	132	11H6	F	9/8	B6v3p2
BIRKS OF ENDERMAY	5552	226L6L	Bb	2/2	S7v1p47
BIRKS OF INVERGARY, THE	1535	2662	A	2/2	H3p4
BIRKS OF INVERMAY, THE	5552	226L6L	A Bb G	4/4	T6v2p98 B5p8 P4p20 Mc23p4,5
					Mc8v1Bp36 Mc8v2Ap20 O1v5p35
					C13v3p4,5 C20p2,3 N1v2p47
					(J3) G17p14 (C25) Mc12v2p2,3
BIRKS OF INVERMAY, THE	5H5H5H2H	2H2H66	D	4/4	C19p9 C5v2p24 E1v2p13 G1v1p18
BIRKS OF INVERMAY, THE	5H6H5H2H	2H2H66	D	4/4	B7p5
BIRNAM WOOD	1H1H1H5	11H2H6	D	4/4	G11v2Cp6
BIRNES HORNPIPE	1H362	31H1H7	D	4/4	A7v5p20 A7v4p7
BIRNOM WOOD	1H1H65	11H2H6	D	4/4*	D15v1p16 G8p29 P1v1p11
BIRTH NIGHT, THE	1H2H3bH2H	1H2H75	D	4/4	S7v1p98
BIRTH OF KISSES, THE	4156	537L2	G	6/8	O1v1Jp99
BISHOP OF ARGYLE'S LAMENT	113b	444	A	9/8	D14v2p35
BISHOP, THE	1542	7bL7bL27bL	A	4/4	C33p11 (II)
BLACK AT THE (BANE) BONE	5L111	216L6L	G	4/4*	Mc9v1p25 G10v6p26,27 C18p30,31
BLACK AT THE BONE	5L111	215L6L	G	2/2	H3p3
BLACK BEARD	1H3H1H3H	2H675	E	2/4	C22p24
BLACK BUT LOVELY	51H3bH2H	7b2H7b1	E	6/8	C5v1p26 A1v5p26
BLACK DANCE, (THE)	1253	1253	G	2/4	H3p29 C13v2p58 Mc9v2p1 R12v2p8
					S7v1p18
BLACK DANCE, THE	1253	1251	G	2/4	A1v1p18
BLACK EAGLE, THE	3555	5555	D	4/4	O1v4p17
BLACK EGLE, THE	3555	1H555	D	4/4	O1v1Ep17
BLACK EY'D SUSAN	325L2	35L41	Bb	3/8	S16p18,19
BLACK EYED MILKMAID, THE	1515	4342	G	2/2	R12v2p4
BLACK EYED SUSAN	51H2H	3bH2H1H	E	3/4	E1v2p5 O1v1Kp115
BLACK GIRL IS NOT CHEERFULL, THE	1552	1127bL	G	4/4	D14v2p26
BLACK HAIR'D DEAR LADDIE, THE	1H1H6	51H1H	D	3/4	C5v2p26
BLACK HAIRED GIRL WITH THE BLUE EYES	47b44	3bL7b44	E	2/4	Mc1v1p116
BLACK JOCK	5L122	3222	G A	6/8	A1v2p27 R4p11,12
BLACK JOCK	5L122	3322	G A	6/8	W7p16 Mc7p10 D13p16
					G11v2Dp10 B15v2p14,15
BLACK JOCK	6L122	3322	A	6/8	C13v3p52,53
BLACK JOCK	5L5L6L	111	G	3/4	O1v5p8
BLACK LASSIE'S NO CANTY, THE	1552	1127bL	G	4/4	A1v6p19
BLACK MAN IS THE BRAVEST, THE	5232	7L6L5L3	G	4/4	C5v2p45
BLACK MAN IS THE BRAVEST, THE	5232	7L6L5L6	D	2/2	C29p17
BLACK MARE, THE	1542	1541	A	2/2	Mc9v3p19
BLACK MARY	1H1H1H1H	1H755	C	4/4	G10v4p14
BLACK MARY	5L122	3231	G	6/8	A1v5p50
BLACK STOOL, THE	135	142	G	9/8	B20p13
BLACK STRAP	3b422	3b456	G	2/2	M12p24
BLACKAMOORE'S JIG, THE	1H13b3bH	2H7b3bH4H	D	6/8	Mc9v2p22
BLACKAMOOR'S JIG	1H13b3H	2H7b5H4H	D	6/8	C22p21
BLACKHALL HOUSE	3151	25L7bL2	D	6/8	P5v2p12
BLACKMOORS JIG, THE	1H13b3bH	2H7b5H4H	D	6/8	Mc7p18 H3p35
BLAIR DRUMMOND	1315	1322	A	2/2	G11v2Dp35 (II)
BLAIR DRUMMOND'S REEL	1335	1322	G	2/2	Mc21v3p13
BLAIR DRUMMOND'S REEL	1355	1322	A	4/4	B15v1p87
BLANCHARD'S HORNPIPE	1H345	3345	D G	4/4	W4v1p11 (II) A1v4p37
[FISHER'S HORNPIPE]					
BLANDFORD HOUSE	1H1H31	437L2	F	2/2	C14v27p10
BLAR LEINE	13b4	456b	G	3/4	F2v2p14(3)
BLATHRIE O'T, THE	31H52	1551	G D	4/4	A1v3p163 C5v2p24 C20p3
					N1v2p49 (J3) (C25) Mc8v1Dp112
BLEAK WAS THE MORN	1355	61H53	G	2/4	A1v6p24
BLENHEIM HOUSE	1352	437L5L	A	2/4	G8p27
BLENHEIM HOUSE	1113	2223	A	2/2	S7v1p76
BLEST AS TH'IMMORTAL GODS	1H3H1H1H	2266	D	4/4	T6v1p9
BLEWITT'S JIG	355	351H	D	9/8	C8v2p34 C8v1p55
BLIND BEGGAR	3H1H5H5H	1H2H66	D	2/4	S7v1p81
BLIND LOVER, THE	1516	521H1H	G	4/4	O1v1Ip75
BLIND SAILOR, THE	3H2H5H5H	3H3H1H1H	D	4/4	A1v4p69
BLINK O'ER THE BURN	3H3H5H	552H	C	3/4	T6v1p30
BLINK O'ER THE BURN SWEET BESSY	333	5L5L2	Bb	3/4	S16p50,51
BLINK O'ER THE BURN, SWEET BETTY	3H3H3H	552H	D	3/4	C4p38 Mc8v1Ap14,15 Mc8v2Bp14
BLINK OVER THE BURN SWEET BETTY	3H3H3H	553H	D	3/4	O1v2p20,21 O1v3p8 O1v1Ap19
BLINK OVER THE BURN SWEET BETTY	3H3H3H	54H2H	D	3/4	P8v2p17
BLOSSOM OF THE RASPBERRY, THE	3H3H4H2H	5H3H55	D	4/4	O1v1Dp17
BLOW ZABELLA	5343	5321	G	6/8	A1v2p45
BLUCHER'S TRIUMPH	1H1H1H1H	1H1H5H2H	D	2/4	F1p33
BLUE AND BUFF	51H3H1H	4H2H3H3H	E	2/4	C14v5p1
BLUE BELLS OF SCOTLAND, THE	1H51H5	3210	C D	4/4	(J3) C5v3p72
BLUE BELL(S) OF SCOTLAND, THE	1H756	3411	E G	4/4*	C6p4 E1v1p50 C8v2p21
					C8v1p53 (II)
BLUE BELLS OF SCOTLAND, THE	3H2H76	637L2	Eb	2/2	C14v16p12
BLUE BONNETS	1H2H2H5	1H664	C D	4/4	(J3) Mc8v1Ap10 Mc8v2Bp21
					O1v4p5 O1v1Bp34

BLUE BONNETS	111H1H	1H66H3H	D	6/8	C5v2p28
BLUE BONNETS	1111	16L64	G	6/8	G1v1p9
BLUE BONNETS OVER THE BORDER	1355	2466	A	4/4	G10v5p23
BLUE BONNETS OVER THE BORDER	1H1H1H1H	1H66H2H	D	6/8	C8v2p63
BLUE BONNETS OVER THE BORDER	1L1L11	16L62	Bb	6/8	G11v1Ap12
BLUE BONNETS OVER THE BORDER	1111	16L62	Bb	6/8	C8v1p40
BLUE BONNETS OVER THE BORDER	111H1H	1H66H2H	D	6/8	E1v2p3
BLUE BRITCHES	1533	27b22	A	4/4	B15v1p67
BLUE JOAK	1352	6527L	G	6/8	W7p16
BLUE RIBBON SCOTTISH MEASURE, THE	3112	5225	F	4/4	G11v2Bp4 K1v2p4,5
BLUE RIBBON, THE	1H1H3H3H	5H5H3H1H	D	2/4	C1v1p10 P8v1p9
BLUE STOCKING, THE	5533	1233	G	6/8	B7p25
BLYTH (BLYTH AND MERRY) WAS SHE	5142	5141	A D E	4/4*	C5v3p66 (J3) G1v1p8
	1353	3H3H65	G	4/4	C5v2p69
BLYTHE HAE I BEEN WHEN I STRAY'D WI' MY LOVE					
BLYTHE JOCKEY	3112	4223	D	2/2	(J3) (C25)
BLYTHE WAS SHE BUT AND BEN	5142	5251	E	2/2	E1v2p97
BLYTHSOME BRIDAL, THE	111	356	F	6/4	T6v1p76
BLYTHSOME MAY I SEE THEE	1265	3110	F	2/4	C10v2Ap11
BOAT MAN, THE	5555	4255	D	4/4	C29p34,35 S16p38,39 Mc8v1Bp46 Mc8v2Bp8
BOAT OF BOG, THE [BRIDGE OF SPEY, THE]	5L17L1	526L6L	D	2/2	Mc9v3p13
BOAT OF LOGY, THE	1326L	1323	G	4/4	A7v6p21 A7v2p6
BOATIE ROWS, THE	3552H	5230	E	2/4	C6p18
BOATIE ROWS, THE	3551H	3H3H2H1H	D	2/4	C8v2p11 C8v1p31
BOATIE ROWS, THE	1546	5321	G	2/4	C5v2p3
BOATIE ROWS, THE (THIRD SETT)	3546	5322	D	2/4	C5v1p61 A1v5p61 (J3)
BOATMAN OF PITNACREE, THE	3H52H5	3H2H1H6	D	2/2	G11v2Cp33 (II)
BOATMAN, THE	5554	4255	D	4/4	N1v2p12 P4p4,5 G17p7
BOATMEN'S SONG, THE	1154	1154	A	2/2	D14v2p10
BOATTIE ROWS, THE	3552H	5330	G	2/4	E1v2p5
BOATY ROW'S WELL, THE	3546	3521	D	4/4	A7v6p65 A7v3p13
BOB AN' JOHN	411	3b22	A	3/2	P5v4p7
BOB IN THE BED	17L6L1	3434	G	6/8	R12v1p91
BOB O' DOOLY, THE	1533	1542	A	2/2	Mc21v3p39
BOB OF DUMBLANE, THE	7b57b6b	7b57b1	E	6/8	T6v1p101
BOB OF DUNBLANE	7576b	7571	G	6/8	S16p64,65
BOB OF FETTERCAIRN, THE	5151	5575	G	4/4*	G7p12,13 G11v1Bp34 A1v4p30 Mc12v1p26 G10v3p34 Mc7p5 C14v11p21 (II)
BOBBY'S FANCY	113b3b	4227bL	G	4/4	C7p7
(BOBER'S/ROBBERS) OF BRECHIN, THE	51H1H5	47b54	G	2/2	E1v1p104 G11v2Ap10 K1v1p12 (II)
BOBIN JOHN	511	3b22	A	3/2	K1v2p24,25 C14v21p11 G11v2Bp22
BOB'S WHIM	1527bL	1565	D	2/2	R12v1p60
BOCAGE QUE, L'AURORE	1H553	3420	G	2/4	E1v2p42,43
BOCHD LIATH NA'N GOBHAR	1541	2427L	A	6/8	Mc1v1Ap7
BOCHUIDDAR [BOCHUIDEAR]	6133	6132	F	4/4	F2v2p38(28)
BODACHAN A GARIDH	3H1H4H2H	3H1H2H5	D	2/2	C5v1p71
BODACHAN A GARIDH	3H1H5H2H	3H1H2H5	D	4/4*	A1v4p71 Mc22p16 A7v6p55
BODACHAN A GARIE	3564	1H542	D	2/2	P5v4p8
BODAICH NA 'M BRIGIS	1624	1655	A	6/8	Mc1v1p102-105
BODHAN AN EASSAIN [BOTHAN AN EASAN]	356	66L1	G	3/4	F2v2p80(70)
BODHAN ARIDH M'BRAIGH RANNOCH [BOTHAN AIRIDH 'M BRAIGHE RAINEACH]	157b	654	G	3/4	F2v2p29(19)
BOG AN LOCHAN	1115	1124	E	4/4	K1v1p18 G11v2Ap16 A1v6p14
BOG OF GIGHT, THE	5511	6L6L22	G A	4/4*	A7v2p11 A7v6p25 Mc9v3p28 G11v2Bp24 M4v3p20 K1v2p26 Mc12v1p58 (II)
BOGANUADH, THE (NEW BOB, THE)	13b54	247b4	B	2/2	K1v1p39 G11v2Ap37 (II)
BOGANUADK	13b54	5424	A	4/4	Mc9v3p41
BOGEN LOCHAN	1114	217bL4	E	4/4	A7v2p10,11
BOGNOR ROCK	1313	1347L	Bb	2/2	C14v18p23
BOGNOR ROCKS	1H51H5	61H75	F	2/2	C14v17p20 P6v1p5
BOHD NA HESUDH	5351	5355	D	6/8	O1v1Kp117
BOHEMIAN WALTZ	3354	3351H	G	3/8	B7p10
BOLD DRAGOON, THE	51H1H1H	2H2H1H1H	D	2/4	E1v1p95
BOLD ROBIN HOOD	6L47L5L	1533	G	4/4	A1v3p170
BOLOGNA'S MARCH	1H1H72H	1H1H1H2H	D C	4/4	A1v4p33 W4v1p2
BON TON or NEW YEAR'S GIFT	3354	2243	F	2/4	S7v1p74
BON TON, (THE)	3122	3125L	A G	2/4	B16v3p5 A1v2p49
BONAPARTE IN A KNAPSACK	1H535	61H75	F	2/4	C14v22p14,15
BONAR BRIDGE, THE	116L5L	3521	G	4/4	G10v4p38
BONDUCA	4541	6523	G	6/8	S7v1p31
BONIE KIRSTY	525L1	3111	G	2/2	Y1p3
BONINTOWN WELL	1H3H2H6	6753	C	4/4	B15v1p96
BONNET MAKERS OF DUNDEE, THE	11H1H7b	7b2H1H7b	E	4/4	B15v1p46
BONNETS O' BONNIE DUNDEE, THE	551H5	3322	G	6/8	C8v2p57
BONNIE BESSIE LEE	5155	1H1H66	F G	4/4	C8v1p64 C8v2p53 (II)
BONNIE BLACK EAGLE, THE	5555	5155	D	4/4	Mc8v1Cp72 C20p78
(BONNIE) BLACK EAGLE, (THE)	5L5L5L5L	5L1L5L5L	Bb	4/4	(J3) Mc8v2Cp15

BONNIE DUNDEE	5L122	5451	G A	6/8	C6p22 E1v2p9
BONNIE DUNDEE	5L11	113b	A B	3/4*	C8v2p27 C8v1p27 G1v1p17
BONNIE HOUSE OF AIRLY, THE	1245	3244	G	4/4	G10v6p14
BONNIE JEANIE GRAY	346L1	5L121	G	2/4	C8v2p20 C8v1p60
BONNIE LADDIE, HIELAND LADDIE	1343	3232	G	2/4	C6p1
BONNIE LASSIE CANNIE LASSIE	5566	5533	A	2/2	R6v2p20
BONNIE PRINCE CHARLIE	3153	321H6	D G	6/8	C8v2p51 E1v2p121 (II)
BONNIE PRINCE CHARLIE	3153	323H1H	D	6/8	C6p24
BONNIE RAN THE BURNIE DOWN	1H663	5555	C	4/4	C6p16
BONNIE WEE THING(, THE)	5H2H61H	5H2H6H5H	D	4/4	C5v2p60 O1v11p63
BONNIEST LASS IN A' THE AULD TOWN	1527L	6547L	G	6/8	S5p22
BONNIEST LASS IN A' THE WARLD, (THE)	35L6L1	226L5L	G F	4/4*	Y1p5 S16p36,37 P8v2p17
BONNIEST LASS IN A' THE WARLD, THE	35L6L1	426L5L	F G	4/4*	C8v1p57 Mc8v1Cp61 Mc8v2Ap1
					Mc7p34 P11v2p21 Mc9v2p10
					C19p11 C20p11 E1v2p111 O1v3p27
					O1v1Bp9
BONNIEST LASS IN A' THE WORLD, THE	15L6L1	426L5L	G	4/4	C5v2p5 C4p68
BONNY ANNIE	115L7bL	113b5	B A	4/4*	G1v2p86 K1v1p24 Mc21v4p34
					G11v2Ap22 D14v3p18 A1v3p209
					D15v1p20
BONNY BANKS OF AYR, THE	4255	1H3H1H1H	D	4/4	C13v4p33
BONNY BANKS OF CLYDE, THE	61H52	422H2H	C	2/2	R5p54
BONNY BANKS OF UGIE, THE	1L13L3L	2L225L	Bb	4/4	C18p36
BONNY BELL	113	551H	A G	3/4	C5v2p36 C5v1p31 A1v5p31 (J3)
BONNY BESSY	1315	6422	D	4/4	(J3) N1v2p36
BONNY BETTY	1H2H75	31H26	G	2/2	R12v1p56
BONNY BLACK LADIE	1H3H53H	2H3H65	D	2/2	S12v1p70
(BONNY) BOAT MAN (THE)	5564	4255	D	4/4	O1v1Bp28 O1v3p6,7 C20p40,41
BONNY BOAT MAN, THE	5664	4255	C	2/2	W7p17
BONNY BRAES OF CLYDE, THE	1H1H55	3bH4H2H1H	E	4/4	C5v3p65
BONNY BRAES OF SKELMORLY, THE	311H5	51H22H	C	2/2	R5p44
(BONNY) BREAST KNOT(S), (THE)	4635	22H76	G	4/4*	A1v1p25 C14v10p23
BONNY BRUCKET LASSIE, THE	31H5	551	G D	3/4	O1v1Ap15 O1v2p17 (J3)
					Mc8v1Dp107 Mc8v2Bp1 C19p23
					C20p78
BONNY CASTLE GORDON	1H3bH2H5	1H2H7b5	E	4/4	C5v3p54
BONNY CHARLIE	113b3b	543b4	D	4/4	G11v2Cp5
BONNY CHARLIE	113b3b	553b3b	E	4/4	A1v2p40
BONNY CHRISTIE	525L1	3114	G	2/2	Mc8v1Bp33 Mc8v2Ap18 E1v2p126
BONNY CHRISTY	525L1	3214	G F	4/4*	O1v1Bp10,11 C29p43 (J3)
					S16p2,3 T6v1p23 P4p32
BONNY CHRISTY	535L1	3214	G	2/2	O1v3p4,5
BONNY CHRISTY	525L1	1214	G	4/4	P8v2p43
BONNY CROWDY	1H1H2H5	6542	D	6/8	C1v1p5
BONNY DUNDEE	5L11	117bL	E A	3/4	N1v2p24 O1v1Cp4
					Mc8v1Bp39(?) Mc8v2Bp7 C29p22
					C20p6,7
BONNY EARL OF MURRAY, THE	113	15L5	G	3/4	C5v3p66 B5p14 Mc8v1Dp104 (J3)
					O1v1Ep14 T6v2p8
BONNY GRAY EY'D MORN, THE	1H1H3H2H	3H5H5H5H	C D	4/4*	O1v1Gp1 P4p9 C5v3p69 G17p16
[OLD GRAY EY'D MORN, THE]					Mc8v1Dp99(?) A1v5p11 P8v2p19
BONNY GREEN OF GLASGOW, THE	3H3H55	662H2H	D	2/2	R5p36 A1v5p53
BONNY GREY-EY'D MORN, THE	1132	3555	Bb	4/4 2/	(J3) S16p54,55
BONNY HIGHLAND HILLS, THE	3313	2H36L6	G	2/2	G10v5p20,21
BONNY HIGHLAND LADDIE, THE	5135	6421H	D	4/4	G11v2Cp6
BONNY HOUSE O' AIRLY, THE	1244	2215	Bb	4/4	C6p15
BONNY ISOBEL ROBERTSON	31H4H2H	72H55	D	4/4	D6p38
BONNY JAMIE O'	1H554	22H2H2H	D	4/4*	B16v1p10
BONNY JANE	115L5L	1132	G	4/4	O1v1Bp11 O1v4p18,19 C19p12
BONNY JEAN	135L5L	1132	F	4/4	T6v1p36 P8v2p5
BONNY JEAN	3546	347L2	F	2/2	H6v23p1
BONNY JEAN	115L5L	1131	F	4/4	B5p11
BONNY JEAN OF ABERDEEN	315L5L	1132	G	4/4	C29p27
BONNY JEAN (OF ABERDEEN)	115L5L	1132	F Bb D	2/2*	S16p88,89 D15v2p14 (J3)
					T7v1p18,19 N1v2p30 Mc8v1Cp71
					Mc8v2Ap17 P4p33 G17p18
					Mc23p8,9 C5v2p23 C13v3p6,7
					M14p20-24 C8v1p38 C8v2p12
					C20p48,49
BONNY JEAN OF ABERDEEN	115L5L	1142	G	2/2	E1v2p113
BONNY JEAN OF St. ANDREWS	5L111	3b3b54	A	4/4	C5v3p53
BONNY KATE OF EDINBURGH	5551H	2H2H66	D C	4/4*	C5v3p66 Mc8v1Ap3 Mc8v2Ap8
					Y1p13
BONNY KATE OF EDINBURGH	5551H	5H2H66	C	4/4	O1v1Ep5
BONNY KITTY	1H4H1H3	621H7	F	6/8	A1v6p52
BONNY LAD LAY YOUR PIPES DOWN	112	3b3b5	D	3/4	O1v2p23 O1v1Ap20 O1v1Dp18
BONNY LADS OF AIR	7552	751H1H	F	2/2	D15v1p19
BONNY LASS OF ABERDEEN, THE	4433	4521	F	2/2	O1v1Lp142
BONNY LASS OF BRANKSOME, THE	3H2H1H1H	3H3H76	C	4/4	T6v2p78 P8v2p45
BONNY LASS OF FANNHIVEN, THE	3132	531H1H	G	2/2	C4p26 B15v1p20
BONNY LASS OF FISHERROW	51H65	1526	D C	4/4*	A1v5p12 D14v1p22 S12v1p65
					D14v4p2 G9v5p30 G11v2Cp21 C7p2

					(II)
(BONNY) LASS OF LIVINGSTON, THE	1133	5552	G F	4/4	A7v6p23 A1v2p30 (J3)
					G11v2Dp13
BONNY LASS OF LUSS, THE	5L13b4	47b47bL	G	2/2	B15v1p51
BONNY LASS TO MARRY ME, A	1323	5L326L	G	4/4*	A1v2p9 B15v1p24
BONNY LASS WI' THE TOCHER, THE	151H2	151H6	C	2/2	Mc22p16
BONNY LASS WILL YOU LYE IN A BARRACK	5L122	5L111	D	6/8	C13v2p80
BONNY LASSES OF ABERDEEN	1351	27L47L	D	2/2	S5p13
BONNY LASSI TAKE A MAN	1122	2122	F	2/2	W7p17
BONNY LASSIE TAKE A MAN	1133	4212	G	2/2	O1v1Kp128
BONNY LASSIE TURN YOU	316L2	3535	G	2/2	C18p14
BONNY MARY	3551H	6531H	G	4/4	C5v3p57 O1v1Ap24 O1v2p15
BONNY MARY	115L7bL	113b5	A	4/4	A7v5p21
BONNY PEGGY	336L5L	1221	G	4/4	C5v3p68
BONNY PEGGY KISS'D ME	111H1H	2H3H1H1H	D	4/4	D14v2p26
BONNY SALLY	3352	7L222	G	2/2	O1v1Jp100
BONNY SCOT, THE	5564	2355	D	4/4	P8v2p41
BONNY SUSIE	555	511H	D C	3/4	O1v1Ep26,27 O1v5p10
BONNY TOWN OF EDINBURGH, THE	1112	4231	A	4/4	W4v2p24
BONNY TWEED SIDE	5524	3b43b2	G	6/8	C10v2Ap16
BONNY WEE THING, THE	526L1	5265	Bb	4/4	(J3) E1v2p135 (II)*
BONNY WI THING, THE	1H31H3	1H344	F	6/8	B15v1p40
BONNY WIDOW OF WIGTON, THE	1H1H3H2H	1H672H	D	4/4*	C5v3p68 O1v1Lp145
BONNY YOUNG LAD IS MY JOCKEY, A	332	554	G	3/4	A1v5p34 C5v1p34 O1v1lp84
BOOLONZIE	51H1H1H	2H71H6	D	2/4	A1v4p29
BOOLONZIE, THE	51H1H1H	2H676	D	2/4	G11v1Bp34
BOOLONZIE, THE	51H1H1H	2H776	D	2/4	G10v3p35
BORDER CHIEFTAINS, THE	5L353	5L526L	G	4/4	P9p26
BORLAM'S (RANT/REEL/STRATHSPEY)	51H56	51H26	F	4/4*	Mc21v4p26 H3p33 B17p17 K1v1p28
[BORLUM'S RANT/REEL]					Mc9v1p23 G11v2Ap26 (II)
BORLUM'S REEL	1526	151H3	G	4/4*	R12v1p99 A1v1p56
BOTH SIDES OF THE TWEED	1332	135L3	G	4/4	K1v1p2 G11v2Ap2
BOTHWELL CASTLE	3L5L3L1	3L5L7F2	Bb	4/4	G11v1Ap12 (II)
BOTHWELL CASTLE	3531H	357L2H	G	2/2	E1v2p116
BOTTLE OF PUNCH	1524	1523	D	6/8	A1v6p54
BOTTLE OF PUNCH, THE	1523	1523	D	6/8	G10v3p22
BOTTLE OF WHISKY, THE	11H2H2H	3H1H1H2H	D	6/8	G10v6p24
BOTTOM OF THE PUNCH BOWL, THE	111H1H	1H135	D	4/4*	O1v3p23 A1v1p33 Mc8v1Cp81
					Mc8v2Ap9 O1v1Ap29 Mc9v2p4,5
					E1v2p139 C20p56 (II)
BOULD SOGER BOY, THE	3H51H7	2H1H3H1H	D	4/4	C8v2p45
BOUNDING ROE, THE	1113	31H1H5	A	4/4	O1v1Kp128,129
BOUQUET, THE	1H3H3H5	671H1H	C	2/4	A1v6p24
BOUROUGH FAIR	1L1L3L	5L17L	Bb	3/2	W7p22
BOWMAN'S FANCY	3142	3512	D	6/8	A1v5p14
BOWMEN OF THE BORDERS REEL, THE	1631H	3125L	F	2/2	L3p7
BOYNE WATER	1557b	427bL1	E	4/4	C7p7
BOYNE WATER	5L547bL	3b515L	A	2/4	C8v2p5
BOYS OF KILKENNY, THE	3H1H51H	4H2H5H2H	C	6/8	C8v1p49
BRAES ABOON BONAW, THE	1555	1532	G	2/4	C6p22 (II)
BRAES ABOON BONAW, THE	1555	1H532	D	2/4	G1v1p13
BRAES OF ABERARDER STRATHSPEY, THE	5336	5522	D	4/4	D16p35
BRAES OF ABERARDER, THE	5435	5632	G	4/4	A1v4p4
BRAES OF ALDCLUNE, THE	5L135	6L5L62	A	6/8	Mc10p6
BRAES OF ALDELUNE, THE	51H3H5H	656H2H	D	6/8	Mc10p15
BRAES OF ANGUS, THE	13b27b	427bL2	E	2/4	A1v1p54
BRAES OF ATHOLE, THE	3235	3122	G	2/2	Mc9v1p15
BRAES OF ATHOLE, (THE)	3236	3122	G	4/4*	N1v1p27 G11v2Bp18 B15v1p78,79
					K1v2p20 (II)
BRAES OF AUCHTERTYRE, THE	1135	1H3H1H5	C D	2/2	G11v2Ap20 P5v2p24 C13v2p4
					C13v1p36 N1v1p30 S12v1p45
					Mc13v2p34 C14v21p21 K1v1p22
					B10p34 (II) A1v2p54
BRAES OF BALANDINE, THE	3H5H5H	5H5H6H	D	3/4	O1v1Ep4
BRAES OF BALANDINE, THE	355	556	Bb	3/4	Mc23p32 O1v2p25 O1v5p3
					C13v3p66,67 P4p17 Mc8v1Ap21
					Mc8v2Ap22
BRAES OF BALLANDINE	355	656	D A G F	3/4	C6p13 C4p25 (C25)
					N1v2p42 (J3) C20p62,63
					Mc12v2p19,20
BRAES OF BALLENDEAN, THE	3H5H5H	6H5H4H	D	3/4	C19p8
BRAES OF BAL(L)ENDEN, THE	3H5H5H	6H5H6H	D	3/4	G17p20 G1v1p10
BRAES OF BALLENDINE	3H5H5H	6H5H6H	D	3/4	E1v2p34
BRAES OF BALLINDALLOCH, THE	147L2	1453	A	2/2	C14v6p22
BRAES OF BALLOCHMYLE, THE	541H7	6432	G Eb	4/4	C5v2p53 (J3)
BRAES OF BALQUHIDDER, THE	13bL5L5L	17bL5L4L	B	2/2	S11v1p9
BRAES OF BALQUHIDER	3133	6532	F	4/4	B15v1p37
BRAES OF BALQUHITHER, THE	5522	5547bL	E	2/2	Mc16p14
BRAES OF BALQUIDDER, THE	3133	3132	G F	4/4*	G1v2p50 Mc9v3p37 G11v2Ap27
					Mc21v3p9 K1v1p29 C14v12p22
					(II)
BRAES OF BALQUITHE, THE	6533	6533	F	4/4	C6p8

12

BRAES OF BALWHEDAR	3133	6532	G	4/4	A1v2p67
BRAES OF BALWHITHER, THE	6133	6532	F	4/4	P5v3p9
BRAES OF BOYNDLIE, THE	5631	5633	G	4/4	C18p13
BRAES OF BRAEDALBANE	5L13b1	53b53b	A	2/4	S7v2p9
BRAES OF BRANKSOM, THE	3H2H1H1H	3H5H76	D	2/2	O1v1Fp7
BRAES OF BROTHERTOWN, THE	16L7L67L	5L123	G	6/8	C10v1p2
BRAES OF BUSHBIE, (THE)	5L13b1	4L7bL23b	A G	4/4*	A1v6p35 A7v6p63 G1v1p47
					G9v5p8,9 Mc7p15 B11p5 G10v6p27
					Mc12v1p22 A7v3p4,5
BRAES OF CRAIGE, THE	3142	31H25L	A	2/2	C21p16
BRAES OF GLENDOCHERT, (THE)	3565	2427bL	D	4/4	Mc9v1p5 (II)
BRAES OF GLENDOCHERT'S REEL, THE	3565	2427L	D	4/4	B17p18
BRAES OF GLENORCHY, THE	3111	5L132	G	2/2	Mc9v1p12
BRAES OF GLENORCHY, THE	5157b	27bL3b4	G	6/8	Mc16p3
BRAES OF GLENTURROTE, THE	3561H	3H3H2H5	C	6/8	B11p16
BRAES OF KILLIECRANKY, THE	3H3H4H2H	4H4H5H3H	D	4/4	C5v3p75
BRAES OF LAINE, THE	13b3b1	27bL7bL2	G	4/4	C10v1p1
BRAES OF LITTLE MILL, THE	1552	1551H	G	2/2	C18p31
BRAES OF MAR, THE	3L13L1	247L7L	Bb	2/2	C14v17p7
BRAES OF MARR	1113	2L6L6L2L	G	4/4	W2v2p9
BRAES OF MARR	351H3H	1H61H6	D	4/4	G9v5p32,33
BRAES OF MARR	351H3H	2H61H6	D	4/4	C23p15
BRAES OF MARR, THE	355H2H	4H2H66	D	4/4	A7v6p47 A7v5p11
BRAES OF MARR, THE	1H1H1H1H	2662	D	4/4*	G1v2p50
BRAES OF MARR, (THE)	1H1H1H1H	2666	D	4/4	G9v5p32 A7v6p54 Mc9v3p37
					B15v1p34 A1v4p18
BRAES OF MARR, THE	1H1H1H1H	6662	D	2/2*	D15v1p23 Mc21v3p9 C14v12p14
					(II)
BRAES OF MARR, THE	1H1H1H3H	2662	D	4/4*	G11v2Bp35 K1v2p37
BRAES OF TULLIEMET	2555	7bL242	G	2/2	P5v4p3
BRAES OF TULLYMET, THE	557b2H	7b444	G	2/2	H3p8
BRAES OF TULLYMET, THE	2555	2454	G	4/4	C8v1p45 K1v1p10 G11v2Ap8
[BRAES O' TULLYMET]					N1v1p5
BRAES OF TULLYMET, THE	2555	4444	D G	4/4*	Mc13v2p19 C13v1p19 Mc9v1p29
					C13v2p30 S12v1p64
BRAES OF TULLYMET, THE	51H1H1H	57b1H7b	D	2/2	C14v7p11 (II)
BRAES OF WAUGHOPE, THE	1531H	53H1H5H	D	2/2	P9p14
BRAES OF YARROW, THE	5L6L5L1	426L0	Bb	4/4	T6v2p34
BRAES OF YARROW, THE	5651H	4H2H6O	D	4/4	P8v2p34
BRAES OF YARROW, THE	1365	2424	G A	6/8	C19p15 C4p71
BRAHAN CASTLE	136L5L	4L3L2L4	A	4/4	M12p30
BRAIGHE BHANBH	5531	5533	F	4/4	F2v2p22(12)
BRAIGHE LOCHIALL	5L5L7L	113b	A	3/4	F2v2p26(16)
BRANCH OF THE WILLOW, THE	1H53b5	3bH2H16b	E	6/8	A1v5p11
BRANDER, THE	1H3H1H3H	5772H	C	2/2	C18p18
BRAVE LADS OF GALLAWATER	3211	31H52	D	4/4	C20p81 O1v1Hp62
BRAW, BRAW LADS (OF GALLA WATER)	3211	5552	D G	4/4	(J3) C8v2p42 C5v2p21 G1v1p36
BRAYS OF ANGUS, THE	113b1	3b3b7b7b	D	4/4	R12v1p87
BREACHDAN UR FHIR GHORTALEIC	1531	7b442	E	4/4	F2v2p104(94)
[BREACAN UR FHIR GHORTUILEIC]					
BREAD AND CHEESE	3H1H1H7b	6461H	D	2/4	R12v1p95
BREAD AND CHEESE TO ROARY	3111	311H6	G	4/4*	A7v6p70,71 A7v5p39 A7v3p26
BREAST KNOT, THE (LADY'S)	4635	22H76	D	2/2	B15v1p31 Mc21v3p10
BRECHIN CASTLE	1115	117L7L	Bb A	4/4*	C8v1p12 C14v20p16 K1v1p34
					G11v2Ap32 (II) N1v1p36
BRECHIN CASTLE	13b15	13b7bL4	E	6/8	D15v1p21
BRECHIN LILT, THE	1122	1151H	A	2/2	O1v1Lp146
BREDAGAD	1H1H76	5522	G	2/2	W7p23
BREECHAN LASSES [BRECHIN LASSES]	5L134	3427L	G	4/4	W2v2p12 (II)
BREECHES (BRITCHES) MAKER THE	3b23b1	3b7b27bL	G	6/8	G10v4p30,31
BREECHES LOOSE	3b43b1	3b427bL	G	6/8	R12v1p13
BRES OF BIRNAM, THE	3356	1H765	G	4/4	O1v3p39 O1v1Bp6
BRES OF EWES, THE	3H1H5	442H	D	3/4	O1v3p40 O1v1Bp7
BREST FLEET, THE	1H2H61H	4525L	D	6/8	B16v1p6
BRIDE HAS A BONNY THING, THE	5562	5551	A	6/8	O1v1Hp55
BRIDE IS A BONNY THING, THE	5562	5555	A	6/8	B15v1p34 G11v2Cp25
BRIDE NEXT	1H1H5	61H6	D	6/4	P7p8
BRIDE OF LAMERMUIR'S REEL	1H1H72H	3H4H3H4H	D	2/2	P9p13
BRIDE, THE	1156	1156	G	2/2	C33p9
BRIDEGROOM GREETS	6652	5223	F	4/4	G15p26
WHEN THE SUN GAES TEE, THE					
BRIDE'S GARTER, THE	13b53b	1H3b1H3b	G	4/4	O1v1Lp161
BRIDESMAIDS' CHORUS, THE	1H3H1H3H	2H2H53	D	2/4	E1v2p50
BRIDGE OF ANAS, THE	13b27b	427bL2	D	2/2	B15v1p58
BRIDGE OF BRECHIN, THE	1H1H3b3b	7b7b24	C	2/2	D15v1p29
BRIDGE OF CRAIGE, THE	1535	47b27bL	A	4/4	Mc13v2p18 C13v1p18 A7v2p14
					A7v6p26
BRIDGE OF CROSK, THE	5346	5342	A	2/2	Mc10p6
BRIDGE OF DEE, THE	3155	4542	C	4/4	Mc13v1p6 Mc13v2p6 (II)
BRIDGE OF DON, THE	5151H	3H4H2H2	C	4/4	G8p17
BRIDGE OF DYE, THE	1155	6643	D	4/4	D15v1p18
BRIDGE OF FOCHABERS, THE	1355	4366	F	2/2	A7v4p24

Title					
BRIDGE OF FORTH, THE [BRIDGE OF FOSS, THE]	5353	4224	A	2/2	C13v2p65 H3p1 B10p1
BRIDGE OF GARRY, THE	1535	2662	A	2/2*	Mc9v3p32 G11v2Dp34 (11)
BRIDGE OF KILLAROW, THE	1153	26L15L	A	2/2	Mc16p29
BRIDGE OF KYNNACHAN	5353	4224	A	4/4	Mc19v1p9
BRIDGE OF LODI	11H1H7	2H51H1H	C	2/2	C14v20p23
BRIDGE OF LYON, THE	5L343	2427L	G	2/2	Mc4v1p22/23
BRIDGE OF PERTH	1565	351H3	A	4/4	A7v6p43
BRIDGE OF PERTH, (THE)	1546	351H3	A	4/4*	G11v2Dp28 D14v4p9 C8v2p49 Mc7p32 D14v1p29 Mc9v3p27 C13v2p34 Mc12v1p6 (11)
BRIDGE OF SPEY, THE	1H57b1H	57b55	A	4/4	G8p1
BRIDGE OF SPEY, THE	5L17L1	526L6L	D	4/4	M4v3p33
(BRIDGE/BANKS) OF NAIRN, THE	1566	5122	G	2/2	B15v1p109 G15p3
BRIGG OF BALATER, THE [BRIG O' BALLATER, THE]	151H6	5H5H2H2H	C	4/4	G11v1Ap8 C13v4p1 G10v1p27 (11)
BRIGHT CYNTHIA'S POWER	3235	2666	F	4/4	T6v2p71 P8v2p47
BRIGHTON WALTZ, THE	3527L	3551	Bb	3/8	H6v2p2
BRIGIS LACHLAINN	11H1H3bH	57b42	D	2/2	Mc16p18
BRIGUS MHIC RUARIDH [BRIOGAIS MHIC RUARAIDH]	3b57b1H	7b53b1	C	6/8	F2v2p69(59)
BRISK	1H1H3H1H	557b6	D	4/4	Mc5p12
BRISK	51H7	1H35	G	9/8	O1v1Dp10
BRISK	1H56	62H7	C	9/8	D15v2p8
BRISK BOB	3b55L1	3b53b7bL	B	4/4	K1v1p40 G11v2Ap38 (11)
BRISK YOUNG LAD, THE	13b52	7bL244	G	6/8	(J3) E1v2p124
BRITANGUE	112	3b13b	A	3/4	Mc9v2p24
BRITISH BOY'S	13H1H3	4442	D	4/4	A1v4p61
BRITISH BOYS	1L313L	4L4L4L2L	D	4/4	Mc12v1p55
BRITISH CONQUESTS	3142	5622	G	2/4	S7v2p12
BRITISH GRENADIERS MARCH, THE	1H1H3H2H	5H3H1H1H	D C	2/4	C8v2p10 C8v1p30 (11)
BRITISH HERO, THE	3343	3322	G	6/8	C14v5p9 S12v1p30
BRITISH NAVY, THE	3H1H1H5H	2H72H4H	D	2/2	C21p13
BRITISH TARRS, THE	351H5	6552	D	2/2	D14v3p10/11
BRITISH TARS CAN DO IT	11H53b	46b7b5	B	4/4	W2v2p4/5
BRODIE HOUSE	1H3H1H5	4642	F	2/4*	S11v1p7 (11)
BROKEN BRIG OF STIRLING, THE	5631	566L6L	F	4/4	C14v13p16
BROOM (OF) (COWDENKNOWES), THE	1155	5211H	D G	4/4	C8v2p52 C4p16 N1v2p10 (C25) G17p19 (J3) E1v1p103 Mc12v2p33,34 G1v1p10
BROOM (OF) COWDENKNOWS, (THE)	2255	5211H	D F G	4/4	S16p26,27 O1v5p27 P4p33 T6v1p18 Mc8v1Cp17 Mc8v2Ap22 B5p13 O1v1Fp21 C20p56 P8v2p1
BROOM'S HUMOUR	5241	1216L	Bb	2/4	B16v3p52
BROSE AND BUTTER	3b11	3b12	A	9/8	B15v1p32
BROSE AND BUTTER	3b11	3b14	A	9/8	E1v1p47 A7v6p37 A7v2p22
BROSE AND BUTTER	3b13b	3b14	A	9/8	K1v1p24 G11v2Ap22
BROSE AND BUTTER	533	536	G	9/8	G1v2p51
BROTHERS, THE	1343	237L5L	G	4/4	A1v2p60
BROUGHTON INVINCIBLES, THE	1H51H5	1H51H2	A	4/4	Mc19v2p22
BROUGHTY CASTLE	113b5	2422	A	2/2	C21p21
BROWN MILKMAID, THE	117b	511	A	3/4	Mc5p16
BROWNIE OF BODSBECK, THE	1H653	1H653	G	4/4	P9p26
BROWN'S REEL or [DUILLATER HOUSE]	1H3H2H6	6753	D C	4/4*	A7v6p17 A7v2p26 Mc9v3p29 S12v1p41 C13v2p36 G11v2Bp20 K1v2p22 (11)
BRUACHAN LOCH NEISH [BRUACHAN LOCH NIS]	5L13b5	7bL7bL7bL7bL	G	4/4	F2v2p16(6)
BRUNSWICK WALTZ, THE	3553	352H1H	F G	3/8	C8v1p51 C8v2p23
BUALIDH MI U AN SA CHEANN [BUAILIDH MI THU ANNS A' CHEANN]	5554	3b3b44	G	4/4	F2v2p17(7)
BUCHAN MAIDS ARE BRAW AN' BONNY	1427L	145L5L	A	4/4	C18p23
BUCHANANS REEL	3152	351H1H	A	2/2	C13v2p1
BUCK OF THE CABRACH, THE	3565	11H2H2	D	2/2	M4v3p36
BUCKET, THE	57b3b	1H7b3b	E	9/8	A1v2p46
BUCKINGHAM HOUSE	3b15L1	3b145	D	4/4	Mc21v3p27 (11)
BUCKINGHAM HOUSE	13L35L	447L2	Eb	4/4	A7v3p7
BUCKLAND DOWNS	1215L	6L7L13	Bb	6/8	S7v1p5
BUCK'S OF ST. JAMES'S	3125L	6L435	A	6/8	S7v1p60
BUFF AND BLUE	3344	3322	A	2/2*	R6v2p5 A7v3p28
BUFFOON DANCE, THE	1H1H3H2H	4H4H4H3H	D	4/4	A1v2p66
BUGLE HORN	5H3H1H5	1H2H3H3H	D	2/4	C14v13p18
BUGLE WALTZ, THE	1H1H1H	351H	D	3/4	B7p3
BULLERS OF BUCHAN, THE	5351	1H46L5L	D	4/4	G8p32
BULL'S HEAD, THE	126L5L	4L3L2L7L	G	6/8	R12v1p60
BUNCH OF GREEN BUSHES	5353	5316L	A	6/8	E1v2p91
BUNG YOUR EYE	13b52	7bL244	A	6/8	G11v2Ap21* C8v2p24 C8v1p10 H3p1 K1v1p23 A1v1p6 Mc7p12 C14v12p24
BURLESQUE ON BLACK JOAK	5L6L1	111	G	3/4	O1v1Gp18,19
BURLESQUE, THE	1153	657L2	F	2/2	C14v27p2

14

BURLIEGH PARK	5H3H1H5	6754	D	4/4	A1v5p47
BURN OF CARNIE, THE	5L5L5L1	2226L	A	4/4*	A7v6p83 B15v1p53 (II)
BURNS' PUNCH BOWL	1H522	1H51H1H	E	4/4	G10v6p16
BURNSIDE HOUSE	3b116b	27bL25	G	2/4	A4v2p2
BURNSIDE OF TYNET	3531	47bL7b7bL	F	4/4	M4v3p13
BURNTWOOD ASSEMBLY	1H3H72H	6753	C	2/2	S7v1p65
BURSTING SIGH, THE	5433	5432	A	4/4	O1v1Kp131
BURTON HOUSE	5H1H56	5H1H2H1H	D	2/4	C14v24p7
BUSH ABOON TRAQUAIR, (THE)	351H1H	2H2H2H2H	D	4/4*	C4p44 C5v2p3 C5v1p70 C29p30
					B5p7 C13v3p42,43 Mc8v1Cp65
					Mc8v2Ap1 A1v4p70 S16p4,5
					O1v1Bp17 O1v4p20 N1v2p2 C20p4
BUSH ABOON TRAQUAIR, THE	351H1H	2H2H3H2H	C E D	4/4	C6p10 C19p23 G17p4
BUSH ABOON TRAQUAIR, (THE)	351H2H	2H2H2H2H	D	4/4	P4p26 T6v1p5 P8v2p4
BUSH ABOON TRAQUAIR, THE	351H1H	1H1H2H2	D	4/4	E1v1p20
BUSH AT THE FOOT OF THE GARDEN, THE	3151	3H3H2H2	D	4/4	G9v5p12
BUSK O BUSK MY BONNY BONNY BRIDE	5555	4H2H66	D	4/4	O1v1Fp12
BUSK YE, BUSK YE	561H0	4H2H1H0	D	4/4	C19p25
BUSK YE, BUSK YE	5L6L5L5L	426L6L	A Bb	4/4	G17p13 N1v2p21
BUSK YE, BUSK YE	5L6L10	4210	A	4/4	D15v2p30
(BUSK YE) BUSK YE MY BONNY BRIDE	5655	4H2H66	D	4/4	O1v4p35 Mc8v1Bp48 Mc8v2Bp9
					B5p4 C5v2p21 C20p66
BUTCHER BOY, THE	1361H	3H316L	G	4/4	G1v2p73
BUTTER'D EGGS	5147L	1212	G	2/2	R12v1p80
BUTTER'D PEASE	3546	3542	D	2/4	A1v1p68
BUTTER'D PEASE	3554	4665	G	2/2	W7p8
BUTTLER'S REEL, THE	1335	4661H	G	4/4*	A7v5p12 A7v6p9 A7v2p31
BUTTON HOLE, THE	1H127bL	1H147bL	A	2/4	A1v2p37
BUXOM JOAN	133H6	1H66L2	G	6/8	S7v1p34
BUY A BROOM	5H3H2H3H	5H3H2H1H	D	3/8	G1v1p1
BY BRAIDS WEE LIMPID STREAM	321H1H	5322	G	4/4	C5v2p58
BY JOVE I'LL BE FREE	3535	62H32	D	3/8	A1v3p191
BY THE DELICIOUS WARMNESS OF THY MOUTH	1H1H5H2H	531H3H	C	4/4	C5v3p64
CA' THE EWES	4L17bL7bL	5L3bL24	B	4/4	A1v5p51 E1v2p20
CA' THE EWES TO THE KNOWES	1544	27bL61H	E	2/4	C5v2p9
CA' THE WETHERS TO THE HILL	11H61H	11H24	A	2/2*	G11v2Dp34 (II)
CABER FEIGH	1H1H1H5	1H531	C	2/2*	Mc23p16,17 C20p64,65 (II)
CABERFEIGH	1H3H1H5	6541	C	4/4	C8v1p20
CABINET, THE	2H1H75	1H2H3H3H	D	2/4	H6v23p2
CACHOCHA DANCE, THE	1H3H55	24H54	F	3/8	C8v1p50
CACINA	3311	4422	G	6/8	A1v1p35 Mc9v2p42
CADDLE ROBBIE	5355	5322	A	4/4	R6v2p19
CADGER WATTY	3265	3262	A	2/2	O1v1Lp150
CADGERS OF (THE) CANNONGATE, (THE)	1151H	51H22	G	2/2*	B15v1p51 G9v5p22,23 G11v2Ap12
					C4p61 K1v1p14 (II)
CAGARAN O	7b411	7b421	A	4/4	Mc5p19
CAIDIL GU LA	531	1H1H3H	D	3/4	F2v2p83(73)
CAIDIL GU LO	523	1H1H3H	C	3/4	Mc5p26
CAILLEACH AN FHRAOICH	5551	5547bL	A	6/8	Mc16p23
CAILLEACH OUER	1133	227b7b	D	4/4	G9v1p22,23 Mc23p25
CAILLEAGAN A BHAIL MHOIR	1H535	1H535	F	2/2	C8v1p36 F2v2p63(53)
[CAILEAGAN A' BHAILE MHOIR]					
CAIRNEY MOUNT, THE	5135	6421H	D	4/4	E1v2p129
CAIRNGORAM MOUNTAIN	5L5L5L5L	6L6L13	A	6/8	G10v4p11
CAISTAL DUNROBHAIN	15L15L	15L1L5L	Bb	4/4	F2v2p16(5,6)
[CAISTEAL DHUNROBAINN]					
CAISTAL INN'RARA [CAISTEAL INBHER-AORA]	5L15L3b	5L13b5	F	4/4	F2v2p21(11)
CAISTAL URCHUDAIN [CAISTEAL URCHUDAINN]	1L3L5L3L	37L5L3L	Bb	4/4	F2v2p28(18)
CAISTEAL DUNAIDH	1L3L31	27L5L3L	A	2/2	F2v2p49(39)
CAKE SHOP, THE	5H4H3H2H	1H2H3H2H	D	6/8	C1v1p12
CALABRIA	51H1H2H	1H2H72H	F	2/2*	C14v24p2 (II)
CALABRIA	51H3H2H	3H2H72H	D F	4/4*	G1v2p69 P6v1p22
CALABRIAN WALTZ	1H541H	1H541H	D	3/8	B7p40
CALAM CRUBACH ANN'S A GHLENN	1525	4242	A	4/4	Mc1v1Ap8
CALDER FAIR	1H663	5555	C G	4/4*	H6v22p2 B7p37
CALEB QUOTEM'S FREAK	137L	127L	G	9/8	H1p12
CALEDONIAN BEAUTY, THE	1H2H1H2H	1H2H3H4H	D C	2/4	A1v4p14 W4v1p3
CALEDONIAN CANAL, THE	11H3bH2H	7b7b7b7b	D	4/4	G10v4p38
CALEDONIAN HUNT ('S STRATHSPEY), THE	31H65	4562	D	4/4	C4p65 P5v3p14 G10v1p9
					Mc12v1p56,57 G7p8
CALEDONIAN HUNT, THE	31H67	4562	D	4/4	A1v4p12
CALEDONIAN HUNT, THE	31H65	3462	D	4/4	C5v1p12
CALEDONIAN HUNT, THE	11H65	4562	D	4/4	G11v1Ap31 (II)
CALEDONIAN HUNT, THE	315L1	247b5	A	2/2	H3p6 (II)
CALEDONIAN HUNT'S DELIGHT	1H2H3H2H	3H1H52H	D	6/8	A7v6p3
CALEDONIAN HUNT'S DELIGHT, THE	1232	315L2	D	6/8	Mc12v2p56
CALEDONIAN MAID, THE	1H3H5H2H	4H2H1H7	D	2/4	A1v6p36
CALEDONIAN MARCH, THE	1151H	5551H	F	4/4	C8v1p50
CALEDONIAN QUADRILLES (SECOND SET)	5L5L22	5L6L12	Bb	6/8	C8v1p62
CALEDONIAN SPAW	1433	6L6L21	A	2/4	D16p7
CALEDONIAN, THE	5561H	5532	C	6/8	C26v1p11
CALIMBO	1115	2226	G	2/4	A1v2p64

CALL A DANCE	5L7L12	3111	A	2/2	B16v3p61
CALL IT WHAT YOU PLEASE	1122	1125	A	6/8	H1p31
CALLAM BROGACH	7bL5L4L7bL	3b212	A	4/4	A1v6p43
CALLAM BROUGACH [CALUM BREUGACH]	7bL5L4L7bL	153b5	A	4/4*	Mc7p31 C24v2p11 G11v1Bp18,19
					G10v2p28 A7v2p4 (II)
CALLAM SHIARGHLAS	1H37L2	1H31H1H	F	4/4	G11v1Cp4 G10v3p25
CALLAM SHIARGHLAS	1H47L2	1H31H2H	F	4/4	Mc12v2p10,11,12 (II)
CALLAM'S FROLLOCK	15L7bL4L	3bL5L15L	G	4/4	Mc4v2p5 Mc12v1p16
CALLENDER HOUSE	513b2	2425	E	2/2	C14v15p24
CALLER HERRING	1H1H71H	3H2H76	D	4/4	B7p22 H6v10p1 C8v2p36 A7v5p12
					E1v2p23 G1v1p46
CALLER HERRING'	117L1	327L6L	Bb	4/4	C8v1p12 G11v1Bp22 C6p5 (II)
CALLUM A GHLINNE	15L6L	111	G	3/4	Mc5p23
CALLUM FIDHDAIR	1353	1H353	G	4/4	A1v5p56
CALLUM FIDHDAIR [CALUM FIGHEADAIR]	3353	1H353	F	2/2	F2v1p11 (II)
CALLUM FIODHDAIR [CALUM FIGHEADAIR]	51H7b5	3bH57b5	D	2/2	F2v2p19(9)
CALTON HILL, THE	13L1L1	13L7F2L	Bb	6/8	P9p4,5
CALUM A GHLINNE	5L153	6L41H6	Eb	6/8	F2v2p103(93)
CALVER LODGE	1H2H55	1152	G	2/4	C14v27p12,13
CAM' YE BY ATHOL	3155	321H6	D	6/8	G1v1p1
CAMBDELMORE	3366	5311	G	4/4	B15v1p92
CAMBRIAN MINSTREL, THE	1H1H35	1H2H3HO	F	4/4	F1p35
CAMBRIDGE LIGHT DRAGOONS, THE	1233	4453	Bb	2/4	G9v4p2
CAMDALE MORE	3366	5321	G	4/4	A7v6p9
CAMELEON, THE	3b15L1	27bL47bL	A	6/8	C26v1p14
CAMERON HAS GOT HIS WIFE AGAIN	1H655	1H622	D	4/4*	Mc7p23 C4p7 Mc21v3p7 B15v1p4
					C14v12p14,15
CAMERON HOUSE, A STRATHSPEY	5L121	7bL7bL23b	A E	4/4	A1v5p74 W4v2p25
CAMERON OF LOCHIL'S REEL	5335	351H5	A	2/2	C14v24p6
CAMERONIAN RANT	5154	5153	F	2/2*	(W3) (II)
CAMERONIAN RANT	3135	3154	F	4/4	P10p20
CAMERONIAN RANT, (THE)	5153	51H53	F	4/4*	K1v1p32 G11v2Ap30 G7p18,19
					C8v1p22 Mc7p29
CAMERONIAN'S	5153	5153	G F	4/4*	A1v1p38 A7v6p4 A7v2p11
(RANT/STRATHSPEY/REEL), (THE)					C13v2p16 S12v1p6 B15v1p82
					Mc9v1p16 C13v1p12,13 G9v5p2
					(II)
CAMERONIAN'S RANT	5155	3153	F	2/2	R12v1p24
CAMERONIAN'S RANT, THE	3153	5153	F	2/4	O1v1Kp112,113
CAMERONIAN'S RANT, THE	5153	5163	F	4/4	B10p38
CAMERON'S GOT HIS WIFE AGAIN	1H555	1H522	D	4/4	A1v4p68 C8v1p14 C8v2p18
					G11v1Bp33 C5v1p65 G7p7 K1v2p9
					G10v3p17 (II)
CAMLARG LODGE	531H5	2H542	C	4/4	H1p28
CAMMOLAN	533	534	G	9/8	C14v10p22
CAMP AT COXHEATH	1H1H53	6631	G	6/6	S7v1p31
CAMP, THE	1H1H4H1H	1H1H5H5H	D	2/4	B16v3p86
CAMPBELL INN	5437L	1366	F	2/2	B20p19
CAMPBELL'S ALLEMAND	1314	527L5L	Bb	2/4	C12p9
CAMPBELL'S ALLEMANDE	1H3H1H4H	5H2H75	D	2/4	A1v2p50
CAMPBELLS ARE COMING (O HO), (THE)	3522	3533	F G	6/8	(J3) G11v2Ap15 K1v1p17
					C14v17p14,15 B15v1p83
CAMPBELLS ARE COMING, THE	2533	2522	G	6/8	Mc16p8
CAMPBELLS ARE COMING, THE	3522	3553	G	6/8	A1v1p8
CAMPBELLS ARE COMING, THE	3532	3553		6/8	O1v1Cp12
CAMPBELLS ARE COMING, THE	3533	3522	D G	6/8	C6p30 C8v2p20 C5v2p71
					C8v1p60 E1v2p18 (II)
CAMPBELL'S REEL	35L3L1L	4L242	Bb	2/2	Mc13v2p28 C13v1p48
CAMPEL'S FROLICK	1230	1H670	G	6/8	R12v1p49
CAMPERDOWN GERMAN WALTZ, THE	5125L	423L1	Bb	3/8	W4v2p32
CAN YE SEW CUSHIONS	11H51	11H55	G	4/4	A1v4p69
CAN YE SEW CUSHIONS	11H53	11H55	G	4/4	C5v1p69
CANADIAN BOAT SONG, THE	5552	1363	G	6/8	E1v2p44
CANTIE CRECKET	51H51	51H72	D	2/2	S12v1p16 (II)
CANTY BODY	3331	2227bL	A	4/4*	B17p22 Mc9v1p27
CAOIDH NA H'ALBA AIRSON NIAL GHOBHA	3bL1L3bL5L	7bL5L3bL7bF	B	4/4	F2v2p70(60) (II)
[CALEDONIA'S WAIL...]					
CAPE BRETON MARCH	1H1H1H1H	2H2H1H1H	D	4/4	A1v6p65
CAPE TRAFALGAR	1H1H2H2H	3H1H2H5	C	6/8	P6v1p4
CAPE TRAFALGAR	1122	3125L	Bb	6/8	C14v21p23
CAPER FEY	1H3H1H5	1H531	C	4/4*	G10v4p26 C13v2p54 G9v5p6
					Mc13v2p17 Mc16p21 C14v21p5
					B15v1p102,103 C24v2p6,7 A7v6p96
CAPER FEY	3H3H1H5	1H531	C	4/4	M12p2
CAPn COOK	3153	3142	F	4/4	C26v1p7
CAPRICIOUS LOVERS, THE	1531H	7L527	Bb	2/2	P9p36
CAPT ARCHd. DOUGLASS' STRATHSPEY	151H3H	6642	D	4/4	A4v2p3
CAPT BAILLIES MARCH	5555	3H511	D	2/2	L3p1
CAPT BLAIR (OF THE ROYALS') QUICKSTEP	1324	131H5	F	2/4	W4v2p34
CAPT CAMPBELL OF AIRD'S QUICK STEP	51H3H2H	4H3H1H1H	D	2/4	A1v1p62
CAPT CAMPBELL OF BLYTHSWOOD'S FAV.	1351H	1321	D	4/4	Mc15p34
CAPT CAMPBELL OF CARPHEN'S STRATHSPEY	113b2	7bL7bL42	A	2/2*	Mc4v2p8 (II)

Title					
CAPT CAMPBELL (OF LOCHNELL'S) Q/STEP	5H3H6H4H	5H3H77	C	6/8	Mc21v2p24
CAPT CAMPBELL OF MELFORD	1H345	4542	A	6/8	L1p18
CAPT CAMPBELL OF ORMIDALE'S REEL	1353	2427bL	D	2/2	Mc12v1p36
CAPT CAMPBELL OF SHAWFIELD'S VALTZ	1H13H3	5H5H4H1H	C	3/8	G9v4p6,7
CAPT CAMPBELL OF SUNDERLAND'S REEL	316L5L	316L2	A	2/2	Mc16p36
CAPT CAMPBELL'S REEL	5H551H	2H3H1H6	D	2/2	Mc15p34
CAPT CHARLES CRAWFORD'S FAREWELL	13b47bL	13b57b	A	6/8	D16p23
CAPT CHARLES GORDON, R.N. HUNTLY	117L7L	1133	A	4/4	M4v4p30
CAPT CHARLES STEWART'S JIGG	1131H	5216L	G	6/8	Mc4v1p5
CAPT COLLIN CAMPBELL OF SHAWFIELDS REEL	5142	517b4	A	2/2	Mc16p29
CAPT CUNINGHAM OF CORSEHILL'S REEL	5417b	47b47bL	G	6/8	R5p13
CAPT CUNNINGHAM OF AUCHINSKEIGH'S REEL	1H3bH1H7b	47b2H7b	G	2/2	R5p40
CAPT DAVID STEWART, 42nd ROYAL HIGHLANDER'S REEL	11H35	27b22	D	2/2	Mc4v4p9
CAPT DOUGAL CAMPBELL KILMARTIN'S STR.	1363	662H2	D	2/2	Mc16p27
CAPT DOUGLAS'S STRATHSPEY	5L13b5	27bL7bL4	E	4/4	Mc16p11
CAPT FLEMING'S REEL	1H1H1H1H	2H71H6	C	4/4	A7v5p11
CAPT FLETCHER'S REEL	3542	351H5	A	4/4	G9v5p31
CAPT GORDON, SCOTS GREY'S JIG	1317	4742	A	6/8	Mc22Cp1
CAPT GRAEME INCHBRAKIE'S STRATHSPEY	5231	2522	F	2/2	B11p14
CAPT GRANTS STRATHSPEY	3561H	1H3H2H2H	C	4/4	A7v3p14,15
CAPT H. MUNRO(OF NEWTOWN'S REEL)	3b15L3b	427bL4	G	2/2	M12p23 (II)
CAPT HILLMAN'S MARCH	1H1H1H3H	2H2H2H4H	D	4/4	A1v3p207
CAPT HOME'S JIG	5115	7bL747bL	E	6/8	Mc22Cp1
CAPT JAMES ABERCRUMBIE'S REEL	3b13b1	2427bL	G	4/4	W2v1p10
CAPT JAS ROBERTSON 76th REGt's REEL	15L13	25L24	A	4/4	Mc22p10
CAPT JIPHSON'S WHIM	3354	2211	G	2/4	A1v3p159
CAPT JOHNSTON'S LAMENT	3322	1131H	G	4/4	C5v3p54
CAPT KEELERS REEL	1H3H5H1T	1H3H72H	D	4/4	G1v2p84
CAPT KELLER'S REEL [CAPt. KEELER]	1351H	117L2	Bb	2/2	S12v1p47 (II)
CAPT LOCKHART	1H542	22H4H2H	D	4/4	A7v6p53 (II)
CAPT MACINTOSH	1115L	1155	A	2/4	G10v2p35
CAPT MACKENZIES REEL	3344	3327bL	G	2/2	S12v1p36
CAPT MACKENZIE'S REEL	3565	27bL27bL	D	2/2	C14v19p3
CAPT MARSHALL'S FANCY	1113	5312	A	2/2	M4v3p14
CAPT McDONALD'S FANCY	5L35L4	5L37L7L	F	2/2	C14v7p9
CAPT McDONALD'S REEL	3453	6L5L32	D	2/4	C14v9p11
CAPT McDUFF'S FAREWELL TO PARLIAMENT HOUSE	513b5	2424	E	2/2	Mc4v4p10
CAPT McDUFF'S FAREWELL TO THE PARLIAMENT HOUSE	3133	652H2	F	2/2	Mc13v1p4 Mc13v2p4
CAPT McDUFF'S REEL	3b53b5	27bL24	G	2/2	S12v1p68 (II)
CAPT MONTGOMERY'S FANCY	1H1H2H7	3H3H4H2H	Eb	6/8	C12p2
CAPT PARK OF PARKHALL'S JIGG	3L13L1L	4L5L4L2L	Bb	12/8	C13v4p4,5
CAPT PARK OF PARKHALL'S STRATHSPEY	3L13L5L	4L6L4L2L	Bb	4/4	C13v1p34,35
CAPT PATRICK McKENZIE'S STRATHSPEY	1L1L5L1	6L6L22	A	4/4	P5v1p17
CAPT ROBERT GRANT'S REEL	1H515	3H4H2H2H	F	4/4	Mc15p25
(CAPT) ROBERTSON OF BALGARVIE'S REEL	1L5L16L	6L5L4L2L	Bb	2/2	Mc22Ap2
CAPT RONALD FERGUSON'S QUICK STEP	572H3H	4H5H2H5	C	6/8	W2v1p4,5
CAPT ROSE OF KILRAVOCK'S STRATHSPEY	314L3L	2L222L	Bb	4/4	L1p10
CAPT ROSS KENDEAS'S QUICK STEP	31H74H	3H1H2H5	C	2/4	J2p7
CAPT SIMON FRASER OF KNOCKY'S FAV.	5L113b	5L111	A	4/4	G11v2Dp18
CAPT SINCLEAR'S STRATHSPEY	1L353	4327bL	G	4/4	A7v3p19
CAPT SMYTH'S FAVOURITE	51H51	51H62	D	2/2	Mc21v3p4
CAPT WALTON CAMPBELL'S STRATHSPEY	5L5L5L7L	3422L	Bb	4/4	C14v19p23
CAPT WHITE 73rd REGt's STRATHSPEY	315L3	5347L	F	4/4	L1p12
CAPT WILLIAM LOGAN'S REEL	3b13b5	7b7b42	G	2/2	C13v4p32
CAPT WILLIAM McLEOD'S FANCY	1H531	2H3H75	F	6/8	M4v3p54
CAPT YOUNG OF BANFF'S REEL	1H515	3H72H2	C	2/2	M12p4
CAPT YOUNG OF THE ROYAL PERTH VOLUNTEERS QUICK STEP	1H71H7	1H2H2H2H	F	2/4	C23p10
CAPTAIN BAILLIES QUICK STEP	5655	513H2H	D	6/8	L3p1
CAPTAIN BISSET'S STRATHSPEY	15L5L1L	2426L	Bb	2/2	J1p22
CAPTAIN BYNG'S REEL	71H31	42H75	G	2/2*	G10v4p4 (II)
CAPTAIN CAMERON'S VOLUNTEERS MARCH	1111	5314L	E	4/4	M4v3p25
CAPTAIN CAMPBELL OF ARGARTER'S MARCH	3322	1113	D	2/2	D16p8
CAPTAIN DASH'S REEL	1333	7L27L7L	G	2/2	P9p28
CAPTAIN FIFE'S STRATHSPEY	1155	4326L	F	4/4	D16p26 (II)
CAPTAIN FLEMING	1111	27L11	Bb	2/4	P6v1p27
CAPTAIN FLETCHER'S FAVORITE	15L11	5622	F	4/4	G10v5p34
CAPTAIN FRANCIS WEMYSS DELIGHT	113b5	7b427bL	A	2/2*	B11p7 (II)
CAPTAIN FRANCIS WEMYSS STRATHSPEY	31H61H	6522	D	2/2*	B11p7 (II)
CAPTAIN HUGH MUNRO'S STRATHSPEY	1H6L5L3L	5L47L2	Eb	2/2	Mc15p6
CAPTAIN JAMES BLACK OF THE 98th QUICKSTEP	11H65	437L2	G	6/8	S5p5
CAPTAIN JOHNSTON'S MARCH	1113L	1322	A	4/4	L3p6
CAPTAIN JOHNSTON'S QUICK STEP	1133	5521	A	6/8	L3p7
CAPTAIN KEELER'S REEL	1351H	137L4	Bb	2/2	G11v2Ap9
CAPTAIN KELLER'S REEL	1351H	137L2	Bb	4/4*	Mc13v2p13 Mc7p4 C8v1p44 G8p5 K1v1p11 A7v2p29 C13v1p3 C13v2p1 Mc12v1p30 (II)
CAPTAIN LEITH HAYS REEL	1L3L13	437L7L	Bb	2/2	D15v2p42

CAPTAIN LOCKHART (OF THE TARTAR)	1H532	22H4H2H	C	2/2	C13v2p8 B15v1p27 N1v1p28
CAPTAIN MacDONALD'S STRATHSPEY	1131	1132	Bb	2/2	G8p27 P1v1p8
CAPTAIN MACDUFF ('S DELIGHT)	137L2	3422	G	2/2 4/	Mc21v1p31 C14v1p12
CAPTAIN MACINTOSH'S STRATHSPEY	1115L	1355	A G	4/4	A7v2p13 A7v6p5
CAPTAIN MACKDONALD	1L5L31	6L5L4L3L	Bb	2/2	P6v2p18
CAPTAIN MAC(K)INTOSH('S FAVOURITE)	117L5L	1155	A	2/4	C5v1p12 C4p19 A1v4p12 P10p9
CAPTAIN McDUFF'S REEL	5215L	1522	A	2/2	D14v3p6/7 G11v2Cp27 Mc9v3p28
CAPTAIN MOUNSEY'S STRATHSPEY	3565	4L217bL	A	2/2	A7v1p4
CAPTAIN NAPIERS MARCH	1H135	1H1H3H4H	D	4/4	Mc12v2p8,9
CAPTAIN O KAIN	5L3b27bL	3b55L1	G	6/8	Mc13v2p29 K1v2p9 G10v4p23
					Mc12v2p9
CAPTAIN O' KAIN(E)	5L12	3b3b2	G	3/4	A1v3p190
CAPTAIN OAKHAIN	5L3b27bL	3b45L1	G	6/8	Mc9v3p36
CAPTAIN OAKHAIN	6bL3b27bL	3b55L1	G	6/8	Mc7p6
CAPTAIN PRYCE GORDON or	3513	6L27L5L	Eb	4/4	Mc21v3p15
GLEN LOCKARTS STRATHSPEY					
CAPTAIN R. MARTIN'S REEL	1H1H31	2466	D	2/2	B20p12
CAPTAIN RACKET	1H11H2H	3H5H2H7	D	6/8	B16v3p69
CAPTAIN RIDDELL'S STRATHSPEY	13b47bL	13b55	G	4/4	A7v1p1
CAPTAIN ROBERTSON LUDES STRATHSPEY	5L135	51H46L	D	4/4	B11p10 (II)
CAPTAIN ROSS('S REEL)	5L5L26L	1353	G A	4/4*	A1v2p17 N1v1p18 G11v2Cp26
					C13v2p3 C4p20 B15v1p8
CAPTAIN SHALL NOT GET THEE, THE	136L5L	7L223	G	2/2	Y1p1
CAPTAIN SINCLAIR'S REEL	1355	5362	A	2/2	A1v5p12 D14v1p35 D14v4p13
(CAPTAIN/MR ROBERT) KENNEDY'S REEL	1565	1H542	F	2/2	B15v1p5 K1v2p31 N1v1p19
					G11v2Bp29
CAPTAIN'S LADY, THE	1355	1564	G F	4/4*	C5v2p7 (J3)
CAPTAIN'S LADY, (THE)	3b23b2	4L7bL4L7bL	G A	6/8	A7v2p18 A7v5p35 A7v6p35
CAPTAIN'S LADY, THE	3b23b2	7bL7bL7bL7bL	A	6/8	D15v1p20
CAPTURE OF SERINGAPATAM, THE	351H6	537L7L	F	2/2	C14v16p1
CAPUCHIN, THE	1H1H2H2H	3H1H2H5	D	6/8	A1v2p5
CAPUCHIN, THE	151H	552	G	9/8	R12v1p55
CARD ASSEMBLY	5142	5145L	D	6/8	D16p19
CARD ROOM	3H1H3H1H	1H1H2H7	F	2/4	D6p26
CARDING O'T, THE	1133	51H52	A G	4/4	C8v1p47 C8v2p17 E1v2p117
CARE THOU CANKER	5H5H5H1T	5H5H4H3H	D	4/4	A1v3p204
CARLAND'S DEVOTION	5L5L17bL	2144	A	2/4	O1v1Hp61
CARLE AN' THE KING COME	3211	115L5L	F G	4/4*	(J3) C5v3p63 E1v2p128
CARLE AN THE KING COME	3212	115L1	F G	2/2	S16p16,17 O1v1Fp15
CARLE AN' THE KING COME	3113	115L1	G	4/4	G11v2Dp20
CARLE AND THE KING COME	3213	115L1	G	4/4*	Mc8v1Cp63 Mc8v2Cp10
CARLE CAN YE WHISTLE	3152	311H1H	D	2/2	C24v2p10,11
CARLE HE CAME O'ER THE CRAFT	1133	7b422	A	4/4*	B15v1p30 A1v1p19 P5v3p25
(WI' HIS BEARD NEW SHAVEN), THE					S12v1p4 G11v2Bp28 G8p16
					K1v2p30 (II)
CARLE HE CAME O'ER THE CRAFT, THE	1155	6542	F	2/2	(J3) T6v1p102
CARLE HE CAME O'ER THE CRAFT, THE	113b5	7b422	A	4/4	A7v5p20
CARLE HE CAME O'ER THE CRAFT, THE	1133	7422	A	4/4	P1v1p7
CARLE HE CAME O'ER THE CROFT, THE	1135	7b422	A	2/2	A7v2p30,31
CARLEN IS YOUR DAUGHTER READY	1553	27bL24	A	2/4	A1v1p9
CARLES RANT, THE	1531	1542	A	4/4	K1v1p6 G11v2Ap6
CARLETON HOUSE	5H5H1H1H	671H1H	D	2/4	A7v6p73 A7v5p38
CARLETON HOUSE	1H51H5	2H4H2H7	C	6/8	C1v1p11
CARLETON HOUSE	15L15L	2427L	Bb	6/8	C14v7p10
CARLETON HOUSE HIGH DANCE	5511	6L7L11	Bb	2/4	D15v2p25 A7v3p7
CARLIN IS YOUR DAUGHTER READY	1533	1542	A	2/2	Mc21v3p39
CARLIN OF THE GLEN, THE	1H1H1H2H	7b2H2H3bH	E	4/4	C20p70
CARLIONE	1H6b6b4	13b3b3bH	C E	4/4	G10v3p21 A1v5p18
CARLIONE	6442	6L111H	G Eb	4/4	C5v1p18 Mc12v2p6,7
CARLISLE YETTS	3H3H1H6	64H3H1H	C	4/4	C6p23
CARLTON HOUSE	1315	5511	Bb	2/4	C14v4p1
CARNIVAL DI VENEZZA	6452	3641	G	6/8	C8v2p47
CARNIVAL OF VENICE	6452	3631	A	6/8	E1v2p10
CARO DOLCE	136L2	7L531	Bb	2/4	C14v21p14
CARO DOLCE	1H673H	1H671H	C	2/4	H6v5p3 P6v1p20
CAROLANES PURSE	1H1H6	553	F	3/4	C24v2p7
CAROLAN'S DEVOTION	3bH2H1H	1H57b	G	3/4	A1v6p48
CAROLAN'S FAREWELL TO MUSIC	113b2	247b5	G	4/4	H1p16
CAROLAN'S LAMENT	5L5L5L	114	A	3/4	O1v1Hp48
CAROLAN'S RECEIPT FOR DRINKING (WHISKY)	6442	6L111H	Eb	4/4*	G11v1Bp20,21 A7v3p30
CARPET WEAVER, THE	1H3H1H2H	631H6	D	2/4	E1v2p58
CARRICK'S (RANT/REEL)	1155	51H33	D	4/4*	Mc9v1p9 E1v1p2 P5v2p18
					G11v2Ap3 K1v1p3 B15v1p94,95
					(II)
CARRICK'S REEL	1155	51H32	D	2/2	N1v1p34
CARRIL'S LAMENT	3211	326L1	G	6/8	O1v1Kp135
CARRON SIDE	326L1	5L422	G	4/4	C5v2p34 G1v2p49 O1v1Hp44
					O1v5p17
CARRON'S REELL	5L17bL2	5L143	G	2/2	C33p17
CARSE HOUSE	3311	4522	D	2/2	R6v1p1
CARY OWEN [GARRY OWEN]	6333	6322	G F	6/8	A7v5p22 C14v16p2,3 C8v2p53
					A7v4p22 K1v2p32 C8v1p64 (II)

Title					
CARY OWEN [GAR(R)Y OWEN)	1H555	1H544	D E	6/8	G11v2Bp30 E1v1p114
CARYSFORT, THE	1153	27L27L	Bb	6/8	P6v1p11
CASCADE, THE	1H71H2H	3H3H3H3H	D	2/2	S7v1p92
CASSAC	1554	1551	G	2/4	Mc9v2p21
(CASSEL/CASTLE) REEL, (THE)	1565	1542	D	2/2	A7v4p18 D15v1p7
CASTLE BAR	135	156	F	9/8	C14v15p16
CASTLE CAMPBELL	5515	4542	F	2/2	B20p13
CASTLE CAMPBELL	3H1H51H	351H3	C	2/2	G11v2Dp33
CASTLE DOWN	1343	326L6L	G	6/8	C14v17p10,11
CASTLE GRANT	31H61H	6542	C	2/2	C14v9p21
CASTLE GRANT	151H5	151H1	D	4/4	Mc9v3p8
CASTLE GRANT	1135	4131	Bb	6/8	G15p22
CASTLE GUTHRIE	3123	1H61H5	D	6/8	A7v6p77 D16p8
CASTLE POOL, THE	13b51	13b47bL	E	6/8	D15v1p21
CASTLE SWIEN	1H1H1H	3H3H3H	D	3/4	O1v1Lp151
CAT IN PATTENS, THE	5L5L5L4L	337L7L	Bb	6/8	B16v3p26
CATCH AS CATCH CAN	1531H	5132	G	2/4	S7v1p90
CATCH HER IF YOU CAN	3556	3552	A	6/8	R12v1p3
CATCHES AND GLEES	1H5H4H7	1H5H4H1H	D C	6/8	Mc9v2p2 S7v1p68
CATHARINE OGGIE	5L13b3b	123b2	A	4/4	C29p20,21
CAULD KAIL	5152	5154	A	4/4	Mc21v4p34
CAULD KAIL (IN ABERDEEN)	31H52	3561	G D	2/4	C5v2p3 A1v5p48 (J3)
CAULD KAIL IN ABERDEEN	351H1H	5321	G	4/4	C8v2p40
CAULD KAIL IN ABERDEEN	31H52	3651	G	2/4	E1v1p81
CAUP O' YE'R TIPPANY KATE, A	1H3b7bL	1H3b1H	D	9/8	F3p2
CAVE OF CORK, THE	5315	261H2H	F	3/8	G10v2p14
CAVE OF ENCHANTMENT	3131	1H1H1H3	G	2/4	S7v1p88
CAW HAWKEY THROUGH THE WATER	3b3b44	3b3b27bL	A	2/2	R12v1p94
CAW THE WITHER TO THE HILL	1155	5126L	G	4/4	P5v3p25
CAWDOR FAIR	1H663	5555	D G	4/4	E1v1p8 G1v2p65 (II) C5v2p62
CAWDOR FAIR	1H663	5655	D	4/4	G11v2Dp9
CEANN AN FHEIDH	3L3L5L4L	3L3L5L3	Bb	2/2	F2v2p59(49)
CEANN DUBH DILEAS	51H3bH2H	7b2H7b1	E	6/8	G10v2p30 Mc12v2p1
CEANN DUBH DILEAS	51H3bH2H	7b2H1H1	E	6/8	G11v1Bp24
CEANN NA DROCHAID BIG	1111	1111	G	4/4	Mc1v1p38-47
CEANN NA DROCHAID MHORIDH	1355	2355	G	4/4	Mc1v1p111-115
CEANRARA [CEANN RARA]	113L5L	6L133	F	2/2	F2v2p56,57(46,47)
CEASE YOUR FUNNING	1H3H4H7	3H62H1H	D	6/8	E1v1p63 O1v1Fp13
CELEBRATED GERMAN MINUET, THE	332	143	D	3/4	G11v1Cp38 G10v3p34
CELEBRATED HUNTERS' CHORUS, THE	1H1H5H3H	2H2H3H1H	D	2/4	E1v2p49
CELEBRATED MEDLEY WALTZ, THE	553	1H1H6	Eb	3/4	G9v3p14
CELEBRATED MEDLEY WALTZ, THE	553H	531	Eb	3/4	G9v3p14
CELEBRATED MEDLEY WALTZ, THE	4H2H7	553	Eb	3/4	G9v3p13
CELEBRATED STORM WALTZ, THE	111	111	Eb	3/4	G9v3p12
CELEBRATED SWISS WALTZ, THE	1543	1543	G	3/8	E1v2p42
CELEBRATED TRUMPET TUNE, THE	333	15L1	A	3/4	G10v5p22
CELEBRATED VALTZ RONDO, THE	1H5H53H	1H5H5H1H	D	3/8	G9v4p22,23
C'EST L'AMOUR	3H2H3H5H	3H2H1H5H	D	6/8	A7v6p92
C'EST L'AMOUR	5555	1H1H1#H2H	F	6/8	E1v2p82
CEUD SORAIDH UAM D'ON AILLEAGAN	16L15L	36L11	A	4/4	Mc5p13
CHA BHAS THIG AIR LOACH ACH CADAL	13b2	13b2	D	9/8	F2v2p86(76)
CHA BHI MI M'IASGAIR	1H1H1H7b	7b51H3b	E	4/4	Mc5p9
CHA CHEILINN SUGRADH VILEAM	3351	5347bL	G	4/4	Mc5p16
CHA D'THEID MI GU LOCH BHRAOIN NO GHEARRLOCH	1141	1152	A	6/8	Mc5p5
CHA MO LEANNAN NUN 'THAR SAL [CHAIDH MO LEANNAN NULL THAR SAL]	1H352	3673	C	6/8	F2v2p93(83)
CHA N EIL FONN AIRA NIGHEAN DUIBH	1552	1127bL	G	4/4	D14v2p26
CHA TILL MI TUILLE	5555	5555	A	6/8	Mc5p41
CHAGAIR, CHAGAIR, CHAGAIR A' GHRUAGACH	1H1H3bH	5H5H5H	D	3/4	Mc5p10
CHAIDH AN TORAN MU THOM	1H1H6	556	D	3/4	Mc5p30
CHAIDH MI LA DO'N BHADTRAILEACH	1H3H1H1H	51H65	D	6/8	Mc5p11
CHAMI MA CHATTLE	6L11	111	G	3/4	(S16)
CHAPEL KEITHACK	332	115L	Bb	3/4	M4v3p6
CHAPLE SHADE HOUSE	1H3H2H5	61H51	F	4/4	C21p6
CHAPLET, THE	5H3H4H2H	3H52H5	D	2/2	A1v3p205 R12v1p31
CHAPTER OF KINGS	51H2H5	52H5H1H	D	6/8	C5v1p25 A1v5p25
CHAPTER OF KING'S, THE	5L125L	5L251	Bb	6/8	C22p44
CHARITY BOY, THE	5H5H6H5H	4H71H1H	C	6/8	A1v6p26
CHARLES DUFF'S COMPLEMENTS	1316L	5L352	Eb	6/8	D15v2p47
CHARLES GRAY ESQr OF CARSE'S STRATHSPEY	1356	5642	F	2/2	D15v1p9
CHARLES LESLIE (OF FINDRASSIE'S STRATHSPEY)	1353	5353	D	4/4	G15p14 (II)
CHARLES LILT	1353	11H22	G	2/2	O1v1Hp40
CHARLES SHARPE ESQr. OF HODDOM'S FAVORITE	1425	437L2	A	6/8	A7v1p3
CHARLES STREET BATH	1H1H1H3	61H65	G A	4/4*	A1v4p58 A1v1p29 C13v2p34 G11v2Dp34 Mc7p13 H3p29 P11v2p6 Mc12v1p28
CHARLIE, HE'S MY DARLING, ORIGINAL SET	13b57b	427bL2	D	4/4	G11v2Dp1
CHARLIE HE'S MY DARLING, THE YOUNG ...	657b2H	657b7b	E	4/4	C5v3p63

Title			Key	Time	References
CHARLIE IS MY DARLING, (OH!), MODERN SET	13b51H	6b1H51H	E D A	4/4*	C6p18 C8v1p17 C8v2p26
					G11v2Dp1 C5v2p56 E1v2p7
CHARLIE STEWART TEARLACH STIUBHARD	13b57b	7b423b	E	4/4	A1v5p67 Mc5p24
CHARLIE STUART	5244	5222	D	2/2*	G11v2Dp29 (11)
CHARLIE, YE ARE WELCOME	1351H	61H51H	F	4/4	C6p27
CHARLOTE COTTILION, THE	3455	61H65	Bb	2/4	C7p10
CHARLOTE, THE	3H5H5H5H	6H1T6H6H	D	2/4	A7v6p71
CHARLOTTE AND WERTER	347L5L	1L432	A	4/4	P9p30
CHARLOTTE, THE	3555	61H66	Bb	2/4	A7v3p6,7
CHARLOTTE'S RANT	1H1H1H7	1H7b55	A	4/4	S7v1p98
CHARMS OF KILDARE, THE	1H5H66	2H4H75	C	6/8	C14v17p14
CHARMS OF THE FAIR, THE	316L5L	7L425L	Bb	4/4	C14v24p6,7
CHASE, THE	1H3H53	1H3H52	D G C	4/4*	H3p26 P5v2p20 B10p28
					K1v2p22,23 G11v2Bp20 C14v26p10
					G9v5p6 C13v2p5
CHASSE MARINE	1H34H1H	54H3H2H	C	6/8	A1v3p195
CHATSWORTH HOUSE	5H3H1H3H	64H75	D	2/4	B16v2p12
CHATSWORTH, THE	351H4	2416L	G	4/4	B16v2p6
CHEAP MEAL	521H2	2662	D	2/2*	G11v2Dp38 Mc21v3p11 C13v2p36
					G15p15 (11)
CHEAP MUTTON	5L127bL	5L121H	G	4/4	G10v4p31
CHEAPUICH NA FASOCH	113b	53b7bL	F	9/8	F2v2p21(11)
[(A') CHEAPACH NA FASACH]					
CHELSEA STAGE	1335	61H55	F	6/8	S7v1p90
CHERRY RIPE	3565	1H3H1H7	G	4/4	G1v1p26
CHESHUNT STATUTE	5357L	2442	A	2/4	B16v3p27
CHESTER CASTLE	5555	4322	F	2/4	Mc9v2p18
CHESTER CASTLE	5551	5751	D	4/4	A1v2p7
CHESTER RACES	5115	47L7L4	Bb	2/4	A7v3p18
CHESTHILL HOUSE	1524	511H5	F	6/8	Mc19v2p11
CHESTHILL'S FAVORITE AIR	1566	7623	G	6/8	Mc19v2p16,17
CHEVY CHACE	51H1H	2H1H6	D	3/4	O1v4p28,29 O1v1Ep31
CHEVY CHASE	5L11	25L5L	G	3/4	Mc8v1Dp108
CHI MI BEAN SAN TRAIGH 'NA SUIDHE	1H1H3bH	5H3bH1H	E	3/4	Mc5p10
CHILING O GUIRY	133	144	G	3/4	T7p32,33
CHINESE DANCE	1411H	1411	D	6/8	S7v1p12
CHISHOLMS FROLICK	315L1	3151H	G	4/4	E2p23
CHIT CHAT	5431	1H637L	A	6/8	B16v4p90
CHIU RI RUO	1H1H1H	3bH3bH3bH	E	3/4	Mc5p1
CHIVEY CHACE	311	311	Bb	3/4	C19p28
CHOARA CHROM [A' CHAORAN CHROM]	5L17bL2	5L13b2	G	4/4	F2v2p17(7)
CHORUS IN ATALANTA	2H5H1H2H	2H2H4H5H	D	4/4	R12v3p14
CHORUS JIG, (THE)	5153	5156	D	6/8	A1v2p48 Mc9v2p30
CHORUS JIG, THE	3151	3156	D	6/8	K1v2p37 G11v2Bp35 B10p39 (11)
CHRISTMAS DAY IN THE MORNING	5L133	3322	G	6/8	A1v3p171
CHRISTMAS EVE	15L41	15L41	Bb	6/8	S7v1p95
CHRISTMAS TALE, A	3H1H1H5	5522	D	2/2	S7v1p19
CIA IAD NA DEE 'SNA DUILE TREUN	1115L	5L5L10	A	4/4	Mc5p31
CIA IAD NA DEE 'SNA DUILE TREUN	1115L	5L5L11	A	4/4	F2v2p93(83)
CIA MAR IS URRA' SINN FUIREACH O'N DRAM	1155	136L1	G	6/8	F2v2p31(21)
CILLE CHASSIDH [CILL A CHASSAIDH]	5513	5642	G	4/4	F2v2p76(66)
CIOD E BHIODH TU 'GIARRAIDH	1133	2215L	G	4/4	C4p56 Mc5p31
[St. KILDA SONG AND DANCE, A]					
CIRCASSIAN CIRCLE	1313	1313	Bb A	4/4*	C8v1p40 (11)
CIRCASSIAN CIRCLE	1H3H1H3H	1H3H1H3H	D	2/4*	C8v2p58
CIRCUS REEL, THE	1153	1142	F	4/4*	Mc22p11 P5v3p15
CIRCUS WALTZ	1555	61H55	G	3/8	B7p39
CITTY SPOON AND TREEN LADLE	1131	4427L	G	2/2	Y1p17
CIVILITY	5642	1232	Bb	2/4	C14v25p6
CLACH NA CUDAIN [CLACHNACUDAINN]	5L3L4L2L	427L5L	G	2/2	F2v2p41(31)
CLAN RANALD'S MARCH TO EDINr	5521	5555	A	6/8	D14v2p39,40,41
CLANRANNALD'S REEL	113b1	7b7bL24	E	2/2*	C13v4p6 G10v2p7 (11)
CLANRONALD HOUSE	1527bL	157b5	E	4/4	R7v2p1
CLAN'S GATHERING, THE	1111	1111	G	4/4	Mc1v1p38-47
CLARINET, THE	5H3H2H1H	1H2H3H3H	D	4/4	R12v3p30
CLARK'S HORNPIPE	13b5	151	E	3/2	Mc9v2p32,33
CLARK'S REEL	1L1L35L	5L12L2L	Bb	2/2	C13v2p62
CLEAN PEAS STRAW	1H3H4H3H	2H577	D	2/2	C14v17p8
(CLEAN) PEASE STRAE	1H3H4H3H	2H57b7b	C D	4/4*	(J3) C8v2p10 G9v5p23
					S12v1p2 B15v1p65 G11v2Cp36
					C8v1p30 G1v2p73 G7p7 (11)
CLEEK HIM INN	151H6	4522	F	4/4	B15v1p66
CLEGHORN'S RANT	51H3H1H	4H3H67	D	4/4	A1v3p211
CLERKENWELL ASSEMBLY	3523	1H527L	A	12/8	B16v3p32
CLIFTON HOUSE	1561H	1561H	D	2/4	W6p17
CLINKIN O'T, THE	1H1H1H5H	1H1H72H	C	2/2	C18p28
CLOAK BAG	1324	51H52	G	2/4	B16v3p57
CLOAK BAGG, THE	1655	27b27bL	D	2/2	R12v1p72
CLODUN REEL	1531	1527bL	G	2/2	B15v1p19
CLOUDEN BRAES	313L1L	3L132	Bb	4/4	R6v1p6
CLOUT THE CALDRON	61H1H5	1H1H1H3H	D	2/2	Mc8v1Bp45

CLOUT THE CAULDRON	1H1H1H1H	2H776	C	4/4	T6v2p58 P8v2p9
CLOUT THE CAULDRON	51H1H1H	2H776	D	4/4	B5p12
CLOUT THE CAULDRON	61H1H1H	2H775	D	2/4	O1v1Gp32,33
CLUB, THE	5L13b1	415L6bL	G	6/8	D6p22,23
CLURIE'S REELL	1155	51H33	D	4/4	C33p19
CLYDE RIVER	1151	4642	A	4/4	A7v1p6
CLYDESDALE LASSES, THE	3565	3535	F	4/4	C8v1p7 G7p17 G10v6p31 G13p14 (II)
CO A NI MIREADH RI MAIRI	133	135	G	9/8	F2v2p81(71)
COALLIER'S DAUGHTER, THE	3115L	7bL7bL24	G	2/2	S12v1p43
COATTER WIFE, THE	1551H	57b27bL	A	2/2	Mc9v3p42
COBLER OF CASTLEBERRY, THE	316L	5L3L7L	Bb	3/4	E1v2p136
COBLER OF CASTLEBERY, THE	315L1	2535	Bb	6/8	G9v3p36
COBLER, THE	1H565	62H4H2H	C	6/8	D16p11
COBURG WALTZ	1H3H71H	1H3H71H	G	6/8	B7p29
COCK IN THE AIR, THE	1535	1535	G	4/4	E2p10
COCK LAIRD (FU' CADGIE), (A/THE)	5553	5553	F G	6/8	(J3) T6v1p54 C5v3p58 C5v1p23 A1v5p23
COCK LAIRD, THE	7b51H	7b56	E	3/4	O1v1Bp33 O1v4p16
COCK OF THE NORTH, THE	15L13	51H62	A	2/2	G9v2(p13)
COCK UP YOUR BEAVER, (JOHNNY)	551	331	F G	6/4	(J3) Mc8v2Cp13 C5v2p53 G1v2p71 Mc8v1Bp49
COCKS LOUNS WALIE HOYN	3551H	3H3H2H1H	D	4/4	Y1p4
COILEACH AN TOABH TUADH	11L5L3L	13L21	Bb	4/4	F2v2p50(40)
COILSFIELD HOUSE	311L1L	437L5L	G	4/4	G10v5p7
COIR A' CHEATHAICH	17bL1	3b3b3b	A	3/4	Mc5p20
COIR' A GHEARRAIG	2L5L7bL7bL	7bF4L2L7bF	B	2/2	F2v2p79(69)
COIR A MHONI [COIRE MHONAIDH]	5L3L1L3L	5L3L6L3L	A	4/4	F2v2p49(39)
COL. ALEXr GRANT'S STRATHSPEY	11H3bH1H	57b42	C	4/4	G15p34
COL. ARCHd CAMPBELL'S QUICK STEP	1H3H4H1H	671H1	D	6/8	A1v1p58
COL. BOYLE OF SHEWALTON	5L36L2	5L36L1	Bb	6/8	G10v6p9
COL. CAMPBELL'S REEL	1353	2466	D	2/2	Mc13v2p27
COL. CATHCART'S REEL	151H5	2424	E	2/2	R5p59
COL. DALRYMPLE'S MARCH	1H535	1H1H3H4H	C	4/4	G3p22
COL. E. WILDMAN'S QUICK STEP	1352	3234	Bb	6/8	Mc19v3p17 Mc19v2p10
COL. FARQUHARSON'S STRATHSPEY	5L13b5	5L7bL24	G	2/2	J2p8
	15L5L1	3356	G	4/4	Mc10p10
COL. FERRIER OF THE SCOTS BRIGADE'S MARCH					
COL. FERRIER'S MARCH	1H555	6453	Eb	4/4	G3p13
COL. GARDEN'S BIRTH DAY	1343	436L7L	G	4/4	P5v2p15
COL. GARDINER'S LAMENT	7bL7bL1	3b10	A	3/4	O1v1Jp91
COL. GRAHAM'S FAVORITE	1H1H4H1H	3H5H2H2H	C	6/8	C21p4
COL. GRANT OF GRANT'S STRATHSPEY	151H2	151H3H	D	4/4	G15p10
COL. HAMILTON OF PENCAITLAND	12H51H	11H72H	C	4/4	G11v1Bp20
COL. K. McKENZIE 52ND REGts STRATHSPEY	5565	5521#	C	4/4	M1p2
COL. LENOX'S MARCH	1H1H1H5	1116	Bb	2/2	M2p32
COL. LESLIE'S MARCH	3113H	7555	D	4/4	M2p12
COL. MacLEOD OF RASAY'S STRATHSPEY	1L3L13	16L5L3L	Bb	4/4	Mc22Ap2
COL. McDONALD'S STRATHSPEY	3b17bL3b	41H6b1H	E	4/4	A1v5p26
COL. McDONALD'S STRATHSPEY	7bL5L4L7bL	153b5	A	4/4	C5v1p26
COL. MONTGOMERY'S QUICK STEP	1515	1524	F	6/8	C14v9p6
COL. MUNRO'S QUICK STEP	3342	1732	Bb	2/4	J2p13
COl. NICHOLSON	116L5L	1136	Bb	4/4	H1p1
COL. WARDLE	51H4H4H	3H53H1H	C	6/8	H6v5p3
COLBECK HOUSE	3531H	3542	C	2/2	Mc4v3p10 (II)
COLD AND RAW	111	3b3b4	E	6/4	C4p1
COLD FROSTY MORNING, (A)	5L11	111	G F	3/4	O1v1Dp16 P4p29 Mc8v1Dp119 O1v5p5 K1v2p4 G11v2Bp4 (J3)
COLD FROSTY MORNING, THE	6L11	111	A	3/4	C13v3p16,17
COLD IS THIS NIGHT	3H3H5	3H3H3H	C	3/4	Mc5p15
COLDSTREAM MARCH	11H35	44H4H2H	D	4/4	A1v6p66
COLDSTREAM MARCH, THE	1H1H3H3H	5H4H3H2H	D	2/2	M2p28
COLIN'S REQUEST	1112	16L7L2	G	4/4	P8v2p41
COLI MERCER OF ALDIE'S STRATHSPEY	1555	7bL7bL7bL7b	D	4/4	Mc4v2p9
COLLA CITEACH	3331H	3336	G	6/8	Mc16p29
COLLAR-GREEN	3331	7bL27b7b	G	4/4	M4v3p42
COLLEGE HORNPIPE	1H115	31H1H3H	D	2/2	C8v2p60
COLLEGE HORNPIPE, THE	11L1L5L	3L113	Bb	4/4*	C8v1p13 Mc21v4p7 Mc9v2p33 B10p8 (II)
COLLEGE OF St. ANDREWS, THE	115L5L	247L2	G	4/4	Mc13v1p7 Mc13v2p7
COLLEGIAN, THE	1133	5532	G	6/8	S7v1p30
COLLIE CAN	5L113b	27bL24	A	2/2	P5v4p4
COLLIER'S BONNY LASSIE, THE	4115L	7bL7bL20	F	2/4	(J3) N1v2p71
COLLIER'S BONNY (LASSIE/DAUGHTER), THE	3115L	7bL7bL20	G	4/4*	Mc8v1Dp120 T6v1p99 (II)
COLLIER'S DAUGHTER, THE	3115L	7bL424	G	4/4	G9v5p25
COLLIER'S (DAUGHTER/LASS), THE	3311	115L5L	G	2/2	O1v1Ep17 P7p5
COLLONEL, THE	5551H	51H4H2H	F	2/4	B16v3p17
COLLr. Wm. SIMSON'S STRATHSPEY	1135	1H4H62H	F	4/4	Mc16p35
(COL./MR) ROBERTSON (OF STROWAN) 'S STRATHSPEY	5551	457bL4	E	4/4	A1v6p8 A7v2p9 G10v2p12 E1v1p34 (II)
COLn ROBERTSON'S STRATHSPEY	5551	4442	E	4/4	G11v1Ap22 A7v2p9

COLONEL BAIRD	5555	5411	F	6/8	G10v4p18
COLONEL BAIRD'S STRATHSPEY	1H13b5	243b2	E	4/4	A7v4p13 (II)
COLONEL BELCHES FAVORITE STRATHSPEY	3b13b5	2454	A	4/4	A7v6p50
COLONEL BYNG'S FAVORITE	1H1H31	42H75	D	4/4	G10v4p34
COLONEL CAMPBELL OF KINGSBURGH'S STRATHSPEY	1255	7b542	E	4/4	R7v2p1,2
COLONEL CAMPBELL OF SHAWFIELD'S STRATHSPEY	13L1L3L	2L47L2	A	4/4	Mc21v4p40
COLONEL CAMPBELL'S REEL	315L1	247b2	A	2/2	C13v2p68
COLONEL CHRISTIE'S MARCH	3H2H3H1H	1H1H2H2H	D	4/4	A1v6p68
COLONEL CRAWFORD'S STRATHSPEY	15L13	2426L	G	4/4	A7v6p83
COLONEL CRAWFORD'S (STRATHSPEY/REEL)	13L13	2426L	F	2/2	B15v1p49 B17p9
COLONEL CUMMING OF ALTYRE	1253	1666	F	6/8	L1p8
COLONEL DAVID STEWART OF GARTH'S REEL	5153	4522	A	4/4	G10v6p4 Mc19v1p11
COLONEL FRASER OF KNOCKY'S STRATHSPEY	5315	4362	G	4/4	L1p1
COLONEL GEDDES'S GRAND MARCH	1HO2HO	3H1H1HO	D	4/4	F1p30
COLONEL HAMILTON OF PENCAITLAND'S WELCOME HOME	1L5L7L	1L5L6L	Bb	9/8	G10v4p32
COLONEL HAY'S STRATHSPEY	35L42	35L5L3	A	4/4	A7v3p18,19
COLONEL H.F. CAMPBELL'S STRATHSPEY	1555	6525L	G	4/4	L1p9
COLONEL MACDONALD'S STRATHSPEY	7bL5L4L7bL	1535	A	4/4	Mc12v1p47
COLONEL MACDONELL'S STRATHSPEY	7bL5L4L7bL	1535	A	2/2	Mc9v3p6
COLONEL MACDOWALL OF LOGANS STRATHSPEY	5L5L5L1L	2L5L4L7bF	A	4/4	G9v5p14,15
[COLONEL MACKAY'S] JIGG	1H11H5	6527bL	C	12/8	Mc13v2p35
COLONEL MACKAY'S STRATHSPEY	1H155	6527bL	C	4/4	Mc13v2p34,35 C13v1p36,37
COLONEL MACKENZIE'S REEL	53b51	53b47bL	G	2/2	C14v12p15
(COLONEL McBAIN'S) (REEL)	3b13b5	27bL24	A G	4/4*	A7v6p42 G1v2p87 A7v5p30
					G9v5p11 Mc7p3 Mc13v2p32,33
					C14v19p17 C8v1p45 B15v1p101
					H3p19 K1v1p10 D15v2p42 A7v2p30
					C13v2p54 G11v2Ap8 Mc9v3p18
					N1v1p12 P5v2p14 C13v1p32,33
					Mc12v1p29 B10p25 (II)
COLONEL MCDONALD OF LOCHGARIE'S STRATHSPEY	351H3H	1H522	E	4/4	Mc4v2p5/6
COLONEL MCDOWALL'S MARCH	1122	1115L	Bb	4/4	C12p2&11
COLONEL McLEAN'S MARCH	1H1H1H2H	3H3H3H4H	D	4/4	A1v6p75
COLONEL McLEOD OF RASA'S REEL	1H3H53	4642	F	4/4	R7v1p2
COLONEL McLEOD'S REEL	1315L	6L6L4L2L	Bb	4/4	C14v21p16
COLONEL McLEOD'S STRATHSPEY	5L353	5L362	F	2/2	G8p31 P1v1p12
COLONEL MONT[G]OMERIE'S FAVORITE STRATHSPEY [JAMIE ROY]	5522	5526L	D	2/2	Mc9v3p36
COLONEL MONTGOMERIE'S COMPLEMENTS TO ORANGFIELD	1113	1162	F	6/8	E2p2
COLONEL MONTGOMERIE'S WELCOME HAME	1H311	47bL42	G	6/8	R5p19
COLONEL MONTGOMERY'S STRATHSPEY	1H522	1H526L	D	4/4	G10v1p17 Mc12v1p46 (II)
COLONEL MONTGOMRIE'S MARQUIE	1122	1542	D	2/4	E2p24
COLONEL MURRAY'S MARCH	552H7	62H2H7	Eb	4/4	B12p2
COLONEL NOEL'S FANCY	5511	661H1H	G	4/4	S13p2,3
COLONEL ROBERTSON OF LAWERS STRATHSPEY	1111	2235	D	4/4	Mc4v4p8
COLONEL ROBERTSON OF STREWAN'S WELCOME HOME	13b24	13b51H	E	6/8	G11v1Ap22 G10v2p12
COLONEL ROBERTSON OF STROWAN'S MARCH	1131	5535	Eb	4/4	B11p27
COLONEL ROBERTSON'S STRATHSPEY	5L3L7F2L	5L3L5L3	Bb	4/4	C14v16p5
COLONEL ROSE OF KILRAVOCK'S STRATHSPEY	5315	1H52H2	F	4/4	L2p21
COLONEL SHARP OF THE PERTH VOLUNTEERS QUICK STEP	1H1H1H1H	1H3H6H4H	C	6/8	C23p8
COLONEL SIR ROBERT H. DICK'S MARCH	13L4L3L	1L113	G	2/2	Mc19v3p9
COLONEL SMALL'S STRATHSPEY	1H1H1H1H	1H1H2H2H	F	2/2	G8p8 P1v1p14
COLONEL SMALL'S STRATHSPEY	1L1L5L1L	4326L	A	2/2	J1p4
COLONEL TARLETON'S QUICK MARCH	5H5H6H5H	6H2H1H7	D	6/8	S12v2p6
COLONEL THORNTON('S STRATHSPEY)	1L5L3bL3bL	2L4L5L4L	A	4/4	G11v1Cp22 G10v2p14,15
COLONEL W. MARSHALL OF THE 79th REGt OF FOOT	5555	1H3H62	C	4/4	M4v4p14
COLONEL WEBSTER'S MARCH	1H1H1H3H	2H2H2H3H	C	4/4	S12v2p7
COLONEL WEMYS'S REEL	1H532	7L242	G	2/2	C5v1p10 A1v4p10 Mc9v3p22
					Mc12v1p45
COLONEL W.F. MACBEAN	1H3H5H3H	6H4H2H7	D	6/8	L2p18,19
(COLONEL/GENERAL) CAMPBELL OF MONZIE'S FAVOURITE	1H1H6b6b	5547bL	C	4/4	G10v3p8,9 G11v1Ap19
(COLONEL/GENERAL) McKAY'S REEL	1H155	6327bL	C	4/4*	D14v4p12 C14v10p18 B15v1p112
					P5v2p22 C13v2p54 D14v1p32
					G11v2Cp22
COMA LEAM, COMA LEAM COGADH NO SITH	3215	2324	A	12/8	Mc5p43
COME AND RANGE THE FIELDS WI' ME	5H6H5H5H	5H6H3H2H	D	2/4	C5v2p46
COME ASHORE JOLLY TAR AND YOUR TROUSERS ON	3b3b3bH2H	7b3b6b5	E	4/4	A1v1p66
COME DANCE AND SING AND LET US BE MERRY	51H3H1H	4H3H2H5	D	6/8	F1p33
COME HAP ME WITH THY PETTICOAT	5522	6L6L6L1	G	2/2	Mc8v1Bp42
COME HAP ME WITH THY PETTICOAT	526L6L	5555	G	4/4	A1v1p65
COME HAP ME WITH THY PETTICOAT	7b543b	17bL13b	E	2/2	Mc8v2Cp16
COME KISS ME COME CLAP ME	5151	5575	G	2/2	S16p118,119 P8v2p46

COME KISS WI' ME COME CLAP WI' ME	1H1H1H3bH	7b7b3b4	E	4/4	C5v3p70
COME MY BRIDE, HASTE, HASTE AWAY	1115L	3b3b42	A	2/2	C10v2Ap67
COME NOW FOR JEST AND SMILING	1H1H2H2H	3H3H3H2H	D	4/4	A1v3p191
COME O'ER THE STREAM, CHARLIE	115	536	G	3/4	G1v1p3
COME SWEET LASS	1355	5226L	G	4/4	A1v3p197
COME SWEET LASS	1533	5226L	G	4/4	C4p41 O1v1Bp33 O1v4p13
COME TELL TO ME MY MAIDENS FAIR	3H3H5H	2H2H5	D	3/4	B7p47
COME (THEN/NOW) ALL YE SOCIAL POWERS	5535	61H65	G D	6/8	A1v3p157
COME UNDER MY PLAIDY	5353	5316L	G Eb	6/8	C5v3p62 (11) (J3)
COMELY GARDEN(S)	331H5	67b27bL	A	2/2	D14v4p10 D14v1p30 C13v2p62
					G11v2Cp24 (11)
COMELY, THO' BLACK-O'-BLEE	1611	1632	F	6/8	C10v2Bp76
COMERS OF LARGO A REELL, THE	1H56	1H51H	D	9/4	P7p8
COMICAL JACK	1H532	6L242	G	2/2	S7v1p36
COMIN' THRO' THE RYE	5L5L22	5L6L11	A Bb	6/8*	C6p10 (11) T8p2
COMIN' THROUGH THE RYE	552H2H	561H1H	D	4/4	E1v2p58
COMING THRO THE BROOM MY JO	5L117bL	1255	A	2/2	O1v1Hp40
COMING THROUGH THE HEATHER	5L455	6L1H22	F	4/4	B11p15
COMING THROUGH THE RAYE	1122	1155	Eb	4/4	P5v3p11
COMING THROW THE BROOM MY JO	123b5	47b15L	A	2/2*	B15v1p25 (11)
COMMA LEAM FEIN A MINISTEIR	355	351H	C	9/8	F2v2p25(15)
COMMIN' THRO' KILBLEEN	117bL2	557b2H	D	4/4	C18p19
COMODORE MITCHELLS' STRATHSPEY	5654	537L2	F	2/2	G8p27 P1v1p8
COMPLAINING MAID	3116	5114	F	12/8	S7v1p79
COMPOSED AND DANCED BY MR McDONALD	155	5L44	A	3/4	D16p4
CONAL AND FLORA	51H1H	1H1H5	E	3/4	C5v2p57
CONCERT ROOM	3331H	3H2H1H6	G	4/4	D6p26,27
CONCERTO	5640	3420	G	2/4	R12v3p15
CONNEL & FLORA	51H7	1H1H5	E	3/4	B7p42
CONQUEST, THE	1H1H1H1H	3H3H4H3H	D	2/4	B16v4p91
CONTENDING PARSONS, THE	3b151H	427L5L	G	4/4	B16v3p31
CONTENTED COTTAGERS	1H1H1H1H	4H3H72H	C	4/4	S7v2p11
CONTENTED WI' LITTLE AND CANTY WI' MAIR	3b3b3b	11H1H	E	6/4	G1v1p24
CONTRE DANCE	1H565	1H5H2H3H	D	6/8	C22p47
CONTRIDANZE	31H3H1H	4H2H75H	D	6/8	B7p34
CONTRIVANCE, THE	356L6L	5L57L2	A	6/8	G10v6p18
CONTRIVANCE, THE	356L6L	5L67L2	A	6/8	B11p12
CONVENTION, THE	1313	5252	G	2/4	W4v2p10
COOL O' GURRO	1H3H2H1H	662H2H	G	6/8	C14v18p15
COOLUN	1H1H2H	1H31	G	3/4	C5v1p29 A1v5p29
COOLUN	1H1H2H	1H51	D	3/4	E1v1p3
COOLUN	1H1H3H	1H51	D	3/4	K1v2p12 G11v2Bp10
COOPPER IN FIFE	353H2H	2H225	C	2/2	P7p18,19
COPENHAGEN WALTZ, THE	4H3H2H	3H1H3H	D	3/4	B7p35 C8v2p50
CORBEY AND THE PYETT, THE	51H1H7b	7b27b4	C	4/4	O1v1Gp5
CORDWAINER'S MARCH, THE	117bL5L	3b3b27bL	B	4/4	A1v1p61
CORELLIS GIGGA	1H1H1H1H	7b6b55	G	12/8	C13v3p76,77
CORIMONIE'S (STRATHSPEY/RANT)	151H5	1524	D	2/2*	C14v1p16 G11v2Cp37 D14v3p21
					(11)
CORN CUTTERS, THE	5566	1H642	D	2/2	Mc9v2p35
CORN CUTTERS, (THE)	1H11H7	2H22H1H	C	2/4*	D16p29 G9v3p27 (11)
CORN RIGGS	1132	7L7L25L	A	4/4	(J3) C20p51
CORN RIGGS	137L2	1315	A	2/4	C6p4
CORN RIGGS	1131	7L7L25L	A	4/4	E1v1p28
CORN RIGGS (ARE BONNIE)	1H1H3H2H	772H2H	D	4/4	B7p31 C5v2p4 P8v2p6
CORN RIGGS (ARE BONNY)	1132	7L7L25L	A G	4/4	G17p10 (J3) Mc8v1Ap28 Mc8v2Ap13
					Mc23p12,13 N1v2p72 C13v3p62,63
					C20p51 C29p42 Mc12v2p25,26
					B5p5
CORN RIGGS (ARE BONNY)	1H1H3H2H	772H5	D	4/4*	O1v4p42,43 O1v1Bp22,23 C8v2p44
					C4p1
CORN RIGGS ARE BONNY	1H1H4H2H	772H2H	D	4/4	T7p22,23
CORNHILL DANCE	3565	3642	F	4/4	C7p12
CORONATION STRATHSPEY, THE	1353	1653	D	4/4	P9p12
CORPORAL CASSEY	35L35	46L46	G	6/8	A7v6p33
CORPORAL, THE	3155	2227bL	A	2/4	A1v1p4
CORPORAL, THE	3135	2427bL	G	4/4	B15v1p79
CORRILLE REVIV'D	3217L	6L237L	Bb	6/8	G8p7
CORRIMONIES REEL	1332	1323	G	4/4	C33p10
CORRIMONY'S STRATHSPEY	551H5	5524	D	4/4	P5v2p13
CORYDONS COMPLAINT	3332	5556	G	4/4	P8v2p42
COSEN COLE'S DELIGHT	3L5L5L5L	6L6L66	Bb	2/2	P7p15
COSSACK DANCE	3115	3532	A	2/4	G9v3p33
COSSACK DANCE, A	3H1H3H1H	661H5	D	6/8	G1v2p65
COSSACK WALTZ	1T5H51H	1T5H51H	C	3/8	B7p33
COSSACK'S DANCE, THE	1555	1551	Bb	2/4	C14v27p12
COSSY('S) JIGG, (THE)	4323	5L123	G	6/8	G10v2p23 A1v3p162 C14v5p10
COTERIE, THE	53b13b	243b5	G	4/4	S7v1p53
COTILLION	1122	3125L	Bb	2/4	C22p36
COTILLION	5165	4225L	A	2/4	C22p38
COTILLION	1231	6L27L2	Bb	2/4	C22p39
COTILLION	1H1H66	4347L	D	2/4	C22p38

COTILLION	3H1H2H5	72H4H3H	C	4/4	C22p42
COTILLION	5653	4322	A	2/4	C22p34
COTILLION	11H67L	3L4L32	Bb	2/4	C22p36
COTILLION	13L13L	1233	Bb	2/4	C22p37
COTILLION	1H564H	3H3H77	D	6/8	C22p38
COTILLION	1H1H2H5	3H5H2H7	C	6/8	C22p40
COTILLION	1363	237L5L	A	6/8	C22p41
COTILLION	3L1L3L5L	6L5L2L7L	Bb	6/8	C22p41
COTILLION	1111	1H525L	Bb	6/8	C22p37
COTILLON	1123	1H233	G	2/4	A1v2p15
COTILLON	1231	1H642	G	2/4	A1v2p29
COTILLON	1H3H61H	5311	E	2/4	P5v1p17
COTILLON	1565	4225L	G	2/4	A1v2p45
COTILLON	17L43	2115L	Bb	2/4	D15v2p40
COTILLON	1H1H1H5	2311H	D	6/8	S12v2p30
COTILLON	1H2H71H	3H4H2H3H	D	6/8	S12v2p30,31
COTILLON	1351H	5231	G	6/8	S12v2p31
COTILLON	1H2H54H	5H5H2H1H	D	6/8	S12v2p32
COTILLON	3b211	523b1	A	6/8	S12v2p37
COTILLON, A	1H542	4311	G	2/4	P5v1p19
COTTAGE BOY, THE	1363	6564	F	4/4	P9p2,3
COTTAGE, THE	3565	1H3H1H1H	D	2/4	G9v3p5
COTTAGER'S DAUGHTER, THE	5535	22H1H6	D	4/4	E1v1p108,109
COTTILION	31H61H	1H425L	G	2/4	S11v2p5
COTTILION	1166	51H2H5	F	2/4	S11v2p7
COTTILION	131H1	2H2H75	D	2/4	S11v2p7
COTTILION	1H2H65	2467L	D	6/8	S11v2p18
COTTILLION 1st	11H55	3623	Bb	2/2	Mc17p1
COTTILLION 2nd	115L5L	3L5L3L3L	Bb	6/8	Mc17p2,3
COTTILLION 3rd	1H1H1H3H	5531	D	2/4	Mc17p4
COTTILLION 4th	1H2H3H1H	5531	F	2/2	Mc17p5
COTTILLION 5th	3H2H1H1H	3H1H2H7	D	2/4	Mc17p5,6
COTTILLION 7th	51H54	52H1H1H	D	2/2	Mc17p8
COTTILLION 8th	115L5L	3L5L3L1L	Bb	2/2	Mc17p9
COTTILLON	1H321	2423	G	2/4	A1v1p19
COTTILON	123b7L	1H6b21	G	2/4	S11v1p24
COTTILON	1H2H3H5H	3H6H2H2H	C	2/4	A1v3p202
COTTILON	5H3H5H3H	5H4H1H1H	C	2/4	A1v3p199
COUNT BROWN'S MARCH	1H1H1H2H	1H751H	D	2/2	A1v6p30
COUNT WARTENSLEBEN	1H31H5	1H3H72H	C	4/4	C26v1p5
COUNTESS OF AIRLY('S STRATHSPEY)	5353	6527L	G	4/4	D16p28 (II)
COUNTESS OF ANCRAM'S (STRATHSPEY/BIRTHDAY), THE	1147L	1115	D G	4/4	G10v5p14 G1v2p78
COUNTESS OF ANTRIM, THE	1H1H55	3H1H4H3H	D	6/8	C14v16p22
COUNTESS OF BREADALBANE'S FAVORITE STRATHSPEY	113L1	4L6L4L2	Bb	4/4	Mc4v4p1 (II)
COUNTESS OF BREADALBANE'S JIG, THE	17L31	1H641H	A	6/8	Mc19v2p16
COUNTESS OF BREADALBANE'S REEL	113L5L	4L226L	Bb	2/2	Mc4v4p1
COUNTESS OF BUCHAN'S STRATHSPEY	13L1L3L	5L6L2L2	A	2/2	C14v26p9
COUNTESS OF BUCHAN'S STRATHSPEY, THE	1135	662H1H	D	2/2	S5p8
COUNTESS OF CASSILLI'S REEL	5L1L5L5L	1322L	A	2/2	G10v4p2,3 (II)
COUNTESS OF CASSILLI'S STRATHSPEY	1113	112L2	A	4/4	G10v4p2
COUNTESS OF DALHOUSIE	551H2H	6542	F	2/2*	G11v1Bp30 (II)
COUNTESS OF DALHOUSIE'S FAVORITE, THE	117L5L	1153	G	2/2	G9v2p1
COUNTESS OF DALKEITH'S FAVORITE, THE	13b55	7b7b42	E	6/8	S4v2p8
COUNTESS OF DALKEITH'S STR., (THE)	115L6L	1122L	Bb	4/4	G10v4p5 P5v3p7
COUNTESS OF DUMFRIES JUNr's REEL	311H1H	3122H	C	2/2	R5p52(60)
COUNTESS OF DUNMORE'S FAVORITE, THE	3b3b15L	3b57b7b	C	2/2	B20p1
COUNTESS OF DUNMORE'S STRATHSPEY, THE	13b55	7b427bL	C	2/2	B20p1
COUNTESS OF EGLINTON'S STRATHSPEY, THE	1331	5522	D	4/4	G11v1Ap3 G10v1p12
COUNTESS OF EGLINTOUN'S DELIGHT	3L5L23	3L5L26L	Bb	6/8	G10v4p1
COUNTESS OF ERROL'S REEL	1H531	427L5L	C	4/4	D6p21
COUNTESS OF FITZWILIAM'S STRATHSPEY	1L133	6532	A	2/2	J1p18
COUNTESS OF GLASGOW'S FAVORITE, THE	5515	3H2H1H6	F	2/2	G9v2p18
COUNTESS OF HADDINGTON('S STRATHSPEY)	3L13L1	6L5L2L2	Bb	4/4	C14v4p15 G11v1Cp15 G10v2p9 (II)
COUNTESS OF HOPETON'S ALLEMAND, THE	1H61H5	62H1H3	D	2/4	Mc9v2p29
COUNTESS OF KINNOUL'S DELIGHT, THE	137L7L	11H65	Bb	2/4	B11p1
COUNTESS OF LAUDERDALE'S REEL, THE	1H565	2H253	A	4/4	C14v13p10
COUNTESS OF LEVEN AND MELVILLE'S FANCY, THE	61H53	547L2	A	2/2	G9v2p7
COUNTESS OF LOUDEN	5L131	2242	A	4/4	F3p8
COUNTESS OF LOUDON'S REEL.	1H3H1H5	64H3H7	D	6/8	Mc21v3p22
COUNTESS OF LOUDON'S REEL, THE	1H1H35	22H76	D	2/2	A1v5p16 B11p18 Mc12v1p23
COUNTESS OF LOUDOUN & MOIRA'S STRATHSPEY, THE	35L6L5L	35L6L2	Bb	4/4	S4v2p16
COUNTESS OF MANSEFIELD'S STRATHSPEY, THE	15L6L1	15L6L2	Bb	2/2	J1p12
COUNTESS OF MANSFIELD, THE	1H13b5	7b7b27bL	D	4/4	S4v2p3
COUNTESS OF MOIRA, THE	116L4	5126L	A	4/4	C14v21p3
COUNTESS OF PERCY'S REEL	51H3H2H	3H2H62H	D	2/2	R5p25 (II)
COUNTESS OF ROTHES'S STRATHSPEY, THE	1531H	2646	F	4/4	Mc21v3p14 (II)

COUNTESS OF SEAFIELD, THE	115	2L24	Bb	9/8	M4v4p20
COUNTESS OF SELKIRK'S FAVORITE, THE	13b42	13b55	C	4/4	G10v5p9
COUNTESS OF SUTHERLAND'S STRATHSPEY, THE	1L5L15L	1L5L6L2L	A	2/2	S13p1 Mc9v3p45
COUNTESS OF SUTHERLAND'S REEL, THE	3b11H3bH	7b521	D	2/2	D14v3p24 (II)
COUNTESS OF SUTHERLAND'S REEL, (THE)	1H565	4322H	D C	4/4*	A1v4p10 E1v1p102 C5v1p10 G1v2p91 (II)
COUNTESS OF SUTHERLAND'S REEL, THE	15L6L5L	4L3L2L2	Bb	4/4*	G10v1p30 G11v1Ap30,31 P5v3p24 N1v1p10 C14v5p18 Mc7p33 Mc21v4p8 C13v4p1
COUNTESS OF UXBRIDGE'S STRATHSPEY, THE	1151H	436L2	G	2/2	J1p24
COUNTESS OF WEMYSS' REEL	5353	26L7L5L	A	2/2	Mc19v3p11 Mc19v2p7
COUNTRY CLUB, THE	3H3H3H2H	1H1H2H6	D	2/4	E1v2p70,71
COUNTRY COTTAGE	1H1H1H1H	2533	F	6/8	S7v1p84
COUNTRY DANCE	3H3H6H3H	2H2H5H2H	D	2/4	N2p15
COUNTRY DANCE	4#H4#H5H1H	72H5H2H	D	2/4	N2p25
COUNTRY FARMER	6L122	37L11	G	6/8	R12v1p18
COUNTRY FARMER, THE	61H72H	3H2H1H1H	D	6/8	C20p73 O1v1Hp39
COUNTRY LASS, (THE)	11H1H	2H77	D	3/4	T6v2p85 P4p17 Mc8v1Dp96 P8v2p45
COUNTY HALL REEL	1343	2427bL	G	2/2	D16p19
COUPAR ANGUS JIGG	1566	1525L	C	6/8	D16p20
COURTSHIP, THE	3H1H2H6	751H3H	D	6/8	S7v1p57
COVE OF CORK, THE	5315	2653	F	3/8	G11v1Cp4,5
COVENTRY DANCE, THE or FEATHERS, THE	115L5L	1321	Bb	2/4	S7v1p58
COW BEHIND THE HAYCOCK, THE	54H3H7	3H3H2H7	D	6/8	A1v1p18
COW KEEPER	1144	5527L	G	6/8	S7v1p50
COXHEATH CAMP	1H1H53	6631	G	6/8	B16v3p19
COX'S MUSEUM	1H1H1H1H	7774H	G	2/2	B16v3p62
COX'S MUSEUM	1H3H3H2H	2H4H4H3H	D	4/4	S7v1p96
CRACKENBERG CASTLE	3213	27L15	G	2/4	P6v1p29
CRAFTS MAN, THE	1H3H1H1H	1H72H2H	F	2/2	W7p21
CRAIG ELACHIE	1351	1355	D	2/2	C33p1 A1v6p12
CRAIG OF BARN'S, THE	5411	4442	G	4/4	K1v2p15 G11v2Bp13 (II)
CRAIGELLACHIE BRIDGE	131H3	27b44	D	4/4	M4v3p30 C8v1p15 G11v2Dp28 (II)
CRAIGELLACHIE LASSES, THE	1H1H53	1H1H2H7	D	6/8	M4v4p4 (II)
CRAIGEY ROCK, THE	57b6	402	G	3/4	O1v1Kp119
CRAIGIE HOUSE	3b113b	27bL27bL	G	6/8	D16p21
CRAIGIEBURN(WOOD)	3265	1H525	F G D	6/8	(J3) C5v2p5 A1v5p45 G1v1p23 E1v2p126,127
CRAIGILLACHY	532	562	A	3/4	Mc1v1p61-67
CRAZY JANE	1H72H	2H3H5H	C D	3/4	D15v2p8 C22p30
CREACH NA CIADAINN	6L5L4	351H	G	3/4	F2v2p41(31)
CREAM CHEESE	1H51H1	1H52H2	G	6/8	R12v1p53
CREAM POT, (THE)	1356	1352	G	6/8	R12v1p25 H3p21 A1v1p25
CREWE HALL	5L16L6L	1342	A	2/2	C14v16p23
CRICHTON CASTLE	1531	2226L	D	2/2	H3p25
CRIEF FAIR	3313	5555	F	4/4*	A1v3p194 B15v1p69
CRIEFF MEETING, THE	5511H	2427bL	A	2/2	B11p7 (II)
CRIES OF EDINBURGH, THE	525	523	G	9/8	O1v1Jp100
CRIPPLE MALCOM IN THE GLEN	1525	4242	A	4/4	Mc1v1Ap8
CRITIC, THE	3352	37L11	A	6/8	B16v4p85
CRO NAN GOBHAR	3535	351H6	F	6/8	F2v2p8(2Ed.)
CROAGH PATRICK	552H3H	5622	D	6/8	B15v1p112
CRODH LAOIDH NA'M BODACH	1H1H7	1HO5	E	3/4	F2v2p36(26)
CROMLET'S LILT	1H56	663	G D	3/4	C5v3p74 O1v2p30 O1v1Ap25 N1v2p49 (J3) T6v2p1 P8v2p12
CROMLET'S LILT	1H1H5	664	D	3/4	B5p11 Mc8v1Dp104
CRONAN MAIRI NIGHEAN ALASTAIR RUADH [LUINNEAG MHIC LEOID]	5333	5321	D	6/8	F2v2p71(61)
CRONA'S VALE	3511	2543	G	2/4	O1v1Kp132
CRONSTOUNE	3551H	1H3H2H2	C	2/2	P7p3
CROOKED HORN	5L127bL	5L143b	G	4/4	R6v1p21,22
CROOKED HORN EWE, THE	5L17bL2	5L143	G	2/2	Mc9v3p29
CROOKED HORN'D EWE, THE	5L17bL2	5L343	G	4/4*	A7v6p14,15 A7v2p3
CROP THE CROPIES	1H31H3	1H72H2H	G F	4/4*	G1v2p71 C14v25p3
CROPPIES LIE DOWN	5122	6542	G	6/8	C14v14p14
CROPPIES LIE DOWN	5122	651H1	G	6/8	C5v1p70
CROSS OF BOWMORE, THE	5L353	5L36L2	G	2/2	Mc16p19
CROSS WELL OF EDINBURGH, THE	551H6	551H2	D	2/2	B15v1p110
CROUGHLY	51H3bH1H	2H7b5H7b	D	4/4	M4v3p54 (II)
CROWHILLOCK'S STRATHSPEY	1153	5L5L47L	A	2/2*	D15v1p11 (II)
CRUIMEACHADH CHLAUN RAONUILL	1111	1155	G	2/4	Mc1v1p68-70
CUBE MARCH	1130	2240	Bb	4/4	C7p13
CUCKOO, THE	3532	3132	G	6/8	L4p10 E1v2p61
CUDDIE'S WEDDING	13b43b	13b53b	A	2/2	H3p6
CUDDY CLAW'D HER	137L7L	137L1	E	6/8	A1v3p193
CUDDY CLAW'D HER	3552	3553	G	6/8	O1v1Ep9
CUDDY CLAWED HER	137L7L	137L7L	Eb	6/8	G10v6p34,35
CUDGELL, THE	11H3	11H4	G	9/8	A1v3p172
C'UIN A THIG THU ARS AM BODACH	1434	5422	A	4/4	Mc1v1Ap7
CUIR A GHAOILDILEAS THARRUM DO LAMH [CUIR A CHION DILIS...]	361H7	5756L	G	6/8	F2v2p54(44)

[CUIR A CHION DILIS...]

CUIR A NALL AM FEILE' BHEAG IS CUR NALL AN ARMACHD	5553	5533	C	4/4	F2v2p60,61(50,51)
CUIR AIR DO SHON FHEIN UILLIAM	1344	1322	A	4/4	Mc1v1Ap7
CUIRIBH SREANG AIR NA BODAICH	3565	3566	G	2/2	Mc16p10
CULCAIRN'S STRATHSPEY	1555	1563	G	4/4	Mc1v1Ap8
CULLEN HOUSE	5551H	5542	D	2/2*	G15p10 (II)
CULLEN HOUSE	1L3b7bL2	1115	A	4/4	M4v3p58,59
CULLODEN FIGHT	1352	137L2	G	6/8	B16v3p58
CULLODEN MUIR	1L124	5232	A	6/8	M12p32
CULLODEN WALTZ	4333	4331	A	3/8	M12p28
CULLODEN WELL	173bH1H	2H7b2H4H	C	4/4	M12p2
CULLODON HOUSE	11H51H	7b525	C	4/4	M12p2 (II)
CUMBERLAND COTTAGER, THE	57L5L1	4266	D	6/8	P9p27
CUMBERLAND RANT, THE	11L1L2L	3L4L5L7L	Bb	4/4	C14v21p15
CUMBERLAND REEL, THE OR UNAS LOCH [CUMBERNAULD REEL]	11H52	7L232	Bb	2/2	C14v6p7 N1v1p5 (II)
CUMERNAD HOUSE [CUMBERNAULD HOUSE]	3352	6L6L23	G	4/4	O1v4p6 O1v1Bp32
CUMH CHLAIBH	1323	6355	G	2/4	Mc1v1p71,72
CUMH DHUC HAMILTON	5542	1111	A	2/4	Mc1v1p23-29
CUMH NA PEAHAIR	2235	3336	G	4/4	Mc1v1p53-55
CUMH PHARIC MOR MHIC CRUIMMEN	1323	11H1H1H	G	4/4	Mc1v1p84-88
CUMHA MHIC A H ARASAIG	3H3H3H	3H2H1H	D	3/4	Mc5p38,39,40
CUMHA ROTHA	100	665	Eb	3/4	F2v2p69(59)
CUMHADH DUBH SHOMHAIRLE	3566	6663	G	4/4	Mc1v1p98
CUMHADH RAOINUILL MHIC AILEAIN OIG	332	1H1H6	G	3/4	Mc1v1p94-97
CUMNOCK FAIR	136L2	1353	G	4/4	F3p11
CUPID IN IRELAND	3543	1H553	A	6/8	N1v1p35
CUPID'S RECRUITING SERGEANT	5212	47L5L2	G	2/4	A1v1p34
CURE FOR THE GOUT, A	1H3H62H	1H3H4H3H	D	2/2	R12v1p51
CURIOSITY, THE	1H71H2H	5H3H75	D	6/8	C26v1p24
CURRI KOUN DILICH	557	1H1H1H	E	3/4	T7p40,41
CUSHION DANCE, THE	5652	6L5L42	A	6/8	G11v2Cp27
CUT AND DRY	3135	247bL2	A	4/4	K1v2p28 S12v1p68 G11v2Bp26 (II)
CUT AND DRY DOLLY	1H51H3	4315	A	2/2	R6v2p2
CUTTING FERNS	11H7b7b	527bL2	A	4/4	Mc19v1p4 (II)
CUTTYMUN & TREELADLE	5553	5542	A	2/2	G11v2Bp26 G7p4 K1v2p28 (II)
CUTTY'S (COUTIES) WEDDING	13b53b	13b53b	A	4/4*	G10v1p13 G11v1Ap6 Mc7p12 Mc9v3p22
CYPRUS GROVE, THE [CYPRESS GROVE, THE]	3b211H	7701H	A G	4/4	O1v1Fp8 O1v2p22,23
DA MIHI MANUM	5L11	115L	G	3/4	D14v2p24 O1v1Hp50
DAFT ROBIN	326L1	5L6L22	B A	4/4	G10v1p36 C4p48
DAFT ROBIN	26L6L1	5L6L22	B	4/4	D14v2p25
DAINTY BESOM MAKER, THE	1H555	1H2H3H2H	D	4/4	A1v1p42
DAINTY DAVIE	5311	1313	F G	4/4	C7p15 C8v1p12 C24v2p19 D15v2p7 G7p18 K1v1p29 G11v2Ap27 Mc7p17 (II) A7v6p67
DAINTY DAVIE	5332	16L11	D	2/2	S16p44,45
DAINTY DAVIE	5532	27L11	G F	4/4*	A1v1p46 Mc8v1Cp72 Mc8v2Bp16 C19p25 C13v3p50,51 C20p67
DAINTY DAVIE	5321	1313	G	2/2	E1v2p111
DALKEITH HOUSE	1H51H3	42H75	D	2/2*	Mc9v3p39 G11v2Dp37 (II)
DALKEITH HOUSE	113b5	7b644	G	6/8	A7v3p5
DALKEITH MAIDEN BRIDGE	1132	2255	G	2/2	A1v3p171
DALKEITH VOLUNTEER'S MARCH	5H5H3H2H	1H1H1H3H	C	4/4	G3p5
DALMENY HOUSE	3151H	3H4H3H2H	C	4/4	G9v2p4
DALMORE PARK	1655	1642	F	4/4	C14v6p16
DALNAGLARE'S RANT	1353	5433	G	2/2	A1v4p71 Mc22p18 C5v1p71
DALRY HOUSE	1535	6542	D	4/4	G11v2Cp36 (II)
DALSWINTON HOUSE	123b4	4217bL	A	4/4	A7v1p3
DAMON	433	443	G	3/4	S5p28
DAN DHEIRG DARGO	13b14L	13b14L	A	4/4	Mc5p18
DAN FEINNE [FONN AIR DAIN FEINNE]	1H1H5	1H1H1H	C	3/4	F2v2p61(51)
DAN FHRAOICH	6L522	315L5L	G	4/4	Mc5p18
DAN LIUGHAIR	555	442	G	3/4	Mc5p18
DAN OSSIAN [DAN OISEIN]	1131	2664	F	2/4	F2v2p19(9)
DANC'D BY ALDRIDGE	5H1H2H5	3675	C	2/4	Mc9v2p37
DANCE, A	5H1H75	64H2H2H	C	6/8	A1v6p20
DANCE, A	123	123	F	9/8	E2p12
DANCE, BOATMAN, DANCE	6565	6521	G	2/4	C8v2p44
DANCE IN QUEEN MAB	3542	56L7L1	G	6/8	A1v1p16
DANCE TO YOUR DADDY & C. WITH VARIATIONS	333	427L	Bb	3/4	P11v2p22
DANCE TO YOUR DADDY MY BONNY LADDIE	3H3H3H	4H2H7	D	3/4	C5v3p53
DANCED BY 14	11H52	1234	Eb	6/8	N2p12,13
DANCED BY ALDRIDGE	1H345	3345	D	2/2	Mc9v2p34
DANCED BY ALDRIDGE	13L25L	47L13L	B	2/4	Mc9v2p35
DANCED BY MASTER D. ALISON	1133	2244	F	4/4	N2p29
DANCED BY MASTER GRAHAME	1H1H1H1H	2H2H2H2H	C	4/4	N2p10
DANCED BY MASTER McEWEN AND MASTER DUNCAN	3555	5564	F	2/2	N2p9

DANCED BY MISS CHALMERS	3H2H3H1H	2H5H5H3H	E	6/8	N2p26,27
DANCED BY MISS MILLER	1H1H5H5H	1H3bH75H	D	2/4	N2p22,23,24
DANCED BY MISS NEISH AND MISS HACKNEY	135	664	F	3/4	N2p16
DANCED BY THE MISSES BOWER	1H1H2H2H	5H4H72H	D	2/4	N2p4,5
DANCED BY THE MISSES JOBSON	5L5L22	347L7L	A	2/4	N2p10
DANCED IN HARLEQUIN HIGHLANDER	3412	3411	G	6/8	Mc9v2p29
DANCING SETT	1562	1561H	D	6/8	G10v3p12,13
DANDALEITH	3631	5522	F	4/4	M4v3p56
DANDLING O' THE BAIRNS, THE	5211	1214	D	6/8	R6v2p8
DANDY DINMOTTE	335L3	1H1H1H6	A	4/4	H1p32
DANNSA GAELACH	5354	5324	A	4/4	Mc1v1Ap7
DANSE BASSE	1555	1555	G	2/4	C14v10p11
DANSE CIVIQUE	1H71H5	64H1H7	C	6/8	S7v2p4
DARNWAY CASTLE	516L5L	6L5L3L5L	F	4/4	G15p27
DARTFORD LODGE	1111	1155	Bb	2/4	C14v11p16
DASHING SERJEANT	1155	1H662	D	2/4	G1v1p12
[DASHING WHITE SERJEANT]					
DAUPHIN MINUET, THE	132	243	G	3/4	C22p19
DAVID EARL OF CASSIL'S REEL	3b413b	447bL2	G	2/2	R5p21
DAVID HUME'S LAMENTATION	13b54	246b5	G	4/4	L9p2
DAVID STEWART IRVINE ESQr's REEL	3546	221H6	D	2/2	Mc19v3p21
DAVIE RAE	13b55	7bL7b7bL4	E	2/2	Mc9v1p14
DAWNING OF DAY, THE	113b2	127L7L	A	4/4	C24v2p1
DAWNING OF THE DAY, THE	116L5L	51L34	G	4/4	A1v3p193
DAWTIE, THE	1H71H	61H5	G	3/4	C5v2p41
DAY RETURNS (MY BOSOM BURNS), THE	5332	6221H	G D E	4/4	C5v2p21 (J3)
DAY, THE	5346	5346	A	4/4	C26v1p6
DAYS O' YORE, THE	1H13b	7b47bL	D	9/8	G11v2Dp2
DAYS OF LANGSYNE, THE	3H1H52H	3H1H51H	D	6/8	C5v2p16
DEACON OF THE WEAVERS, THE	5656	5622	F	4/4	B15v1p104
DEAD AN' YE SHANT	7L243	7L241	A	6/8	H1p31
DEAD MARCH, THE	1117bL	3b554	E Bb	4/4*	C8v1p16 C8v2p25
DEAL STICK THE MIN(I)STER, THE	111	3b3b5L	A	3/4	P7p16
DEAR DUBLIN	3565	3567	D	6/8	C1v1p4
DEAR DUBLIN	514	512	D	9/8	C14v16p8
DEAR HIGHLAND LADDIE, THE	1154	1121	B	2/4	B7p2
DEAR LAMB, THE	5L326L	5L321	A	4/4	S13p1
DEAR SILVIA NO LONGER	2H1H3H	4H3H1H	D	3/4	P8v1p6,7
DEAR TO ME IS MY HERO	1123b	5L5L5L3bL	B	4/4	A1v5p71
DEAR TOM THIS BROWN JUG	5H5H3H	2H1H7	D	3/4	E1v2p104
DEATH OF ADMIRAL BENBOW	135	531	G	3/4	A1v5p41
DEATH OF DERMID	553	311	G	3/4	Mc5p9
DEATH OF NELSON, THE	3b7L11L	3b7L15	A	6/8	C24v2p16
DEATH OF THE FOX, THE	1L11	311	A	3/4	A7v3p24,25
DEE WATER	5L13b5	2427bL	G	4/4	A7v3p33
DE'EL TAK THE WAR	1H1H3H2H	1H664	D C	2/4	G17p15 VC25
DEEL TAK THE WAR'S	1H1H3H1H	1H664	C	2/4	R4p3
DE'EL TAKE THE GEAR AND THE BLADRIE O'T	53bH7b4	57b7b3b	E	2/2	Mc8v2Cp9
DE'EL TAKE THE WAR	1H1H2H2H	1H653	D	2/2	C4p41
DEIL AMANG THE TAILORS, THE	1H51H5	1H564	A	4/4*	C8v1p46 G7p3 C8v2p16 C14v15p1
					G11v1Bp27
DE'IL AMONG THE MANTUA-MAKERS, THE	3353	5764	A	2/2	M4v3p19
DEIL STICK THE MINISTER	1125L	3b227bL	A	2/4	O1v1Gp30,31
DE'IL TAK' THE WAR(S)	1H1H2H2H	1H664	D C	4/4*	C5v2p70 N1v2p62 (J3)
DEIL TAKE THE GAIR AND THE BRAGRIE O'IT	1315L	7bL222	G	2/2	O1v1Ep23
DEILS AMONG THE TAYLORS, THE	1H51H5	1H554	A	4/4	P5v3p18 (II)
[DEIL AMONG THE TAILORS, THE]					
DEIL'S DEAD, THE	3546	3551H	A	2/2	B17p10 C14v12p3
DELACHAPLE'S REEL	1126L	1151	D	2/4	C33p3
DELGATY CASTLE	5125L	6L7L13	A	2/4	Mc21v2p18 P5v1p15
DELGATY ICE HOUSE	1331	5632	D	4/4	P5v2p21
DELGATY KENALL	1H3b11	47b47bL	G	6/8	P5v2p9
DELIGHT OF THE PANTHEON, THE	1H1H55	427L2	D	6/8	B16v3p71
DELRACHNAY'S RANT	1322	136L6L	G	4/4	G15p3 (II)
DELVEN HOUSE	1115	1116	D	6/8	G11v1Ap25
DELVEN SIDE	57b7b4	57b7b5	E	4/4	G10v1p11
DELVEN SIDE [DELVIN SIDE]	17b7b5	7b7b7b4	E	4/4	K1v1p17 G7p10 G11v2Ap15
					E1v1p101 (II)
DELVIN CAMP	13b53b	247b2	E	6/8	G8p12 P1v1p4
DELVIN HOUSE	1H51H5	22H76	D C	4/4*	A7v4p19 A7v5p31 G11v1Bp28
					G7p14,15 Mc16p12 (II)
DELVIN HOUSE	556L6L	6L5L2L2L	A	6/8	G8p1 G8p1 Mc4v3p12
DELVIN SIDE	1555	157b5	E	2/2	H3p15
DELVIN SIDE	17b55	17b7b4	E	4/4*	C13v1p16 A7v2p17 Mc9v1p33 (II)
DELVIN SIDE	17b7b5	17b7b4	E	4/4*	P5v2p20 C14v15p2 P6v1p2
					A7v2p17
DENMARK DANCE	1111	5555	G	4/4	B16v3p51
DENNY'S HORNPIPE	1115	1115	Bb	2/2	C14v22p19
DEOCH SLAINNTE DO'N AIRMAILT	1511	1535	F	6/8	F2v2p62(52)
THA FLANNRIOSE SA CEANNAS					
DEOCH SLAINT' AN RIGH	111	13b3b	B	3/4	F2v2p52(42)
DEPARTED WORTH	1L3L6L5L	1L3L22L	Bb	4/4	Mc16p34

DEPARTURE OF A FRIEND, THE	1H135	1H351H	D	4/4	L1p11
DEPARTURE, THE	3342	16L15	Bb	2/4	C14v26p8
DER FREISCHUTZ WALTZ	6H3H1H	6H3H1H	D	3/4	C8v2p48 G13p5 E1v2p51
DESERTER, THE	1111	2231	Bb	2/4	W6p13
DESERTS OF TULLOCH, THE	31H2H1H	5542	D	6/8	G15p10
DESTRUCTION OF THE BASTILE	1H533	1233	G	2/4	C5v1p45 W4v1p19
DESTRUCTION OF THE BASTILE	1H5H3H3H	1233	G	2/4	A1v4p45
DEUKES DANG OWER MY DEDDIE, THE	1H1H5	331	D	3/4	O1v2p4,5 O1v3p32,33 O1v1Ap1
DEUK'S DANG O'ER MY DADDIE	1H327	1H331	C D	6/8	(J3) E1v1p27 C5v2p8 Mc8v1Ap5 A1v1p24 (II)
DEUKS DANG O'ER MY DADDIE, THE	1H327	1H431	D	6/8	C8v1p14 C8v2p18
DEVIL AMANG THE MEAL MEN, THE	1H531	6L7L15	G	6/8	Mc7p2
DEVIL IN DENMARK	155	154	D	9/8	(D2) P6v1p9
DEVIL UPON TWO STICKS JIG	55L6L5L	6L5L6L5L	A	6/8	P9p30
DEVILS DREAM	1H51H5	1H564	A	2/2	B17p19
DEVIL'S HOP, THE	1H1H5H	6H4H2H	C	9/8	C14v18p23
DEVONSHIRE HOUSE	1122	1121	D	2/4	S7v1p20
DEVONSHIRE HUNT, THE	5356L	6L5L53	Bb	6/8	C14v25p10
DEVONSHIRE MINUET AND GAVOT, THE	553	553H	Eb	3/4	C22p15,16
DEVONSHIRE, THE	1124	1232	G	6/8	C14v27p7
DH'EIRICH MI MOCH	6b57b1	443b1	B	4/4	Mc5p11
DH'FHAG THU MI FO BHRON	376	1H52	D	3/4	F2v2p74(64)
DI PIACER MI BALZA IL COR	5H5H7H	1T01T	D	3/4	E1v2p96
DI TANTI PALPITI	3H3H3H5H	4H2H3H1H	D	2/4	C8v2p34 E1v2p98,99
DIAMOND REEL, THE	3b3b6b7b	557b2	G A	2/2	Mc21v1p30 A7v5p15
DIBDINS FANCY	113L5L	4L6L22	G	2/4	C14v3p12,13
DIBDINS FANCY	1H1H35	644H2H	C	2/4	A7v3p12
DICK A DOLLIS	3653	47b47b	A	2/2	P7p9
DICK O' THE COW	5L131	5L153	G	6/8	C10v2Bp30
DICKY GOSSIP	1H1H2H5	1H451	D	4/4*	A7v5p4 A7v4p26
DIEL'S AWA' WI THE EXCISEMAN	1552	5135	G	6/8	C6p29
DILL STICK THE MINISTER	1127bL	3b247bL	A	2/2	R12v1p94
DI-MOLADH AN UISGE-BHEATHA	116L	352	G	9/8	F2v2p31(21)
DING DONG, DING DONG	117L2	1110	G	4/4	A1v6p59
DING'S MUSIC SHOP	1H313	1H622H	D	4/4	A7v6p82
DINNA THINK BONNIE LASSIE I'M GAUN TO LEAVE YOU	1H3H1H1H	5531	D	4/4	C8v2p48
DINNA THINK BONNIE LASSIE (I'M GAUN TO LEAVE YOU)	1H3H2H1H	5531	D	4/4*	(J3) C5v2p51
DISPATCH, THE	1H1H53	64H1H7	F	6/8	H1p2
DIVISION ON AN OLD GROUND BASS FOR VIOLINS, A	133	522	Bb	3/4	O1v4p38,39
DO CHINNEADH BHI GUN CHEANN	13b21	427L0	G	4/4	F2v2p17(7)
DO YOU KNOW JACK ADAMS'S PARISH	1H33H2H	1H335	D	6/8	B16v3p33
DOCTOR GORDON'S COMPLIMENTS TO JOHN MORISON	1L126L	1L125	Bb	4/4	M11v2p18
DOCTOR LAING	1354	5L47L2	Eb	4/4	M4v3p26
DOCTOR, THE	15L3L1L	4522	Bb	4/4	G11v2Cp32 (II)
DOCTOR, THE	5123	5552	G	6/8	A1v2p69
DOCTORS DREAM, THE	5351	5453	D	4/4	A7v3p28
DOCTOR'S FANCY, THE	5346	5216L	G	4/4	B16v3p18
DOD HOUSE	1L5L13	16L22L	A	4/4	D16p24 (II)
DOGE OF VENICE STRATHSPEY, THE	5351H	5322H	C	4/4	P9p6
DOIDEAG MHUILEACH	5313	5755	C	6/8	Mc16p16
DOLLIE'S THE GIRL FOR ME	31H1H	652	D	9/8	A1v3p190
DON SIDE	1326L	1323	G	4/4*	Mc9v1p21 B15v1p63 G9v5p21 G11v2Ap11 P5v4p8/9 K1v1p13 (II)
DONALD	3311	6L5L5L0	Bb	4/4	C19p16
DONALD	3311	7L5L5L0	Bb	4/4	G17p9 VC25
DONALD	3H3H1H1H	7550	D	4/4	E1v2p6
DONALD BUTCHER'S BRIDAL	1111	5642	D	4/4	G9v1p8,9
DONALD BUTCHER'S BRIDAL	1111	5632	D	4/4	B15v2p16 D13p18
DONALD CAIRD'S COME AGAIN	1515	1427bL	D	2/4	C10v2Bp80
DONALD CLEIREACH or NEAT SHOE, THE [DOMHNULL CLEIREACH]	3152	311H1H	D	4/4	Mc21v3p19 (II)
DONALD COUPER AND HIS MAN	13b14	13b6b4	B	2/4	A1v2p4
DONALD DHU	5653	5652	A	6/8	G9v1p32,33
DONALD DOW('S STRATHSPEY)	5651	51H52	F	4/4	G11v2Cp28 (II)
DONALD McQUEEN	5L7bL7bL7bL	3b111	A	2/2	A1v6p3
DONALD O CREADY	1H555	1353	F	6/8	C14v22p6
DONALD OF DUNDEE	3H1H53	352H2H	D	2/4	A1v5p20 C5v1p20
DONALD QUAICH	3b524	3b51H5	A	4/4	K1v2P25 G11v2Bp23 (II)
DONALD ROBERTSON, ESQr's STRATHSPEY	3b13b1	7b7b44	D	4/4	Mc19v3p15
DONALD SIMON	13L15L	4L2L22	Bb	2/2	C18p36
DONCASTER RACES	5151	51H42	G	6/8	C14v8p15 Mc15p13
DONEL COOPER'S STRATHSPEY	1H327b	1H331H	A	4/4	A7v3p25
DONNACHA MAC SHUINE	5L111	543b7bL	A	4/4	F2v2p42,43(32,33)
DOROTHEA OF HYDRABAD	5353	3122	D	3/8	L2p22
DORSET:SHIRE MARCH	3153	1H53H1H	D	4/4	A1v6p72/73
DOUBLE DEFEAT, THE	351H5	5431H	Eb	6/8	B16v1p12
DOUBLE ENTENDRE	3542	3542	G	2/4	R12v1p2

DOUBLE HORNPIPE	365	652	E	9/8	C22p35
DOUBLE HORNPIPE	131	267L	Bb	6/4	S11v2p6
DOUBLE HORNPIPE NO. 1	1H57L	367	Eb	9/8	S11v1p13
DOUBLE HORNPIPE NO. 2	11H2H	7b44	C	9/8	S11v1p14
DOUBLE HORNPIPE NO. 3	351H	2H24	F	9/8	S11v1p14
DOUBLE HORNPIPE No. 4	565	62H7	F	9/8	C22p21 S11v1p14
DOUBLE JIG	1H362	36L27L	Bb	6/8	C22p43
DOUBLE JIG	1363	7L127L	Bb	6/8	C22p45
DOUBLE JIG	1233	6537L	Bb	6/8	C22p39
DOUBLE JIG	1234	56L27L	A	6/8	C22p39
DOUBLE JIG	15L15L	2427L	Bb	6/8	C22p37
DOUBLE JIG	31H55	4542	D	6/8	C22p42
DOUBLE JIG	357L1	6L5L4L2L	Bb	6/8	C22p28
DOUBLE JIGG	31H51	6275	Eb	6/8	S11v2p5
DOUBLE KISSES	1H51H1H	1H52H2	C	4/4*	A1v2p69 C13v2p18 A7v5p34 A7v6p29
DOUBLE KISSES	1H51H2H	1H52H2	C	4/4*	B15v1p75 C8v1p49 Mc21v4p13 Mc21v3p14 (II)
DOUBTFUL SHEPHERD, THE	1H542	7L222	G	2/2	B16v3p90
DOUN THE BURN DAVIE	116L1	3211	F	4/4	C13v3p20
(DOWN) FALL OF PARIS, (THE)	1H1H1H4H	2H2H2H5H	D C	2/4	E1v2p100,101 A1v6p57 C8v2p38 C7p17 C23p20
DOWN THE BURN DAVIE	315L1	3211	F	4/4	S16p92,93
DOWN THE BURN DAVIE	5L5L11	3211H	G	4/4	W7p7
DOWN THE BURN DAVIE	116L1	3213	G F	4/4*	C5v2p19 N1v2p23 T6v1p113 Mc8v1Bp36 Mc8v2p11 (J3) G17p13 P4p3 C20p1
DOWN THE BURN DAVIE	116L1	3313	G	4/4	O1v1Dp18,19
DOWN THE BURN, DAVIE (LAD)	3H1H52	351H1H	D	4/4	C8v2p48 G10v6p23 (II)
DOWN WITH THE PEEBLES	5333	5326	D	4/4*	A1v5p2 C5v1p2
DOWNIE'S RIGADON	1H1H2H5	4231	F	6/8	Mc9v2p23
DOWNSHIRE (CAMPERDOWN) QUICK STEP, THE	3115	7552H	F D	4/4*	G9v3p24 C7p20
Dr. CROMAR	3H1H53	5322	C	2/4	D6p39
DR FOWLER'S CLOCKBAG	1655	27b7bL2	G	4/4	C10v2Bp98
Dr GREGORY GRANT'S STRATHSPEY	5126L	5566	D	4/4	Mc21v3p36 (II)
DR GUTHRIE'S (Junr) STRATHSPEY	5511	7bL242	A	4/4	C18p22
DR HAYDN'S STRATHSPEY	1313	136L2	F	4/4	G10v5p26,27
Dr IRVINE'S STRATHSPEY	116L3L	1L37L2	G	4/4	Mc19v3p9
Dr. JAMES HAMILTON'S QUICK STEP	15L25L	1231	A	6/8	Mc21v2p28
Dr JOHN McLAGAN'S STRATHSPEY	5151H	6522	D	2/2	Mc4v1p10
DR McKAY	51H72H	3H1H35	D	2/4	C5v1p39 A1v5p39
Dr McNICOL'S REEL	5531H	6535	G	2/2	Mc16p8
Dr ROSS OF DORNOCH	5L15L4L	2L27L2	Bb	2/2	M12p21
Dr RUTHERFORD OF CRAIGOW'S STRATHSPEY	1313	11H64	D	4/4	P11v2p8
Dr STEWART'S REEL	3b17bL4L	3bL7bL3b7bL	A	2/2	C18p11
DR W.A. ROSE'S FANCY	1H535	22H2H6	D	2/2	Mc16p35
DR Wm GRANT'S REELL	1125L	3b247bL	D	4/4	C33p9 B15v1p71
Dr Wm GRIGOR OF ELGIN'S REEL	3b13b5	7b7b24	G	2/2	G15p37
DRAPER'S FANCY, THE	5341	2233	F	2/2	B6v4p2
DRAWING ROOM, THE	1131	657L2	Eb	6/8	A7v3p8
DRAYCOT HOUSE	637L5L	31H46	D	2/2	C14v26p14,15
DREAM, THE	1H651	2H62H5	F	6/8	P9p39
DRIBBLES OF BRANDY	13b57b	46b52	E	6/8	A1v3p160
DRIMEN DUFF	3b3b2	17bL1	A	3/4	T7p38,39
DRIMEN DUFF	3b3b2	15L1	A	3/4	O1v1Hp46
DRIMINDOO	3b3b2	17L1	B	3/4	A1v6p37
DRINK TO ME ONLY	3452	5311	A	6/8	A1v6p59 E1v2p7
DRINK TO ME ONLY WITH THINE EYES	3H4H5H2H	5H3H1H1H	D	6/8	C8v2p36
DROPS OF BRANDY	133	11H5	G	9/8	C14v11p22,23
DROPS OF BRANDY	533	534	G	9/8	C8v2p51 E1v1p113 (II)
DROPS OF DRINK	1151	2462	G	6/8	A1v2p10
DROUTH	31H33	4231H	D	6/8	O1v1Ap33 O1v4p17
DROWN DROUTH	3L13L3L	4L2L3L1	Bb	6/8	K1v1p34 G11v2Ap32 C22p22 P5v1p21
DROWN DROUTH	3L13L	3L4L2L	Bb	9/8	B15v1p65 (II)
DROWN DROUTH	31H3	342	D	9/8	A1v3p192
DRUB THE ROGUES	1245	1241	G	6/8	A1v2p63
DRUCHEN LAIRD'S STRATHSPEY, THE	113L1	226L2	Bb	2/2	B20p9
DRUIMIONN DUBH	117bL3b	43b7bL7bL	B	4/4	Mc5p13
DRUM HOUSE	1364	5543	D	2/2	S5p23
DRUM HOUSE [or KEEP IT UP]	3142	3151H	G	2/4	G10v4p24
DRUMBAIN'S REEL	11H55	4542	F	2/2	M4v3p55
DRUMEDDIE, A	1H655	553H4H	D	6/8	P5v3p23
DRUMER, THE [DRUMMER, THE]	1H3bH55	7b7b2H4H	D	4/4	R12v3p18
DRUMIN'S STRATHSPEY	1516	5542	D	4/4	M4v3p36 (II)
DRUMLANRIG CASTLE	5L133	536L6L	G	2/2	G11v2Dp30
DRUMMCHARY HOUSE	1H3H4H3H	5327bL	D	2/2	Mc4v1p16
DRUMMER, THE	135L5L	7bL7bL24	G	2/2	S12v1p28
DRUMMER, THE	13b5L5L	7bL7bL24	G	2/2	H3p32 R12v1p30
DRUMMER, THE	13b5L5L	7bL7bL47bL	A	4/4*	A1v1p45 A7v5p21 A7v6p44
DRUMMER, THE	13b5L5L	7bL247bL	A	4/4*	G11v2Bp23 C8v1p10 C8v2p24 C14v19p10 K1v2p25 (II)

DRUMMOND CASTLE	11H1H7b	3b524	A	6/8	E1v1p3 G11v1Bp4 G10v2p8
DRUMMOND CASTLE	11H1H7b	3b544	B A	6/8	G1v2p61 A7v5p17 A7v6p7 A7v2p22,23
DRUMMORE'S RANT	3565	357bL4	G	2/2	B15v1p11
DRUMNAGOUR	1361	3562	D	4/4	S5p22
DRUMSHUGH [DRUMSHEUGH]	311H1H	2H2H22	D	2/2	B15v1p106 (11)
DRUMUACHDAIR [DRUIM-UACHDAIR]	5353	5335	G	2/2	F2v2p76,77(66,67) (11)
DRUNK AT NIGHT AND DRY IN THE MORNING	3H3H2H	3H1H3H	D	3/4	C5v2p52
DRUNK AT NIGHT AND DRY IN THE MORNING	332	313	A	3/4	G11v2Cp1
DRUNK AT NIGHT AND DRY IN THE MORNING	115L	5L3L5L	A	3/4	R6v2p30
DRUNKEN DOCTOR, THE	5415L	3L127L	Bb	6/8	B16v3p53
DRUNKEN DRUMMER, THE	3113	316L6L	G	6/8	A1v2p63
DRUNKEN FRIDAY	1H3bH1H5	7b7b47bL	D	2/2	P5v2p17
DRUNKEN FRIDAY	1H3H1H5	7b7b47bL	D	2/2	S12v1p38
DRUNKEN GAUGER, THE	36L6L	36L2	G	9/8	H1p31
DRUNKEN MAG YOUNG	313	554	D	3/4	O1v5p21
DRUNKEN MAGG YOUNG	323	554	D	3/4	O1v1Kp136
DRUNKEN WIFE OF GALLOWAY, THE	111	555	G	6/4	C5v3p54 O1v1Jp94
DRUNKEN WIFE, THE	3524	3551H	A	2/2	Mc19v1p13 Mc19v2p20
DRUNKEN WIFIE, THE	3547b	3511H	A	4/4	B15v1p48
DRUNKEN WIVES OF ABERDEEN, THE	151H5	1H52H2	G	2/2	R12v1p71
DRUNKEN WIVES OF CARLISLE, THE	1H31H5	1H372	G	2/2	R6v2p16
DRUNKEN WIVES OF FOCHABERS, THE	113b5	446b5	E D	4/4	A1v6p4 G11v1Cp19 C13v1p22 G10v1p10 (11)
DRUNKEN WIVES OF FOCHABERS, (THE)	3b13b5	46b7b5	D	4/4	A7v5p40 A7v6p86
DRURY HILL	5H1H6H2H	5H2H75	D	6/8	A1v6p25
DRURY LANE	3131	2427L	F	6/8	A7v3p12
DRURY LANE HORNPIPE	15L3L1	1522	Bb	4/4	S7v1p56
DUBH AIG CHREABH	5L111	237L6L	G	4/4	P5v4p21
DUBLIN KEY	3b212	4L7bL12	A	6/8	C24v2p12,13
DUBLIN VOLUNTEERS QUICK MARCH	151H2H	4531	G	2/4	A1v2p51
DUC D'ANGOULEME'S STRATHSPEY, LE	11L3b1	157bL4	G	4/4	Mc21v3p33
DUCHESS D. OF RICHMOND'S STRATHSPEY THE	1555	54H2H2	E	4/4	M4v3p37
DUCHESS OF ARGYLE, THE	5L121	4L6L2L2	Bb	4/4	M6p1
DUCHESS OF ATHOL(L)'S (DELIGHT/FAVORITE), THE	11L13	11L2L2	A	6/8	G11v1Bp17 G10v2p20,21 (11)
DUCHESS OF BEDFORD'S CAIRN, THE	5642	567L2	F	4/4	M4v4p10,11
DUCHESS OF BEDFORD'S STRATHSPEY	535L3L	5324	F	2/2	C14v20p18
DUCHESS OF BEDFORD'S WALTZ, THE	117L4	117L1	G	3/8	P6v1p15
DUCHESS OF BEDFORD'S WALTZ, THE	5323	5321	F	3/8	H6v10p3
DUCHESS OF BUCCLEUCH, THE	3131	3162	F	2/2	M4v4p1
DUCHESS OF BUCCLEUCH'S WELCOME TO SCOTLAND, THE	6L16L5L	6L47L2	G	2/2	G9v2p13
DUCHESS OF BUCCLEUGH('S FAVORITE), THE	5L6L5L3L	5L15L5L	Bb	4/4	G10v4p5 (11)
DUCHESS OF BUCCLEUGH'S REEL, THE	3332	331H1H	A	2/2	Mc19v3p18 Mc19v2p2
DUCHESS OF BUCCLEUGH'S REEL, THE	3135	1H542	F	4/4	G9v2p8
DUCHESS OF GORDON, (THE)	5551	5424	E	4/4	G11v2Cp19 (11)
DUCHESS OF GORDON, THE	1552	1127bL	G	4/4	G11v1Cp13
DUCHESS OF GORDON, THE	111	335	Bb	3/4	M4v4p18
DUCHESS OF GORDON'S BANQUET, THE	1331	5662	D	2/2	P1v2p6 J1p11
DUCHESS OF GORDON'S DELIGHT, THE	1H3b1H2H	1H7b52	C	2/4	Mc21v2p2
DUCHESS OF GORDON'S FAVORITE, THE	11H3H1H	161H2	Eb	2/2	G9v2p14
DUCHESS OF GORDON'S NEW STRATHSPEY, THE	113L5L	6L26L2	F	4/4	Mc21v2p37
DUCHESS OF GORDON'S REEL, THE	5L122	151H5	A	2/4	S7v1p73
DUCHESS OF GORDON'S STRATHSPEY	5162	5L7bL44	F	2/2	Mc19v3p16
DUCHESS OF GORDON'S STRATHSPEY, THE	33H1H6	51H2H2	Eb	2/2	G9v2p14,15
DUCHESS OF HAMILTON, THE	317L2	313L1L	G	4/4	G11v1Cp36 G10v1p27 (11)
DUCHESS OF HAMILTON'S REEL	527L2	6L16L1	G	2/2	S7v1p37
DUCHESS OF HAMILTON'S REELL, THE	5333	5322	D	4/4	C33p3
DUCHESS OF MANCHESTER'S STRATHSPEY, (THE)	1133	6522	F	4/4	G11v2Cp30
DUCHESS OF MANCHESTER'S STRATHSPEY, THE	3565	4322	C	4/4	J1p25
DUCHESS OF MANCHESTER'S STRATHSPEY, THE	3H5H1H3H	4H3H2H2H	C	4/4	E2p3
DUCHESS OF RICHMOND, THE	4211	361H3	Bb	4/4	M4v4p18,19
DUCHESS OF ROXBURGHE'S STRATHSPEY, THE	156L1	1513H	Eb	4/4	M4v3p58
DUCHESS OF YORK('S WALTZ), THE	5125L	423L1	Bb	3/8	G9v3p2,3 C14v6p6
DUCHESS OF YORK'S FANCY, THE	1522H	1565	D	6/8	A7v3p3
DUCHESS OF YORK'S REEL	3L5L15L	6L5L7L2	Bb	2/2	C14v11p1
DUCHESS OF YORK'S WELCOME TO LONDON	5L121	51H62	E	2/4	J1p3
DUCHESSES OF RUTLAND'S REEL, THE	1155	42H2H6	C	4/4	B17p14
DUCKERS OF DOWN, THE	3b53b1	27b27bL	G	2/2	C13v2p72
DUCKS AND GREEN PEASE	1L1L1L5L	1315	Bb	4/4	P9p19
DUCK'S DANG O'ER MY DADIE, THE	1H1H5	331	D	6/4	Mc8v2Cp5
DUDDINGSTON CASTLE	3H52H2H	3H2H1H6	D	4/4	Mc21v3p23
DUDHOPE BARRACKS	5555	5551	A	3/8	B6v1p2
DUEL STRATHSPEY, THE	1H331H	7675	D	4/4	P9p29
DUENNA, THE	1H423	4225	F	6/8	S7v1p22
DUETTO	1H1H3H2H	1H001H	D	4/4	F1p28,29
DUFF HOUSE	511H3	4642	F	4/4	C24v1p10
DUFF HOUSE	35L3L5L	4L5L2L2	Bb	2/4	C14v9p16
DUFF HOUSE	513b5	4642	E	4/4	Mc11p6
DUFF HOUSE	1155	1125L	Bb	6/8	D15v2p14

Title			Key	Time	References
DUGI CAMPBELL ESQr. OF BALLINABY'S JIG	5L122	7bL5L7bL4L	A	6/8	Mc16p4
DUKE OF ARGYLE('S STRATHSPEY)	5L121	1321	D	4/4	G11v1Cp18,19 G10v1p32
DUKE OF ATHOLES DELIGHT, THE	1121	1111	G	4/4	G10v1p33,34
DUKE OF ATHOLE'S FORREST, THE	1535	2422	A	2/2	Mc9v3p16
DUKE OF ATHOLE'S RANT, THE	5515	6626	D	2/2	Mc9v1p32
DUKE OF ATHOLL ('S STRATHSPEY), THE	1111	7bL7bL47bL	A	4/4	G11v1Cp33 G10v2p28 (II)
DUKE OF ATHOLL'S MARCH	1543	2532	A	4/4	D14v2p44
DUKE OF ATHOL'S FORREST LODGE GLEN TILT	11H61H	61H24	A	2/2	Mc9v3p42
DUKE OF ATHOL'S RANT, THE	1H3H2H1H	6522	D	2/2	S12v1p31 S7v1p42
[DUKE OF ATHOL'S REEL, THE]					
DUKE OF BRUNSWICK'S MARCH	1H1H3H4H	5H1T5H5H	D	4/4	A1v6p61
DUKE OF BRUNSWICK'S MARCH	116L2	7L6L11	A	2/4	Mc21v2p21
DUKE OF BUCCLEUCH, THE	131H3H	1H526L	F	4/4	M4v4p1
DUKE OF BUCCLEUGH	13b57b	427bL2	E	2/2	C13v2p55
AND HIS FENCIBLES, THE					
DUKE OF BUCCLEUGH, THE	1L17L2	1355	A	4/4	G10v6p34
DUKE OF BUCCLEUGH'S MARCH	1H1H1H1H	1H2H3HO	D	4/4	A1v6p62
DUKE OF BUCCLEUGH'S MARCH, THE	5L315	5225	Bb	4/4	G9v3p1
DUKE OF CLARENCE'S FANCY, THE	1335	7L5L3L1	G	2/4	P1v2p7
DUKE OF CLARENCE'S FANCY, THE	1335	637L5L	G	2/4	J1p10
DUKE OF CLARENCES FANCY, THE	1335	627L5L	G	2/4	C14v5p3
DUKE OF CLARENCES HORNPIPE	1351H	46L16L	Bb	2/2	C14v24p15
DUKE OF CLARENCE'S MARCH	1H156	1H2H54	F	2/2	M2p10
DUKE OF COTILLON	51H2H2H	1H61H7	D	6/8	A7v6p85
DUKE OF CUMBERLAND'S REEL, THE	1655	27b27bL	D	2/2	Mc13v2p17 G9v5p12
DUKE OF CUMBERLAND('S STRATHSPEY, THE)	1655	47b27bL	D	4/4	K1v2p38 G11v2Bp36 (II)
DUKE OF GLOUCESTER'S MARCH	5H1H1H1H	2H753	C	4/4	M2p31
DUKE OF GLOUCESTER'S QUICK MARCH, THE	31H72H	3H72H5	D	2/4	A1v1p5
DUKE OF GLOUCESTERS REEL	5334	5342	G	2/2	C14v10p10
DUKE OF GORDON AND HIS VOLUNTEERS, THE	15L6L5L	1322L	Bb	6/8	C13v2p50
DUKE OF GORDON, THE	1111	51H32	G	2/2	N1v1p4
DUKE OF GORDON('S BIRTH DAY), (THE)	1111	51H22	G	4/4*	C13v1p47 A7v2p2,3 A7v6p12 G11v2Ap12 K1v1p14 M4v3p38 A1v4p1 Mc12v1p46 C2v8p8 Mc7p20 Mc13v2p27 C8v1p24 Mc12v1p46 C14v7p1 (II)
DUKE OF GORDON'S FANCY, THE	1H2H1H1H	5H4H3H7	Eb	6/8	Mc21v2p30
DUKE OF GORDON'S FAVORITE, THE	15L3L2L	4637L	Bb	6/8	Mc21v4p2
DUKE OF GORDON'S (FAVORITE/STRATHSPEY)	16L15L	436L6L	D	4/4	G11v1Ap24 G10v1p19
DUKE OF GORDON'S RANT, THE	5351	5355	D	2/2	Mc9v1p7
DUKE OF GORDON'S REEL, THE	3331	2227bL	A	2/2	A7v3p15
DUKE OF GORDON'S (REEL/STRATHSPEY), THE	1H353	6322	D	4/4	M4v1p10 M4v3p31
DUKE OF GORDON'S STRATHSPEY	3H1H15	662H2H	D	4/4	G8p36
DUKE OF GORDON'S STRATHSPEY	1511H	53H2H2H	E	4/4	Mc21v2p19
DUKE OF HAMILTON AND HIS VOLUNTEERS	1351H	1325L	Bb	6/8	C13v2p51
DUKE OF HAMILTON'S REEL	1331	27bL27bL	G	4/4	B15v1p86
DUKE OF KENT'S REEL	1351H	4246	F	4/4	G9v3p6,7 (II)
DUKE OF MANCHESTER'S FANCY, THE	5L16L1	327L5L	Bb	4/4	Mc21v4p2
DUKE OF PERTH'S REEL (THE)	151H5	1H52H2	G	4/4*	K1v1p17 A1v2p74 C13v2p1 N1v1p23 S12v1p4 G11v2Ap15 B15v1p8 P5v2p6 E1v1p3 G9v5p23 (II)
DUKE OF QUEENSBURY'S SCOTCH MEASURE, THE	331H4	321H3	D	2/2	Y1p9
DUKE OF REICHSTADT'S WALTZ	706	504#	A	3/4	G13p6
DUKE OF RICHMOND, THE	547L5L	5L352	Bb	4/4	M4v4p16
DUKE OF RICHMOND'S MARCH	1H1H1H5	1H1H1H3H	D	4/4	A1v6p70/71
DUKE OF RICHMOND'S WELCOME TO GORDON CASTLE, THE	13L1L3L	16L2L2	A	4/4	T1v1p6
DUKE OF ROXBURGH'S REEL	1535	7bL7bL24	D	2/2	S7v1p42
DUKE OF WELLINGTON, THE	555	51H2H	D	3/4	G9v3p23
DUKE OF WELLINGTON'S NEW WALTZ	1146	5421	Bb	3/8	E1v4p3
DUKE OF WELLINGTON'S NEW WALTZ	3541H	5541H	G	3/8	B7p5
DUKE OF WELLINGTON'S QUICKSTEP	3H1H2H5	353H1H	D	6/8	G1v2p82
DUKE OF WELLINGTON'S STRATHSPEY	3L5L6L5L	3L5L26L	Eb	4/4	P9p36
DUKE OF YORK AT BERLIN	3H1H51H	3H1H3H3H	C	2/4	S7v2p1
DUKE OF YORK IN BERLIN, THE	1355	1241	Bb	3/8	J1p9
DUKE OF YORK'S BIRTHDAY	1351H	547L2	Bb	2/4	C14v20p7
DUKE OF YORK'S CAMP, THE	1H531	4325L	F	6/8	C21p18
DUKE OF YORK'S COTILLION	5L122	16L17L	Bb	6/8	C14v4p5
DUKE OF YORK'S FANCY, THE	5H2H1H5	6542	D	6/8	A7v1p15
DUKE OF YORK'S FAVOURITE	1551	7L425L	G Bb	2/4	A1v4p50 W4v1p30
DUKE OF YORK'S FAVOURITE	1551	7L4#25L	G	2/4	C5v1p50
DUKE OF YORK'S MARCH	1133	5515	D G F	4/4*	M2p8 C8v2p42 A1v4p23 C23p1
DUKE OF YORK'S QUICK STEP, THE	3155	4211	G	2/2	C14v6p18
DUKE WILLIAM'S MARCH	1112	3332	G	4/4	R12v3p12
DUKERS OF DOON, THE	3b53b1	3b527bL	G	2/2	C24v2p19 A7v3p5
DUKE'S BIRTH DAY, THE	1473H	144H1H	D	2/4	R12v1p46
DUKE'S REEL, THE	1322	1343	G	2/2	R12v1p40
DUMB GLUTTON, THE	3144	327L4	G	2/4	A1v1p50
DUMB WAITER	3144	327L4	G	2/4	R12v1p26

DUMBARTON CASTLE	1L5L32	15L22L	Bb	2/2	C13v2p77
DUMBARTON DRUMS	3332	1555	F	4/4	C13v3p24,25
DUMBARTON DRUMS	3332	1664	G	4/4	P8v2p21
DUMBARTON'S DRUMS	3333	1554	F D	4/4*	B5p1 T6v2p16 C20p34 N1v2p70 (J3)
DUMFRIES HOUSE	1151	46L25L	G	6/8	K1v1p15 Mc9v3p28 R5p32 G11v2Ap13 A1v4p19 (II)
DUMFRIES HOUSE	1151	4525L	G	6/8	A7v5p26 A7v6p25 A7v2p18,19 (II)
DUMFRIES RACES	5451	7654	G	4/4	C5v2p25 G10v5p7
DUMFRIES THEATRE	5231	1H675	G	6/8	A7v1p2
DUMFRIES-SHIRE HUNT, THE	15L13	6523	A	2/2	R6v2p20
DUMOND'S JIGG	1H53b1	13b45	D	6/8	R12v1p48
DUMOURIERS ESCAPE IMITATING A GALLOP & A TROT	531H3	3H355	G	2/4	G9v5p7
DUNBAR VOLUNTEER'S MARCH	1H1H34	5553	F	4/4	G3p2
DUNCAN DAVIDSON	1155	1152	E	2/2	Mc9v1p14
DUNCAN DAVIDSON	1155	1162	D	4/4	A7v5p35
DUNCAN DAVIDSON	1555	1551	D	4/4	C8v1p54
DUNCAN DAVIDSON	1555	1552	D	4/4	C8v2p33
DUNCAN DAVIDSON	1555	11H62	E	2/2	C4p69
DUNCAN DAVIDSON	1555	11H52	E D	2/2*	G11v1Bp4,5 G10v1p15,16 G7p11 G11v2Ap34 E1v1p8 K1v1p36 P5v2p16 (J3) Mc7p14 (II)
DUNCAN DAVIE	1555	1562	D	4/4	C13v2p31
DUNCAN GRAY	127L1	237L7L	G	2/2	C13v3p30,31
DUNCAN GRAY	572H7	1H2H3H1H	D	4/4*	Mc8v2Cp1 C8v2p46 C5v2p5
DUNCAN GRAY	5L7L27L	1231	Bb A G	4/4*	C19p22 G11v2Dp18 (J3) E1v2p9 A1v2p41 Mc8v1Ap1 O1v1Cp8 C20p44
DUNCAN GRAY	572H1H	1H2H3H1H	D	2/4	G1v1p28
DUNCAN GRAY CAM' HERE TOO WOO	5L7L21	1231	A	2/4	C6p7
DUNCAN MACQUEEN('S STRATHSPEY)	5L13b1	543b7bL	A	4/4	G1v2p85 A7v6p16 A7v2p2
DUNCAN McDUFF	1547bL	153b5	G	4/4	W4v2p31
DUNCAN McLEERIE	521H1H	2H72H2H	G	4/4	C5v2p72
DUNCAN McQUEEN	5L13b1	5417bL	A	4/4*	A1v6p8 W4v2p21
DUNCAN SWINE'S WIFE	3b17bL4	3b13b5	A	4/4	C18p27
DUNCAN'S COMPLAINT	333	235	Bb	3/4	O1v11p85
DUNCAN'S DANCE	31H31H	362H2	G	6/8	A1v1p26 O1v1Hp41
DUNCAN'S LILT	11H1H3H	2H223	F	2/4	O1v1Hp48
DUNDARY	1353	5L135	A	2/2	C18p8
DUNDEE LASSIE	1H1H3H2H	1H667	D	4/4	A1v5p29 C5v1p29
DUNDEE VOLUNTEERS MARCH	1122	3334	G	4/4	C5v1p1
DUNDEE VOLUNTEERS MARCH, THE	1122	3334	G	4/4	A1v5p1
DUNFERMLINE RACES	3333	7b7bL44	A	4/4*	G10v4p8 (II)
DUNGARVEN	1123	1166	G	6/8	C18p24
DUNIRA LODGE	3551H	526L2	D	4/4	S13p4 B11p17 G11v2Cp11
DUNKELD BRIDGE	1H3H75	1H3H2H7	F	4/4*	G10v5p26 (II)
DUNKELD HERMITAGE	153b5	2424	E	2/2	G10v1P25
(DUNKELD) HERMITAGE BRIDGE, (THE)	114L1	7bL55L7bL	B	6/8	G11v1Ap24 G10v2p24
DUNKELD HOUSE	1515	1H526L	E	2/2	Mc9v3p10
DUNKELD HOUSE	13b53b	7bL242	E	6/8	N1v1p8
DUNKELD HOUSE	13b53b	247b4	E	6/8	G11v1Ap6 G10v1p20
DUNKELD STEEPLE	1L5L36	1H642	A	4/4	G11v1Bp19
DUNNICHEN HOUSE	3155	3142	D	2/2	D15v1p18 (II)
DUNNIKEER HOUSE	1235	1620	A	4/4	W2v1p5
DUNNSTER CASTLE	1L155	2427bL	B	2/2	D15v1p30
DUNROBIN CASTLE	113b5	4455	D	2/2	H3p26
DUNROBIN CASTLE	3232	536L6	G	4/4	A7v6p74 A7v3p27
DUNSE CASTLE	51H53	51H2H2	G	2/2	Mc13v1p2 Mc13v2p2 (II)
DUNSE DINGS A'	351H3	351H1H	A	4/4*	G11v1Ap35 G1v2p79 G7p1 A1v4p64 C14v12p20
DUNSE DINGS A'	3b51H3b	3b51H1H	A	2/2	S12v1p43
DUNSKY	13b27bL	123b1	A	4/4	F3p17
DUNT THE GRUND AT LEISURE	1121	1151H	G	4/4	P5v3p25
DUPLIN CASTLE	1132	7L223	E	4/4	B11p5
DUPLIN HOUSE	111H1H	1H66H2H	D	6/8	G1v2p81 A7v6p17
DUPLIN HOUSE	1L1L11	16L62	Bb	6/8	G10v2p5 A7v2p7
DURANDARTE AND BELERMA	3H3H1H	531H	C	3/4	B7p47
DURIE HOUSE	3546	52H1H1H	D	2/4	W4v2p13
DUSKY NIGHT, THE	1H531	6432	D	6/8	B16v3p23
DUSKY NIGHT, THE	1H531	6430	D	6/8	S7v1p22
DUSTY MILLER, (THE)	335	321	G	6/4*	G9v5p32 (J3) B15v1p27 C5v2p15 P6v1p6 W7p9 C8v2p32 C14v11p24 C8v1p52
DUTCH LADY, THE	1122	3211	Bb	6/8	S7v3p3
DUTCH SKIPPER, (THE)	1H1H77	6656	D	4/4	G10v4p35 A1v3p180
DUTCH TROT, THE	5451H	4432	D	2/2	A1v4p61
DUTCH TROT, THE	5451H	447L2	C	4/4	Mc12v1p52
DUTCHES OF ATHOLE'S STRATHSPEY, THE	53H2H6	53H5H3H	D	4/4	A1v3p216
DUTCHES OF GORDON'S STRATHSPEY, THE	1552	1127bL	G	4/4	G10v1p24
DUTCHES OF HAMILTON'S NEW STRATHSPEY	5513	1524	E	4/4	C13v1p1
DUTCHES OF RICHMOND'S ALLEMAND, THE	3H3H4H3H	3H3H4H3H	D	2/2	B16v3p67

Name			Key	Time	References
DUTCHESS OF ARGYLE, THE	15L3L1L	4L242	Bb	2/2	C13v2p78
[DUCHESS OF ARGYLL, THE]					
DUTCHESS OF ARGYLE'S STRATHSPEY	5551	5524	E	4/4	C13v1p1
DUTCHESS OF ATHOLE'S REEL	1353	2366	A	4/4	P5v2p21
DUTCHESS OF ATHOLE'S REELL	5135	5522	F	4/4	C33p4,5
DUTCHESS (OF ATHOLE)'S SLIPPER, (THE)	5L353	5L36L2	G F	4/4	A1v4p57 E1v1p58 G11v1Ap18
					S11v1p11 G10v2p19 G7p19
					Mc12v1p43 (11)
DUTCHESS OF ATHOLL	5L326L	5L353	A	4/4	G11v1Ap5 G10v1p1 (11)
('S STRATHSPEY), (THE)					
DUTCHESS OF ATHOLL'S REEL	1H1H1H3H	72H75	C	2/2	D14v3p25
DUTCHESS OF BEAUFORT'S REEL	513bH2H	7b547bL	D	6/8	B10p12
DUTCHESS OF BEDFORD'S FANCY, THE	1131	6252	Bb	2/4	L2p23
DUTCHESS OF BEDFORD'S REEL	5H1H3b5	247b7bH	C	6/8	Mc21v4p40
DU(T)CHESS OF BEDFORD'S STRATHSPEY, THE	1L115L	2245L	Bb	4/4	M4v3p5 (11)
DUTCHESS OF BUCCLEUCH'S REELL	1342	16L6L5L	D	2/2	C33p4
DU(T)CHESS OF BUCCLEUCH('S STR., THE)	311H1	27bL44	A	4/4	G11v1p4,5 G10v1p23 (11)
DUTCHESS OF DEVONSHIRE'S REEL	5L13b1	4L7bL22	G	2/2	B10p19
DUTCHESS OF DORSET'S REEL, THE	113b5	2427bL	C	2/2	Mc21v4p44
DUTCHESS OF GORDON, THE	1545	4362	A	3/8	L2p24
DUTCHESS OF GORDON'S MINUET, THE	554	346	Eb	3/4	C22p4
DUTCHESS OF GORDON'S REEL	1135	1122	D	4/4	M4v1p11
DUTCHESS OF GORDON'S REEL	1H355	1H3H2H2	D	4/4	A1v6p11
DUTCHESS OF GORDON'S REEL, THE	1226L	1211H	A	2/2	R5p17 B10p17
DUTCHESS OF GORDON'S REELL	1H355	1H3H2H2	C	4/4	C33p4
DUTCHESS OF GORDON'S STRATHSPEY (REEL)	5551	5524	D G E	4/4*	A1v6p14 G1v2p73 C14v1p13
					K1v2p6/7 D14v3p1 Mc9v3p18/19
					(11)
DUTCHESS OF HAMILTON'S GIGG	5127bL	513b6b	A	6/8	B10p18
DUTCHESS OF HAMILTON'S NEW STRATHSPEY	5513	1524	E	4/4	C13v4p15
DUTCHESS OF HAMILTON'S REEL	5127bL	513b5	A	6/8	R5p9
DUTCHESS OF HAMILTON'S REEL, THE	1535	27bL7b4	D	2/2	D14v3p11 H3p18
DUTCHESS OF MANCHESTER, THE	3135	3622	E	4/4	L1p17
DUTCHESS OF MANCHESTER'S FAREWELL	113L5L	112L2L	Bb	4/4	M4v3p4
TO THE HIGHLANDS OF SCOTLAND, THE					
DUTCHESS OF MANCHESTER'S FAVORITE	1217L	6L237L	Bb	6/8	Mc21v4p1
DUTCHESS OF MANCHESTER'S NEW STRATHSPEY	1365	552H2H	F	4/4	Mc21v4p36
DUTCHESS OF MONTROSE'S REEL	1353	1355	G	4/4	A1v4p46 W4v1p22 C5v1p46
DUTCHESS OF PORTLAND'S REEL	3b421	4L27b2	Bb	2/2	B10p3
DUTCHESS OF YORK, THE	5551H	5522	D	4/4	C26v1p20
DYESTER LADDIE, THE	4264	2445	D	4/4	Mc9v2p32
DYSART HORNPIPE	556	464	A	6/4	G3p4
DYSART HOUSE STRATHSPEY	1112	2223	Bb	4/4	W2v1p7
DYSART MASSON LODGE HARMONY	1121	3343	A	6/8	W2v1p12
DYSART VOLUNTEERS MARCH	1343	3411	G	4/4	W2v2p14
DYSART VOLUNTEER'S MARCH	3355	3113	Bb	4/4	G3p18
DYSART VOLUNTEERS QUICK STEP	3355	3532	G	6/8	W2v2p14
E HO RO, MO GHORM SHUILEAG DHUBH	47b44	3bL7b44	E	2/4	Mc1v1p116
EARL & COUNTESS OF ERROL'S WELCOME	5551	6662	F	4/4	M11v2p13
TO SLAINS CASTLE					
EARL CORNWALLISE'S MARCH	1115	33H1H5	G	4/4	S12v2p5
EARL DOUGLAS'S LAMENT	3H3H1H	61HO	D	3/4	O1v1Gp30
EARL DOUGLAS'S LAMENT(ATION)	331	6L10	A Bb	3/4	Mc8v1Dp101 C4p5 O1v5p31
EARL FITZWILLIAM'S STRATHSPEY	5351H	5326L	A	2/2	J1p19
EARL MOIRA	1135	437L7L	F G	4/4	C8v1p23 C8v2p60
EARL MOIRA ('S STRATHSPEY)	1135	4327L	F G	4/4	A7v4p12 A7v5p16
EARL MOIRA'S RETURN TO ENGLAND	5L3L5L3L	227L2	G	4/4	A7v4p12
EARL OF ANGUS AND ARRAN, THE	1531	427L6L	C	4/4	M4v4p33
EARL OF BALCARRAS'S MARCH	1H554	3333	G	4/4	C5v1p49 A1v4p49
EARL OF BRADALBANE'S DELIGHT	3355	4517L	G	2/4	Mc22p9
EARL OF BREADALBANE'S (HERMITAGE/REEL)	1155	7b424	E	4/4*	G10v2p10 G11v1Cp36,37 (11)
EARL OF BREADLABAN(E)'S BIRTH DAY	53b3b7b	4224	E	2/2	A1v6p18 Mc4v2p1 (11)
EARL OF BUCHAN'S STRATHSPEY, THE	5L333	5L344	G	4/4	S5p7
EARL OF CARLISLE'S REEL	1H535	1H522	D	2/2	S7v1p37
EARL OF CASSLES'S REEL	57L12	536L2	A	4/4	E2p8
EARL OF DALHOUSIE'S HAPPY RETURN	147L5L	141H5	F	4/4	G9v2p22
TO SCOTLAND, THE					
EARL OF DALHOUSIE'S MARCH	15L6L4L	5L5L5L3	Bb	4/4	G10v5p1
EARL OF DALHOUSIES REEL	1H3H53H	2H3H1H6	Eb	4/4*	G10v4p15 (11)
EARL OF DALHOUSIE'S WELCOME	5L17L2	3561H	F	4/4	G10v4p37
FROM THE PYRENEES, THE					
EARL OF DALKEITH'S MARCH, THE	1H1H2H7	2H3H2H2H	C	4/4	G9v3p8,9
EARL OF DALKEITH'S REEL	13L13	2426L	F	4/4	G10v3p20 (11)
EARL OF DUNMORE, THE	13b51H	3bH7b42	C	6/8	B20p20
EARL OF DUNMORE'S REEL, THE	15L11	2242	Bb	2/2	B20p5
EARL OF EGLINTON'S STRATHSPEY	1513H	1H562	E	4/4	G10v1p16
EARL OF ELGIN'S (FAVORITE/STRATHSPEY)	1555	54H2H2	E	4/4	G11v1Ap21 G10v3p5
EARL OF ELGIN'S FAVOURITE	15L6L5L	6L27L2	E	2/4	G10v3p5
EARL OF ELGIN'S STRATHSPEY, (THE)	1142	1141H	D	4/4	S13p2 Mc4v2p4
EARL OF ERROL'S STRATHSPEY	1131	11H7L2	C	2/2	D6p21
EARL OF FIFE, THE	5324	5366	Bb	4/4	M4v4p16,17
EARL OF FIFE'S BIRTH DAY, THE	113b5	7b427bL	A	4/4	T1v2p16

Title					
EARL OF FIFE'S FIRESIDE, THE	315L1	3342	F	4/4	P5v4p14 (II)
EARL OF FIFE'S REEL	3135	6542	F	2/2	P5v4p6
EARL OF FIFE'S STRATHSPEY, THE	1122	1113	A	4/4	M4v3p16
EARL OF GALLOWAY'S REEL	17bL3b4L	17bL3b5	A	2/2	S7v1p41
EARL OF GLENCAIRN'S STRATHSPEY, (THE)	111L1L	436L2	G	4/4*	P5v3p12 Mc9v3p12 Mc12v1p10/11
EARL OF GLENCAIRN'S, THE	3b13b1	3b7bL7bL7bL	E	2/2	Mc9v1p6
EARL OF HADDINGTON ('S STRATHSPEY), THE	31H66	1H5H6H3H	C	4/4	G11v1Ap9 G10v1p9
EARL OF HYNDFORD'S REEL	13b1H3bH	7b427bL	C	2/2	G10v3p32
EARL OF KINNOULL'S REEL	1H531	27bL7b2	D	2/2	G11v2Dp37
EARL OF KINTORE, THE	1127L	1144	Bb	4/4	D6p5
EARL OF LAUDERDALE ('S REEL)	1347L	1554	G	2/2	G11v1Bp35 G10v3p19 (II)
EARL OF LEVEN'S FAVORITE, THE	3555	3551H	Eb	4/4	G10v6p36
EARL OF LOUDON'S STRATHSPEY, (THE)	5515	6L662	G F	4/4	A1v3p198 A7v6p31 C4p9 A7v2p15 C13v1p28 G10v1p3 G11v1Cp21 (II)
EARL (OF) MARSHALL ('S REEL) [EARL MARISCHAL'S REEL]	1153	3153	G F	4/4*	A1v3p224 G1v2p85 A7v6p22 P5v2p4 K1v1p30 G11v2Ap28 Mc7p4 G9v5p34 C14v14p5 B15v1p73 N1v1p28 (II)
EARL OF MOIRA'S WELCOME TO SCOTLAND	1135	4327L	D G	4/4*	E1v1p15 G1v1p43
EARL OF MORAY'S REEL, THE	3564	54H72H	F	2/2	G15p30
EARL OF MORTON'S JIG(G)	31H71H	432H2	C	6/8	G11v1Ap37 G10v3p18
EARL OF ROSEBERY'S REEL, THE	1H3H2H3H	3H676	F	2/2	G9v2p9
EARL OF SEAFIELD, THE	1H1H7	3H3H2H	F	3/4	M4v4p8
EARL OF SEAFIELD'S REEL, THE	1H531	227L5L	D	2/2	G15p7
EARL OF SEAFIELD'S STRATHSPEY, THE	31H3H1H	5122	D	4/4	G15p7
EARL OF SEAFORTH'S REEL, THE	5L5L26L	1353	A	2/2	Mc9v1p19
EARL OF WIGTON'S LAMENT	11L3L5L	6L123	G	2/2	D14v2p2,3,4,5
EARLE OF CASSLES'S FAVORITE	3H1H2H2H	3H1H3H2H	D	4/4	E2p7
EARLY HORN, THE	1H31H1	1H2H5H5H	G	6/8	R12v3p24,25
EAS NA SMUID	3365	31H66	C	4/4	F2v2p90(80)
EAST NEUK OF FIFE (No. 5), THE	1113	5151	G	4/4*	C8v1p63 B15v2p17 E1v2p19 G9v1p12,13 R4p9,10 D13p19 Mc8v1Cp89 Mc8v2Cp17 Mc9v2p8 C20p16,17 (II)
EAST NOOK OF FIFE, THE	1155	2266	G	2/4	A1v1p20
EASTER ELCHIES	1152	1153H	F	2/2*	M4v3p58 (II)
EBDEN'S QUICK STEP	1351H	5122	F	4/4	C7p12
ECCENTRIC REEL, THE	5653	5357	D	2/2	B6v4p1
ECLYPSE, THE	1H1H1H	535	A	3/4	B6v4p2
EDIN CASTLE	1111	14L2L2	Bb	4/4	M11v2p10
EDINBURGH CASTLE	1342	5L342	F	4/4	P9p25
EDINBURGH CASTLE	3H2H3H1H	5H5H3H2H	C	6/8	E2p3
EDINBURGH JIGG	5L135	1H652	G	6/8	R12v1p57
EDINBURGH MUSICAL FUND, THE	1H765	437L5L	G	6/8	G9v3p16
EDINBURGH SCOTCH MEASURE, THE	3235	1554	A F	4/4	O1v1Cp11 O1v5p1
EDINBURGH THEATRE ROYAL	15L21	5216L	Eb	6/8	P9p10
EDINBURGH VOLUNTEER'S MARCH	1155	661H3H	G	4/4	A1v5p19
EDINBURGH WAITS, THE	3335	1H523	G	2/4	C6p30
EDINR DEFENSIVE BAND'S MARCH, THE	1H533H	5H5H4H2H	C	4/4	S12v2p8
EDINr VOLUNTEER'S MARCH	1155	661H3H	G	4/4	C5v1p19
EGLINTON CASTLE	315L2L	3L5L6L6L	A	4/4	G8p30
EGLINTON CASTLE	15L6L2L	16L11	Bb	4/4	G10v4p1
EIGHT MEN OF MOIDART, (THE)	1135	2227bL	A G	2/2	C14v22p18 B15v1p88 S12v1p23
EIGHTH OF DECEMBER, THE	3546	72H1H3H	D	2/2	G10v5p15
EIGHTY THIRD REGts MARCH, THE	12L12L	1114	G	4/4	R6v1p9
EILAN MO ROON	567	1H1H1H	D	3/4	C20p58
EILEAN AIGEIS	3bH53b1	1451H	C	6/8	F2v2p98(88)
EILIDH DHUGHLAS	5217bL	6bL5L3b1	A	3/8	F2v2p64(54)
EIRIDH NA FINNEACHA' GAIDHEALACHD	3321	131H0	D	4/4	F2v2p11(1)
EISD MO CHAILEAG EISD	3b224	3b56b5	B	6/8	F2v2p52(42)
ELBA WALTZ, THE	1215	1256L	D	3/8	G9v3p22
ELEVENTH OCTOBER, THE	1H1H1H1H	6542	A	2/2	Mc16p19
ELGIN ACADEMY, THE	1131	2246	D	4/4	T1v2p11
ELGIN TRINITY LODGE'S STRATHSPEY, THE	1L5L4L2L	1L5L6L1	A	4/4	G15p20
ELLECTION REEL, THE	6L165	4662	F	2/2	R6v1p3
ELOUIS, THE	3562H	75H4H3H	D	2/2	C14v21p6
ELSIE MARLY	3111H	317bL7b	G	6/8	P5v4p22,23 G11v2Dp38 B15v1p26
ELTHAM ASSEMBLY	1375	637L7L	Bb	6/8	R12v1p23
EMIG	3H1H2H5	1H1H2H5	C	2/4	C14v26p6
EMON O KNUCK	135	31H6	G	3/4	A1v6p37
EMPEROR OF GERMANY'S MARCH	1H1H1H5	1H3H1H1H	D	4/4	A1v6p72
EMPEROR OF HAYTI, THE	5436	5522	G	6/8	H6v2p3 P6v1p18
EMPEROR OF RUSSIA'S WALTZ, THE	1H2H3H1H	661H1H	C	3/8	G9v3p9
EMPTY PURSE, THE	53b53b	5L15L1	B	6/8	G10v2p22
EMPTY (PURSE/POCKETS), (THE)	1542	1511H	A	4/4	C5v1p18 A1v5p18 Mc12v1p37
ENCE CROUDIE TWICE CROUDIE, &C.	1113	2121	G	2/2	C20p22
END OF THE GREAT BRIDGE, THE	1355	2355	G	4/4	Mc1v1p111-115
ENFIELD CHACE	1H535	61H2H7	D	6/8	G8p24
ENGLAND'S GLORY	5L131	5L242	A	2/4	S7v2p8
ENGLISH BRING TO GRATNEY GREEN, THE	521H7	1H136	G	2/2	R6v2p17
ENGLISHMAN IN PARIS	551H1H	6531	F	2/4	S7v1p85

EPPIE ADAIR [MY APPIE]	554	512	E G	3/4	(J3) C5v2p44 O1v1Kp129
EPPIE McNAB	6622	5511	G F	6/8	A1v2p60 B15v1p111
EPPIE McNAB	1126L	11H53	A	6/8	G11v1Bp17
EPPIE McNAB	554	542	G E	3/4	O1v4p46 C5v2p50 (J3)
EPPING CHACE	3535	1H543	F	6/8	C14v2p10,11
EPPING FORREST	1H1H2H5	6651	F	6/8	B16v4p92
ERE AROUND THE HUGE OAK	5454	3211	G Eb	6/8	A1v6p14
ESKE SIDE	1H1H1H	2H1H6	D	3/4	O1v3p41 O1v1Bp8
ESSEX BAND, THE	1H1H33	2243	D	2/4	C7p22
ETRICK BANKS	3b3b15	1H51H1H	D E	4/4	O1v1Bp16 Mc8v1Ap13 Mc8v2Ap15
					C13v3p1 E1v2p39 C20p15
					G1v1p44
ETRICK BANKS	3b3b15	1H51H3bH	D	4/4	N1v2p74 A1v6p45
ETTRICK BANKS	3b3b13bH	1H1H53bH	E D	4/4	T6v2p102 B5p2 O1v5p19
ETTRICK BANKS	3bL3bL1L3b	115L3b	B	4/4	O1v2p28,29
ETTRICK SHEPHERD, THE	51H63	64H1H5	D	6/8	P11v2p5
EUROPEAN WALTZ	1H564	3H1H3H1H	G	3/8	H1p30
EVAN BANKS	117bL3b	543b3b	F	4/4	C5v2p56
EVELEEN'S BOWER	1H1H1H6	51H1H6	D	4/4	B7p29
EVELEEN'S BOWER	51H1H6	51H1H6	C D	4/4	C8v1p20 C8v2p59
EVENING BRUSH, THE	1H543	1H541	G	6/8	C14v4p11
EVENING STAR, THE	3515	353H5	F	4/4	H1p20
EVERARDS FAVORITE HORNPIPE	1H3H4H1H	1H3H1H6	C	4/4	A7v3p31
EW-BUGHTS MARION	1251	6L5LO5L	G	4/4	T6v2p32 P8v2p22
EW(I)E WI' THE CROOKE'D HORN, THE	5L17bL2	5L143b	G	4/4	G10v1p11 (II)
EWIE WI' THE CROOKED HORN, THE	5L17L2	5L143b	G	4/4	C8v1p44
EWIE WI' THE CROOKED HORN, THE	5L17L2	5L143	G	4/4*	H3p16 (J3) G10v6p14
EXCAMBEY, THE	1H61H3	4362	D	6/8	A1v3p224
EXETER CHANGE	3332	1115	G	2/2	S7v1p88
EXILE OF ERIN, THE	1H1H1H7	6663	G D	4/4	C8v2p23 E1v2p57
EXILE, THE	3H1H1H5	72H4H2H	C	2/4	P6v1p33
EXPRESS, THE	151H3	26L16L	Bb	4/4	B16v1p4
EXTRAORDINARY GAZETTE, THE	1L1L6L5L	1L1L57L	Bb	6/8	B16v1p5
F. GARDEN CAMPBEL	11H66	547L2	Eb	4/4	P5v4p16
FAILTE BHEAG MHIC LEOID	137L6L	5L7L3L2L	G	6/8	D14v2p8
FAILTE FIR BHOISDAIL	256	255	G	3/4	Mc1v1p56-60
FAILTE MHIC CAONNICH	1531	2326L	F	6/8	D14v2p1
FAILTE MHIC DHONAIL GHUIRM	3155	4266	D	2/2	D14v2p6,7
FAILTE NA BAN MHARC	13L5L3L	5L3L24L	F	4/4	F2v2p97(87)
FAILTE NA MIOSG	1H1H2H	661H	D	3/4	O1v2p39 O1v3p46 O1v1Ap22
FAILTE PHROINSA	1542	7bL7bL7bL4	A	4/4	Mc1v1p1-6
FAINT AND WEARILY	1H1H76	1H3H5H2H	C	2/4	E1v1p53
FAIR AFRICAN, THE	53H1H6	6566	F	2/4	C14v24p3
FAIR AN' LUCKY	35L7bL2	3213	G	6/8	C18p39
FAIR, BEAUTIFUL AND CHEARFUL MAID	3b243b	127bL6	A	4/4	Mc5p12
FAIR FIELD HOUSE	51H6b4	3b57b3b	A	4/4*	R5p11 (II)
FAIR HELEN	133	36L6L	Bb	3/4	N1v2p65
FAIR IS THE BROWN MAID OF MY HEART	1L5L6bL5L	1L5L4L7bF	A	6/8	Mc5p7
FAIR KITTY	1H53H3H	1H71H1H	G	2/2	O1v1Ip67
FAIR METHODIST, THE	1L3L1L3	2L242	A	6/8	P9p28
FAIR SALLY LOV'D A BONNY SEAMAN	3bH2H7	2HO5	E	3/5	O1v1Kp125
FAIRIES MARCH, THE	5553H	5331H	D	4/4	G9v3p34
FAIRIES, THE	1H347L	4L2L7L6L	Bb	4/4	S7v1p49
FAIRLY SHOT OF HER	1115	117bL4	A F E	6/8	G1v2p89 S11v1p10 D16p34
					G10v2p24 Mc12v1p13
FAIRLY SHOT ON HER	1H1H3H	1H3H1H	D	6/4	W7p19
FAIRWELL, THE	1155	1H642	F	2/4	D16p35
FAIRY DANCE, THE	3H3H3H3H	3H3H75	D	2/4*	H6v1p2 P6v1p24 (II)
FAIRY DANCE, (THE)	3H3H3H3H	3H3H72H	D	4/4*	E1v1p14 C8v2p14 C14v23p12,13
					C8v1p42 G13p14 A7v4p19
FAIRY KING	1133	2466	G	2/2	A1v5p27 C5v1p27
FAIRY QUEEN, THE	115L	115L	G	3/4	O1v2p41 O1v3p47 O1v1Ap23
FAITH I DEFIE THEE	113	1H53	G	3/4	O1v1Ep32
FAITHFULL SHEPHERD, THE	1212	3215	G	2/4	A1v1p24
FAL LA LA	5311	437L2	A	2/4	E1v1p114
FAL LAL LA	5H3H1H1H	4H3H72H	D	2/4	A1v6p37
FALCONER'S LAMENT, THE	1136	5622	F	4/4	E2p4
FALCONERS TWA DAUGHTERS, THE	1H51H3	1H52H2	A	2/4	E2p15
FALCONERS WHIM, THE	3331	6421	A	4/4	E2p11
FALL OF FYERS, THE	3b55L3b	4544	C	4/4	G8p14
FALLAIN GUN DITH 'THAINAIG E	51H1H	2H1H1H	D	3/4	F2v2p45(35)
FALLEN HERO (NELSON), THE	315L5L	5L122	A	4/4	G11v2Cp8
FALLS OF FOYERS, THE	3333	6453	C	4/4	C8v1p58
FALMOUTH ASSEMBLY	3142	5521	G	6/8	B16v3p92
FANCY OF THE MOMENT, THE	351H3H	1H1H1H1H	D	4/4	L1p12
FANCY, THE	3L111	427L2	Bb	4/4	A7v1p5
FANNY'S FANCY	31H74H	2H531H	D	2/4	A1v5p4
FANNY'S FANCY	31H74H	2H531H	D	2/4	C5v1p4
FAOILEAGAN SGARBA	1553	6523	D	6/8	Mc5p25
FARE THEE WEEL THOU FIRST AND FAIREST	3b13b5	3b11H5	B	6/8	C5v3p55
FAREWELL	551HO	5530	F	4/4	F1p35
FAREWELL BUT REMEMBER THE HOUR	1341	1553	G	2/2	B7p21

Title					
FAREWELL MY PRETTY MOGGY	1H1H1H5	2211	G	4/4	O1v4p36 O1v1Ep8
FAREWELL MY PRETTY WITTY MAGGY	1H1H1H5	2215	G	4/4	Mc8v1Cp6 C20p10
FAREWELL MY PRETTY WITTY PEGGY	1H1H1H5	2216	G	4/4	Mc8v1Bp40
FAREWELL MY PRETTY WITTY PEGGY	1H3H1H5	226L5	G	4/4	C5v2p27
FAREWELL MY WEE COT HOUSE	1H1H1H	531	G	3/4	C5v2p44
FAREWELL, THE	5313H	2H4H2H2	E	4/4	M4v4p35
FAREWELL, THE	5652H	51H32	D C	4/4	A7v6p28 A7v2p5
FAREWELL, THE	1H313	1H362	D	6/8	A1v2p74
FAREWELL TO EDINBURGH	5121	1234	G	4/4	O1v1lp86
FAREWELL TO WHISKY	11H2H6	12H5H3H	D	4/4	B7p3 E1v1p98
FAREWELL TO WHISKY	1L126L	1L253	Bb	4/4	C8v1p41 G11v1Ap2 G10v5p36
FARMERS OF THE BORDER, THE	5365	51H3H2H	D	6/8	C7p20
FARMER'S WISH, THE	3H1H5	432	D	3/4	O1v1Lp154
FARR AWA' WEDDING, THE	311	312	A	9/8	G11v2Bp27 K1v2p29
FARTHER BEEIN THE WELLCOMER, THE	3363	7b7b7bL7bL	D	2/2	Y1p21
FA'S SAE MERRY'S THE MILLER WHEN A' HIS POCKS ARE FU'	533	532	A	9/8	C18p28,29
FASHION, THE	3H4H2H7	62H75	D	6/8	B16v2p5
FASHIONABLE LEVITIES	1H2H1H1H	4H3H2H2H	C	6/8	C1v1p7
FASKALLY HOUSE	1356	7b7bL45	A	2/2	Mc19v3p1,2,3 Mc19v2p6,7
FASQUE HOUSE	5354	536L2	A	6/8	D15v1p12
FATHER MOTHER AND SUKE	5H4H1H6	553H2H	D	6/8	S7v2p9
FAUSAN'S MAGGOT	1324	3421	D	2/2	R12v1p22
FAV. STRATHSPEY, A	5142	5151H	Bb	2/2	Mc16p15
FAVORITE, A	2221	25L7L5L	A	6/8	P5v4p2
FAVORITE AIR, A	317L6L	6L211	G	2/4	A7v6p51
FAVORITE ARIETTA	1H3H65	5H4H2H2H	C	6/8	F1p31
FAVORITE DANCE, A	1H3H1H1H	62H76	D	2/4	A7v6p54
FAVORITE DANCE, A	1H345	3345	F	2/2	Mc13v2p16
FAVORITE HORNPIPE, A	1H7H6H4H	4H71H6	D	4/4	A7v5p17
FAVORITE HORNPIPE, A	1H1T5H3H	3H61H6	C	4/4	F1p33
FAVORITE IRISH TUNE, A	11H7b4	11H1H3bH	C	2/2	G9v5p20
FAVORITE JIGG, A	3b51H7b	6b543b	D	6/8	P5v4p15
FAVORITE MARCH	1H1H1H4H	2H555	D	4/4	E1v2p50,51
FAVORITE MARCH, A	3335	1122	Bb	4/4	E2p20
FAVORITE MINUET, A	112	331	A	3/4	N2p1,2,3,4
FAVORITE POLLACCA, THE	551H	2H50	D	3/4	E1v2p59
(FAVORITE) QUICK STEP (,25th REGt), (A)	1H531	1231	G	2/4	A1v1p1 A7v6p96
FAVORITE QUICK STEP, A	1111	6L432	Bb	2/4	E2p20
FAVORITE REEL, A	1H51H5	1H2H3H7	C	6/8	C23p4
FAVORITE SCOTCH DIVERTIMENTO	5H5H5H2H	5H5H2H3H	D	6/8	G1v1p27
FAVORITE SLOW TUNE, A	13b15L	7bL5L4L7bF	A	4/4	Mc16p28
FAVORITE SLOW TUNE, A	1H1H53	5432	Eb	4/4	B12p5
FAVORITE TUNE FROM MOTHER GOOSE, A	1365	1362	D	6/8	A7v4p28
FAVORITE TUNE FROM MOTHER GOOSE, A	1123	16L7L5L	Bb	6/8	A7v4p27
FAVORITE TUNE FROM MOTHER GOOSE, A	555	556	D	9/8	A7v5p15 A7v4p28
FAVORITE TUNE FROM MOTHER GOOSE, A	3H3H2H	3H3H2H	D	9/8	A7v4p28
FAVORITE WALTZ	53H2H1H	1H6H2H1H	D	3/8	H1p29
FAVOURITE AIR, A	5H3H1H1H	4H3H1H2H	C	2/4	A1v6p20
FAVOURITE AIR, A	3H1T5H	3H1T6H	D	9/8	A1v6p38
FAVOURITE AIR BY MR BASTIN, A	1H2H3HO	3H4H2HO	D	2/4	R12v3p19
FAVOURITE BALLAD FROM ROBIN HOOD, A	534	223	G	3/4	A1v3p223
FAVOURITE GERMAN AIR, A	135	531	G	3/4	C7p14
FAVOURITE HIGHLAND AIR, A	1151H	6651H	D	4/4	A1v3p226
FAVOURITE HIGHLAND QUICKSTEP, 73rd REGt, A	6666	3232	G	4/4	A1v2p25
FAVOURITE HIGHLAND STRATHSPEY, A	151H5	2H1H22	D	2/2	D15v1p23
FAVOURITE HORNPIPE, A	511H5	4321	F G	2/4	C8v1p50 C8v2p54
FAVOURITE STRATHSPEY, A	5135	5522	D	4/4	A1v2p18
FAVOURITE WELCH AIR, A	1322	115L1	G	3/8	C23p17
FEADAN GLAN A PHIOBAIR	3b111	3b57b3b	A	2/2	F2v2p27(17)
FEAR CHUL CHARN	1555	1563	G	4/4	Mc1v1Ap8
FEATHERS, THE	1H1H55	3H3H2H1H	D	4/4	A1v2p47
FEATHERS, THE	115L5L	3321	Bb	4/4	Mc9v2p2
FEATHERS, THE	111H5	427L5L	G	6/8	A1v3p161 S7v1p46
FEE HIM FATHER FEE HIM	1253	1250	G	4/4	A1v5p50 Mc8v1Dp98
FEET WASHING, THE	5126	6562	A	6/8	G11v2Cp27
FEIDAG GHORACH AN T'SLEIDH	157b	652	G	3/4	M12p26
FEMALE HERO, THE	3343	3327L	G	6/8	A1v1p23
FEMALE LOVER'S CHALLENGE, THE	1113	15L12	A	2/4	Mc1v1p116
FEMALE RAKE, THE	1H1H43	362H7	D	6/8	A1v1p30
FERGUSON'S RANT	325L3	7L55L3	G	4/4	A1v3p181
FERNY BED, THE	13b4	556	G	3/4	O1v1Lp152
FERTISH HILL, THE	1H3H5H3H	4H2H3H6	E	6/8	P11v2p19
FETE CHAMPETRE MINUET, THE	112	154	F	3/4	C22p4
FETTERESSO HOUSE	1346	3432	F	6/8	M11v1p3
FEUDAL TIMES	116L1	116L1	Bb	2/4	B17p5
FHEARAIBH MO RUIN NA DIULTAIBH IOMART	1333	1376	C	6/8	F2v2p92(82)
FHIR A BHATA [FEAR A' BHATA]	165	6L11	Bb	3/4	F2v2p50(40)
FHUAIR MI LITIR O'N GHOBHADH	132	551	A	9/8	Mc1v1p116
FICKLE JENNY	543	354	G	3/2	P8v2p19
FIDDICH-SIDE LASSES, THE	5551	5547bL	A	4/4	M4v3p15 (ll)

Title			Key	Time	Sources
FIDLERS' CONTEMPT	15L6L6L	1123	D	4/4	D14v2p45
FIELDS OF ODIN, THE	5L5L1	133	G	3/4	L2p17
FIENT A CRUM O' THEE SHE FA'S, THE	11H52	13bH1H1H	A	6/8	C5v2p43
FIERVELS MINUET	1H42	223	D	3/4	C22p19
FIFE AND ALL ABOUT IT	6L111H	5451	G	4/4	Mc8v1Dp108(?)
FIFE AND ALL THE LANDS ABOUT IT	6L111H	5551	F G	4/4*	(J3) B5p8 C5v3p52 O1v2p7
					O1v3p3 Mc8v2Bp18 O1v1Ep2,3
					O1v1Ap5
FIFE DOCKS	5L112	7bL222	A	6/8	W2v2p11
FIFE HUNT, (THE)	3H1H53	22H2H2H	D C	4/4*	A7v6p2 E1v1p92 A1v4p18
					A1v3p157 C13v1p38 N1v1p30
					A7v2p30 G10v1p10 P10p5 C14v4p13
					A7v5p24 C8v1p59 G11v1Ap36
					G7p16 (II)
FIFE NESS	13b53b	7b527bL	G	2/2	G8p34
FIFTEENTH Regt. 2ND. QUICKSTEP	1H64H3H	1H64H1H	D	6/8	A1v1p49
FIFTH OF DECEMBER	1515L	6L542	A	2/2	A1v3p211
FIG FOR A KISS, A	155	244	E	9/8	B15v1p74 A7v6p50
FIGARO	1H1H1H1H	2H5H4H1H	D	2/4	C14v27p2,3
FIGHT ABOUT THE FIRE SIDE	5322H	5353	D C	4/4*	G1v2p78 C8v1p21 C14v16p21
					E1v1p4 Mc21v4p15 G11v2Ap19
					G7p15 K1v1p21 (II)
FIGURE DANCE	3H1H4H7	1H1H2H5H	D	2/4	D15v2p43
FILE-BEK IS AY READY, THE	3531H	3524	G	4/4	B15v1p77
FILL THE STOUP	53b41	53b57bL	B	2/2	A1v4p25
FILL THE STOUP	5351	5362	A	4/4*	H3p36 K1v1p27 G11v2Ap25
					P5v2p21 G7p2 (II)
FILL THE STOUP	6451	6462	A	2/2	Mc9v3p14/15
FIN CH' HAN DAL VINO	1T1T3T1T	5H5H1T5H	C	2/4	E1v2p84
FINALE FROM "LA NIEGE"	5555	1H1H55	C	6/8	G13p11
FINALE IN INKLE AND YARICO	1H2H3H1H	62H75	G	2/4	E1v1p120
FINALE, THE	1H1H2H3H	1H1H67	E	2/4	C18p40
FINALE, THE	5365	4322	G	2/4	W4v2p34
FINALI, THE	5353	4433	D	4/4	W4v1p30
FINE FLOWERS IN THE VALLEY	115L5L	115L5L	G B	4/4	(J3) C5v2p14
FINGALL'S LAMENTATION	3b51	3b53b	F	3/4	G10v4p17
FINGAL'S CAVE	1321	1362	E	4/4	G8p26 K1v2p6 G11v2Bp6 P1v1p9
FINGAL'S HORNPIPE	1H154	22H2H6	C	4/4	Mc16p9
FINLAY IS HIS FATHER'S DARLING	5521	6661H	D	4/4	D14v2p33
FINLAYSTON HOUSE	5555	1H56L3	C	4/4	R5p47(55)
FIR TREA, THE	311H7b	27bL7b2	D	4/4	C4p50 G10v1p17 G11v1Ap16
FIR TREE, THE	311H6	27bL7b2	D	4/4	G9v5p36 B15v1p38 C33p1
FIRE DRAKE	1H513	445L2	F	6/8	B16v3p63
FIRR TREE, THE	3b1H7b5	643b5	A	2/2	R12v1p100
FIRST MEDLEY DANCE	3H4H2H5H	3H1H2H7	D	6/8	G3p10,11
FIRST OF APRIL, THE	5252	5521	A	6/8	B16v3p91
FIRST OF DECEMBER, THE	3H5H4H2H	2H4H1H6	D	2/2	R12v2p10
FIRST TURKS MARCH	5554	3332	G	4/4	A1v2p3
FISHER'S (HORNPIPE/FAVORITE DANCE)	1H345	3345	F G	4/4*	A7v3p9 C8v1p51 A7v6p72
					C8v2p54 A7v5p36
FISHERS RANT, THE	51H51H	7b2H4H7b	D	4/4	C7p22
FITZ WILLIAM, THE	1133	2211	A	2/4	B16v4p94
FIVE MILES OFF	5151	4244	C	2/2	H1p9
FIVE TIMES BY THE TAPER'S LIGHT	1H1H1H1H	2H2H2H2H	D	4/4	E1v2p93
FLAG DANCE, THE	3H1H3H1H	2H4H2H7	C D	6/8	W4v1p19 A1v4p45
FLAGGON, THE	3135	3111H	G	4/4*	G11v1Ap27 A7v6p88 Mc16p18
					G10v1p5 (II)
FLEASGAICH OG A'S CAILEAGAN	37L5L3L	4L2L4L6L	F	2/2	F2v2p97(87)
FLEE OVER THE WATER	5454	7L254	A	2/4	G10v1p35
FLIGHT, THE	1H1H1H5	362H2H	D	6/8	A1v2p59
FLIGHTS OF FANCY	1H1T5H4H	1H1H1H5	C	4/4	P6v1p32
FLINTO	1516	1542	D	4/4	W4v2p14
FLITCH OF BACON	1H664	4335	G	2/2	B16v3p19 S7v1p34
FLITCH OF BACON, THE	1H1H2H2H	3H3H77	D	6/8	B16v3p2
FLODDEN FIELD	3H3H2H2H	1H3H77	D	2/4	P6v1p36
FLORINO	3355	2244	G	4/4	H1p7
FLOW ON THOU SHINING RIVER	1H653	4530	G	2/4	E1v2p15
FLOW THOU REGAL PURPLE STREAM	1122	3131	D	4/4*	E1v2p66,67
FLOWER GARDEN	1H2H3H3H	3H3H5H5H	D	6/8	S7v1p85
FLOWER OF EDINBURGH, (THE)	5L5L11	3332	G	4/4*	O1v1Cp19 (W3) (II)
FLOWERS OF EDINBURGH, THE	5L5L11	3532	F G	4/4*	(J3) E1v1p91 C4p21
					Mc8v1Bp59 C20p32
FLOWERS OF EDINBURGH, THE	5L5L11	3542	G	4/4	C8v2p8 C8v1p24 G11v2Dp16
FLOWERS OF EDINBURGH, THE	5L134	7L5L26L	G	2/4	C6p12
FLOWERS OF THE FOREST, THE	5551H	4H2H65	D	4/4	C8v2p61
FLOWERS OF THE FOREST, THE	5551H	4H2H66	D	4/4	C5v2p11 G1v1p7
FLOWERS OF THE FOREST, THE	5552H	3H2H66	D C	4/4*	Mc8v1Ap23 Mc12v2p27 C4p22
					C20p23 O1v1Ip80 E1v1p108
FLOWERS OF THE FOREST, THE	5L5L5L1	326L6L	Bb	4/4	(J3)
FLOWERS OF THE FOREST, THE	5L5L5L1	426L5L	Bb	4/4	C8v1p28
FLOWERS OF THE FOREST, THE	5L5L5L1	426L6L	Bb	4/4	C6p11
FLOWERS OF THE FOREST, THE	5L5L5L2	326L6L	Bb	4/4	N1v2p56

FLOWERS OF THE FOREST, THE	3453	2432	A	2/4	E1v2p63
FLY BY NIGHT	3H1H3H1H	4H2H75	C	2/4	P6v1p7
FLY NOT YET	1135	572H7	G	6/8	B7p28 E1v1p113
FLY, THE	71H65	71H65	G	6/8	B16v4p96
FOCHABER'S RANT, THE	1H3H2H1H	1H3H2H1H	G	2/2	M4v3p41 (11)
FOLEY HOUSE	3534	427L5L	F	2/4	C14v23p3
FOLEY HOUSE	3535	427L5L	F	2/4	P6v1p5
FOLKSTONE CAMP	1111	1H51H5	F	4/4	E2p4
(FOLLOW HER) OVER THE BORDER	533	535	F	9/8	E1v1p57 Mc7p9 G11v1Cp5 G10v2p14 S11v1p11 Mc12v1p60
FOLLY AS IT FLIES	3535	7L27L2	F	2/2	P9p21
FONAB HOUSE	351H5	5142	D	6/8	G9v2p16,17 G10v6p24,25
FONCASTELLE HOUSE	331H6	432h2	C	2/2	Mc4v1p11
FONN LIONARACHD DO BHRIARABH OSSIAN [FONN GNATHAICHTE...OISEIN]	55L43	4321	A	6/8	F2v2p20(10)
FOOTE'S MINUET	5H3H5H	5H4H3H	D	3/4	E1v1p17
FOOT'S MINUET	5H3H5H	4H4H3H	D	3/4	R12v3p27
FOOTS VAGARIES	1331	2462	G	2/2	R12v1p22
FOR A' THAT AN' A' THAT	1H1H62H	3H4H66	D	2/2	Mc7p22 (11)
FOR A' THAT AND A' THAT	3H5H4H2H	3H5H66	D	2/4	A1v1p7
FOR BONNIE ANNIE LAURIE	11H70	5230	D	4/4	C6p21
FOR (LAKE/SAKE/LACK) OF GOLD	1L1L5L1	6L221	Bb A	4/4	N1v2p5 (J3) (C25) C24v2p2
FOR OLD LONG GINE MY JOE	1H1H1H3H	5554	F	2/2	P7p11
FOR OUR LANG BIDING HERE	1255	4411	A	4/4	C5v2p48
FOR OUR LANG BIDING HERE	1541	47b66	D	4/4*	S16p58,59 T6v2p20
FOR OUR LANG BIDING HERE	5L215L	1433	G	4/4	P8v2p3
FOR TENDERNESS FORM'D	1H71HO	1H63H2H	C	2/4	E1v1p116
FOR (THE) LACK/SAKE OF GOLD (SHE LEFT ME/I LOST HER)	1151H	62H2H1H	C D	4/4	C13v3p74,75,76 Mc8v2Cp2 edv1Cp2 A1v3p220 Mc8v1Cp90,91 R12v3p11 C5v2p7 C13v3p2,3 E1v2p11 C20p14,15 G1v1p18
FOR THE LOVE OF GEAN	17L5L	122	G	3/2	O1v1Hp49
(FOR THE SAKE O') SOMEBODY	1H5H2H2H	1H3H6H5H	D	4/4*	B7p44 G1v2p76
FOR THE SAKE OF SOME-BODY	1353	461H6	G	4/4	O1v1Dp30
FORBES'S RANT, THE	1327L	1323	G	4/4	C33p11
FORDELL HOUSE	331H1H	3342	G	2/2	H3p22 (11)
FOREIGN AIR, A	51H65	671H3H	G	2/4	A1v3p197
FOREST OF BONDY, THE	5553	661H5H	C	2/4	H6v23p2
FOREST OF GA-ICK, THE [FOREST OF GARTH]	11H1H1H	7b2H7b7bL	D	4/4	M4v3p52 (11)
FORFAR ASSEMBLY	1151H	656L2	D	6/8	D16p28
FORFAR BEEF STEAK CLUB, THE	1H3H53	1H3H72H	D	2/2	A4v2p3
FORFAR INSTRUMENTAL BAND'S LAMENT FOR THE DEATH OF WILLIAM PEART, THE	13b53b	56b47bL	C	4/4	A4v1p4
FORGLEN HOUSE	1H1H6b6b	5547bL	C	4/4	M4v3p28
FORNETH HOUSE	3555	1H3H1H6	D	4/4	P5v1p7 P5v3p14 G8p15
FOR(R)EST(, THE)	131H1H	1352	D	6/8	G10v2p6 B10p36
FORT GEORGE	3H2H1H5	47bL44	D	4/4	A7v2p16
FORT GEORGE ASSEMBLY	1555	152H2	D	4/4	A1v6p13
FORTINGALL FAIRS	153b1	5424	E	2/2*	Mc4v1p22 (11)
FORTRESS, THE	3551	5451	G	2/4	C14v23p8
FORTY SECOND QUICKSTEP	5541	7bL427bL	A	6/8	C8v2p49
FORTY-SECOND Regt. 2ND QUICKSTEP	1554	3525L	G	6/8	A1v1p48
FOSS DYKE, THE	5653	6532	G	2/2	G8p34
FOSS' RECOVERY	113b3b	47b47bL	D	2/2	Mc19v2p3 Mc19v3p19
FOSS'S LAMENT	1H653	2511H	D	6/8	Mc19v3p20
FOSTER MEADS	3135	6542	G	6/8	R12v1p29
FOULLER'S RANT, THE	117bL7bL	117bL5L	A	2/2	Mc9v1p3
FOUR AND TWENTY HIGHLANDMEN	1353	27b27bL	A	2/2	Mc16p23,24
FOUR QUAKERS	351H5	4325L	G	6/8	R12v2p7
FOUR SEASONS	3H5H2H1H	2H3H1H5H	D	6/8	S7v1p18
FOURTEEN OF OCTOBER, THE	3352	3552	G F	4/4	A1v2p56 C5v3p56 O1v1Cp9 C20p45 Mc8v1Dp99 Mc8v2Bp15 S16p30,31
FOURTEENTH OF FEBRUARY, THE	1H135	461H5	F	2/4	C14v18p22
FOURTEENTH REGt's NEW QUICK STEP	1133	2247L	G	4/4	S5p6
FOURTH DRAGOON'S SLOW MARCH, THE	1113	5114	G	4/4	C8v2p43
FOURTH MEDLEY DANCE	5H3H5H3H	6H3H72H	C	6/8	G3p26,27
FOURTH OF JULY, THE	1H1H2H2H	3H1H1H5H	D	4/4	Mc21v4p36
FOX (CHAC'D), THE	3153	5764	G A	4/4*	G1v2p88 Mc13v2p16 S11v1p4 W4v2p25 (11)
FOX CHASSE, THE	156L2	1533	E	6/8	S11v1p10
FOX HUNTERS JIG	334	332	D	9/8	H1p34
FOX HUNTER'S JIG, THE	3H2H1H2H	3H2H1H1H	D	6/8	A1v3p222
FOX OUTWITED, THE	1314	156L7L	G	6/8	A7v3p2
FOX, THE	5323	536L7L	G	4/4	C14v7p15
FOX-HUNTER'S JIG	1H3H3H3H	1H61H6	D	6/8	R12v1p34
FOYER'S STRATHSPEY	13b42	13b1H1H	G	4/4	F2v1p5
FRA TANTE	3H2H75	1H2H3H2H	G	2/4	E1v2p94
FRANCIS GARDEN ESQr. JUNr's FAVORITE	16L6L3	1126L	Bb	4/4	P5v3p2
FRANCIS GORDON, ESQr. OF KINCARDINE	1H513	4322	D	4/4	T1v1p4
FRANK WALKER'S STRATHSPEY	1156	22H62H	D	4/4	A7v5p25
FRASERBURGH VOLUNTEER'S MARCH	1H51H1H	4H2H1H6	D	4/4	M11v1p19
FRASER'S QUICK STEP, THE	116L5L	5L142	G	6/8	S5p4

FREE AND EASY	5H2H5H2H	62H3H2H	D	6/8	R12v1p9
FREE MASONS ANTHEM, THE	121	6b7L1	G	3/4	O1v2p34
FREE MASON'S MARCH, THE	137L2	1335	G	6/8	A1v1p60
FREEMASON'S ANTHEM, THE	121	57L1	A	3/4	A1v3p204
FRENCH AIR	27L24	16L11	A	4/4	A1v3p215
FRENCH LIBERTY	1233	4111	Bb	2/4	A7v3p17
FRENCH MARINE'S MARCH	5H5H3H3H	1H1H1H5	D	4/4	A1v6p73
FRENCH TAPTOO	1253	6422	G	2/4	A1v2p10
FRENET HA'	112	555	G A	3/4	(J3) C5v1p24 A1v5p24
FRESH AND STRONG THE BREEZE, & C.	1H1H3H3H	3H2H2H2H	D	4/4	E1v2p12
FRIEND IN NEED, A	1H5H2H4H	5H3H75	D	6/8	A1v2p72
FRIEND TO THE POOR, A	11H2H5	31H2H5	C	2/4	C14v14p24
FRIENDLY ASSEMBLY	5515	3H5H2H5	E	2/4	C14v21p13
FRIENDLY VISIT, THE	1H523	5L5L23	Eb	2/4	S7v1p94
FRIENDSHIP	115	215	G	3/4	O1v1lp85
FRIENDSHIP IS ALWAYS THE ENTRY TO LOVE	1346	5211	G	4/4	C5v2p46
FRIOMH IS CROAGH TIGH CHALLADAIR	3b115L	7bL7L7bL7bL	A	4/4	F2v2p64(54)
[FREUMH A'S CRAOBH TAIGH CHALLADAIR]					
FRISK IT	3423	1211L	G	2/2	R12v1p86
FRISKY, THE	3523	3521	A	6/8	B16v3p7 S7v1p17
FRITH OF CROMORTIE, THE	3b53b1	2424	E	2/2	G8p9
FROG HE WOULD A WOOING GO, A	1H531	1H3H70	D	6/8	E1v2p64
FROLICK, THE	3H1H51H	351H3	C	2/2	R12v1p61
FROLICK, THE	315L1	3L5L13L	Bb	2/2	C13v1p5 C13v2p14
FROM NIGHT TILL MORN	3H3H3H3H	2H2H1H2H	D	4/4	E1v1p49
FUADH NA MFILAIRAN	15L6L6L	1123	D	4/4	D14v2p45
FULL MOON, THE	1321	6L131	G	2/4	B16v3p28
FUMBLER, THE	1H1H1H1H	1H1H24	F	6/8	A1v3p199 R12v1p58
FUNERAL MARCH	5331	2422	F	2/4	A1v6p38
FURTHER BENN THE WILCOMER, THE	111H3	7b7bL7bL3	D	2/2	C20p41
FUTTERAT WI' THE GRAY TAIL, THE	1551	427bL5L	A	2/2	C18p30 (II)
FY GAR RUB HER O'ER WI' STRAE	3b3b11	4427bL	G	2/2	T6v1p60
FY GAR RUB HER O'ER WI STRAE	3b3b11	43b27bL	B	2/2	P8v2p42
FY GAR RUB HER (O'ER WITH STRAW)	3b3b15	43b21	B A	4/4*	O1v1Ap32,33 A1v2p32
					Mc8v1Bp58 Mc8v2Cp14 S16p148,149
					Mc12v2p62,63 C20p82
FY LET US A' TO THE WEDDING	135	226	G F	9/8*	C5v2p23 K1v2p11 G11v2Dp12
					Mc8v2Cp19
FY ON THE WARS	1H3H4H	2H2H3H	C	3/4	O1v2p26,27 O1v1Ap7
FY ON THE WARS	134	223	Bb	3/4	O1v3p30
FYE LET US A' TO THE BRIDAL	115	326	F G	9/8	C8v1p6 C8v2p56
FYE LET US AW' TO THE BRIDAL	115	226	G	9/8	C4p54 A1v1p43
FYE ON THE WARS	1H1H2H2H	1H653	D	2/4	Mc8v1Dp117
FYKET (STRATHSPEY), THE	651H1	6527bL	A	4/4	C13v4p7 G10v1p29 G11v1Ap10
					(II)
FYKET, THE	351H3H	1H666	D	2/2	G1v2p56
FYKET, THE	6561	6527bL	A	4/4*	A1v1p28 S12v1p7 C13v2p24
					B15v1p6
FYKET, THE	6567b	6527bL	A	2/2	C4p28
FYKET, THE	651H5	6527bL	A	4/4*	G7p5 G13p15 G11v2Cp25 (II)
GABERLUNZIE MAN, THE	51H1H	1H1H7b	E C	3/4	O1v1Ep13 T6v1p95
GABERLUNZIE MAN, THE	5L11	117bL	A	3/4	C29p19 (J3) N1v2p41 C4p10
GACH TINNEAS ACH GOAL	51H53	51H32	C	6/8	F2v2p60(50)
GAE TO THE KYE WI' ME JAMIE	553b	3b52H	D	9/8	E1v2p119
GAELIC AIR, A	3331	3361H	D	2/4	G11v2DP9
GAELIC SOCIETY OF PERTH, THE	1653	1H642	F	4/4	P5v4p18
GAFFER GRAY	1H51H3b	3bH73bH3bH	D	6/8	A1v6p36
GAIRM NA 'N COILEACH	3236	3222	A	6/8	Mc1v1Ap6,7
GAIRTH HOUSE	5555	6522	D	6/8	Mc4v1p14/15
GALLANT GRAHAM(S), (THE)	5L11	7bL22	A	3/4	G9v3p3 C5v2p38
GALLANT WEAVER, THE	5534	6655	D	4/4	C5v3p70 (J3)
GALLAWAY GIRLS	1H3bH7b5	6b47b5	E	2/4	A1v2p57
GALLAWAY TOM	1H3H1H6	1H3H5H2H	C D	6/8	O1v1Fp25 C5v2p66
GALLAWAY'S LAMENT	51H1H	1H1H7b	G	3/4	O1v1Hp53
GALLOP TO KINROSS, A	1356	5125L	A	6/8	M12p32
GALLOW SHIELS	3333	5222	G	4/4	G17p11
GALLOWAY'S HORNPIPE	1155	2445L	F	2/2	Y1p10
GALOP	4#37L5L	4#416	Bb	2/4	G13p8,9
GALOP	2H755	3551H	F	2/4	G13p7
GALOP	4H3H2H7	576H5H	D	2/4	G13p8
GALOP	5#H2H5H6	1H1H5H1T	F	2/4	G13p7
GALSHILS GRAY	1516	31H42	D	4/4	C7p12
GAME COCK, THE	31H61H	6522	D	4/4	A1v6p6
GANNACHIE BRIDGE	3351	336L6L	A	6/8	D15v1p11
GARB OF OLD GAUL ([IN] THE)	1H1H1H3H	1H31H2H	D	4/4	E1v1p44 C5v2p25
GARB OF OLD GAUL, THE	1H1H1H3H	1H31H1H	C D	4/4*	C8v1p48 C8v2p44
GARDEN SHIEL	11L5L1L	11L5L5L	Bb	4/4	P5v3p2/3
GARDEN WELL, GLEN CALLATTER	511H1H	5125L	G	6/8	P5v2p22
GARDENER'S MARCH, THE	1234	5644	G	4/4	A1v1p61
GARDNER, THE	3353	2232	Bb	6/8	C26v1p9
GARDNER WI' HIS PAIDLE, THE	1H1H3H4H	5H6H4H4H	D	4/4	C5v3p62
GARDNER'S HORNPIPE	5541	127L5L	A	2/2	C12p9

Title					
GARLAND OF ROSES	1H531	1132	G	6/8	S7v1p81
GARLAND, THE	3555	5322	G	4/4	H1p12
GARLAND, THE	1357	1H355L	D	6/8	B16v3p65
GARRET FIELD	1L5L31H	3H526L	G	4/4	R6v1p5
GARSCUBE HOUSE	5L3L5L1L	4L5L4L2L	Bb	4/4	G10v4p13
GARTHLAND HOUSE (STRATHSPEY)	5L5L1L5L	5L5L6L2L	Bb	4/4	Mc21v2p18
GARTHLAND ('S STRATHSPEY)	1331H	137L2	G	4/4*	G10v2p1 C14v24p12 G11v1Ap28,29 G1v2p79 (II)
GARTHLAND'S STRATHSPEY	135L3	137L2	G	4/4	C13v1p40
GARTHLAND'S STRATHSPEY	1331H	147L2	G	4/4	A1v4p8 Mc12v1p12 (II)
GARTHLANDS (STRATHSPEY)	1431H	147L2	G	4/4	A7v2p15 A7v6p23
GARTH'S FIRE-SIDE	13b3b3b	7bL222	G	2/2	P5v4p8
GASAN FINEALT	5355	6355	C	4/4	Mc5p6
GATES OF EDINBURGH, THE	5L7L41H	5221	F	4/4	R12v1p1
GATHER AND GO	5555	6664	G	6/8	C18p32
GAVISIDE	5L15L5L	1426L	G	4/4	C10v1p4
GAVOT	5466	5455L	A	2/4	C22p41
GAVOT	5121	6421	A	2/4	C22p14
GAVOT	3452	5543	G	2/4	C22p34
GAVOT	31H75H	3H1H2H5	D	6/8	C22p17
GAVOT BY MR MACLEAN	1234	5556	G	2/2	S12v2p10
GAVOT LA ROSE	1124	27L25L	Bb	2/4	C22p13
GAVOT OF VESTRIS	1H1H1H1H	4H2H77	F	2/4	E1v2p118
GAVOTT	1233	3455	Bb	2/4	C13v3p78,79
GAVOTT	1H6b50	1H2H75H	E	2/4	Mc21v1p8
GAVOTTA	517L1	4331	Bb	2/4	Mc21v1p14,15
GAVOTTA	1H1H3H2H	1H1H1H5	Eb	2/2	Mc21v1p19
GAVOTTA	1H2H53	1H2H3H4H	E	2/4	N2p6,7
GAVOTTA	1H3H75	31H3H2H	Eb	2/4	Mc21v1p22
GAVOTTA	1H71H2H	7771H	D	4/4	Mc21v1p6
GAVOTTA	1H5H5H4H	3H2H1H3H	Eb	4/4	Mc21v1p29
GAVOTTA	15L25L	37L25L	Bb	2/4	Mc21v1p13
GAVOTTA	1347L	6L17L2	Bb	2/4	Mc21v1p16
GE DO THA MI M'AONAR SNA GLEANNAIBH	1256	2H52H1H	D	6/8	Mc5p7
GE DO THEID MI DO M'LEABAIDH 'S BEAG MO SHUND RIS A CHADAL	554	27bL3b	A	3/4	Mc5p15
GELD HIM LASSES GELD HIM	1H1H5	61H1	D	3/2	O1v1Fp23 C5v3p61
GENERAL ACTION	1355	3122	G	6/8	B16v1p9
GENERAL ATTACK	153H	152H	D	3/4	W4v1p26
GENERAL CAMPBELL (OF MONZIES') STRATHSPEY	136L5L	5L432	A	4/4	Mc21v3p8
GENERAL CAMPBELL OF MONZIES WELCOME HOME	3142	3151H	G	2/4	Mc4v4p3
GENERAL CAMPBELL'S JIGG	151H5	11H24	C	6/8	Mc13v2p30
GENERAL CAMPBELL'S STRATHSPEY	151H5	1525	C	4/4	Mc13v2p30
GENERAL ELLIOT	5L13b1	7bL7bL43b	A	2/4	C14v3p15
GENERAL ELLIOT'S MARCH	1H1H1H3H	5553H	D	4/4	M2p4,5
GENERAL GORDON CUMING SKENE'S STRATHSPEY	117bL5L	1115	G	4/4	M11v2p3
GENERAL GORDON CUMING SKENE'S MARCH	1H51H3	1113	D	4/4	M11v2p1
GENERAL GORDON CUMING SKENE'S QUICKSTEP	3H546	31H62H	D	2/4	M11v2p2
GENERAL GORDON CUMING SKENE'S REEL	3b13b5	2454	G	2/2	M11v2p4
GENERAL GRANT'S REELL	3236	3122	G	4/4	C33p11
GENERAL GRANT'S STRATHSPEY	1155	6642	D	4/4	G15p8
GENERAL HILL	3H3H1H1H	2H2H5H3H	D	6/8	C1v3p3
GENERAL HOPE'S QUICK MARCH	6565	62H3H7	F	6/8	C14v24p13
GENERAL MACDONALD'S REEL	3H1H51H	3H1H3H5H	C	4/4	G10v5p10 (II)
GENERAL MACDONALD'S STRATHSPEY	13b53b	7b422	C	4/4	G10v5p9 (II)
GENERAL Mc BEAN'S STRATHSPEY	5215L	1333	A	4/4	L1p7
GENERAL McDONALD'S STRATHSPEY	1H1H35	24H72H	F	4/4	B6v1p1
GENERAL ROBERTSON OF LAWAR'S	5551H	51H22	C	4/4	G11v1Bp8,9
GENERAL SIR HECTOR MUNRO'S REEL	5L347L	5L342	G	2/4	J2p2
GENERAL STEWART OF GARTH'S REEL	11H3b5	1524	G	2/2	G9v2p12
GENERAL STEWART, (WEST PARK, ELGIN)	1H531	1H1H1H1H	C	4/4	M4v4p12,13
GENERAL SUWAROWS WALTZ	5H5H5H5H	5H5H2H1H	C	3/8	B17p3
GENERAL TEST, THE	1411	3625	G	6/8	S5p26
GENERAL TOAST, THE	11H63	11H65	G	6/8	A1v3p196
GENERAL WASHINGTON'S MARCH	1115	2221	G	4/4	A1v3p212
(GENERAL/COLONEL) WEMYSS (OF WEMYSS)'S REEL	1335	357L2	G F	4/4	E1v1p59 G9v5p2,3 (II)
(GENERAL/COLONEL) WEMYSS (OF WEMYSS) (STRATHSPEY)	5H3H2H7	432H2	C	4/4	G10v1p27 G11v1Ap21 (II)
GENl. CARLETON'S QUICK MARCH	1H2H71H	2H3H1H2H	D	6/8	A1v2p57
GENl. DRUMMOND'S REEL or HASTINGS CAMP	3135	31H2H2	G	2/2	Mc21v3p1 (II)
GENTLE ANN	1155	1154	D	2/4	A1v1p11
GENTLE LOVE	3352	5551H	D	4/4	O1v1Hp52
GENTLE SHEPHERD, THE	5L5L5L5L	6L6L6L5L	Bb	4/4	(C25)
GENTY TIBBY	5L17bL2	3b17bL5L	G	2/2	S16p144,145
GEOFFREY CRAYON	1L3L5L3L	1L5L31	Bb	4/4	P9p18
GEORDIE AFFLICK	3511	27L53	Eb	2/2	M12p34
GEORDY AGAM	13b55	4427bL	G	4/4	C10v2Bp22
GEORGE KINLOCH	35L6L5L	35L6L1	Bb	6/8	C14v14p15

GEORGE ROBERTSON, ESQr's STRATHSPEY	136L5L	2L247L	A	4/4	Mc19v3p14
GEORGE SKENE DUFF, OF MILTON	1H1H1H1H	1H3H2H2	C	2/2	M4v4p13
GEORGE SKENE ESQr OF SKENE'S STRATHSPEY	5542	5515	F	2/2	D15v1p28
GEORGE'S SQUARE	5551H	5562	F	2/2	M4v1p2
GEORGIA GRENADIER'S MARCH, THE	1356	1H113	G	4/4	A1v3p217
GEORGINA, THE	5L5L5L2	5L5L21	Bb	6/8	G9v3p2
GERMAN AIR	1547L	152H5	G	2/4	B7p32
GERMAN DANCE	5551H	6661H	G	2/4	A1v4p33 W4v1p2
GERMAN DANCE	1111	2222	Eb	2/4	S7v1p45
GERMAN HORNPIPE	1H51H6	547L5L	F G	2/4	W4v1p9 A1v4p3
GERMAN MARCH	5553	1113	G	4/4	A1v6p30
GERMAN QUICK MARCH, A	3H2H1H7	671H1H	D	2/4	A1v2p2
GERMAN SPA WALTZ, THE	5551	5551	Eb	3/8	C1v1p6 C14v7p20
GERMAN VALTZ	145L1	145L1	Bb	3/8	W4v1p7
(GERMAN) WALTZ	1145	1125L	G	3/8	B7p21 D15v2p36
GERMAN WALTZ	1H2H3H2H	1H2H1H7	F	3/8	C26v1p21
GERMAN WALTZ	1H4H51H	1H4H51H	C	3/8	A1v4p21
GERMAN WALTZ	53H1H	555	D	3/4	B7p36
GET UP AND BAR THE DOOR	1212	1535	G	6/8	C5v2p38
GHILLEADH DHUINN S'TOIL LEAM U	1427bL	17b55	G	4/4	F2v2p33(23)
[A' GHILLE DHUINN IS TOIGH LEAM THU]					
GHOID IAD MO BHEAN (UAM AN REIR)	53b3b1	3b7bL7bL5L	A	4/4	Mc5p3 C4p25
GI' THE LASSES MAIR O'T	551H1H	1H522	D	4/4	F3p6,7
GIBRALTAR MARCH	1H1H1H3H	2H557	Eb	4/4	M2p6
GIBRALTER BALLOONS	1H52H3H	5H6H5H2H	D	6/8	A1v3p228
GIDEN HALL	1412	32H1H1H	F	6/8	B16v3p1
GI'E ME A LASS WI' A LUMP O' LAND	1565	157b4	A	6/8	A1v3p185
GIE THE CANTY CARLE MEAR O'T	1H153	7726	G	2/2	C20p26 O1v1Cp27
[GI'E THE MAWKING MAIR O'T]					
GI'E THE LASSES MAIR O' IT	551H3H	1H522	D	4/4	A1v3p211
GIG	1H2H35	457L2	A	6/8	C13v2p71
GIG	1H55	62H7	D	9/8	(R12v3)
GIGA	1555	5542	G	6/8	A1v2p43
GIGA	3210	6L7L30	A	12/8	G9v3p30,31
GIGG	15L5L2	15L11	A	6/8	G10v1p36
GIGG	15L11H	157L2	F	6/8	C13v2p28
GIGG	3527L	1232	G	6/8	R12v3p23
GIGG	1H3H2H	1H75	D	9/8	S12v2p21
GIGG BY MR ARNE	1H1H2H7	1H1H2H1H	D	6/8	S12v2p17
GIL MORICE	3323	6531	F	4/4	N1v2p16
GIL MORICE	332	653	G F	3/4	C5v2p14 Mc8v1Dp106 (J3)
GIL MORRIS	331	653	G	3/4	G17p16
GILDEROY	113b3b	5443b	A G	4/4	O1v4p30 O1v1Ep20 Mc8v1Cp70
					Mc8v2Ap17 Mc23p34,35 S16p94,95
					T6v2p106 G17p5 N1v2p8 C6p24
					C13v3p60,61 B5p15 C5v2p8
					E1v2p8 C20p35 P4p29 (J3)
					(C25)
GILDEROY	113b3b	3b443b	A	4/4	C8v2p27 C8v1p27
GILL MORICE	3323	6532	F	4/4	P4p33 C20p10
GILL MORRIS	3323	6542	G	4/4	O1v1Lp147
GILLAN NA DROVER	11H1H1H	5353	G	6/8	B11p24,25 Mc12v2p31,32 Mc22Ap4
GILLE CALLUM [GILLE CALUIM]	1342	1343	A	2/2*	G11v2Dp35 Mc9v3p26 Mc19v1p12
					Mc19v3p13 R12v1p70 G7p1 (II)
GILLEAN BAN A MHUILFHEAR	1313	2366	F	4/4	F2v2p39(29)
[...A' MHUILLEIR]					
GILLIBH NA FELA	3b13b3b	3b11H5	B	6/8	A1v6p39
GILLIE CALLUM DA PHEITHEIN	1332	1333	A	4/4	C13v1p8,9 G11v1Cp6,7 G10v1p1,2
GILLIECRANKIE	5555	54H72H	C D	4/4*	Mc8v2Cp11 Mc8v1Bp37
GILLY CRANKY	5553	5553	D C	2/2	O1v1Cp26,27 C20p8 P7p3
GIMBLET, THE	1H555	1H2H3H2H	D	2/4	O1v1Jp103
GIN A BODY MEET A BODY	552H2H	561H1H	D	4/4	C8v2p33 C5v2p2 E1v2p4 G1v1p48
GIN A BODY MEET A BODY	5L5L22	5L6L11	G Bb	4/4	C5v1p2 A1v5p2 K1v2p4
					C8v1p28 G11v2Bp4
GIN A BODY MEET A BODY	552H2H	561H1H	F	6/8	G13p1
GIN LIVING WORTH	1142	2253	E	4/4	C6p11
GIN YE WONNE TAKE ME	111	313	G	3/2	Mc8v1Bp52
GIN YE WONNE TAKE ME YE MAY LET ME BE	131	313	G	3/2	Mc8v1Cp7
GINGLING GEORDIE	1H1H1H2	1H1H1H1	G	6/8	Mc8v2Cp15
(GIN/IF I HAD/HE THAT HAS) A BONNY LASS	3b53b5	2427bL	G	4/4*	F2v1p6 Mc21v3p26 P5v3p16 (II)
(LITTLE SLEEP WOU'D SERVE ME)					
GINLEING GEORDE	1H1H3	1H1H3	G	6/4	P7p5
GIPSY CHORUS	3H2H1H0	3211	G	4/4	E1v2p54
GIRL I LEFT BEHIND ME, THE	5426L	1153	G	2/4	C8v2p56
GIRVAN WATER	1H51H5	1H562	D	6/8	F3p15
GIULLAN NAM BO	1363	1366	Eb	6/8	F2v2p14(4)
GIVE ME A DONALD	5H3H5H3H	5H3H1H6	D	6/8	A7v5p21
GIVE ME LOVE AND LIBERTY	3531	1321	G	2/4	R12v1p83
GLAD TRUMPET SOUNDS A VICTORY, THE	1H1H3H1H	5355	D	2/4	E1v2p12
GLAMMIS CASTLE	13b55	7b7b27bL	C E	4/4	D15v1p10 A7v4p15
GLANCING OF HER APRON, THE	1H665	44H2H2H	C	4/4	(J3) C20p49
GLANCING OF HER APRON, THE	1H61H5	44H2H2H	D	4/4	T6v2p95 P4p14 P8v2p47

Title			Key	Time	Sources
GLANCING OF HER APRON, THE	1H61H5	44H3H2H	D	4/4	O1v1Kp133
GLASGOW BELLS	15L15L	2L5L42	Bb	6/8	C13v2p32
GLASGOW COLLEGE	3L13L5L	4L5L4L2L	Bb	2/2	C13v2p74
GLASGOW FLOURISH	1353	7L6L3L2	Bb	2/2	C13v2p65
GLASGOW FLOURISH	113L1	5226L	A	4/4	C13v1p20
GLASGOW LADIES (REEL)	15L6L5L	4L3L22L	Bb	2/2	G9v5p2 Mc13v2p31 C13v1p4 C13v2p3
GLASGOW LASSES	1155	1142	F	2/2	S12v1p49 (W3)
GLASGOW LASSES, THE	1153	1142	F	4/4	G11v2Cp28 (II)
GLASGOW THEATRE HORNPIPE	1346	3316L	Bb	4/4	A7v4p6
GLASGOW TONTINE	15L3L3	4522	Bb	4/4	C13v1p20
GLASSA HOUSE	1H2H1H5	4522	D	2/2	C24v1p10 (II)
GLASSERTON HOUSE	3b15	7bL42	G	9/8	F3p1
GLEAN' MOR NA H'ALBAIN [GLEANN MOR NA H-ALBAINN]	5153	5336	D	6/8	F2v2p44(34)
GLEN LYONS RANT	313L1	4L27L2	G	4/4	G8p9 P1v1p14 (II)
GLEN LYON'S (STRATHSPEY/REEL/RANT)	11H55	6547bL	D	4/4*	A7v2p29 S12v1p18 Mc9v1p20 G11v2Cp37 B15v1p99 (II)
GLEN MORISONE'S REELL	5266	5222	D	2/2	C33p12
GLEN STEWART	3333	427L6L	G	2/2	P9p14
GLENARA	3333	6531	E	2/4	C6p25
GLENBUCKET'S BREEKS	3555	1H3H2H2H	C	4/4	G11v2Dp32
GLENBURNIE RANT, THE	1111	7bL247bL	E	4/4	G10v5p32 (II)
GLENCAIRN'S STRATHSPEY	1111	436L2	G	4/4	G1v2p83
GLENFIDDICH (STRATHSPEY)	1353	5L322	A	4/4	M4v3p18 M4v1p4
GLENGARRIE'S REELL	1655	27b27bL	D	4/4	C33p18,19
GLENGARRY'S STRATHSPEY	136L1	37L42	Bb	4/4	Mc11p5
GLENKELRY STRATHSPEY	143b7bL	147bL4	A	4/4	P5v3p10
GLENKILRY'S STRATHSPEY	51H54	51H51H	D	4/4	D16p23
GLENLYON HOUSE	5542	31H22	D	6/8	Mc4v1p20
GLEN-RIDDELL'S REEL	31H33H	31H62	D	2/2	R6v1p2
GLENTROMIE	5H3H1H1H	5H6H72H	C	4/4	M4v3p45
GLINQUICH'S BUSH	5552	5552	A	4/4	O1v1Jp109
GLOAMIN', THE	35L6L	106	Eb	3/4	B12p11
GLOOMY WINTER ('S NOW AWA')	1H1H1H5	3bH3bH4H2H	D E	4/4	E1v1p22 G1v2p80 C5v2p57 C8v2p24 B7p6
GLOOMY WINTER'S NOW AWA'	1115L	3b3b42	A	4/4	C8v1p10
GLORIOUS APOLLO	3H3H1H1H	2H2H2H2H	D	4/4	E1v2p56,57
GLORIOUS FIRST OF AUGUST, THE	1H3H1H3H	72H4H2H	C	2/2	G9v3p28
GLOUCESTER HOUSE	1H1H4H4H	5H2H1H1H	D	2/4	S7v1p67
GO GEORGE I CAN'T ENDURE YOU	5H5H6H0	5H5H6H0	C	2/4	E1v2p82,83
GO TELL HER I LOVE HER	1H4H1H1H	5H7H4H1H	D	2/4	E1v2p38 E1v2p60
GO TO BERWICK JOHNNY	516	513	F	3/4	E1v1p46 N1v1p21
GO TO BERWICK, JOHNNY	511	564	G D F	3/2*	O1v1Fp22,23 C20p55 (J3) K1v2p32 G11v2Dp22 G11v2Bp31 C8v1p7 C14v11p17
GO TO THE DEVIL & SHAKE YOURSELF	51H55	51H3H6	D	6/8	(B21) G11v2Bp21
GO TO THE DEVIL AND SHAKE YOURSELF	51H55	1H2H3H6	C	6/8	N1v1p21 (II)
GO TO THE DEVIL AND SHAKE YOURSELF	1H3H1H3H	1H3H1H6	C	6/8	C14v13p22
GO TO THE DEVIL AND SHAKE YOURSELF	5H3H5H3H	5H3H1H6	C	6/8	C5v1p5
GO TO THE DEVIL AND SHAKE YOURSELF, [THE ORIGINAL SET OF]	3b53b1	2427bL	E	6/8	G9v5p14
GO TO THE DEVIL AND SHAKE YOURSELF, [NEW SET OF]	3b53b5	3b53b1	A	6/8	G9v5p14
GO TO THE DEVIL AND SHAKE YOURSELF	5353	5316L	A	6/8	Mc13v2p12 P5v3p25 A7v4p20 C23p8
GO TO THE DEVIL AND SHAKE YOURSELF	1316L	7L27L5L	A	6/8	W4v2p19
GO WHERE GLORY WAITS THEE	125	465	G	3/4	B7p28
GO WHERE GLORY WAITS THEE	1H2H5H	4H6H5H	F	3/4	E1v2p70
GO WHERE YOU WILL I WILL FOLLOW	1115	2226	G	4/4	G1v2p66
GOBY (0), THE	3b15L1	27bL47bL	A	6/8	A1v4p38 D16p23 C14v4p21
GOD PRESERVE THE EMPEROR	3H2H4H3H	2H1H6H5H	C	2/2	E1v2p105
GOD SAVE THE (KING/QUEEN)	1H1H2H	772H	D C	3/4	C8v2p5 E1v1p44 C8v1p5 C7p1
GODDESSES, THE	1575	52H3H1H	D	2/4	A1v3p215
GODFREY, LORD MACDONALD'S WELCOME TO THE ISLE OF SKYE	32H56	53H2H1H	D	2/2	G9v2p16
GOLDEN AGE, THE	5531	437L2	G	6/8	S7v2p12
GOLDEN ISLAND, THE	1566	11H51	D	6/8	S5p24
GOLF CLUB, THE	151H5	4341	G	6/8	D6p22
GOLLOCHY'S FAREWEL	15L3L1L	4522	Bb	4/4	M4v1p2 (II)
GOOD LUCK	315L1	357L2	F	2/2	F3p19
GOOD MORROW TO YOUR NIGHT-CAP	13b5L5L	7bL243b	B	2/4	G10v2p36
GOOD NEWS FROM LEGHORN	1H1H33	6L213L	G	2/4	S7v1p71
GOOD NIGHT AND GOD BE WITH YOU	1H1H55	665H5H	C	2/2	P7p4
GOOD NIGHT AND JOY	3b3b7bL7bL	111H1H	A	4/4	C13v3p26,27
GOOD NIGHT AND JOY BE WI' YE A'	1H1H55	666H6H	D C	4/4*	C5v2p72 C8v2p58 A1v2p74 Mc8v1Dp20(?) G11v2Bp38 O1v1Dp32 K1v2p40
GOOD NIGHT AND JOY BE WI' YOU A'	111	111	G	3/4	C18p36
GOOD THING, THE	1H52H7	3H3H77	D	6/8	A1v2p53
GOOD THOUGHT, A	5666	5632	A	2/4	E2p14
GOODEN WELL	315L1	437L2	A	4/4*	W2v1p14 (II)

GOODNIGHT AND GOD BE WI YOU A'	1H1H51H	666H6H	C	2/2	Mc8v2Cp19
GORANS, THE	537L2	221H7	G	2/2	P5v4p2
GORDIAN KNOT, THE	1555	1552	D	2/2	B16v2p4
GORDON BANK HOUSE	1H3H1H5	1H3H4H2H	D	2/2	Mc13v1p5 Mc13v2p5
GORDON CASTLE	5326	5355	A	4/4	K1v1p26,27 G11v2Ap24 (II)
GORDON CASTLE	3561H	351H2H	C	4/4	M4v3p44
GORDON CASTLE	3b3b11H	3bH1H1H7	E	4/4	Mc8v1Bp31 Mc8v2Bp2 A1v5p73
					Mc12v2p48
GORDON CASTLE	3366	5311	G	4/4	Mc9v1p26
GORDON CASTLE	3536	3542	G	2/2	R12v1p97
GORDON CASTLE	3b3b11H	3bH1H1H1H	E	4/4	O1v1Jp88,89
GORDON OF LESSMOR'S STRATHSPEY	15L35	1H522	A	4/4	A7v3p20
GORDONS HA'E THE GUIDIN' O'T	1H31H1	1H32H2	D	2/4*	T1v1p1 (II)
GORDONS HAS THE GIRDING O'T, THE	1H31H1	1H32H2	D	4/4	P5v3p7 K1v1p8 (II)
(or MY LOVE SHE'S BUT A LASSIE YET)					
GOSSIP JOAN	1H52	22H7	D	3/4	Mc16p7
GOSSIP JOAN	1H134	5554	G	2/2	O1v1Lp150
GOUD A GOUPENS	53b3b4	3b122	A	6/8	S12v2p19
GOUGH HOUSE	527L2	4235	G	2/2	C14v20p22
GOWAN BANK, THE	3152	3532	G	6/8	S5p16
GOWD IN GOWPINS	3H1H2H5	353H1H	C	6/8	K1v2p23 G11v2Bp21
GRACE'S FAREWELL	11H1H5	11H1H2	G	6/8	A1v1p57
GRACE'S FAREWELL	113	1H61H	G	6/4	R12v1p73
GRACES, THE	1135	671H1H	Bb	2/4	Mc9v2p42 S7v1p23
GRACES, THE	1H51H5	1H5H2H3H	D	6/8	C7p18
GRACES, THE	1152	3122	Bb	6/8	D15v2p20
GRACES, THE	1321	7L221	G	6/8	G1v2p69
GRAIDHEAN DONN	1245	4245	A	2/4	Mc5p5
GRAMACHREE	5561H	5122	D	4/4	S7v1p44
GRAMACHREE IS A SUP OF GOOD DRINK	1H3bH2H5	1H3bH5H1H	D	12/8	A1v6p40
GRAMACHREE (MOLLY)	5561H	5210	F D	4/4	C8v1p64 VC25
GRAND BALLOT DANCE, THE	5125L	3L6L27L	Bb	6/8	W4v2p26
GRAND FRENCH MARCH	1H1H3H3H	5H4H3H2H	Eb	4/4	G9v3p11
GRAND MARCH, A	1T5H5H3H	1H2H1H3H	D	4/4	G1v2p61
GRAND MARCH, THE	1112	3334	D	4/4	R12v3p26
GRAND PARADE, THE	1H5H2H4H	3H2H1H3	D	6/8	A1v1p4
GRANT LODGE	1122	1155	G	4/4	M4v3p40 (II)
GRANTS RANT	5551	51H51	D	2/2	R12v2p6
GRANT'S (RANT/OF STRATHSPEY), THE	1331	2662	G	4/4*	Mc9v1p12 B15v1p64 C33p1
					A7v6p68
GRANT'S REEL	151H6	432H2	C	2/2	R12v1p58
GRANT'S STRATHSPEY	3335	1H61H6	C	4/4	Mc13v2p18 C13v1p18
GRAY EY'D MORNING, THE	1H1H2H	3H4H2H	C	3/4	O1v3p34,35 O1v1Bp13
GRAY STONE OF ARDNAHOW, THE	1H1H62H	1H642	D	2/2	Mc16p3
GRAY'S FAVORITE JIG	131H2H	4324	D	6/8	A7v4p25
GREAT NEWS FROM CAMPERDOWN	5L5L31	5L5L2L2L	Bb	4/4	G9v5p1
GREEN & GOLD	1H5H5H3H	4H2H3H1H	D	2/4	S7v1p63
GREEN GARTERS, THE	3115	4226	G	6/8	A1v3p218
GREEN GROW THE RASHES O'	1131	2662	G	2/4	C6p16
GREEN GROW THE RASHES (O!)	1331	2662	F G	4/4*	(J3) P5v4p6,7 G7p13 K1v1p14
					N1v1p30 G11v2Ap12 C8v1p9
					C8v2p7 E1v1p83 P5v2p22 P5v3p13
					(II)
GREEN GROWES THE RASHES	117bL3b	3b43b3b	B	4/4	Mc8v1Bp41
GREEN GROWS THE RASHES	3324	5655	G	4/4	O1v1Ap18,19
GREEN GROWS THE RASHES	3325	5655	G	4/4	Mc8v2Ap12 O1v2p42 O1v3p46,47
GREEN GROWS THE RASHES	3335	5655	G	4/4	Mc12v2p29
GREEN LEAVES WERE US BETWEEN	13b52H	1H1H1H5	A	4/4	C5v2p30
GREEN PARK PALLISADES, THE	5L351H	51H53	F	2/2	B16v3p15 S7v1p25
GREEN PEASE	3175	651H1	G	6/8	B16v2p3
GREEN PURSE, THE	131H1H	3H2H1H5	D	4/4	C10v2Bp72
GREEN RIBON, THE	3112	5225	F	2/2	Y1p14
GREEN SHADES OF GASK, THE	131H7	532H2	G	6/8	B11p6 (II)
GREEN SLEEVES	3b3b47bL	3b17bL5L	A	6/8	A1v1p46
GREEN SLEEVES	3b3b47bL	3b17L5L	G	6/8	S16p82,83
GREEN SLEEVES	3b3b47bL	3b125L	G	6/8	(J3) G11v2Dp7 O1v1Hp38
G(R)EEN TREE, THE	1H122	4H3H2H6	D	2/2	K1v2p36 G11v2Bp34
GREENEND PARK	13L13	527L2	Eb	2/4	Mc4v2p10 (II)
(GREENOCK) GROGG	1H553	5362	A	6/8	H3p2 A7v3p28
GREENWICH HILL	5H1H71H	1H2H3H2H	D C	2/4	E1v1p37 G10v2p34 W6p12
GREENWICH HILL	5H1H71H	1H2H3H3H	C	2/4	A7v2p35
GREIG'S PIPES	5351	5326L	A	4/4*	A7v2p26 G11v2Ap24 B16v3p56
					K1v1p26 C13v2p11 C14v14p17
					N1v1p17 (II)
GREIG'S PIPES	5353	5326L	A	4/4*	S12v1p44
GREIG'S PIPES	5351	5325L	A	2/2	G9v5p15
GREIG'S STRATHSPEY	351H5	631H5	C	4/4	C13v1p5
GREIG'S STRATHSPEY	351H5	1H61H5	C	4/4	G11v1Ap17 G10v2p20
GREY DAY LIGHT	1353	227b7b	D	4/4	A7v5p36 A7v6p73
GREY DAY LIGHT [GRAY DAY LIGHT]	1353	227bL7bL	D	2/2	A7v3p27
GRIEG'S STRATHSPEY	3L5L15L	16L15L	Bb	2/2*	A7v2p4 C24v2p10 (II)
GRIM MALCOLM	1H47L2	1H31H2H	G	4/4	A1v4p42 C5v1p42

Title			Key	Time	References
GRIMALDIE	1365	1362	G	6/8	C14v24p2,3
GRINDER, THE	1H63	1H65	G A Eb	9/8	Mc7p16 C14v15p5 D15v2p10
GROANS OF THE WOUNDED	3H3H1H6	562H2H	D	4/4	A1v4p16 C5v1p16 W4v1p27
GROVE HOUSE, THE	1H5H4H7	62H5H7	C	6/8	B16v3p18
GROVE, THE	15L12	15L6L1	Bb D	6/8	H3p5 Mc9v2p2
GU MO MAIDH A THIG AN CRUN DHUIT A THEARLUICH (OIG)	1H761H	3553H	D	4/4	F2v2p53(43)
GU MO MEAR A CHARAID	1135	1135	A	2/2	F2v2p48(38)
GU MO SLAN A CHI MI MO CHAILINN DILEAS DONN	1265	36L10	F	4/4	F2v2p39(29) (II)
GUARDIAN ANGELS	1347L	127L5L	G	4/4	S7v1p57
GUDE FORGIE ME FOR LIEIN	1321	3165	G	6/8	C5v2p5
GUDE NIGHT AND JOY BE WI' YOU A'	1H566H	3H3H3H1H	C	2/4	E1v1p80
GUDEWIFE OF PEEBLES	37L6L5L	326L2	Bb	6/8	G11v2Dp14
GUESS AGAIN	1561H	1561H	D	2/4	R12v1p10
GUIRACHA, THE	6H5H4H1H	6H5H1H1H	D	3/8	B7p28
GUN BHRIS MO CHRI O'N DH('FH)ALBH THU	3553	51H3H2H	F	4/4	F2v2p56(46) (II)
GUN DUINE AIG A' BHAILE	51H3H1H	5351H	F	6/8	F2v2p97(87)
GUR BOIDHEACH, BOIDHEACH AN CNOCAN	1112	147b1	A	6/8	Mc5p5
GUR BOIDHEACH NIGHEAN DONN MO CHRIDHE	1L5L6bL5L	1L5L4L7bF	A	6/8	Mc5p7
GUR EUTROM AN T AISEAG	61H1H	2H66	G	3/4	Mc5p2
GUR LIONAR GOBHLAN DUBH FRAOICH ANN	1566	1562	G	6/8	Mc5p8
GUR MIS THA GU CRAITEACH O'N 'UIRIDH	1H52	13b6b	E	9/8	F2v2p72(62)
GUR MISE THA SO MHULAD E O UIM O	115L3bL	7bF1L7bL7bF	A	6/8	Mc5p6
GUR MULADACH A THA MI	7bL5L13b	5554	A	4/4	F2v2p43(33)
GUR MULADACH THA MI, 'SMI GUN MHACNUS GUN MHANRAN	61H1H1H	6611	G	4/4	Mc5p19
GUR TROM AN DEIGH MO THURAIS MI	3b27bL5L	3b211	E	4/4	F2v2p88(78)
GUR TROM LEAM MO CHEUM	1H3bH3bH	7b1H3b	E	3/4	Mc5p19
GURAGUAG, THE	5526	5311	G	2/2	Mc16p31
GUSENDALL BAY	1H51H2H	1H51H2H	F	6/8	C14v14p2
GUSTAVUS GALOP, THE	51H51H	551H5H	D	2/4	G13p8 C8v2p61
GUSTAVUS GALOP, THE	5L15L1	5L5L15	Bb	2/4	C8v1p28
GUTHRIE CASTLE	111H3	422H4H	C D	2/2	A7v4p15 A7v5p7
GUY MANNERING	1H73H7	6543	F	2/2	H6v22p2
GUZZLE TOGETHER	355	357b	A	9/8	B15v1p85 G11v2Cp26
H. GARDINE'S WALTZ	51H1H	1H3H3H	D	3/4	B7p15
H R H THE PRINCESS CHARLOTTE'S FAVORITE	3565	3125L	A	2/2	C14v18p1
HA A CHAILLICH AIR MO DHEIDH	5211	5622	A	4/4	D14v2p12
HA! BIDAG ER MAC HOMAISE [THA BIODAG AIR MAC THOMAIS]	3131	2427bL	A	2/2	D15v1p29
HA DA LOLAL O	1111	7bL13b2	A	2/2	Mc5p5
HA TOLL AIR A BHATA	5555	551H1H	G	2/2	Mc16p14
HABBIE'S HOW	113b4	553b7bL	A	4/4	G10v6p21
HACKNEY ASSEMBLY	3331H	5522	F	2/2	S7v1p1
HAD A WAD HAME	51H1H7b	51H51	E	6/8	C14v19p8
HAD AWA' FRAE ME DONALD	3b3b7bL7bL	3b3b54	G	4/4	P9p22,23
HAD AWA' FRAE ME DONALD	1H61H1H	5255	C D	4/4	O1v1Cp17 C20p20 C5v3p58
HAD AWA' (FRAE ME), DONALD	1H61H1H	5355	C	4/4*	T6v2p104 Mc8v1Dp101 Mc8v2Cp5 C8v1p48 C4p37 G1v1p33
HAD AWA FRAE ME DONALD	315L5L	35L34	A	2/4	Mc23p1
HAD I A HEART (FOR FALSEHOOD FRAMED)	5561H	5210	G	4/4	C8v2p35 E1v1p54
HAD I THE WATE SHE BADE ME	5151	5175	G	4/4	O1v1Gp20
HAD I THE WYTE SHE BAD ME	5151	5575	F	4/4*	(J3) C20p18,19
HA'D THE CRADLE ROCKIN'	1551	2662	D	2/2	C18p21
HA'D THE LASS TILL I WIN AT HER	1565	157b2	A	4/4*	C4p39 A1v1p14
HAD THE LASS TILL I WINN AT HER	1565	1544	A	2/2	B15v1p12
HADDINGTON ASSEMBLY	3565	351H5	A	6/8	D14v3p6
HADDINGTON ASSEMBLY	5151	6276	G	6/8	A7v2p19
HADDINGTON ASSEMBLY	5151	6271H	G	6/8	E1v1p60 A7v5p33 G11v1Bp36 A7v6p26 G1v2p60
HADDINGTON LASSES	3H2H1H5	31H2H2	D	2/2	H3p25
HAGGIES O' DUNBAR, THE	315L7bL	7bL427bL	A	2/2	K1v2p29 G11v2Bp27 (II)
HALLOW E'EN	3211H	3H2H66	F G	4/4*	Mc9v2p6 S16p22,23 O1v5p11 C5v3p55 Mc8v2Bp18 O1v1Cp21 P8v2p46
HALLOW EVEN	3111H	2H2H61H	F	2/2	Y1p9
HALLOW FAIR	5432	27b42	A	6/8	S12v1p21
HALLOWEEN	5555	51H24	A	4/4	C14v16p17
HAMBURG DANCE	1753	37L25L	Eb	2/2	B16v3p50
HAMILTON HOUSE	1313	7bL7bL47bL	E	4/4*	Mc9v3p10/11 C13v1p40,41
HAMILTON HOUSE	1313	7bL247bL	E	4/4	C13v4p12,13
HAMILTON HOUSE	5551H	51H26	D	2/2	C14v1p10
HAMILTON HOUSE	51H32	62H75	G	4/4	O1v3p39 O1v1Bp6
HAMILTON HOUSE	1H542	327L5L	G	6/8	C14v4p4
HAMILTON RACES	11H2H5	6542	D	6/8	G11v2Dp29 A7v2p22
HAMILTON RACES	31H2H5	6542	D	6/8	Mc9v3p40
HAMILTON'S RANT	3664	4646	A	4/4	C5v1p39 A1v5p39
HAMMERMEN'S MARCH, THE	61H1H5	1H1H1H3H	B	4/4	A1v1p60
HAMPSTEAD ASSEMBLY	155L3	15L3L1L	Bb	6/8	S7v1p78
HAND ORGAN, THE	1122	31H52	Bb	6/8	S11v2p11
HANDEL'S HORNPIPE	3215L	7L211	G	4/4*	R12v1p35 (W3)

44

HANDEL'S WATER PIECE	1HO3H3H	3HO5H5H	D	4/4	R12v3p28,29
HANDSOME JEWESS, THE	1531	247L5L	G	2/4	B16v3p20
HANNAGAN MUGGANS	553H5	3522H	F	6/8	G9v3p6
HAP AN' ROW THE FEETY O'T	31H2H1H	31H2H2	G	4/4	C5v2p48
HAP ME WI' THY PETTICOAT, (COME)	526L6L	5555	F G	2/2	T6v1p21 (J3) Mc9v2p9 P8v2p14
HAP ME WITH THY PETTICOAT	5311	5555	F	4/4	N1v2p51
HAP ME WITH THY PETTICOAT	5322	5355	D	4/4	S16p60,61
HAPPY CLOWN	1355	7542	G	6/8	A1v2p57
HAPPY CLOWN, (THE)	1355	7531	G F	6/8	C5v2p61 O1v1Gp8 (J3)
HAPPY MILK MAID, THE	1H53H1H	4H2H77	D	2/4	A1v5p35 C5v1p35
HAPPY NIGHT, THE	3521	3562	G	6/8	O1v1Fp27
HAPPY RETURN, THE	1T1T3H1H	2H5H1H6	D	4/4	C23p18
HAPPY TIMES	1H3H2H4H	3H5H2H6	D	2/2	S7v1p70
HAPPY WEDDING	3H1H2H2H	3H1H75	D	6/8	S7v1p89
HARD TO THE BONE	5L111	216L6L	G	4/4	G15p2
HARDY KNUTE	113b	57b4	B A	3/4	O1v1Ep31 (J3) O1v4p7
HARE IN THE CORN, THE	3563	4342	A	6/8	R6v2p22
HARE IN THE CORN, THE	341H3	4542	G	6/8	C5v1p25 A1v5p25
HARE IN THE CORN, THE	5563	4542	G	6/8	O1v1Gp12
HARK I HEAR SWEET MARY COMING	5H3H2H3H	2H4H6H2H	D	4/4	C5v2p40
HARK THE COCK THAT CROW'D	3175	2H62H5	D	6/8	O1v1Jp87
HARK! THE LARK	1HO2HO	3H2H1HO	C	6/8	E1v2p102
HARK 'TIS A VOICE FROM THE TOMB	3b51H	3bH3b4	E	3/4	O1v1Kp116,117
HARLEQUIN	1151H	137L2	F	2/4	C13v2p28
HARLEQUIN NEPTUNE	1H31H3	1H322	D	2/2	B16v4p89
HARLEQUIN RANGER	1H5H3H1H	1243	D	6/8	S12v2p3
HARLEQUIN (REEL/STRATHSPEY), THE	1H3H5H3H	2H4H2H7	E	2/2	C24v2p5 C24v1p8
HARLEQUIN TUNE	1H1H55	4443	A	6/8	S12v1p53
HARLEQUIN TUNE	1531	1L2L4L3L	Bb	6/8	S12v1p56
HARLEQUIN TUNE	5651	5625L	G	6/8	S12v2p3
HARLEQUINS LAMENT FOR THE LOSS OF COLOMBINE	111	7L7L5L	G	6/4	W4v1p15
HARMONICS IF PERFORMED ON A VIOLIN	3H1H3H1H	2H61H3H	A	2/4	N2p11
HARPER OF MULL, THE	51H53	62H1H5	D	6/8	C5v2p60
HARPER'S FANCY	3131	72H1H1H	D	2/4	A1v3p176
HARRIET'S, THE	1H6H4H2H	72H76	D	4/4	G1v2p93
HARRIETT & SOPHIA'S WALTZ	53H71H	53H71H	F	3/8	C14v27p15
HARRIOT, THE	3142	7L5L13	Bb	2/4	A7v2p34
HARRIOT, THE	1H3H5H2H	2H4H1H6	D	2/4	B16v3p94
HARRIOT, THE	3H1H4H2H	751H3H	C	2/4	G10v2p34 P10p13
HARRIS DANCE	1H5H5H6H	5H3H5H3H	C	4/4	Mc5p37
HARRIS DANCE	7b61H5	7b444	A	4/4	Mc5p37
HARROGATE ASSEMBLY	1545	22H76	D	2/2	C14v24p14,15
HARRY'S FROLICK	5223	1155	A	4/4	B16v3p30
HASTE TO THE CAMP	415L1	3b155	G	2/4	C14v8p9
HATTON OF BUCHROMB'S REEL	11H7b2	11H57b	F	2/2	M4v3p29
HAUGHS OF CROMDALE, THE	5152	517bL2	A E	4/4*	(J3) C8v2p55 G11v1Ap6 Mc7p19 E1v1p20 (II) C33p15 (II)
HAUGHS OF CROMDALE, THE	1H155	27bL22	A	4/4	G15p1
HAUGHS OF DEVLIN, THE	513b5	5124	E	4/4	G10v6p15
HAUNTED TOWER, THE	1542	3132	Bb	2/4	C14v4p9
HAVE AT THE BONNIE LASSIE	1H5H2H4H	3H1H2H2H	D	6/8	C5v2p35
HAVE YOU HEARD OF THE TAX	1H1H2H5H	1H1H2H5H	D	6/8	A1v6p23
HAWICK, A STRATHSPEY	3553	2442	G	4/4	P11v2p16
HAWICK LASSES, A REEL	5313	2424	D	2/2	P11v1p17
HAWK WHOOPS ON HIGH, THE	111H	335	G	3/4	C10v2Ap56
HAWTHORN (THATS BLOOMS), THE	1551H	3H750	D	2/4	C5v2p14 A1v5p12
HAY MAKERS, THE	1H1H72H	1H554	F	2/2	W7p20
HAY MAKERS, THE	1H2H3H2H	1H2H3H2H	C	6/8	G13p12
HAY MAKERS, THE	1232	1231	G	6/8	G11v2Cp38 Mc7p1 G7p20 A1v1p15 Mc9v2p15 (II)
HAY STACK, THE	3131H	3542	C	4/4	P9p7
HAYDEN'S SURPRISE	1353	427L5L	Bb	2/4	F1p34
HAYDN, THE	117L5L	3432	Bb	2/4	C14v3p8 P10p18
HAYDN, THE	3211	5625L	A	2/4	W4v2p18
HAYDN'S CELEBRATED MOVEMENT	3215L	5622	A	2/4	E1v1p115
HAYDN'S FANCY	1H1H75	3H4H3H2H	C	2/4	A7v3p16
HE HIRPLED TILL HER	5351	4522	A	2/2	C4p30 B15v1p12
HE LOVES AND HE RIDES AWAY	1H3H3H1H	2H2H3HO	C	6/8	E1v2p99
HE MAN DU I O RO U	13b43b	13b55	A	4/4	Mc5p21
HE NA BODDACHIN	1122	111H6	G	6/8	G11v1Cp12 G10v1p19
HE TIL'T AND SHE TIL'T	533H1H	537L2	F	4/4	O1v1lp74
HEALTH TO BETTY, A	17L3b2	547b5	G	6/8	T6v1p51
HEARTS OF OAK	1H1H1H3H	1H750	D	4/4	A1v4p35 C8v1p42 C8v2p14
HEARTS OF OAK	1H1H1H3H	1H755	C	4/4	E1v1p63
HEATHCOT'S HORSE RACE	1H1H1H	776	D	6/4	W7p23
HEATHER BRAES	13L13	5216L	Bb	2/2	A7v3p18
HEATHER HOUSE, THE	13b4L4L	3b3b7bL6bL	A	4/4	W2v2p1
HEAVENS ARE TELLING, THE	1H1H1H1H	2H2H2H2H	D	2/2	E1v2p106,107
HEAVING OF THE LEAD	3324	17L10	G	4/4	A1v6p29 E1v2p40/41
HEBRIDEAN DANCING MEASURES & C	513b2	1164	A	4/4	C10v2Bp98
HEBRIDEAN DANCING MEASURES & C NO. 5	1155	7b654	B	4/4	C10v2Bp98

HEBRIDEAN DANCING MEASURES & C No. 1	1H655	1H655	D	4/4	C10v2Bp98
HEBRIDEAN DANCING MEASURES & C No. 3	1H1H53bH	4H2H1H3bH	E	4/4	C10v2Bp98
HEBRIDEAN DANCING MEASURES & C No. 2	1H1H7b5	7b7b7b7b	D	4/4	C10v2Bp98
HEGH HOW THE BALLOP	1H1H1H5	3357	G	2/2	O1v1Fp20
HEITHER TOPS, THE	3b21	543b	A	3/4	O1v1Lp141
HEMP DRESSERS	1542	5135	G	6/8	A1v2p38
(HENDRIE'S) HORNPIPE	3353	1764	Eb	4/4*	C22p44 P11v2p8
HENRY B. STEWART, Esqr.	113b5	2227bL	E	2/2	Mc19v3p81
OF BALNAKELLIE'S REEL					
HENRY McLIESH'S COMPLEMENTS	17L6L5L	347L2	A	4/4	L4p4
TO A. LEBURN					
HENRY PATERSON ESQr	3215	6444	G	4/4	D6p13
HENRY'S COTTAGE MAID	3353	3315L	G A	6/8	E1v1p77,78
HEN'S MARCH, THE	1H51H3H	5H4H2H2H	D	4/4	G9v3p20,21 (II)
HEN'S NEST, THE	3116L	5L26L2	G	2/4	D16p15
HER ABSENCE WILL NOT ALTER ME	321H1H	526L5L	F G	4/4*	(J3) Mc8v1Ap4 Mc8v2Cp4
HER ANSWER WAS I'M TOO YOUNG	1H1H1H5	3557	D	4/4	A1v5p46
HER ANSWER WAS MUM	1H61H1H	7557	G	4/4	O1v1Jp91
HER GRACE THE DUTCHESS OF BUCCLEUGH	551H7	5543	F	6/8	W4v2p17
HERBERTS DELIGHT	5L15L3	3637L	A	6/8	B16v1p10
HERBERT'S FROLICK	5555	1353	D	2/4	S7v1p25
HERE AWA' THERE AWA'	5123	5136L	G	6/8	Mc8v1Dp108
HERE AWA', (THERE AWA')	553	111	G C F	3/4	C6p7 C20p81 O1v1Hp35
(WANDERING) WILLIE					E1v1p26 (J3) N1v2p27
HEREFORDSHIRE LASSES, THE	1415	4321	G	2/4	B16v3p58
HERE'S A HEALTH TO MY TRUE LOVE	1H1H2H	7b53bH	C E	3/4	(J3) C5v3p58
HERE'S A HEALTH TO THEM THAT'S AWA'	1H653H	1H63H2H	C D	6/8	C6p1 C5v1p5 C8v2p50 C5v2p72
					(J3)
HERE'S A HEALTH TO THEM THAT'S AWA'	O3H1H6	53H1H6	D	6/8	A1v5p5
HERE'S A HEALTH TO THEM THAT'S AWA'	3H1H65	3H1H62H	D	3/8	G11v2Cp24
HERE'S A HEALTH TO THEM THAT'S AWA'	1H650	1H62H3H	G	6/8	G1v1p116
HERE'S HIS HEALTH IN WATER	5155	5422	G F	4/4*	C5v2p68 (J3)
HERMET IN LONDON'S REEL, THE	11H1H1H	2H72H4H	C	2/2	P9p6
HERNITE, THE	3142	7L5L11	Bb	2/4	C7p9
HERO AND LEANDER	116	551	G	3/4	T6v2p90
HEROES OF CIUDAD RODERIGO, THE	1115	642H5	F	2/4	C1v2p1
HEROES OF WATERLOO	5241	7L415	F	2/4	C1v4p10
HE'S AYE KISSING ME	5651	5222	D	2/4	K1v2p14
HE'S BONNY, HE'S O'ER THE HILL	3b15L1	3b57bL7bL	B	4/4	C5v2p54 G10v5p15
THIS NIGHT (THAT I LOE WEEL ETC]					
HE'S DEAR TO ME THO' HE'S FAR FRAE ME	3312	1H521	F	4/4	G11v2Bp10 K1v2p12
HESSIAN ALLEMANDE	3217L	6L27L5L	A	2/4	B16v3p7
HESSIAN'S MARCH, THE	51H3H3H	3H3H2H2H	D	2/4	C18p20
HEY DING A DING	1H2H3H7	1H2H3H2H	D	12/8	B16v3p94
HEY HO JOHNIE LAD	1122	15L22	A Bb	4/4	C8v2p49 Mc21v4p6
HEY HOW JOHNNIE LAD	1122	15L22	A G	4/4	C6p25 (J3)
HEY JENNY COME DOUN TO JOCK	3b3b3b	457b	E	6/4	Mc8v2Cp7
HEY JENNY COME DOWN TO JOCK	1262	1266L	D G F	6/8	(J3) Mc8v1Cp85 C5v2p16
					C20p1 G1v1p23 K1v2p13
					E1v1p5 G11v2Bp11
HEY ME NANNY	1H55	1H52	D	9/8	A1v5p38 C5v1p38
HEY MY NANNY	633	632	D A	9/8	O1v1Ep8 B15v1p46 G11v2Cp24
					C4p54
HEY THE HEDRIE FALIE	533	536	F	9/8	G15p28
HEY TO C(O)UPER	1355	4327L	G D	6/8	A1v3p171 C4p60 G11v2Bp35
					C14v13p12 K1v2p37 B15v1p89
HEY TO RUCKHOLT	1H2H1H5	3452	F	6/8	R12v1p76
HEY TO THE CAMP [HAY TO THE CAMP]	1H2H62	31H3H2H	C	6/8	K1v2p21 G11v2Bp19
HEY TO THE CAMP	1H2H62	351H2H	D	6/8	O1v1Gp1
HEY TUTI TATEY (TATETY)	5551H	6661H	D	4/4	Mc8v1Bp55 Mc8v2Cp18 C20p36
HEY TUTTI TAITI	3H3H3H5H	2H2H2H4H	C D	4/4	(J3) O1v1Cp13
HEY TUTTIE TETTIE	5L5L5L1	6L6L6L1	Bb	4/4	K1v2p1 G11v2Bp1
HI RI RI RI HO	1H1H1H3b	7b57b5	D	4/4	O1v1Lp155
HIBERNIA	3H1H55	354H2H	C D	6/8	G9v3p28 E1v1p40 B7p7
HIE OVER HUNT	3154	15L7L2	Bb	4/4	G10v5p28
HIE OVER HUNT (STRATHSPEY)	113L5L	1322L	Bb	4/4	G10v5p28
HIGH DANCE	1H1H3H3H	5H5H4H7	A	6/8	S11v1p24,25
HIGH ROAD TO LINTON, THE	351H1H	661H1H	A G	4/4*	Mc21v3p14 G11v2Bp24 D15v1p28
[HIGHWAY TO LINTON, THE]					K1v2p26 A1v4p3 C8v1p18 C8v2p29
					G7p3 (II) A7v6p56
HIGH ROAD TO LINTON, THE	351H1H	661H2	A	4/4	Mc10p4 G9v5p17
HIGH ROCKS, THE	1H4H62H	1H763	F	6/8	B16v4p95
HIGH WAY TO DUBLIN, THE	54H3bH2H	7b7b54H	D	6/8	A1v2p71
HIGH WAY TO DUBLIN, THE	6351	6347bL	A	6/8	K1v2p29 A1v1p15 G11v2Bp27
HIGH WAY TO EDINBURGH, THE	3L5L5L5L	15L5L5L	Bb	4/4	O1v1Cp28
HIGH WAY TO GREENVALE, THE	311	316	F	9/8	R5p35
HIGH WAY TO NEWFIELD, THE	1311H	3H652	G	6/8	R5p11
HIGH WAY TO WARINGTON, THE	171H	513	F	9/8	Mc9v2p24
HIGHLAND AIR	51H2H1H	51H2H1H	C	2/4	C4p47
HIGHLAND AIR	1H61H5	1H2H3H3H	D	6/8	C4p53
HIGHLAND AIR	1H1H56	1H1H65	C	6/8	M2p31
HIGHLAND AIR	3422	362H1H	D	6/8	C4p67

HIGHLAND BATTLE, A	1326	1353H	D	2/4	O1v11p68,69
HIGHLAND BONNET, THE	1H2H1H5	31H2H2	C	2/2	C14v11p20
HIGHLAND BRIGADE AT WATERLOO, THE	5154	5152	A	6/8	G11v2Dp2
HIGHLAND CHEESE IS RARE LASSES	1331	5632	D	4/4	G1v2p74
HIGHLAND CHIEFTAIN, THE	3H1H53	5533	D	4/4	G11v1Bp2 A1v4p27 G10v3p1
HIGHLAND CHIEFTAIN, THE	111L1	4327L	G	6/8	P9p17
HIGHLAND COTT, THE	1115	31H42	C	2/2	S7v3p11
HIGHLAND COTTAGE	5324	5324	G	2/2	C14v23p14
HIGHLAND DANCE	1H5H5H6H	5H3H5H3H	C	4/4	A1v5p72
HIGHLAND DANCE	3H52H1H	3H51H6	D	4/4	A1v5p72
HIGHLAND DANCE	1554	7bL442	A	6/8	A1v5p72
HIGHLAND DANCE, A	5135	5126	G	4/4	A1v5p65
HIGHLAND DANCE, A	1531	4327bL	A	4/4	A1v5p65
HIGHLAND DANCE, A	3211	7bL7b27bL	A	6/8	A1v5p65
HIGHLAND DRESS, THE	313L5L	2L222	G	2/2	S12v1p61
HIGHLAND FAIR	5551H	4H2H72H	D	4/4	A1v4p39
HIGHLAND HILLS	5151	5575	G	2/2	C13v2p20
HIGHLAND JUBILEE, THE	5H3H1H5	62H3H2H	D	6/8	B16v2p6
HIGHLAND KING	3b213bH	2H1H1H1H	G	4/4	O1v1Kp130
HIGHLAND LAD MY LOVE WAS BORN, A	3333	5332	Eb	2/4	C6p6
HIGHLAND LADDIE	5354	6262	A	2/2	C13v2p70 G9v5p16,17
HIGHLAND LADDIE [cf: WAVERLEY]	1353H	1H453	D	6/8	S7v1p54
HIGHLAND LADDIE, THE	1122	5522	D G C	4/4	C5v2p16 T6v1p28 O1v1Ap36
					O1v4p26,27 P8v2p15 (J3)
HIGHLAND LADDIE, (THE)	5353	6262	A F G	4/4*	B15v1p47 G11v2Dp34 R6v1p16-19
					(J3) N1v1p29 A1v1p12
HIGHLAND LADDIE, THE	5135	6422	D	4/4	B5p3
HIGHLAND LADDIE, THE	1212	1623	F	2/4	G9v1p26,27,28
HIGHLAND LADDIE, THE	3235	6422	D	2/2	Mc8v1Cp84 Mc8v1Ap9 N1v1p29
					N1v2p75
HIGHLAND LADDY	1132	4433	G	2/2	W7p9
HIGHLAND LADIE	1122	1322	G	2/2	A7v6p5
HIGHLAND LAMENTATION, THE	1H1H3H	1H1H3H	D	3/4	O1v1Cp24
HIGHLAND (LASSES) FAIR, THE	5L5L5L1	427L2	A	4/4*	G10v6p33 C14v9p13 W4v1p23
					Mc12v1p57
HIGHLAND LASSIE	1122	1322	G	4/4	A7v5p26
HIGHLAND LASSIE O, THE	1122	5223	D C	4/4	C5v3p52
HIGHLAND LASSIE, THE	3235	6422	D	4/4	O1v1Ap12,13 O1v2p37 O1v3p45
HIGHLAND MARCH, THE	1H1H1H3H	1H51H2H	D	4/4	M2p29
HIGHLAND MARY	5L111	3b212	A B	4/4	C8v1p26 C5v2p2
HIGHLAND PLAID, THE	5H5H5H5H	5H5H6H2H	C	4/4*	C14v3p1 P10p14 N1v1p23
HIGHLAND PLAID, THE	15L13	436L6L	G	2/2	Mc9v1p30 (II)
HIGHLAND PORT. BY RORY DALL, A	1352	135L2L	G	6/8	O1v5p30,31
HIGHLAND PRESIDENT, THE	5L113b	2455	G	4/4*	G11v2Cp3 J1p21
HIGHLAND QUEEN, (THE)	31H1H1H	61H22	D	2/4	C5v2p8 O1v1Kp120 (J3)
HIGHLAND QUEEN, THE	31H1H1H	61H32	G	2/4	B7p12
HIGHLAND RANT, THE	6L326L	6L331	G	6/8	C5v2p28
HIGHLAND REEL	1L1L1L1L	7bL4L7bF7bF	G	2/2	S7v1p40
HIGHLAND REEL, A	3313	4324	A	4/4	C4p14
HIGHLAND REEL, A	1H3H1H6	41H22	D	2/2	A1v5p5 C5v1p5
HIGHLAND REEL, A	2H576	2H576	D	2/2	C4p19
HIGHLAND REEL, A	3H555	3H52H6	D	4/4	A1v5p67
HIGHLAND REEL, A	336L2	1515	G	6/8	C4p5
HIGHLAND REEL, THE	1353	5353	G	2/2	H1p15
HIGHLAND REEL, THE	1H1H35	3424	D	2/2	R12v1p65
HIGHLAND SANTE, THE	531	222	G	3/4	O1v1Lp154
HIGHLAND SECRETARY, THE MR MACKENZIES STRATHSPEY	53b53b	4242	G	2/2	J1p22
HIGHLAND SECRETARY, THE	5111	5155	A	4/4	G11v2Dp11
HIGHLAND SKIP, THE	5555	5555	F	2/2	C14v12p13 D14v3p22/23 G11v2Cp31
					(II)
HIGHLAND SOLO	5566	5533	D	4/4	D14v2p18,19,20,21,22
HIGHLAND SOLO	1352	1352	G	6/8	H1p14,15
HIGHLAND WATCH (NOW THE 42nd REGt or ROYAL HIGHLANDERS), THE	3b13b1	3b17bL7bL	E A	4/4	K1v1p1 G11v2Ap1 Mc19v1p14 C5v2p67
HIGHLAND WATCH, THE	3b13b1	3b7bL7bL7bL	E A	4/4*	D14v2p42 E1v1p99
HIGHLAND WATCH, THE [HIGHLANDER'S FAREWELL TO IRELAND, THE]	1L1L1L1L	7bL4L7bF7bF	D A	4/4*	Mc13v2p29 S12v1p27 G11v2Bp5 Mc9v3p5 Mc7p6 K1v2p5 H3p10/11
HIGHLAND WEDDING, THE	1353	6L6L22	Bb	2/2	C14v7p13
HIGHLAND WHISKY [HIGHLAND WHISKEY]	1113	2246	A	4/4	C8v1p19 C8v2p28 G11v2Dp26 (II)
HIGHLANDER, THE	311H5	3142	D	6/8	P6v2p22
HIGHLANDERS FAREWELL TO IRELAND	1111	7b47bL7bL	A	4/4	G1v2p55 (II)
HIGHLANDERS KNEE BUCKLE, THE	3751	437L2	Eb	2/2	C1v4p8
HIGHLANDERS' MARCH, THE	1452	4331	D	6/8	O1v1Gp32
HIGHLANDERS WELCOME HOME, THE	5551	4447bL	A	4/4	K1v2p6
HIGHLANDMAN KISS'D HIS MOTHER, THE	1H5H5H5H	1H5H2H5	D C	4/4*	G1v2p52 C4p26 K1v1p23 G11v2Ap21 B15v1p10 C8v1p48 G9v5p19 (II)
HIGHLAND-MAN KISS'D HIS MOTHER, THE	1555	1525L	G	2/4	A1v1p32
HIGHWAY TO BOURTRIE HILL, THE	513bH2H	7b547bL	D	6/8	R5p42
HIGHWAY TO COILSFIELD, THE	1H111	1H126L	G	4/4	R5p16
HIGHWAY TO COLAIN, THE	31H3	652	F	9/8	R5p18

HIGHWAY TO CRAIGIE HOUSE, THE	1H12	1H14	D	9/8	R5p31
HIGHWAY TO DUBLIN, THE	1523	1523	G	6/8	G8p35
HIGHWAY TO EDINBURGH	5L115	7b3b3b7bL	E	6/8	A1v3p158
HIGHWAY TO EDINBURGH, THE	1354	1362	Bb	2/2	C14v15p21
HIGH-WAY TO EDINBURGH, THE	5551H	3H522	D	2/2	C13v2p75
HIGHWAY TO EGLINGTON, THE	1H1H1H1	1H1H2H2	C	6/8	R12v1p44
HIGHWAY TO EGLINTOUNE, THE	1H51H1	1H52H2	C	6/8	R5p27
HIGH-WAY TO LONDON, THE	3L37L6L	3L35L1	Bb	6/8	C13v2p76
HIGHWAYMAN, THE	5H4H2H5H	3H1H2H3H	D	3/8	R12v1p17
HILL OF BURNIE, THE	5327L	15L4L2L	Bb	2/2	G8p14 P1v1p5
HILLAND TUNE	153b5	7b47bL4	A	2/2	Y1p24
HILLOCH OF HAY, THE	5552	3555	D	4/4	O1v1Lp148
HILLS OF CROMDALE, THE	1551	427bL5L	A	2/2	G15p1
HILLS OF CROOK HAVEN, THE	31H3H3	31H2H2	G	6/8	S7v3p10
HILLS OF GLENORCHY, THE	5157b	47bL47b	E	6/8	C8v2p25 C8v1p16 G10v6p16 (II)
HILTON LODGE	5H5H4H2H	5H5H1H5H	D C	4/4	A1v4p2 C5v1p51 G10v3p6 Mc21v4p13 G11v18p28 C14v10p4 (II)
HIS GRACE THE DUKE OF ATHOLE'S MARCH	15L35L	3352	A	4/4	D16p1
HIS GRACE THE DUKE OF BUCCLEUCH'S STRATHSPEY	1144	3347L	G	2/2	Mc19v2p4,5 Mc19v3p10,11
HIS GRACE THE DUKE OF GORDON'S RECOVERY	1L5L5L1	1L5L6L2L	A	4/4	G15p18
HIS MAJESTY'S RECOVERY	3211H	357L2	G	6/8	A7v6p8 A7v2p28
HIS MAJESTY'S WELCOME TO SCOTLAND	1L1L3bL5L	1L1L2L7bF	A	2/2	Mc19v2p17 Mc19v3p22
HISTORICAL WAR SONG	1355	4655	D	6/8	C10v2Bp68-71
HIT HER (UP)ON THE BUM(E)	537b4	531H5	A	6/8	D13p13 G9v1p6,7 O1v1Fp17 B15v2p11
HIT OR MISS	1H2H1H2H	63H5H1H	D	2/4	H6v10p2
HITHIL UIL AGUS	5336	1H631	G	2/2	C4p11
HO CHA CHEILLIN NACH TU B'FHEARR LEAM	6L232	6L236L	Bb	6/8	F2v2p95(85)
HO CHA N'EIL MULAD OIRNN'	5L126L	5L151H	Eb	4/4	F2v2p102(92)
HO CUIR A NALL AM BODACH	5L17bL6L	5L3b42	G	4/4	F2v2p95(85)
HO MO CHAILEAGAN	1H353	1H352	G	6/8	Mc16p12
HO RIN O I RI O HO NIGHEAN AN AIRICH	13b57bL	13b54	A	4/4	Mc5p21
HO RO GU'M B'AOBHUIN LEAM,etc.	1147bL	2545	A	2/4	Mc1v1p116
HO (RO) GUR COMA LEAM H'UILE NI (A) TH'ANN	1H655	1H622	D	6/8	F2v2p75(65)
HO RO HOI HUG ORIONNAN, EC	1515L	7bL427bL	B	2/4	Mc1v1p116
HO RO MO BHOBAN AN' DRAM	351	1H51	G	9/8	F2v2p77(67)
HO RO MO NIGHEAN DONN BHOIDHEACH	53b11	3b57b5	E	4/4	F2v2p66(56)
HOB OR NOB	1533	1522	G	6/8	R12v1p15
HOBLE ABOUT	31H1H7	6542	D	6/8	N1v1p15 B15v1p59
HODDOM CASTLE	3431H	647L2	G	4/4	A7v1p1
HODDOM CASTLE	1H1H4H7	1H1H5H4H	D	6/8	G1v2p54 C5v1p51 A1v4p51
HODDOM CASTLE	1147L	1154	Bb	6/8	G11v1Bp21 G10v3p6
HOIRRIONN O(!) AIR NIGHEAN AN AIRICH	13b57bL	13b55	E	4/4	F2v2p67(57)
HOLE IN THE RIDDLE, THE	521H1H	2H72H5	G	4/4	O1v1Jp102
HOLIN GREEN HOLIN	13b2	211	E	3/4	C10v2Bp5
HOLLOW DRUM, THE	1113	2211	G	4/4	A1v5p5
HOLY EVEN	3211H	2H2H61H	F	2/2	P7p16
HOME, SWEET HOME	3453	4433	G	2/4	C8v2p21
HOME, SWEET HOME	3453	4430	G	6/8	C8v1p51
HON. JAMES RAMSAY'S REEL, THE	1H1H31	427L5L	A	2/2	G9v2p2
HON: MISS CHARLOTTE McKINZIE'S FAVORITE, THE	1113	15L13L	A	6/8	M12p31
HON: MR MAULE OF PANMURE'S MARCH, THE	1155	2416L	Bb	4/4	G9v3p17
HON: MR McKINZIE OF SEAFORTH'S BIRTH DAY, THE	1535	627L2	A	2/2	M12p33
HON: MRS MAULE'S STRATHSPEY, THE	11H3H1H	61H62	C	4/4	G9v2p4,5
(HONbl) MRS DUNDAS OF ARNISTON'S REEL	1H1H2H5	6451	C	4/4*	G10v3p18 G11v1Ap37
HONble CAPt ELPHINSTONE OF THE TARTAR, THE	1H532	22H4H2H	C	4/4	G9v5p20
HONble CAPTAIN ELLIOT'S QUICK STEP	1215	436L7L	Bb/Eb	2/4	P11v1p12
HONble CAPTN ELPHINSTON ('S STRATHSPEY)	1515L	1153b	G	4/4	G11v1Bp37 G11v1Cp37 G10v3p23
HONble CAPTn MAITLAND'S STRATHSPEY	1347L	1353	G	4/4	Mc4v2p10 G11v2Bp14 K1v2p16 (II)
HONble CHARLES BRUCE'S REEL, THE	13L6L5L	4L3L2L2L	Bb	2/2	S13p4 B11p20 (II)
HONble COL. HAMILTON'S DELIGHT	1H542	327L5L	G	6/8	G10v2p6
HONBle COLONEL HAMILTON'S QUICK STEP	1133	5331H	Bb	4/4	L3p2
HONble COLONEL HAMILTON'S STRATHSPEY	5531	1H3H3H2H	D	2/2	L3p6
HONBle COLONEL (Wm) WEMYSS	1335	357L2	F	2/2*	G10v2p25 (II)
HONble EARL OF BREADALBINE'S STRATHSPEY	11H53	51H3H2H	D	2/4	A1v5p54
HONble EDWARD SPENCER COWPERS	5L111	3253	G	2/2	C14v18p21
HONble FOX MAULE'S FAVORITE, THE	3163	3124	A	6/8	Mc19v3p14
HONble FRANCIS GRAY'S STRATHSPEY	5557b	4442	G	4/4	C13v1p30
HONble GEORGE BAILLIE ('S STRATHSPEY)	5551H	5522	F	2/2	G11v1Cp21 G10v1p21
HONble GEORGE CARNEGIE'S STRATHSPEY, THE	13b5L1	27bL27bL	G A	4/4	Mc22p5 (II) A7v6p52
HONble GEORGE MELVILL LESLIE MELVILL'S STRATHSPEY	31H53	31H42	C	2/2	L4p2
HONble GEORGE MELVILL LESLIE'S ALAMANDE	31H2H5	3525L	G	2/4	L4p12

Title			Key	Time	Source
HONble HENRY ERSKINE'S FAVORITE, THE	1231	4525L	Eb	6/8	P11v2p9
HONble JOHN LESSLIE MELVILLE('S STRATHSPEY, THE)	1H3bH2H1H	5427bL	D	4/4	G10v5p13 (II)
(HONBle) (LADY/MRS/MR) (F.) GRAY'S STRATHSPEY	51H3H1H	51H2H4	D F	4/4	A1v5p64 C5v1p64 G10v5p10,11 P5v2p10 (II)
HONble MARGARET ERSKINE'S REEL, THE	5753	4316L	G	2/2	P11v2p17
HONble MISS BAGOT'S STRATHSPEY	1335	5662	F	4/4	J1p33
HONble MISS CATHERINE ELLIOT'S REEL	3215L	6L452	A	2/2	P11v1p9
HONble MISS CATHRINE ABERCROMBEY'S STRATHSPEY	1L5L5L1	4526L	A	4/4	S4v2p5
HONble MISS COURTENAY'S REEL	5L353	4322	A	2/2	G8p8 .P1v1p13
HONBLE MISS DRUMMOND OF PERTH'S MINUET	111	222	G	3/4	W4v2p15
HONble MISS EARDLEY'S MINUET	1H53	115	C	3/4	S7v3p14,15
HONble MISS ELIZA MURR(A)Y ELIBANK'S STRATHSPEY	5L5L1L5L	147L5L	G	4/4	W4v1p12
HONble MISS ELLIOT'S STRATHSPEY	1351	247L5L	F	4/4	P11v1p1
HONble MISS ELPHINSTONE'S FANCY, THE	546L6L	5L5L32	Bb	2/4	Mc15p2
HONble MISS ELPHINSTONE'S REEL, THE	1353	5L37L2	Bb	2/2	Mc15p2
HONble MISS ELPHINSTON'S STRATHSPEY	1131	247L2	D	4/4	W4v1p10
HONble MISS ELPHINSTON'S STRATHSPEY	1H1H3H1H	2H4H72H	D	4/4	A1v4p51
HONble MISS GEORGINA ELPHINSTON'S STRATHSPEY	15L13	6562	A	2/2	B20p2
HONble. MISS H. ELLIOT'S DANCE, THE	5313	427L7L	G	2/4	P11v2p14
HONble MISS H. ELLIOT'S REEL	3546	72H1H3H	F	2/2	P11v1p1
HONble MISS HAMILTON'S REEL, THE	131H3	4362	E	2/2	P1v2p4
HONble MISS HAMILTON'S REEL, THE	15L3L5L	2L4L6L4L	Bb	2/2	B20p1
HONble MISS JANE RUTHVEN'S JIGG	1H5H6H2H	3H1H2H5	C	6/8	L4p9
HONble MISS JESSIE A. RUTHVEN'S STRATHSPEY	11H3b5	7bL7b22	C	4/4	L4p6 (II)
HONble MISS JESSIE A. RUTHVEN'S FAVOURITE	5L457L	37L31	A	6/8	L4p10
HONble MISS K. ELPHINSTON'S	1331	5L5L22	G	4/4	A1v6p7
HONble MISS KEITH ELPHINSTONE'S FAVOURITE, THE	1H1H35	61H32	C	2/4	Mc15p5
HONble MISS KENNAIRD'S REEL, THE	3565	4322	C	2/2	C14v4p19
HONble MISS KINNAIRD'S STRATHSPEY, THE	1H135	22H4H7	F	4/4	B6v2p1
HONble MISS MACKINZIE ELPHINSTONE'S FAVOURITE, THE	1461H	1362	F	2/4	Mc15p18
HONble MISS P. ELPHINSTONE'S STRATHSPEY, THE	315L3L	436L2	G	2/2	J1p32
HONble MISS PETRIE'S STRATHSPEY	5L131	5426L	E	2/2	J1p30
HONble MISS PRIMROSE ELPHINSTONE'S STRATHSPEY, THE	1H535	4H3H72H	E	4/4	Mc15p11
HONble MISS ROLLO('S REEL), THE	3H1H2H1H	6522H	C	2/2*	B11p10 (II)
HONble MISS RUTHVEN'S REEL	5L353	5247L	A	2/2	L4p4
HONble MISS RUTHVEN'S STRATHSPEY	151H3	15GL2	C	4/4	L4p8,9
HONble MISS SEMPILL'S REEL	1H515	2H626	G	2/2	Mc21v2p8 (II)
HONble MISS STUART, BLANTYRE'S STRATHSPEY, THE	1135	6561H	F	2/2	Mc15p18
HONble MR BAILLIES STRATHSPEY	115L5L	15L22	E	2/2	L3p4
HONBle Mr F. GRAY'S STRATHSPEY	537L2	5354	F	4/4	Mc21v2p12
HONble MR FRASER (OF LOVAT) 'S REEL	543b1	247b2	B	2/2	Mc21v2p24 (II)
HONble MR FRASER OF LOVAT'S STRATHSPEY	5526L	5513H	F	4/4	F2v1p2
HONble MR J.T.L. MELVILLE'S, THE	1H1H55	4433	Eb	2/4	L2p17
HONble MR MAULE'S FROLICK, THE	1H531	5L5L6L7L	F	6/8	G10v4p20
HONble MR RAMSAY MAULE'S FAVORITE	3b111	3b6b54	E	6/8	G11v1Cp24 G10v3p10
HONble MR RAMSAY MAULE'S REEL	3b15L3b	47bL24	G	2/2	P5v2p4
HONble MR RAMSAY MAULE'S STRATHSPEY	5527bL	5555	E	4/4	G11v1Cp24 G10v3p10
HONble MR W. MELVILLE'S, THE	3135	457L2	F	6/8	L2p10
HONble MRS ANDREW RAMSAY'S STRATHSPEY, THE	1H1H31	6542	G	4/4	C14v18p3
HONble MRS BUCHANAN'S FAVORITE, THE	1231	457L2	D	6/8	S4v2p4
HONble MRS CAMPBELL (OF LOCHNELL'S) REEL	1H535	1H3H2H2	C	2/2	Mc21v2p23
HONble. MRS. CHARTERIS' STRATHSPEY	5342	537L5L	G	4/4	Mc10p1
HONble MRS CHARTERIS'S VALTZ, THE	5H5H5H5H	5H5H2H1H	C	3/8	G9v4p8
HONble MRS DRUMMOND OF PERTH'S STRATHSPEY	1311H	5326L	D	4/4	G10v2p17 Mc12v1p42 (II)
HONble MRS DRUMMOND OF PERTH'S DELIGHT, THE	1L155	6L242	A	6/8	Mc4v3p5 G8p6
HONble MRS FRASER OF LOVAT'S STRATHSPEY	51H63	51H42	D	4/4	F2v1p7
HONble MRS GRAY'S STRATHSPEY	5515	5642	F	2/2	M11v1p10
HONble MRS JOHN RAMSAY'S REEL, THE	3L5L15L	6L5L7L2	Bb	2/2	G10v4p33
HONble MRS JOHN RAMSAY'S STRATHSPEY	36L5L3L	157L2	F	4/4	S4v2p7
HONble MRS LESLIE CUMING, THE	1352	1353	F	6/8	G11v2Dp16
HONble MRS MAULE OF PANMURE'S FAVORITE	536L2	3535	F	6/8	G10v4p9
	5526L	5515	F	4/4	G10v4p9 W4v2p2
HONble MRS MAULE (OF PANMURE'S) STR. THE					
HONble MRS MAULE'S REEL, (THE)	1H535	2462H	A	4/4*	P5v2p3 C14v13p7 A7v5p3 A7v6p21 Mc21v4P32
HONble MRS MURRAY ELLIBANK'S STRATHSPEY	16L5L3L	5L37L4	Bb	4/4	S4v2p22

Title					
HONble MRS OGILVY OF CLOVA'S FAVOURITE, THE	1H531	1H536	D	6/8	B6v2p1
HONble MRS OLIPHANT MURRAY'S REEL	1H1H35	6522H	D	4/4	G10v5p25
HONble MRS PETRIE'S STRATHSPEY, THE	351H3H	4H3H2H5	Eb	2/2	J1p30
HONble MRS RAMSAY MAULE OF PANMURE'S STRATHSPEY	5526L	5515	F	2/2	G9v5p1
HONble RAMSEY MAULE'S MARCH	1H1H5H5H	2H4H1H6	D	4/4	A1v5p17 C5v1p17
HONEST DUNCAN	1H151	1H155	D	4/4	G1v2p64
HONEST DUNCAN	11L5L1L	11L5L5L	Bb	4/4	K1v2p1 G10v5 (11)
HONEST MEN AND BONNY LASSES	113L5L	112L2L	Bb	4/4	G10v5p27
HONEY MOON, THE	51H1H3H	4H2H75	D	4/4*	E1v1p11 A7v5p5 N1v1p3 (11)
HONEY MOON, THE	51H1H3H	4H2H72H	D G	4/4*	G1v2p74 A7v4p11 P11v2p10 C14v21p19 P6v1p4
HONle MRS DRUMMOND OF PERTH'S FAVORITE, THE	5L155	6L242	G	6/8	A7v6p46
HONORABLE MISS WARD'S FANCY, THE	351H6	5542	F	2/2	C14v19p6,7
HONORABLE MRS DUFF OF ECHT'S REEL, THE	3L1L3L1	3L1L2L2L	G	2/2	S5p11
HONOURABLE COLONEL HAMILTON'S MARCH	1115L	225L2	Bb	4/4	L3p2
HONOURABLE GEORGE MURRAY, THE	3L7L14	5416L	A	6/8	Mc19v3p6
HON(oura)ble MISS CHARTERIS' REEL, THE	1H3bH1H7b	47b2H7b	G	2/2*	G11v1Bp36 G10v3p15 (11)
HONOURABLE MISS FRANCESS HAY'S Q/STEP	3b211H	3bH7b42	E	6/8	W2v1p14
HONOURABLE MISS FRANCESS HAY'S REEL	13b5L3b	247bL2	E	2/2	W2v1p14
HONOURABLE MR DRUMMOND BURREL, THE	1111	447bL2	E	4/4	G11v1Bp6
HONOURABLE MRS MAULE, THE	1L5L3bL5L	7bL4L2L7bF	A	2/2	Mc19v3p4
HONOURABLE MRS MAULE'S MEDLEY, THE	1L1L2L1L	7bL17bL7bF	A	4/4	Mc19v3p4
HONOURABLE PEACE(, THE/AN)	1515L	7bL247bL	E	2/2	C14v1p20 D14v3p4/5 G11v2Cp19 (11)
HOOLY AND FAIRLY	1324	151H5	G	6/8	Mc8v1Dp109 G1v1p37
HOOLY AND FAIRLY	111	345	F	6/4	(J3) (C25)
HOOLY AND FAIRLY	111	535	G	6/4	C4p35
HOOP HER AND GIRD HER	1313	1124	G	6/8	G10v4p12,13
HOOPERS JIGG	157b4	11H54	G	6/8	R12v1p53
HOPE TOLD A FLATTERING TALE	3210	5620	G	6/8	E1v1p69
HOPETOUN HOUSE	157b5	7b47bL2	E	4/4*	S12v1p11 A1v6p7 A1v1p22
HOPETOUN HOUSE	1551	7b47bL3b	E	2/2	R6v2p33
HOPETOUN HOUSE	1555	7b7b7bL2	E	4/4	G3p27
HOPETOUN HOUSE	157b1	7b47bL2	E	2/2	C4p24 B15v1p9
HORATIO, THE	3H4H1H7	553H2H	D	6/8	C14v25p9
HORNPIPE	1113	27L5L3L	Bb	4/4	C22p50
HORNPIPE	1127L	5L3L1L5L	Bb	4/4	C22p40
HORNPIPE	1131	1115L	Bb	2/2	Mc9v2p29
HORNPIPE	1131H	5L5L7L4	F G	4/4	C8v1p23 C8v2p60
HORNPIPE	337L7L	1155	Eb	4/4	C22p33
HORNPIPE	1L5L36	1H642	A	4/4	G10v2p29
HORNPIPE	3L5L17L	2444	Bb	4/4	C22p50
HORNPIPE	113L3L	1531	A	4/4	C22p33
HORNPIPE	5645	36L53	Bb	4/4	S11v2p4
HORNPIPE	1H3H6H	3H5H2H	D	3/2	S12v2p13
HORNPIPE, A	5315L	4L3L41	G	2/4	P5v1p13
HORNPIPE, A	1764	47L16L	Bb	4/4	A7v4p7
HORNPIPE, A	15L6L1	5L6L4L2L	Bb	2/2	M4v1p8
HORNPIPE BY MR FESTING	1H2H3H	1H1H5	D	3/2	S12v2p11
HORNPIPE, DANC'D BY ALDRIDGE'S	3112	7L445	F	4/4	Mc9v2p37
HORSE-MAN'S PORT	331	15L1	D	6/4	B15v2p8,9 D13p10
HORUINN O U ORO	143b5	7b53b1	G	6/8	M12p25
HOSSIER'S GHOST	342	123	G	3/4	O1v1Fp10
HOT BATH, THE	1H4H1H4H	1H677	D	6/8	S7v1p69
HOTT MUTTON PYES	3b11	27bL4	A	9/8	A1v6p53
HOUSE OF ACHLUNCART, THE	1H1H3H5H	1H1H2H5	C	4/4	M4v3p46 (11)
HOUSE OF BUCHAN	1H642	3535	D	6/8	A7v3p35
HOUSE OF CAIRNFIELD, THE	151H5	52H3H1H	E	4/4	M4v3p24
HOUSE OF CANDACRAIG, THE	1L3L1L1	547L2	A	4/4	M4v3p18
HOUSE OF CLUNY, THE	1331	7L227L	F	4/4	M4v3p57 (11)
HOUSE OF CRAIG, THE	5L132	5216L	G	2/2	S5p9
HOUSE OF GLAMS	1554	6b423b	E	4/4	Mc8v2Bp18
HOUSE OF GRAY, THE	13b44	13b55	A G	6/8	A1v3p173 (11) B15v1p101 R12v1p48 P11v1p13
HOUSE OF LETTERFOURIE, THE or [LASSES LOOK BEHIND YOU]	5326L	531H1H	D	2/2	M4v3p33 (11)
HOUSE OF NEW, THE	11H31H	51H72H	C	4/4	M4v3p47 (11)
HOUSE OF PARK, THE	3546	5122	F	4/4*	M4v3p51 (11)
HOUSE OF REW, THE	1H515	1H562	D	2/2	R5p45
HOUSE UNDER THE HILL, THE	351H1H	1H1H72	A	2/4	O1v1Hp51
HOW BLEST THE MAID	5555	61H1H0	D	6/8	E1v2p47
HOW CAN I BE SAD ON MY WEDDING DAY	5337	64#4#1H	G	6/8	O1v1Ep12
HOW CAN I BE SAD ON MY WEDDING DAY	5517	6641H	G	6/8	C5v3p69
HOW CAN I &C	1131	2266	G	4/4	W4v2p21
HOW FAIR SHINES THE MORNING	3H1H65	51H52	D	6/8	C5v2p63
HOW IMPERFECT IS EXPRESSION	5H5H6H4H	3H3H4H2H	C	4/4	A1v3p202
HOW LONG AND DREARY IS THE NIGHT	11H1H	1H55	G E	3/4	C5v3p67 (J3)
HOW SHE'LL NE'ER BE GUIDED	313	314	A	9/8	R6v2p18
HOW SWEET IN THE WOODLANDS	1H3H3H	1H1H2H	C	3/4	E1v2p90

HOW SWEET IT IS LOVE	3b111	3b554	G	2/2	O1v11p66
HOW SWEET THE LOVE (THAT MEETS RETURN)	551H5	3111	G	4/4*	A1v6p48
(HOW SWEET THIS) LONE VALE, (THE)	5L36L1	5L321	Bb A	6/8	G11v2Cp14 E1v2p120 (J3)
HOW TO BE HAPPY	51H2H3H	51H3H2H	C	6/8	S7v2p3
HUGAR MU FEAN	561H	2H2H2H	D	3/4	T7p44,45 O1v1Kp113
HUGH GILMOUR'S LAMENT FOR NIEL GOW	3b211	443b1	G	4/4	G10v5p6
HUM DRUM, THE	1231H	3H72H5	D	2/4	B16v3p29
HUME CASTLE	3153	6532	F	2/2	D14v3p20/21
HUME CASTLE	3333	6532	G	4/4	C7p9
HUME CASTLE	361H6	1H362	C	6/8	G8p33 P1v1p13
HUMOROUS LIEUTENANT, THE	5566	5522	A	6/8	P9p32
HUMORS OF HILLSBROUGH, THE	13b55	7bL244	E	6/8	R12v1p73
HUMOURS OF BURROW, THE	131H1H	1352	D	6/8	C14v2p4
HUMOURS OF COVENT GARDEN, THE	61H61H	62H75	G	6/8	B16v1p11
HUMOURS OF CULLEN, THE	5L155	47bL54	E	6/8	C18p38
HUMOURS OF DUBLIN, (THE)	1H352	1H342	D G	6/8	K1v1p38,39 Mc21v3p20,21
					G11v2Ap36 Mc9v2p31 S12v2p34
HUMOURS OF GLEN	113b3b	114L1	A D	6/8	Mc23p31 Mc12v2p13,14 C20p50
HUMOURS OF GLEN, THE	115L3b	114L1	A	6/8	K1v2p14
HUMOURS OF GRAIGNAMANOCH, THE	1H362	1H31H1H	D	6/8	A1v2p70
HUMOURS OF KILDARE, THE	3366	3355	D	6/8	C14v5p15
HUMOURS OF KILKENNY, THE	3155	3161H	A	6/8	Mc9v2p36 C13v2p63 G9v5p16
					Mc7p35,36 K1v2p30 G11v2Bp28
					B10p2
HUMOURS OF LIMERICK, THE	1H31H3	4542	G	6/8	A1v3p179
HUMOURS OF LIMERICK, THE	1123	5L162	G	6/8	C13v2p66
HUMOURS OF LISTIVAIN, THE	5L127bL	5127b	A	6/8	A1v3p182 B11p28
HUMOURS OF NAIRNSHIRE, THE	5535	662H2	A	6/8	L1p8
HUMOURS OF PANTEEN, THE	1454	1457b	D	6/8	B11p31
HUMOURS OF [THE] GLEN	115L3b	115L1	A	6/8	G11v2Bp12
HUMOUR'S OF THE POINT, THE	1H652	1H621	G	2/4	A1v3p170
HUNDRED YEARS SINCE, A	5L5L11	2226L	Eb	2/2	P9p4 (II)
HUNGARIAN MARCH, THE	1H2H3H5H	4H3H2H5	D	2/4	R12v1p19
HUNGARIAN WALTZ	1T76H5H	1T76H1H	C	3/8	E1v2p88
HUNT THE SQUIRREL	1553	1212	G	6/8	O1v1Kp115
HUNTINGTONE CASTLE	13b52	13b57b	E	6/8	B11p18
HUNTLY LODGE	1121	2243	Bb	4/4	M4v3p3
HUNTLY LODGE	31H42	31H4H7	D	4/4	G10v6p6,7
HUNTLY LODGE	1H3H72H	3H2H75	F	4/4	P5v3p4
HURLY BURLY, THE	13b53b	247b4	E	6/8	C14v2p8
HURRAH! FOR THE BONNETS OF BLUE	1H3H55	1H5H2H2H	D	6/8	C8v2p61
HURRAH! FOR THE BONNETS OF BLUE	135L5L	1522	Bb G	6/8	C8v1p29 G1v1p6,7
HUZZA	1H3bH5H5H	6bH5H5H5H	D	2/2	W7p14
I AM DISPOSED TO MIRTH	4L5L1L3bL	4L5L7bF1L	A	4/4	Mc5p7
(I AM) O'ER YOUNG TO MARRY YET	351H3H	1H52H2H	C	4/4*	G9v5p19 Mc21v4p14
I CANNOT WIN AT HER FOR HER BIG BELLY	16L24	1636	G	6/8	O1v1Ep6,7
I CANNOT WINSULL HER FOR HER BIGG BELLY	1H1H5	665	F	3/4	P7p20
I CAN'T FOR MY LIFE	351H1H	3553	D	6/8	R4p2
I CONNA' BUCKLE TO	3b3b54	4511	G	2/2	C4p52
I DINNA KEN	311	314	G	9/8	H1p13
I DON'T CARE WHITHER OR NO	1H765	4327L	F	6/8	R12v1p12
I FIX MY FANCY ON HER	3235	2665	F	2/2	P7p15
I FIXT MY FANCY ON HER	3235	2666	F	4/4*	Mc8v2Cp2 S16p68,69
I GAVE A WAEFU' GATE YESTREEN	1H1H1H3H	1H665	D	4/4	E1v2p31
I HAD A HORSE AND I HAD NAE MAIR	111H	522	F G	3/4	(J3) C5v2p15
I HA'E LAID A HERRING IN SA'T	3L5L6L6L	5L135	A	6/8	C4p39 (II)
I HAVE A WIFE OF MY AIN	113b	557b	E	3/4	O1v1Jp90
I HA(V)E A (WIFE/HOUSE) O' MY AIN	13b5	13b5	E	9/8	C8v2p25 G1v2p70 C8v1p16
					C14v14p22 B15v1p45 C4p52
					K1v1p19 G11v2Ap17 (J3)
					S12v1p12 C13v4p73 (II)
I HAVE BEEN COURTING AT A LASS	1H1H2H2H	551H1H	D	4/4	A1v6p47
I KNOW SOMETHING	3H3H2H3H	3H3H2H1H	D	2/4	R12v1p47
I LO'E NA A LADDIE BUT ANE	1166	5122	G D	6/8	C6p21 (J3) (II)
I LO'E NE'ER A LADDIE BUT ANE	1160	5230	G	6/8	G1v1p31
I LOO'D A BONNY LADY	1H62H6	21H65	D	6/8	S16p70,71
I LOST MY HEART ON FRIDAY	651H2	651H3H	C	2/2	G15p34
I LOST MY LOVE	113b3b	557b5	A	6/8	A7v6p36 A7v2p21 C8v1p10
AND I (DINNA KEN HOW/CARE NOT)					C8v2p24 (II)
I LOVE A BONNY LASS	6551H	651H2	A	2/2	H3p23
I LOVE MY LOVE FOR SHE LOVES ME	13b3b	7bL7bL4	A	9/8	K1v2p25 G11v2Bp23
I LOVE MY LOVE IN SEACREIT	3H2H1H1H	62H2H6H	C	2/2	P7p2
I LOVE MY LOVE IN SECRET	3211	6L225	Bb A	4/4*	Mc8v1C66,67 C20p12,13
					C5v3p64 (J3)
I LOVE MY LOVE IN SECRET	3H2H1H1H	62H2H5H	C	2/2	O1v3p14,15 O1v1Bp26,27 Mc8v1Ap2
I LOVE MY LOVE IN SECRET	4215L	6L225	G	4/4	E1v2p137
I LOVE THE YOUTH	5L117bL	3b443b	A B	4/4	A1v6p40 D14v2p17
I MADE LOVE TO KATE	553b	3b7b7b	E	9/8	C4p23
I MET IN OUR VILLAGE	3H6H3H3H	51H2H3H	D	3/8	P8v1p2
I MET THEE IN THE MORN OF LIFE	1H1H1H	3bH2H0	C	3/4	C10v2Bp89
(I SATE UPON) THE PEER OF LEITH	6L155	4222	C A	4/4	C29p14 O1v5p24
I SAW AN EEL CHASE THE DEEL	1355	4357L	F	4/4	C10v2Bp33

I STILL MAY BOAST MY WILL IS FREE	1135L	1332	F	2/4	C10v2Ap12
I STOOD UPON THE PIER OF LEITH	5L155	4222	A	4/4	C5v3p60
I THINK THE CARLIE'S WUD THE NIGHT	551H6	551H5	D	4/4	C18p33
I WAS NOT-SINCE MARTINMASS	1527bL	1551	G	2/4	O1v1Fp21
I WINNA GAE TO BED (UNTIL I'M MARRIED)	3H551H	2266	D	2/2	K1v2p36 G11v2Bp34 (II)
I WISH I MAY DIE IF I DO	31H2H1H	31H1H1H	D	6/8	A1v2p14
I WISH MY LOVE WAS IN A MIRE	1H3H1H1H	2265	D C	4/4	O1v1Fp9 P4p27
I WISH MY LOVE WERE IN A MIRE	1311	2L2L6L5L	Bb	4/4	(J3) N1v2p15
I WISH MY LOVE WERE IN A MIRE	1H1H1H1H	2265	D	4/4	Mc8v1Cp84 S16p28,29 G17p16 C29p31 Mc8v2Ap17 C20p76
I WISH YOU A HAPPY NEW YEAR	51H2H2H	3H4H3H2H	D	6/8	A1v2p8
I WISH YOU WOULD MARRY ME NOW	5L13b3b	427bL2	A	4/4*	B15v1p58 C8v2p27 C8v1p27 G9v5p29 A7v6p81 A7v5p4Z (II)
I WOUD HAVE MY GOWN MADE	3b215	1H1H1H7b	D	2/2	Y1p6
IAN AN CIOBAIR [IAIN AN CIBEIR]	5L2L5L6L	5L2L3L6L	Bb	3/8	F2v2p28(18)
I'D RATHER HAVE A PIECE THAN A KISS OF MY JO	4H2H4H4	4H2H1H5	D	6/8	A1v1p28/29
IF E'ER YE DO WELL IT'S A WONDER	135	556	D	3/4	O1v2p5 O1v3p33 C5v2p61 O1v1Ap27 (J3) Mc8v1Ap27 Mc8v2Bp12
(IF I HAD/HE THAT HAS) A BONNIE LASSIE (LITTLE SLEEP WOU'D SAIR ME)	3535	2427bL	G	4/4*	C8v2p6 C8v1p8 K1v2p21 Mc4v2p5 G11v2Bp19
IF LOVE IS THE CAUSE OF MY MOURNING	133	321	F	3/4	P7p10
IF LOVE'S A SWEET PASSION	443b	43b5	G	3/4	O1v1Dp29
IF THOU WERE MINE OWN THING	551H3H	2H2H65	D	2/2	Y1p5
I'LL BID MY HEART BE STILL	115L4L	7bL7bL7bL3b	B	4/4	C10v2Ap40
I'LL DRINK A HEALTH TO CHARLIE	1212	1535	A	6/8	C6p29
I'LL GANG NA MAIR TO YON TOWN	11H31	3131	G	4/4	C1v2p2
I'LL GANG NAE MAIR TO YON TOWN	11H31	3132	D G F	4/4*	G9v1p1,2,3 A7v5p22 E1v1p7 A1v1p13 O1v1Jp101 K1v1p30 G7p18 G1v1p25 N1v1p10 P5v2p15 C13v2p17 P5v3p10 B11p26 G11v2Ap28 B15v1p6 C8v1p6 Mc7p3,4 G9v5p35 C4p6 (II)
I'LL HAE A PIPER TO MY GUDEMAN	33H3H6	33H1H5	D	6/8	C18p26
I'LL HAE HER AWA' IN SPITE O' HER MOTHER	1333	1342	G	6/8	C5v2p69
I'LL HAE HER AWA' IN SPITE O' HER MINNIE	113	323	G	6/4	C20p42,43
I'LL KISS THE WIFE SHE BAD ME	5151	5575	G	4/4*	A7v6p11 D13p14,15 B15v2p12,13 G1v2p82
I'LL KISS THE WIFE SHE BADE ME	5151	5575	G	2/2	A7v5p23
I'LL LOVE NO MORE	3H3H1H	5H5H3H	D	3/4	O1v1Kp137
I'LL MAKE YOU BE FAIN TO FOLLOW ME	31H2H2	31H71H	D C	6/8	C5v2p27 G1v2p58 E1v1p104,105 (J3) G11v2Ap20 N1v1p31 Mc21v3p6 B15v1p24 C13v2p12 S12v1p10 K1v1p22 C14v13p2 G9v5p5 Mc7p16 B10p7 (II)
I'LL MAKE YOU BE FOND TO FOLLOW ME	351H3H	2H222	D	4/4	O1v1lp72
I'LL NE'ER RETURN MORE	35L5L5L	6L16L6L	Bb	3/8	C10v2Ap51
I'LL NEVER GO TO FRANCE	1151H	5542	D	4/4	G9v5p22
I'LL NEVER LEAVE THEE	133	333	D	3/4	O1v4p36 C1v3 O1v1Ep14 S16p108,109
I'LL NEVER LEAVE THEE	135	331	G A D	3/4	C5v2p21 G17p20 P4p11 (J3)
I'LL NEVER LEAVE THEE	135	333	D	3/4	N1v2p7 Mc8v1Cp77 Mc8v2Ap22 C20p79
I'LL NEVER LOVE MAIR THO' LIVE TO THREESCORE	3H3H1H	5H5H3H	D	3/4	C5v2p35
I'LL NEVER SEE HIM MORE	5552	4423	D	2/2	O1v1Fp16
I'LL TELL YOU WHAT	5L135	6216L	G	2/4	A7v6p64
I'LL TELL YOU WHAT	3L135	6216L	F	2/4	A7v3p9
I'LL TOUZLE YOUR KURCHY	13b51H	3bH7b45	E	6/8	A1v1p2
ILL WIFE, THE	1H1H66	5322	D	4/4	C5v3p71
ILLUMINATION (NOVEMBER THE 5th, 1788), THE	115L5L	7bL47bL7bL	A	4/4	A7v6p7 A7v2p2
ILLUMINATION (9TH) FEBR. 1781, THE	1H3H2H1H	1H3H2H1H	G	2/2	M4v1p8 Mc9v3p8
IMIR FEIN, A CHOINNICH CHRIDHE	57b1H1H	1H7b51	E	4/4	Mc5p18
IN INFANCY OUR HOPES AND FEARS	1H1H1H2H	3H3H3H4H	C	4/4	E1v2p33
IN MY COTTAGE NEAR A WOOD	5566	501H2H	G	4/4	E1v1p67
IN THE GARB OF OLD GAUL	1H1H1H3H	1H51H1H	D	4/4	C5v3p73 (II)
IN THE STYLE OF AN OPERA DANCE	131H1	27L27L	D	6/8	G10v3p35
IN WINE THERE IS ALL	335	111H	D	3/4	A1v3p187
IN YOUTH WHEN THE HEART IS WARM	13b51	7bL4L7bL7bL	G	2/4	C10v2Bp37
INCH OF GARTH	1H151	23H3H6	D	4/4	A1v5p55
INCH OF GARTH	1H151	24H3H6	D	2/2	Mc4v1p4
INDEPENDENTS MARCH, THE	1H113H	3H115H	D	4/4	R6v1p9
INDIAN CHIEF	5141H	527L5L	Bb	2/4	C14v2p14,15
INDIANS MARCH	1113	25L5L7L	A G	4/4	W4v1p14 A1v4p39
INN OF KILLIN, THE	3b5L7L5L	7bL644	G	2/2	P9p15
INNES'S JIG	1356	636L2	G	6/8	A1v3p209
INNOCENT MAID, THE	5151	6L7L32	A	6/8	B16v3p88

52

INSH OF PERTH	5357b	4246	A	4/4	B15v1p69
INSTALLATION, THE	1115	227L7L	Bb	2/2	C14v21p12,13
INSTALLATION, THE	1H1H65	1H523	D	6/8	B16v3p95
INVERCALLDS REEL [INVERCAULD'S REEL]	11H51H	22H66	D	2/2	S12v1p54
INVERCAULD'S SCOTS MEASURE	425L3	7bL45L3	G	2/2	Mc9v2p26
INVERCAULD'S STRATHSPEY	1551H	152H2	D	4/4	Mc21v2p29
INVERCAULD'S STRATHSPEY	4L5L15L	5L6L3b3b	A	4/4	A7v6p39 S7v1p39 (II)
INVERCAULD'S(REEL/RANT/STRATHSPEY)	5L6L26L	5L6L44	G A D	4/4*	Mc9v1p26 S12v1p31 A7v2p29
					C33p10 P5v2p24 (II)
					B15v1p107
INVERESHIE	1L3L11	526L6L	Bb	4/4	M4v3p8
INVERESK HOUSE	3452	1232	Bb	6/8	G9v3p20
INVEREY'S OR CAPTAIN MCKENZIE'S	13b53b	7bL27bL7bL	A	4/4*	H3p2 A1v6p5 P5v2p9
(REEL/STRATHSPEY)					
INVEREYS RANT	1531	2427bL	A	2/2	D14v3p22 (II)
INVEREY'S STRATHSPEY	1L153	2L246L	A	4/4	P5v1p21
INVERNESS or [NORTHERN MEETING, THE]	5L3L1L3	437L2	A	2/2	M12p30
INVERNESS NORTHERN MEETING	3546	3561H	F	2/4	J2p3
INVERNESS SCOTS MEASURE, THE	1122	5223	D	2/2	O1v1Fp28
INVERNESS SCOTS MEASURE, THE	1122	6223	D	4/4	A1v2p35
INVERNESSHIRE HUNT	7L5L32	1353	Bb	2/2	C14v18p17
INVERNYTY'S (REEL/RANT)	1H1H35	67b24	D	2/2	Mc9v1p17 S12v1p28
INVERUGIE CASTLE	1H1H31	5L364	D	2/2	M11v1p17
IOMAN NAN GAMHNA	531	536	F	9/8	F2v2p57(47)
IOMRADH EADAR ILA 'S UIST	13b22	156b5	A	6/8	F2v2p26(16)
IORRAM IOMRUIGH [IORRAM IOMRAIMH]	3342	11H3H1H	D	6/8	F2v2p71(61)
IRISH	3322	3411	Bb	6/8	C22p40
IRISH AIR	17L6L1	3434	G	6/8	A1v6p50
IRISH AIR	3211	6542	G D	6/8	A1v6p42 Mc7p9
IRISH AIR	113	16L5L	G	3/4	A1v6p44
IRISH AIR	113	465	G	3/4	A1v6p39
IRISH AIR	111	7L7L5L	G	6/4	A1v4p21
IRISH AIR, AN	1H1H3H3H	2H1H55	G	4/4	A1v6p21
IRISH AIR, AN [IRISH GIRL, THE]	5L5L5L5L	6L6L13	G	6/8	Mc5p32 (II)
IRISH AIR, AN	1111	7bL3b7bL5L	A	6/8	Mc22p12 C5v1p66 A1v4p66
IRISH BILLY	13b52	13b55	A	6/8	A1v1p21
IRISH BLANKET, THE	1116	51H4H7	D	6/8	Mc9v2p30,31
IRISH CRY, THE	5H2H5H	1T1T2T	D	3/4	T7p46,47
IRISH DANCE	3335	2224	G	6/8	A1v6p44
IRISH DANCE	315	422H	D	9/8	C22p46
IRISH DANCE	1H56	62H7	D	9/8	C22p49
IRISH DANCE	1H3H4H	3H4H7	D	9/8	C22p32
IRISH DUMP, AN	5551	3b3b44	E	4/4	A1v6p46
IRISH FOOTMAN, THE	13b52	13b55	B	6/8	O1v1Dp14
IRISH GIRL	1H355	1H353H	D	6/8	A7v6p15
IRISH GIRL, (THE)	5L133	3323	G A	6/8	A7v5p9 E1v1p36 G11v1Bp27
					A7v2p21 G10v2p15
IRISH HAUTBOY, THE	5L133	4336L	G	4/4*	H1p33 A1v1p5
IRISH HEROES, THE	134	512	F	9/8	C1v4p7
IRISH HOBOY	5L133	4437L	A	2/4	B16v2p10
IRISH HOP, THE	1H1H5H	6H4H2H	C	9/8	H1p19
IRISH LAMENTATION	333	331	G	3/4	W7p14
IRISH LASSES	11H2H2H	6b554	E	6/8	A1v2p11
IRISH LASSES, THE	3151	25L7L2	D	6/8	C24v2p13
IRISH LASSIE, THE	3352	6L6L25L	G	6/8	A1v3p228
IRISH LILT	3142	1H531	D	6/8	A1v1p68
IRISH LILT, THE	2H2H2H7	1H3H72H	D	6/8	O1v1Jp103
IRISH MILKMAID, THE	35L33	35L31	A	6/8	C1v1p4 C14v7p3
IRISH MORSHAW	1H3H3H5H	5H5H5H3H	D	6/8	A1v3p200
IRISH PELT	5152	5157b	E	6/8	A1v3p203
IRISH POT STICK, THE	351H	356	D	9/8	O1v1Ip77
IRISH QUICK STEP, THE	315	422H	D	9/8	C14v12p10,11
IRISH SHANTRUSE	15L1	666	Bb	9/8	P5v4p14
IRISH SHELALEY, THE	3122	3153	D	6/8	E2p23
IRISH TROTT	46b46b	543b5	D	6/8	A1v1p52
IRISH TUNE, AN	3333	5331	G	4/4	Y1p24
IRISH WASHER WOMAN, THE	35L35	45L46	G	6/8	C14v5p4
(IRISH) WASHER WOMAN, (THE)	35L35	46L46	F G	6/8	D16p20 G10v3p31 A1v4p8
					H6v22p1 Mc7p8 C8v2p47 Mc12v1p7
					(II)
(IRISH) WATERMAN, THE	5312	5L5L5L2	A G	6/8	A7v2p20 S7v1p59 A7v6p20
IRISH WEDDING(A FAVOURITE DANCE), THE	1H565	1H2H3H1H	C	6/8	G11v2Cp20 C24v2p12 P11v1p14
IRISH WHIM	2H2H71H	1H3bH2H2H	D	6/8	R12v1p42
IRISH WHISKY	1551	2662	F	6/8	C1v1p2
IRISH WIDOW	556L6	5217L	F	6/8	S7v1p97
IRON CHEST, THE	3H4H1H1H	346H1H	C	2/4	A1v6p16
IRON TOWER	1541H	547L2	Bb	2/2	C14v22p9
IRVIN STIPLE [IRVINE STEEPLE]	1H1H35	67b24	D	4/4*	B15v1p36 (II)
IS MOR MO MHULAD 'S CHA LUGHA	1H66	3H2H1H	C	3/4	Mc5p14
M'EASLAINT					
IS YOUR GRAITH IN ORDER	1552	1555	D	4/4	K1v1p4 G11v2Ap4
ISLA REEL	5153	61H53	G	2/2	G8p35

Title			Key	Time	Sources
ISLA REEL, THE	3111	5L132	A	2/2	Mc9v3p33 C14v17p12
ISLAND OF LOVE	5212	47L5L2	G	2/2	S7v1p44
ISLAND OF MULL, THE	315L5L	3132	A	6/8	G11v2Dp10
ISLAY BACHELOR'S STRATHSPEY	15L2L2	15L1L5L	Bb	4/4	Mc16p36
ISLAY HOUSE	1H1H55	1H2H3H6	C D	6/8	Mc7p1 G1v2p80
ISLE OF MAN	1525	2424	A	2/2	C14v15p15
ISLE OF MULL, THE	313L5L	4L422	Bb	2/2	G8p3 P1v1p1
ISLE OF SKY	5142	5142	D	4/4*	K1v2p12 A1v3p164/165 G11v2Bp10
(THE PRINCE'S WELCOME TO THE)					C20p69
ISLE OF SKY, THE	1H31H3	422H6	D	4/4*	A1v4p60 A7v5p26 G1v2p72 A7v6p3
ISLE OF SKY, (THE)	13L13L	4L2L26L	Bb	4/4*	Mc21v4p7 K1v1p34,35 N1v1p22
					A7v2p17 C13v2p5 B15v1p7
					P5v2p23 P5v3p9 G11v2Ap32
					Mc9v3p30 G9v5p30,31 Mc12v1p48
					C14v7p3 (II)
ISLINGTON ASSEMBLY	3142	427L5L	G	6/8	S7v1p73
ISOBAIL NI CAOIDH	1142	57bL7bL4	A	4/4	D14v2p40
IT WAS O'ER IN YON SOA	112	315L	G	3/4	C10v2Ap28
IT WINNA DO	121H2H	7b427bL	D	2/2	Mc22p6
ITALIAN DANCE	5H5H1H1H	5565	D	4/4	H1p23
ITALIAN DANCE	5H1H56	5H1H2H1H	D	2/4	S7v1p55
ITALIAN MONFRINA	1321	7L221	G	6/8	B7p34
ITALIAN PEASANTS	5555	561H5	G	2/2	S12v2p10,11
IT'S NAE AY FOR WANT O' HEALTH	5H564	53H1H6	A D	2/2	C18p37 (II)
THE LADIES GANG TO PANNANICH					
IT'S NOUGHT BUT THE LOVE O' THE TOCHER	1H5H2H	1H5H2H	C	9/8	C5v2p38
I'VE KISS'D AND I'VE PRATTLED	51H75H	661H1H	C	6/8	E1v2p88,89
I'VE MADE A VOW	5L5L5L2	3L6L46L	Bb	3/8	C10v2Ap32
I'VE NOT SAID HOW MUCH I LOVE HER	51H3H5H	1H2H4H1H	G	3/8	B7p27
I'VE SEEN MID-WINTERS DREARY HOURS	5L5L11	225L5L	F	4/4	C10v2Bp6
IVY BUDS, THE	3H2H1H6	3H2H51H	D	6/8	O1v1p78
J. LEE ALLAN ESQ OF ERROL'S STR.	1355	4423	F	2/2	B6v3p1
JACK HOLME'S REEL	3535	3524	A	6/8	R12v1p39
JACK IN THE BOX	1565	4225L	G	2/4	R12v1p3
JACK IN THE WEST	113b	7bL7bL4	E	9/8	G1v2p74
JACK O' THE GREEN	112	7bL7b4	D	9/8	A7v3p22
JACK OF THE GREEN	7L12	523	D	9/8	O1v1Lp140
JACK ON THE GREEN	112	353	D	9/4	R12v1p32
JACK RATLIN	5551H	51H2H2	G	4/4	C26v1p23
JACK RATLIN	1H1H3H4H	71O1H	D	4/4	A1v5p15
JACK THE SAILOR	5166	5132	Bb	6/8	W4v1p3
JACKEY LAITEN [JACK LATTIN]	1353	5353	G	4/4	A7v6p70 (II)
JACKIE LATIN	1553	5353	D G	4/4*	C14v2p13 Mc23p27 A7v5p37
					Mc8v1Dp110,111 C20p57
					O1v1Lp144,145
JACK'S ALIVE	1324	3432	G	6/8	G11v2Cp17
JACK'S DELIGHT	1H2H76	326L6L	G	2/2	R12v1p41 (W3)
JACK'S DELIGHT	311H1H	2H2H22	D	4/4	S7v1p66
JACK'S GRATITUDE	1H3H5H5H	3H1H2H2H	D	4/4	A1v4p73
JACKSON OVER THE WATER	3b3b44	5544	D	6/8	A1v3p177
JACKSON OVER THE WATER, 1780	3344	5544	G	6/8	A1v6p51
JACKSON'S BOUNER BOUGHER	5231	5261H	D	6/8	A1v3p208
JACKSON'S COG IN THE MORNING	5L127bL	7bL7bL7bL5L	G	6/8	H1p16
JACKSON'S DREAM	1153	5322	D	6/8	C14v14p20 A1v2p20 C23p11
JACKSON'S FOLLY	1343	1356	D	6/8	C24v2p14
JACKSON'S FROLICK	5333	4322	D	6/8	H1p5 A1v3p191
JACKSON'S HOBBY	3b215L	3b214L	A	6/8	C24v2p14
JACKSON'S MORNING BRUSH	1215	61H3H2H	D	6/8	A1v1p8
JACKSON'S MORNING BRUSH	1215	61H4H2H	D	6/8	H1p11
JACKSON'S NIGHT CAP	1H763	1H71H2	D	6/8	C14v5p11 A1v3p161
JACKSON'S QUANDERY	5355	47b66	D	6/8	H1p34
JACKSON'S RAKES OF KILKENNY	113	116	D	9/8	H1p6
JACKSON'S RAMBLE	35L32	35L37L	A	6/8	C24v2p14
JACKSON'S ROLLER	135L4	1356	D	6/8	H1p29
JACKSON'S TUNET	1H1H1H3H	2H2H2H4H	D	2/4	A1v6p51
JACKY STEWARTS REELL	5151	47bL7b7bL	E	2/2	B15v1p7
JACKY TAR [JACK A' TAR]	1H1H1H3bH	7b557b	E	4/4	C8v2p25 C8v1p16 (II)
JACKY TARR	1H1H3bH2H	7b554	E	4/4	A7v5p13
JACQUETTA AGNETTA MARIANA JENKS	35L3L5L	2L27L6L	G	4/4	P9p20
JAMAICA	1113	6361H	G	2/2	Mc8v2Bp17 Mc9v2p7
JAMES B. DUNBAR'S STRATHSPEY	1353	2416L	D	4/4	T1v2p1
JAMES DUFF M.P.	1H564	4H2H75	F	2/2	M4v4p6
JAMES FERGUSSON ESQr W.S.'S REEL	3151H	3162	D	2/2	Mc19v2p19
JAMES HADDEN, ESQr's HORNPIPE	3555	3555	Bb	4/4	D6p33
JAMES PORTEOUS'S FAREWELL TO WHISKY	5165	51H3H1H	F	4/4	P9p40
JAMES PORTEOUS'S FIDDLE	5653	5324	F	2/2	P9p40
JAMES ROBERTSON, ESQr's STRATHSPEY	53b11	57b11	E	4/4	Mc19v3p7
JAMIE BOICK, A STRATHSPEY	3b527bL	3b51H5	E	4/4	P11v2p6
JAMIE COME TRY ME	113	661H	Eb G	3/4	(J3) C5v3p60 O1v4p26
JAMIE ROY	5522	5526L	D	2/2	Mc9v3p36 Mc12v1p49
JAMY COME TRY ME	113	667	G	3/4	O1v1Bp34
JANETT DRINKS NO WATTER	1H51H1H	2H223	C	2/2	Y1p13

Title			Key	Time	References
JANNY CAMERON'S REEL	3H1H2H5	2H52H2H	D	4/4	C13v1p14,15
JANNY NETTLES	3b211H	57b42	A	4/4	Mc21v4p41
JARNOVICHI'S HORNPIPE	4162	5675	E	2/4	G10v4p25
JARNOWICK, THE	5H3H2H3H	4H3H2H2H	D	2/4	W4v2p5
JEANETTE AND JEANNOT	3333	5133	G	2/4	C8v2p64
JEANIE IS FAUSE AN' UNKIND	3b13b1	3b7b50	A	6/8	C5v2p42
JEAN'S THE BEST OF (ANY/MY LOVE'S)	1H111	3551H	D C	4/4*	C5v3p54 Y1p22
JEANY LATIN	1565	151H1H	D	4/4	Mc9v3p33
JEM OF ABERDEEN	3331	2245	Bb	4/4	C19p11
JENKINS(' HORNPIPE)	1357L	671H7L	Bb	4/4*	C8v1p29 (II)
JENKINS'S DUSTY MILLER	1H1H1H	3H1H5	E	3/2	J1p31
JENKINS'S SHANTRUSE	5532	1H553H	E	2/2	J1p45
JENNY AND I	365	642	G	3/4	O1v4p15 O1v1Ep27
JENNY CAMERON ('S REEL)	3H1H2H5	2H52H2H	D	4/4	Mc13v2p14,15 A7v6p94,95
JENNY COME TYE MY GRAVAT	313	554	D	3/4	O1v1Fp14,15
JENNY DANG THE WEAVER	1H555	1H53H2H	D	4/4*	C8v1p14 E1v1p45 C8v2p18 G7p10
					K1v1p36 S12v1p13 Mc21v3p21
					N1v1p14 C13v2p23 C14v7p14
					G11v2Ap34 (II)
JENNY DANG THE WEAVER	3H555	1H53H2H	D	2/2	B15v1p54
JENNY DANG THE WEAVER	3H555	3H53H2H	D	2/2	R12v1p36
JENNY DANG THE WEAVER	5H555	51H3H2H	D	4/4	A7v6p40
JENNY DANG THE WEAVER	1H111	1465	A	4/4*	A7v5p33 A7v2p32,33
JENNY DRINKS NAE WATER	1H61H1H	2H226	D	2/2*	Mc8v2Bp12 Mc9v2p5 C5v2p29
					E1v2p139 (II)
JENNY JONES	1H53	123	D	3/4	C8v2p10 C8v1p30
JENNY LIND POLKA	3453H	42H31H	G	2/4	C8v2p52
JENNY LIND POLKA	3L4L5L3	4L23L1	Bb	2/4	C8v1p28
JENNY MY BLITHEST MAID	351H	3H2H6	G	3/4	O1v1Gp25
JENNY NETTLES	3b3b11H	57b47bL	Bb G	4/4*	(J3) C19p21
JENNY NETTLES	3b211H	5547bL	A	4/4	B15v1p80
JENNY NETTLES	3b211H	57b47bL	A	4/4*	C8v2p30 C8v1p11 G1v2p55 G7p14
					G9v5p22 C14v8p12 A1v2p31 Mc7p8
					G11v1Bp27 G10v3p16 (II)
JENNY SUTTON	1155	1147L	G A	4/4*	A1v4p15 G11v1Cp33 C24v2p19
					G10v2p4 P10p10 C14v1p1 (II)
JENNY SUTTON	1155	1137L	G	2/2	C5v1p15
JENNY'S BABEE [JENNY'S BAWBEE]	3H5H3H1H	4H675	D	2/2	C13v2p79 (II)
JENNY'S BAWBEE	5H5H3H1H	62H75	C D	4/4*	C19p5 A7v5p37 A7v6p49
					Mc21v3p25 D15v1p25 A1v4p29
					E1v1p13 G9v5p13
JENNY'S BAWBEE	5H5H3H1H	4H675	D	2/2	Mc10p2
JENNY'S BAWBEE	5H5H3H1H	4H2H75	D	4/4*	(D2) G11v2Ap36 N1v1p32 C8v2p50
					C14v9p17 C1v1p8 K1v1p38
					Mc17p7 (II)
JENNY'S BAWBIE	5H3H67	5H3H61H	D	2/4	Mc7p7
JENNY'S BAWBIE	5531	427L5L	G Bb	2/4	(J3) C6p26
JENNY'S HORNPIPE	3L5L35	1H765	Eb	4/4	P9p17
JENNY'S JOE	4245	521HO	G	4/4	O1v1Lp146
JENNY'S WHIM	3111	351H7	F	4/4	S7v1p82
JESS McFARLANE	3310	1H62H5	G	4/4	A1v5p55
JESSAMINE BOWER, THE	3b111H	3bH7b43b	E	4/4	O1v1Lp162
JESSIE, THE FLOWER OF DUMBLANE	3H2H1H2H	531H2H	D	6/8	C5v2p40 C8v2p44
JESSONDA	554#6	1H42#4	F	4/4	T8p1
JEW, THE	3531	1332	G	2/4	C26v1p17
JIG	11H53	1327L	Bb	6/8	D15v1p2
JIG	15L5L5L	7L245	G	6/8	C22p47
JIG	5311H	7755	F	6/8	Mc9v2p3
JIGG	11H36	3527L	Bb	6/8	Mc21v1p10,11
JIGG	11H2H7	6231	Eb	6/8	Mc21v1p18
JIGG, A	1155	7b547bL	A	6/8	C5v1p28 A1v5p28
JIGG, A	13b3b5	23b12	B	6/8	A1v5p71
JIGG, A	3324	3335	A	6/8	A1v5p68
JIGG, A	1H1H1H1H	4H3H72H	F	6/8	W4v2p27
JIGG, A	111H1H	1H542	F	6/8	W4v2p30
JIGG, A	1H33	1H32	G	9/8	A1v5p71
JIGG TO THE IRISH CRY	1H1H1H3H	1H1H72H	D	6/8	T7p48,49
JINGLIN' JOHNNY	1122	1122	G	4/4	C5v2p34
JINK ABOUT	5453	5524	A	6/8	A1v3p189
JINKING OF THE LOOM, THE	1131	7L7L27L	D	2/2	S5p12
JINKINSON'S HORNPIPE	1364	2H765	G	4/4	W4v2p31
Jn. GOW'S COMPLIMENTS TO THE MINSTRELS OF SCOTLAND	13bL15	63b3b7bL	A	4/4	G10v6p33
JOB OF JOURNEY WORK, THE	5155	5421	G	2/4	A1v3p155
JOCK O' HAZELDEAN	5215L	1432	Eb G F	4/4*	C6p29 E1v2p69 C8v1p22
JOCK O' HAZELDEAN	5H2H1H5	1H4H3H2H	D	2/4	C8v2p40
JOCK O' THE SIDE	5L115L	1140	G	6/8	C10v2Bp29
JOCKEY AND JENNY	351H	642	G	3/4	P8v2p20
JOCKEY AND PEGGIE	5151	5575	G	2/2	C4p65
JOCKEY CLUB, THE	3H1H2H5	1H542	D	2/2	Mc21v2p1 (II)
JOCKEY LATIN [JACK LATIN] [JACKIE LATIN]	1553	5354	G	2/2	G11v2Cp18

JOCKEY TO THE FAIR	1355	3122	G	6/8	S7v1p3
JOCKEY'S DREAM	3b221	113b3b	G	2/2	O1v1Jp99
JOCKEY'S RETURN FROM DOVER	15L6L5L	1135	A	6/8	D15v2p21/22
JOCKIE AND SANDIE	13b5	1H1H7b	E D	3/4	(J3) P4p28
JOCKIE BLYTH AND GAY	342	666	D	3/4	P4p13 O1v1Ap2,3 O1v2p2,3
					O1v3p10,11
JOCKIE BLYTH AND GAY	352	666	G D	3/4	C5v3p69 Mc8v1Ap20 Mc8v2Ap20
					(J3)
JOCKIE WAS THE BLYTHEST LAD	3bH3bH4H1H	1H1H55	C D	4/4*	Mc23p36,37 Mc8v1Dp113 Mc8v2Bp20
(IN ALL OUR TOWN)					O1v1Gp8
JOCKIE'S FOU & JANNIE'S FAINE	1352	131H5	G	4/4	C29p25
JOCK'S LODGE	3135	247bL2	A	4/4	B15v1p93
JOCKY AND JENNY	356	542	F G	3/4	O1v4p11 O1v1Ep31
JOCKY FOU AND JENNY FAIN	1142	5122	G	4/4	C5v2p45
JOCKY SAID TO JEANY	131	313	F G	3/2	(J3) O1v1Cp15
JOCKY SAID TO JENNY	111	313	G	3/2	S16p142,143 C20p36,37
JOCKY SAID TO JENNY	111	315	G	3/2	T6v2p14 P8v2p2
JOCKY TO THE FAIR	1355	3122	G	6/8	A1v2p2 E1v2p48
JOCKY'S DANCE	561H6	5663	G	2/4	W4v1p6 A1v4p36
JOCKY'S GRAY BREECHES	554	117bL	B	3/4	O1v4p6,7 O1v1Bp32
JOCULAR, THE	5511	27L11	Bb	2/4	S7v3p12
JOHN ANDERSON, ESQr's HORNPIPE	572H3H	4H2H75	F	4/4	D6p34,35
JOHN ANDERSON MY JO	5L111	3b3b3b4	A	2/2	S16p114,115
JOHN ANDERSON MY JO	5L111	3b3b54	G	4/4	O1v1Dp22,23
JOHN ANDERSON, MY JO	5L122	3b3b3b4	G B A	4/4*	C8v1p45 C5v3p70 C8v2p64
					(J3)
JOHN ANDERSON, MY JO, JOHN	5L13b3b	27bL7bL7bL	A G	2/4	C6p5 A1v2p61/62
JOHN ANDERSON MY JOE	5L112	3b3b3b4	A	2/2	E1v2p114
JOHN ANDERSON'S (AULDEST) DAUGHTER	3b25L7bL	7bL7bL13b	A	2/4	G11v1Cp6 G10v3p36 A1v4p29
JOHN BARLYCORN	1524	151H5	D	12/8	F3p4,5
JOHN BULL'S REEL	3H511	437L2	C	2/2	P9p33
JOHN BURTON	4#231	3522	G	2/4	R12v1p14
JOHN CHEAP THE CHAPMAN	153b3b	1527bL	G	4/4*	K1v2p15 G11v2Bp13 (II)
JOHN COME ALONG	1H71H1H	3H2H3H3H	D	2/4	A1v3p166
JOHN COME KISS ME NOW	1112	4443	G	4/4	G9v1p34,35,36 Mc8v1Dp94,95
					B15v2p6,7 Mc7p11 A1v4p31
					D13p8,9
JOHN COME KISS ME NOW	1132	4443	G F	4/4	C5v2p35 O1v1Fp2,3 (J3)
JOHN CUMINE ESQr OF AUCHRY'S STRATHSPEY	1532	6L5L4L3	Bb	4/4	C18p12
JOHN FRENCH'S COMPts TO MR NATH. GOW	5316L	5L132	Eb	4/4	F3p18
JOHN GULLIVER'S REEL	1313	1H2H75	D	2/2	P9p28
JOHN HAY'S BONNIE LASSIE	5L11	113	F G D	3/4	T6v1p74 O1v1Cp20 Mc8v1Ap7
					P8v2p44 N1v2p50 (J3) P4p5
					S16p132-135
JOHN HAY'S BONNY LASSIE	133	113	D	3/4	C29p2,3
JOHN HIGHLANDMAN	51H1H5	52H2H2H	C	6/8	C10v2Bp75
JOHN KNOX	137L4	46L11	Bb	2/4	O1v5p18
JOHN McGREGOR'S STRATHSPEY	1565	1366	D	4/4	Mc19v1p8
JOHN MENZIES, ESQr OF CHESTHILL'S STRATHSPEY	1H2H1H6	5642	F	2/2	Mc19v1p10
JOHN MORISON'S COMPts TO MR NATHI. GOW	1126L	1151H	D	2/2	M11v1p3
JOHN O' BADENYON(D)	15L15L	3b3b7bL7bL	Bb G B	4/4*	A1v3p212 C8v1p45 Mc7p32
					Mc9v3p23 (J3) E1v2p115
JOHN OCHILTREE	1H2H4H7	1H2H1H5	D	6/8	Mc8v1Dp104 T6v2p109
JOHN OF BADENYON	15L15L	3b417bL	A	4/4	A7v3p12,13
JOHN ROY STEWART	5313	5551	F	2/2	Mc7p19 H3p40
JOHN ROY STEWART	6313	5553	F	4/4	A7v2p13
(JOHN) ROY STEWART ('S REEL)	5313	5353	F G	4/4*	G11v2Ap26 C13v1p17 Mc9v1p30
					B17p24 K1v1p28 P5v2p19
					D15v1p19 C8v1p17 E1v1p54 (II)
					A1v3p176
JOHN ROY STEWART'S STRATHSPEY	6313	5353	G	4/4	A7v6p13
JOHN ROY'S FAREWEL	1H1H1H5	7b2H2H3bH	E	4/4	G8p36
JOHN SMALL'S MINUET	1326	1321	G	3/8	A1v3p181
JOHN STEWART ESQr. OF GARTH'S FAVORITE STRATHSPEY	1653	1H642	F	4/4	P5v4p18
JOHN TOD	1111	1111	A	6/8	C6p27
JOHNIE BLUNT	1212	1535	G	6/8	(J3) A1v5p18 C5v1p18
JOHNIE GORDON	1H535	6622H	C	4/4	H1p4
JOHNNIE FAA	1144	2255	A G E	4/4	C5v3p55 Mc8v1Dp107 Mc8v2Bp11
					(J3) G17p17 G11v2Dp11
					N1v2p13
JOHNNIE FAA	551H1H	662H2H	C	4/4*	B5p6 C20p10
JOHN(N)IE FAA	551H3H	6L6L2H2H	C	4/4	O1v1Gp23
JOHNNIE'S GREY BREEKS	3H4H61H	3135	C D	4/4*	A7v4p16 E1v1p27 C5v2p23
JOHNNY AND MARY	551H2H	551H2H	D C	4/4	A1v6p46 (J3)
JOHNNY AND NELLY	113	223	F G	3/4	T6v1p42 P8v2p21
JOHNNY COCK UP THE BEAVER	5324	5213	G	6/8	C4p44
(JOHNNY) COCK UP YOUR BEAVER	5324	5313	F G	6/8	R6v2p4 E1v2p119 O1v1Gp2,3
JOHNNY COPE	1112	5117bL	B A G	4/4*	C5v2p14 (J3) O1v1Ip73
JOHNNY COPE	1113b	5117bL	A	4/4	A1v2p19
JOHNNY COPE	1152	7bL7bL42	G A B	4/4*	Mc23p23 G9v1p29 Mc12v2p30

					E1v2p30 C20p54
JOHNNY GROAT'S HOUSE	1H1H1H1H	71H22	F	2/4	R12v1p5
JOHNNY IN THE NETHER MAINS	1113	6361H	F	4/4	G8p32 K1v2p2 Mc4v4p4 G11v2Bp2
JOHNNY LAD	1H3bH4H7b	1H3bH2H1H	D E	4/4*	A7v6p95 C18p19 (II)
JOHNNY MCGILL ('S JIG)	5353	5316L	G F	6/8	A1v2p44 (II) Mc9v2p33
					C13v2p31 B10p4
JOHNNY PRINGLE	5L153	5L153	G	4/4*	C14v24p16 G11v2Cp15 (II)
JOHNNY'S FRIENDS ARE NE'ER PLEASED	1133	3316L	G	2/2*	G11v2Dp30 (II)
JOHNNY'S GRAY BREECKES	5544	113b3b	A	4/4	Mc9v2p3
JOHNNY'S GRAY BREEKS	3342	6L6L11	Bb	4/4	N1v2p43
JOHNNY'S GRAY BREEKS	3H3H4H2H	661H5	D	4/4	C19p14
JOHNNY'S GREY BREEKS	346L1	3L1L3L5L	G Bb	2/4	A1v1p21
JOHNNY'S MADE A WADDING O'T	3531	2427bL	G	4/4*	C13v2p6 Mc9v3p18 S12v1p42
					G11v2Dp30 G9v5p11 Mc7p28
					Mc12v1p28 (II)
JOHNSON'S MUSIC SHOP	11H3H1H	6262	D	2/4	A7v6p69
JOHNSON'S MUSIC SHOP	1L131	6L2L6L2L	Bb	2/4	A7v3p6
JOHNSTON'S MOOR	5551	7bL647bL	E	2/2	A7v3p5
JOHNSTON'S REEL	1311H	5H2H2H6	E	2/2	M4v1p10
JOLLITY	1H531H	1H2H75	D	6/8	A1v1p7
JOLLITY	15L3L1	127L5L	Bb	6/8	R12v1p24
JOLLY BEGGAR, THE	1351	11H76	D F G	4/4	(J3) C8v1p57 C8v2p53
					C5v2p40 (II)
JOLLY BOAT	136L4	527L6L	A	4/4	C14v17p18
JOLLY RINGER'S, THE	7531	2H751	G	2/4	A1v4p73
JOLLY TOPER	3134	4245	A	4/4	S7v1p83
JORUM, (PUSH ABOUT [THE])	527L2	331H7	G	4/4*	G9v5p8 C14v18p12 A7v5p36
JORUM, (THE/PUSH ABOUT THE)	527L2	331H7	G	4/4*	C13v2p33 A7v6p30 A1v1p39
JOSEPH EST BIEN MARIE	751H2H	3bH3bH4H3bH	D	4/4	A1v6p49
JOSEPH'S FROLIC	5663	6542	D	6/8	A1v2p16
JOY GAE WI MY LOVE	7b152	7b151	A	6/8	K1v2p5
JOY GAE WI' MY LOVE	4H52H6	4H52H5	A	6/8	G11v2Bp5
JOY GO WITH MY LOVE	3H51H6	3H2H1H5	D	6/8	S12v1p24
JUBILEE OF 1810, THE	5125L	6L15L3L	Bb	6/8	D15v2p47
JUBILEE, THE	1316L	1314	A	4/4	Mc16p7
JUBILEE, THE	3H1H2H5	1H533	D	2/4	A1v2p33
JUDY OF FLANIGAN	1323	5L152	A	6/8	E1v1p48
JULIANA	5L131	5542	Bb	6/8	C14v25p1
JULIANA'S WALTZ	15L1	15L1	D	3/4	H1p27
JULIA'S COTTAGE	1H3H4H5H	5H2H1H7	C	6/8	C14v26p2
JUMPIN JOHN	3322	3212	G	6/8	C5v2p70
JUMPING JOAN	1H513	6L27L5L	G	2/2	C5v1p15 A1v4p15
JUMPIN(G) JOHN [JUMPING JOAN]	3322	3211	F Ab G	6/8	(J3) C6p23 O1v11p72,73
JUNTA OF SEVILLE, THE	1231	27L15	Bb	6/8	P6v1p28
JUST A GOING	3H3H3H3H	4H74H7	D	2/2	R12v1p79
JUST AS I WAS IN THE MORNING	1H327	1H351H	D	6/8	B15v1p64 R12v1p84
JUST AS I WAS IN THE MORNING	1H327	1H353H	D	6/8	O1v1Kp114
JUST SO	13b13b	427L2	E	2/4	S7v1p61
JUST SO IN THE NORTH	11H55	11H66	G	4/4	S7v1p91
KAIL REETS OF FITTIE, THE	5147bL	5154	A	6/8	C18p29
KATE AMANG THE CLOVER	3b3b13b	556b4	E	4/4	C5v2p66
KATE KEARNEY	51H2H1H	1H5H3H2H	D	6/8	B7p23
KATE OF ABERDEEN	1H1H3H7	3H555	E	4/4	C19p9
KATE OF ABERDEEN	553H2H	62H4H3H	D	4/4*	C5v2p39 O1v1Jp100
KATE OF KINROSS	122	541	A	3/4	O1v1Lp148
KATE'S DELIGHT	1H37L5L	1237L	G	6/8	B16v3p25
KATHERINE OGIE	5L110	3b212	G	4/4	T6v1p44
KATHERINE OGIE	5L111	3b217bL	A	4/4	S16p136,137 O1v1Dp2,3
KATH'RINE OGGIE	5L117bL	2112	A	4/4	C4p35
KAT(HRINE) OG(G)IE	5L111	3b212	G A B	4/4	(J3) N1v2p52 O1v5p6,7
					P8v2p23 G17p12 P4p23 Mc8v1Bp44
					Mc8v2Ap13 B5p1 C20p13
					E1v2p31
KATRIN HOGGIE	5L117bL	2112	A	4/4	Y1p12
KATTY DARLING	3427L	5L5L5L1	Bb	4/4	C8v1p40
KATTY O' LYNCH	1H565	1H54H5	D	6/8	E1v2p81
KATY MOONEY	1H111	3565	G	6/8	C8v1p9 C8v2p7
KATY'S COMPLAINT	552	111H	G F	3/4	O1v1Ep15 P4p25 O1v4p14
KEAPACH 'NA FASACH	111	3b17bL	E	9/8	Mc5p9
KEAPPOCH'S FAREWELL	5L113b	427bL1	G	4/4	C10v1p3
KEBBUCKSTANE WEDDING, THE	5152	5141	A	6/8	C5v2p49
KEEP THE COUNTRY BONNY LASSIE	5324	5353	A	2/2*	K1v2p27 G11v2Bp25 (II)
KEEP THE COUNTRY BONNY LASSIE	5324	531H3	A	2/2	C13v2p10
KEEP THE COUNTRY BONNY LASSIE	1324	1353	A	4/4*	P5v2p12 Mc7p24 G9v5p29 G9v5p26
					B15v1p32 S12v1p2 Mc9v3p41
					N1v1p14 B10p10
KEETHS REEL	3111	3152	G	6/8	B16v1p7
KEITH MORE	1561H	5222	Bb	4/4	P5v3p17
KEITH-HALL	5L5L15L	1311	Bb	4/4	D6p5
KEITHMORE	1553	1553	Eb	4/4	M4v3p59
KELO HOUSE	1L1L3bL5L	7bL5L2L2L	G	2/2	Mc13v1p9 Mc13v2p9 (II)
KELRAVOCK'S STRATHSPEY	1L11L1	2L26L6L	A	4/4	G11v1Bp3

Title					
KELSO BOWLINGREEN	1511	1522	D	12/8	C7p19
KELSO LASSES	1H33	1H32	G	9/8	S12v2p21
KELSO RACES	1H3H2H3H	1H3H3H6	D	6/6	G11v1Ap15
KELSO RACES	1323	1336L	D	6/8	E1v1p103
KELSO VOLUNTEERS MARCH, THE	1111	3356	A	4/4	C7p3
KELSO VOLUNTEERS QUICK STEP, THE	1122	3326L	A	6/8	C7p3
KELVIN GROVE	3216L	6L221	A	4/4	C6p13
KEMPSHOT HUNT	5333	3342	G	4/4	A7v6p91
KEMPSHOT(T) HUNT	5333	3442	A G	2/4	E1v1p86 G10v3p26 A1v4p64
KENILWORTH CASTLE	331H1H	337L7L	F	2/2	P9p3
KENMURE'S ON AN' AWA (WILLIE)	11H54	11H22	G	6/8	C5v2p66 (II)
KENMURE'S ON AND AWA' (WILLIE)	11H55	11H22	Eb G F	6/8	G11v2Dp4 B7p25 C8v2p63 E1v2p2 H1p10 (J3)
KENNET'S DREAM	332	16L5L	A	3/4	O1v1Jp106
KENTISH CRICKETERS, THE	51H51	51H72	D F	2/2	R12v1p88 Mc17p10
KENTISH MARCH	11H1H3	6L112	G	4/4	A1v3p209
KEPPEL'S DELIGHT	3566	637L7L	A	6/8	B16v3p91
KEPPOCH'S RANT	5155	4522	A	2/2	R12v1p63
KETTLEBENDER	3H3H1H1H	72H2H5H	D	4/4	O1v1Kp136,137
KEW GARDENS	3H2H72H	3H52H6	D	4/4	S7v1p71
KEY OF KINDNESS, THE	11H11H	22H66	D	4/4	A1v3p167
KEY OF THE CELLER, THE	3b11	5L11	G	3/2	G11v1Cp31
KEYS OF LOVE, THE	5536	5312	G	4/4	C5v2p48
KHEELLUM KHALLUM TAA FEIN	1342	1353	A	2/2	B15v1p108
KICK THE (ROGUES/SCRUBS) OUT	315	316	D	9/8	R12v1p37 B15v1p36 S12v2p27
KICK THE WORLD BEFORE YOU	315	316	D	9/8	O1v1Jp101
KIDS, THE	1H51H5	1H51H2	A	4/4*	Mc19v1p6 (II)
KILCRAIGIE	5565	2216L	E	4/4	G3p31,32
KILDRUMMIE CASTLE	1111H	356L2	G	6/8	S5p17
KILECRANKIE	3H3H4H4H	3H3H3H5H	D	4/4*	G11v1Cp16 G10v1p26 A7v6p87
KILLIN	4511	4527bL	A	2/2	Mc19v1p10 (II)
KILLWORTH VOLUNTEERS' QUICK MARCH, THE	3551H	3551H	G	2/4	A1v2p50
KILLYCRANKIE	5555	2155	D	4/4	A1v2p7
KILRACKS REEL	1L11L1	2L26L6L	A	4/4	Mc9v1p16
KILRACK'S STRATHSPEY	1L15L1	2L222	A	4/4	G10v1p29
KILRAVOCK VOLUNTEER'S MARCH, THE	1H1H1H3	5553H	D	4/4	L1p22
KILRAVOCK'S REELL	51H51H	22H2H6	D	2/2	C33p17
KILRAVOCK'S STRATHSPEY	1L15L1	2L26L6L	G	4/4	A7v3p23
KILWINAN LODGE	3131	1H342	F	4/4*	N1v1p19 B15v1p38,39
KINCALDRUM'S REEL	1H532	7L242	G	4/4*	K1v2p20 P5v3p13 G11v2Bp18 (II)
KIND GOODWIFE OF KETTICH'S MILL, THE	3132	3142	G	6/8	S5p20
KIND KIMMER	1565	1565	G	2/4	G11v1Cp13
KIND ROBIE COME AGAIN	3L5L15L	5L325L	A	2/2	C18p29
KIND ROBIN LO'ES ME	1111	226L6L	G F	4/4*	G11v2Dp5 C5v2p6 (J3)
KIND ROBIN LO'ES ME	1111	226L5L	G	4/4	C8v1p9 C8v2p7 G1v1p24
KIND ROBIN LO'ES ME	1H1H1H1H	2H2H65	C	4/4	E1v2p16
KINDNESS FOR EVER MAIR	3H3H1H1H	3H1H2H2H	D	4/4	C5v3p71 G11v2Cp13
KINEGAD SLASHERS	1H1H55	1H1H22H	C	6/8	H1p19
KINFAUN'S HOUSE	353	211H	F	3/4	G10v5p10
KING CRISPIN	5322	5331H	Bb	2/2	P9p36
KING OF CORSICA, THE	15L31	46L7L5L	G	6/8	C1v1p2
KING OF FRANCE HE RUN A RACE, THE	1343	2427bL	G	2/4	O1v1Hp60
KING OF FRANCE, THE	1343	27b27bL	A	2/2	C13v2p73
KING OF POLAND'S ALLEMAND	5231H	5211H	A	2/4	S7v1p2
KING OF PRUSSIA'S HORNPIPE	1H1H3H1H	1H1H1H5	D	2/2	S12v2p1
KING[OF PRUSSIA]'S MARCH	5H5H5H4H	3H3H3H2H	D	4/4	R4p15
KING OF PRUSSIA'S REEL	11H52	31H52	D	6/8	B15v1p25
KING OF PRUSSIA'S WALTZ, THE	1H3H2H1H	1H3H1H1H	F	3/8	G9v3p36
KING OF SWEDEN'S MARCH	3H3H1H3H	4H4H4H5H	D	2/2	A1v3p168/169
KING OF THE CATTI	5436	5522	G	6/8	C14v23p10,11
KING SHALL ENJOY HIS OWN AGAIN, THE	551H1H	2H4H3H2H	D	4/4	G9v3p4
KING SHALL ENJOY, THE	1H1H2H4H	3H2H4H6	D	4/4	O1v1Bp20
KING SHALL ENJOY, THE	0055	1H1H2H4H	D	4/4	O1v4p8,9
KING STREET FESTINO	1134	1423	G	6/8	S7v1p43
KING'S ANTHEM, THE	1H1H2H	772H	D	3/4	A1v3p200
KINGS ARMS, THE	1555	51H2H5	D	6/8	W7p3
KING'S BIRTH DAY	1H3H4H2H	3H3H77	C	2/4	S7v1p15
KING'S BIRTH DAY, THE	5313	437L7L	Bb	2/2	C21p19
KING'S JIG, THE	1H2H3H2H	7662H	D	6/8	Mc9v2p22
KING'S JIG, THE	3565	25L35	D	6/8	C22p20
KING'S PARK, THE	1L3L1L3L	1L116L	A	4/4	P9p11
KING'S WELCOME TO SCOTLAND, THE	5L13b3b	427bL1	A	2/2	B20p21
KINGSBRIDGE ASSEMBLY	3H3H1H5	6543	D	6/8	B16v3p86
KININVIE HOUSE	351H2	351H1H	C	4/4	M4v3p46
KINLOCH OF KINLOCH [KINLOCH'S FAVORITE]	3H565	3H561H	D	6/8	B7p35 C8v2p63 G1v2p66 (II)
KINMONT WILLIE	1122	3322	F	4/4	C10v2Ap78
KINNAIRD CASTLE	1124	1127L	Bb	6/8	D15v1p3
KINNOUL PEEBLE HORNPIPE	5H4H1H7	2H1H55	D	2/4	A7v4p26
KINRARA	11H1H5	11H1H2	D	4/4	G1v2p63
KINRARA	1L115L	1L322L	Bb	4/4	P5v3p7
KINRARA	1L115L	1L122L	Bb	4/4	M4v3p2

KINRARA COTTAGE	1L115L	1L112L	Bb	4/4	A7v4p4
KINRARA(STRATHSPEY)	115L6L	1122L	Bb	2/2*	M4v3p2 (11)
KIRKALDY MERCHANT'S HALL	151H1H	51H22	D	2/2	W2v1p7
KIRKFORTHER	333	554	A	3/4	O1v1Jp108,109
KIRKMICHAEL PLOUGHS	15L13	15L22L	Bb	4/4	P5v1p4
KIRKOSWOLD REEL, THE	31H53H	4H3H2H7	D	4/4	A1v6p23
KIRN, THE	1315	3H562	G	4/4	F3p3
KISS FOR NOTHING, A	136	152	F	9/8	B15v1p74
KISS ME FAST MY MINNIE'S COMING	1324	1315	D	6/8	K1v2p39 G11v2Bp37 (11)
KISS ME FAST (MY MOTHER'S COMING)	1324	1313	D	6/8	A1v2p36 A7v5p27 A7v6p34
					A7v2p23 S12v1p14
KISS ME SWEETLY	6H1H3H1H	6H1H3H2H	C	4/4*	Mc21v4p14 G9v5p30 B15v1p4
					G11v2Dp32 (11)
KISS ME SWEETLY	6131	6132	G	2/4	A1v1p34
KISS MY BONNY MOW	3131	1H2H50	D	2/4	A1v6p50
KISS MY LADY	1H1H2H2H	3H5H1H1H	D	2/4	C5v1p23 A1v5p23
KISS MY LADY	1H1H3H3H	5H3H1H1H	D	2/4	W4v2p8
KISS THE LASS YE LIKE BEST	5362	5313H	D	2/2	C18p33 B15v1p55
KISS UNDER THE STAIRS	3L1L3L5L	6L5L2L7L	Bb	6/8	R12v1p4
KISSING'S BEST OF ALL	3112	331H6	G	4/4	G9v5p24 (11)
KITTIE OF CRILE	3335	6665	G	2/2	O1v1lp81
KITTY OF COLERAINE	51H2H7b	51H4H1H	D	6/8	C8v1p63
KITTY OF COLERAINE	51H2H1H	51H4H1H	D	6/8	C8v2p53
KITTY TYRREL	5L6L1	111	G Eb	3/4	E1v1p84 C24v2p3 P5v2p9
					G11v2Bp8 K1v2p10
KNECT THE POCKIE	11H1H4H	7b53b3b	D	4/4	A7v3p26
KNIGHT, THE	1H1H1H5	362H2H	D	6/8	C5v1p25 A1v5p25
KNIT THE POCKY	11H1H3bH	7b53b2	D E	4/4*	B15v1p84 (11) G1v2p67
KNIT THE POCKY	11H1H3bH	7b542	D	4/4*	T8p3 P11v2p7
KNITT THE POCKEY	1557b	4242	G	4/4*	Mc7p4 G9v1p24,25
KNOCKANDO ('S REEL/HOUSE)	1155	1152	D	4/4*	Mc9v3p14 M4v3p34 (11)
KNOCKANDOE'S (STRATHSPEY/REEL)	3b7bL7bL7bL	3b111	A	2/2	A1v6p9 C33p8
KNOLE PARK	3374H	361H7	F	2/4	C14v23p5
LA BAGATELLIER	1432	1432	Bb	6/8	B16v3p9
LA BALLARDE	361H6	1H535	G	2/4	P6v2p12,13
LA BALLET HOLLANDOISE	3215	3215	G	6/8	S7v1p48
LA BELL AMAZONE	3625	147L5	G	2/4	P6v2p4,5
LA BELL GUIMORE	1535	35L11	G	6/8	P6v2p8,9
LA BELLA ROSA	1355	2466	Bb	2/4	C14v20p19
LA BELLE ALLIANCE	3511	4327L	Bb	6/8	C1v4p2
LA BELLE ARSENE	5321	1453	G	6/8	C14v2p15
LA BELLE ASSEMBLEE	5544	15L43	Bb	6/8	B16v4p86
LA BELLE CATHERINE	1H3H3H1H	62H75	C D	4/4*	A7v2p34 G10v2p36 E1v1p58 W6p16
					P10p21 A1v4p13 A7v6p6
					C5v1p13
LA BELLE COUQUETTE	1H3H5H2H	761H7	C	2/4	C14v3p16
LA BELLE ISABELL	1313	5252	G	2/4	C14v4p17
LA BELLE JEANNETTE	1342	5313	G	2/4	P10p1
LA BELLE LAITIERE	1H1H67	1H1H5H2H	D	6/8	C14v21p2
LA BISSETTE	3450	61H65	G	2/4	A1v2p56
LA BLANCHIFFEAU	3H4H1H2H	3H4H1H1H	D	6/8	S12v2p51
LA BOULANGER	51H1H1H	2H676	D	2/4	C14v4p16
LA BRUNETTA	51H53	1251	G	4/4	B16v3p87
LA BRUNETTE	51H53	1251	G	2/4	Mc9v2p19
LA CAMERGO	553b3b	4522	A	6/8	S12v2p44,45
LA CARMAGNOLE	3545	4312	G	6/8	S7v2p2
LA CI DAREM LA MANO	1H3H62H	71H53H	G	2/4	E1v2p76,77
LA COMTESSE DU NORD	1H2H51H	3H71H1H	G	2/4	C14v2p16,17
LA CONSTANTE	5531	5L421	G	6/8	W6p2
LA COUNTERFAITTE	1123	427L5L	G	6/8	A1v2p29
LA DEP	1H1H55	1H1H2H2H	D C	6/8	A7v6p62 A7v3p4
LA DHOMH 'SMI DIREADH BEALAICH	551H3bH	5551H	E	6/8	Mc5p8
LA DORIVAL	1347L	153H5	G	4/4	C22p20
LA DOUBLE INCONSTANCE	11L12	22L23	Bb	6/8	Mc9v2p28
LA DOUBLE INCONSTANCE	2H3H1H1H	2H3H1H1H	D	6/8	S7v1p75
LA DUCHES(SE)	5H5H4H3H	5H5H4H1H	D	3/8	C14v7p22
LA FAFORITTE	3316	527L5	A	6/8	P6v2p1
LA FETTE DE VILLAGE	5H3H4H3H	3H1H2H5	D	2/4	A1v2p24
LA FINALE	5L153	5555	G	2/4	E1v2p134
LA FLORICOURT	553H1H	472H5	G	2/4	N2p31
LA FRANG	3355	1H313H	F	4/4	C22p43
LA GRANDE MARCHE DU FAMEUX GEN. BUONAPARTE	3334	3323	C	4/4	W4v2p9
LA HIER AU SOIR	5431	3422	G	6/8	S12v2p30
LA JARNOVIK	1H71H5	6233	E	2/4	C14v5p2
LA JULIE	351H5	671H1H	F	2/4	Mc9v2p28
LA JUPON ROUGE	5322	4215L	G	6/8	A1v3p187
LA LESGERE	2222	427L1	G	2/4	P6v2p2,3
LA LUCILLE	1H2H1H1H	661H5	D	6/8	S7v1p50
LA MALTA	71H3H5H	1H71H5	D	6/8	W6p1
LA MARESCHAL	1H1H5H5H	3H1H2H2H	C	2/4	C14v26p4
LA MARQUISE	1H3H74H	3H71H3	F	6/8	Mc9v2p27

LA MARQUISE DOUBLE JIG	137L4	37L13L	Bb	6/8	C22p28
LA MEGARDE	3211H	4H3H55H	Eb	6/8	N2p32
LA MIGNONETTE	3355	5532	F	6/8	Mc9v2p18
LA MIGNONETTE FRANCOISE	1355	5531	G	6/8	S12v2p22
LA MONACA	7L5L11	5L311	G	2/4	W6p3
LA NEIGE	5H3H1H5	5H5H6H3H	D	6/8	E1v2p79
LA NEUVENNE	3243	5523	G	6/8	S12v2p39
LA NEVELL HOLLANDOIS	1234	52H1H1H	F	2/4	Mc9v2p20
LA NINA	1423	127L3	G	2/4	P6v2p10,11
LA NINETTE	12H3H5H	2H4H2H1H	D	6/8	S7v1p56
LA NONIME	1H3H2H2H	1H3H2H1H	D	6/8	S12v2p39
LA NONIME	3b221	3b211	A	6/8	S12v2p45
LA NOUVELLE ANGLOISE	1415	4321	G	2/4	A1v1p56
LA NOUVELLE HOLLANDOISE	3351	2253	A	6/8	W6p6,7
LA NOUVELLE MARIE	1H5H4H3H	1H5H61H	D	2/4	C14v1p9
LA NOVELLE HOLENDOISE	1531	427L5L	G	2/4	A1v3p165
LA NOWELLA BALLANDOISE	1324	3525L	A	6/8	Mc9v2p26
LA PAPILLON	1122	3413	G	6/8	B16v3p14 S7v1p33
LA PETITE PARISIANE	1231	6L215L	G	6/8	W6p4
LA PIPE TABAC	5H6H6H5H	3H2H1H1H	C	2/4	E1v2p92,93
LA PLASIR L'ETE	1542	3532	F	2/4	C14v3p10
LA POLONESE	17L17L	5421	G	2/4	A1v2p18
LA POULE	5755	5552	G	6/8	E1v2p26,27
LA POULE	5H2H1H5	2H2H2H4H	C	6/8	E1v2p132
LA POULE from MASANIELLO	53H56H	3H4H1H5	D	6/8	G13p10,11
LA QUATRE COMPLOSSE'A	5533	1115	Bb	2/4	Mc9v2p14
LA RACROCHEUSE	3311	3211	G	6/8	S12v2p42
LA REVEIL DU PEUPLE	3H3H2H3H	1H1H51H	D	4/4	A1v5p62 F1p29 C5v1p62
LA ROCHELLE	5H3H5H3H	6H2H1H1H	D	2/4	A1v2p55
LA ROSALIA	311H5	637L2	G	6/8	A1v2p37
LA ROYAL LOVERIE GAVOT	1H2H1H3	3H4H3H5	D	2/4	A1v3p188
LA SAGATAIRE	561H4	27L5L1	G	2/4	P6v2p14,15
LA SAUBE	1H553	3111	A	2/4	B16v3p55
LA SCIMBALLE	1133	5411	G	6/8	S12v2p13
LA SECULERE	1L7L35	647L1	Bb	2/4	Mc9v2p4
LA SIMPLICITA	3111	3111	G	2/4	Mc9v2p10
LA SOIRRE DU VAUXHALL	5411	1231	G	6/8	S12v2p37
LA SUISESSE DU BORD DU LAC	3H2H1H1H	3H3H5H3H	C	6/8	E1v2p75
LA TAISON DOR	117L4	6425	G	2/4	P6v2p6,7
LA TALIA	1H53H1H	4H71H5	F	2/4	N2p34
LA TERZA	331H1H	3322	A	2/4	H6v22p3 C14v25p11
LA TOISON D'OR	53b11	12b42b	G	6/8	C14v21p6,7
LA TRENISE	151H6	53H4H2H	C	2/4	T1v2p14
LA TRENISE	1113b	427L2	B	2/4	E1v2p133
LA TRENISE	5H5H5H5H	5H4H2H5H	D	2/4	E1v2p27
LA TRENISE	11H33H	3H2H2H1H	A	6/8	G13p11
LA TRIUMPHE	5342	5765	G	2/4	C14v9p18
LA TROMPE	3345	427L7L	G	2/4	S7v1p97
LA VILLETTE	2353	5523	G	6/8	S12v2p51
LA VISITE	1H1H4H6H	5H4H72H	C	2/4	C14v3p3 A1v6p34 P6v2p21
LA ZEMIRE	5H4H1H1H	2H71H5	D	6/8	N2p30
L'ABBE	1H1H1H3H	4H2H5H1H	D Eb	2/4	A1v4p34 W4v1p5
LABORIE'S DANCE	3L13L1	7L447L	A	4/4	C22p27
LABYRINTH	3344	2230	G	6/8	C14v23p1
LABYRINTH, THE	3354	2230	G	6/8	H6v1p1 P6v1p23
LACHLAIN DUDH [LACHLAN DUBH]	1H53bH2H	1H53bH2H	E	6/8	F2v2p55(45)
LAD IF YOU LO'E ME	1H1H1H2H	3H3H3H4H	C D	6/8	W4v1p15 C5v1p41 A1v4p41
LADDIE LIE NEAR ME	51H7	1H1H1H	E D	3/4	C5v2p15 (J3)
LADDIE LIE NEAR ME	51H7	1H1H3bH	G Bb	3/4	Mc8v1Dp116 E1v2p110 O1v1Lp143 A1v5p47
LADIES AMUSEMENT, THE	5311	27L5L5L	A	6/8	B16v3p64
LADIES OF ABERDEEN	1355	5532	G	6/8	D6p28
LADIES OF ARGYLE, THE	13b55	7b422	C	2/2	C13v2p60
LADIES OF DINGWALL, THE	1H3H3H1H	4H61H6	D	2/2	M12p8
LADIES OF EDINBURGH, THE	1515	1616	D	4/4	P9p38
LADIES' RAMBLE	3653	2236	G	6/8	S7v1p35
LADIES REGIMENTALS, THE	1L3L13	4113L	Bb	2/4	B16v3p21
LADS AND THE LASSES, THE	1541	3452	Bb	6/8	B16v3p33
LADS OF BOOT, THE	1565	157b2	A	2/2	R12v1p100
LADS OF DUNSE, THE	5116	6562	D	6/8	G10v2p33 A1v1p19 Mc21v3p3 G11v1Cp34,35 W7p8 (II)
LADS OF ELGIN, THE	1353	26L7bL2	A	2/2	B15v1p59
LADS OF GLASGOW	1H535	1H442	G	2/4	S7v1p59
LADS OF LEITH, THE	5427L	1411	G	6/8	O1v1Dp31
LADS OF NAIRN, THE	1562	1561H	D	6/8	O1v1Lp149
LADS OF THE PRINTFIELD, THE	1353	2466	D	2/2	C13v2p26
LADS OF THE SHAWS, THE	13b3b4	2424	G	2/2	C13v2p16
LADS OF THE VILLAGE, THE	11H63	237L7L	G	2/4	A1v1p1
LADS WITH THE KILTS, THE	3b13b3b	3b11H5	A	6/8	D14v2p23
LADY ABERCROMBY'S STRATHSPEY	5L5L6L1	5L13L2L	Bb	4/4	M11v1p12
LADY ADMIRAL GORDON'S	1115L	526L6L	A	4/4	G8p2 N1v1p12
LADY AGNES DUFF, THE	1H1H31	1H1H2H2H	F	4/4	M4v4p8,9

Title			Key	Time	References
LADY AGNES PERCY'S HORNPIPE	53b1	53b1H	C	6/4	Mc15p37
LADY AGNES PERCY'S REEL	3453	6L5L32	D	2/2	C14v19p12
LADY ALEXr RUSSELL	11H35	652H2H	F	4/4	M4v4p3
LADY AMELIA KER'S MINUET	11H3H	2H75	Eb	3/4	S11v1p20 Mc21v1p16 C13v4p42
LADY AMELIA MURRAY'S REEL	3133	627L2	F G	2/2	Mc4v2p4 A7v4p16
LADY AMELIA MURRAY'S STRATHSPEY	5662	5653H	D	4/4	G10v5p3
LADY ANN BOTHWEL'S LAMENT	311	15L5L	G	3/4	T6v2p40 P8v2p22
LADY ANN CARNEGIE'S FAVORITE	3155	321H6	F	6/8	G9v2p17 G10v6p30,31
LADY ANN ERSKIN'S REEL	112H1H	31H42	C	4/4	B15v1p86 (II)
LADY ANN HAMILTON'S REEL	331H1H	332H2	F	6/8	R5p29
LADY ANN HOPE'S FAVOURITE	5151	51H22	G	4/4	G11v1Ap14 C5v1p51 G10v3p4 A1v4p51
LADY ANN HOPE'S FAVOURITE	5151	51H22	G	4/4	Mc7p7
LADY ANN HOPE('S STRATHSPEY)	316L5L	7L37L5L	G	4/4	G11v1Bp35 G10v3p4,5 A1v4p25 (II)
LADY ANN HOP'S STRATHSPEY	1115L	446L2	G	4/4	A7v6p8,9
LADY ANN HOPS STRATHSPEY	111L1L	446L2	G	4/4	A7v2p23
LADY ANN MAITLAND'S MINUET	1H1H5	15L1	Eb	3/4	C22p9
LADY ANN MAITLAND('S REEL)	1H515	1H1H2H6	G	2/2	Mc4v2p4 (II)
LADY ANN STEWART('S STRATHSPEY)	1H553	657L2	A Bb	4/4	(II) G11v1Ap30 A7v4p5
LADY ANN STEWARTS STRATHSPEY	1T5H5H3H	6H5H72H	C	4/4	A7v5p17
LADY ANN WHARTON DUFF'S STRATHSPEY	1L6L2L4L	1L6L5L1	Bb	4/4	M4v3p7 (II)
LADY ANNE BOTHWELL'S LAMENT	411	6L5L5L	G	3/4	N1v2p6
LADY ANNE GORDON('S REEL)	5326L	531H1H	D	2/2	K1v2p40 M4v1p10 P5v2p14 Mc9v3p7 Mc12v1p13,47
LADY ANNE HOPE'S REEL	111L1L	436L2	G	4/4	M4v2p2
LADY ANSTRUTHER'S REEL	1151	427L2	G	4/4	G9v5p24
LADY ARBUTHNOTT'S FAVORITE	1351H	547L2	D	2/2	P5v4p12,13
LADY ARCHd CAMPBELL'S REEL	1321	5L122L	Bb	2/2	C13v1p1
LADY ASHBURTON('S STRATHSPEY)	1H135L	6L122	Eb	4/4	G10v5p8 (II)
LADY AUCKLANDS REEL	3L3L11	3L122L	Bb	2/2	C14v8p21
LADY AUGUSTA FITZCLARANCE	3H5H1H2H	51H53H	C	2/2	G9v2p19
LADY AUGUSTA HAY'S MINUET	1H1H5	321	Bb	3/4	D15v2p5 C22p6
LADY AUGUSTA MURRAY'S REEL	137L2	331H5	F	2/2	D14v1p26 D14v4p5 G9v5p3
LADY AUGUSTA MURRAY'S STRATHSPEY	5511	6L6L22	A	2/2	C14v6p17
LADY AUGUSTA'S DELIGHT	1H3H1H3H	4H3H4H5	D	2/4	R12v1p62
LADY AUGUSTUS MURRAY OF AUCHTERTYRE	5527bL	5555	A	4/4	Mc4v2p7
LADY BAIRD OF SAUGHTONHALLS REEL	51H53H	6562	D	2/2	D14v3p13
LADY BAIRD'S DELIGHT	5L343	2347bL	G	4/4	G10v1p4
LADY BAIRD'S MINUET	111H	447L	Eb	3/4	S7v3p18,19
LADY BAIRD'S NEW REEL	543b1	5427bL	B	2/2	Mc21v3p27 (II)
LADY BAIRD'S NEW REEL	137L2	3365	F	2/2	Mc21v2p20
LADY BAIRD'S REELL	1313	2216L	A	2/2	Mc4v1p1
LADY BAIRD'S STRATHSPEY	5H3H1H1H	6565	D	4/4	C5v2p36
LADY BAIRD'S (STRATHSPEY/REEL)	5311	6L5L6L5L	A G	4/4*	G11v1Ap34 A7v2p16,17 E1v1p57 C14v13p21 Mc12v1p410 A7v6p35 A1v4p1
LADY BALCARRAS'S REEL [LADY BALCARRES'S REEL]	3151H	3126L	D	2/2	R5p57
LADY BARBARA ASHLEY COOPERS STRATHSPEY	1151H	637L7L	Eb	4/4	C14v16p7
LADY BARONESS KEITH	153b1	27b24	G	2/2	G9v2p10
LADY BATH'S STRATHSPEY	15L6L2	15L2L6F	Bb	2/2	J1p30
LADY BEATRICE HAMILTON	151H5	1564	F	4/4	M4v4p2
LADY BELHAVEN'S DELIGHT	1125L	1322	G A	6/8	C5v2p70 G10v4p34,35
LADY BERKLEY'S WHIM	3L5L33	246L7L	A	2/2	R12v1p20
LADY BERNARD'S LAMENT	5L5L1	322	Bb	3/4	O1v5p34
LADY BERNARD'S LAMENT	551H	3H2H2H	D	3/4	O1v1Gp24
LADY BERTIE'S ALLEMAND	3H5H3H2H	1H1H55	D	2/2	S7v1p35
LADY BETTY BOYLE'S MINUET	1H1H1H	1H1H2H	E	3/4	C13v4p44
LADY BETTY BOYLE('S REEL)	13L4L5L	157L2	Bb	2/2*	S12v1p63 G11v2Cp32 Mc21v1p32 (II)
LADY BETTY COCHRAN'S REEL	1155	42H2H6	C	4/4	B15v1p72
LADY (BETTY) COCHRAN'S REEL	3155	42H2H2	C	2/2	D14v4p4 C14v11p10,11
LADY BETTY COCHRAN'S REEL	3155	42H2H6	D C	2/2	G8p22 G9v5p30 S12v1p11 D14v1p24
LADY BETTY COCHRAN'S REEL	331H5	657L2	F	2/2	C13v2p35
LADY BETTY COCHRAN'S REEL	5L31H5	657L2	F	4/4*	Mc13v2p28 C14v1p14 Mc21v1p32 S12v1p58 C13v1p48
LADY BETTY HAMILTON'S REEL	5656	5245	F	2/4	S7v1p100
LADY BETTY HAY'S REEL	1555	7b47bL2	G	2/2	B15v1p106
LADY BETTY MAITLAND'S MINUET	1H51H	2H75	F	3/4	D14v1p5
LADY BETTY RAMSAY'S REEL	1351	5532	D	2/2	D14v3p16/17
LADY BETTY WEMYSS'S REEL	31H31H	2H1H22	C	2/2	B15v1p21 (II)
LADY BEWMONT'S GIG	13b52	7bL244	A	6/8	B10p31
LADY BINNIE'S MINUET	113	557	F	3/4	Mc21v1p23
LADY BINNING('S STRATHSPEY)	1233	427L5L	A	4/4	G11v2Dp23 (II)
LADY BOSWELL OF AUCHENLECK	1L3L6L2L	1L3L11	Bb	4/4	G10v6p8
LADY BROMES STRATHSPEY	3b1H1H1	22H7b7bL	C	4/4	Mc21v4p39 (II)
LADY BRUCE OF SCOTSTON	3551	27L11	Bb	4/4	D6p1
LADY BRUCE'S HORNPIPE	1L3L16L	3311	Bb	4/4	D6p2
LADY BURDIT'S REEL	15L3L5L	137L2	Bb	2/2	J2p1
LADY BURNSIDE'S (BIRTH DAY)/(STRATHSPEY)	1H1H3b3b	7b7b24	D C	4/4	A7v6p78 D16p13 (II)

LADY BYRON'S WALTZ	1H1H61H	1H1H62H	F	3/8	C1v4p4
LADY C. BRUCE'S REEL	5354	5324	D	2/2	C1v1p11
LADY C. MONTAGUE'S VALTZ	3H1H3H	5H3H5H	C	3/4	G9v4p23
LADY CAMPBELL ARDKINLASS'S STRATHSPEY	5L13b4	2422	G	4/4	Mc12v1p50
LADY CAMPBELL OF ARDKINGLASS'S JIGG	3b211H	3bH7b44	C	6/8	S4v1p8
LADY CARLISLE'S REEL	15L16	6326L	A	6/8	B10p13
LADY CARMICHAEL (OF CASTLECRAIG'S STRATHSPEY)	1H3H65	652H2H	C	4/4	C8v1p20 G10v5p18 (11)
LADY CARMICHAEL	15L3L1L	1432	Bb	4/4	S4v2p1
LADY CARMICHAEL'S STRATHSPEY	3L5L7L2	437L2	Bb	4/4	S4v2p1
LADY CARNEGIE OF SOUTHESK'S STRATHSPEY	3b13b5	2454	G	4/4	D15v1p3
LADY CAROLINE BERTIE	52H75	5527L	Eb	2/4	C14v27p14
LADY CAROLINE DOUGLAS'S FAVORITE	1231	427L5L	A	6/8	S4v2p10
LADY CAROLINE ELIZABETH DOUGLAS'S REEL	3H531H	3H5H72H	D	2/2	G9v2p16
LADY CAROLINE LEE	3624	3H1H51H	D	3/8	P6v1p33
LADY CAROLINE MONTAGUE'S STRATHSPEY	5H3H1H5	5H3H72H	C	4/4	G10v4p7 A7v4p17 (11)
LADY (CAROLINE/HARRIET) LEE'S WALTZ	3623	3H1H51H	D F	3/8	C14v19p1 H6v10p3
LADY CASSLES'S FAVORITE	5515	5531	G	4/4	E2p10
LADY CATHCART OF EARLSTON'S REEL	1155	5522	G	2/2	R5p21
LADY CATHCART'S STRATHSPEY	116L1	247L2	Bb	2/4	J1p13 P1v2p4
LADY CATHERINE BLIGH'S REEL	313L5L	4L422	Bb	4/4	Mc21v4p35
LADY CATHERINE BLYTH	1353	4242H	F	2/2	C14v17p6
LADY CATHERINE PELHAMS REEL	1H3bH2H1H	6b57L2	G	4/4	Mc21v4p30
LADY CATHERINE STEWART (STRATHSPEY) or [HAUGHS O' CROMDALE, THE]	5152	517bL2	E	4/4	A1v6p4 G10v1p20 Mc21v4p20,21 (11)
LADY CHARLES SPENCER'S FANCY	5H3H5H3H	4H4H3H0	D	2/4	S7v1p20
LADY CHARLOTE'S DELIGHT	1565	157L2	G	6/8	A1v1p37
LADY CHARLOTTE BENTINCKS REEL	313L1	157L2	Bb	2/2	C14v11p8
LADY CHARLOTTE BENTINCKS WALTZ	554H7	554H1H	C	3/8	C14v13p5
LADY CHARLOTTE BRUCE (FAVOURITE/STRATHSPEY)	3342	357L2	G F	6/8	C5v2p64 A1v4p28 G10v3p2 E1v1p82 G11v1Bp12
LADY CHARLOTTE BRUCE'S REEL	5354	5324	D	2/2	C14v9p5
LADY CHARLOTTE BRUCE'S STRATHSPEY	1351	6L47L2	A	4/4	S4v1p18 (11)
LADY CHARLOTTE CADOGAN'S REEL	3b53b1	2424	E	4/4	Mc21v4p39
LADY CHARLOTTE CAMPBELL	137L2	331H5	F	2/2	C14v6p15
LADY CHARLOTTE CAMPBELL ('S STRATHSPEY)	5323	536L7L	G	4/4	E1v1p95 C8v2p41 G11v1Bp34 C8v1p61
LADY CHARLOTTE CAMPBELL'S (REEL/MEDLEY/NEW REEL) REEL, (THE)	1135	427L2	Bb	4/4*	D15v2p33 Mc21v4p9 G11v2Bp31 C24v2p4,5 K1v2p33 (11)
LADY CHARLOTTE CAMPBELL'S ([NEW]STRATHSPEY/MEDLEY)	3L5L4L6L	7L531	Bb	4/4	K1v1p33 G11v2Bp31 Mc21v4p10 (11)
LADY CHARLOTTE CAMPBELL'S REEL	1H1H3H5H	4H2H72H	D	2/2	A7v5p8
LADY CHARLOTTE CAMPBELL'S REEL	1353	5L37L2	Bb	4/4	C14v8p11
LADY CHARLOTTE CAMPBELL('S STRATHSPEY)	5323	536L7L	G	4/4	G1v2p78 A1v4p58 G10v3p19 (11)
LADY CHARLOTTE CAMPBELL'S STRATHSPEY	1313	136L2	F	2/2	Mc15p1
LADY CHARLOTTE CAMPBELL'S STRATHSPEY	3546	75H3H1H	D	2/2	A7v5p8
LADY CHARLOTTE CAMPBELL'S VALTZ	1112	7L7L7L1	Bb	3/8	G9v4p1
LADY CHARLOTTE CAMPBELL'S WALTZ	3343	2121	Bb	3/8	C14v14p1
LADY CHARLOTTE CHOLMONDELEY'S FANCY	3141	31H51	Bb	2/4	C14v27p14,15
LADY CHARLOTTE DUNDAS'S STRATHSPEY	1H531	2461H	F	2/2	J1p26
LADY CHARLOTTE DURHAM	11H1H3	116L6L	G	4/4	A7v5p1 E1v1p81 B7p1 K1v2p8 G10v5p30 D15v2p49 (11)
LADY CHARLOTTE DURHAM'S STRATHSPEY	5327bL	5337b	A	4/4	G10v4p8 (11)
LADY CHARLOTTE FLETCHER OF SALTON	1125L	427L2	A	2/2	Mc19v3p18,19 Mc19v2p2,3
LADY CHARLOTTE GOOLD'S REEL	3b145	3b527b	E	4/4	Mc21v4p21
LADY CHARLOTTE GORDON'S REEL	1H543	1H3H2H2	F	2/2*	M4v3p56 M4v1p3 (11)
LADY CHARLOTTE HAMILTON'S REEL	1553	2542	A	2/2	C14v15p11
LADY CHARLOTTE LENNOX REEL	1H51H6b	7b527b	E	4/4	Mc21v4p22
LADY CHARLOTTE LEN(N)OX'S STRATHSPEY	5654	547L2	F	2/2	C14v6p3
LADY CHARLOTTE LENOX	3H1H2H5	1H2H3H2H	C D	2/4	A7v3p3 A7v6p62
LADY CHARLOTTE LENOX'S REEL	1133	1132	Bb	2/2	J1p22
LADY CHARLOTTE LEVESON GOWER'S STRATHSPEY	15L13	5426L	E	2/2	B10p41
LADY CHARLOTTE LEVESON GOWER'S REEL	1L147L	3422L	A	2/2	B10p16
LADY CHARLOTTE MENZIES REEL	31H65	432H2	F	2/2	Mc4v4p4 (11)
LADY CHARLOTTE MURRAY ('S FAVORITE) (JIG)	311H5	27bL7b7bL	D	6/8	G11v1Bp2,3 G10v1p6 Mc12v1p52,53
LADY CHARLOTTE MURRAY'S REEL	1H3H55	44H2H2H	D	2/2	Mc4v2p2 (11)
LADY CHARLOTTE MURRAY'S REEL	5651	51H52	F	2/2	D14v3p23
LADY CHARLOTTE MURRAY'S REEL	315L1	247b5	A	2/2	Mc9v3p38
LADY CHARLOTTE MURRAY'S STRATHSPEY	1562	151H5	D	4/4	A1v6p17
LADY CHARLOTTE PERCEY'S FANCY	1H3H2H5H	1H3H75	C	2/4	C14v20p14,15
LADY CHARLOTTE PERCY'S REEL	1H515	47bL24	G	2/2	C14v8p13
LADY CHARLOTTE PERCY'S SCOTCH MEASURE	1142	3556	Eb	2/2	Mc15p7
LADY CHARLOTTE PRIMROSE'S STRATHSPEY	1H51H1H	1H51H2	D	4/4	G10v4p18 (11)
LADY CHARLOTTE RAWDONS STRATHSPEY	1522	153b5	E	2/2	S4v2p24
LADY CHARLOTTE RAWDOW'S MINUET	1H1H1H	555	Eb	3/4	C22p8
LADY CHARLOTTE VILLERS REEL	1H542	3551H	A	2/2	C14v11p18,19
LADY CHOLMONDLEY'S WALTZ	5671H	5671H	F	3/8	B17p2 C14v12p17
LADY CLEMENTINA	1L3L11	1125L	Bb	4/4	P6v1p12
LADY CLIFFORD'S GIG	1H1H65	457L2	A	6/8	B10p29
LADY CLINTON'S FANCY	1351H	246L2	Eb	2/4	C14v9p9

LADY CLINTON'S FANCY	1351H	246L2	Eb	2/4	C14v9p9
LADY COVENTRY'S MINUET	111	321	A G	3/4	C13v3p70,71 C5v1p27 A1v5p27
LADY CRAWFURD'S MINUET	3H3H2H	3H1H2H	D	3/4	R5p1
LADY CRAWFURD'S REEL	311H1	312H2	D	6/8	R5p34
LADY CUMMING OF ALTYRE'S STRATHSPEY	1H51H5	1H526L	C	4/4	T1v2p1
LADY CUNNINGHAM (OF LIVINGSTONE) ('S STRATHSPEY)	11L5L5L	237L2	A	4/4	G11v1Ap16 G10v2p2
LADY CUNNINGHAM OF LIVINGSTON'S FAVORITE	1H2H1H5	454H2H	Eb	6/8	S11v2p8
LADY CUNNINGHAM'S REEL	1H122	4H3H2H6	D	2/2	S12v1p37 C13v2p64 S7v1p11
LADY CUNNINGHAM'S STRATHSPEY	11L5L5L	247L2	A	4/4	A7v2p14 Mc12v1p12
LADY DALRYMPLE (OF NORTH BERWICK'S FAVOURITE)	1L13b1	7bL7bL43b	A	2/4	G11v1Cp8 G10v3p12
LADY DALRYMPLE HAMILTON'S REEL	1H1H31	5L342	G	4/4	F3p3
LADY DALRYMPLE HAY'S STRATHSPEY	5555	1H3H62	C	4/4	P11v2p18
LADY DICK LAUDER'S STRATHSPEY	116L5L	5L332	Bb	4/4	T1v2p2
LADY DOLL SINCLAIR'S REEL	1343	27b27bL	A	2/2	B15v1p1
LADY DOUGLAS OF BOTHWELL	53b51	53b47bL	E	6/8	G11v2Cp19
LADY DOUNE	1H1H1H1H	2H2H66	F	4/4	G11v1Bp31 C8v1p56 B12p10,11 (II)
LADY DOUNE (DOWNE)	53H2H7	1H653	Eb	4/4	G10v4p6
LADY DOUNE'S REEL	3135	3542	D	2/2	Mc21v3p37
LADY DOWNE'S ALLAMANDE	1233	5755	Bb	2/4	G9v4p11
LADY DOWNE'S FANCY	5L23L2L	5L23L1L	Bb	6/8	E2p19
LADY DOWNE'S STRATHSPEY	551H3	551H6	A	4/4	E2p18
LADY DOWN'S REEL	1H1H31	427L5L	C	2/2	Mc4v4p11 (II)
LADY DUFF OF DELGATY	5L6L5L3L	2L4L6L4L	Bb	2/2	M4v4p22
LADY DUMFRIES'S MINUET	3H3H3H	571H	D	3/4	R5p2
LADY DUMFRIES'S REEL	1153H	1H522	F	2/2	R5p43 K1v2p32 G11v2Bp30 (II)
LADY DUNBAR OF BOATH'S STRATHSPEY	5622	536L5L	Eb	4/4	G15p6
LADY DUNBAR OF BOATH'S STRATHSPEY	5632	536L5L	F	4/4	T1v2p4
LADY DUNBAR OF NORTHFIELD'S REEL	1316L	6L431	Bb	2/2	C18p22
LADY DUNBAR OF NORTHFIELD'S STRATHSPEY	1131	1122	Bb	4/4	G15p22
LADY DUNBAR OF NORTHFIELD'S STRATHSPEY	15L27L	16L2L4	Bb	4/4	C18p21
LADY DUNCANNON'S REEL	1135	1H642	F	2/2	B10p15
LADY EGLINTON'S REEL [LADY EGLINTOUNE'S REEL]	111H1H	632H2	C	4/4*	Mc7p13 H3p19 R5p41(42)
LADY EGLINTON'S REEL	1H3bH3bH5H	2H7b2H4H	E	12/8	B10p11
LADY ELCHO'S	151H7	5351H	G	2/2	Mc19v3p12 Mc19v2p1
LADY ELCHO'S MEDLEY	11H53	51H3H1H	G	2/2	Mc19v3p12 Mc19v2p1
LADY ELEANOR CAMPBELL OF SHAWFIELD'S REEL	1H1H33	6542	A	2/2	Mc19v2p5
LADY ELEANORA DUNDASS'S REEL	11H76	5H1H2H2H	D	2/2	G11v1Ap33
LADY (ELENORA) HOME'S REEL	3653	47b27bL	D	2/2	D14v4p5 G9v5p12 C14v11p14
LADY ELGIN	1H345	1H36L7L	G	2/4	C5v2p26 G11v1Cp12
LADY ELGIN'S REEL	1126L	1151	D	2/2	B15v1p62 Mc9v1p32
LADY ELIBANK'S FAVO(U)RITE	115L7bL	113b5	G	4/4	G10v3p15 G11v1Cp31
LADY ELINOR CAMPBELL'S REEL	16L13	27L24	A	2/2	Mc16p10
LADY ELINORA HOME'S REEL	3653	47b27bL	D	2/2	G11v2Dp37 D14v1p25
LADY ELISABETH MONCREIFFE'S REEL	131H1H	5542	F	2/2	L4p5
LADY ELISABETH MONTAGUE'S JIG	3b125L	3b144	A	6/8	Mc21v4p33
LADY ELISABETH MONTAGUE'S REEL	3b16b4	57b42	A	4/4	Mc21v4p33
LADY ELIZA CALLANDER'S FAVOURITE	3H765	3H761H	D	6/8	C5v1p48 A1v4p48
LADY ELIZA CALLANDERS FAVOURITE	37L6L5L	37L6L1	Bb	6/8	W4v1p23
LADY ELIZA LINDSAY'S HORNPIPE	111H1H	2H755	C	2/2	W4v1p28
LADY ELIZA LINDSAY'S MINUET	112	112	F	3/4	W4v1p24
LADY ELIZABETH BUTLERS FANCY	5521	5521	Bb	3/8	J1p48
LADY ELIZABETH CAMPBELL'S REEL	4635	43b27L	A	4/4	Mc19v2p22
LADY ELIZABETH CAMPBELL'S REEL	4635	43b27bL	A	4/4	Mc19v1p6 (II)
LADY ELIZABETH CRICHTON'S MINUET	112	315L	Eb	3/4	C22p2,3
LADY ELIZABETH CRICHTONS REEL	137L5L	6L4L5L1L	Bb	2/2	H3p22
LADY ELIZABETH HERONS REEL	1155	42H2H6	C	4/4	G9v5p20
LADY ELIZABETH LINDSAY'S STRATHSPEY	5316L	5L3L5L3L	Bb	4/4	G11v1Ap30 (II)
LADY ELIZABETH MARGARET CARNEGIE	3l.13L1	6L47L5	Bb	2/4	G9v3p2
LADY ELIZABETH PERCY'S FANCY	151H5	1542	G	4/4	C14v22p1
LADY ELIZABETH PRINGLE'S REEL	4635	43b27L	A	4/4	Mc19v3p13
LADY ELIZABETH STANLEY'S JIG	5L122	5L152	F	6/8	C14v6p14
LADY ELPHINSTONE'S FAVORITE	25L13L	3L322L	G	4/4	G11v1Ap13
LADY ELPHINSTON'S REEL	3b421	4L27b2	G	2/2	Mc13v2p23
LADY ELPHISTON'S STRATHSPEY	11L5L5L	247L2	A	4/4	C13v1p31
LADY EMELLIA KER'S REEL	13b51	27b27bL	E	2/2	S12v1p72
LADY ERSKINE'S REEL	113b2	27b27bL	A	2/2	W2v1p2 (II)
LADY FITZGERALD'S REEL	515	656	D	9/8	C14v17p2,3
LADY FLORA CHARLOTTE HASTING'S STRATHSPEY	47L15L	6L15L3L	Bb	4/4	G10v5p35
LADY FLORA MACDONALD	1151	1137bL	E	4/4	P6v1p34
LADY FORBES OF NEW AND EDINGLASSIE	5552H	7533	Bb	4/4	M4v4p20
LADY FORD'S STRATHSPEY	1L1L5L1L	4327L	A	2/2	P1v2p7
LADY FORD'S STRATHSPEY	1L354	5622	Bb	2/2	J1p31
LADY FRANCES SCOT'S REEL	53b51	53b47bL	E	6/8	D14v3p26
LADY FRANCES SOMERSET'S REEL	531H5	437L2	Bb	2/2	Mc15p24 (II)
LADY GARDINER'S STRATHSPEY	5353	6444	D	2/2	P1v2p5

LADY GARDINER'S STRATHSPEY	5353	6464	D	2/2	J1p16
LADY GEORGE BEAUCLARK'S REEL	311H3	4542	C	4/4*	B15v1p33 (II)
LADY GEORGE MURRAY	136L5L	5L322	A	4/4	J1p38
LADY GEORGINA GORDON'S (REEL/STRATHSPEY)	1133	6522	F G	4/4*	M4v3p49 Mc9v3p2 (II) G1v2p75
LADY GEORGINA GORDON'S REEL	3bH1H3b1H	2H7b27b	D	2/2	Mc21v3p31 (II)
LADY GEORGINA GORDON'S STRATHSPEY	315L3	422L4	F	2/2	J1p27
LADY GEORGINA RUSSELL'S REEL	1L1L5L1	6L6L22	Bb	2/2	M4v3p2 (II)
LADY GILFORD'S REEL	1361H	51H32	F	2/2	J2p12
LADY GLASGOW'S FAVORITE	113L1	4522	F	4/4	E2p8
LADY GLASGOW('S STRATHSPEY)	1565	1535	A	4/4	E2p2 (II)
LADY GLENCAIRN'S MINUET	344	515	F	3/4	R5p4
LADY GLENORCHY'S REEL	1H1H1H1H	113b1H	D	2/2	G9v2p19
LADY GLENORCHY'S REEL	1H632	311H5	A	4/4	Mc19v1p6 Mc19v2p22 (II)
LADY GORDON CUMMING'S STRATHSPEY	1353	1332	F	4/4	G15p28
LADY GORDON OF GORDONSTOWN'S REEL	3b13b5	2424	C	4/4	M12p3
LADY GORDON OF GORDONSTOWN'S STRATHSPEY	11H1H5	7b427bL	C	4/4	M12p3
LADY GOWERS FANCY	1H1H42	62H65	F	2/4	C14v4p6
LADY GOWERS STRATHSPEY	116L4	51H26L	D	2/4	G8p18 P1v1p7
LADY GRACE DOUGLAS'S REEL	5347L	15L4L2L	Bb	2/2	G10v3p6
LADY GRACE DOUGLAS'S REEL	5H3H2H7	1H542	D	2/2	C5v1p52 A1v4p52
LADY GRACE DOUGLASS'S REEL	5327L	15L4L2L	Bb	4/4*	G11v1Ap30 Mc12v1p2 (II)
LADY GRACE DOUGLASS'S VALTZ	561H1H	561H1H	F	3/8	G9v4p18
LADY GRACE STEWART'S MINUET	115L	133	Eb	3/4	C22p7
LADY GRACE STEWART('S STRATHSPEY)	1L13b7bL	1L13b3b	B	4/4	G10v2p11 (II)
LADY GRACE STUART'S MINUET	1H53	17L1	F	3/4	S7v3p20,21
LADY GRANT OF DALVEY'S REEL	1522	5426L	D	2/2	C14v2p6 C33p6
LADY GRANT OF GRANT'S REELL	1115	1124	E	4/4	C33p2
LADY GRANT OF MONYMUSK'S REELL	1126L	1111	G	2/2	C33p6
LADY GRANTLEY'S STRATHSPEY	15L1L5L	15L6L2L	Bb	2/2	J1p14
LADY GRANT'S STRATHSPEY	5511	2231	Bb	2/4	P1v2p4
LADY GWYDIR	1311H	5326L	D	4/4	G11v1Cp32 (II)
LADY HADDO ('S STRATHSPEY)	351H6	1H1H22	C D	4/4	A7v2p28 G11v1Bp9 G10v2p13 A1v6p18 A7v6p38
LADY HADDO'S STRATHSPEY	351H6	1H1H22	D	4/4	E1v1p33
LADY HAMILTON	5L15L1	2L27L6L	G	2/2	C14v21p18
LADY (HAMILTON) DALRYMPLE ([OF] NORTH BERWICK)'S STRATHSPEY	3b15L1	2452	A G	4/4	A7v5p32 K1v2p9 G10v4p23 Mc21v2p7 (II)
LADY HAMILTON'S REEL	15L6L5L	4L3L2L2	Bb	2/2	J1p20 (II)
LADY HAMILTON'S REEL	35L5L1	6L27L2	G	2/2	C14v12p23
LADY HAMPDEN'S STRATHSPEY	1L153	2L226L	A	2/2	Mc4v3p6
LADY HAMPDON'S REEL	3b13b5	27bL27bL	G	6/8	C14v16p18,19
LADY HARIOT HOPE'S REEL	1564	1H2H2H2	F	2/2*	C13v2p2 Mc12v1p27 (II)
LADY HARRIET HAY'S STRATHSPEY	3b11L3b	27bL42	G	2/2	J1p28
LADY HARRIET SUTTIE'S STRATHSPEY	153b5L	3b3b7bL4	E	4/4	Mc19v2p4 Mc19v3p10
LADY HARRIOT CAVENDISH'S TRIP	3131	447L5L	Bb	2/4	C14v19p21
LADY HARRIOT HAY'S STRATHSPEY	1115	117L7L	Bb	4/4	P5v2p8 P5v3p8
LADY HARRIOT HOPE ('S REEL)	1554	1H3H2H2	D F	4/4*	A1v2p38 G9v5p33 C4p31 K1v1p33 G11v2Ap31 N1v1p20 B15v1p10 P5v2p10 P5v3p10 C8v1p37
LADY HARRIOT HOPE'S REEL	1554	1H2H2H2	F	2/2	S12v1p3
LADY HARRIOT HOPE'S REEL	1564	1H3H2H2	F G	2/2	A7v2p31 E1v1p18 A7v5p9 A7v6p13
LADY HARRIOT MONTAGUE'S FAVORITE	1H3H1H6	5622H	D	6/8	G10v4p34
LADY HARRIOT SPENCER'S FANCY	1H4H1H2H	1H4H1H1	D	6/8	B16v2p11
LADY HEATHCOT'S FANCY	116L5L	5L5L12	Bb	2/4	J1p1
LADY HELEN DALRYMPLE'S NEW REEL	551H6	551H2	D	2/2	R5p23
LADY HELEN DOUGLAS'S REEL	3b53b5	1H2H7b7bL	D	2/2	S12v1p69 (II)
LADY HELEN WEDDERBURN'S REEL	3555	351H1H	D	4/4*	Mc19v1p9 (II)
LADY HELENORA HOME'S MINUET	115	331	Bb	3/4	Mc21v1p13
LADY (H)ELENORA HOME'S REEL	3L13L5L	4L3L4L2L	Bb	2/2	S12v1p57 Mc21v1p34
LADY HELONORA HOME'S REEL	11H76	5H1H2H2H	D	2/2	G10v1p13
LADY HERIET GEORGINA HAMILTON	5366	5362	F	4/4	M4v4p2
LADY HERRIOT CUNNINGHAM'S MINUET	111	133	F	3/4	D14v1p8
LADY HOME('S JIG)	1H5H5H5H	1H5H2H4H	D C	6/8	G1v2p53 E1v1p10 C14v21p10 G11v2Ap21 (II)
LADY HOOD'S FAVORITE	1356	4347L	A	2/4	M12p28
LADY HOPE OF PINKIE'S STRATHSPEY	11H76	5437L	Bb	4/4	G10v6p9
LADY HOPE'S FAVORITE WALTZ	3343	2121	Bb	3/8	Mc22Ap4
LADY HOPE'S STRATHSPEY	1L5L11	3L122L	Bb	4/4	Mc22Ap2
LADY HUNTLY'S STRATHSPEY	33H1H6	51H2H2	Eb	2/2	G10v6p1
LADY INVERURY'S REEL	1H565	4532	F	2/2	M11v1p7
LADY ISABELLA THYNNES MINUET	553	57L1	Bb	3/4	S7v3p16,17
LADY ISABELLA WEMYSS'S STRATHSPEY	1256L	5L121	D	4/4	M4v3p32 (II)
LADY JANE BELSCHES'S ALAMANDE	5346	5321	G	2/4	L4p12
LADY JANE DOUGLAS' STRATHSPEY	1H61H1H	1H522	F	4/4	C14v12p4
LADY JANE DUNDAS'S REEL	1565	157L2	G	2/2	L4p6
LADY JANE MONTAGUE'S STRATHSPEY	1L4L4L2L	1L4L3L1	Bb	4/4	M12p17
LADY JANE MONTGOMERY ('S STRATHSPEY)	5524	5551H	F	4/4	G7p17 A7v4p23 (II)
LADY JANE MONTGOMERY'S REEL	3135	4542	A	4/4	S4v2p6
LADY JANE MURRAY'S RANT	1133	227b7b	D	2/2	R12v1p70

Tune	Code 1	Code 2	Key	Time	References
LADY JANE NEVILL(E)('S REEL)	1H535	352H2H	G	2/2*	M4v3p40 (II)
LADY JANE TAYLOR('S STRATHSPEY)	31H31H	31H2H2	C	4/4	M4v3p46 (II)
LADY JARDINE OF APPLEGIRTH'S NEW STRATHSPEY	3L1L42	5L6L11	Bb	4/4	P11v2p14
LADY JARDINE'S REEL	3111	2347L	Bb	2/2	P9p1
LADY JARDINE'S STRATHSPEY	5115	5124	G F	4/4	A7v4p14 G11v2Cp29 (II)
LADY JARDINE'S STRATHSPEY	1L3L5L5L	1322L	Bb	4/4	P9p1
LADY JEAN DUNDASS'S STRATHSPEY	1155	5162	F	2/2	E2p18
LADY (JEAN) HUME ('S REEL/JIG)	1H5H5H5H	1H5H2H3H	C	6/8	K1v1p23 N1v1p32 B15v1p50
LADY JEAN LINDSAY('S MINUET)	112	351H	F G	3/4	D14v1p1 D14v4p11
LADY JEAN MONTGOMERIE'S STRATHSPEY	5524	5551H	F	4/4	G10v4p27
LADY JEAN MURRAY'S RANT	1133	2277	D	4/4	B15v1p35
LADY JEMIMA CORNWALIS' REEL	11H1H1H	1H364	A	2/2	M4v3p20 (II)
LADY JEMIMA JOHNSTON'S STRATHSPEY	3535	31H42	C	4/4	G10v4p26 (II)
LADY JERSEY'S REEL	5L3L1L3L	1L3L6L2L	A	2/2	B10p14
LADY JOHN SCOTT	1122	5226L	A	4/4	M4v4p28
LADY KEITH'S STRATHSPEY	13L11	6L242	Bb	2/2	B20p5
LADY KETTIE GORDON'S MINUET	1H31	5L7L4	Eb	3/4	D14v1p4
LADY KINLOCH OF GILMERTON'S STRATHSPEY	131H1H	3H3H5H2H	D	4/4	P5v4p20
LADY L. RAMSAY'S REEL	3542	3565	Bb	2/2	G10v3p11
LADY LAUDER DICK'S JIGG	5157	5122	F	6/8	Mc4v1p21
LADY LAWRIES REEL	113b5	47bL37b	A	2/2	R6v1p6
LADY LOUDON'S FAVORITE	1111	2316L	Bb	4/4	E2p18
LADY LOUDON'S STRATHSPEY	5H5H5H5H	5H5H6H2H	D C	4/4	A7v6p1 C5v1p9 A1v4p9 G1v1p45 G10v2p3 A7v2p8 E1v1p32 C8v1p59 G11v1Ap35 Mc12v1p11 (II)
LADY LOUDOUN'S REEL	5L353	47L7L6L	A	4/4	B12p3
LADY LOUGHBOROUGH'S REEL	5L13b5	247b4	E	2/2	B10p33
LADY LOUISA ANN DOUGLAS, A MEDLEY WALTZ	555	51H1H	C	3/4	G9v3p26,27
LADY LOUISA ANN DOUGLAS, A MEDLEY WALTZ	1H3H1H	51H3	C	3/4	G9v3p27
LADY LOUISA ANN DOUGLAS, A MEDLEY WALTZ	333	333	C	3/4	G9v3p26
LADY LOUISA CORNWALLIS' STRATHSPEY	1453	6L247L	Eb	4/4	M4v3p24 (II)
LADY LOUISA GORDON	31H64	31H53	F	2/2	C14v11p3
LADY LOUISA GORDON'S FANCY	1335	6662	G	2/4	P1v2p2
LADY LOUISA GORDON('S REEL)	5L133	6L244	F	4/4	M4v1p7 (II)
LADY LOUISA GORDON'S STRATHSPEY	5331	6542	A	2/2	J1p48
LADY LOUISA GORDON'S STRATHSPEY	3b113b	27bL25	E	4/4	Mc21v2p27
LADY LOUISA HAMILTON	5551H	5562	F	2/2	M4v4p7
LADY LOUISA MACDONALD STRATHSPEY	1155	1142	F	2/4	B10p32
LADY LOUISA MacDONALD'S STRATHSPEY	3bH2H1H1	3b6b27b	E	4/4	Mc21v4p22
LADY LOUISA PAGET'S STRATHSPEY	15L15L	131H2	E	2/2	J1p35
LADY LOUISA RAMSAY'S STRATHSPEY	3H5H5H1H	5H6H3H2H	C	4/4	Mc21v4p15
LADY LOUISA RUSSELL'S JIG	5511	4325L	Bb	6/8	M4v3p5
LADY LUCINDA RAMSAY('S NEW STRATHSPEY)	53b5L1	424L7bL	G	4/4	Mc21v3p32 (II)
LADY LUCY LESSLIE MELVILLE'S REEL	1H511	22H62H	F	4/4*	G10v5p5 (II)
LADY LUCY LESSLIE MELVILLE'S WALTZ	5L132	5L131	Bb	3/8	G9v3p18,19
LADY LUCY RAMSAY	3H5H5H1H	5H6H72H	C	4/4	D15v2p48
LADY LUCY RAMSAY ('S STRATHSPEY/FAVORITE)	3H5H5H1H	5H6H3H2H	D C	4/4*	A7v4p28 C14v15p4 G10v4p16 (II)
LADY LUCY RAMSAY'S REEL	1327L	1331H	C	4/4	C14v18p19
LADY LUCY RAMSAY'S STRATHSPEY	1353	237L7L	F	4/4	S4v2p1
LADY LUCY RAMSAY'S STRATHSPEY	3H5H5H1H	3H6H3H2H	D	4/4	A7v5p29
LADY LUCY RAMSAY'S VALTZ	1H641	1H641	Bb	3/8	G9v4p2,3
LADY MACBETH'S DREAM	3H5H3H1H	3H6H5H2H	D	6/8	O1v3p37 O1v1Bp4
LADY MACKENTASHES REEL	1H1H66	4H3H66	C	2/2	(W3)
LADY MACKINTOSH'S REEL	1H1H62H	1H4H66	D	2/2	B15v1p52 G11v2Bp36 K1v2p38
LADY MACKINTOSH'S REEL	1H1H62H	3H4H66	D	2/2	Mc21v3p6
LADY MADALINA SINCLAIR'S REEL	11H76	5127L	A	4/4	L2p22
LADY MADELINA GORDON'S REEL	5L35L4	5L37L7L	F	2/2	M4v3p54 M4v1p6
LADY MADELINA PALMER'S STRATHSPEY	5H3H3H6H	5H6H2H2H	D	2/2	A7v5p15
LADY MADELINA PALMER'S STRATHSPEY	5654	547L2	F	4/4	M4v3p50
LADY MADELINA (PALMER/SINCLAIR) 'S BIRTH DAY	1H535	1H4H72H	D	4/4*	E1v1p39 A7v5p5 (II)
LADY MADELINA SINCLAIR	331H1H	6542	E	6/8	L1p12
LADY MADELINA SINCLAIR ('S STRATHSPEY)	5336	5522	A	4/4	G10v3p3 G11v1Bp26 C14v8p18 Mc7p7
LADY MADELINA SINCLAIR'S BIRTH DAY	15L3L5L	137L2	Bb	4/4	G10v4p6
LADY MADELINA SINCLAIR'S BIRTH DAY	1H535	1H3H72H	D	4/4	G1v1p46
LADY MADELINA SINCLAIR'S REEL	13L4L5L	157L2	Bb	4/4	Mc21v4p38
LADY MADELINA SINCLAIR'S REEL	15L3L4L	2L242	A	2/2	Mc4v3p7 (II)
LADY MADELINA SINCLAIR'S STRATHSPEY	5336	5622	A	4/4	P5v3p18 (II)
LADY MARGARET STEWART ('S REEL)	513b5	5424	B	4/4*	E1v1p35 G11v1Cp32 G10v2p22,23 (II)
LADY MARGRET CARNEGIE'S MINUET	116	1H71H	Eb	3/4	C13v4p38
LADY MARGRET MACDONALD	527L2	331H7	F	2/2	S12v1p34
LADY MARGt STEWART'S MINUET	11L1	112	Bb	3/4	C22p3
LADY MARIA PARKER	3233	427L5L	A	4/4	B12p2,3
LADY MARIA PARKER'S STRATHSPEY	3233	427L2	A	2/2	C14v20p11
LADY MARY ANN	3342	5555	C D	4/4	(J3) A1v5p56
LADY MARY ANN CARN(E)GIE'S FAVOURITE	3112	311H1H	D	2/2	Mc22p8
LADY MARY ANN CARNEGIE'S MINUET	1H52H	755	Eb	3/4	Mc21v1p22

LADY MARY ANN CARNEGIE'S STRATHSPEY	3b551	3b127bL	G	4/4	D16p18
LADY MARY BENTINCK'S FANCY	1131	1H5H4H2H	D	2/4	C14v20p20 P6v1p3 P10p17
LADY MARY BRUCE'S STRATHSPEY	5551H	4H3H2H2H	D	2/2	G9v2p21
LADY MARY DOUGLAS'S FAVORITE	3565	353H2H	D	6/8	E1v1p52,53
LADY MARY HAY'S ALLAMANDE	1H1H1H5H	5H3H71H	C	2/4	G9v4p6
LADY MARY HAY'S FAVOURITE	1335	1362	Bb	6/8	S11v1p1
LADY MARY HAY'S MINUET	115L	553	Bb	3/4	S11v1p16
LADY MARY HAY'S REEL	5353	53H2H2	F	4/4	F3p3
LADY MARY HAY'S REEL	5H3bH1H3bH	4H2H7bH2H	C	2/2	S11v1p1
LADY MARY HAY'S SCOTCH MEASURE	1155	151H3bH	D	4/4	G10v3p27
LADY MARY KEITH'S MINUET	113	553	Eb	3/4	C22p1
LADY MARY LESSLEY'S MINUET	1H1H3	515L	Eb G	3/4	D14v1p3 D14v4p10
LADY MARY LINDSAY'S ALLAMANDE	5H5H5H5H	5H5H1H1H	C	2/4	G9v4p6
LADY MARY LINDSAY'S JIG	13b1H1H	7b424	G	6/8	F3p8
LADY MARY LINDSAY'S REEL	1H515	3H4H2H2H	F	2/2	(B21)
LADY MARY LINDSAY'S REEL	3H1H1H1H	2266	C	2/2	R5p33 (II)
LADY MARY LINDSAY'S STRATHSPEY	13b13b	2427b	G	4/4	A7v1p6
LADY MARY LINDSAY'S STRATHSPEY	115L3L	1142	F	4/4	E2p9
LADY MARY LYONS REEL	1H1H22H	1H1H1H1H	D	2/2	Mc9v3p39
LADY MARY MENZIE'S REEL	5351H	5362	F	4/4*	B15v1p82 C4p63 (II)
LADY MARY MONTAGUES REEL	51H53	6542	D	4/4*	Mc21v4p19 B11p19 Mc21v3p18
					A1v6p9 (II)
LADY MARY MONTGOMERY'S REEL	5L31H5	657L2	F	4/4	Mc21v4p24
LADY MARY MURRAY'S ALLAMANDE	3H4H5H4H	3H2H1H5H	C	2/4	G9v4p20
LADY MARY MURRAY'S STRATHSPEY	13b13b	2427b	E	2/2	G8p28
LADY MARY MURRAY'S STRATHSPEY	5L153	2427L	G	4/4	G10v4p3 (II)
LADY MARY POWIS'S MINUET	113	154	D	3/4	R12v3p12
LADY MARY PRIMROSE('S FAVORITE)	5L3L5L1	16L2L2L	Bb	4/4	G10v4p13 A7v4p9 (II)
LADY MARY RAMSAY ('S STRATHSPEY)	1153	5653	D Eb G	4/4*	C8v1p43 C14v17p17 G10v4p15
					B12p8,9 C8v2p15 (II)
LADY MARY RAMSAY'S VALTZ	1345	1341	Bb	3/8	G9v4p11
LADY MARY STOPFORD'S REEL	51H53	6542	D	4/4*	G10v4p19 C14v12p18 (II)
LADY MATILDA BRUCE('S REEL)	3H3H1H7	532H4H	F	4/4*	G11v2Dp21 C14v26p6,7
LADY MAXWELL OF MONREATH'S REEL	1H511	22H2H2H	F	2/2	R5p32
LADY MAXWELL'S REEL	1H511H	1H52H2	C	6/8	Mc13v2p31 C13v2p25
LADY MAXWELL'S REEL	1H551H	1H52H2	C	6/8	C13v1p4 C13v2p25
LADY MAY FROWN,	3362	35L31	G	6/8	W4v2p19
AND BE KIND ENOUGH TOO, A					
LADY McDUFF'S LAMENT	552	315	D .	3/4	O1v3p35 O1v1Bp4
LADY McINTOSHES REEL	1H1H62H	1H4H1H6	D	2/2	G1v2p64
LADY McINTOSHE'S REEL	11H1H3bH	7b53b2	D	2/2	S12v1p57
LADY McINTOSH'S RANT	51H62H	3H1H55	D	2/2	R12v1p65
LADY McINTOSH'S REEL	51H1H3bH	7b542	D	4/4*	G9v5p36 C33p5
LADY McKENZIE OF COUL	5564	751H5H	C	4/4	G11v1Bp28 (II)
LADY McNEIL	15L6L1	5L6L4L2L	Bb	4/4	M4v4p19
LADY MELVILLE'S FAVORITE	5451	537L5L	Bb	6/8	G9v2p2,3
LADY MENZIES OF CASTLE MENZIES'	5L5L5L3L	5L5L11	Bb	4/4	Mc19v1p1 Mc19v2p13
STR./MEDLEY					
LADY MENZIES OF CASTLE MENZIES	1H3H72H	1H3H4H6H	C	6/8	M4v4p12
LADY MENZIES OF CASTLE MENZIES(REEL)	115L5L	6L5L6L5L	Bb	4/4	Mc19v1p1 Mc19v2p13
LADY MILNER'S REEL	1151	1354	A	2/2	B10p5
LADY MINTO'S FAVOURITE	116L5L	1132	A	6/8	P11v1p2
LADY MONTAGUE'S STRATHSPEY	13b11	7bL7bL42	A	4/4	S4v2p14
LADY MONTGOMERIE('S REEL) [LADY	113L5L	117L2	Bb	4/4*	C8v1p12 C14v20p2 P6v1p15
MONTGOMERY]					A7v4p10 G11v2Dp15 N1v1p24 (II)
LADY MONTGOMERIES STRATHSPEY	5L5L5L5L	5L1L26L	A	4/4	N1v1p34
LADY MONTGOMERY'S REEL	1H1H35	1H1H72H	C D	4/4*	A7v5p14 E1v1p71 G1v2p72
LADY MONTGOMERY'S STRATHSPEY	136L5L	1462	A	4/4	S4v2p15
LADY MORPETH'S WALTZ	5544	5541	Bb	3/8	C14v17p5
LADY MUIR MACKINZIE	1H531	427L6	D	4/4	G11v1Cp2
LADY MUIR McKENZIE'S FAVORITE	5L111H	6416L	D	2/4	G10v5p2
LADY MUNRO'S REEL	5L322	5L326L	Bb	2/2	J2p1
LADY MURRAY'S REEL	5131	26L7L5L	A	2/2	G9v2p21
LADY NELLY WEMYSS('S (JIG/REEL)	3535	3524	A	6/8	K1v1p21,27 B17p21 C13v2p6
					G11v2Ap25 B15v1p13 C8v2p29
					C8v1p18 (II)
LADY NELSON'S REEL	1H564	2H775	G	4/4	H1p33
LADY NIVEN LUMSDEN	1H513	6L241	Eb	4/4	M4v3p22
OF ACHINDOIR'S STRATHSPEY					
LADY NORTH'S FANCY	3517L	2431	F	6/8	B16v3p64
LADY OF THE DESART, THE	1H51H	766	G	3/4	B11p30,31 Mc12v2p15,16
LADY OF THE FLOW'RY FIELD, THE	112	3b3b2	G	3/4	O1v5p23 O1v1Dp4,5
LADY OF THE LAKE	316L1	316L2	A	6/8	C14v27p13
LADY OF THE LAKE	3335	1H652	G	6/8	B7p42
LADY OF THE LAKE, THE	316L1	3125	G	6/8	C8v2p6 C8v1p8 E1v2p45 (II)
LADY OF THE LAKE, THE	3335	1H653	G	6/8	H6v22p1
LADY OF THE MANOR	11H5H3H	4H2H3H1H	D	6/8	B16v3p85
LADY OF THE MANOR, THE	5353	537L2	F	4/4	B16v3p2
LADY ORMINSTON	311	5L3L3L	Bb	6/4	C22p22
LADY PEEL	116L2	1351H	Eb	4/4	M4v4p33
LADY PENNYMAN'S ALLEMAND	1342	7L242	Bb	4/4	S7v1p26
LADY PENUEL GRANT'S STRATHSPEY	13L12	13L4L2L	A	4/4	T1v2p5

LADY PERTH'S STRATHSPEY	1525	2422	A	4/4	Mc21v4p41
LADY PORTMORE'S FANCY	3555	4646	G	2/2	C14v6p21
LADY RACHAEL RUSSELL	1151H	2246	F	4/4	M4v4p7
LADY RAMSAY OF BALMAINS MINUET	112	665	Eb	3/4	D15v2p1
LADY RAMSY'S FANCY	1H1H1H3H	1H1H22H	C	6/8	B11p10
LADY ROBERT KERR'S STRATHSPEY	5514	27bL42	G	2/2	G9v2p9
LADY ROSS OF BALNAGOWAN'S REEL	31H31H	31H42	C	2/4	J2p7
LADY S. MONTGOMERY'S REEL	1H76b5	43b27b	E	4/4	Mc21v4p22
LADY SALISBURY'S FANCY	1H1H2H5	5H2H2H5	D	2/4	C14v3p14
LADY SALTON'S GAVOTT	5353	2247L	G	2/2	S5p18
LADY SCOTT'S REEL	17L5L1L	17L6L2	Bb	2/2	P11v2p1
LADY SCOTT'S STRATHSPEY	16L15L	147L2	Bb	4/4	P11v2p1
LADY SHAFT(E)SBURY	15L13	547L2	Eb	2/4	C14v6p1
LADY SHAFTSBURY ('S STRATHSPEY)	1H31H3H	5H2H72H	D	4/4*	A1v5p21 E1v1p22 C5v1p21
LADY SHAFTSBURY('S STRATHSPEY)	13L13	527L2	Eb	4/4*	G11v1Bp21 D16p31 K1v2p10
					Mc12v1p3 (II)
LADY SHAFTSBURY'S STRATHSPEY	13L13	547L2	G	2/4	N1v1p3
LADY SHAFTSBURY'S STRATHSPEY	1352	7L213L	Eb	2/4	Mc12v1p4
LADY SOPHIA CECIL'S FANCY	1125L	6L5L4L2L	Bb	6/8	C14v22
LADY SOPHIA KEPPEL	1231	4322	Bb	2/4	H1p22
LADY St. CLAIR DYSART'S STRATHSPEY	5232	551H1H	D	4/4	W2v1p1
LADY St. CLAIRS ERSKINE'S REEL	525L5L	136L2	A	2/2	W2v2p1
LADY STAMFORD'S REEL	5353	27b27bL	D	4/4	B10p30
LADY STOPFORD'S REEL	4251H	3122	A	4/4	W4v1p18
LADY STOPFORD'S REEL	4H2H5H1T	3H1H2H2H	D	4/4	A1v4p44 C5v1p44
LADY STORMONT'S STRATHSPEY	1131	6447L	A	2/2	Mc19v2p2 Mc19v3p18
LADY STORMOUNT'S GIGG	1H61H1	1H652	G	6/8	B10p20
LADY STORMOUNT'S STRATHSPEY	3b154	2424	G	2/2	G8p28 P1v1p8
LADY SUSAN GORDON'S QUICK STEP	1215L	2437L	Bb	6/8	Mc21v2p6
LADY SUSAN GORDON('S REEL)	1353	6L5L4L2L	Bb	2/2	M4v1p5 M4v3p10 (II)
LADY SUSAN GORDON'S STRATHSPEY	5L1L5L1L	5L322L	Bb	4/4	Mc21v2p29
LADY SUSAN GORDON'S STRATHSPEY	5L3b53b	4L242	G	2/2	S4v1p22
LADY SUSAN HAMILTON	5L3L5L3L	547L2	Bb	4/4	P6v1p19
LADY SUSAN STEWART'S STRATHSPEY	15L11	436L2	G	4/4	Mc4v2p13
LADY SUSAN STEWART'S STRATHSPEY	13b1H2H	7b427bL	D	2/2	B10p24
LADY SUTTIE'S REEL	5151H	5162	D	2/4	E2p7
LADY TANKERVILLE'S GIG	1H1H1H1H	2H62H5	C	6/8	B10p21
LADY TEMPLE'S STRATHSPEY	136L6L	1166	A	4/4	Mc11p3
LADY TERFICHEN'S RANT [LADY TORPHICHEN]	13b44	13b6b6b	E	4/4*	W7p6 (II)
LADY TOWNS	1H1H1H1H	1H1H2H2H	F	2/2	C14v20p5
LADY TOWNSEND'S WHIM	1H3H2H5	671H5H	C	2/4	C14v2p1
LADY VIRGINIA MURRAY'S FANCY	3112	3122	G	6/8	C14v6p19
LADY VISCOUNTESS DUNCAN'S STRATHSPEY	5622	5651H	D	4/4	G10v5p25
LADY WALKER DRUMMOND'S STRATHSPEY	3H2H1H6	5565	F	4/4	G9v2p22
LADY WALLACE	3b1L3bL1L	4527b	G	4/4*	K1v2p16 G11v2Bp14
LADY WALLACE	5L113b	5L111	A	4/4	A7v3p29
LADY WALLACE REEL	3b1L3bL5L	4524	G	2/2	A7v4p4
LADY WALLACE'S MINUET	51H4	320	Eb	3/4	S11v1p20
LADY WALLACE('S REEL)	1H513	2466	F	2/2*	R5p16 Mc7p12 H3p5 (II)
LADY WALLACE'S REEL	3b1L3bL5L	4527b	G	4/4*	Mc21v4p30,31 Mc21v12
LADY WALLACE'S REEL	3b5L6bL5L	4422	A	4/4	A7v5p25
LADY WARWICK'S REEL	3b3b43b	3b3b42	G	6/8	B10p6
LADY WHITEFOORD'S REEL	131H3	27bL27bL	D	2/2	Mc9v3p6
LADY WHITEFORD'S REEL	3b23b2	47bL47bL	G	6/8	R5p38
LADYKIRK HOUSE	113L	114	A	9/8	G10v5p22
LADY'S DELIGHT, THE	51H42	2416L	A	4/4	C7p5
LADY'S FAVOURITE, (THE)	3344	337L2	A	2/4	R12v1p19 (W3)
LADY'S PLAY THING, THE	3322	1132	G	6/8	A1v1p2
LAING AND HENDRY'S BIRTHDAY	532H2H	2H3H1H6	C	4/4	M12p4
LAIRD O' COCKPEN(, NO.3), THE	13b27bL	11H75	G	6/8	C8v1p62 G1v1p40
LAIRD O' COCKPEN, THE	13b27bL	11H7b5	E A	6/8	C6p25 (II) E1v2p121
LAIRD OF COCKPEN'S SCOTCH-MEASURE, THE	3255	3551H	F	2/2	P7p13
LAIRD OF FOVERAN, THE	511	417bL	A	3/2	C18p26,27
LAIRD OF GLENBUCKIE'S HIGHLAND FLING, THE	13b27bL	13b55	B	2/2	B20p15
LAIRD OF MACFARLANE, THE	1H531	3H2H3H2H	C	4/4	G11v1Ap20
LAIRD OF MAC(K)INTOSH ('S STRATHSPEY(, THE)	5353	7L27L2	G	4/4*	G11v2Cp16 (II)
LAIRD OF McNAB'S FAVORITE, THE	1524	17b41	A	6/8	G10v4p38
LAIRD OF STOW, THE	51H65	3H2H72H	E	4/4	G10v6p17
LAKES OF KELLARNIE, THE	3H2H5H5H	6H2H6H2H	D	6/8	A1v4p63
LAKES OF KILLARNEY (KELLARNIE) THE	3255	6262	Bb	6/8	G11v1Cp16 G10v3p31
LAKES OF KILLARNEY, THE	3255	6252	Bb	6/8	E1v1p86
LAKES OF WICKLOW, THE	51H2H6	551H7	D	6/8	C14v21p22
L'ALLEGRANTE	3H2H76	5650	C	2/4	P10p11
L'ALSACIENNE	1355	72H1H1H	G	2/4	Mc9v2p27
LAMAIR'S FROLICK	5443	3113	A	2/2	B16v3p68
LAMBERTON RACES	153H2H	1H542	G F	4/4	C5v1p10 A1v4p10 E1v1p30
					G11v1Cp21 G10v2p11 Mc12v1p38
					(II)
LAMBERTON RACES	1232	315L2	D	6/8	C13v1p28,29
LAMENT	5555	5555	F	6/8	C10v2Bp54

LAMENT FOR A FRIEND, A	1H72H2H	5H3bH1H2H	E	4/4	G1v2p92	
LAMENT FOR KING JAMES	3355	6632	G	2/4	Mc1v1p89-91	
LAMENT FOR LORD BALLENDEN, A	132	6L5L5L	A	3/4	P11v1p18	
LAMENT FOR MR RAMSAY OF BARNTON	316L5L	5353	G	4/4	G10v6p25	
LAMENT FOR MRS TULLOCH, KIRKMICHAEL, A	3221	6651	G	4/4	T1v2p8	
LAMENT FOR SIR HARRY NIVEN LUMSDEN BARt. OF ACHINDOIR	35L1L1	532L2	Bb	6/8	M4v3p60	
LAMENT FOR THE DEATH OF LADY DUNBAR OF NORTHFIELD	3b117bL	3b115	G	6/8	C18p37	
LAMENT FOR THE DEATH OF HUGH ALLAN	3b215L	3bL4L5L1	A	4/4	C18p34	
LAMENT FOR THE DEATH OF JANE, DUCHESS OF GORDON	1H72H2H	5H3bH1H2H	C	4/4	M12p34	
LAMENT OF FLORA McDONALD	16L21	35L31	A	6/8	G10v6p20	
(LAMENT OF) MARY, QUEEN OF SCOTS (LAMENT)	3313	6621	F D	4/4*	C6p29 (J3)	
LAMENT OF WALLACE(, AFTER THE BATTLE OF FALKIRK), THE	3335	3H3H3H6	C G	6/8	C6p28 G1v1p20	
LAMENT ON THE DEATH OF PATRICK MORE McCRUIMMEN	1323	11H1H1H	G	4/4	Mc1v1p84-88	
LAMENT, THE	316L5L	5L2L31	Bb	6/8	L3p4	
LAMENTATION FOR MCGRIGOR (OF RORO)	112	35L5L	A	3/4	K1v2p2 Mc5p13 G11v2Bp2	
LAMENTATION FOR THE FALLEN HEROES OF WATERLOO	31H63	3752	Eb	4/4	G11v2Dp4	
LAMMERMUIR LILT	1435	2425L	G	4/4	L3p6	
LAMOTT'S JIG	3L6L36	7563H	G	6/8	Mc9v2p22	
LAMOTT'S RIGADON	1H3b11	3bH53b3b	D	6/8	Mc9v2p23	
L'AMOUR DE VILLAGE	1162	35L13L	Bb	6/8	C14v2p3	
LANCERS QUADRILLE, THE [LANCIERS]	5553	1111	G	4/4*	C8v2p32 C8v1p52 G1v1p14	
LANCERS QUADRILLE, THE	5H5H1H1H	3H3H2H2H	C	2/4	G7p21	
LANCERS STRATHSPEY, THE	31H65	31H2H2	F	4/4	P9p35	
LANCIER'S QUADRILLE, THE	5H5H5H3H	1H1H1H1H	C	4/4	G13p3	
LAND O' CAKES, THE	1H324	1H326L	F	2/2	B20p16,17	
LANDLADY OF INVER INN, THE	317L2	3135	F	2/4	G11v1Ap18	
LANG LIFE TO NEIL GOW	1111	6L213	D	4/4	D15v1p16	
LANG LIFE TO NEIL GOW	1H1H1H1H	62H1H3H	D	4/4	A7v6p58	
LANGO LEE	1H3H2H3H	51H5H2H	D	6/8	A1v1p24	
LANGO LEE	5L144	35L31	G	6/8	E1v1p91 A1v1p9	
LANGOLIL [LANGO LEE]	1323	5L152	A	6/8	O1v1lp70	
LAOIDH AN AMADAIN MHOIR	3H3H2H1H	1H61H1H	C	4/4	Mc5p18	
LAOIDH AN T'SLANUIGHEAR	1315L	1210	G	4/4	F2v2p30(20)	
LAOIDH GHARA 'SNAM BAN	121	3b3b4	A	3/4	Mc5p18	
LARGO ANDANTE	1H2H3H5H	3H2H1H1	D	2/4	P8v1p12	
LARGO LAW	15L13	6522	A	4/4	G11v2Cp24 (II)	
LARGO'S FAIRY DANCE	3H3H3H3H	3H3H72H	C D	2/4*	G10v5p19 (II)	
LARICKILLE	1353	2366	D	2/2	Mc9v1p8	
LARK MINUET, BY HAYDN	17L1	201	G	3/4	G9v3p14,15	
LAR(R)Y GROGAN	3322	3411	G	6/8	A1v1p54 O1v1Jp98	
LARY GROGAN	3H3H2H2H	3H4H1H1H	D	6/8	A1v4p11 C5v1p11	
LARY GROGAN	3H3H2H2H	3H4H2H2H	D	6/8	Mc12v1p56	
LAS CHASSE DE LA GARDE	531H7	5H3H1H2H	D	6/8	S12v2p14	
LASHLEYS MARCH	1H1H1H	1H1H1H	D	6/4	W7p24	
LASLY'S MARCH	1H1H1H5	1H532	D	6/8	A1v4p16 O1v4p33 O1v1Bp36	
LASS AMONG THE EATNOCH, THE	3b3b11	3b3b15L	A	4/4	P5v3p26 Y1p15	
(LASS AMONG) THE ETNOCH'S, (THE)	4L7bL11	3b13b5L	A	4/4	A7v6p16 A7v2p5	
LASS AMONGST THE ACTENOCH, THE	7bL3b11	3b3b15L	A	4/4*	A1v6p13 Mc9v1p27 C33p9	
LASS IF I COME NEAR YOU	13b27bL	13b1H5	A	4/4	C5v2p67 A1v1p63 C4p18	
LASS O' GOWRIE, THE	3L5L11	6L6L22	Bb	2/4	C6p22	
LASS OF BALLANTRAE, THE [LASSES OF BALLANTRAE]	5367	5326L	F G	2/2*	G11v2Dp22 (II) G1v2p68	
LASS OF BALLOCHMYLE, THE	4433	6426L	G	4/4	C5v2p33	
LASS OF HUMBER SIDE, THE	15L1	366	G	3/4	G10v5p20	
LASS OF LEVING-STONE, THE	3115	1H1H3H3H	F	2/2	P7p14/15	
LASS OF LEVINGSTONE, THE	1133	5552	G	2/2	W7p10	
LASS OF LEWENEY, THE	4311H	1H756	G	2/2	O1v1Kp123	
LASS OF LIVINGSTON, THE	1131H	5552	F G	2/2	Mc9v2p8,9 T6v1p107	
LASS OF LIVINGSTON, THE	1133	5552	G	2/2	C20p26,27	
LASS OF LIVINGSTONE, THE	1136	5552	Eb F G	4/4*	H1p28 S16p102,103 Mc8v2Bp15 O1v1Cp7	
LASS OF PATIE'S MILL, THE	4235	1H1H55	D	2/2	Mc9v2p12,13	
LASS OF PATIE'S MILL, THE	4235	1H1H3HO	D	4/4	G17p1	
LASS OF PATIE'S MILL, THE	4235	1H1H3H3H	C	4/4	C6p3	
LASS OF PATIES MILL, THE	3235	1H1H55	D	4/4	O1v1Bp14,15 O1v3p16,17 C13v3p38,39 S16p80,81 Mc8v1Ap24 B5p3 C20p74,75	
LASS OF PATIES MILL, THE	3235	1H1H1H5	G D	4/4	C19p7 T7p10,11	
LASS OF PATIES MILL, THE	3235	1H1H3HO	G D C F	4/4	C8v2p45 C4p47 E1v1p79 C5v2p24 N1v2p19 (C25) (J3) Mc12v2p21,22	
LASS OF PATIE'S MILL, THE	3335	1H1H55	D	4/4	Mc8v2Ap11	
LASS OF PATY'S MILL, THE	3235	1H1H3H5	D	4/4	T6v1p1 P4p8 P8v2p7	
LASS OF PETTIE'S MILL, THE	331H5	6622	F	4/4	C29p24	
LASS OF RICHMOND HILL, THE	51H1H2H	3H61H7	D	2/4	C8v2p50	

Title					
LASS OF THE HILL, THE	542	7L7L2	G	3/4	O1v1Lp160,161
LASS THAT STOLE MY HEART AWA, THE	1315L	7bL220	G	4/4	C5v3p65
LASS WI' A LUMP O' LAND, THE	1565	1544	A	6/8	A7v2p20
LASS WI' THE GOLDEN HAIR, THE	1H1H76	72H1H1H	G	6/8	C4p3
LASS WITH A LUMP OF LAND, (A)	1H1H72H	1H1H55	D F	6/8	(J3) T6v2p26 P8v2p24
LASSES LIKES NAE BRANDY	5333	47bL1H3H	A	2/2	Mc23p18,19
LASSES LIKE(S) NAE BRANDY	51H65	27b46	A	4/4	B15v1p83 (II)
LASSES LIKES NAE BRANDY	5333	47bL46	A	2/2	C20p59
LASSES OF ANCRUM, THE	51H51H	7b2H4H7b	D	4/4	C7p22
LASSES OF BERWICK	11H63	637L2	D	6/8	R12v1p92
LASSES OF DUNCE, THE	5H2H1H5	6522	D	6/8	R12v1p96 A1v1p55
LASSES OF IRVIN, THE	1H1H35	67b24	D	2/2	C13v2p4
LASSES OF MELROSS, THE	3142	3125L	G	6/8	A1v2p34
LASSES OF STEWARTON, THE	3H2H1H5	3155	D	2/2	Mc7p14
LASSES OF STEWARTON, THE	3H2H1H1H	3155	D	4/4*	G1v2p59 C14v9p19 A7v6p90 G8p16
					K1v1p37 S12v1p46 G11v2Ap35
					(II)
LASSES OF THE BARN, THE	1515	427L2	D	4/4	Mc16p2
LASSES OF THE BORDER, THE	151H5	6522	D	6/8	C7p6
LASSES OF THE FERRY, THE	1122	15L22	A	2/2	S12v1p33
LASSES OF THE WEST, THE	5331	2453	F	4/4	C7p2
LASSIE AN' SILLER AN' A'S MY AIN	351H5	352H2	D	6/8	C18p20
LASSIE GAE MILK ON MY COW HILL	663	1H52	G	3/2	R6v2p9
LASS(IE) GIN YE LO'E ME (TELL ME NOW)	3566	51H3H5H	D	6/8	C5v2p30 C5v3p63 A1v2p4 E1v2p32
LASSIE I LO'E BEST OF A', THE	3352	35L05L	G	2/2	G1v1p21
LASSIE I'LL COME NEAR YOU	13b27bL	11H1H5	G	4/4	G11v2Bp6
LASSIE IN THE YELLOW COATIE, THE	1157b	61H66	G	2/2	R12v1p93
LASSIE LOST HER SILKEN SNOOD, THE	3426	5551	Eb	4/4	G10v4p15
LASSIE LOST HER SILKEN SNOOD, THE	112	553	G	3/4	O1v1Lp160
LASSIE WI' THE YELLOW COATIE, (THE)	1151H	61H66	A D G	4/4*	O1v1Hp47 G11v2Ap7 A1v1p68
					B15v1p76 E1v1p12 N1v1p7
					K1v1p16 C4p63 (II)
LASSIE WIE THE LINT WHITE LOCKS	3335	1H61H6	D	4/4	B7p36
LASSIE WITH THE YELLOW COATIE, THE	1151H	7b7b66	D	4/4	Mc7p15
LASSIE WITH THE YELLOW COATY, THE	1151H	662H2H	D	4/4	Mc9v3p34/35
LASSIES OF STEWARTOWN, THE	764#5	7L5L22	G	2/2	C13v2p53
LAST CRADLE SONG, THE	3234	226L6L	Bb	4/4	C10v2Ap31
LAST MAY A BRAW WOOER, &c.	1321	3165	G	6/8	G1v1p22
[LOTHIAN LASSES]					
LAST MERRY NIGHT, THE	313	556	G	6/4	R12v1p76
LAST PINT ALE, THE	1122	6547bL	D	4/4	B15v1p37
LAST PINT ALE, THE	1526	3521	G	4/4	O1v1Ip74
LAST PINT OF ALE, THE	1122	6522	D	4/4	A7v6p74
LAST PINT OF ALE, THE	1H3H4H2H	6547bL	D	2/2	Mc21v3p2,3
LAST PINT OF ALE, THE	1122	6527bL	D	2/2	A7v3p26,27
LAST PINT, THE	1126L	1155	D	2/2	C33p15
LAST ROSE OF SUMMER, THE	31H7	531	G	3/4	C8v2p13 C8v1p39
LAST ROSE OF SUMMER, THE	31H6	531	G	3/4	E1v2p43
LAST TIME I CAME O'ER THE MOOR, THE	421H1H	3H2H1H6	E D	4/4	C6p13 G17p2
LAST TIME I CAME O'ER THE MOOR, THE	321H1H	1H2H76	D	4/4	C13v3p8,9
LAST TIME I CAME O'ER THE MOOR, THE	321H1H	3H2H76	F G D	4/4	T6v1p10 P4p16 T7p16,17
					C4p66 C5v2p17 O1v4p34
					(J3) S16p78,79 Mc8v1Cp80
					Mc8v2Ap21 N1v2p55 O1v1Bp24
					B5p4 Mc12v2p17,18 C20p3 P8v2p5
LASTRUMPONY	3335	3324	A	6/8	O1v1Kp123
LATHA SUIBHAIL (SLEIBH DHOMH)	11H7b5	3b420	E	4/4	C4p24 Mc5p19
LATHER AWA' WI' YOUR OAK STICK	3155	3161H	G	6/8	A1v1p43
LAUCHLAN'S LILT	553b1	3b427bL	G	2/2	O1v1Jp102
LAUDER LILT, THE	1122	3547L	G	4/4	O1v1Lp155
LAURETTA	1H1H2H5H	1H1H2H5	E	2/4	D15v2p9
LAWER'S HOUSE	4215	427b7b	A	4/4	G10v5p33
LAWERS HOUSE	3b215	3b27b7b	A	4/4	Mc4v2p11 Mc12v1p25
LAWLAND LADS THINK THEY'RE FINE, THE	1355	1H453	F	6/8	E1v2p97
LAWLAND LADS WI' HIGHAND KILTS, THE	1552	1555	D	2/2	H3p18
LAWLAND MAIDS, THE	351H	1H1H1H	G	6/4	P8v1p3
LAWREL OF VICTORY, THE	333	542	A	3/2	H1p26
LAY BY YOUR WHEEL BETTY	331	432	G	3/4	A1v5p63
LAY BY YOUR WHEEL BETTY	331	432	G	3/4	C5v1p63
LAY DOWN IN THE BROOM	5255	222H1H	D	4/4	K1v1p8
LAY TO THE ROYAL HIGHLANDERS,	321H7	5620	D	2/4	C10v2Bp67
OR 42 REGt					
LAY'S OF LUNKERTY, THE	1343	27b47bL	G	2/2	C24v2p25
LAZY MIST, THE	51H1H	1H1H3H	C	3/4	O1v1Lp158
LE BAGATELLE	1H2H75	651H1H	D	6/8	B16v2p8
LE BRUNETTE	51H53	1257L	G	2/4	B16v2p8 B16v4p85
LE CRITIQUE	3352	3211	A	6/8	B16v2p1
LE DEROUTTE DE PALATINE or	1111	15H4H2H	D	2/4	C14v6p4
MISS BENTINCK'S FANCY					
LE DIABLE AN LAIR	5531H	72H51	G	6/8	S12v2p47
LE FONTAINBLEAU	3232	3211	G	6/8	S12v2p1
LE GARCON VOLAGE	1122	31H2H2H	G	6/8	G13p4 E1v2p28,29

LE PANTALON	3H1H55	5553H	G	2/4	E1v2p130
LE PANTALON	1H1H2H1H	3H4H2H5H	G	6/8	E1v2p25
LE PETIT BOSSU	1343	7L225L	G	6/8	A1v5p47
LE PETIT TAMBOUR	1H31H1H	2H2H2H2H	C	2/4	E1v2p87
LE PLAISIRE DE PLOMBIERE	5H4H5H4H	5H5H2H5	C	6/8	C14v7p17
LE PULLEYS ALLEMAND	1H634	1H631	G	2/4	B16v3p95
LE PULLEY'S FANCY	1H653	1H652	A	6/8	B16v4p88
LE SPAGNOLETTE	5515L	2631H	G	2/4	W6p10,11
LE VERTIGO	17L12	4212	G	6/8	B16v3p6
LEA RIG, THE	35L11	2436L	A	4/4	G9v1p16,17 R4p7,8 C20p28,29
LEADER HAUGHS AND YARROW	357b	640	G	3/4	Mc8v1Dp116
LEADER HAUGHS AND YARROW	357b	644	G A F	3/4	T6v2p21 C5v2p14 (J3)
LEAM IS AITHEARR AN T SUAIN	7bL3b3b	3b51	A	9/8	Mc5p20
LEANDER ON THE BAY	116	551	G F	3/4	Mc8v1Dp96 N1v2p69 (J3)
LEAP OVER THE GARTER	5511	27L11	Bb	2/4	W4v1p16
LEAP OVER THE GARTER	5H5H1H1H	2H71H1H	D	2/4	A1v4p40
LEAVE THEE, LOTH TO LEAVE THEE	426L1	5L6L22	G	2/4	C10v2Ap44
LEE MILLS	35L6L5L	35L26L	A	4/4	B11p23
LEE RIGG	3H51H1H	2H4H3H6	D	2/4	G1v1p28
LEE RIGG, THE	15L11	1227L	G	2/4	A1v1p16 (II)
LEE RIGG, THE	15L11	3426L	A	2/2	R6v2p28
LEE RIGG, THE	15L5L6L	1113	A	2/2	O1v1Hp54
LEES OF LUNCARTIE, THE	5L343	2347bL	G	4/4	Mc21v3p12 G10v1p4 (II)
LEES OF LUNCARTIES STRATHSPEY, THE	5L343	2427L	G	4/4	C13v1p27
LEEZIE LINDSAY	113	51H5	F	3/4	C6p23
LEGACY, THE	1H1H5H5H	1H3H61H	D	6/8	E1v1p36 C8v2p34
LEGACY, THE	1155	136L1	Bb	6/8	C8v1p29
LEIPSIC WALTZ	553	1H1H6	G	3/4	B7p16
LEITH SCOTS MEASURE, THE	1554	2665	A	2/2	O1v1Lp157
LEITH WYND	5326L	5555	D	4/4	C29p16
LEITH WYND	5322	5555	D	4/4	C20p77 Mc8v1Cp82 Mc8v2Ap8 O1v1Bp18,19 O1v3p28,29
LEITH WYND	526L6L	5555	G F	4/4*	C5v3p55 (W3) (J3)
LEITH-HALL	5L133	5L146L	F	4/4	M4v3p55
LEIUt COL: BAILLIE OF LEYS STRATHSPEY	131H3	227L7L	D	4/4	G15p11
LENNOX LOVE	1H131	2366	F	4/4	P5v2p11
LENNOX LOVE TO BLANTYRE	1131	22H66	F	2/2	C13v2p13
LENNOX'S LOVE TO BLANTYRE	1131	2366	F G	2/2	G11v2Ap29 K1v1p31 C14v21p10,11 (II) E1v1p56
LENOX LOVE TO BLANTYRE	1131	2266	F	2/2	S12v1p9 G9v5p31 B15v1p17 N1v1p6
LES BOIS	561H1H	7651	G	6/8	S12v2p17
LES DRAPEAUX	5532	1143	G	4/4	A1v3p177
LES FETES CHAMPETRE	5H3H1H5	62H2H7	D	6/8	B16v3p17
LES FEUX D'ARTIFICE	1142	3364	A	6/8	A7v6p51
LES FILEE DE TEMP'E	1H3H5H5H	4H4H3H5H	C	2/4	Mc9v2p25
LES NOUVELLES E'TRENNES	2H515L	7L32H1H	F	2/4	C22p49
LES PIEDMONTESE [LES PIADMONTESE]	15L15L	1525L	Bb	6/8	G10v2p34,35
LES PLAISEURS DES DAMES	5251	427L3	G	6/8	A1v3p159
LES PLAISIRS CHINOISE	1H3b6b7b	5425	G	6/8	W6p5
LES PLAISIRS DE BASQUE	1H515L	7L145	G	2/4	W6p8,9
LES PLASCER'E DE METZ	3455	61H65	A	2/4	Mc9v2p25
LES SOAIRS	1H235	5231H	G	6/8	S12v2p47
LESLEY HOUSE [LESSLEY HOUSE]	5L15L2L	4L5L6L2L	Bb	6/8	P5v1p2 Mc21v2p17
LESSLIE'S MARCH	1H1H1H5	1H542	D	6/8	C4p70 A1v1p64
L'ESTELLE	3H6H1H1H	2H5H3H1H	C	6/8	N2p33
LET ME ALONE	137L6L	6L47LO	A	2/2	A1v3p214
LET ME IN THIS AE NIGHT	3b11H1H	7b7b55	D E	2/4	(J3) G1v2p66
LET THAT STAND THERE	1H651	357b7b	D	4/4	A1v3p175
LET THAT STAND THERE	1555	3666	F	2/2	C18p4
LET US HASTE TO KELVIN GROVE	3H2H1H6	62H2H1	D	4/4	E1v2p37
LET US TO THE AIRD	5135	5532	F G	4/4*	G11v2Ap28 B15v1p62,63 K1v1p30,31 N1v1p25 Mc9v1p18 C4p28
L'ETE	3H1H2H4H	72H1H3H	C	2/4	G13v10
L'ETE	346L5L	5L432	A	2/4	T1v2p13
L'ETE	5L5L5L3	2215	G	2/4	E1v2p131
L'ETE	7654	3235	G	2/4	E1v2p26
LETHE	1H521	3652	G	6/8	A1v3p176
LETHEN'S REEL(L)	115L7bL	113b5	A	4/4	C33p19,20 A7v6p44
LET'S BE JOVIAL	1H751H	2H4H3H1H	D	4/4	S16p12,13
LET'S SHAK HER WEALL	5324	5363	G	2/2	W7p19
LEUt COLONEL MONTGOMRIE OF SKERMORLIE'S STRATHSPEY	313L1	31L22	F	4/4	E2p4
LEVEN HOUSE	13b3b5	7b427bL	G	2/2	G8p34,35
LEWIE GORDON	1H3H1H2H	1H3H6H1T	D	2/4	G9v1p30,31
LEWIE GORDON	1312	1361H	G	4/4	E1v1p8
LEWIE GORDON STRATHSPEY	5354	5362	D	4/4	C14v1p2,3 G8p23
LEWIS AIR, A	1117bL	3b3b7b2	A	6/8	Mc5p4
LEWIS GORDON	1312	1336	A	4/4	M12p29
LEWIS GORDON	1312	1351H	F G	4/4	(C25) C5v2p6 N1v2p53
LEWIS GORDON	1312	1361H	G	4/4*	G11v2Ap2 K1v1p2 C6p11

Title			Key	Time	References
LEWIS RICARDO, M.P.	15L5L3	5432	Eb	4/4	M4v4p19
LEWt GEORGE RAE'S MARCH	1H1H1H1H	3H553H	C	4/4	M11v1p20
LICK THE LADLE SANDIE	51H65	27b46	A	2/2	Mc13v2p26 S12v1p21
LICK THE LADLE SANDY	5353	7bL7b46	A	2/2	G11v2Bp26 G7p5 K1v2p28 (II)
LIDDEL BOWER, THE	3536L	25L36L	G	3/8	C10v2Ap39
LIEUT. A. STEWART, 94th REGt's REEL	3127L	3146	A	4/4	Mc19v2p14
LIEUt. A. STEWART(, 94th REGt's REEL)	3127bL	3146	A	4/4*	Mc19v1p4 (II)
LIEUt ABERCROMBY('S REEL)	1565	4327L	Bb	2/2	C24v1p1 (II)
LIEUT. BARRY'S REEL	315L3	7L531H	F	2/4	N2p27
LIEUT: COL: LUMSDEN'S REEL	13bL13b	227b2	G	2/2	Mc15p23 (II)
LIEUt COLONEL DAVID STEWART'S STRATHSPEY	5L3L5L3L	227L2	A	4/4	G10v5p23
LIEUT. COLONEL MAXWELL'S (7th Dr GUARDS) FANCY	531H5	642H7	F	2/4	G10v5p5
LIEUt COLONEL MONTGOMERY'S REEL	3b3b3b1	3b527bL	G	6/8	Mc21v3p26
LIEUt DUNBAR 22nd REGIMENTS WALTZ	553	553	F	3/4	T1v2p12
LIEUt DUNBAR (22nd REGt's) REEL	315L1	3135	G	2/2	T1v2p5
LIEUT. GRANT OF THE 10th FOOT'S STRATHSPEY	5331	5347bL	A	2/2	Mc15p16
LIEUt. HOWARD DOUGLAS'S STRATHSPEY	11H51H	7bL7b47bL	D	4/4	Mc21v3p34
LIEUt. JAMIESON'S QUICKSTEP	546L1	5622	G	2/4	W2v2p7
LIEUt MORISON'S (DUMFRIES MILITIA) REEL	1355	6753	G	2/2	W2v2p2
LIEUt. WHITEFORD BELL'S MARCH	331H1H	3H1H5H5H	D	4/4	M11v1p21
LIFE LET US CHERISH	3451H	1232	F G	6/8	E1v1p43 C8v2p6 C8v1p8
LIFE WE LOVE, THE	1546	5521	G	6/8	A1v3p177 O1v1Dp27
LIFE'S A PUN	54H3H2H	1H527	D	6/8	A1v4p73
LIGHT AND AIRY	5311H	5324	F G	6/8	H3p13 G11v1Cp27 P5v2p19 G10v2p25 (II) G1v1p44
LIGHT AS THISTLEDOWN	51H60	72H3HO	D	4/4	E1v2p91
LIGRUM CUS	5531	5561H	D	6/8	A1v5p39 C5v1p39
LIKE LIGHTNING GLEAMS	125L6L	2231	G	4/4	C10v2Ap24
LILLA'S A LADY	3635	41H65	G	3/8	C8v2p32 C8v1p52
LILLIE BULERA	1324	3421	G	6/8	A1v3p186 O1v1Gp13 S12v2p2
LILLIES OF FRANCE, THE	1H514	6277	D	4/4	A1v3p225
LILLIGNONETH FRANCOISE	3311	5532	F	4/4	A1v3p167
LILLING HALL	1235	6L427L	Bb	6/8	B16v3p13
LILLY, THE	51H4H4H	3H4H75	D	6/8	W4v1p7 A1v4p37
LILLY, THE	1H1H65	3222	D	4/4*	(D2) A1v2p53 C14v15p6
LINCOLN RACES	1143	56L11	G	6/8	B16v3p4
LINK HIM DODDIE	1533	27b22	A	4/4	G11v1Bp4 G10v1P13 (II)
LINK HIM DODIE	1531	27b22	A	4/4	G7p3
LINKS OF KILLAROW, THE	5H1H3H2H	3H5H3H2H	C	2/2	Mc16p15
LINKS OF LEITH	3313	27b27bL	A	2/2	B15v1p57
LINKY LANKY	153b4	153b5	E	6/8	A1v1p38
LINLITHGOW LOCH	1135	1122	D	4/4	M4v4p25
LINNA MACHREE	35L32	35L37L	G	6/8	G9v5p24
LINNEN HALL	1235	6L427L	G	6/8	A1v2p46
LIRA LIRA LA	51H1H1H	72H1H1H	D	2/2	A1v4p70
LITTLE ASSEMBLY, THE	1345	1352	A	2/4	C14v10p19
LITTLE GLEANER, THE	5415L	6L217L	G	6/8	S7v2p7
LITTLE HOUSE UNDER THE HILL	351H1H	1H1H62	G	2/4	A1v1p27
LITTLE LEAPER, THE	1122	3413L	G	6/8	B16v3p69
LITTLE LOVE, A	1H1H1H4	6421	D	6/8	R4p2,3
LITTLE MEN OF THE MEARNS, THE	1H1H22	1H1H1H1H	D	4/4	Mc21v4p42
LITTLE MEN OF THE MEARNS, THE	1H1H62H	1H1H3H3H	D	2/2	Mc9v1p20
LITTLE NABOB, THE	5311	61H65	Bb	2/4	W4v1p24
LITTLE NABOB, THE	5H3H1H1H	6H1T6H5H	D	2/4	A1v4p59
LITTLE PEGGY'S LOVE	1366	51H2H2H	G	4/4	A1v6p23
LITTLE PEGGY'S LOVE	1355	1551H	G	4/4	C5v1p6
LITTLE PEGGY'S LOVE	5L133	6L244	F	2/2	C14v13p8
LITTLE SKIRMISH	31H42H	3H72H5	D	6/8	A1v2p52
LIVERPOOL ASSEMBLY, THE	547L2	4315L	Bb	4/4	H6v23p3
LIVERPOOL HORNPIPE, THE	331H5H	4H2H1H6	D	2/2	C8v2p33 C8v1p54 (II)
LIVERPOOL PRIZE	1H2H1H4	4542	G	2/4	B16v3p11
LOCAL ATTACHMENT	1234	3542	Eb	4/4	L1p9
LOCH ALOIE	5L5L5L5L	5L1L26L	A	4/4	C14v17p1
LOCH BHRAOIN	1261H	1H61H6	D	6/8	Mc5p7
LOCH CATHRINE	113b5	7b7b24	D	4/4	P9p34
LOCH EARN (REEL)	1H513	6L27L5L	G	4/4*	A7v6p14 G11v1Ap29 C8v1p38 C8v2p12 E1v1p34 A7v2p30 G10v2p2 A7v5p9 (II)
LOCH EIREACHD SIDE [LOCH ERICHT SIDE]	351H1H	662H2H	C D	4/4	C13v1p26,27 A7v2p16 (J3) G10v2p7 N1v1p27 Mc9v3p46 G11v1Ap20 P6v1p1 (II) C19p18 A1v4p26 A1v3p207 A7v6p6
LOCH ERROCH (SIDE)	351H1H	1H1H2H2	F D C	4/4	E1v1p31 C14v2p2 C8v2p37 B7p34 Mc7p25 C8v1p21 Mc21v4p12,13
LOCH FYNE SIDE	453b1H	7b427bL	G	4/4	Mc15p3
LOCH KATRINE	5131	3131H	G	4/4	G10v6p13
LOCH LOMOND	1H1H1H3	1H31H3	D	4/4	S11v1p25
LOCH LOMOND	3L131	3L5L3L2L	Bb	2/2	P9p5

LOCH LOMOND SIDE	3b13b5	2427bL	G	4/4	K1v1p9
LOCH MADEY	5313	6562	D	2/2	M12p9
LOCH NESS	11H7b4	3b7bL7bL3b	B A	4/4*	A1v2p15 A1v6p7 B15v1p29
					G9v5p29 (II)
LOCH OF FORFAR, THE	15L3L5L	15L13	A	4/4	C18p7 (II)
LOCH OF STRATHBEG, THE	53H2H1H	5327	C	4/4	C18p18
LOCH RANNOCH SIDE	315L3L	24L27bL	F	4/4	C14v7p6
LOCH RUADHAN [LOCH RUADHAINN]	3bH1H53b	7b424	C	4/4	F2v2p15(5) (II)
LOCH TAY	1535	1H522	A	2/2	G8p35
LOCH VACH	5155	6522	F G	4/4*	Mc9v3p13 Mc12v1p14 A1v4p9
					C5v1p9
LOCHABER	3H3H3H	3H2H3H	C	3/4	E1v1p25
LOCHABER	135	333	G	3/4	T6v2p50
LOCHABER NO MORE	333	324	F	3/4	C8v1p57
LOCHABER (NO MORE)	333	331	G	3/4	P4p28 O1v4p32 O1v1Bp15 P8v2p3
LOCHABER (NO MORE)	333	333	F G	3/4	(C25) (J3) N1v2p3 C6p26
					B5p2 C29p26 C4p20 C5v2p1
					G17p6 Mc8v1Bp29 Mc8v2Bp1
					C20p25
LOCHABER RANT	5131	31H62	D	2/2	C14v6p11
LOCHAIL'S AWAY TO FRANCE	5154	27bL24	A	4/4	Mc21v4p34
LOCHEIL'S MARCH	5653	5652	A G	6/8	R4p13,14 A1v4p22
LOCHGARY'S STRATHSPEY	3b7L1L1	3b155	G	4/4	A7v3p25
LOCHGERY'S RANT	1126L	1111	G	2/2	Mc9v1p13
LOCHIEL'S AWA TO FRANCE	5154	117b4	A	4/4	G11v1Ap17 G10v2p14
LOCHIEL'S RANT	5154	27bL24	A	4/4*	A1v3p183 B15v1p44 R12v1p64
					(II)
LOCHLEVEN SIDE	1234	5235L	A	6/8	B11p20
LOCHNAGAR	1155	1H3H1H1H	Eb D	4/4	C6p9 E1v2p1
LOCHNESS	11H7b4	3b7bL7bL7bL	A	4/4	A7v6p42
LOCHNESS SIDE	5L7bL11	3b53b7bL	G	2/2	Mc4v3p9
LOCHNESS SIDE	5L111	3b53b7bL	G	2/2	G8p6 P1v1p3
LOCHRYNACH	1347L	1344	G	2/2*	M4v3p38 (II)
LOCHSPEY SIDE	5562	5565	D	2/2	C14v15p7
LOCKET, THE	3H2H1H5	3231	D	2/4	B16v3p49
LODOISKA	1111	1325L	Bb	2/4	C14v19p24
LODOISKA	1H1H1H6	1H1H1H6	D	4/4	E1v2p28
LOGAN BANKS	3423	1131H	G	4/4	C5v2p68
LOGAN WATER	3b211	7bL4L7bL7bL	G A	4/4	T6v2p56 (J3) S16p56,57
					G17p14 Mc8v1Ap21 Mc8v2Ap21
					Mc23p14,15 N1v2p17 C5v2p17
					B5p9 E1v2p46 C20p68,69
LOGAN WATER	3b211	7bL4L7bL5	A	4/4	C8v2p30 C8v1p11 O1v1Ep18
					O1v4p21
LOGAN WATER	5433	26L22	G	2/2	P8v2p37
LOGIE O' BUCHAN	3L5L16L	3L5L31	Bb	6/8	C19p4
LOGIE O' BUCHAN	351H6	353H1H	D	6/8	C5v2p4 A7v6p69 A7v3p14
LOGIE O' BUCHAN	335	53H2H	G D	3/4	C8v2p22 C8v1p55 A1v4p44
					E1v2p3 (II)
LOGIE O' BUCHAN	335	53H3H	D	3/4	G1v1p17
LOISG IAD GUAL IO UO	4H3H5H6	4H3H5H6	D	4/4	Mc5p11
LONA'S VALE	5221	31H52	G	2/4	O1v1Kp138
LONDON ASSEMBLY	1H652	41H51	F	2/4	S7v1p9
LONDON ASSOCIATION	1H335	1H37L2	G	6/8	B16v3p7
LONDON CAMP, THE	1H4H3H2H	1H4H3H1H	D	6/8	S12v2p23
LONDON HIGHLAND SOCIETY, THE	15L16L	2L47L2	G	4/4	G11v1Cp30,31 G10v3p9
LONDON MARCH (THE)	3332	1565	D G	4/4	A1v4p21 C8v2p21
LONDON MILITARY ASSOCIATION DANCE, THE	3H2H1H1H	5H72H2H	D	2/2	B16v4p88
LONDON NAIRNSHIRE MEETING, THE	13b55	7b2H7b5	E	4/4	Mc11p6
LONDON NEW MARCH	1223	3322	G	2/2	W7p12
LONDON REEL, THE	3H753	1515	D	2/2	P11v2p3
LONE WANDERER, THE	512	445	Eb	3/4	C10v2Bp14
LONG AM I IN SOLITUDE	41H3b1	47b57b	E	4/4	Mc5p14
LONG LIFE TO STEPMOTHERS	116L1	116L1	D	2/4	G10v4p4
LONG ROOM OF SCARBROUGH, THE	113	112	G	9/8	A1v1p45
LOOK BEFORE YOU	1313	27b27bL	D	2/2	G11v2Bp37
LOOK BEHIND YOU	5326L	531H1H	D	4/4	G7p11 G11v2Bp38 (II)
LORD ABOYNE	3333	5521	D	4/4	K1v2p3 G11v2Bp3
(LORD ABOYNE'S WELCOME) or CUMBERNAULD HOUSE	3332	6L6L23	G	4/4	B5p6 C5v2p2 Mc8v1Cp70
					Mc8v2Ap15 E1v2p32 C20p11
					G1v1p38
LORD ABOYN'S STRATHSPEY	3153	2427bL	C	4/4	A7v3p16
LORD ADAM GORDON'S REEL	3564	3127bL	G	2/2	S7v1p40
LORD AIRLY'S REEL [LORD AIRLIE]	537L2	5353	G F	4/4*	A7v6p46 Mc4v3p3 G10v4p28
					(II)
LORD ALBREMARLE (REEL/'S DELIGHT)	1353	7bL7bL24	D	2/2	R12v1p67 S12v1p32
LORD ALEXANDER GORDON'S (REEL/STRATHSPEY)	1L153	5642	A	4/4*	G11v2Ap23 M4v2p3 Mc9v3p38
					M4v3p17 A7v2p17 K1v1p25
					C13v1p42 Mc7p24 Mc12v1p26,27
					(II)
LORD ALEXANDER RUSSELL'S JIG	1H1H71H	1H522	C	6/8	M4v3p59
LORD ALEXr GORDON'S REEL	11H5H3H	5H6H4H2H	D	2/2	A1v4p58 G1v2p57

Name	A	B	Key	Time	References
LORD ALEXr. GORDON'S STRATHSPEY	31H5H3H	5H6H4H2H	C	4/4	A7v6p29
LORD ANTRIM'S DELIGHT	1117bL	7bL27bL5L	A	2/4	O1v1Lp139
LORD ARBUTHNOT	3b113b	13b45	G	4/4	G10v6p10,11
LORD BALGONIE'S FAVORITE	1115L	3b3b42	A	4/4	G10v4p36
LORD BALGOWNIES MINUET	112	351	F	3/4	Mc21v1p3
LORD BANFF	15L11	5326L	D	2/2	C24v2p4
LORD BANFF'S STRATHSPEY	15L13	5326L	E	2/2	C24v2p8
LORD BANFF'S STRATHSPEY	15L13	5422	E	4/4	G11v2Ap7
LORD BANFF'S STRATHSPEY	15L13	6426L	E	4/4	A7v2p23 A7v6p8
LORD BANFF'S (STRATHSPEY/REEL)	15L13	5426L	G E	4/4*	A7v5p19 L2p10,11 G8p19 Mc4v3p12 C24v1p1 C24v2p8 P1v1p6
LORD BATEMAN'S FANCY	5311	2226L	Bb	2/2	S7v1p27
LORD BATH'S GATE	1H565	1H565	D	2/4	A1v5p4 C5v1p4
LORD BATH'S GATE	1H565	1H543	D	2/4	S7v1p17
LORD BERNARD'S MARCH	1H1H1H4H	2H2H2H3H	C	4/4	A1v3p221
LORD BINNING'S REEL	13b51	7b427bL	E	2/2	G11v2Cp20
LORD BINNY'S MINUET	1H1H1H	3H1H1H	C	3/4	D14v1p20
LORD BINNY'S REEL	13b54	247b4	E	2/2	D14v1p31
LORD BINNY'S REEL	13b54	247b4	E	2/2	D14v4p11
LORD BLANTYRE'S STRATHSPEY	3131H	67b27bL	A	4/4	G10v5p33 (II)
LORD BREADALBAN'S MARCH	1624	1615	A	6/8	D14v2p32,33
LORD BREADALBANE'S DELIGHT	1115	1126	D	6/8	Mc4v4p8
LORD BUCHAN	1H65	53H2H	D	3/4	G11v2Cp2
LORD CASSEL'S REEL	651H2	651H3H	C	2/2	S12v1p26
LORD CASSILL'S REEL	7b51H2	761H3H	C	2/2	R5p51
LORD CASSILS JIGG	651H2	651H3H	C	12/8	R5p14
LORD CATHCART('S WELCOME HOME)	5L552	3417L	Bb	6/8	P6v1p27 A7v4p27
LORD CHARLES MURRAY'S STRATHSPEY	13b22	13b13b	D	4/4	G10v5p4
LORD CHICHESTER SPENCER'S REEL	1515	432H2	G	2/2	C12p7
LORD CHIEF BARON'S FAVORITE	11H7b4	3b7bL7bL2	A	4/4	Mc21v4p32
LORD COLLINGWOOD	1115	1136	D	6/8	P6v1p13 C14v21p24
LORD COLLINGWOOD'S HORNPIPE	5653	6225L	Bb	2/4	C14v23p16
LORD CORNWALLIS OR RODNEYS MARCH	1113	6L6L6L1	Bb	4/4	C7p16
LORD CORNWALLIS'S MARCH	1H1H2H2H	5H5H1H5	D	4/4	A1v6p61
LORD DALHOUSIE	1H3H2H3H	2H3H1H6	D	4/4	C8v1p43 (II)
LORD DALHOUSIE	13H2H3H	2H3H1H6	D	4/4	C8v2p15
LORD DOUNE ('S STRATHSPEY)	547bL2	5557b	G	4/4	G11v1Cp25 G10v2p18 (II)
LORD DOUNE'S REEL	351H5	3542	F	2/2	Mc21v2p38
LORD DOWN'S STRATHSPEY	1551	7bL447bL	G	4/4	Mc4v4p1 (II)
LORD DRIGHORN'S QUICK STEP	1H51H3	1H62H7	D	6/8	Mc21v2p37 (II)
LORD DUMFRIES'S BOWLING GREEN	3H1H71H	3H1H3H6	C	6/8	R5p15
LORD DUMFRIES'S BRIDGE	1H1H63H	1H1H22	C	2/2	R5p34
LORD DUNCAN	15L33	62H54	A	4/4	L1p5
LORD DUNCAN'S FLAG	5365	1364	C	4/4	G11v1Bp9
LORD DUNCAN'S GERMAN WALTZ	3H1H2H5H	3H1H2H1H	D	3/8	W4v2p32
LORD DUNCAN'S GRAND MARCH	5151	61H53	G	2/4	W4v2p4
LORD DUNCAN'S VICTORY	1655	1642	F	4/4	C14v13p1
LORD DUNDEE'S LAMENTATION	555	3b52	A	9/8	D14v2p7
LORD DUNMORE'S DELIGHT	3251H	1H61H1H	D	2/2	O1v1Kp111
LORD DUNMORE'S QUICK STEP	1H1H4H5H	1H2H4H1H	D	6/8	A1v5p31 C5v1p31
LORD DUPLIN'S JIGG	1H353	1H622	D	6/8	B11p9
LORD EGLINTON'S REEL	5511H	6522	D	4/4	B15v1p95
LORD EGLINTON'S REEL	5L35L3L	5L322L	Bb	4/4*	C14v15p22 G9v5p31 N1v1p10 Mc9v3p30 A7v2p32 R5p33 C13v2p59 G10v4p1 P5v2p8 B10p37 (II)
LORD EGLINTOUNE'S REEL	53H53	53H2H2	D	2/2	R5p38
LORD EGLINTOUN'S AULD MAN	5451	5455	D	4/4	K1v1p4 G11v2Ap4 (II)
LORD ELCHO	5L115	553b7bL	G	6/8	G11v1Cp25
LORD ELCHO'S FAVOURITE	5L115	53b3b7bL	G	6/8	A7v2p20 Mc7p15
LORD ELCHO'S MARCH	15L31	5333	Bb	4/4	Mc19v2p10 Mc19v3p17
LORD ELCHO'S REEL	1H546	3547L	G	4/4	Mc21v2p13
LORD ELCHO'S STRATHSPEY	11L5L5L	247L2	Bb	4/4	N1v1p20
LORD ELGIN'S FAVORITE STRATHSPEY	5526L	5513H	G	4/4	A7v6p55
LORD ELGIN'S REEL	1126L	1154	D	4/4	(B21)
LORD ELGIN'S STRATHSPEY	3L5L5L5L	147L2	Bb	2/2	C14v9p2
LORD ELPHINSTONE('S STRATHSPEY)	1355	1351H	F	4/4	Mc15p25 (II)
LORD ELPHINSTONS FAVORITE	51H72H	3H2H55	F	2/4	W4v2p6
LORD ELPHINSTON'S REEL	5H3H2H5H	5H3H2H7	C	2/2	Mc21v3p31
LORD ELPHINSTON'S STRATHSPEY	1L5L13	16L22L	A	4/4	C13v1p38,39
LORD ERROLL'S MINUET	554	211	Bb	3/4	C22p10
LORD FALCONBERG'S MARCH	1H1H3H2H	2H2H4H3H	D	4/4	A1v6p71
LORD FIFE'S REELL	351H3H	1H62H2H	D	2/2	C33p16
LORD FIFE'S WALTZ	51H65	51H64	F	3/8	C18p3
LORD FIFE'S WELCOME TO ELGIN	3542	36L7L5L	A	4/4	G15p19
LORD FINCASTLE'S REEL	1133	6522	F	2/2	B20p14
LORD FINLATER'S REEL	1H3H1H5	662H2H	D	2/2	A1v6p13 C33p8
LORD FRANCIS RUSSELL	1155	5542	F	4/4	M4v4p7
LORD FREDERICK AND HIS FENCIBLES	313L1L	5L7L52	Bb	2/2	C13v2p51
LORD FREDERICK AND HIS FENCIBLES	313L2L	5L7L52	Bb	2/2	C13v1p13
LORD GARLIES REEL	1H2H7b5	527bL4	G	6/8	R5p18

LORD GARLIS DELIGHT	5362	531H3H	D	4/4	S7v1p76
LORD GEORGE GORDON'S REEL	1H3H53H	4327L	C	2/2	M4v1p1
LORD GLENCAIRN'S QUICK STEP	1H73H1H	64H5H3H	D	2/4	A1v1p63
LORD GLENCAIRN'S STRATHSPEY	115L2	436L2	G	2/2	Mc16p22
LORD GLENLYON'S REEL	113b5	27b47bL	C	2/2	G9v2p10,11
LORD GLENORCHA'S STRATHSPEY	1H3H1H6	51H22	F	4/4	Mc4v4p12 (II)
[LORD GLENORCHY]					
LORD GRANTHAM'S WHIM	315	422H	D	9/8	C14v19p4 P6v1p12
LORD GREGORY	551	7L7L5L	A	3/4	C5v2p24
LORD HADDO'S (FAVOURITE) STRATHSPEY	1225	47b3b5L	G A	4/4	A7v2p10 A7v6p36
LORD HARDWICK'S MARCH	3333	331H4	G	4/4	C8v2p22
LORD HARRINGTON'S VOLUNTEERS	1357	7750	A	2/4	S7v1p10
LORD HAY('S STRATHSPEY)	5627bL	5655	D	4/4	P5v3p8 (II)
LORD HENRY	545	57b5	G	3/4	O1v2p9
LORD HINCHINBROOKS REEL	3L13L5L	4L3L4L2L	Bb	4/4	Mc21v4p38
LORD HUM'S REEL	5524	5565	G	4/4	A7v6p92
LORD ISLE'S SALUTATION	1H2H1H5	61H63	G	6/8	D14v2p9
LORD JAMES MURRAY'S REEL	1H51H3	22H76	D	4/4	G10v5p3 (II)
LORD JOHN	555	552	D	3/4	O1v2p35 O1v3p42
LORD JOHN	111	115L	A	3/4	O1v1Ap25
LORD JOHN CAMPBELL'S NEW STRATHSPEY	1135	4427L	F	2/2	C14v18p6,7
LORD JOHN CAMPBELL'S REEL	131H1H	2H2H2H2	F	2/2	Mc15p1 (II)
LORD JOHN CAMPBELL'S STRATHSPEY	137L2	1353	D G	4/4	G10v4p10 (II) C5v2p36
LORD JOHN RUSSELL	4211	6L5L2L2L	Bb	4/4	M4v4p21
LORD JOHN SCOTT'S STRATHSPEY	551H3H	1H1H32	C	2/2	G9v2p3
LORD KELLY'S REEL	5L3b53b	O27bL2	G	2/2	N1v1p11
LORD KELLY'S REEL	5L3b53b	4L27bL3b	A G	4/4	A7v5p37 A7v6p80 (II)
LORD KELLY'S REEL	5L3b53b	7bL27bL3b	E	4/4	A1v1p59
LORD KELLY'S REEL	5L3b53b	227bL2	G	2/2	Mc13v2p13 C13v1p3
LORD KELLY'S (REEL/STRATHSPEY)	5L3b53b	4L27bL2	G	4/4*	G9v5p11 K1v1p10 C13v2p1 P5v3p16
					G11v2Ap8 S11v1p11 B15v1p57
					Mc12v1p29 (II)
LORD KILDARE'S REEL	1H57L2	1H565	Bb	2/2	C14v18p20
LORD KILMAUR'S (REEL)	117bL2	113b5	E	2/2	G11v2Ap17 R5p12 K1v1p19 (II)
LORD KINAIRD'S REEL	1H1H1H2	1H565	D	4/4	G11v2Cp34 G9v5p13 S12v1p17
[LORD KINNAIRD('S REEL)]					B15v1p81 (II)
LORD KINARD'S REEL [LORD KINNAIRD]	1H1H1H3	6565	D	4/4*	A7v6p89 (II)
LORD KIRKCUDBRIGHT	365	1H52	D	3/4	G10v6p23
LORD LEWIS GORDON'S REEL	3332	3323	G	2/2	H3p34,35 Mc9v1p1
LORD LEWIS GORDON'S STRATHSPEY	3152	311H1H	D	4/4	A7v2p25
LORD LINDSAYS MARCH	1H1H1H3H	2H2H2H4H	D	4/4	C5v1p57 A1v5p57
LORD LOVAT	3122	3361H	G	4/4	G10v6p13
LORD LOVATE'S REELL	5555	6666	D	2/2	C33p5
LORD LOVAT'S STRATHSPEY	1122	1151H	G	4/4	A7v2p11 A7v6p4
LORD MACDONALD ('S REEL)	5551H	51H2H2	G	4/4*	G8p36 A7v6p60 P6v1p6 G11v1Ap29
					C8v1p61 C14v8p19 Mc7p5
					C8v2p41 E1v1p12 Mc4v3p2 A1v4p7
					N1v1p12 G10v3p9 Mc12v1p8,9
					A7v3p32 (II)
LORD MACDONALD'S FAVOURITE	15L13	4332	F	6/8	R7v1p1
LORD MACDONALD'S REEL	1H3H1H5	662H2H	D	2/2	Mc9v1p19
LORD MACDONALD'S STRATHSPEY	15L16L	2L27L2	G	2/2	G8p26
LORD MAUCHLINE'S REEL	5L13b5	247b4	E	4/4	G10v5p17
LORD McDONALD('S OLD REEL)	355H2H	4H2H66	D	2/2*	G11v2Cp35 (II)
[LORD MACDONALD]					
LORD McDONALD'S STRATHSPEY	1353	1H622	F	2/2	J1p23
LORD McKENZIES STRATHSPEY	5351	5364	A	4/4	A7v3p31
LORD McLEOD'S STRATHSPEY	3551H	1H651	G	4/4	A7v3p32
	1H555	3H2H5H3H	C	4/4	B12p1
LORD MELVILLE'S WELCOME TO STRATHEARN 18 06					
LORD MILLINGTON'S STRATHSPEY	53b13b	4242	A	4/4	C14v8p3
LORD MILTON'S STRATHSPEY	5351H	6562	F	2/2	J1p15
LORD MINTO'S WALTZ	5612	5631H	F	3/8	P11v1p13
LORD MOIRA ('S WELCOME TO SCOTLAND)	1135	4327L	F	4/4	B17p6 D15v2p16 P6v1p21 (II)
LORD MOIRA'S MARCH	1H3bH2H5H	4H3bH2H5H	D	4/4	L2p24
LORD MOIRA'S WELCOME TO EDINBURGH	51H53H	1H5H3H2H	F	2/4	L2p20,21
LORD MOIRA'S WELCOME (TO SCOTLAND/HOME)	1135	4427L	F	2/2 4/	C14v22p2,3 N1v1p26
LORD MONTGOMERIE'S REEL	3H1H53	51H2H2	C	2/2	C14v22p12
LORD MONTGOMIRIE'S STRATHSPEY	1111L	2L7bL4L2L	G	4/4	G10v4p31
LORD MURRAY	1126L	4453	G	4/4	C8v2p7 C8v1p9
LORD NELSON	15L3L5L	6L5L2L2	Bb	4/4	C7p11
LORD NELSON'S VICTORY	1H2H53H	64H1H6	F	2/4	P6v1p14
LORD NELSON'S WALTZ	1111	11H5H1H	C	3/8	C14v14p3
LORD NELSON'S WALTZ	1212	11H4H1H	C	3/8	P6v1p2
LORD NORTH'S JIGG	1H5H1H6H	1H5H2H7	C	6/8	B16v3p15 S7v1p26
LORD OF COCKPEN'S SCOTCH-MEASURE, THE	31H11	3332	G	2/2	P7p4
LORD OGILVY	1321	6L5L2L2	Bb	2/2	A4v1p1
LORD PALMERSTON'S FAVOURITE	536L5L	5L5L42	A	6/8	P11v1p9
LORD RAE'S SALUTATION	1L1L3bL3bL	5L5L1L1L	A	4/4	D14v2p15
LORD RAMSAY'S FAVORITE	4#413	7L556L	Bb	2/2	G9v2p2
LORD RAMSAY('S STRATHSPEY)	3555	31H52	Bb	4/4	A7v4p9 G10v5p1 (II)

LORD ROBt MURRAY'S STRATHSPEY	1L132	1L122L	Bb	4/4	Mc4v2p13
LORD ROLLO'S MARCH	1112	3334	D	4/4	B11p27
LORD ROLLO'S REEL	5431	51H62	D	2/2	Mc21v3p24
LORD RONALD	21H1H1	2H1H52	D	3/8	C10v2Bp45
LORD SALTON'S GAVOTT	1331H	6633	G	2/2	S5p18
LORD SEAFORTH('S STRATHSPEY/REELL)	15L13	436L6L	G	4/4*	C8v2p12 C8v1p38 G1v2p72
					P11v2p1 G11v2Cp15 C33p8 (II)
LORD SEYMOUR'S REEL	1335	4651H	G	2/2	C14v15p14,15
LORD SPENCER CHICHESTER'S STRATHSPEY	116L1	136L2	F	4/4	G10v4p27
LORD SPENCER'S STRATHSPEY	1H31H3	1H622	D	4/4	C5v1p56 A1v4p56
LORD SPENCERS STRATHSPEY	116L1	116L2	F	4/4	A7v4p23
LORD SPENCER'S STRATHSPEY	13L13L	16L2L2L	Bb	2/2	Mc12v1p40
LORD STRATHAVEN'S STRATHSPEY	1365	1364	F	4/4	P5v3p14/15 (II)
LORD STRATHMOR'S STRATHSPEY	1525	243b2	G	2/2	A7v3p35
LORD TORPHICHEN'S FAVORITE	3546	51H32	E	2/4	G10v4p3
LORD TORPHICHEN'S STRATHSPEY	3546	51H22	E	4/4	S13p3
LORD WELLINGTON'S WALTZ	1H115	71H51	Bb	3/8	C14v25p13
(LORD/EARL OF) HOME	5564	5565	F	4/4	G11v1Bp29 G10v3p7 C14v20p12
('S STRATHSPEY/REEL)					
(LORD/EARL) OF KELLY'S REEL, (THE)	5L3b53b	7bL7b7bL3b	G	2/2	S12v1p17 Mc9v1p34
L'ORDI'ANCE	3455	1H1H42	A	6/8	A1v3p217
LOSS OF BETTIES MILLS, THE	3235	1H1H75	F	2/2	Y1p7
LOTHARIA	5264	3135	G	3/8	R12v3p11
LOTHIAN LASSES	5L13b5	247b4	E	2/2	H3p17 (II)
LOTHIAN LASSIE, THE	1321	3165	F A	6/8	C8v1p37 C6p18
LOTS OF KISSES	13b45	1H1H3b3b	G	6/8	H1p8
LOTTERY TICKET, THE	1H1H51	2425L	G	2/2	H1p2
LOUDON, THE	5522	4461H	G	2/4	A1v3p156
LOUDOUN CASTLE	3522	3531H	E	2/4	G10v5p16
LOUIS'S ADIEU	5355	1H1H65	D	4/4	C5v1p64 A1v5p64
LOUVRE, THE	331	111	F	3/4	C22p18,19 Mc9v2p34
LOVE & WHISKEY	53b3b	53b2	A	3/4	P6v1p20
LOVE AND FICKLE FORTUNE	5L111	5542	F	4/4	C10v2Bp10
LOVE AND GLORY	504	203	G	3/4	E1v2p15
LOVE AND HONOUR	1H356	2H675	D	6/8	S12v2p28
LOVE AND OPPORTUNITY or	3b11H1H	7b7b55	D	4/4	Mc21v3p2
LET ME IN THIS AE NIGHT					
LOVE AND OPPORTUNITY	51H53	1251	G	2/4	A1v2p58
LOVE IN A TUB	1H1H1H1H	5H4H3H2H	D	2/2	B16v3p35
LOVE IN A VILLAGE	5L13b1	7bl27bL4L	G	4/4	P9p24
LOVE IN A VILLAGE, (A REEL IN)	1133	117L7L	G	4/4*	P5v3p12 G11v2Cp17 S12v1p60
					S12v2p2
LOVE IS THE CAUSE OF MY MOURNING	133	333	F G	3/4	O1v2p1 O1v1Ap27
LOVE IS THE CAUSE OF MY MOURNING	135	331	F G D	3/4	T6v1p34 C4p69 C5v3p53
					G17p18 P8v2p18 N1v2p57 (J3)
LOVE IS THE CAUSE OF MY MOURNING	135	333	F G	3/4	O1v3p21 Mc8v1Cp64,65 Mc8v2p4
					C20p1
LOVE IS THE CAUSE OF MY MOURNING	113	333	D	3/4	S16p32-35
LOVE LOCK, THE	5557	5557	G	2/2	H1p7
LOVE MAKES A MAN	1L3L5L3L	1L3L2L2	Bb	4/4	P9p37
LOVE SICK JOCKY	15L13	5555	G	2/2	O1v1lp78
LOVE SICK POLLY	1H13b3b	3bH3bH1H6b	E	2/2	A1v3p187
LOVE SLIP, THE	3555	4H2H7O	D	2/4	O1v1Hp57
LOVE SONG, A	1553bH	1H7b54	D	2/4	C10v2Bp10
LOVE WILL FIND OUT THE WAY	555	351H	D	3/4	C5v3p59
LOVE WILL FIND OUT THE WAY	555	451H	D	3/4	A1v5p60 C5v1p60
LOVE WILL FIND OUT THE WAY	5L5L5L	3L5L1	Bb	3/4	(J3) Mc12v2p35,36
LOVELY FANCY	1216L	1232	F	2/2	B16v3p71
LOVELY JEANIE	3b3b13b	556b4	E	4/4	A1v3p227
LOVELY LASS OF INVERBERVIE, THE	3642	3521	G	4/4	C5v3p59
LOVELY LASS OF INVERNESS, THE	1H531H	2H1H21	D	4/4	(J3) O1v1Ap9 O1v2p12 O1v3p23
LOVELY LASS OF MONORGON, THE	3642	2521	A	4/4	O1v1lp82
LOVELY LASS TO A FRIAR CAME, A	4221	4221	G	2/4	A1v1p48
LOVELY LASS TO A FRYAR CAME, A	4321	2212	G	4/4	S16p74,75
LOVELY MALLY	11H52	31H52	D	6/8	A1v2p49
(LOVELY) MISS WEIR	3b21	542	G A	3/4	(J3) C5v3p56
LOVELY NANCY	111	222	G	3/4	O1v3p2,3 O1v1Bp2,3
LOVELY SPRIGHTLY GALLANT TAR	1H1H1H3H	2H2H2H5H	D	4/4	G1v2p75
LOVER'S STREAM	1341	1341	G	6/8	S7v1p79
(LOW) DOWN IN THE BROOM	5255	222H2H	C D G	4/4	N1v2p64 (J3) Mc8v1Dp112
					P4p14 C20p45 O1v1Gp6
					C5v2p63
LOW DOWN IN THE BROOM	5256	222H2H	C	4/4	(C25)
LOW DOWN IN THE BROOM	131H6	662H2H	D	2/4	C19p15 (II)
LOW LANDS OF HOLAND, THE	3313	5554	A	4/4	O1v4p25 O1v1Bp36
LOW LIES THE MIST ON MALLAVURICH	1H1H3bH1H	3bH1H3bH3bH	D	4/4	C4p11 Mc5p10
LOWE'S HORNPIPE	516L1	516L2	Bb	4/4	M4v3p13
LOYAL BORROWSTOUNNESS VOLUNTEERS	1H565	1H421	F	4/4	C23p16
SLOW MARCH, THE					
LOYAL BORROWSTOUNNESS VOLUNTEERS	1H1H72H	3H5H1H7	F	2/4	C23p16
QUICK MARCH, THE					
LOYAL EDINBURGH SPEARMEN'S MARCH, THE	1113	3113	Bb	4/4	P11v2p20

LOYAL FARMER, THE	5353	532H2	F	4/4	C7p14
LOYAL FARMER'S STRATHSPEY, THE	5353	532H2	G	4/4	G1v2p58
LOYAL KIRKCALDY VOLUNTEERS SLOW & QUICK MARCH, THE	3342	4667	G	4/4	C23p6
LOYAL NORTH BRITONS	31H1H1H	31H2H2	G	6/8	C14v19p20
LOYAL SOLDIER, THE	5327L	15L4L2L	Bb	2/2	C14v8p17
Lt. COLONEL GUTHRIE (OF THE FORFARSHIRE SHARP SHOOTERS) REEL	5327L	227L6L	Bb	4/4	B6v2p2
Lt. COLONEL RIDDOCH'S (OR 4th BATTN FORFARSHIRE VOLUNTEER'S) SLOW MARCH	1H3H4H7	1H5H1H1H	D	4/4	B6v1p1
Lt. RIDDOCH'S QUICK MARCH	3366	4H2H75	D	6/8	B6v1p2
LUCKY MINUTE, THE	113b3b	551H1H	G	4/4	O1v1Jp98
LUCY LONG	3H1H72H	4H61HO	D	2/4	C8v2p43
LUCY'S DELIGHT	5164	641H4	G	2/2	R12v1p28
LUDE'S LAMENT	3H3H2H	663	D	3/4	O1v1Ip65
LUDE'S SUPER	27bL5L2L	15L22	A	6/8	D14v2p43
LUDE'S SUPPER	555	3b11	E	3/4	O1v1Jp92,93
LUG OF THE SPADE, THE	1122	71H26	D	6/8	H1p5
LUINNAG FERRAMH BATA	1154	1154	A	2/2	D14v2p10
LULLABY OF AN INFANT CHIEF	51H53	51H36	C	3/8	C10v2Ap23
LULLABY, THE	1H5H65	51H3H2H	G	6/8	B7p42
LUMPS OF PUDDINGS	3b151	27bL47bL	A	6/8	C20p34 O1v1Gp4
LUNARDI	351H	2H24	F	9/8	C22p29
LUNDIE'S DREAM	1H2H52	23H1H5	F	2/4	O1v1Ip70
LURG'S REELL	15L13	6622	A	2/2	C33p15
MA CHERE AMIE	1H1H5H2H	3H5H1H7	D	2/4	E1v2p101
MA HURRAMAN	1153	5355	G	2/2	Mc16p36
MAC A' BHAILLIDH A UIST	5331H	3H526	D	2/2	F2v2p35(25)
MAC AOIDH	3bH2H1H5H	7b4H2H7b	D	4/4	F2v2p18(8)
MAC CAOIDH CHONASAIN	113b1	3b17bL5L	A	2/2	Mc5p3
MAC DHONAILL MOR NAN EILLAN [MAC DHOMHNUILL MOR NAN EILEAN]	1H2HO	1H2HO	C	3/4	F2v2p99(89)
MAC FOSET'S FAREWELL	1122	116L5L	F	2/2	W7p4
MAC MHIC AILLEAN [MAC 'IC AILEIN]	3316L	1353	F	4/4	F2v2p87(77)
MAC (MH)'IC ALASTAIR	5L3L1L5L	5L3L26L	A	4/4	F2v2p20(10)
MAC MO RIGH S'DOL NA EIDEADH	1121	3223	A	2/4	Mc1v1p116,117
MAC S'HIMI MOR A BASACHA(DH)	3316L	6L233	G	4/4	F2v2p31(21)
MACARIA	3b3b11H	53b15L	A	6/8	S7v3p8
MACARONI FOP, THE	1353	5L242	G	2/4	B16v3p66
MACARONI'S ALLEMAND, THE	1H53H1H	2H2H1H1H	D	2/4	B16v3p66
MACDONELL SONG, A	1555	1H57b1	E	3/8	C10v2Ap81
MACFARLANE'S RANT [MCFARLANE'S RANT]	3H52H6	3H52H1H	D	2/2*	G7p9 G11v2Dp37 (11)
MACFARLANE'S REEL	6152	6154	A	2/2	Mc9v3p17 (W3)
MACFARLANE'S STRATHSPEY	1H531	3H2H3H2H	C	4/4	G10v2p21
MACGREGOR OF RUARU/RORO, ETC.	112	26L5L	Bb	3/4	C10v2Bp18 (11)
MACGREGORS' GATHERING, THE	3121	6531	G	2/4	C10v2Ap91
MACGRIOGAIR A RUARO	112	35L5L	A	3/4	K1v2p2 Mc5p13 G11v2Bp2
MACHINE WITHOUT HORSES, THE	1515	4327L	G	6/8	R12v2p5
MACHLACHLANE'S SCOTS MEASURE	1122	5223	D	2/2	Mc7p36 (11)
MACKENZIE'S RANT	1353	7bL27bL7bL	A	4/4*	K1v1p24,25 G11v2Ap22
MACKINTOSH'S LAMENT	3311	2226L	A	6/8	R6v2p32
MACLACHLAN'S RANT [McLACHLAN'S REEL]	315H3H	2H3H2H2	D	2/2	S12v1p29 Mc9v1p18 S7v1p38
MACLACHLAN'S (STRATHSPEY/REELL)	3551H	1H3H2H2H	D C	4/4*	A1v6p15 C33p16 (11)
MACLEOD'S REEL	5551H	51H26	D	2/2	C13v1p11 Mc9v1p8
MACLEOD'S REELL	5551H	5526	D	4/4	C33p12
MACPHERSON'S FAREWELL	1122	116L5L	G	4/4*	O1v1Gp14,15 (11)
MACPHERSON'S LAMENT	1113	2221	F	4/4	K1v1p4,5 G11v2Ap4
MACPHERSON'S LAMENT	1122	17L6L5L	F	4/4	Mc7p19,20 Mc9v3p1
MACPHERSON'S RANT	313H2H	2H3H2H2	D	2/2	C33p12
MAC'S FANCY	1516	5125L	F	6/8	C14v6p10
MAD CAP	135L3L	247L6L	Bb	2/2	M12p23 (11)
MAD (OR POOR) BOY, THE	5L327L	5L321	Bb	4/4	G11v1Cp14
MAD OR POOR BOY, THE	5L31	5L21	Bb	9/8	G11v1Cp14
MADAINN CHIUIN CHEITEIN	1153	1H531	G	6/8	C4p49 Mc5p24
MADAINN CHIUN CHEITEIN	1153	1H631	G	6/8	F2v2p55(45)
MADAM ANGIOLINI	1H523	7L123	G	6/8	P6v1p35
MADAM CASSEY	3b17bL7bL	3b13b5	E	6/8	A7v2p19 G10v2p35 A7v5p31 A7v6p41
MADAM DEL CARO'S REEL	1575	5335	Bb	2/4	C14v10p6
MADAM DIDELOTS REEL	3L5L13	115L2L	A	4/4	C14v13p4,5
MADAM FREDRICK('S DANCE)	1L3L5L5L	1L5L5L1	A	4/4*	M4v3p15 Mc7p2 (11)
MADAM HEINEL	1H1H5H5H	562H1H	D	2/4	C22p29
MADAM HEINEL	51H65	3532	Eb	6/8	C22p45
MADAM HEINEL'S GAVOT	1H1H1H5H	5H5H4H3H	C	2/2	S7v1p60
MADAM HYNEL'S MINUET	334	546	D	3/4	S11v1p21
MADAM PARRISOT'S HORNPIPE	1342	3211	Bb	2/4	P5v3p24
MADAM SEFOTH'S SCOTCH-MEASURE	111H1H	5236	F	2/2	P7p12
MADAM THEODORE'S MINUET	1H51H	2H55	F	3/4	W6p19
MADAMOSELLE [LA DAMOSELLE]	5564	5311	D G	6/8	B16v3p60 S7v1p15 A1v1p38
MADHAIR SPEA [MATHAIR UISGE SPE]	3b13b5	7b53b5	E	4/4	F2v2p36(26)
MADle HEINEL'S FANCY	5352	2242	G	2/4	A1v3p173
MADle HILLISBERG'S FAVORITE SCOTCH DANCE	1L3L5L5L	1L5L5L1	Bb	4/4	C26v1p2

Title			Key	Time	Sources
MADRIGAL, THE	1H1H55	671H1H	C	6/8	A1v3p163 C22p23
MAGGIE GAE BACK AN' TAK' UP YOUR SCULLIE	5133	5122	A	6/8	C18p23
MAGGIE LAUDER	1H1H1H1H	2H4H72H	C D A	4/4*	C6p14 C5v2p31-33 C29p38-40 G9v1p18-21 A1v2p47 C19p6 Mc8v1Ap16,17 Mc8v2Ap16 O1v1Ap30,31 E1v1p80 O1v3p24 C4p4 Mc12v2p46,47 C20p24,25 (II)
MAGGIE LAUDER	1H3H54H	3H5H14H	D	4/4	O1v4p40
MAGGIE OF DRUMLANRIG	5551	6L113	G	2/2	O1v11p86
MAGGIE('S LAMENTATION)	11H2H2H	1H755	D	4/4	O1v1Hp46 O1v5p17
MAGGIE'S TOCHER	3b43b	7L27L	A G	9/8	C5v3p60 E1v2p136,137 T6v1p84 (J3)
MAGGY LAUDER	1111	247L2	D	4/4	R4p18,19,20
MAGGY SHANKS	5H5H4H4H	5H5H5H5H	D	4/4	A7v5p39 A7v6p75 A7v3p27
MAGGY'S WAME IS FU' I TRUE	5353	5324	D	4/4*	A1v2p4 B15v1p85
MAGIC MIROR, THE	13b51	47bL42	G	6/8	C14v2p5
MAGY'S TOCHER	11H1H	513	F	9/8	S16p48,49
MAID IN BEDLAM, THE	5561H	5210	F G	4/4	(J3) E1v2p1
MAID IN THE MILL, THE	3561H	5222	D	2/2	O1v1Gp27
MAID OF BATH, THE	1322	6651	A	2/4	B16v3p50
MAID OF CRAIGMADHE, THE	5L53b1	22H27bL	G	6/8	G10v5p29
MAID OF DORNOCK, THE	5564	5332	G	2/2	O1v1Lp156
MAID OF EDIN, THE	111	14L4L	A	3/4	Mc5p14
MAID OF ELGIN, THE	3467	5222	D	2/2	O1v1Kp137
MAID OF FORFAR, THE	5312	61H1H7	G	4/4	O1v1Lp140
MAID OF ISLA	1555	151H3	F	4/4	C8v1p23
MAID OF LODI, THE	137LO	3210	G	6/8	E1v1p50
MAID OF PALAISEAU, THE	3315L	1532	Bb	6/8	C1v4p1
MAID OF THE MILL, THE	1L5L6L5L	6L5L2L2	A	4/4	P9p32
MAID OF THE MILL, THE	5175H	661HO	D	6/8	A1v6p31
MAID OF THE MILL, THE	51H75H	661H1H	D	6/8	A1v3p159
MAID THAT TENDS THE GOATS, THE	5L13b4L	5L3b22	B A	4/4	A1v6p45 C5v2p17 K1v2p14 (J3) G11v2Bp12 Mc5p21
MAIDS COMPLAINT, THE	1H1H1H1H	3bH3b3b3bH	D	4/4	O1v1Dp30 O1v2p14
MAIDS IN THE MORNING, THE	13b55	13b3b3b	E	6/8	A1v6p53
MAIDS OF ARROCHAR, THE	3335	3H3H2H6	F D	6/8	B11p23 E1v1p111 G10v4p30 (II)
MAIDS OF KILEARNEY, THE	3121	5555	A	2/2	H1p26
(MAID[S]/LASS) OF ISLA, THE	1555	1563	G A F	4/4*	A7v5p18 G1v1p9 G11v2Cp22 E1v1p90 Mc16p12 G10v4p20,21 C22p25 (II)
MAIL COACH, THE	3144	5435	G	6/8	A7v6p78
MAIR 'S MO LUAIDH	551H2H	3H52H1H	D	6/8	P5v4p20
MAIR THE MORN	3H3H2H	3H3H2H	D	9/8	A7v5p6
MAIREAR(A)D NIGHEAN DHOMHNUILL	1H3bH1H1	3b3b20	D E	4/4	C4p59 F2v2p55(45) Mc5p19
MAIRI BHAN OG	13b54	517LO	A	6/8	F2v2p27(17)
MAIRI BHEADARACH	5L3b3b1H	7b422	B	2/2	F2v2p53(43)
MAIRI GHREANNAR	5L5L11	3216L	Bb	6/8	F2v2p94(84)
MAIRI NIGHEAN DHEORSA	1335	6521	A	2/4	F2v2p12(2)
MAIS' AN TOABH TUADH	3L135	6L27L5L	Eb	4/4	F2v2p84(74) (II)
MAJOR ALVES QUICK STEP	1H763	1H562	A	6/8	Mc21v2p21
MAJOR ARCHd CAMPBELL OF ASKOMELL'S STRATHSPEY	3L5L13	2422	A	2/2	C13v1p35
MAJOR BAILLIE OF DUNAIN'S STRATHSPEY	11H53bH	7bL7b7b5H	C	4/4	F2v1p9
MAJOR BROOKS'S STRATHSPEY	1565	1H47L2	G	4/4	F1p34
MAJOR CHURCHILL'S DANCE	151H4	22H76	D	2/2	A1v3p219
MAJOR CRICHTON'S DELIGHT	1H3H1H3H	5H2H5H2H	D	2/4	C5v1p24 A1v5p24
MAJOR DAVID STEWART'S STRATHSPEY	5L3L5L5L	227L2	A	4/4	C14v23p6
MAJOR FRASER OF CULDUTHIL'S STRATHSPEY	3b17bL7bL	113b5	G	4/4	F2v1p6
MAJOR FRASER OF KNOCKY'S FAREWELL	3b13b1	7bL427bL	F	6/8	F2v1p2
MAJOR GRAHAM (OF INCHBRAKIE)	5L111H	5222	G D	4/4	E1v1p92 A1v3p210 C13v1p46 G11v1Ap3 G10v1p6 (II)
MAJOR GRAHAM'S STRATHSPEY	5L111H	6422	G D	4/4	A7v6p18 A7v2p7
MAJOR JAMES MONRO('S STRATHSPEY)	3b5L3b5	2425	D	4/4	Mc21v2p22 (II)
MAJOR JAs CAMPBELL'S QUICKSTEP W.F.R.	1H3H1H5	31H2H5	D	2/4	A1v1p51
MAJOR JOHN BRUCE'S QUICK STEP	1165	456L2	G	6/8	A1v2p26
MAJOR J.S. KER'S MARCH	5535	6665	F	4/4	L3p2
MAJOR KER'S QUICK STEP	111H1H	357L5L	F	2/4	L3p3
MAJOR(L.) STEWART('S REEL)	11H2H1H	5353	G	4/4	M4v3p42 (II)
MAJOR LOGAN'S FAVORITE	1L113	1L326L	Bb	4/4	G10v4p32
MAJOR LOGAN'S FAVORITE	1H3H1H6	5622H	D	6/8	A7v5p24
MAJOR LOGAN'S FROLLICK	53H2H3H	53H2H6	F	4/4	F3p11
MAJOR MACBEAN 6TH REGt's MARCH	1122	1113	Bb	4/4	L1p24
MAJOR MACBEAN'S 14th REGT's STRATHSPEY	1353	662H2	A	4/4	L1p18 (II)
MAJOR MACDONALD'S RANT	15L3L5L	5L2L7L2	Bb	2/2	C14v20p21
MAJOR McLEAN	4L13b1	4L7bL7bL4L	E	2/4	G10v5p16,17
MAJOR McLEAN(OF 60th. REGt.) 'S REEL	1331H	7b424	A G	2/2	Mc10p12 A1v5p8 C5v1p8
MAJOR MOLLE'S (OF THE 9th REGt OF FOOT) REEL	153b1	153b2	B	4/4	G10v5p15 (II)
MAJOR MONTGOMERIE'S QUICK STEP	1155	51H1H1H	D	4/4	A1v1p41

Title	A	B	Key	Time	Sources
MAJOR MONTGOMERIE'S QUICK STEP	1155	51H1H1H	D	4/4	A1v1p41
MAJOR MONTGOMERY'S REEL	51H15	51H2H2	D	2/2	C13v2p68
MAJOR PATON OF THE PERTH VOLUNTEERS QUICK STEP	2H71H5	2H71H5H	D	6/8	C23p11
MAJOR RAY'S STRATHSPEY	3b115L	2424	E	4/4	G15p37
MAJOR ROBERTSON'S STRATHSPEY	5551H	51H22	C	4/4	G10v2p2,3 Mc12v1p39
MAJOR, THE	3112	3542	A	6/8	T7p36,37
MAJOR, THE	3152	3142	A	6/8	A1v1p49
MAJOR WEBSTERS DELIGHT	35L7L2	3542	G	4/4	F3p10
MAJOR'S MAGGOT	1H565	1H1H53	A	6/8	A1v1p17
MAKER TOWER	1H5H4H1H	3453	D	6/8	S7v1p4
MAL BROUKE	3343	2231	G	6/8	A1v3p179
MALBROOK	3H3H4H3H	2H2H3H1H	G	6/8	E1v2p78
MALT MAN (COMES ON MONDAY), (THE)	6L15	7L27L	D G	9/8	B15v2p18,19 D13p20 O1v1lp71 G11v2Bp17 B15v1p47 R4p10 K1v2p19
MALTESE DANCE, THE	1H531	4326L	F	2/2	P9p35
MAN HAS GOT HIS MARE AGAIN, THE	556	1H1H2H	D	3/4	O1v1Lp162
MAN IN, THE	3565	4303	G	2/2	P8v2p30,31
MANAGERS LAST KICK, THE	1547L	1574	Bb	2/4	C1v2p2
MANDERSTON HOUSE	1115	127L5	G	4/4	Mc13v1p2 Mc13v2p2
MANLY HEART, THE	25H3H5	37L45	G	6/8	E1v1p64-67
MAN'S A MAN FOR A' THAT, A	1H1H62H	3H1H66	D	2/4	C8v1p42 E1v2p17
MAN'S A MAN FOR A' THAT, A	5536	7533	G	2/4	C8v2p14
MAN'S GANE GYTE, THE	1212	11H52	A	4/4	L9p5
MANUS	13b54	5222	E	4/4	Mc5p18
MAOL DONAIDH	3555	3566	G	6/8	Mc5p7
MAOL NAN CROGAN	1311	5L5L22	D	2/2	Mc16p25
MARAIDH BHAN OG	13b54	427bL0	A	6/8	Mc5p21
MARCH	1324	3513	G	2/2	A1v6p64
MARCH	551H3H	51H2H5	D	2/4	C8v2p51
MARCH	5566	1H111	F	4/4	Mc21v1p40
MARCH	5H4H5H4H	3H1H3H1H	D	4/4	E1v2p53
MARCH 30th REGt BY MR ALPHY	1H31H2H	1H31H2H	D	4/4	A1v3p208
MARCH 3d REGT DRAGGOON GUARDS	1H334	5112	G	4/4	A1v3p210
MARCH 3d RIGt OF GUARDS	3332	1565	D	4/4	A1v3p216
MARCH 3rd REGt OF GUARDS	5H5H3H2H	1H1H1H5	D	4/4	A1v6p31
MARCH 6th REGt	1H13H1	61H1H1H	D	2/4	A1v6p61
MARCH, A	1H1H3H2H	2H2H4H3H	C	4/4	W2v1p8
MARCH, A	3513	1H2H55	D	4/4	A1v5p66
MARCH, A	5H3H3H1H	2H2H1H1H	C	2/4	A1v6p21
MARCH BY McGIBBON	1H1H55	3551H	D	4/4	M2p18
MARCH DES GENS D'ARMES	1353	1511	G	2/4	A1v1p50
MARCH FOR THE CLANS, A	15L34	15L13	C	4/4	M12p5
MARCH (FROM "BLUE BEARD")	5H5H3H2H	1H1H2H2H	C D	4/4	E1v1p105,106 C8v2p37
MARCH IN DEMOSOONTE	1H1H1H2H	71HO2H	Eb	2/2	M2p21
MARCH IN MASANIELLO	5313	5556	G	4/4	E1v2p140,141
MARCH IN MONTEZUMA	1H2H3H5H	4H4H1H1	C	2/4	M2p34
MARCH (IN THE BATTLE OF PRAGUE)	1H1H1H2H	5553H	F G	4/4	E1v1p93,94 A1v6p62 C8v2p39
MARCH IN THE WATER PIECE	5555	1H1H1H3H	D	4/4	R12v3p30
MARCH, MARCH, ETTRICK AND TEVIOTDALE	1111	16L63	Bb	6/8	C6p9
MARCH OF LORD McDONALD'S HIGHLANDERS	11H3H4	22H4H5	D	4/4	A1v6p67
MARCH OF THE 15 REGt	5H5H5H6H	3H3H3H1H	C	4/4	M2p30
MARCH OF THE 17 REGt	1351H	6553	G	2/4	M2p26 S12v2p12
MARCH OF THE 21 REGt	1H1H55	3501H	D	4/4	M2p27
MARCH OF THE 22nd REGt	1H1H3H2H	2H551H	D	4/4*	A1v6p68 M2p16
MARCH OF THE 25th REGt.	1133	5121	G	4/4	M2p25 A1v6p63
MARCH OF THE 37th REGt	5554	1112	G	4/4	A1v3p218
MARCH OF THE 44th REGT.	5342	3127L	G	2/2	A1v6p67
MARCH OF THE CAMERON MEN, THE	51H3H1H	5322	D	6/8	C8v2p55
MARCH OF THE RENFREWSHIRE MILITIA	5533	25L5L4L	Bb	4/4	C12p8,12
MARCHE	3332	1113	Bb	2/2	B4p2,3
MARCHE	1T1T5H5H	3H1HO5	C	4/4	B4p9,10
MARCHE FRANCOISE	5H3H4H2H	3H1H5H5H	D	2/4	A1v2p51
MARCHES DES MARSEILLOIS	1H1H2H2H	5H3HO1H	D	4/4	A1v4p2
MARCHIONESS CORNWALLIS'S STRATHSPEY, THE	3L5L15L	5L532	Eb	4/4	D15v2p47,48
MARCHIONESS OF BLANDFORDS REEL	3H1H53	27b27bL	C	2/2	C14v10p7
MARCHIONESS OF BREADALBANE, THE	1H1H55	436L7L	C	4/4	M4v4p15
MARCHIONESS OF BREADALBANE'S REEL, THE	1H632	311H5	A	4/4	Mc19v3p13
MARCHIONESS (OF) CORNWALLIS'S STRATHSPEY	3L5L13L	5L56L5L	Eb	4/4	M4v3p22 G11v2Dp4
MARCHIONESS OF HUNTLY'S FAVORITE, THE	1H1H55	427bL7bL	C	4/4	M4v3p27
MARCHIONESS OF HUNTLY'S FAVORITE, THE	11H3H1H	161H2	Eb	2/2	G10v6p1
MARCHIONESS OF HUNTLY'S FAVORITE JIG	1H3bH2H4H	1H3bH5H5H	C	6/8	M4v3p27
MARCHIONESS OF HUNTLY'S JIG, THE	315L3L	1L57L2	Bb	6/8	M4v3p27
MARCHIONESS OF HUNTLY'S STRATHSPEY, THE	151H6	662H2H	C	4/4	G15p32
MARCHIONESS OF HUNTLY('S STRATHSPEY)	1L5L4L5L	6L247L	Bb A	4/4	M4v3p1 G7p4 K1v2p11 (II)
MARCHIONESS OF NORMANBY, THE	3131	6L237L	Bb	6/8	M4v4p17
MARCHIONESS OF QUEENSBERRY'S FAVORITE WALTZ, THE	1H3H4H1H	51H32	C	6/8	G9v3p10
MARCHIONESS OF TWEEDDALE	1153	26L7L5L	A	4/4	Mc19v3p6,7

Name			Key	Time	Sources
MARCHIONESS OF TWEEDDALE, THE	17L3L5L	5L7L13	Eb	4/4	M4v3p23
MARCHIONESS OF TWEEDDALE'S DELIGHT	3b11	5L11	G	6/4	G10v2p30
MARCHIONESS OF TWEEDDALE'S VALTZ	354H1H	354H1H	F	3/8	G9v4p9
MARCHIONESS OF WORCESTER'S FAVORITE, THE	1H3H53H	4327L	C	2/2	C14v6p12
MARCHIONESS, THE	1125	317L5L	A	6/8	P5v1p13
MARCHMONT HOUSE	311H1	312H2	D	6/8	B15v1p23 C13v2p69 G11v2Cp34
MARGARET'S FANCY	3H5H4H1H	3H5H4H3H	D	6/8	B16v3p5
MARGATE ASSEMBLY	1H535	627L5L	F	2/4	W4v1p21
MARGATE CLIFFS	5L13b5	2454	A	2/4	C14v23p14,15
MARGATE HUNT	1H3H74H	3H71H3	D	6/8	C5v1p7 A1v5p7
MARI NIGHEAN DEORSA	112	565	G	3/4	A1v6p41
MARIAN DOW	1H1H1H5	4H3H3H6H	C	4/4	D16p33
MARIANNE OF WALTHAMSTOW	351H5	3H2H4H5H	D	6/8	L2p26
MARIA'S FROLIC	3565	22H75	D	6/8	A1v2p1
MARINERS, THE	5643	4435	G	4/4	C5v1p61 A1v5p61
MARION DUNN	3b13b1	27b27bL	F	4/4	F3p10
MARIONETS	1565	4321	G	6/8	A1v1p40
MARK IN THE DUMPS	15L15L	6L211L	G	6/8	B16v3p30
MARK YONDER POMP	1H1H3H1H	1H664	C	4/4	C6p12
MARKET CHORUS	53H2H1H	763H5	D	2/4	C8v2p40 (II)
MARLY HOUSE	1551H	3H1H52	D	4/4	B11p13
MARNOCH'S STRATHSPEY	3b13b1	2L7bF2L7bF	A	4/4	M4v3p43 (II)
MARQUES OF TULLYBARDIN'S REEL, THE	5351	5364	A	2/2	Mc9v3p16 Mc12v1p58,59
MARQUESS OF TWEEDDALE'S STRATHSPEY, THE	5L5L5L5L	5L1L26L	A	4/4	Mc4v2p11
MARQUIS OF BOWMONT'S REEL	5L4L3L5L	3L422L	Bb	4/4	M4v3p1
MARQUIS OF GRANBY	1562	1561H	G	6/8	A1v1p34
MARQUIS OF GRANBY'S DELIGHT	3325L	4431	G	2/4	A1v1p23
MARQUIS OF HASTINGS, THE	1135	4327L	F	4/4	G11v2Dp21 (II)
MARQUIS OF HUNTLEY'S MARCH	1H1H1H4H	7551H	E	2/2	J1p47
MARQUIS OF HUNTLEY'S WELCOME TO THE CHAIR	16L15L	2426L	A	2/2	J1p29
MARQUIS OF HUNTLY (NEW STRATHSPEY)	151H6	1522H	F	4/4	Mc21v4p23 (II)
MARQUIS OF HUNTLY'S HIGHLAND FLING, (THE)	1H3H4H3H	62H75	D	4/4*	P1v2p3 C14v24p4 C8v1p30 C8v2p10 C24v2p17 G7p9 K1v2p38 G11v2Bp36 D15v2p44 C22p28 J1p17 (II)
MARQUIS OF HUNTLY'S BIRTHDAY	1H3H2H6	54H2H2	F	4/4	P5v3p3
MARQUIS OF HUNTLY'S FAREWELL, THE	1155	1H1H1H1H	D	4/4	A7v6p1
MARQUIS OF HUNTLY'S FAREWELL, THE	1L1L5L5L	1111	A	4/4	A7v2p1
MARQUIS OF HUNTLY'S FAREWELL, (THE)	1L1L5L5L	1311	A	4/4	C8v1p32 Mc7p22 G7p6 K1v1p26 G11v2Ap24 M4v3p14 M4v2p1 C13v1p42 Mc9v3p38 N1v1p16 Mc12v1p15 (II)
MARQUIS OF HUNTLY'S FAREWELL, THE	1L1L5L5L	1321	A	4/4	G8p13 P1v1p5
MARQUIS OF HUNTLY'S FAVORITE, THE	111	112	Bb	9/8	M4v3p3
MARQUIS OF HUNTLY'S MARCH	1H556	5331	D	4/4	L2p25
MARQUIS OF HUNTLY'S MARCH, THE	1555	4666	D	4/4	S5p6
MARQUIS OF HUNTLY'S NEW REEL	1H3H2H4H	3H3H77	C	2/2	Mc21v2p38
MARQUIS OF HUNTLY'S REEL, THE	1H3H67	1H36L7L	C	2/2	G15p32
MARQUIS OF HUNTLY'S SNUFF MILL, THE	5L126L	5L151H	G F	4/4*	A7v5p22 A7v4p22 G10v4p2 (II)
MARQUIS OF HUNTLY'S (STRATHSPEY/REEL)	5L15L1	7bL247bL	A G	4/4*	A1v6p9 G1v2p52 A1v2p37 A7v5p38 A7v6p34,35 A7v2p13 K1v1p11 Mc13v2p32 Mc21v4p41 M4v1p6 C8v1p44 G9v5p8 Mc7p28 Mc9v3p17 C13v1p32 M4v3p11 D15v2p49 G11v2Ap9 (II)
MARQUIS OF HUNTLY'S WELCOME TO THE ROYAL HIGHLANDERS	3155	3542	F	2/2*	Mc4v3p3 (II)
MARQUIS OF HUNTLY'S WELCOME HOME, THE	1351H	547L2	Bb	2/4	G11v1Cp14,15
MARQUIS OF LORNE'S STRATHSPEY	3211	567L2	F	4/4	Mc21v4p23
MARQUIS OF LORN'S FANCY	3b11	3b12	A	9/8	A7v3p30
MARQUIS OF LORN('S REEL, THE)	5353	4542	G	2/2*	Mc12v1p50,51 (II)
(MARQUIS OF) LORN('S) STRATHSPEY, THE [LORN STRATHSPEY, THE]	3H2H1H1	27bL44	D	4/4*	G10v1p25 G11v1Cp18 (II)
MARQUIS OF LOTHIAN'S REEL	5555	7b47bL2	E	2/2	S7v1p41
MARQUIS OF TULLIBARDINE('S GIGG), (THE)	13b5	7bL24	G	9/8	C4p8 G11v1Bp7 G10v1p18
MARQUIS OF TULLYBARDINE('S REEL)	1351	5164	A	2/2*	G11v2Dp15 (II)
MARQUIS OF WELLINGTON	5342	15L5L4L	G	2/2	M12p16
MARQUIS WELLINGTON	5451H	53H2H5	F	6/8	C1v3p5
MARQUISS OF HUNTLEY'S QUICK STEP	31H1H1H	3H3H2H2	C	6/8	C14v22p8
MARQUISS OF LORN'S STRATHSPEY	1L3L5L3L	1L3L6L2L	Bb	4/4	C14v14p11
MARQUISS OF LORN'S STRATHSPEY, THE	11H46L	5L136	Eb	4/4	Mc15p37
MARR HILLS	1555	1553	G	4/4	P5v3p24
MARR HILL'S STRATHSPEY*	1565	1562	G	4/4	P5v1p8
MARRIAGE KNOT, THE	4L3L3L1L	116L2	G	4/4	G11v2Cp4
MARRIAGE MORN, THE	3453	2121	Eb	6/8	P11v2p17
MARRIAGE OF FIGARO	1240	5620	F	2/4	M2p11
MARRY KETTAY	3133	3132	G	4/4	P5v3p12
MARRY KETTY, (WILL YOU GO AND)	1133	1132	G	4/4*	G10v2p6 A7v6p86 G11v1Ap29 Mc9v1p20 Mc7p35 S12v1p22 (II)

79

Title			Key	Time	References
MARSAIL LOCHINALIE	114	551	A	3/4	O1v1Kp124,125
MARSEILLOIS HYMN, THE	1H1H2H2H	5H5H1H1H	C D	4/4*	C8v1p5 C8v2p2 E1v2p144
MARSEILLOIS, THE	1122	5511	G	4/4	S7v2p4
MARSHAL SAX(E)'S MINUET	111	222	Eb G	3/4	S11v1p22,23 R12v3p27
MARSHALL FANCY	1325L	1322	A	4/4	C14v3p4
MARSHALL'S FAVORITE	1H1H6b6b	5547bL	C	2/2	G8p31
MARSHALL'S STRATHSPEY	1311H	5H2H2H6	E	4/4	C13v1p39
MARSHALL'S STRATHSPEY	1H53b1	3b3b55	C	2/2	J1p32
MARSHALL'S STRATHSPEY	11H1H5	22H2H6	D	4/4	A1v6p5
MART DO CHRO' A MHEINANICH	315L3L	3135	Bb	2/2	F2v2p50,51(40,41)
[MART DHE CRODH A' MHEINEIRICH]					
MARTHA	1H3H5H3H	4H61H6	E	2/4	S7v3p4
MARTINI'S MINUET	1H1H2H	2H2H3H	D	3/4	S11v1p20,21
MARY AND DONALD	1H1H51H	51H4H3H	C	2/2	A1v3p179
MARY GRAY	5342	531H3	G	4/4*	S12v1p14 G11v2Ap13 C13v2p25
					K1v1p15 B15v1p81 A7v6p94
					E1v1p33 G9v5p25 C14v21p9 (II)
MARY HUDSON	51H2H5H	71H63	Eb	4/4	L2p16,17
MARY KETTY	1133	1132	G	4/4	E1v1p40
MARY OF GLENFYNE	151	4L7bL4	G	3/4	C10v2Bp50
MARY SCOT	113	223	G	3/4	M14p4,5
MARY SCOT(T)	113	556	G D	3/4	R12v3p18 T6v1p38 Mc8v1Bp60
					Mc8v2Ap6 (J3) O1v1Ap4 N1v2p48
					O1v2p6,7 O1v3p12,13 T7p8,9
					C4p48 C13v3p40,41 C20p29
					P8v2p1
MARY SCOT(TS THE FLOWER OF YEARON)	113	555	D	3/4	C29p33 S16p72,73
MARY THE DAUGHTER OF GEORGE	112	565	D	3/4	D14v2p23
MARY'S DREAM	5113b	5553b	B F	4/4	C5v2p19 (J3)
MARY'S DREAM	1133	5553	G	4/4	G1v1p14,15
MARY'S DREAM, (NEW SET OF)	1233	5555	G Eb	4/4	A1v5p59 C5v1p59 E1v1p43
					(J3)
MARY'S LAMENT	5L13b1	3b6b24	G	4/4	W4v2p11
MARY'S PRAISE FOR HER GIFT	153	135	A	3/4	Mc1v1p73-79
MASON LADDIE, THE	3111	5L132	G	4/4*	A1v5p52 Mc7p13 H3p9
MASON'S APRON, THE	3111	5L132	A	4/4*	G11v2Bp24 K1v2p26,27 G1v2p87
					C8v1p33 (II)
MASON'S MARCH, THE	1H1H1H3H	1H3H1H3	D	4/4	D6p15
MASONS RANT	3H1H35	7b7b22H	D	2/2	R12v1p95
MASQUERADE DANCE	1151	47L7L6L	Bb	2/2	C14v23p11
MASTER ERSKINE'S HORNPIPE	5757	3H5H6H5H	D C	4/4	A7v5p28 A7v4p8 G10v4p26,27
MASTER FOX MAULE (OF PANMURE)'S	3H51H1H	3H3H4H2H	C	4/4	P5v3p4 A7v4p14
BIRTHDAY					
MASTER F(RANCIS) SITWELL('S REEL)	5364	54H72H	C	4/4	A7v5p11 (II)
MASTER F(RANCIS) SITWELL('S STRATHSPEY)	5L3L6L4L	5L47L2	Bb	4/4*	E1v1p112 C8v1p13 P6v1p1
					A7v4p10 B17p1 N1v1p22 G10v4p33
					D15v2p48
MASTER FRANK ROMILY	5155	6522	F	4/4	M4v4p11
MASTER JAMES ROSE'S HORNPIPE	1155	1155	Bb	4/4	D15v2p45,46
MASTER JOHN ROMILY	31H31	2H4H2H2	F	4/4	M4v4p11
(MASTER JOHN TURNER'S) HORNPIPE	11H1H7	2H51H1H	C D	4/4*	D15v2p45 C8v1p34 C8v2p61
MASTER JOHNSTONE'S HORNPIPE	5432	135L1	Bb	2/2	M1p3
MASTER MASON'S MUSICK, THE	112	351	G	3/4	O1v2p32,33
MASTER McDONALD St MARTIN'S STRATHSPEY	5L153b	4L7bL42	G	4/4	P5v1p19
MASTER PINTO	3L6L16L	3L6L15L	Bb	2/4	G11v1Bp22,23 (II)
MASTER THOMAS BEST'S HORNPIPE	1112	7L556	Bb	4/4	D15v2p46
MASTER THOs BUCHAN'S	13L17L	25L21	Bb	4/4	D15v2p45
(MASTER WILLIAM DUGUID'S) HORNPIPE	13L12	3333	Bb	4/4	D15v2p46 C22p45
MATTHEW BRIGGS	11H7b7b	3b524	A	6/8	A1v2p59 O1v11p65
MAUT'S ABOON THE MEAL, THE	51H3H2H	5555	D	4/4	C5v2p39
MAVIS BANK	131H1	132H2	G	2/2	R6v1p1
MAXWILL'S RANT	1H37L2	1H31H1H	F	2/2	R12v1p42
MAY IS MY LOVE	115L	115L	A	3/4	D14v2p34
MAY IS MY LOVE	115L	113b	B	3/4	C5v2p42
MAY MORNING, THE	1H1H1H5	3557	D	4/4	C5v2p50
MAZURKA	5L121	5L121	Bb	3/8	G13p9
MAZURKA	51H4#1H	51H4#1H	F	3/8	G13p9
MAZZINGHIS FANCY	3332	5331	G	2/4	A1v6p27
M'BAILE M'BEIL MO LEANNAN FEIN	3321	3361H	G	4/4	F2v2p36(26)
McBEAT	5L133	6642	G	2/2	P5v4p11,12
MCCRAE'S FANCY	31H1H7	72H55	D	2/2	A1v2p5
McDONALD OF KEPPACH'S LAMENTATION	113b	3b77bL	A	9/8	D14v2p6
McDONALD OF THE ISLES SALUTATION	3155	4266	D	2/2	D14v2p6,7
MCDONALD'S RANT	355H2H	4H2H66	D	2/2	R12v1p59
McDONOGH'S LAMENTATION	3b21	111	G	3/4	O1v1Hp53
McDUFF'S SCOTS MEASURE	1H511	31H1H6	G	2/2	O1v1Kp129
McFARLANE'S STRATHSPEY	3H52H7	3H52H1H	D	4/4	A1v6p19
McFARLAN'S DELIGHT	5162	512H5	D	6/8	A1v5p14
McGILPIN'S STRATHSPEY	5L13b2	7bL7bL43b	G	4/4	S7v3p13
McGREGOR MURRAY IN THE CELTIC CHAIR	5153	47bL46	D	4/4	G10v6p36
McGREGOR'S GATHERING, (THE)	1H2H55	1H1H4H2H	D C	2/4	C8v2p54 G1v1p6 C8v7p49
McGRIGOR'S LAMENTATION, THE	51H1H	2H1H6	D	3/4	D14v2p16

MCGRIGOR'S SEARCH	155	542	A	3/4	D14v2p9
McINTOSH'S LAMENT	3333	3211	A	4/4	G10v6p2,3
McINTOSH'S LAMENT	333	321	A	3/4	O1v1Jp104,105
McINTOSH'S MAGGOT	1315L	1L122L	Bb	2/4	D15v1p5
McINTYRE'S FAREWELL	3b115	543b7bL	G	4/4	G10v6p36
McKINNON'S REEL	11H1H5	7b7b47bL	A	2/2	H3p36
MCLACHLAN'S SCOTTISH MEASURE	1122	5223	D	4/4*	K1v2p3 G11v2Bp3 Mc9v2p12
					Mc8v2Cp6 C20p61
McLEAN'S BONNY LASSIE	3336	51H22	A	4/4	W2v1p2,3
McLEOD'S LESS SALUTATION	137L6L	5L7L3L2L	G	6/8	D14v2p8
McLOUD'S SALUTE	1H1H7b7b.	5555	D	6/8	B11p33
McNEIL'S MAGGOT	1H3H1H1H	51H22	D	2/2	A1v3p192
McNIEL'S STRATHSPEY [McNEILL'S RANT]	5L5L13	6316L	D	4/4*	G15p16 A7v3p8 O1v1Kp122
MCPHERSON'S FAREWELL	1122	17L6L6L	G	4/4*	Mc8v1Cp92 O1v1Jp96,97
McPHERSON'S FAREWELL	1122	125L5L	G	2/4	N1v2p45
McVICAR'S STRATHSPEY [MACVICAR'S]	5353	51H22	C	4/4	K1v2p22 G11v2Bp20
MEASON'S OF YORK	1135	2431	F	6/8	P5v2p14
MEDLEY COTTILION	312H5	6561	F	2/4	S11v2p17
MEDLEY COTTILION	1H1H5H5H	2H2H2H7	C	2/4	S11v2p10
MEDLEY OVERTURE	3254	5551H	G	4/4	C19p1
MEDLEY OVERTURE	155	154	G	9/8	(C19)
MEDLEY OVERTURE (10)	356	1H1H3H	G	3/4	(C19)
MEDLEY OVERTURE (12)	1554	6b423b	G	4/4	C19p3
MEDLEY OVERTURE (13)	1262	1266L	G	6/8	(C19)
MEDLEY OVERTURE (2)	3342	5331H	G	4/4	C19p1
MEDLEY OVERTURE (3)	1H1H1H3H	1H1H1H3H	G	4/4	C19p1
MEDLEY OVERTURE (5)	1122	1122	G	4/4	C19p2
MEDLEY OVERTURE (6)	3121	6113	G	6/8	(C19)
MEDLEY OVERTURE (7)	1324	151H5	G	6/8	(C19)
MEDLEY OVERTURE (9)	351H1H	2H2H3H2H	G	4/4	C19p2
MEDLEY OVERTURE(4)	51H71H	2H3H77	G	4/4	C19p1
MEDWAY	1H71H5	4327	C	6/8	R12v1p85
MEG MERRILEES	5357	6553	A	4/4	C8v2p29 C8v1p18 (II)
MEILLIONEN O FERIONY'DD	1H3H74H	3H4H72H	D	2/2	W7p19
MELBOURNE HOUSE	311H1H	427L2	D	4/4	C14v11p7
MELVIL HOUSE	1H1H1H1H	1H755	C	4/4	G8p32
MEMORY OF DEPARTED WORTH, THE	3b113b	56b47bL	C	4/4	G10v5p8,9
MEMORY OF INVER, THE	1H57b5	2427bL	G	4/4	G10v6p10
MEMORY OF JOYS THAT ARE PAST, THE	1H654	4322H	D	4/4	A7v6p76
MEMORY OF JOYS THAT ARE PAST, THE	16L5L4L	4L3L2L2	Bb	4/4	D16p11 G10v6p28
MENTAL BEAUTY	1H1H67	2H71H1H	D	4/4	A1v6p33
MERN'S STRATHSPEY, THE	1L332	5L323	G	4/4	A7v3p21
MERRILIE DANC'D THE QUAKER'S WIFE	15L43	15L6L1	G	6/8	C6p4
MERRILY DANCE(D) THE QUAKER('S WIFE)	15L26L	15L6L1	G	6/8	G9v5p21 K1v2p19 B15v1p53
					G11v2Bp17
MERRY AT THE FAIR	5351	5364	A	2/2	Mc19v1p13 Mc19v2p20
MERRY BEGGARS, THE	13b7L	124	G	9/8	O1v1Ip76
MERRY COBLERS	331H1H	1H3H2H2	D	2/2	S7v1p7
MERRY COUNCILLORS, THE	5165	42H22	G	2/2	R12v1p74
MERRY DANCERS	333	416L	G	6/4	R12v1p33
MERRY DANCERS, (THE)	3411	345L5L	G	6/8	A1v1p52 B15v1p94 B10p26
MERRY FIDLER, THE	151H1H	2H2H4H2H	F	2/2	B20p17
MERRY FIFERS, THE	1H1H11	1H1H41	A	6/8	S7v1p49
MERRY GIRLS OF (EPSOM/YORK), THE	5L5L5L5L	2125L	G Bb	6/8	Mc9v2p16 R12v1p6
MERRY GIRLS OF YORK, THE	5555	2H1H2H5	D	6/8	A1v2p32/33
(MERRY) LADS OF AYR, (THE)	3H1H1H5	3H1H4H3H	C	4/4*	C14v23p2,3 B15v1p15
					Mc21v3p14,15 R5p10
(MERRY) LADS OF AYR, (THE)	3H1H1H5	3H1H4H4H	C	4/4*	Mc7p16 A7v5p28 A7v6p89 K1v1p21
					G7p15 G11v2Ap19 (II)
MERRY LADS OF BANFF, THE	1H1H2H7	1H1H66	F	2/2	H3p14
MERRY LADS OF CLYDE, THE	5326L	5366	D	2/2	C24v2p20
MERRY LADS OF FOSS, THE	3565	1H542	D	2/2	Mc9v3p15 A1v4p25 (II)
MERRY LADS OF HUNTING TOWER, THE	3256	51H27L	G	2/2	R12v1p54
MERRY LADS OF KILLAROW, THE	1122	161H5	G	2/2	Mc16p13
MERRY MAID'S WEDDING, THE	5152	517bL2	A	2/2	Mc9v1p31
MERRY MEETING, THE	1342	671H6	G	2/4	A1v2p24
MERRY MEETING, THE	1H3H5H3H	1H3H72H	C	2/2	C14v24p10
MERRY MEETING, THE	5331	2H72H5	D	6/8	O1v1Gp5
MERRY MILKMAID	1H53H3H	1H566	C	6/8	S7v1p28
MERRY MINX, THE	1H565	4111	G	4/4	A1v3p214
(MERRY) PLOWMAN, THE	3552	3551	G	2/4	A1v2p15 O1v1Dp6
MERRY QUAKERS	537L5L	3L4L5L2	Bb	6/8	S7v1p21
MERRY SCOT, THE	1132	51H1H7	D	2/2	R12v1p16
MERRY SHEPHERD, THE	1343	3313L	A	2/4	B16v3p62
MERRY SHERWOOD or STRAW BONNET, THE	1135	3122	Bb	2/2	C14v12p19
MERRY SWABBS, THE	51H31	2327L	G	2/4	B16v2p9
MERRY TAYLORS	3331	4442	G	2/2	R12v1p90
MERRY TODAY	1355	6L237L	F	12/8	F3p10,11
MERRY WAKEFIELD	31H1H	52H2H	G	9/8	R12v1p34
MERRY WIVES OF WINDSOR, THE	16L25L	16L25L	C	3/8	B17p8
MERTOUN HOUSE	5364	5342	D	2/2	C14v26p15
METHVEN CASTLE	3546	3642	A	4/4	C21p10

M'EUDAIL, IS M'ULAIDH, IS M'AITHIR	327L4	327L3	G	4/4	Mc5p24
'MHOIDH	1H3H53	462H6	C	2/2	F2v2p61(51)
MI M'SHUIDH 'N EIREADH BATA	116L5L	3521	G	4/4	F2v2p76(66) A1v5p49 F2v1p4
MICHAEL WIGGINS	3H3H1H5	3H3H4HO	F G	6/8	P6v1p31 E1v1p120
MICHAEL WIGGINS IN IRELAND	1H1H55	11H6H2H	D	6/8	C14v25p2,3
MID LOTHIAN	5342	3526L	D	2/2	G8p11 P1v1p4 C14v10p9
MIDNIGHT HOUR, THE	1351H	5527L	G	6/8	A1v6p55
MILE TAING' AN U(GH)DAIR	3L5L15L	3L5L33	Eb	4/4	F2v2p103(93)
MILE TO RIDE, A	51H71H	3551H	G	6/8	Mc16p22
MILITARY MOVEMENT	1H1H2H2H	1H351H	C	4/4	B7p37
MILK MAID, THE	1H2H3H5H	4H3H2H1H	D C	6/8	A1v2p48 B16v3p9
MILK MAID, THE	1332	551H1H	A	2/2	O1v1Gp24,25
MILK MAID'S HORNPIPE, THE	1322	3325L	G	6/8	B16v3p22
MILK POT, THE	1351H	5226L	F	2/2	S7v1p72
MILKING PAIL, THE	53H3H1H	1H1H3H6	C	4/4	O1v1Jp103
MILKMAIDS OF BLANTYRE, THE	1343	25L7bL2	G	2/2	B15v1p2
MILL, MILL O, THE	5550	2H2H2HO	C	4/4	T6v1p40
MILL, MILL O, THE	3H555	662H1H	D	4/4	C8v2p15 C8v1p43 C5v2p1 B5p15
					Mc8v1Cp76 Mc8v2Bp4 O1v1Cp2,3
					Mc12v2p64 C20p8,9 P8v2p4
MILL (MILL) O, THE	35L5L5L	6L6L21	Bb A	4/4	O1v5p37 G17p1 (J3) P4p30
MILL MILL O, THE	35L5L1	6L6L21	Bb D	4/4	C19p20 E1v2p94
MILL, MILL O, THE	15L5L5L	6L6L21	G	4/4	S16p154,155
MILL O' TIFTIE'S ANNIE	521	254	D	3/4	C18p20
MILL OF LAGGAN(, THE)	151H7	2H4H2H2	F	2/2	M4v3p52 (II)
MILLAR OF DRONE, THE	5322	5L1H66	D	2/2*	C24v2p26 (II)
MILLAR OF FIFE, THE	337L5L	31H22	G	2/2	O1v1Fp24
MILLER IS CANTY, THE	1H542H	1H51H3	G	4/4	A1v6p2
MILLER O' DRONE, THE	1H655	552H2H	D	4/4	C8v2p37
MILLER OF DEE, THE	1H73bH2H	4H3bH1HO	C	6/8	G11v2Cp8
MILLER OF DRON(E)	16L5L5L	1L423	A	2/2	A7v4p20
MILLER OF DRONE, THE	1H655	112H2H	D	4/4*	A7v5p10 E1v1p1 G1v1p48
MILLER OF DRONE, THE	16L5L5L	1L1L22	A	4/4	H6v5p2 G11v2Bp25 C8v1p33
					K1v2p27 P11v1p2
MILLER OF DRONE, THE	16L5L5L	2L422	A	2/2	P6v1p28
MILLER'S DAUGHTER, THE	5534	3165	A	2/2	C13v2p35
MILLER'S DAUGHTER, THE	5535	3165	G A	4/4*	A1v2p18 G9v5p16 S12v1p45
MILLER'S DAUGHTER, THE	1122	5L6L11	D	2/2	Mc7p35 Mc9v1p5
MILLER'S DAUGHTER('S STRATHSPEY), THE	6L122	5L6L11	D	4/4	G11v1Ap15 G10v1p22 (II)
MILLER'S FAVOURITE, THE	13b53b	7bL27bL7bL	A	2/2	D15v1p20
MILLER'S RANT, THE	3b53b7bL	3b541	A	6/8	A1v1p16
MILLERS WEDDING, THE	1122	5L6L11	D G	4/4*	A7v2p6,7 B15v1p41 N1v1p1
					C33p17,18 A7v6p20
MILLINER'S HOUSE, THE	4535	27L16L	G A	4/4	C5v1p49 A1v4p49 W4v1p25
MINERS OF WICKLOW, THE	3565	6251	D	6/8	A1v4p11 A1v1p9 C5v1p11 C14v5p8
					Mc12v1p54
MINIKIN FENCIBLE MARCH, THE	3035	3035	F	2/4	G9v3p24
MINION, THE	1H351H	1H523	G	6/8	B16v3p1
MINORS WALTZ, THE	3H4H73H	3471H	C	3/8	C14v11p13
MINTO HOUSE, A STRATHSPEY	51H63	51H42	D	4/4	P11v2p2
MINUET	1H2H2H3H	362H3H	D	3/8	R12v3p22
MINUET	3H4H1H3	62H6H7	D	3/8	(R12v3)
MINUET	5H1H5H1H	5H1H5H1H	D	3/8	Mc9v2p20
MINUET	1T3H3H7	1H2H3H2H	D	3/8	R12v3p24
MINUET	5316	42H1H1H	D	3/8	R12v3p22
MINUET	556	642	Bb	3/4	C13v3p6
MINUET	5H3H5H	771H	D	3/4	R12v3p17
MINUET	114	7L14	Eb	3/4	C13v3p81
MINUET	133	211	Bb	3/4	C13v4p45
MINUET	11H7	671H	Eb	3/4	Mc21v1p18,19
MINUET	14H2	35H4	D	3/4	(R12v3)
MINUET	512	355	G	3/4	(R12v3)
MINUET	511H	775	G	3/4	R12v3p26
MINUET	5L11	5L22	Bb	3/4	C13v3p79,80
MINUET	111	113	Eb	3/4	C13v4p41
MINUET	113	554	Eb	3/4	N2p13
MINUET	113	6L4L4	Bb	3/4	Mc21v1p27
MINUET	334	15L0	A	3/4	W4v2p18
MINUET	555	311	G	3/4	P8v1p9
MINUET BY DR BOYCE	5H3H4H2H	3H2H1H1H	D	3/8	P8v1p4
MINUET BY FELTON	332	117L	A	3/4	S11v1p18,19
MINUET BY MR ARNE	3H71H	654H	D	3/4	P8v1p8
MINUET DANCED BY THE MISSES BAXTER	1H1H2H	5HO2H	E	3/4	N2p6
MINUET DE LA CHASSE	3H3H3H	3H2H1H	D	3/4	C22p16
MINUET DE LA COUR	335	543	A Bb	3/4	D15v2p1 R4p17 C22p13
MINUET IN PORUS	1215	1256L	A	3/8	R12v3p26
MINUET IN SAMPSON	5755	3321	G	3/8	R12v3p23
MINUETTO	1H7b5	515	E	3/4	Mc21v1p7
MINUETTO	5H5H4H	1H1H5	C	3/4	Mc21v1p4
MINUETTO	111	7L5L2	A	3/4	G9v3p8
MINUETTO	542	7L7L1	Bb	3/4	Mc21v1p14
MIRRY NIGHT AT TUMBLE BRIDGE, THE	1326L	1535	A	2/2	Mc4v1p6

MISER, THE	1113	117L2	G	6/8	R12v1p78
MISS A. BROWN'S MINUET	556	51H3H	Eb	2/4	S11v2p25,26
MISS A. HEDDERWICK'S STRATHSPEY	5L16L2	5346L	Bb	4/4	Mc16p35
MISS ABERCROMBIE'S FANCY	115L3L	1122L	Bb	6/8	L4p11
MISS ABERCROMBY	146L7L	1435	G	4/4	S4v1p1
MISS ABERCROMBY OF TULLIBODY'S ALLAMANDE	1H1H5H3H	2H2H1H5H	C	2/4	G9v4p4
MISS ABERCROMBY'S REEL	1H1H5H6H	4H2H75	C	2/2	C24v1p8
MISS ABERCROMBY'S REEL	1531	247L5L	A	2/2	Mc19v3p5
MISS ABERCROMBY('S REEL)	3b13b5	43b24	C	2/2	M4v3p23 (II)
MISS ABERCROMBY'S REEL	3b13b5	44£4	C	2/2	M4v1p5
MISS ABERNETHIE OF MAYHEN'S REEL	1343	1322	A	2/2	C24v1p6
MISS ADAMINA DUNCAN'S STRATHSPEY	16L11	5632	F	2/2	E2p21
MISS ADAMS FAVORITE WALTZ	1123	1121	Eb	3/8	H6v10p1
MISS ADAM'S HORNPIPE	1H553H	2H554H	F	2/2	C14v18p4
MISS ADAM'S JIG	1H155L	3542	Eb	6/8	D14v1p33
MISS ADAM'S MINUET	1H1H3	433	Eb	3/4	D14v1p10
MISS ADAM'S REEL	1133	6542	A	2/2	J1p43
MISS ADAMS STRATHSPEY	1363H	1H542	F	4/4	C14v16p16
MISS ADAMS'S REEL	1H3H72H	3H62H7	C	2/2	P11v1p6
MISS ADMIRAL GORDON'S (REEL/STRATHSPEY)	1H1H1H1H	5H2H66	D	4/4	A1v6p16 G1v2p77
MISS ADMIRAL GORDON'S (STRATHSPEY/REEL)	1111	526L6L	A	4/4*	K1v1p5 M4v3p16 M4v1p3 G11v2Ap5 Mc9v3p4 Mc7p26 Mc12v1p62,63
MISS ADMIRAL GORDON'S WALTZ	1166L	1155	A	3/8	G9v3p8
MISS ADMIRALL GORDON'S STRATHSPEY	1111	5416L	G A	4/4	A7v6p27 A7v2p15
MISS AGNES GORDON'S MINUET	154	17L1	Bb	3/4	Mc21v1p10
MISS (AGNES) ROSS('S REEL/STRATHSPEY)	1313	27b27bL	D	4/4*	K1v2p39 M4v1p10 Mc9v3p21 M4v3p33 Mc12v1
MISS AGNES WILLE'S STRATHSPEY	1H1H65	4322H	C	2/2	D16p31
MISS AINSLIE'S STRATHSPEY	113b5	4444	G	4/4	F3p6
MISS AITKEN'S SINGLE HORNPIPE	1H55	355	F	6/4	D16p31
MISS ALICIA HEGGE'S STRATHSPEY	53b53b	2427bL	G	2/2	Mc22p3
MISS ALLISON CHALMERS REEL	3131H	5342	D	2/2	C23p17
MISS ALSTON STEWART OF URRARD'S REEL	313L5L	547L2	A	2/2	Mc19v3p6
MISS ALSTON'S STRATHSPEY	3L13L1	247L7L	Bb	4/4	Mc12v1p34
MISS ALVES'S VALTZ	5H1H2H3H	5H1H2H1H	C	3/8	G9v4p20
MISS AMELIA CLARKE'S STRATHSPEY	1121H	5326L	D	2/2	Mc22p14
MISS AMELIA FLEMING'S STRATHSPEY	5124	513H1H	F	2/2	P5v4p11
MISS AMELIA HUNTER'S SINGLE HORNPIPE	1H1H3H	1H1H2H	D	3/2	D16p14
MISS AMELIA MARY DUFF OF MUIRTOWN'S STRATHSPEY	1527L	6L136L	Bb	4/4	M12p19
MISS AMELIA MENZIES' REEL	3565	437L2	F	2/2	Mc19v2p9
MISS AMELIA OLIPHANT GASK'S STRATHSPEY	5326L	5361H	D	4/4	B11p12 (II)
MISS AMELIA STEWART MENZIES' REEL	1H1H65	7b427bL	C	4/4	Mc19v2p12
MISS ANDERSON'S FAVORITE	1125L	1354	Bb	6/8	S4v2p17
MISS ANDERSON'S FAVOURITE	37L62	7L152	F	6/8	P11v1p14
MISS ANDY CAMPBELL'S SCOTS MEASURE	4255	3551H	F	4/4	Mc9v2p10
MISS ANGUS, BOTRIPHNIE'S REEL	1L115	27L5L3L	Bb	2/2	M4v3p10
MISS (ANN) (AMELIA) STEWART ('S) (STRATHSPEY)	1353	3H1H32	G F	4/4	A7v6p81 A7v4p18 G11v2Ap30 Mc21v4p24,25 Mc7p17 P5v2p5 K1v1p32 (II)
MISS ANN AMELIA STEWART'S STRATHSPEY	1327L	1353	F	4/4	C14v13p13
MISS ANN AMELIA STUARTS ALLAMAND	3454	7L415	A	2/4	G9v4p13
MISS ANN BAIN'S FANCY	1352	7L5L7L5L	G A	4/4	A1v4p40 W4v1p16
MISS ANN BISSET LOGIERAIT	3bH3bH4H4H	3bH3bH2H4H	E	2/2	Mc4v4p9
MISS ANN CAMERON'S JIG	152	155	Bb	9/8	M4v3p9
MISS ANN CARNEGIE OF SOUTHESK'S REEL	3572H	3H72H5	Eb	2/2	Mc13v2p22
MISS ANN CARNEGIE'S ALLAMANDE	1H531	7L411	G	2/4	D15v1p15
MISS ANN CARNEGIE'S FAVOURITE VALTZ	1552	46L11	G	3/8	D15v1p15
MISS ANN CARNEGIE'S HORNPIPE	5236L	3L142	Bb	2/4	D15v1p6
MISS ANN COCKBURN'S FANCY HIGH DANCE	561H3	6L27L2	Bb	6/8	G3p31
MISS ANN CUMING'S STRATHSPEY	51H26L	51H62H	Eb	4/4	R9p14
MISS ANN DALRYMPLE'S STRATHSPEY	1H1H72H	1H3H4H3H	F	4/4	S4v2p7
MISS ANN DAVIDSON'S JIG	113L3	1H67L2	Bb	6/8	M11v1p10
MISS ANN DEWAR FRAZER OF TORBRECK'S REEL	5L5L11	5L5L55	A	2/2	C23p5
MISS ANN DONALDSON'S REEL	5357	3H524	F	2/2	C24v2p4
MISS ANN DOUGLASS BRIGTON'S JIGG	3H2H1H5	61H2H2	C	6/8	B11p13
MISS ANN DRUMMOND SMYTH'S REEL	1356	5432	F	6/8	C23p13
MISS ANN DRYSDALE'S KIRKALDY REEL	13b53b	4242	G	4/4	W2v2p5
MISS ANN GRAHAM OF FINTRY'S STRATHSPEY	117L2	1313	Bb	4/4	S4v2p12
MISS ANN GREIG'S REEL	1353	2466	F	2/2	C24v2p4
MISS ANN HAY ('S REEL)	5411H	6422H	D	2/2	G11v1Cp35 P11v1p19
MISS ANN MACKAY'S FAVORITE	31H31	42H42	C	6/8	Mc21v4p44
MISS ANN McNEE'S REEL	3b5L3b5	2454	B	2/2	B20p15
MISS ANN MOIR'S BIRTHDAY	1115	1126L	G	4/4	D16p27
MISS ANN MONRO('S QUICK STEP)	1543b	7bL47b2	B	6/8	Mc21v2p24 (II)
MISS ANN MURRAY'S STRATHSPEY	5L14L6L	4L326L	Bb	2/2	R9p25
MISS ANN ROBINSON'S STRATHSPEY	1H51H3	62H72H	C	4/4	M12p4
MISS ANN ROSS'S REEL	1152	7bL47b4	A	4/4	C23p8
MISS ANN STEWART (EASTCRAIGS STRATHSPEY)	11H1H3bH	7b43b7bL	G	4/4	G10v2p26 G11v1Cp26 (II)

Title					
MISS (ANN) STEWART, EAST CRAIGS REEL	5L13b5	247bL2	A G	2/2	A7v4p16 G10v2p26
MISS ANN STEWART'S REEL	5L15L1	6L5L2L2L	Bb	4/4	M4v2p4 (II)
MISS ANN STEWART'S STRATHSPEY	5513	661H6	C	2/2	R9p20
MISS ANN WILLIAMSON'S FAVORITE JIG	1H1H66	557L2	F	6/8	R9p13
MISS ANNA MUNRO	5446	3432	F	2/2	J2p14
MISS ANNE CAMPBELL BALMARTIN'S REEL	3131	7L27L2	Bb	2/2	Mc16p23
MISS ANNE CAMPBELL'S STRATHSPEY	1H61H6	31H22H	C	2/2	Mc16p11,12
MISS ANNE CARNEGIE'S HORNPIPE	5127L	35L6L2L	Bb	4/4	A7v4p3
MISS (ANNE) CARRE'S REEL	3131H	3542	F	2/2	Mc21v1p35 S12v1p57
MISS ANNE GORDON	1153	1136L	F	4/4	M4v4p32
MISS ANNIE LIVINGSTON'S REEL	1H3H2H5	61H51	D	2/2	S12v1p47
MISS ANNIE ROBERTSON (DINGWALL)	3335	4446	F	2/4	Mc21v2p12
MISS ANNIE WATSON'S REEL	3561H	3542	G	2/2	Mc13v1p10 Mc13v2p10
MISS ANNY FORBES REEL	1113	6522	A	2/2	C24v1p3
MISS ANNY STEWART BOHALLY'S REEL	1535	47b27bL	A	2/2	Mc4v1p11 (II)
MISS ANSONS REEL	3152	311H6	A	2/2	J1p43
MISS ASHURST'S REEL	5353	2362	G	2/2	J1p20
MISS ATHILL'S REEL	1H562	3125L	Bb	2/2	C14v14p10
MISS AUGUSTA CHARTEIR'S STRATHSPEY	13b53bH	7b542	C	4/4	S4v2p18
MISS AUGUSTA MURRAY	5L5L5L5L	2226L	Eb	4/4	B12p4
MISS AUGUSTA MURRAY'S REEL	1L1L3L1L	1L5L4L2L	Bb	4/4	B12p4
MISS B. CAMPBELL OF SHAWFIELD'S FAVORITE	551H5	2352	G	6/8	S11v2p2
MISS B. CAMPBELL OF SHAWFIELD'S WALTZ	136L7L	136L1	A	3/8	S11v2p15
MISS B. CAMPBELL'S BUMPKIN	1324	3527L	Bb	6/8	S11v2p2
MISS BABIE GRAY'S MINUET	111	115	F G	3/4	D14v1p6 D14v4p9
MISS (BABY) MONTGOMERY('S) REEL	1L5L15L	3L122L	Bb	2/2	C13v2p19 S12v1p53
MISS BAILLIE'S MARCH	1H1H1H1H	3H3H5H4H	D	4/4	A1v5p19 C5v1p19
MISS BAINE'S STRATHSPEY	5L111	7bL541	G	4/4	W4v1p14
MISS BAIN'S REEL	5157	1H2H2H2H	D	4/4	A1v5p55
MISS BAIN'S STRATHSPEY	113b5	7bL424	E	4/4	A1v5p54
MISS BAIRD OF SAUGHTON HALL'S ALLAMANDE	1313	5252	G	2/4	G9v4p16
MISS BAIRD OF SAUGHTONHALL	5553	5655	F	4/4*	G10v5p34 C14v27p6,7 (II)
MISS BAIRD OF SAUGHTONHALL'S HORNPIPE	5L13	17L2	A	6/4*	G11v1Bp17 G10v3p26
MISS BAIRD'S MINUET	131	6H1H3	Bb	3/4	Mc21v1p11
MISS BAIRD'S STRATHSPEY	13b51H	7b7b22	D	4/4	S4v2p3
MISS BAKER'S HORNPIPE	3112	7L445	F	2/2	A1v3p174 S7v1p45
MISS BALCARRAS LINDSAY'S FAVOURITE	1H3H5H1H	62H1H6	D	2/4	S4v1p9
MISS BALCETTI'S REEL	3344	331H1H	A	2/2	Mc15p14
MISS BALFOUR WHITEHILL'S REEL	1H3H1H5	11H2H2H	G	4/4	F3p14,15
MISS BALFOUR'S JIG	5L133	5233	Eb	6/8	G3p34
MISS BALFOUR'S REEL	137L5L	3637L	G	2/2	S12v1p71
MISS BALFOUR'S STRATHSPEY	5L16L2	1316L	G	4/4	P11v2p10
MISS BALFOWR [MISS BALFOUR]	1H1H66	6422	D	4/4	W2v2p10
MISS BARBARA ARGO'S JIG	1122	4125L	Bb	6/8	M11v1p8
MISS BARBARA CAMPBELL'S JIGG	536L6L	415L5L	G	6/8	P11v1p12
MISS BARBARA CAMPBELL'S MINUET	1H54	622	F	3/4	S11v2p27
MISS BARBARA CAMPBELL'S STRATHSPEY	135L3L	137L2	F	4/4	S4v2p2
MISS BARBARA CUNNINGHAM('S STRATHSPEY)	1513	6L27L5L	G	4/4	Mc21v2p38 (II)
MISS BARBARA DONALD'S STRATHSPEY	5353	3127bL	D	4/4	A7v2p25
MISS BARBARA HAY'S FAVORITE	11H51	427L5L	G	6/8	Mc21v3p38
MISS BARBARA MUNRO'S REEL	1316L	5L6L4L2L	Bb	2/4	J2p15
MISS BARBARA STEWART	1H535	2H646	C	2/2	M4v4p13
MISS BARBARA STEWART	5L13b5	2527bL	E	6/8	S4v1p2
MISS(BARBARA) STEWART'S REEL	3H1H1H1H	3155	D	2/2	M4v1p8 C14v7p16
MISS BARCLAY'S REEL	5337b	4242	A	2/2	W2v1p3
MISS BARINGTON'S FANCY	1H3H1H6	4622H	E	2/2	C14v4p20
MISS BARSTOW'S REEL	15L3L5L	6L27L6L	G	2/2	Mc21v3p16
MISS BARTLET('S REEL)	37L6L5L	37L42	F G	2/2	Mc10p3 (II)
MISS BARTRAM'S STRATHSPEY	1132	3366	Bb	4/4	G3p28
MISS BASS WALTZ	37L37L	37L31	Bb	3/8	C14v23p4
MISS BEATON'S REEL	1316L	5L5L3L1L	Bb	2/4	J2p16
MISS BECK'S MEASURE	4211	16L6L1	Bb	4/4	G3p4
MISS BEGBIES REEL	331H1H	6542	D	2/2	A7v3p29
MISS BELFIELD'S STRATHSPEY	1H3H62H	1H3H64H	D	2/2	J1p49
MISS BELL CAMPBELL OF KINGSBURGH'S SCOTS MEASURE	1311	6L36L2	Bb	4/4	R7v3p2
MISS BELL KENNEDY'S REEL	123b6b	527bL4	A	6/8	R5p58
MISS BELL'S FAVOURITE	152H6	61H22	D	2/2	S7v1p3
MISS BELL'S REEL	1155	51H22	D	2/2	C14v15p13
MISS BELSCHE'S WHIM	5125	5541	F	2/4	L4p11
MISS BELSCHES'S STRATHSPEY	1333	62H66	G	4/4	L4p8
MISS BENHAM'S STRATHSPEY	51H64	4626L	D	2/2	J1p40
MISS BENNETS JIGG	1H1H1H3	11H3H2H	C	6/8	C14v8p16
MISS BENTINCK'S FANCY	1131	1H5H4H2H	G	2/4	A1v6p35
MISS BETSEY CAMPBELL OF SHAWFIELD'S MINUET	113	335	Bb	3/4	S11v2p19,20
MISS BETTSAY MURRAY'S JIG	5542	356L7L	Bb	6/8	R9p9
MISS BETTSY ROBINSON'S REEL	1151H	647L5L	F	2/2	C24v1p4
MISS BETTSY WILSON'S REEL	1H3H4H7	1H347L	D	2/2	C24v1p4
MISS BETTY CAMPBELL OF FAIRFIELD'S STRATHSPEY	1H51H5	6522	F	4/4	E2p13

MISS (BETTY) CAMPBELL ('S REEL)	3b13b1H	7b522	C	2/2	C14v1p18 S12v1p62 Mc21v1p34
					P10p25
MISS BETTY CATHCART'S REEL	3151H	662H2H	D	4/4	R5p49
MISS BETTY FORBES' REEL	1122	3347L	A	2/2	C24v1p5
MISS BETTY HUNTER	1H311	4215L	Eb	6/8	D16p10
MISS BETTY HUNTER('S REEL)	3H1H1H5	6532	C	2/2*	D16p12 (II)
MISS BETTY KERR'S REEL	1H564	537L7L	Bb	6/8	Mc21v3p17
MISS BETTY McDONALD'S REEL	15L13L	1322	G	4/4	B15v1p99
MISS BETTY McLEAN'S REEL	5H3H1H5	6535	C	2/2	Mc16p4
MISS BETTY McLEAN'S STRATHSPEY	1H335	22H2H6	C	4/4	Mc16p4
MISS BETTY MUNRO'S REEL	1366	1325L	Bb	2/4	J2p12
MISS BETTY PLUMMER'S REEL	1H3H1H5	662H2H	D	4/4	S12v1p64
MISS BETTY ROBERTSON	51H35	22H76	G	2/2	A7v4p13
MISS BETTY SCOTT'S FAVORITE	136L5L	4L5L2L2L	Bb	4/4	R9p5
MISS BETTY SHAW'S REEL	3151H	1H7b24	G	2/2	S12v1p62
MISS BETTY WATERSTON'S REEL	5353	437L2	C	2/2	C21p21
MISS BEWMENT'S MINUET	556	1H15	Eb	3/4	Mc21v1p28
MISS BIGGAR'S STRATHSPEY	5311H	5322H	G	4/4	B11p22
MISS BIGG'S FANCY	5325L	536L5L	F	2/2	C12p4
MISS BIGG'S (OF NEWCASTLE'S) DELIGHT	1133	227L7L	Bb	4/4	W4v2p6
MISS BISSET LOGIERAIT'S REEL	1H2H1H5	7b422	E	2/2	Mc4v4p5 (II)
MISS BLACK'S REEL	1H565	6562	D	6/8	W2v2p3
MISS BLACK'S WALTZ	1H2H2H3H	5H5H5H1H	C	3/8	D15v2p37
MISS BLACKWOOD'S FANCY	3b13b1	2427bL	F	6/8	J1p36
MISS BLAGROVE'S STRATHSPEY, THE	1326L	1346	A	2/2	J1p44
MISS BLAIR'S REEL	1H1H1H1H	1H1H72H	C	4/4	G8p33 P1v1p13
MISS BLAIR'S REEL	3H3H2H1H	3H3H66	D	2/2	B15v1p5 C4p12
MISS BLAIRS REEL	1L7L5L3	1L7L22L	Bb	4/4	C14v5p6
MISS BLAIR'S SCOTS MEASURE	5516	1H1H1H6	D	4/4	D16p16
MISS BLAKE'S STRATHSPEY	136L2	1353	A	2/2	J1p38
MISS BLAND'S ALLEMAND	1232	3511	Bb	2/4	B16v4p95 B16v2p2
MISS BOGLE (OF GLASGOW'S) FAVORITE	351H5	352H2	D	6/8	W4v2p20
MISS BONNAR'S REEL	1H5H4H3H	1H5H4H2H	D	2/2	P11v2p11
MISS BOOKER'S REEL	31H63	4322	D	2/2	C24v2p9
MISS BOONES FANCY	5511	2231	Bb	2/4	J1p9
MISS BOSSWELL OF AUCHINLECK'S VALTZ	333	555	A	3/4	G9v4p21
MISS BOSWELL'S REEL	1H522	1155	D	4/4	F3p15
MISS BOTHWICK'S REEL	153b5	7bL424	E	4/4	F2v1p8
MISS BOWIS OF INVERNESS	5L3L6L2L	5L3L5L3	Bb	4/4	M12p20
MISS BOWLS'S MINUET	1H1H3H	3H2H2H	D	3/4	R12v3p27
MISS BOW'S DANCE	1132	7L7L25L	Bb	4/4	C22p26,27
MISS BOYCE'S REEL	1151H	3H4H2H2	D	4/4	S11v1p10
MISS BOYD'S STRATHSPEY	5515	247L2	D	2/2	C18p21
MISS BOYN	3374H	361H7	F	2/4	P6v1p17
MISS BRANDER OF SPRINGFIELD	5313	1632	D	4/4	T1v2p8
MISS BRANDER'S REEL	15L3L5L	2L27L2	Bb	2/2	G15p23
MISS BRIDGES' STRATHSPEY	1H155	1H122H	D	2/2	A1v5p8 C5v1p8 Mc10p5
MISS BRODIE OF BRODIE'S REEL	5L126L	5L161H	A	2/2	J2p4
MISS BRODIE OF LATHAN'S FAVORITE	1H1H2H5	1H1H5H5H	C	2/4	W4v2p3
MISS BRODIE'S FANCY, THE	3511	62H65	F	2/4	J1p41
MISS BROOK'S DANCE	334H7	333H2H	G	2/4	F1p27
MISS BROWERS STRATHSPEY	3H1H3H1H	3H1H4H2H	C	4/4	C14v10p15
MISS BROWN OF KELLY-BANK'S REEL	1122	4524	A	2/2	B20p2
MISS BROWN OF LINKWOOD'S STRATHSPEY	3335	6624	F	4/4	G15p31
MISS BROWN'S FAVOURITE	3151H	3122	D	6/8	S4v1p9
MISS BROWN'S JIG	5633	267L7L	Eb	6/8	G3p35
MISS BROWN'S JIG	15L6L1	457L2	A	6/8	R9p16,17
MISS BROWN'S REEL	317L2	311H4	G	4/4	A1v5p56
MISS BROWN'S STRATHSPEY	5L3L5L3	16L6L2L	A	4/4	R9p16
MISS BRUCE OF KINROSS'S REEL	113b5	7b7bL24	E	2/2	S12v1p33
MISS BRUCE'S JIG	5565	3H3H2H2H	C	6/8	R9p22
MISS BRUCE'S REEL	1H557	1H642	F	2/2	S12v1p70 (II)
MISS BRUCE'S STRATHSPEY	1H3H1H5	4H5H2H2H	C	4/4	R9p21
MISS BUCHAN OF AUCHMACOY'S HIGH DANCE	3436	5532	F	2/4	D15v2p26
MISS BUCHAN OF KELLOS	1H515	1H527	D	4/4	S4v2p4
MISS BUCHAN OF KELLY'S STRATHSPEY	137L2	1335	F	4/4	G3p9
MISS BUCHANAN OF CAMBUSMORE'S JIGG	3b111	3b6b54	E	6/8	S4v1p16 (II)
MISS BUCHANAN OF DULLATER'S STRATHSPEY	1111	3232	Eb(G)	2/4	Mc10p12/15
MISS BULLOCK'S FANCY	1133	5322	Bb	2/4	J1p10
MISS BULMAN'S FAVORITE	311H3	422H4	D	6/8	C14v19p15
MISS BUNBURY'S JIG	11H65	3532	Eb	6/8	G3p22
MISS BURBRIDGE'S FANCY	15L6L7L	1547L	Eb	2/2	Mc15p17
MISS BURGOYNE'S FANCY	1135	4131	Bb	6/8	J1p25
MISS BURNET OF MONBODDO'S REEL	113b5	2427bL	C	2/2	Mc21v1p31
MISS BURNETS OF MONBODO'S STRATHSPEY	3L5L5L1	4L6L6L4	A	4/4	C10v1p2,3
MISS BURNET'S REEL	5L153	5L153	G	4/4	M4v2p3
MISS BURNETT FASQUE'S STRATHSPEY	16L3L1L	2L232	Bb	4/4*	A7v4p4 D15v1p3
MISS BURNETT OF LEYS MINUET	1H1H3H	1H1H6	Eb	3/4	D15v2p5
MISS BURNETT'S MINUET	113	224	Eb	3/4	C22p10
MISS BURNS STRATHSPEY	115L3L	1L3L6L3	G	4/4	R9p19
MISS BURN'S WALTZ	3H2H1#H1H	325#1H	C	3/8	G9v2p8
MISS BURRINGTON'S FANCY	1H1H1H6	4622H	E	2/2	J1p28

85

Title					
MISS BURROWS REEL	531H3	437L2	D	2/2	C14v11p15
MISS BUSHBY'S ALLAMANDE	1H1H1H3H	2H2H3H1H	F	2/4	G9v4p17
MISS BUTT'S FAVORITE	1565	6L6L7L1	G	6/8	S7v1p89
MISS C. BARTLET'S STRATHSPEY	3146	1H37L2	G	4/4	Mc10p6/7
MISS C. CLARK'S STRATHSPEY	31H61H	31H22H	C	4/4	Mc16p18
MISS C. DALRYMPLE'S JIG	3211	5532	Eb	6/8	G3p1
MISS C. ELPHINSTONE('S STRATHSPEY)	15L11	4L5L2L2L	A	2/2*	Mc15p14 (II)
MISS C. GEDDES'S WALTZ	115	1H1H3	G	3/4	F1p35
MISS C. HONYMAN OF ARMADALE'S HIGH DANCE	3H3H2H	1H71H	E	3/4	S11v2p13,14
MISS (C.) LITTLE'S FANCY	1H2H3H1H	4H2H75	C	6/8	P1v2p2 J1p15
MISS C. McDUFFIE'S STRATHSPEY	5L13b5	7b2H7b7bL	G	2/2	Mc16p34
MISS C. PHIN'S REEL	1H1H35	1H1H72H	C	4/4	G3p23
MISS C. RAMSAY'S FANCY	1H53H1H	4H1H1H5	D	2/4	A1v4p38
MISS C. RAMSAY'S FANCY	15L31	4115L	Bb	2/4	W4v1p13
MISS CALDWALL'S FAVORITE	3123	351H4	F	6/8	P11v2p3
MISS CALEY	322	011	A	3/4	L1p5
MISS CALLANDER'S MINUET	554	335	G	3/4	W4v1p6 A1v4p36
MISS CALL'S REEL	15L3L5L	137L2	F	2/4	C14v9p15
MISS CALL'S REEL	15L5L1	5226L	Bb	2/2	J1p5
MISS CAMERON OF GLENEVIS STRATHSPEY	13b53b	27b47bL	G	4/4	R7v3p2
MISS CAMERON'S REEL	1H1H64	642H4	A	4/4	M4v3p15
MISS CAMERON'S REEL	3115L	7L245	Bb	2/2	M4v3p3
MISS CAMPBELL FAIRFIELD'S STRATHSPEY	1L132	5522	Bb	4/4	E2p19
MISS CAMPBELL JURA'S REEL	1515	6633	D	2/2	Mc13v2p22
MISS CAMPBELL LOCH-END'S REEL	551H1H	2H2H2H6	C	2/2	Mc4v1p9 (II)
MISS CAMPBELL OF COMBIE	1H11H1H	2H2H75	D	6/8	M6p3
MISS CAMPBELL OF JURRA'S ALLAMNDE	3317L	2221	Bb	2/4	G9v4p9
MISS CAMPBELL OF KILBRIDE'S STRATHSPEY	1153	6526L	G	4/4	Mc10p11
MISS CAMPBELL OF MELFORD	3H3H2H3H	52H3H2H	G	6/8	L1p15
MISS CAMPBELL (OF) MONZIE ('S STRATHSPEY)	5551H	3H2H2H2	C D	4/4	B11p9 K1v1p7 Mc12v1p20 (II) A1v4p55 C5v1p55 (II)
MISS CAMPBELL OF MONZIE'S(REEL)	1H53H5	432H2	C	2/2*	G10v3p24 (II)
MISS CAMPBELL (OF MONZIE'S) REEL	3L5L4L6L	7L235	Bb	6/8	Mc21v3p6
MISS CAMPBELL OF MONZIE'S STRATHSPEY	1113b	3b422	G	4/4	Mc4v4p10
MISS CAMPBELL (OF SADDELL'S) REEL	3b1H3b5	27b24	D	2/2*	Mc21v3p16 (II)
MISS CAMPBELL (OF SADDELL'S) STRATHSPEY	1311	6L27L5L	Bb	4/4	Mc21v3p20 (II)
MISS CAMPBELL OF SADDEL'S REEL	1H31H3	7L7L1H3	G	2/4	A1v4p5 C5v1p48
MISS CAMPBELL OF SHAWFIELD'S	311H7	1H542	C	6/8	C14v6p13
MISS CAMPBELL OF SHAWFIELD'S STRATHSPEY	13b53b	7bL27b2	G	4/4	Mc10p7
MISS CAMPBELL OF SHAWFIELD'S VALTZ	1H1H1H1H	1H1H1H1H	C	3/8	G9v4p7
MISS CAMPBELL OF SMIDDY GREEN'S JIGG	5437L	6L542	Bb	6/8	Mc10p13
MISS CAMPBELL OF SMIDDY GREEN'S STR.	5L353	5L426L	Bb	4/4	Mc10p13
MISS CAMPBELL PARK PLACE'S REEL	3H2H1H1H	31H31	D	2/2	S4v1p21
MISS CAMPBELL SILVER CRAIG'S REEL	1H3H5H6H	5H3H2H2H	C	2/2	Mc15p5
MISS CAMPBELL SUNDERLAND'S STRATHSPEY	3L13L3	3L14L2L	Bb	4/4	F2v1p9
MISS CAMPBELL'S FANCY	3L1L3L1L	5L1L4L2L	Bb	2/2	C14v12p5
MISS CAMPBELL'S JIG	5437L	6L542	G	6/8	C5v1p40 A1v5p40
MISS CAMPBELL'S MINUET	1H1H1H	1H1H5	Eb	3/4	G3p3
MISS CAMPBELL'S REEL	1351H	537L7L	Eb	2/2	Mc13v2p35
MISS CAMPBELL'S REEL	1H565	2H253	G	2/2	A7v4p13
MISS CAMPBELL('S REEL)	536L5L	4L3L22L	F	4/4	Mc21v4p25 (II)
MISS CAMPBELL'S STRATHSPEY	3576	5H5H2H2H	C	2/2	R9p7
MISS CAMPBELL'S STRATHSPEY	1153	6526L	G	4/4	A1v5p34 C5v1p34
MISS CAMPBELL'S STRATHSPEY	5L326L	5L526L	Bb	4/4	R9p25
MISS CANTOUR'S REEL	1H51H3	42H72H	D	2/2	Mc21v4p10
MISS CARMICHAEL'S JIG	1H1H4H2H	751H1H	F	6/8	S4v2p15
MISS CARMICHAEL'S STRATHSPEY	1H322H	1H353	D	4/4	Mc10p2
MISS CARNEGIE (OF SOUTHESK)'S HORNPIPE	1H11	235	G	6/4	C5v1p32 D15v1p4 A1v5p32
MISS CARNEGIE'S ALLAMANDE	5433	27L11	F	2/4	D15v1p13
MISS CARNEGIE'S FAVOURITE VALTZ	3332	1121	Bb	3/8	D15v1p13
MISS CARNEGIE'S MINUET	554	652	G	3/4	Mc21v1p5
MISS CARNEGY OF LOWER'S STRATHSPEY	1653	5322	F	4/4	M1p1
MISS CAROLINE GRANT'S STRATHSPEY	113L5L	1111	Bb	4/4	S4v1p18
MISS CAROLINE THOMSONS REEL	1H3H2H4H	1H3H2H5	C	2/2	L4p6
MISS CARSINA GORDON GRAY'S FAVOURITE	1565	4622H	D	4/4	A4v1p3
MISS CATHARINE REDDIE'S STRATHSPEY	31H71H	457L2	A	4/4	D16p32
MISS CATHERINE ANSON'S STRATHSPEY	1354	1326L	A	2/2	J1p29
MISS CATHERINE BISSET'S STRATHSPEY	131H1H	2H4H62H	D	2/2	J1p46
MISS CATHERINE FORSYTH'S REEL	1213L	17L22L	Bb	2/2	T1v2p10
MISS CATHERINE HALES JIG	1562	3125L	G	6/8	C22p47
MISS CATHERINE HAYWOOD'S JIG	13H74	3542	D	6/8	C22p31
MISS CATHERINE MILLER'S REEL	3H1H2H7	1H65#3	C	6/8	W2v1p3
MISS CATHERINE STEWART	1527L	1551H	F	12/8	M4v4p9
MISS CATHERINE STEWART OF DESKY'S REEL	1355	4326L	G	2/2	T1v2p8
MISS CATHne SHIRREFF'S FAVORITE	311H1H	3142	F	6/8	W4v2p31
MISS CATHRINE ABERCROMBY'S DELIGHT	1311H	64H72H	D	2/4	S4v1p3
MISS CATHRINE CAMPBELL ARDMORE'S STRATHSPEY	13b53b	13b52	B	2/2	Mc16p2
MISS CATHRINE CHALMERS (REEL)	3445	327L6L	G	4/4	G10v3p29 G11v1Bp23 (II)
MISS CAVE'S REEL	3H1H4H6H	3H1H2H6	D	4/4	J1p49
MISS CAY'S JIGG	1335	1337L	A	6/8	P11v1p18

MISS C.H. BAIRD'S STRATHSPEY	1H535	1H3H72H	F	4/4	S4v2p16
MISS CHALMER'S JIGG	1144	5527L	G	6/8	H3p24 S12v2p9
MISS CHALMERS JIG(G)	5122	5156	D	6/8	G11v1Ap32,33 G10v3p17
MISS CHALMERS REEL	1H1H1H1H	665H3H	D	2/4	N2p15
MISS CHAMER'S REEL	5555	7b47bL2	E	2/2	S12v1p27
MISS CHARLES HAMILTON SCOTTS JIGG	3565	6542	F	6/8	Mc13v1p4 Mc13v2p4
MISS CHARLES MURRAY'S REEL	331H4	4542	D	2/2	Mc22p8
MISS CHARLOTE HOPE OF CRAIGIEHALL	537L7L	15L4L3L	Bb	2/4	B11p2
MISS CHARLOTE KER'S MINUET	111	222	D	3/4	R5p6,7
MISS CHARLOTE ROSSE'S MINUET	1H53	115L	D	3/4	S11v1p23
MISS CHARLOTE ROSS'S REEL	316L2	331H5	D	2/2	S11v1p7
MISS CHARLOTE ROSS'S STRATHSPEY	3135	1H622H	D	2/2	S11v1p6,7
MISS CHARLOTE STEWART'S FAVOURITE	1H53b1	22H4H2H	C	6/8	S11v1p2
MISS CHARLOTE STIRLING	1516	5311	F	2/4	B11p4
MISS CHARLOTE STIRLING'S JIGG	5151H	5125	D	6/8	A1v5p41
MISS CHARLOTTE ALSTON STEWART'S REEL	3127bL	1356	A	2/2	Mc19v3p5
MISS CHARLOTTE BRODIE'S REEL	361H3H	3H3H75	C	2/4	J2p7
MISS CHARLOTTE CARRUTHERS'S FAVORITE	5L5L5L1L	316L3L	G	6/8	P11v2p16
MISS CHARLOTTE COX'S FANCY	53bH4H7b	53bH5H3bH	C	4/4	Mc15p21
MISS CHARLOTTE DUNDAS'S REEL	3H1H1H5	2H4H2H6	C	2/2	J1p18
MISS CHARLOTTE DUNDAS('S STRATHSPEY)	1L47L2	1L353	Bb	4/4	S4v1p11 (II)
MISS CHARLOTTE ELLIOTT'S REEL	3H535	3H572H	C	4/4	S4v2p2
MISS CHARLOTTE GORDON OF CLUNY'S STRATHSPEY	1H535	4H5H6H2H	C	4/4	L2p25
MISS CHARLOTTE HALL'S STRATHSPEY	13L13L	6L47L2	Bb	2/2	P5v4p23
MISS CHARLOTTE MONRO'S ALLAMANDE	1215	427L5L	Bb	2/4	G9v4p14,15
MISS CHARLOTTE ROSS('S REEL)	6424	5353	Eb D	2/2*	G15p6 (II)
MISS CHARLOTTE STIRLING'S JIGG	5151H	5125L	D	6/8	B11p15 Mc12v1p24
MISS CHARLOTTE STIRLING'S REEL	351H5	1H522	G	6/8	W2v1p4
MISS CHARLOTTE TOLL'S STRATHSPEY	1H3H65	2632	E	4/4	C12p4
MISS CHARTERE'S REEL	15L13	2242	Bb	2/2	Mc4v1p7
MISS CHARTER'S MINUET OF AIMSFIELD	111	331	F	3/4	D14v1p11
MISS CHARTER'S REEL	5122	5155	D	2/2	D14v3p7
MISS CHAt STEWART'S REEL [MISS CHARLOTTE STEWART]	13b55	7b422	C D	2/2*	S11v1p5 (II)
MISS CHISHOLM'S STRATHSPEY	3bL1L2L7bF	3bL5L3bL5L	A	2/2	Mc19v2p11
MISS CHRICHTON'S REEL	1566	1542	G	4/4	G3p19
MISS CHRISTIAN BUCHAN OF KELLIES FAVORITE	536L7L	16L27L	G	6/8	E2p22
MISS CHRISTIAN DUFF'S FAVORITE	5353	1243	Eb	4/4	M12p33
MISS CHRISTIAN RIDDELL'S STRATHSPEY	5326	5353	A	4/4	S4v2p6
MISS CHRISTIE OF DURRIE	1H757	2H4H1H6	C	4/4*	W2v2p4 (II)
MISS CHRISTIE'S STRATHSPEY	1426L	1553H	Eb	4/4	R9p4
MISS CHRISTINA ABERCROMBY'S HIGH DANCE	1575	5335	A	2/4	D15v2p33,34
MISS CHRISTINA STEWART'S REEL	1131	2461H	G	2/2	C14v11p12
MISS CHRISTY STEWART'S REEL [MIS CHIRSTY STEWART]	2H565	3522H	C	2/2	Mc4v1p8 (II)
MISS CHURCHILL'S STRATHSPEY	1155	6661H	D	2/2	B12p3
MISS CLARK'S DOUBLE JIGG	1H3H2H5	1H532	Eb	6/8	S11v2p3
MISS CLARK'S STRATHSPEY	315L1	227L4	Bb	4/4	G3p34
MISS CLAVERING'S FANCY	5L3b47bL	3b51H5	A	6/8	Mc15p16
MISS CLAVERING'S STRATHSPEY	13L13	7L27L5L	Bb	4/4	M6p1
MISS CLEMENTINA ELPHENSTONE'S REEL	1H1H31H	2H2H72H	C	2/2	B11p11
MISS CLEMENTINA IRVINE'S STRATHSPEY	3566	5342	A	4/4	Mc19v1p3
MISS CLEMENTINA LOUGHMAN ('S STR.)	51H55	1H522	F	2/4	G11v1Ap10 G10v3p6,7
MISS CLEMENTINA SARAH DRUMMOND OF PERTH'S STRATHSPEY	3125L	3142	A	2/2*	B11p11 (II)
MISS CLEMENTINA STEWART OF GARTH'S JIGG	1H1H2H5	6542	D	6/8	Mc4v3p10/11
MISS CLEMENTINA STEWART'S JIGG	113b3b	3b7bL24	G	6/8	Mc4v1p19
MISS CLEMENTINA STEWART'S REEL	1351H	6652	G	2/2	D16p21 (II)
MISS CLEMENTINA STEWART'S REEL	311H3	432H2	C	2/2	Mc4v1p13
MISS CLEMENTINA STEWART'S REEL	131H3	337L7L	G	2/2	Mc4v2p5 (II)
MISS CLEMENTINA STEWART'S STRATHSPEY	5L13b5	2424	E	2/2	S4v1p2
(MISS CLEMIE STEWART'S) MINUET	111H	655	Bb	3/4	C13v4p40 Mc21v1p30
MISS COCHRAN MERCER	1H31H3H	6562	D	2/2	Mc4v2p3
MISS COCHRAN'S JIG	35L6L5L	357L2	A	6/8	G3p9
MISS COCKBOURNE'S ALLEMAND	1H3H54	4111	G	2/4	B16v3p63
MISS COCKBURN HOPE PARK'S STRATHSPEY	147L7L	147L2	Bb	2/2	S4v1p5
MISS COLCROFTS FAVORITE	1H3H4H2H	3H72H2H	D	2/4	C14v9p8
MISS COLQUHOUN'S REEL	1126L	1143	G	2/2	P11v2p15
MISS COLQUHOUN('S REEL)	1355	457L2	F	6/8	B15v1p98 L2p14,15 C13v2p54
MISS COLSTON'S STRATHSPEY	3b13b1H	7b527bL	A G	4/4*	A7v5p7 G1v1p47 G10v4p31 (II)
MISS COLT OF SEACLIFF'S STRATHSPEY	1114	7bL27bL4	E	4/4	S4v1p16
MISS COMBE'S FANCY	5533	1311	G	2/4	J1p10
MISS COOK'S FANCY	3342	37L25L	A	6/8	J1p27
MISS COOPER'S FANCY	1565	1541	Bb	6/8	S7v1p2
MISS CORBET'S FANCY	1H3H64H	4H1H1H1H	D	2/2	C12p4
MISS CORBET'S REEL	1353	2427b	D	4/4	A1v5p8
MISS CORBET'S REEL	1353	2427	D	4/4	C5v1p8
MISS CORBETT'S REEL	1353	2427bL	D	4/4	Mc10p5
MISS CORBETT'S STRATHSPEY	1351H	147L5L	G	4/4	Mc21v3p16

MISS COULL OF ASHGROVE	1H531	5L3L32	F	4/4	T1v2p9
MISS COUTTS'S REEL	31H35	31H2H2	C	2/4	J2p2
MISS COX(E'S STRATHSPEY)	1H6L5L3L	5L47L2	Eb	4/4	G10v5p22 (II)
MISS COX'S FAVOURITE	316L2	3151H	Eb	4/4	Mc15p17
MISS CRAGIE OF DUMBARNIE'S STRATHSPEY	136L5L	147L5	G	4/4	S4v2p14
MISS CRAUFURD'S REEL	1151	4H3H2H6	E	2/2	J1p2
MISS CRAWFORD'S FAVORITE	1212	4522	Eb	6/8	S4v2p9
MISS CRAW'S FAVORITE STRATHSPEY	35L46	547L2	F	4/4	R9p12
MISS CRICHTON'S SCOTT'S MEASURE	1113	16L6L4L	Bb	4/4	D16p18
MISS CRUDENS REEL	5L5L4L2	15L4L2L	Bb	2/2	Mc13v1p3 Mc13v2p3
MISS CRUICKSHANK'S REEL	5L144	5226L	Bb	2/2	M4v3p12
MISS CRUIKSHANKS' STRATHSPEY	5H5H5H1H	5H5H2H7b	Bb	2/2	C14v12p9
MISS CUMINE OF AUCHRY'S STRATHSPEY	1366	5353	F	4/4	C18p3
MISS CUMINE OF LOGIE'S REEL	37L6L1	5L3L5L5L	G	2/2	C18p33
MISS CUMINE OF LOGIE'S STRATHSPEY	317L3L	1L3L11	G	4/4	C18p32
MISS CUMIN'S GERMAN WALTZ	3421	3421	Bb	3/8	W4v2p7
MISS CUMMING BRUCE	131H5	2366	D	4/4	T1v2p2
MISS CUMMINGS FANCY	153H2H	1H7b27bL	D	2/2	C14v8p10
MISS CUMMINGS FANCY	5L236L	5L144	A	6/8	C14v13p17
MISS CUMMING'S REEL [MISS CUMING]	1L3L13L	1522	Bb	4/4	F3p6
MISS CUMMINGS STRATHSPEY	1H37L2	131H3H	D	2/2	Mc15p33
MISS CUMMYN'S REEL	1353	2366	A	2/2	J1p37
MISS CUNNINGHAM OF LAINSHAW'S FAVOURITE	357L2	437L6L	Bb	2/2	C12p5
MISS CUNNINGHAM'S FANCY	1H565	1H543	F	6/8	C22p48
MISS CUNNINGHAM'S FANCY	3423	3421	F	6/8	G3p2
MISS D. COOPER'S MINUET	133	551H	Bb	3/4	G3p25
MISS DALLAS('S REEL)	5L126L	5L122	G	4/4	M4v2p1 (II)
MISS DALLAS'S STRATHSPEY	1H3H5H4H	1H3H77	D	4/4	P11v2p10
MISS DALRYMPLE HAY'S REEL	1H551	3b427bL	E	2/2	P11v1p7
MISS DALRYMPLE OF FORDEL'S STRATHSPEY	5L13b5	7bL7b2H3bH	D	4/4	S4v1p21
MISS DALRYMPLE OF NORTH BERWICK'S ALLAMAND	5H5H3H3H	1H4H2H2H	C	2/4	G9v4p16,17
MISS DALRYMPLE (OF NORTH BERWICK'S) QUICK STEP	317L2	311H1H	G	6/8	Mc21v2p13
MISS DALRYMPLE'S JIG	15L15L	2427L	Bb	6/8	D14v4p7 D14v1p27 (II)
MISS DALRYMPLE'S (N(th) BERWICK) JIG	5H3H2H1H	1H2H4H2H	C	6/8	G3p29
MISS DALRYMPLE'S REEL	1353	6L464	Bb	4/4	C14v2p12
MISS DALZELL'S STRATHSPEY	116L5L	5562	F	4/4	L4p7
MISS DALZIEL'S STRATHSPEY	5315L	4L3L41	A	4/4	G3p24
MISS DARRELL'S FANCY	1353	2464	A	2/2	J1p37
MISS DAVIDSON OF TULLOCH'S JIGG	3323	3324	D	6/8	C14v5p13
MISS DAVIDSON'S JIG	1H1H75	1H1H4H4H	D	6/8	C14v6p8
MISS DAVIDSON'S REEL	1H3H1H3H	1H3H2H6	F	2/2	C8v1p56 G10v4p2 (II)
MISS DAVIE'S WALTZ	1575	4332	G	3/8	D6p12
MISS DAWSON'S JIG	1135	2246	Bb	6/8	Mc15p40
MISS DAWSON'S WHIM	5151	5522	G	6/8	C5v1p31 A1v5p31
MISS DE VISMES DELIGHT	1H2H3H1H	62H75	G	2/4	C26v1p22
MISS DEANS'S FAVORITE	3L4L7L1	656L7L	Bb	6/8	S4v2p11
MISS DEFFELL'S STRATHSPEY	15L3L1L	2L226L	Bb	2/2	J1p20
MISS DEVEREUX REEL	1H1H35	22H76	D	2/2	C14v10p23
MISS DEVON'S REEL	1H515	432H2	C	2/2	C14v10p17
MISS DIANA SINCLAIR'S STRATHSPEY	15L35L	346L1	D	4/4	P11v1p15
MISS DICKINSON'S REEL	5L133	6562	F	4/4	P1v2p5 J1p19
MISS DICKSON'S REEL	1H565	1H51H2H	D	6/8	Mc21v3p4
MISS DICKSON'S STRATHSPEY	147L2	5551H	G	4/4	S4v1p1
MISS DIGBY	1H553	2435	Bb	2/2	C14v26p11
MISS DINNING OF NEWLAND'S STRATHSPEY	13b13b	7bL27bL2	E	4/4	S4v2p8
MISS DINWIDDIE'S REEL	1353	242H4H	F	2/2	C13v2p78
MISS DINWIDDIE'S REEL	3542	7L237L	Bb	2/2	P9p24
MISS DIROM'S (STRATHSPEY/REEL)	1111	2255	D	4/4*	C24v1p9 C24v2p8 P5v3p20
MISS DISHINGTON'S FANCY	1H3H4H7	1H3H5H7H	C	2/2	C14v12p6
MISS DOBBIE'S STRATHSPEY	3162	3125L	F	4/4	W4v2p29
MISS DONALDSON'S STRATHSPEY	3546	547L2	Eb	4/4	M4v3p25
MISS DOROTHEA S. CHEYNE OF EDINr	5L13b5	4L7bL27bL	G	4/4	C21p15
MISS DORSET	1155	5522	D	2/2	W2v2p9
MISS DOUGLAS	3131	6L27L5L	G	4/4	Mc21v3p30
MISS DOUGLAS BRIGTON'S JIGG	311H5	4562	D	6/8	B11p18
MISS DOUGLAS OF BRIGTON'S STRATHSPEY	1115	117L7L	Bb	2/2*	Mc4v3p4 (II)
MISS DOUGLAS OF BRIGTON'S STRATHSPEY	1H1H1H5H	1H1H77	C	2/2	A1v6p31
MISS DOUGLAS'S FANCY	1126	5211	G	6/8	A1v6p28
MISS DOUGLAS'S JIG	1542	356L7L	G	6/8	R9p19
MISS DOUGLASS MONCRIEF'S REEL	3531	427L5L	G	2/2	Mc21v3p3
MISS DOUGLAS'S STRATHSPEY	5353	6L27L5L	G	4/4	Mc21v3p11 (II)
MISS DOUGLAS'S STRATHSPEY, THE	1H531	22H2H6	C	2/2	J1p41
MISS DOUGLASS'S REEL	5L3L5L3	6L5L4L2L	Bb	2/2	S12v1p55
MISS DOWNIE'S STRATHSPEY	11L5L1L	11L5L5L	Bb	2/2	Mc15p40
MISS DR. GRANT'S MINUET	111	131	Eb D	3/4	D14v1p2 D14v4p3
MISS (Dr) GRANT'S QUICK STEP	1H555	1H522	D	6/8	Mc21v2p10
MISS DRAK'S DELIGHT	1354	4431	G	2/4	R12v1p78
MISS DRUMMOND FORBES'S HORNPIPE	1H313	1H3H1H6	C	4/4	G3p30
MISS DRUMMOND FORBES'S MINUET	1H1H3H	2H1H6	Eb	3/4	G3p17
MISS DRUMMOND MEGGINSH'S STRATHSPEY (MISS DRUMMOND OF MEGGINCH]	1H61H6	31H22H	C	2/2*	Mc4v3p5 (II)

MISS DRUMMOND OF DRUMTOCHTY'S STRATHSPEY	351H3H	2H1H52	F	4/4	G10v4p37
MISS DRUMMOND OF KELTIE'S REEL	15L5L3	15L6L2L	Bb	2/2	B11p15 (11)
MISS DRUMMOND OF LOGIEALMOND'S STRATHSPEY	3b3b15	3b7b24	E	4/4*	P5v3p22/3 S4v1p7 (11)
MISS DRUMMOND OF PERTH'S FAVORITE SCOTS MEASURE	3b211	3b3b54	G	4/4	Mc4v4p2
MISS DRUMMOND OF PERTH'S REEL	5337b	4224	A	2/2	G8p5 Mc4v3p1
MISS DRUMMOND OF PERTH'S REEL	5336	4224	A	2/2	P1v1p2
MISS DRUMMOND'S FAVORITE	13b1H1H	3bH1H45	E	2/2	P5v4p12
MISS DRYSDALE'S FAVORITE REEL	3231	1575	A	4/4	Mc13v2p12
MISS DRYSDALE'S JIG	1H1H55	4542	D	6/8	B20p12
MISS DUFF OF FETTERESSO'S STRATHSPEY	1531	7bL427bL	D	4/4	Mc4v4p6/7
MISS DUFF OF LOACH	31H4H2H	4H2H72H	F	2/2	C21p4
MISS DUFF OF MUIRTON'S JIG	121H3bH	5H2H54	D	6/8	G15p30
MISS DUFF OF MUIRTOWN'S REEL	317L2	311H4	G	4/4	A1v4p74 F2v1p4
MISS DUFF'S STRATHSPEY	3562	3H5H77	C	4/4	P11v1p6
MISS DUMBRECK'S REEL	4213	6361H	A Bb	2/2*	C8v1p13 G10v6p29 (11)
MISS DUNBAR OF NORTHFIELD'S FAVORITE	1313	6342	Bb	2/2	C18p12,13
MISS DUNBAR OF NORTHFIELD'S HORNPIPE	331	35L3	A	3/2	C18p6
MISS DUNBAR OF NORTHFIELD'S STRATHSPEY	3H3H1H6	53H3H2H	F	4/4	G15p29
MISS DUNBAR'S STRATHSPEY	3553	5362	D	4/4	T1v2p3
MISS DUNDAS OF MELVILLE'S STRATHSPEY	1L13bL6bL	2L7bL2L7bF	A	4/4	S4v1p23
MISS DUNDAS'S GIGG	5H1H2H2H	5H5H2H1H	D	6/8	S12v2p9
MISS DUNDAS'S MINUET	1L3L3L	3L5L5L	Bb	3/4	D14v1p14
MISS DUNDAS(S) OF ARNISTON('S REEL)	3527bL	3565	D	4/4*	G10v4p19 (11)
MISS DUNDASS OF DUNDASS'S STRATHSPEY	13b52	4427b	G	2/2	A7v1p7
MISS DUNDASS OF KERSE STRATHSPEY	5213	7L5L2L2L	A	4/4	W4v1p17
MISS DUNDASS OF KERSE'S STRATHSPEY	5H2H1H3H	7522	D	4/4	C5v1p43 A1v4p43
MISS DUNDAS(S REEL)	1555	7b47bL2	G	2/2*	D14v1p34 D14v4p14 (11)
MISS DUNKANSONS JIGG	5333	47bL7b7bL	A	6/8	P5v2p24
MISS DUNLOP'S REEL	13L13	13L26L	Bb	2/2	Mc13v2p23 C13v1p23 C13v2p9
MISS DURY'S REEL	1H1H1H1H	2H4H71H	D	2/4	J1p13
MISS E. BAILLIE'S STRATHSPEY	6L5L6L5L	5L332	Bb	4/4	L3p5
MISS E. BELL'S FAVORITE STRATHSPEY	3b15L1	3b155	G	4/4	D16p30
MISS E. CAMPBELL'S STRATHSPEY	1L3L5L6L	5L3L6L6L	Bb	2/2	Mc16p32
MISS E. CARNEGIE'S HORNPIPE	1112	1112	Bb	4/4	A7v4p6
MISS E. ELDER(S REEL)	1L16L5L	4L5L2L2	Bb	2/2	P5v1p4 (11)
MISS E. ERSKINE	3362	6355	C	4/4	W2v2p6/7
MISS E. FERGUSON'S HIGH DANCE	5147L	3216L	A	4/4	S11v2p4
MISS E. GRANT, LOSSYMOUTH'S REEL	3L5L6L5L	3L16L2	A	4/4	T1v2p6
MISS E. MacLEOD'S REEL	11L5L1	15L6L7L	A	4/4	Mc21v4p32
MISS E. WADE'S REEL	1H535	6522H	C	2/2	P11v2p20
MISS EASTWOOD'S FANCY	1353	6L5L4L3L	Bb	2/2	C14v15p17
MISS EDMONDSTONE OF NEWTON'S STRATHSPEY	151H5	54H72H	D	4/4	S4v1p14 (11)
MISS EDMOND(STON)'S REEL [MISS EDMONDSTON]	11H52	7L232	Bb	2/2	S12v1p41 C13v2p19 S7v1p7 (11)
MISS ELDERS	1353	6432	A	4/4	Mc4v2p12
MISS ELDERS REEL	1535	3527	D	4/4	A7v5p28
MISS ELDER(S REEL)	153b5	3b527bL	E	4/4*	P5v1p22 (11)
MISS ELDERS REEL	1535	3527L	D	4/4	A7v4p8
MISS ELEANORA HAMILTON'S REEL	17bL3b5	3b547bL	A	2/2	R5p52
MISS ELEANORA KER'S REEL	113b4	5247bL	A	12/8	R5p50
MISS ELEANORA ROBERTSON'S FAVOURITE	11H3b5	27b22	C	6/8	G10v3p32
MISS ELEONORA CAMPBELL OF KILBRIDE'S REEL	3H1H35	67b21	D	4/4	C5v1p3 A1v5p3
MISS ELEONORA CAMPBELL OF KILBRYDE'S STR.	3H1H35	67b27bL	D	4/4	Mc10p4
MISS ELEONORA ROBERTSON'S REEL [MISS ELENORA ROBERTSON]	137L7L	137L5	Bb	2/2	Mc21v3p10 (11)
MISS ELEXA SCOTT'S STRATHSPEY	1553	547L2	A	2/2	D15v1p12
MISS ELEZBATH OSWALD'S REEL	5213	5216L	D	2/2	W2v1p10,11
MISS ELISA SKENE'S REEL	1111	4326L	G	2/2	S5p15
MISS ELISABETH COPLAND'S STRATHSPEY	5555	2462	A	4/4	C13v1p25
MISS ELISABETH COPLAND'S STRATHSPEY	5555	2462	A	4/4	Mc13v2p25
MISS ELIZA ANDERSON'S FANCY	3H2H1H1H	4H2H75	C	6/8	A7v1p14
MISS ELIZA BRODIE	3b216b	6b554	F	2/2	J2p13
MISS ELIZA BRODIE'S STRATHSPEY	111H1H	1H542	F	4/4	W4v2p30
MISS ELIZA FORSYTH('S STRATHSPEY)	5122	4513	G	2/2*	M11v1p6 (11)
MISS ELIZA LOW'S HIGH DANCE	51H65	3532	Eb	6/8	D15v2p19,20
MISS ELIZA M. TOD'S HORNPIPE	13L1L5L	1322L	Bb	2/4	B20p18
MISS ELIZA ROBINSON'S REEL	1542	1357	Bb	4/4	Mc19v3p16
MISS ELIZABETH CAMPBELL'S REEL	137L5L	1333	G	2/2	P11v1p8
MISS ELIZABETH CARNEGIE'S FAVOURITE VALTZ	5311	5311	D	3/8	D15v1p14
MISS ELIZABETH CARNEGIE'S ALLAMANDE	1H71H1H	3H2H1H1H	C	2/4	D15v1p14
MISS ELIZABETH CARNEGIE'S HORNPIPE	1111	4425L	Bb	2/4	D15v1p5
MISS ELIZABETH DEWAR'S REEL	5322	1357	A	2/2	P11v1p2
MISS ELIZABETH FERGUSON'S FAVORITE	5651	1H37L2	A	6/8	P5v3p21
MISS ELIZABETH FLEMYNG'S STRATHSPEY	5L3L11	6L5L4L3L	Bb	4/4	Mc19v1p5 Mc19v2p21
MISS ELIZABETH GLEGG'S STRATHSPEY	5354	546L2	G	2/2	D15v1p24
MISS ELIZABETH HAMILTON'S	5121	5121	Bb	3/8	R9p2,3

MISS ELIZABETH HAMILTON'S FAVORITE WALTZ	5121	5121	Bb	3/8	R9p2,3
MISS ELIZABETH MAGd FORDYCE STRATHSPEY	117L5L	1122	A	4/4	Mc21v2p28
MISS ELIZABETH MURRAY'S JIG	516L7L	357L2	Eb	6/8	R9p4
MISS ELIZABETH MYLNE'S STRATHSPEY	11H3b5	7bL7b27bL	D	4/4	S4v2p4
MISS ELIZABETH ROBERTSON'S REEL	5535	22H76	G	2/2	A7v5p18 Mc21v4p37 Mc21v2p39
MISS ELIZABETH TOWART'S STRATHSPEY	1H1H31	42H2H6	C	4/4	K1v2p7
MISS ELLIOT'S FAVOURITE	3426L	16L15L	A	2/4	Mc15p10
MISS ELLIOT'S REEL	353H4H	3H4H2H2	C	2/2	Mc21v1p33
MISS ELLIOT'S REEL	353H4H	3H4H2H3	C	2/2	S12v1p63
MISS ELLIOTT'S STRATHSPEY	1353	1322H	C	4/4	S4v2p2
MISS ELPHINSTONE'S STRATHSPEY	151H5	1566	C	2/2	J1p18
MISS ELPHINSTONE'S STRATHSPEY	15L16L	4L5L2L2	A	4/4	G11v2Cp23
MISS ELTON'S STRATHSPEY	1353	5622	F	2/2	J1p40
MISS ERSKINE OF ALVA('S REEL)	5135	67b27bL	A	2/2	D14v3p4 G11v2Dp36 (II)
MISS ERSKINE OF BARJARG'S REEL	51H3H2H	1H526L	D	2/2	R5p53
MISS ERSKINE OF MARR'S FAVOURITE	537L2	3561H	E	2/4	S4v1p19
MISS ERSKINE OF TORRY('S STRATHSPEY)	315L3L	24L27bL	F	4/4*	G11v1Cp20 A7v2p8,9 G10v2p19 (II)
MISS ERSKINE OF TORY'S STRATHSPEY [MISS ERSKINE OF TORRY]	3b13b1	2427bL	A	4/4	W2v1p12 (II)
MISS ERSKINE WADE'S JIGG	136L7L	1673	G F#	6/8	G1v2p91 P11v1p8
MISS ERSKINE'S MINUET	1H1H5H	3H2H1H	C	3/4	D14v1p16
MISS ESTER OSWALD (OF AUCHINCRUIVE'S) STRATHSPEY	137L2	1515	G	4/4	Mc21v3p30
MISS EUPHEMIA LOWE'S JIG	1171H	1H16L7L	C	6/8	M4v3p44
MISS EVERILDA FRASER	1122	5543	A	4/4	G10v6p5
MISS EVERILDA FRASER	113b	514	G	9/8	G9v2p11
MISS EWING'S REEL	11H1H3bH	2H424	D	2/2	C13v2p67
MISS EYRE'S REEL, THE	131H3	4362	E	2/2	J1p3
MISS F. BAIRD'S JIG	3142	7L5L35L	Bb	6/8	G3p23
MISS FAIRFAX'S STRATHSPEY	151H5	13H2H2	D	4/4	S4v2p13
MISS FALCONER'S STRATHSPEY	13b55L	13b11	E	4/4	P11v1p7
MISS FANNY HOW'S SCOTCH MEASURE	5335	4642	D	2/2	B20p4,5
MISS FANNY STEWART'S STRATHSPEY	1L5L13	6L222	Bb	4/4	S4v1p14
MISS FARQUHAR'S STRATHSPEY	3b11L1	227b2	A	2/2	J1p33
MISS FARQUHARSON BALDOVIE'S DELIGHT	3b41H2H	1H7b7b4	D	6/8	Mc22p21
MISS FARQUHARSON OF BALDOVIE('S STR.)	31H35	31H62	C	4/4	D16p9 (II)
MISS FARQUHARSON OF INVERCAULD (STR.)	5L133	6L243	F	4/4	M4v4p6
MISS FARQUHARSON OF INVERCAULD'S STR.	5555	447L2	Bb	2/2	P5v4p10
MISS FARQUHARSON OF INVERCAULD'S STR.	1H57L2	1H51H5	Bb	4/4	G10v6p28
MISS FARQUHARSON OF INVERCAULD'S STR.	5L122	5551H	D	4/4	S4v1p3
MISS FARQUHARSON (OF INVERCAULD)'S STR.	5L133	6L244	F	4/4*	C14v13p8 P5v2p7
MISS FARQUHARSON (OF INVERCAULD'S) R.	1H53b5	2424	C	4/4	Mc21v2p22
MISS FARQUHARSON OF INVERCAULD'S JIGG	11H7b4	11H1H3bH	C	6/8	Mc4v4p13 P5v1p15
MISS FARQUHARSON'S REEL	1H31H1	1H362	D	2/2	C4p33 B15v1p19
MISS FERGUSON OF KILKERRAN'S REEL	1151H	1165	G	2/2	R5p40
MISS FERGUSON OF RAITH'S STRATHSPEY	3b13b1H	7b527bL	G	4/4	Mc4v2p9
MISS FERGUSON OF RATH'S DELIGHT	1L5L5L1	147L2	A	4/4	A7v4p21
MISS FERGUSON'S REEL	3H2H1H3	4522H	F	4/4	Mc21v4p23
MISS FERGUS'S REEL	61H51	2253	D	2/2	W2v2p3
MISS FERGUSSON OF REITH'S STRATHSPEY	15L5L1	4322	G	4/4	W2v1p6
MISS FERRIER'S MINUET	5L5L4L	113	Bb	3/4	G3p19
MISS FIELDING'S REEL, THE	1111	1164	Bb	2/2	J1p7
MISS FIELD'S STRATHSPEY	1L13L1	2L27L6L	G	4/4	Mc21v2p13
MISS FINCH'S REEL, THE	1H3H1H5	662H2H	D	2/2	J1p44
MISS FINLAY'S STRATHSPEY	3151H	27bL44	C	4/4	G3p9
MISS FLEMYING OF MONESS'S STRATHSPEY	5513	5642	G	4/4	A1v4p74 F2v1p4
MISS FLEMYNG'S REEL [MISS FLEMING OF KILLIECHASSIE]	1L1L11	5216L	A	4/4*	Mc19v1p3 Mc19v2p18 (II)
MISS FLEMYNG'S REEL	1H3H51	1H3H2H3H	Eb	2/2	C23p19
MISS FLOCKHARTS GERMAN VALTZ	151H5	4321	Bb	3/8	W4v2p26
MISS (FLORA) MACDONALD'S (REEL/RANT/QUICK-STEP)	1151	117b7bL	A E	4/4*	G1v2p94 R12v1p97 B15v1p21 S12v1p15 Mc9v3p29 A1v1p31 G11v2Ap16 C14v25p16 K1v1p18 (II)
MISS (FLORA) McLEOD (OF COLBECK)'S MINUET	151H	776	Eb	3/4	S11v1p18 C22p5
MISS FLORA MCLEOD OF COLBECK'S REEL	351H3H	1H542	E	2/2	S11v1p2
MISS FOGO (KILLORN'S REEL)	3155	3142	G	2/2	C23p16 (II)
MISS FORBES	3565	3542	C	2/2*	C8v1p35 (II)
MISS FORBES' FAREWELL	3342	3561H	Eb G	4/4*	G11v2Dp5 (II)
MISS FORBES' FAREWELL TO BANFF	3H4H3H6H	5H5H3H2H	C	2/4	G13p1
MISS FORBES OF EDINGLASSIE'S STRATHSPEY	131H3	46L7L5L	F	4/4	Mc11p4
MISS FORBES OF PITSLIGO'S STRATHSPEY	5L353	5L362	F	4/4	G10v4p29 (II)
MISS FORBES'S FAREWELL TO BANFF	3542	3561H	G	4/4	C8v1p60 C8v2p20 (II)
MISS FORBES'S REEL [LADY FORBES'S REEL]	3565	3542	C	4/4*	C14v1p21 D14v3p2 A7v4p14 G10v4p7
MISS FORBES'S REEL	3H2H1H5	6543	F	2/2	G9v2(p12)
MISS FORBES'S STRATHSPEY	5646	5642	Eb	2/4	G3p35
MISS FORD'S FANCY	3521	4521	A	6/8	J1p29
MISS FORDYCE OF CULSH REEL	5L133	5222	G	2/2	S5p16

MISS FORDYCE OF AYTON'S FAVORITE REEL	3141H	31H2H2	F	4/4	Mc21v4p25
MISS FORDYCE'S (OF AYTON'S) REEL	1513b	247b2	E	2/2	Mc21v2p25 (II)
MISS FORSYTH'S REEL	5L13b3b	7bL247bL	A	2/2	M4v3p43 (II)
MISS FOTHERINGHAM'S STRATHSPEY	5L351H	5642	F	4/4	D15v1p19
MISS FOWLER'S DELIGHT	1357	5315L	A	4/4	S7v1p86
MISS FRANCES DRUMMOND'S JIGG	3b15L1	3b124	E	6/8	S4v1p7
MISS FRANCES RUSSELL	1212	1234	Bb	2/4	D15v2p16
MISS FRANCKLYN'S REEL	52H3H1H	4H3H75	D	4/4*	C1v1p5 C14v9p7
MISS FRASER OF BROOMHILL'S REEL	1111	72H4H7	C	2/2	S5p15
MISS FRASER OF FRASERFIELD'S REEL	5L151	2427L	G	2/2	S5p10
MISS FRASER OF STONEYFIELD'S REEL	1H131	1H126L	G	2/2	G15p3
MISS FRASER'S FAVORITE	51H64	447L2	A	2/4	R9p17
MISS FRASER'S REEL	1H111	1H126L	G	2/2	G11v2Cp16 S12v1p5 B15v1p18
					C13v2p8
MISS FRENCH'S REEL	41H54	247b2	A	2/2	C13v2p66
MISS FULLARTON'S MINUET	1H1H1H	531	D	3/4	R5p9
MISS FYFFE'S STRATHSPEY	535L3L	7L244	Eb	4/4	M4v4p24
MISS G. GORDON	15L3L5L	25L7L5L	Bb	2/2	M4v3p12
MISS G. MACKAY'S FAVORITE	3232	11H1H2	A	6/8	E2p7
MISS GARDEN CAMPBELL OF TROUP'S HORNPIPE	335	422	F	3/2	C18p1
MISS GARDEN (DELGATY'S) STRATHSPEY	53b53b	2427bL	G	4/4	P5v2p13
MISS GARDEN OF TROOP'S REEL	1H3H5H3H	4H3H72H	C	2/2	P5v4p11
MISS GARDEN OF TROOP'S STRATHSPEY	1353	27L7L7L	F	2/2	P5v4p6
MISS GARDEN OF TROUPS FAVORITE	5L321	6L5L6L2L	Bb	4/4	Mc21v4p4
MISS GARDEN OF TROUP'S REEL	5L35L2	331H3	G	4/4	Mc11p9
MISS GARDINER'S JIG	351H5	6547L	F	6/8	D14v1p36
MISS GARDNERS FANCY	11H72H	3H1H4H7	D	2/4	A7v3p14
MISS GAUSSEN'S FANCY	3b11L1	3b142	G	6/8	J1p31
MISS GEDDES'S STRATHSPEY	5513	6636	G	2/2	Mc22p14 C5v1p66 A1v4p66
MISS GEDDES'S STRATHSPEY	1L13b3b	2L7bL43b	A	4/4	S4v1p13
MISS GENERAL BROWNRIGG'S REEL	351H6	537L7L	F	2/2	G10v6p30
MISS GEORGIANA FORBES'S FAVORITE	1234	3642	A	4/4	M12p27
MISS GEORGINA B. STEWART	15L3L5L	5122	F	4/4	M4v4p9
MISS GEORGINA CARNEGIE	3b1L3b5	7b427bL	G	2/4	A4v1p3
MISS GEORGINA MACKAY'S REEL	1L15L3bL	2L7bL4L2L	G	4/4	F3p14
MISS GEORGINE SCOTT OF SEA BANK'S WALTZ	16L11	16L11	G	3/8	R9p10,11
MISS GEORGINE SCOTT OF SEA BANK'S WALTZ	1H1H67	1H1H41	F	3/8	R9p4
MISS GEORGINE SCOTT (OF SEABANK) 'S REEL [MISS GEORGINA SCOTT]	1H1H35	42H76	F G	4/4*	R9p13 (II) G1v2p83 A7v4p17
MISS GIBSON CRAIG	116L2	1351H	Eb	4/4	M4v4p31
MISS GIBSON'S JIG	3L16L5L	3L2L3L1	Bb	6/8	G11v2Bp4 K1v2p4
MISS GIBSON'S STRATHSPEY	31H63	531H4	D	2/2	Mc19v3p7
MISS GLEN'S STRATHSPEY	551H5	5524	D	2/2	Mc22p15
MISS GORDON, (LIVERPOOL)	115	7L27L	F	9/8	M4v4p10
MISS GORDON OF ABERGELDIE'S JIGG	3H2H1H5	22H2H4H	C	6/8	P5v1p9
MISS GORDON OF BELLIE'S REEL	3H3H2H1H	64H2H5	D	2/2	M4v1p10
MISS GORDON OF BRAID	3546	557L2	F	6/8	L1p14
MISS GORDON OF BRAID'S REEL	5331H	7b427bL	A	4/4	F3p12,13
MISS GORDON OF CAIRNFIELD'S REEL	3L1L5L1	3L5L4L2L	Bb	2/2	M4v1p4
MISS GORDON OF CLUNY	1351H	5222	G	2/4	L2p22,23
MISS GORDON OF GIGHT('S REEL)	5L3b1H3bH	7b7b47bL	C	2/2	C24v1p10 (II)
MISS GORDON OF GLASTIRUM('S REEL)	3b15L3b	27bL24	G	2/2	M4v1p6 (II)
MISS GORDON OF LASMORES FAVORITE	1L315L	7bL4L4L7bF	A	2/2	P5v4p4
MISS GORDON (OF LESMORE) 'S REEL	13b51	7b427bL	E	4/4*	H3p9 G15p38
MISS GORDON OF LESMORE('S STRATHSPEY)	1351	2626	F	4/4	Mc22p11 P5v3p5 (II)
MISS GORDON OF NETHERMUIR'S STRATHSPEY	1361H	5327L	D	2/2	C24v2p23
MISS GORDON OF PARK	1516	5125L	F	6/8	M4v4p5
MISS GORDON OF PITLURG'S REEL	1H535	6422H	D	2/2	M11v2p8
MISS GORDON OF SHIELDAGREEN'S REEL	151H3	427L5L	C	2/2	C24v1p9
MISS GORDON (ROCKVELL'S) REEL	5153	227b7b	A	2/2	Mc21v2p20
MISS GORDON'S STRATHSPEY	3555	353H1H	D	4/4	M4v3p34
MISS GOULDING'S STRATHSPEY	1L1L1L1L	246L2	A	2/2	J1p28
MISS GOW OF LONDON	537L1	234#5	G	6/8	G10v6p14,15
MISS GRACE ABERCROMBY OF BIRKENBOG'S STRATHSPEY	5L13b5	247bL4	G	2/2	M11v1p11
MISS GRACE CAMPBELL'S STRATHSPEY	1L5L31	3L142	A	4/4	A7v2p24
MISS GRACE GORDON'S STRATHSPEY	5337b	4224	A	4/4	Mc21v2p28
MISS GRACE GRANT'S REEL	1562	1155	G	2/2	C14v20p4 Mc15p9
MISS GRACE HAY'S DELIGHT	1356	1352	G	6/8	G10v3p33
MISS GRACE HAY'S REEL	15L16L	27L36	G	6/8	Mc21v3p34
MISS GRACE LESLIE'S REEL	5631	5631	D	2/2	S5p12
MISS GRACE MENZIES	5555	5555	F	2/2	M4v4p4
MISS GRACE SPEIR'S (OF ELDERSLIE'S) REEL	1H753	237L7L	Bb	2/2	Mc21v3p35
MISS GRACE SPEIRS STRATHSPEY	151H5	151H1H	D	4/4	S4v1p4
MISS GRACE STEWART'S MINUET	1H51	233	F	3/4	D14v1p19
MISS GRACE STEWART'S MINUET	113	1H55	D	3/4	Mc21v1p7
MISS (GRACE) STEWART'S REEL	1H1H31	22H62H	F	4/4*	Mc21v1p35 S12v1p54 C14v1p17
MISS GRACE STEWART('S STRATHSPEY)	5L13b5	247bL7bL	G	4/4	E2p6 (II)
MISS GRAHAM OF AIRTH'S STRATHSPEY	113b5	7b4b7L4	E	2/2	B20p6,7
MISS GRAHAM (OF GARTMORE'S) STRATHSPEY	1L5L2L2	7L235	G	4/4	Mc21v3p10

Title			Key	Time	Sources
(MISS) GRAHAM (OF INCHBRACKIE) ('S STRATHSPEY)	1H3H1H5	11H2H2	C D	4/4*	C8v1p20 G11v1Ap20 C24v2p6 G10v2p9 Mc12v1p8 A1v4p53 C5v1p53 B7p32 E1v2p45
MISS GRAHAM OF INCHBRAKIE'S STRATHSPEY FOR THE HARPSICHORD	1315L	1L222L	Bb	4/4	D16p25
MISS GRAHAM OF INCHBRAKIE'S STRATHSPEY	1H1H1H5	11H2H2	D C	4/4	G1v2p53 A7v6p10 A7v2p3
MISS GRAHAM OF INCHBRAKIE'S STRATHSPEY	1315L	1L122L	Bb G	4/4	L2p12,13 (II)
MISS GRAHAM OF INVERARAY'S REEL	5136	5522	F	2/2	Mc15p39
MISS GRAHAM OF MOSSKNOW'S FAVORITE	1325L	1312	Bb	4/4	G10v6p8
MISS GRAHAM OF ORCHILL'S REEL	151H1H	2H1H22	G	2/2	Mc4v2p6
MISS GRAHAM OF ORCHILLS STRATHSPEY	11H55	11H2H2	G	2/2	Mc4v3p2
MISS GRAHAM'S DELIGHT	5L136	5136L	G	6/8	Mc4v2p13
MISS GRAHAM'S HORNPIPE	1355	1H316L	Bb	4/4	A7v4p26 D15v1p22
MISS GRAHAM'S JIGG	3432	6L232	G	6/8	S4v1p6
MISS GRANT OF ELCHIES	1L131	2L242	Bb	4/4	M4v4p21
MISS GRANT OF ELCHIE'S STRATHSPEY	1H1H31	42H75	C	4/4	G15p33
MISS GRANT (OF GRANT) ('S REEL)	3113	6532	F	2/2	D14v3p14 G11v2Cp29
MISS GRANT OF (GRANT/MONYMUSK) ('S REEL)	1547L	151H1H	G	4/4*	C14v2p9 Mc21v1p34 (II)
MISS GRANT OF GRANT'S FAVORITE	16L27L	16L36	Bb	6/8	G15p21
MISS GRANT OF GRANT'S REELL	557b2H	7b444	G	4/4	C33p16
MISS GRANT OF GRANT'S STRATHSPEY	5313	5366	Bb	4/4	G15p22,23
MISS GRANT OF GRANT'S STRATHSPEY	1316L	5L6L3L2L	Bb	4/4	T1v2p3
MISS GRANT OF KINAIRD'S REEL	3b3b3b1H	7b524	D	2/2	Mc4v3p9 (II)
MISS GRANT OF KNOCKANDO'S REEL	5555	2462	A	2/2*	M4v2p1 (II)
MISS GRANT OF MONYMUSK'S JIGG	1H71H1	1H71H1H	C	6/8	P5v1p14
MISS GRANT'S FAVOURITE	13b24	1251	E	6/8	Mc22p1
MISS GRANT'S JIG	1L111	1L16L2	Bb	6/8	M4v3p4
MISS GRANT'S REEL	3H1H53	4322H	C	2/2	J1p46
MISS GRANT'S REEL [MISS GRANT OF CULLEN HOUSE]	5531H	6424	F	2/2*	M4v3p49 (II)
MISS GRANT'S STRATHSPEY	531H3H	1H632	D	4/4	A1v5p35 C5v1p35 Mc10p8,9
MISS GRANT('S STRATHSPEY)	5115	47bL7bL2	E	2/2*	Mc22p1 (II)
MISS GRANT'S STRATHSPEY	1456	1H522	F	4/4	M4v3p49
MISS GRIERSON'S STRATHSPEY	1135	447L7L	F	4/4	C22p29
MISS GRIZIE KENNEDY'S REEL	1H1H1H3H	1H522H	C	2/2	R5p53
MISS GUNNING	4H2H75	31H2H5	D	4/4	A7v6p79
MISS GUNNING('S REEL)	427L5L	3L125L	A	2/2*	C14v5p20 Mc9v3p44
MISS GUNNING'S (REEL/DELIGHT)	327L5L	3L125L	G A	4/4*	A1v1p46 Mc13v2p26 P5v2p9 R12v1p2
MISS GUTHRIE OF CRAIGIE'S JIGG	1355	4237L	G	6/8	D16p28
MISS GUTHRIE OF GUTHRIE'S STRATHSPEY	53b53b	53b42	G	4/4	D16p25
MISS GUTHRIE OF GUTHRIE'S STRATHSPEY	1321	1362	E	4/4	D15v1p17
MISS GWYNNE'S FANCY	1H1H55	6651	A	6/8	J1p32
MISS H. ERSKINE'S STRATHSPEY	4226L	1515	A	4/4	P11v2p4
MISS H. HUNTER OF BLACKNESS'S VALTZ	51H43	51H21	G	3/8	G9v4p21
MISS H. HUNTER'S OF BLACKNESS(REEL)	3H2H1H3H	62H75	Eb	2/2	G10v3p16 (II)
MISS H. SCOTT'S STRATHSPEY	51H24	51H66	F	4/4	P11v2p18
MISS H. WAUCHOPE'S FAVOURITE	3b5L3b3bL1L	27bL27bL	G	6/8	S4v2p21
MISS HACKET'S FAVORITE	6H1H3H1H	6H1H3H2H	C	4/4	A7v6p53
MISS HACKHARTS STRATHSPEY	5L37bL2	1115	G	4/4	A7v6p40
MISS HACKHART'S (STRATHSPEY/REEL)	1L37bL2	1115	A	4/4	M4v2p3 A7v2p36
MISS HAGGART'S ALLAMANDE	3455	3450	Bb	2/4	G9v4p15
MISS HAGGART'S STRATHSPEY	1H155	2H266	D	4/4	S4v1p10
MISS HAIG OF BEMMERSIDE	13b53b	7bL27bL5	E	2/2	C14v26p2,3
MISS HAIG OF DOLLARFIELD'S STRATHSPEY	5L13b5	27bL27bL	G	2/2	B20p10
MISS HALDAN GLENEAGLES	1H31H3H	2H4H75	C	4/4	Mc4v2p3
MISS HALDANE OF GLENEAGLES ('S STRATHSPEY)	3142	3125L	C	4/4	S4v1p17 (II)
MISS HALDANE'S JIGG	1365	6L225L	G	6/8	P11v2p16
MISS HALKET CRAIGIE'S REEL	3135	1H542	F	4/4	G10v6p32
MISS HALL OF DUNGLASS'S REEL	535L5L	1L5L5L5L	Bb	4/4*	G9v2p18 G10v6p28,29
MISS HALLIFAX'S FAVOURITE	11H45L	351H4	Eb	6/8	Mc15p20
MISS HAMERSLEY'S ALLMAND	531H5	2H72H5	E	2/4	C14v1p8
MISS HAMILTON OF BANGOWRE ('S STRATHSPEY)	5555	31H22	F	4/4	G11v1Cp4 G10v3p19 (II)
MISS HAMILTON OF BANGOWRE'S STRATHSPEY	5555	31H32	G F	2/2	A1v4p53 C5v1p53 Mc12v1p5
MISS HAMILTON OF BLANDFIELD'S STRATHSPEY	35L31	6622	D	4/4	Mc10p8
MISS HAMILTON OF SUNDRUM'S REEL	53b13b	7bL5bL7L3b	A	2/2	R5p49(51)
MISS HAMILTON OF WISHAW'S ALLAMANDE	5H3H5H5H	5H7H5H5H	C	2/4	G9v4p12
MISS HAMILTON OF WISHAW'S STRATHSPEY	3155	3532	F	2/2	E2p21
MISS HAMILTON'S DELIGHT	3H3H4H2H	5H3H55	D	4/4	Mc8v1Bp18 C13v3p46,47
MISS HAMILTON'S FANCY	5555	5562	G	4/4	A7v6p84
MISS HAMILTON'S REEL, THE	15L3b2	27bL53b	B	2/2	J1p33
MISS HAMMERSLY'S FANCY	1H2H1H4	2675	D	2/4	C14v9p12
MISS HANBURY'S FANCY	5L5L32	7L242	Bb	2/2	Mc15p4 (II)
MISS HANNAH'S JIG	1313	22H75	G	6/8	M4v3p41
MISS HARDIE'S MEASURE	3211	247L2	Bb	2/4	G3p8
MISS HARIOT MACDONALD'S REEL	51H51	5522	F	2/2	D14v3p18/19
MISS HAY MACKENZIE'S FAVORITE	1154	4321	Bb	2/4	S4v2p25
MISS HAY OF DRUMELZIER'S MEDLEY	1133	117L7L	Bb	4/4	G9v3p16

Title			Key	Time	Reference
MISS HAY OF DRUMELZIER'S MEDLEY	1531	1L2L4L3L	Bb	6/8	G9v3p16
MISS HAY OF LEY'S STRATHSPEY	1327bL	1313	D	4/4	S4v2p19
MISS HAY OF LYES'S STRATHSPEY	51H3H3H	4H4H3H6	C	2/2	L4p9
MISS HAY OF YESTER'S ALLAMANDE	11H3H3H	52H1H1H	F	2/4	G9v4p5
MISS HAY(OF YESTER'S REEL)	1H3H2H4H	3H3H77	D	2/2*	G10v4p4,5 (II)
MISS HAYNE'S MINUET	553	531	A	3/4	C22p7
MISS HAY'S DOUBLE JIGG	1355	6L237L	Bb	6/8	S11v2p6
MISS HAY'S FAVOURITE	5151H	4362	G	4/4	A1v4p35
MISS HAY'S REEL	1226L	1211H	A	2/2	Mc9v3p21
MISS HAY'S REEL	3131	1H342	F	2/2*	S12v1p5 S7v1p4
MISS HAY'S REEL	5L13b4	2454	G	2/2	P5v2p10
MISS HEDGE'S MINUET	113	423	G	3/4	R12v3p14
MISS HELAN WILLIAMSON'S REEL	1366	53H2H6	C	4/4	R9p21
MISS HELEN CAMPBELL ARDMORE'S JIG	1111H	5125L	F	6/8	Mc16p26
MISS HELEN GRANT'S REEL	5551H	5522	D	2/2	C5v1p37 A1v5p37 Mc10p3
MISS HELEN McCALL'S STRATHSPEY	151H5	6542	D	2/2	C12p8
MISS HELEN McINNES	5L17L2	5L145	A	6/8	M4v4p29
MISS HELLEN BOWER	5561H	57L24	D	6/8	D16p16
MISS HELLEN RENNY'S SCOTCH MEASURE	111H1H	51H51	F	2/2	D15v1p9
MISS HENDERSON OF FORDEL('S REEL)	5315	437b2	A	2/2	D14v3p9 (II)
MISS HENDERSON OF STEMPSTER'S REEL	1H1H1H3	61H65	A	2/2	G15p20
MISS HENDERSON, TRINITY'S FAVORITE	153b3b	47b27bL	E	6/8	G9v2p6
MISS HENDERSON'S MINUET	1H1H6	555	Bb	3/4	C22p8
MISS HENDERSON'S MINUET	13b2	15L1L	G	3/4	Mc21v1p12
MISS HENDERSON'S MINUET	115L	553	Bb	3/4	C13v4p37
MISS HENNY MITCHELSON REEL	153b1	2427bL	E	2/2	S12v1p49
MISS HENRIETTA ABERNETHIE('S REEL)	1H3H2H1H	5322	C	2/2*	C24v1p1 (II)
MISS HENRIETTA DUFF'S FAVORITE	5L3b53b	4542	G	2/2	C21p13
MISS HERON (OF HERON) 'S REEL	537L2	31H66	G F	4/4*	A7v5p19 A7v4p23 G10v4p9
[MISS HERRON'S REEL]					C7p7 W4v2p23 (II)
MISS HERRAN OF INGLISTON'S FAVOURITE WALTZ	1332H	1331H	F	3/8	G9v3p5
MISS HERRIES FORBES REEL	1351	427L5L	F	2/2	C24v1p9
MISS (HERRIES) FORBES'S FAREWELL (TO BANFF) [MISS FORBES' FAREWELL]	3436	5532	D F E G	4/4*	E1v1p17 G9v5p34 C24v2p24,25 A1v4p1 C5v3p68 A7v4p13 T1v1p1 (II)
MISS HERRON OF HERRON'S VALTZ	5335	5331	F	3/8	G9v4p18
MISS HIPPISLEY'S REEL	351H5	6562	A	2/2	J1p37
MISS HOBART'S (FANCY/FAVOURITE)	3H1H2H1H	63H1H5H	C	4/4*	B16v4p92 B16v2p10
MISS HOG (OF NEWLISTON'S) REEL	3b23b1	3b427bL	G	2/2	Mc21v3p28,29 (II)
MISS HOLDER'S FAVORITE AIR	5415L	1343	A	2/4	J1p42
MISS HONEYMAN'S STRATHSPEY	1515	1524	D	4/4	S4v2p18
MISS HONYMAN OF ARMADALE'S MINUET	1H1H3H	5H5H1T	C	3/4	S11v2p23,24
MISS HONYMAN OF ARMADALE'S WALTZ	127L1	127L1	Bb	3/8	S11v2p15,16
MISS HOPE	O3H1HO	4H2H75	C	4/4	B12p6
MISS HOPE OF PINKIE HOUSE'S STRATHSPEY	511H6	5153H	D	4/4	S4v1p20
MISS HOPE'S REEL	5131	25L7L2	A	4/4	B12p13
MISS HOPE'S (REEL/STRATHSPEY)	1326L	4463	D	4/4*	C14v25p7 P11v1p3
MISS HOPE('S STRATHSPEY)	1126L	4463	G	4/4	G11v2Dp30 (II)
MISS HOPGOODS REEL, THE	3565	6562	A	2/2	J1p48
MISS HOPKINS(REEL)	5L144	5226L	Bb	2/2	M4v1p11 G11v2Cp32 (II)
MISS HORN'S STRATHSPEY	15L6L1	15L6L2	Bb	2/2	G8p31 P1v1p11
MISS HOUSTON OF JORDONHILL'S ALLAMANDE	5553	62H53	F	2/4	G9v4p10
MISS HUME'S REEL	15L5L1L	2L226L	A	2/2	D16p14
MISS HUME'S REEL	1151H	5142	F	4/4	W4v2p11
MISS HUNTER (BLACKNESS) 'S STRATHSPEY	1116L	5L6L4L2L	Bb	2/4	G3p23
MISS HUNTER BLAIR'S REEL	1H1H51H	2H1H24	F	4/4	F3p2,3
MISS HUNTER BLAIR'S SLOW JIG	1H1H3bH1H	7b4H2H7b	C	6/8	G3p36
MISS HUNTER BLAIR'S STRATHSPEY	13L1L3L	136L2	Bb	4/4	S4v2p17
MISS HUNTER (OF BURNSIDE) 'S STRATHSPEY	3546	337L2	G F	4/4	A7v6p60 D16p21
MISS HUNTER'S JIGG	52H1H3	456L7L	Eb	6/8	S11v2p6
MISS HUNTER'S MINUET	111	334	A	3/4	G3p28
MISS HUNTER'S STRATHSPEY	51H61H	51H24	Eb	4/4	R9p25
MISS HUTTON'S STRATHSPEY	15L3L5L	3L6L13	Bb	4/4	B11p23 (II)
MISS I. McLEOD'S REEL	15L13	4326L	F	2/2	J1p19
MISS IN HER OWN HAIR	1212	11H65	A	2/2	R12v1p66 (W3)
MISS INNES OF EDINGIGHT('S REEL)	1155	1327L	G	2/2*	C24v1p7 (II)
MISS IRVINE'S REEL	1H1H3b1	27bL7b7b	D	2/4	Mc19v3p19 Mc19v2p3
MISS ISAAC FORSYTH, (ELGIN)	1311H	557L2	F	6/8	M4v4p3
MISS (ISABELLA) CAMPBELL'S DELIGHT	3115	7552H	F	4/4*	C23p12 W4v2p19
MISS ISABELLA ELLIS'S JIG	1H1H2H5	1H551	C	6/8	M11v1p9
MISS ISABELLA HEGGIE	1H2H42	2266	D	4/4	W2v2p10
MISS ISABELLA HUTCHISON'S JIG	1366	1663	G	6/8	M11v1p2
MISS ISABELLA McKENZIE'S STRATHSPEY	15L3L1L	427L2	Bb	4/4	Mc21v2p11
MISS ISABELLA McPHERSON GRANT'S STRATHSPEY	5531H	6662H	F	4/4	M4v3p51
MISS ISABELLA PATERSON'S REEL	53b13b	427bL2	G	2/2	B20p11
MISS ISABELLA REID'S REEL	5342	7L232	Bb	2/2	C24v2p20
MISS ISABELLA ROBERTSON'S HORNPIPE	1H75	1H72H	F	9/8	Mc21v2p20
MISS ISABELLA ROBERTSON'S REEL	11H52	7bL7b41	D	6/8	Mc21v3p36
MISS ISABELLA SCOTT'S SINGLE HORNPIPE	335	31L5L	Bb	3/2	D16p15
MISS (ISABELLA/J.) MURDOCH'S REEL	331H6	31H2H2	C D	2/2	Mc12v1p20 A1v4p55 A7v4p17

MISS ISOBEL CLARK'S FAVORITE	1H11H1H	4H2H75	C	6/8	C21p1
MISS J. CLARKE'S REEL	1H3H5H3H	62H4H5H	D	4/4	C14v19p14
MISS J. CUMING'S REEL	1H535	22H76	D	4/4	F3p2
MISS J. DALRYMPLE'S STRATHSPEY	11H53bH	27b42	D	4/4	S4v2p24
MISS J. RENNY'S STRATHSPEY	5551	44H27bL	E	2/2	D15v1p8
MISS J. ROSE'S REEL	5364	5327L	F	6/8	Mc21v3p33
MISS J. SOMERVELL'S FAVOURITE STRATHSPEY	1122	1151H	G	2/2	Mc22p12 A1v4p66
MISS J. TOD'S STRATHSPEY	3H3H3H3H	4H3H72H	D	4/4	G3p30
MISS JACKSON'S REEL	5335	6542	G	2/2	S12v1p67
MISS JAMIESON'S JIG	1131H	2H4H2H5	D	2/4	A1v2p12
MISS JANE BRUCE'S JIG	31H53H	5H5H72H	D	6/8	A1v3p183
MISS JANE CAMPBELL (OF MONZIE'S) STRATHSPEY	1323	5L335	G	4/4	Mc21v3p18
MISS JANE CAMPBELL'S STRATHSPEY	5426L	5353	D	4/4	G15p15
MISS JANE CAMPBELL'S STRATHSPEY	5L133	5L133	G	4/4	P11v1p4
MISS JANE CARNEGIE OF SOUTHESK'S STRATHSPEY	1326L	1355	Eb	4/4	Mc13v2p22
MISS JANE CARNEGIE'S ALLAMANDE	1135	54#31	G	2/4	D15v1p15
MISS JANE CARNEGIE'S FAVOURITE	51H2H1H	3H4H2H3H	E	6/8	D15v1p6
MISS JANE CARNEGIE'S FAVOURITE VALTZ	37L35	657L2	Eb	3/8	D15v1p14
MISS JANE D. GRANT'S FAVOURITE	1H516	1H664	G	2/4	Mc15p9
MISS JANE DOUGLAS'S FAVORITE	3126L	7L5L12	G	6/8	Mc21v3p2
MISS JANE DUNBAR'S REEL	3L13L1	3L12L2L	Bb	2/2	G15p22
MISS JANE FRAZER'S MINUET	135	1H1H5H	C	3/4	C22p6,7
MISS JANE GORDON'S REEL	1151	427L5L	A	2/2	C24v2p22
MISS JANE GRANT OF GRANT'S REEL	3112	7L245	A	4/4	G15p18
MISS JANE GRANT('S REEL)(,LYNMORE)	1133	1142	F	2/2	M4v3p57 (II)
MISS JANE HUNTER BLAIR'S JIG	5135	4524	D	6/8	S4v2p26
MISS JANE HUNTER'S REEL	31H2H2	4H2H75	C	2/2	P11v2p18
MISS JANE MARSHALL'S REEL	1H3H2H4H	1H3H2H5	C	2/2	B20p20,21
MISS JANE McINNES	5L5L7bL7bL	1151	A	4/4	M4v4p29
MISS JANE McINNES(,DANDALEITH)	1151H	1126L	D	2/2	M4v3p30 (II)
MISS JANE STEWART('S REEL)	1353	5L37L2	Bb	2/2*	G15p24 (II)
MISS JANE STEWART'S STRATHSPEY	1133	5L133	G	2/4	M4v3p42
MISS JANE STIRLING'S STRATHSPEY	5L15L1	427L7L	Bb	4/4	M1p2
MISS JANE TYTLER'S FAVOURITE	56L5L1L	5467L	F#	6/8	P11v1p4
MISS JANE WEDDERBURN('S REEL)	3b1H1H5	27b7b4	A	2/2	Mc21v3p38 (II)
MISS JANE WEDDERBURN'S STRATHSPEY	1122	1H151H	D	4/4	S4v1p9
MISS JANE WOOD McKINZI'S STRATHSPEY	136L5L	1366	F	4/4	R9p10
MISS JANE YOUNG (BANFF)	31H64	2462H	A	2/2	M4v3p18
MISS JANET McKERRELL'S REEL	15L3L1	2637L	Eb	2/2	C12p3
MISS JANET McKERRELL'S STRATHSPEY	131H6	1H422	F	4/4	C12p8
MISS JEAN ABERDEIN('S REEL)	3b53b5	27bL24	C	2/2	A7v2p28 (II)
MISS JEAN ALVES'S REEL	3b15L1	247b4	F	4/4	F2v1p3
MISS JEAN CAMPBELL ARDMORE'S JIG	11H2H1H	5353	G	6/8	Mc16p28
MISS JEAN CAMPBELL ARDMORE'S REEL	13L13	436L2	F	2/2	Mc16p13
MISS JEAN CAMPBELL OF AIRD'S REEL	3632	3662	G	2/2	Mc16p20
MISS JEAN DALRYMPLE'S STRATHSPEY	1555	1522	Bb	4/4	E2p10
MISS JEAN DONALDSON'S HORNPIPE	1H757	1H2H2H5	C	2/4	W2v1p11
MISS JEAN DOUGLAS'S FAVORITE	115L5L	116L6L	A	4/4	G9v5p27
MISS JEAN DOUGLAS'S VALTZ	5L5L5L	331	Bb	3/4	G9v4p23
MISS JEAN HAMILTON OF SUNDRUM'S STRATHSPEY	353H2H	662H2	D	4/4	E2p1
MISS JEAN JOHNSTON'S STRATHSPEY	13b47bL	13b55	E	2/2	B20p14
MISS JEAN KERR'S STRATHSPEY	5513	5642	G	4/4	A1v5p51
MISS JEAN LOGAN'S STRATHSPEY	31H1H1H	31H32	A	4/4	E2p12
MISS JEAN MAXWELL OF MONREITH'S REEL	13b27bL	13b13b	E	4/4	F3p9
MISS JEAN MILLERS REEL	15L3L1L	4562	A	4/4	R6v1p9
MISS JEAN ROBERTSON'S REEL	131H3	1342	D	4/4	A1v5p13 C21p7
MISS JEAN ROBERTSON'S STRATHSPEY	13L1L3L	16L2L2	A	4/4	R9p16
MISS (JEAN) SCOTT'S REEL	3L3L11	3L122L	Bb	4/4*	Mc21v1p33 S12v1p59
MISS JEAN SHERRIF'S REEL [MISS JEAN SHIRREF'S REEL]	1H31H5	1H3H72H	D C	4/4*	C5v1p36 A1v5p36 M10p3
MISS JEAN STEWART OF BOHALLY('S REEL)	137L5L	1353	G	2/2	Mc4v1p17 (II)
MISS JEAN STEWART('S REEL)	3L126L	1155	A	4/4	M4v2p2 (II)
MISS JEAN WATERSON'S FANCY	15L16	5162	Bb	6/8	C21p20
MISS JEAN WOOD McKINZIES FAVORITE	5514	567L2	D	4/4	R9p18
MISS JEANIE MERCER'S REEL	5525	7bL7b47bL	E	2/2	S12v1p34
(MISS) (JEANIE/JENNY) CAMERON ('S REEL)	3H1H2H5	5H52H2H	D	2/2	A7v5p6 Mc16p31
MISS JEANNY ROSS'S REEL	3H1H1H5	31H4H2H	C	2/2	M4v1p10
MISS JEANNY WILLIAMSON('S REEL)	1353	2464	F	2/2*	M4v1p7 (II)
MISS JEANY ABERNETHIE('S REEL)	1H31H3H	2H3H4H2H	C	2/2*	C24v1p4 (II)
MISS JEANY CAMERON'S STRATHSPEY	5L15L1	7bL7bL22	G	2/2	C14v27p3
MISS JEANY GRANT'S REEL	1151H	662H2H	D	2/2	S5p17
MISS JEANY SANDEMAN'S REEL	15L13	437L2	F	2/2	B11p11
MISS JENNER'S FAVORITE	115L5L	1162	Bb	6/8	J1p24
MISS JENNY DUFF'S REEL	131H1	41H2H2	C	6/8	R5p26
MISS JENNY ELLIOT'S STRATHSPEY	11H72H	3H761H	D	4/4	Mc21v3p22
MISS JENNY GORDON'S STRATHSPEY	15L13	2226L	Bb	4/4	E2p10
MISS JENNY GUTHRIE'S (STRATHSPEY)	11L5L5L	5646L	A	4/4	D16p17 (II)

94

MISS JENNY LINDSAY'S STRATHSPEY	5364	5642	D	2/2	Mc22p4 C5v1p67 A1v4p67
MISS JENNY WEDDERBURN'S REEL	5551H	3H523	D	2/2	H3p13
MISS JESS CAMPBELL'S REEL	5353	2372	D	2/2	A7v1p11
MISS JESSIE CUMMINGS ALLAMANDE	2121	7L252	Bb	2/4	G9v4p10
MISS JESSIE DUN'S STRATHSPEY	3135	3535	D	2/2	M11v1p8
MISS JESS(IE) HUNTER'S STRATHSPEY	116L2	1115	A	2/2	D15v1p11 A7v4p21
MISS JESSIE REID'S STRATHSPEY	1355	1342	A	4/4	Mc22p13
MISS JESSIE ROSE'S STRATHSPEY	13b57b	552H1H	D	2/2	M11v1p4
MISS JESSIE SCALES HORNPIPE	136L1	5L5L3L2L	Bb	4/4	Mc13v1p11 Mc13v2p11
MISS JESSIE STEWART GARTH'S REEL	13b3b3b	427bL2	D	2/2	Mc4v3p7
MISS JESSY BAIRD'S REEL	4542	7L232	F	4/4	G3p19
MISS JESSY BELL'S JIG	3L3L5L5	423L3L	Bb	6/8	G3p5
MISS JESSY CAMPBELL'S REEL	5226L	5266	D	2/2	Mc9v3p3
MISS JESSY CAMPBELL'S REEL	1356	1H642	F	2/2	C13v2p59
MISS (JESSY) CAMPBELL'S REEL	1351H	537L7L	C	2/2	C13v1p37 C13v2p50
MISS JESSY CRAWFORD'S STRATHSPEY	3b125L	3b13b5	G	4/4	W4v2p17
MISS JESSY CUMING'S STRATHSPEY	5151	5422H	D	4/4	Mc21v3p37
MISS (JESSY) DALRYMPLE'S REEL	1353	6L464	Bb	2/2*	S12v1p51 Mc21v1p35 C13v1p23
[[MISS JESSIE DALRYMPLE]					C13v2p9 Mc13v2p23 (II)
MISS JESSY DEWAR'S FAVOURITE	37L45	1H653	D	6/8	P11v1p3
MISS JESSY GRAHAM	531H1H	567L2	D	4/4	R9p11
MISS JESSY HUME'S REEL	1542	151H5	G	4/4	G3p4
MISS JESSY HUNTER'S REEL	1H535	3H4H72H	F	4/4	H1p22
MISS JESSY MILLERS REEL	15L35L	4L5L4L4	Bb	2/2	Mc13v2p31 C13v2p2 C13v1p4
MISS JESSY ROBERTSON'S REEL	15L3L5L	6L47L2	Bb	2/2	C14v27p11
MISS JESSY SCOTT'S REEL	3H2H1H5	6542	D	2/2*	P11v1p3 (II)
[MISS JESSIE SCOTT]					
MISS JESSY STEWART'S JIGG	1313H	1H522	D	6/8	Mc4v1p18
MISS JESSY STEWART'S JIGG	5151H	5123	D	6/8	Mc22p15
MISS JESS(Y) STEWART'S REEL	5L13b4	2454	A G	4/4*	A7v5p7 A7v4p11 Mc9v3p23
[MISS JESSIE STEWART]					(II)
MISS JESSY STEWART'S STRATHSPEY	5L13b5	2454	G	2/2	Mc4v1p10
MISS JESSY WALLACE REEL	1635	47b27bL	A	2/2	W2v1p6
MISS JOAN DALRYMPLE OF HAILES	1H335	1H342	D	4/4	C10v1p1
MISS JOAN KIERS STRATHSPEY	5L3L5L1	15L3L2L	Bb	4/4	C23p5
MISS JOAS'S STRATHSPEY	1L3L2L4L	1L3L5L1	Bb	4/4	S4v1p5
MISS JOHNSON (OF BYKER'S) REEL	5226L	5266	D	4/4*	Mc21v3p26 (II)
[MISS JOHNSTON]					
MISS JOHNSON(,PITWORTH)	137L5L	1353	Bb	2/2	W2v2p6 (II)
MISS JOHNSTON	3551H	3H1H3H1H	G	4/4	P6v1p10
MISS JOHNSTON (LATHRISK'S) STRATHSPEY	1L12L2	1L16L7L	G	4/4	Mc21v2p38
MISS JOHNSTON (OF) HIL(L)TON	11H7b2	11H3bH2H	D C	4/4	G11v1Ap4 G10v2p5 A7v2p27
('S STRATHSPEY)					(II)
MISS JOHNSTON OF HIL(L)TON('S REEL)	1H155	7b424	E	4/4*	G10v1p29 (II)
MISS JOHNSTON (OF HILTON) 'S REEL	1H535	6522H	C	2/2	D14v1p34 C13v2p57 D14v4p14
					C13v1p34
MISS JOHNSTON OF HILTON'S FANCY	3355	1H57L2	Eb	6/8	G10v3p22
MISS JOHNSTON OF HILTON'S REEL	5551H	5542	F	2/2	D14v3p24/25
MISS JOHNSTON (OF HILTON'S) REEL	3535	4646	G	2/2	Mc21v3p1
MISS JOHNSTON OF TWICKENHAM'S REEL	1H1H1H3	432H2	C	2/2	Mc10p14
MISS JOHNSTON(E)	3553	51H3H1H	G	4/4*	C14v21p12 (B21) G10v5p30 (II)
(OF HOUGHTON HALL) ('S REEL)					
MISS JOHNSTON''S JIG	5151H	5162	C	6/8	R9p23
MISS JOHNSTON'S MINUET	115L	331	Eb	3/4	S11v1p16,17
MISS JOHNSTON('S REEL)	13b53b	7bL242	E	2/2	Mc4v1p6 (II)
MISS JOHNSTON'S REEL	1353	6L5L4L2L	Bb	2/2	C14v7p8
MISS JOHNSTON'S STRATHSPEY	31H66	5H3H2H2H	C	4/4	R9p24
MISS JUBB'S MINUET	333	15L1	G	3/4	S11v1p22
MISS JUDWINS WALTZ	1H5H71H	1H5H1H1H	D	3/8	C14v14p6
MISS JUILIETT RANNIE'S MINUET	554	215	Bb	3/4	S11v2p20,21
MISS JULIA SINCLAIR'S FAVORITE	3b13b1H	3bH7b7b4	G	6/8	P11v2p13
MISS JULIET MORISON	151H5	4632	F	2/2	M11v1p1
(OF FETTERESSO'S) STRATHSPEY					
MISS KATHARINE MILLER'S BIRTH DAY	15L31H	7532	D	4/4	G10v5p14
MISS KATHARINE STEWART FORBES	1124	1151H	F	4/4	M4v3p57 (II)
(' STRATHSPEY)					
MISS KATHRINE MELVEL'S REEL	311H5	432H2	A	2/2	S11v1p3
MISS KATIE HALL'S REEL	5222	526L6	G	6/8	A1v1p29
MISS (KATTY) GORDON	151H5	6522	D	2/2*	R5p24 S12v1p37 (II)
(OF EARLSTON) 'S REEL					
MISS KATTY HALL'S(JIG)	1H553H	1H523H	D	6/8	Mc21v3p18 C14v12p12
MISS KATTY MAXWELL'S REEL	1H3H1H3	1H3H2H2	C	2/2*	R5p30(60) (II)
MISS KATTY MONTGOMERIE'S MINUET	135	1H75	D	3/4	R5p5
MISS KELMAN'S REEL	13b5L3b	7bL24L2	G	2/2	C18p38
MISS KELMAN'S STRATHSPEY	113bL5	7bL27bL7bL	G	4/4	C18p37
MISS KEMP'S JIGG	517bL3b	56b47bL	B	6/8	Mc22Ap2
MISS KENNEDY FRASER'S REEL	5151	5142	D	6/8	S5p21
MISS KENNEDY'S MINUET	116L	3L3L1	Bb	3/4	R6v1p11
MISS KETTY ALLAN'S REEL	5551	6662	C	4/4	M4v2p3
MISS KETTY HALL	1H551	1H527	D	6/8	G11v1Cp28,29 G10v2p27 C4p53
MISS (KETTY) TROTTER'S REEL	335L3	427L2	G	2/2	H1p18 S12v1p59 Mc21v1p31
MISS KINLOCH OF GILMERTON('S REEL)	3565	3542	D	2/2	S4v1p20 (II)

Title					
MISS KINLOCH OF GOURDIE'S DOUBLE JIG	5L16L5L	4367L	Bb	6/8	B6v3p2
MISS KINLOCH'S REEL	5226L	5266	D	4/4	P5v3p20
MISS KIRKWOOD'S STRATHSPEY	1L3b53b	7bL242	G	4/4	Mc10p1
MISS KITTY CAMPBELL OF SHAWFIELDS REEL	1347L	131H5	G	2/2	C14v14p12
MISS KITTY CAMPBELL'S STRATHSPEY	1353	7L225L	F	2/2	C14v14p4
MISS KITTY FARQUHAR'S REEL	361H1H	357b2	A	2/2	B10p22
MISS KNOWLES	1H667	1H62H2	D	6/8	L1p16
MISS KNOX'S FANCY	3555	31H2H2	F	6/8	C14v19p9
MISS L. JOHNSTONE'S COMPLIMENTS TO NIEL GOW	1H1H46	3542	C	4/4	G11v1Cp10 G10v3p5
MISS L. MONTGOMERIE OF SKERMORLIE	1L1L16L	6L6L22L	Bb	4/4	G10v3p17 (II)
MISS L. MONTGOMERY OF SKERMORLIE'S STRATHSPEY	111H6	662H2	D	4/4	A1v4p72 C5v1p72
MISS LAING'S FAVORITE	3H4H5H5H	1H4H2H5	C	6/8	C22p42
MISS LAIRD'S ALAMANDE	1335	671H3H	F	2/4	D16p26
MISS LAKE'S REEL	1115	1H562	Bb	2/2	J1p12
MISS LAMONT OF LAMONT'S REEL	3H2H1H5	11H22	D	4/4	S4v2p19
MISS LAMONT OF LAMONT('S STRATHSPEY)	1346	3627L	G	4/4	S4v1p22 (II)
MISS LAURENSON OF INVEREIGHTY'S STRATHSPEY	5L13b5	5427bL	E	4/4	A4v2p1
MISS LAWDER	1H3H54H	3H5H14H	D	4/4	O1v1Dp10-12
MISS LAY'S REEL	13b53b	7bL242	G	2/2	Mc16p34
MISS LESLIE OF BERRYDEN'S STRATHSPEY	1135	4652	A	2/4	Mc13v1p11 Mc13v2p11
MISS LESLIE OF ROTHY'S REEL	1135	7424	D	2/2	S5p11
MISS LESLIE OF St ANDREWS REEL	1H3H2H5	61H51	D	2/2	G15p12
MISS LESLIES FANCY	5L136	2H2H1H6	D	4/4	Mc15p32
MISS LIDDEL'S GERMAN VALTZ	1H2H3H2H	1H2H3H1H	F	3/8	W4v2p12
MISS LILIAS CUNNINGHAM'S DANCE	551H6	6432	D	2/2	P11v1p15
MISS LILLIE RITCHIE'S REEL	517bL2	513b5	E	2/2	R5p36
MISS LINDSAY STEUART OF STEUART LODGE'S STRATHSPEY	3344	3325L	F	6/8	L4p3
MISS LINDSAY'S JIGG	1H765	6542	F G	6/8	D14v1p36 C5v1p7 A1v5p7
MISS LINDSAY'S REEL	5116L	5L4L5L3L	Bb	4/4	A7v4p4
MISS LINDSAY'S REEL	5H1H1H6	5353	C	2/2	A7v5p8
MISS LINDSAY'S STRATHSPEY	5L13b2	5L13b5	G	2/2	S4v1p25
MISS LITTLES FANCY, THE	5655	436L2	A	6/8	J1p9
MISS LLOYD'S FAVORITE REEL	15L2L2	15L5L3	Bb	4/4	Mc21v4p3
MISS LLOYD'S REEL	5555	2362	A	2/2	J1p7
MISS LOGAN, AYR	313H1H	2H4H2H2	D	4/4	F3p2
MISS LOGAN'S JIG	13b44	5527bL	G	6/8	H1p21
MISS LOGAN'S STRATHSPEY	1L3L13	2422	Bb	4/4	E2p17
MISS LOUGHNAN'S FAVORITE	311L1	3156	A	6/8	J1p38
MISS LOUISA BROWN'S REEL	5115	27bL7b4	D	2/2	C18p30
MISS LOUISA CAMPBELL'S STR./(DELIGHT)	5556	5562	D	4/4*	C13v1p7 Mc9v1p2 H3p28,29
MISS LOUISA DRUMMOND (LOGIE ALMOND)'S REEL	1H53b5	2424	C	2/2	C14v10p16 Mc22p22
MISS LOUISA DRUMMOND LOGIEALMOND'S DELIGHT	1L3b15L	7bL4L4L7bF	A	4/4	Mc10p4
MISS LOUISA DUFF	3b15L3b	27bL24	G	4/4*	M4v4p2 (II)
MISS LOUISA JOHNSTON'S FANCY	541H5	4665	G	2/4	G10v2p31
MISS LOUISA RUSH'S REEL	1313	31H22	D	2/2	C14v17p11
MISS LOWIS'S REEL	3L1L43	6L27L5L	G	2/2	P11v1p4
(MISS) LUCY CAMPBELL ('S DELIGHT)	5555	5562	D	4/4*	Mc7p11-12 G11v1Cp3 C4p34 N1v1p2 (II)
MISS LUCY CAMPBELL('S REEL)	35L35L	5142	A	4/4*	S12v1p51 (II)
MISS LUCY GORDON'S STRATHSPEY	5L3L1L3L	5L3L2L2L	A	4/4	T1v1p4
MISS LUMSDANE'S STRATHSPEY	1H3H1H6	4542	C	4/4	R9p20
MISS LUNDIE'S JIG	155	154	A	9/8	S4v2p11
MISS LYLE'S REEL [MISS LYALL] [MRS GRANT OF LAGGAN]	15L3b2	5L4L2L4L	A	2/2*	C8v1p26 (II)
MISS LYLE'S STRATHSPEY [MISS LYALL]	11L3bL5L	4L27bL7bL	A	4/4	H1p4 (II)
MISS LYLLE OF GARDYNE'S STRATHSPEY	5L1L5L1	5L132	G	2/2	D15v1p25
MISS LYNOTT'S REEL	1526	3542	F	4/4	Mc11p2
MISS LYONS' HORNPIPE	561H2H	3H67L5L	F	2/4	B6v3p1
MISS M. CADENHEAD'S REEL	1H531	427L2	F	2/2	Mc16p33
MISS M. DUNDAS' REEL	1H531	2466	F	2/2	B20p6
MISS M. McL. MENZIES' REEL	1153	26L7L5L	A	4/4	Mc19v1p4 Mc19v2p14
MISS M. ROSE'S REEL [MISS M. ROSS]	1H13b5	7b524	E	2/2	Mc21v3p15 (II)
MISS M. TAIT'S JIGG	1365	6527L	Eb	6/8	S11v2p3
MISS M. WHITE OF BRACHLOCH	1253	6L7L27L	A	6/8	L1p3
MISS MAC INTOSH'S FAVOURITE	1364	1313H	F	2/4	Mc15p29
MISS MAC INTOSH'S REEL	1362	1361H	F	2/2	Mc15p29
MISS MACDONALD BUCHANAN'S STRATHSPEY	1362	1366L	D'	4/4	P11v2p13
MISS MACDONALD KENLOCHMOIDART	1324	31H54	G	2/4	G9v5p7
MISS MACDONALD KINLOCHMOIDART'S FAVOURITE	112	556	D	3/4	Mc22p17
MISS MACDONALD OF BARRODALES FAVORITE	1155	5151H	C	4/4	P5v4p24
MISS MACDONALD OF POWDER HALL'S REEL	3131	627L5L	F	4/4	P5v4p22
MISS MACDOWAL GRANT('S STRATHSPEY) (OF ARNDILLY)	51H3bH3bH	4H2H7b2H	C	4/4	M4v3p27 (II)
MISS MACDOWALL GRANT'S REEL	1142	3442	A	2/2	G15p19
MISS MACINTOSH'S JIGG	1562	1511H	F	6/8	Mc15p29

Title					
MISS MACKENZIE OF AVOCH'S REEL	15L4L5L	7L431	A	2/2	Mc11p7
MISS MACKENZIE OF AVOCH'S STRATHSPEY	5L3L1L3	447L2	Bb	4/4	Mc11p5
MISS MACKENZIE OF COULS WALTZ	5355	3131	Bb	3/8	G9v3p6
MISS MACKENZIE OF CROMARTIE'S STR.	3335	4422	E	4/4	L1p15
MISS MACKENZIE OF STRATHGARVE'S STR.	31H63	31H42	G	4/4	Mc11p9
MISS MACKENZIES REEL	15L13	2226L	Bb	2/2	J1p8
MISS MACKENZIE'S STRATHSPEY	5211	6L224	D	4/4	Mc21v2p29
MISS MACKENZIE'S STRATHSPEY	3215L	3565	F	2/2	C14v19p22
MISS MACKINTOSH'S REEL	131H3	427L5L	G	2/4	J2p5
MISS MACKINZIE'S REEL	3341H	337L7L	F	2/2	Mc21v3p29
MISS MACKWORTH'S STRATHSPEY	3L1L3L5L	15L6L2L	B	2/2	J1p23
MISS MACLACHLAN'S REEL	15L3L5L	4L436L	Bb	2/2	P11v1p5
MISS MACLEAN OF DUART'S REEL	15L5L3	15L2L2	Bb	2/2	D14v3p19
MISS MACLEOD OF DALVEY'S FAVORITE	5134	3356	G	4/4	C18p18
MISS MACLEOD OF DALVEY'S WALTZ	1113	1111	G	3/8	C18p19
MISS MACLEOD OF GEANIES	17L32	3522	A	6/8	L1p2
MISS MACLEOD OF MACLEOD'S REEL	3bH2H2H4#	6b7b7b2	G	4/4	Mc21v4p29
MISS MACMURDO'S FAVOURITE (STRATHSPEY)	1H1H1H5	7b2H2H3bH	E	4/4	G10v3p25 Mc12v1p23
MISS MACNEIL'S FAVORITE	1343	6L27L5L	Bb	2/4	S4v2p25
MISS MACRAE OF INVERINAT'S REEL	13b51	53b51	E	2/2	F2v1p5
MISS MACWHINNIE'S FAVOURITE	112	156	Bb	9/8	Mc15p24
MISS MADALINA MAXWELL'S STRATHSPEY	1H1H35	2246	D	4/4	S4v1p20
MISS MADELINA MAXWELL OF MONRIETH	1522	151H5	F	6/8	E2p15
MISS MAINY BELL'S STRATHSPEY	3b215L	3b247bL	A	4/4	G3p29
MISS MAITLAND (OF FREUGH) REEL	315L3	6L27L5	D	2/2	Mc21v3p28
MISS MAJOR MACLEOD	1566	5125L	F	6/8	L1p6
MISS MALCOLM'S HORNPIPE	1353	2464	Eb	2/2	M4v3p22
MISS MALCOMB'S REEL	1162	1165	A	6/8	P1v2p2
MISS MANAGIES HORNPIPE	3212	4323	G	4/4	A7v5p29
MISS MANNERS'S FANCY	1H1H1H7	1H1H2H2H	E	2/4	J1p34
MISS MAr MARSHALL'S SCOTCH MEASURE	5553	51H1H3	D	4/4	W2v1p13
MISS MARGARET BROWN('S FAVOURITE)	516L6L	25L11	G	6/8	E1v1p55 G11v1Bp23 G10v3p29 A1v4p63
MISS MARGARET BUCHAN'S STRATHSPEY	13b53b	7bL27bL2	D	4/4	S4v2p5
MISS MARGARET CAMPBELL (OF SADDELL'S) REEL	1351H	6542	A	2/2	Mc21v3p8 (II)
MISS MARGARET DRYSDALE'S STRATHSPEY	125L4L	1236L	Bb	4/4	R9p6
MISS MARGARET DUNBAR'S STRATHSPEY	1632	1313	D	4/4	T1v2p4
MISS MARGARET EWING'S STRATHSPEY	11H61H	6562	D	4/4	Mc13v2p36 C13v1p44
MISS MARGARET GORDON (OF LESSMORE'S) STRATHSPEY	3b17bL4	3b13b5	G	4/4	Mc21v3p22
MISS MARGARET GORDON (OF LESSMORES) AVOURITE REEL	1H535	44H2H2H	C	2/2	Mc21v3p27
MISS MARGARET GORDON OF LESSMORE'S REEL	3342	7L27L5L	G	2/2	Mc10p1 (II)
MISS MARGARET GRAHAM (OF GARTMORE) 'S STRATHSPEY	3565	1H642	D	4/4	Mc21v3p32
MISS MARGARET GRAHAM OF GARTMORE'S STRATHSPEY	1353	137L1	G	2/2	S4v1p6
MISS (MARGARET) GRAHAM OF INCHBRAKIE ('S STRATHSPEY)	5551	4442	G	4/4	G10v1p18 G11v1Bp7 (II)
MISS MARGARET GRAHAM'S (OF GARTMORE'S) FAVORITE	1H563	537L7L	Bb	2/2	Mc21v3p17
MISS MARGARET GRANT'S REEL	5551H	51H26	D	2/2	C14v16p13
MISS MARGARET GRANTS REEL	317L5L	351H6	A	2/2	Mc15p10
MISS MARGARET MCGREGOR'S FAVOURITE	31H7	652	D	9/8	C5v1p67 Mc22p4 A1v4p67
MISS MARGARET MOIR'S STRATHSPEY	5316L	5L642	A	4/4	D16p9
MISS MARGARET NICOLS HIGH DANCE	3L6L17L	3L6L15L	Bb	2/4	D15v2p27
MISS MARGARET OSWALD (OF SCOTSTOWN'S) REEL	15L3L5L	26L4L6L	A	2/2	Mc21v3p12
MISS MARGARET RENNYS STRATHSPEY	1H3H2H1H	51H22	F	2/2	D15v1p25
MISS MARGARET ROBERTSON'S JIGG	4231	6L7L33	G	6/8	S4v1p26
MISS MARGARET SETON'S STRATHSPEY	535L3L	1326	F	4/4	S4v2p12
MISS MARGARET SMITH'S WALTZ	37L53	36L2H1H	Bb	3/8	R9p26
MISS MARGARET THOMSON'S STRATHSPEY	5151H	152H1H	C	2/2	Mc19v2p15
MISS MARGRET HAMILTON SUNDRUM'S STRATHSPEY	1111	2222	G	4/4	E2p6
MISS MARGRET McINTOSH'S JIG	1H653	3565	A	6/8	M11v1p4
MISS MARGRET RANKINE'S REEL	5L5L31	6L420	Eb	2/2	C23p5
MISS MARGRET ROBERTSON'S JIG	1122	1253	D	6/8	R9p18
MISS MARGRET STEUART OF STEUART LODGE'S REEL	5L133	4426L	A	2/2	L4p5
MISS MARGRETT DALRYMPLE'S JIG	1324	11H52	Bb	6/8	M11v1p15
MISS MARGRETT DAVIDSON'S STRATHSPEY	1H642	4515	F	2/2	M11v1p3
MISS MARGRETT SKELTON'S JIG	5135	363H7	F	6/8	M11v1p11
MISS MARGt. BALFOUR'S FANCY	3424	316L7L	G	6/8	G3p3
MISS MARGt BLAIR'S STRATHSPEY	3L5L3L5L	4L6L7L5L	Bb	4/4	Mc21v2p21
MISS MARGT CHRISTIE'S VALTZ	3155	311H5	F	3/8	W4v2p12
MISS MARGt. DRUMMOND FORBES'S JIG	1H543	25L1H5	A	6/8	G3p16
MISS MARGt GORDON'S REEL	1H535	1H53H2H	D	2/2	G15p8
MISS MARGt GREIG OF QUEBEC	35L36	4646	F	4/4	C21p2
MISS MARGt. HONYMAN'S DOUBLE JIGG	351H1H	6527L	E	6/8	S11v2p12
MISS MARGt McDOUGAL OF ARDBEG STRATHSPEY	5L3bL5L3b	4242	G	2/2	Mc16p3

STRATHSPEY

Title	Code1	Code2	Key	Time	Reference
MISS MARGt St. CLAIR REDDIES FANCY	5651H	562H2	C	6/8	W2v1p8
MISS MARGt STEWART MENZIES REEL	3b15L5L	7bL242	E	2/2	Mc19v2p3
MISS (MARIA) DUNDAS('S REEL)	5153	6753	G F	4/4*	A7v5p19 G1v1p39 (II)
					G10v4p21 A7v4p22 (II)
MISS MARIA STEWART'S JIGG	1H1H1H2H	6542	F	6/8	P11v2p12
MISS MARIANE OLIPHANT	1L5L6L4L	5L231	G	4/4	Mc21v2p26 (II)
(ROSSIE'S) STRATHSPEY					
MISS MARKBY'S FANCY	3315L	6L422	A	2/4	J1p8
MISS MARRION CAMPBELL	3H2H3H2H	62H62H	G	6/8	Mc16p30
ARDMORE'S FAVORITE					
MISS MARRION CAMPBELL ARDMORE'S REEL	15L11	5352	G	2/2	Mc16p4
MISS MARTINE'S REEL	5L36L5L	4L5L22L	Bb	2/2	R9p26
MISS MARY ABERCROMBY'S STRATHSPEY	326L5L	2L47L2	G	4/4	S4v1p6
MISS MARY ANN GORDON	35L33	5755	Bb	4/4	L1p18
MISS MARY ANN HAIG'S STRATHSPEY	1353	2464	F	2/2	B20p14
MISS MARY ANN HUNTER	13L4L3L	47L42	Bb	2/4	D16p11
OF BURNSIDE'S HORNPIPE					
MISS MARY ANN JOHNSTON'S FAVOURITE	1114	7L224	E	2/4	S4v1p19
MISS MARY ANN JOHNSTON'S REEL	3L13L5L	4L24L6L	Bb	2/2	Mc21v2p6
MISS MARY ANN JOHNSTON'S STRATHSPEY	51H51H	2427bL	D	2/2	Mc22p5
MISS MARY ANN URQUHART'S HIGH DANCE	1124	27L25L	Bb	2/4	D15v2p19
MISS MARY ANN WHITEFOORD'S STRATHSPEY	5L133	6L242	D	4/4	P5v3p6
MISS MARY BALFOUR'S STRATHSPEY	1111	117bL3b	E	4/4	G10v5p31
MISS MARY BANNERMAN'S REEL	1L133	5122	Bb	2/2	C23p19
MISS MARY BOWER OF KINCALDRUM'S REEL	1353	437L7L	F	2/2	M1p1
MISS MARY BUCHANAN'S STRATHSPEY	137L4	131H3	F	4/4	S4v2p10
MISS MARY CAMPBELL ARDMORE'S JIG	1131H	637L2	G	6/8	Mc16p17
MISS MARY DOUGLAS'S ALLAMAND	3310	5530	Bb	2/4	G9v4p19
MISS MARY DOUGLAS'S JIG	551H7	557L2	Eb	6/8	R9p3
MISS MARY DOUGLAS'S REEL	3b11H5	46b7b5	A	4/4	G9v5p28
MISS MARY DOUGLAS'S REEL	3H5H3H2H	2H3H72H	D	2/2	C4p6
MISS MARY DOUGLAS'S STRATHSPEY	1L36L5L	1L36L2	Bb	4/4	Mc21v3p19
MISS MARY DOUGLAS'S WALTZ	156L7L	16L21	Bb	3/8	R9p8,9
MISS MARY DOUGLASS('S REEL)	3532	237L2	Bb	4/4*	G10v2p31 G11v1Cp36
MISS MARY DUFF OF HATHORN'S JIG	5L13b5	2425	G	6/8	M11v1p14
MISS MARY G: ABERNETHIE'S STRATHSPEY	13b53b	7bL242	G	2/2	C24v2p22
MISS MARY GARDEN (DELGATY) 'S REEL	531H3	2424	A	2/2	P5v2p15
MISS MARY GARDEN OF TROUP'S REEL	1H53b1	247b2	E	6/8	Mc21v4p21
MISS MARY GILESPIE'S STRATHSPEY	5L326L	5L353	A	4/4	G3p31
MISS MARY GORDON OF BRAID	1351H	5542	A	6/8	L1p2
MISS MARY GORDON OF CLUNY	1H563	0027L	E	3/8	L2p20
MISS MARY GRANT'S REELL	657b1	6527bL	A	4/4	C33p20
MISS MARY JARVI'S REEL	3362	331H1H	F	2/2	C21p3
MISS MARY JEAN HOME'S STRATHSPEY	3b15L1	3b17bL4	A	4/4	S4v1p23
MISS MARY JOHNSON'S QUICK STEP	73b53b	247b2	E	6/8	Mc21v2p25
MISS MARY JOHNSTONE HOPE'S BIRTH DAY	3352	7L6L11	Bb	2/2	G9v3p20
MISS MARY JOHNSTON'S STRATHSPEY	5315	4522	G	2/2	M11v1p16
MISS MARY L. ROBERTSON	351H1H	2H4H2H2	C	4/4	M4v4p14,15
MISS MARY LEE'S DELIGHT	16L5L1	3432	Bb	4/4	Mc13v1p3 Mc13v2p3
MISS MARY LUMSDANE'S FAVORITE	511	17L2	G	3/2	G10v5p30
MISS MARY LUMSDEN'S FAVORITE	51H1H	1H72H	C	3/2	C5v2p65
MISS MARY LUMSDEN'S FAVOURITE	5L11	17L2	G	3/2	C8v1p53 K1v2p8
MISS MARY MACDONALD	1H53b1	1H527bL	D	2/2	Mc21v3p30
(OF CLANRONALD'S) REEL					
MISS MARY MacDONALD'S REEL	1327bL	1323	G	4/4	G11v1Bp36 G10v2p31 E1v1p28
MISS MARY MACKAY'S REEL	1H655	1H662	C	6/8	Mc21v4p14
MISS MARY McDONALD'S REEL	1345	1327L	A	2/2	Mc19v1p10
MISS MARY MONCREIF'S DANCE	4564	7L122	F	2/4	C22p25
MISS MARY MURRAY'S JIG	15L12	3125L	Bb	6/8	B12p7
MISS MARY MURRAY'S REEL	131H6	672H2	A	2/2	Mc13v1p3 Mc13v2p3
MISS MARY OGSTON'S STRATHSPEY	5L13b5	7b422	A	2/2	M11v1p15
MISS MARY RAM'S FANCY	5151	5147bL	B	6/8	C14v17p13
MISS MARY SHAND'S REEL	5H5H5H1H	5H5H2H2H	D	2/2	G15p9
MISS MARY STEWART OF DERCLUICH'S GIGG	351H2H	6542	Eb	6/8	S11v1p8,9
MISS MARY STEWART'S STRATHSPEY	5165	7b547bL	D	2/2	S4v1p4
MISS MARY URQUHART'S REEL	3L5L6L2	4326L	Bb	2/2	C24v1p6
MISS MASTERTON'S FAVORITE	1545	47b27bL	A	2/4	S11v1p8
MISS MASTERTON'S GIGG	3451H	5432	A	6/8	S11v1p8
MISS MATILDA GRANT'S STRATHSPEY	116L5L	4L4L7F2L	Bb	4/4	Mc10p9
MISS MATILDA LOCKHART'S REEL	3565	3542	D	2/2	A1v4p60 Mc12v1p51
MISS MAULE OF PANMURE'S REEL	127bL5L	7bL5L7bL5L	B	4/4	A1v5p1
MISS MAULE OF PANMURE'S REEL	6753	5353	D	4/4	C5v1p1
MISS MAULE OF PANMURE('S REEL)	62H53	5353	C	4/4*	G9v5p4 G10v4p16 (II)
MISS MAULE'S STRATHSPEY	316L5L	316L2	A	4/4	Mc21v4p32 P5v2p3 (II)
MISS MAULES WALTZ OR COUNTRY DANCE	1527L	137L2	Bb	6/8	G9v3p17
MISS MAXWELL GORDON'S REEL	3511	27L53	D	2/2	P11v2p5
MISS MAXWELL OF MONRIETH'S	1111	3L111	Bb	4/4	E2p6
FAREWELL TO THE W.L. FENCIBLES					
MISS MAXWELL OF MONRIETH'S REEL	551H5	3H1H22	F	4/4	E2p16
MISS MAXWELL OF MORISTON	3b13b1H	3bH7b44	C	6/8	S4v1p12
MISS MAXWELL OF MORRESTON'S REEL	1L1L5L5L	1542	A	4/4	W4v1p21

MISS MAXWELL'S FANCY	1516	5125L	F	6/8	G8p14
MISS MAXWELL'S REEL	3155	12H2H2	A	4/4	C14v15p19
MISS MAXWELL'S STRATHSPEY	151H1H	64H72H	D	4/4	S4v1p10
MISS MAY HAY('S REEL)	13b51	7b427bL	E	2/2	D14v3p20 (II)
MISS McCLOUD'S FANCY	1525	1666	E	2/2	C14v10p22
MISS MCDONALD OF BOROUGHDALE'S JIG	1565	61H32	F	6/8	R7v1p1,2
MISS MCDONALD OF LEYNDALE'S REEL	13b7bL3b	13b41	A	2/2	R7v3p1
MISS McDONALD St. MARTIN'S JIGG	1H351	1H325L	A	6/8	B11p22
MISS McDONALD St. MARTINS STRATHSPEY	5L13b3b	427bL2	G	4/4	B11p21
MISS McDOUALL'S MINUET	11H3H	2H54	F	3/4	D14v1p18
MISS McDOUGAL'S STRATHSPEY	16L13	16L22	F	4/4	E2p21
MISS McINNES' FANCY	1L11L1	1L144	A	4/4	M4v4p26,27
MISS McINNES' REEL	5164	2464	F	2/2	M4v3p55
MISS McKENZIE OF COULS REEL	113b5	7b7bL24	E	2/2	H3p27
MISS McKENZIE'S REEL	1H51H3bH	4H7b42H	D	2/4	N2p28,29
MISS McKINLAY'S DANCE	5325L	3L232	A	6/8	C22p34
MISS McKINNON OF LIVERIES REEL	1322	537L7L	Bb	2/2	R7v3p2
MISS McKINZIE'S REEL	35L3L5L	7L27L2	Bb	2/2	H1p1
MISS McLAINE OF TARLOISK'S STRATHSPEY	15L5L5L	16L6L6L	A	4/4	C10v1p2
MISS McLAUCHLAN('S REEL)	1531	227L5L	A	4/4*	B11p21 (II)
MISS McLEAN OF INVERSCADLE(S REEL)	3b5L3b5	24L24	G	2/2	Mc4v4p10 (II)
MISS McLEAN OF LOCHBOWIE'S STRATHSPEY	1135	1H1H1H6	F	4/4	R7v1p2
MISS McLEOD (OF COLBECK)'S (FAVORITE/STRATHSPEY)	5L133	6L244	D	4/4*	G11v2Dp16
MISS McLEOD OF COLBECK'S STRATHSPEY	5555	6662	F	4/4*	K1v2p31 Mc4v3p9 (II)
MISS McLEOD OF DELVEY'S REEL	1L13b3b	6bL243b	A	2/2	T1v2p11
MISS McNEAL'S REEL	53H1H6	432H2	F	2/2	S11v1p4
MISS McNEILL'S [STRATHSPEY]	1H1H35	4242H	D	4/4	A1v6p6
MISS McNEIL'S FANCY	5652	7L27L2	G A	2/4	A1v4p37 W4v1p12
MISS McNIELLS REEL	113L5L	4L2L4L2	A	2/2	H3p23
MISS McPHERSON GRANT'S JIG	5L17L2	3125L	A	6/8	M4v3p21
MISS McPHERSON'S REEL	3L1L5L1	3L5L4L2L	Bb	2/2	M4v3p12
MISS McQUEEN'S REEL [McQUEEN'S REEL]	1456	1H522	F	4/4	M4v1p5 C14v7p4
MISS McQUEIR'S REEL	1135	27L5L7L	F	2/2	R5p24(26)
MISS McREADY OF PERSTON'S FAVOURITE	3456	3562	A	2/2	C12p3
MISS MELVEL DYSART	1315	1316L	A	4/4	W2v2p4
MISS MENZIES OF CULDARE('S REEL)	5157	1H2H2H2H	D	2/2	Mc4v1p4 (II)
MISS MENZIES OF CULDARES' REEL	1L1L3bL5L	7bL4L2L7bF	A	4/4	Mc19v2p9
MISS MENZIES OF MENZIES' REEL	1H51H5	1H52H2	G	2/2	Mc19v1p11 Mc19v2p15
MISS MERCER ELPHINSTONE'S REEL	5555	5524	G	2/2	J1p36
MISS METHUEN'S REEL, THE	136L2	1353	G	2/2	J1p40
MISS MEYNELL'S REEL	11H76	5H1H2H2H	D	2/2	H3p12
MISS MILLAR'S STRATHSPEY	3551	5166	D	4/4	P11v2p11
MISS MILLER OF DALSWINTON'S FANCY	1316	2422H	Eb	4/4	A7v1p11
MISS MILLER OF DALSWINTON'S STRATHSPEY	1555	1522	D	4/4	R6v1p8 (II)
MISS MILLER OF GLENLEE'S REEL	3155	1322	A	4/4	F3p16
MISS MILLER OF GLENLEE'S STRATHSPEY	3b3b1H5	7b544	C	2/2	S4v1p16
MISS MILLER'S REEL	113b3b	4427bL	E	4/4	B20p7
MISS MILLER'S REEL	113L5L	4L5L2L2	Bb	4/4	G3p33
MISS MILLIKEN'S REEL	1113	526L6L	F	2/2	Mc9v3p2
MISS MILNERS DELIGHT	31H2H1H	2H1H75	D	6/8	B16v4p87
MISS MILNE'S STRATHSPEY	3b15L3b	27bL44	G	4/4	G3p29
MISS MITCHEL'S STRATHSPEY	1362	1366	D	4/4	G3p33
MISS MOLLY DAKER'S REEL	5L1L5L5L	1322L	A	2/2	S12v1p65
MISS MOLLY GRANT'S REEL	156b2	3b3b7L7L	B	2/2	Mc21v1p33
MISS MOLLY SCOT'S RANT	17L26L	1151	D	2/2	R12v1p67
MISS MONCREFF OF REEDY'S REEL	11H3H5H	2H4H2H6	D	2/2	S11v1p7
MISS MONCRIEFF OF PITLOWER'S REEL	5L5L31	5562	A	2/2	L4p7 (II)
MISS MONCRIEFF OF REEDIE'S STRATHSPEY	1565	1562	E	4/4	L4p1
MISS MONCRIFF OF REEDY'S FAVORITE	1H565	4362	D	6/8	S11v1p6
MISS MONEYPENNY OF PITMI(L)LY'S REEL	113b2	7bL5L7b2	G	2/2	Mc4v4p11 (II)
MISS MONRO'S DOUBLE HORNPIPE	31H5	552	A	9/8	G3p16
MISS MONRO'S STRATHSPEY	1353	2366	G D	4/4	A7v6p32 A7v2p8
MISS MONTGOMERIE OF SKELMORELIE'S STRATHSPEY	5324	5351H	F	2/2	G8p5
MISS MONTGOMERIE OF SKELMORLIE ('S STRATHSPEY)	5524	5551H	F G	4/4*	Mc4v3p1 (II) A1v6p18
MISS MONTGOMERIES REEL	5524	5351H	F	2/2	C14v20p6
MISS MONTGOMERY'S MINUET	111	112	Eb	3/4	C22p5
MISS MONTGOMERY'S REEL	5342	5351H	D	2/2	W4v1p17 A1v4p39
MISS MONTGOMRIE OF ANNICK LODGE	1345	1642	F	4/4	E2p2
MISS MONTGOMRIE OF SKERMORLIE'S STRATHSPEY	311H1H	3126L	Bb	4/4	E2p5
MISS MOODIE'S HORNPIPE	1131H	7351	Eb	2/4	C18p35
MISS MOODY'S FAVORITE	3H545	3H542	D	2/4	C23p13
MISS MORE OF RAEDEN'S FAVORITE DANCE	1H1H55	671H1H	C	6/8	D15v2p19
MISS MOREHEAD'S REEL	113b3b	543b2	B	2/2	B20p9
MISS MORISON'S REEL	5353	2462	F	2/2	S12v1p50
MISS MORISON'S REEL	31H2H1H	641H5	G	2/2	A7v3p21
MISS MORRISON'S JIG	5211	6L5L5L1	Bb	6/8	G3p12
MISS MOYSEY'S REEL	1351H	5326L	G	2/2	J1p11
MISS (M./POLLY) SKINNER'S REEL	1322	1313	D	4/4*	C13v2p29 B15v1p2 C4p27

99

MISS M.S. REDDIE'S REEL	5535	62H75	D	2/2	W2v2p12
MISS MUIR MACKENZIE'S FAVORITE	1H345	64H1H7	D	6/8	S4v2p26
MISS MUIR MCKENZIES STRATHSPEY	1H1H1H1H	2H3H66	E	4/4	G10v5p16 (II)
[MISS MUIR MACKENZIE]					
MISS MUNRO DINGWALL'S REEL	3535	3547L	D	2/4	J2p5
MISS MUNRO OF DORNOCH'S REEL	1H535	22H76	D	2/2	G15p18
MISS MUNRO'S REEL	11H66	11H53	F	2/4	J2p12
MISS MURE'S REEL	331H5	4H3H72H	F	2/2	M6p2
MISS MURRAY LINTROSE	316L5L	3215	Bb	2/4	B11p2
MISS MURRAY OCHTERTYRE	1111	1127L	Bb	2/4	B11p3
MISS MURRAY OF ABERCARNEY('S REEL)	5L13b1	4L242	G	2/2	Mc4v2p7 (II)
MISS MURRAY (OF AUCHTERTYRE)	31H61H	31H66	G F	4/4*	A7v6p56 G11v2Ap30 A7v4p25
'S STRATHSPEY					C14v12p11 (II)
'S MURRAY OF AUCHTERTYRE'S FAVORITE	1H3H55	61H53	F	2/4	G9v3p28
MISS MURRAY (OF AUCHTERTYRE'S) STR.	31H61H	31H66	G	4/4*	G1v2p59 A7v5p18
MISS MURRAY OF AUCHTERTYRE'S STRATHSPEY	31H61H	31H66	F	4/4	K1v1p32,33
MISS MURRAY OF ELLIBANK'S FAVORITE	126L1	3422	A	6/8	S4v2p23
MISS MURRAY OF HENDERLAND'S VALTZ	1H6H54H	1H6H51H	C	3/8	G9v4p3
MISS MURRAY OF MURRAYFIELD'S STRATHSPEY	315L3L	437L2	F	4/4	S4v1p24
MISS MURRAY OF POLMAIZE'S REEL	1135	1125L	G	2/2	B20p4
MISS MURRAY'S HORNPIPE	13L13	25L24	Bb	4/4	G3p1
MISS MURRAY'S JIG	1H31H3	1H344	F	6/8	A1v3p184
MISS MURRAY'S REEL	5513	227L6L	Eb	2/4	N2p28
MISS MURRAY'S REEL	311L1	3152	A	2/2	J1p38
MISS MURRAY'S REEL	3L13L1	15L2L2L	A	2/2	Mc9v2p21 C13v1p6 C13v2p30
MISS MURRAY'S REEL	511	3b22	A	3/2	C4p45 B15v1p11
MISS MURRY'S REEL	4H64H6	4H677	C	6/8	R12v1p38
MISS NANCIE LOW('S REEL)	51H51	1355	F	2/2	D16p20 (II)
MISS NANCY CAMPBELL'S REEL	5351H	7366	E	2/2	Mc9v3p42/43
MISS NANCY CAMPBELL'S SCOTS MEASURE	3313	551H1H	D	2/2	Mc9v2p12
MISS NANCY DICK'S REEL	1H3H5H5H	1H3H72H	C	6/8	Mc21v3p35
MISS NANCY GIBSON'S MINUET	111	135	Eb	3/4	D14v1p9
MISS (NANCY) GIBSON'S REEL	11H52	7L232	Bb	4/4*	K1v2p33 G11v2Bp31 P5v3p2 Mc7p3
(OR THE CUMBERLAND REEL)					Mc16p19
MISS NANCY KENNEDY'S REEL	1H551H	1H772H	C	2/2	R5p48
MISS NANCY RAMSAY'S FAVORITE	1313	5252	Bb	2/4	C23p7
MISS NANCY ROBINSON'S REEL	153H2H	1H552	E	2/2	C24v1p6
MISS NANCY STEWART Frs. WALTZ	1H1H5	3H3H1H	D	3/4	F1p29
MISS NANCY WATERSTON'S FANCY	153H3H	4H3H72H	E	2/2	C21p20
MISS NAPIER OF MERCHISTON HALL('S REEL)	1H2H1H3b	1H7b42	D	6/8	Mc21v3p7 (II)
MISS NAPIER'S MINUET	132	115	Eb	3/4	D14v1p7
MISS NAPIER'S REEL	111L5	437L2	G	2/2	P11v1p12
MISS NAPIER'S (REEL/FANCY)	115L5	437L2	G	2/2	C14v4p12 D14v1p23 D14v4p3
MISS NELLY BELL'S DOUBLE JIG	1L135	17L24	Bb	6/8	G3p8
MISS NELLY FERGUSON'S REEL	1H535	1H1H2H2	C	2/2	R5p43
MISS NELLY KENNEDY'S REEL	61H22H	61H53H	C	2/2	R5p37
MISS NELLY WATSON'S STRATHSPEY	536L5L	5367	F	2/2	A7v4p22 Mc22p11
[MISS N. WATSON'S STR.]					
MISS NICHOLAS ARBUTHNOT'S JIG	1H761H	2H3H2H3H	F	6/8	M11v1p6
MISS NICHOLSON'S REEL	31H64	5125L	F	2/2	G15p27
MISS NICOL OF STONEHAVEN'S MINUET	554	101	Eb	3/4	D15v2p6
MISS NICOL'S STRATHSPEY	3133	27bL44	G	4/4	A7v6p57
MISS NICOL'S STRATHSPEY	3333	2144	A	2/2	A7v3p15
MISS NIEL OF BARNWIEL'S REEL	1H1H3H1H	51H42	F	2/2	H1p32
MISS NISBET OF DIRLETON ('S REEL)	1527bL	1535	A	4/4*	G11v1Bp26 G10v3p3 (II)
MISS NISBET OF DIRLETON'S STRATHSPEY	1513b	7bL27b2	G	2/2	S4v1p22
MISS NISBET'S STRATHSPEY	1123	247L7L	A	4/4	P11v2p19
MISS NORRIS'S FANCY	116L5L	6L5L22	Bb	6/8	J1p35
MISS NORTON OF NORTON'S STRATHSPEY	1366	51H2H2H	D	4/4	P5v4p19
MISS NORTON'S REEL	137L5L	1343	Bb	2/2	P11v2p7
MISS NORTON'S REEL	1H1H35	72H4H3H	D	4/4	P5v4p19
MISS O' NEIL'S WALTZ	1H5H2H1H	1H5H2H1H	C	3/8	C1v4p9
MISS OATS'S STRATHSPEY	15L3L1L	2L27L6L	G	2/2	J1p27
MISS OGILVIE OF CLOVA'S STRATHSPEY	61H62	61H31	D	4/4	B6v3p2
MISS OGILVIE'S REEL	1353	5L347L	Bb	2/2	J2p6
MISS OGILVIE'S REEL	3155	42H2H2	G	4/4	C21p10 A1v5p13
MISS OGILVY OF CLOVA'S FAVOURITE	16L5L6L	16L2L2	Bb	4/4	A4v1p2
MISS OGILVY OF ISLABANK'S JIGG	15L11	4542	A	6/8	D16p32
MISS OGILVY'S WALTZ	5351	5351	Bb	3/8	W4v2p7
MISS OGLEVES FANCY	1164	7L7L6L2	Bb	2/4	C14v10p24
MISS OLIPHANT OF GASK'S DELIGHT	1132	231H1H	G	2/2	B11p24
MISS OLIPHANT (ROSSIE'S) STRATHSPEY	3L153	7L5L7L2	G	4/4	Mc21v2p10
MISS OLIPHANT'S REEL	3515L	6L7L12	Eb	2/2	T8p2
MISS OMMANNY'S REEL	3555	4362	D	6/8	Mc21v3p25
MISS ONSLOW'S REEL	3535	227L2	G	2/2	C14v10p8
MISS OR MAJOR SPICER	3H4H5H1T	5H1H2H5	C	6/8	P6v1p25
MISS OSWALD	3366	6362	A	2/2	W2v2p8/9
MISS OSWALD OF AUCHINCRUIVE	117bL7bL	113b5	A	4/4	G10v4p8
MISS OSWALD (OF DUNAKEER) 'S REEL	3b3b54	2427bL	G	2/2	C14v1p15 D14v3p3 (II)
MISS OSWALD (OF SCOTSTOWN'S) REEL	1H151	1H62H7	D	6/8	Mc21v3p37
MISS OSWALD'S BASS MINUET	155L	151H	G	3/4	O1v2p27
MISS OUSTEIN'S (FANCY/STRATHSPEY)	1H53b1	3b525L	G	4/4*	Mc4v3p8 G8p13 P1v1p5

Title			Key	Time	References
MISS PARKER'S REEL	3112	2252	G A	4/4*	A7v5p23 P5v4p15 A7v4p21
MISS PARKER'S REEL, THE	5132	531H3H	G	2/2	J1p24
MISS PARKINSON'S STRATHSPEY	1316	1342	F	4/4	P6v1p17
MISS PARK'S REEL	3b13b5	7b7b42	G	2/2	C13v2p57
MISS PATERSON'S REEL	1342	7bL47b7b	D	2/2	Mc15p28
MISS PATERSON'S REEL	3H3H1H3H	6H3H72H	D	2/4	N2p25
MISS PATTISON'S JIG	516L5L	1332	A	6/8	G3p17
MISS PEARSON OF KIPPENROSS'S STRATHSPEY	3L3L11	3L3L22L	Bb(D)	4/4	Mc10p9/15
MISS PEGGY CAMPBELL'S STRATHSPEY	1311H	5326L	D	4/4	C13v1p35
MISS PEGGY GORDON'S REEL	1565	1547L	G	2/2	S5p12
MISS PEGGY McKENZIE'S REEL	1351	4323	D	4/4	A1v6p17
MISS PEGGY MONTGOMERIE'S HORNPIPE	13b5	151	E	3/2	R5p54
MISS PEGGY WILLIAMSON STRATHSPEY	1H1H76	567L2	C	2/2	R9p21
MISS PEMBERTON'S REEL	3566	5322H	F	4/4	C14v13p24
MISS PENNY McKINNON'S REEL	5161H	5322	F	2/2	H3p30
MISS (PENSY) MACDONALD (NOW LADY BALHAVEN)('S REEL)	3151H	3147bL	G C	4/4*	G10v2p4 G11v1Ap28 A7v4p15 (II)
MISS PENUEL GRANT OF GRANT'S STRATHSPEY	3L16L1	3L16L2L	Bb	4/4	G15p24
MISS PENUEL GRANT OF GRANT'S STRATHSPEY	5411	4242	G	4/4	Mc10p7
MISS PERKIN'S REEL	537L7L	3451H	F	4/4	Mc11p4
MISS PETRIE'S FANCY, THE	3144	57L25L	A	6/8	J1p46
MISS PILLANS'S STRATHSPEY	3111	3142	G	2/2	L4p12
MISS PITT'S REEL	5555	2466	A	2/2	J1p42
MISS PLASKETT'S REEL	5L13b3b	553b1	D	2/2	J2p14
MISS PLATOFF'S MINUET	633	522	F	3/4	G9v3p25
MISS POINTZRICKET'S FANCY	1162	1162	A	6/8	J1p8
MISS POLE'S REEL	1121	1H532	Bb	2/2	J1p6
MISS POLLOCK'S STRATHSPEY	1H322	6L5L21	G	4/4	G3p16
MISS POLLY WELSH ('S REEL)	113b5	2427bL	C	2/2	S12v1p56 A7v2p32
MISS POURIE OF RESWALLIE'S FAVOURITE	11H66	6322	F	6/8	A4v1p5
MISS PRATT'S REEL	1335	662H2	F	2/2	C14v17p9
MISS PRESTON FERNTON('S REEL)	5531H	2362	D	2/2*	B11p14 (II)
MISS PRESTON OF FERNTON'S STRATHSPEY	1L5L1L1	137L2	A	2/2	S4v1p18
MISS PRINGLE'S REEL	3H2H1H1	4522H	C	2/2	S12v1p58 Mc21v1p32
MISS PRINGLE'S REEL	6365	2466	F	2/2	B20p17
MISS PRINGL'S MINUET	1H1H3H	1H3H5H	C	3/4	D14v1p15
MISS PROUD	5531H	3522	G	4/4	A7v6p93
MISS PROUD'S REEL	3531H	3514	G	2/2	S12v1p48
MISS PROUD'S REEL	3531H	3524	G	2/2	C13v2p21
MISS PROUD('S REEL)	3531H	5524	G	2/2*	Mc9v3p46 (II)
MISS PURSE'S JIG	5L3L1L1	1H527L	Bb	6/8	Mc15p4
MISS PYPS'S FANCY	1H52H5	3H5H67	E	6/8	J1p34
MISS RABINA BOSWELL'S REEL	1135	1H642	G	2/2	C5v1p52 A1v4p52 Mc12v1p2
MISS RAE (OF ESKGROVE)'S JIG(G)	11H1H1	11H2H2	C	6/8	G11v1Ap38 G10v2p29
MISS RAE OF ESKGROVES VALTZ	1H3H2H1H	1H3H2H1H	C	3/8	G9v4p8
MISS RAE'S (FAVORITE/STRATHSPEY)	3b13b6b	2454	C	2/4	G11v1Ap19 G10v3p8
MISS RAE'S JIG	1311H	1H3H72H	D	6/8	G1v2p93
MISS RAE'S STRATHSPEY	3b5L5L1	27bL3b7bL	G	4/4	S4v1p25
MISS RAMSAY OF BARNTON	1111	2237L	F	6/8	G9v3p25
MISS RAMSAY OF CRAIGLEITH'S FAVORITE	56L5L3L	4L222	Bb	6/8	S4v2p21
MISS RAMSAY'S REEL	3H1H31	4326L	G	4/4*	C4p9 G11v2Cp16 A1v1p27 B15v1p3 (II)
MISS RANDON'S DANCE	11H1H1	2L23bH4	G	6/8	G8p25
MISS RANKEN'S REEL	3155	3142	D	2/2	Mc4v4p12
MISS RATTRAY OF DALRULLZIAN	1H31H2H	1H531	G	6/8	P5v1p8
MISS RAY	3H1H51	337L0	F	6/8	P6v1p26 H6v1p2
MISS READ'S REEL	1151	2236L	Eb	2/2	C14v16p3
MISS REDDIES REEL	5L31H3H	2H2H2H6	F	4/4	W2v1p1
MISS REMINGTON'S DOUBLE HORNPIPE	351H	62H7	F	9/8	S11v2p7
MISS RICHARD'S REEL	5142	3126L	A	2/2	J1p4
MISS RICHARDSON'S STRATHSPEY	5353	51H32	C	4/4	A7v4p16
MISS RICHARDSON'S STRATHSPEY	13b51	27b47b	D	4/4	A7v1p13
MISS RIDDLE'S FANCY	5342	3125L	Bb	6/8	C12p6
MISS RIGG OF MORTON'S JIGG	1351	1342	A	6/8	Mc22Ap3
MISS RITCHIE('S REEL)	1115	5142	F	2/2*	S11v1p5 (II)
MISS ROBERTS FANCY	1516	5125L	F	6/8	B17p6
MISS ROBERTSON	117L2	317L2	A	4/4	M4v3p20
MISS ROBERTSON KILTEARN'S REEL	1113	7L7L7L2	Bb	2/4	J2p16
MISS ROBERTSON OF BODDOM'S STRATHSEPEY	11H55	6547bL	D	4/4	M11v2p5
MISS ROBERTSON OF CLAVERSTON'S JIGG	3152	7L5L15	A	6/8	P5v4p15
MISS ROBERTSON OF TULLYBELTON'S (REEL/STRATHSPEY)	1L1L26L	5L12L2L	Bb	4/4*	G11v1Ap2 G10v1p7 (II)
MISS ROBERTSON'S FANCY	116L2	7L6L11	A	2/4	Mc21v2p22
MISS ROBERTSON'S FAVORITE	4225L	31H62	A	4/4	C21p15
MISS ROBERTSON'S MINUET	333	553	D	3/4	C22p9
MISS ROBERTSON('S REEL)	5L3L6L6L	7L7L13	A	2/2	Mc21v3p29 (II)
MISS ROBINSON OF CLERMESTON'S REEL	315L1	3142	G	2/2	C18p3
MISS ROLLO'S STRATHSPEY	116L4L	2L47L5L	G	4/4	P11v1p8
MISS ROSE BLACKHALL'S STRATHSPEY	1L3L5L5L	1L5L5L1	A	4/4	P5v2p7
MISS ROSE OF DRANIE'S REEL	15L13	437L2	F	2/2	G15p25
MISS ROSE OF TARLOGIE('S REEL)	3L3L15L	6L6L4L2L	Bb A	2/2*	G15p23 (II)
MISS ROSE'S FANCY OF JAMAICA	1122	3527L	A	6/8	C14v8p14

MISS ROSE'S JIG	11H7b4	11H1H1H	G	6/8	Mc15p36
MISS ROSE'S REEL	5H1T3H1H	6H4H4H2H	C	2/4	N2p28
MISS ROSE('S STRATHSPEY)	1345	4542	A	2/2*	C24v2p24 (11)
MISS ROSS ANKERVILLE	3b423b	127L5L	G	2/4	J2p15
MISS ROSS OF ROSSIE'S STRATHSPEY	51H51	2216L	D	2/2	D15v1p21
MISS ROSS'S HORNPIPE	1H31H2H	1H31H3H	G	4/4	F1p35
MISS ROSS'S JIG	1H1H51	1H62H7	Eb	6/8	R9p14
MISS ROSS'S JIG	1H2H3H7	5353	F	6/8	Mc15p39
MISS ROSS'S REEL	11H55	4542	F	2/2	M4v1p11
MISS ROSS('S STRATHSPEY)	351H6	1H1H22	A	4/4	L1p6 (11)
MISS ROSS'S STRATHSPEY	156L2	1565	Eb	4/4	G15p5
MISS ROSS('S STRATHSPEY)	5L5L5L1	2326L	Bb	4/4	G10v4p22 (11)
MISS RUNNINGTON'S REEL	113L1L	1554	G	2/2	P1v2p3 J1p12
MISS RUSSEL OF BLACKHALL'S JIG	551H1H	5562	F	6/8	D15v1p28
MISS RUSSELL OF BLACK HALL'S FAVORITE DANCE	1321	3535	F	2/4	D15v2p7
MISS RUSSELL OF BLACKHALL('S REEL)	13b15L	7bL7b47bL	G	6/8	Mc21v4p29 P5v2p16
MISS RUTHERFOORD'S JIGG	5L155	2L242	A	6/8	P5v1p17
MISS RUTHERFORD KINGHORN'S STRATHSPEY	5L17bL2	3b3b47bL	A	4/4	W2v1p2
MISS S. CAMPBELL OF SADDLE'S ALLAMANDE	1355	5755	Bb	2/4	G9v4p19
MISS S. McLEOD'S HORNPIPE	31H2H5	6242	Eb	4/4	S11v2p3
MISS S. THOMAS	1H1H2H2H	3H1H75	D	2/4	C14v27p9
MISS SACKVILE'S FANCY	5561H	1H64H1H	D	2/4	A1v2p71
MISS SALLY BARTLET'S JIGG	1H751	2425L	G	6/8	Mc22p7
MISS SALLY BARTLETT'S REEL	3235	4H2H2H2	D	4/4*	A1v5p36 C5v1p36 Mc10p7(15)
MISS SALLY EGLISON'S REEL	5555	3H1H2H2H	C	4/4	M4v2p2
MISS SALLY HUNTER OF THURSTON('S JIGG)	11H61H	62H2H7	D	6/8	A1v4p30 G11v1Bp16 G10v3p33 (11)
MISS SALLY McDONALD'S MINUET	115	115L	A	3/4	D15v1p26
MISS SALLY MCLEAN	5154	57bL3b7bL	G	6/8	W2v2p5
MISS SANDFORD'S JIGG	1343	5L142	Eb	6/8	P11v1p11
MISS SANDWICH COTILLON	1142	3364	F	6/8	A7v3p11
MISS SARAH DRUMMOND OF PERTH ('S STRATHSPEY)	1111	447bL2	E	4/4	G10v2p7 (11)
MISS (SARAH) DRUMMOND OF PERTH ('S STRATHSPEY)	1525	4242	A	4/4*	G11v1Ap35 G8p10 Mc4v2p1 G10v3p16 E1v1p85 (11)
MISS SARAH GEORGIANA DUFF OF MUIRTOWN'S STRATHSPEY	5L6L1L3L	4L622L	Bb	4/4	M12p22
MISS SARJENT LIVINGTON'S REEL	115L5L	247bL7bL	A	4/4	W2v2p2
MISS SAUNDER'S FANCY	1156	1H411	Bb	3/8	J1p10
MISS SCAFFE	1155	6355	G	4/4	W2v2p8
MISS SCOT OF HARDEN	125	127L	Eb	9/8	C14v26p14
MISS SCOT'S REEL	1H3H75	1H3H3H3H	D	2/2	S4v2p20
MISS SCOTT	15L1	26L2	Bb	9/8	G9v2p13
MISS SCOTT OF ANCRUM'S REEL	1H515	432H2	C	2/2	P11v2p21
MISS SCOTT OF BALWILLIE'S REEL	113b5	5427bL	E	4/4	A4v2p1
MISS SCOTT OF BELVEAU'S ALLAMANDE	5H6H5H6H	5H5H1H1H	C	2/4	G9v4p13
MISS SCOTT OF BELVUE('S REEL)	3H1H53	3H1H2H4H	C	2/2*	S4v1p17 (11)
MISS SCOTT OF LOGIE'S STRATHSPEY	31H2H1H	31H22	D	2/2	D15v1p18
MISS SCOTT OF SINTON'S STRATHSPEY	5361H	5324	D	4/4	P11v1p5
MISS SCOTT OF USAN('S REEL)	1551H	1562	F	2/2*	D16p10 (11)
MISS SCOTT'S FAVORITE	3142	3125L	G	4/4	E2p22
MISS SCOTT'S FAVORITE	3525L	351H1H	D	6/8	G9v3p22
MISS SCOTT'S STRATHSPEY	35L3L5L	367L2	F	4/4	R9p13
MISS SCOTT'S WALTZ	1H62H1H	1H63H1H	C	3/8	R9p20
MISS SERVICE'S STRATHSPEY	1L121	5326L	A	4/4	G8p29 P1v1p11
MISS SEYMOUR'S REEL	5L3L5L3	15L4L2L	Bb	2/2	C14v19p7
MISS SHAND'S STRATHSPEY	15L11	5L122	D	4/4	G15p8
MISS SHANK'S STRATHSPEY	116L1	5232	A	2/2	D15v1p12
MISS SHARPE OF HODDOMS REEL	353H1H	53H2H2	F	2/2	C14v10p26
MISS SHARPES FANCY	1H565	1H525L	D	6/8	G10v3p4
MISS SHARP'S FANCY	1H565	1H525	D	6/8	A1v4p43 C5v1p43
MISS SHAW STEWART'S STRATHSPEY	331H1H	6542	G	2/2	B20p3
MISS SHERRIFF'S STRATHSPEY	1313	1H661H	A	4/4	P11v2p6
MISS SIBBALDS WALTZ	1141	1141	Bb	3/8	C14v14p8
MISS SIMPSON'S REEL	51H35	42H46	D	4/4	Mc11p3
MISS SITWELL'S STRATHSPEY	1362	1351H	D	4/4	A1v5p74
MISS SITWELL('S STRATHSPEY)	1L3L6L2L	1L3L11	Bb	4/4	G10v4p22,23 (11)
MISS SMITH	153b1	27bL47bL	A	6/8	W2v2p6
MISS SMOLLET'S ALLAMANDE	1H531H	2H3H2H5	F	2/4	G9v4p8,9
MISS SMOLLET'S FANCY	5551	5547bL	A	2/2	B17p13
MISS SMOLLET'S STRATHSPEY	13b7L2	13b7b6b	E	2/2	W4v2p13
MISS SMYTH OF METHVEN	51H4H7	51H4H5H	C	2/4	L1p13
MISS SMYTH (OF METHVEN'S) FAVOURITE	3L5L4L1	3L5L3L2L	Bb	6/8	Mc21v3p5
MISS SMYTH OF METHVEN'S REEL	15L5L1L	2L226L	A	2/2	G10v4p28,29
MISS SOPHIA CAMPBELL (OF SADDELL'S) REEL	51H53b	47b42	G	6/8	Mc21v3p24 (11)
MISS SOPHIA CUMMING'S REEL	4231H	4H3H1H6	F	2/2	G15p28
MISS SOPHIA DIROM'S REEL	1346	5327L	D	2/2	C24v1p7
MISS SPANKIE'S MINUET	51H1H	1H1H2H	Eb	3/4	G3p12
MISS SPENCE'S FAVORITE	3H1H2H5	4324	D	2/4	S4v2p25
MISS SPENS'S REEL	5315L	6L5L2L2	Bb(C)	2/2	Mc10p9/15

MISS SPIER'S REEL	3142	3542	A	2/2	B20p3
MISS SPIERS'S JIGG	1H1H5H1H	2H2H4H7	Eb	6/8	L4p2,3
MISS SPROT'S WALTZ	1H1H1H3H	1H61T2H	C	3/8	R9p23
MISS St CLAIR ERSKINE OF SINCLAIR	1355	1H2H53	A	2/2	W2v2p1
MISS ST. GEORGE'S DOUBLE JIGG	3251	437L7L	A	6/8	S11v2p18
MISS STAGG'S STRATHSPEY	5555	54H72H	Eb	4/4	C22p31
MISS STAGS FANCY	155	22H7	D	9/8	A7v1p10
MISS STANHOPE'S REEL	136L5L	4L3L2L2	G	2/2	J1p23
MISS STEEL OF NORWICH'S REEL	3b3b6b7b	557b2	G	4/4	Mc21v4p41
MISS STENHOUSE'S FAVORITE	1155	4415L	Bb	2/4	W4v2p24
MISS STEPHENS DELIGHT	13L10	2423	Bb	4/4	C23p7
MISS STEUART OF STEUART LODGE'S REEL	1333	137L7L	A	2/2	L4p4
MISS STEVENS OF BROADLAND'S REEL	151H2H	151H2H	D	6/8	S5p19
MISS STEVENSON'S REEL	1353	6L464	Bb	4/4	Mc21v4p38
MISS STEVENSON'S STRATHSPEY	1H531	627L5L	F	4/4	P11v1p19
MISS STEVENSON'S VALTZ	71H4H5H	71H5H1H	C	3/8	G9v4p24
MISS STEWART DEMPSTER'S MINUET	1H54	345	F	3/4	D14v1p13
MISS STEWART DERCULLOCH'S REEL	1H1H2H2H	3H4H2H2	D	2/2	P5v1p14
MISS STEWART DOWALLY'S JIGG	3b15L1	27bL47bL	A	6/8	P5v1p5
MISS STEWART FLEMYING OF KILLIEHASSY'S STRATHSPEY	1L37L2	1L353	A	4/4	S4v1p13
MISS STEWART MENZIES OF CULDAR'S FAVORITE	1346	5327L	D	2/2	P5v4p13
MISS STEWART MITCHELL'S REEL	131H3	4362	E	4/4	P5v1p22
MISS STEWART OF ALLANBANK'S STRATHSPEY	3b13b5	27b27bL	C	4/4	S4v1p8 (II)
MISS STEWART OF BALLECHEN'S FAVOURITE	116L6L	2232	G	6/8	S4v1p1
MISS STEWART OF DERCULUH'S REEL	311H5H	4H3H72H	D	2/2	S11v1p6
MISS STEWART OF EDERADEYNAT'S JIGG	1L135	2252	Bb	6/8	P5v4p18
MISS STEWART OF FASNACLOICH'S(REEL)	1555	6562	A	2/2*	G11v2Dp26 (II)
MISS STEWART OF FOSS' REEL	1H511	4462	D	4/4	Mc19v1p3 Mc19v2p18
MISS STEWART OF GARTH('S REEL)	1131H	2242H	D	2/2	Mc4v4p8 (II)
MISS STEWART OF GARTH'S REEL	3333	27bL44	G A	2/2	A1v5p16 Mc10p12
MISS STEWART OF GARTH'S STRATHSPEY	1353	2422	D	2/2	S4v1p3
MISS STEWART OF GARTH'S STRATHSPEY	3b13b6b	2423b	D	2/2	Mc19v1p2
MISS STEWART (OF) GRANDTULLY ('S STRATHSPEY)	1333	2247bL	A	4/4	G11v1Ap33 G10v1p7 (II)
MISS STEWART OF GRANDTULLY'S REEL	1H513	7b427bL	A	2/2	D14v3p2/3
MISS STEWART (OF GRANTULLY) 'S REEL	1353	7bL242	A	4/4*	G11v1Ap34 G10v1p8
MISS STEWART OF PHYSGILL'S FAVORITE	1H1H53	62H51H	D	6/8	G10v6p7
MISS STEWART OF URRARDS REEL	5331H	537b2	D	2/2	D14v3p16
MISS STEWART STENTON'S REEL	331H5	4542	C	2/2	B11p16
MISS STEWARTS	131H6	436L2	G	2/2	A7v4p10
MISS STEWART'S FAVORITE	1542	4527L	A	3/8	R9p15
MISS STEWART'S GIG	5125L	6L15L3L	Bb	6/8	A7v2p26,27
MISS STEWART'S JIG	1H151	6L27L5L	D	6/8	M4v3p32
MISS STEWART'S JIG	3342	3311H	G	6/8	Mc15p38
MISS STEWART'S MINUET	111	3H51	Eb	3/4	C13v4p39
MISS STEWART'S REEL	6142	3126L	A	2/2	P1v2p7
MISS STEWART'S REEL	15L3b2	5L5L2L4L	A	2/2	H1p4
MISS STEWART'S REEL	115L1	6L5L6L5L	Bb	2/2	Mc16p32
MISS STEWART('S STRATHSPEY)	1133	227L7L	Bb	4/4	Mc13v1p11 Mc13v2p11 (II)
MISS STEWART'S STRATHSPEY	5513	5541H	F	2/2	Mc19v2p11
MISS STEWART'S STRATHSPEY	111L1L	436L2	G	4/4	M4v3p41
MISS STEWART'S WALTZ	5H3H4H3H	5H1H3H1H	C	3/8	R9p22
MISS STIRLING'S REEL	1H3H2H6	1H3H4H3H	D	2/2	Mc21v3p4
MISS STORY'S FAVOURITE	1H3H1H1H	2262	D	2/2	J1p13
MISS STRONACH OF MARNOCH'S STRATHSPEY	5551H	5522	D	4/4	M4v3p35
MISS STRONG'S JIG	333L3	427L2	G	6/8	S4v2p14
MISS STUART OF ALLANBANK'S STRATHSPEY	1342	1343	D	4/4	P11v1p11
MISS SUSAN BOGG'S STRATHSPEY	3135	1H3H2H2	F	2/2	P5v4p22
MISS SUSAN BROWN'S STRATHSPEY	5151	2227bL	D	4/4	C18p30
MISS SUSAN CAMPBELL MONZIES (' STRATHSPEY)	51H52	2436L	D	2/2*	B11p8 (II)
MISS SUSAN ELLIOT('S REEL)	1H3H2H1H	51H2H2	G	2/2	Mc15p8 (II)
MISS SUSAN GORDON('S REEL)	1135	3H535	F	4/4*	M4v3p50 (II)
MISS SUSAN SPALDING'S JIGG	5151	7b427bL	E	6/8	P5v1p6
MISS SUSANNA BAIRD('S REEL)	513b5	27bL24	E	2/2	Mc4v1p9 (II)
MISS SUSANNA CUMMING'S MINUET	552H	1H1H3H	Eb	3/4	S11v2p22
MISS SUSANNA RENTON'S REEL	3135	4246	G	4/4	C7p5
MISS SUTTON'S FAVORITE	123b2	123b1	A	6/8	S4v2p15
MISS SWANSON'S STRATHSPEY	3566	5342	A	4/4	Mc19v2p18
MISS SWINTON'S MINUET	112	37L1	F	3/4	C13v4p43
MISS SWINTON'S REEL	3L3L15L	5L6L4L2L	Bb	2/2	S12v1p52 C13v2p20
MISS SWINTON'S STRATHSPEY	3L3L15L	6L6L4L2L	Bb	4/4	Mc13v2p27 C13v1p47
MISS SYME WILSON	3H1H1H5	31H4H2H	C	4/4	M4v4p14
MISS SYME'S REEL	1353	15L4L2L	Bb	4/4	G3p30
MISS T. WILSON	1H2H1H1H	3622	C	2/4	C26v1p10
MISS TAIT	37L6L1	325L2	Bb	6/8	S4v1p12
MISS TAIT'S FAVORITE	1H3H5H5H	2H71H5	G	6/8	S11v2p16
MISS TAIT'S MINUET	1H1H7	654	A	3/4	S11v2p24
MISS TAYLOR'S FAVORITE, THE	115L5L	2L426L	A	2/2	J1p42
MISS TAYLOR('S REEL)	1H1H1H3H	5H3H1H6	C	2/2*	M4v3p48 (II)

MISS TAYLOR'S REEL	3H1H1H5	44H2H2H	F	2/2	G15p27
MISS THOMPSONS REEL, THE	1111	51H52	Bb	2/2	J1p48
MISS THOM'S REEL	131H1H	5232	G	2/2	D15v1p24
MISS THOMSON	1565	1527L	A	6/8	W2v2p8
MISS THOMSON OF LECKYBANK'S STRATHSPEY	15L13	26L24	A	4/4	P11v2p2
MISS THOMSON'S FAVORITE	115L1	116L2	A	2/4	G10v6p5
MISS TILNEY LONG'S WALTZ	3343	3321	G	3/8	C1v2p2
MISS TINKER('S REEL)	1H565	4522H	F	2/2	D15v1p9 (11)
MISS TODD'S STRATHSPEY	3H5H5H1H	5H6H3H2H	C	2/2	Mc15p31
MISS TOD'S (GEORGES SQUARE) ALLAMADE	1115	5211	G	2/4	G9v4p14
MISS TROTTERS (OF BUSH'S) REEL	5315L	4L3L22L	Bb	2/2	Mc21v2p10
MISS TROTTERS REEL	1H3H52	22H4H3H	D	4/4	C14v19p10,11
MISS TYTLER'S STRATHSPEY	3111	465L2	F	4/4	P11v1p13
MISS URQUHART OF MELDRUM('S REEL)	1361H	5327L	D	2/2*	C24v1p2 (11)
MISS VEARIE HAY('S REEL)	15L2L2	15L5L3	A Bb	4/4*	G8p22 D14v4p8 G9v5p2
					Mc13v2p16 Mc9v3p27 A7v2p32
					G11v2Ap32 D14v1p28 C14v20p16
					K1v1p34 P1v1p9 (11)
MISS VICKOR'S DELIGHT	1H3H61H	5452	D	2/2	C14v2p10
MISS W. DALRYMPLES FANCY	331H5	4425L	Eb	6/8	W4v1p10
MISS WADE'S DELIGHT	5H5H3H3H	4H2H3H1H	D	2/4	A1v3p186
MISS WADE'S MINUET	113	557	Eb	3/4	C22p1,2
MISS WALKER'S STRATHSPEY	1547L	151H3	Bb	4/4	P11v1p5
MISS WALKER'S STRATHSPEY	15L13	246L6L	Bb	4/4	J1p14
MISS WALLACE'S FANCY	3322	16L7L5L	A	2/4	J1p17
MISS WALLACE'S REEL	1565	3H542	F	2/2	C13v2p26
MISS WALLACE'S REEL	1565	4H642	F	2/2	C13v1p6 Mc13v2p21
MISS WARDLAW'S ALLAMANDE	5H5H5#H6H	5H3H1H1H	C	2/4	G9v4p5
MISS WARDLAW'S FAVORITE	3342	3621	A	6/8	S4v2p22
MISS WARDLAW'S REEL	1335	137L7L	G	4/4*	A1v4p49 C5v1p49 W4v1p24
MISS WARDLAW('S STRATHSPEY)	1364	1313H	F	4/4	G10v4p21 (11)
MISS WARDLAW'S STRATHSPEY	116L6L	1113L	Bb	4/4	E2p14
MISS WATSON'S FAVORITE	1351H	5442	Eb	6/8	W4v1p13
MISS WATSON'S REEL	1L113b	27bL47bL	B	4/4	M4v2p4 (11)
MISS WATT'S JIG	3434	37L27L	D	6/8	M4v3p31
MISS WATT('S REEL)	135L3L	1225L	Bb	4/4	D16p18 (11)
MISS WATT'S REEL (NETHER CLUNY)	1353	6L6L22	Bb	2/2	M4v3p9 (11)
MISS WEDDERBURN COLVILL'S FAVORITE	1155	2243	Bb	2/4	S4v2p16
[MISS WEDDERBURN'S] JIGG	5L5L5L1	2231	A	6/8	Mc13v2p24
MISS WEDDERBURN'S REEL	5555	1H3H62	C	4/4	M4v2p4
MISS WEDDERBURN('S REEL)	5L5L5L1	2226L	A	4/4*	N1v1p13 C13v2p75 C14v3p17
					G9v5p15 Mc13v2p24 Mc7p9
					C13v1p24 G11v2Dp27 Mc12v1p32
					(11)
MISS WEDDERBURN'S REEL	5L5L5L1	2216L	A	2/2	B10p23
MISS WEDDERBURN'S (STRATHSPEY/REEL)	5515L	5542	Eb	4/4*	A7v2p28,29 G15p6
MISS WELLESLEY'S FAVORITE	3L4L11	3L6L41	Bb	2/4	C14v26p12
MISS WELLWOOD'S FANCY	315L5L	5L122	A	4/4	Mc13v2p36 Mc9v3p45 C13v1p44
MISS WELSH	531H1H	5353	F	4/4*	G10v5p34,35 (11)
MISS WELSH'S FANCY	313H2H	6562	D	2/2	C14v9p4
MISS WEMYS OF WEMYS'S SCOTS MEASURE	53b13b	53b3b5	D	2/2	Mc4v4p9
MISS WEMYSS OF CUTTELHILLS STRATHSPEY	51H77	1H5H6H5H	C	4/4	W2v2p3
MISS WEMYSS OF DUNDEE('S REEL)	13L4L5L	13L4L2L	Bb	2/2*	W2v1p7 (11)
MISS WEMYSS OF WEMYSS	11H52	1116L	Eb	4/4	G11v1Cp11 G10v3p27
MISS WEMYSS OF WEMYSS FAVORITE	5L33	552	D	3/4	G9v3p34
MISS WEMYSS OF WEMYSS'S REEL	11H35	427L2	F	2/2	S4v1p24
MISS WETHERELL'S STRATHSPEY	1H3H5H5H	4H3H62H	D	2/2	J1p44
MISS WHARTON DUFF	1237L	4L3L2L3	Bb	2/2	M4v3p6
MISS WHARTON DUFF'S JIG	1H654	5L5L5L7L	Bb	6/8	M4v3p6
MISS WHITE OF BRACHLOCH'S STRATHSPEY	11H1H3	137L2	G	4/4	L1p6
MISS WHITEFORD'S JIGG	5651H	5243	G	6/8	H3p15
MISS WHITEFORD'S REEL	3151H	51H22H	C	2/2	R5p57
MISS WHITELOCK'S DELIGHT	13b55	3b115L	G	4/4	R12v2p11
MISS WHITE'S JIG	3L5L15L	6L6L27L	Bb	6/8	G3p24
MISS WIESES WALTZ	1H543	1H551	F	3/8	C14v14p7
MISS WILCKE'S ALLEMAND	1H5H1H5H	4H2H4H6	D	2/4	C1v1p9
MISS WILHELMINA McDOWAL'S REEL	5H6H5H6H	5H3H2H2H	C	2/2	M4v3p44,45
MISS WILLES OF LESLIES BIRTHDAY	1H1H33	1H1H62H	C	2/2	W2v1p8,9
MISS WILLIAMS	1315	2266	Bb	4/4	W2v2p6
MISS WILLIAMS FANCY	511H6	517L2	F	6/8	C14v23p13
MISS WILLIAMSON OF OLDFIELD'S JIGG	1H2H1H5	4525L	D	6/8	G15p13
MISS WILLIAMSON OF POLMONT'S REEL	1133	2244	F	2/2	Mc4v4p7
MISS WILLIAMSON'S JIGG	1L12L2	537L7L	Bb	6/8	S4v1p14
MISS WILLIAMSON'S REEL	357L2	3522	G	4/4	A1v5p36 C5v1p36 Mc10p14
MISS WILLIAMSON('S STRATHSPEY)	3146	51H22	D	2/2*	Mc4v1p12 (11)
MISS WILLISON'S REEL	31H64	42H2H6	D	2/2	Mc10p2
MISS WILLIS'S STRATHSPEY	151H6	1542	G	4/4	C14v10p14
MISS WILLY ALEXANDER	5L133	5522	G	2/2	C5v1p53 A1v4p53 Mc12v1p4
MISS WILSON OF CULLIN'S REEL	5526L	5555	D	2/2	Mc9v3p3 Mc12v1p53
MISS WOODCOCK'S REEL	1113	51H52	G	2/2	J1p6
MISS WOOD'S MINUET	112	321	Bb	3/4	R6v1p10
MISS WRIGHT OF LATON('S REEL)	1H535	2424	D	2/2	B11p17 (11)

Title					
MISS YORK'S HORNPIPE	1513b	7L47L2	C	2/2	B16v3p68
MISS YOUNG('S STRATHSPEY)	5555	3H1H2H2H	C	4/4	M4v3p47 (II)
MISS YOUNG'S STRATHSPEY	5555	2462	A	4/4	C23p14
MISS Z. LOUGHNAN ('S STRATHSPEY)	3555	236L6L	C	4/4	G11v1Cp9 G10v3p23
MISS ZOFFANY WEIPPERT WALTZ	5L5L5L1	5L5L21	Bb	3/8	C14v12p8
MISSES FIDDES' WALTZ, THE	1H1H1H5H	5H4H2H1H	D	3/8	D6p11
MISSES FORBES' WALTZ, THE	1127L	1121	Bb	3/8	D6p10
(MISS/LADY) CUNNINGHAM'S STRATHSPEY	1H155	2H4H72H	D	4/4	A1v4p54 C5v1p54 A7v6p24 A1v6p5
(MISS/LADY) MARY DOUGLAS('S FAVORITE)	3L5L6L5L	3L5L32	Bb	6/8	Mc21v4p3 C14v18p2 N1v1p9
MISTAKE, THE	11H11H	657L2	A	6/8	R12v1p74
MITTINS DANCE, THE	1155	671H1H	G	2/2	W7p23
MNATHAN CHROSPUIL IS BHAILE MHUIRICH	1565	6653	G	6/8	Mc5p9
MNATHAN TRODACH OBAIR-THAIRBH	53b3b7b	4226	G	2/2	F2v2p28(18)
MO CHAILIN DONN OG	1565	6225	D	6/8	Mc5p7
MO CHAILIN OG THOIR LE TOIGH	3333	3655	Eb	4/4	F2v2p102(92)
AN AIRE DHOMH					
MO CHEAN AIR AN UR GHIBHT [MO CHION...]	215L	212	A	3/4	F2v2p91(81)
MO CHRUINNEAG GHREANNAR	1H51H1H	3H2H1H1H	D	4/4	Mc5p11
MC DHUCHAS [MO DHUTHCHAS)	5313	5316L	D	4/4	F2v2p34(24)
MO GHAOL AN COLGAIRNEACH SPRAICEIL	113b	422	A	9/8	Mc1v1p117
MO GHRADH FODH LEON	345	211	G	3/4	F2v2p41(31)
MO LEANNAN FALAICH	3555	31H3H6	G	4/4	F2v2p30(20)
MO NIGHEAN DHUBH NA TREIG MI	3b3b53bH	7b6b51	E	4/4	F2v2p67(57)
MO RUN AN DIUGH MAR AN DE THU	3516L	61H53	G	6/8	F2v2p77(67)
MO RUN GEAL OG	1315L	5L335	G	12/8	Mc5p28
MO RUN GEAL OG	131	5L33	Bb	9/8	F2v2p95(85)
MOAR NEIN I GIBERLAN	1154	1425L	A	2/4	A1v2p61
MOCH MADAINN CHEITEIN	13b27bL	7b422	A	6/8	Mc5p24
MOCK DOCTOR, THE	51H1H1H	3bH7b53b	D	2/2	P9p37
MODERATE	3b23b1	5550	A	4/4	Mc5p4
MODERATE	5L13b4	5522	E	6/8	Mc5p9
MODERATE	5L11	222	A	3/4	Mc5p5
MODERATE	17bL7bL	23b2	A	9/8	Mc5p6
MODERATE	1H1H5	7b41	E	9/8	Mc5p12
MODERATO	1H3H2H1H	1H3H2H1H	D	2/4	M2p5
MOLADGH MARI	153	135	A	3/4	Mc1v1p73-79
MOLE CATCHER'S DAUGHTER, THE	111	7L6L5L	Bb	3/4	G11v1Cp26
MOLL IN THE WAD [MOLL ITH WAD]	316L1	3125L	G	6/8	C14v12p10 Mc13v2p12
MOLL IN THE WADD	13b13b	13b47bL	E	6/8	K1v1p20
MOLL IN THE WAD(D)	53b13b	53b47bL	G E	6/8	P5v3p22 A1v5p44 G11v2Ap18
					G9v5p18 Mc7p21 C23p13
MOLL ROSS	1H327	1H351H	C	6/8	R12v1p23
MOLLY APPLE PYE	1111	4415	A	2/4	B16v3p54
MOLLY'S DELIGHT	17L13b	243b1	G	2/2	R12v1p45
MOLONIE'S GIG	3555	6562	C	6/8	Mc9v2p38
MOMENTS APPROACHING, THE	335	531H	D	3/4	C10v2Ap60
MONAGHAN JIG, THE	3b13b5	3b124	E	6/8	G10v5p31
MONALTRIES(REEL)	11H51	437L2	F	2/2	P5v1p4 (II)
MONALTRIE'S STRATHSPEY	517b1H	53H2H2	F	4/4	Mc21v2p18 P5v1p18
MONALTRIE'S WELCOME HOME TO BALLATERS	1353	1324	F	2/2	P5v4p9
MONEY IN BOTH POCKETS	1H355	1H353H	D	6/8	A7v5p20 A7v3p29
MONEY IN BOTH POCKETS	1H355	1H354H	D	6/8	G11v1Cp30 C14v5p5 G10v3p30
					Mc4v3p8 P5v1p11 Mc12v1p60
MONKTON LASSES, THE	1524	12H3H2H	D	4/4	F3p18
MONMOUTH STREET	1131	4650	G	4/4	A1v6p21
MONSIEUR PANTIN	5454	1H423	G	6/8	R12v1p68
MONSIEUR THE COUNT D'ARTOIS'S REEL	3H2H65	5565	C	2/2	Mc21v3p31
MONTRILE	1215	5431	Bb	6/8	C14v24p17
MONTROSE ASSEMBLY	1L113b	24L2L2L	B	2/2	D15v1p30
MONTROSE ASSEMBLY	1355	26L27	G	6/8	A7v1p7
MONTROSE BRIDGE	13b11	27bL42	E	6/8	D15v1p8
MONTROSE RACES	3b5L3b6b	24L25	G	4/4	P5v2p2
MONTROSE SCOTS MEASURE	5L111	3366	G	4/4	O1v1Jp94
MONYFIETH RANGERS REEL	15L21	15L23	Bb	2/2	M1p2
MONYMUSK	5354	5324	G A F	4/4*	A7v2p3 P10p23 A1v4p33
					K1v1p12,13 G7p13 A7v6p10,11
					C13v1p41 G11v2Ap10 N1v1p10
					D15v2p49 C8v2p9 C8v1p25
					G9v5p10 W6p15 C5v1p14 P5v2p11
					(II)
MOON WALTZ	332H6	572H1H	D	3/8	G1v1p40,41
MOONLIGHT ON THE GREEN	1115	11H66	D	2/2	O1v1Dp26,27
MOONMORE'S STRATHSPEY	5155	1H3H2H2	C	4/4	G15p33
MOOR LAND WILLIE	112	3b3b4	G	6/4	Mc8v1Bp54
MOOR SO WETT, THE	1331	1327bL	G	12/8	B11p8
MOORINGS	3H74H1H	3H1H1H3H	D	4/4	A1v6p55
MOORLAND BALLAD	17L15L	5333	F	2/4	C10v2Bp49
MOORLAND WILLIE [cf: MUIRLAND WILLIE]	3b3b1	3b3b4	D A	6/8	Mc8v1Cp17 C20p75
MOORLAND WILLY	13b55	27b42	D	6/8	A7v2p22
MOR NIAN A GHIBARLAN	1154	17bL25L	G	4/4	F2v2p96(86)
[MOR NIGHEAN A GHIOBARLAIN]					
MOR NIAN A GHIOBALAIN	1154	1121	A	4/4	Mc5p21 (II)

Name			Key	Time	Sources
MORAG	1H3bH2H5	1H2H7b5	E	4/4	A1v5p52 G1v1p11
MORAG	1H3bH2H7	1H2H7b6b	D	2/4	F2v1p11
MORAG	1H53b4	6b511	D	4/4	F2v2p57(47) D14v2p46 G10v4p33
MORAY'S FROLICK, THE	3b41H2H	1H7b55	D	6/8	G10v5p3
MORAY-SHIRE FARMER'S CLUB, THE	136L7L	131H3	G	2/2	M4v3p39
MORDELIA	5L123	5L6L6L5L	Bb	6/8	G9v3p1
MORDINGTON HOUSE	113bL5L	2L4L2L4L	A	2/2	Mc13v1p7 Mc13v2p7
MORE N'INGHEAN GHIBERLAN	5L117bL	2214	A	4/4	O1v2p35 O1v3p45 O1v1Ap17
MORFA RHUDDLAN	113b	443b	A	3/4	C5v1p17 A1v5p17 Mc12v2p49
MORFHEAR SHIMM [MORAR SIM]	3121	5L151H	F	4/4	C8v1p37 F2v2p63(53)
MORGAN RATTLER, (THE)	5231	5266	C D	6/8	P6v2p19 P10p15 A1v5p41 A7v6p80
					C14v3p7 P5v1p5/6 G10v3p30
					Mc12v1p31 A7v3p33
MORGIANA	51H1H5	51H2H2H	F	6/8	D15v2p50
MORGIANA	53H1H5	51H4H1H	F	6/8	H6v5p1 P6p25
MORGIANA IN IRELAND	5L123	5L133	Bb G	6/8	D15v2p50 E1v2p34,35
MORGIANA IN RUSSIA	1H3H2H2H	1H3H2H7	G	2/4	G1v2p68
MORISON'S FANCY	1113	3113	Eb	4/4	M11v1p16,17
MORMOND	5L122	5L123	A	4/4	C18p9
MORN RETURNS, THE	5H3bH5H1T	5H2H1H4H	D	4/4	E1v2p92
MORNING SERENADE	1116L	5L213	Bb	2/4	W4v2p5
MORNING STAR STEAM BOAT, THE	5142	5145L	A	6/8	B20p18,19
MORNING THOUGHT, THE	1355	5555	D	2/2	H1p5
MORNING WALK TO BERRY-DEN, A	151H5	6L237L	G	6/8	S5p23
MORPETH RANT	1H533	6677	D	4/4	A7v6p47
MORPETH RANT	15L3L3L	6L6L7L7L	G Bb	4/4*	C14v10p13 (D2) G9v5p25 P5v2p17
					(11)
MORPETH RANT, THE	13L6L7L	357L2	Bb G	2/4	Mc4v3p8 L1p20
MORTLACH REEL, THE	1353	2464	F	2/2	K1v2p31 M4v3p53
MOSCOW	3455	64H2H2H	D	2/4	C14v27p1
MOSS HOUSE, LOGIEALMOND, THE	3211	3522	Eb	6/8	Mc22p22
MOSS PLATE	3551H	3H3H2H1H	C	4/4	R4p5,6
MOTHER GOOSE	551	6L22	Bb	9/8	P6v1p20
(MOTHER) GOOSE, (THE)	5H5H5H6H	2H2H5H	C	4/4*	A7v4p5 A7v5p4
MOTHER MIDNIGHT'S TASTE	5437L	6L237L	Bb	6/8	B16v3p31
MOTHER QUOTH HODGE THE NEW WAY	51H2H3H	4H72H1H	D	6/8	R12v1p18
MOTHER'S LAMENT	17b17bL	4445	A	4/4	Mc5p30
ON THE DEATH OF HER CHILD, A					
MOUNT SION	1H1H11	1H1H41	A	6/8	S7v1p48
MOUNT STEWART HOUSE	5313	6542	F	2/2	Mc12v1p36,37
MOUNT YOUR BAGGAGE	1355	1564	D	4/4	G10v2p16,17 G11v1Bp14,15
					A1v2p27
MOUNT YOUR BAGGAGE [MOUNT MY BAGGAGE]	1516	3215	A G	2/4	R4p23,24,25,26 O1v1Gp26,27
MOUNT YOUR BAGGAGE	1516	4215	D	2/4	O1v5p36,37 C20p74
MOUNT YOUR BAGGAGE	115	515	F	3/2	B15v1p109
MOUNT YOUR HORSES	1115	4111	Bb	2/4	W4v1p14
MOUNTING OF THE AIR BALLOON, THE	1323	1321	G	6/8	S5p14
MOURNFUL AM I	1256	52H65	D	6/8	Mc5p7
MOURNFUL IS MY STORY	51H65	57b7b6	E	4/4	C10v2Bp42
MOWBRAY CASTLE	1313	247L2	G	2/4	H6v10p3
MOZART'S GRAND WALTZ	555	555	G	3/4	B7p13
MR A. CAMPBELL'S STRATHSPEY	316L5L	3L142	Bb	4/4	P5v4p19
MR A. CUMMING'S FANCY	551H1H	5525L	D	2/2	C14v16p10
MR A. JAFFRAY'S STRATHSPEY	3365	1H542	F	4/4	Mc10p2/3
MR A. MACWHINNIE'S REEL	3543	2427bL	G	2/2	Mc15p38
MR A. OSWALD'S JIG	157bL4	151H5	E	6/8	F3p8,9
MR A. PEARSON'S (FAVOURITE) STRATHSPEY	1H57b4	1H553bH	B E	4/4	A1v5p49 A1v4p70 F2v1p3
MR A. PURSE'S REEL	351H5	432H2	A	2/2	Mc15p15
MR A. R. SUTHERLAND'S REEL	1H531	4327L	D	2/2	P11v1p10
MR ADAM FERGUSON'S FAVORITE REEL	13b53b	7bL224	B	2/2	Mc22Ap3
MR ADAM ROBERTSON'S FAVORITE	13b55	27bL7b2	A	6/8	C21p9
MR ADm SHIRREFF'S VALTZ	1L15L2	35L31	Bb	3/8	W4v2p28
MR ALDRIGES FAVORITE HORNPIPE	13L25L	47L27L	Bb	2/4	Mc21v4p4,5
MR. ALEXANDER DOWNIE'S WALTZ	5541	551H5	Bb	3/8	A4v2p2,3
MR ALEXANDER LAING'S HORNPIPE	1H3H1H6	61H64	E	2/2	M4v3p37
MR ALEXANDER OSWALD'S REEL	1155	2H2H4H2H	C	2/2	W2v1p4
MR ALEXr. CAMPBELL'S STRATHSPEY	136L1	1355	G	4/4	P11v1p17
MR ALEXr CUNNINGHAM('S STRATHSPEY)	146L2	1435	D	4/4*	G10v3p36 G11v1Cp1
MR ALEXr GRAHAM'S REEL	3H3H2H1H	3H3H22H	D	2/2	A7v1p12
MR ALEXr. HUNTER OF BLACKNESS'S	111	6L5L5L	A	3/4	D16p2,3
FAVORITE MINUET					
MR ALEXr IRVINE'S STRATHSPEY	1H651	436L6L	D	4/4	Mc19v1p2 Mc19v2p19
MR ALEXr LESLIE'S STRATHSPEY	15L3bL5L	15L11	A	2/2	G15p2
MR ALEXr McDOUGALL ARDBEG'S REEL	1551	1562	D	2/2	Mc16p13
MR ALEXr MINZIE'S HORNPIPE	5551H	51H51	G	2/2	D16p26
MR ALEXr. MITCHEL, CRAIGS REEL	5313	6542	F	2/2	Mc22p21
MR ALEXr MONTGOMERIE'S REEL	13b3b1	247b2	G	2/2	R5p59
MR ALEXr. PATERSON'S STRATHSPEY	5364	5361H	D	2/2	B20p12
MR ALEXr THOM'S HORNPIPE	3115	4224	F	4/4	D6p34
MR ALEXr. THOM'S HORNPIPE	15L1L4	27L2L1	Bb	4/4	D6p4
MR ALLAN GRANT'S STRATHSPEY	1111	236L6L	D	4/4	G15p13
MR AND: LAUGHLAN'S WELCOME TO BANFF	115L5L	2L236L	Bb	2/2	(C24v2)*

MR AND W HENDERSON'S FAVORITE	5551H	3H4H2H2	D	4/4	Mc16p7
MR ANDERSON'S STRATHSPEY	131H3	7bL27bL7bL	D	4/4	P5v2p23
MR ANDREW NICOLL'S REEL	316L5L	2462	Bb	2/2	A4v1p2
MR ANDREW THOMSONS REEL	15L5L3b	27bL7bL4	A	4/4	W2v2p11
MR ARCHd CAMPBELL ARDMORE'S REEL	15L3L5L	6L2L7L2	Bb	2/2	Mc16p21
MR ARCHd CAMPBELL BALMARTIN	3L3L11	3L6L4L2L	Bb	4/4	Mc16p23
MR ARCHD DOW OF PERTH'S QUICK STEP	1H1H2H5	1H1H5H5H	C	2/4	C23p9
MR ARTHUR THOMSON'S WALTZ	3427L	3421	Bb	3/8	D6p9
MR BAILLIE OF MELLERSTON'S STRATHSPEY	557bL2	5513b	E	4/4	G10v3p25 (II)
[MR BAILLIE OF MELLERSTAIN]					
MR BAIRD OF NEWBYTH'S JIGG	5155	27bL44	E	6/8	Mc4v1p18
MR BAIRD OF NEWBYTH'S REEL	1535	2424	D?	2/2	Mc4v1p7
MR BALLANTYNE'S JIG	3H1H11H	3H1H22H	C	6/8	B2p6
MR BARCLAY DUN'S HORNPIPE	1324	3544	Bb	2/2	M11v1p9
MR BERNARD'S REEL	15L37L	6L5L3L5L	F	4/4	G10v5p11 (II)
MR BERRY'S REEL	113b5	1H7b27bL	E	2/2	Mc15p12
MR BINDEN'S FANCY	1115	1126	G	6/8	A1v5p51
MR BINDON'S QUICK STEP	137L2	1332	Bb	6/8	W4v2p17
MR BLACK'S STRATHSPEY	1346	51H46L	Eb	4/4	R9p14
MR BOSWELL OF AUCHINLECK'S REEL	13b51	247b2	G	4/4	F3p11
MR BRANDER OF PITGAVNEY'S STRATHSPEY	3316L	5L132	Bb	4/4	G15p23
MR BRANDER OF SPRINGFIELD'S STRATHSPEY	16L5L3	16L4L2L	A	4/4	G15p20
MR. BRISBANE'S STRATHSPEY	331H5	2H4H72H	D	4/4	M6p3
MR BRODIE OF BRODIE'S FAVOURITE	4321	7L242	F	2/4	J2p12
MR BRODIE OF BRODIE'S REEL	6452	31H76	A	2/2	T1v2p6
MR BRODIE OF BRODIE'S STRATHSPEY	5L15L1	5122	D	4/4	L1p1
MR BRODIE'S REEL	1546	1542	Bb	2/4	J2p16
MR BROWN OF KELLYBANK'S MARCH	1133	5342	A	4/4	B20p15
MR BRUCE'S REEL	1353	5L7L27L	Eb	4/4	C18p15
MR BRUCE'S STRATHSPEY	3153	25L27L	Eb	4/4	C18p15
MR BUCHAN OF AUCHMACOY'S REEL	1H535	2662	D	2/2	M11v2p6
MR BUIST'S FROLIC	315L1	437L2	A	4/4	W2v1p14
MR BUSBY MAITLANDS REEL	3b13b1	3b7bL7bL7bL	E	4/4	Mc21v3p13
MR BUSHBY MAITLAND'S REEL	351H1H	1H1H2H2	D	2/2	C5v1p65 G10v3p8 A1v4p68
					G11v1Bp33 E1v1p21
MR C. CAMPBELL'S REEL	15L13	4542	F	2/2	Mc22Bp2
MR CAMPBELL OF ACHNABREACK'S SALUTATION	2H2H1H1H	6636	G	6/8	D14v2p13
MR CAMPBELL OF GLENLYON'S REEL	3453	47b27bL	A	2/2	Mc4v1p13
MR CAMPBELL OF KINLOCH	5555	2462	A	2/2	Mc4v2p8
MR CAMPBELL YOUNGER OF CRAIGNISH'S REEL	3531H	3542	F	2/2	Mc4v4p4/5
MR CAMPBELL'S HORNPIPE	113L1	6L216L	Bb	2/2	R9p7
MR CHARLES GIBSON,	1152	7b427bL	E	2/2	Mc19v3p8
PITLOCHRY'S STRATHSPEY					
MR CHARLES GRAHAM(S STRATHSPEY)	15L3L1L	227L2	A	2/2*	B11p19 (II)
MR CHARLES MONTGOMERY'S STRATHSPEY	1L3L5L1	5426L	A	4/4	B2p3
MR CHARLES OLIPHANT	1H1H1H5H	1H762H	C	2/2	G9v5p4
MR (CHARLES) SHARP OF HODDOM('S GIGA)	5653	6542	D	6/8	G11v1Cp17 G10v1p26
MR (CHARLES) SHARP (OF HODDOM)'S REEL	3b15L3b	247b2	G	2/2	C13v1p38 C13v2p67
MR CHARLES STEWART (PETTYVAICH)	1353	6L427L	Bb	2/2	M4v4p16
MR CHAs GORDON'S STRATHSPEY	5162	5153H	D	4/4	G15p15
MR CHAs GRAHAM'S WELCOME HOME	5L121	4427bL	A	6/8	G10v2p20
MR CHAS GRAHAM'S WELCOME HOME	5L121	4427bL	A	6/8	G11v1Cp23
MR CHURCHILLS REEL	3L112	6L26L2	Bb	2/2	B12p5
MR CLARK'S FAVOURITE	53b53b	3b7b42	A	2/4	Mc22p8
MR COLIN CAMPBELL'S STRATHSPEY	1313	6L27L5L	F	2/2	Mc22Bp2
MR COMPTON OF CARHAM-HALL'S REEL	1351H	1326L	A	4/4	G11v2Dp4 (II)
[MR COMPTON OF COMPTON HALL]					
MR CONNEL'S STRATHSPEY	15L13	6522	A	4/4	Mc16p26
MR CRAWFURD OF ARDMILLAN'S REEL	3135	4642	F	2/2	R5p12
MR CREAGH'S IRISH TUNE	5L113b	51H1H1H	B	4/4	T7p42,43
MR CREECH'S STRATHSPEY	5L247bL	5L251	A	4/4	W4v2p23
MR CROOK'S FAVOURITE	1124	6521	Eb	6/8	S4v1p12
MR CUMING'S STRATHSPEY	1L3L13	6L526L	Bb	2/2	R9p24
MR D. BRIDGES REEL	331H3H	6522	D	2/2	A1v5p37 C5v1p37 Mc10p8
[MR D. BRIDGES JNR'S REEL]					
MR D. STEWART OF GARTH'S JIGG	11H7b1H	7b47b7bL	C	12/8	F2v1p8
MR DANL McFARLANE'S DELIGHT	5162	5125L	D	6/8	C21p16
MR DAVID BLACK'S FAVOURITE	13b42	11H3bH1H	E	6/8	D15v1p8
MR DAVID DUNCAN'S REEL	63H1H1H	6526L	D	6/8	W2v1p9
MR DAVID DUN'S HORNPIPE	1132	5531	Bb	2/2	M11v1p16
MR DAVID DUN'S STRATHSPEY	5L351H	5642	F	2/2	M11v1p9
MR DAVID MAXWELL'S FAVOURITE	1562	3431	A	6/8	P11v1p6
MR DAVID McDOWALL'S STRATHSPEY	1H354	4522H	D	2/2	B11p8
MR DAVID STEWART('S REEL)	5333	2427bL	A	2/2	Mc4v1p17 (II)
MR DAVID SUTTER'S REEL	5354	5324	F	2/2	Mc16p26
MR DAVIDSON OF CANTRAY'S STRATHSPEY	16L5L5L	1532	D	4/4	P11v1p10
MR DAVIDSON'S STRATHSPEY	146L2	1423	G	2/2	A1v5p42
MR DAVIDSON'S STRATHSPEY	1423	146L2	G	2/2	D15v1p4
MR DAVIE PIRIE'S HORNPIPE	5551H	7532	Bb	4/4	D6p30
MR DON'S FAVORITE	553H	2H61H	D	3/4	G9v3p34,35
MR DOUGAL CAMPBELL OF BALLINABY'S	5L5L1L5L	2L1L2L4L	Bb	2/2	Mc16p16
STRATHSPEY					

MR DOUGAL McDOUGAL'S FAVORITE	1H1H31	4462	G	2/2	Mc16p15
MR DOUGLAS(S) OF BRIGTON('S STRATHSPEY)	3L3L11	4L6L4L2L	Bb	4/4	D16p36 (II)
MR DRUMMOND OF PERTH'S STRATHSPEY	1515	54H2H2	E	2/2	Mc4v3p7
MR DRUMMOND YOUNGER OF PERTH'S STRATHSPEY	1555	1562	G	4/4	A1v4p62 G10v3p31
MR DUFF (OF FETTERESSO'S) BIRTH DAY	5653	5342	F	4/4	P5v2p16
MR DUFF (OF FETTERESSO'S) BIRTHDAY	1H3H1H5	1H3H2H2	F	2/2	M11v1p1
MR DUFF (OF FETTERESSO'S) STRATHSPEY	5L135	526L1	G	2/2	M11v1p2
MR DUFF'S FAVOURITE MINUET	111	222	Eb	3/4	D15v2p8
(MR) DUFF'S (FAVOURITE) SCOTS MEASURE	5553	5553	D	4/4	A1v5p42 D15v1p7
MR DUGALD CAMPBELL ARDMORE'S FAVORITE	3b3b44	3b13b5	A	2/2	Mc16p6
MR DUGALD CAMPBELL ARDMORE'S JIG	313	316	A	9/8	Mc16p24
MR DUNCAN FORBES DUFF OF MUIRTOWN'S R.	1627L	15L6L2L	Bb	2/2	M12p19
MR DUNCAN OF GARMOUTH'S STRATHSPEY	5L152	4L7bL42	G	2/2	G15p36,37
MR DUNCAN'S DELIGHT	3135	4246	D	6/8	Mc13v1p4 Mc13v2p4
MR DUNDAS MCQUEEN('S REEL)	13b3b5	7b422	C	2/2	G10v2p30 (II)
MR DUNn CAMPBELL ROCKSIDE'S REEL	2556	2563	G	2/2	Mc16p8
MR DUN'S FAVOURITE	15L5L5L	16L22L	Bb	2/4	M11v1p13
MR DUN'S FROLICK	5153	5153	F	2/2	G10v3p13 G11v1Bp30 (II)
MR E. CAMPBELL ARDMORE'S REEL	1333	227L2	A	2/2	Mc16p21,22
(MR E. MARJORIBANKS'S) HORNPIPE	1342	26L16L	Bb	2/2	P11v1p7 C22p32
MR E. MARJORIBANKS'S QUICKSTEP	13L6L6L	1446L	Bb	2/4	P11v2p11
MR EDMONDSTONE OF NEWTON'S STRATHSPEY	1513b	1522	A	2/2	S4v1p23
MR EDMONDSTOUNE OF NEWTON'S FAVORITE	5531	3L4L27L	F	6/8	S4v2p10
MR EDWARD SANDER'S STRATHSPEY	5353	547L2	F	2/2	D15v1p25
MR EDWARD SIMPSON'S FANCY	1153	112H7	F	2/2	M4v3p53
MR EDWARD WAGSTAFF'S FANCY	5H5H1H6H	4H2H1H6	C	4/4	M4v3p47
MR EDWARD WARDEN'S FAVORITE	331H3	27bL24	A	4/4	C21p5
MR EDWARD'S HORNPIPE	1H1H33	671H6	F	2/2	C14v15p10
MR F. G. CAMPBELL OF TROUP AND GLENLYON'S REEL	37L35	1H365	F	2/2	C18p2
MR F. H. BINDON'S MARCH	5551H	4231	G	4/4	A1v5p43
MR FAIRBANKS MINUET	1H55	321	G	3/4	W7p26
MR FAIRBANKS RIGADOON	1111	3352	G	6/8	W7p26
(MR) FAIRVIELLES MINUET	334	553	A	3/4	C22p11 D15v2p2
MR FARQUHAR CAMPBELL'S STRATHSPEY	3b215	47bL47bL	A	4/4	Mc16p31
MR FERGUSON OF RAITH'S STRATHSPEY	1115	2246	G	2/2	G9v2p10
MR FISHER'S HORNPIPE	1115	7531	G	4/4	F1p34
MR FLEMYNG'S REEL	3b3b47L	3b125L	G	4/4	Mc19v2p21
MR FLEMYNG'S REEL	3b3b47bL	3b125L	G	4/4	Mc19v1p5
MR FLETCHER'S REEL	1327L	1355	G	2/2	C18p40
MR FLETCHER'S STRATHSPEY	3153	5432	G	4/4	C18p40
MR FOOTES REEL	31H61H	31H62	A	2/2	C23p11
MR FORTATH'S REEL	1H3H1H6	51H3H2H	Eb	2/2	G15p5
MR FRANCISCO D'SOUZA'S FAVORITE	1131	2462	A	2/4	R9p15
(MR) FRANK WALKER('S) STRATHSPEY	1L1L5L6L	2L26L2	Bb	4/4	G11v1Cp35 A7v4p5
MR FRASER'S FANCY	1525	1523	G	6/8	C14v5p17
MR FRASER'S FAVORITE	553bH2H	1H7b47bL	E	4/4	G10v4p25
MR F-----'S BIRTH-DAY	113b5	7bL7bL7bL2	A	4/4	M11v2p12
MR G DOUGLASS OF TILIWHILLY'S STRATHSPEY	5351H	5122	F	4/4	Mc4v4p7
MR G. KENNEDY'S MINUET	333	351H	F	3/4	R6v1p10
MR G. PATERSON'S REEL	1155	4326L	A	2/2	W2v2p10
MR GARDEN JUNr (OF TROUP'S) STRATHSPEY	151H3	6532	F	4/4	P5v2p4
MR GARDEN JUNr's RETURN AND WELCOME TO TROOP HOUSE	11H1H3bH	47b7b2H	C	6/8	P5v4p1
MR GARDEN (OF TROUP'S) FAREWELL TO FRANCE	1353H	1H422	F	4/4	P5v2p1
MR GARDEN (OF TROUP'S) REEL	11H3bH1H	5427bL	C	4/4	P5v2p12
MR GARDEN OF TROUP'S RETURN HOME FROM BATH	3b513b	247b2	E	4/4	Mc21v4p35
MR GARDEN OF TROUP'S STRATHSPEY	5151H	3H4H2H2	C	4/4	Mc21v4p8
MR GARDEN (OF TROUP'S) STRATHSPEY	5L3b53b	7bL242	G	4/4	P5v2p3
MR GARDEN'S WELCOME HOME TO TROUPE HOUSE	51H65	3642	F	4/4	P5v2p1
MR GEO. BROWN'S HORNPIPE	1H644	2H531H	D	4/4	D6p14,15
MR GEO. F. MACKENZIE OF ALLANGRANGE'S STR.	3144	357L2	D	4/4	Mc11p11
MR GEO THOMPSON'S JUNr's WALTZ	1H5H2H1H	1H5H2H1H	D	3/8	D6p20
MR GEO. THOMSON JUNr'S HORNPIPE	3535	31H75	G	4/4	D6p14
MR GEORGE A. YOUNG	45L45	354H2H	Eb	4/4	M4v4p32
MR GEORGE ANDERSON'S STRATHSPEY	5L343	5L347L	G	4/4	D16p19
MR GEORGE CHRISTIE'S DELIGHT	5356	537L2	F	4/4	C21p6
MR GEORGE FORBES Yr OF NEW AND EDINGLASSIE	113b2	227b2	F	2/2	M4v4p34
MR GEORGE GOODON'S REEL [MR GEORGE GORDON]	52H1H5	47b54	G	2/2	Mc9v3p13 (II)
MR GEORGE GORDON'S STRATHSPEY	5L31H3	5522	A	2/2	M11v1p10
MR GEORGE GRANT'S STRATHSPEY	3542	3455	E	4/4	G10v4p36
MR GEORGE HOGARTH'S FAVORITE	17L6L6	2H71H6	A	2/2	G9v2p20
MR. GEORGE HUNTER'S REEL	1H535	1H366	D	4/4	M6p3
MR GEORGE JENKIN'S REEL	1115	27b27bL	E	2/2	G9v2p7

Title					
MR GEORGE JENKIN'S SCOTISH MEASURE	6L4L5L1	3327L	A	4/4	G10v6p18,19
MR GEORGE JENKIN'S STRATHSPEY	153b1	1H2H7b7bL	E	2/2	G9v2p6
MR GEORGE MUNRO'S REEL	11H53b	7bL7b27bL	G	2/2	J2p1
MR GEORGE NEWTON'S JIG	113b1	27bL44	D	6/8	Mc22p5
MR GIBB'S JIG	1351	2252	Bb	6/8	M12p20
MR GIBSON'S FAVORITE	3211	5625L	A	2/4	C23p9
MR GILLAN'S REEL	5L5L5L1	3427L	A	2/2	C18p4
MR GILLAN'S STRATHSPEY	3L5L5L1	3211	A	4/4	C18p4
MR GORDON OF HALLHEAD'S STRATHSPEY	13L13L	137L2	G	4/4	M4v3p40 (II)
(MR) GRAHAM OF ORCHILL'S (STRATHSPEY/REEL)	5553	5522	F G	4/4*	G10v1p3 (II) A7v4p18 A1v6p4 G1v1p45
MR GRAHAM STIRLING OF AIRTH'S STRATHSPEY	151H1H	6542	F	2/2	B20p6
MR GRANT OF GLENQUICH'S STRATHSPEY [MR GRANT OF GLENQUAICH]	1155	2266	D	4/4	D16p17 (II)
MR GRANT OF KINAIRD('S REEL)	5327L	15L4L2L	Bb	2/2	Mc4v3p4 (II)
MR GRANT OF KINNEARD'S REEL	1355	1H522	F	2/2	D16p33
MR GRANT OF PITNACHREE'S STRATHSPEY	1H353	4622H	D	4/4	Mc4v4p5
MR GRANT OF ROTHYMURCHUS STRATHSPEY	535L6L	5L462	D	4/4	Mc21v2p7
MR GRAY OF CARSE REEL	5H3H2H7	1H542	C	2/2*	D16p22 (II)
MR GUN MONRO POYNTZFIELD('S REEL)	1353	532H2	C	4/4*	L1p4 (II)
MR H. BROWN OF FULHAM FANCY	3H535	3H3H4H2H	C	6/8	C14v22p16
MR HADDEN'S HORNPIPE	5432	1117L	Bb	4/4	D15v2p45
MR HAIGES FAVOURITE	2565	2552	A	2/2	Mc22p7
MR HAMILTON OF BARGENNY'S MINUET	112	3b15	A	3/4	R5p8
MR HAMILTON OF PENCAITLAND'S STRATHSPEY	12H61H	11H72H	C	4/4	G10v2p13 Mc12v1p61
MR HAMILTON OF WISHAW'S REEL	3H1H1H5	2H4H2H2	D	2/2	A1v4p72 C5v1p72
(MR HAMILTON OF) WISHAW('S) (REEL)	3115L	2422L	Bb	4/4*	C13v4p32 G11v1Bp32 G8p10 C14v8p8 G10v3p18 P1v1p14
MR HAMILTON OF WISHAW'S REEL	3115L	2426L	Bb	2/2	Mc4v2p1
MR HANNY OF BARGALY('S REEL)	5165	6542	D	2/2	Mc13v1p10 A1v4p32 A1v6p32 Mc13v2p10 (II)
MR HARRY ANGELO JUNrs FAVORITE	112	123	G	9/8	C14v16p9
MR HENRY ERSKINE'S REEL	3143	311H6	A	2/2	P11v2p4
MR HOBHOUSE'S FAVORITE	1355	6653	E	2/4	J1p35
MR HOGERT'S HORNPIPE	3513	6L15L1	G	4/4	C7p9
MR HOPE'S JIG	316L6L	457L2	F	6/8	R9p10
MR HOPE'S WALTZ	5641	561L1L	Eb	3/8	R9p6
MR HORN	5115	447bL7bL	G	4/4	G10v6p10
MR HORN'S STRATHSPEY	3b13bL1L	247b2	G	4/4	G8p3
MR HORN'S STRATHSPEY	3b13bL1L	246b2	G	4/4	P1v1p2
MR HOUSTON (OF JORDANHILL) 'S REEL	543b1	43b27bL	E	2/2	Mc21v2p27
MR HOY	1H3H2H	1H55	F	3/4	M4v3p51
MR H.R. DUFF'S FAVORITE	3127L	1647L	Eb	2/4	M12p33
MR HUGH GRAY'S STRATHSPEY	5153	61H53	G	2/2	Mc22p12
MR HUNTER (OF BURNSIDE'S) STRATHSPEY	1H1H6b6b	5547bL	C E	4/4	D16p29 A7v6p61
MR HUNTER'S REEL	3b13b5	1H7b52	G	4/4	Mc22p20
MR HUNTER'S REEL	151H3	4542	Bb	2/2	R9p24
MR I. ROSE'S STRATHSPEY [MR J ROSE]	5L321	5L37L2	Bb	2/2*	Mc15p36 (II)
MR J. AITKEN'S FAVOURITE	5L131	4326L	A	6/8	Mc22p10
MR J. BROWN'S WALTZ	1H5H4H6H	1H5H5H1H	C	3/8	F1p32
MR J. J. HENRY'S STRATHSPEY	1351H	61H32	D	4/4	C12p10
MR J R COUTTS'S STRATHSPEY	1111	4227bL	E	4/4	L1p16
MR J. WALKER'S FANCY	1H5H2H3H	1H5H51H	C	6/8	C14v22p5
MR JAFFREY'S (JUNr) STRATHSPEY	13b7bL7bL	13b57b	A	4/4	C18p34
MR JAMES BELFOUR'S FANCY	3333	362H2	D	6/8	W2v1p9
MR JAMES BENNET'S REEL	1H1H65	3222	G	2/2	M4v4p24
MR JAMES BOSWELL'S JIG	3135	227b2	D	12/8	F3p9
MR JAMES BUCHANAN'S STRATHSPEY	11H1H3bH	7b424	G	4/4	C13v1p40
MR JAMES CAMPBELL'S STRATHSPEY	31H61H	5362	D	4/4	P11v2p12
MR JAMES DALLAS' STRATHSPEY	3H1H64	5362	F	2/2	Mc19v2p8,9
MR JAMES FAIRLEY'S STRATHSPEY	3b427bL	13b55	G	2/2	B20p21
MR JAMES FRASERS REEL	1H1H35	427L5L	A	4/4	W2v2p11
MR JAMES GEORGE('S STRATHSPEY)	3131H	6642	C	4/4	D16p22 (II)
MR JAMES HAMILTON'S VALTZ	1H1H53H	1H1H51H	Eb	3/8	R9p1
MR JAMES HECTOR MACKENZIE'S STRATHSPEY	3L5L34	447L2	Bb	4/4	R9p5
MR JAMES JENKINS FAVORITE	5L135	5L322	D	4/4	G10v5p24,25
MR JAMES JENKINS'S STRATHSPEY	36L3L1L	35L2L2	G	4/4	P11v2p15
MR JAMES MONTGOMERY'S JIG	15L3L5L	4L3L2L2	Bb	6/8	B2p3
MR JAMES MONTGOMERY'S REEL	15L3L5L	6L5L4L2L	Bb	4/4	B2p2
MR JAMES RAMSY'S STRATHSPEY [MR JAMES RAMSAY]	5L343	5L47L2	A	4/4	A7v1p4 (II)
MR JAMES RENTON'S REEL	3H1H53	3H1H2H4H	C	2/2	B2p6
MR JAMES STEWART'S REEL	1H551H	2H2H4H2H	E	2/2	B20p8
(MR) JARNOVICHI'S REEL	1H51H5	61H75	F	4/4*	C24v2p10 A7v4p6 N1v1p26 Mc7p21
MR JAs. CAMPBELL BALMARTIN	1153	1142	G	2/2	Mc16p5
MR JAs GRANT'S STRATHSPEY	1H122	1H12H2H	D	4/4	Mc21v2p30
MR JAs. McLACHLAN'S RANT	1153	51H46L	D	4/4	Mc16p33
MR JAS McNICOL INVERARAY'S STRATHSPEY	1H31H3H	1H322H	C	4/4	Mc16p2
MR JAs THOMSON'S STRATHSPEY	5524L	5553H	D	4/4	G15p12
(MR) JENKINS SHAN TRUISH	1125L	1322	A	6/8	C14v18p10 N1v1p16
MR JO. REID'S REEL	3b5L1L3b	47bL4L2	G	2/2	Mc22p3

Title			Key	Time	Reference
MR JOHN ALLISON'S WALTZ	1H17L1	1H17L5	G	3/8	F1p34
MR JOHN ANGUS' REEL	1311H	5H2H2H6	E	2/2	M4v3p37
MR JOHN BEGG'S FAVOURITE	35L6L1	35L6L2	Bb	6/8	S4v1p5
MR JOHN CAMPBELL ARDMORE'S FAVORITE	3155	3153	G	2/2	Mc16p28
MR JOHN CAMPBELL ARDMORE'S STRATHSPEY	113L1L	427L2	Bb	2/2	Mc16p13
MR JOHN CUNNINGHAM'S STRATHSPEY	1353	61H53	D	4/4	R9p11
MR JOHN DYKES REEL	3531H	227b4	A	2/2	W2v1p12
MR JOHN GEORGE CAMPBELL'S REEL	1324	137L7L	Bb	4/4	Mc21v4p38
MR JOHN GORDON'S REEL	3H2H1H1H	3H3H5H5H	D	4/4	D6p7
MR JOHN GORDON'S STRATHSPEY	1H3H2H3H	4H3H66	D	4/4	D6p7
MR JOHN GOW'S DELIGHT	13bH7b4	3b53b7bL	C	2/2	G9v2p20
MR JOHN GRAHAM	315L3	4642	F	4/4	R9p11
MR JOHN GRAHAM'S FAVORITE	13H62H	13H2H3H	D	2/2	A7v1p10
MR JOHN GRAY'S WALTZ	1H5H3H5H	1H5H3H1H	C	3/8	F1p33
MR JOHN McDOUGALL ARDBEG'S REEL	1H515	1H522H	D	2/2	Mc16p24
MR JOHN REDDIE'S STRATHSPEY	5555	4247bL	C	2/2	W2v1p14
MR JOHN ROBERTSON'S JIG	51H62	562H7	ZF	6/8	R9p16
MR JOHN SCOTT'S REEL	1H531	22H75	D	2/2	P11v2p12
MR JOHN SHAW STEWART'S STRATHSPEY	1H31H3H	2H4H75	C	4/4	C13v1p30,31
(MR JOHN) SHAW STEWART('S STRATHSPEY) [SIR JOHN SHAW STEWART'S]	5L13b4	2454	G	4/4*	C14v24p4,5 G10v1p4 (11)
MR JOHN SIMSON LARGY'S JIG	5122	5151H	G	6/8	Mc16p5
MR JOHN SMITH'S REEL [MR JOHN SMITH]	131H3	2216L	Eb	4/4*	D16p31 (11)
MR JOHN SMITH'S STRATHSPEY	13b53b	47bL27bL	G	2/2	Mc22p20
MR JOHN SMITH'S STRATHSPEY	11H1H3bH	7b7b47bL	C	4/4	D16p13
MR JOHN SMYTH'S REEL	5L5L6L6L	7L533	Bb	2/2	C23p10
MR JOHN STEWART OF GARTH'S REEL	3151H	3162	D	2/2	Mc19v1p2
MR JOHN STEWART OF GRANTUL(L)Y('S REEL)	1353	7bL7bL47b	A	2/2	D16p17 (11)
MR JOHN STEWART('S REEL)	1135	1132	F	2/2	Mc4v1p2 (11)
MR JOHN STEWART'S REEL	1H1H51	42H76	C	2/2	R9p20
MR JOHN STEWART'S REEL	153H1H	1H642	D	2/2	M4v3p34
MR JOHN TROTTER OF CASTLELAW'S HORNPIPE	3545	3112	F	4/4	Mc21v2p1
MR JOHN TROTTER'S REEL	3b151H	27bL7b7bL	D	6/8	Mc21v2p23
MR JOHN WALKER'S FAVOURITE	546L5L	151H5	D	2/2	W2v1p10
MR JOHNSON('S REEL)	1351H	6522	A	2/2	M4v1p1 (11)
MR JOHNSTON GRANT'S STRATHSPEY	113b3b	56b55	B	4/4	Mc22p16
MR J.R. COUTTS	1351H	557L2	G	6/8	L1p15
MR LAUDER DICK'S STRATHSPEY	1L5L15L	16L2L4L	Bb	4/4	G15p24,25
MR LAUDER'S STRATHSPEY	1H1H5H1H	4H2H77	D	4/4	Mc13v1p8 Mc13v2p8
MR LAWRENCE AINSWORTH'S MARCH	11L1L3L	5L6L11	A	4/4	A4v1p4,5
MR LEID'S REEL	53b13b	2427bL	E	2/2	C18p17
MR LEID'S STRATHSPEY	113b5	247b5	E	4/4	C18p16,17
MR LINDSAY('S REEL)	13b15	247bL2	E	2/2	Mc22p18 (11)
MR LIVINGSTON OF PARK HALL'S STRATHSPEY	113b1	27bL42	A	4/4	Mc4v4p3
MR LUMSDEN(OF BLAINEARN'S STRATHSPEY)	5654	547L2	F G	4/4	Mc21v4p25 (11) A1v4p3
MR LUMSDEN (OF BLANERNE) 'S STRATHSPEY [cf: COMMODORE MITCHELL]	5654	537L2	F	4/4*	N1v1p24 G10v3p13 G11v1Bp29 Mc4v3p3
MR MACBEAN OF ROARING RIVIE'S STRATHSPEY	5515	1562	D	4/4	L1p2
MR MacCULLOCH'S STRATHSPEY	45L6L5L	4326L	D	2/2	Mc19v2p12
MR MACDONALD OF STAFFA('S STRATHSPEY)	3b125L	3b13b3b	G	2/2	Mc22Bp1 (11)
MR MACDONALD'S REEL [MR MACDONALD OF STAFFA]	3b142	7bL424	G	4/4*	Mc22Bp1,2 (11)
MR MACINTYRE OF GLENOE('S STRATHSPEY)	11H51	4326L	D	2/2*	Mc15p35 (11)
MR MACINTYRES REEL	1H454	1H47bL2	Bb	2/2	C14v18p14
MR MACKAY'S REEL	1531	2427bL	A	2/2	Mc4v1p16
MR MACKENZIE MILLBANK'S REEL	5L365	437L5L	Bb	4/4	Mc11p11
MR MACKINZIES STRATHSPEY	3b1H1H1	22H7b7bL	C	4/4	G8p20
MR MACLEOD OF GEANIES' STRATHSPEY	1551H	3H5H3H2H	E	4/4	L1p14
MR MACMURDO'S STRATHSPEY	5354	6266	D	4/4	A7v1p9
MR MACNEILL OF COLLONSAY'S REEL	5555	4562	D	2/2	Mc9v3p39
MR MAITLAND OF FREUGH REEL	351H3	4562	A	4/4	Mc21v4p31
MR MALCOLMS REEL	113L5L	4L24L6L	Bb	4/4	G8p7 P1v1p3
MR MALCOLM'S STRATHSPEY	1121	16L22	Bb	2/2	J1p14
MR MARSHALL'S CELEBRATED PANORAMA WALTZ	3637	3671H	F	3/8	D6p29
(MR) MARSHALL'S COMPLIMENTS TO NIEL GOW	1111	116L2	G A	4/4*	G1v2p88 M4v3p21 G11v2Cp9 Mc7p23 Mc9v3p14 (11)
(MR) MARSHALL'S (FAVORITE/STRATHSPEY)	1L115L	2L226L	A	4/4	G11v1Ap26 G10v2p12 (11)
MR MARSHALL'S GRAND MINUET	111	222	Eb	3/4	C7p21
MR MARSHALL'S REEL	3364	5342	D	2/2	G9v2p15
MR MARSHALL'S REEL	131H3	2464	D	2/2	M4v4p25
MR MARSHALL'S STRATHSPEY, EDINr	1353	7L727L	D	4/4	T1v2p10
MR MASSON, MANSE OF BOTRIPHNIE	1L131	6L5L3L1L	Bb	4/4	M4v4p22
MR MATTHEW'S REEL	15L32	16L5L3L	Bb	2/2	C18p14
MR MATTHEW'S STRATHSPEY	1231	1237L	Bb	4/4	C18p14
MR McANDREW'S STRATHSPEY	531H3	4346H	D	4/4	G15p11
MR McCLAUKLAINE'S SCOTCH-MEASURE	5551H	511H1H	C	2/2	P7p1
MR McDONALD	1515	1562	D	4/4	M4v3p31
MR McDONALD OF GORDON CASTLE'S STR.	11H3bH1H	51H2H1H	C	4/4	G15p35
MR McDONALD'S FAVORITE	1H1H2H7	5555	G	2/2	E1v1p16
MR McGHIE'S STRATHSPEY	1L13b5	53b27bL	A	2/2	Mc22p6
MR McINNES'S STRATHSPEY	1L3L5L7L	1L3L6L2L	Bb	4/4	R9p5

MR McINTOSH OF McINTOSH'S STRATHSPEY	3551H	53H2H2	C	4/4	L1p11
MR McINTOSH'S REEL	5L531	6L642	D	2/2	C18p32
MR McINTOSH'S STRATHSPEY	5L132	5L135	D	4/4	C18p31
MR McINTOSH'S WHIM	5311	51H2H2H	G	6/8	L2p23
MR McLAE'S FAREWELL	5L36L5L	247L2	G	4/4	A1v5p10
MR McLAINE'S SCOTCH MEASURE	1122	5223	C	2/2	P7p1
MR McPHADDEN'S FAVORITE	112	7L64	D	9/8	G15p14
MR MELDRUM'S REEL BANFF	1H535	72H4H5H	D	2/2	M12p8
MR MENZIES (OF CULDAIR'S) STRATHSPEY	1111	6L27L6L	D	4/4	Mc21v3p28
MR MERRICK'S REEL	1H1H42	7L232	A	2/2	B2p4
MR MILLER'S HORNPIPE	1H533	4433	D	4/4	C14v25p14
MR MILLER'S STRATHSPEY	3b215	427bL7bL	A	2/2	Mc22p9
MR MONRO BINNING'S STRATHSPEY	1565	4362	D	4/4	F3p15
MR MOORE('S STRATHSPEY)	513b5	4427bL	C	4/4	Mc15p6 (II)
MR MORISON OF BOGNIE	1114	356L6L	A	6/8	M4v4p26
MR MORISON'S JIGG	1122	315L3L	Bb	6/8	D16p30
MR MORRISON SUPERVISOR DINGWALL	1333	5L27L2	G	2/2	M12p17
MR MORTHLAND ('S REEL)	113b5	2224	A G	4/4*	A7v5p14 G11v1Bp37 G11v1Cp37
[MORTLAND'S REEL]					G10v2p31 P5v2p18
MR MORTHLAND'S FAVORITE(STRATHSPEY)	5L111	443b7bL	A	4/4	G10v2p8 G11v1Bp16,17
MR MORTHLAND'S REEL	113b5	2224	A G	4/4	A7v5p14 G11v1Bp37
MR MUNRO OF POINTSFIELD'S REEL	1133	561H1H	F	2/2	J2p6
MR MURRAY (OF ABERCAIRNEY)('S STR.)	13b53b	7bL242	G	4/4	C13v1p48 G10v1p26 Mc13v2p28
					G11v1Bp37 (II)
MR MURRAY OF SIMPRIMS FAVORITE	3112	5225	F	4/4	Mc4v4p4
MR N. DUFF'S DOUBLE JIGG	1H2H5H2H	5H1H2H7	D	6/8	S11v2p14
MR NAIRNE'S STRATHSPEY	1115L	3b3b42	A	2/2	Mc22p20
MR NcNIEL ELISTER'S FAVORITE	3b211	27bL47bL	E	4/4	Mc16p27
MR NEIL MACBRAYNS JIGG	1235	1H532	Bb	6/8	Mc12v1p24
MR NISBET OF DIRLETON'S FAVORITE	13b55	3b111	A	4/4	G10v6p6
MR O. GALLAGHER	1H1H7	1H1H4H	D	9/8	C14v22p4
MR OFFICER'S STRATHSPEY	11L3L1	47L43	A	4/4	C18p6
MR OLIPHANT OF CONDIE'S STRATHSPEY	3131	6L27L5L	G	4/4	B11p17
MR OLIPHANT OF CONDIE'S WILLCOME HOME	3111	357L2	A	6/8	B11p6
MR ORQUHART'S STRATHSPEY	53b13b	4422	E	2/2	P5v4p7
MR OSWALD'S (OF AUCHINCRUIVE'S) STR.	1333	527L2	G	4/4	Mc21v3p20
MR OSWALDS OF DUNNIKIER'S REEL	31H51	2316L	A	2/2	W2v1p5
MR OSWALD'S REEL	13b55	427bL2	G	4/4	F3p6
MR P. BROWN OF LINKWOOD'S STRATHSPEY	5551H	7b47bL7bL	E	4/4	G15p38
MR P. P. SHIRREFF'S FAVORITE	3265	3H652	D	6/8	C5v1p6 A1v5p6 Mc10p5
MR P. ROBERTSON'S REEL	1H533H	1H32H2	C	2/2	Mc10p14
MR PATRICK DUFF JUNr's STRATHSPEY	1131	3555	F	4/4	G15p28,29
MR PATRICK DUFF'S FAVORITE STRATHSPEY	5365	1364	C	4/4	D16p22
MR PATRICK DUFF'S STRATHSPEY	1351H	51H3H2H	D	2/2	D15v1p26
MR PETER ANDERSON'S REEL	1325L	1353	Bb	2/2	C21p12
MR PETER DUFF'S FAVORITE	3H2H1H5	2H2H4H2H	C	6/8	C21p17
MR PETER McLEAN'S HORNPIPE	1H2H1H6	6753	F	4/4	C21p3
MR PETER PATTISON'S REEL	316L5L	6L5L22L	Bb	2/2	Mc16p33,34
MR PIRIE OF WATERTON'S HORNPIPE	13L13	1214	Bb	4/4	D6p32,33
MR PITT'S MINUET	5H2H7	111	D	3/4	R12v3p14
MR POPE'S STRATHSPEY	3155	4324	F	2/2	B20p13
MR R. CAMPBELL OF SHAWFIELD'S ALLAMANDE	1H3H5H1T	2H2H5H3H	C	2/4	G9v4p7
MR R. CATTO JUNr's HORNPIPE	51H35	4621	Bb	4/4	D6p32
MR R. DOWNIES FANCY	5L354	51H62	A	4/4	C14v17p3
MR R. MENZIES' STRATHSPEY	5333	5336	A	4/4	Mc19v1p13 Mc19v2p20
MR RAE'S JIGG	1L3L1L1	137L2	Bb	6/8	S4v1p11
MR REID OF ELGIN ACADEMY'S STRATHSPEY	1H3H1H6	1H3H66	F	2/2	G15p31
MR REID'S REEL	11H3b1H	7b424	E	2/2	B2p5
MR REID'S REEL	131H3	1H2H1H6	D	2/2	G15p17
MR REINAGLE'S FAVORITE	1H3bH55L	7bL247b	C	4/4	G10v6p2
MR RENTON'S JIG	1155	47bL27bL	E	6/8	B2p5
MR RICHd. CAMPBELL'S REEL	3b3b15	27bL7b2	G	2/2	F3p19
MR RICHIE'S HORNPIPE	1H1H35	6416L	F	4/4	R9p12
MR RIEDHEAD'S REEL	1H3H2H6	2427bL	D	2/2	S12v1p1
MR RITCHIE'S REEL	1551H	1H522	F	2/2	C18p28
MR RITCHIE'S STRATHSPEY	1355	4642	F	4/4	C18p28
MR ROBERT AITKEN'S REEL	3135	42H75	G	2/2	B20p16
MR ROBERT BISSIT'S STRATHSPEY	3b13b6b	2423b	D	2/2	Mc19v2p19
MR ROBERT FERGUSON OF RAITH'S REEL	3427L	2432	F	2/2	J2p6
MR ROBERT GORDON'S REEL	131H5	4562	D	2/2	M11v1p5
MR ROBERT HENDERSON'S WALTZ	113	551h	Bb	3/4	D6p8
MR ROBERT HUNTER'S STRATHSPEY	1353	2226L	D	4/4	P11v1p19
MR ROBERT STEWART REEL	4L1L3L1	3L6L4L2L	Bb	2/2	D16p30
MR ROBERTSON OF LADYKIRK ('S STR.)	351H2	351H3H	C	4/4	G10v3p28 K1v2p7 G11v13p20
MR ROBERTSON OF LAW'S (LUDES) STR.	5551H	5522	D	4/4*	A1v6p2 G10v1p28
MR ROBERTSON OF LUDE('S STRATHSPEY)	5651H	5622	D	4/4	G11v1Ap24,25 (II)
MR ROBERTSON'S STRATHSPEY	153b1	27bL47bL	A	4/4	Mc22p12,13
MR ROBINSON'S JIG	5L13b5	247b4	E	6/8	Mc15p12
MR ROBt ADAMSON JUNr REEL	311H5	7427bL	A	4/4	C21p14,15
MR ROBt BAIN'S STRATHSPEY	1H1H1H5	7b57b7bL	C	4/4	G15p34,35
MR ROBt BOWMAN'S FANCY	3142	357L2	D	6/8	C21p19
MR ROCHEAD'S MINUET	113	135	F	3/4	D14v1p17

Name					
MR RONALD CRAWFORD OF FRESKIEHALL'S STRATHSPEY	1351H	157L7L	A	4/4	C13v1p20,21
MR ROSS CRAWFORD('S STRATHSPEY)	3b13b5	7bL27bL2	F	2/4	G11v1Bp10,11 G10v3p24,25
MR ROSS'S STRATHSPEY	11H51	2462	D	4/4	B2p7
MR S. MONCRIEFF'S STRATHSPEY	3b113b	27bL7bL4	G	4/4	Mc22Ap3
MR SAMl. HEPBURN'S FAREWELL	123b2	1255	A	6/8	Mc22p6
MR SAMl ROSES REEL	3231H	527L2	A	2/2	C14v8p22
MR SAMUEL MACKNIGHT'S FAVOURITE	1414	16L23	Bb	6/8	P11v1p16
MR SHARP'S FAVOURITE (DUNSE DINGS A')	351H3	351H1H	A	2/2 4/	G10v3p21 Mc21v3p12,13
MR SHARP'S REEL	1H51H1H	3H2H4H2H	D	4/4	W2v2p12
MR SHARP'S STRATHSPEY	1H531	6L242	Eb	2/2	Mc19v3p22 Mc19v2p17
MR SHEPHERD'S STRATHSPEY	131H6	6542	C	4/4	R9p22,23
MR SINCLAIR YOUNGER OF BARRACK'S REEL	53H4H3H	2H2H4H7b	D	2/2	G15p15
MR SLOAN'S REEL	1531H	5126L	F	4/4	F3p12
MR SMITON'S HORNPIPE	15L5L5L	3L4L5L5L	Bb	4/4	W4v2p28
(MR) STABILINI'S FAVOURITE	1H576	527L2	Eb	2/4	G11v1Cp11 G10v3p28
MR STEUART'S JUNr STRATHSPEY	5L5L5L1L	2L226L	A	2/2	J1p43
MR STEUART'S OF DEVONSHIRE STREET'S FAVORITE	3b13b1	3b53b7bL	F	6/8	J1p39
MR STEWART DOWALLY'S REEL	3H1H5H1H	2H7b4H7b	D	2/2	P5v1p14
MR STEWART JUNR OF CARNOCK'S REEL	15L6L1	7L531	Bb	4/4	G10v5p27
MR STEWART OF BALECHIN'S STRATHSPEY	315L1	447L2	A	4/4	Mc4v4p6
MR STEWART OF BALLAICHIN'S STRATHSPEY	1326L	1344	F	2/2	J1p15
MR STEWART OF BALLECHEN'S WELCOME HOME	13b15L	7bL5L4L7bF	A	4/4	S4v1p13
MR STEWART OF DALGUISE	51H51H	47b42	D	2/2*	Mc4v3p6 (II)
MR STEWART (OLIPHANT) OF ROSSIE(S REEL)	1151	427L7L	F	2/2	Mc4v3p2 G8p19 P1v1p10 (II)
MR STEWART TROTTER'S REEL or CAPTAIN'S FANCY, THE	1H3H2H1H	1H4H4H2H	E	2/2	Mc21v2p39
MR STEWART'S REEL	1H31H5	4646	D	2/2	Mc13v1p9 Mc13v2p9
MR STIRLING OF KEIRS REEL	1353	2561H	A	4/4	S13p2
MR STIRLING OF KEIR'S REEL	151H5	1542	G	2/2	G9v5p4
MR STIRLING'S JIG	3L5L6L5L	3L122L	Bb	6/8	R9p6,7
MR STRANG OF LOPNESS'S REEL	11H3b5	2427bL	C	2/2	Mc15p19
MR TAIT'S STRATHSPEY	131H6	1H4H72H	Eb	4/4	R9p1
MR THOs JARVIS REEL	3115L	2462	A	4/4	C21p1
MR W. JOPP'S HORNPIPE	335L3	1H1H31H	C	4/4	D6p35
MR W. LESSLIE'S STRATHSPEY	11H1H1H	2H3H1H6	F	4/4	M1p3
MR W. THOM'S HORNPIPE	15L3L	5L4L2L	Bb	3/2	D6p39
MR WAGSTAFF'S FAVORITE	31H35L	7L47L2	Bb	4/4	M12p18
MR WATSON CARNEGIE OF LOWER AND TURN	351H6	2451	F	3/8	A4v1p7
MR WATT'S REEL	31H71H	631H3	G	2/2	G15p4
MR WELCH'S MARCH	1H1H1H2H	3H3H3H1H	D	4/4	B12p6
MR W.F. THOMSON'S REEL	5L3L5L3L	2226L	Bb	2/2	Mc16p32
MR WHITE'S STRATHSPEY	116L5L	117L2	A	4/4	R9p17
MR WILLIAM FERGUSON'S REEL	5L153	61H65	D	2/2	J2p4
MR WILLIAM FRASER'S FAVORITE	551H1H	2H4H2H6	D	4/4	G10v6p7
MR WILLIAM JARDINE'S STRATHSPEY	1165	1H4H72H	F	4/4	P11v1p14
MR WILLIAM KILMAN'S STRATHSPEY	15L11H	5322	A	2/2	M11v1p5
MR WILLIAM STEWART'S STRATHSPEY	1551H	6522	D	4/4*	A1v5p52 Mc4v1p2
MR WILLIAM TOWER'S QUICK STEP	3H1H65	3H1H2H4H	D	6/8	S5p5
MR WILLm FERGUSON OF REATHS REEL	116L2	4433	A	4/4	W2v2p4
MR WILLm FORDYCE'S STRATHSPEY	1H1H3H5H	4H3H2H2H	C	2/2	(C24v2)*
MR WILLm ROBERTSON'S REEL	3H2H1H6	357L2	D	2/2	S4v1p15
MR WILLm. SKENE QM ABERDEENSHIRE REGT.'S FAVOURITE	1316L	5L3L6L6L	Bb	4/4	D15v1p22
MR WILL'S FAVOURITE	3H545	3H542	D	2/4	A1v4p71 Mc22p18 C5v1p71
MR WILLS'S STRATHSPEY	3H1H3H5H	4H5H4H2H	C	2/2	J1p49
MR WILLS'S STRATHSPEY	1512	1512	A	4/4	C14v15p18
MR WILSON'S HORNPIPE	532	532	F	9/8	Mc21v4p24
MR Wm. CAMPBELL ARDMORE'S REEL	16L7L5L	1753	G	2/2	Mc16p6
MR Wm CAMPBELL BALMARTIN'S REEL	331H5	662H2	A	2/2	Mc16p27
MR Wm. CLARK'S FAVOURITE	1347L	1351	G	6/8	Mc12v1p18,19
MR Wm ETTLES FAVORITE	3L16L4L	3L112L	Bb	4/4	M12p20
MR Wm HAIG'S STRATHSPEY	1515	427L4	D	2/2	Mc16p17
MR Wm. TENNANT'S FAVORITE	3b147bL	3b141	E	6/8	B20p19
MR Wm YOUNG'S REEL	1H53b1	7b427bL	A	2/2	G15p21
MR WORK'S REEL	536L2	1566	G	2/2	Mc15p13
MR YEAMAN OF MURIE'S MARCH	3333	15L5L5L	G	2/2	D16p6
MR YOUNG OF MARY HILL'S STRATHSPEY	1H535	1H522H	F	4/4	G15p26,27
MR YOUNG'S STRATHSPEY	5555	247b5	E	4/4	B2p4
MRS A. GRANT'S STRATHSPEY	1L111	7bF7bL7bL7bL	A	4/4	Mc12v1p19
MRS A. MACGLASHAN('S JIGG)	111L3b	7bL242	G	6/8	Mc10p11 (II)
MRS A. ROSE OF KILLRAVOCK'S STRATHSPEY	5L353	6522	F	4/4	F2v1p2
MRS ABERCROMBY (OF GLASSA) 'S (STRATHSPEY/REEL)	113b5	7b547bL	G A	4/4*	A7v2p12 C24v1p5 A7v6p37
MRS ABERNETHY'S STRATHSPEY	1353	27bL47bL	D	2/2	C24v2p20
MRS ADYE('S STRATHSPEY) [MRS ADIE]	1125L	127L5L	Bb	4/4	G10v5p6 (II)
MRS ALEX(ANDE)R BRODIE('S REEL)	4H3H2H7	4H3H66	D	2/2*	G15p14 (II)
MRS ALEXANDER OF BALLAMILES STRATHSPEY	3L5L11	1H532	F	4/4	E2p16
MRS ALLAN OF ERROL'S FAREWELL TO LONDON	351H2	351H3H	C	4/4	D16p29
MRS ANDERSON OF BALGAY('S REEL)	1531H	1H542	C	2/2	Mc13v1p6 Mc13v2p6 (II)
MRS ANDERSON OF KINCRAIG'S STRATHSPEY	3H3H1H6	5122	F.	4/4	G15p31

Name					
MRS ANDERSON'S REEL	1H535	427L5L	G	2/2	Mc21v3p39
MRS ANDERSON'S STRATHSPEY	5555	2462	A	4/4	M4v3p21
MRS ANDREW'S STRATHSPEY	3537	1H537	G	4/4	M12p16
MRS ANDw SIVEWRIGHT OF EDINr	3155	437L2	G	4/4	C21p14
MRS ANN SUTHERLAND'S STRATHSPEY	136L5L	447L2	Bb	2/2	R9p9
MRS ARCHd CAMPBELL OF ASKOMELL'S STR.	3215L	2422L	Bb	4/4	C13v4p35
MRS ARNOT'S REEL	1H2H1H5	661H2H	C	2/2	R5p60
MRS BAILLIE COOPER'S STRATHSPEY	1551H	5326L	D	2/2	M11v1p17
MRS BAILLIE OF DUNAIN'S STRATHSPEY	17L13	15L22	Eb	4/4	F2v1p10
MRS BAILLIES REEL	3H3H4H3H	3H3H4H7	D	2/2	R6v1p8
MRS BAIRD(HILL'S REEL)	3b215L	7bL242	G	2/2	Mc4v4p2 (II)
MRS BAIRD OF NEW BYTHS STRATHSPEY	5527bL	5656	D	4/4	G11v1Cp34 G10v1p9
MRS BAIRD OF NEWBYTH ('S STRATHSPEY)	351H3H	1H562	C	4/4	G11v1Bp19 G10v2p9 (II)
MRS BAIRD (OF NEWBYTH) 'S STRATHSPEY	5555	7b427bL	E	4/4*	C5v1p59 A1v5p59 Mc4v1p1 (II)
MRS BAIRD OF NEWBYTH'S JIGG	5L5L5L3	6L6L23	A	6/8	Mc4v1p21
MRS BAKER'S FANCY	1H1H1H2	1351	D	2/4	B16v1p11
MRS BALLANTINE'S REEL	1L151	6L5L2L2	A	4/4	F3p13
MRS BEARD'S STRATHSPEY	1322	51H26L	A	4/4	J1p25
MRS BELL'S STRATHSPEY	1H31H3	432H2	D	4/4	C5v1p62 A1v5p62
MRS BILLINGCROFT'S WALTZ	1512	1551	Bb	3/8	C14v22p4,5 P6v1p10 (B21)
MRS BIRCH'S REEL	11L2L2L	5L123	Bb	2/2	R6v1p4
MRS BISHOP'S WALTZ	1H62H5	1H62H5	C	3/8	C14v12p16
MRS BISSET'S STRATHSPEY	1113	5322	Bb	2/2	M11v1p7
MRS BLAIR OF AVONTOWN'S FAVORITE	5551H	3H2H2H5	D	2/4	G10v4p18
MRS BLAIR OF BLAIR'S FAVORITE	1133	5522	Bb	2/4	E2p17
MR(S) BLAIR OF BLAIR'S JIGG	5125L	6L237L	G	6/8	A1v5p21 C5v1p21 Mc12v1p3
MRS BLAIR OF BLAIR'S REEL	1H3H5H3H	62H76	D	4/4	F3p17
MRS BLAIR OF BLAIR'S REEL	1515	47bL37bL	A	4/4*	C14v16p15 E2p3
MRS BLAIR OF BLAIR'S STRATHSPEY	15L6L1	4531H	A	4/4	Mc21v3p12
MRS BLAIR OF MERCHISTON	114L5	3L4L3L2L	Bb	6/8	L2p26
MRS BOSWELL OF AUCHINLECK'S REEL	137L5L	6L4L5L3L	Bb	4/4	F3p1
MRS BOSWELL OF AUCHINLEEK'S FAVORITE	111H1	6L217L	Eb	6/8	S4v2p18
MRS BOYD OF PINKIE'S STRATHSPEY	153b1	2424	G	4/4	F3p14
MRS BRODIE OF BRODIE'S STRATHSPEY	1L3L1L1	5426L	Bb	4/4	T1v2p6
MRS BRODIE'S DELIGHT	3322	1332	E	2/2	J2p4
MRS BROWN OF KELLY-BANK'S STRATHSPEY	116L4	527L2	A	2/2	B20p2
MRS BROWN (OF LINKWOOD'S) (REEL)	13b55	7b424	E	2/2	M4v3p60 C8v1p17 C8v2p26
MRS BRUCE OF KINNAIRD'S FAVORITE	5122	5125L	F	6/8	S4v2p12
MRS BUCHAN OF AUCHMACOY	1111	3122L	Bb	4/4	M4v4p22
MRS BURN CALLANDER'S REEL	3b7L5L7L	3b13b5	D	2/2	Mc19v3p15
MRS BURNS' REEL	3113	51H34	G	2/2	B20p3
MRS BUTTER OF FASKALLY	7531	2342	A	4/4	Mc19v3p5
MRS BUTTER OF FASKALLY'S MEDLEY	5L3L6L5L	4347L	A	4/4	Mc19v3p4
MRS BUTTERS' REEL	131H6	3347L	G	2/2	Mc19v2p5
MRS CAMPBELL ARDMORE'S JIG	1133	146L2	G	6/8	Mc16p25,26
MRS CAMPBELL ARDMORE'S REEL	1H535	1564	Bb	2/2	Mc16p9
MRS CAMPBELL OF BALINABY'S REEL	3531	2422	G	2/2	Mc16p5
MRS CAMPBELL OF ORMIDALE'S STRATHSPEY	5L13b5	7bL7bL7bL2	A	4/4	Mc12v1p35
MRS CAMPBELL OF TREESBANK'S REEL	3H1H53	4542	C	4/4	F3p13
MRS CAMPBELL'S REEL	1H3H65	33H67	F	4/4	Mc21v4p26
MRS CAPt CAMPBELL	5H3H1H1H	5H3H3H3H	D	4/4	L1p16
MRS CAPt. CHARLES GORDON	1H1H61H	62H75	A	4/4	M4v4p30
MRS CAPt McBARNET'S STRATHSPEY	3153	1H61H7	Eb	4/4	M4v3p25
MRS CAPT REID'S STRATHSPEY	1113	6522	A	2/2	C24v2p21
MRS CAPt SKENE'S STRATHSPEY	11H52	16L6L2	Eb	4/4	M4v3p58
MRS CAPt STEWART'S STRATHSPEY	5555	6662	F	4/4	P5v1p16
MRS CAPTAIN ROSS	3b13b1H	7b522	C	2/2	Mc21v4p44
MRS CAPTn STEWART OF FINCASTLE'S STR.	1126L	1561H	E	4/4	S4v1p15
MRS CARMICHAEL OF SKIRLING'S STRATHSPEY	5L122	5L126	D	4/4	G10v4p34
MRS CARRUTHERS'S REEL	5H5H1H5H	5H5H6H2H	C	2/2	R6v1p2
MRS CARTER'S STRATHSPEY	1353	7L5L47L	A	2/2	C14v11p4
MRS CARTWRIGHT'S DELIGHT	72H67	4327L	G	6/8	S7v1p61
MRS CASEY	3b17bL7bL	116b5	E	6/8	C14v1p5 P10p16
MRS CHARLES FERGUSSON'S REEL	151H5	461H6	D	2/2	R6v1p6
MRS CHARLES GRAHAME'S STRATHSPEY	5L5L5L1	1346L	A	4/4	B11p12
MRS CHARLES MENTEATH OF CLOSE-BURN'S JIG	5L12	7bL7b4H	E	9/8	R6v2p18
MRS CHARLES STEWART	5653	7L244	F	2/2	M4v4p5
MRS CHAs DALRYMPLE'S REEL	3135	7L5L7L2	G	2/2	Mc21v2p8
MRS CHEAPE OF ROSSIE'S STRATHSPEY	5353	5342	A	4/4	L4p7
MRS CHISHOLM(OF CHISHOLM'S STRATHSPEY)	1326L	1353	A	4/4	G10v4p11 (II)
MRS CHOLMONDLEY'S REEL	1H765	153H2H	C	6/8	C14v9p10
MRS CHRISTIE'S RANT	5551	5557bL	A	4/4	A1v4p7
MRS CHRISTIE('S) (RANT/STRATHSPEY)	5551	5547bL	A	2/2*	Mc9v3p3 G11v2Cp23 Mc12v1p9 (II)
MRS C.K. JOHNSTON'S REEL	1326L	1361H	G	4/4	T1v1p5
MRS CLARK'S STRATHSPEY	1H1H31	5322H	C D	4/4	A7v4p5 Mc12v1p17 A1v4p54 C5v1p54
MRS CLARK'S STRATHSPEY	1H1H35	5322H	C	2/2	A7v5p5
MRS CLARKSON'S FAVOURITE	31H3H1H	33H72H	D	6/8	C23p18
MRS. COL. CAMPBELL'S OF BALLOCHYLL REEL	15L3L5L	2L27L2	Bb	2/2	M6p2
MRS COL: GRANT OF GRANT'S STRATHSPEY	51H22	51H55	Eb	4/4	G15p5

Title	Code 1	Code 2	Key	Time	References
MRS COL: GRANT'S REEL	1H535	1H3H72H	Eb	2/2	G15p5
MRS COL. HAY OF MAYNE'S STRATHSPEY	5622	5353	F	4/4	G15p30
MRS COL: SINCLAIR OF FORSS'S STRATHSPEY	5L31H3	51H4H6	D	4/4	G15p17
MRS COLI ROSS'S REEL	1H342	2463	A	2/2	P11v2p19
MRS COLL:FARQUHARSON'S FAVOURITE	13b57b	7bL246b	G	2/2	J2p8
MRS COLONEL FORBES(' STRATHSPEY)	1H522H	1H61H1H	C	4/4	M4v3p45 (11)
MRS COLONEL GORDON OF LEITCHIESTON'S REEL	13L13	4522	A	2/2	M4v3p17
MRS COLQUHOUN GRANTS STRATHSPEY	1122	347L2	Bb	2/2	C24v2p23
MRS CONDIE'S REEL	13L6L1	2343	G	2/2	Mc19v3p12
MRS COUTS TROTTER'S FAVORITE	125L5L	1236L	Bb	2/4	G10v5p6
MRS CRAWFORD OF LITTLETON'S REEL	5353	5335	A	4/4	G10v6p20,21
MRS CRAWFORD('S) (FAVORITE STRATHSPEY) [FORNEATH HOUSE]	3565	1H3H1H6	D	4/4	A7v4p18 K1v2p8 G10v4p30 (11)
MRS CRAWFORD'S REEL	51H65	1H51H3	C	2/2	Mc16p20
MRS CRAWFURD OF ARDMILLAN'S REEL	5154	27bL24	E	2/2	R5p20
MRS CRAWFURD OF DONESIDE'S MINUET	1H3H5H	3H3H2H	C	3/4	R5p4,5
MRS CRAWFURD OF DONSIDES REEL [MRS CRAWFORD OF DONSIDE]	5L13b4	47b47bL	G	2/2*	R5p25 (11)
MRS CROMBIE'S REEL	1H3H53	4H2H75	D	2/2	C24v2p25
MRS CRUICKSHANK'S FANCY	565	452	D	9/8	C14v14p16
MRS CUMINE OF AUCHRY'S STRATHSPEY	1151	4642	G	4/4	C18p2
MRS CUMING'S MINUET	1H1H3H	551H	Eb	3/4	S11v1p17
MRS CUMMING BRUCE'S STRATHSPEY	3L5L11	3432	Bb	4/4	T1v2p4
MRS CUNINGHAM OF CORSEHILL'S REEL	1H123b	1H147bL	A	6/8	R5p20
MRS CUNNINGHAM OF BONNINGTONE'S STR.	1151H	6326L	Eb	4/4	L4p11
MRS CUTHIL OF JOCK'S LODGE FAVORITE	1316L	4L6L2L2	Bb	2/4	C23p19
MRS DALRYMPLE OF ORANGEFIELD'S REEL	1H1H55	1H1H77	F	2/2	R5p41
MRS DALRYMPLE'S REEL	1L1L3L3L	7L47L2	Bb	4/4	L2p25
MRS DALZELL OF DALZELL LODGE	5213	126L6L	Eb	4/4	G10v5p8
MRS DARLEY OF TIBERMORAY'S REEL	13b54	2442	G	2/2	R7v2p2
MRS DAVID GORDON'S MINUET	555	553	F	3/4	D16p5
MRS DAVID PATRICK'S FAVORITE	13b3b4	27bL52	G	2/2	C21p11 (11)
MRS DAVID STEWART'S FAVORITE	5351	1H46L5L	D	2/2	Mc4v3p4
MRS DAVIDSON'S REEL	5564	5342	F	2/2	Mc15p27
MRS DEMPSTER OF DUNNICHEN'S MINUET	556	17L5L	Bb	3/4	D16p3
MRS DINGWALL OF BROCKL(E)Y'S STRATHSPEY	35L3L5L	3342	F	2/2*	P5v4p4,5 (11)
MRS DINGWALL OF BRUCKLAY'S REEL	1H1H1H5	1353	A	2/2	C18p9
MRS DINGWALL OF BRUCKLAY'S WALTZ	1H4H3H1H	1H4H3H1H	C	3/8	C18p17
MRS DOCTOR ABERNETHIE'S REEL	1353	2247bL	D	2/2	C24v1p3
MRS DONALDSON'S STRATHSPEY	13b27bL	13b55	F	4/4*	Mc15p19 Mc7p3
MRS DONALDSON'S STRATHSPEY	11H1H1H	1H522	D	4/4	A7v6p34
MRS DONALDSON'S STRATHSPEY	1L111	15L2L2L	Bb	2/2	A7v2p18
MRS DONALDSON('S STRATHSPEY)	1L113	15L2L2L	Bb	4/4	G11v1Ap11 G10v2p5 Mc12v1p42
MRS Dr. FORBES' REEL	115L5L	1142	A	2/2	Mc19v3p11 Mc19v2p7
MRS Dr. GORDON, ELGIN	13b57b	7b427bL	E	2/2	T1v2p7
MRS Dr NICOL'S REEL	3b53b5	3b7b24	G	2/2	M12p27
MRS DR STEPHEN'S REEL	31H1H5	31H1H6	F	2/2	G15p31
MRS Dr STEWART'S REEL	5551	5522	E	2/2	Mc4v2p12
MRS Dr STEWART'S REEL	15L3bL1L	7bL27bL4L	A	2/2	C18p27
MRS Dr. STEWART'S STRATHSPEY	1141	1145	A	4/4	C18p27
MRS DR TORRENCE OF THURSO'S REEL	1H525	1H61H6	C	2/2	G15p34
MRS DRUMMOND OF LOGIEALMONDS REEL	1H3bH75	7b542	E	4/4	G10v4p3
MRS DRYSDALE'S JIG	1355	4527L	G	6/8	B20p10,11
MRS DUFF OF CARNUCIE'S REEL	5322	16L3L1	Bb	2/2	C18p10
MRS DUFF OF CARNUCIE'S STRATHSPEY	1313	26L4L2	Bb	4/4	C18p10
MRS DUFF (OF FETTERESSO'S) BIRTHDAY	16L15L	16L13	A	2/2	M11v1p6
MRS DUFF (OF FETTERESSO'S) MARCH	5155	27bL24	E	2/2	M11v1p1
MRS DUFF (OF FETTERESSO'S) STRATHSPEY	1353	432H2	G	4/4	P5v2p6
MRS DUFF OF MUIRTOWN'S WALTZ	5342	35L5L1L	Bb	3/8	M12p21
MRS DUFF'S RECOVERY	1135	2255	D	4/4	M12p8
MRS DUFF'S REEL	15L16L	27L15	Bb	4/4	Mc21v4p9
MRS DUNCAN CHRISTIE'S STRATHSPEY	5431H	547L2	A	2/2	B20p18
MRS DUNCAN'S FANCY	313L5L	4L422	Bb	2/2	C14v1p19
MRS DUNCAN('S REEL)	1H5H3bH5H	3bH5H2H7b	D C	2/2	A7v4p24 L4p5 Mc4v2p10 G10v4p14 (11)
MRS DUNCAN'S REEL	1H5H3bH5H	3bH5H3bH5H	C	2/2	G8p21
MRS DUNCAN'S REEL	1H5H3H5H	3H5H2H7b	D	2/2	A7v5p6
MRS DUNDAS McQUEEN('S REEL)	3546	3551H	G A	4/4*	A1v5p54 G9v5p14 Mc21v3p7 P5v3p21 (11)
MRS DUNDAS OF ARNISTON'S STRATHSPEY	1143b	5L16b5	E	4/4	S4v1p2
MRS DUNDASS McQUEEN'S STRATHSPEY	1H3H2H2H	1H3H2H6	D	4/4	E2p11
MRS DUPREE'S REEL	5531	4421	G	4/4	Mc21v4p43
MRS EDWARDS OF WOODEND'S JIG	511H5	4362	D	6/8	A1v4p38 W4v2p25
MRS ERNEST LESLIE'S STRATHSPEY	3232	7L7L55	F	4/4	C18p16
MRS FALCONER'S REEL	1H51H5	2222	G	4/4	M4v4p23
MRS FARQUHAR'S REEL	15L35	26L7L7L	F	4/4	C18p35
MRS FARQUHAR'S STRATHSPEY	1343	1362	F	4/4	C18p34
MRS FARQUHARSON (OF INVERCAULD)'S REEL	5351	532H2	D	4/4	Mc21v2p30
MRS FARQUHARSON OF INVEREY('S STR.)	351H1H	3572	C	4/4	P5v1p22 (11)
MRS FARQUHARSON OF MONALTRIE'S DELIGHT	1115	7bL4b72	C	4/4*	Mc21v2p14 P5v1p1
MRS FARQUHARSON (OF MONALTRIE'S) STR.	1316L	5L462	Bb	4/4	P5v2p5

Name			Key	Time	References
MRS FARQUHARSON'S JIGG OR QUICK STEP	1H51H3bH	1H542	C	6/8	Mc21v2p17 P5v1p2
MRS FERGUSON OF RAITH'S STRATHSPEY	3155	3542	F	4/4	P5v1p20
MRS FERGUSON OF REATH('S STRATHSPEY)	5L121	7bL7b47bL	G	4/4	G11v1Bp24 G10v2p26
MRS FERGUSON'S STRATHSPEY	116L6	5222	G	4/4	A1v6p10
MRS FERGUSSON OF CRAIGDARROCHS REEL	1H13b5	7b7b47bL	D	2/2	R6v1p6
MRS FERGUSSON OF RAITH'S DELIGHT	1L5L5L1	1422	A	4/4	P5v1p13
MRS FLEMING OF MONESS	3L3L12	5L6L4L2L	Bb	4/4	G11v1Ap13 (II)
MRS FLEMING OF MONESS(STRATHSPEY)	3L3L17L	5L6L4L2L	Bb	4/4	G10v1p30 (II)
MRS FLEMING STRATHSPEY	3L3L11	5L6L4L2L	Bb	4/4	C14v7p19
MRS FOGG'S FANCY	11H1	7bL7b7bL	C	9/8	Mc15p7
MRS FOLJAMBE, ELGIN	3L135	3L16L2L	Bb	4/4	T1v2p9
MRS FORBES OF BOHARM'S STRATHSPEY	1L131	6L5L2L4L	Bb	2/2	M4v3p7 (II)
MRS FORBES OF SHIVERS' FANCY	1H51H5	671H5	D	2/4	A1v4p60 W4v1p28
MRS FORBES' REEL	1H542	3125L	Bb	2/2	M4v3p8
MRS FORDYCE'S (OF AYTON'S) STRATHSPEY	1L113L	2L27L6L	Bb	4/4	Mc21v2p6
MRS FORSYTH'S STRATHSPEY	1L5L7bL7bF	1L5L7bL7bL	A	4/4	M4v3p43
MRS FORTATH'S STRATHSPEY	5515L	5L332	Eb	2/2	G15p6,7
MRS FRANK WALKER	3H2H1H6	5565	F	4/4	G10v6p32
MRS FRASER OF BELLADRUM'S REEL	467b5	1H631	D	2/2	G15p12
MRS FRASER OF CULBOCKIE'S JIG	315	316	D	9/8	G15p12
MRS FRASER OF CULDUTHEL'S STRATHSPEY	13b27bL	13b53b	F	4/4	F2v1p3
MRS FRASER OF FOYERS'S STRATHSPEY	11H3bH2H	7b7b7b7b	D E	4/4	F2v1p10 A7v6p49
MRS FRASER OF GORTULEG'S FAVOURITE	1524	17b47L	A	6/8	F2v1p7
MRS FRASER OF LOVAT'S STRATHSPEY	5L5L5L1L	2L5L4L7bF	A	4/4*	Mc21v4p33 G11v1Ap17 P5v1p5
					P5v3p5
MRS FRASER'S CULDUTHOL'S FANCY	3335	656L2	F	6/8	A7v1p13
MRS FRASER'S REEL	1353	7L242	Bb	2/2	M4v3p7 (II)
MRS FRASER'S STRATHSPEY	11L3bL1L	27bF2L7bF	A	2/2	G8p30 P1v1p12
MRS FULLARTON OF FULLARTON	5L16L2	5L153	A	4/4	F3p4
MRS FULLARTON OF FULLARTON'S MINUET	556	535	D	3/4	R5p3
MRS FULLARTON OF FULLARTONS REEL	1H1H1H5	1H11H1	F	6/8	R5p22
MRS FULLARTON OF FULLARTON'S STRATHSPEY	1L3L13L	15L2L2L	Bb	4/4	E2p5
MRS FULLARTON OF ROSEMOUNT'S REEL	113b5	7b47bL2	E	2/2	R5p48
MRS G. FORBES, ASHGROVE	5651H	6632	D	4/4	T1v2p15
MRS GARDEN CAMPBELL OF TROUP	5221H	3H1H63	C	4/4	C18p4,5
AND GLENLYON'S STRATHSPEY					
MRS GARDEN OF DALGETY'S REEL	3b13b5	2424	D	2/2	S4v1p26
MRS GARDEN OF TROOP	3146	6L27L5L	F	2/2	P5v4p3
AND GLENLYON'S STRATHSPEY					
MRS GARDEN (OF TROUP)('S REEL)	31H3H1H	6542	F	4/4*	P5v2p1 (II)
MRS GARDEN (OF TROUP/E)('S STRATHSPEY)	1156	7L5L7L5L	F G	4/4	P5v2p2 P5v3p10 G11v2Ap31 C7p6
					C8v1p6 Mc7p21 C14v14p9 A7v4p10
					B12p14,15 K1v1p33 (II)
					E1v1p68
MRS GARDEN OF TROUP'S REEL	1H564	537L7L	Bb	4/4	Mc21v4p2
MRS GARDEN OF TROUP'S STRATHSPEY	1155	7L5L7L5L	G	4/4	A7v5p27
MRS GENERAL CAMPBELL'S REEL	3b15L1	247b5	A	4/4	A7v4p14 (II)
MRS GENERAL CAMPBELL'S REEL	315L1	247b5	A	4/4	G11v2Cp28
MRS GENERAL HAY'S STRATHSPEY	5563	5532	F	2/2	M11v1p8
MRS GENERAL MAXWELL	1H3H2H7	1H3H2H6	C	2/2	Mc4v4p7 (II)
OF PARKHILL('S REEL)					
MRS GENERAL STEWART'S STRATHSPEY	5L111	115L4L	G	4/4	G15p36
MRS GEO. ABERCROMBY'S REEL	5L5L13	436L6L	A	2/2	C24v1p3
MRS GEORGE BUCHANAN'S STRATHSPEY	1H3H1H5	11H2H2	C	4/4	C13v1p31
MRS GEORGE JOHNS(T)ON (OF BYKER)	13b54	247b4	B	2/2	Mc21v3p25 (II)
'S REEL					
MRS GEORGE ROBERTSON GREENOCK'S STR.	11H11H	7b524	C	4/4	Mc12v1p33
MRS GEORGE ROBERTSON'S REEL	1L5L15L	357L2	Bb	2/2	M4v3p4
MRS GIBBON'S REEL	51H33	4233	D	2/2	C18p26
MRS GIBBON'S STRATHSPEY	1565	1542	D	4/4	C18p26
MRS GILLESPIE'S REEL	15L11	4326L	A	2/2	R6v1p8
MRS GILLIES('S STRATHSPEY)	1L5L32	15L4L2L	Bb	4/4	Mc21v4p7 (II)
MRS GLASS	315L3L	3122	A	2/4	Mc19v2p6
MRS GLENNIE'S REEL	1131H	224#2H	D	2/2	M4v3p33
MRS GORDON CAMPBELL OF TROUP	531H1H	3H2H1H2	C	2/2	C18p5
AND GLENLYON'S REEL					
MRS GORDON OF ABERDOUR('S REEL)	1562	1155	G	4/4	P5v3p24 (II)
MRS GORDON OF ABERDOUR'S STRATHSPEY	1H2H55	661H1H	A	4/4	C18p9
MRS GORDON OF ABERDOURS'S STRATHSPEY	113b5	7b547bL	G	2/2	C24v2p17
MRS GORDON OF ABERGELDIE'S STRATHSPEY	1322	51H26L	A	4/4	P5v1p11
MRS GORDON OF ABERGELDIE'S STRATHSPEY	1H1H51	2416L	D	4/4	T1v2p7
MRS GORDON OF BELLIE'S REEL	3631	5522	F	4/4	M4v1p9
MRS GORDON (OF BELLIE)'S STRATHSPEY	51H53b	7b7b44	D	4/4*	G11v2Cp7 C14v7p7 (II)
[MRS GORDON OF BELSIES]					
MRS GORDON OF CAIRNESS' REEL	135L1	4L3L2L2	A	2/2	C18p25
MRS GORDON OF CAIRNESS' STRATHSPEY	3L5L3L5L	3L5L6L2L	A	4/4	C18p25
MRS GORDON OF KINCARDINE'S REEL	51H55	11H3H1H	C	4/4	T1v1p4
MRS GORDON OF KNOCKESPOCH	1135	7b2H24	F	4/4	M4v5p10
MRS GORDON OF MOONMORE'S STRATHSPEY	3b17bL2	3b13b5	G	2/2	G15p36
MRS GORDON OF PARK	3L5L5L5L	3L5L12L	A	4/4	M4v4p27
MRS GORDON OF PITLURG'S STRATHSPEY	51H3H1H	51H3H2H	F	2/2	M11v1p11
MRS GORDON OF PITLURG'S STRATHSPEY	51H3H1H	6542	F	4/4	M11v2p7

MRS GORDON OF WHITEHILL('S STRATHSPEY)	5322	526L6L	G	4/4	C23p7 (II)
MRS GORDONS FANCY	1555	1552	D	2/4	A7v3p31
MRS GORDON'S FAVORITE	1152	517bL5L	E	2/4	G11v2Dp20
MRS GORDON'S REEL [MRS GORDON, UVIE]	1H575	72H4H7	D	2/2	M4v3p35 (II)
MRS GOW'S STRATHSPEY	153H2H	1H7b27bL	D	2/2	Mc15p30/31
MRS GRAHAM (OF BALGOWAN'S) REEL	5335	4362	D	4/4	P5v2p23
MRS GRAHAM OF BALGOWAN'S REEL	5335	437b2	D	2/2	H3p39 G11v2Cp38 D14v3p8/9
MRS GRAHAM OF GARTMORE'S STRATHSPEY	1H313	1H322H	D	4/4	S4v2p13
MRS GRAHAM OF ORCHILL'S REEL	5336	537b2	A	2/2	D14v3p14/15
MRS GRAHAM OF ORCHILL'S STRATHSPEY	1225	7b547bL	D	4/4	Mc4v2p8
MRS GRAHAM'S DELIGHT	5335	437b2	D	2/2	C14v2p6,7
MRS GRANT	1122	347L2	A	2/2	C24v2p25
MRS GRANT OF BUGHT'S JIG	1H327	1H351H	D	6/8	G15p7
MRS GRANT OF LAGGAN'S FAVORITE	1H3H3H7	1H562	D	6/8	G15p16
MRS GRANT OF LAG(G)AN('S STRATHSPEY)	47L11L	3bL5L7bL7bL	A	2/2*	G11v2Dp26 (II)
MRS GRANT OF SEABANK'S STRATHSPEY	3b113b	27bL47bL	A	4/4	G15p1
MRS GRANT OF VIEWFIELD'S REEL	3b53b5	27bL24	C	2/2	G15p35
MRS GRANT'S FANCY	1513H	1H522	D	2/2	P1v1p6
MRS GRANT'S REEL	52H1H5	47b54	G	2/2	G8p22
MRS GRANT'S STRATHSPEY	11H74H	3H4H2H5	F	4/4	M4v3p54,55
MRS GRANT'S STRATHSPEY	1513H	1H522	D	2/2	G8p15
MRS GREGORY'S STRATHSPEY	3551H	3H4H66	D	4/4	L1p10
MRS GREIG OF QUEBEC [MRS GRAY OF QUEBEC]	1H531	427L2	A	4/4*	C21p2 (II)
MRS G.S. MONTEATH'S STRATHSPEY	1H551	22H2H6	E	2/2	J1p34
MRS GUN MONRO OF POYNTZFIELD'S FANCY	1235L	1236	G	4/4	L1p7
MRS GUNN'S STRATHSPEY	3b513b	247b2	E	4/4	G8p18 P1v1p10
MRS GUTHRIE OF GUTHRIE CASTLE	1H1H2H1H	1H1H2H1H	F	3/8	A4v1p6
MRS GUTHRIE OF GUTHRIE'S STRATHSPEY	51H3bH2H	57b7b	D	4/4	A7v4p24
MRS GUTHRIE OF GUTHRIE'S STRATHSPEY	51H3bH2H	7b7b7b7b	D	4/4	D16p9
MRS H. INGLIS	5551	6662	C	4/4	M4v4p15
MRS HAMILTON OF BARGENEY	5326L	5L132	A	4/4	E2p8
MRS HAMILTON OF BARGENNY'S REEL	1131	1126L	G	2/2	R5p44
MRS HAMILTON OF PENCAITLANDS STRATHSPEY	3566	3532	C	4/4	G11v1Bp10 G10v3p14
MRS HAMILTON OF PENTCAITLAND	342H1H	342H7	D	2/4	S4v1p10
MRS HAMILTON OF PITCAITHLAND	3565	4522	C D	2/4	C8v1p35 C8v2p62
MRS HAMILTON OF SUNDRUM	5L121H	5562	Eb	4/4	E2p5
MRS HAMILTON OF SUNDRUM'S (JUNr) REEL	13b52	7bL27b2	A	4/4	F3p16,17
MRS HAMILTON OF SUNDRUM'S MINUET	1H33	321	D	3/4	R5p2
MRS HAMILTON OF SUNDRUM'S REEL	3b17bL5L	3b13b5	A	2/2	R5p49
MRS HAMILTON (OF WISHAW) 'S STRATHSPEY	1125L	1322	A G	4/4	G11v1Bp16 G8p21 Mc4v2p11 G10v3p20 M4v3p19 C13v4p33 A7v3p22 C5v1p72 A1v4p72 A7v6p68 P1v1p10
MRS HARDIE'S STRATHSPEY	13L13L	2L27L6L	Bb	4/4	P11v2p7
MRS HARVEY (OF BROADLAND'S) STRATHSPEY	5551	3642	Bb	4/4	P5v2p6
MRS HASWALL(INVERARAY'S STRATHSPEY)	1555	51H55	Eb	4/4	Mc15p20 (II)
MRS HASWALL'S FAVOURITE	3b55L1	3b53b7bL	B	4/4	Mc15p35
MRS HAY OF HAYSTON'S FAVORITE	51H6b5	3b525	D	6/8	G9v2p21 G10v6p32
MRS HAY OF WESTERTOWN'S STRATHSPEY	5313	5366	D	4/4	T1v2p2
MRS HENDERSON OF AIMSTER'S FAVORITE	1H311H	2H2H1H4	F	6/8	G15p29
MRS HENRY LUMSDEN OF TILLWHILLY'S STR.	1311	6L5L32	Bb	4/4	M4v3p9
MRS HEPBURN BELCHES	1122	347L5L	Bb	2/4	B11p1
MRS HEPBURN OF CLERKINGTON'S REEL	1H535	27b27bL	D	4/4	F3p4
MRS HERMITAGE'S FANCY	1H3H5H3H	4H3H62H	C	2/2	C14v10p12
MRS HOGGAN'S STRATHSPEY	3b13b5	247b4	E	4/4	S4v2p23
MRS HOUSTON OF ROSEHALL ('S FAVOURITE)	11H1H3bH	7b3b47bL	D	4/4	G11v1Bp25 G10v3p26
MRS H.R. DRAYTON'S REEL	351H1H	44H2H2H	F	4/4	Mc21v3p32
MRS HUGH LUMSDEN'S STRATHSPEY	125L1L	5L122L	A	4/4	M4v3p60
MRS HUGHES	425L3	4542	F	4/4	F3p12
MRS HUNTER OF BLACKNESS STRATHSPEY	5622	5651H	D	2/2	D16p12
MRS HUNTER'S REEL	2H1H31	4326L	G	2/2	R5p28
MRS INGLIS'S STRATHSPEY	1L17L7L	6L6L5L5L	Bb	4/4	P11v2p4
MRS IRVINE'S REEL	3b15L5L	7bL242	E	2/2	Mc19v3p19
MRS J. BISHOP'S STRATHSPEY	11H1H6	3532	F	4/4	M4v3p52
MRS J. F. GORDON OF BALMUIR'S STR.	5325L	5351H	G	4/4	L1p7
MRS J. GRANTS STRATHSPEY	3531	4326L	G	2/2	Mc15p8
MRS J. ROSE'S FANCY	3bH1H51H	2H2H4H7b	D	6/8	Mc15p26
MRS J. ROSE('S STRATHSPEY)	3bH1H51H	2H4H2H7b	D	2/2*	Mc15p26 (II)
MRS JA(ME)S CAMPBELL('S REEL)	1H535	6522H	F	2/2	Mc4v4p11 (II)
MRS JAMES DUFF(S') (STRATHSPEY/REEL)	1L5L35	4322	A	4/4*	C24v1p5 C24v2p21 (II)
MRS JA(ME)S ERSKINE OF KIRKWALL('S REEL)	3b55L1	2427bL	G	2/2	Mc15p3 (II)
MRS JAMES McINNES' STRATHSPEY	5L343	4322L	G	4/4	M4v3p39
MRS JOHN ANDERSON'S FAVOURITE	137L2	3456	Eb	6/8	S4v1p19
MRS JOHN CLARK'S DELIGHT	15L14	5432	Bb	6/8	C21p8
MRS JOHN LEISTER'S FAVORITE	1H351	427L5L	D	2/2	C21p11
MRS JOHN STEWART'S STRATHSPEY	5353	4322	D	4/4	M4v3p32
MRS JOHN STIRLING'S JIG	1H1H2H5	6532	D	6/8	C5v1p55 A1v4p55
MRS JOHN STIRLING'S JIGG	1125L	6L5L3L2L	Bb	6/8	Mc12v1p18
MRS JOHN WELLING'S FANCY	5451	5462	D	6/8	Mc11p10
MRS JOHN WELLING'S STRATHSPEY	1355	11H62	F	4/4	Mc11p2

MRS JOHNSON	5551	5542	F	6/8	L1p8
MRS JOHNSTON OF WOODHILLS REEL	15L5L1	5226L	Bb	2/2	P5v1p9
MRS JOHNSTON'S REEL	1H3H62H	761H3	D	2/2	G15p11
MRS J.W. BOURKE'S REEL	137L2	331H5	F	2/2	G10v4p30
MRS KEIR OF MILLBANK'S REEL	113b4	2427bL	A	4/4	C7p8
MRS KEIR OF MILLBANK'S STRATHSPEY	113b5	4247bL	A	4/4	C7p18
MRS KELSO OF DANHEITH'S REEL	1313	2662	Eb	4/4	F3p5
MRS KELTY AUCHTERMUCHTY'S FAVOURITE	1155	2266	G	2/4	L4p10
MRS KENNEDY OF DUNURE'S REEL	1H51H3H	4H3H72H	C	2/2	R5p45
MRS KENNEDY OF GREENAN('S REEL)	1H1H54	7b47b2H	E	2/2	R5p58 (11)
MRS KENT'S DANCE	5511	447L5L	A	6/8	B16v3p6
MRS KEPLING'S STRATHSPEY	3b11H1H	7b7b45	G	2/2	Mc22p4
MRS KERR'S MINUET	1H1H7	650	Eb	3/4	C22p3
MRS KINLOCH OF GOURDIE'S DELIGHT	1L124	5125L	Bb	6/8	B6v2p1
(MRS) KINLOCH (OF KINLOCH)	35L6L5L	35L6L1	Bb	6/8	C8v1p41 G10v4p35 P6v1p22
					W4v2p11
MRS L. STEWART'S REEL	1H3H53H	4327L	C	2/2	M4v3p45 (11)
MRS LAING'S STRATHSPEY	1515	156L2	Eb	2/2	M4v3p26
MRS LAIRD OF STRATHMARTINS STRATHSPEY	116L4	51H26L	D	4/4	Mc13v1p10 Mc13v2p10
MRS LAIRD OF STRICKMERTENS FAVORITE	1322	115L1	G	3/8	Mc4v4p3
MRS LAIRD'S HORNPIPE	1122	3344	A	2/2	D16p24
MRS LANDLE'S DELIGHT	5531H	5532	E	4/4	Mc4v2p7
MRS LEIS HORNPIPE	5H5H1H3H	2H2H54	D	4/4	C7p10
MRS LEITCH'S STRATHSPEY	5555	512H6	D	4/4	A1v4p59
MRS LEITCH'S STRATHSPEY	5L5L5L5L	5L1L26L	Ab	4/4	Mc12v1p34,35
MRS LEITH (OF GLENKENDY)'S(REEL)	35L5L3	46L6L4	A	4/4*	P5v2p17 (11)
MRS LESTER	3553	352H1H	F	3/8	C14v10p20
MRS LIEUt. MARISON'S FANCY	5127L	3366	G	6/8	W2v2p7
MRS LINLEY('S REEL)	1H515	2H47bL4	C	2/2*	Mc15p21 (11)
MRS LOCH'S FAVORITE	5651	2122	Eb	6/8	G10v4p22
MRS LOCKHARTS STRATHSPEY	1L1L35L	6L12L2L	Bb	4/4	C13v1p45
MRS LOUGHNAN'S STRATHSPEY	15L1L5L	2L27L2	A	2/2	J1p26
MRS LUMSDEN OF ACHINDORE'S REEL	1H513	6L237L	Eb	4/4	M12p34
MRS LUNDIE'S MINUET	333	11H7	Eb	3/4	D15v2p6
MRS M. SUTTON'S STRATHSPEY	53b3b7b	4224	E	4/4	Mc16p14
MRS MACDONALD	3H1H55	3H1H3H2H	A	6/8	E1v2p44
MRS MACDONALD OF CLANRANALD'S REEL	153b7bL	153b5	E	4/4*	E1v1p29 G10v2p24
MRS MACDONALD OF STAFFA'S REEL	5311	1313	A	4/4	C10v2Ap100
(PERTHSHIRE DANCING MEASURES &c No14)					
MRS MACDOUALL GRANT ('S STRATHSPEY)	3546	337L2	G F	2/4*	A1v4p4 G10v3p2 E1v1p76
[MRS MACDOUGAL GRANT]					G11v1Ap11 (11)
MRS MACDOWALL GRANT'S NEW STRATHSPEY	3556	317L2	Eb	2/4	W4v2p3
MRS MACINTOSH OF BLACKHEATH'S REEL	1H542	7L232	D	2/2	Mc15p28
MRS MACINTYRE ('S STRATHSPEY)	1353	3H1H32	F	2/2	C14v20p3 Mc15p27
MRS MACKAY'S STRATHSPEY	5L353	4542	D	4/4	L1p13
MRS MACKENZIE	15L3L5L	6L15L2	Bb	2/2	C14v24p5
MRS MACKINZIE OF CROMARTY'S STRATHSPEY	5L111	5L222	A	4/4	L1p4
MRS MacLEOD OF GEANIES'S	5H5H4H2H	5H5H2H5	D	2/4	L2p18
MRS MACLEOD OF MACLEODS STRATHSPEY	1H53b1	7bL242	G	4/4	Mc21v4p30
MRS MAITLAND OF FREUGH'S REEL	5651	53H2H2	C	4/4	Mc21v4p16
MRS MAITLAND (OF RANKEILLOR'S) REEL	1513	6L237L	G	6/8	Mc21v3p36
MRS MAJOR HAMILTON'S REEL	1H3H4H3H	5H3H75	C	2/2	C14v11p18
MRS MAJOR L. STEWART	5L3L1L1	516L2	A	4/4	M4v3p17
OF THE ISLAND OF JAVA					
MRS MAJOR MITCHELL'S STRATHSPEY	1315L	1311	F	4/4	M4v3p50
MRS MAJOR RAY'S FAVORITE	3b554	3b51H2H	D	6/8	G15p38
MRS MAJOR SHAW	315L4	547L2	Bb	4/4	H1p1
MRS MARSHALL'S REEL, EDINr	131H3	427L7L	D	2/2	T1v2p10
MRS MARY GRANT McINNES	5551H	5522	F	4/4	M4v4p1
MRS MASSON'S REEL	3661H	5351H	F	2/2	G15p30
MRS McADAM OF CRAIGENGILLAN'S REEL	1H1H11H	2H1H22	G	2/2	R5p47
MRS McCARDIE'S STRATHSPEY	5322	5376	F	2/2	C13v4p33
MRS McCOMBIE OF TILLIFOUR'S STRATHSPEY	16L5L3L	5L6L5L3L	A	4/4	T1v1p6
MRS McDONALD OF CLANRANALD('S STR.)	3L3L15L	3L16L2L	Bb	4/4	K1v2p33 G11v2Bp31 (11)
MRS McDONALD'S FAVORITE	5757	2H62H6	D	2/4	A7v5p24
MRS McDONELL OF LOCHGARRY'S REEL	1H531	5633	G	4/4	Mc19v1p8
MRS McDOWAL GRANT(OF ARNDILLY)	3546	347L2	F	4/4	C8v1p36 (11)
MRS McDOWAL GRANT OF ARNDILLY'S STR.	146L2	1415	Eb	4/4	M4v3p24
MRS McGHIES REEL	13b51	47bL42	G	6/8	R5p28
MRS McGRIGOR'S REEL	1H13b5	7b422	D	2/2	S12v1p61
MRS McINNES OF DANALIETH'S REEL	1353	671H3	F	2/2	G15p29
MRS McINNES STRATHSPEY	1H3H13	1H3H62H	Eb	2/2	R9p4
MRS McINROY, LUDE'S REEL	11H7b5	56b7b5	E	2/2	Mc19v3p8
MRS McINTYRE	1353	3H1H32	F	2/2	C8v1p7
MRS MCKENZIE OF KILCOWIE'S JIG	1H1H55	1H72H5	C	6/8	R7v1p2
MRS McKENZIE'S STRATHSPEY	113L1L	2L27L5L	G	2/2	C14v20p8
MRS McKINLAY'S FAVOURITE	137L4	37L6L7L	Bb	6/8	S4v1p15
MRS McLEA'S FAREWELL	5L36L5L	247L2	G	4/4	Mc10p11
MRS McLEOD OF COLBECK'S FAVOURITE	5331	247L5L	F	2/4	S11v1p2,3
MRS MCLEOD OF COLBECK('S REEL)	1156	31H2H2	F	2/2	S11v1p3 (11)
MRS McLEOD OF COLBECK'S STRATHSPEY	1311H	662H2	D	4/4	S4v1p21
MRS McLEOD OF COLBECKS STRATHSPEY	115L5L	7bL47bL7bL	A	2/2	Mc4v3p10

MRS McLEOD OF COLBECKS VALTS	1531	5L221	Bb	3/8	G9v4p12
MRS McLEOD OF DELVEY'S STRATHSPEY	113b3b	27bL27bL	A	4/4	T1v2p11
MRS McLEOD OF DUNVIGGEN CASTLE'S REEL	1527bL	157b1	E	2/2	R7v2p2
MRS McLEOD OF ELANREOCH('S STRATHSPEY)	1H3H1H5	61H62	D	4/4	E1v1p87 G11v1Ap32 A1v4p62
					G10v3p33 (II)
MRS McLEOD OF GEASTOW'S STRATHSPEY	3535	6442	F	4/4	M12p26
MRS McLEOD OF RASA[Y] ('S REEL)	11H66	3333	G A	4/4*	B7p6 E1v1p6 C8v1p47 G1v2p92
					C8v2p17 G10v5p36 C14v27p5
MRS McLEOD OF RASEY'S STRATHSPEY	3b111	7b424	G	4/4	M12p27
MRS McLEOD OF RAZA'S STRATHSPEY	5116L	5L132	Bb	4/4	R7v3p2
MRS McLEOD OF TALISCAR'S REEL	1H1H3H3H	1H1H2H2H	D	2/2	R7v2p2
MRS MCPHERSON	1H1H1H1H	1H1H2H2H	C	2/2	M4v4p12
MRS McPHERSON'S REEL	1H3bH1H5	7b542	C	2/2	M4v3p28
MRS McQUHAE'S STRATHSPEY	5L13b1	5L14L7bL	E	4/4	H1p20
MRS McREADY'S STRATHSPEY	5322	5376	G F	4/4	C5v1p54 A1v4p54 Mc12v1p16
MRS MELVILL DYSART REEL	3b13b5	7b7bL24	E	2/2	W2v1p13 (II)
MRS MENZIES OF COUFARES REEL	5L37L2	221H5	F	2/2	P5v4p2
MRS MENZIES OF CULDARE'S REEL	3131	3542	G	2/2	Mc13v1p7 Mc13v2p7
MRS MENZIES (OF CULDARE'S) STRATHSPEY	1H61H1H	1H622	C D	4/4	C4p12 C5v1p56 A1v4p56
					A1v3p218
MRS MENZIES'S, DUNKELD	11H64	547L2	D	2/2	Mc19v3p21
MRS MINZIES (OF CALDAIR) 'S STRATHSPEY	531H3	246L2	D	4/4	Mc21v3p34
MRS MINZIES OF CULDARE'S STRATHSPEY	16L11	16L2L2L	Bb	4/4	C13v1p21 G10v1p7 G11v1Ap2
					Mc12v1p38 (II)
MRS MITCHELL OF STOW	1H61H1H	1H1H4H7	C	4/4	M4v4p27
MRS MITFORD'S FANCY	1111	5565	D	2/4	J1p44
MRS MONCRIEFF OF REEDIE'S DELIGHT	5L131	6L243	D	4/4	L4p1
MRS MONRO BINNING'S FAVORITE	1147L	1165	Eb	6/8	S4v2p9
MRS MONTGOMERY OF COILSFIELD'S REEL	11H1H1	11H2H2	F	6/8	R5p39
MRS MONTGOMERY'S JIG	11H65	216L2	Bb	6/8	B2p2
MRS MONTGOMERY'S REEL	3135	7L5L7L2	Bb	2/2	B2p1
MRS MONTGOMRIE OF ANNICK LODGE	3112	7L225	F	4/4	E2p9
MRS MONTGOMRIE OF ANNICK'S STRATHSPEY	1H1H1H3	1H1H53H	F	4/4	E2p13
MRS MONTGOMRIE OF SKERMORLIE'S STR.	316L2	346L6L	Bb	4/4	E2p1
MRS MONTGOMRIE OF STAIR'S STRATHSPEY	113L1	6L5L3L2L	Bb	4/4	E2p18
MRS MONYPENNY('S REEL)	3H2H1H5	3572H	C	4/4	P5v3p4 (II)
MRS MORAY (MURRAY) OF ABERCAIRNEY	1353	2422	D	4/4	G11v1Cp18 G10v1p5 (II)
('S STRATHSPEY)					
MRS MORAY OF ABERCAIRNEYS STRATHSPEY	13b53b	1353	G	4/4	E1v1p106,107
MRS MORTHLAND'S REEL	3H2H51H	4H3H4H3H	C	2/2*	E1v1p21 A1v4p62 G10v3p28,29
					(II)
MRS MOSMAN'S STRATHSPEY	1345	137L2	G	4/4	Mc21v3p17
MRS MOSMAN'S STRATHSPEY	11H53	11H22	D	4/4	G11v1Ap26 G10v2p25 (II)
MRS MUIR MACKENZIE'S DELIGHT	17L11	3434	G	6/8	Mc4v3p12
MRS MUIR MACKINZIES DELIGHT	16L5L5L	5L36L6L	A	4/4	B11p14
MR(S) MUIR MACKINZIE'S FAVOURITE	1H531	427L6	D C	4/4*	G10v3p3 A7v3p3
[MR. MUIR MACKENZIE'S FAVOURITE]					
MRS MUIR McKENZIES FANCIE	1565	6527L	A	6/8	Mc4v2p12
MRS MUIR OF CALDWELL ('S STRATHSPEY)	5551H	5555	D	4/4*	G11v1Cp2,3 C5v1p65 A1v4p68
					G10v3p7 (II)
MRS MUIR OF CALDWELL'S REEL	1343	427L7L	Bb	4/4	F3p5
MRS MUIR (OF WARRISTON'S) REEL	3453	6L17L5L	G	2/2	Mc21v2p37
MRS MUIR OF WARRISTON'S STRATHSPEY	1122	1112L	Bb	4/4	E2p19
MRS MURRAY OF ABERCARNEY'S REEL	3155	51H22	D	2/2*	G10v1p6 G11v1Ap31 (II)
MRS MURRAY OF ABERCARNY	5L35L3	436L6L	A	4/4	Mc4v2p9 (II)
MRS NORMAN(D) LOCKHART('S REEL)	1351H	627L7L	F	4/4*	G10v5p27 (II)
MRS OSWALD (OF ACHINCRUIVE'S)	6565	653H2H	D	4/4	Mc21v3p1
(NEW) STRATHSPEY					
MRS OSWALD OF AUCHENCRUIVE'S JIG	1151	437L2	F	6/8	E2p16
MRS OSWALD [OF AUCHINCRUIVE]	5311	5362	G F	4/4*	A7v4p17 Mc21v2p1 (II)
'S (NEW) STRATHSPEY					
MRS OSWALD (OF AUCHINCRUIVE'S)	3411	6L237L	G	6/8	Mc21v2p26
FAVOURITE QUICK STEP					
MRS OSWALD OF AUCHINCRUIVE'S FAVOURITE	3H655	3H53H2H	D	6/8	E2p1
MRS OSWALD (OF AUCHINCRUIVE'S) NEW REEL	1135	7L27L2	G	2/2	Mc21v3p11 (II)
MRS OSWALD OF DUNNIKEERS MINUET	115	153	Eb	3/4	D14v1p12
MRS OWEN'S FANCY	1H521	362H7	F	6/8	C14v23p10
MRS P. CAMPBELL'S STRATHSPEY	1315	2422	D	4/4	S4v2p24
MRS PARKER'S DANCE	1H51H5	1H572H	D	2/4	A7v5p2
MRS PARKER'S FANCY	5351H	6562	F	2/2	P1v2p1
MRS PARKER'S REEL	15L3b2	27bL53b	B	2/2	P1v2p1
MRS PARKER'S STRATHSPEY MINUET	5532	1H553H	E	2/2	P1v2p5
MRS PATRICK STERLING	37L6L5L	7F2L4L6L	A	4/4	Mc11p8
OF KIPPENDAVIE'S REEL					
MRS PENDER'S STRATHSPEY	1531	4347L	G	2/2	Mc19v2p12,13
MRS PETERKIN OF GRANGE HALL'S STR.	3125L	6L3L7L2	F	4/4	C18p39
MRS PHILIP DUNDAS'S REEL	351H6	662H2	C	2/2	S4v1p26
MRS PITCAIRN'S REEL	5H3H4H2H	5H3H53H	C	2/2	M1p2,3
MRS PITTINDRIGH'S WALTZ	1H1H2H2H	1H1H2H1H	D	3/8	D6p10,11
MRS PRYCE GORDON'S REEL	3bH3bH1H1H	4H4H2H2H	D	2/2	Mc21v4p10
MRS R. CATTO'S HORNPIPE	1131	27L5L5L	Bb	4/4	D6p4
MRS R. JOHNSTON'S REEL	113b5	427bL2	E	2/2	P11v2p9

MRS RACHAEL GIBSON'S DELIGHT	4H2H4H3H	1H425L	D	2/4	S11v1p24
MRS RACHAEL GIBSON('S REEL)	3135	461H6	A	4/4	S11v1p24 (II)
MRS RAMSAY	1555	1632	F	2/2	M11v1p2
(OF INVERNETTIE LODGE'S) STRATHSPEY					
MRS RAMSAY OF BARNTON'S FAVORITE	1313	1632	Bb	4/4	E2p13
MRS RAMSAY OF BARNTON('S STRATHSPEY)	13b51H	7b427bL	E F	2/2*	Mc15p15 (II)
MRS RAMSAY OF BARNTON'S STRATHSPEY	3L122	1126L	Bb	2/2	G10v3p10,11
MRS REAS REEL	3b13b7b	4247bL	E	4/4	W2v1p13
MRS REID OF ADAMTON'S FAVOURITE	1577	337L7L	G	2/2	C12p6
MRS REID OF KILCALMKILL'S STRATHSPEY	1431H	5426L	D	4/4	G15p16,17
MRS RENNY TAILYOUR'S MINUET	114	551H	D	3/4	D15v2p4
MRS RICHARD WALPOLE'S REEL	1H1H35	6522H	C	4/4	Mc21v4p15
MRS RICHARDSON PITFOUR'S REEL	35L1L5L	351H3	A	2/2	Mc19v3p14,15
MRS RIDDELL'S HORNPIPE	1351H	6442	D	2/2	R6v1p4
MRS RIDDELL'S MINUET	112	321	Bb	3/4	R6v1p22
MRS RIDDELL'S OF WOODLY PARK'S REEL	521H2	526L2	D	2/2	R6v2p16
MRS RIDDELL'S REEL	351H5	5L32H2	D	2/2	R6v1p1
MRS RIGG JUNr	13b7bL7b	13b11H	G	6/8	G10v5p29
MRS RITCHIE'S REEL	551H6	551H2	D	4/4	R5p10
MRS. ROBERT CAMPBELL OF SKIPNESS STR.	131H3	7L272	F	4/4	M6p2
MRS ROBERT CHAMBERS	5133	172H2	G	4/4	M4v4p23
MRS ROBERTSON	51H35	1233	A	2/4	Mc19v2p6
MRS ROBERTSON OF LADYKIRK'S FAVORITE	3b3b55	4213b	D	4/4	G10v5p13
MRS ROBERTSON OF LAWERS DELIGHT	1123	5L166	G	6/8	Mc4v3p11 G8p19
MRS ROBERTSON OF LAWERS STRATHSPEY	116L4	5326L	D	2/2	Mc4v2p2
MRS ROBERTSONS OF LAWERS REEL	315L1	437L2	A	2/2	Mc4v4p6
MRS ROBERTSON'S REEL	11H52	7L232	Bb	2/2	Mc9v3p30
MRS ROBERTSONS STRATHSPEY	3L5L5L5L	4L5L7L2	Bb	2/2	C14v21p17
MRS RONALD('S REEL)	3H535	3H52H2H	F	2/2	D16p26 (II)
MRS ROSE FEUGHSIDES (REEL)	1H535	6522H	D C	4/4*	A7v5p25 A7v4p3 P5v3p6
MRS ROSE (MOUNT COFFER) (REEL/STR.)	5555	662H2H	D	4/4*	C24v2p21 A7v6p66 C24v1p2
MRS ROSE OF KILRAVOCK'S JIGG	11H63	637L2	D	6/8	G15p13
MRS ROSE OF KILRAVOCK'S STRATHSPEY	1136	53H22	G	4/4	L1p1
MRS ROSE('S REEL)	1151H	51H22	G	2/2	M4v3p39 (II)
MRS ROSE'S STRATHSPEY	5L3b7bL5L	5L3b53b	A	4/4	C18p11
MRS ROSS, DOWAGER OF KILRAVOCK'S	531H5	5632	G	4/4	M12p15
FAVORITE					
MRS ROSS'S RANT	3131	3147bL	G	2/2	Mc9v3p12
MRS ROSS'S REEL	13L13	4522	A	2/2	M4v1p4
MRS ROSS'S REEL	1H765	4562	D	6/8	B15v1p20 C4p32
MRS ROY (OF NENTHORN'S) FAVORITE	1H71H3	26L27L	Bb	6/8	Mc21v3p35
MRS RUSSEL (OF BLACKHALL) 'S STRATHSPEY	5364	5327L	F	4/4	Mc21v3p29
MRS RUTHERFORD OF EGERSTON	5151	5142	E	12/8	C7p8
MRS RUTHERFORD'S JIG	15L13b	5222	B	6/8	B20p9
MRS SAMUEL ANDERSON'S STRATHSPEY	13b22	5L3b1H3bH	E	4/4	S4v1p17
MRS SEVEWRIGHT'S REEL	3155	437L2	G	4/4	A1v5p13
MRS SEWELS DELIGHT	1H555	6550	Eb	2/2	B16v3p12
MRS SHEARER OF BUCHROMB	5L13b1	5L124	F	4/4	M4v3p29
MR(S) SHEARER (OF BUCHROMB'S) STR.	5L121	447bL7bL	F	4/4	M4v3p29 C22p43
MRS SHERRIF CAMERON	535L3L	7L244	Eb	4/4	M4v4p32
MRS SIM'S STRATHSPEY	5322	16L22	A	2/2	M11v1p5
MRS SITWELLS VALTZ	5H5H1T6H	5H5H71H	C	3/8	G9v4p4,5
MRS SKINNER OF DRUMINS' STRATHSPEY	16L5L3L	5L3L6L2L	Bb	4/4	T1v2p7
MRS SMALL OF DIRNANEAN DELIGHT	113L3	657L2	Bb	6/8	P5v1p9
MRS SMALL OF DIRNANEAN'S JIGG	1122	351H1H	D	6/8	P5v1p11
MRS SMITH'S STRATHSPEY	5314	5366	D	4/4	Mc16p24
MRS SMITON'S STRATHSPEY	13L13	427L5L	F	4/4	W4v2p27
MRS SMOLETS FAVORITE	5L3L11	2211H	Eb	4/4	Mc12v1p1
MRS SMYTH (OF METHVEN'S) FAVOURITE	1H751	4326L	Bb	2/2	Mc21v3p5
MRS SPENCE'S STRATHSPEY	5L115L	3522	A	4/4	G15p21
MRS SPENS MONRO'S JIG(G)	1236	1236L	G	6/8	A1v4p9 C5v1p9 Mc12v1p17
MRS SPICER'S FANCY	3451H	5135L	Bb	6/8	C14v23p9
MRS STENNET'S QUICKSTEP	1L17L6L	1L16L7L	Bb	6/8	Mc21v2p11
MRS STEWART ALLEAN'S REEL	116L5L	4L5L4L2L	A	2/2	Mc19v2p8
MRS STEWART, BENCHILL'S REEL	335L5L	5553	Eb	2/2	Mc10p13
MRS STEWART, BUN RANNOCH'S REEL	1153	4253	G	4/4	Mc19v1p8
MRS STEWART FRENICH OF FOSS	1H31H3	432H2	D	2/2	Mc4v1p12
MRS STEWART (KIRKMICHAEL'S) REEL	1515L	7bL247bL	E	4/4	P5v2p20
MRS STEWART KYNNACHAN'S STRATHSPEY	5351H	5322	D	2/2	Mc4v1p8
MR(S) (STEWART) MENZIES	3565	2427bL	D	2/2	Mc4v1p15 G11v1Cp34 G10v1p17
OF CULDARE ('S REEL)					
MRS STEWART NICHOLSON('S STRATHSPEY)	316L2	15L15	Eb	4/4	G10v4p6 (II)
MRS STEWART NICOLSON'S STRATHSPEY	51H7b7b	51H3bH5H	D	2/2	B20p6
MRS STEWART OF ALLENBANK('S STRATHSPEY)	1L147L	2322L	A	4/4*	G11v1Cp23 G10v2p21
MRS STEWART OF BINCHILL'S REEL	113b3b	7bL242	A	2/2	C21p17
MRS STEWART OF FOSS' STRATHSPEY	5L3L31	5L3L5L3L	Bb	2/2	Mc19v2p9
MRS STEWART'S REEL	1153	2462	D	2/2	C14v12p21
MRS STEWART'S STRATHSPEY	131H3	6246	D	4/4	M4v3p35
MRS STEWART'S STRATHSPEY	5L5L5L1L	2L5L4L7bF	A	4/4	G8p15
MRS STIRLING'S REEL	1H1H33	447L7L	A	2/2	C13v2p70
MRS STRACHAN'S STRATHSPEY	551H6	3H522	F	4/4	B6v2p2
MRS SYME'S REEL	1H1H2H2H	4H3H72H	C	2/2	B20p20

MRS T. BENSON'S REEL	116L2L	111L3L	A	4/4	Mc11p7
MRS THOM'S FAVOURITE JIG	1H1H2H5	1H551	D	6/8	M11v1p14
MRS TROTTER (OF CASTLELAW'S) QUICK STEP	11H74	157L2	F	6/8	Mc21v2p12
MRS TULLOH'S JIG	5333	47bL7b7bL	A	6/8	Mc4v2p2
MRS WALKER OF URQUHART'S STRATHSPEY	53b42	13b53bH	G	4/4	G15p37
MRS WALLACE'S REEL	427L2	351H3	A	2/2	C13v1p38 C13v2p79
MRS WALLACE'S REEL	1L5L11	1L5L22L	Bb	4/4	Mc21v2p11
MRS WALTER WEMYS'S FAVOURITE	5135	5116	D	4/4	D16p13
MRS WARDEN OF PARKHILL	536L5L	5L6L3L2L	G	4/4	T1v2p3
MRS WARREN HASTINGS ANDERSON	351H6	5437L	G	4/4	G10v6p12
MRS WARREN'S STRATHSPEY	1H565	22H4H2H	F	4/4	M1p3
MRS WATT'S STRATHSPEY	11H35	11H2H2	G	4/4	G15p4
MRS WEMYSS OF CUTTLEHILL'S STRATHSPEY	1H636	1H63H3H	D	2/4	G1v2p54
MRS WEMYSS OF CUTTLEHILL('S STRATHSPEY)	3b15L1	3b155	G	2/4	E1v1p97 G11v1Bp8 G10v3p23 Mc7p5 (II)
MRS WHITEFOORD'S REEL	15L5L1	5226L	Bb	2/2	S12v1p69 G11v2Cp31
MRS WILDMAN'S STRATHSPEY	5124	5141H	D	4/4	Mc21v4p19
MRS WILLm ELLIS OF LONDON'S MINUET	1H1H2H	3H4H1H	D	3/4	D15v2p4
MRS WILLm MARSHALL'S REEL	1362	317L5L	Bb	4/4	C21p9
MRS WILSON('S REEL)	15L3L5L	16L4L2L	Bb	2/2*	G15p25 (II)
MRS Wm ELLICE'S REEL	1H3bH2H7b	47b2H7b	G	4/4	D15v2p50
MRS Wm. MURRAY OF POLONAISE	131H1H	2H2H2H2	C	4/4	F3p13
MRS WRIGHT OF LATON ('S STRATHSPEY)	5555	7b47b4	E	4/4	G11v1Ap8 G10v1p14 (II)
(MRS YOUNG'S) STRATHSPEY	11H55	11H22	C	4/4	M4v3p48 C22p48
MRS YOUNG'S STRATHSPEY	3L16L1	3L12L6L	Bb	2/2	Mc19v3p16
MRS/LADY) MUIR MACKENZIE'S REEL	11H31	27b27bL	C	4/4*	G11v1Ap36,37 Mc4v4p13 G10v2p22 (II)
MUCH TO DO ABOUT NOTHING	1114	1112	G	6/8	R12v1p98
MUCKING OF GEORDIE'S BYRE, THE	3b11	111	G B	3/4	(J3) Mc8v1Ap2 Mc8v2Ap10 C5v2p15 A1v5p50 C20p43
MUCKING OF GEORDY'S BYRE, THE	3b11	117bL	B	3/4	O1v4p10,11 O1v1Bp35
MUFFIN, THE	126L5L	4L3L2L7L	G	6/8	R12v1p55
MUGDRAM HOUSE	1H3H5H3H	2H4H6H4H	C	4/4	L4p2
MUIRLAND WILLIE	13b57b	3b7b47bL	E A G	6/8	(J3) P8v2p15 C5v2p22 W7p15
MUIRLAND WILLIE	13b57b	3b7b42	G	6/8	P11v2p15
MUIRLAND WILLIE	13b47b	3b1H47bL	E	6/8	T6v1p56
MUIRLAND WILLIE	13b57b	47b47bL	E	6/8	S16p14,15
MUIRLAND WILLIE	13b57b	47b42	G	6/8	E1v2p135
MUIRLAND WILLIE	13b57b	47b47L	G	6/8	C29p45 O1v1Gp11
MUIRTOWN HOUSE	1113	5753	C	2/2	M12p6
MULCHARD'S DREAM	3133	3132	G	2/2	C33p17
MULLIN DU, THE	557b6	4447bL	A	2/2*	G11v2Cp23 (II)
MULLIN DU, THE [MUILEANN DUBH]	557b6	4444	A	2/2	Mc7p30 Mc9v3p20 (II)
MULLINDOUGH	557b6	4547bL	A	2/2	A1v6p3
MULLONIE'S JIG	3555	4362	D	6/8	C24v2p13 G11v2Cp38
MUNGO	51H52H	54H2H2H	D	2/2	B16v3p36
MUNRO'S RANT, (THE)	1353	2366	G D	4/4*	A1v6p15 G15p9 C33p15
MUNSTER SWITCH, THE	1H534	3422	A	6/8	H1p31
MURPH(E)Y DELANEY	1113	116L7L	Bb	6/8	M12p22 G11v2Cp32 (II)
MURPHY DELANEY	1113	115L7L	Bb	6/8	C14v20p1
MURPHY DELANEY	1113	1127L	G	6/8	N1v1p29
MURRAY'S MARCH, (THE)	6415L	5L5L5L5L	G	4/4	O1v1Ep27 O1v3p13 O1v2p18
MURT GHLINN-COMHAIN [MORT GHLINNE COMHAINN]	5L121	5L333	G	6/8	F2v2p30(20)
MUSES, THE	3362H	751H3H	Eb	6/8	C14v27p8
MUSES, THE	3362H	751H5H	D	6/8	G1v2p65
MUSETTE	1H1H2H5H	1H4H77	D	4/4	R12v3p20
MUSETTE	1125	147L7L	Bb	4/4	Mc21v4p8
MUSHATT'S CAIRN	1L5L3L1	5L35L3L	G	2/2	P9p11 (II)
MUSHET, THE	5551	2247bL	A	2/2	Mc16p27
MUSICAL SOCIETY OF FORFAR'S MARCH, THE	1355	1H2H65	F	4/4	D16p6/7
MUSICAL SOCIETY'S MARCH	1351H	5555	D	4/4	C7p6
MY AIN FIRESIDE	3H652H	3H651H	D	6/8	C8v2p35
MY AIN KIND DEARIE	3H51H1H	2H4H3H6	C D	4/4*	C19p5 E1v1p18 C8v2p62
(MY) AIN KIND DEARIE	15L11	1226L	A	2/2	C13v2p18 G7p4 G11v2Cp24
MY AIN KIND DEARIE	15L11	2326L	A	2/2	B15v1p76
MY AIN KIND DEARIE O	15L11	2416L	A	2/2	Mc23p2,3
MY AIN KIND DEARY	15L12	1226L	G	4/4*	W7p15 S7v1p65
MY AIN KIND DEARY (O)	35L11	2436L	G A	4/4	(J3) C8v1p33 Mc7p9,10 G9v5p28 C5v2p20 Mc12v2p4,5,6
MY APRON DEARIE	1H1H3H	1H56	C D	3/4	Mc8v1Cp88 Mc8v2Ap4 T6v1p68 S16p66,67 G17p19 O1v3p26 C29p32 O1v1Dp13
MY APRON DEARIE	1H5H3H	1H56	D	3/4	C13v3p22,23
MY APRON DEARIE	113	15L6L	Bb A	3/4	O1v5p32,33 P4p19 (J3) N1v2p29
MY APRON DEARIE	1H1H3H	156	D	3/4	C20p80
MY BONNIE LADDIE'S LANG O GROWIN'	551H7b	7b1H55	E	4/4	G1v2p76
MY BONNY LADDIE HAS MY HEART	151	417bL	E	3/4	C18p16
MY BONNY MARY	1356	1H633	D C	4/4	C5v3p61 (J3)
MY BONNY YOUNG LAD WAS THE FAIREST OF A' [OUR BONNY SCOTCH LADS]	3H5H2H3H	1H65H2H	D	6/8	C5v2p37 G1v1p30

OF A' [OUR BONNY SCOTCH LADS]

Title			Key	Time	References
MY BOY TAMMY	13b57b	4420	D E	4/4	(J3) C8v1p17 E1v2p11 C8v2p26
MY CHEEKS ARE FURROWED	3H5H6H	5H2H2H	C	3/4	Mc5p2
MY DAD WAS AN IRISH BLADE	5L223	16L16L	G	6/8	C10v2Ap69
MY DADDIE LEFT ME GEAR ENOUGH	5135	427bL7bL	G	4/4	C5v2p45
MY DADDY'S A DELVER OF DYKES	3b115	3b7bL3b1	A	6/8	T6v1p69
MY DEAR I DOW NE DO NE MAIR	1H1H7b4	7b445	D	2/2	O1v1Ep22,23
MY DEARIE AN THOU DIE	1H555	3H666	C	2/4	A1v2p70
MY DEARIE AN YE DIE	15L5L1	5L5L5L1	A	4/4	O1v2p37,38
MY DEARIE AND THOU DIE	15L5L5L	1111	A	2/2	C29p11
MY DEARIE AND THU DIE	1H555	5553H	C	2/2	Y1p11
MY DEARIE IF THOU DIE	15L5L5L	5L5L5L3	A	4/4	S16p110,111
MY DEARIE, IF THOU DIE	15L5L1	5L5L5L1	A G	4/4	O1v3p44 O1v1Ap10,11 (J3) N1v2p67
MY DEARY IF THOU DIE	35L5L1	2L2L5L5L	A	4/4	T6v2p4
MY FAIR YOUNG LOVE	1315L	5L335	G	12/8	C4p72
MY FATHER SAID THAT HE WOULD HIRE ME TO A MAN	51H1H3H	4H2H67	D	4/4	A1v3p157
MY FRIEND AND PITCHER	1155	51H22	A	2/2	E1v2p80
(MY HEART IS SAIR FOR) SOMEBODY	1522	1365	Bb F	4/4*	G10v5p35 C6p14
MY HEART IS SAIR FOR SOMEBODY	1155	2223	Bb	4/4	C8v1p12
MY HEART WITH LOVE IS BEATING	1H3H76	3H2H1H1	D	6/8	B7p17
MY HEART'S IN THE HIGHLANDS	1H1H2H	671H	D	3/4	C5v2p16
MY HEARTY WANTON CARLIE	5L353	4326L	G	4/4	C18p13
MY HIGHLAND LASSIE O	1H327	1H331	C	6/8	C6p6
MY JO JANET	61H72H	3H1H35	D	2/2	S16p112,113
MY JO JANET	51H72H	3H1H35	D C	4/4*	O1v1Cp16 T6v2p80 C5v2p15 C20p5 (J3) C6p20
MY JO JANET	51H72H	3H2H35	D	4/4	P8v2p38
MY JOE JANNET	61H1H2H	772H4H	D	2/2	Mc8v1Cp91 Mc8v2Cp3
MY JOY AND MY LOVE	551H2H	3H52H1H	D	6/8	P5v4p20
MY LADDIE IS A SAILOR	13b6b4	47bL24	D E	4/4	F3p16
MY LADY HOPES SCOTCH MEASURE	351H1H	351H1H	D	2/2	P7p7
MY LODGING IS ON THE COLD GROUND	1141H	5230	G F	6/8	C8v2p39 VC25
MY LODGING IS ON THE COLD GROUND	1141H	5233	F	6/8	C8v1p6
MY LODGING IS ON THE COLD GROUND	1161H	5122	D	6/8	A1v1p41
MY LODGING IS ON THE COLD GROUND	1H1H6HO	5H1H2HO	C	6/8	E1v2p16
MY LORD SEFOTH'S SCOTCH-MEASURE	1133	51H52	G	2/2	P7p4/5
MY LOVE ALASS IS DEAD AND GONE	1H3H2H	555	D	3/4	O1v1Gp33
MY LOVE ANNIE'S VERY BONNY	1131H	5221	G	4/4	C5v2p22
MY LOVE HAS FORSAKEN ME KEN YE FOR WHY	16bL3b	3b13b	B	3/4	C5v3p59
MY LOVE IS LIKE A RED RED ROSE	121H6	662H1H	D G	4/4*	C8v1p15 E1v2p6 C8v2p38
MY LOVE IS LIKE THE RED, RED ROSE	121H7	662H1H	D	2/4	C6p17
MY LOVE IS LOST TO ME	3b25L1	3b254	A G	2/2	O1v1Ep25 O1v5p14,15
MY LOVE SHE'S BUT A LASSIE YET	1H31H1	1H362	D	4/4	G9v5p13
MY LOVE SHE'S/IS BUT A LASSIE YET	1H31H1	1H32H2	Eb G D	2/4	C6p2 E1v1p101 C5v2p3 (J3) C8v2p46 A1v2p1 (II)
MY LOVE'S A BONNY NAETHING	3234	5L111	G	4/4	C5v3p63
MY LOVES A BONNY NAITHING	3235	5L111	G	2/2	O1v1Hp37
MY LOVE'S BONNY WHEN SHE SMILES ON ME	5L5L11	3332	G	4/4	O1v4p13
MY LOVE'S IN GERMANY	1H1H54	3bH2H2H5H	E	2/4	C5v2p13
MY LOVE'S IN THE BROOM	121H5	222H2H	G	4/4	O1v1Ep3
MY LOVE'S THE FAIREST CREATURE	51H3bH1H	1H1H76b	E	2/2	A1v6p49
MY MARY DEAR DEPARTED SHADE	5651H	5323	G Eb	4/4	C5v2p30 E1v2p22 G1v1p20 (J3)
MY MARY'S SMILE IS LIKE THE MORN	3b221	113b3b	A	4/4	C5v2p29
MY MOTHER BIDS ME BIND MY HAIR	1H1H76	1H5H2H2H	C	6/8	E1v2p108
MY MOTHER SAYS I MANNA	361H6	4210	D	6/8	A1v3p189 (J3)
MY MOTHER SAYS I MANNOT	361H6	4211H	D	6/8	O1v1Hp37
MY MOTHER'S AY GLOWRIN' O'ER ME	17L3b2	547b5	A G	6/8	C5v3p56 K1v1p16 B15v1p87 G11v2Bp14 S16p124,125
MY MOTHER'S AY GLOWRING O'ER ME	113b2	547b5	G	6/4	Mc9v2p8
MY MOTHER'S AY GLOWRING O'ER ME	111	7bL7bL5L	G	6/4	Mc8v1Cp62,63
MY MOTHER'S AY GLOWRING O'ER ME	111	7L7L5L	G	6/4	Mc8v2Cp8 C20p6
MY MOTHER'S AYE GLOWRING O'ER ME	17bL3b2	547b5	E G	6/8	A1v1p22 E1v2p124,125
MY NANNIE O!	1H3H1H6	5542	D	2/4	C5v1p22 A1v5p22 (J3)
MY NANNY, O	5155	3b217bL	E D C	4/4	G17p11 Mc8v1Cp71 O1v1Ep3 C8v2p55 C13v3p10,11 E1v1p24 C20p60,61 Mc23p26 S16p86,87 Mc8v2Ap17 O1v3p17 (J3)
MY NANNY O	5155	3b212	E	4/4	C6p21
MY NANNY O	3333	17L6L5L	F	4/4	T6v1p82
MY ONLY JO AND DEARIE (O)	1H1H3bH1H	1H555	E D	4/4	C5v2p7 G11v2Cp12
MY OWN DEAR SOMEBODY	6655	3322	G	6/8	E1v2p95
MY PEGGY IS A YOUNG THING	5L117b	415L4L	A	4/4*	C4p14 A1v1p47
MY PEGGY THOU ART GANE AWAY	3b13b1	3b17bL7bL	E	4/4	C10v2Bp25
MY PEGGY'S FACE (,MY PEGGY'S FORM)	13b55	7b7b27bL	E C	4/4*	C5v2p38 (J3)
MY PRIDE IS TO HOLD	5H4H6H7H	7H6H1TO	D	2/2	P8v1p20
MY SILLY AULD MAN	5353	5316L	F	6/8	R6v2p10
MY TIME O YE MUSES	113b	551H	B	3/4	A1v5p46
MY TOCHER'S THE JEWEL	5L115	53b3b7bL	A B G	6/8	C5v2p67 G1v1p25 C8v1p44
MY TRIM-BUILT WHERRY	1H1H6	353	G Eb	3/4	A1v3p208

MY WIFE IS A WANTON WEE THING	1H1H1H5	7b7b7b2	D	6/8	K1v1p36,37 G11v2Ap35 B10p35 (II)
MY WIFE SHE DANG ME	357b2	353H1H	D	2/2	Mc8v1Ap6 Mc8v2Cp8
MY WIFE SHE'S A WANTON WEE THING	1H71H5	7b7b7b3bH	D	6/8	A7v4p8
MY WIFE SHE'S TA'EN THE GEE	1H51H5	7b244	C	4/4	G10v5p32
MY WIFE'S A WANTON WEE THING	1H61H5	7b7b7b2	D	6/8	G1v2p90 S12v1p30 O1v1Fp12 A1v1p15
MY WIFE'S WALTZ	1H654	3637L	F	3/8	D6p20
MY WINSOM JOHN	1H71H2H	1H765	D	6/8	C20p79
MYRES CASTLE, THE	7564	357L2	F	2/2	L4p1
MYRTLE SPRiG	51H53	6L15L1	F	6/8	S7v1p51
'N ANN AIR MHIRE THA SIBH	2233	6666	A	4/4	Mc1v1p92,93
'N CARN GORM	5L5L5L5L	6L6L13	G	6/8	F2v2p72(62)
'N CUALA SIBH MAR THACHAIR DHUIN	3b57b5	1H3bH44	C	4/4	F2v2p68(58)
'N DEAN THU RUIDH AIR FALBH LEAM	3b3b54	2424	A	2/2	F2v2p65(55)
N LEATH SHUIL CHAOIG	1H51H1H	3H663H	C	2/2	D14v2p16
N' TROOPA GHAELACH ['N TRUPA GHAIDHEALACHD]	5L121	5L154	G	6/8	F2v2p40(30)
NA COMPUICH A'G'OL [NA CCMPAICH AG OL]	1253	1266	Eb	6/8	F2v2p85(75)
NA LOGAISEAN	2531	4251	F	2/2	Mc16p9,10
NACH BEIR THU AIR A' BHAN' MHEARLACH	113b3b	61H2H6	G	2/2	F2v2p25(15)
NACH BOCHD A BHI'M FALACH	3526L	13L3L5L	Bb	6/8	F2v2p58(48)
NACH TRUAGH MO CHAS	35L5L3	3211	Bb	4/4	F2v2p59(49)
NAE FAIRER BLOOMS THE DAISY	13b1H3bH	7b443b	E	4/4	C5v2p43
NA'ER A BOTTOM, THE	3344	5523	G	6/8	R12v1p89
NAMELESS, THE	53H1H6	53H1H6	F	4/4*	H6v1p1 P6v1p23 C14v23p4,5
NANCY DAWSON	1H1H5H1H	2H2H2H7	D	6/8	E1v1p88
NANCY DAWSON	1151	2227L	G Bb	6/8	A1v1p40 G11v2Cp5
NANCY STUART	1316L	151H2	G	2/2	S7v3p7
NANCY UNDER THE HILL	1H3H2H7	61H53	D	12/8	B16v3p32
NANCY'S CHOICE	1234	527L5L	G	12/8	B16v3p25
NANCY'S FANCY	1H3H4H2H	3H72H2H	D	2/4	P5v3p24
NANCY'S TO THE GREEN-WOOD GANE	5L5L5L4L	4L2L6L6L	Bb	4/4	(J3) N1v2p25
NANNY O	5555	3b217bL	E	4/4	P8v2p13
NANSY'S TO (THE GREEN WOOD GANE)	5554	2166	D	4/4	Mc23p10,11
NANSY'S TO THE GREEN WOOD GANE	5554	4266	D	4/4	Mc8v1Bp56 Mc8v2Bp13 O1v1Ap3 G17p7 S16p40,41 O1v2p10,11 O1v3p18,19 C13v3p28,29 C20p48
N'AOICHE ROIDH NA PHOSADH ['N OIDHCHE RO'N PHOSADH]	3bH1H1H5	7b2H4H4H	C	2/2	F2v2p15(5)
NAPLES DANCE	5H3H3H1H	1H555	D	2/2	S7v1p96
NARRATOR, THE	3555	3521	A	6/8	S7v3p6
NATH. GOW'S COMPLIMENTS TO HIS BROTHER	1L5L5L1	2326L	A	4/4	G10v6p19
NATH: GOW'S COMPLts TO MR W.K. JENKINS	3354	6423	Eb	4/4	G10v5p21
NATH. GOW'S LAMENT FOR (HUGH) EARL OF EGLINTOUN	1326L	131H6	D	4/4	G10v6p21
NATHANIEL GOW	1L3L5L3L	1L3L6L2L	Bb	4/4	G10v5p35 (II)
NATHANIEL GOW'S COMPLts TO MR GRANT	5332	5351H	D	4/4	G10v5p24
NATHANIEL GOW'S LAMENT FOR MRS OSWALD OF AUCHINCRUIVE	53b11H	3bH751H	C	4/4	G10v4p14
NATHANIEL GOW'S LAMENT FOR (THE DEATH OF) HIS BROTHER	3b53b1	3b527bL	A	6/8	C8v1p11 C8v2p30 G10v3p11
NATIVE LAND, ADIEU	511H1H	1541	E	2/4	C10v2Bp90
NAVAL REVIEW, THE	1H1H27	1H1H21H	C	2/4	C14v4p10
N'COMUN RIOGHAIL GAELACH ['N COMUNN RIOGHAIL GAIDHEALACHD]	15L5L5L	15L2L2L	A	4/4	F2v2p12,13(2,3)
NEAT SHOE, THE	3342	331H1H	A	2/2	Mc9v3p24
NEEPS LIKE SUCKER, WHAE'LL BUY NEEPS	5345	5321	Bb	6/8	P11v2p23
NEGLECTED TAR, (THE)	1H1H66	5530	F E	4/4	A1v6p33
NEGROE, THE	3211	3211	G	2/2	R12v1p49
(NEIL) NIEL GOW'S LAMENTATION FOR (JAS MORAY ESQr OF) ABERCARNEY	1L5L6L5L	246L6L	G	4/4*	G11v1Ap1 G10v1p3 (II)
(NEIL) NIEL GOW'S LAMENTATION FOR THE DEATH OF HIS BROTHER (DONALD)	5L127b	47b47bL	E	6/8	G11v1Bp6,7 G10v2p18
NEIL GOW'S FANCY	3135	3111H	G	2/2	C14v11p14,15
(NEIL) GOW'S LAMENT(ATION) FOR ABERCA(I)RNEY	1565	2H4H66	D	4/4	B7p44 A1v3p206
NEIL GOW'S SNISHEN MILL	1H57b2	1H513H	D	4/4	F2v1p6
NEITHER SHALL I GO TO LOCH BROOM NOR GAIRLOCH	1141	1152	A	6/8	Mc5p5
NELL OF CONNAUGHT	1H1H1H	3bH3bH4H	D	3/4	O1v1Ip84,85
NEOPOLITAN THRESHERS	3565	1H2H1H1	D	6/8	A1v2p17
NEOPOLITAN WALTZ	1H3H5H	6H5H5H	C	3/4	E1v2p41
NESS RIVER	5326	5353	C	2/2	A7v3p15
NESS SIDE	5L126L	5L143	A	2/2	H3p5
NETHER BOW HAS VANISHED, THE	1L353	47bL7b7b	G	4/4	B15v1p104
NETHERBY HOUSE	3b5L3bL2L	5L7b47bL	G	4/4	P9p26,27
NEVER MORE SHALL I RETURN	5555	5555	A	6/8	Mc5p41
NEW ACADEMY, THE	1342	547L5L	Eb	6/8	B16v1p8
NEW ALLEMAND	1531	2H71H1H	F	2/4	S7v1p91
NEW ALLEMAND, THE	351H4	2H4H75	D	2/4	B16v4p96
NEW ALLEMAND, THE	5561H	1H3H3H2H	D	2/4	B16v3p96

Title					
NEW BARRACKS, THE	3112	311H6	G	2/2	C14v11p11
NEW BRIDGE OF AYR, THE	351H3H	2H1H32	C	2/2	C14v16p11
NEW BRIDGE OF BALLATERS	3165	31H42	C	2/2	P5v4p9
NEW BRIDGE (OF) DUMFRIES, THE	13b53b	7bL242	G	2/2	A7v1p16 (II)
NEW BRIDGE (OF EDINBURGH), THE	1H531	22H75	D	2/2	C13v2p60 H3p7
NEW BRIDGE OF GLASGOW, THE	1H51H5H	1H542H	C	2/2	C13v2p24
NEW BRIDGE OF LAGAVUILLIN, THE	4235	6661H	D	2/2	Mc16p11
NEW BRIDGE OF RUTHERGLEN, THE	113b5	2454	C	2/2	C13v2p71
NEW BRIDGE OF SPEY, THE	1353	2326L	A	4/4	T1v1p5
NEW BRIGHTON WALTZ, THE	4#37L3	4#2#7L1	G	3/8	P6v1p16
NEW BROOM, THE	5355	51H1H3H	D	2/2	O1v1lp79
NEW BUMPKIN	1H542	327L5L	G	6/8	G11v1Ap38 A7v6p87
NEW CASTLE TROOP	1H2H3H2H	1H2H3H1H	D	3/8	A1v5p3 C5v1p3
NEW CHRISTMAS	3155	1H3H2H2	G	4/4	G11v2Bp16 K1v2p18 (II)
NEW CHRISTMASS	3155	1H2H2H2	G	4/4	B15v1p91 A7v5p34 A7v6p77
NEW CHRISTMASS	3155	12H2H2	G	4/4	A7v3p20
NEW CLARET	133	132	G	9/8	H6v2p3 P6v1p26
NEW CLARET	133	133	G	9/8	K1v2p20 C14v22p13 B15v1p70 (B21) G11v2Bp18 (II)
NEW CORN RIGGS	5566	5530	D	2/2	S7v1p8
NEW COTILLON, THE	327L2	3427L	A	6/8	B16v3p35
NEW DUKE OF YORK'S MARCH	1H1H1H2H	3H3H3H4H	D	2/4	W4v1p8,9
NEW FAIR, THE	3b3b11	7bL46b4	E	2/2	C14v2p5
NEW FANDANGE, THE	17L12	4312	A	6/8	B16v3p24
(NEW) GERMAN SPA (DANCE), THE	3512	3432	A G	4/4*	Mc9v3p40 Mc12v1p64 A1v3p205 A7v2p35 A7v6p12
NEW GERMAN WALTZ	3153	311H5	F	3/8	C26v1p3
NEW GERMAN WALTZ, (THE)	3155	311H5	G F	3/8	A1v6p25 C14v10p5 Mc7p27
NEW GYPSIE, THE	1545	2411	G	2/4	C14v6p9
NEW HIGHLAND LADDIE, THE	1122	1132	G A	2/2	A1v4p46 C5v1p46 W4v1p20
(NEW) HIGHLAND LADDIE, (THE)	5L131	4242	Bb	2/2	B17p7 Mc9v2p16
(NEW) HIGHLAND LADDIE, (THE)	1353H	1H453	D	6/8	R12v3p14 (J3)
NEW HONEY MOON, THE	5353H	64H1H6	D	2/2	H1p19
NEW IRISH JIG, THE	355	351H	F	9/8	G9v3p7
NEW ISLA REEL, THE	51H4H2H	51H4H3bH	D	2/2	C14v11p22
NEW JOHNNY COPE	1144	7bL7bL47b	E	2/2	R6v2p36
NEW LANGO LEE	5L144	35L31	A	6/8	S7v1p55
NEW LONDON, THE	1361H	3532	F	2/2	C14v6p5
NEW LONG ROOM AT SCARBOROUGH, THE	133	132	G	9/8	R12v1p75
NEW MADRIGALL, A	1H71H1	3H675	Eb	6/8	D15v1p10
NEW MAGGIE LAUDER	1H53H1	2H4H72H	D	4/4	Mc8v1Bp114,115
NEW MAGGIE LAUDER	15L31L	247L2	G	4/4	B15v2p10 D13p12
NEW MARCH, A	1111	2222	G	4/4	A1v6p34
NEW MARKET	31H31H	31H31	F	6/8	G11v2Bp8
NEW MARRIED WIFE, THE	3551	5152	E	2/2	B20p8
NEW MERRY DANCERS, THE	1H534	2425L	G	2/2	S7v1p64
NEW MILLER'S DAUGHTER	3312	227L6L	Bb	2/4	S7v1p32
NEW MILLS HOUSE	1523	151H5	D	6/8	B15v1p72 B17p16
NEW MINUET DE LA CHASSE AND GAVOT	3H5H5H	5H4H3H	D	3/4	C22p17,18
NEW OPERA DANCE, THE	5651	2122	Eb	6/8	G10v4p22
NEW PEIR OF PETERHEAD	5533	5522	D	2/2	M11v1p14
NEW PERRO	1H1H76	5561H	D	2/2	W7p12
NEW POLONES, THE [POLONESE DANCE]	17L17L	5327L	A	2/4	B16v3p88 S7v1p46
NEW POST, THE	1H353	3753	D	2/2	C14v2p11
NEW RIGG'D SHIP, (THE)	1H1H1H1H	2H52H5	D C	6/8	C8v2p54 E1v1p37 G11v1Cp10 C8v1p48 G10v2p8 C14v7p18 (II)
NEW ROAD TO BRECHIN CASTLE, THE	1H2H1H6b	53b7L5L	A	4/4	G9v2p5
NEW ROYAL QUICK STEP, THE	1155	6L427L	Bb	6/8	C14v19p19
NEW RUSSIAN WALTZ, THE	3L37L3	3L37L1	Bb	3/8	C14v27p4
NEW SCOTCH AIR, A (or MRS NEIL FERGUISON'S DELIGHT)	1H1H3H3H	4H2H66	E	4/4	J1p45
NEW SCOTCH MEASURE, A	5555	5151H	C	2/2	P7p13
NEW SCOTCH MEASURE, A	3H3H66	1H2H66	F	2/2	P7p13
NEW SCOTCH-MEASURE, A	321H1H	2H2H2H6	F	2/2	P7p9
NEW SETT OF AULD ROBIN GRAY	3565	61H6O	D	4/4	(C25)
NEW SHIELDS	123b	221	D	6/4	R12v1p82
NEW SIMON BRODIE	5353	5342	A	4/4	A7v3p19
NEW SPAW MINUET	1H3H5H	1HO5H	C	3/4	W6p18
NEW STEPNEY MARCH	51H76	557L2	G	6/8	A1v3p205/206
NEW STRATHSPEY REEL, A	551H6	1H5H6H3H	C	4/4	O1v1Cp23
NEW STRATHSPEY REEL, A	3313	2H36L6	G	4/4	O1v1Cp23
NEW TAMBOURIN, THE	61H1H7	6655	D	2/2	R12v1p16
NEW TARTAN PLAIDIE, THE	531H7	2H231	F	4/4	C14v13p11
NEW THEATRE, THE	151H5	64H1H6	F	2/4	C14v25p8,9
NEW TOON OF EDINBURGH, THE	5551H	5551H	F	4/4	P9p2
NEW TOWN OF EDINBURGH, THE	1L147L	3322L	A	2/2	B15v1p97
NEW TOWN OF EDINBURGH, THE	1L147L	3422L	A	2/2	C13v2p27
NEW TOWN OF EDINBURGH, THE	1L147L	3622L	A	4/4	C13v1p46
NEW TRUMPET MINUET	1H3H1H	1H53	D	3/4	W7p13
NEW TURRIFF HUNT, THE	1356	4635	Bb	2/2	M11v2p11
NEW WALTZ	4H3H2H1H	4H3H2H1H	D	3/8	G1v2p57
NEW WATER KETTLE, THE	5111	5127L	F	6/8	G11v2Dp22

NEW WAY OF WOOING	3551H	3H3H2H1H	D	2/2	W7p5
NEW WAY OF WOOING, THE	1135	3311	G	4/4	O1v1Ep28
NEW WAY TO EDINr, THE	1111	1111	F	4/4	Y1p16
NEW YEARS DAY	11H1H1	11H2H2	F	6/8	R4p17 K1v2p31 P5v2p5 G11v2Bp29
					A1v3p173
NEW YEAR'S DAY	1564	5532	G	6/8	S7v1p12
NEW YEAR'S GIFT	1122	1122	Eb	2/4	S7v1p99
NEW YORK GIRLS	3142	5352	G	6/8	A1v2p52
NEWBYTH HOUSE	513b5	27bL7b4	E	2/2	D14v3p17 (II)
NEWBYTH HOUSE	3555	6362	D	6/8	Mc4v1p24
NEWCASTLE BRIDGE	3125L	3522	A	6/8	Mc13v1p2 Mc13v2p2
NEWCASTLE VOLUNTEERS QUICK STEP	3565	353H2H	D	6/8	C7p18
NEWFIELD COTTAGE	1L115L	2L226L	A	4/4	M4v3p19
NEWGATE BROTH	11H53	11H75	A	6/8	R12v1p31
NIAL BROCDHAIR [NIALL BROCHDAIR]	1113L	1516L	Bb	6/8	F2v2p16(6)
NIAN BODDACH AN ROAINAITIN	31H66	1H61H3	C	4/4	F2v2p27(17)
[NIGHEAN BODACH AN ROAINAITINN]					
NIAN DONN RO' BHEADARACH [NIGHEAN...]	553b1	551H1H	F	4/4	F2v2p101(91)
NIAN DOUN A BUAIN NAN DEARCAG	3b17bL4	3b11H5	G	4/4	F2v2p29(19)
[NIGHEAN DONN...]					
NIAN DOUN AN T'SUGRIDH	3b212	5414	A	4/4	F2v2p26(16)
[NIGHEAN DONN AN T-SUGRAIDH]					
NIAN NAN COARACH [NIGHEAN...]	5L53b1	3b53b7bL	F	12/8	F2v2p101(91)
NIAN TORMAID [NIGHEAN THORMAID]	3b157bL	7bL5L7bL7bL	G	4/4	F2v2p33(23)
NIEL GOW ('S STRATHSPEY)	51H62	51H66	Eb G D	4/4*	Mc15p17 C5v1p1 A1v5p1
					G10v4p36 E1v1p16 K1v2p26
					P6v1p9 G9v5p26,27 C8v1p46
					C8v2p16 Mc7p28 G11v2Bp24
					Mc21v3p39 P5v3p19 C14v12p2
					(II)
NIEL GOW'S COMPLIMENTS	13H5H3H	14H72H	D	4/4	A1v6p6
RETURN'D TO MR MARSHALL					
NIEL GOW'S COMPLIMENTS	1L353	1L47L2	A	4/4	G11v1Ap26 G10v2p13 (II)
RETURNED TO MR MARSHALL					
NIEL GOW'S FIDDLE	1H527bL	1H61H1H	D	4/4	G10v4p19
NIEL GOW'S LAMENT	5L126	5236L	D	6/8	G10v5p2,3
FOR THE DEATH OF HIS 2d. WIFE					
NIEL GOW'S RECOVERY	3L5L31	6L5L4L2L	Bb	4/4	G11v1Bp32 (II)
NIEL GOW'S WIFE	3b127bL	3b13b3b	G	4/4	K1v2p15 G11v2Bp13 (II)
NIGHEAN BHUIDH BHOIDHEACH	57b11	47b7bL7bL	B	2/2	F2v2p71(61)
NIGHEAN DONN NAN GABHAR	5L13b4L	5L3b22	A	4/4	Mc5p21
NIGHTINGALE, THE	1H2H1H5H	1H2H1H5H	D	2/4	C8v2p58
NIGHTS OF PLEASURE	1H3H5H2H	1H6H3H1H	D	2/4	S7v2p11
NINE-PINT COGGIE, THE	3115L	7bL424	G	2/2*	C18p10,11 (II)
NINETEENTH OF FEBRUARY, THE	1H3H2H1H	1H3H2H1H	G	4/4	C14v7p2
NINETEENTH OF MAY	1342	37L25L	G	6/8	S7v1p14
NINETY-SECOND, THE	5353	27bL47bL	A	2/2	C14v19p18
NIRE NORE	3b51H1H	3b57b2	A	4/4	A7v3p10
NIS O RINNEADH AR TAGHADH	5651	1321	G	12/8	Mc5p14
NITHIAN A GHREISICH	16L15L	1332	D	4/4	G10v1p21,22 Mc12v2p54,55
NIVEN'S SCOTS MEASURE	3b113b	5553b	G	2/2	A1v3p185
NO CATCHEE NO HAVEE	1313	1322	G	6/8	R12v1p5
NO SURE	3423	3333	G	6/8	R12v1p64 (W3)
NO. TWO MARCH TO THE BATTLE FIELD	3H3H1H6	51H3H2H	C	2/4	C8v1p62
NOBLE RACE WAS SHENKIN, A	3bH2H72H	1H111	C	4/4	W4v2p3
NOBLE SQUIRE D'ACRE COMES	3112	4246	A	6/8	G1v2p60 R6v2p15
OVER THE BORDER					
NOBODY COMING TO MARRY ME	351H0	3H1H2H2H	F	6/8	E1v2p89
NOCHD FUR FAOIN (MO CHADAL DOMH)	1366L	1133	G	4/4	Mc5p21(?) C4p29
NON MUNTON HUNT	6L15L1	327L2	D	2/2	B16v3p57
NONE LIKE IT	3146	6531	A	6/8	R12v1p43
NONE SO PRETTY	1H1H65	13H75	D	2/4	C1v1p9 C14v9p22
NONE SO PRETTY	1H3bH4H2H	1H3bH7b5	E	6/8	R12v1p87
NOORAH CREENAH	113b5	1124	A	6/8	C14v15p20 P6v1p3
NORAH CREENA	1T1H3H5H	1T1H2H5H	D	6/8	C8v2p56
NORA'S VOW	31H63	3552	Eb	4/4	C10v2Ap20
NOREA'S LOST TO ME	51H2H7	6643	D	2/4	O1v1Ep16
NOREA'S SCOTS MEASURE	1115	2665	G	2/2	O1v1Ep6
NOREA'S WISH	37L6L5L	37L6L5L	G	2/4	O1v1Kp116
NORICKYSTIE	1H3H4H3H	1H3H72H	D	6/8	A1v1p50
NORRY'S CAKE	37L5L7L	227L2	G	6/8	C14v18p11
NORTH BERWICK LAW	566L6L	5653	Bb	4/4	G10v6p29
NORTH BRIDGE OF EDINBURGH, THE	5L113b	27bL47bL	B A	4/4	K1v1p39 G11v2Ap37 (II)
NORTH BRIDGE, THE	1H3H53	22H2H2	C	2/2	A7v1p14
NORTH HIGHLAND 1	1554	7bL442	A	6/8	Mc5p33
NORTH HIGHLAND 10	61H1H3H	72H67	D	6/8	Mc5p34
NORTH HIGHLAND 12	3211	7bL527bL	A	6/8	Mc5p35
NORTH HIGHLAND 13	3b3b2	155	B	9/8	Mc5p35
NORTH HIGHLAND 14	5135	5126	G	4/4	Mc5p35
NORTH HIGHLAND 15	1531	4327bL	A	4/4	Mc5p35
NORTH HIGHLAND 16	5132	5133	A	4/4	Mc5p35
NORTH HIGHLAND 17	3111H	7b524	A	4/4	Mc5p35

Title					
NORTH HIGHLAND 18	3535	7b47b2	A	4/4	Mc5p36
NORTH HIGHLAND 19	3313	4324	A	4/4	Mc5p36
NORTH HIGHLAND 2	1313	1324	A	6/8	Mc5p33
NORTH HIGHLAND 20	1434	1422	A	4/4	Mc5p36
NORTH HIGHLAND 21	6154	6142	A	4/4	Mc5p36
NORTH HIGHLAND 22	1H7b27bL	27bL22	A	4/4	Mc5p36
NORTH HIGHLAND 23	3555	3566	G	4/4	Mc5p36
NORTH HIGHLAND 24	3b43b7bL	3b3b51	A	6/8	Mc5p36
NORTH HIGHLAND 3	311	312	A	9/8	Mc5p33
NORTH HIGHLAND 4	1113	1142	A	6/8	Mc5p33
NORTH HIGHLAND 5	31H66	37b1H2	A	6/8	Mc5p33
NORTH HIGHLAND 6 (REEL), (A)	3b547bL	3b541	A	6/8	A1v5p69 Mc5p33
NORTH HIGHLAND 7	3324	3335	A	6/8	Mc5p34
NORTH HIGHLAND 8 (FENCIBLES)	1H33	1H32	G	9/8	Mc22p9 Mc5p33 A1v4p48
NORTH HIGHLAND 9	1553	1524#	G	6/8	Mc5p34
NORTH HIGHLAND II	3H564	3H51H1H	D	6/8	Mc5p34
NORTH HIGHLAND REEL, A	1347L	1353	G	2/2	Mc16p22
NORTH HIGHLAND REEL, A	1H567	1H51H5	G	2/2	Mc16p25
NORTH HIGHLAND REEL, A	1113	1342	A	6/8	A1v5p69
NORTH HIGHLAND REEL, A	31H66	351H2	A	6/8	A1v5p69
NORTH HUNT, THE	13L13	527L2	Eb	4/4	A7v3p7
NORTH LOCH, THE	3535	2427bL	G	4/4	B15v1p44
NORTH OF THE GRAMPIANS	3553	3532H	C	4/4	M12p4 (II)
NORTH OF THE GRAMPIANS	3553	351H2H	C	4/4	C8v1p35
NORTH REEL, THE	1113	2333	G	2/2	R12v1p99
NORTH STREET THEATRE, THE	3H2H1H3H	4H4H75	C	2/4	A7v3p4
NORTHAMPTON FROLICK	1H2H61H	1H3H2H5	C	6/8	R12v1p10
NORTHERN LASS	3225	1H2H66	D	4/4	Mc8v1Dp100
NORTHERN LASS, THE	3225	3H2H66	G D	4/4	C5v2p17 (J3) O1v1Ap5 O1v2p11 O1v3p19
NORTHFIELD HOUSE, DUFFUS	1L3L1L1	6516L	A	2/2	T1v2p5
NORTHLAND JOCKEY	1132	6532	F	2/2	R12v1p6
NORTH'S (MILLES MACPHAIL) FAREWELL TO THE CALEDONIAN HUNT	52H3H2H	3H651H	C	6/8	G10v4p16
NOS CALEN	5532	1231	G	4/4	A1v3p224
NOS GALEN	5H5H3H2H	1H1H3H1H	C	4/4	E1v2p83
NOSEGAY, THE	3654	2515L	G	6/8	S12v2p49
NOTHING AT ALL	1H524	3214L	Bb	4/4	S7v1p95
NOTTINGHAM CASTLE	1H3H53	1243	G	2/4	A1v2p31
NOTTINGHAM RACE(S)	1H1H66	427L2	G D	4/4*	A1v2p41 Mc9v2p23 S7v2p24
NOVAR HOUSE	131H3	1H345	F	2/2	J2p14
NOW WAT YE WHA I MET YESTREEN	1115	47b15L	A	4/4	C5v3p58
NOW WINTER'S WIND	1356	1221	Eb	2/4	C10v2Ap48
NUAGHALACHD [NUADHALACHD]	5L3L5L3L	5L5L33	Eb	2/2*	F2v2p84,85(74,75) (II)
NUMBER THREE	151H7	6543	D	6/8	W7p9
NUNC EST BIBENDUM	561H2H	3H2H2H1H	D	4/4	O1v1Kp127
NURSE'S LAMENTATION FOR THE LOSS OF HER FOSTER CHILD, A	1120	3210	G	12/8	Mc5p13
NYMPH OF THE DANUBE, THE	1552	47L17L	G	2/4	B7p43
NYMPH, THE	1H1H1H5H	4H1H1H1H	D C	2/4	C5v1p13 A1v4p13 G10v2p36 P10p24 E1v1p30
O AS I WAS KISS'D TH'STREEN	1151	27bL47bL	A	6/8	O1v1Ep5 (II)
O AS I WAS KISS'D YE'STREEN	1151	7bL7bL47bL	A	2/4	T1v1p3
(O AS/SAE WEEL AS/SAE BRALEY AS) (I WAS) KISS'D YESTREEN	1151	27bL27bL	G A	6/8	(J3) A7v5p40 A7v6p82 G11v2Bp22 K1v2p24 B15v1p75 C8v2p27 C8v1p27 (II)
O BEAUTY, WHY SHOULD'ST THOU COMPLAIN	1H533	1355	F	4/4	B7p27
O BONNY LASS	5L5L7L	113	G	3/4	C4p55
O BOTHWELL BANK(S, THOU BLOOMEST FAIR)	556	1H1H1H	Eb	3/4	C6p15 (J3)
O BUSY FOLK AND IDLE FOLK	5421	27bL24	A	4/4	C10v2Bp94
O BUT YE BE MERRY [O SHE'S COMICAL]	5564	5531	A	2/2*	Mc9v3p9 (II)
O CHIADAINN AN LO	3H5H5H	6H1H1H	C	3/4	F2v2p92(82) Mc5p2
O DEAR MOTHER WHAT SHALL I DO	331	356	D	3/4	C13v3p14,15
O (DEAR) MOTHER (WHAT SHALL I DO)	111	356	C D	3/4	(J3) Mc8v1Ap11 Mc8v2Bp20 N1v2p76 P4p34 O1v1Cp10,11 O1v1Ap9 O1v2p28 B5p13 C4p18
O DEAR WHAT CAN THE MATTER BE	5555	4444	G	6/8	C8v2p9 C8v1p25 H1p17,18 (J3) A1v4p6 (II)
O DEAR WHAT CAN THE MATTER BE	5H5H5H5H	4H4H4H4H	D	6/8	E1v2p79
(O) GAE TO THE KY WI' ME JOHNNY	531	536	G F	9/8	C5v3p52 D14v2p42 (J3)
(O GIN I WERE) FAIRLY SHOT O' HER	3b3b3b5	3b3b24	E	6/8	(J3) O1v1Gp28
O GIN MY LOVE WERE YON RED ROSE	51H7b4	53bH7b4H	E	6/8	C5v3p67
O GIN YE WERE DEAD GUDE MAN	1151	3222	D G	4/4*	A1v1p53 A1v2p49 O1v1Dp24
O GIN YE WERE DEAD GUDEMAN	1151	3223	F G	4/4*	(J3) C8v1p7 C8v2p55 (II)
O GIN YE WERE DEAD GUDEMAN	1532	1535	F	2/4	G13p2
O GIN YE WERE DEAD GUDEMAN	1151	3225L	F	2/2	E1v2p125
O HE DE NO'S [AR HYD Y NOS]	16L15L	1310	A	4/4	A1v3p222
O HI EILE, O HO HI RI	1453b	1453b	F#	4/4	Mc1v1p117
O I HAE SEEN THE WILD FLOWERS BLA'	5L113b	427bL1	E	4/4	C10v2Bp39
O IF I WERE WHERE GADIE RUNS	51H3H3H	3H3H2H2H	D	2/4	C18p20
O IF JOCKEY WOU'D BUT STEAL ME	351H6	357b2	G	2/2	C18p8,9
O JEAN I LOVE THEE	3b212	3b3b54	G	4/4	P4p1 C19p13p

Title					
O' KELLY'S RANT	115L	5L3L5L	A	3/4	R6v1p11,12,13
O LA MY DEAR	2H2H53H	4H2H1H1H	D	2/4	A1v2p59
O LET ME IN THIS AE NIGHT	3b3b15	1H1H3bH3bH	E	4/4	C5v2p7
O LET ME IN THIS AE NIGHT	3b11H1H	7b7b45	G	4/4	G11v2Cp14
O LET ME IN THIS AE NIGHT	3b13b5	46b7b5	E	4/4	E1v2p36
O LOGIE O' BUCHAN	351H6	353H1H	C	3/8	C6p17
O MARY IS MY ONLY JOY	5312	5520	F	4/4	C10v2Bp46
O MERRY MAY THE MAID BE	3331	6L6L12	G	4/4	C5v2p18 A1v6p51
O MERRY ROW THE BONNIE BARK	351H6	3120	G	2/4	G1v1p41
O MITHER DEAR, (I GIN TO FEAR)	1H555	51H3H2H	C D	4/4	(J3) T6v2p83 P8v2p39
O MO CHUID CHUIDEACHDA	3b154	23b11	G	4/4	M12p25
O MY LOVE! LEAVE ME NOT	323	321	Bb	3/4	C10v2Ap43
O NANNY WILT THOU GANG WI' ME	5753	5525	D F G	4/4	C6p7 C8v1p56 E1v1p74-76
					B7p40 C8v2p22
O ONCE I LOV'D (A BONNY LASS)	321H1H	5221	F G	4/4	(J3) C5v2p66
O PESCATOR	1H2H3H2H	1H01H2H	F	2/4	E1v2p109
O ROWAN TREE, THOU'LT AYE BE DEAR	3335	6660	F	2/4	C6p19
O SAW YE MY FATHER/(MOTHER)	1355	62H76	G D	4/4*	C5v2p12 (J3)
O' SHE'S COMICAL	5566	5531	A	2/2	G11v2Cp22
O! SING YE CHILDREN OF THE BRAVE!	1H651H	1H611	Eb	4/4	C10v2Ap59
O! 'SMIS THA FO LEON	333	26L6L	C	3/4	Mc5p14
O SWEET IS THE FEELING	356	17L7L	G	3/4	C10v2Bp2
O THIS IS NO MY AIN LASSIE	353H2H	6542	D	4/4	C5v2p29 (II)
O THOU MY CHOICE OF COMPANIONS	3b154	23b11	G	4/4	M12p25
O WALY, WALY, LOVE IS BONIE	51H5	47b6	G	3/4	C5v3p53
O WALY, WALY, UP YON BANK	351H	2H3H2H	C	3/4	C6p16
O WERE I ON PARNASSUS HILL	3b211H	3bH1H1H7b	D	4/4	E1v2p33
O WHAT A BEAW MY GRANNY WAS	153H2H	1H542	D	4/4	A7v3p2,3
O WHAT NEEDS I MY APRON WASH	1253	6221	Eb	4/4	C18p14,15
O WHAT WILL I DO	5L33	26L1	A	3/4	C10v2Bp17
O WHISTLE AND I'LL COME TO YOU MY LAD	3H522H	3H561H	D	6/8	C8v2p63 E1v1p23 (II)
(O) WHISTLE AND I'LL COME TO YOU MY LAD	35L2L2	35L6L1	B	6/8	C8v1p41 G11v2Cp12 (J3)
OAK STICK	1H1H75	1H2H3H5H	D	6/8	A1v2p65
OAK STICK	3H1H75	2H2H4H5H	D	6/8	A1v2p51
OAK TREE	3125L	31H22	G	6/8	S7v1p87
OBSERVER, THE	1H3H5H6H	2H1H1H5H	C	2/4	C26v1p16
OCH A BHODAICH NA BI RIUM	5313	5353	G	2/2	Mc16p29,30
OCH IS OCH MAR ATA MI	6L11	337	G	3/4	C4p17
OCH IS OCH MAR ATA MI	6L11	331H	G	3/4	Mc5p16
OCH IS OCHAN MO CHARADH	1447bL	5511	F	3/8	F2v2p47(37)
OCH O RO U	112	110	A	3/4	Mc5p15
ODE DE PINDARE	5555	443b3b	E	2/2	W4v2p15
O'ER BOGGIE	1H1H1H5	1H1H51H	C	4/4*	G9v5p5 N1v1p31 B15v1p90
O'ER BOGIE	1H1H1H5	1H2H60	C	4/4	T6v1p104
O'ER BOGIE (WI' MY LOVE)	1H1H1H5	1H1H55	C	4/4*	S12v1p16 G11v2Bp21 D15v2p48
					C14v19p16 A7v6p85 G7p16
					K1v2p23 S16p126,127 (II)
O'ER THE DYKE	131H6	1H661H	G	4/4	A1v5p46
O'ER THE HILLS	5H3H1H6	5H3H3H2H	D	2/4	T1v1p3
O'ER THE HILLS AND FAR AWAY	1113	16L6L5L	Bb G	4/4	C6p26 A1v2p11
O'ER THE HILLS AND FAR AWAY	1H1H1H3H	1H665	D C	4/4	Mc8v1Dp97 (J3)
O'ER THE HILLS AND FAR AWAY	1H3H1H3H	1H665	D	2/2	C4p58
O'ER THE MOOR AMANG THE HEATHER	1111	2222	D	2/2	H3p17
O'ER THE MOOR AMANG THE HEATHER	111H1H	1H3H1H5	D	2/4	A1v5p58 C5v1p58
O'ER THE MOOR AMANG THE HEATHER	5L111	6L222	G	4/4*	G11v2Cp15 C8v2p47 G9v5p10
					G7p12 S12v1p9 P5v3p26 C13v2p15
O'ER THE MOOR, AMONG THE HEATHER	5L111	6L242	F D G	4/4*	(J3) Mc7p30 A7v2p12
					N1v1p4 E1v1p67 A7v6p30
					B15v1p77 (II)
O'ER THE MOOR FOR A' THAT	61H62H	1H1H66	D	4/4	C7p1
O'ER THE MOOR TO KATIE	5533	11H66	D	4/4	O1v4p1
O'ER THE MOOR TO MAGGIE	531H3	22H2H7	G D	4/4	D13p4 G9v1p10,11 A1v2p72
					Mc8v1Dp118,119 C20p31 (J3)
O'ER THE MOOR TO MAGGIE	531H1H	22H2H7	G	2/2	Y1p2
O'ER THE MOOR TO MAGGIE	531H3	22H2H7	G	4/4	B15v2p3
O'ER THE MUIR TO KETTY	1155	51H1H1H	D G	4/4*	G11v2Cp3 Mc9v2p14 E1v2p127
					C5v2p26
O'ER THE MUIR TO MAGGIE	51H22H	51H55	G	4/4	S16p130,131
O'ER THE MUIR TO MAGGIE	5311	22H2H1H	G	2/2	O1v1Gp16,17
O'ER THE WATER TO CHARLIE	1562	1561H	G D	6/8	C5v3p73 C8v2p47 G1v1p37,37
					(J3) Mc21v3p21 E1v1p82,83
					G11v1Bp25
O'ER YOUNG TO MARRY (YET), (SHE'S/I'M)	351H3H	1H52H2H	C	4/4*	S12v1p7 B15v1p28 Mc9v3p46
					N1v1p24 R12v1p4 (J3)
					G11v1Bp28,29
OF A' THE AIRTS THE WIN' CAN BLAW	1111	526L6L	A	2/4*	C6p15 C8v1p19
OF A' THE AIRTS (THE WIN' CAN BLAW)	1H1H1H1H	5H2H66	D C	4/4	C8v2p28 E1v1p118
OF ALL COMFORTS I MISCARRY'D	51H1H6	1H2H3bH3b	D	4/4	O1v1Lp147
OFF SHE GOES	3451H	3452	D	6/8	E1v1p35 C8v2p11 C8v1p31
					C14v20p10 A7v4p20 P6v1p3 C7p15
					C22p46 (II)
OFF SHE GOES	533	535	F	9/8	C14v19p6

Title					
OFF TO PARIS	1H516	2H3H75	D	6/8	P9p29
OFT IN THE STILLY NIGHT	3H3H1H6	51H3H2H	C	2/4	C6p8
OFT IN THE STILLY NIGHT	3H3H1H6	51H2H3H	C	2/4*	E1v2p4 G1v1p32
OH! CARRY ME BACK TO OLE VIRGINNY	5353	5322	F G	6/8	C8v1p57 C8v2p23
OH GRAIN AIR NA BRIOGAISEAN	1H71H3	61H53	D	2/2	F2v2p75(65)
OH LADDIE I MAUN LO'E THEE	333	113	D	3/4	N1v2p73 (J3)
OH NO WE NEVER MENTION HER	1135	2210	Bb D	2/4	E1v2p73 G1v1p42
OH ONOCHIE O	334	221	G	3/4	O1v2p19 O1v1lp66
OH OPEN THE DOOR LORD GREGORY	551	7L7L5L	A	3/4	N1v2p22 (J3)
OH 'SE MO RUN AN T-OIGEAR	1511	157bL7bL	E	4/4	F2v2p66(56)
OH! SUSANNAH	3551	3222	G	2/4	C8v2p42
(O/HAY) JENNY COME DOWN TO JOCK	11H76	6231	G	6/8	O1v4p5 O1v1Bp31 (W3)
OIG FHEAR A CHULDUINN	511H1H	1541	G	4/4	M12p24
[BROWN HAIR'D YOUTH, THE]					
OLD AGE AND YOUNG	113b	43b4	G	3/2	A7v3p35
OLD BARD, THE	1H752H	3H3HO2H	D	4/4	O1v1Lp148
OLD BUFFS MARCH, THE	3333	3335	F	4/4	R4p16
OLD COLLIN'S COMPLAINT	17L1	3b21	G	3/4	O1v1Dp20
(OLD) COUNTRY BUMPKIN, THE	4327L	1313	G	6/8	G1v2p63 G11v2Ap38 S12v1p71
					K1v1p40 C14v14p18 B10p40
(OLD) DUMBARTON DRUMS (BEAT BONNY [O])	3332	1554	G F	4/4*	O1v4p43 O1v1Bp1 C4p17
					K1v2p13 A1v3p192 Mc8v1Cp78
					Mc8v2Bp14 S16p98,99 G11v2Bp11
					(II)
OLD ENGLAND FOREVER	1H1H1H3H	1H755	D	4/4	A7v6p91
(OLD) HIGHLAND LADDIE, THE	1122	1122	G Eb F	2/2	O1v1Fp1 R12v1p17 A7v3p1
					O1v5p26 C23p2-4
OLD HIGHLAND LADDIE, THE	1133	4233	Bb	4/4	Mc21v4p5
OLD IRELAND REJOICE	1H1H7b	1H1H7b	E	3/4	Mc23p30
OLD JEW, THE	551H	1H1H2H	E	3/4	O1v1Ep19
OLD LEE RIGG	1H555	1H2H3H2H	C	4/4	G11v1Bp19 G10v2p29
OLD MAN WILL NEVER DIE, THE	1566	5122	G	4/4*	K1v2p17 G11v2Bp15 A1v2p21
					S12v1p67 Mc9v1p34 (II)
OLD PLANTATION GIRLS	3b25L	7bL7bL2	A	9/8	A1v1p52
OLD REEL OF TULLOCH STRATHSPEY	4144	4144	G	4/4	D16p27 A7v3p1
(OLD) SIMON BRODIE	13b22	13b53b	E	4/4*	A1v2p55 A7v2p12 G10v2p19
					G11v1Ap22
OLD SIR SIMON THE KING	13b3b	13b6b	A	9/8	O1v1Gp6,7
OLD SIR SYMON THE KING	1H1H1H	61H4H	C	9/4*	B15v2p2 D13p3 Mc8v1Dp102,103
OLD SPEDLING CASTLE'S GHOST'S DANCE	1L32L4	1L363	A	6/8	P9p10,11
OLD STUARTS BACK AGAIN	327L2	3246L	G	4/4	B15v1p88
OLD TOWLER	1H635	673H3H	D	6/8	E1v1p51 A1v5p9 C8v2p46
OLD UNCLE NED	3451	3420	G	2/4	C8v2p45
OLD WIFE HAUNTS AFTER ME, THE	5211	5622	A	4/4	D14v2p12
OLD WITCH OF OCHILTREE, THE	5L117bL	53b3b3b	A	2/2	O1v1Lp159
OLD WOMAN IN THE GLEN, THE	1H1H3bH2H	7b2H4H3bH	E	4/4	Mc23p22,23
OLIVE BRANCH, THE	2H1H2H1H	4H3H2H5	G	2/4	C1v1p2
OLIVER CROMWELL'S MARCH	O1H1H1H	2H2H3H3H	D	2/2	Mc8v2Cp10
OMAI	1H1H11H	3bH7b3b2	D	4/4	C14v2p14
OMNIA VINCIT AMOR	1255	5255	G	4/4	C20p79 O1v1Hp41
ON A BANK OF FLOWERS	3b556	1H553bH	C D	2/2	(J3) E1v2p122
O'N A THA THU FALBH	51H1H	1H55	D	3/2	F2v2p96(86)
ON DIT QU IA QUINZE ANS	1H2H1H1H	661H5	D	6/8	A1v2p60
ONE BOTTLE MORE	1516	3525L	G	3/8	A1v6p40
ONE CHOPPIN MAIR	5L353	4362	D	4/4	F3p9
ONE DAY AS I CLIMBED THE HILL	551H3bH	5551H	E	6/8	Mc5p8
ONE DAY I HEARD MARY SAY	135	331	D	3/4	T6v2p28
ONE EVENING AS I LOST MY WAY	1355	7531	G	6/8	O1v1Jp99
ONE WINKING EYE, THE	1H51H1H	3H663H	C	2/2	D14v2p16
ONOCHIE OH	3b3b3b	554	E	3/4	(C25)
OOH NEVER NEVER MAIR WILL I RANGE	1H31H1H	2H2H1H1T	D	4/4	C5v2p62
O'ER THE PLAIN					
O.P. DANCE, THE	1142	1125L	Bb	2/4	A7v4p27
O.P. HAT	3H53H5	4H3H2H5	C	2/4	A7v5p31
O.P. HAT, THE	35L35L	4325L	Bb	2/4	A7v4p27
OPEN THE DOOR TO THREE	132	134	G	9/8	A7v5p35 A7v6p28
OPEN THE DOOR TO THREE	134	134	G	9/8	G11v2Bp16
OPEN THE DOOR TO THREE	142	134	G	9/8	C4p33 O1v1Hp61
OPERA DANCE	1242	1H522	Bb	6/8	C22p35
OPERA HAT, THE	1H1H55	671H2H	D	6/8	B7p41
OPERA HORNPIPE, THE	51H51H	61H53	D	4/4	C14v24p8
OPERA POLKA, THE	5L125L	2465	Bb	2/4	C8v1p29
OPERA REEL, THE	1133	1122	D	4/4*	G8p24 N1v1p33 C14v1p4 P1v1p9
					(II)
ORAN AN AOIG	1451	53b7bL7bL	E	6/8	(J3) Mc5p27
ORAN GAOIL	53b2	3b51	G	9/8	C10v2Bp87
ORANGE AND BLUE	3H1H53	3H3H1H1H	D C	6/8	E1v1p19 G11v2Dp32 (II)
ORANGEFIELD HOUSE	5322	5376	F	2/2	G11v1Cp20
ORANGEFIELD HOUSE	5147bL	511H1H	G	6/8	Mc12v1p5
ORCHALL	5553	5542	F	4/4	A1v3p193
ORCHILL GRAHAM	5553	5522	F	4/4	G11v1Ap11
ORCHILL HOUSE	1326L	1353	D	4/4	B11p19

Title					
ORCHILL HOUSE	7bL5L4L7bF	7bL5L7bL1L	A	4/4	G11v1Cp6 (II)
ORCHILL'S DELIGHT	1113	6361H	F	4/4	G8p32 K1v1p2 Mc4v4p4 G11v2Bp2
ORCHILL'S FAVOURITE	5315	261H2H	F	3/8	G10v2p14
ORDINANCE, THE	3455	1H1H53	F	6/8	B16v2p4
ORECK'S SCOTCH-MEASURE	3551	1H33H5	D	2/2	P7p7
ORIGINAL AIR TO WHICH THE POEMS OF OSSIAN WERE SUNG IN STRATHSPEY TIME	3b3b53b	41H1H6b	D	4/4	G10v5p12
ORIGINAL DUTCH WALTZ, AN	1H3H3H2H	1H3H3H1H	D	3/8	B7p20
ORIGINAL GALLIC AIR, AN	335	211	D	3/4	G10v5p24
(ORIGINAL) HIGHLAND LADDIE, THE	1343	3232	Bb A	2/4	Mc7p31,32 E1v1p11 K1v2p2,3 G11v2Bp2
(ORIGINAL) HIGHLAND LADDIE(, THE)	1H3H4H3H	3H2H3H2H	D	2/4*	B7p26 G1v1p12,13
ORIGINAL LANGO LEE, (THE)	1323	5L152	A	6/8	G11v2Cp13
ORIGINAL POLKA, THE	4253H	74H1H3H	F	2/4	C8v1p37
ORIGINAL SETT OF KILLIECRANKIE, THE	5555	5155	D C	4/4	E1v1p94 K1v1p7 G11v2Ap7
ORIGINAL SETT OF THE BRAES OF MARR, THE	351H3H	1H666	D	4/4	G11v2Cp10
ORKNEY(REEL)	1311	5L5L22	D	4/4	Mc19v1p7 (II)
ORKNEYS, THE	1H53b5	2424	C	2/2	G8p25
ORTON HOUSE	1353	432H2	G	4/4	G15p4
OSCAR & MALVINA	5333	3342	G	2/4	S7v2p5
OSCAR'S GHOST	1H1H5	1H1H1H	C	3/4	Mc5p15
OSMOND'S RECOVERY	3L3L5L1L	1351	A	4/4	L1p3
OSSIAN 'AN DEIGH NAM FION	217bL	7bL5L1L	A	9/8	Mc5p18
OSSIAN'S HALL	3565	227b2	A	4/4*	D14v3p10 G10v4p17 D15v1p29 A7v4p25 A7v5p3 A7v6p95 (II)
OSWALD'S COMPLAINT	1H52	356	D	3/4	O1v1Jp94
OSWALD'S DREAM	1353	3H3H65	G	2/2	O1v1Lp141
OSWALD'S FAREWELL	3H2H61H	561H1	D	4/4	O1v1Kp130
OSWALD'S SCOTCH MEASURE	1H554	3216	G	2/2	O1v1Dp25
OSWALD'S SCOTS MEASURE [McKEENY'S...]	1155	51H1H1H	D C	4/4*	C4p3 O1v1Ep30 P7p2
OSWALD'S WISH	3311	2332	G	4/4	O1v1Kp134
OUR AIN COUNTRIE	3211H	5231	D	4/4	C6p28
OUR HEROES RETURN	555	365	D	3/4	C10v2Ap52
OVER MY SPIRIT ARE SHADOWS FLITTING	511	111	E	3/4	C10v2Bp86
OVER THE BORDER	331H	565	G	9/8	R6v2p7
OVER THE HILLS AND FAR AWAY	5757	5333	G	2/2	O1v1Gp23
OVER THE MOOR SHE RAN	5135	5542	F	2/2	C14v20p13
OVER THE WATER	5L13b2	7bL27bL2	A	6/8	B17p4
OVER THE WATER (TO CHARLIE)	5531	5561H	F D	6/8	R12v1p20 G10v3p12 B15v1p16 O1v1Dp7 A1v2p12 G11v1Bp25 C4p37
OVERTURE TO THE DESERTER	1H1H3H2H	1H565	D	4/4	R4p1,2
OWEN GLENDOUR, WALTZ, THE	531H	642	Eb	3/4	G9v3p12,13
OX MINUET, THE	1H1H1H	333	C	3/4	G9v3p10,11
OXFORD CASTLE	151H5	657L2	F G	6/8	W4v1p23 A1v4p48 C5v1p48
OXONIAN BALL, THE	1111	3333	G	4/4	B12p7
OYSTER WIVES RANT, THE	5551	447bL2	A	4/4*	A1v1p3 B15v1p80 (II)
P. BAILLIE'S STRATHSPEY	11H76	5H1H2H2H	D	4/4	B2p7
PADDEEN O RAFARDIE	15L5L2	15L11	G	6/8	A1v3p184
PAD(D)IE'S RESOURCE	15L16	6326L	A F	6/8	Mc9v2p21 A1v2p25
PADDIE'S RESOURCE	1H51H6H	6H3H2H6	C	6/8	S12v2p10
PADDY CAREY	51H3H1H	62H4H7	C	6/8	E1v1p26
PADDY CAREY	51H3H1H	62H4H1H	C	6/8	C8v1p59
PADDY FROM IRELAND	5152	5155	E	6/8	Mc16p19
PADDY O' BLARNEY	1H1H51H	2H5H3HO	D	6/8	A1v6p56
PADDY O' CARRAL	3233	51H22	D	6/8	A7v4p11 E1v2p46
PADDY O' CAR(R)OL	3333	51H22	G D	6/8	F1p27 (II) (B21) C8v2p33 C8v1p54 C14v22p21 P6v1p19 (II)
PADDY O CONNER	1H1H3H	2H2H7	C	9/8	P6v1p18 H6v2p3
PADDY O' FLANAGAN	35L12	35L11	G	6/8	C14v17p4
PADDY O RAFERTY	35L5L2	35L11	A	6/8	C14v19p2
PADDY O' RAFFERTY	5L5L5L2	5L5L11	A	6/8	Mc7p2
PADDY O' RAFFERTY	15L5L2	15L11	A	6/8	E1v1p93 P6v1p8 C24v2p15
PADDY O'CONNOR	35L35	51H22	D	6/8	C24v2p12
PADDY WHACK	11H63	11H75	G	6/8	Mc7p13 H3p7 A1v1p37 B16v3p49 S7v1p16
PADDY WHACK	11H64	1675	G	6/8	E1v1p85 (II)
PADDY WILL YOU LOVE ME	1H36L6	7L73H1H	G	2/4	C8v2p56
PADDYS FANCY	117bL	117bL	A	3/4	A7v3p13
PADDY'S FLIGHT	133	555	D	9/8	H1p26
PADEEN O BASARDEE	15L6L2	15L17L	G	6/8	B17p20
PADLOCK, THE	1H71H3	2365	A	6/8	H3p31
PAINTERS' RANT, THE	151H5	11H62	D	2/2	B20p16
PAISLEY LADIES	3b13b5	1H7b52	G	2/2	C13v2p72
PANDEUR, THE	1H521	1H521	F	6/8	C26v1p4
PANDOURS DANCE, THE	1313	1312	A	2/4	B16v3p3
PANGS OF LOVE, THE	113	531H	G	3/4	O1v1Hp49
PANMURE HOUSE [MISS LYALL]	11L3bL5L	7bL27bL7bL	A	4/4	G11v2Dp15 (II)
PANTALON	51H1#H6	1H54H1H	F	6/8	G13p10
PANTALOONS, THE	315L1	3136L	A	2/2	Mc16p20
PANTHEON, THE	5533	1233	G	6/8	A1v2p41 S12v2p28,29 S7v1p13
PARCEL OF ROGUES IN A NATION, THE	1H7b1H1H	3bH7b3b4	D	4/4	Mc8v1Bp54 Mc8v2Cp12 O1v1Dp26

Title					
PARISH OF DALMAILING	1152	7L27L2	Eb	4/4	P9p4
PARISIAN GUARDS MARCH, THE	1H3H2H1H	54H1H1H	C	6/8	W4v2p33
PARKES OF GLAMES SINGLE HORNPIPE, THE	111	364	D	6/4	D16p15
PARKHILL HOUSE	1324	11H52	Bb	6/8	M11v2p9
PARKS OF DUNLOP, THE	3166	513H1H	D	6/8	R5p30
PARKS OF EGLINTON, THE	537L2	351H5	E	4/4	F3p18
PARKS OF FOCHABERS, THE	353H1H	5642	F	2/2	G11v2Cp30
PARKS OF KILBURNIE, THE	353H1H	5642	F	4/4*	B15v1p3 C4p8 G9p5p3 (W3) (II)
PARKS OF YESTER, THE	355	467	D	9/8	G10v3p1
PARKS OF YESTER, THE	356	351H	D	9/8	A1v4p28 G11v1Cp29
PARLALAW	1353	4211	G	4/4	A1v2p28
PARLOUR, THE	5652	6L5L42	G	6/8	A1v3p170
PARODY ON CAWDER FAIR	1H763	3555	C	6/8	H1p25
PARODY ON JESSIE OF DUMBLANE	3325	1121	Bb	4/4	P5v4p17
PARSON AND HIS BOOTS, THE	1133	136L3	G	6/8	B15v1p15
PARSON AND HIS BOOTS, THE	1133	236L2	G	6/8	B17p12
PARSON IN BOOTS, THE	1133	136L2	G	6/8	K1v2p17 G11v2Bp15
PARSON IN HIS BOOTS, THE	5553	4635	D	6/8	A1v1p44
PARSON IN (THE/YE) SUDDS, THE	1H532	7L242	G	2/4	R12v1p50 A1v1p47
PARSON OF BRENTFORD, THE	3456	1H754	A	2/2	R12v2p9
PARTANT POUR LA SYRIE	5567	1H1H7O	D	4/4	E1v2p19
PARTING KISS, THE	3322	1126L	G	4/4	A1v2p69
PAS DEUX MISSES GRANT OF MONYMUSK	3215L	5620	G	2/4	D15v2p25,26
PAS DI TROIS MISSES GLENNIE	427L7L	1235	G	2/4	D15v2p42
PAS DI TROIS	3524	1232	Bb	2/4	D15v2p41
PAS DUOX [DEUX]	1H62H1H	6423	F	6/8	D15v2p31
PAS REDOUBLE	3H4H1H1H	2H4H5H3H	C	2/4	B4p12,13,14
PAS REDOUBLE	1522	16L15L	Bb	2/4	B4p20
PAS REDOUBLE	5555	357L5L	Bb	6/8	B4p6,7
PAS SEUL MISS ANN MITCHELL	5432	6422	F	2/4	D15v2p15
PAS SEUL MISS ELIZA ROBERTSON	1215L	1232	A	2/4	D15v2p17
PAS SEUL	1H1H2H5H	1H1H2H5	C	2/4	D15v2p8
PAS SEUL	1H1H65	4575	E	2/4	D15v2p9
PAS SEUL	3131	5322	A	2/4	D15v2p21
PAS SEUL	51H3H3H	1H1H53	C	2/4	D15v2p37
PAS SEUL	137LO	3220	Bb	6/8	D15v2p11
PAS SEUL	1316	5536L	Eb	6/8	D15v2p10
PAS SEUL MISS ELIZA INNES	351H6	353H1H	F	6/8	D15v2p34
PAS SEUL MISS ELSY HADDEN	332	113	Bb	3/4	D15v2p23,24
PAS SEUL MISS HELEN HADDEN	1115	1110	A	6/8	D15v2p22
PAS SEUL MISS ISABELLA SIMPSON	3L5L11	2222	Bb	4/4	D15v2p32
PAS SEUL MISS JANE FORBES	117L1	327L6L	Bb	2/2	D15v2p13
PAS SEUL MISS JANE HECTOR	1353	4325L	F	6/8	D15v2p38
PAS SEUL MISS JANE ROBERTSON	555	516L	A	3/4	D15v2p39
PAS SEUL MISS MARGARE(T) RUSSEL OF ADEN	111	521	A	3/4	D15v2p29
PAS SEUL MISS MARY ADAMSON	3H1H53	2231	E	6/8	D15v2p31
PAS SEUL MISS MARY NICOL	5564	3342	G	2/4	D15v2p36
PAS SEUL MISS SHERRIFS	552	7L5L3	Bb	3/4	D15v2p33
PAS SEUL MISS SHIVAS	1H3H5H3H	4H2H3H1H	C	2/4	D15v2p27,28
PAS SEUL MISS SOPHIA GRANT	5L27L	5L21	Bb	9/8	D15v2p18
PASS OF GLEN TILT, THE	5L311	51H2H2H	E	4/4	G8p34
PASS OF KELECRANKIE, THE	35L35L	5142	A	2/2	Mc9v1p18
PAST ONE O'CLOCK	5L6L1	111	G	3/4	T7p30,31
PASTHEEN FUEN	1H1H2H	751H	D	6/4	A1v6p42
PASTORALE	5H6bH5H2H	3bH1H2H1H	C	6/8	B4p8,9
PAT IN THE CORNER	1L13	432	G	9/8	H1p33
PAT RIOT	3b3bH1H1H	6b7b53bH	G	2/2	Mc21v3p24
PATIE & PEGGY	1531	5L5L14	A	2/2	S16p150-153
PATIE AND PEGGY	1H5H3H1H	551H4H	D	4/4	O1v1Fp6
PATIE AND PEGGY	1652	5L5L13	A	4/4	T6v2p76
PATIE'S WEDDING	527L	112	A	9/8	C5v1p32 C5v2p42 (J3) A1v5p32
PATRICK GEORGE MONCRIEFF ESQr OF REEDIE'S JIGG	1351H	57L22	G	6/8	L4p8
PATRICK SARFFIELD or NEW LANGO LEE	1323	5L5L52	A	6/8	B16v3p90
PATTIE AND PEGGY	16H5H2H	551H3H	C	4/4	P8v2p48
PATTSY FROM CORK	3b117b	3b13b4	E	6/8	R12v1p56
PATTY'S DELIGHT	1111	5433	G	6/8	S7v1p82
PATTY'S WHIM	51H51	5411	Bb	6/8	R12v1p69
PATTY'S WHIM	1H31H5	4541	A	6/8	S7v1p69
PAUVRE JACQUE	3H3H5H4H	2H4H1HO	G	2/4	E1v2p68
PAVILION, THE	1H53H1H	72H4H1H	F	2/4	H6v23p1
PEACE AND PLENTY	1H553	471H1H	F	2/4	W4v2p2
PEACE UPON A TRENCHER	1133	2244	G	2/4	A1v1p58
PEACOCK, THE	3b117bL	3b3b43b	B	4/4	A1v2p6
PEARL, THE	1351H	5426L	A	4/4	T1v2p16
PEARLIN' PEGGIE'S BONNY	511	417bL	A	3/2	C18p26,27
PEASANTS, THE	35L6L5L	35L23	Bb	6/8	C14v25p8
PEASE BRIDGE	1H3b1H3bH	7b542	D	4/4	Mc13v1p5 Mc13v2p5 (II)
PEEP (A/OF) DAY,(THE)	1353	2366	D G	4/4*	P5v3p19 H3p33
PEEP AT THE JUBELEE, A	3535	1H325L	Bb	2/4	B16v3p27
PEEP OF DAY	1353	2361H	G	2/2	A1v2p64
PEGEY'S LAMENT	133	556	G	3/4	O1v1Bp29 O1v3p1

PEGGIE I MUST LOVE THEE	6L111	226L5L	G	4/4	S16p104,105
PEGGIE'S DREAM	5555	651H2	A	6/8	O1v1Lp157
PEGGIE'S WEDDING [LADY'S FANCY]	1H1H1H5H	1H1H72H	C	6/8	C4p60 B15v1p54 G11v2Cp21 (II)
PEGGY BAWN	1H3H7	1H65	G	3/4	F1p27
PEGGY BAWN	1H3H2H	1H43	D	3/4	C5v1p63 A1v5p63
PEGGY BAWN	1H3H2H	1H45	D	3/4	G11v2Cp12
PEGGY I MOST LOVE THEE	3555	6633	D	4/4	C20p78
PEGGY, I MUST LOVE THEE	6L111	226L6L	A G	4/4*	C29p18 Mc8v1Ap2 Mc8v2Ap10
					Mc12v2p37,38 N1v2p4 (J3)
					(C25) P4p1 P8v2p7
PEGGY I MUST LOVE THEE	6L111	426L6L	G	4/4	O1v4p24 T6v1p62 O1v1Ap31 C4p46
PEGGY IN DEVOTION	1351H	5533	C D	2/2	(J3) Mc8v2Cp4
PEGGY OF DARBY	1H1H1H6	1H1H1H6	D	4/4	A1v3p166
PEGGY OF THE GREEN	5642	5641	A	2/4	B16v3p96
PEGGY OF THE GREEN	1H1H66	5122	G	2/2	O1v1Hp52
PEGGY PERKINS	1H3H5H5H	4H3H2H2H	D	2/4	A1v4p13 P10p4 C5v1p13 C14v4p7
PEGGY WAS THE PRETIEST LASS IN AW THE TOWN	5555	522H2H	D	2/2	P7p8
PEGGY WITH THE GOWDEN HAIR	3355	1H522	D	4/4	A1v5p68
PEIR OF BOWMORE, THE	1H1H5	1H2H3H	D	9/8	Mc16p11
PEMBROKE'S MAGGOTS	137L5L	4L3L2L7L	Bb	6/8	B16v3p54
PENNY WEDDING REEL, THE	1524	1551H	D	4/4	G10v5p13
PENNYCUICK HOUSE	311H5	1H3H1H2	C	6/8	G9v2p4
PENTLAND HILLS	115	431H	G	3/4	Mc8v1Dp113 O1v1Lp157
PENTONVILLE ASSEMBLY, THE	1356	1347L	A	4/4	C14v16p19
PEOPLE'S JIG, THE	117	762H	D	9/8	H1p24
PERRIE WERRIE, THE	3111	311H6	G	4/4*	G11v2Bp16,17 K1v2p18,19
PERSIAN DANCE	3211	4622	G	2/4	C8v2p41 C8v1p61 (II)
PERSIANS FAREWELL, THE	1H3H5H2H	4H73H1H	D	2/4	C14v25p4,5
PERSIANS REVEILLE, THE	3211	4322	G	2/4	C14v25p12
PERSIE HOUSE REEL	153b1	2427bL	E	4/4	P5v1p20
PERTH BARRACKS	1155	427L5L	Eb	2/2	C21p12
PERTH BARRACKS	1H51H5	1H51H2H	D	4/4	A7v6p59
PERTH HUNT	5313	1362	D	4/4	A7v5p27 (II)
PERTH HUNT	5L3L1L3L	1L3L4L2L	A	2/2*	A7v2p31 (II)
PERTH HUNT, THE	1353	2466	D	2/2	C13v1p47
PERTH RACES	1355	457L2	A	6/8	Mc4v3p6
PERTH REEL	1155	1142	F	2/2	N1v1p19
PERTHSHIRE DANCE	3b23b4	3b217bL	A	6/8	C10v2Bp98
PERTHSHIRE DANCING MEASURES & C	125L6L	6L211	A	4/4	C10v2Ap98-100
PERTHSHIRE DANCING MEASURES & C No. 11	5L121	5L16L5L	A	6/8	C10v2Ap99
PERTHSHIRE DANCING MEASURES & C No. 14 (MRS MACDONALD OF STAFFA'S REEL)	5311	1313	A	4/4	C10v2Ap100
PERTHSHIRE DANCING MEASURES & C No. 1	5326	5512	G	4/4	C10v2Ap98
PERTHSHIRE DANCING MEASURES & C No. 8	3676	3663	D	4/4	C10v2Ap99
PERTHSHIRE DANCING MEASURES & C No. 9	361H7	3673	D	4/4	C10v2Ap99
PERTHSHIRE DANCING MEASURES & C No. 17	1311	5L5L22	D	4/4	C10v2Ap100
PERTHSHIRE DANCING MEASURES & C NO. 16	3332	1122	Bb	4/4	C10v2Ap100
PERTHSHIRE DANCING MEASURES & C No. 4	1H672H	1H675	D	4/4	C10v2Ap98
PERTHSHIRE DANCING MEASURES & C No. 3	3554	4322	D	4/4	C10v2Ap98
PERTHSHIRE DANCING MEASURES & C No. 15	1552	7bL427bL	A	4/4	C10v2Ap100
PERTHSHIRE DANCING MEASURES & C No. 2	1566	5122	G	4/4	C10v2Ap98
PERTHSHIRE DANCING MEASURES & C No. 10	15L13	15L11	G	4/4	C10v2Ap99
PERTHSHIRE DANCING MEASURES & C No. 7	17bL6bL7bL	17bL3b5L	B	4/4	C10v2Ap98
PERTHSHIRE DANCING MEASURES & C No. 12	11H2H1H	5353	F	6/8	C10v2Ap100
PERTHSHIRE DANCING MEASURES & C No. 5	1324	1313	D	6/8	C10v2Ap98
PERTHSHIRE DANCING MEASURES & C No. 13	3322	3356	C	6/8	C10v2Ap100
PERTHSHIRE HIGHLANDERS, THE	5515	1564	D	2/2	C14v11p2
PERTH(SHIRE) HUNT	5313	1362	D	4/4*	A7v6p38 A1v6p17
PERTHSHIRE HUNT, (THE)	5L3L1L3L	1L3L6L2L	A	4/4*	C13v4p6,7 G11v1Ap34,35 G10v2p2
					C14v4p3 G7p2 S13p4 Mc12v1p6
PERTHSHIRE LASSES	3H1H53	353H2H	C	2/2	C14v18p8
PERTHSHIRE VOLUNTEERS (STRATHSPEY, THE)	1L331	447L2	A	4/4*	C14v13p9 C23p18
PERTHSHIRE VOLUNTEERS (STRATHSPEY)	5L331	447L2	A	4/4	G7p5 P5v4p16,17 P5v2p8
					G10v4p28 (II)
PETER REID(ESQr KINARDY)	1H515	1H566	D	4/4	M12p7 (II)
PETER STREET	1353	51H76	A	4/4	G13p14
PETERHEAD ARTILLERY VOLUNTEERS MARCH	1H1H1H1H	3H3H3H1H	C	4/4	M11v1p22
PETERHEAD ASSEMBLY	3H1H53	3H1H2H4H	C	2/2	M11v1p4
PETERHEAD BATH	1565	1562	D	6/8	M11v1p15
PETERHEAD LADIE'S STRATHSPEY	3136	1642	F	2/2	M11v1p13
PETERHEAD VOLUNTEER'S MARCH	1H1H1H3H	2H4H1H6	D	4/4	M11v1p18
PETRARCH AND LAURA'S STRATHSPEY	1H1H1H1H	2H2H72H	F	4/4	P9p27
PETRIE'S FROLICK	1H3H5H3H	2H4H2H7	E	2/2	P5v4p13
PETRONELLA	3211	127L5L	F	2/4	C8v1p22 (II)
PETRONELLA	3211	1H2H1H5	G D	2/4	G13p12 G7p20 (II)
PETTICOAT, THE	3355	1H522	D	6/8	A1v3p183
PETTICOAT TIGHT	3361H	61H62	D	6/8	R12v1p21 (W3)
PETTICOAT('S) LOOSE, (THE/MY)	3b23b2	7bL7bL7bL7bL	A G	6/8	G1v2p87 N1v1p28 (W3)
					G11v2Ap10 K1v1p12 R12v1p13
					Mc21v4p31 C14v17p19 (II)
PHEBE	113b	551H	A	3/4	O1v1Dp19

PHEBILLIA	3L4L5L1	7L5L7L5L	Bb	2/4	C14v26p13
PHILLIS' COMPLAINT	1H3H2H0	3H61H0	D	6/8	O1v11p71
PHILLY McCUE	1H3H4H	3H4H7	D	9/8	C14v13p4
PHILOSOPHER'S JIGG, THE	1H2H3H7	6543	D	6/8	B16v3p29
PHIURAG NAN GAOL	3b3b3b	555	A	3/4	Mc5p1
PIBROCH	5552	5523	G	6/8	C5v2p41
PIBROCH OF DONALD DHU	5353	5252	G	6/8	E1v2p114,115
PIBROCH OF DONUIL DUBH	5352	5552	F	6/8	C10v2Ap82
PIC NIC, THE	1H36L5L	7L317L	C	2/4	G10v5p18
PIER OF LEITH, THE	352H2H	1H666	D	4/4	Mc8v1Bp38 Mc8v2Bp19 O1v1Cp24,25
					C20p76
PIERROT	3H1H5H5	1H1H1H1H	D	2/2	W7p22
PINKEY HOUSE [PINKIE HOUSE]	3342	5551H	D	4/4	G17p6 Mc12v2p23,24
PINKIE HOUSE	3332	5551H	Eb G D	4/4*	Mc23p6,7 C13v3p64,65 C5v2p1
					C20p47 O1v2p13 O1v3p25
					O1v1Ap11 Mc8v1Ap13 Mc8v2Ap9
					R12v3p11 B5p10 (J3) (C25)
					P4p1 N1v2p31
PINKY HOUSE	3332	5556	G	4/4	S16p120,121
PIOBAIREACHD DHOMHNUILL DUIBH	5352	5353	A	6/8	Mc1v1p106-110
[PIBROCH O' DONALD DUBH]					
PIOBAIREACHD MHIC DHONUIL	5352	5253	A	6/8	O1v1Lp152
PIPE REEL, A	3131	3134	A	2/2	G8p15 P1v1p6
PIPERS MAGGOT	315	31H6	G	9/8	C5v1p2 A1v5p2
PIPERS MAGGOT, (THE)	315	31H5	G	9/8	K1v2p18 G11v2Bp16 B15v1p29
PIPPINGO REEL, THE	53b53b	53b42	E	6/8	R5p37
PIQUE'S SCOTS MEASURE	3L5L5L1	6L166	Bb	2/2	Mc9v2p29
PIT THIEVELESS CASTLE	5313	5367	D	4/4	G1v2p68
PITHER IN ENOUGH	3366	3355	D	6/8	A1v3p225 B11p28
PITKERIE'S REEL	1332	1323	G	4/4	B15v1p66
PITLOWER HARMITAGE	13L11	546L2	A	6/8	L4p3
PITLOWER HOUSE	315L5L	7bL235	G	2/2	L4p6,7
PIZARRO	5757	5341	A	2/2	C14v16p6
PLATE RANT, THE	1H3H77	1H3H3H3H	D	2/2	A1v4p65 Mc22p21 C5v1p68
PLEASURE GROUNDS AT MONYMUSK, THE	5533	226L5L	G	4/4	S5p24
PLEASURES OF MEMORY	1L3L3L	6L11	G	3/4	L2p19,20
PLEYEL	5555	1331	Bb	2/4	D15v2p24
PLEYEL'S DANCE	1H1H62H	1H51H5	D	6/8	C26v1p12
PLEYEL'S FANCY	3H2H1H5	2H2H5H3H	C D	2/4	C14v4p8 A1v4p57
PLOUGH BOY, THE	3H5H1H3H	6651H	D	4/4	E1v2p74
PLOUGH BOY'S REEL, THE	316L5L	5L47L2	Bb	4/4	C14v18p9
PLOUGHMAN (JOLLY), THE	3542	351H5	F D G A	4/4*	(J3) C4p26 A7v6p57
[JOLLY PLOUGHMAN, THE]					G8p8 G10v4p28 B15v1p89
PLOUGHMAN SAILOR, A	3334	3356	G	4/4	A1v6p22
PLOUGHMAN'S DANCE, THE	5L7L13	51H52	D	4/4	F3p7
PLSH LE FAWNA	1555	27b67b	D	6/8	C14v18p18
POLENESE, CHE GLORNO DI CONTENTO	551H	3H5H5H	C	3/4	B7p24
POLTALLOCH or MALCOLM'S MANSION	13b55	47b43b	D	2/2	J1p39
POLTOGUE JIGG, THE	555	556	C	9/8	P11v1p16
POLWART ON THE GREEN	3155	551H2H	D	4.4	O1v1Ap6,7
POLWART ON THE GREEN	3253	551H1H	D	4/4	G17p10 Mc8v1Cp81 Mc8v2Ap5
POLWART ON THE GREEN	3254	5551H	D	2/2	T6v1p49
POLWART ON THE GREEN	3254	551H1H	D	4/4*	P4p14 S16p6,7 C20p44,45
POLWART(ON THE) GREEN	3255	551H1H	D	4/4	C29p36 O1v2p30,31
POLWART ON THE GREEN	3313	551H1H	D	2/2	E1v2p138
POLYGON, THE	5H2H1H3	162H7	D	6/8	A1v1p53
POLYSTONS HORNPIPE	3H3H2H	3H1H1H	D	3/2	S12v2p2,3
POMPEY RAN AWAY	331	6L7L1	G	3/4	A1v1p57
PONEY RACE, THE	1H51H3H	2H2H3H2H	E	12/8	Mc15p11
PONEY RACES	1235L	4L211	Bb	2/4	W4v1p5
POOR JOE THE MARINE	1H1H53	761H7	C	6/8	E1v2p64
POOR LAWRIE	3b11	27bL2	G	9/8	H1p21
POOR LITTLE GYPSY, THE	51H52	3671H	G	3/8	A1v6p29
POOR MARY ANN	1H62H7	671H1H	C	2/4	E1v1p100
POOR OF PURSE BUT ROUTH O' CREDIT	1H5H3H3H	1H5H4H2H	D	4/4	H1p24 A1v2p34
POOR SOLDIER, THE	5H3H4H2H	3H1H2H7	D	4/4	C7p12
POOR SOLDIER, THE	17L6L1	3434	G	6/8	A7v6p32
POOR TOWN	1H363	1H62H7	F	6/8	B16v4p94
POP GOES THE WEASEL	1231	1231	G	6/8	C8v2p32 G7p21 C8v1p52 (11)
POP HER AWAY	1H13b5	243b2	E	4/4	P5v3p22
POP THE QUESTION	51H53	1251	G	4/4	B16v3p87
PORT A BHODICH	3542	3531	A	2/2	Mc9v1p28
PORT A BHODICH	1531	1542	A	4/4	K1v1p6 G11v2Ap6
PORT ATHOL	113b3b	51H1H1H	G	4/4	O1v1Hp45
PORT ATHOLL	133	333	G	3/4	B11p35
PORT ATHOLL	333	333	G	3/4	D14v2p11
PORT GLASGOW ASSEMBLY, THE	13b52	5244	A	4/4	A7v2p14
PORT GORDON	1132	2356	F	4/4	D14v2p27
PORT GORDON	5H555H	5H4H4H3bH	D	4/4	B11p34
PORT GORDON	1132	2353	F	4/4	O1v1Hp59
PORT LENNOX	1H1H1H1H	2H2H2H2H	C	4/4	D14v2p10 B11p33
PORT LENOX	1111	2222	D	2/2	A1v6p60

PORT NA FAINNE	1313	157L5L	Bb	4/4	F2v2p6(16)
PORT PATRICK	5142	5145L	A G	6/8	A1v1p32 B15v1p55
PORT PATRICK	5212	4222	A	4/4	O1v1Lp153
PORT RORIE DALL	11H1H1H	1H3bH7b4	E	4/4	A1v3p174
PORTEOUS MOB, THE	1353	427L5L	G	2/2	P9p12
PORTRAIT CHARMANT	5554	4303	G	4/4	E1v2p10
PORTUGUESE WALTZ	5H3H53H	5H3H2H1H	D	3/8	B7p46
POSADH PEATHAR (IN BHAIN)	311H5	3142	D	6/8	C4p51 Mc5p31
POSIE, THE	1H1H3bH2H	5H4H2H2H	E	4/4	C5v2p12
POT STICK, THE	13b52	13b55	E	6/8	O1v1lp76
POTATOE DIGGER, THE	13b51H	27b15L	G	2/2	H1p8
POTTER HILL HOUSE	13L4L2L	13L15	Bb	4/4	C21p8
PRAY GOODY (AS SUNG BY MR SINCLAIR)	5542	3115	G	4/4	B7p16 E1v1p4
PREAMBLE, THE	3H2H1H1H	4H3H2H5	D	6/8	G1v2p67 M12p7
PRESTO	1H52H4H	3H4H77	D	2/4	A1v3p160
PRESTO	5H5H3H3H	4H2H72H	C	2/4	M2p35
PRESTO	11H22	31H47L	G	2/4	M2p25
PRESTO	1565	1527L	A	6/8	D15v2p17
PRETTY BELL	1H652	2466	D	2/2	R12v1p27
PRETTY MILLINER, THE	51H43	3111	Bb	2/4	B16v3p65
PRETTY PEG(G) [PRETTY PEGGY]	1H3H51	1H3H2H3H	D	4/4	G11v2Cp34 (II)
PRETTY PEGGY	1H3H52	1H3H2H3H	D	4/4*	C8v1p55 P5v4p23
PRIEST IN HIS BOOTS, THE	2H2H2H7	1H3H72H	D	6/8	C14v15p9
PRIEST IN HIS BOOTS, THE	2227L	117L2	G	6/8	H1p2
PRIME OF LIFE	531H1	2253	F	2/4	P6v1p27
PRIME OF LIFE	5535	1H511	F	2/4	C14v24p1
PRIMITIVE, THE	1H72H1H	4H1H1H1H	F	2/4	S7v3p9
PRINCE & OLD ENGLAND FOR EVER	1H1H1H6H	1H1H1H4H	C	6/8	S7v2p1
PRINCE ADOLPHUS' FANCY	5H5H1H1H	2H4H3H3H	D	2/2	A1v5p16
PRINCE CHARLIE'S FAREWELL TO SCOTLAND	1555	1524	A	6/8	G11v2Cp2
PRINCE DOLGORUCKI	3131	2531	Bb	2/4	P6v1p30 A7v4p25
PRINCE EDWARD'S FANCY	3331H	2215L	Eb	2/4	C14v8p1
PRINCE ERNEST'S VALTZ	1111	3333	G	3/8	G9v4p24
PRINCE EUGENE'S MARCH	3355	1H1H1H3H	D	2/2	A1v5p28 C5v1p28
PRINCE FERDINAND'S QUICK STEP	3H3H4H2H	55H1H3	D	2/4	A1v2p43
PRINCE FREDRICK'S MARCH	1H1H1H3H	2H555	D	4/4	A1v6p70
PRINCE HOHENZOLLERN'S WALTZ	15L3	427L	Bb	3/4	H1p10
PRINCE OF SAXECOBOURG'S FAVOURITE MARCH	1HO11	1154	D	4/4	A1v6p69
PRINCE OF TUNIS, THE	1133	6222	G	4/4	A1v3p172
PRINCE OF WALES DELIGHT, THE	1H1H1H3H	1H1H55	D	2/2	Mc9v2p7 Mc8v2Cp19
PRINCE OF WALES MINUET	3H3H2H	1H6H5H	C	3/4	C22p14
PRINCE OF WALES MINUET, THE	332	165	Bb	3/4	D15v2p3
PRINCE OF WALES STRATHSPEY, THE	5L133	546L6L	Bb	2/2	J1p1
PRINCE OF WALES STRATHSPEY, THE	5151	6262	D	4/4	A7v3p2
PRINCE OF WALES, THE	131H3	337L7L	G	2/2	C26v1p18
PRINCE(OF WALES)'S (FAVORITE/FANCY)	113L5L	4L6L43	G Bb	2/4	W4v1p7 P11v2p14
PRINCE OF WALES'S (OR 13th Regt) MARCH	1H2H1H2H	1H2H3H4H	D	4/4	A1v6p63
PRINCE OF WALES'S REEL, THE	31H3H1H	31H42	C	2/2	S7v3p2
PRINCE OF WALES('S) STRATHSPEY, (THE)	5L5L1L5L	5L5L6L2L	Bb	4/4*	N1v1p4 G8p1 Mc21v4p9 G11v1Bp31
					P1v1p1
PRINCE REGENT, THE	1H1H5H5H	3H1H2H2H	C	2/4	C1v2p1
PRINCE REGENT'S FAVORITE	11H31	3131	G	4/4	C1v2p2
PRINCE REGENT'S FAVORITE	11H31	3131	G	4/4	C1v2p2
PRINCE REGENTS FAVORITE, THE	316L6L	315L5L	C	4/4	G10v6p35
PRINCE REGENT'S STRATHSPEY	5151	5262	D	4/4	G1v2p84
PRINCE WILLIAM	1111	2431	A	6/8	B16v3p70
PRINCE WILLIAM HENRY'S RETURN	1H655	553H4H	D	6/8	A1v6p65
PRINCE WILLIAM OF GLOUCESTERS FAVORITE	537L5L	31H46	Eb	2/4	C14v10p2
PRINCES FAVORITE, THE	113L5L	4L6L42	G	2/4	C14v4p2 P10p8
PRINCE'S FAVOURITE, THE	1H1H35	61H4H2H	D	2/4	A1v6p34
PRINCES FETE, THE	5513	227L6L	Bb	2/2	C14v26p1
PRINCE'S REEL, THE	5536	61H33	G	2/2	R12v1p69
PRINCE'S SALUTE, THE	1542	7bL7bL7bL4	A	4/4	Mc1v1p1-6
PRINCE'S WELCOME TO INVERNESS, THE	1322	136L6L	G	2/2	Mc9v1p19
PRINCES WELCOME TO INVERNESS, THE	51H3H3H	3H3H2H6	D	2/4	P5v4p17
PRINCESS AMELIA'S FANCY	5L121	5L121	A	6/8	P1v2p3 J1p8
PRINCESS AUGUSTA	5351	1H46L5L	D	2/4	G11v1Bp13 G10v3p32,33
PRINCESS AUGUSTA'S REEL	5466	5426L	A	2/4	J1p4
PRINCESS CHARLOTTE OF WALES WALTZ	4321	4321	Bb	6/8	C14v25p6,7
PRINCESS ELIZABETH'S FANCY	1111	2242	Bb	2/4	J1p5
PRINCESS MARY'S FANCY	1335	5662	G	2/4	J1p6
PRINCESS OF WALES'S MINUET	1H1H1H	551	G	3/4	A1v6p56
PRINCESS OF WALES'S REEL	315#6	1642	F	2/4	J2p3
PRINCESS OF WALES'S REEL	1H51H5	1H522	D	2/2	A1v6p56
PRINCESS OF WALES'S STRATHSPEY, THE	1L5L5L5L	2L16L6L	Bb	2/2	C14v10p1
PRINCESS OF WALES'S WALTZ, THE	51H2H7	51H2H1H	D	3/8	P6v1p36 Mc5p12
PRINCESS OF WIRTEMBURG'S DEPARTURE FROM ENGLAND, THE	3135L	1351H	Bb	4/4	L1p16
PRINCESS ROYAL	3b215	3b115	G	2/2	W7p14
PRINCESS ROYAL, THE	3b215	3b211	G	4/4	G11v2Bp7
PRINCESS ROYAL, (THE)	3b215	3b215	G	4/4*	Mc9v2p13 C22p31 P5v3p17
PRINCESS ROYAL, THE	11H1H1H	2H2H4H2H	E	2/4	J1p2

PRINCESS ROYAL, THE	16L3L5L	6L6L42	G	2/4	C14v9p1 C1v1p1	
PRINCESS ROYAL'S MINUET	5H5H3H	4H4H2H	D	3/4	A1v5p22 C5v1p22	
PRINCESS SOPHIA'S REEL	1155	1H522	Bb	2/2	J1p7	
PRIONNS' TEARLACH [PRINCE CHARLES]	1155	7b427bL	E	2/2*	F2v2p89(79) (II)	
PRIOR'S OR MR MALIE'S STRATHSPEY	113b5	7b7b7b7b	C	4/4	G15p35	
PRIZE OR 325, THE	1135	51H57	G	2/2	P9p26	
PROMENADE, THE	1111	5562	F	4/4	R6v1p5	
PROPHECY OF DANTE, THE	5L3L5L3L	1L426L	A	4/4	P9p6	
PROVANCE	5553	5433	G	2/4	A1v3p185	
PUBLIC THANKS	1133	5561H	Bb	4/4	B16v1p3	
PUBLICK UTILITY	17L32	6L232	Bb	6/8	B16v1p8	
PUDDING MAGGIE	1551	1562	D	2/2	B15v1p50	
PUMP ROOME, THE	1111	531H1H	F	2/2	W7p16	
PUNCH BOWL, THE	3H1H33	2266	F	2/2	R12v1p57	
PUNCH IS DONE, THE	5151	47bL47bL	A	6/8	C18p7	
PURIE'S FAREWELL	315L	1L3L1	A	3/4	O1v1Jp106,107	
PURSUIT, THE	1H155L	11L5L5L	G	6/8	W4v1p11	
PUSH ABOUT THE JORUM	537L2	3367	G	4/4	C8v2p9 C8v1p25 G10v5p20 (II)
PUSH ABOUT THE JORUM	317L2	331H7	G	2/4	B16v3p16 S7v1p32	
PUT THE GOWN UPON THE BISHOP	5L111	2231	G	4/4	C5v2p47 G11v2Cp9	
PUT THE GOWN UPON THE BISHOP	5L122	5L111	G	2/2	Mc8v2Ap16	
PUT THE GOWN UPON THE BISHOP	5L133	2221	G	4/4*	(J3) Mc8v1Cp15(?)	
PUT THE GOWN UPON THE BISHOP	1133	2221	G	4/4	O1v1Gp21	
PUTNEY BOWLING GREEN	151H5	1542	A	6/8	R12v1p80	
PYD HORSE, THE	5111H	6666	D	2/2	W7p20	
QUAKER'S WIFE	15L42	15L6L1	A	6/8	B12p12,13	
QUAKER'S WIFE, THE	15L53	15L6L1	G	6/8	E1v1p5	
QUAKER'S WIFE, THE	1H53H2H	1H561H	D	6/8	G1v1p26	
QUEEN MAB	1335	1322	G	2/4	Mc9v2p15	
QUEEN MARY'S LAMENTATION	553	234	G Eb	3/4	A1v4p20 VC25	
QUEEN OF HEARTS, THE	5531	427L5L	G	2/4	A1v1p5	
QUEEN OF MAY, THE	1H1H1H	3H1H5	D	3/4	O1v1Fp24	
QUEEN OF PRUSSIA'S WALTZ	1H1H1H	1H1H6H	D	3/4	B7p30	
QUEEN OF THE MAY, THE	3355	5433	G	4/4	O1v1Jp97	
QUEEN SQUARE HOUSE or	5351H	5326L	D	2/2	J1p47	
MRS STEVENSON'S STRATHSPEY						
QUEEN'S FANCY, THE	1H5H6H5H	1H4H3H7	D	6/8	Mc9v2p35	
QUEENS (GRAND) MARCH (THE)	1H1H55	3135	D	4/4	M2p20 A1v6p63	
QUEEN'S OR 2d REGt QUICK STEP	5H5H1H1H	2H4H3H1H	D	2/4	A1v3p178	
QUEEN'S PALACE	3153	1H543	G	2/4	S7v1p87	
QUEENSBERRY HOUSE	5244	5222	D	4/4*	B15v1p40 R12v1p37 A1v1p35
QUICK	1515	7L247L	A	2/4	D15v2p30	
QUICK	1515	4427L	Bb	2/4	D15v2p18	
QUICK	155	354	A	9/8	D15v2p23	
QUICK DREAM, THE	3b51	3b43b	F	3/4	D14v2p45	
QUICK MARCH	551H3	1H2H3H3H	D	2/4	W4v2p4	
QUICK MARCH	373H7	6562	F	6/8	C12p1	
QUICK MARCH, 19th REGt	1355	7L245	G	2/4	A1v1p59	
QUICK MARCH. 1st BATTN. ROYALS	1H31H3	2462	D	6/8	A1v2p22	
QUICK MARCH 2d BATTn OF ROYALS	6323	5535	D	6/8	A1v2p6	
QUICK MARCH BY MR HANDEL	3215L	7L211	G	2/4	A1v1p45	
QUICK MARCH EAST YORK MILITIA	3411	3411	G	6/8	A1v2p68	
QUICK STEP	351H6	6425L	Bb	2/4	G3p18	
QUICK STEP	5571H	2H4H72H	E	2/4	S11v1p25	
QUICK STEP	1H1H3H3H	2H2H4H4H	D	4/4	L1p22	
QUICK STEP	1H2H5H3H	1H2H5HO	C	2/4	M11v1p23	
QUICK STEP	1H3H66	5H2H2H2H	C	2/4	M11v1p20	
QUICK STEP	1H72H1H	2H4H2H5	D	2/4	Mc21v4p36,37	
QUICK STEP	1H1H33H	64H2H1H	D	2/4	M11v1p19	
QUICK STEP	5H3H2H1H	1H2H4H1H	D	2/4	M11v1p18	
QUICK STEP	3113	51H25	G	4/4	L1p23	
QUICK STEP	1751	4215L	Bb	2/4	P11v2p20	
QUICK STEP	5L121	5326L	A G	2/4	W4v1p32 A1v4p17	
QUICK STEP	5654	4543	G	2/4	W4v2p22	
QUICK STEP	5552	5523	A	6/8	G9v3p29	
QUICK STEP	54H2H1H	6542	Eb	6/8	B12p2	
QUICK STEP	1H155L	11L5L5L	Bb	6/8	Mc21v1p27	
QUICK STEP	1H322	537L7L	F	6/8	G3p2	
QUICK STEP	1H565	637L7L	Eb	6/8	G3p13	
QUICK STEP	1H62H5	61H3H4H	C	6/8	M11v1p22	
QUICK STEP	5H1T5H5H	5H5H2H2H	C	6/8	G3p5	
QUICK STEP	1351H	5544	F	6/8	G3p22	
QUICK STEP	1251	46L25L	Bb	6/8	L1p24	
QUICK STEP	1122	3125L	Bb	6/8	C7p13	
QUICK STEP	5151H	6522H	D	6/8	D15v1p27	
QUICK STEP	3361H	5535L	Bb	6/8	C12p7	
QUICK STEP	3H4H2H2H	71H2H3H	D	6/8	S11v2p12	
QUICK STEP	1H5H6H7H	6H5H2H7	C	6/8	S12v2p8,9	
QUICK STEP 10 REGT.	32H1H5	362H5	D	4/4	A1v3p198	
QUICK STEP 10th REGt	1H1H4H1H	1H1H57b	E	12/8	A1v2p33	
QUICK STEP 12th REGt	1H363	57L25L	G	2/4	A1v2p39	
QUICK STEP, 15th REGt	11H1H5	432H1H	D	6/8	A1v1p33	

Title			Key	Time	Reference
QUICK STEP 17th REGt	1237L	1255L	G	6/8	A1v1p3
QUICK STEP, 21st REGt	3565	1H631	D	2/4	A1v1p3
QUICK STEP, 22nd REGt	1221	1247bL	A	2/4	A1v1p7
QUICK STEP. 23rd REGt.	1H71H5	6331	G	6/8	A1v2p28
QUICK STEP 25th. REGt	1231	4321	G	2/4	A1v2p9
QUICK STEP 26th. Regt.	5324	5313	G	6/8	A1v2p39
QUICK STEP, 2d BATn ROYALS	1H31H3	47bL7b2	A	2/4	A1v1p58
QUICK STEP, 30th REGt	3H5H4H2H	3H4H72H	D	2/4	A1v1p55
QUICK STEP, 32d. REGt	1H1H55	4433	G	6/8	A1v1p67
QUICK STEP, 37th REGt	1H4H3H7	1H4H3H1H	D	6/8	A1v1p30
QUICK STEP, 40th REGt	3H11H1	1H2H3H2H	D	6/8	A1v2p30
QUICK STEP, 42nd REGt	1313	5226L	G	2/4	A1v1p44
QUICK STEP 44 REGt	1H344	5542	G	2/4	A1v2p36
QUICK STEP, 45th REGt	1143	56L17L	G	6/8	A1v2p19
QUICK STEP, 4th REGt.	1H367L	1352	G	6/8	A1v1p31
QUICK STEP 55th REGt	5321	5321	G	6/8	A1v2p42
QUICK STEP 71st REGt	1H2H1H4H	1H2H1H1H	D	6/8	A1v1p6
QUICK STEP 8th REGT.	1H555	1H51H2	G	6/8	A1v1p14
QUICK STEP, A	111H5	6531	G	4/4	A7v6p31
QUICK STEP, (A)	1351	6252	G	4/4*	C5v1p50 A1v4p50 A1v6p66
QUICK STEP, A	3325L	3325L	Bb	6/8	P5v3p17
QUICK STEP, FENCIBLES	1327L	1344	G	2/4	A1v1p59
QUICK STEP FUSILEERS	71H2H2	71H51	G	6/8	A1v1p35
QUICK STEP GEN. BURGOYNES	3H5H5H2H	3H72H5	D	6/8	A1v1p20
QUICK STEP LA PROMINADE	1H3H3H3H	1H3H2H1H	D	6/8	A1v1p26
QUICK STEP, OLD BUFFS	3H2H1H5	31H22	D	2/4	A1v1p6
QUICK STEP SOUTH FENCIBLES	15L33	25L7L7L	G	2/4	A1v2p20
QUICK STEP, THE TROUPERS	1H1H51H	2H3H2H5	D	6/8	A1v1p13
QUICK STEP, WEST FENCIBLES	1H1H64H	3H1H2H5	D	2/4	A1v1p63
QUICKSTEP	1H533	5311	G	2/4	A1v6p66
QUICKSTEP	3b3b57b	3b7b42	E	6/8	A1v6p64
QUICKSTEP	5546	337L5L	G	6/8	MC10p10
QUICKSTEP 13th REGt.	1333	1331H	G	2/4	A1v2p44
QUICKSTEP 2nd REGt	5552	7L223	G	2/4	A1v2p43
QUICKSTEP 33rd REGt	3H1H75	6431	D	2/4	A1v2p28
QUICKSTEP, 43rd REGt.	321H5	1H61H5	G	6/8	A1v1p40
QUICKSTEP IN THE BATTLE OF PRAGUE	5H3H3H1H	2H2H1H1H	D	2/4	A1v6p62
QUICKSTEP OF THE W LOWLAND FENCIBLE REG	3336	3316L	A	4/4	E2p2
QUICKSTEP, SCOTS ROYALS	1H533	2422	D	2/4	A1v1p54
QUICKSTEP, TURKISH	3311H	335L1	G	6/8	A1v1p26
QUIET AND SNUG	1231	25L4#2	G	2/2	R12v1p9
QUITE PRODIGIOUS	1H531	62H3H2H	F	2/2	R12v1p43
QUOTH THE MASTER TO THE MAN	1H1H3bH2H	4H2H3bH3bH	D	2/2	P7p15
R. JOHNSTON, ESQR'S HORNPIPE	4515	1H2H52H	D	4/4	D6p38
R. PETRIE'S LAMENT FOR THE LATE MR GARDEN OF TROUP	1H1H3bH3bH	5H3bH3bH1H	C	4/4	P5v4p1
RAB THE RANTER	151H5	1562	D	2/2	B20p16
RACHEL RAE	131H5	1H3H2H5	D	4/4	C8v1p15 (II)
RACK OF SILLY, THE	3142	1H2H4H2H	G	6/8	A1v6p27
RAECHEAL REA'S RANT [RACHEL RAE]	131H5	1H3H2H7	D	2/2	D15v1p22
RAGGED SAILOR, THE	11H52	6211H	G	6/8	O1v4p6 O1v1Bp20 S12v2p26
RAGGED SAILOR, THE	11H5	262	G	6/8	A1v3p181
RAIN RINS DOWN THRO' MIRRY LAND TOWN	52H3H2H	3H61H1H	D	6/8	C5v2p64
RAINBOW, THE	1565	4321	A	2/4	B16v3p14
RAINBOW, THE	1432	1432	Bb	6/8	B16v3p56
RAITH HOUSE	15L6L0	7L5L10	A	2/4	G9v3p33
RAKES OF ADAIR, THE	11H71H	6522	G	6/8	R12v1p7
RAKES OF BRESTNEATH, THE	51H3	51H4	D	9/8	B17p23
RAKES OF KILKENNY	1131	1511	D	6/8	C5v1p40 A1v5p40
RAKES OF KILKENNY, (THE)	113	115	D	9/8	A1v5p40 Mc22p14
RAKES OF LONDON, THE	1115	7L7L7L4	G	2/2	R12v1p90
RAKES OF MALLO, THE	1115	7L7L7L5	G	2/4	A1v2p8
RAKES OF ROCHESTER, (THE)	316L5L	7L425L	G A	2/4	A1v3p203 (W3) R12v1p15
RAKES OF WESTMOUTH	1H1H3	1H1H4	D	9/8	A1v5p9
RAKISH HIGHLAND MAN, THE	153b1	27bL27bL	E	6/8	A1v3p175 Mc22Ap4
RALPH'S FROLICK	1133	51H33	F	2/2	W2v1p2
RALPH'S RAMBLE IN LONDON	1H3H5H2H	2H61H6	D	4/4	S7v1p84
RAMAH DROOG	3H2H1H1H	2H4H76	C	2/4	C14v15p14
RAMS HORNS	557bL2	5L121	D	2/2	B15v1p30
RAMS HORNS	557bL2	557b2H	D	2/2	S12v1p42
RANELAGH GARDEN	1252	5652	A	6/8	H1p23
RANGER'S FROLICK	1134	1124	G	6/8	A1v1p62
RANGERS FROLICK	111	115	G	6/4	R12v1p29
RANTING HIGHLANDMAN, THE	3332	3331H	G	2/2	C4p40 A1v1p1
RANTING (ROARING) HIGHLANDMAN, THE	1535	47bL7b2	A	4/4*	A1v1p39 C4p36 K1v1p25 B15v1p31 C13v2p7 G11v2Ap6 S12v1p6 (II)
RASAY HOUSE	11H64	22H4H1H	E	4/4	G11v2Dp20
RASAY'S FAVORITE	5555	3b3b44	A	2/2	G11v2Dp36
RASHES, THE	1H1H1H3bH	7b53b4	D	4/4	O1v1Ep26
RATHA FAIR	5H5H2H4H	5H5H5H5H	D	2/2*	K1v2p35 G11v2Bp33 B15v1p1 (II)
RATHA FAIR	51H57b	51H3bH2H	E	4/4	A1v6p15
RATHER SLOW	11H3H1H	51H3H1H	D	4/4	Mc5p22

Title					References
RATHER SLOW	1621	4445	A	6/8	Mc5p25
RATHER SLOW	3b23b5L	3b23b5L	A	6/8	Mc5p3
RATHER SLOW	111	17bL7bL	A	3/4	Mc5p5
RATTLE THE BOTTLES	1H763	1H765	D	6/8	P5v1p12
RATTLING ROARING WILLIE	513	7b24	D A	9/8	R6v2p3 G10v3p36 C8v2p17
					G11v1Bp26 C8v1p47
RATTLING ROARING WILLIE	313	7b44	A	9/8	O1v1Gp9
RAVING WINDS AROUND HER BLOWING [MACGREGOR A RUARO]	1H1H2H	3H55	C D	3/4	(J3) A1v4vp14
RAYAN'S RANT	1H5H6H5H	1H5H2H5	D	4/4	A1v5p7 C5v1p7
RAZA'S REELL	1H544	7b57b5	D	2/2	C33p12
RAZA'S RELL	6322	5353	F	2/2	C14v1p22
REABART MORE	1534	3147L	A	2/2	Mc16p8
READY MONEY	1H1H31H	2H2H72H	C	4/4	H1p9
READY PENNY, THE	5L342	5L353	G	4/4	G11v1Cp13
RECOVERY, THE	1355	1522H	D	4/4	N1v1p32
RECOVERY, THE	1355	1551H	D	4/4	A7v4p19 (II)
RECOVERY, THE	552H2H	5H2H1H1H	D	2/4*	B7p38 G1v2p89 C1v3p4 (II)
RECOVERY, THE	5L5L22	5211	Bb	2/4	C14v26p5 G9v3p35
RECRUITING OFFICER, THE	1H2H1H5	4522	D	6/8	A1v1p12
RED FLAG, THE	3453	427L5L	F	6/8	H1p22
RED JOCK, THE	1H2H1H3	5553H	G	4/4	A1v3p213
RED, RED ROSE, THE	2H73H2H	6427	G	4/4	G1v2p80
RED STAR, THE	513L1	357L2	F	4/4	P9p39
REEL	1324	1353	A	2/2	C4p2
REEL	1H51H5	22H76	C	2/2	D15v2p38
REEL	11H64	22H75	A	4/4	N2p11
REEL OF BOGIE, THE	351H1H	6422	D	4/4	C19p7
REEL OF CAITHNESS	5415L	7bL7bL47bL	A	4/4	C5v1p62 A1v5p62
REEL OF CAITHNESS	1H7b41	3b3b7b3b	E	4/4	A1v5p62
REEL OF FIFE	51H3H1H	31H42	D	4/4	C5v1p38 A1v5p38
REEL OF HARDEN, THE	313	314	A	9/8	O1v1Lp141
REEL OF THE MEARN'S, THE	1332	1323	G	4/4	C18p8
REEL OF TULLOCH, THE [RIELLE HULUCHEN] ETC.	5151	5147bL	A	4/4*	K1v1p27 G11v2Ap25 S12v1p8
					C13v2p12 C33p13,14 D13p5,6,7
					B15v1p84 B15v2p4,5 G7p1 E1v1p4
					Mc1v1Ap6 Mc19v1p14-17 (II)
REEL OF TULLOCH, THE	5551	5527bL	E	2/2	H3p30
REEL OF TULLOCH, (THE) (OLD SETT)	3331	3347bL	A	2/2	C5v1p68 A1v4p65 Mc22p2,3
REEL OF TYRIE, THE	5L36L5L	4L3L5L3L	A	2/2	C18p24
REEL, THE	1122	15L22	Bb	4/4	Mc21v4p5
REFRESHMENT, THE	5651H	427L5L	D	2/4	C1v3p6
REGENTS BRIDGE, THE	1H1H5H7	1H1H5H7	D	2/4	G9v3p35
REGISTER OFFICE, THE	3555	1H3H1H5	D	2/2	P9p13
REJOICING NIGHT, THE	1357	1525L	G	4/4	B16v1p5
REPLEYS DELIGHT	1214	3431	G	6/8	R12v1p96
RETREAT	1H3H2H6	5361H	D	4/4	A1v4p17 W4v1p27
RETREAT, THE	1452	4351	D	6/8	R12v1p26
RETURN, THE	1H1H1H	62H7	D	9/8	C14v22p15
REVd PATRICK McDONALD OF KILMORE	1115L	3b3b42	A	4/4	C10v1p2
REVIEW, THE	5544	3325H	A	2/4	B16v2p2
RIBHINN ALAINN, AOIBHINN OG [...EIBHINN OG]	3b253b	517L6bL	B	4/4	F2v2p79(69)
RIBHINN, ALUINN, AOIBHINN OIG	3b243b	127bL6	A	4/4	Mc5p12
RICHER'S HORNPIPE	5H5H1H3H	2H2H54	D	4/4	E1v1p119
RICHER'S HORNPIPE	5513	225L4L	Bb	2/2	C14v12p7
RICHMOND GREEN	3H2H1H1	47L44	D	2/2	R12v1p85
RICHMOND PARK	5124	5542	G	6/8	A7v3p36
RIDDING RACES	1H531	6432	D	6/8	Mc9v2p17
RIDE A MILE	513	516	A	9/8	P6v1p18
RIDE A MILE	51H7	1H35	F G	9/8	G9v5p3 C14v17p2 G1v2p83
RIDICULE, THE [RETICULE THE]	3131	3331	F	4/4*	P6v1p29 C14v23p2 G11v1Bp29
					A7v4p23 G7p17 (II)
RIDICULE, (THE/LA)	1354	1325L	F	6/8	C14v22p20 H6v1p3
RIEFIELD LODGE	3b53b3b	2247bL	G	4/4	M12p24
RIGADOON	1H11H2H	2H22H3H	D	2/2	S12v2p12
RIGADOON BY PHILPOT	1H2H3H5H	2H755	D	6/8	S12v2p16,17
RIGS OF BARLEY, THE	5651H	51H22	D	4/4	C5v3p75
RINAWAY BRIDE, THE	3215	6422	G D	6/8	C5v2p63 (J3)
RING DOVE, THE	1H3H5H3H	4H2H1H1H	D	6/8	C5v1p44 A1v4p27
RING DOVE, THE	1353	427L1	Bb	6/8	W4v1p16
RING, THE	53b44	53b44	C G	6/8	S7v1p5 S12v1p32
RINN M'EUDAIL MO MHEALLADH	342	321	G	3/4	Mc5p23
RINN M'EUDAIL MO MHEALLADH	15L6L	522	G	3/4	F2v2p81(71)
RIPE THE RIBS	1L5L5L5L	1L422L	A	4/4	F3p16
RISE AND FOLLOW CHARLIE	5L111	6L222	G	4/4	C10v2Ap63
RISE LAZY LUBBER	117bL7bL	3b511	A	4/4	A1v6p10 C33p8 (II)
RISE (YE) LAZY LUBBER	117bL7bL	3b511L	A	4/4*	K1v2p24 G11v2Bp22 (II)
RISING BREEZE, THE	117b5	1H3b55	G	4/4	O1v1Lp156
RISING OF THE LARK, (THE)	1H535	461H1H	F C	2/4	E1v1p106 Mc7p27 C24v2p18,19
RISING SUN, THE	3H3H2H	3H75	F	6/4	W7p22
RIVAL CANDIDATES	1111	1111	G	2/4	S7v1p74

RIVEN RANT, THE	3255	3322	G	4/4*	A7v2p8 A7v6p22
RIVER TAY, THE	5342	3125L	A	6/8	C21p5
ROAD TO BERWICK, THE	3565	11H2H2	D	2/2	M4v1p3 (II)
ROAD TO CLERK-SEAT, THE	1353	1327L	D	2/2	S5p14
ROAD TO DOWN, THE	1516	3322	A	2/2	C24v1p7
ROAD TO DROCHE(R)DAY, THE	3b15L1	27bL47bL	A	6/8	A7v5p29 A7v6p45 A7v3p10
ROARING JELLY	131H2H	4324	D	6/8	G11v2Cp34 (II)
ROAST BEEF	1H73H2H	1H765	D	6/8	A1v1p27
ROASTED EMPEROR, THE	1H1H1H4	2632	G	2/4	C1v1p8
ROB DOUN [ROB DONN]	3b23b1	5550	D	4/4	F2v2p18(8)
ROB: DOWN	6353	6342	G	6/8	A1v1p10
ROB DOWN	6353	6542	G	6/8	H1p15
ROB ON LUGY [ROB AN LUGI]	1353	1342	A	4/4	Mc19v1p12 (II)
ROB ROY	1H522	1H526L	D	4/4	G11v1Ap16
ROB ROY	3b115L	13b54	D	4/4	A7v3p21
ROB ROY'S CAVE (LOCH LOMOND)	1H13b5	7b1H47bL	E	4/4	G10v6p17
ROB ROY'S RANT	5L122	326L2	Bb	2/2	B20p17
ROB RUADH MACGHRIOGAIR	3b115L	13b53b	E	4/4	F2v2p88,89(78,79) (II)
ROBERTSON('S HORNPIPE)	3113	25L5L1	Bb	4/4*	C8v1p41 (II)
ROBIE DONNA GORACH	326L1	5L6L22	A B	4/4	G11v1Bp3 Mc12v2p56,57
					G10v1p36
ROBIN ADAIR	567	1H1H3H	C D G	3/4	C8v1p59 C8v2p35 B7p38
ROBIN ADAIR	5L6L7L	113	Bb	3/4	E1v1p70
ROBIN CUSHIE	1111	226L5L	G	4/4*	Mc8v1Cp77 Mc8v2Ap22 C20p7
ROBIN FILL THE DRINK ABOUT	13b17bL	3b53b7bL	A	2/2	C18p34
ROBIN HOOD'S DELIGHT	661H5	2222	D	2/2	O1v1Kp111
ROB(IN) SHEAR'D IN HER'ST	351	355	G F	3/2	O1v1Ep11 B15v1p103
ROBIN'S COMPLAINT	561H	553	D	3/4	O1v1Hp39
ROBINSLAW	1H1H2H2H	3H61H7	C	6/8	P11v2p21
ROCK AND A WEE PICKLE TOW	1H2H6H2H	3H3H3H1H	D	6/8	G1v1p29
ROCK AND A WEE PICKLE TOW, A	6L362	3331	A	6/8	C5v2p56
ROCK AND A WEE PICKL(E) TOW, (THE)	5L352	3331	F	6/8	G11v2Dp17
ROCK AND A WI PICKLE TOW, A	6L12	335	G	3/4	Mc8v1Bp55 Mc8v2Cp18 O1v1Ap8
					(J3) O1v2p16,17 O1v3p9 C20p9
ROCKET, THE	1335	427L5L	F	2/4	P6v1p35
ROCKS OF CASHEL	31H3H1H	31H2H4	F	2/2	C14v11p9
ROCKS OF CASHEL	1H5H6H5H	1H5H6H2H	D	2/2	C5v1p11 A1v4p11
ROCKS OF CASHEL, THE	1565	1542	D	4/4	K1v2p36 G11v2Bp34 (II)
ROCKS OF CASHELL	1565	1562	D	4/4*	Mc7p8 P5v4p24 Mc12v1p54,55
ROCKS OF MELROSS, THE	6555	653H2H	C	2/2	C18p16
RODERICH DHU [RUARI DUBH]	3b213b	51H1H3bH	D	2/2	F2v2p38(28)
ROGER'S FAREWELL	1122	1155	G	4/4	A1v3p201
ROLE THE RUMPLE SAWNY	5555	5222	D	4/4	W7p15
ROLL DRUMS MERRILY	3H3H2H1H	72H1H3H	C	6/8	F1p33
ROMANCE	5333	2253	G	2/4	A1v3p158
ROMP, THE	3H1H51H	2H4H2H2H	F	4/4	P9p39
ROMP, THE	4L2L3L1	6L5L32	A	4/4	C10v1p3
ROMPING FANNY	5651H	5225L	A	6/8	B16v3p53
RONDO	3H2H1H3H	74H75	D	2/4	S11v2p11
RONDO, A	51H2H2H	1H61H7	D	6/8	A1v6p19
RONDO D' HENRY 4th	5564	5542	G	4/4	A1v3p219
ROODULUM, (THE)	653	653	D	9/8	C14v14p21 C23p17
ROPE DANCE, THE	51H53	637L5L	G	6/8	A1v3p197
RORIE DALL'S SISTER'S LAMENT	111	7bL7bL2	D	3/4	D14v2p14
RORY DALL'S PORT	1352	1352	G	6/8	O1v1Hp58
RORY DALL'S SISTER'S LAMENT	222	113	G	3/4	A1v6p41
RORY MACNAB	5151	47bL7b7bL	E	2/2*	K1v1p20 G11v2Ap18 (II)
ROSA LEE	1H5H6H5H	6H3H3H2H	D	2/4	C8v2p57
ROSA WALTZ, THE	5L12	310	Bb	3/4	G13p5
ROSABELL	3451	5131	C	4/4	G10v5p17
ROSE BUDD, THE	135L3	4542	Bb	2/2	R12v2p3
ROSE BUDS IN MAY, THE	5653	51H4H2H	D	6/8	C5v2p63
ROSE OF ALLANBANK, THE	351H1H	3H5H2H2H	D	4/4*	C5v3p74 O1v1Ip86
[MAID OF ALLANBANK]					
ROSE, THE	1H1H3H3H	5H4H1H1H	C	6/8	S7v1p23
ROSE TREE, THE	1H555	1H2H3H2H	C D	4/4*	E1v1p25 (II)
ROSE TREE, THE	1H555	1H3H3H2H	D	2/4	C8v1p14 C8v2p18
ROSE TREE, THE	15L5L5L	1332	Bb	2/4	Mc22p19
ROSEBERRY HORNPIPE	1H1H33	671H6	Eb	2/4	A7v1p5
ROSEBUD BY MY EARLY WALK, A	2115	27bL7bL2	A	4/4	C5v3p56
ROSEBUD BY MY EARLY WALK, A	1351H	6527L	G	6/8	C8v2p38
ROSENEATH CASTLE	5651H	5632	D	4/4	K1v1p8
ROSETTE QUICK STEP	1111	2231	G	6/8	A1v2p13 S12v2p4
ROSIN THE BOW	1H3H3H6H	5H1H66	D	6/8	C8v2p58
ROSINA	1H2H1H1H	661H2H	C	6/8	C22p23
ROSLIN CASTLE	1554	6b423b	A D C E	4/4	C4p15 N2p19,20 O1v5p20
					(J3) O1v1Dp3 N1v2p33
					Mc8v1Bp35 E1v1p23 P4p21
					C5v2p13 C13v3p54 C20p71 G1v1p4
ROSLIN CASTLE	1554	6b43b3b	C E	4/4	C6p9 G17p9
ROSS CASTLE	3214	7L232	G	2/4	A1v2p46
ROSS HOUSE	1H535	1H522	D	2/2	B15v1p97 S12v1p26 S7v1p67

ROSS LODGE	3b13b5	227b2	G	2/2	K1v1p9
ROSSIE HOUSE	5555	6L27L5L	G	6/8	A1v5p42 D15v1p4
ROSY MORN, THE	5551H	5443	G	4/4	A1v6p20
ROTHEMURCHES (RANT/STRATHSPEY/REEL)	3335	1H61H6	D C	4/4*	A7v6p2 A7v5p32 E1v1p53 A1v6p10
					G7p16 K1v1p20 G11v2Ap18
					Mc21v4p11 C8v1p58 C4p50,51
					Mc7p34 G9v5p19 C33p7 B15v1p42
					N1v1p22 A7v2p10 Mc9v1p17 (II)
ROTHESAY CASTLE	1H126L	1H153H	D	4/4	G8p12 P1v1p4
ROTHIEMAY	11L11H	1H542	G	2/2	S7v3p5
ROTHIEMURCHUS	2H2H1H6	5H4H1H6	C	4/4	G15p32,33
ROTHSAY AND CAITHNESS FENCIBLES	1H1H1H6	2H4H7O	D	2/4	A1v5p73
ROTTERDAM FAVORITE WALTZ	1215	1256L	Bb	3/8	P9p3
ROUDLUM	1H1H7	1H3H3H	D	9/8	H1p16
ROUGH AND HARDY	3H3H5H1H	2H1H1H1H	D	4/4	A1v3p175
ROUND THE WORLD FOR SPORT	3b3b44	5527bL	E	6/8	G9v5p18
ROUND THE WORLD FOR SPORT	3b3b44	5551	E	6/8	P5v3p23
ROUND TOWER, THE	1H3H2H3H	2H3H4H2H	D	6/8	C14v20p17
ROUSSEAU'S DREAM	3311	2233	D	4/4	G9v3p3
ROUSSEAU'S DREAM	3H3H1H1H	2H2H3H1H	D	4/4	C8v2p19 E1v2p48
ROUTE IS COME, THE	5351	2451	F	6/8	L2p8,9
ROW DOW DOW	5553	5555	G	2/4	A1v3p223
ROW THOU, DEAREST KENNETH	57b1H1H	1H7b51	E	4/4	Mc5p18
ROW YOUR RUMPLE SAUNCY	3H1H5H1H	3H5H3H3H	D	2/2	O1v1Dp28
ROXBURGH CASTLE(HORNPIPE)	1155	4452	A	4/4	C7p6 (II)
ROXBURGH CAVALRY'S QUICK STEP, THE	51H62H	751H3	D	6/8	C7p4
ROXBURGH HOUSE	1H2H3H1H	2H3H1H5	D	6/8	S7v1p10
ROXBURGHSHIRE CAVALRY'S MARCH, THE	1354	6440	D	4/4	C7p4
ROY STEWART'S REEL	3156	4642	F	4/4	C14v15p23
ROYAL ARTILLERY WHIM, THE	1542	1525L	G	6/8	C14v13p14
ROYAL BOARDING SCHOOL , THE	1515L	6L542	A	2/2	A1v3p211
(ROYAL) CALEDONIAN HUNT'S DELIGHT	1232	315L2	G D	6/8	A1v4p52 C5v1p52 G10v2p1
					G11v1Bp1 A7v2p6 C13v4p2,3
ROYAL CIRCUS	3546	3542	F	6/8	G10v2p34
ROYAL CIRCUS, THE	1H1H72H	1H1H2H7	D	4/4	P9p31
ROYAL EDINBURGH VOLUNTEERS, THE	3b421	4L27b2	G	2/2	C13v2p49 C13v1p23
ROYAL EXCHANGE	1331	1321	G	6/8	S7v1p80
ROYAL FLIGHT TO BRIGHTON	3H3H1H1H	2H4H1H6	D	2/4	J1p16
ROYAL FUSILLIER'S NEW QUICK STEP	5H1H2H7	6523	D	6/8	S5p19
ROYAL GLASGOW VOLUNTEERS FAREWELL	1122	1153	G	6/8	A1v1p41
ROYAL GLASGOW VOLUNTEERS JIG, THE	1H552	5125L	G	6/8	A1v1p17
ROYAL GLASGOW VOLUNTEER'S MARCH	1H1H55	1115	Eb	4/4	C12p1
ROYAL GLASGOW VOLUNTEERS, THE	1H3H53	1H5H52	C	6/8	C13v4p31 C13v2p49 C13v1p45
ROYAL HIGHLANDERS WELCOME FROM WATERLOO	5555	6666	G	4/4	G11v2Dp6
ROYAL HUNT, THE	3243	6532	Bb	6/8	C14v25p5
ROYAL JOAK	1L122	337L2	Bb	6/8	W7p21
ROYAL MARQUEE	1H325	6527L	G	6/8	S7v1p29
ROYAL MONTROSE VOLUNTEER'S MARCH, THE	1H753	1113H	D	4/4	D15v1p27
ROYAL NAVY, THE	1526	4257L	G	6/8	B16v1p6
ROYAL PAIR, THE	1H3H1H3	3H5H3H5	D	2/2	B16v3p28
ROYAL PAISLEY VOLUNTEER'S MARCH, THE	1112	37L15L	Bb	4/4	C12p7
ROYAL PERTH VOLUNTEERS QUICKSTEP	3H1H35	3H4H72H	D	4/4	A7v6p94
(ROYAL) RECOVERY, THE	1L3L5L5L	1L5L5L1	A Bb	4/4	K1v2p10,11 G8p10 G11v2Bp8
					Mc4v2p3 P1v1p3 (II)
ROYAL SALUTE, THE	1546	3542	D	6/8	B16v1p4
ROYAL SCOTS MARCH, THE	1H1H33	1115L	G	2/2	A1v3p194
ROYAL SOVEREIGN, THE	5562	5555	A	6/8	R12v1p40
ROYAL TAR'S WELCOME TO OLD ENGLAND, THE	3H1H1H2H	2H554	D	4/4	C10v1p4
ROYAL TERRACE, THE	1153	51H3H2H	F	2/2	P9p2
ROYAL VICTORY, THE	1125L	3543	A	2/2	C14v21p4
ROYAL WEDDING, THE	1H51H5	1H531	D	6/8	C14v10p25
ROYAL(L) LAMENT, THE	331H	642	G	3/4	O1v1Hp36
ROYALTY	117bL7bL	113b4	B	6/8	G11v1Cp32
ROYALTY, THE	3211	2232	Bb	2/4	C14v3p9
ROY'S WIFE (OF ALLDIVALLOCH)	5333	5322	CDFG Eb	4/4*	(J3) A7v6p88 A1v4p40
					C8v2p23 G11v1Bp12 G10v3p13
					E1v1p1 C5v2p4 C8v1p64
					G1v1p11 (II) C6p5
RT HON EARL(E) OF BR(E)ADALBINE'S STR.	11H53	51H3H2H	D	2/2	Mc4v1p23
RT HON LADY ELIZABETH GREVILLE'S WALTZ	1H1H53	1151	C	3/8	C14v16p24
RT HON LADY SALTOUN'S REEL, THE	5L3b11	27bL4L7bL	A	2/2	C18p5
RT HON LADY SALTOUN'S STRATHSPEY, THE	5L3b17bL	4L424	A	4/4	C18p5
(RT HON) LORD BALLENDEN ('S STRATHSPEY)	5532	5553H	E	4/4	G10v1p24 G11v1Ap8
RT HON LORD ELCHO, THE	153b5	1524	E	4/4	Mc19v2p4 Mc19v3p10
RT HON LORD JOHN SCOTT, THE	3253	3111	A	2/4	Mc19v3p20
RT HON LORD TORPHICHEN'S MARCH	1115L	4422	Bb	4/4	L3p7
RT HON LORD TORPHICHEN'S QUICK STEP	1632	1321	Bb	6/8	L3p7
RUAIG GHLENNE FRUIN	1131	3331	A	4/4	Mc1v1p48(?)
RUFFIAN'S RANT, THE	5333	5322	D	4/4*	N1v1p14 B15v1p43 K1v1p35 C4p57
					G11v2Ap33 A1v2p42 Mc9v1p22
					C14v12p1
RUGANTINO	1H765	1H765	A	6/8	C14v22p11

Title			Key	Time	References
RULE A WIFE AND HAVE A WIFE	337b2	3131H	A	2/2	P9p33
RULE BRITANIA	1115	2243	Bb	4/4	D15v2p18
RULE BRITANNIA	1H1H1H5H	2H2H3H0	D	4/4	C8v2p15 C8v1p43
RULE BRITANNIA	1H1H1H5H	2H2H3H3H	D	4/4	E1v1p45
RULE BRITANNIA	1H1H1H5H	2H4H3H0	D C	4/4*	A1v3p200
RUMBLING BRIDGE, THE	5336	5327bL	A	2/2	G8p4 P1v1p2
RUN DOWN THE TOWN IN HASTE	1353	6L6L22	Bb	2/2	M4v1p2
RUNAWAY BRIDE, THE	3H2H1H5H	6H4H3H2H	D	6/8	E1v2p128
RUNAWAY, THE	33H76H	33H4H1H	D	2/4	P6v1p26
RUNAWAY, THE	5566	5527L	Bb	6/8	H3p27
RUNING FOOTMAN	1H1H6	553	D	6/4	W7p13
RURAL ASSEMBLY, THE	1565	4321	A	2/2	B16v4p93
RURAL FELICITY	5555	52H30	D	4/4	L2p18
RURAL FELICITY	552H3H	5622	D	6/8	A1v1p30 E1v1p48 C8v2p48
RURAL THOUGHT, THE	5522	4653	G	6/8	A1v3p221
RUSSIAN AIR	4H2H3H1H	2H1H2H5H	D	4/4	C22p48
RUSSIAN AIR	15L35L	15L35L	A	2/4	G9v3p33
RUSSIAN AMBASSADOR'S WALTZ, THE	1H4H73H	2H3H1H1H	C	3/8	C14v22p10
RUSSIAN DANCE	3H3H3H3H	671H1H	D	2/4	H1p23
RUSSIAN DANCE, (THE)	35L35L	4325L	Bb	2/4	C14v24p17 H6v10p2
RUSSIAN DANCE, THE	1115	5#1#51	Bb	3/8	C14v10p21
RUSSIAN MARCH	1H1H2H2H	3H3H3H1H	D C	4/4	A1v4p36 W4v1p6
RUSSIAN SONG, A	1H1H1H2H	7771H	E	4/4	G1v2p91
RUSSIAN TIPPET, THE	5531	2231	A G	2/4	W4v1p19 C5v1p47 A1v4p47
RUSSIAN WALTZ, THE	1355	1351	Bb	3/8	C14v21p20
RUTHVEN'S RANT	5L155	5L132	G	4/4	A1v6p11
RYE-HEAD'S	1L15L1	6L226L	A	2/2	R6v1p7
('S) ANN AGAM THA BHEANAG IS MAISICHE SUILE	1331H	2H1H52	D	6/8	F2v2p82(72)
'S ANN AGAM THA 'M BODACH A'S MEASA AIR AN T SHAOGAL	5142	5145L	A	6/8	Mc1v1Ap8
S' BEAG MO SHUNND' RIS A CHADAL	5H5H4H	2H7b3bH	E	3/4	F2v2p37(27)
'S CIANAIL M'AIGNE	1H332	2366	C	4/4	Mc5p26
'S E COINNEACH OG A FHUAIR AN TOGAIL	1321	6161	G	6/8	Mc5p8
'S EAGAL LEAM A MBAS	446b	511	A	3/4	D14v2p31
'S FAD THA MI M'ONARAN	41H3b1	47b57b	E	4/4	Mc5p14
'S FLUICH AN OIDHCHE NOCHD 'SGUR FUAR I [FAREWELL TO LOCHABER]	333	323	G	3/4	Mc5p1
'S MATH AN LA FHUAIR M'EUDAIL	1121	7bL446	G	4/4	Mc5p17
'S MI AIR CRAGAN NA SGURRA	533	611	C	3/4	Mc5p14
'S MI GA M'IOMAGAN A'M' LEABAIDH	532	16L5L	D	3/4	Mc5p30
'S MITHICH DHOMH BHI TOGAIL ORM	2H2H2H6	3H53H1H	D	4/4	Mc5p25
'S NEONACH LE CLANN DONAIL MI	5L11	222	A	3/4	Mc5p6
'S TOIGH LEAM FEIN MO LAOCHAN (DEAR TO ME IS MY LITTLE HERO)	1123b	5L5L5L3bL	A	4/4	Mc5p27
'S TU MO LUAIDH NA'M FAIGHINN THU	111	27L7L	Bb	3/4	F2v2p32(22)
SA MHUIR NI DILIS EILIN OG	1H1H1H7	6663	D	4/4	A1v6p54
SACK POSSETT	11H76	6231	G	6/8	R12v1p86
SAE MERRY AS WE HAE BEEN	1H1H3H	113	D	3/4	T6v2p6 P8v2p2
SAE MERRY AS WE (TWA') HAE BEEN	1H1H3H	543	D C	3/4	Mc8v1Cp64 Mc8v2Ap4 G17p3 O1v1Bp21 O1v4p28 C5v2p11 C29p1 (C25) (J3) N1v2p58
SAILOR LADDIE, THE	156L2	1531H	G	6/8	A1v3p196
SAILOR LADDIE, (THE)	3122	6113	G	6/8	C13v2p17 A1v2p26 G9v5p10 S12v1p15
SAILOR LASSIE, THE	31H7	652	C D	9/8	B15v1p107 A1v3p198
SAILOR'S ALLEGORY, THE	1H1H1H6	1H1H33	D	2/2	A1v5p11
SAILORS DANCE IN CAPt COOK	5512	217L6L	Bb	4/4	D16p33
SAILOR'S DELIGHT, THE	16b5	43b7bL	C	9/8	S7v1p62
SAILOR'S JOURNALE	1H76	357	D	3/4	A1v6p22
SAILORS LEAD A MERRY LIFE	1H1H1H2H	1H766	G	2/2	O1v1Gp10,11
SAILOR'S RANT	1H565	1H527L	G	6/8	A1v1p69
SAILORS RETURN	1H2H1H5	7b7b27bL	D	4/4	P9p37
SAILOR'S WIFE, (THE)	121H3bH	5H2H54	D F	6/8	H3p24 G11v2Bp32 K1v2p34,35 (II)
SAILOR'S WIFE, THE	121H3bH	5H2H7b4	D	6/8	A7v2p27
SAILOR'S WIFE, THE	121H3bH	5H2H1H5	D	6/8	A7v2p27
SALAMANCA	1H3H1H5	4322	F	2/4	C14v27p16
SALISBURY CRAGGS	5337b	7bL7b27bL	D	4/4	P9p14
SALISBURY CRAIGS	351H2	351H3H	C	4/4	G8p33
SALLY GRANT'S RANT	5355	52H2H	D	2/2	S7v1p77
SALLY IN OUR ALLEY	005	1H72H	D	3/4	A1v4p18
SALLY IN OUR ALLEY	51H7	4H1H7	F	3/4	E1v2p90
SALLY KELLY	11H1H1H	2H7b2H4H	D	2/2*	G11v2Bp32 C14v14p23 K1v2p34 (II)
SALLY KELLY ('S REEL)	1H1H3bH3bH	2H7b2H4H	D	4/4*	G9v5p13 H3p40
SALLY KELLY'S REEL	51H1H1H	2H7b2H4H	D	4/4	P5v3p8
SALLY MCGIE	5L127bL	3b27bL5L	A	6/8	C23p6
SALLY ROBINSON'S FAVORITE	3451	35#17L	F	2/4	P11v2p5
SALLY'S WISH	3115	61H52	A	4/4	S7v1p83
SALT FISH AND DUMPLINS	1133	5552	G	4/4	A1v3p188
SAM JONES	1131	3433	G	4/4	A1v1p53

SAMSON DUNCAN'S COMPts TO CHAs DUFF	11L5L1	6L6L22	A	4/4	D16p24
SAMUEL FERGUSON, ESQr's REEL	3H1H53	13H72H	C	4/4	Mc19v3p22
SANDERS (BRANE/RANIES) (STRATHSPEY)	3b13b1	427bL2	D	4/4	K1v2p34 A7v4p24 G11v2Bp32 (II)
SANDFORD LODGE	5L122	3125L	A	6/8	M11v2p14
SANDIE O'ER THE LEE	5522	4461H	G A	4/4	A7v6p52 Mc22p13
SANDS OF PORTOBELLO, THE	1L5L6L5L	6L5L6L5L	A	4/4	P9p7
SANDWICH, THE	1H1H3H1H	4H2H77	F	2/4	C14v3p6
SANDY & JENNY	554	335	C	3/4	B7p47
SANDY GOW'S THREE PINTS	1H3H2H2H	1H3H2H3H	D	4/4	D14v2p17
SANDY IS MY DARLING	11H7b4	3b7bL7bL3b	B A	4/4*	G1v2p94 K1v2p24 G11v2Bp22
					(II)
SANDY LADDY	7656	1H1H1H3H	C	2/2	W7p7
SANDY O'ER THE LEE	1155	2266	G A	2/4	A1v2p26 (J3) S7v1p19
SANDY O'ER THE LEE	1353	5222	D	4/4*	G11v1Ap32 G10v2p1
SANTO CARLO DI NAPOLI	1321	1321	G	6/8	C23p14
SARAH WILLIAMSON'S LAMENT	3352	3315L	Bb	2/4	C18p12
SAUNY'S DELIGHT	327L2	3434	G	2/2	R12v1p51
SAVAGE DANCE, THE	1131	25L11	G	4/4	A1v2p66
SAVOURNA DELIGH	1H1H1H7	6663	D	4/4	E1v1p109,110 G10v4p10
SAVOYARD'S HOLIDAY	1H5H2H3H	1H5H51H	C	6/8	S7v1p33
SAW A'WAY 'LIAS SCRAPE AWAY	5351	4242	G	12/8	A1v3p210
SAW YE A LASSIE OF FIFTEEN YEARS	351H5	352H2	D	3/4	O1v1Hp51
SAW YE JOHNNY COMING?	1253	1250	F	4/4*	G11v2Bp2 C6p25 K1v2p2 E1v1p68
SAW YE JOHNNY COMING CO SHE	1253	1240	G	4/4	A1v2p54
SAW YE JOHNNY COMING (QUO SHE)	1253	1253	F G	4/4*	C8v1p37 C8v2p37 (J3) C5v2p24
SAW YE MY FATHER?	1355	62H1H6	E	2/4	C6p6
SAW YE MY FATHER	1355	64H1H6	D	2/4	C4p72
SAW YE MY PEGGY	1H1H1H	7b7b4	E D	3/2	O1v1Cp22,23 Mc8v2Bp12
					S16p46,47
SAW YE NAE MY PEGGY	1H1H1H	3bH7b4	E G	3/2	C5v2p10 Mc8v1Cp79 A1v3p182
					C20p20 E1v2p120
SAW YOU MY FATHER	1355	64H1H6	D	2/4	S7v1p63
SAWNY'S PIPE	355H5H	4H2H66	D	4/4	C5v3p61 O1v1Ip82
SAXON DANCE	3H6H2H2H	5H2H4H1H	D	2/4	E1v2p24
SCARBROUGH WHIM	5342	351H3	G	6/8	R12v1p89
SCARLET PETTICOAT, THE	5322	4215L	G	6/8	A1v3p187
SCHOTTISCHE, THE	5431H	7L513	G	2/4	C8v2p13 C8v1p39
'SCIAN FADA FADA O'N UIRIDH	551H3bH	5551H	E	6/8	Mc5p8
'SCIAN 'SGUR FAD THA MI M'THAMH	3H2H3H	1H55	D	3/4	Mc5p22
SCONE PALACE	151H5	4622	D	4/4	A7v4p15
SCONE PALACE	1L5L33	427L2	A	2/2	C21p18
SCOON HOUSE	1H2H2H1H	6522	D	4/4	O1v1Bp7 O1v3p40,41
SCORNFU' NANCY	5554	4266	C D	4/4*	W7p11 C4p62 T6v1p25 P8v2p15
SCOTCH COLLOPS	17L11	3434	G	6/8	C1v1p3
SCOTCH GIG	5262	5266L	G	6/8	O1v1Dp8,9
SCOTCH HERO'S REEL, THE	3343	3322	G	6/8	S7v1p39
SCOTCH JENNY	551H6	553H2H	D	4/4	S7v2p10
SCOTCH MARCH	1151H	5551H	D	2/2	G1v1p2,3
SCOTCH MEASURE	3255	5255	F	2/2	Y1p14
SCOTCH MEASURE, A	3H536	1H535	F	2/2	Y1p19
SCOTCH MEASURE, A	11H11	526L6L	F	2/2	Y1p21
SCOTCH MEASURE, A	5L111	3b3b54	G	2/2	Y1p20
SCOTCH MEASURE, A	111	7L5L1	G	3/4	Y1p20
SCOTCH MILITIA, THE	331H1H	6362	A	4/4	C7p15
SCOTCH MINISTER, A	13b54	3b3b13b	G	2/2	Y1p16
SCOTCH REEL	5514	5427bL	A	4/4	(C25)
SCOTCH REEL	5532	16L13	Eb	4/4	(C25)
SCOTCH SCOLLOPS	151H5	443b1	E	2/4	R12v1p45
SCOTCH TUNE	113	555	F	3/4	Y1p22
SCOTLAND YARD	3165	3522	G	2/2	R12v1p93
SCOTS BONNET	1354	2466	G	2/2	R12v1p14
SCOTS BONNET, (THE)	1355	2466	G	2/2	B17p11 B15v1p28 C4p29 (II)
SCOTS CAME O'ER THE BORDER, THE	131H1H	663H6	C	6/8	H6v23p3
SCOTS JENNY	355	1H1H5	G	3/4	O1v1Ep7 O1v4p31
SCOTS LAMENT	355	551H	D	3/4	O1v4p12 O1v1Bp19
SCOTS MARCH	6442	115L1	F	4/4	W4v2p16
SCOTS MEASURE	3561H	2H3H5H5H	D	4/4	S12v2p5
SCOTS MEASURE, (THE GLASGOW)	1132	2666	G	4/4 2/	O1v1Ep10
SCOTS QUEEN, THE	3b251H	7b555	E A G	4/4	A1v5p45 C5v3p62 O1v1Lp139
SCOTS RECLUSE, THE	1H1H66	5211	D	4/4	O1v1Ap13 O1v2p14,15 C5v3p62
SCOTS THISTLE, THE	1113	2224	G	4/4	B20p11
SCOTS TUNE	331	15L6L	G	6/4	Y1p23
SCOTS WHA HAE WI' WALLACE BLED	5551H	6661H	C D	4/4*	C6p1 C8v2p5 E1v2p7 C5v2p9
					(II)
SCOTS WRIGGLE, THE	133	136	G	9/8	O1v1Fp25
SCOTT OF YARROW, THE	1111	5632	G D	2/4	C5v3p57 O1v1Gp28,29
SCOTTS GAVOT, THE	3254	2211	G	4/4	O1v1Hp44
SE GAOL A BHOBAIN FIONNLLA	5521	6661H	D	4/4	D14v2p33
SE' N RIGH A' TH'AGAINN IS FEARR LEINN	3b3b55	3b3b55L	A	6/8	F2v2p65(55)
'SE SO MARBH RANN MO CHARAID	3b13b1	7bL427bL	F	3/8	F2v2p46(36)
SEA MEW, THE	6L133	3321	G	6/8	C10v2Ap55
SEA QUADRILLE, THE	1H2H1H5	7531H	D	6/8	G1v1p32,33

Title			Key	Time	References
SEAFORTH HIGHLANDERS, THE	11H15	11H31	A	2/2	A7v3p22 (II)
SEAFORTH'S FAREWELL	1H1H55	31H3H3H	G	4/4	O1v1Kp117
SEAFORTH'S SALUTATION	1531	2326L	F	6/8	D14v2p1
SEAL-FISHER'S SONG, THE	3555	3566	G	6/8	C4p16
SEALG IS SUGRADH NAN GLEANN	3b1H3b4	3b1H14	F	3/8	F2v2p80(70)
SEAN TRUIDH'S UILLACHAN	5L125L	3b227bL	D	2/2	F2v2p86,87(76,77)
[SEANN TRIUBHAIS UILLEACHAIN]					
SEANN GHILLE NA 'N CAR	11H66	3333	A	4/4	Mc1v1Ap8
SEATON HOUSE	5312	61H1H7	F	4/4	O1v1Gp13
SECOND BATTn SCOTCH BRIGADE, THE	11L17L	25L43	Bb	6/8	L1p10
SECOND MEDLEY DANCE	1152	7L5L11	Bb	6/8	G3p14,15
SECOND QUICK STEP SECOND BATTn. ROYALS	5H3H4H2H	3H2H1H1H	D	6/8	A1v2p14
SECOND QUICKMARCH 10th REGt	3H1H2H5	353H1H	D	6/8	A1v2p58
SECOND TURKS MARCH	3112	4225	G	4/4	A1v2p3
SECRET KISS, THE	1355	1H633	D	4/4	O1v1Dp23
SECRET STREAM, THE	1242	6b425L	G	4/4	O1v1Kp126
SEE THE CONQUERING HERO COMES	5351	2432	G	2/4	E1v1p46
SEE THE CONQUERING HERO COMES	5533	5511	G	4/4	C8v2p9 C8v1p25 A1v3p199
SEIGE OF BELGRADE	1H51H5	624H1H	Eb D	2/4	W4v1p22 C5v1p46 A1v4p46
SEME RUNE TALLANACH	117bL7bL	117bL5L	A	4/4	C33p2
SEMENZATI	5421	4553	G	2/4	A1v3p195
SEND US WHISKY	515L5	4362	F	12/8	F3p12
SEVENTH OF NOVEMBER, THE	5332	6221H	D	2/2	R6v1p5
SEVENTH REGt	5H1H2H7	6523	D	6/8	S5p19
SEVENTY THIRD (REGt's) MARCH, THE	15L3L5L	1112	G	4/4	L1p23
SFHADDE MAR SEO THA SINN	1111	2221	A	4/4	Mc1v1p34-37
SHADDIE	3H1H51	337L0	F	6/8	P6v1p26 H6v1p2
SHAKE YOURSELF	5L155	5L1H3H6	C	6/8	K1v2p23
SHAKE YOURSELF	5351	5316L	G	12/8	C7p19
SHAM FIGHT, THE	3343	1H525L	G	6/8	B16v3p85
SHAMBO BREECKS	3564	3127L	G	4/4	A1v2p10 A7v5p13 A7v6p48
SHAMBOE BREECHES	3564	3127bL	G	2/2	S12v1p35
SHAN DOL GRIGRUGH	3b225L	7bL247bL	A	2/2	R6v2p14
SHANBUIE	1565	1561H	G	6/8	O1v1Kp131
SHANE'S CASTLE	1565	1H542	G	4/4	C14v5p12
SHANTRUISH	1127bL	3b247bL	A	4/4	A1v1p55
SHARP AND FLAT	1112	3b525	G	2/4	H1p34
SHAVELING GABBIT BROCK, THE	5544	31H66	D	4/4	L9p4
SHAWL DANCE	123b2	1755	A	2/4	N2p18,19
DANCED BY THE MISSES KIRKALDY					
SHE GRIPED AT YE GREATEST ON'T	1111	5151	G	2/2	O1v1Dp5
SHE HAD SOMETHING ELSE TO DO	3255	61H55	G	4/4	A1v3p227
SHE ROSE AND LET ME IN	1551H	7754	D E	4/4	O1v2p8,9 O1v3p20 Mc8v2Cp1
					O1v1Ap21 G17p8 C20p82
SHE ROSE AND LET ME IN	1551H	7756b	B D E G	4/4	O1v1Ap21 O1v2p29 (J3)
					N1v2p35 P8v2p24 T6v2p30
					Mc8v1Ap9 P4p3 C6p14 C13v3p73
					E1v2p110
SHE ROSE AND LET ME IN	1551H	7756	D	4/4	(C25)
SHE ROW'D HIM IN HER APRON	1153	1255	F	4/4	C5v2p12 (J3)
SHE STOOPS TO CONQUER	13L3L1	13L7F2L	Bb	4/4	P9p38
SHE WADNA HAE ME BUT WAD HAE ANITHER	7b152	7b151	A	6/8	C5v3p71
SHE WOU'D NOT DIE A MAID	521H1H	5233	G	4/4	O1v1Lp158
SHEELA NA GIGG	351H3	561H1H	D	6/8	A1v5p37
SHEELAN O' GEARY	1H3H3H	2H4H4H	C	3/4	E1v1p116,117
SHELAH O' NEAL	1552	1551	F	6/8	G10v5p11
SHELDON HOUSE	5155	3572H	C	4/4	H1p28
SHENVALL, THE	1126L	1111	G	4/4	A7v6p48
SHEPHERD ADONIS, THE	5L17bL	13b5	G B	3/4	(J3) C5v3p57
SHEPHERD ADONIS, THE	111	17bL1	B	3/4	A1v3p186
SHEPHERD OF NEATH, THE	1H1H51H	7756	F	2/2	O1v1Lp145
SHEPHERD ONCE HAD LOST HIS LOVE, A	5311	4321	G	2/4	A1v5p4 C5v1p4
SHEPHERD, THE	3555	3572	D	2/4	G9v3p21
SHEPHERDS OF YARROW, THE	111	113b	A	3/4	O1v1Ep12
SHEPHERD'S PIPE, THE	112	331	G	3/4	O1v4p4 O1v1Bp31
SHEPHERD'S SON, THE	5L111	2244	G	4/4	G11v2Dp15
SHEPHERD'S WIFE, THE	1351H	6527L	Eb	6/8	G10v4p22
SHEPHERD'S WIFE, THE	1351H	6521	G	6/8	C5v2p39
SHE'S FAIR AND FAUSE	5427L	1411	A E F	6/8	C5v3p67 E1v2p2 G1v1p22
(THAT CAUSES MY SMART)					G11v2Cp9 (J3)
SHE'S GONE! WHILE WE WONDER	3H3H2H	751H	D	3/4	C10v2Bp41
SHE'S SWEETEST WHEN	1526L	1511H	G	2/2*	G15p4 (II)
SHE('S NAKED/SMILES)					
SHE'S SWEETEST WHEN SHE'S NAKED	115	53b5	A	3/4	O1v2p35 O1v3p47 O1v1Ap26
SHILLING O' GAIREY	1214	3431	G	6/8	A1v1p51
SHIPPARD'S WIFE, THE	1357	6527L	Eb	6/8	P5v3p11
SHIUBHAIL MI ILE'S CEANN-TIRE	137L1	6L6L5L1	G	4/4	Mc5p24
SHIVAS HOUSE	1355	671H1H	G	4/4	S5p25
SHOE MAKERS DAUGHTER	1342	16L6L5L	D	2/2	S12v1p72
SHOELA NA GIGG	351H3	5635	D	6/8	C5v1p37
SHOGALLIE'S REELL	13b53b	13b53b	A	4/4	C33p20
SHORT APRON, (THE)	51H3H5	51H3H6	F	6/8	G9v5p35 B15v1p9 C13v2p7

					G11v2Cp30
SHORT APRON, THE	7b55	553bH	E	3/4	O1v1Jp90
SHORT FOLLY, THE	1127L	1127L	Bb	2/2	B16v3p70
SHORT LIFE TO (ALL) STEPMOTHERS	5L5L5L5L	6L213	D G	4/4	G1v2p62 G9v5p27
SHORT LIFE TO ALL STEPMOTHERS	5L111	2247bL	D	4/4	G9v5p27 Mc4v4p12/13
SHORT LIFE TO STEPMOTHERS	116L3	116L1	D	2/4	C8v1p54
SHREWSBURY RAKES	1122	1154	F	2/2	R12v1p75
SHURLEY'S FANCY	3127L	3151H	G	4/4	A1v2p23
SI' NAILL SO DHUISG MI	1244	4221	A	6/8	Mc5p2
SIBYL	17L15L	17L5L6L	F	2/2	G9v1p33
SIC A WIFE AS WILLIE HAD	1132	227b6	F A	4/4	(J3) C5v2p53
SIC A WIFE AS WILLIE HAD	1142	227b6	F	4/4	G10v6p31
SICH A GETTIN' UP STAIRS	3535	6424	G	2/4	C8v1p53
SICH A GETTIN' UP STAIRS	3H5H3H5H	6H4H2H4H	D	2/4	C8v2p64
SICILIAN AIR	5511	2217L	G	2/4	H1p7
SICILIAN AIR	3H4H5H3H	4H4H3H3H	D	2/4	E1v2p69
SICILIAN MARINERS HYMN	5653	5653	F	2/4	E1v1p102
SICILIAN PEASANT, THE	3H2H5H7	342H2H	D	6/8	B16v3p3
SICILIAN WALTZ	3555	6124	G	3/8	B7p15
SICILIAN WALTZ	1H53H1H	5H5H1H1H	C	3/8	H1p8
SIEGE OF MANHEIM	1121	1H1H2H1H	D	3/8	C14v11p19
SIGH, THE	5543b	5551	G	2/4	R12v1p50
SIGr FIDDLIDEE	1566	5122	G	2/2	R12v1p54
SILESIAN WALTZ, A	1H17L4	5671H	G	3/8	B7p17
SILKEN-SNOODED LASSIE, THE	3213	5552	D	4/4	C4p43
SILLER CROWN, THE	332	135	G F	3/4	C5v2p18 N1v2p40 (J3)
SILVER MINERS WALTZ, THE	3553	352H1H	G	3/8	G1v2p69
SIMON BRODIE	3353	3322	A	4/4*	G11v1Ap5 G10v1p23 C13v2p76
					Mc9v3p23
SIMPLICITY	3453	3110	D	6/8	G9v3p3
SIMPSONS REEL	3L3L11	5L5L4L2L	Bb	2/2	C14v13p6
SINCE THEN I'M DOOM'D	1H2H1H0	1H63H2H	D	2/4	A1v5p33 C5v1p33
SINCE THIS I'M DOOM'D	5H3H3H3H	2H2H5H3H	C	2/4	E1v1p62
SINGLE COMBAT	1H1H3H	1H1H2H	D	3/4	W4v1p26
SINGLE HORNPIPE	5L11	17L2	G	6/4	D15v2p44
SINGLE HORNPIPE	554	6b54	D	6/4	S11v1p15
SINGLE HORNPIPE	531	642	F	6/4	S11v2p9
SINGLE HORNPIPE, A	111	131	Bb	3/2	G3p31
SINGLE HORNPIPE NO. 1	1H1H5	61H1	D	6/4	S11v1p14,15
SINGLE HORNPIPE No. 2	311	5L3L3L	Bb	6/4	S11v1p15
SINGLE JIG	71H52	7571H	D	6/8	C22p21
SINGLE JIG	1H542	7L5L15L	G	6/8	C22p20
SINGLE JIG	4H2H1H6	751H5	Eb	6/8	C22p23
SINGLE JIG	3L16L5L	7F2L3L1	Bb	6/8	C22p22
SINGLETON HALL	1212	1234	Bb	2/4	W6p14
SIR A. FERGUSSON'S STRATHSPEY	5353	5532	F	4/4	A7v1p12
SIR ALEX DONS STRATHSPEY	1122	1155	D	4/4	C13v1p45
SIR ALEXANDER DON	3146	3542	F	4/4	G11v1Cp27 (II)
SIR ALEX(ANDE)r DON('S STR.)	3b13bL1L	247b2	G	4/4	Mc21v2p9 (II)
SIR ALEXr DON'S MEDLEY (JIG)	5313	1336	D	6/8	G10v6p22
SIR ALEXr DON'S MEDLEY (REEL)	1H3H1H6	1H3H1H6	D	4/4	G10v6p22,23
SIR ALEXr DON'S STRATHSPEY	1122	1155	D	4/4	G11v1Ap3
SIR ALEXr DUNBAR'S STRATHSPEY	1347bL	1353	D	2/2	Mc9v3p7
SIR ALEXr McDONALD'S REEL	355H2H	4H2H66	D	4/4	A1v1p25 S12v1p1 B15v1p22
					C13v2p29 C33p6 C4p55 Mc12v1p30
SIR ALEXr. MUNRO'S REEL	1316L	5L132	G	2/4	J2p2
SIR ALLAN MCLEAN'S REEL	1122	1111	G	2/2	H3p37
SIR ARCHd CAMPBELL'S JIGG	1351H	1325L	Bb	6/8	Mc13v2p20 C13v1p2
SIR ARCHd DUNBAR OF NORTHFIELD'S STRATHSPEY	1126L	111H6	F	4/4	G15p25
SIR ARCHd DUNBAR	1347bL	1353	D	4/4	G11v2Cp36 (II)
SIR ARCHd DUNBAR OF NORTHFIELD'S STRATHSPEY	1613	1627L	F	4/4	C18p1
SIR ARCHd DUNBAR BARt OF NORTHFIELD'S STRATHSPEY	331H6	333H2H	C	4/4	T1v2p9
SIR ARCHd GRANT (OF MONYMUSK'S)(REEL)	5354	5324	G	2/2*	D14v3p5 Mc7p23 Mc9v3p19
					Mc12v1p43 (II)
SIR ARCHIBALD CAMPBELL'S FAVORITE	5L155	236L6L	D	2/2	G8p4
SIR CHARLES DOUGLASS'S STRATHSPEY	5351	5331H	D	4/4	G10v4p4
SIR CHARLES FORBES OF NEW AND EDINGLASSIE	13b3b5	13b55	F	4/4	M4v4p34
SIR CHAs DOUGLAS	5451	5331H	D	2/2	Mc16p15
SIR CHAs ROSS OF BALNAGOWAN'S HORNPIPE	14L3L2	347L5L	Bb	2/2	J2p11
SIR DAVID CARNEGIE OF SOUTHESK BARt's STRATHSPEY	1L133	2L247L	Bb	4/4	D15v1p2
SIR DAVID HUNTER BLAIR	7555	53H53H	F	2/4	D15v2p39
SIR DAVID HUNTER BLAIR ('S REEL)	1H555	53H53H	F	4/4*	E1v1p2 C14v16p2 G11v1Bp30
					Mc21v4p24 N1v1p6 (II)
SIR DAVID HUNTER BLAIR'S NEW REEL	15L13	2L242	A	4/4	F3p4
SIR DAVID HUNTER OF BLAIR'S NEW REEL	3541H	357L2	F	2/2	C14v24p14
SIR GEO: MURRAY'S FAVORITE	1H31H1	337L5L	D	6/8	G9v3p23
SIR GEORGE CLERK (OF PENNYCUICK)	3H1H53	4422	G	4/4*	G11v1Ap23 C5v2p62

SIR GEORGE MACKENZIE(OF COUL)('S REEL)	5346	5342	A	2/2*	G10v4p11 (11)
SIR GEORGE MCKENZIE OF COUL'S FAVORITE	31H52	31H53	C	4/4	G10v5p32
SIR GEORGE McKENZIES REEL	6346	5342	A	2/2	A7v5p2
SIR GEORGE RAMSAY'S LAMENT	315L5L	5122	E	2/2	W4v1p29
SIR GILBERT STIRLING'S STRATHSPEY	3b13b5	7b47bL4	E	2/2	B20p4
SIR HARRY INNES'S REELL	151H3	247L2	A	4/4	C33p18
SIR HENDRY'S STRATHSPEY	5L3L5L1	15L3L2L	Bb	4/4	C7p11
SIR HENRY TROLLOPE'S FANCY	137L6L	5L343	D	4/4	C14v13p3
SIR HEW DALRYMPLE Bt.(N BERWICK'S) REEL	1133	7L27L2	G	2/4	Mc21v2p8
SIR HUGH MUNRO OF FOWLES REEL	5333	3342	A	2/2	C14v5p16
SIR HUGH MUNRO OF FOWLIS'S FAVOURITE	3b5L3bL5L	3b556b	G	2/4	J2p3
SIR Ja: GRANT'S STRATHSPEY*	3535	357L2	Eb	4/4	A7v1p8
SIR JAMES BAIRD ('S STRATHSPEY)	5551	5642	G	4/4	G10v2p2 A7v2p7 E1v1p38
					G11v1Bp8 A7v6p19
SIR JAMES BAIRD'S (FAVORITE/STRATHSPEY)	15L5L5L	16L6L6L	A	4/4	G11v1Ap4 G10v1p8 (11)
SIR JAMES BAIRD'S NEW STRATHSPEY	3b53b1	2427bL	G	4/4	Mc21v3p28
SIR JAMES [B]ASON	111	234	C	6/4	W7p21
SIR JAMES CAMPBELL'S JIGG	13b1H1H	4522	G	12/8	Mc13v2p33
SIR JAMES CAMPBELL'S STR.(AND GIGG)	13b3b4	2424	G	4/4	Mc13v2p33 C13v1p33
SIR JAMES COLQUHOUN'S REELL	3b13b1	3b7bL7bL7bL	E	2/2	C33p7
SIR JAMES G. BAIRD BART('s STRATHSPEY)	1111	6L27L2	G	4/4	Mc21v2p26 (11)
SIR JAMES ST CLAIR ERSKINE	1122	3366	G	4/4	W2v2p2/3
SIR JAMES St CLAIR'S MARCH	1H3H1H5H	1H550	D	4/4	W2v1p1
SIR JOHN CATHCART'S REEL	1H3H1H5	2326L	C	2/2	R5p27
SIR JOHN HENDERSON('S JIGG)	3153	6562	F G	6/8	G10v2p15 G11v1Bp34,35
SIR JOHN HOPE'S MARCH	1H1H55	3515	F		G9v3p36
SIR JOHN LOCKHART ROSS('S STR./REEL)	13b3b4	2424	G	4/4*	G11v2Bp14 A7v2p9 K1v2p16 (11)
SIR JOHN MALCOLM	51H3H2H	5555	C D	4/4	(J3) A1v2p73 B15v1p96 (11)
SIR JOHN MAXWELL'S REEL	351H3	42H4H2H	C	2/2	C13v2p74
SIR JOHN MAXWELL'S STRATHSPEY	5L133	6632	D	4/4	Mc13v2p25 C13v1p25
SIR JOHN MCGREGOR MURRAY'S STRATHSPEY	1356	2467	D	4/4	Mc11p10
SIR JOHN MOORE'S REEL	3131	2424	A	4/4	P6v1p29
SIR JOHN SCOTT'S FAVOURITE	126L	124	G A	9/8	A1v4p64
					G10v3p20
SIR JOHN SINCLAIR	321H1H	5320	Eb	4/4	G10v5p8
SIR JOHN SINCLAIR OF STEVINGSTOUN	3456	71H1H2	G	2/4	L2p16
SIR JOHN STEWART OF GRANDTULLIE'S REEL	3H2H1H5	27bL44	D	2/2	Mc9v3p6
SIR JOHN STEWART (OF GRANDTULLY)	3131	1H342	G F	4/4	A1v4p56 C5v1p56 G10v1p30
('S STRATHSPEY)					G11v1Cp5 C4p30 Mc12v1p40 (11)
SIR JOHN STEWART OF GRANDTULLY'S STR.)	5532	5752	D	4/4	C14v1p11
SIR JOHN STEWART OF GRANTULLY'S REEL	5151	47bL7b7bL	E	4/4	Mc21v4p20
SIR JOHN STEWART'S FAVOURITE	1115	1116	G	6/8	D15v1p24
SIR JOHN STEWART'S STRATHSPEY	3b15L1	3b145	D	4/4	A7v3p16
SIR JOHN STUART OF GRANTULLIE'S RANT	1H535	2424	D	2/2	S12v1p29
SIR JOHN WHITEFOORD('S STRATHSPEY)	116L1	526L6L	G Eb	4/4	A1v3p214 C4p56 E11v1Cp10,11
					G10v1p12 C13v1p43
SIR (JOHN/GEORGE) STEWART	116L5L	1315L	A	4/4	D14v3p15 G10v4p16,17
OF GRAN(D)T(UL)LY'S (STRATHSPEY/REEL)					
SIR L. DUNDAS'S REEL	1H1H35	67b24	D	2/2	S7v1p38
SIR MICHAEL BRUCE'S MARCH	31H1H1H	5445	F	4/4	D6p2
SIR NEIL MENZIES BART'S STRATHSPEY	1L3L46L	4347L	A	2/2	Mc19v2p8
SIR NORMAN McLEOD'S LAMENT	335	531H	C	3/4	C4p23 Mc5p626
SIR PATRICK MURRAY'S MARCH	1H1H1H6	1H3H1H5	C	4/4	B12p1
SIR PATRICK SPENS	1111	27L7L2	Bb	4/4	C10v2Bp63
SIR PATRICK SPENS	1H51H5	7b7b45	C	2/4	C10v2Bp63
SIR RICHARD STRACHAN	1351H	61H55	Bb	2/4	C14v23p8,9
SIR RICHARD STRACHAN	1565	3512	Bb	2/4	H6v1p3 P6v1p24
SIR ROBERT PEEL	15L3L5L	2L27L2	Bb	2/2	M4v4p21
SIR ROGER DE COVERLEY	115	6L27L	D	9/8	C14v18p5
SIR RONALD McDONALD'S REEL	1555	7b47bL2	G	2/2	K1v1p11 G11v2Ap9
SIR WALTER SCOTT	5L31H1H	5556L	F	6/8	G9v2p12
SIR WALTER SCOTT BART.	11H62	11H3H6	Bb	4/4	M4v3p13
SIR WILLIAM BLACK'S LAMENT	3b527bL	3b211L	A	6/8	Mc15p31
SIR WILLIAM DICK'S REEL	1313	1362	D	2/2	Mc21v3p33
SIR WILLIAM HOPE'S SCOTCH-MEASURE	31H1H5H	3H3H1H7	D	2/2	P7p6
SIR WILLIAM STIRLING'S STRATHSPEY	31H61H	61H22	D	2/2	S13p3
SIR Wm GORDON CUMMING'S REEL	11H3H1H	1H553	G	2/2	G10v5p21
SIR Wm JARDINE'S REEL	6453	662H7	A	2/2	P9p34
SIR Wm JARDINE'S STRATHSPEY	1L5L33	5453	A	4/4	P9p34
SISTER OF LOVES	3b3b3b	555	A	3/4	Mc5p1
SISTERS LAMENT, THE	2235	3336	G	4/4	Mc1v1p53-55
SISTERS, THE	1H1H44H	1H1H35	D	2/2	A1v5p27 C5v1p27
SIUBHAL AN T'SNEACHD TRA OIDHCHE	3bH1H7b	3bH1H3bH	C	9/8	F2v2p14(4)
SIXPENCE UNDER MY THUMB, A	3432	5221	G	6/8	A7v6p70 A7v3p23
SIXTEEN REGts MARCH, THE	1112	3334	G	4/4	M2p14
SKENE HOUSE	3311	5532	F	6/8	D15v2p29
SKENE OF SKENE('S STRATHSPEY)	5L143	137L2	G	4/4	D16p32 (11)
SKENE'S ELECTION	1511H	1542	D	2/2	S5p10
SKENE'S QUICK STEP, THE	5L147L	5L145	G	6/8	S5p4
SKIRMISH OF FOOT SOLDIERS	3H3H4H4H	3H2H1H1	D	6/8	W4v1p26
SKIVER THE QUILT	1H1H7b7b	1H1H7b4	G	6/8	A1v3p155

```
SKY AIR                                     1H342      6555        D     4/4     A1v5p70
SKY AIR                                     17L15L     1211        G     4/4     A1v5p70
SKYE AIR (No.168)                           1135       5326L       G     4/4     A1v5p70   Mc5p29
SKYE AIR                                    111        123         F     3/4     Mc5p27
SKYE AIR, A  (O HITHIL O HORINO)            5336       1H631       G     4/4     A1v5p66   Mc5p28   G11v2Cp10   (II)
(HITHIL UIL AGUS)
SKYE AIR, A                                 236L1      5562        G     6/8     Mc5p29
SKYE DANCE                                  5565       1H655       A     4/4     Mc5p37
SKYE DANCE                                  5554       3b3b3b4     A     4/4     Mc5p37
SKYE DANCE                                  5542       3b17bL2     A     4/4     Mc5p37
SKYE DANCE, (A)                             1532       2246        A     4/4*    C4p15   Mc5p37   A1v5p68
SLAN GUN TIG MO RUN A NALL                  156L1      1H57L2      Eb    4/4     F2v2p84(74)
SLAUNT RI PLULIB                            117L       124         G     3/4     T7p34,35
SLEEP ON TILL DAY                           51H51      51H56       G     6/8     G1v2p94
SLEEP ON TILL DAY                           51H53      51H36       D     3/8     C5v3p66
SLEEP ON TILL DAY                           523        1H1H3H      C     3/4     G11v2Cp8
SLEEPY BODY                                 3352       3351        F A   6/8     G11v2Cp6         Mc8v1Cp62   Mc8v2Cp7
SLEEPY BODY                                 3352       3651        G F   6/8     O1v1Cp17         T6v2p112
SLEEPY MAGGIE                               53b53b     53b42       B     2/2     Mc9v3p35   Mc21v3p38
SLEEPY MAGGY/IE [SLEEPING MAGGIE]           5153b      5142        B     4/4*    G7p11   K1v1p40   R6v2p34   C13v2p13
                                                                                 G11v2Ap38   B15v1p48   E1v1p59
                                                                                 C14v17p15   Mc7p14   O1v1Jp95   (II)

SLINGSBIE'S PROVINCE                        5553       5411        G     2/4     Mc9v2p17
'SLIONAR EUBH' AGUS IOLACH                  111        633         G     3/4     Mc5p1
SLOW                                        1117L      5L5L5L3     A     4/4     D15v2p22
SLOW                                        111H1H     2H7b2H1H    G     4/4     Mc5p10
SLOW                                        355        656         Bb    3/4     C22p26
SLOW                                        112        222         A     3/4     Mc5p10
SLOW                                        122        554         A     9/8     Mc5p6
SLOW                                        653        231         D     9/8     Mc5p12
SLOW AND DISTINCT                           5333       5322        F     4/4     D15v2p35
SMALL PIN CUSHION, THE                      552H3H     5622        D     6/8     O1v1Jp94
SMALL REEL, THE                             3H2H64     3H2H5H2H    D     4/4     A7v6p65
SMALL REEL, THE                             6527bL     651H5       A     2/2     A7v3p20
SMASH THE WINDOWS                           1155       6677        A     2/2     H6v5p2
SMASH THE WINDOWS                           131H2H     4324        D     6/8     H6v10p2
SMEORACH CLANN DONAILL                      111        222         A     3/4     F2v2p42(32)
[SMEORACH CHLAINN DOMHNUILL]
'SMI GABHAIL AN RATHAID                     111        425L        A     3/4     Mc5p16
SMILIN' KATIE                               1551H      7b547bL     E     2/2     C18p38   H3p11
SMITH HE'S BLACK AN' BRUCKET, THE           5L11       531         G     3/2     C18p10
SMITH OF KILLECHASSIE, THE                  1155       4422        A     4/4*    Mc19v1p5   (II)
SMITH'S A GALANT FIREMAN, THE               1155       51H42       D     4/4     A7v6p67   (II)
SMITH'S A GALANT FIREMAN, THE               1155       51H32       D     2/2     A7v3p36
SMITH'S MAGGOT, THE                         1135       3631H       G     2/4     D15v1p16
SMITH'S ORANGE & FORK                       3H1H3H1H   5H3H1H5      E     6/8     C14v16p20
SNAIM A' PHOSAIDH                           5147bL     5127b       E     6/8     F2v2p73(63)
SNAKES LANE                                 1352       5L7L25      G     2/2     S7v1p72
SNAW FOURTEEN                               116L5L     1136        Bb    4/4     H1p1
SNUG PARTY, THE                             1H1H2H2H   3H3H2H7     D     6/8     B16v3p21
SO MERRY AS WE HAVE BEEN                    1H1H1H     543         D     3/4     C20p43
SO MERRY AS WE TWA' HAVE BEEN               1H1H3H     553         D     3/4     T7p6,7
SOCIETY'S FAVOURITE, THE                    117bL3b    113b5       A     2/2     F2v1p7
SODGER LADDIE, (MY/THE)                     3122       6113        F G   6/8     (J3)   T6v2p63         G11v2A14   W7p5
                                                                                 C4p70   K1v1p16   B15v1p22   P8v2p38
                                                                                 (II)
SOFT MAY MORN                               1153       1H531       G     6/8     C4p49   Mc5p24
SOFT, SOFT WHISPERED THE MAID               1H1H3bH    5H5H5H      D     3/4     Mc5p10
SOFTLY SWEET IN LYDIAN MEASURES             6063       3HO2HO      C     4/4     E1v2p71
S'OLC A CHUIR A MHIREADH RIUM               31H53      31H52       Eb    4/4     F2v2p103(93)
'SOLC A FHUAIR MI TUS A GHEAMHRAIDH         1162       1127L       G     6/8     Mc5p8
SOLDIER AND A SAILOR, A                     1H1H1H5    3H3H3H1H    D     6/8     O1v1lp74
SOLDIER LADDIE, THE                         3122       3113        G     6/8     P5v3p13
SOLDIER MAC                                 1H3H75     61H52       D     2/2     S7v1p28
SOLDIER'S ADIEU                             1H1H2H7    5533        F     4/4     E1v1p72,73
SOLDIER'S ADIEU, THE                        1H1H1H7    5530        G     4/4     A1v5p10
SOLDIER'S DANCE                             1125       317L5L      A     6/8     W4v1p5   A1v4p35
SOLDIER'S DANCE AFTER THE BATTLE            5651       51H52       G     4/4     A1v4p17   W4v1p32
SOLDIER'S DREAM                             561H       1H1H1H      C     3/4     B7p45
SOLDIER'S FROLICK                           1H544      1H522       F     12/8    C7p19
SOLDIER'S JOY                               5151       11H1H7      D     2/2     S7v1p77
SOLDIER'S JOY(, THE)                        5151       51H1H7      D     4/4*    A1v1p39   Mc9v2p32   B10p27   (II)
SOLDIER'S JOY, THE                          5151       51H1H1H     D     2/2     C8v2p51
SOLDIER'S JOY, THE                          5151       571H7       D     2/2     C13v2p56   G9v5p9
SOLDIER'S RETURN(, THE)                     3H555      662H1H      D     4/4*    E1v1p61   G1v1p30   (II)
SOLDIER'S RETURN, THE                       35L5L5L    6L6L21      Bb    4/4     C6p19
SOLDIERS TAKE AWAY THE WOUNDED              3231H      56L6L2      D     6/8     W4v1p27
SOLDIER'S WEDDING, THE                      51H71H     2H1H1H1H    D     2/4     A1v6p57
SOLITUDE, THE                               13b1       51H1H       E     3/4     O1v1Ep18,19
SOLITUDE, (THE)                             13b1       51H3bH      E     3/4     O1v4p9   P4p34
SOLO                                        553b3b     1117b       G     4/4     Mc21v1p36-40
SOMEBODY                                    1H1H7b7b   5544        E     6/8     A1v6p36
```

143

Title					
SONG OF DEATH, THE	6L236L	315L5L	G	6/8	C4p31
SONNAN MO GHAOIL	5L1L5L5L	5L1L4L7bF	A	6/8	Mc5p6
SORAIDH LEIS AN T'SEANA BHLIADHNA	3L13L3L	3L122L	A	4/4	F2v2p13(3)
SORAIDH SLAN DO'N AILLEAGAN	16L15L	26L11	A	4/4	F2v2p12(2)
SOUR PLUMBS IN GALLASHIELS	3333	3221	A	4/4	C29p6-9
(SOUR PLUMS [IN]) GALLA SHIELS	3331H	5222	G	4/4	C13v3p48,49 M14p28-32 N1v2p18
					O1v1Bp30,31 O1v4p2,3 P4p31
					T6v1p91
SOUR PLUMS OF GALLOW-SHIELS	3333	5222	G	4/4	Mc8v1Cp86 Mc8v2Ap14 C20p75
SOUTERS OF SELKIRK, THE	356	531H	F G	3/4	(J3) W7p4 C5v2p47 B5p10
					O1v4p44,45 O1v1Ap34,35
					Mc8v1Cp79 Mc8v2Bp19 A1v2p73
SOUTERS OF SELKIRK, (THE)	556	557	A	9/4	Mc23p19 E1v2p123
SOUTERS OF SELKIRK, THE	355	357	A	9/4	G9v1p4,5
SOUTERS OF SELKIRK, THE	365	367	G	9/8	S12v2p29
SOUTH AND NORTH	1332	135L3	G	4/4	K1v1p2 G11v2Ap2
SOUTH DOWNS	1H1H75	4331	F	2/2	C14v24p11
SOUTH DOWNS	1H1H64	4331	F	2/2	H6v2p2 P6v1p16
SOUTH SEA	771H1H	7555	F	2/4	S7v1p93
SOUTHAMPTON ROOM	5432	1411L	Bb	6/8	S7v1p53
SOUTHESK RIVER	1L124	1L135	Bb	6/8	D15v1p8
SOUTHWARK GRENADIER'S MARCH	1H1H2H2H	3H1H1H5H	D	2/2	A1v3p228
SOW'S TAIL, THE	117L5L	1111	D	4/4	G11v1Bp38
SOWS TAIL, THE	5524	151H3H	D	4/4	C20p52
SOW'S TAIL (TO GEORDIE), THE	5524	5551H	D	4/4*	G10v2p32,33 Mc9v2p39,40,41
					A1v2p67 C4p5
SPA (DANCE), (THE)	11H3H3H	5H5H1H1H	C D	2/4	Mc9v2p42 A1v2p23
SPA PROMENADE, THE	5121	5121	Bb	2/4	C14v7p21
SPACE AND COMPASS	111H3	422H4H	C	2/2	H3p4
SPAIDSEARACHD DHONUILL CHRUAMAICH	1433	2222	A	4/4	Mc1v1p13-22
SPANISH AIR	3355	3211	A	6/8	E1v2p53
SPANISH BARBER	5L132	4242	G	2/2	S7v1p47
SPANISH COUNTRY DANCE	1H72	651	F	3/4	G13p13
SPANISH DANCE	3H2H1H3H	4H4H75	C D	2/4	W4v1p4 A1v4p34
SPANISH FANDANGO	1123	1121	G	3/8	B7p29 G1v2p70
SPANISH JIG, A	3325	3325	G	6/8	A1v1p27
SPANISH MARCH	5355	5543	D	2/4	M2p22,23
SPANISH MARCH, A	1H3H4H4H	1H1H2H5	D	2/4	A1v1p64
SPANISH PATRIOT	1355	2461H	F	6/8	P6v1p32
SPANISH PATRIOTS, THE	351H5	461H1H	F	4/4	G9v3p7
SPANISH PATRIOTS, THE	1H1H33	1H1H31H	D	2/2	P6v1p31
SPARK'S RANT	5L133	536L6L	G	2/2	S12v1p22
SPAW, THE	11H3H3H	5H5H1H1H	C	2/4	S7v1p70
SPEED THE HARROW	37L6L5L	4L3L2L2	A	2/2	P9p30
SPEED THE PLOUGH	1155	5555	G B A	4/4*	A7v5p23 D15v2p14 A7v4p3
					C8v1p19 C8v2p28 G7p6 N1v1p35
					(II)
SPELL, THE	131H3	1347L	C	4/4*	G11v2cp20 S12v1p39 B15v1p73
SPELL, THE	131H5	1347L	C	2/2	C24v2p22
SPEY RIVER	1111	427L2	Bb	2/2	A7v1p16
SPEY SIDE	1H1H31H	54H2H2H	C	4/4	G8p17
SPINNING O'T, THE	5L6L1	335	G	3/4	C5v2p13
SPINNING WHEEL, THE	3356	51H1H3	G	2/2	O1v1Jp96
SPINNING WHEEL, THE	11H52	11H1H1	E	6/8	A1v2p72
SPLASH'D PETTICOAT	1255	457L2	G	6/8	R12v1p12
SPOIGAN	1H33	1H1H2	F	9/8	H3p8
SPORT, THE	1525	1555	E	4/4	C33p10
SPORTSMAN, THE	535	447L	G	9/8	B16v2p12
SPRIG OF SHILLELAH, THE	51H2H2H	1H5H2H2H	D	6/8	C8v2p19
SPRIG OF SHILLELAH, THE	5L122	1522	G Bb	6/8	C8v1p53 E1v2p14 (II)
SPRING FIELD	3b15L1	47bL44	G	4/4	Mc13v1p9 Mc13v2p9 (II)
SPRING FOR ME REVIVES IN VAIN, THE	16L15L	26L11	Bb	2/4	C10v2Ap47
SPRING, THE	1H321	1H35L1	G	2/4	S7v1p6
SQr PARSONS MARCH	115L1	3331	G	2/2	W7p18
SQUARE AND COMPASS, THE	131H3	422H3H	C	4/4	C8v1p58 (II)
SQUITAL BRIDGE	3L1L6L2	4426L	A	4/4	M12p30
Sr ADAM FERGUSON'S REEL	5L112	4L7bL7bL1	E	2/2	R5p14
Sr. SIDNEY SMITH'S WALTZ	1H131	1H131	Bb	3/8	C14v15p12
Sra MARANERI E Sr BUGIENI PAS DE DEUX	1243	1231	G	3/8	P8v1p14-16
SRATH MHUISIDH [STRATH MHATHAISIDH]	5316L	5L15L5L	Eb	4/4	F2v2p89(99)
ST ANDREWS ASSEMBLY, THE	1111	4466	G	6/8	C23p12
ST ANN'S FANCY	1H533	26L16L	G	4/4	C14v11p10
ST BRYCE'S DALE	31H3H1H	5642	D	2/4	C23p12
ST. HELENA	1H1H2H7	2H2H2H4H	C	4/4	C1v4p5
ST JAMES'S	1351H	3H1H1H1H	G	2/4	R12v1p72
St. KILDA GIRL'S LAMENT (ATION ON THE DEATH OF HER LOVER), A	5631	572H6	G	6/8	C4p68 Mc5p31
St KILDA SONG AND DANCE, A	51H65	57b66	D	2/2	C4p43
St. KILDA (SONG/AIR), (A)	115L6L	1322	F C	4/4	(J3) Mc5p31
St. KILDARE	5531	5531	Bb	2/2	P6v1p9
St. KILDA('S) REEL, (THE)	5531	5531	Bb	2/2	G11v1Bp32 C14v19p11
St. MARTIN'S CHURCH YD.	53bH7b	443b	G	3/4	O1v1Cp25

St. PATRICK'S DAY	1155	316L6L	G	6/8	E1v1p39
St. PATRICK'S DAY	1155	336L6L	G	6/8	R12v1p1
ST. PATRICK'S DAY	5L112	5552	G	4/4	O1v1Kp132,133
St. PATRICK'S DAY(IN THE MORNING)	1155	236L6L	G	6/8	G11v2Cp18 (II)
St. PATRICK'S DAY IN THE MORNING	1155	326L6L	G	6/8	A1v1p18
ST. PATRICK'S DAY IN THE MORNING	5L155	236L6L	G	6/8	C8v1p24 C8v2p8
ST PIERRES HORNPIPE	1122	36L7L5L	Bb	2/4	C22p32
STACK IN VIRGO	35L6L	111	A	3/4	B11p29 Mc12v2p28
STADHOLDERS, THE	135	1H53	Bb	3/4	C13v4p46-48
STAG CHACE	5437	2H51H1	D	2/4	S7v1p68
STAR, THE	3142	1H531	F	6/8	R12v1p33
STATEN ISLAND HORNPIPE [BURNS HORNPIPE]	3355	1H3H75	D	4/4	A1v2p30 (II)
STAY AND TAKE YOUR BREECHES WITH YOU	1H1H22	1H1H13H	D	2/2	Y1p17
STAY MY CHARMER, CAN YOU LEAVE ME	1H754	4565	C D	4/4	(J3) C5v3p57
STEAM BOAT, THE	3L15L2	1324	Bb	4/4	P9p5
STEER HER UP AND HAD HER GAUN	1H1H3H3H	1H3H5H5	C D	4/4	(J3) O1v3p22 R4p21,22
					Mc8v1Cp57 Mc8v2Ap5 A1v1p42
					G11v2Dp8 Mc9v2p11 O1v1Bp25
STEER HER UP AND HAD HER GAUN	1H1H33	1H632	D	2/2	P7p6,7
STEER THE GILL	1H1H1H4	1H1H2H3H	D	2/2*	K1v2p38 B15v1p13 G11v2Bp36
					(II)
STEUART LODGE	13b6b3b	11H6b4	E	2/2	L4p2
STEWARD'S LODGE SONG, THE	3H1H1H1	3551H	D	4/4	A1v2p9
STEWART CUMMING	3355	4244	A	4/4	C14v13p20
STEWART ROBERTSON'S STRATHSPEY	13b57b	47b47bL	G	4/4	P5v1p7
STEWARTS MARCH, THE	1142	57bL7bL4	A	4/4	D14v2p40
STEWART'S RANT, THE	3653	462H6	A	4/4	G11v2Dp24 (II)
STEWART'S RANT, THE	3654	462H6	A	2/2	N1v1p15
STEWART'S RANT, THE	3664	462H6	A	4/4	P5v4p21
STEWART'S RANT, THE	3664	47b1H7b	A	2/2	Mc9v3p20
STIRLING VALE	3212	5367	A	4/4	C5v3p58
S'TOIL LEAM FEIN AN SIOSALACH	1115	1166L	F	4/4	F2v2p56(46)
['STOIGH LEAM...]					
STOILEADH NIAL GOBHA	5551	557b7bL	B	4/4	F2v2p70(60)
[STOILE NEILL GHOBHA]					
STOLEN KISS, THE	1142	1H633	G	4/4	O1v1Jp95
STONEHAVEN ASSEMBLY	1145	1H532	Bb	6/8	M11v1p7
STONEHAVEN VOLUNTEER MARCH, THE	1H535	1H1H5H6H	C	4/4	M11v1p23
STOOL OF REPENTANCE, THE	1H31H5	1H666	A	6/8	G1v2p76 G10v5p36 (II)
STORACE	1313	27L11	Eb	2/4	P10p6,7
STOREMONT LADS, THE	5515	6626	F	4/4	E1v1p38
STORM, THE	431	123	G	3/4	E1v2p55
STORMONT BRAES, THE	1451H	5H1H2H2H	D	4/4	G8p20
STORMONT LADS, THE	5515	6626	F	4/4	G11v1Bp13 G10v2p10
STORMONT'S GHOST	16L1L3	3342	A	4/4	O1v1Jp110
STORMO(U)NT LADS(IS WALKING), THE	1515	6661H	G	4/4	P5v3p5 (II)
STORNWAY LASSIES	1542	1565	G	2/2	W2v2p8
STOUR LODGE	3H555	74H2H2H	D	2/4	C14v5p19
STRABURG WALTZ, THE	1H1H2H1H	1H1H2H1H	D	3/8	C14v21p7
STRADH FARGAIC [S(T)RATH FHARAGAIC]	5L5L3L2L	5L5L5L2	Bb	4/4	F2v2p59(49)
STRADH SPEA [SRATH SPE]	1115L	3bL5L7bL7bL	E	4/4	F2v2p73(63)
STRASBURGH DANCE, THE	1337L	3553	Bb	2/4	C14v26p3
STRATH EARN SIDE	1135	1H1H62H	D	4/4	G8p29
STRATH SPAY REEL	5353	3127L	D	2/2	R12v1p11
STRATHALLAN'S LAMENT	1H56	513	G D	3/4	C5v3p52 (J3)
STRATHBOGIE TOAST, THE	52H1H5	47b54	G	4/4	M4v3p11 (II)
STRATHBOGIE WALTZ, THE	31H54	3451	Eb	3/8	G9v3p12
STRATHDOWN	1516	5542	D	4/4	M4v1p10
STRATHEARN	1551H	7b542	G	4/4	G10v5p19 (II)
STRATHGLASS HOUSE	1135	51H22	D	4/4*	G11v2Ap34 C33p19 Mc9v1p8/9
					B15v1p100 (II)
STRATH-NITH	1323	1326L	D	2/2	R6v1p7
STRATHSPEY	1131	6L27L7L	Eb	4/4	N2p14
STRATHSPEY	5L16L2	5L16L7L	G	2/2	D15v2p37
STRATHSPEY, A	1111	11H52	G	2/4	G10v4p24,25
STRATHSPEY, A	1531H	2525	Bb	4/4	G9v5p1
STRATHSPEY REEL, A	136L6L	1323	G	2/2	S12v1p50
STRATHSPEY WRIGGLE, THE	1563	1326L	G	2/2	O1v1Jp93
STREET MARCH	1H1H1H3H	5H5H5H6H	C	4/4	C7p18
STRILY VALE	3212	5367	A	4/4	O1v1Bp5 O1v3p38
S'TROM TROM A THA MI	3H5H1H1H	3H5H3H6	C	4/4	M12p1
STRUAGH NACH'EIL BODAICH (AN DOMHAIN)	1H2H55	1H2H55	G	6/8	C4p13 Mc5p7
(STRUAN)ROBERTSON'S RANT	13b55	7bL27bL4	E	4/4*	C8v1p17 C8v2p26 K1v1p2
					B15v1p17 G11v2Ap2 G1v2p62
					G9v5p18 (II)
STRUAN ROBERTSON'S RANT	1H4H6H2H	4H1H61H	D	2/2	S12v1p19
STRUAN ROBERTSON'S RANT	3135	2424	A	2/2	Mc9v3p20 A1v4p25
STUART'S RANT, THE	3654	47b1H7b	A	4/4	B15v1p45 Mc21v3p23 (II)
STUMPIE(STRATHSPEY)	31H1H1H	31H2H2	A	4/4	G11v1Cp8,9 (II)
STUMPIE (STRATHSPEY), (REEL O')	31H2H1H	31H2H2	A G D	4/4*	G10v1p35 G7p2 Mc12v1p44,45
					(II) A1v2p16 A1v4p59
					(J3)

SUCKIE BIDS ME	15L11	5126L	G	4/4	Mc21v3p19
SUCKY BIDS ME	15L16	5126L	G	2/2*	K1v2p19 (11)
SUCKY BIDS ME	15L56	5126L	G	4/4	G11v2Bp17
SUD AIR M'AIGNE SO GHRUAIM	551	27bL5L	A	9/8	Mc5p2
SUD AN GLEANN 'S AM BI NA FEIDH	51H7b5	3bH545	D	4/4	F2v2p19(9)
SUD MAR CHUIR MI'N GEAMHRADH THARUM	3H555	3H52H6	D	4/4	Mc5p32 (11)
SUGAR BANKS	3L111	6L5L4L2L	Bb	4/4	F3p5
SUGARCANDY	3H1H6H5H	6H5H64H	C	4/4	B15v1p91
SUIHEL SHEMES	3355	6632	G	2/4	Mc1v1p89-91
SUKEY BIDS ME	15L16	5226L	G	4/4*	R12v1p25 A1v1p49 (D2)
SUL MARGINE D'UN RIO	1H1H5H2H	3H2H2H5	D	2/4	B7p6
SUL MARGINE DUN RIO	1H1H5H2H	3H2H2H1H	F	2/4	E1v2p74
SULLIVANS FANCY	113	116	A	9/8	C14v18p16
SUMMER APPROACHES, THE	1H1H1T1T	6H5H3H3H	D	4/4	B7p46
SUMMERS AMUSEMENT	1347L	6L7L13L	G	2/2	B16v3p11
SUN BEAM, THE	5126	6562	A	6/8	O1v1Lp151
SUN SHINING BRIGHTLY, THE	5552	4121	E	3/8	C10v2Bp53
SUNDERLAND MUSICAL SOCIETY, THE	5511	2231	A	2/2	J1p36
SUNDRUM HOUSE	11H45	2642	D	4/4	H1p27
SUNDRUM HOUSE	5L3b5L3b	247b3b	A	4/4	F3p8
SUNY BRAE, THE	3H3H1H5	4731	D	2/4	L3p4
SUPPER'S READY	135	11H5	C	9/8	H1p9
SURINAM BIRDS, THE	3b142	17L13b	A	4/4	L2p15
SURLY GALLOPE, THE	5555	5H5H5H3H	C	2/4	T1v2p15
SURPRISE, THE	1H51H5	1H51H2H	D	2/2	A7v3p17
SURRENDER OF CALAIS	1H533	1H72H1H	G	2/2	A1v4p42 C5v1p42 W4v1p18
SUSANNA	5331	1232	Bb	6/8	C14v25p4
SUSIE BRODIE	5342	5353	G	4/4	G10v5p20 (11)
SUSIE, (CUT HIM DOWN), (A STRATHSPEY)	5124	5151H	D	4/4*	P11v1p17 S12v1p35 A1v2p20
SUTTERS OF SELKIRK	351H	351H	G	3/4	C29p28,29
SUTTERS OF SELKIRK, THE	555	531H	A	3/4	C20p60
SUTTOR'S DAUGHTER, THE	16L15L	1332	D	4/4*	G10v1p21,22 P5v3p20 Mc9v1p6
[SUTOR'S DOCHTER, THE]					G11v1Ap14,15 C13v4p7
SWALLOW, THE	331H1H	1H3H2H2	D	2/2	S12v1p36
SWALLOW, THE	331H1H	3H1H2H2	D	4/4*	C13v2p64 P5v3p21 G11v2Bp37
					G9v5p9 K1v2p39 (11)
SWARD HOUSE	311H5	4327L	G	6/8	C21p14
SWEET ANNIE (FRAE THE SEA BEACH CAME)	13b55	523b1	G	4/4	O1v5p29 (J3) P4p10 O1v1Fp6,7
SWEET BELLS OF GLASGOW, THE	15L13	157L2	F	6/8	Mc13v2p21 C13v1p6
SWEET DAWNS THE DAY	13b57bL	7bL4L7bL7bL	A	4/4	C5v3p63
SWEET IS THE LASS THAT DWELLS	3L5L5L1	5216L	A	4/4	G11v2Bp5 Mc9v3p31 Mc12v2p60/6
AMONG (THE) HEATHER					
SWEET IS THE LASS THAT DWELLS	3L5L5L1	5211	A	4/4	K1v2p5
AMONG THE HEATHE					
SWEET LITTLE BARBARA	111	113	G	3/4	E1v2p109
SWEET MALLY [SWEET MOLLY]	11H1H7b	7b2H1H7b	E	2/4*	A1v1p44 (11)
SWEET MOLLY	157b5	7b47bL2	E	2/2*	K1v1p19 G11v2Ap17 (11)
SWEET MOLLY	157b1	7b47bL2	E	2/2	G9v5p23
SWEET RICHARD	5L17L2	1324	G	2/2*	A1v3p219 C14v6p2
SWEET WILLY O	1H33H5H	4H66H1T	D	6/8	A1v2p68
SWEETEST LASSIE	3H4H5H1H	2H4H2H7	D	2/4	A1v2p52
SWEET'S THE LASS THAT LOVES ME	5L7bL7bL7bL	111H1H	G	4/4	O1v1Ep10
SWEET'S THE LASS THE LOE'S ME	3555	666H6H	C	4/4	C5v3p65
SWINLEY CAMP	351H1H	647L2	F	2/2	C14v15p18,19
SWISS BOY	5551H	52H1H5	D	2/4	G1v1p42
SWISS BOY, THE	5551H	52H1H1H	G	2/4	C8v2p21
SWISS BOY, THE	5551H	5211	G	2/4	E1v2p73
SWISS WALTZ	1123	1121	Bb	3/8	G13p6
SWORD KNOT, THE	1H544	337L5L	G	4/4	S7v1p94
SYLPH, THE	3115	3142	G	2/4	C14v23p7
SYMINGTON LODGE	521H1H	5222	D	4/4	W4v2p13
SYMON BRODIE [SIMON BRODIE]	1522	3b51H5	E	2/2*	R6v2p1 (11)
SYMON BRODIE	113b3b	27bL24	E	2/2*	C20p72 O1v1Hp42
TABOR BOY, THE	5H3H55	72H4H3H	C	2/4	A1v6p26
TACK AND TACK	1H2H1H5	3433	G	2/4	A1v4p69
TADIE'S WATTLE	1335	4461H	G	2/2	A1v2p5
TAIGEIS AGUS DEALG INNT' [HAGGIS, THE]	3553	351H1H	C	2/2	F2v2p25(15) (11)
TAIL TODDLE	1341	1327L	G	4/4	A1v2p36
TAIL TODDLE	1342	1353	A	4/4	G10v1p32 G11v1Ap9
TAIL TODDLE	13H4H3H	1H3H2H7	D	4/4*	A7v6p72 A7v4p20 A7v3p26 (11)
TAIL TODLE	1H3H4H1H	1H3H2H7	D	4/4*	K1v1p39 G11v2Ap37 Mc23p20,21
					Mc21v3p10 C20p52,53
TAK' YOUR AULD CLOAK ABOUT YE	3b3b3b	422	A	3/4	C5v2p12
TAK' YOUR AULD CLOAK ABOUT YE	110	27L0	A G	3/4	Mc8v1Dp109 (J3) N1v2p28
TAK' YOUR AULD CLOAK ABOUT YE	111	27L7L	Bb	3/4	G11v2Dp14
TAK YOUR AULD CLOAK ABOUT YOU	13b3b	422	A	3/4	O1v1Bp29
TAKE CARE OF MY CAP	13bL11	3b147bL	G	6/8	H1p32
TAKE ME JENNY	3224	3252	F	4/4	S7v1p52
TALAVERA	1H535	62H75	F	2/2	C14v25p2
TALISMAN, THE	551H1H	2H71H5	C	6/8	(B21)
TAM GLEN	3b11	111	B A	3/4	A1v6p39 E1v2p18
TAM GLEN	5L11	53b6b	A	9/8	G1v1p22

146

Title					
TAM NA HURITH STRATHSPEY	13b42	13b53b	G	2/2	C14v9p14
TAMBORINE DANCE	3H3H3H3H	4H2H75	D	4/4	S7v1p9
TAMBOURINE	3H2H3H2H	1H2H76	D	2/2	A1v3p189
TANK, THE	1H1T66H	2H5H3H1H	D	2/2	B7p19
TANK, THE	16L23	3451H	Bb	2/4	C14v26p10,11
TAOBH' TUADH NAN GARBH BHEANN	3553	351H2H	C	4/4	F2v2p90(80)
TAR FOR ALL WEATHERS, THE	1H57L	367	Eb	9/8	C22p36
TARBAT HOUSE	1H71H1	562H2H	C	6/8	L1p11
TARGET, THE	3555	4666	D	6/8	B16v1p12
TARR WATER	3H1H51H	3H1H3H5H	C	4/4	R12v1p82
TARRY A WHILE	15L5L5L	4332	Bb	6/8	P11v2p23
TARRY WOO	1132	6L6L22	G F	4/4	A1v5p53 C5v2p10 Mc8v2Bp13
					O1v1Cp3 C20p23 N1v2p32 (J3)
TARRY WOOL	326L6L	2211	G	4/4	Mc8v1Dp106
TARS OF THE VICTORY	551H1	25L15	Bb	6/8	C14v23p12
TARS OF THE VICTORY, THE	5551	25L15	Bb	6/8	P6v1p13
TARTAN BONNET, THE	3b51L3b	43b4L2	G	4/4	C14v4p14
TAST, THE	1H1H3H5H	1T5H2H2H	D	6/8	S12v2p14,15
TASTE LIFE'S GLAD MOMENTS	3451H	1232	G	6/8	C5v1p69
TAY MOUTH	536L5L	4L3L22L	F	2/2	G8p11
TAY SIDE	1H341H	51H4H2H	D	6/8	B6v4p3
TAYLOR'S MARCH, THE	6L642	6L641	A	6/8	A1v1p60
TAYMOUTH	3b13b1	543b7bL	F	2/2	D14v3p12
TAYMOUTH HERMITAGE	5547bL	5555	D	6/8	Mc4v1p3
TAYMOUTH HOUSE [TAYMOUTH CASTLE]	3565	6562	A	2/2*	A1v4p24 Mc9v3p10 (II)
TAYNADALOCH HOUSE	1515	1562	D	2/2	Mc4v1p13
TEA ROOM, THE	1H2H65	457L2	F	6/8	R12v1p91
TEAGUES RAMBLE	555	556	C	9/8	C24v2p15
TEANN A NALL IS CUM' DO GHEALLADH	5315	5336	Eb	4/4	F2v2p68(58)
TEARS OF SCOTLAND, THE	13b5	1H3bH2H	E	3/4	(J3) O1v1Dp14,15
TEIN AIGHAIR AIR GACH BEANN DHIUBH	5553b	7b427bL	G	4/4	F2v2p32(22)
TEKELI	1H765	51H4H7	F	6/8	E1v1p70
TEKELI	1H1H65	51H4H7	G F	6/8	C8v2p36 A7v5p16 A7v4p7
					P6v1p8 (B21)
TELEGRAPH, THE	3411	5L325L	Eb	6/8	S11v1p25
TELL TODDLE [TAIL TODDLE]	1H3H4H3H	1H3H2H2H	D	2/2	A7v5p3
TEMPEST, THE	1555	152H5	G	2/4	S12v2p7
TEMPETE, LA	1H53H1H	2H61H5H	G	2/4	G7p21
TEMPLE, THE	3115	427L2	F	4/4	H1p30
TEMPO DI MINORE	3H2H1H	765	D	3/4	L2p19
TENANT OF MY OWN, A	3b13b2	4243b	A	2/4	O1v1Ip77
TENDER IS MY AFFECTION	1H332	2366	C	4/4	Mc5p26
TENTH OF JANUARY, THE	5117	6527L	Bb	6/8	P6v2p20
TENTH OF JUNE, THE	5L13b3b	427bL2	A	2/2	A1v2p8
TERROR OF DEATH, THE	446b	511	A	3/4	D14v2p31
TEVIOT BRIDGE [TEVIOT BRIG]	55L6L5L	5L5L42	A	6/8	G11v2Dp24 (II)
THA BHUAIDH AIG AN FHIODHDAIR	15L5L5L	5L134	Bb	6/8	F2v2p94(84)
THA BIODAG AIG MAC THOMAIS	3331	2427bL	A	2/2	G11v2Dp36
[McHOMAS HAS A DIRK]					
THA CEO MOR AIR MEALL A' MHUIRICH	1H1H3bH1H	3bH1H3bH3bH	D	4/4	Mc5p10
THA CRODHAIGH MACALLAN	335	211	D	3/3	P5v3p6
THA FONN GUN BHI TROM	4L5L1L3bL	4L5L7bF1L	A	4/4	Mc5p7
THA GRUAGACH SAN AODAN	111	14L4L	A	3/4	Mc5p14
THA GUILLAN AGAM FHIN	51H65	57b66	D	4/4	Mc5p31
THA LOINGEAS FO BREIDE	1120	3210	G	12/8	Mc5p13
THA M'AIGNE FODH GHRUAIM	623	16L3	A	3/4	F2v2p48(38)
THA MI FODH GHRUAIM	331H7	63H3H7	D	6/8	F2v2p100(90)
THA MI MO CHADAL	5L11	113	F	3/4	F2v2p22(12)
THA MI TINN LEIS A GHOAL	131H1H	71H66	D	4/4	F2v2p11(1)
THA MISE FO MHULAD	1256	52H65	D	6/8	Mc5p7
THA MO CHION AIR AN UR GHIBHT	215L	211	A	3/4	Mc5p16
THA MO DHAOINE FLUICH FUAR,	1H3H1H	1H1H5	D	9/8	Mc5p11
THA MO GHRADH AIR A' CHUAN					
THA MO GHAOLS' AIG DONAL	1153	1255	G	4/4	Mc5p8
THA MO GHOAL AIR A NIGHEAN	13b23b	5L7bL7bL5	B	4/4	F2v2p78(68)
THA MO GHRUAIDHEAN AIR PREASADH	3H5H6H	5H2H2H	C	3/4	Mc5p2
THA MULAD, THA SGIOS ORM	111	13b4	A	3/4	Mc5p16
THA 'N OIDHCHE NOCHD FUAR	3H3H5	3H3H3H	C	3/4	Mc5p15
THA NIGHEAN AIG A BHREABADAIR	3b13b7bL	3b16b6b	G	4/4	F2v2p17(7)
THA SGEUL BEAG AGAM AIR FIONN	531	36L6L	G	3/4	Mc5p18
THA TAIRM ANNS A' GHLEANN	1H2HO	3bH2HO	C	3/4	F2v2p99(89)
THA TIGH'N FODHAM EIRIDH	5L111	6L242	Eb	4/4	F2v2p102(92)
THADDY YOU GANDER	3H2H3H2H	62H62H	D	6/8	C8v2p39
THA'N DOARACH SA BHAILIE SO	5531	7bL7bL47bL	A	2/2	Mc16p30
(THE MOON AND) SEVEN STARS	1H545	62H3H7	D	6/8	R12v1p11 A1v1p4
THEADORE, THE	5346	1H2H53	G	2/4	A7v2p34 A7v6p21
THEATER, THE	15L15	6521	Bb	2/4	C7p16
THEATRE ROYAL	553H1H	2H71H5	C	6/8	D6p24
THEID, SGUN D'THEID MI THAIRIS	112	1H1H5	A	3/4	Mc5p20
(THEN) GUDE WIFE COUNT THE LAWIN	1H1H72H	1H653	G D	4/4	C5v2p65 G1v2p71 (J3)
THEODORE	3146	551H1H	F	4/4	P10p26
THEODORE MINUET, THE	111	331	A	3/4	C22p12

THERE ARE FEW GOOD FELLOWS WHEN JAMIE'S AWA'	1H2H7	71H6	C	3/4	O1v1Ap20
THERE ARE FEW GOOD FELLOWS WHEN JAMIE'S AWA'	3b42	23b1	G	3/4	O1v1Fp19 O1v2p22 O1v3p36
THERE CAME A GHAIST TO MARGRET'S DOOR	116L	7L7L6L	Bb	3/4	N1v2p77
THERE CAME A GHOST TO MARGARET'S BOWER	1H76	3H2H7	D	3/4	C5v3p70
THERE IS NO LUCK ABOUT THE HOUSE	1344	1322	A	4/4	Mc21v4p35
THERE WAS A LAD AND A LASS IN A KILOGIE	113	223	G	3/4	O1v1Fp26,27
THERE WAS A MAID & SHE WENT TO THE MILL	1H3H1H3H	1H3H2H2H	D	4/4	O1v1Ip76,77
THERE'LL NEVER BE PEACE TILL JAMIE COMES HAME	3b42	23b1	G	3/4	G11v2Dp6 Mc8v1Cp86,87 Mc8v2Ap18 C20p77
THERE'S BRAVE BEER AT SUDBURY'S	5331	5331	D	2/2	R12v1p79
(THERE'S) CAULD KAIL IN ABERDEEN	31H52	31H51	Eb D	2/4	C6p20 G11v2Cp13
THERE'S GRACE IN YOUR GRAY LOCKS	13b54	427bL0	G	6/8	C10v2Bp64
THERE'S MY THUMB	1154	2461H	F	4/4	N1v2p38
THERE'S MY THUMB	1334	2466	G	4/4	S16p140,141
THERE'S MY THUMB	1354	2466	G	4/4	A1v3p162
THERE'S MY THUMB (I'LL NE'ER BEGUILE THEE)	1354	2461H	F	4/4	T6v1p93 (J3)
THERE'S MY THUMB I'LL NE'ER BEGUILE THEE	1351	2461H	G	2/2	P8v2p20
THERE'S MY THUMB I'LL NE'ER BEGUILE YOU	1155	2466	F G	4/4	O1v5p25 O1v1Cp18 Mc8v1Cp69 Mc8v2Bp17 C29p44 C20p39
THERE'S NAE HARM DONE GOODWIFE	1131H	224#2H	D	2/2	M4v1p7
THERE'S NAE LUCK ABOUT THE HOUSE	3344	3322	G	2/4	C8v2p41 C8v1p61
THERE'S NAE LUCK ABOUT THE HOUSE	1H544	1H520	D	2/4	(J3) C4p2 A1v4p19 S7v1p43
THERE'S NAE LUCK ABOUT THE HOUSE	1H544	1H522	G F D	4/4*	C5v2p20 C6p12 G11v2Dp29 G7p8 M11v2p16,17
THERE'S NAE LUCK ABOUT THE HOUSE	1H1H62H	3H1H66	D	2/2	E1v1p88,89
THERE'S NAE LUCK ABOUT THE HOUSE	3H1H2H5	2H52H2H	G	4/4	A1v1p69
THERE'S NAE LUCK ABOUT THE HOUSE	116L2	316L6L	Bb	4/4	G11v2Cp4
THERE'S NOTHING SO FATAL AS WOMAN	3b1H1H7b	433bH4H	D	3/8	C10v2Ap64
THERE'S NOUGHT SAE SWEET AS LOVE	1155	1126L	G	4/4	L9p4
(THERE'S) THREE GOOD FELLOWS (DOWN IN YON GLEN)	15L3b	7bL4L4	A G	9/8	C5v2p59 Mc8v1Bp50 O1v1Ep1 C20p66,67 Mc8v2Bp11 C19p24 (J3) G10v5p19
THEY TOOK FRAE ME MY WIFE	5551	4442	A	4/4	A7v6p64
THEY TOOK FRAE ME MY WIFE	5551	4447bL	A	4/4	A7v3p10
THEY TOOK FRAE ME MY WIFE YESTREEN	5151	27bL27bL	A	2/2	A1v6p3
THIRD (CAMPERDOWN) MEDLEY DANCE	3211	61H22	Eb	2/4	G3p20,21
THIRD OF MAY, THE	1H7H5H3H	1H4H4H1H	C	2/4	C14v7p5
THIRD QUICK MARCH 15th REGt	5H5H5H5H	3H2H1H3	D	2/4	A1v2p39
THIRTIETH Regt. 2ND QUICKSTEP	51H52H	3H5H77	D	2/4	A1v1p57
THIS IS (NAE) MY AIN HOUSE	353H2H	6562	D	4/4*	A1v2p65 N1v1p33 (II)
THIS IS NO MINE AIN HOUSE	353H2H	657b2	D	4/4	O1v1Kp118
THIS IS NO MY AIN HOUSE	313H2H	6662	D	4/4	G11v1Bp33 Mc21v4p16
THIS IS NO MY AIN HOUSE	353H2H	6542	D	4/4	C1v2p8
THIS IS NO MY AIN LASSIE	513H2H	6562	D	4/4	C8v2p11
THIS IS NOT MY AIN HOUSE	313H2H	6562	D	4/4*	C8v1p31 C14v18p13 G7p7 G10v1p31
THO' FOR SEVEN LONG YEARS	113	224	G	3/4	T7p14,15
THO' I AM NOW A VERY LITTLE LAD	3413	6432	G	2/4	A7v3p34
THOMAS AND SALLY	1H3H3H2H	2H676	C	4/4	S12v1p66
THORN, THE	5356	1H530	Eb	4/4	D15v2p10
THOSE LILLY LIPS	546b6b	43b55	B	2/4	P8v2p32
THOU ART GANE AWA'	1H1H1H1H	5353H	C	4/4	E1v2p29
THOU ART GANE AWA' FRAE ME, MARY	1H1H1H1H	5553H	C D	4/4	C6p19 C5v2p6
THOU ART GANE AWA FROM ME MARY	1H1H1H7	5553H	D	4/4	B7p8
THOU ART GONE AWA' (MARY/,NEW SETT)	1111	5L5L5L3	Bb A	4/4	C4p38 (J3)
THOU LING'RING STAR!	5651H	5333	G	4/4	C6p24
THOUGH I AM ALONE IN THE VALE	1256	2H52H1H	D	6/8	Mc5p7
THOUGHTLESS, THE	551H5	347L1	F	3/8	H1p33
THRE WEEKS AFTER MARRIAGE	35L3L5L	35L2L2	F	4/4	P9p21
THREE CAPTAINS, THE	1347L	1351	G	6/8	C7p14
THREE FINGER'D JACK	3135	671H6	D	2/2	H1p27
THREE GIRLS OF PORTREE, THE	5551	5526	F	4/4	G10v6p30
THREE GRACES, THE	3H73H1H	1H1H3H2H	C	6/8	C13v2p63
THREE HALFPENCE	555L	514	D	9/8	A7v2p21
THREE HALFPENCE	555	514	D	9/8	A7v5p30
THREE SHEEP SKINS	1354	4352	G	2/4	O1v1Gp10
THREE SHEEP SKIN'S, THE	1355	4452	G	4/4	A1v1p61
THREE SIFTERS REEL, THE	1353	4362	A	4/4	Mc21v4p42
THREE SISTERS	347L1	347L1	Bb	3/8	C14v23p15
THREE TIMES THREE	351H5	2H53H5	F	6/8	B6v4p3
THRO' THE LANG MUIR	51H1H7b	51H51	E	6/8	A1v1p12
THRO' THE LANG MUIR I FOLLOW'D HIM HAME	5H4H1H	3bH1H5	E D	3/4	C5v2p55 O1v1Gp30
THRO' THE MOOR SHE RAN	5135	5522	F	2/2	H3p20,21
THRO' THE MOOR SHE RAN	5135	5532	F	4/4	A7v3p10,11
THRO' THE MUIR AT NIGHT	113b	7bL7b4	E	9/8	C5v2p44
THRO' THE WOOD LADDIE	6L12	331H	A D G F	3/4	C19p26 (J3) P8v2p8 Mc8v1Ap26,27 G17p17 O1v4p19 O1v1Bp24 T7p20,21 C5v2p10

Title					References
					C4p42 Mc12v2p44,45 C20p38
					Mc8v2Bp5 G11v2Dp12 N1v2p39
					P4p7 T6v1p7 C29p23 C13v3p56
					B5p12 S16p90,91
THRO' THE WOOD LADDIE	61H2H	3H3H1T	C	3/4	E1v2p112,113
THRO' THE WOOD (OF FAVIE/FYVIE)	5324	5353	G A	4/4*	A7v6p27 C14v21p8,9 K1v1p13
					G11v2Ap11 G11v2Bp17(Some Edns.)
					A7v2p33 (II)
THRO' THE (WOOD/MOOR) SHE RAN	1H3H1H6	5522	F	2/2*	G11v2Bp29 K1v2p30 (II)
THRO' THE WORLD WOU'D I GAE WE THE LAD I LIKE	1H1H62H	1H1H3H3H	D	4/4*	K1v2p40 G11v2Bp38
THRO' THE WORLD WOU'D I GANG WI' THE LAD THAT LOVES ME	7b411	4542	A	2/2	C18p22
THROID MO BHEAN IS THROID I RIUM	117bL7bL	113b5	G	4/4	F2v2p32(22)
THUAIR MACSHIMI N'OIGHREACHD [FHUAIR MAC SHIMI 'N OIGHREACHD]	1H3H2H3H	62H72H	D	4/4	F2v2p34(24)
THUG A' MULT A MONNADH AIR	1155	5126L	G	2/2	D16p36
THUG NA MNATHAN GAOL DO M'CHODHALT	57bL7bL4	117bL7bL	A	4/4	Mc5p5
THUSSEL LODGE, THE	1531	7b427bL	D	2/2	Mc4v1p3
TIBBIE FOWLER OF THE GLEN	117bL7bL	117bL5L	A	2/2	H3p14
TIBBY FOULLER O' THE GLEN	113b5	4455	D Bb	2/2	Mc9v1p3 (II)
TIBBY FOWLER	1117bL	117bL5L	A	4/4	A7v6p45
TIBBY FOWLER IN THE GLEN	5L17bL2	517bL7bL	A	4/4	A1v3p155
TIBBY FOWLER O' THE GLEN	1117bL	217bL5L	A	4/4	A7v5p34
TIBBY FOWLER (O' THE GLEN)('S RANT)	117bL2	5147bL	A	4/4	K1v1p7 K1v1p6 G11v2Ap6
TIBBY FOWLER'S GRAND DAUGHTER	1124	153b1	G	4/4	M12p23
TIDE CAME IN, THE	1554	4663	G	4/4	C7p22
TIGH AN DROM [TAIGH AN DROMA]	113b	5L5L5	B	6/4	F2v2p78(68)
TIGH BHEALLADRUM [TAIGH BHEALLADRUM]	1353	5322	D	4/4	F2v2p74(64)
TIGH EOIN GROAT [TAIGH IAIN GROT]	51H3H2H	72H72H	C	2/2	F2v2p91(81) (II)
TIGHEARNA BHRODHI	1311	1521	D	4/4	F2v2p83(73)
TIGHEARNA CHULODAIR [...CHUIL FHODAIR]	5L3b7bL3bL	5L3b55	F	4/4	F2v2p101(91)
TIGHEARNA GLINNAMORISTOIN [...GHLINNE MOIREASTUINN]	5L15L3L	1L132	G	4/4	F2v2p40(30)
TIGHT ROPE DANCER	1H1H55	4443	D	6/8	S7v1p54
TIMBER TOE	1H1H2H2H	3H4H3H2H	D	2/2	S7v1p30
TIMES A TELL TALE	1H1H5H5H	1H1H2H5	D	6/8	H6v2p1
TIMES, THE	1231H	6621	F	2/4	B16v2p7
TIMOUR THE TARTAR	1353	7651H	A	4/4	C8v1p32
TIMOUR THE TARTAR	1557	5524	A	2/4	G9v3p31
TIMOUR THE TARTAR	1353	51H76	A	4/4	C8v2p31 (II)
TINK A TINK	1515	4427L	F G	4/4*	C8v1p57 C8v2p53 C5v1p69
TINK A TINK	1H5H1H5H	4H4H2H7	D	2/4	E1v2p95
TINKAR'S OCCUPATION, THE	61H1H5	1H1H1H3H	C	2/2	Mc8v2Cp18
TINKLING HARP, THE	1H5H7H5H	3H4H6H5H	C	2/4	F1p31
TIPSTAFF STRATHSPEY	31H5L1	42H6L2	G	4/4	P5v1p3
TIREE AIR, A	5551	1323	G	4/4	Mc5p29
TIROLIEN AIR	135	51H3	G	3/4	B7p1
'TIS THE DIRGE OF KEEN SORROW	661H5	21H54	D	3/8	C10v2Bp21
TIT FOR TAT	1H565	1H2H4H3H	D	6/8	A1v2p31
TIT FOR TAT	5565	111H5	G	6/8	S7v1p8
TIVIOT BANKS	1111	6L6L22	F	6/8	P11v1p1
TIVOT BRIDGE	55L6L5L	1142	A	6/8	C7p11
TO BIDE MY LANE FULL LOATH AM I	1242	3415L	F	2/4	C10v2Bp34
TO DANTON ME [TO DAUNTON ME]	5114	217bL7b	E G A	4/4	C13v3p13 (J3) O1v1Ap16,17
					O1v2p38,39 O1v3p42 C5v2p13
					C20p4,5 (II) Mc8v1Bp51
					Mc8v2Bp15 B5p7 A1v2p22
TO HIS CRUTCH	1566	11H51	D	6/8	S5p30
TO M. HEINEL	1H1H4H2H	3H1H2H5	D	6/8	C22p35
TO MARRY OR NOT TO MARRY	13L3L1	437L5L	G	4/4	P9p20
TO MY BED I WONA GANG	3H551H	2266	D	4/4	P5v3p15
TO RODNEY WE WILL GO	1342	3550	G	2/4	A1v3p160
TO RODNEY WE WILL GO	1342	3555	G	2/4	A1v6p64
TO ROSLIN BANK WE'LL GO MY LOVE	51H51H	6522	D	6/8	C5v2p28
TO SERVE A GALLANT LADY	3333	1555	F	4/4	Y1p8
TO THE BROOK AND THE WILLOW	51H6O	5520	G	4/4	B7p44
TO THE GREENWOOD GANG WI' ME	1H3H61H	521H1H	D	4/4	A1v6p47
TO THE WEAVER GIN YE GO	5332	5333	G	2/4	A1v2p6
TOAST, THE	1H1H1H	7b7b4	D	6/4	T6v1p80
TODLEN BUTT AND TODLEN BEN	11H7b7b	11H7b4	E	6/8	T6v2p93 P8v2p34
TODLEN HAME	36L5L2	36L5L1	A	6/8	G11v2Dp19 (J3)
TODLIN HAME	3H652H	3H651H	C D	6/8	D15v2p28 C5v1p70 C5v2p22
					A1v4p74
TOKEN, THE	64H3H	1HO1T	D	3/4	A1v6p32
TOM BOWLING	1H454	4632	F	2/4	E1v1p78
TOM JONES	5H4H3H2H	1H2H1H2H	D	6/8	A1v5p33 C5v1p33
TOM THUMB	1H51H5	1H2H1H6	C	4/4	G13p13 (II)
TOM TULLUS'S HORNPIPE	5165	427L6L	G	2/4	A1v1p43
TOMBREACKACHIE'S STRATHSPEY	5526L	5555	D	4/4	M4v3p36
TOMMY PRINGLE	5L153	5L153	G	4/4*	P6v1p24 H6v1p2
TON, THE	51H35	1233	A G	2/4	W4v1p17 A1v4p44 C5v1p44

TOO LONG IN THIS CONDITION	1111	2221	A	4/4	Mc1v1p34-37
TOO OLD TO MARRY	1131	3353	F G	2/4	W4v1p4 A1v4p34
TOP OF BALVENIE, THE	1313	5L7L45	G	4/4	M4v4p23
TOP OF THE LAW, THE	1527L	1555	D	6/8	C21p7
TOPSAILS SHIVER IN THE WIND, THE	1H1H1H3H	1H111H	D	4/4	A1v6p43
TOPSY TURVY	1H1H1H3H	7772H	F	2/2	R12v1p77
TORE OF TROUP, THE	115L3L	1142	F	4/4	P5v2p2
TORPHICHEN'S RANT	1135	3313	G	2/2	R6v2p6
TORRY BURN	1335	4661H	G	4/4*	K1v2p17 G11v2Bp15 (11)
TOUCHSTONE, THE	1H1H4H1H	1H1H5H5H	D	2/4	B16v3p93
TOWLERS LAMENT	5555	6532	C	6/8	E2p24
TOW'RING TINTO	13L1L5L	2215	A	4/4	W4v2p33
TRAFALGAR	5L132	3H1H32	F	2/2	C24v2p16
TRAFALGAR HORNPIPE	35L43	15L5L1	Bb	2/4	H6v2p1
TRAVELLERS, THE	1H1H7	1H1H4H	D	9/8	P6v1p11
TREBAN MORGANOUGH	1355	4432	G	2/2	W7p18
TREEBLE HORNPIPE	1H367L	3L4L27L	F	2/4	C22p46
TREEBLE HORNPIPE NO. 1	1H345	3345	F	2/2	S11v1p12
TREEBLE HORNPIPE NO. 2	1H535	627L5L	F	2/2	S11v1p12
TREEBLE HORNPIPE, No. 4	113L1	27L5L2	Bb	2/2	S11v1p13
TREEBLE HORNPIPE No.3	5312	3416L	Bb	2/2	S11v1p12,13
TRIFLER, THE	1H71H7	671H2H	D	6/8	C26v1p15
TRIHODYAN	3245	3253	G	6/8	C10v2Ap73
TRIO	3343	2217L	Bb	6/8	H1p3
TRIP TO BRISTOL	11H22H	3H4H74	D	6/8	S7v1p14
TRIP TO CLUMBER	551H7	62H1H1H	F	2/4	A7v3p34
TRIP TO CLUMBER, A	551H7	61H1H1H	D F	2/4	A1v2p13 Mc9v2p38
TRIP TO DERRY, A	1H1H55	1H1H27	D	6/8	K1v2p13
TRIP TO DUBLIN	3565	3567	Bb	6/8	C14v7p12
TRIP TO DUNKIRK, A	5312	4242	G	2/4	C5v1p33 A1v5p33
TRIP TO EASTON	3H5H72H	61H52	D	2/4	B16v3p87
TRIP TO EDINBURGH	5L353	5L326L	Bb	2/2	B16v3p4
TRIP TO FARLEIGH, A	5H3H4H3H	572H2H	D	2/2	R12v1p81
TRIP TO FORNETH, A	156L5L	1543	G D	6/8	A1v5p48 W4v2p14
TRIP TO GLASGOW	35L1L3L	5L222L	Bb	2/2	B16v2p3
TRIP TO GLASGOW	25L1L3L	5L222L	Bb	2/2	C14v7p1
TRIP TO GUILSLAND, THE	5535	5562	A	2/2	R6v1p3
TRIP TO GUNNING HILL WELLS	1H1H1H2H	1H2H3H1H	D	6/8	S12v2p11
TRIP TO HANAU, A	3355	3111L	A	6/8	S7v1p66
TRIP TO HATFIELD HOUSE	1H51H5	1H525L	D	6/8	C14v3p2
TRIP TO HAWKHURST	5125L	6L15L4L	Bb	6/8	C14v4p18
TRIP TO HINKSTON	1546	5411	F	6/8	B16v3p8
TRIP TO HOLLAND, A	5336	5362	A	4/4	C14v8p4
TRIP TO INCHCOMB, A	3546	337L2	G	4/4	A1v4p6
TRIP TO ISLINGTON, A	1H1H1H5	6535	G	2/2	W7p24
TRIP TO KELSO	1353	2464	A	6/8	C7p4
TRIP TO LIVERPOOL	17L17L	17L42	A	2/4	C14v24p9
TRIP TO LIVERPOOL	1H531	47L13L	Bb	6/8	S7v1p75
TRIP TO LONDON, A	3L37L6L	3L35L1	Bb	6/8	B15v1p18
TRIP TO OATLAND, A	5555	1H562	G	6/8	A7v6p19 A7v2p20
TRIP TO OATLAND(S), A	5555	1H542	D F	6/8	Mc9v2p1 Mc7p33,34 A7v2p20 S7v1p24
TRIP TO OSTEND, A	1H31H3H	5H1H72H	D	2/4	C1v4p6
TRIP TO PANCRASS, A	1351H	7756	G	2/2	W7p20
TRIP TO PLYMOUTH	1H2H65	362H7	D	6/8	B16v3p8
TRIP TO PORTSMOUTH, A	1H2H3H4H	5H3H1H5H	C	2/2	S7v1p99
TRIP TO RANALAGH, A	3H1H6	3H1H4	C	9/8	R12v1p83
TRIP TO RICHMOND	1352	61H52	A	2/2	S7v1p78
TRIP TO SHORTS, A	1353	6543	G	6/8	W7p21
TRIP TO SKYE, A	3562	351H3	F G	4/4	M12p26 (11)
TRIP TO SLIGO, A	5L6L5L2	1H653	G	6/8	A1v2p64
TRIP TO SPA(, A)	1352	5L6L11	Bb	2/4	C1v1p6 C14v7p24
TRIP TO SPA, A	1H15L1H	2H25L2H	C	6/8	B16v3p61
TRIP TO St. ANDREWS, A	111H5	1125L	A	6/8	L1p4
TRIP TO STRATFORD UPON AVON, A	1H565	6342	D	2/4	B16v3p26
TRIP TO STRATHBOGIE, A	1353	6L27L6L	A	2/2	M12p32
TRIP TO THE CAMP	1H347L	1525L	G	2/4	B16v2p11
TRIP TO THE CAMP, A	1131	26L7L5L	Bb	2/4	Mc15p22,23 C14v8p20
TRIP TO THE FALLS OF THE CLYDE, A	5121	5126	F	6/8	P9p35
TRIP TO THE JERSEYS	1H12H5	3H72H2H	D	6/8	S7v1p51
TRIP TO THE JUBILEE	1532	1532	G	2/4	R12v1p28
TRIP TO THE LAWNDRY, A	1232	47L42	A	2/4	W7p8
TRIP TO THE PANTHEON	1342	7L226L	A	2/2	B16v3p60
TRIP TO THE ROTUNDA, A	1H1H33H	6H7H72H	D	6/8	A1v3p201
TRIP TO VAUXHALL	51H3H3H	653H2H	D	6/8	B16v1p7
TRIP TO WESTON, A	1H3H1H7	2H4H2H1H	C	2/4	B16v3p52
TRIP TO YORK, A	111H1H	4522	G	6/8	A1v6p25
TRIP UP STAIRS, A	1H3H2H1H	63H63H	D	6/8	R12v1p92
TRIP UP THE STAIRS, THE	3175	327L5L	G	6/8	S12v2p29
TRISTRAM SHANDY	51H2H2H	3H1H2H1H	D	6/8	A1v1p66
TRISTRAM SHANDY	3164	4225L	A	2/4	S7v1p62
TRIUMPH, THE	5417	5411	G	2/4	G7p20

Title					
TRIUMPH, THE	5342	1765	G	2/4	P6v1p30
TRIUMPH, THE	5342	11H76	A	4/4	C8v2p16 C8v1p46 (II)
TRIUMPH, THE	5H4H1H6H	5H4H1H1H	D	2/4	G13p12
TROON HOUSE, THE	112	3b3b3b	A	3/4	R5p56
TROOP	3H1H3H5	1H6H2H2H	D	3/8	M11v1p21
TROOPS MARCHING DOWN THE ROCKS, THE	1H1H1H5	1H532	D	6/8	W4v1p31
TROUBADOUR, THE	3H5H1H1H	2H1H3H0	D	2/4	C8v2p57
TROUP HOUSE	1314	1632	Bb	4/4	P5v2p11
TRUE SPORTSMAN, THE	1H3H72H	1T3H3H2H	C	6/8	S7v2p8
TRUMPET AIR, A	1354	3522	G	6/8	A1v1p67
TUATH IS DEAS	1342	135L3	G	2/2	A1v4p67 Mc22p7 C5v1p67
TULLOCH CASTLE	5342	5361H	D	4/4	M12p9
TULLOCH GOIRM	157b2	1535	G	4/4	Mc9v1p4
TULLOCH GORUM [CORN BUNTING, THE]	3542	3535	F G	4/4*	(J3) C8v2p6 P5v4p5 G11v1Ap27 G13p15 G7p12 C13v1p12 C14v11p6 C14v11p6 E1v1p9 G10v1p18 C33p3 C13v2p5 Mc22Ap1 R6v1p20 (II)
TULLOCH GORUM	3542	3561H	A	4/4	Mc1v1Ap6
TULLOCH GORUM	3544	3535	G	4/4*	A7v2p2 A7v6p14
TULLOCH GORUM	1H5H4H2H	3H5H3H5H	D	2/4	A1v1p30
TULLOCH GORUM	3522	3536	A	4/4	A7v3p24
TULLOCHGORUM	1542	3535	C G	4/4*	C8v1p8 B15v1p16 C4p32
TULLYMET HALL	3b554	2424	A	4/4	G10v5p33 (II)
TURKISH AIR	3H4H5H1H	71H2H5	D	2/4	B7p26
TURKISH MARCH	3311	2231	G	6/8	A1v1p10
TURK'S HEAD	1315	3647L	F	6/8	S7v1p100
TURN AGAIN THOU FAIR ELIZA	31H5	551	G	3/4	G1v1p35
TURN IN THE PARK, A	17L5L6L	6L211	A	2/4	B16v3p67
TURNPIKE GATE	3H4H5H1H	2H671H	D	6/8	B7p12
TURRIFF HUNT	1525	7b542	G	4/4	P5v1p4
TUZZIMUZZY	1H3H2H	1H1H5	D	3/4	R12v1p63
TWA CORBIES, THE	1351H	5542	F	2/4	C10v2Bp26
TWAS A MARECHAL OF FRANCE	51H1H1H	2H2H1H1H	G	4/4	B7p43
'TWAS AT THE SHINING MID-DAY HOUR	3561H	5222	D	4/4	(J3) C5v2p47
('TWAS) WITHIN A FURLONG TO EDINBURGH	13b54	43b11	G B	4/4	O1v1Dp32 C5v3p69
TWEED SIDE	1122	3321	A	6/8	M14p25
TWEED SIDE	1H56	1H1H3H	D	3/4	E1v1p52 T7p12,13 O1v1Ap28,29 C5v2p23
TWEED SIDE	15L6L	111	A	3/4	S16p8,9
TWEED SIDE [MEDLEY OVERTURE (8)]	15L6L	113	G A	3/4	A1v4p57 (J3) (C19) (C25) C4p45 N1v2p9 C5v1p42 Mc8v1Cp68 Mc8v2Ap7 O1v4p22 C19p19 P4p6 T6v1p32 G17p2 C24v2p2,3 C6p20 C13v3p44,45 C29p12,13 Mc12v2p50,51 C20p80
TWEED SIDE	16L6L	113	A	3/4	M14p26,27
TWEED SIDE	1H56	1H1H1H	D	3/4	P8v2p6
TWEEDDALE CLUB, THE	51H63	51H2H2	C	4/4	C8v1p49 G11v1Ap36 G10v3p14,15 (II)
TWINE WEEL THE PLAIDEN	3426	5651	D	4/4	A1v6p49
TWINE (YE) WEEL THE PLAIDEN	3326	5551	D	4/4	C5v2p13 N1v2p26 (J3)
TWINKLING STAR, THE	15L13	657L2	F	6/8	B16v3p51
TWO MISERS	17L12	17L32	G	2/4	S7v1p58
TWO TO ONE	3b15L3bL	247b2	G	2/2	H1p13
TYNE SIDE STRATHSPEY	1L3L13	15L2L2L	Bb	4/4	G3p24
TYRIE RANT	1H1H3H6	5362	D	6/8	C23p10
TYRISH RUIN, THE	17L5L3L	5L132	Bb	2/2	J2p13
TYROLEN DANCE	5564	2541	G	2/4	B7p33
TYROLESE SONG OF LIBERTY	135	3H1H1H	D	3/4	E1v2p68
U GU VI U, PORT NA MAIGHDINN CHUAIN	2H5H2H1H	2H5H2H1H	D	4/4	Mc5p11
UAIGH A' BHAIRD	5L5L5L	111	A	3/4	F2v2p49(39)
UDNY ACADEMY	1353	1362	A	2/2	M11v1p12
UGI NAN GU 'SMO THRIALL DACHAIDH	13b11	3b15L7bL	A	4/4	Mc5p3
UILLEACHAN 'N TIG THU CHAOIDH	5115	5136	F	4/4	F2v2p96(86)
UILLIAM 'S CALUM'S MORAG	3b11	3b14	B	9/8	Mc1v1Ap6
UNA OF ULVA	1663	6522	E	6/8	C10v2Bp13
UNANIMITY	1H1H45	1562	G	2/4	A1v2p73
UNA'S LOCK	53b11	13b53b	G	4/4	C14v4p22 W4v2p15
UNDER THE GREEN WOOD TREE	5H5H3H1H	2H61H1H	D	6/8	O1v1Kp126
UNDER THE ROSE	11L27F	3522	Bb	6/8	B16v3p34
UNFORTUNATE JOAK	1H1H1H3H	61H67	D	12/8	R12v1p88
UNION GROVE	315L3L	4L3L5L3L	F	4/4	D6p6
UNION, THE	3252	3562	G	6/8	C14v16p4
UNTITLED	1111	2313	G	4/4	Mc5p24
UNTITLED	13b24	6b57bL1	E	4/4	Mc5p17
UNTITLED	127L7L	1515	G	4/4	Mc5p8
UNTITLED	3232	3434	G	4/4	Mc5p10
UNTITLED	51H44	5324	Eb	2/2	F2v1p11
UNTITLED	3b13b4	51H1H5	E	4/4	Mc5p8
UNTITLED	35L3L5L	3642	G	2/4	J2p5
UNTITLED	5L3L1L1	352L2	Bb	2/2	F2v1p10

Title			Key	Time	References
UNTITLED (No.35)	15L15L	117bL7bL	A	4/4	Mc5p6
UNTITLED	15L11	2223	G	4/4	Mc5p29
UNTITLED	5353	536L6L	F	2/2	Mc17p11,12
UNTITLED	5353	5L347bL	G	2/2	Mc17p12
UNTITLED	3H5H53	4233H	D	2/4	P8v1p12
UNTITLED	3532	1121	G	4/4	P8v1p10
UNTITLED	51H55	1H2H3H6	C	6/8	C14v13p23
UNTITLED	1H1H1H5	1H532	D	6/8	C5v1p16
UNTITLED	5H6H1T6H	5H6H1T5H	C	6/8	Mc5p4
UNTITLED	3b451H	3b455	A	6/8	Mc5p4
UNTITLED	3b53b1	2427bL	E	6/8	C14v13p23
UNTITLED	1153	1126L	G	6/8	Mc5p8
UNTITLED	117b7b	117b7b	A	6/8	Mc5p25
UNTITLED	13b22	156b5	A	6/8	Mc5p4
UNTITLED	13b53b	57bL5L4L	A	6/8	Mc5p5
UNTITLED	1321	1326L	G	6/8	Mc5p7
UNTITLED	1344	1341	A	6/8	(R6v2)
UNTITLED	5217bL	5210	A	6/8	Mc5p16
UNTITLED	5353	5316L	G	6/8	C14v13p23
UNTITLED	3422	362H1H	D	6/8	Mc5p12
UNTITLED	1H51H3H	1H543	F	6/8	Mc17p11
UNTITLED	3b3b5	213b	A	3/4	Mc5p20
UNTITLED	333	211	G	3/4	Mc5p17
UNTITLED	16L1	5L5L3	G	3/4	Mc5p17
UP AND DOWN	5523	5L142	F	6/8	C26v1p13
UP AND WAR THEM A' WILLIE (/WULLIE)	1344	1322	G Bb A	4/4*	(J3) C5v3p64 A7v5p14 G1v1p36
					(II) C8v1p62 E1v1p5
					O1v1Cp1 Mc1v1Ap7 Mc23p29
					B15v1p60 G11v2Cp26 R12v1p36
					G7p6,7 G9v5p17 O1v5p18,19
					C4p64 C14v22p16,17 C20p32,33
UP IN THE AIR	113b3b	443b3b	A	2/2	S16p146,147
UP IN THE AIR	311H7	27bL7b2	D	2/2	B10p9
UP IN THE MORNING EARLY	13b7bL4	13b15	G	6/8	B15v2p1 D13p2 Mc8v1Ap8
UP IN THE MORNING EARLY	13b7bL4	1515	G	6/8	Mc8v2Cp9
UP IN THE MORNING EARLY	13b57bL	1515	G A	6/8	G11v2Cp4 E1v1p90
UP IN THE MORNING EARLY	112	3b3b4	B G	6/4	A1v5p44 (J3)
UP IN THE MORNING EARLY	111	3b3b5	A	3/4	O1v1Lp143
UP THE TOWN IN HASTE	3564	27L5L3L	A	2/2	C24v1p8 C24v2p5
UP WI 'T AILLY NOW	155	154	A	9/8	A1v1p47
URQUAHART'S SCOTTS MEASURE	351H1H	561H6	D	2/2	O1v1Hp45
VAGA'RY, THE	1232H	2H2H3H2	Eb	6/8	L3p5
VALE OF KEAPPOCH	5L5L5L5L	236L6L	A	4/4	C10v1p4
VALENTINE, THE	1H664	557L2	G	6/8	S7v2p10
VALENTINES DAY IN THE MORNING	363	362H	D	9/8	R12v2p12
VALLENCIENNES MARCH	1H2H3H5H	4H2H75	D	2/4	A1v6p52
VALLIANT SCOTCHMAN	347L5L	1232	G	6/8	S7v2p7
VAN DIEMEN'S LAND	3b7bL3b5	3b127bL	G	6/8	P9p18
VAN ROTTERDAM OP DORT	1H2H3bH4H	5H4H2H3bH	D	2/2	S7v1p92
VAUHALL'S MINUET	113	215L	Bb	3/4	C22p2
VEDRAI CARINO	1H3H77	1H3H1H7	D	3/8	E1v2p81
VENERABLE, THE	1111	2222	G	4/4	C14v13p19
VERTIGO	17L12	3327L	G	6/8	Mc9v2p1
VICAR, THE	1H3H5H2H	1H2H74H	D	2/4	H6v5p3
VICTORY, THE	5353	61H52	G	4/4	B16v3p93
VICTORY, THE	5L344	537L7L	F	2/2	C24v2p16,17
VICTORY, THE	1353	427L2	Bb	2/2	S7v1p29
VILLAGE BELLS, THE	1115	41H64	G	2/2	B6v4p2
VILLAGE MAID, THE	1121	3343	G	2/4	A7v6p79 C14v1p6,7 P10p2,3
VILLAGE REEL, THE	3L131	3L14L2L	Bb	4/4	C14v8p2
VIOTTI'S POLLACCA	111	521	A	3/4	E1v1p112,113 A1v6p58
VIRGINS FROLICK, THE	151H3	427L2	A	2/4	B16v3p34
VISCOUNT HAMILTON	1113	526L6L	F	4/4	M4v4p3
VISCOUNT MANDEVILLE	5671H	67L16L	Bb	2/2	M12p18
VISCOUNT REIDHAVEN	5353	52H75	F	4/4	M4v4p6
VITE MARCHE	5H5H1T1T	4H4H6H6H	C	6/8	W4v2p10
VITTORIA MARCH	531H3H	2H505	D	4/4	B7p4
VIVE HENRI QUATRE	1H1H7b7b	2H757b	D	2/4	E1v2p72
VOCAL SHELL, THE	351H5	527L6L	G	4/4	O1v1Lp159
VOI CHE SAPETE	1H52H5	3H1H3H2H	G	2/4	E1v2p86,87
VOICE OF MY LOVE, THE	5533	5432	A	4/4	O1v1Kp118
VOULEZ VOUS DANCEZ	3H3H2H1H	72H1H3H	C D	6/8	C14v26p7 (II)
VOULEZ VOUS DANSER MADEMOISELLE	3321	7L213	Bb	6/8	G9v3p19
VOULEZ VOUS DANSEZ	3H3H2H1H	72H1H2H	D	6/8	C8v2p19
VOWS OF ENDLESS LOVE, THE	3453	151H1H	G	4/4	O1v1Hp61
VULCAN'S FORGE	1T3H4H7	1H2H3H7	C	6/8	C5v1p47 A1v4p47
VULCAN'S MARCH	1H05H5H	3H2H1H1H	C	2/4	A1v4p47 C5v1p47
W. MORRISON OF CULODEN'S COMPLIMENTS TO JOHN MCGREGOR	1L47L6L	5L47L2	A	4/4	Mc11p8
W. MORRISON'S COMPLIMENTS TO MR SCOTT 78th REGt. BAND	1151	47L31	Bb	2/4	M12p18
W. MORRISON'S FAVORITE	3211	4532	D	4/4	M12p6

W. ROBISON, ESQr's HORNPIPE	1H3H55	4627L	F	4/4	D6p36
WAAKING OF THE FAULD, THE	5L117b	415L4L	A	4/4*	Mc8v1Dp105 O1v1Cp20 (II)
WAEFU' HEART, THE	1132	2243	G	4/4	C4p36 (J3)
WAE'FUL HEART, THE	1142	2253	G	4/4	G1v1p31
WAGER, THE	5L132	5L146	A	4/4	S13p2
WAGGLE CAIRN, THE	3L5L6L5L	3L5L24	A	4/4	C18p29
WAGS OF WINDSOR	1H361H	1H5H5H2H	C	2/2	C14v17p16
WAKEFIELD HUNT	5356L	6L5L42	A	6/8	B16v3p13
WALKER'S FAVOURITE	3216L	5L5L12	A	6/8	W2v1p6
WALKER'S HORNPIPE	51H33	4433	F	4/4	H1p25
WALLACE'S LAMENT	3335	3H3H2H6	G	6/8	B7p25
AFTER THE BATTLE OF FALKIRK					
WAL(L)ACE'S LAMENT	112	6L6L5L	G	3/4	O1v1Gp7
WALLACE('S) MARCH	11H53	115L5L	G	4/4*	O1v1Fp22 R6v2p26 T7p24,25
WALLEY HONEY	1H51H	1H51H	C	9/8	W7p7 O1v1Gp3 O1v5p34
WALLI'S HUMOUR IN TAPPING THE ALE	6L6L6L5L	1113	F	2/2	P7p12/13
WALLY, WALLY	351H	2H2H2	D	3/4	O1v2p12,13 O1v3p26 O1v1Ap5
WALTZ	1152H	1151H	A	3/8	H1p6 D15v2p39
WALTZ	11#35	11#31	A	3/8	N2p21
WALTZ	1437L	1451	Bb	3/8	D15v2p24
WALTZ	1H1H1H4H	7771H	D	3/8	B7p14
WALTZ	1H2H45	1H67L1	G	3/8	H1p30
WALTZ	1H3H2H1H	1H3H2H1H	C	3/8	H1p9
WALTZ	1H4H3H7	1H4H5H1H	D	3/8	B7p22
WALTZ	1H5H2H3H	1H5H4H1H	Eb	3/8	N2p14
WALTZ	5H5H1H2H	5H5H1H1H	D	3/8	B7p2
WALTZ	5H5H5H7	5H5H2H1H	D	3/8	B7p19
WALTZ	5554	4443	F	3/8	N2p16,17
WALTZ	51H53	1242	Bb	3/8	D15v2p33
WALTZ	575	575	G	3/4	B7p23
WALTZ	4H2H5H	3H1H1H	D	3/4	B7p30
WALTZ	5H5H3H	2H1H1H	D	3/4	B7p10
WALTZ A WEIR	51H1H1H	2H5H4H3H	D	6/8	B7p39
WALTZ BY MOZART	1H1H1H	2H2H2H	G	3/4	G9v3p15
WALTZ DANCED BY MISS SCRYEMSURE	1112	1112	F	3/8	N2p8
AND MISS LINDSAY					
WALTZ DANCED BY THE MISSES HUNTER	1H2H3H6H	5H4H5H1H	C	3/8	N2p7
WALTZ OF BIONDINA	51H71H	51H71H	G	3/8	B7p43
WALTZ OF LEIPSIC	1H1H5H2H	1T5H1H1H	D	3/8	B7p31
WALTZ OF MAIENCE	561H1H	561H1H	D	3/8	B7p31
WALTZ, THE	3b154	3b17b5	A	3/8	G9v3p32
WALTZE	1H1H5H2H	1H2H71H	Eb	3/8	B4p18,19
WALTZE	5H5H3H7	4#H5H6H2H	C	3/8	B4p11,12
WALTZE	55H5H5H	55H4H1H	Eb	3/8	B4p4,5
WALY WALY	662H	2H2H3	G	3/4	B5p5
WALY WALY	355	2H2H2H	D F	3/4	Mc8v1Cp87 Mc8v2Ap15 E1v2p141
WALY WALY (UP THE BANK)	351H	2H2H2H	F D	3/4	(J3) T6v1p71 N1v2p60
					A1v5p29 (J3) C5v1p30 C5v2p9
WALZE A LA REINE	2H4H4H	1H1H1H	C	3/4	B7p45
WANDERER, THE	3H2H1H	531H	D	3/4	C5v3p75
WANDERING WILLIE	553	111	F	3/4	G11v2Dp17
WANTON WIFE OF HULL, THE	31H3H3	31H2H2	G	6/8	C14v14p13
WANTONESS FOR EVER MAIR	3H3H1H1H	2H1H66	D	4/4	A1v3p172
WANTONESS FOR EVER MORE	13b55	5255	E	4/4	P5v1p10
WAP AT THE WIDOW	3122	3121H	D	6/8	W7p17
WAP AT THE WIDOW MY LADDIE	3122	3111H	G	6/8	Mc9v2p6
(WAP AT) THE WIDOW (MY LADDIE)	3122	3131H	F G	6/8	(J3) C5v2p18 Mc8v1BCp53
					Mc8v2Bp16 O1v1Cp18,19 T6v2p10
					C20p27
WAPPAT THE WIDOW MY LADY	333	131	G	6/4	P7p10
WARKWORTH CASTLE	1355	4327L	D	6/8	A1v1p14
WARLD'S GANE O'ER ME NOW, THE	532	534	A	9/8	C18p36,37
WARLEY CAMP	3231	6543	G	6/8	S7v1p36
WARLEY COMMON	1H5H2H3H	1H5H2H1H	C	2/4	B16v3p1
WARLEY COMMON	5H3H1H5	62H2H7	D	6/8	B16v3p24
WARS ALARM, THE	3352	1H1H3H2H	D	4/4*	C20p7 O1v1Hp36
WAR'S ALARMS	5322	36L7L6L	G	2/2	S7v1p21
WARST CARLE IN A' THE WORLD, THE	5142	5145L	A	6/8	Mc1v1Ap8
WARWICK CASTLE	3b13b1	2427bL	E	6/8	C14v5p71
WAS YE AT THE BRIDAL	3554	47b47b	A	2/4	O1v1Hp41
WAS YOU AT THE WEDDING	3564	462H6	A	2/2	G9v5p16
WAS YOW AT THE WADDING	3764	462H6	A	2/2	C13v2p22
WASHER WOMAN(, THE)	35L35	42L46	F	6/8	P5v1p7
[IRISH WASHERWOMAN, THE]					
WASP, THE	1567	1H532	A	6/8	B16v2p5
WAT YE WHA I MET THE STREEN	1225	47b25L	B	4/4	G10v2p11
WAT YE WHA I MET YESTREEN	13b3b5	47b15L	G	4/4	S16p122,123
WAT YE WHA I MET YESTREEN	1225	47b3b5L	B	4/4	G11v1Ap23
WAT YE WHO YOU MET THE STREEN	1225	47b15L	A	4/4	Mc21v4p43
WATE YOU HOW THE PLAY BEGAN	5152	517bL2	A	4/4	O1v1Kp134
WATER PARTED FROM THE SEA	112	343	F G	3/4	(J3) A1v3p220
WATERLOO MARCH	1H1H1H7	5534	G	4/4	B7p20

WATER-MAN, THE	5312	5L5L32	G	6/8	C13v2p58
WATERMAN, THE	5312	5L5L42	A	6/8	Mc9v2p15
WATERMEN'S RANT, THE	15L13	447bL2	G	2/2	B15v1p105
WATERS OF ELLE	1H71H2H	3H4H1H7	D	4/4	E1v2p20
WATIE LAING	1524	1515	A	2/2	G11v1Cp33 G10v1p14
WATLEN'S HORNPIPE	1H555	3115L	F	4/4	W4v2p16
WATSON'S CLASS	13b11H	7b43b7bL	E	4/4	G10v2p10 G11v1Bp6
WATSON'S SCOTCH MEASURE	1151	3225L	G F	2/2	C5v2p68 K1v1p5 G11v2Ap5
					Mc9v2p7
WATSON'S SCOTS MEASURE	1151	3221	G	2/2	C4p64 C20p65 Mc8v2Cp6(?)
WATTIE LANG	1322	1313	G	4/4	A1v3p180
WAUKING OF THE PLAIDEN, THE	15L15L	15L22	F	4/4	G11v1Ap18 G10v1p21
WAWKING OF THE FAULDS, THE	5L111H	526L5L	F	2/2	T6v2p12 P8v2p33
WAY TO AIR, THE	117bL2	113b5	E	2/2	Mc9v3p8
WAY TO ELGIN, THE	1135	3531	G	2/2	Mc9v3p11
WAY TO GET MARRIED, THE	356	71H2	G	9/8	A1v6p27
WAY TO GROW RICH, THE	1121	2154	G	4/4	(S7v2)
WE ARE ALL MERRY	1H1H2H7b	1H1H64	E	2/2	S12v1p40
WE ARE ALL RIGHT AT CANTERBURY	1H3H4H3H	1H3H2H6	D	2/2	R12v1p7
WE MET	331	331	G	3/4	C8v1p63
WE WILL DOWN WITH THE FRENCH	5H5H1H3H	4H4H2H7	D	6/8	B16v3p92
WEAPON SHAW, THE [WAPPINSHAW, THE]	13b3b3b	427bL2	D	4/4*	K1v2p34 G11v2Bp32 (II)
WEARY PUND O' TOW, THE	1H1H1H	1H2H2H	D	3/4	E1v1p89
WEARY PUND O' TOW, THE	111	122	Bb G	3/4	G11v2Cp11 C5v2p50 C20p9
					O1v1Hp38
WEAVER, THE	3b421	4L23b1	G	4/4	F3p7
WEAVER'S MARCH, THE	5534	6655	D	4/4	A1v1p60
WEAVER'S MARCH, THE	5534	61H55	C	4/4	C6p27
WEAZLE, THE	1355	7231	A G	6/8	R12v1p52 A1v2p17
WEBER'S LAST WALTZ	1H74	651	A	3/4	E1v2p140
WEDDERBURN HOUSE	1H1H3b1	27b27bL	D	2/2*	Mc13v1p5 Mc13v2p5 (II)
WEDDING CAKE, THE	1H1H55	1H1H4H7	C	6/8	H6v22p2
WEDDING, THE	15L11	2326L	A	2/2	C33p9
WEE ANNIE'S HORNPIPE	1H35L3	5L35L3	F	4/4	P9p10
WEE BOBBIT BLANCH OF MIDDLEBIE	3565	357b4	A	6/8	R6v2p21
WEE MAN, THE	3H3H4H2H	2H2H3H1H	D	3/8	G9v3p4,5
WEE WEE MAN, THE	1H61H1	1H652	G F	6/8	C8v2p43 (J3)
WEE WILLIE'S STRATHSPEY	5L131	6L27L6L	G	4/4	P9p12 (II)
WEEL MAY THE BOATIE ROW	3552H	5332	D	2/4	G11v2Dp8
(WEEL MAY) THE KEEL ROW	3142	3125L	A	4/4*	C8v2p16 C8v1p46 D6p16,17
					G15p20
WEEL MAY THE KEEL ROW	3142	3127L	A	2/2	A7v5p4
WEEL MAY THE KEEL ROW	3142	327L5L	G	2/2	Mc23p21 G9v1p23 C20p70
[LASSIE'S PETITION TO NEPTUNE, THE]					
WEEL MAY YE A' BE	5L5L5L1	6L6L6L1	Bb	4/4	P11v2p23
WE'ER NO VERY FOU BUT WE'ER GAYLY YET	51H57b	51H51H	D	6/8	G11v2Cp11
WEIPPERT'S FANCY	3131	3124	A	2/4	C14v7p23
WELCH AIR, A	1122	327L5	G	2/4	G9v3p15
WELCH AIR, A	1H2H3H5H	1H2H50	C	2/4	Mc7p27
WELCH FUSILEERS' MARCH	1H1H33	5552H	D	4/4	M2p22
WELCH HARPER, THE	1235	37L5L5L	Bb	6/8	E1v1p79
WELCOME FROM VIGO	1515	157L2	G	6/8	O1v4p37
WELCOME TO ALL STRANGERS	3b17L2	3b15L1	D	6/8	Mc9v2p21
WELCOME TO YOUR AIN HOUSE	113b5	7bL242	G	2/2	B20p10
WELCOME TO YOUR FEET AGAIN, (YOU'RE)	151H2	151H6	F C	4/4*	E1v1p24 G11v2Ap19 B15v1p14
					K1v1p21 S12v1p10 (II)
WELL A DAY	351H1H	5222	G	4/4	O1v1Jp102
WE'LL A' TO KELSO GO	11H71H	6524	F G	6/8	B15v1p105 R4p16 A1v2p34
					O1v1Fp11
WELL DONE JOCK	5H4H3H2H	5H4H3H2H	D	6/8	A1v1p32
WE'LL GANG NAE MAIR TO YON TOUNE	11H31	3142	F	4/4	C6p16
WE'LL KISS THE WORLD BEFORE US	3bH2H5	3bH4H1H	D	9/8	O1v1Lp142
WE'LL PUT THE SHEEP-HEAD IN THE PAT	115L	7bL7bL2	A B	9/8	(J3) C5v2p39
WELL-A-DAY, LACK-A-DAY	3561H	5310	G	6/8	A1v6p59
WELLCOME FROM VIGO	1515	357L2	G	6/8	O1v1Ep8
WELLCOME TO THE COUNTRY	11H31	3132	F	2/2	R12v1p71
WELLINGTON AND VICTORY	3535	64H75	D	2/4	C14v27p6
WELLINGTON DANCE, THE	3364	7L7L51	G	2/4	H1p12
WELSH DANCE, A	1H1H77	6653	G	4/4*	A1v4p50 C5v1p50
WELSH DANCE, A	117L7L	6L6L5L3L	G	2/2	W4v1p28
WELSH JIG, THE	7L222	1313	Bb	6/8	P10p22
WEMYS CASTLE	1351H	5322	F	4/4	G3p25
WEMYSS CASTLE	1335	357L2	F	4/4	G11v1Bp31
WEMYSS CASTLE REEL	11H55	4323	A	6/8	W2v1p11
WEMYSS CASTLE(STRATHSPEY)	116L4L	4L426L	Bb	4/4	P5v1p20 (II)
WE'RE A FORSAKEN FOR WANT O' SILLER	3632	4636	G	6/8	S12v2p26,27
WE'RE A' FORSAKEN FOR WANT O' SILLER	3H76	1H3H7	D	9/8	C5v2p55
WE'RE A' KISS'D SLEEPING	15L7bL2	15L11H	G	2/4	O1v1Kp114
WE'RE A' NODDIN'	3223	3231	G	2/4	C6p3
WE'RE A' NODDIN'	3H2H2H3H	3H2H3H1H	D	2/4	E1v2p14
WERE NA MY HEART(S) LIGHT I WAD DIE	6L351	6L353	F	6/8	(J3) T6v1p88
WERTEMBURG WALTZ, THE	1356	1H521	G	3/8	C14v13p15

WEST BARNS BREWERY	3b15L1	3b51H1H	G	2/2	G3p7
WEST LOTHIAN CAVALRY'S MARCH, THE	1T5H3H5H	1T5H3H5H	D	4/4	W4v2p22
WEST LOWLANDS STRATHSPEY	131H3H	1H532	F	4/4	E2p8
WEST STREET ASSEMBLY	1H516	51H52	F	6/8	R12v1p8
WESTBURN	1113	5551H	Bb	4/4	D6p30,31
WESTERN ISLE AIR, A	5542	3b17bL2	A	4/4	C5v1p59
WESTERN ISLE AIR, A	1H1H7b5	6b43b5	E	4/4	A1v5p59
WESTERN ISLE DANCE	5153	5136	G	4/4	Mc5p37
WESTERN ISLE DANCE	1153	117L5L	G	4/4	Mc5p37
WESTMINSTER BRIDGE	1H1H1H1	2H3H2H2	F	6/8	R12v1p8
WESTMINSTER VOLUNTEERS	1H1H1H1H	471H2H	D	6/8	B16v3p10
WESTMINSTER VOLUNTEERS MARCH	1H1H2H2H	3H1H1H2H	D	4/4	A1v6p74/75
WESTS HORNPIPE	1H1H1H5	11H2H2	D	4/4	A7v6p10
WEST'S HORNPIPE	1H355	1H355	D	4/4	A7v2p33 C8v2p14 C8v1p42 (II)
WET AND WEARY	31H62H	31H63	G	6/8	R12v1p39 S12v1p25
WET QUAKERS, THE	537L5L	3L4L5L2	Bb	6/8	B16v3p23
WEYDIMANS AIR	1H5H7b0	1H2H3bH0	E	2/4	R12v3p19
WEYDIMAN'S MINUET	5H6H4H	2H1H1H	D	3/4	R12v3p24
WEYMOUTH FETE	15L13	5142	A	6/8	N1v1p36
WEYMOUTH FETE, THE	1215L	5L37L2	Bb	2/2	C14v20p9
W.F. CAMPBELL ESQr. OF ISLAY AND SHAWFIELD'S STRATHSPEY	16L5L3L	547L2	A	2/2	Mc16p10
WHA CAN HELP IT	1L5L6L1	3422L	A	6/8	G10v6p2
WHA WADNA' FIGHT FOR CHARLIE?	1133	1132	G	2/4*	C6p28 (II)
WHA'LL BE KING BUT CHARLIE	1H1H3H3H	1H1H3H3	C	6/8	E1v2p21 (II)
WHA'LL BE KING BUT CHARLIE	1H1H3H3H	1H1H3H5	D	6/8	G1v1p8
WHA'LL HAE MY DAINTY WHITE PUDDINGS	3530	2420	G	6/8	C5v2p34
WHAT A BEAU (MY/YOUR) GRANNY WAS	3H2H1H5	31H2H2	D	2/2	A1v4p6 W4v1p20 P10p19
WHAT A BLUNDER	13L5L3L	2L47L2	G	4/4	P9p19
WHAT BEAUTEOUS SCENES	1H1H2H6	1H543	G	4/4	O1v1Kp119
WHAT CARE I FOR WHOM SHE BE	1H13H1	2527L	F	6/8	S7v1p6
WHAT NEXT	3H3H65	3H3H2H5H	D	2/4	C14v27p10,11
WHAT SHALL I DO TO SHOW HOW MUCH I LOVE HER?	3bH1H2H	771H	D	3/4	O1v5p4 O1v1Dp1
WHAT SHOU'D A LASSIE DO WI' AN AULD MAN	1H3bH4H2H	1H3bH7b5	E	6/8	O1v1Fp5
WHAT THE DEVIL AILS YOU	7b52H	5H5H2H	D	3/4	O1v1Jp89
WHAT THE D...L AILS YOU	3b11H5	46b7b5	B A	4/4*	C5v2p57 G11v2Ap22 B15v1p67 K1v1p24 C14v22p14
WHAT WILL I DO GIN MY HOGGIE DIE	3551H	3H3H2H1H	D C	4/4	Mc9v2p11 A1v5p43 (J3)
WHAT YOU PLEASE	3572H	5H3H72H	D	6/8	S7v1p1
WHAT'S A' THE STEER, KIMMER?	3H3H3H3H	3H3H3H0	D	4/4	C8v2p45
WHAT'S THAT TO YOU	1H2H2H6	6752	F	4/4	S7v1p80
WHEEM, THE	1H3H5H5H	4H4H3H3H	C	2/4	H3p12 Mc9v2p38
WHEEM, THE	5533	515L5L	G	2/4	A7v2p33
WHEN ABSENT FROM THE NYMPH (I LOVE)	3b211	3b3b54	E	4/4	(J3) N1v2p59
WHEN ABSENT FROM THE NYMPH I LOVE	321H1H	526L6L	G F	4/4	O1v1Ep30 P8v2p36 O1v2p24 O1v3p31 T6v2p54
WHEN ARTHUR FIRST AT COURT BEGAN	3H3H4H6H	5H4H3H3H	D	6/8	E1v2p85
WHEN FAIRIES DANCE ROUND	1374H	3H2H34	G	6/8	P8v1p17
WHEN FIRST MY FOND DAMON	534	516	G	3/4	R12v3p13
WHEN FIRST THIS HUMBLE ROOF I KNEW	5566	5430	G	6/8	E1v1p71
WHEN I FOLLOWED A LASS	3322	3211	G	6/8	A1v2p35
WHEN I PARTED	157bL4	153b1H	E	6/8	A7v3p6
WHEN I WAS A WEE THING	1143	447bL4	F	2/4	C10v2Bp78
WHEN I'VE GOT SAXPENCE UNDER MY THUMB	3432	5421	F	6/8	C19p27
WHEN PENSIVE I THOUGHT OF MY LOVE	551H0	61H1H7	G	6/8	E1v2p77
WHEN PENSIVE I THOUGHT ON MY LOVE	551H1H	61H1H7	G	6/8	B7p11
WHEN PETTIE CAME OVER THE GLEN	3b11	27bL2	G	9/8	P5v4p16
WHEN SHE CAM BEN SHE BOBBED	13b27bL	11H75	A G	6/8	C5v3p61 (J3)
WHEN SHE CAM BEN SHE BOBBIT	111	3b3b4	G	6/4*	C5v2p64 O1v1Bp43
WHEN SHE CAM BEN SHE BOBBED	111	3b3b2	G	3/4	O1v2p40,41 O1v1Ap14,15
WHEN SHE CAME BEN SHE BOBBED	111	3b3b5	G	6/4	S16p96,97
WHEN SHE CAME BEN SHE BOBED	1227bL	11H7b5	A	6/8	A1v2p29
WHEN SHE CAME BEN SHE BOBED	111	3b3b3b	G	6/4	Mc8v1Ap22 Mc8v2Ap19
WHEN SOL HAD LOOS'D	1542	5135	G	6/8	O1v1Hp55
WHEN THE HOLLOW DRUM	1113	2211	G	2/2	E1v1p107
WHEN THE KINE HAD GIVEN A PAIL FULL	113b2	423b1	G	4/4	O1v1Lp146
WHEN THE KING CAME O'ER (THE) [BOYNE] WATER	1H1H1H3bH	7b7b3b4	E D	4/4*	A1v2p44 E1v2p143 Mc8v1Bp40 Mc8v2Cp5 G11v2Cp2 C20p69
WHEN THE KING CAME O'ER THE WATER	1H1H1H3bH	7b53b4	D	4/4	O1v1Kp133
WHEN THE ROSY MORN APPEARING	5551H	5443	A	4/4	E1v2p104,105
(WHEN) WAR'S ALARMS (ENTIC'D MY WILLY)	5322	36L16L	G	4/4	A1v3p226
WHEN WILL YE WED ME WITH A RING	15L15	426L5L	G	4/4	C18p2
WHEN YOU GO TO THE HILL TAKE YOUR GUN	5L343	2347bL	G	4/4	G11v1Ap28
WHERE HELEN LIES	51H2H	3H3H2H	D	3/4	Mc8v1Dp93
WHERE HELEN LIES	122	332	Bb	3/4	(J3)
WHERE HELEN LIES	5L12	332	Bb	3/4	B5p14
WHERE IS MY LOVE	121	554	A	3/4	P8v2p29
WHERE THE BEE SUCKS	5H6H2H5H	3H3HO3H	C	4/4	E1v2p40
WHERE WAD BONIE ANNIE LY	11H53	27b42	A F G	4/4*	C5v2p25 (J3) E1v2p37

Title			Key	Time	References
WHERE WILL OUR GOODMAN LIE	11H53	21H42	A	2/4	A1v1p33
WHERE WILL (Y)OUR GOODMAN L(A)YE	11H1H7	5533	G	2/2	Mc8v2Cp14 O1v1Gp22
WHEREFOR CAME YOU HERE ISE WARRANT	335	535	G	6/4	Y1p23
WHIGS OF FIFE(, THE)	5132	511H3H	G F	4/4*	A7v6p90 B15v1p98 K1v1p31
					S12v1p24 G11v2Ap29 Mc13v2p26
					S7v1p64 (II)
WHILST I FONDLY VIEW YE CHARMER	15L13	5531	G	4/4	O1v4p4
WHIM, THE	1H353	4246	D	2/2	H1p6
WHIM, THE	1565	437L4	Bb	6/8	C14v24p18
WHIM WHAM, THE	1H121	237L5L	G	6/8	B16v3p22
WHIP HER AND GIRD HER	1113	1124	G	6/8	S12v2p24,25
WHIP THE CAT	1135	1H41H4	G	2/2	R12v1p66 (W3)
WHIPMAN LADDIE, THE	5H3H4H2H	5H3H4H1H	D	6/8	A1v1p65
WHIPMAN'S RANT, THE	1552	1555	D	4/4	K1v1p4 G11v2Ap4 (II)
WHIRLIE-WHA, THE	51H2H5	321H1H	D	6/8	A1v3p195
WHISKY BOTTLE, THE	11H2H2H	3H1H1H2H	D	6/8	Mc15p30
WHISKY, THE	5L13b3b	217bL5L	A	4/4	D14v2p46
WHISKY WELCOME BACK(AGAIN)	1L122	16L5L2L	Bb	4/4	G10v5p36 (II)
WHISTLE O'ER THE LAVE O'T	1133	5326L	G	4/4	C33p10,11
WHISTLE O'ER THE LAVE O'T	16L23	4326L	G	4/4	A7v6p33
WHISTLE O'ER THE LAVE O'T	16L23	5326L	G	2/2	Mc7p36 Mc9v1p31
WHISTLE O'ER THE LAVE O'T	16L33	5326L	F G	4/4*	(J3) C8v1p24 C4p46
					K1v1p14,15 P5v3p26 G11v2Ap12
					C8v2p8 O1v1Lp153 (II)
WHISTLE O'ER THE LEAVE O'T	15L33	5326L	G	4/4	G9v5p21
WHISTLE O'ER THE LEAVE O'T	16L33	5126L	G	4/4	B15v1p56
WHITE COCKADE	5333	5332	G	2/4	Mc7p10
WHITE COCKADE, THE	5332	3331H	G F	4/4	C5v2p34 (J3)
WHITE COCKADE, THE	3333	537L2	G	2/4	A1v4p15 C5v1p15 P10p12 C14v3p5
WHITE COCKADE, THE	3333	547L2	G	2/4	K1v2p21 G11v2Bp19 (II)
WHITE COCKADE, THE	3342	3331H	G	4/4	C8v2p13 C8v1p39
WHITE COCKADE, THE	5333	5322	G	2/4	E1v1p14 B7p27
WHITE JOAK, THE	1H3H75	6651	D	6/8	W7p18
WHITE JOCK	1H3H1H5	6651	D	6/8	Mc7p19 A1v1p13 H3p38
WHITTINGTON'S CAT	354H3H	354H1H	C	3/8	P6v1p34
WHO CAN HELP IT	1561H	3H3H2H2	C	6/8	G8p21 Mc4v2p6
WHO'D HAVE THOUGHT IT	15L5L	13b4	G	3/2	H1p25
WHO'S THE DUPE	1H535	4H2H75	F	4/4	B16v3p10
WHY DOES LADY LINLEY WEEP	7bL7bL6L	6L5L1	A	3/4	C10v2Bp9
WHY HANGS THAT CLOUD	3211H	3H2H66	F D	4/4	T6v2p74 (J3)
WHY LEFT I MY HAME?	5L111	436L1	G	2/4	C8v1p53 C8v2p64
WHY SHOULD I NOT LIKE MY LOVE	13b3b	7bL7bL4	A	9/8	A1v2p172
WHY SHOULD I SIT AND SIGH	11H7b7b	53b7bL2	E	2/4	C10v2Ap15
WIDOW ARE YE WAKING	1133	6231	Eb	4/4	G11v2Bp7
WIDOW ARE YE WAUKIN'	1133	6221	G F	4/4	C5v3p68 Mc8v2Bp3 O1v1Cp12
					C20p63 (J3) O1v5p16,17
WIDOW GIN THOU BE WAKING	1133	3221	F	2/2	P7p14
WIDOW WAD MAN, THE	1H3H2H5	6767	D	2/2	B16v3p16
WIDOW'S LILT, THE	5L131H	5122	Bb	2/4	O1v1Hp43
WIDOW'S RANT, THE	1565	1522	A	6/8	A1v1p10
WIDOWS SHALL HAVE SPOUSES, THE	1H51H5	2266	A	2/2	O1v1Kp126
WILD GOOSE, THE	3546	3547L	D	2/2	R12v1p52
WILD IRISHMAN, THE	1H3H4H3H	1H3H72H	D E	6/8	Mc9v2p36 C14v7p2 C24v2p15
					R12v2p2
WILKE'S WRIGLE	521H6	5235	D	6/8	A1v1p51
WILKESS RELEASE	1H2H3H5H	3H2H1H3	D	2/4	A1v2p53
WILL THE WEAVER	11H63	237L7L	G	2/4	W4v2p21
WILL WITH A WISP	1H2H3H1H	2H61H1H	D	2/2	R12v1p59
WILL YE COME TO THE BOWER	5555	5750	F G	2/4	E1v1p47 C8v2p31
WILL YE GO THE BROOM	335	212	G	3/4	C18p24
(WILL YE GO TO) SHERRIFF MUIR	5535	2424	F A	4/4*	G11v2Cp2 O1v1Fp10,11 C8v2p16
					C8v1p46
WILL YE GO TO THE EWE BUGHTS MARION	1H2H1T7H	6H61H2H	C	2/4	C5v2p4
WILL YE GO (TO) (THE) (EWE-BUGHTS)	121H7	66L12	G F E	4/4*	C4p7 (J3) E1v2p39 (C25)
(MARION?)					C6p22 N1v2p61 A1v3p184
WILL YE GO TO THE FOREST MY BONNIE LASS	1133	6361H	G	4/4	C5v2p37
WILL YE GO TO THE HIGHLANDS	5555	61H32	G	4/4	C5v2p46
AND CHACE THE FLEET ROE					
WILL YE LEND ME YOUR LOOM LASS	17L6L3	661H5	G	4/4	O1v1Dp21
WILL YOU GO TO FLANDERS	5555	6666	A	4/4	C13v3p32-36
WILL YOU GO TO FLANDERS	5553	6661H	G	2/2*	B15v2p20 D13p22 Mc8v1Bp30
					C20p30,31
WILL YOU GO TO FLANDERS	5553	5566	F	2/2	Mc8v2Bp2
WILL YOU GO TO SHERIFF MOOR	5L122	5L144	G	2/2	B15v1p49
WILL YOU TO FLANDERS	1561H	5211	G	4/4	O1v1Ap36 O1v4p37
WILLIAM AND MARGARET	1H3H2H	1H56	G D	3/4	C5v3p70 O1v1Ap9 O1v2p25
WILLIAM AND MARGARET	5L11	25L0	G	3/4	T6v1p109
WILLIAM AND MARGARET, (THE OLD TUNE OF)	1H76	3H2H6	C	3/4	O1v4p27 C4p57 O1v1Ep28
WILLIAM BROWN ESQr's WALTZ	367L3L	367L1H	G	3/8	D6p18,19
WILLIAM GIBSON CRAIG, M.P.	15L5L3	5422	Eb	4/4	M4v4p31
WILLIAM'S GHOST	1355	6776	D	4/4	Mc8v1Dp97
WILLIAM'S GHOST	3355	6775	D	4/4	O1v1Ep25 O1v4p33 P4p30

WILLIAM'S LOVE	151H6	3557	A	2/2	C18p6,7
WILLIE ARE YE WAUKIN	3355	62H65	G	2/2	C18p25
WILLIE BREW'D A PECK O' MAUT	51H64	62H1H6	F G	4/4	C8v1p36 C8v2p39 E1v2p116,117
WILLIE BREW'D A PECK OF MAUT	51H64	661H6	D	4/4	C5v2p19 G1v1p34 (J3)
WILLIE CAMERON	1122	1311H	D	2/4	T8p3
WILLIE DUNCAN	1133	22H22H	C	4/4	G11v2Cp20 (II)
WILLIE HAS GOTTEN A WIFE	3b11	3b12	B	9/8	C5v2p43
WILLIE PRINGLE, A STRATHSPEY	1H53b1	3b6b25L	G	4/4	P11v2p13
WILLIE STAYS LANG AT THE FAIR	3H1H5H	2H52H	D	9/8	R6v2p9
WILLIE WAS A WANTON WAG	351H1H	352H6	D C	4/4	C4p49 C5v2p61 A1v1p17 E1v1p57 G1v1p34 (II) (J3) T6v2p60 P8v2p35
WILLIE WAS A WANTON WAG	351H1H	355H6	D	2/4	C8v2p59
WILLIE WAS A WANTON WAG	311H1H	31H3H6	D	4/4	Mc23p24
WILLIE WAS A WANTON WAG	3556	1H1H1H5	D	4/4*	01v5p22 01v1Ep24 R6v2p24 Mc8v1Ap12 Mc8v2Cp9 Mc9v2p6 C20p54,55
WILLIE WAS A WANTON WAG	351H1H	354H6	C	2/4	C8v1p21
WILLIE WINKIE ('S TESTAMENT)	5351	5326L	F	2/2*	Mc21v3p9 G11v2Bp29 S12v1p19 K1v2p30 (II)
WILLIE WINKIE'S TESTAMENT	5135	47bL7bL7bL	F	2/2	T6v2p104
WILLIE WINKS (STRATHSPEY)	5651	5326L	F	4/4*	G9v5p33 C14v22p17 B15v1p61 N1v1p18
WILLIE'S AWA'	13L13L	16L2L2L	Bb	2/2	G11v2Cp31
WILLIE'S DROWN'D AT GAMRY	3b17bL	4L7bL0	A	3/4	C18p15
WILLIE'S RARE AND WILLIE'S FAIR	1H3H2H	544	C D	3/4	(J3) C5v2p21
WILLm SWANSON, ESQr's REEL	1336	1H37L2	D	2/2	Mc19v2p16
WILLY WINKS	5551	5326L	F	2/2	A7v3p12
WILLY WINKY'S TESTAMENT	5651	5526L	F	2/2	Mc22p10
WILLY'S RARE AND WILLY'S FAIR	51H3H3H	653H2H	D	6/8	B16v4p89
WILLY'S RARE(AND WILLY'S FAIR)	1H3H2H	644	C D	3/4	T6v2p110 P8v2p44
WILLY'S THE LAD FOR ME	3556	1H133	D	4/4	01v1Kp127
WILT THOU BE MY DEARIE	1H61H5	1H4H3H2H	D	4/4	C5v2p49
WILT THOU BE MY DEARIE	16L15L	1332	G	4/4	A1v5p53
WILT THOU BE MY DEARIE	16L15L	1432	G A	4/4*	C6p17 (J3) E1v2p129 E1v2p13
WILTON LODGE, A STRATHSPEY	1335	2461H	E	4/4	P11v1p10
WIND BOUND SAILOR, THE	1515L	7bL427bL	B	2/4	Mc1v1p116
WINDING OF THE STREAM, THE	1H1H3bH2H	1H6bH55	E	4/4	01v1Kp122
WINDMILL DANCE, THE	1H1H2H3H	3H3H3H7	D	6/8	W7p3
WINDSOR CHACE	1H565	5542	F	6/8	B16v2p12
WINDSOR FORRESTERS MARCH, THE	1H51H5	1H5H1H5H	C	4/4	C23p15
WINDSOR HUNT	3H1H51H	3H1H4H5H	C	2/2	C14v9p3
WINE CANNOT CURE	3333	2212	G	4/4	A7v6p84
WINTER	1H1H4H2H	5H4H2H0	C	6/8	A1v3p194
WINTER IS PAST	1H2H76	61H64	D	4/4	C10v2Bp85
WINTER IT IS PAST, THE	3311H	5222	F G	2/4	(J3) C5v3p59
WINTER IT IS PAST, THE	3311H	5212	G	2/4	01v1Jp95
WIT WITHOUT MONEY	16L7L1	2432	C	4/4	P9p33
WITCHES HILL, THE	13b15L	7bL2L7bL2	A	4/4	Mc13v1p6 Mc13v2p6
WITH BROKEN WORDS	5555	6665	D	4/4	P8v2p14
WITH VERDURE CLAD	1H2H4H4H	72H2H1H	D	6/8	E1v2p103
WITHIN A MILE OF EDINBURGH	5211	6L5L5L1	Bb	6/8	G3p12
WITHIN A MILE OF EDINBURGH(TOWN)	5213	6L5L5L1	A G F B	4/4	C1v1p10 C8v1p18 (II) C19p19 C6p2 (J3) G3p6,7
WITHIN A MILE OF EDINBURGH(TOWN)	5H2H1H3H	6551H	D G	4/4*	E1v1p10 A1v4p32 G1v1p19 (II)
WIVES OF KILWINNON, THE	7b547bL	7b57b2H	A	2/2	B15v1p111
WIVES OF TORPHICAN, THE	3124	3113H	D	6/8	R12v1p44 B15v1p42,43
Wm. SHEPHERD'S LAMENTATION FOR THE DEATH OF SIR RALPH ABERCROMBY	3b212	4112	G	6/8	S4v2p20
WOE IS ME WHAT MAN ! DO	555	531	G	3/4	01v1Gp15
WOE'S MY HEART (THAT WE SHOU'D SUNDER)	5555	6665	D C	4/4	C5v2p9 C5v1p60 A1v5p60 Mc8v1Ap20 Mc8v2Ap20 G17p5 T6v1p16 N1v2p44 C20p72,73
WOES MY HEART THAT WE SHOULD SUNDER	3255	6665	C	4/4	S16p10,11
WOE'S MY HEART THAT WE SHOULD SUNDER	5L2L5L5L	6L6L6L5L	Bb	4/4	01v5p28,29
WOE'S MY HEART THAT WE SHOU'S SUNDER	5255	6665	C	4/4	01v1Cp5
WOLDS OF SUSSEX, THE	551H1H	61H55	D	4/4	P6v1p22
WOMAN'S DANCE IN OMBRES CHINOISES	5511	447L5L	G	6/8	A1v3p163
WONDER, THE	1133	5432	G	2/4	A1v1p48
WOOBURN ABBEY	15L22	3637L	Bb	6/8	B16v4p93 B16v2p9
WOO'D AN' MARRY'D AN A'	331	155	G	9/8	C19p21
WOO'D AND MARRIED AND A'	531	355	G F	9/8	A1v2p63 C5v2p22 E1v1p29 K1v1p31 G11v2Ap29 (J3)
WOO'D AND MARRIED AND A'	531	315	F	9/8	C13v4p52
WOO'D AND MARRIED AND A'	531	555	F	9/8	B15v1p52 C4p58 (W3) (II)
WOO'D AND MARRIED AND A'	553b	7b7b7b	E	9/8	01v1Jp91
WOOD CUTTERS, THE	1111	2235L	G	6/8	R12v3p20,21
WOOD NUNRICH FAIR	351H5	4642	G	6/8	A1v1p11
WOODHILL	1H3H51H	3512	G	4/4	D6p31
WOOD-HOUSE REEL, THE	51H61H	6522	A	2/2	R6v1p7
WOODPECKER'S MARCH	1H1H2H2H	3H1H2H5	D	2/4	C8v2p57

WOOD'S HORNPIPE	1113	5552	G	4/4	A1v6p26		
WOODS OF BARGENNY, THE	1H51H3	1H52H7	F	6/8	R5p31		
WOUNDED HUSSAR	5L3b27bL	3b55L1	G	6/8	E1v1p111		
WRIGHT'S RANT, THE	3535	467b5	A	6/8	A1v1p62		
WRIGHT'S RANT, (THE)	3535	47b1H6	A	6/8	G1v2p51	B15v1p92	
YANKE DOODLE	1H2H1H2H	1H2H1H1H	D	2/4	A7v3p34		
YANKEE DOODLE	1H2H1H7	1H2H1H7	C D	4/4*	C8v1p5	C8v2p56	(II)
YANKIE DOODLE	1H2H1H2H	1H2H1H7	D	2/4	A1v1p36	Mc21v4p37	
YARROW VALE	51H1H2H	62H2H1H	D	4/4	C5v1p57	A1v5p57	
YE BANKS AND BRAES (O' BONNIE DOON)	1H2H3H2H	3H1H52H	C D	6/8	C8v1p34	C8v2p19	G1v1p15
(YE) BANKS (AND BRAES) O' (BONNIE) DOON	1232	315L2	Bb A G	6/8	C6p2	C5v2p20	E1v1p32
					(J3)		
YE GODS, WAS STREPHON'S PICTURE BLEST	3352	3552	F D G	4/4	T6v2p18	(J3)	P8v2p33
YE KEN WHAT	1H51H5	1542	D	4/4	F3p17		
YE NYMPHS OF THE PLAIN	3H2H1H2H	675#0	G	2/4	P8v1p18,19		
YE SONS OF FREEDOM	1122	5511	A	4/4	E1v2p65		
YEAL YEAL	17b7b4	1555	E	4/4*	B15v1p68	C13v2p22	
YEAR OWER YOUNG, A	5L5L11	226L5L	A	4/4	C10v2Ap27		
YE'LL AY BE WELCOME BACK AGAIN	113	556	D	3/4	O1v1Jp87		
YE'LL AYE BE WELCOME BACK AGAIN	1555	11H52	D	2/2	B15v1p56		
(YE'LL NEVER BE LIKE MY) AULD GOODMAN	1H71H2H	1H765	C D	6/8	(J3)	C5v3p67	O1v1Cp15
YELL YELL	557b5	5551	E	4/4	G11v1Ap7	G10v1p27,28	
YELL YELL	1525	1555	E	2/2	C13v1p10	Mc9v1p11	
YELLOW HAIR'D LADDIE, THE	156	1H1H1H	D	3/4	C13v3p18		
YELLOW HAIR'D LADDIE, THE	356	1H1H1H	A D	3/4	C19p10	O1v3p29	N1v2p66
					Mc8v1Cp85	Mc8v2Ap19	O1v1Bp12
					S16p84,85	C29p15	C20p5
YELLOW HAIR'D LASSIE, THE	3b53b1	3b527bL	A	6/8	C5v3p75		
YELLOW JOKE	1H311H	3H2H1H3	F	6/8	W7p20		
YELLOW-HAIR'D LADDIE, (THE)	356	1H1H3H	G D	3/4	C8v2p36	C5v2p6	G1v1p16
					E1v1p13	C8v1p63	T7p4,5 C6p10
					C4p54	A1v6p45	P4p7 G17p8
					T6v1p12	(J3)	P8v2p12
YEMON O NOCK	154	465	G	3/4	T7p28,29	O1v1p120,121	
YEO YEO	1536	4225	G	4/4	A1v6p29		
YE'RE WELCOME CHARMING CHARLIE	5L13b1	417bL2	A	4/4	C5v2p55		
YES OR NO	1153	51H2H2	F	2/2	P9p21		
YESTER HOUSE	5542	5557b	A	4/4*	Mc4v3p1	G10v4p17	(II)
YON WILD MOSSY MOUNTAINS	113b	551H	A G	3/4	C5v2p65	(J3)	
YORK FANCY, THE	1H1H75	1H1H71H	D	4/4*	A1v3p206	H1p24	
YORK HORNPIPE, THE	151H6	6555	F	4/4	G3p8		
YORK HOUSE	1H544	1H532	D	2/4	A7v3p8		
YORK HOUSE	1121	4365	Bb	2/4	C14v6p20		
YORKSHIRE LASSES(, THE)	1H367	1H2H3H7	C	6/8	B16v3p20	S7v1p27	
YOUNG BENJIE	11H7b	541	E	3/4	C10v2Ap35		
YOUNG CHORISTER, THE	3561H	5542	D	6/8	C1v1p7		
(YOUNG) COLIN STOLE MY HEART AWAY	1H3H5H5H	4H4H3H0	D	4/4*	A1v5p30	C5v1p30	E1v1p118,119
YOUNG COLIN THE PRIDE OF THE PLAIN	3b1H3bH3b	554H2H	E D	2/4	O1v1Dp9	O1v5p33	
YOUNG COLLIN	3H3H5H4H	1H2H3H2H	D	4/4	O1v1Jp93		
YOUNG INVERCAULD'S STRATHSPEY	13b27bL	13b51H	G	2/2	P5v4p10		
(YOUNG) JOCKEY WAS THE BLYTHEST LAD...	3b3b41	115L5L	A	4/4*	(J3)	G11v2Cp13	
YOUNG LADY'S PANEGYRICK ON HER LOVER, A	6L66	511	A	3/4	Mc5p30		
YOUNG MAID WITH THE GOLDEN LOCKS	1565	6225	D	6/8	Mc5p7		
YOUNG MAIDENS I TO YOU CONSIGN	1155	3b3b55	F	4/4	C10v2Bp38		
YOUNG MAY MOON, THE	1H1H65	1H2H3H1H	C D G F	6/8	C8v1p34	S9p26 (II)	G1v1p21
					C8v2p40	E1v2p54	
YOUNG MYRTLE, THE	327L5L	5L5L52	A	6/8	G3p13		
YOUNG SIMON STRATHSPEY	3b6b27bL	3b51H1H	E	2/2	C14v11p5		
YOUR BONNY FACE WHERE BLOOMS THE ROSE	3b113b	43b15	A	6/8	C5v3p72		
YOUR WELCOME INTO BERVIE	5331	5362	A	2/2	H3p16		
YOU'RE WELCOME HOME	3511	4622H	G	2/2	C14v10p25		
YOU'RE WELCOME TO YOUR FOOT	151H2	151H1H	C	4/4	Mc21v4p16		
YOUTH THAT I LOVE, THE	5L122	47b47bL	A	6/8	C5v2p49		
YOU'VE BEEN LONG AWAY	135	155	D	3/2	S12v1p20		
ZITTI, ZITTI, PIANO, PIANO	5451	4255	G	2/4	E1v2p35		

5

TUNE TITLE INDEX (A-Z) (II)

The music of the period 1844-1922, from Joseph Lowe's Collections (Books 1-6) to Scott Skinner's "Cairngorm" Series

TITLE	CODE A	CODE B	KEY SIG	TIME SIG	SOURCE CODE/S

Title			Key	Time	Source
A BHEAN AN TAIGH NACH LEIG THU STEACH	1111	516L6L	Bb	2/4	Mc3v1p191
AM FEAR A THA AIR FOGAIRT					
[GOOD WIFE, ADMIT THE WANDERER]					
A CHO-DHALTA MO RUIN	1554	5454	C	4/4	M10v2p26
A CHO-DHALTA MO RUIN! SEACAINN AN DUN!	154	242	G	3/4	M10v2p12
A' CHRIDHEALACHD [MERRY MAKING, THE]	3531H	357b2	F	2/2 R	R10p231
A' CHUACHAG	3H1H1H5	2H2H3H2H	D	2/2 R	R10p106
A DHOMHNUILL, A DHOMHNUILL	1135	5126L	G	2/2 R	R10p161
A. F. IRVINE ESQ.	1L2L3bL4L	5L6bL4L7bF	A	4/4 SS	S8v3p42
A MHISG A CHUR AN NOLIG OIRN	5127bL	1642	A	4/4 R	Mc3v1p14
[CHRISTMAS CAROUSING]					
A' THE WAY TO GALLOWAY	1H3bH7b5	6b47b5	E	4/4 R	K2v3p10
ABBEY CRAIG, THE	536L5L	356L2	E	4/4	W1p43
ABERARDER RANT	1H5H3H2H	1H1H1H1H	D	4/4 PR	Mc3v1p70
ABERCAIRNY HOUSE	11H1H3bH	7b7b47bL	C	4/4 S	R10p273
ABERDEEN HUNT	5L13b5	7b422	G	4/4 S	R10p197
ABERDEENSHIRE VOLUNTEERS	1353	6647L	D	4/4 S	Mc3v1p53 S8v3p9
ABERGELDIE	1H535	471H7	D	4/4	B9p2
ABERGELDIE CASTLE	3151	26L7L2	A	2/2	W1p6
ABERLOUR RIFLE VOLUNTEER MARCH	1353	4437L	F	4/4 M	G14p28
ABERLOUR'S SQUEEZE	1H1H2H1H	51H2H4H	C	4/4 S	K2v2p13 Mc3v1p118 R10p82
ABOYNE CASTLE	1336L	1362	D	2/4	W1p29
ACADEMY, THE	5531	227L5L	A	2/4	S8v6p107
ACHMONY	311H5	3127bL	A	4/4	S8v6p74
ACROSS THE MEADOWS	16L6L6L	3L5L5L3	Bb	4/4	P3p20
ADNIL'S MAZURKA	34#5	722	F	3/4	S8v5p23
AGGIE AND INA (JAFFREY)	551H5	662H2	D	2/2 R	S8v5p12
AGUS HO "MORAG"	3326L	6L231	F	4/4	M10v2p6
AIR [UNTITLED]	6216L	1511	E	6/8	M10v1p2
AIRCHIE BROWN	531H5	2462	A	2/2*R	Mc3v1p20 S8v3p32
AIRCHIE SYMON	1L5L7L5L	3L5L2L2L	A	2/2 R	S8v3p36
AIRIDH NAN BADAN	5153	3261H	C	6/8	M10v2p15
ALASDAIR MACALISTER	3b15L1	3b155	A	4/4 S	Mc3v1p119 R10p45
[ALASDAIR MAC ALASDAIR]					
ALBERT	1135	2246	A	4/4	S8v6p70
ALDIVALLOCH	5333	5322	D	4/4 S	K2v3p5
ALDIVALLOCH or	5L111	6L242	D	4/4	Mc3v1p157
O'ER THE MUIR AMANG THE HEATHER					
ALEXANDER BRODIE	4H3H2H7	4H3H66	D	2/2 R	R10p115
ALEXANDER DAVIDSON ESQ. OF DESSWOOD	1H651	1H3H22	F	4/4	W1p49
ALEXANDER RAMSAY ESQ.'S REEL	3135	6542	G	2/2	W1p60
ALEXANDER TROUP	1151	516L2	D	4/4 S	S8v5p20
ALEXANDER WALKER'S REEL	5551	2466	D	2/2	W1p31
ALEXANDRA PARK	5353	462H7	A	2/2 R	K2v4p6
ALFORD WEAVER, THE	1H51H5	6451	D	2/2 R	S8v5p13 S8v6p94
ALI BOBO	3136	5122	A	4/4 S	S8v3p34
ALICE'S DOLLIE	5531	4640	A	4/4 S	S8v7p8
ALICK YOUNG	153bH1H	6b547L	D	2/4 HP	S8v8p134
ALISTER MCALISTER	3b15L1	3b155	A	4/4 S	K2v2p9
ALLEY CROCKER [ALLY CROCKER]	51H1H1H	2H72H4H	D	4/4 CD	K2v1p22
ALLOWA' KIRK [ALLOA KIRK]	1526L	1551H	G	4/4 S	L8v1p12 L8v8Bp12
ALLT A' GHOBHAINN [SMITH'S BURN, THE]	3564	6327bL	A	2/2 R	R10p5
ALLT GHIUSACH	3342	331H3H	C	4/4 S	L8v8Ap18
ALLY CROKER	51H1H1H	2H72H4H	D	4/4 R	L8v2p6
ALVA HOUSE	315L5L	3522	Bb	4/4	P3p6
AM BODACH LUIDEACH ODHAR	1353	2366	D	4/4 S	R10p155
AMERICAN AIR	1H3H4H3H	552H1H	D	2/4 CD	K2v1p21
AMERICAN AIR	1H635	1H631	D	2/4 CD	K2v1p21
AMERICAN, THE	5L321H	5236L	G	2/2 R	K2v4p13
AMONG THE HEATHER	1L3L5L3L	6L15L1	A	4/4 S	K2v3p13
AMONG THE OCHILS	15L3L2L	15L13	Bb	4/4	P3p6
AMULREE [AMBULREE]	3344	3327bL	G	4/4*R	K2v2p16 L8v6p14 R10p155
					S17p38
AN GABH THU BEAN DHO'ILL BHIG?	5L113b	5L111	A	2/2 R	Mc3v1p111 R10p43
[LITTLE DONALD'S WIFE]					
AN GEARRAN	351H5	3542	D	4/4 S	R10p84
AN GILLE DUBH MO LAOCHAN	1H1H62H	2H3H65	D	2/2 R	R10p84
AN NOCHD GUR FAOIN MO CHODAL DHOMH	6L125L	6L123	G	4/4	M10v2p11
AN OIDHCHE A BHA BHANAIS ANN	15L11	1226L	A	2/2 R	R10p10
[LEA RIG, THE]					
AN OIDHCHE BHA NA GABHAIR AGAINN	5153	61H53	G	2/2 R	R10p168
[NIGHT WE HAD THE GOATS, THE]					
ANDERSON'S RANT	151H1H	5122	C	2/2 R	G6v2p19
ANDREW CARR	355	467	D	9/8 J	R10p139
ANE AN' TWENTY TAM	5262	5266L	G	6/8	K2v1p32
ANGUS CAMPBELL	15L1H6	4325L	A	2/4 R	S8v8p94
ANGUS CAMPBELL	15L1H6	4327L	A	2/4 R	S8v7p13
ANGUS MACRAE	5313	427bL2	A	4/4 S	S8v7p13
AN(N) GILLE DUBH CIAR DUBH	15L5L6L	314L6L	Bb	6/8	M10v1p2
ANNA IS MY DARLING	113L1	3216L	A	4/4* R	K2v2p5 R10p19
ANNIE ALLAN	3b3b1H5H	227b4H	D	2/4 HP	S8v3p48
ANNIE DALGARNO	1H3b11	3b51H1H	C	4/4 SS	S8v3p62

Title					References
ANNIE IS MY DARLING	113L1	3216L	A	4/4 R	Mc3v1p31
ANNIE LAURIE	11H76	5222	D	4/4 S	K2v4p7
ANNIE O' FIDDOCHSIDE	5L153	3226L	A	4/4	S8v6p51
ANTIQUARY, THE	51H1H1H	2H4H5H4H	D	4/4 R	L8v8Bp27
APPIN HOUSE	3133	26L22	A	2/2 R	R10p2
APPIN HOUSE	5L5L15L	5L5L12L	G	2/2 R	Mc3v1p94
APPLE TREE, THE	11H64	1764	A	4/4 R	K2v2p5
ARBEADIE	5313	6424	D	4/4 S	S8v7p6
ARCHDUKE JOHN OF AUSTRIA	3bH1H51H	2H4H2H7b	D	4/4 R	R10p214
ARCHIE MENZIES	15L37L	361H3	F	4/4 R	L8v1p20 L8v8Ap24
ARDCLACH	15L3L5L	4L3L2L6F	Bb	2/2	W1p16
ARGYLE BOWLING GREEN (THE)	11H1H3H	1H1H53	C	4/4*R	K2v2p12 L8v1p17 L8v8Ap21
[ARGYLL BOWLING GREEN]					Mc3v1p120 R10p66 S17p71
ARGYLE IS MY NAME	1H1H3H2H	3H3H51H	D	6/8	K2v1p32
ARKANSAS TRAVELLER	16L5L1	2326L	A	2/4 CD	K2v1p22
ARRAN BOAT, THE	1544	1521	E	6/8 A	K2v1p47
ARRAN LILT, AN	5133	61H22	G	2/4	K2v1p47
ARTHUR SEAT	1H7L3L3	4#316L	Bb	2/4 HP	S8v9/6
ARTHUR'S SEAT	15L3b3b	2453b	B	2/2 R	R10p133
AS A THOISEACH [BE OFF MACINTOSH /	7b57b5	7b527bL	E	2/2*R	Mc3v1p83 R10p253 S17p133
KEEP IT UP]					
ATHOLE BROSE	315L1	3145	D	4/4 R	K2v2p17 L8v8Bp10 Mc3v1p73
					R10p118
ATHOLE BROSE or BUCKINGHAM HOUSE	3b15L1	3b145	A	4/4 S	S8v8p113
ATHOLE BROSE	415L1	4165	D	4/4 R	Mc3v1p74
ATHOLE CUMMERS, (THE)	1115	1124	A E	4/4 S	K2v3p24 K2v1p5 R10p252
ATHOLE HIGHLANDERS' FAREWELL	5515	557bL4	A	2/4*M	S8v7p32 S8v8p46
TO LOCH KATRINE, THE					
ATHOL(E) HOUSE	5356	537L2	F	2/2*R	G6v2p25 L8v5p17 Mc3v1p151
					R10p211 S17p69
ATHOLE LADS	3551	3552	A	2/2 R	R10p12
ATHOLE'S BONNY LASSES	15L3L5L	2L6L26L	G	4/4 R	K2v3p7 Mc3v1p96 R10p180
ATHOLE'S HONEST MEN	15L5L3L	2L4L6L4L	G	4/4 S	K2v3p7 Mc3v1p95 R10p180
AUCHINDOUN CASTLE	1115L	7bL3bL4L1L	B	2/2	W1p21
AUCHTERTYRE HOUSE	5562	5551H	D	4/4 S	R10p123
AULD BIRK TREE, THE (BANCHORY)	5L131	6L244	A	4/4 SS	S8v5p19 S3v6p65
AULD BRIG O' AYR, THE	5L5L11	326L5L	F	4/4 S	K2v3p18
AULD BRIG O' DON, THE	137L1	4L3L25L	Eb	4/4 SS	H5p1
AULD HOUSE, THE	3226L	5L121	G	4/4 SC	K2v3p24
AULD INN, THE	15L6L5L	1232	A	6/8	K2v4p28
AULD KIRK OF MACALLAN, THE	135L3L	13L55	G	2/2 R	G14p5
AULD KIRK, THE	1H545	427L7L	G	4/4 S	K2v4p16
AULD LANG SYNE	1122	1166	A	4/4 S	R10p1
AULD LANG SYNE	1122	1366	G	2/4	S9p18
AULD LUCKIE	1H3H5H3H	5535	C	4/4 S	K2v3p15
AULD MAN, THE	31H65	31H27L	F	4/4	S8v6p110
AULD ROAD TO TOWIE, THE	6665	3232	G	4/4 S	M7p9
AULD STEWART'S BACK AGAIN, THE	6535	6562	D	4/4 R	L8v6p7 R10p102
AULD STEWART'S BACK AGAIN, THE	6535	6542	D	4/4 R	S17p74
AULD STEWARTS OF FOTHERGILL	131H3H	6H3H2H6	C	2/2 R	R10p65
AULD STYLE'S AWA', THE	1L3L1L3	16L5L4L	A	4/4 A	S8v8p13
AULD TOUN O' AYR, THE	131H1H	61H53	D	4/4 S	K2v2p19 M7p17 R10p111
AULD WHEEL, THE	1H535	62H75	D	4/4*R	Mc3v1p67 S8v3p1 S8v7p7
AULD WIFE AYONT THE FIRE, THE	326L4	3211H	G	4/4 R	L8v3p8
AULD WIFE AYONT THE FIRE, THE	427L2	4211H	G	4/4 R	K2v2p14
AULD-BELL ROBBIE	1H127bL	1124	A	4/4 S	M7p11
AURORA	3333	31H64	G	4/4	S8v6p56
AVIMORE [AVIEMORE]	3365	2427L	A	4/4 S	L8v6p5 Mc3v1p21
AWA' AWA'	3317L	7L6L5L5L	A	4/4	S8v6p33
AYRSHIRE LASSES, (THE)	532H2H	1H3H1H6	C	4/4 S	K2v2p11 L8v2p16 L8v8Bp15
					Mc3v1p112 R10p64 S17p24
BABES IN THE WOOD	1557	5523	A	2/4 CD	K2v1p22
BABIE'S SCHOTTISCHE	5351	6L7L11	F	4/4	S8v6p109
BACK OF THE CHANGE HOUSE, THE	552H6	551H1H	D	4/4 R	K2v1p4 L8v2p9 Mc3v1p39
					R10p101 S17p23
BACK TO THE HILLS	13b46b	5217L	D	4/4 A	S8v7p41
BAG OF PRATIES, THE	1H1H1H5	7b7b65	D	4/4 CD	K2v1p22
BAGPIPE, THE	1H1H53	2466	A	4/4 S	L8v4p3 M7p29
BAILE NA GRANNDACH	5555	5562	D	4/4 SS	R10p119
BAILIE NICOL JARVIE	1H753	61H73H	F	4/4 R	K2v3p19
BAKER, THE	33L47L	33L43	A	2/4 R	S8v8p102
BAKER, THE	35L3L1	427L5	A	4/4 R	S8v7p5
BALLANGEICH	3152	61H62H	D	4/4	P3p14
BALLECHIN RANT	3142	3152H	D	2/2 R	R10p96
BALLETERACH STRATHSPEY	1215L	16L22	Eb	4/4	W1p36
BALLINDALLOCH CASTLE	1545	1452	A	4/4 QS	S8v8p48/9
BALLINDALLOCH'S DREAM	3b151H	7b7b7bL4	A	2/2 R	R10p51
BALLOCHMYLE BRIG	5L5L5L3L	126L5L	A	4/4 S	K2v3p11
BALLOCHMYLE BRIG	425L3	5525	A	4/4 R	K2v3p11
BALLOCHMYLE BRIG	1L3L6L3L	126L5L	A	4/4 S	S8v7p17
BALMENACH	5313	5351H	B D	4/4 S	S8v5p11 S8v6p93
BALMORAL BRIDGE	5L13b5	2422	G	4/4 S	L8v8Bp28

2

Title					
BALMORAL CASTLE	11H53	51H3H1H	G	4/4 S	R10p168
BALMORAL CASTLE	135L3L	4L216L	A	4/4 M	S8v7p34 S8v8p27
BALMORAL CASTLE	3b15L3bL	1L3bL5L1	G	4/4 S	L8v8Ap2
BALMORAL CASTLE	13b15L	7bL4L7bL2	F	2/2	W1p54
BALMORAL GILLIES	3b5L5L3b	3b53b1	E	4/4 S	L8v8Bp14
BALMORAL HIGHLANDERS, THE	1155	7bL7bL7bL4	A	4/4 QS	S8v7p3 S8v8p39
BALMORAL HORNPIPE	35L32	2465	Bb	2/2	W1p19
BALMORAL REEL, THE	1353	671H3	F	4/4	B9p6
BALMORAL SCHOTTISCHE	5153H	1H644	D	4/4 SC	S8v5p3
BALMORAL STRATHSPEY, THE	1353	5L322	F	4/4	B9p6
BALNAGOWN	3b151	27bL47bL	D	2/2 R	S8v3p3
BANFF BAILLIES, THE	1H3H1H5	1H3H2H2H	C	4/4	P3p2
BANFFSHIRE VOLUNTEERS, THE	3316L	6L5L7bL6L	Bb	4/4	P3p19
BANKS	137L2	4L64#4	Eb	4/4 HP	S8v7p43 S8v8p141
BANKS O' CLYDE, THE	1565	671H5	G	4/4 SC	K2v1p20
BANKS O' LOSSIE, THE	13b13b	53b22	A	4/4 S	S8v5p14
BANKS O' YTHAN, THE	1H1H72H	1H1H2H5	D	2/2 R	S8v3p12
BANKS OF AVON, THE	5326L	5L132	D	2/4	W1p33
BANKS OF BOGGIE, THE	5L131	4327L	D	2/2	W1p29
BANKS OF CLYDE, THE	3111	311H5	A	4/4 PS	Mc3v1p11
BANKS OF DON, THE	5551H	2H3H66	E	4/4	W1p40
BANKS OF EARN	13b53b	2452	G	2/2	W1p67
BANKS OF GARRY, THE	5551H	5522	D	4/4 S	Mc3v1p71 R10p113
BANKS OF LOCH NESS, THE	513b5	7bL7bL7bL7bL	G	4/4 S	R10p189
BANKS OF LOMOND, THE	1132	236L5L	A	2/4	M10v2p29
BANKS OF SPEY, THE	1126L	1155	D	4/4 R	S17p142
BANKS OF THE ALLAN, THE	3335	6565	D	6/8	K2v1p31
BANNERMAN'S RANT	5431H	6522	D	4/4 S	S8v3p16
BARGENNY'S BOWLING GREEN	1147bL	112H2H	D	6/8	G6v1p21
BARN DANCE	3b123b	11H1-	G	4/4	S9p15
BARNS OF CLYDE, THE	1H13b5	7b7b24	D	4/4 R	G6v1p22
BARONY O' BRACKLEY, THE	3455	3444	A	2/4 QS	S8v8p34
BARREN ROCKS OF ADEN, THE	3H3H1H5	753H1H	D	2/4*	M10v2p22 S8v7p31 S8v8p54
BATTLE OF FALKIRK, THE	557b5	557b7b	A	4/4 QS	S8v8p26
BEAN NA GABHAR	1352H	1353	D	4/4	M10v2p11
BEAUFORT CASTLE	1L3L31	27L5L3L	A	4/4 R	K2v2p7
BEAUTY OF THE NORTH, THE	3L135	6L27L5L	Eb	4/4 S	R10p267
BECAUSE HE WAS A BONNIE LAD	3642	3641	A	2/4 R	S8v8p92
BECAUSE HE WAS A BONNY LAD	3165	4522	A	4/4*R	K2v2p4 L8v2p3 Mc3v1p9 R10p13
BEDDING OF THE BRIDE, THE	1535	1527bL	D	2/2 R	R10p117
BELFAST ALMANAC, THE	17L6L1	3434	G	6/8 J	R10p156
BELLADRUM	113b5	7bL424	E	4/4 S	G6v2p48
BELLADRUM HOUSE	1453	5322	D	4/4 S	K2v1p17
BELLADRUM HOUSE	1353	5322	D	4/4 S	R10p102
BELLS O' LOCH LOMON	1133	115L5L	G	4/4	S9p16
BELLS OF DUBLIN BAY	1H125	1251	G	6/8	S9p16
BELTED PLAID AND HEALTH TO WEAR IT, THE	3535	357b7bL	E	2/2 R	R10p275
BELTED PLAID, THE	1215L	5L5L11	A	2/2	W1p13
BEN ALLIGEN	35L3L1	6L27L7L	F	2/2	S8v6p110
BEN LOMOND	5555	662H2H	D	4/4 S	K2v2p17 L8v2p8 Mc3v1p47 R10p90 S17p72
BEN NEVIS	1155	1152	D	4/4 S	K2v2p18 R10p102 S17p86
BEN NEWE	1H3H1H3	1H2H2H2	C	2/2	W1p23
BEN-A'CHIE	1535	5L27L2	Eb	2/2	W1p36
BENRINNES	51H1H5	7b427bL	D	4/4 S	G14p23
BETTY'S APRON	1L1L3bL3bL	5L3b11	A	4/4 QS	K2v4p17
BHA MI'N DUIL	1347L	1342	F	4/4	M10v2p14
BIDE YE YET	3134	3136	G	6/8	K2v1p32
BIG CAPTAIN OF CARTLEHAUGH, THE	1H51H6	5125L	D	4/4 S	S8v8p77
BIG KIRSTY	1H3bH7b5	6b47b5	E	4/4 S	K2v1p12
BILLY MACKINNON	5366	527L2	A	4/4 S	K2v4p6
BILLY'S REVERIE	1333H	1H652	D	4/4 S	S8v3p11
BIODAG AIR MAC ALASDAIR [MACALISTER WEARS A DIRK]	2532	317bL2	A	2/2 R	Mc3v1p15 R10p30
BIODAG AIR MAC THOMAIS [BIODAG AIN M' OMISH]	3331	2427bL	A	4/4*R	K2v1p18 Mc3v1p9 R10p8
BIODAG DHO'ILL 'IC ALASDAIR, OR GLENGARRY'S DIRK	5L3L1L5L	5L3L26L	A	4/4 S	R10p23
BIRK HALL	3115	3147bL	A	4/4 PS	Mc3v1p10
BIRK HALL	5H3H75	1H3H73H	C	4/4 R	L8v8Ap18
BIRKS OF ABERFELDIE, (THE) [BIRKS OF ABERGELDIE, THE]	131H1H	1H1H71H	D F	4/4 S	K2v3p4 L8v4p23 L8v8Ap22
BIRKS OF ABERFELDY	131H1H	1H1H2H2H	F	2/2 R	R10p209
BIRKS OF DELHANDY, THE	1354	4653	D	4/4	W1p29
BIRNAN HALL	3231	7675	D	6/8	W1p34
BIRTHDAY 1790, THE	131H6	22H75	D	2/4 S	G6v2p8
BISHOP, THE	1542	7bL427bL	A	4/4 S	G6v1p24
BISHOP'S MITRE, THE	1L5L13	16L6L2L	A	2/2	S8v6p98
BIT OF HEATHER, A	3422	1113	F	4/4	S8v8p168
BLACK BUT COMELY	1H3H53H	2H3H66	D	4/4 R	K2v2p18
BLACK BUT COMELY	1H3H53H	2H3H65	D	2/2*R	Mc3v1p52 R10p97 S17p159
BLACK CAT O' BENRINNES, THE	3651H	1H2H2H6	D	4/4 S	S8v3p5

Title			Key	Type	Sources
BLACK HAIR'D LAD, THE	11H7b6	7b47bL4	A	4/4 PR	Mc3v1p81
BLACK JOCK O' SKELLATER	1H73H6H	4H2H76	C	2/2 R	S8v3p45
BLACK SHEPHERDESS, THE	11H65	57b42	A	4/4 PR	Mc3v1p88
BLACK WATCH, THE	3431	37b27bL	A	2/4	S8v6p78
BLACKBIRDS, THE	1125	1125	A	2/4	S8v6p70
BLACKSMITH O' BOTRIPHNIE, THE	341H7L	3463H	F	2/4 R	S8v8p125
BLAIR ATHOLE	1115L	13b53b	A	4/4 R	K2v3p17
BLAIR ATHOLE	5L13b1	247b2	B	2/2	W1p23
BLAIR DRUMMOND	1315	1322	A	4/4 R	K2v1p16
BLAIR DRUMMOND	13b3b5	13b22	G	2/2 R	R10p200
BLAIRNANE'S RANT	3551H	2H2H66	D	4/4 S	Mc3v1p65 S8v3p12
BLANCHARD'S HORNPIPE	1H345	3345	D	4/4 HP	Mc3v1p172 M7p36
[FISHER'S HORNPIPE]					
BLIN' JAMIE	5631H	2H1H62	D	4/4 S	S8v7p2
BLOOMS OF BON-ACCORD, THE	3321	4432	A	2/4 A	S8v7p32 S8v8p156
[COCKERS ROSES]					
BLUE BELLS (OF SCOTLAND, THE)	1H756	3411	G	4/4*S	K2v4p13 S9p15
BLUE BONNETS	1111	6L6L63	Bb	6/8	S9p24
BLUE BONNETS OVER THE BORDER	1355	2466	A	2/2 R	Mc3v1p23 R10p24
BLUE BONNETS OVER THE BORDER	1L1L11	16L62	Bb	6/8	Mc3v1p162 R10p145
BOATIE ROWS, THE	3352H	5322	A	4/4 SC	K2v3p24
BOATMAN OF PITNACREE, THE	3H52H5	3H2H1H6	D	4/4 R	S17p48
BOB MORRIS	13L13	427L2	Bb	2/2 S	K2v4p18
BOB OF FETTERCAIRN, THE	5151	5575	G	4/4*R	K2v1p24 Mc3v1p99 R10p163
BOB SIMMS	316L5L	4L2L4L6L	G	4/5 R	K2v3p8
BOB WILLIAMSON	14#27L	6L15L3L	Bb	2/4 R	S8v8p127
BOBERS O' BRECHIN [BOBBERS OF BRECHIN]	51H1H5	47b54	G	4/4 R	L8v5p22 S17p160
BOG AN LOCHAN, or ATHOLE CUMMERS	1115	1124	E	4/4 S	L8v4p16 Mc3v1p90
BOG O' GIGHT, THE	5511	6L6L22	A	4/4 S	K2v2p4 Mc3v1p31 M7p26 R10p16
BOG OF RANNES, THE	1H565	1H562	E	6/8	W1p43
BOGANNACH, THE	13b54	247b4	B	2/2 R	Mc3v1p62
BOGNIEBRAE	5L131	5L132	A	4/4	S8v6p95 S8v7p8
BONFIRE, THE	5553b	7b427bL	G	4/4 S	R10p193
BONNETS O' BLUE	1H3H55	1H5H2H2H	D	6/8	K2v2p34
BONNIE ANN, THE	5531	4466	D	4/4	S8v6p12
BONNIE ANNIE	115L7bL	113b5	A	4/4*R	K2v2p9 G6v1p23 L8v8Bp21 Mc3v1p112 R10p43 S17p114
BONNIE ANNIE ANDERSON	5231H	64#1H5	D	4/4 S	S8v9/1
BONNIE BANCHORY	3155	3125H	A	2/4	S8v3p36 S8v7p46
BONNIE BANKS O' LOCH LOMOND	1113	226L5L	G	4/4	K2v3p45
BONNIE BESSIE LEE	5155	1H1H66	G	4/4 S	K2v3p9
BONNIE BIRKS OF BALMORAL, THE	331H5	6542	D	4/4 R	L8v8Ap7
BONNIE CHARLIE	136L5L	5532	A	4/4 S	K2v3p11 K2v4p16
BONNIE CHARLIE	1H3H65	31H2H2H	C	4/4 S	S8v3p46
BONNIE DOON	1232	315L2	G	6/8	K2v4p28
BONNIE DUNDEE	551H5	3322	G F	6/8	K2v2p34 S9p26
BONNIE DUNDEE	5556	2H755	A	2/2 R	K2v4p4
BONNIE GLENFARG	1255	6L7L33	A	12/8 A	S8v9/1
BONNIE KATE	51H65	1522	D	2/2 R	K2v4p7
BONNIE LASS O' BONACCORD, THE	1313L	1522	A	4/4 SS	Mc3v1p152 S8v6p28,9 S8v7p1 S8v8p2,3
BONNIE LASS OF BALLANTRAE, (THE)	5367	5326L	F	4/4*R	L8v1p18 L8v8Bp24 R10p206
BONNIE LOSSIE	3H1H76	5222	F	4/4 SS	S8v3p51
BONNIE NELLIE	3135	27bL24	A	2/2 R	S8v3p34
BONNIE PRINCE CHARLIE	3153	321H6	G	6/8	K2v4p28
BONNIE THACKIT HOOSIE, THE	5752	4651H	F	4/4	S8v8p159
BONNIE/BONNY LASS OF FISHERROW, (THE)	51H65	1526	C	4/4*R	K2v3p14 L8v4p19 R10p70
BONNY BROOM, THE	553b1	4427bL	E	4/4 S	K2v4p16
BONNY LASS O' ROTHIEMAY, THE	5L122	5522	G	4/4	W1p60
BONNY LASSIE O'	5313	51H62	Eb	2/2 R	R10p266
BONNY LINKS OF ABERDEEN, THE	1H535	22H2H6	Eb	2/2 R	G6v2p31
BONNY TOUN O' KENMORE, THE	5555	61H66	G	4/4 S	K2v3p8 R10p163
BONNY WEE THING	526L1	5245	A	4/4 SC	K2v3p23
BONNYBRIDGE	1H531	427L5L	A	4/4 S	K2v3p14
BONNYGATE FIDDLER, THE	1112	36L4L1	A	2/4	S8v6p100
BORLUM'S RANT	51H56	51H26	F	4/4 R	Mc3v1p146 S17p141
BOTHAN AIRIDH 'M BRAIGHE RAINEACH	57b6	541	G	3/4	Mc3v1p191
[SHIELING IN THE BRAES OF RANNOCH, THE]					
BOTHWELL CASTLE	3L5L3L1	3L5L7F2	Bb	4/4 S	Mc3v1p189
BOTTOM OF THE PUNCH BOWL, THE	111H1H	1H135	D	4/4*CD	Mc3v1p168 R10p148
BOTTOM OF THE PUNCHBOWL	11H1H3	22H2H5	D	2/4 R	K2v1p26
BOVAGLIE'S PLAID	6L5L13	4526L	A	4/4 SS	S8v5p21 S8v7p36 S8v8p5
BOW TO FATE	3bH1H1H1	3b57b5	C	4/4	S8v6p39
BOYS OF OUR TOWN, THE	1H651	4522	D	4/4 S	K2v4p11
BRAES ABOON BONAW	1555	1522	D	4/4 S	K2v1p9
BRAES O' AUCHTERTYRE, THE	1L1L3L5L	1315L	A	4/4 A	S8v7p37 S8v8p6
BRAES O' MAR REEL	1H1H1H3H	6662	D	4/4 R	M7p13
BRAES O' MAR, THE [OLD SET OF]	351H3H	1H61H6	D	4/4 SC	K2v1p19 Mc3v1p64 S9p10 R10p89
BRAES O' MAR, THE	351H3H	1H666	D	4/4 S	Mc3v1p63 M7p13 R10p85 S8v8p86
BRAES O' TULLYMET or BIRNIEBOOZLE	2555	2454	Bb G	4/4*S	M7p27 Mc3v1p134 R10p185

4

					S17p12
BRAES OF ATHOLE, THE	3236	3122	G	2/2 R	R10p301
BRAES OF AUCHTERTYRE, THE	1135	1H3H1H5	C	4/4*S	K2v1p14 L8v3p11 Mc3v1p106
					M7p5 R10p62
BRAES OF BALQUHITHER, THE [BALQUHIDDER]	3133	3132	G F	4/4*S	K2v1p11 L8v1p21 R10p212
BRAES OF ELCHIES, THE	51H3H1H	54H3H2H	C	6/8 J	G14p1
BRAES OF GLENDOCHERT [GLENDOCHART]	3565	2427bL	D	2/2 R	G6v1p6
BRAES OF LETTERFOURIE, THE	3546L	5L5L2L2L	A	4/4	W1p4
BRAES OF MARR	1111	2662	C	4/4 R	S17p157
BRAES OF MAR(R), THE	1H1H1H1H	6662	D	4/4*S	L8v3p6 R10p85
BRAES OF MARR, THE	1H1H1H1H	2H6H6H2H	D	4/4 R	K2v2p17
BRAES OF MAYEN, THE	3b27bL3bL	3b241	A	6/8	W1p13
BRAES OF MORVEN, THE	5L115L	4L5L2L4L	G	2/2	W1p65
BRAES OF NEWE, THE	136L5L	136L2	F	4/4	W1p50
BRAES OF RHYNIE, THE	1327L	1153	D	4/4	W1p30
BRAES OF TULIMET [BRAES OF TULLYMET]	1555	2454	E	4/4 SC	K2v1p19
BRAES OF TULLYMET	51H1H1H	57b1H7b	Bb	4/4 S	K2v2p23
BRAES OF TULLYMET	1555	2454	G	4/4	S9p9
BRANDLINGS	5153	5764	A	4/4*R	K2v3p13 R10p31
BRAVE LEWIE ROY	1H653H	1H651H	C	2/4	K2v3p45
BRAW LADS	5656	51H3H3H	D	4/4 S	K2v4p8
BREACAN MAIRI HUISTEAN	1321	11H65	C	4/4*	M10v1p6
[MARY HUISTEAN'S PLAID]					
BRECHIN CASTLE	1115	117L7L	Bb	4/4 S	S17p4
BRECHIN CASTLE	1115	1127L	Bb	4/4 S	K2v1p17 L8v1p22 L8v8Ap29
					Mc3v1p125 R10p278
BRECHIN LASSES	5L134	3427L	G	2/2 R	G6v2p17
BREEKS ARE LOOSE	3b3b3b1	3b227bL	G	12/8 J	R10p141
AND THE BUTTONS AWA', THE					
BREEM DOG, THE	1H3H62	1153	D	2/4 R	S8v8p81
BRIDE'S REEL, THE	1H36L7L	1H473H	D	2/4 R	S8v7p7 S8v8p72
BRIDGE OF ALFORD, THE	13bL13b	7bL27bL7bL	G	4/4	W1p67
BRIDGE OF BALLINDALLOCH (See			A	4/4	G14p10
CRAIG-AN-CHROCHAN)					
BRIDGE OF BAMORE	1L553	26L7L5L	A	2/2 R	R10p3
BRIDGE OF BANFF, THE	1L5L15L	2L4L2L7bF	A	2/2	W1p14
BRIDGE OF BRACKLIN, THE	6H1H3H1H	6H1H3H2H	C	4/4 R	S17p70
BRIDGE OF BRECHIN, THE	5L351H	547L2	F	4/4 S	K2v2p22 L8v6p20
BRIDGE OF BUCKET	5L5L5L1L	5L5L26L	A	2/2	W1p7
BRIDGE OF DEE	135L3	4522	D	4/4 R	L8v4p9
BRIDGE OF DEE	3542	4531H	D	4/4 S	L8v4p9
BRIDGE OF DEE, THE	3155	4542	C	4/4 S	G6v1p34
BRIDGE OF GAIRN, THE	316L5L	3562	D	4/4	W1p32
BRIDGE OF GARRY, THE	1535	2662	A	4/4*R	K2v2p5 R10p20
BRIDGE OF INVER, THE	15L3L1L	4L2L3L5L	Bb	2/2 R	Mc3v1p126 R10p286
BRIDGE OF LODI, THE	11H2H1H	3H4H3H2H	D	2/4	S9p28
BRIDGE OF NEWE, THE	41H3bH1H	5422	E	4/4	W1p44
BRIDGE OF PERTH, (THE)	1535	351H3	A	4/4*R	L8v1p5 R10p23
BRIDGE OF PERTH, THE	1536	351H3	A	4/4 R	S17p51
BRIDGE OF PERTH, THE	1546	531H3	A	4/4 R	Mc3v1p15
BRIDGE OF TURK, THE	3111	311H6	G	4/4 R	S17p73
BRIDGE OF YARE, THE	1H3H51H	62H72H	C	4/4 R	L8v8Bp16
BRIG O' ABOYNE	3561H	51H62	D	4/4 S	M7p12
BRIG O' BALGOWNIE, THE	11H63	11H62	F#	4/4 S	S8v5p15
BRIG O' BALLATER, THE	151H6	5H5H2H2H	C	4/4 S	G6v2p17 K2v2p11 Mc3v1p186
[BRIDGE OF BALLATER, THE]					R10p67
BRIG O' DEE	1353	4522	D	4/4 R	M7p12
BRIG O' DEE, THE	3542	3531H	D	4/4 S	K2v2p18 R10p93
BRIG O' DEE, THE	3542	4531H	D	4/4 S	M7p11 S8v8p73
BRIG O' FEUGH	1H3H72H	1H3H4H7	D	4/4 R	M7p12
BRIG O' FEUGH, THE	13bL13b	53b24	G	4/4 S	S8v3p57
BRIG O' KYLE, THE	1L5L5L3L	1342	A	4/4 S	K2v3p10
BRIG O' PERTH, THE	1565	331H3	A	4/4 SC	K2v1p20
BRIG O' PERTH, THE	1565	151H3	A	4/4 S	M7p19 K2v1p20
BRIG O' POTARCH, THE	3b15L3b	47b27bL	E	4/4	S8v6p86 S8v7p23
BRIG O' TILT, THE [BRIDGE OF TILT]	331H5	3342	D	4/4*R	K2v2p18 L8v6p10 Mc3v1p50
					R10p103
BRIOGAN SEAMBO	3564	3127bL	G	2/2 R	R10p158
BRISK BOB	3b55L1	3b53b7bL	B	4/4 S	L8v4p11 R10p130
BRISK BOB	3b53b1	3b53b7bL	B	4/4 S	K2v3p6
BRISTOL HORNPIPE	1H315	6212	A	4/4	S9p27
BRITANNIA THE PRIDE OF THE SEAS	127L0	1240	G	4/4 A	S8v3p19
BRITISH GRENADIERS, THE	1H1H3H2H	5H3H1H1H	C	2/4	S9p17
BRITISH PRESS, THE	15L3b1	3b543b	G	2/4	W1p67
BRODIE HOUSE	1H3H1H5	4642	F	4/4 R	S17p127
BRODIE OF BRODIE	5L15L1	5122	DD	4/4 S	R10p115
BROWN'S REEL, [OR DUILLATER HOUSE]*	1H3H2H6	6753	C	4/4*R	L8v2p17 R10p67
BROWN'S REEL	1L5L7L2	1231	Bb	4/4 R	Mc3v1p192
BRUCE'S LETTER BOX, HUNTLY	15L15L	7L322L	G	2/2 R	S8v5p14 S8v6p83
BRUCE'S MARCH	1321	1H632	D	4/4	S8v8p30
BUCK O' THE CABRACH, THE	3535	31H35	A	12/8	S8v7p28
BUCK OF THE CABRACH, THE	3565	11H2H2	D	2/2 R	R10p127

Title			Key	Time	References
BUCKINGHAM HOUSE or ATHOLE BROSE	3b15L1	3b145	D	4/4 S	G6v2p41 S8v8p118
BUCKINGHAM HOUSE [ATHOLE BROSE]	315L1	311H6	A	4/4 S	S8v7p10
BUCKS O' DROMORE	1H3H2H6	1H3H2H4H	D	4/4 R	K2v3p4
BUCKS OF CRANMORE	5356	5362	D	2/2 R	K2v4p9
BURN O' BUCKET, THE	363H2H	363H1H	D	2/4	S8v6p107
BURN O' CAIRNIE or MISS WEDDERBURN*	5L5L5L1	2226L	A	4/4 S	Mc3v1p7 M7p23
BURN O' FORGUE, THE	3L135	427L5L	A	2/2	S8v6p95
BURNIE O' AUCHRASK, THE	5L131	3126L	G A	4/4 SS	S8v5p18 S8v6p58
BURNIE, THE	1L132	1L14H3	A	2/4 R	S8v8p90
BURNS AND HIS HIGHLAND MARY	5155	25L22	D	4/4 SS	S8v5p4
BURNT LEG, THE	11H2H7b	7b2H1H7b	E	4/4 R	Mc3v1p71
BUSH IN BLOSSOM, THE	5326L	1361H	G	2/2 R	K2v4p15
BUT AND BEN	5311H	3H2H3H5H	D	4/4 S	K2v4p8
CA' HAWKIE THROUGH THE WATER or LORD ELPHINSTON	7b53b5	7b53b1	A	4/4 S	K2v2p10 R10p54
CA' THE STIRKS (FRAE OUT THE CORN)	1225	4215L	A	4/4 S	K2v2p10 L8v5p16 Mc3v1p114 R10p53
CA' THE WETHERS TO THE HILL	11H61H	11H24	A	4/4 S	K2v3p14
CABER FEIGH [CABAR FEIDH]	1H3H1H5	1H531	C	4/4 R	K2v1p14 L8v1p16 L8v8Bp17 Mc3v1p117 R10p60
CADGERS IN/(OF) THE CANONGATE, (THE)	1151H	51H22	G	4/4 S	K2v4p13 L8v5p10 Mc3v1p78
CAILLACH LIATH RASAR [GREY OLD LADY OF RAASAY, THE]	17b1H5	7b1H64	A	4/4 PR	Mc3v1p116
CAILLACH OIDHCHE	1565	7bL47b4	A	4/4 S	Mc3v1p6
CAILLICH ODHAR	5351	5331H	D	4/4 S	Mc3v1p46
CAIRDING O'T, THE	1133	51H51	A	4/4 R	K2v2p3
CAIRNGORM ["CHEAP MEAL"]	531H3	2662	D	4/4 R	K2v1p13 L8v6p7
CAIRNGORM (CHEAP MEAL)	521H2	2662	D	4/4 R	S17p163
CAIRNGORM, THE	3b175	3b3bH47L	G	2/4 R	S8v8p127
CAIRNTOUL	15L3L1L	4L5L6L7L	G	2/2	W1p61
CAISTEAL CHUIMRI	1H563	657L2	G	4/4 S	R10p165
CAITHNESS RANT, THE	1H7b41	3b3b7b3b	C	2/2 R	R10p271
CALABREA [CALABRIA]	51H3H2H	3H2H72H	F	4/4*R	L8v6p21 R10p227
CALEDONIAN HUNT, (THE)	31H65	4562	D	4/4 S	K2v1p13 Mc3v1p54
CALEDONIAN HUNT, THE	315L1	247b5	A	2/2 R	G6v1p3 Mc3v1p54
CALEDONIAN MARCH	5551H	3H3H3H2H	D	4/4	K2v1p49
CALEDONIA'S WAIL FOR NIEL GOW	3bL13bL5	7bL53bL7bL	B	4/4 SS	S8v8p11
CALLAM SHIARGHLAS	1H47L2	1H31H2H	F	4/4 S	S17p124
CALLER HERRING	117L1	327L6L	Bb	4/4	Mc3v1p162
CALLUM BROUGACH	7bL5L4L7bL	153b5	Am	4/4 S	L8v6p19
CALTON HILL	5L315L	6L426L	Bb	4/4 S	K2v3p21
CALUM A GHLINNE	5L153	6L31H6	F	6/8	M10v2p9
CALUM BREUGACH	7bL5L4L7bL	153b5	A	4/4 S	K2v2p10 Mc3v1p110 R10p52
CALUM FIGHEADAIR	3653	1H353	F	2/2 R	R10p230
CALVER LODGE	1H2H55	1142	D	2/4	K2v1p29
CAM' YE BY ATHOL	3153	321H6	D	6/8	K2v3p45
CAMERON HIGHLANDERS, THE	1165	1132	A	2/4	S8v6p79 S8v7p30
CAMERONIAN RANT, THE	3135	5153	A	4/4	S9p5
CAMERONIAN RANT, THE or BLACK WATER	5555	4445	F	2/4 R	S8v8p123
CAMERONIAN, THE	3553	3551H	G	2/2 R	K2v4p16
CAMERONIAN('S) RANT, THE	5153	5153	F G	4/4*R	K2v1p4 L8v2p21 L8v8Ap25 Mc3v1p143 R10p203 S17p79
CAMERON'S GOT HIS WIFE AGAIN	1H555	1H522	D	4/4 S	K2v1p10 L8v1p8 L8v8Bp9 Mc3v1p45 R10p84 S17p122
CAMPBELL OF DUNTROON'S WELCOME	331	445	G	3/4	M10v2p15
CAMPBELLS ARE COMING, THE	1533	1522	G	6/8	K2v1p32
CAMPBELLS ARE COMIN(G), THE	3533	3522	G	6/8 CD	M7p31 S9p22
CAMPSIE GLEN	3L5L6L5L	3L5L13	A	4/4 S	K2v3p14
CANTY AULD MAN, THE	1146	557L2	G	6/8	K2v1p33
CANTY CRECKET	51H51	51H72	D	2/2 R	G6v1p4
CANTY JEANIE MUNRO	316L5L	316L7L	B	4/4 S	S8v8p121
CAOIDH NA H-ALB AIRSON NEILL GHOBHA [CALEDONIA'S WAIL FOR NEIL GOW]	3bL1L3bL5L	7bL5L3bL7bF	B	4/4	Mc3v1p183
CAPE WRATH			D	4/4 S	S8v9/3
CAPt. BYNG	71H31	42H76	G	4/4 R	L8v8Ap15
CAPT. CAMPBELL	5L13b2	4L7bL23b	A	4/4 S	K2v1p9
CAPT. CAMPBELL OF CARPHEN	113b2	7bL7bL42	A	4/4 S	G6v1p46
CAPT. FIFE	1155	4326L	F	4/4 S	G6v1p36
CAPT. FRANCIS WEMYSS	31H61H	6522	D	4/4 S	G6v1p29
CAPT. HUGH MUNRO	1H6L5L3L	5L47L2	Eb	4/4 S	G6v2p31
CAPT. LOCKHART OF THE TARTAR	1H532	22H4H2H	C	4/4 R	G6v1p9
CAPT. McDUFF	3b53b5	27bL24	Bb	2/2 R	G6v1p17
CAPTAIN BARCLAY	1113	5555	A	4/4	S8v6p116
CAPTAIN BYNG	71H31	42H76	G	4/4 R	L8v1p11 Mc3v1p93
CAPTAIN BYNG	1H1H31	42H76	G	4/4 R	K2v2p14
CAPTAIN BYNG	71H31	42H75	G	2/2*R	R10p167 S17p98
CAPT[AIN] CAMPBELL	5L13b2	4L7bL23b	Am	4/4 S	L8v5p16 R10p51
CAPTAIN CHARLES LEITH HAY'S REEL	1H653	51H55	E	2/2	W1p40
CAPTAIN DAVID STEWART 42nd. R. HLRS.	11H35	27b22	D	2/2 R	R10p112
CAPTAIN ELPHINSTON	1515L	1153b	G	4/4 S	R10p134
CAPTAIN FIFE	1155	4326L	F	4/4 S	R10p238
CAPTAIN FRANCIS WEMYSS	31H61H	6522	D	4/4 S	K2v3p3

Title					
CAPTAIN FRANCIS WEMYSS DELIGHT	113b5	7b427bL	A	4/4 S	K2v3p18
CAPTAIN GEORGE HUNTER	5L13b1	5L13b1	B	4/4 S	R10p133
CAPTAIN GILLANS	5L5L5L1	3211	A	4/4 S	Mc3v1p27
CAPTAIN H. MUNRO	3b15L3b	427bL4	G	2/2 R	R10p303
CAPTAIN KEELER	1351H	137L2	G A Bb	4/4*R	K2v1p13 L8v3p19 Mc3v1p123
					M7p27 R10p186 S9p5 S17p42
CAPTAIN KENNEDY	1565	1H542	F	4/4 R	S17p16
CAPTAIN MACDUFF'S FAREWELL	513b5	2424	E	2/2 R	R10p263
CAPTAIN MAITLAND	1347L	1353	G	4/4 S	M7p8
CAPTAIN MCDUFF	5215L	1522	A	4/4*R	K2v2p20 Mc3v1p27 R10p22
					S17p61
CAPTAIN McKENZIE	13b43b	7bL27bL7bL	A	4/4 S	K2v4p17
CAPTAIN MENZIES	1123b	3b57b2	A	2/2 R	S8v3p42
CAPTAIN PRINGLE OF YAIR	5551H	3H4H2H2	D	4/4 S	S17p92
CAPTAIN ROBERTSON, LUDE[S]	5L135	51H46L	D	4/4 S	K2v3p5
CAPTAIN ROSS	5L5L26L	1353	A	4/4*R	K2v3p14 R10p22
CAPTAIN WHITE	11H2H6	5352	D	6/8	K2v1p28
CARDOWNIE	3531	7L27L5L	A	2/4	S8v6p107
CARLE HE CAM(E) O'ER THE CRAFT, THE	1133	7b422	A	4/4*R	L8v3p1 R10p20
CARLISLE LASSES	137L1	3535	F	4/4 S	R10p238
CARMICHAEL'S FANCY	3565	352H2	E	4/4 SS	S8v3p39
CARN DUBH	1353	7bL247bL	A	4/4 S	R10p14
CARNEGIE'S WELCOME TO SCOTLAND	3L5L13L	3L522L	A	4/4 M	S8v8p34
CARNIES CANTER	3564#	34#1H4	F	2/2 R	S8v3p52
CARNIE'S CANTER	3564#	34#1H4	F	2/2 R	Mc3v1p142 S8v3p52
CARRICK FERGUS	552H3H	5522	D	6/8 CD	M7p31
CARRICK'S RANT	1155	51H33	D	4/4 S	R10p104
CARRICK'S RANT or	1135	51H31	D	4/4 S	S8v8p87
SMITH'S A GALLANT FIREMAN, THE					
CARRON	5L13b1	4L7bL27bL	A	4/4 S	S8v3p43
CARRON WATER	5L47L6L	5L47L2	A	4/4 S	M7p19
CASAG LACHDUNN RUAIRDH RUAIDH	1211	7bL7b47bL	A	4/4 S	Mc3v1p81
[RED RODERICK'S DUN COAT]					
CASHMERE SHAWL, THE	1115L	5L13b2	A	2/2 R	K2v4p17
CASTLE FORBES	3b55L1	24L24	E	4/4	W1p46
CASTLE GORDON	311H6	437L2	A	4/4 QS	S8v8p32/3
CASTLE GRANT	2121	2532	A	4/4 QS	S8v8p44
CASTLE NEWE	315L3L	2L226L	A	4/4	W1p2
CASTLE SPYNIE	5431H	3H1H2H2	D	4/4 S	Mc3v1p56 S8v3p4
CATCH AND KISS THE ROMP	557b7b	3H5H6H3H	C	4/4*R	K2v3p16 R10p50
CATHERINE OGIE	2121	427bL2	Am	2/4	M10v2p28
CATHKIN BRAES	5L131	5L5L3L1L	A	4/4 SC	K2v3p23
CAT'S BACK, THE (STRATHPEFFER)	116L1	3632	A	2/4 HP	S8v5p21
CATTERTHUN	135L3L	6L275L	G	4/4 R	L8v4p12
CAULD KAIL	11H7b4	3b112	A	4/4 R	K2v3p18
CAWDOR FAIR	1H663	5555	D C	4/4	L8v1p9 Mc3v1p111 S7p81
CAWDOR FAIR	3bH1H1H5	7b7b7b7b	E	4/4 SC	K2v1p20
CAWDOR FAIR	3b115L	7bL7bL7bL7bL	A	4/4 S	R10p43
CEASE YOUR FUNNING	1131	447L5L	Bb	4/4 R	L8v5p19
CELEBRATED TYROLESE WALTZ, THE	135	51H1H	Eb	3/4	S15p3
CELTIC CHAIR, THE	1H347L	1H353	A	2/4	S8v6p103
CELTIC SOCIETY'S QUICKSTEP, THE	1335	1347bL	A	2/4	K2v3p46
CERES GREEN	1353	2223	A	4/4 S	Mc3v1p19
'CHAILLEACH MHUSGACH [DRUNKEN WIFE]	3524	3551H	A	2/2 R	R10p30
'CHAILLEACH ODHAR [DUNN CARLINE, THE]	5351	5331H	D	4/4 S	R10p85
CHAILLEACH OIDHCHE	1565	7bL47b4	A	4/4 S	K2v2p6 R10p35
'CHAILLEACH OIDHCHE	1565	7bL47b4	A	4/4 S	R10p35
CHALLENGE BREAKDOWN	5L133	5133	G	4/4 HP	M7p37
CHAMPION HORNPIPE	13b50	6b450	E	4/4 HP	M7p37
CHAMPION MARCH, THE [WILLIE MACLENNAN]	1355	5544	A	2/4 M	S8v8p36
CHA'N FHAOD CALLUM CARUCHADH	6535	6522	D	4/4	Mc3v1p184
[MALCOLM DARE NOT MOVE]					
CHA'N IOGHNADH NA GILLEAN	1H651	1H652	C	6/8	M10v1p6
CHARLES JOHN FORBES OF NEWE'S STR.	1L3L5L3L	5L46L2	A	4/4	W1p2
CHARLES LESLIE	1353	5353	D	4/4 S	K2v2p19 R10p114
CHARLESTOWN BREAKDOWN	1353	1761H	A	4/4 HP	M7p37
CHARLIE	1353	51H52	A	4/4 R	K2v4p3
CHARLIE HARDIE	5353	6464	E	2/2 R	S8v3p40
CHARLIE STUART	5244	5222	D	4/4*R	K2v2p17 L8v1p8 L8v8Ap10
[YOU'RE WELCOME CHARLIE STUART]					R10p90 S17p9
CHARLIE STUART	5344	5322	D	2/2 R	M7p17
CHARLOTTE'S REVERIE	1455	5122	A	6/8	S8v6p123
CHARMING MRS. DAVIDSON	351H5	462H6	D	4/4	S8v6p108
CHATIL MACCRIMMAN	5555	4422	A	6/8	M10v1p16
[CHA TILL MAC CRUIMEIN]					
CHEAP MEAL	521H2	2662	D	4/4*R	K2v1p12 L8v5p5 R10p103
CHIEFTAIN'S FROLIC, THE	3H52H2H	3H2H1H6	D	4/4 PR	L8v4p6
CHISHOLM, THE, OR	1115	1166L	F	4/4 S	R10p215
'S TOIGH LEAM FHEIN AN T-SIOSALACH					
CHORUS JIG, THE	3151	3156	D	6/8 J	L8v2p9 Mc3v1p58
CHORUS JIG, THE	4131	4136	D	4/4 R	Mc3v1p58
CHROMATIC HORNPIPE	5555	437L3b	G	2/4	S8v6p85

Title			Key		
CHUIR I GLUN AIR A' BHODACH	1425	1452	A	2/2 R	R10p45
CHUNNAIC MI ON(AN) DAMH DONN ...	3263	1H563	D	4/4	M10v1p3
C'ORSDAN MHOR	1H3bH7b5	6b47b5	E	4/4 S	R10p263
C'ORSDAN MHOR [MISS STEWART BUNRANNOCH]	1153	4253	E	2/2 R	R10p264
CIRCASSIAN CIRCLE	1111	2227L	A	2/4 CD	K2v1p26
CIRCASSIAN CIRCLE	1313	1313	A	4/4	M7p32
CIRCUS REEL	1H1H2H2H	1H1H2H2H	G	4/4 R	L8v3p22
CIRCUS, THE	5L131	436L6L	A	4/4 R	S17p128
CLACH NA CUDAIN	1315L	1363	D	4/4 S	K2v2p18
CLACH NA CUDAIN	1131	1363	D	4/4 S	R10p95
CLACH NA CUDAIN	1311	1363	D	4/4 S	Mc3v1p47
CLACHAN, THE	53H64H	53H72H	D	4/4 S	K2v4p10
CLACHNACUDDIN	1311	1353	D	4/4 S	M7p10
CLACH-NA-CUDDIN	1315L	1353	D	4/4 S	S8v7p6
CLAN CHATTAN	1211	4522	A	4/4 QS	S8v8p40
CLAN FRASER	13b15L	13b11	B	4/4 S	S8v5p22
CLAN MUNRO	1H531	6L5L7L2	A	4/4 S	S8v10p2
CLANRANALD	113b1	7b7bL24	E	2/2 R	Mc3v1p80 R10p263
CLANSMEN'S QUICK STEP, THE	5L3b11	53b42	A	2/4	W1p13
CLARENCE TOUGH	4#L35#4	7L2#25	Bb	2/4 HP	S8v8p138
CLASHNETTIE'S HORNPIPE	5353	1353	Eb	4/4	W1p37
CLEAN PEA(SE) STRAE	1H3H4H3H	2H57b2	D	4/4 R	K2v1p10
CLIFF HORNPIPE, THE	1516	51H3H5	D	4/4	S9p28
CLOCHNABEN*	3135	4322L	G	4/4 S	S8v5p18
CLOG DANCE	3bL3bL2L2L	1L11H0	B	4/4	S9p19
CLOG DANCE, A	1126L	1565	A	4/4	S9p19
CLOUD AND THE CHILL, THE	3b115L	3b53b2	A	6/8	S8v6p50
CLOUT THE CAULDRON	3263	3261H	C	4/4	S8v8p164
CLUNY CASTLE	137L6L	5L432	A	4/4 R	L8v8Ap3
CLUNY CASTLE, INVERNESS-SHIRE	1375	1622	D	4/4 A	S8v8p15
CLUNY MACPHERSON'S LAMENT	5561H	2H3H2H6	D	4/4	S8v8p148
CLUNY ROCK	1H1H64	2466	A	2/2 R	R10p35
CLUNY WATER	3565	2H3H66	C	4/4	W1p24
CLUNY'S GOLDEN WEDDING	1L5L5L5L	5L15L5L	A	4/4 SS	S8v5p5 S8v6p115
CLYDESDALE LASSES [CLYDE SIDE LASSES]	3565	3535	F	4/4*R	K2v1p14 L8v3p15 L8v8Ap26
					Mc3v1p139 R10p204 S9p6 S17p3
COCK O' BENDY	1H663	5555	C	4/4 S	M7p7
COCK O' THE NORTH, THE	3336	3325	G	6/8	K2v2p34
COCK OF THE NORTH, THE	11L5L3L	13L21	Bb	4/4 S	Mc3v1p192 R10p282
COIL-A-CREICH INN, DEESIDE	1H1H2H4	1H1H3bH3bH	C	2/2	W1p26
COILANTOGLE [COILLE AN TOGAIL OR	5L127bL	5L121H	G	4/4 S	R10p188 S17p98
CHEAP MUTTON]					
COIRECHOILLE	5L13b2	2247bL	B	2/2 R	R10p129
COIRSDAN MHOR or	1153	4253	G	2/2 R	Mc3v1p85
MISS STEWART BUN RANNOCH					
COL. CALL'S STRATHSPEY	1316L	512L2L	A	2/2	W1p10
COL. FARQUHARSON OF INVERCAULD'S STR.	5L3b53b	5L3b53b	D	4/4	W1p34
COL H. F. CAMPBELL	3555	6525L	G	4/4 S	G6v2p16
COLBECK HOUSE	3531H	3542	C	2/2 CD	R10p154
COLIN CAMPBELL	5353	5366	G	4/4 S	K2v4p14
COLLAR GREEN	3b3b3b1	7bL27b7b	G	2/2 R	R10p194
COLLEGE HORNPIPE, THE	1H131H	2H275	Bb	2/4	S9p27
COLLEGE (HORNPIPE), (THE)	11L1L5L	3L113	Bb	4/4*HP	Mc3v1p173 R10p299 S8v7p44
					S8v8p136/7
COLLIER'S DAUGHTER, THE	3115L	7bL7bL24	G	2/2 S	G6v1p7
COLONEL BAIRD	1H13b5	243b2	E	4/4 S	R10p247
COLONEL CRAWFURD'S REEL	13L13L	2426L	F	2/2 S	G6v1p12
COLONEL FORBES C.B.	3543	3H1H22	C	4/4 S	S8v3p45
COLONEL FRASER OF KNOCKY	5315	4362	G	4/4 S	Mc3v1p97 R10p171
COLONEL JACKSON	5L155	437L6L	A	2/4	S8v6p114
COLONEL MCBAIN [COLONEL MACBEAN]	3b13b5	27bL24	Gm	4/4*R	L8v3p20 Mc3v1p135 R10p185
					S17p6
COLONEL MONTGOMERY	1H522	1H526L	D	4/4 S	R10p91
COLONEL ROBERTSON	5551	457bL4	E	4/4 S	R10p156
COLONEL SMITH'S LAMENT	1456	5652	A	4/4	S8v8p148
COLONEL THORNTON	1L5L3bL3bL	2L4L5L4L	A C	4/4 R	Mc3v1p104 R10p67
COLONEL WEMYSS	1335	357L2	F	2/2 R	R10p233
COLOSSEUM, THE	1112	3334	A	4/4	S9p28
COLQUHALZIE FIR TREES	1353	51H53	G	4/4 S	K2v3p7 R10p181
COME AGAIN	116L6L	116L2	A	4/4	P3p17
COME ALONG AND KEEP YOUR PROMISE	5315	5336	Eb	4/4 S	R10p267
COME LET US DANCE AND SING	1H3H3H1H	62H75	D	2/4	K2v1p29
COME UNDER MY PLAIDIE·	5353	5316L	G	6/8	K2v1p49
COMELY GARDEN	331H5	67b27bL	A	2/2 R	R10p13
COMELY GARDEN	331H5	6727L	A	4/4 R	Mc3v1p17
COMIN' THRO' KILBLEEN	116L5L	4L5L6L2L	Bb	4/4	W1p17
COMIN' THRO' THE RYE	5L5L22	5L6L11	A	4/4 S	K2v4p3
COMING THROW THE BROOM MY JO	123b5	47b15L	A	4/4 S	G6v1p23
COMPOSER'S FAREWELL	3L4L7L1	4631	A	4/4	S8v8p182
COOKIE SHINE	5357	5353	F	4/4 R	K2v3p20
COOPERS	31H1H7	72H2H1H	D	2/2 HP	R10p296
COPPERBEECH, THE	1H5H6H6H	1H5H73H	E	2/4 R	S8v8p120

Title					
CORDUROY, THE	3313	5551H	A	4/4 S	K2v3p10
CORGARFF CASTLE	15L3bL1L	7bL4L2L2	G	4/4 A	S8v7p39
CORGARFF CASTLE	1L5L6L5L	1L5L47	A	4/4	W1p3
CORHABBIE	1L115L	7bL4L2L7bF	A	2/2 R	G14p6
CORIMONIE'S RANT	551H5	5524	D	4/4 S	K2v2p17 L8v3p5 L8v8Bp7
CORIMONIE'S RANT [CORIEMONIE'S RANT]	151H5	1524	D G	4/4 S	G6v1p6 R10p90 S17p136
CORN CUTTER, THE	1H11H7	2H22H1H	C	4/4 R	K2v2p13 L8v3p12
CORN RIGGS [CORN RIGS]	1H1H3H2H	772H5	D	4/4 R	K2v1p24 S9p4
CORN RIGS	1142	7L7L25L	G	2/2 CD	R10p148
CORN RIGS	147L2	1315	G	2/4	M7p30
CORRIEGILLS	5L5L5L1	3426L	A	4/4 S	K2v3p13
CORRIMONY	5L3L1L3L	5L3L6L3L	A	4/4 S	K2v2p7
CORTES GARDENS	13b53b	5L3b27bL	E	4/4 S	S8v7p14 S8v8p65
COSSACK, THE	31H31H	72H75	F	2/2 CD	S15p21
COTTAGE HYMN, A	115L	123	Eb	3/4	P3p9
COTTAR'S WIFE, THE	1551H	57b27bL	D	2/2 R	R10p99
COULL O' NEWE	351H5	4522	D	4/4	S8v6p90
COUNT D'ARTOIS	3H2H65	5565	C	4/4*R	K2v3p15 R10p78
COUNTESS OF CRAWFORD, THE	125L3L	1L3L5L5L	A	4/4 S	M7p23
COUNTESS OF AIRLY	5353	6527L	G	4/4 S	G6v1p31
COUNTESS OF BREADALBANE	113L5L	4L226L	Bb	2/2 R	G6v2p30
COUNTESS OF BREADALBANE	113L1L	4L6L4L2	Bb	4/4 S	R10p294
COUNTESS OF CASSILLIS	5L1L5L5L	1322L	A	2/2 R	R10p29
COUNTESS OF DALHOUSIE	551H2H	6542	F	4/4 S	Mc3v1p149 R10p226
COUNTESS OF ELGIN, THE	1H535	2463H	D	4/4 R	S17p135
COUNTESS OF FIFE'S STRATHSPEY, THE	3L5L22	1422L	A	4/4	W1p8
COUNTESS OF HADDINGTON, THE	31H31H	6622H	C	4/4 R	S17p108
COUNTESS OF HADDINGTON, THE	3L13L1	6L5L2L2	Bb	4/4 S	Mc3v1p132
COUNTESS OF LOUDON, THE	5555	5562	Bb	4/4 S	S17p2
COUNTESS OF PERCY, THE	51H3H2H	3H2H62H	D	2/2 R	G6v1p5
COUNTESS OF ROTHES, (THE)	1531H	2646	F	4/4 S	G6v2p23 Mc3v1p188 R10p232
COUNTESS OF SEAFIELD'S STRATHSPEY	1L5L5L5L	4322L	A	4/4	W1p6
COUNTESS OF SUTHERLAND, THE	1H565	4322H	C	4/4 R	S17p19
COUNTESS OF SUTHERLAND, (THE) [LADY HAMILTON]	15L6L5L	4L3L2L2	Bb	4/4*R	K2v3p20 L8v2p23 Mc3v1p148 R10p288
COUNTESS OF SUTHERLAND, THE	3b11H3bH	7b521	D	2/2 R	G6v1p21
COUNTRY DANCE	5321	5321	A	2/4 CD	K2v1p21
COUNTRY DANCE	156L5L	5L432	A	6/8	K2v1p27
COUNTRY LASSES	131H3	61H51	Bb	4/4 R	K2v3p20
COUNTY HALL	13b43b	2427bL	G	2/2 R	R10p199
COUTIE'S WEDDING [CUTTIE'S WEDDING]	13b53b	13b53b	A	4/4 S	K2v3p17 M7p7 R10p57 S17p90
CRADLE SONG, THE	1256	5530	A D	4/4	S8v6p27 S8v7p36 S8v8p1 S8v8p166
CRAIG A CHAIT	3H1H51H	4H2H62H	D	2/4	S8v6p76
CRAIG A CHROCHAN OR BRIDGE OF BALLINDALLOCH	515L1L	5L1L6L2	A	4/4 S	G14p10
CRAIG CHATTAN	53H2H1H	51H76	D	4/4	S8v8p164
CRAIG COYNACH	5L13b1	2454	A	4/4	W1p14
CRAIG ELLACHIE BRIDGE	1L5L6L6L	5L5L2L2L	Bb	2/2 S	S15p25
CRAIG OF BARNS, THE	5411	4442	A G	4/4 SC	K2v1p19 Mc3v1p133 R10p192
CRAIGELLACHIE BRIDGE	131H3	27b44	D	4/4 S	K2v1p12 L8v3p4 Mc3v1p32 R10p98
CRAIGENDORAN	5363	1H3H1H1H	G	4/4 S	K2v4p15
CRAIGENROAN	1H3H1H6	652H2H	C	2/2	W1p25
CRAIG-GOWAN REEL	1H1H1H3H	4H3H72H	C	4/4	B9p3
CRAIGIE HALL	5642	5651H	D	4/4 S	L8v8Ap11 R10p110
CRAIGLUG BRIG	5313	3555	A	4/4 S	M7p22
CRAIG-ROY	1466	5126L	G	4/4	P3p12
CRAIL	1352	11H1H6	D	4/4 S	K2v4p9
CRARAE	351H1H	3H4H2H6	D	4/4 R	K2v3p6
CREAG NA POLLAICH	1331H	137L2	C	4/4 S	R10p65
CREAKING DOOR, THE	5532	1352	A	4/4	S8v6p21
CRIEFF FAIR	5553b	7b7b7b7b	D	4/4 S	R10p244
CRIEFF MEETING, THE	5511H	2427bL	A	2/2*R	G6v1p26 K2v3p14
CRIPPLE BRIGADE, THE	3131H	6225	Bb	2/4 HP	S8v5p19
CROALL'S	13b51H	523b1	B	4/4 S	S8v8p79
CRONAN NA LINNE MHUILICH [SOUND OF MULL]	5122	111H6	A	2/2 R	R10p45
CROPIE'S STRATHSPEY	5L17L2	1566	G	4/4 S	M7p8
CROQUET GREEN, THE	1152	6L5L7L2	Bb	4/4 R	S8v3p55
CROSS OF INVERNESS, THE	5L3L6L4L	427L1	G	4/4*R	K2v3p7 Mc3v1p77 R10p179
CROUGHLY	511H3bH1H	2H7b5H7b	D	4/4 S	R10p242
CROWHILLOCK	1153	5L5L47L	A	4/4 S	G6v2p2
CUFFE ST.	5152	7b47bL4	E	2/2 R	K2v4p13
CUIR A CHINN DILEAS [TURN ROUND THY FAITHFUL HEAD]	561H1H	51H66L	A	6/8	M10v1p1
CUIR I GLUN AIR A BHODACH	1425	1452	A	2/2 R	Mc3v1p119
CUIR SA CHISTE MHOIR MI or MISS CRUIKSHANK'S REEL	5L144	5226L	Bb	2/2 R	Mc3v1p137
CULLEN HOUSE	5551H	5542	D	4/4 R	K2v1p17 K2v2p19
CULLEN OF BUCHAN	4L1L3bL1L	4L1L7bL7bL	A	4/4	P3p10
CULLODEN DAY	3b213b	1H557b	A	2/2	K2v3p46

Title					
CULLODEN DAY or INVERNESS GATHERING, THE	411H5	7b7bL7b4	A	2/4 QS	S8v7p33 S8v8p43
CULLODEN HOUSE	11H51H	7b525	C	4/4 S	R10p272
CUMBERLAND REEL	3H1H1H5	4235	D	6/8	K2v1p27
CUMBERLAND, THE OR MISS GIBSON	11H52	7L232	Bb	2/2 R	R10p278
CURRANT BUSH, THE	13b51H	6b1H53b	G	4/4 R	K2v3p22
CURRIE'S RAMBLES	1353	761H1H	D	4/4 S	M7p15 S8v8p81
CURRIE'S RAMBLES	1353	671H1H	D	4/4 SS	S8v7p12
CUT AND COME AGAIN	11H1H4	22H2H6	C	4/4 R	L8v5p13
CUT AND DRY	3135	247bL2	A	4/4 S	K2v2p6 R10p26
CUT AND DRY	3333	1H315	G	4/4 S	K2v3p7 L8v6p15
CUT HIM DOWN SHUSIE [CUT HIM DOWN SUSIE]	5124	5151H	D	4/4 S	G6v1p4 R10p92
CUTTING FERNS	11H7b7b	527bL2	A	4/4 S	K2v1p18 Mc3v1p105 R10p58
CUTTY CLAY	5553	572H7	F	2/2 R	K2v4p18
CUTTY SARK	1315L	1353	G	4/4 R	K2v1p8 L8v1p12 Mc3v1p92
CUTTYMAN AND TRELADLE [CUTTYMUN AND TREELADLE]	3553	3542	A	4/4 R	K2v1p18 S17p153
CUTTYMUN AND TREELADLE	5553	5542	A	2/2 R	R10p27
D. MORISON'S SEVEN THISTLES	5L3L1L3L	5L35L3L	A	4/4 QS	S8v9/2
DAFT WILLIE DAWSON	315L1	3131	D	4/4 S	K2v3p5 L8v1p10 L8v8Bp6
DAINTY DAVIE [DAINTIE DAVIE]	5311	1313	F D	4/4 S	K2v1p4 L8v1p18 L8v8Ap22 Mc3v1p143 R10p209 S17p102
DALDOWNYS	31H36	3155	A	4/4 PR	Mc3v1p12
DALKEITH HOUSE	1H51H3	42H75	D	2/2*R	R10p111 S17p83
DALKEITH'S LAMENT	13b51	5427bL	A	6/8	S8v6p74
DALRY HOUSE	1535	6542	D	4/4 S	R10p106 S17p76
DALWHINNIE	5L13b5	7b427bL	A	4/4 S	L8v8Bp22
DAN DEIRG	57b51	57b51	D	4/4	M10v2p9
DANDALEITH	5551	6662	D	4/4	S8v6p92
DANDY DINMONT	5551	7b425	Em	4/4 S	L8v4p17
DARGAI	3235	3236L	A	6/8	S8v7p42 S8v8p146
DARK HAIR'D MARY	117bL2	5147bL	A	4/4 S	K2v3p9
DARK HAIRED YOUTH, THE	116L1	5563	G	6/8	K2v1p48
DARLING ANNIE	113L1	3216L	A	4/4 R	L8v6p3
DARLING, THE	553b1	551H1H	F#	4/4 S	R10p129
DASHING WHITE SERGEANT	1155	1H562	D F G	2/4	K2v1p30 M7p31 R10p150 S9p18
DAVID ADAMS	17L47L	1253	A	2/4 R	S8v7p9
DAVIE COURAGE	131H5	227L5L	D	4/4 S	S8v10p11
DAVIE TAYLOR	15L15L	3L122L	G	4/4 S	S8v7p14
DAVIE WORK	17L47L	1H643	A	2/4 R	S8v7p9
DAWTED MARY	5L3b3b1H	7b422	B	4/4 S	R10p132
DAYS THAT WE HA'E SEEN, THE	1133	3332	G	4/4	P3p13
DEAN BRIG OF EDINBURGH, THE or MISS GRAY OF CARSE	5553	1115L	Eb	4/4 S	M7p28 S8v7p40 S8v8p20
DEAN BRIG REEL	1363	1366	Eb	2/2 R	M7p28
DEAN, THE	5431H	6523H	D	2/2 R	S8v3p11
DEAR AULD HA', THE	5767	5250	Db	4/4	S8v8p165
DEATH AND DR. HORNBROOK	51H61H	51H62H	D	12/8 J	S8v5p7
DEE CASTLE	5335	6562	A	2/2 R	S8v5p9 S8v6p96
DEER FOREST, THE	51H7b5	7b545	D	2/2 R	R10p229
DEIL AMANG THE TAILORS, THE [DEIL AMONG THE TAILORS, (THE)]	1H51H5	1H564	A	4/4*R	K2v1p6 L8v3p2 L8v8Ap5 Mc3v1p4 R10p11 S8v7p29 S17p28
DEIL AMONG THE TAILORS	5757	5764	F	4/4	S9p4
DEIL AMONG THE TAILORS, THE	1H1H1H6	4447	A	2/4 R	S8v8p108/9
DEIL O' BALDARROCH, THE	3213L	6L17L7L	Bb	2/2 R	S8v3p61
DEIL TAK THE BREEKS	1H71H3	61H53	D	2/2 R	R10p100
DELLAGYLE POOL	3b3b27bL	3b3b3b1H	G	2/2 R	G14p30
DELNABO	13b53b	43b27bL	E	4/4 S	S8v7p49 S8v8p64
DELNADAMPH LODGE	3115L	3562	A	2/2	W1p4
DELRACHNIE'S RANT	1322	136L6L	G	4/4	W1p58
DELVIN HOUSE	1H51H5	22H75	C	4/4 R	L8v2p17
DELVIN HOUSE	1H51H5	22H76	C	4/4 S	K2v2p13 L8v8Ap19 Mc3v1p118 S17p97
DELVIN SIDE	17b7b5	7b7b7b4	E	4/4 S	S17p106
DELVIN SIDE	17b55	17b7b4	E	4/4 S	K2v1p6 L8v2p13 L8v8Ap17 Mc3v1p83 S9p7
DELVIN SIDE	1133	1H51H5	D	2/2 R	K2v4p10
DELVINE SIDE	17b55	57b7b4	E	4/4 S	R10p246 S8v8p62/3
DER FREYSCHUTZ WALTZ	6H3H1H	6H3H1H	D	3/4 W	K2v1p25
DERNCLEUCH	3455	3211	D	4/4 SS	S8v5p25
DERVAIG MEDLEY, THE	5531H	5552	D	6/8	R10p138
DESKRYSHIEL	5L13b1	427b2	E	2/2	W1p44
DEUKS DANG O'ER MY DADDIE, THE	1H326	1H331	D	6/8 CD	R10p146
DEVERON SIDE	5364	51H42	A	4/4 R	M7p19
DEVERONSIDE	5L121	6L27L5L	G	4/4	S8v6p109
DEVIL AND THE DIRK, THE	1557L	1553	D	2/4 R	S8v8p84/5
DEVIL AND THE DIRK, THE	1351H	537L2	D	2/2 R	S8v7p3
DEVIL IN THE KITCHEN, THE	5157b	517b5	A	4/4 PS	S8v8p115
DEVIL IN THE KITCHEN, THE or PRINCE OF WALES JIG, THE	5113	517b5	A	4/4 S	S8v7p11

DEVIL'S DREAM, THE	1H1H1H1H	61H64	A	4/4 R	K2v4p6
DEVIL'S ELBOW, THE	1H61H6	1H643	D	2/4 R	S8v9/3
DHU HILL, THE	1544	51H51	F#	6/8	K2v4p27
DIAMOND, THE	3b3b6b7b	557b2	G Bb	4/4 R	L8v6p23 S17p46
DIAMOND, THE	3b6b57b	16bL4L1	G	2/4 HP	S8v8p135
DOCHGARROCH LODGE	5H3H5H3H	4H2H75	C	4/4 S	S8v3p43
DOCTOR PROFEIT'S STRATHSPEY	1111L	3L5L11	Bb	4/4	W1p16
DOCTOR, THE	13L5L6	13L53	G	2/4 R	S8v8p56
DOCTOR, THE [MISS JANE STEWART]	15L3L1L	4522	Bb	4/4 R	Mc3v1p122 R10p281
DOD HOUSE	1L5L13	16L22L	A	4/4 S	G6v1p27
DOGGIE, THE	51H65	4522	D	4/4	S8v6p94
DOGS BITE CHAPMEN	6527bL	651H1	D	4/4 R	L8v5p5
DOGS BITE CHAPMEN	3H2H64	3H2H5H5	D	4/4*R	Mc3v1p43 R10p99
DOLLS' LEVEE, THE	325L7L	4313	A	4/4	S8v6p59
DOMHNULL CLEIREACH	3152	311H1H	D	4/4 S	R10p117
DOMINIE'S DELIGHT, THE	13b53b	7bL242	E	4/4 S	S8v3p17
DON SIDE	1326L	1323	G	4/4 S	K2v2p15 L8v2p11 Mc3v1p93 R10p166 S17p132
DONALBANE	5535	1365	A	4/4 S	K2v4p4
DONALD DINNIE	5L343	3H5H52	D	4/4	S8v6p91
DONALD DOW	5651	51H52	F	4/4 S	S17p44
DONALD MACGUGAN'S RANT	1H1H1H1H	661H5	D	4/4*R	K2v2p18 Mc3v1p51 R10p107
DONALD MACPHERSON'S LAMENT	3H2H3H2H	1H52H2H	D	4/4	S8v8p147
DONALD McGREGOR	1H323	1H322	C	2/4	S9p4
DONALD QUAICH	3b524	3b51H5	A	4/4*R	K2v2p9 R10p48
DONALD THE PIPER*	131H3	1H642	D	2/2 R	S8v10p14
DONALD TO YOUR SOALS	5L111	5L111	A	4/4 S	K2v3p8
DONSIDE LASSES, THE	5L3L5L1	5L5L6L2L	A	2/2	W1p2
DOON BY THE BURN	5634	5133	F	4/4	S8v6p17
DOON THE WATER	3333	3333	A	2/2 R	K2v4p6
DORNOCH LINKS	5351	5362	A	2/4	K2v1p48
DORSINCILLY	11L5L1	22L7L5L	A	4/4 S	S8v8p98/9
DOUBLE KISSES	1H51H2H	1H52H2	C	2/2 R	Mc3v1p120 R10p66
DOUGAL CREATURE, THE	5151	5162	D	6/8 J	L8v4p9
DOUGAL MORE	3561H	72H1H1H	D	4/4 S	K2v4p8
DOUGLAS	11H1H7	2H51H1H	C	2/2 HP	R10p299
DOUN THE BURNIE	1H3H1H5	2H4H2H6	C	4/4 R	K2v3p16
DOUNE OF INVERNOUGHTY, THE	51H3bH2H	1H7b47bL	E	2/2	W1p47
DOVE COT, THE	3451	117L2	A	4/4 A	S8v7p30 S8v8p160/1
DOWN THE BURN DAVIE LAD	3H1H52	351H1H	D	4/4 A	Mc3v1p182
DR. BAIRD	11L3L5L	1135	A	4/4 S	S8v7p28
Dr. CAMERON'S STRATHSPEY	13b53b	53b42	D	4/4	W1p35
DR. GORDON STABLES(' REEL)	11H62	3H643	D	2/4 R	S8v7p7 S8v8p76
DR. GREGORY GRANT	5126L	5566	D	4/4 S	R10p124
DR. KEITH, ABERDEEN	31H53	6542	F	4/4 S	Mc3v1p142 S8v3p52
DR. MACDONALD	11H51	4532	A	4/4	S8v6p66
DR. MACDONALD'S COMPLIMENTS TO MR. JAMES SCOTT SKINNER	1L3L6L3L	6L216L	G	4/4 S	Mc3v1p94
DR. MAITLAND MOIR	3565	3H562	D	4/4 S	S8v5p6
DR. MANSON	5L122	51H2H6	D	4/4 S	S8v3p15
DR. MANSON OF SPYNIE	13b57b	47b47bL	D	4/4 S	R10p243
Dr. MARSHALL'S HORNPIPE	1353	1H1H64	D	4/4	W1p33
DR. McHARDY	3135	1H636	D	4/4 S	S8v8p80
DR. PROFEIT	15L31	357L2	Bb	4/4 SS	S8v3p60
DR PROFEIT'S STRATHSPEY	31H61H	31H66	C	4/4	B9p2
Dr. ROBERTSON'S REEL	3H1H1H5	532H2	C	2/2	W1p24
DR. SHAW	1351H	7b427bL	D	4/4 S	S8v8p89
DR. SHAW	15L27L	1H4#6L3	A	2/4 R	S8v8p101
DR. WHYTE	15L5L1	227L2	A	4/4 S	S8v3p31
DRAW THE SWORD [FOR] SCOTLAND	3351H	61H51H	G	4/4 R	K2v1p24
DREAM OF LOVE AT LUMSDEN, A	526L1	61H55	F	2/4	S8v6p11
DRIVE HOME THE MAINLANDERS	16b13b	2454	B	2/2 R	K2v4p12
DROGHEDA LASSES	53b13b	427bL2	E	2/2 R	K2v4p8
DROPS OF BRANDY	533	534	G	9/8	S9p25
DROVER LADS, THE [GILLEAN AN DROVER]	11H2H1H	5353	G	6/8	Mc3v1p176
DROVER, THE	3331	3335	D	4/4 S	S8v3p6
DROWN DROUTH	3L13L	3L4L2L	Bb	9/8	G6v1p14
DROWSY MAGGIE	513b5	5154	E	2/2 R	K2v4p12
DRUIM-UACHDAIR	5353	5335	G	2/2 R	R10p159
DRUMIN	11H51	4647L	D	4/4 S	S8v7p6 S8v8p72
DRUMINS	1516	5542	D	4/4 S	K2v2p19 R10p127
DRUMMER, THE	13b5L5L	5L111	A	2/2 R	Mc3v1p111
DRUMMER(S), THE	13b5L5L	7bL247bL	A	4/4*R	K2v1p8 L8v2p20 R10p43 S17p17
DRUMMOND CASTLE	11H1H7b	57b7bL4	A	6/8	K2v4p28
DRUMMOND'S RANT	3565	3524	A	2/2 R	R10p59
DRUMMUIR CASTLE	5431H	7b527bL	A	4/4 QS	S8v8p44
DRUMNAGARRY [cf: FISHER'S RANT]	13L3L1	6L7L16L	G	4/4 S	Mc3v1p74 M7p8
DRUMSHEUGH	311H1H	2H2H22	D	4/4 S	G6v1p5
DRUNKEN PARSON, THE	1234	5431	G	6/8	K2v1p29
DRUNKEN WIVES OF FOCHABERS	113b5	446b5	D	4/4 S	R10p199
DUBH CHNOCAN	3155	1H52H2	D	2/2 R	R10p97
DUBLIN LASSES	74H2H3H	1H3H2H5	D	4/4 R	M7p16

Name					References
DUCHESS OF HAMILTON, THE	317L2	313L1L	G	4/4 S	K2v2p14
DUCHESS OF ATHOLE	5L326L	5L353	A	4/4 S	K2v1p15
DUCHESS OF ATHOLE'S FAVOURITE, THE	11L13	11L2L2	A	6/8	Mc3v1p154
DUCHESS OF ATHOLE'S REEL, THE	3b115L	7bL27bL7bL	B	2/2	W1p20
DUCHESS OF ATHOLE('S SLIPPER, THE)	5L353	5L36L2	F G	4/4*S	G6v2p21 K2v2p21 L8v1p20
[DUCHESS'(S) SLIPPER, THE]					L8v8p26 Mc3v1p77 Mc3v1p145
					M7p7 R10p180 S17p68
DUCHESS OF BEDFORD	1133	6522	F	2/2 R	R10p213
DUCHESS OF BEDFORD'S STRATHSPEY, THE	1L115L	2245L	Bb	4/4 S	Mc3v1p163
DUCHESS OF BUCCLEUCH, THE	5L6L5L3L	5L15L5L	Bb	4/4 S	K2v4p18
DUCHESS OF BUCCLEUGH, THE	311H1	27bL44	A	4/4 S	Mc3v1p17
DUCHESS OF GORDON	5551	5524	E	4/4 S	R10p275 S17p60
DUCHESS OF GORDON, THE	5551	5424	D	4/4 S	L8v2p6
DUCHESS OF GORDON, THE	1L5L4L5L	6L247L	A	4/4 S	S17p22
DUCHESS OF GORDON, THE	5551	5562	D	4/4 S	K2v2p17 Mc3v1p66 R10p106
DUCHESS OF GORDON, THE	1552	1127bL	G	4/4 S	R10p202
DUCHESS OF HAMILTON	317bL2	313L1L	G	4/4 S	R10p161
DUCHESS OF HAMILTON, THE	317L2	313L1L	G	4/4 S	Mc3v1p96 S17p120
DUCHESS OF MANCHESTER, THE	1133	6522	F	4/4 S	Mc3v1p140 S17p156
[LADY GEORGINA GORDON]					
DUCHESS OF RICHMOND'S REEL, THE	1H1H31	4362	E	2/2	W1p39
DUCHESS OF ROXBURGHE, THE	3bH3bH1H1H	3bH1H2H4H	D	4/4 R	S17p1
DUCHESS TREE, THE	3332	46L6L7L	Ab	4/4	S8v6p24
DUCHESS TREE, THE	3H3H3H2H	4H667	A	4/4 A	S8v7p36
DUFF OF MUIRTOWN	3342	31H2H6	G	2/2 R	R10p183
DUILLATER HOUSE	1H3H2H6	6753	C	4/4 R	S17p36
DUKE OF ATHOLE(, THE)	1111	7bL7bL47bL	A	4/4 S	K2v3p17 R10p54
DUKE OF ATHOLE'S STRATHSPEY, THE	1L3bL5L5L	5L5L3bL7bF	B	4/4	W1p20
DUKE OF ATHOLL'S MARCH	5552	5523	A	3/8	M10v1p9
DUKE OF BUCCLEUCH, THE	16L5L1	7L213	Bb	2/2 R	K2v4p18
DUKE OF CUMBERLAND	1655	47b27bL	D	4/4 S	Mc3v1p50 R10p103
DUKE OF FIFE'S WELCOME TO DEESIDE, THE	5L121	4552	A	4/4 M	S8v7p38 S8v8p31
DUKE OF GORDON('S BIRTHDAY, THE)	1111	51H22	G	4/4 S	K2v1p4 L8v5p10 Mc3v1p99
					R10p163 S17p38
DUKE OF KENT, THE	1135	4246	F	4/4*R	L8v6p20 R10p225
DUKE OF PERTH	151H5	1H52H2	G	4/4*R	K2v1p11 L8v3p9 R10p171
					S17p25
DUKE OF RICHMOND'S BIRTHDAY, THE	131H3H	2H1H26L	E	4/4	W1p38
DUKE OF ROXBURGHE, THE	1355	1355	G	4/4 R	S17p40
DUKE OF SUTHERLAND(, THE)	5L3L6L2L	5L3L6L5L	Bb	4/4 S	K2v3p20 L8v2p23
DUKES DANG OWER HIS DADDY, THE	1H327	1H431	D	6/8	K2v1p32
DUMBARTON CASTLE	5L131	3555	A	4/4 S	K2v4p3
DUMBARTON CASTLE	13L5L5L	1532	A	4/4 QS	S8v7p38 S8v8p23
DUMFRIES HOUSE	1151	46L25L	D G	6/8	K2v2p34 L8v2p10
DUMFRIES HOUSE	1151	4525L	G	6/8 J	R10p139
DUNBLANE	1353	61H53	Bb	4/4 S	K2v3p20
DUNCAN BAIN'S BARGAIN	5L155	51H22	G	4/4 S	S8v8p58
DUNCAN DAVIDSON	1555	11H52	D C	4/4 S	K2v1p17 L8v5p6 R10p94 S9p9
DUNCAN MACPHERSON	1L127bL	3b15L4L	A	4/4	P3p21
DUNCAN McQUEEN	5L111	543b7bL	A	4/4 S	M7p6 R10p57
DUNCAN ON THE PLAINSTONES (ELGIN)	3135	7b7b22	D	4/4 R	Mc3v1p56 S8v3p5
DUNCAN QUADRILLE, THE	351H3H	1H632	D	2/4	P3p22
DUNCAN QUADRILLE, THE	1133	6423	A	4/4	P3p24
DUNCAN QUADRILLE, THE	1H531	2357	G	6/8	P3p22
DUNCAN QUADRILLE, THE	1316L	1632	F	6/8	P3p23
DUNCAN QUADRILLE, THE	115L3L	5L5L5L5L	Bb	6/8	P3p23
DUNCAN R. DAWSON'S STRATHSPEY	5L5L5L1	5L5L2L2L	A	4/4	W1p7
DUNCAN'S RANT	5L13b5	4243b	G	4/4 S	S8v3p56
DUNDEE	5L5L1L3L	5L5L4L2L	A	2/2 R	K2v4p4
DUNDEE BURNS CLUB, THE	31H34	31H33	A	2/4	S8v8p51
DUNDERAVE	3215	3212	A	4/4 R	K2v3p10
DUNECHT HOUSE	1363	1547L	A	4/4 S	M7p23
DUNFERMLINE ABBEY	1366	5353	G	4/4 SC	K2v3p24
DUNFERMLINE RACES	3333	7b7bL44	A	2/2 R	R10p18
DUNIE MAINS	1H531	22H75	G	4/4 S	Mc3v1p98 R10p159
DUNIQUAICH	3564	527L2	G	4/4 R	K2v3p8
DUNKELD BRIDGE	1H3H75	1H3H2H7	F	2/2 R	R10p223
DUNKELD HERMITAGE	153b5	2424	E	2/2 R	G6v2p48 R10p259
DUNNECHAN (REEL) DUNNICHEN HOUSE	3155	3142	D	2/2*R	G6v2p10 Mc3v1p55 M7p16
DUNNOTTAR CASTLE	131H3H	1H47L7L	D	4/4 S	Mc3v1p76 M7p18 S8v8p80
DUNROBIN CASTLE	15L13	437L2	F	4/4 R	S17p109
DUNROBIN CASTLE	15L15L	35L1L5L	Bb	4/4 S	K2v3p21 R10p290
DUNS DINGS A'!	151H3	351H1H	A	2/2 R	R10p19
DUNSE CASTLE	51H53	51H2H2	G	2/2 R	G6v1p33
DUNSE DINGS A'	351H3	351H1H	A G	4/4 R	K2v2p3 L8v5p2 L8v8Ap4
					Mc3v1p16 S17p99
DUNT THE GRUND AT LEISURE	1126L	1111	G	4/4 S	K2v2p15 R10p161
DUNTROON	5651	57b27bL	A	4/4 PR	S8v8p53
DUNTULM QUICKSTEP	11H65	11H52	G	4/4	M10v2p18
DUPPLIN CASTLE	5L3b53b	247b2	D	4/4	W1p35
DUTCHESS OF ATHOLE'S SLIPPER, THE	5L353	5L36L2	F	4/4 S	G6v2p21
EAGER'S STRATHSPEY	35L35	46L46	A	4/4 S	L8v8Ap5

Name					
EARL GREY	116L5L	447L2	A	4/4 S	K2v2p3 M7p20 R10p5 S8v8p94
EARL MARISCHAL	1153	3153	F	4/4*R	K2v2p21 L8v3p14 Mc3v1p144
					R10p122 S17p67
EARL O' DEAN, THE	1351H	2H1H65	D	6/8	S8v6p42/3
EARL OF BREADALBANE('S HERMITAGE) (THE)	1155	7b424	E	4/4*R	Mc3v1p96 R10p250 S17p107
EARL OF BREADALBAN'S BIRTHDAY	53b3b7b	4224	E	4/4 S	G6v1p48
EARL OF CRAWFORD'S REEL, THE	1H531	4326	A	2/2 R	M7p24
EARL OF DALHOUSIE	1H3H53H	2H3H1H6	Eb	4/4*R	K2v1p13 R10p269
EARL OF DALKEITH(, THE)	13L13	2426L	F	4/4*R	K2v2p21 Mc3v1p141 R10p234
					S17p150
EARL OF EGLINTON, THE	5L35L3L	5L322L	Bb	4/4 R	Mc3v1p145 S17p131
EARL OF EGLINTON'S BIRTHDAY	1324	3642	F	4/4 S	R10p237
EARL OF FIFE, THE	3L5L3L5L	7L4#L7L5L	Bb	2/2 R	S8v5p5 S8v6p112
EARL OF FIFE'S FIRESIDE, THE	315L1	3342	F	4/4 S	Mc3v1p151
EARL OF FIFE'S WELCOME TO BANFF, THE	1351H	1362	F	2/2 S	S15p18
EARL [OF] HOME	5564	5565	F	4/4 S	L8v3p14
EARL OF HOME	5524	5565	G F	4/4 S	K2v1p10 Mc3v1p142 R10p220
EARL OF HOPETOUN'S REEL	5L5L11	3342	G	4/4	S9p3
EARL OF HYNDFORD('S REEL)	13b1H3bH	7b427bL	C	2/2 R	Mc3v1p196 R10p268
EARL OF LAUDERDALE, THE	1347L	1554	G	4/4*R	K2v1p11 L8v2p10 R10p176
EARL OF LOUDON(, THE)	5515	6L662	F	4/4 S	R10p228 S17p140
EARL OF MARCH	351H5	3542	F	2/2 R	R10p214
EARL OF MARCHES HORNPIPE, THE	1H1H1H3	61H52	D	2/2	W1p27
EARL OF SEAFIELD'S REEL, THE	5L13b1	247b2	A	2/2	W1p12
EAST KILBRIDE	35L6L5L	5L125	A	4/4 S	K2v3p11
EAST NEUK O' FIFE, THE	1155	2261H	G	2/4 R	S8v8p60/1
EAST NEUK OF FIFE(, THE)	1113	5151	G	4/4*CD	K2v1p23 Mc3v1p170 R10p147
					S8v7p22,23
EASTER ELCHIES	1152	1153H	F	4/4*R	K2v3p19 R10p243
EASTER SKENE	136L5L	1322L	F	4/4	W1p53
ECLIPSE	1L11L1	227L6L	G	4/4 SC	K2v2p24
ECLIPSE	1113	1113	Bb	2/2 HP	R10p300
EDGE OF THE EVENING, THE	1357	6562	A	2/2	S8v6p104
EDIE OCHILTREE	1H13b1	7b422	D	4/4 S	L8v8Bp27
EDINBURGH CASTLE	1L131	6L4L4L2L	A	4/4 M	S8v9/7
EDINVILLIE	1L113b	7bL7bF2L7bL	A	4/4 S	G14p29
EDITOR'S FAREWELL, THE	3L5L4L6L	7L213	A	4/4 A	S8v7p48
EDRADYNATE HOUSE	131H3	5L7L44	D	4/4 S	R10p87
EDRADYNATE HOUSE	3565	311H1H	D	2/2 R	R10p87
EDRADYNATE MEDLEY	1H753H	1H1H2H2H	F	2/4 CD	R10p152
EIGHT O'CLOCK TRAIN	3127L	15L7bL4L	A	2/2 R	K2v4p5
ELLON CASTLE	5L321	6L244	F	4/4 SS	S8v3p49
EMSLIE'S FIDDLE	15L1L5L	4L27L5L	A	4/4 S	S8v7p4
EWAN'S HORNPIPE [EVANS]	5753	15L32	G	4/4* H	M7p33 R10p298
EWIE WI' THE CROOKED HORN	5342	5346	A	4/4 S	R10p18
EWIE WI' THE CROOKED HORN	5L17bL2	5L13b2	G	4/4 S	R10p191
EWIE WI' THE CROOKIT HORN, THE	5L17bL2	5L143b	G	4/4 S	K2v3p22
EXCELSIOR	3L4L3L6	4L3L1#1	Bb	2/4 HP	S8v3p56
FAICHFIELD	5353H	6464H	D	4/4 S	S8v3p13
FAILLIRINN 'ILLIRINN	1112	5412	F	4/4	M10v2p1
FAIR FA' THE MINSTREL	315L3L	3135	Bb	4/4*R	Mc3v1p124 R10p280 S17p33
[MART DO CHRO A' MHEINANICH]					
FAIR FIELD HOUSE	51H6b4	3b57b3b	A	2/2 R	G6v1p24
FAIR HAIRED LASSIE	5L5L5L1	5L5L5L1	A	4/4 S	K2v4p4
FAIR WIND TO GREENLAND, A	1H1H31	427L5L	A	2/2 R	K2v4p5
FAIRBAIRN'S(STRATHSPEY)	13L4L3L	4L3L2L2	A	4/4 S	K2v1p15 M7p18 S8v8p20,21
FAIREST FLOWER, THE	6632	226L0	F	4/4	P3p15
FAIRLIE CASTLE	16L5L3L	16L22	Bb	4/4 S	K2v3p21
FAIRY DANCE(, THE)	3H3H3H3H	3H3H72H	D	4/4*R	K2v1p10 Mc3v1p57 R10p113
FAIRY DANCE, THE	3H3H3H3H	3H3H75	D	4/4	S9p4
FAIRY HILLOCK, THE	3b113b	13b1H5	A	4/4	G14p21
FALLEN CHIEF, THE	533	1#64	A	6/4	S8v9/8
FALLS OF CORRYMULZIE, THE	3115L	4L3L6L2L	A	2/2	W1p8
FALLS OF DIVACH, THE	5351	27L25L	D	4/4 S	Mc3v1p24 S8v6p18
FALLS OF TARNASH, THE	3231	3236L	G	6/8	S8v6p18
FANCY BALL, THE	3H2H1H5	35L7L2	D	4/4 R	S8v3p4
FANCY HORNPIPE	1311	5L3L3L5L	A	4/4	M7p33
FANG THE FIDDLERS	1511H	1527bL	A	2/2 R	R10p50
FANNY FARQUHARSON	1323	5L5L22	D	4/4 S	Mc3v1p77 M7p12
FAREWEEL TO WHISKY, O	5L37L6L	6L332	A	2/4	S8v6p36/7
FAREWELL! I MAUN CROSS THE SEAS	15L6L3L	1552	G	4/4	S8v6p22
FAREWELL TO BUTE	53b11	5551H	E	4/4 S	K2v4p12
FAREWELL TO DUNDEE	5L17bL2	5551	B	2/4	M10v1p17
FAREWELL TO GAIRLOCH	3223	6521	F	4/4	S8v6p16 S8v8p170
FAREWELL TO GARTLY	1L5L6L5L	1L5L4L2L	Bb	6/8	S8v8p159
FAREWELL TO HUNTLY	16L6L5L	4L5L2L2	A	4/4 M	S8v7p34
FAREWELL, TO THE GLEN	3H51H3H	2H5H3H1H	D	2/4	S8v6p77
FAREWELL TO THE GLEN	1133	3343	A	2/4 M	S8v10p8
FAREWELL TO THE HIGHLANDS	13L5L1	37L22L	A	4/4 SS	S8v5p2
FAREWELL TO WHISKY	1L126L	5L253	Bb	4/4 S	Mc3v1p136
FARNIE HOUSE	1353	51H3H5	G	2/2 R	K2v4p14
FAVORITE DANCE, A	3351H	547L2	G	2/4	S15p26

Title			Key	Time	References
FAVORITE FRENCH DANCE, A	3321	7L212	Bb	6/8	S15p20
FAVOURITE BAGPIPE JIG	1H565	1H526	A	6/8	L8v5P3
FAY HORNPIPE	1351	1H1H51	G	4/4 HP	M7p37
FEARGAN	3b15L5L	113b5	A	4/4*R	K2v2p9 R10p46
FEASGAR CIUIN [LOVELY EVENING]	1331H	6366L	D	4/4	M10v1p4
FECHT ABOUT THE FIRESIDE	5322H	5353	C	4/4 R	L8v8Bp18
FEET WASHING, THE	3bH1H1H5	7b2H4H4H	C	2/2 R	R10p266
FERNTOSH WHISKY	5L131	47L7L4	D	4/4 S	M7p18
FERRINTOSH [FERINTOSH]	5L131	47bL7bL4	D	4/4 S	Mc3v1p49 R10p103
FERRY, THE	1H635	1H622H	D	4/4 S	K2v4p10
FERRY, THE	3165	1H332	A	6/8	K2v4p28
FHEAR NAN CASUN CAOLA	3176	5531	A	4/4 PR	Mc3v1p10
(REJECTED LOVER, THE)					
FIDDICH BRIDGE	1H1H45	1H1H6L7L	G	4/4	W1p62
FIDDICH-SIDE LASSES, THE	5551	5547bL	A	4/4 S	Mc3v1p28
FIELD OF BANNOCKBURN, THE	3116	3144	A	2/4 M	S8v7p30 S8v8p38 S8v9/7
FIFE HUNT(, THE)	3H1H53	22H2H2H	C	4/4*R	L8v1p15 L8v8Ap20 Mc3v1p107
					R10p72 S17p18
FIGHT ABOUT THE FIRESIDE	5322H	5353	C	4/4 R	K2v2p11 L8v2p15 S9p6 S17p31
FIGHT ABOUT THE FIRESIDE	5362H	5353	C	2/2 R	Mc3v1p112 R10p63
FILL THE STOUP	5351	5362	A	4/4*R	K2v2p6 L8v2p5 Mc3v1p18
					R10p27 S17p50
FILL YOUR GLASSES	1356	1H2H1H7	D	4/4 S	K2v4p11
FINGAL'S CAVE	1221	2547bL	A	2/4	K2v1p48 M10v1p13
FINGAL'S DIRK	3431	37b27bL	A	4/4 QS	S8v8p49
FINNIN' HADDIES	1H53b1	2427bL	E	4/4 S	K2v3p10
FIR A BHATA [1ST.TUNE]	112	556	G	3/4	M10v1p7
FIR A BHATA [2ND.TUNE]	5L11	312	G	3/4	M10v1p7
FIR TREE, THE	311H7b	27bL7b2	D	4/4 S	Mc3v1p49
FIRE AWAY	5566	774H7	F	2/4 HP	S8v3p47
FIRESIDE AT HAME, THE	1117L	5L5L3L5L	Bb	4/4	S8v6p45
FIRTH O' FORTH	51H3H1H	62H4H2H	D	4/4 SC	K2v3p24
FISHERS	1H345	3345	D	2/2 HP	R10p297
FISHERS RANT, THE	14L3L5L	6L7L17L	G	4/4 S	K2v2p15 L8v4p12 Mc3v1p100
					R10p169
FISHER'S RANT, THE or DRUMNAGARRY	13L3L1	6L7L16L	G	4/4 S	S8v8p56
FISHERS' REEL O' BUCKIE, THE	5L135	5L326L	A	2/2	W1p16
FISHER'S WEDDING	1363	5632	F	4/4 R	K2v3p19
FISHER'S WEDDING, THE	1363	6532	F	4/4*R	L8v6p20 R10p217 S17p112
FIVE-MILE CHASE, THE	1522	1551L	G	2/4 R	S8v8p144
FLAGGON, THE [FLAGON, THE]	3135	3111H	G	4/4*R	K2v2p16 L8v1p14 Mc3v1p89
					R10p170
FLAGSTAFF, THE	5L5L5L2L	5L5L13	A	4/4	P3p16
FLAP OF THE EAGLE'S WING, THE	1111	1627b	A	2/4 PR	S8v8p50
FLINT AND FLEERISH, THE	3577	6543	F	2/4 R	S8v8p125
FLOORS CASTLE	3H551H	2266	D	4/4 R	S17p118
FLORA MACDONALD [FLORA McDONALD]	1151	117b7bL	E	4/4 R	K2v1p5 L8v2p13 L8v8Ap17
FLORA'S FROLICS	1215	2H652	D	2/4	S8v6p90
FLOWER O' STRATHBOGIE, THE	3231	3255	G	6/8	S8v6p46
FLOWER O' THE QUERN, THE	117L6L	4435	A	4/4 A	S8v5p16 S8v6p19 S8v7p35
FLOWER OF AUCHATTIE, THE	1H563	6325	D	6/8	S8v6p13
FLOWER OF THE NORTH, THE	536	51H3	D	3/4	S8v5p24
FLOWERDALE	1H735	447L2	D	4/4	S8v6p68
FLOWERS OF EDINBURGH, THE	5L5L11	3342	G	4/4*CD	K2v1p23 Mc3v1p170 M7p30
					R10p146
FOCHABERS RANT, THE	1H3H2H1H	1H3H2H1H	G	2/2 R	Mc3v1p68
FOOT IT FEATLY	1H135	7b427bL	A	4/4 R	Mc3v1p30
FOR A' THAT AND A' THAT	1H1H62H	1H3H66	D	4/4 S	K2v2p17
FORBES LODGE	1H1H35	1H1H22	D	2/2	W1p27
FORBES MORRISON	35L3L1L	4L27L4	A	4/4	S8v6p94 S8v7p10
FORBES' SNEESHIN MULL	331H5	7b447bL	G	4/4 S	S8v8p70
FORDELL HOUSE	331H1H	3342	G	2/2 R	G6v1p7
FOREST OF GARTH, THE	11H1H1H	7b2H7b7bL	D	4/4 S	K2v3p20 R10p240
[FOREST OF GAICK, THE]					
FOREST OF MAR, THE	51H1H3bH	7b3b47bL	D	2/2	W1p35
FORFAR HUNT	113b3b	27bL53b	B	2/2 R	R10p133
FORFAR HUNT, THE	113b3b	247b2	Bm	4/4 R	L8v4p11 Mc3v1p66
FORGE, THE	553b1	2424	E	4/4 S	K2v4p13
FORTH BRIG, THE	31H42H	71H1H5	G	2/4 HP	S8v7p46 S8v8p129
FORTINGALL FAIRS	153b1	5424	E	4/4 S	G6v1p47
FORTY TWA, THE	3L6L11	326L6L	A	2/4	S8v6p20 S9p14
FORTY-SECOND HIGHLANDERS' FAREWELL, THE	3b13b1	3b47bL7bL	B	2/4	K2v3p47
FOX CHASE	331H3	427L2	A	2/2 R	R10p39
FOX CHASE, THE	1H565	2H243	A	4/4 R	L8v6p3 S17p89
FOX, THE	3153	5764	A	2/2 R	G6v2p3
FRANCIS SITWELL [MASTER F. SITWELL]	5L3L6L4L	5L47L2	Bb	4/4 S	G6v2p28 L8v3p18 L8v8Ap30
					Mc3v1p124 R10p283
FRANK GILRUTH	3L411H	4347L	A	2/4 HP	S8v7p43
FRANK WALKER	1L1L5L6L	2L26L2	Bb	4/4 S	L8v8Bp29
FRANK'S	3165	4325	A	2/4 HP	S8v3p38
FRASER ARMS, THE	3L3L5L4L	3L3L5L3	Bb	2/2 R	R10p290
FREE GARDENERS' MARCH, THE	5511	315L5L	D	4/4	W1p27

Title			Key	Type	References
FRENCH AIR	1H1H35	1H1H46	D	2/4 CD	K2v1p22
FRENCH AIR	5H1H3H3H	2H3H3H1H	D	2/4 CD	K2v1p22
FRENCH WALTZ, A	111	5L5L3	Bb	3/8	S15p16/17
FUTTERAT WI' THE GREY TAIL, THE	1551	427bL5L	A	2/2 S	Mc3v1p116
FYKET, THE	651H5	6527bL	A	4/4*R	L8v6p5 Mc3v1p13 R10p38
					S17p75
FYKET, THE	651H1	6527bL	A	4/4 S	Mc3v1p13
FYVIE CASTLE	1451H	3bH6b55	C	4/4	S8v6p63 S8v7p39
FYVIE SENSATION	1363	6L247L	A	4/4 S	S8v9/9
GABERLUNZIE, THE	1H1H3bH2H	772H5	D	4/4 R	K2v3p20
GABHAIDH SINN AN RATHAD MOR	5535	2424	A	2/2 CD	R10p153
[THE STEWART'S MARCH]					
GAELIC AIR, A	3142	3147bL	A	2/4 QS	K2v1p26
GAELIC AIR, A	1122	111H6	G	6/8	K2v1p48
GAIR'S RANT	5L17bL2	5125L	A	4/4 S	L8v8Bp19
GALLATON	1L1H63	6L27L4L	G	4/4 S	S8v7p14
GALOPADE COUNTRY DANCE	6565	3H674	C	2/4	M7p32
GANE IS MY JEAN	126L5L	1155	Ab	4/4	S8v6p26
GARDEN'S STRATHSPEY	17L6L5L	4L3L2L5L	A	4/4 S	M7p24
GARELOCH, THE	15L3L1L	427L5L	G	4/4 S	K2v4p13
GAREY COTTAGE	3331	447L2	F	4/4 S	K2v1p14 L8v2p21 Mc3v1p141
					R10p217
GARIBALDI	131H6	6522	D	4/4 S	M7p15
GARRY HILLS	5L323	5L316L	A	2/4	M10v1p16
GARRY OWEN	6333	6322	F	6/8	S9p23
GARTHLAND HOUSE	5L5L1L5L	5L5L6L2L	Bb	4/4 S	Mc3v1p193
GARTHLAND'S	1331H	147L2	G	4/4 S	K2v2p14 L8v4p12
GARTHLANDS	1331H	137L2	G	4/4 S	Mc3v1p86 R10p174
GATHERIN' O' THE GUNNS, THE	5L123	1461H	A	4/4 JS	S8v8p110
GATHERING, THE	1133	117L7L	G	4/4 R	S17p13
GAVIN J. HAMILTON'S STRATHSPEY	5L351H	537L2	D	4/4 S	S8v8p75
GEANIE'S LAMENT	3b3b24	117bL1	A	4/4 A	S8v3p43
GENERAL BAILLIE	151H3	5L257L	D	4/4	S8v6p75
GENERAL DRUMMOND	3135	31H2H2	G	2/2 R	K2v4p14
GENERAL GATHERING 1745, THE	1H351H	2H1H52	D	6/8 J	K2v2p35 R10p136
GENERAL GRAHAM	3131	437L5L	F	4/4 R	L8v4p21
GENERAL MACDONALD	13b53b	7b422	C	4/4 S	R10p269
GENERAL MCDONALD	3H1H51H	3H1H3H5H	C	4/4*R	L8v4p19 Mc3v1p108 R10p76
GENERAL WEMYSS(OF WEMYSS)	5H3H2H7	432H2	C	4/4 S	R10p65 S17p94
GENERAL WEMYSS OF WEMYSS	1335	357L2	F	4/4 R	Mc3v1p190
GENTLE DARK EYED MARY	1555	553b4	B	4/4	K2v1p48
GEORDIE JACK	1H3H61H	5531	Eb	4/4 R	K2v3p22
GEORDIE MACLEISH	1H715	1H753H	D	2/2 R	Mc3v1p76 M7p17
GEORDIE WALKER	5364	537L5L	D	4/4 S	S8v9/8
GEORGE GORDON ESQr.'s STRATHSPEY	5L13b5	7b427bL	G	4/4	W1p66
GEORGE REID ESQ.	5L153b	53b42	E	4/4	W1p48
GEORGE S. FORBES OF ASLOWN'S HORNPIPE	1L15L3L	2L26L4L	Bb	4/4	W1p15
GEORGE TAYLOR	1113	5751	Bb	4/4 HP	H5p1
GEORGE THE FOURTH	1L1L3bL1L	1L1L2L7bF	A	4/4 S	M7p6
GEORGE THE FOURTH REEL	1L5L6L5L	1L5L3bL1L	A	4/4 R	M7p6
GEORGE THE IV	5L1L3bL1L	5L1L2L7bF	A	4/4 S	K2v1p7 L8v5p15
GEORGE THE IVth's WELCOME TO EDINBURGH	5353	7L27L5L	Bb	4/4 R	Mc3v1p133
GEORGE WRIGHT	3L136L	5L3L6L2L	Bb	4/4 S	H5p7
GERTIE GIBB	1353	1455	D	4/4 SC	S8v8p74
GIBSON'S WHISKY	331H5	6422	D	2/2 R	S8v3p6
GILLAN A DROVER	11H2H1H	5353	G	6/8 J	L8v4p14
GILLE CALUIM	1342	1343	A	4/4 S	R10p9
GILLEAN AN FHEILIDH [LADS IN THE KILT]	1H51H1H	1H65H3H	D	6/8	Mc3v1p177 M10v2p23
GILLIE CALLUM [GHILLIE CALLUM or	1342	1353	A	4/4 S	K2v1p5 L8v2p2 M7p28 S8v8p113
SWORD DANCE]					S17p139
GILLIE CALLUM [GILLIE CALUM]	1332	1333	A	4/4	M10v1p19
GILLIE CALUM	1342	1343	A	4/4 S	Mc3v1p14
GIN HAD A BONNY LASSIE	3b53b5	2427bL	G	2/2 R	R10p190
GIN I HAD A BONNY LASS	3b13b5	7b7b27bL	G	4/4 R	K2v2p23 L8v6p23
(LITTLE SLEEP WAD SAIR ME)					
GIN YE KISS MY WIFE,	5L125L	3b247bL	A	4/4 S	S8v7p21 S8v8p59
I'LL TELL THE MINISTER					
GINNIE PIN YOUR BONNET ON	1122	117bL4	E	2/2 R	K2v4p12
GIORNOVICHI	1H51H5	61H75	F	4/4 R	S17p56
GIRL I LEFT BEHIND ME, THE	6336L	1153	G	2/4	S9p16
GIRLS OF OUR TOWN, THE	1H551H	1H57b7b	E	2/2 R	K2v4p11
GLASGOW LASSES(, THE)	1153	1142	F	2/2*R	R10p219 S17p113
GLASSA HOUSE	1H2H1H5	4522	D	2/2 R	G6v2p7
GLEN COTTAGE	5L111L	526L6L	Bb	4/4	S8v6p113
GLEN ELG	151H5	1H1H22	D	4/4 S	L8v5p5
GLEN FISHIE	1H535	1H522H	A	4/4 R	L8v1p5
GLEN GELDER	3b115L	3b3b53b	E	4/4 R	L8v8Bp14
GLEN GRANT	1L16L3L	5L247L	A	4/4 S	K2v1p8
GLEN GRANT	3L16L3L	3L146L	A	2/2 S	G14p15
GLEN LEAN	3235	1H61H6	A	4/4 S	K2v4p4
GLEN LYON	11H55	6547bL	D	4/4 R	S17p161
GLEN LYON	5152	27bL22	D	4/4 R	K2v1p10

Tune			Key	Time	Sources
GLEN LYONS RANT	313L1	4L27L2	G	4/4 S	Mc3v1p186
GLEN OGLE	1H3H62H	761H3	D	4/4*R	K2v1p24 R10p95
GLEN TILT LODGE	11H61H	61H24	A	2/2 R	K2v4p5
GLEN TRUIM	3b5L3b5	247b5	E	4/4 S	L8v8Ap16
GLEN WHERE MY LOVE IS, THE	5464	5413	A	4/4 PR	Mc3v1p11
GLENAVON FOREST	15L3L1L	15L13	Bb	4/4	W1p65
GLENBUCKET CASTLE	1555	7b542	C	4/4	W1p25
GLENBUCKET LODGE	1353	4542	G	4/4	W1p60
GLENBURNEY RANT, THE	153b5	4427bL	E	2/2 R	R10p246
GLENBURNIE RANT(, THE)	1111	7bL247bL	E	4/4 R	K2v1p5 L8v4p17
GLENCOE	5531	5531H	Eb	4/4 A	S8v7p42 S8v8p147
GLENDUACHIE	1L3L5L3L	5L15L2L	G	4/4	P3p8
GLENELG	151H5	1H1H22	D	4/4 S	R10p99
GLENFIDDICH	1353	5L322	A	2/2 S	G6v1p3
GLENGAIRN	151H3H	11H2H2	F	6/8	W1p52
GLENGARRY'S DIRK	5L3L1L5L	5L3L26L	A	4/4 S	K2v2p20
GLENGARRY'S MARCH	3142	3147bL	A	2/4	K2v3p46
GLENKINDIE	1L153	5642	G	4/4 S	K2v4p15
GLENLIVAT	1L1L5L5L	7bL3bL4L7bF	B	4/4	W1p20
GLENLIVET	11H3b1	27bL7b2	A	4/4 R	K2v1p24
GLENLIVET (WHISKY) [GLENLIVET, THE]	1L5L4L1	5L422L	A	4/4 SC	S8v5p3 S8v6p96 S8v7p8
GLENLYON	11H55	6547bL	D	2/2 R	R10p107
GLENLYON('S PIPER)	5152	27B122	Am	4/4*R	L8v5p15 Mc3v1p186 R10p152
GLENMORISTON	5L15L3L	1L132	G	4/3 S	K2v3p7 R10p179
GLENQUEY	1551	1562	D	4/4*R	K2v1p17 R10p128
GLENRINNES	1L15L5L	4L2L2L7bF	A	2/2 S	G14p6
GLENTANA	53bH2H1H	7b427bL	F#	4/4	S8v6p99
GLENTILT	11H61H	11H24	A	2/2 R	R10p4
GLENTROMIE	5H3H1H1H	5H6H72H	C	4/4 S	K2v3p16 R10p79
GLOOMY WINTER	1115L	3b3b42	A	4/4 S	K2v1p7
GLORIES OF "THE STAR", THE	13L15	7L432	Eb	4/4 SS	S8v5p18
GO TO THE DEVIL AND SHAKE YOURSELF	51H55	51H3H6	C	6/8 IJ	L8v1p17
GOAT FELL	1H3H1H6	5155	C	4/4	K2v3p16
GOBBIE O, THE	3b15L1	27bL47bL	A	6/8	K2v1p33
GOLDEN LOCKS	57b11	47b7bL7bL	B	2/2 R	R10p129
GOLLOCHY'S FAREWELL	15L3L1L	4522	Bb	4/4 S	G6v1p16
GOOD BYE, GRAMIN	51H1H7	7665	D	4/4	S8v6p57
GOOD MORNING, MRS. BARCLAY	1564	5322	D	4/4	S8v6p58
GOOD NIGHT	631HO	637LO	G	4/4	S8v6p128
GOOD NIGHT AND JOY BE WI' YOU	1H566H	3H3H3H2H	D	2/4	K2v1p26
GOODEN WELL	315L1	437L2	A	2/2 R	G6v2p3
GORDON CASTLE (or CASTLE GORDON)	637L7L	131H3	A	4/4 R	L8v4p2
GORDON CASTLE	5326	5355	A	4/4 S	K2v2p5 L8v6p1 R10p20
GORDON CASTLE WALTZ	1H51H	3H1H5H	C	3/4	W1p25
GORDON CROMBIE MUNRO	1H36L4	1H36L1	A	2/4 R	S8v9/2
GORDON HIGHLANDERS, THE	1151H	51H3H1H	C	4/4 S	K2v3p16
GORDON HIGHLANDERS, THE	31H31	27b27bL	A	2/4	S8v6p78
GORDON STEWART FORBES' (H.E.I.C.S.) JIG	5L13b5	7b427bL	E	6/8	W1p48
GORDON, THE [GORDONS THE]	1254	2121	A	4/4 S	K2v3p17 Mc3v1p187
GORDONS HAE THE GIRDING O'T, THE	1H31H1	1H32H2	D	4/4 S	Mc3v1p57 R10p110
GORTHLECK'S HIGHLAND PLAID	1531	7b442	E	4/4 S	R10p276
GOUROCK BAY	325L1	3236	A	4/4 S	K2v3p13
GOUROCK BAY	5555	572H7	A	2/2 R	K2v4p5
GOWAN BRAES, THE	51H53	51H22	D	4/4	P3p14
GOWRIE	351H1H	662H2H	D	4/4 S	K2v4p7
GRACEFUL MOVE, THE	1565	1553	A	4/4 PR	Mc3v1p48
GRAHAM'S RANT	5L342	7L244	G	4/4 S	K2v4p16
GRAMIN	1H67L3L	1#4L7L5	Bb	2/4	S8v6p111
GRAND OLD McINTYRE	3455	4362	A	2/4 PM	S8v8p37
GRANITE CITY, THE	1353	427L2	D	4/4*R	Mc3v1p53 S8v3p9
GRANNY'S HOOSIE I' THE GLEN	51H61H	61H44	A	4/4 S	S8v5p13
GRANT LODGE	1122	1155	G	4/4 S	K2v2p16 R10p181
GRANTS' HORNPIPE, THE	1H531	3131	E	2/2	G14p11
GRANTULLY BRIDGE	1L5L16L	5L5L2L2L	Bb	4/4 S	R10p295
GREEN GROW THE RASHES(O!)	1331	2662	G	4/4*SC	K2v1p19 K2v2p14 L8v1p13 L8v8Ap12 Mc3v1p80 R10p157 S9p10
GREEN SHADES OF GASK, THE	131H7	532H2	G	6/8	K2v2p35
GREENEND PARK	13L13	527L2	Eb	2/4 M	G6v1p41
GREENHOLM	5161H	5122	G	6/8	K2v4p28
GREGG'S PIPES	53b53b	53b25L	E	2/2 R	K2v4p16
GREIG'S PIPES	5351	5326L	A	4/4*R	L8v4p5 Mc3v1p5 R10p16
GREIG'S STRATHSPEY	3L5L15L	16L15L	Bb	4/4 SS	S8v8p16
GREIG'S STRATHSPEY	351H5	1H61H5	C	4/4 S	Mc3v1p101
GREY BUCK, THE	5541	4427bL	A	6/8	K2v4p28
GRINDER, THE	1H65	1H65	G	9/8	S9p25
G.S. MACKAY	153bH1H	6b427L	E	2/4 HP	S8v8p128/9
GU MA SLAN A CHI MI [MAY I SEE YOU HAPPY]	1265	36L11	F	4/4	M10v1p4
GUN BHRIS MO CHRIDH' ON DH'FHALBH THU [MY HEART IS BROKE SINCE THY DEPARTURE)	3553	51H3H2H	F	4/4	Mc3v1p191
H. MACKWORTH	3L133	1153	Bb	4/4 HP	S8v3p59

Title					
HAGGIS OF DUNBAR, THE	315L7bL	7bL427bL	A	2/2 R	R10p154
HAGGIS, THE	3553	351H1H	C	4/4 R	K2v2p11 L8v3p12
HAGGIS, THE	3453	351H1H	C	4/4 R	Mc3v1p109
HAGGS CASTLE	3H1H65	31H3H2H	D	4/4 S	K2v2p19
HAGGS CASTLE	3H653	5357	D	4/4 R	K2v2p19
HALE-WHEEL	3135	3175	A	2/2	S8v6p82
HAMILTON OF WISHAW [MR.]	3115L	2422L	Bb	4/4 R	L8v3p18
HAMILTON'S	5L351H	537L2	D	4/4 S	S8v7p13
'HAP AN' ROW THE FEETIES O'T	31H1H1H	31H42	A	4/4 QS	S8v7p40
HAPPY FRANK	3L411H	4347L	A	2/4 HP	S8v8p131
HAPPY TOM	1L5L15L	3L122L	A	4/4 S	S8v7p4 S8v8p110/1
HAPPY WE'VE BEEN A' THEGITHER	335	556	D	3/4 W	K2v1p25
HAPPY WE'VE BEEN A THE-GITHER	351H1H	352H6	A	4/4 SC	K2v2p24
HARE AMONG THE CORN, THE	351H3	3542	G	6/8 J	L8v5p9
HARE AMONG THE HEATHER, THE	51H2H1H	57b42	E	2/2 R	K2v4p16
HARK! HOW SKINNER'S FIDDLE RINGS	1121	5L235	A	4/4	S8v6p101
HARMONICA, THE	1H362	7L5L15	G	6/8	K2v1p29
HARVEST HOME	111H1H	2H4H2H5	F	2/4	S9p28
HARVEST HOME	1313	1H3H1H6	D	2/2*HP	M7p35 S8v7p44 S8v8p130/1
HARVEST HOME	1313	1H2H1H6	D	4/4*HP	Mc3v1p171 R10p298
HARVEST HOME	1353	5L7L27L	D	4/4 S	L8v8Ap8 Mc3v1p35 R10p83
HASBERRY HOWARD	1H35L2	35L1L5L	G	4/4 HP	S8v7p45
HASTE TO THE WEDDING	552H3H	5532	D	6/8	K2v1p27
HASTE TO THE WEDDING	552H3H	5522	D	6/8 CD	MC3v1p168 R10p145 S9p13
HATTON BURN [TARBOLTON LODGE]	11H1H5	3b43b1	E	4/4 R	Mc3v1p75
HATTONBURN	1563	1563	D	4/4	S8v6p93
HAUD AWA' FRAE ME DONALD	115L5L	1132	G	4/4 S	K2v3p10
HAUD AWA' HAME	51H1H7b	51H51H	F#	6/8	K2v4p27
HAUD THE LASS TILL I COME AT HER	1565	1544	A	2/2 R	K2v4p8
HAUGHS O' SPEY, THE	5L3L11	6L15L5L	A	4/4 S	S8v5p11 S8v6p72
HAUGHS OF CROMDALE	5152	517bL2	E A	4/4 S	K2v1p6 L8v6p16 Mc3v1p85 M7p7 R10p249 S17p112
HAUGHS OF DELBAGIE, THE	5L13b5	3bH2H23b	E	4/4	W1p45
HAUNT OF THE GNOMES, THE	5L7L43	6L6L21	A	4/4 A	S8v7p47 S8v8p154
HAWTHORN HEDGES	325L1	3236	A	4/4 S	K2v3p14
HAYMAKERS' JIG	1212	1231	G	6/8	M7p33
HAY-MAKERS, THE	1232	1231	G	6/8 CD	K2v1p27 Mc3v1p169
HAZELDEAN	5215L	1422	A	4/4 S	K2v3p12
HEATHER BELL	5L15L1	5L13b5	A	4/4 S	K2v3p17
HEATHER BELLS	1313	5655	D	4/4 S	K2v4p11
HEATHER HILLS	352H6	51H5H2H	D	6/8	K2v4p27
HEATHERY BREEZE, THE	5L353	5L252	G	2/2 R	K2v4p15
HEATHER[Y] JOCK (?)	51H51H	51H63	A	4/4 S	K2v4p5
HECKLEBIRNIE	315L5L	31H22	Bb	2/4 HP	S8v9/4
HECTOR MACDONALD	3123	4552	A	4/4 PM	S8v8p40
HECTOR THE HERO	3655	3622	A	6/8	S8v8p152
HECTOR THE HERO	3L6L5L5L	3L6L2L2L	A	6/8 A	S8v7p49
HEIDSET, THE	5551	4447bL	E	4/4 S	S8v5p3
HEIRESS, THE	3bL5L3bL5L	15L3bL1L	Bm	4/4 R	L8v6p12
HENRY A. GRANT ESQ., OF ELCHIES	1L13L1L	1L111	A	4/4 S	G14p25
HEN'S MARCH, THE	1H1H1H3H	3H4H2H5	D	4/4	M7p36
HERR ROLOFF'S FAREWELL	3453	1H751	F	4/4	S8v8p158
HEY THE BONNIE BREAST KNOTS	1346	5125	A	4/4 SC	K2v3p23
HI LO RO! HOG EILE	546L4	5L7L11	Eb	4/4	M10v2p5
HIELAN' BROCHAN	51H51	51H53	G	4/4 R	K2v3p10
HIELAN' TONAL'	53b11H	7b57b5	D	4/4 S	K2v4p18
HIGH LEVEL, THE	13L51	25L7L4	Bb	2/4 HP	S8v7p44 S8v8p44
HIGH ROAD TO FORT AUGUSTUS	2L5L7bL7bL	7bF4L2L7bF	B	2/2 R	R10p131
HIGH ROAD TO LINTON	531H1H	661H1H	A	2/2 R	R10p33
HIGH ROAD TO LINTON(, THE)	351H1H	661H1H	A	4/4 R	K2v1p7 L8v3p2 Mc3v1p22 S17p10
HIGH UP THE GLEN	1H3bH2H7b	47b2H7b	G	2/2 R	R10p195
HIGHLAND BLACK LADDIE	5353	6262	A	2/2 R	K2v4p4
HIGHLAND DONALD	1133	1132	G	4/4 S	M7p8
HIGHLAND DONALD KISS'D KITTY (cf:.WILL YOU GO AND MARRY KETTY)	3133	3132	G	4/4 S	L8v3p9 L8v8Bp11
HIGHLAND DONALD KISSED KITTY	3133	3124	G	4/4 S	K2v3p9
HIGHLAND DRESS AND ARMOUR	5553	5533	C	4/4 S	K2v3p15 R10p74
HIGHLAND EMIGRANTS, THE	5L5L11	315L3L	Bb	4/4	P3p5
HIGHLAND FLING	5551H	61H51H	D	4/4 S	K2v4p10
HIGHLAND LADDIE	1H3H4H3H	3H2H3H2H	D	2/4 CD	K2v1p21
HIGHLAND LADDIE	1343	3232	A	2/4	M10v1p18
HIGHLAND MINSTREL BOY, THE	35L6L5L	6L27L5	G	4/4 S	K2v3p8
HIGHLAND PIBROCH	5151	5141	A	6/8	K2v1p47
HIGHLAND PLAID, THE	15L13	436L6L	G	2/2 R	G6v1p8
HIGHLAND QUEEN, THE	5L17bL2	3b7bL5L3bL	G	4/4	P3p18
HIGHLAND QUICKSTEP	5542	7bL427bL	A	6/8	K2v1p47
HIGHLAND RANT	5152	5147bL	A	2/2 R	K2v4p18
HIGHLAND SKIP, THE	5555	5555	F	2/2*S	G6v1p13 R10p216 S17p111
HIGHLAND SOCIETY OF LONDON, THE	1531	7b527bL	A	4/4 PS	Mc3v1p10
HIGHLAND SOCIETY OF SCOTLAND'S MARCH	1H1H1H3H	1H511	E	4/4	W1p42
HIGHLAND WATCH'S FAREWELL TO IRELAND	1L1L1L1L	7bL4L7bL7bL	A	4/4 S	G6v1p23

Title					
HIGHLAND WHISKEY [HIGHLAND WHISKY]	1113	2246	A	4/4 S	K2v1p7 L8v2p3 Mc3v1p26 R10p6 S17p148
HIGHLANDERS FAREWELL TO IRELAND, THE	1L1L1L1L	7bL4L7bF7bF	A	4/4 S	K2v1p9 Mc3v1p102 R10p48
HIGHLANDERS' FAREWELL TO WATERLOO	5154	5155	A	6/8	M10v1p15
HIGHLANDERS IN PARIS, THE	1127bL	113b5	E	4/4 S	K2v1p12
HIGHLANDER'S KNEE BUCKLE, THE	513b2	47b7bL2	E	2/2 R	K2v4p7
HIGHLANDMAN KISS'D HIS MOTHER, THE	15H5H5H	15H47bL	C	4/4 R	Mc3v1p105
HIGHLANDMAN(KISSED HIS MOTHER), THE	1H5H5H5H	1H5H2H5	C	4/4 R	K2v1p7 L8v2p15 R10p51 S17p37
HIGHLANDMAN'S COWL, THE	5351	3522	A	4/4 SC	K2v3p23
HIGHLANDS OF BANFFSHIRE	5535	5533	F	4/4 S	K2v2p22
HIGHLANDS OF BANFFSHIRE, THE	5531	5533	F	4/4 S	L8v3p16 L8v8B2p24 Mc3v1p161 R10p216 S8v8p123
HIGHLANDS OF BANFFSHIRE, THE	5551	5533	F	4/4 S	S8v7p15
HIGHLANDS OF SCOTLAND, THE	5551H	3bH1H3bH3bH	E	4/4 S	K2v4p14
HIGHWAY TO DUBLIN, THE	6351	6347bL	A	6/8	Mc3v1p177
HILL HEAD	1H133	2H246	G	4/4 R	L8v8Bp12
HILL O' NIGG, THE	3564	532H2	C	4/4 S	S8v5p15 S8v6p83
HILL O RO, HILL O RO	217bL5L	3b3b42	G	4/4	M10v2p16
HILL OF DOUNE, THE	1L527L	6L6L5L3L	G	4/4	P3p8
HILLS OF GLENORCHY, THE	5157b	47bL42	E	6/8	K2v1p47
HILTON LODGE	5H5H4H2H	5H5H1H5H	C	4/4 S	G6v2p19 K2v2p12 L8v2p16 Mc3v1p118 R10p71 S17p96
HIRN DEVIL, THE	1353	427L5L	D	2/2 R	S8v10p10
HO RO GUM B'AOIBHINN LEAM	3315L	1216L	A	4/4	M10v1p8
HOBBLE JENNY	3331	2227bL	A	4/4 S	M7p19
HOCH HEY JOHNNIE LAD	1122	15L22	A	4/4*R	K2v2p6 Mc3v1p14 R10p26
HOGMANAY, OR ADIEU TO THE AULD YEAR	3L13L3L	3L122L	A	4/4 S	K2v2p8
HOKEY POKEY	3H1H1H5	4235	F	6/8	S9p13
HOME BOYS HOME	1H3H1H3H	1H1H55	F	2/4	S9p14
HOME RULE	27L25	27L31	G	2/4 R	S8v8p143
HON. CAPT. MAITLAND	1347L	1353	G	4/4 S	G6v1p31 K2v2p15 R10p170 S17p46
HON. CHAS. BRUCE, THE	13L6L5L	4L3L2L2L	Bb	2/2 R	G6v1p41
HON. MISS ROLLO, THE	3H1H2H1H	6522H	C	2/2 R	G6v1p34
HONble. COLONEL WEMYSS, THE	1335	357L2	F	4/4 R	Mc3v1p145 S17p156
HONble. GEORGE CARNEGIE, THE	13b5L1	27bL27bL	G	4/4 S	R10p202
HONbLE. JOHN LESLIE MELVILLE	1H3bH2H1H	5427bL	D	4/4 S	R10p241
HONBLE. MISS DRUMMOND OF PERTH	5337b	4224	A	2/2 R	R10p17
HONble. MISS DRUMMOND OF PERTH, THE	1311H	5326L	D	4/4 S	R10p109
HONble. MISS JESSIE A. RUTHVEN	11H3b5	7bL7b22	C	4/4 S	G6v2p33
HONBLE MISS ROLLO, THE	3H1H2H1H	6522H	D	4/4 R	K2v3p3
HONble. MISS SEMPILL	1H515	2H626	G	2/2 R	G6v2p12
HONble. MR. FRASER (OF LOVAT)	543b1	247b2	B	2/2 R	G6v2p50
HONble. MRS. CAMPBELL (OF LOCHNELL)	1H535	1H3H2H2	C	2/2 R	G6v2p17
HONble. MRS. F. GRAY	51H3H1H	51H2H4	F	2/2 R	G6v2p24
HONble. MRS. FRASER OF LOVAT, THE	5L5L5L1L	2L5L4L7bF	A	4/4 S	Mc3v1p103
HONble. MRS. GRAHAM OF BALGOWAN, THE	5335	437b2	D	2/2 R	R10p109
HONble. MRS. MAULE OF PANMURE	5526L	5515	F	4/4 S	R10p235
HONble. MRS. MAULE('S STRATHSPEY)	1H535	2462H	A	4/4*R	Mc3v1p181 R10p32
HONble. MRS. RAMSAY MAULE('S STR.)	5527bL	5555	E	4/4 S	Mc3v1p82 R10p261
HONble SEYMOUR EGERTON'S REEL, THE	5L135	6L246	F	2/2	W1p53
HONEST DUNCAN	11L5L1L	11L5L5L	Bb	4/4 SS	R10p289
HONEYMOON, THE	51H1H3H	4H2H75	D	4/4*R	K2v2p17 L8v4p8 R10p118 S9p6
HONOURABLE MISS CHARTERIS, THE	1H3bH1H7b	47b2H7b	G	4/4 R	S17p105
HONOURABLE MRS. DRUMMOND OF PERTH, THE	1311H	5326L	D	4/4 S	Mc3v1p56
HONOURABLE PEACE, AN	1515L	7bL247bL	E	2/2 R	R10p257
HOO DINNA YE PLAY MAIR	315L1	316L2	Bb	2/4	S8v6p113
HORNPIPE	11H2H1H	3H4H5H2H	D	2/4	K2v1p26
HORNPIPE	1H367	3H4H72H	D	2/4	K2v1p26
HO!RO! MO NIGHEAN DONN BHOIDHEACH	16L15L	3423	F	4/4	M10v2p2
HOUSE OF ACHLUNCART, THE	1H1H3H5H	1H1H2H5	C	4/4*R	K2v2p13 R10p81
HOUSE OF BELLABEG, THE	3565	352H2H	C	4/4	W1p25
HOUSE OF CLOVA, THE	17L6L5L	13L6L2L	Bb	6/8	W1p19
HOUSE OF CLUNY, THE	1331	7L227L	F	4/4 S	R10p223
HOUSE OF CRAIG, THE	136L5L	1356	D	2/2	W1p32
HOUSE OF DRUMMUIR, THE	1H3H1H6	5122	D	2/2	W1p31
HOUSE OF EDINGLASSIE, THE	5L13b3b	4422	E	2/2	W1p45
HOUSE OF GLENKINDY, THE	136L7L	1353	G	4/4	W1p57
HOUSE OF GRAY, THE	13b44	13b55	A	6/8	K2v4p28
HOUSE OF INVERCAULD, THE	5266	5226L	E	2/2	W1p41
HOUSE OF INVERERUAN, THE	5L3b11	427b2	B	4/4	W1p22
HOUSE OF LETTERFOURIE, THE [or LASSES LOOK BEHIND YOU]	5326L	531H1H	D	2/2 R	Mc3v1p39
HOUSE OF NEW, THE	11H31H	51H72H	C	4/4 S	R10p81
HOUSE OF PARK, THE	3546	5122	F	2/2 R	R10p240
HOWARD'S	1342	31H64	A	4/4 R	L8v8Bp4
HOWARD'S	5L37L2	5L365	A	4/4 S	L8v8Bp4
HOWE O' ECHT, THE	1L2L3L4L	5L47L2	A	4/4 S	S8v3p35
H.R.H. THE PRINCE OF WALES' WELCOME TO DEESIDE	1115	2247L	A	4/4	B9p1
HUGH DUNLOP	5L31H5	3142	D	4/4 S	K2v3p4
HUNDRED PIPERS, THE	35L6L1	5332	A	6/8	K2v1p31

Title			Key	Time	Refs
HUNDRED YEARS SINCE, A	5L5L11	2226L	Eb	2/2 R	Mc3v1p130
HUNKER HILL	51H2H6	5222	D	4/4	S8v6p64
HUNTINGTOWER	1132	131H6	A	4/4 S	K2v4p4
HUNTLY CASTLE	176b5	3b125L	E	4/4	S8v6p62
HUNTLY'S WEDDING MEDLEY [BANAIS MARCUIS HUNNDFHUINN]	536L5L	3L11H2H	A	4/4 S	K2v2p8 Mc3v1p178 S8v8p95
HURDLE RACE, THE	3115L	1L5L35	A	4/4*R	K2v2p8 L8v4p4 Mc3v1p6 R10p34
HURICHUM HARICHIM	1H61H6	1H2H2H2H	D	6/8	K2v4p27
HURRICANE, THE	313L2	3163	A	2/4 R	S8v7p5 S8v8p112
HYMN OF THE FOOLISH MAN, THE	3321	16L11	Bb	4/2	M10v2p3
HYND'S WEE CABIN	3456	3213	G	4/4	S8v6p54
I DAURNA SAY NO	5L121	4527L	A	6/8	S8v6p32
I HAE A LASS O' MY AIN OR MRS GRANT	5L21	5L24	E	9/8	G14p12
I HA'E A WIFE O' MY AIN	13b5	13b5	E	9/8	K2v2p34
I HA'E LAID A HERRIN' IN SA'T	3L5L6L6L	5L135	A	6/8	K2v2p35
I LO'E NAE A LADDIE BUT ANE	1166	5122	D	6/8	K2v1p31
I LOST MY LOVE	113b3b	557b5	A	6/8	K2v1p31
I THOUGHT THAT SHE WAS MINE	5L7bL15L	5L7bL11	A	4/4	P3p12
I WILL LOVE THEE YET	5555	7676	G	2/4	P3p11
I WILL SING YOU A SONG	5451	547b7bL	A	4/4	P3p7
I WINNA GAE TO BED	3H551H	2266	D	2/2 R	Mc3v1p46 R10p97
I WINNA GANG TAE BED THE NICHT, I CANNA' SLEEP AVA	51H51	3255	D	4/4	S8v6p90
I WISH YOU WOULD MARRY ME NOW	5L13b3b	427bL2	A	2/2*R	G6v1p23 L8v5p16
IF YE HAD BEEN WHERE I HAE BEEN	5H564	5H561H	D	4/4 S	R10p114
I'LL BREAK YOUR HEAD FOR YOU	3332	1122	Bb	4/4 R	K2v3p21
I'LL GANG NAE MAIR TO YON TOUN	11H31	3142	F	4/4 R	K2v2p21 L8v8Bp26 S9p6
I'LL GANG NAE MAIR TO YON TOUN	11H31	3542	F	2/2*R	Mc3v1p140 R10p205
I'LL GANG NAE MAIR TO YON TOWN	11H31	3132	F	4/4 R	L8v2p22 S17p57
I'LL HAP YE IN MY PLAIDIE	526L6L	5555	G	4/4 S	K2v1p9 R10p250
I'LL MAKE YOU BE FAIN TO FOLLOW ME	31H2H2	31H71H	C	6/8 J	L8v3p11 R10p140
I'LL/WE'LL AYE BE FOND O' INGRAM	5L16L1	6L27L5	A	4/4 S	S8v5p12
I'M A YOUNG MAN	552H3H	552H2H	D	6/8	K2v1p31
I'M OWRE YOUNG	5133	5132	G	4/4 R	K2v1p9
I'M OW'RE YOUNG	5133	5132	D	6/8	K2v2p34
IN THE GARB OF OLD GAUL	1H1H1H3H	1H31H1H	C	4/4	K2v3p46
IN THE GLOAMIN'	3565	3542	F	4/4 S	K2v3p19
INVER FIDDOCH	1315L	6L133	A	4/4	S8v6p68
INVER LASSES	5344	5342	A	4/4 R	K2v1p3
INVER LASSES	5346	5342	A	2/2 R	R10p18
INVERARAY	51H3H1H	51H2H2H	D	4/4 S	K2v3p6
INVERARAY CASTLE	5L15L3b	5L13b5	F#	4/4 S	S8v8p102
INVERARAY CROSS	1H3H61H	5531	D	4/4 R	K2v3p6
INVERARAY MARCH	3331	5556	G	4/4	K2v3p46
INVERARY CASTLE [INVERARAY CASTLE]	5L15L3b	5L13b5	F#m Em	4/4 S	L8v6p3 Mc3v1p75
INVERCAULD	4L5L15L	45L3b3b	A	4/4 S	K2v2p9
INVERCAULD	5L6L26L	5L6L44	A	4/4 S	R10p53
INVEREY'S RANT	1531	2427bL	A	2/2 S	G6v1p2 Mc3v1p33
INVERNESS GATHERING(, THE)	4213	1H554	A	4/4 QS	K2v1p47 Mc3v1p178
INVERNESS LASSES	1H535	1H535	F	4/4*R	L8v3p16 R10p221
INVERURIE	551H6	551H2H	D	4/4	S8v6p92
IRISH GIRL, THE	5L133	3323	A	6/8 J	L8v6p2
IRISH GIRL, THE	5L5L5L5L	6L6L13	G	6/8	Mc3v1p183
IRISH WASHERWOMAN(, THE)	35L35	46L46	G	6/8 J	L8v4p13 Mc3v1p175 R10p139 S9p20
IRVINE STEEPLE	1H1H35	67b24	D	2/2 R	R10p126
ISLA BANK	1546	7L122	A	4/4	S8v6p115
ISLA SIDE	1221	5522	G	4/4	S8v6p49
ISLA SIDE LASSES	1L17bL2L	1L113b	B	2/2	W1p21
ISLAND OF JAVA	1H3H53H	4327L	C	2/2 R	R10p79
ISLE OF SKYE(, THE)	13L13L	4L2L26L	Bb	4/4*R	L8v1p22 L8v8Ap28 Mc3v1p122 R10p279 S17p14
IT WINNA DO	121H2H	7b427bL	D	2/2 R	G6v2p41
ITALIAN MONFRINA	1321	57L21	G	6/8	K2v1p27
ITALIAN OPERA DANCE	1321	7L27L2	Bb	6/8	S15p21
IT'S BONNY O'ER THE HILL THE NIGHT	1H1H62H	3H4H66	D	4/4 R	L8v4p7
IT'S NAE AY FOR WANT O' HEALTH O?	5H564	53H1H6	D	2/2 R	Mc3v1p21
IVY HOUSE	551H1H	5525L	G	6/8	K2v4p28
J. SCOTT SKINNER'S COMPLIMENTS TO MR. PETER DAVIDSON	5L126L	5L57L2	A	4/4 SS	S8v3p38
JACK A' TAR	1H1H1H3bH	7b557b	E	4/4*HP	Mc3v1p173 R10p296
JACK LATTIN	1353	5354	A	4/4 R	K2v3p13
JACK'S HALF CROWN	7651	7655	A	2/2	S8v6p82
JACOBITE, THE	51H63	3232	A	4/4 S	K2v4p5
JAMES D. LAW'S REEL	16L3L1	567L2	Eb	2/2 R	S8v7p45
JAMES DOCKAR	153b1	17bL6bL4	E	4/4	P3p4
JAMES LUMSDEN ESQr	1L111	7bL7bL2L1L	B	4/4	W1p21
JAMES McINNES, ESQ., DANDALEITH	1131	6L27L5L	F	4/4 S	G14p19
JAMES McINNES, ESQ., DANDALEITH	15L15L	427L2	F	2/2 R	G14p31
JAMES MCNICOLL	1H31H3H	1H322H	C	4/4 S	K2v2p11 R10p64
JAMES MOIR ESQ.'S STRATHSPEY	5155	5124	G	4/4	W1p62
JAMES MORRISON	3b5L15	24L7bL4	D	4/4 S	H5p5

Title			Key		References
JAMES MORRISON	3bH2H1H5	7b527bL	D	4/4 R	H5p6
JAMES O. FORBES ESQ. OF CORSE	3142	361H1H	D	4/4 S	M7p15
JAMIE AND HIS BONNIE CATTIE	3L5L6L3L	6L126L	A	4/4	S8v6p60
JAMIE GRAY	1H111	3135	A	4/4	S8v6p98
JAMIE HARDIE	11H12	11H33	D	2/4 R	S8v7p21 S8v8p83
JAMIE MACKINTOSH	5L133	5353	A	4/4	S8v6p97
JAMIE RUSSELL	5161H	5125L	D	4/4	S8v6p89
JAMIE SHEARER	1H1H76	3H1H43	D	2/4 R	S8v7p3
JAMIE'S PAPER	1366	137L5L	G	4/4 SC	K2v3p24
JEANIE AND HER LOWLAND LADDIE	3b13b5	3b13b1	E	4/4 A	S8v3p16
JEANIE SKINNER	5366	5322	G	4/4 S	S8v3p25
JEANIE'S BLUE EEN	1H51H2H	3H5H2H7	D	6/8	K2v4p27
JEANIE'S DOLL IS DRESSED AGAIN	3531	4642	F	4/4 S	Mc3v1p146 S8v3p49
JEFFREY'S QUICKSTEP	5L565	1532	A	2/4	S8v6p116
JENKINS	1357L	671H7L	Bb	2/2 HP	R10p299
JENNY BOWSER	351H5	2662	D	4/4 R	Mc3v1p40 S8v3p2
JENNY DANG THE WEAVER	1H555	1H53H2H	D	4/4*R	K2v1p6 L8v1p10 L8v8Ap9
					Mc3v1p35 R10p83 S17p27
JENNY DRINKS NAE BRANDY	1H61H1H	2H226	D	2/2 CD	R10p149
JENNY GEDDES	117L7L	1123	Bb	2/2 R	K2v4p18
JENNY LATIN	1565	151H1H	D	2/2 R	K2v4p10
JENNY NETTLES	3b211H	57b47bL	A	4/4*R	K2v1p9 L8v3p22 Mc3v1p115
					R10p143
JENNY SUTTON	1155	1147bL	A	2/2 R	R10p28
JENNY'S BABEE [JENNY'S BAWBEE]	3H5H3H1H	4H675	D	2/2 R	G6v1p5
JENNY'S BAWBEE	5H5H3H1H	4H2H75	D	4/4*R	K2v1p4 L8v3p5 L8v8Bp7
					Mc3v1p72 R10p88
JESSIE(OF DUNBLANE)	3425	1121	A Bb	4/4 S	K2v4p4 L8v2p23
JESSIE RALSTON'S REEL	1H3H4H2H	7575	D	4/4 R	K2v2p20
JESSIE SMITH	5314	5366	D	4/4 S	K2v1p4 M7p17 R10p86
JIG [cf.SOLDIERS DANCE, the parts reversed]	5366	751H1H	A	6/8	K2v1p28
JIM ALONG JOSEY	1H1H1H1H	1H3H1H3	G	4/4 R	L8v3p23
JINGLIN JOHNNIE	1122	1122	A	2/2 CD	R10p144
J.O. FORBES ESQ. OF CORSE	3142	361H1H	E	4/4 SS	S8v7p37 S8v8p19
JOCKEY CLUB, THE	3H1H2H5	1H542	D	2/2 R	G6v2p9
JOCKEY LATIN	1553	5353	G	4/4 R	S17p95
JOCKS RAP	15L31	6522	G	4/4	S8v6p84
JOHN ABRACH MACKAY	5164	5124	A	4/4 PS	S8v9/7
JOHN ANGUS	1311H	5H2H2H6	E	2/2 R	R10p277
JOHN BEGG ESQ	1563	1322	F	4/4	W1p50
JOHN BROWN or FAITHFUL FRIEND	351H4	3524	A	4/4 SC	K2v1p20
JOHN CHEAP THE CHAPMAN	153b3b	1527bL	G	4/4*R	K2v1p13 L8v3p19 R10p189
					S17p35
JOHN FORBES ESQ.	5211	53b42	E	4/4	W1p46
JOHN HAY DELDONALD	5122	511H3H	D	4/4 S	G14p5
JOHN HOWATS REEL	5H3H4H2H	1H531	D	4/4 R	K2v2p20
JOHN HOWATS STRATHSPEY	3H1H42	35L24	D	4/4 S	K2v2p20
JOHN LAMONT'S REEL	136L7L	5L31H3	G	4/4	B9p5
JOHN MARSHALL	5L3b51H	7b427bL	E	4/4 S	S8v8p67
JOHN McALPIN(E)	3316L	5L132	A	4/4 S	K2v1p3 R10p3
JOHN McCOLL'S REEL	1353	4327bL	A	2/2 R	S8v7p28
JOHN McNEIL	1L2L3L4L	5L6L7L1	A	4/4 S	M7p20
JOHN McNEIL'S REEL	1L3L6L3L	13L6L3L	A	2/2 R	M7p20
JOHN McNIELL'S HIGHLAND FLING [?McNEILL)	511H3	37b27bL	A	4/4 S	S8v8p48
JOHN OF BADENYON	6L3L6L3L	115L5L	Bb	4/4 S	Mc3v1p148
JOHN OF PARIS	3353	41H53	A	6/8	K2v1p27
JOHN ROY STEWART [JOHN ROY STUART]	5313	5353	F	4/4 S	G6v1p22 K2v2p21 L8v1p19
					L8v8Ap23 Mc3v1p150 R10p208
					S8v8p122 S17p130
JOHN STEWART	1H1H51	42H76	C	4/4 R	S17p66
JOHNNIE GIBB O' GUSHETNEUK	1531	5L11L1L	G	4/4	S8v6p85
JOHNNIE LAD	3322	3361H	G	4/4 R	K2v1p10
JOHNNIE LAD	5544	551H3bH	E	2/2 R	R10p249
JOHNNIE PRINGLE	5L153	5L153	G	4/4 S	R10p160
JOHNNIE SMITH MY FALLA FINE	5L6L5L1	2135	A	4/4 S	S8v3p32
JOHN[N]IE STEELE	131H1H	1326L	D	4/4 S	S8v8p82
JOHNNIE'S FRIENDS ARE NE'ER PLEASED	1133	3316L	G	4/4 R	S17p20
JOHNNIE'S HIGHLAND FLING	5L133	6L27L5L	G	4/4	S8v6p86
JOHNNIE'S MADE A WADDIN' O'T [WEDDIN']	3b53b1	2427bL	G	2/2 R	R10p190
JOHNNIE('S) MADE A WEDDING O'T	3531	2427bL	G	4/4* R	K2v3p7 L8v2p11 Mc3v1p131
					S17p136
JOHNNY GALBRAITH	131H6	51H4H2H	C	4/4 S	L8v3p10 Mc3v1p160
JOHNNY GROATS HOUSE	51H3H2H	72H72H	C	4/4 R	K2v3p15
JOHNNY LAD	3322	3361H	Em	4/4 R	L8v2p14
JOHNNY LAD	1H3bH4H7b	13bH2H1H	E	4/4 R	M7p10
JOHNNY McGILL('S JIG)	5353	5316L	G	6/8 J	Mc3v1p175 M7p38 R10p141
JOHNNY PRINGLE	5L153	5L153	G	4/4 S	K2v2p14 L8v3p7 L8v8Ap13
					Mc3v1p88
JOHNNY WON'T YOU MARRY ME	551H3H	1H61H6	D	4/4 S	K2v4p8
JOLLY BEGGAR, THE	1352	11H76	G	4/4 S	K2v4p14

JOLLY BUTCHER, THE	3146	1H322	A	4/4		S8v6p99	
JOLLY SHEPHERDS, THE	3bH1H1H5	57b7b1H	E	4/4	SC	K2v2p24	
JOSEPH HUME	1131	1136L	F	4/4	S	K2v3p18	
JOY BE WITH MY LOVE	3H2H1H6	3H2H1H5	##	2/4		M10v2p25	
JUMPERS	315L3L	1L362	Bb	2/4	HP	S8v3p58	
JUMPING GEORDIE	1H51H5	1H542	G	4/4	R	K2v3p9	
KAFOOZALUM	5H5H3H5H	2H4H2H4H	D	4/4	SC	K2v1p20	
KAFOOZLE-UM	5535	2424	A	4/4	SC	M7p29	
KAIL POT, THE	13b51H	3bH1H2H5	D	4/4	S	K2v3p20	
KATE DALRYMPLE	1122	1122	A	4/4	R	K2v1p24	
KATIE'S BIRTHDAY	15L3L1	6522	A	4/4		S8v6p100	
KAY'S HORNPIPE	1112	3334	D	4/4	HP	M7p36	
KEABOG	51H3bH1H	7b427bL	F#	4/4	S	S8v8p91	
KEEL ROW(, THE)	3142	3125L	A	4/4*S		K2v1p19	K2v3p12 L8v6p4
						R10p11	S17p144
KEEL ROW, THE	3H1H4H2H	3H1H2H5	C	4/4		S9p10	
KEEP IT UP	7b57b1	7b527bL	Em	4/4	R	L8v5p12	
KEEP THE COUNTRY BONNY LASSIE	5324	5353	A	4/4*R		K2v2p4	L8v2p4 Mc3v1p25
						R10p24	
KEITH HALL	51H3H2H	5555	D	4/4		S8v6p71	
KELO HOUSE	1L1L3bL5L	7bL5L2L2L	G	2/2	R	G6v1p44	
KENMURE'S ON AN' AWA WILLIE	11H55	11H22	G	6/8		K2v1p32	Mc3v1p168 R10p145
[KENMORE LADS]							
KERR'S HORNPIPE	35L6L5L	35L1L1	A	4/4		W1p11	
KIDS THE	1H51H5	1H51H2	A	2/2	R	R10p36	
KILCOY CASTLE	1353	1H353	A	4/4	PR	Mc3v1p73	
KILDRUMMIE LODGE	1126L	5L3L3L2L	Bb	2/2		W1p17	
KILDRUMMY CASTLE	1351	6L27L5#L	Eb	4/4		S8v6p73	
KILDRUMMY CASTLE	3bL5L5L1	7bL4L2L7bF	B	4/4		W1p22	
KILLIECHASSIE	5513	5642	G	4/4	S	K2v2p16	R10p174
KILLIECRANKIE	5555	5155	D	2/4		K2v1p49	
KILLIN	4511	4527bL	A	2/2	R	R10p19	
KILTY LADS, THE	13b55	3b7b47bL	E	6/8		K2v1p48	
KINCALDRUM	1H542	7L242	G	4/4	R	S17p82	
KINCALDRUM [KURCALDRUM'S REEL)	1H532	7L242	G	2/2*R		L8v6p15	Mc3v1p92 R10p173
KINERMONY	1H533	64H72H	D	4/4	S	G14p31	
KING GEORGE IV'S WELCOME	1L1L3bL5L	1L1L2L7bF	A	4/4	S	R10p42	
KING GEORGE THE IVth	1L1L3bL1L	1L1L2L7bF	A	4/4	S	Mc3v1p106	
KING ROBERT THE BRUCE	1321	1H632	D	4/4	M	S8v7p32	
KING'S GUN, THE	11H61H	11H31	A	4/4	PR	Mc3v1p11	
KING'S REEL, THE	1L5L6L5L	1L5L3bL1L	A	2/2	R	Mc3v1p106	
KING'S, THE	1L5L6bL5L	1L5L3bL1L	A	4/4*R		K2v2p9	R10p42
KINLOCH OF KINLOCH	3H565	3H561H	D	6/8		K2v1p32	
KINLOCHEWE	11H65	4527L	D	4/4		S8v6p88	
KINRARA	113L5L	6L133	F	2/2	R	R10p211	
KINRARA	115L6L	1122L	Bb	4/4	S	R10p293	
KIRKMICHAEL PLOUGHS	15L13	15L22L	Bb	4/4	S	G6v1p39	
KIRKNEY WATER	1H535	4642	G	2/2		W1p59	
KIRK'S HORNPIPE	3511H	72H53H	D	4/4		M7p34	
KIRN, THE (HARVEST HOME)	1353	5L7L27L	D	4/4	S	S17p144	
KIRSTY MACFARLANE	5551H	3H1H2H6	D	2/2	R	K2v4p8	
KISS ME FAST(MY MINNIE'S COMING)	1324	1315	D	6/8	J	L8v6p6	R10p137
KISS ME SWEETLY	6H1H3H1H	6H1H3H2H	C	2/2	R	Mc3v1p113	
KISS THE LASS YE LIKE BEST	5362	5313H	D	4/4	S	Mc3v1p62	
KISSED YESTREEN	1151	27bL27bL	A	6/8		K2v1p31	
KISSING IS BEST OF A'	3134	311H6	G	4/4	R	K2v3p10	
KISSING IS(THE) BEST OF A'	3111	311H6	G	4/4	R	L8v6p14	Mc3v1p93
KITTLE CATTLE	15L3L1L	2L27L2	Bb	4/4	R	K2v3p21	
KITTY ROBERTSON	51H35	22H76	G	2/2	R	K2v4p14	
KITTY STEWART	5221	6L3L6L2	A	4/4		S8v6p105	
KNIT THE POCKY	11H1H3bH	7b53b2	D	2/2	R	G6v1p20	
KNOCK HIM DOWN SUSIE	5124	5151H	D	2/2	R	K2v4p11	
KNOCKANDO HOUSE	1155	1152	D	4/4	S	R10p127	
KNOCKIE	1H53b5	3bH1H1H5	C	2/2		S8v6p113	
KNOWLES'	3L4L7L1	41H22	A	2/4	HP	S8v8p132	
KYE COMES HAME	1H663	3555	D	4/4	S	K2v4p9	
LA SIESTA	321	7L6L1	Ab	3/4		S8v6p53	
LAD WI' THE JACKET O' BLUE, THE	51H1H3	1555	D	4/4		S8v6p63	
LAD WI' THE KILT, THE	51H3bH1H	2H424	E	4/4	R	L8v8Ap16	
LAD WI' THE PLAIDIE, THE	3H3H1H1H	5572H	D	4/4	SC	K2v1p19	
LADAR MOR A' GHOGAIN	1524	1551	E	2/2	R	R10p251	
LADDIE WI' THE BONNET BLUE, THE	16L5L3L	4L3L2L6F	Bb	2/2		W1p17	
LADS O' DUNS(E, THE)	5116	6562	D	6/8		K2v1p33	L8v1p9 R10p136
LADS O' ELGIN, THE	13b53b	25L7bL2	A	4/4	S	R10p59	
LADS OF FOSS, THE	3565	1H542	D	4/4*R		K2v2p18	R10p93
LADS OF LEITH	5L13b2	4L7bL21	E	2/2	R	K2v4p13	
LADS OF TAIN(, THE)	5364	531H6	D	4/4	S	K2v2p17	L8v3p6 Mc3v1p41
						R10p104	
LADS OF TARLAND, THE	115L5L	1122L	G	6/8		W1p63	
LADS WI' THE KILTS, THE	1H51H1H	665H4H	D	6/8		K2v4p27	
LADY AMELIA MURRAY	5662	5653H	D	4/4	S	L8v6p9	R10p121
LADY ANDERSON	1H531	427L5L	D	2/2*R		S8v3p7	Mc3v1p53

LADY ANN ERSKINE	11H2H1H	31H42	C	4/4 R	L8v6p18	
LADY ANN HOPE	5L126L	4453	G	4/4 S	L8v1p12	L8v8Ap12 Mc3v1p95
LADY ANN HOPE	1126L	4453	G	4/4 S	K2v1p10	R10p157
LADY ANN HOPE	316L5L	7L37L5L	G	4/4 S	R10p175	
LADY ANN MAITLAND	1H515	1H1H2H6	G	2/2 R	G6v1p31	
LADY ANN STEWART	1H553	657L2	A	4/4 S	S17p74	
LADY ANN WHARTON DUFF'S STRATHSPEY	1L6L2L4L	1L6L5L1	Bb	4/4 SS	Mc3v1p164	
LADY ASHBURTON	1H135L	6L122	Eb	4/4 S	R10p170	
LADY AUGUSTA GORDON LENNOX'S STRATHSPEY	15L3bL1L	7b527bL	G	4/4	W1p64	
LADY BAIRD	5311	6L5L6L5L	A	4/4 S	L8v1p3	L8vdBp5 Mc3v1p25
					R10p8	S9p9 S17p142
LADY BAIRD	53b11	6b56b5	A	4/4 S	K2v1p9	
LADY BAIRD'S NEW REEL	543b1	5427bL	B	2/2 R	G6v2p49	
LADY BELHAVEN	3151H	3147bL	G	2/2 R	R10p178	
LADY BETTY BOYLE	13L4L5L	157L2	Bb	4/4 R	S17p68	
LADY BETTY COCHRANE	1H515	42H2H6	C	4/4 R	K2v2p13	L8v6p18
LADY BETTY WEMYSS	31H31H	2H1H22	C	2/2 R	G6v1p11	
LADY BINNING	4233	427L5L	A	4/4 S	S17p42	
LADY BINNING	1233	427L5L	A	4/4 S	K2v2p4	L8v2p2 Mc3v1p9 R10p9
LADY BROME'S STRATHSPEY	3b1H1H1	22H7b7bL	C	4/4 S	Mc3v1p194	
LADY BURNSIDE'S BIRTHDAY	1H1H3b3b	7b7b24	C	4/4 S	G6v1p42	R10p271
LADY CARMICHAEL	1H3H65	652H2H	D	4/4 S	K2v1p3	R10p63
LADY CAROLINE MONTAGUE	5H3H1H5	5H3H72H	C	4/4 S	K2v3p14	L8v6p18 Mc3v1p107
					R10p73	
LADY CATHERINE STEWART or	5552	517bL2	G E	4/4 S	S8v7p12	S8v8p64
HAUGHS O' CROMDALE, THE						
LADY CHARLOTTE BRUCE	1351	6L47L2	A	4/4 S	G6v2p5	
LADY CHARLOTTE CAMPBELL	3546	75H3H1H	C	4/4 S	S17p84	
LADY CHARLOTTE CAMPBELL	1H1H3H5H	4H2H72H	C	4/4 R	S17p85	
LADY CHARLOTTE CAMPBELL	5323	536L7L	G	4/4 S	G6v2p16	K2v2p14 L8v1p11
					R10p173	S17p30
LADY CHARLOTTE CAMPBELL	3L5L4L6L	7L531	Bb	4/4 S	G6v2p26	K2v2p23 L8v6p22
					Mc3v1p190	R10p282
LADY CHARLOTTE CAMPBELL	1135	427L2	Bb	4/4*R	G6v2p26	K2v2p23 L8v6p22
					R10p282	S8v7p15
LADY CHARLOTTE CAMPBELL	1347L	137L3	Bb	2/4 R	S8v8p126	
LADY CHARLOTTE CAMPBELL'S REEL	1135	427L1	Bb	4/4 R	Mc3v1p190	
LADY CHARLOTTE DURHAM	5327bL	5337b	A	4/4 S	R10p18	K2v2p5
LADY CHARLOTTE DURHAM	11H1H3	116L6L	G	4/4	Mc3v1p185	
LADY CHARLOTTE GORDON	1H543	1H3H2H2	F	4/4 R	Mc3v1p146	
LADY CHARLOTTE MENZIES	31H65	432H2	F	2/2 R	R10p220	
LADY CHARLOTT[E] MURRAY	1H3H55	44H2H2H	D	2/2 R	G6v1p28	R10p122
LADY CHARLOTTE MURRAY OR DONALD DOW	5651	51H52	F	4/4 S	R10p228	
LADY CHARLOTTE PRIMROSE	1H51H1H	1H51H2	D	4/4 S	R10p121	
LADY CLARE	5366	5353	F	4/4 S	K2v4p18	
LADY DAVIDSON OF CANTRAY	1551	22H4H7	D	4/4 S	K2v3p4	L8v4p6
LADY DOUNE	1H1H1H1H	2H2H66	F	4/4 S	K2v1p14	L8v4p23 L8v8Bp23
					R10p204	S17p52
LADY DOWN	1H1H31	427L5L	C	2/2 R	Mc3v1p119	R10p82
LADY DUMFRIES	1153H	1H522	F	2/2*R	R10p220	S17p45
LADY ELIZABETH CAMPBELL	4635	4327bL	A	2/2 R	R10p34	
LADY ELIZABETH LINDSAY	5316L	5L3L5L3L	Bb	4/4 S	K2v2p23	L8v3p17 L8v8Ap28
					Mc3v1p135	R10p284 S17p58
LADY ERSKINE	113b2	27b27bL	A	2/2 R	G6v2p44	
LADY FORBES OF NEWE'S REEL	15L3L5L	6L6L6L2L	A	2/2	W1p1	
LADY FRANCES SOMERSET	531H5	437L2	Bb	2/2*R	G6v2p27	Mc3v1p193
LADY GEORGE BEAUCLARK [BEAUCLERK]	311H3	4542	C	2/2 R	G6v1p11	
LADY GEORGINA CAMPBELL	15L11	5352	G	4/4 R	Mc3v1p184	
LADY GEORGINA GORDON	3bH1H3b1H	2H7b27b	D	2/2 R	G6v2p42	
LADY GEORGINA GORDON	3bH1H3bH1H	2H7b27b	D	2/2 R	R10p226	
LADY GEORGINA GORDON'S STRATHSPEY	1133	6522	F	4/4 S	Mc3v1p147	
LADY GEORGINA(RUSSELL'S REEL)	1L1L5L1	6L6L22	Bb	2/2 R	Mc3v1p138	R10p293
LADY GLASGOW	1565	1535	A	4/4 S	G6v2p4	
LADY GLENORCHY	1H631	311H5	A	4/4*R	K2v2p6	R10p33
LADY GRACE DOUGLAS	5327L	15L4L2L	Bb	2/2*R	Mc3v1p136	R10p286 S17p104
LADY GRACE STEWART	1L13b7bL	1L13b3b	B	4/4 S	G6v2p49	R10p132
LADY GWYDER	1311H	5326L	D	4/4 S	Mc3v1p64	S17p160
LADY HALL	115L1	3553	G	4/4 S	K2v2p20	
LADY HAMILTON	15L6L5L	4L3L2L2	Bb	2/2 R	G6v2p29	Mc3v1p128
LADY HAMILTON (OF)DALRYMPLE	3b15L1	2452	G	4/4 S	G6v2p36	K2v3p21 R10p194
LADY HAMPDEN	1L153	2L226L	A	4/4 S	G6v1p27	R10p154
LADY HARRIET HOPE	1564	1H3H2H2	F	4/4*R	K2v1p14	L8v2p22 L8v8Ap27
					Mc3v1p144	R10p216 S17p32
LADY HARRIET SUSAN KER	6L6L5L1	4522	Bb	4/4 R	S17p124	
LADY HELEN DOUGLAS	3b53b5	1H2H7b7bL	D	2/2 R	G6v1p21	
LADY HELEN WEDDERBURN	3555	351H1H	D	2/2 R	R10p123	
LADY HOME	1H5H5H5H	1H5H2H4H	C	6/8 J	L8v5p14	
LADY ISABELLA WEMYSS' STRATHSPEY	1256L	5L121	D	4/4 SS	Mc3v1p156	
LADY JANE MONTGOMERY	5542	5551H	F	4/4 S	R10p236	
LADY JANE NEVILLE	1H535	352H2H	G	4/4*R	K2v2p15	Mc3v1p99 R10p162
LADY JANE TAYLOR	31H31H	31H2H2	C	4/4 S	K2v3p15	R10p80
LADY JARDINE	5115	5124	F	4/4 S	R10p218	

LADY JEMIMA CORNWA(L)LIS	11H1H1H	1H364	A	2/2 R	Mc3v1p27
LADY JEMIMA JOHNSTON	3535	31H42	C	4/4 S	K2v2p12 Mc3v1p108 R10p76
LADY LOUDON	5H5H5H5H	5H5H4H2H	C	4/4 S	K2v2p11 L8v1p15 L8v8p20
					Mc3v1p117 R10p62
LADY LOUISA CORNWALLIS' STRATHSPEY	1453	6L247L	Eb	4/4 S	Mc3v1p130
LADY LOUISA GORDON	5L133	6L244	F	4/4 S	G6v1p14
LADY LUCINDA RAMSAY	53b5L1	424L7bL	G	4/4 S	R10p195
LADY LUCY LESLIE MELVILLE	1H511	22H62H	F	2/2 R	R10p236
LADY LUCY RAMSAY	3H5H5H1H	5H6H3H2H	C	4/4 S	K2v1p14 L8v1p16 Mc3v1p120
					R10p66 S17p64
LADY MACKENZIE OF COUL	5564	751H5H	C	4/4 S	S17p154
LADY MACKENZIE OF SEAFORTH	5557b	4446	A	4/4 PS	Mc3v1p70
LADY MADALINA GORDON	5L35L4	5L37L7L	F	2/2 R	R10p242
LADY MADELINA PALMER('S STRATHSPEY)	1H535	1H4H72H	D	4/4 S	Mc3v1p37 M7p13
LADY MADELINA SINCLAIR	5336	5622	A G	4/4 S	L8v3p2 Mc3v1p4 R10p11 S17p40
LADY MADELINA SINCLAIR	5336	5322	A	4/4 S	K2v2p4
LADY MADELINA SINCLAIR	15L3L4L	2L242	A	2/2 R	G6v1p25
LADY MADELINA SINCLAIR'S BIRTHDAY	15L3L5L	137L2	Bb	4/4*R	K2v2p23 L8v3p17 L8v8Ap29
					Mc3v1p135 R10p284 S17p34
LADY MARGARET STEWART	513b5	5424	B	4/4*R	K2v3p6 L8v4p11 R10p132
					S17p106
LADY MARIA DUNDAS [LADY MARY DUNDAS]	5153	6753	F	2/2*R	K2v4p18 S17p103
LADY MARY HAY	53b13b	427b2	C	2/2 R	G6v2p32
LADY MARY HOPE VERE	1H535	42H76	D	4/4*R	L8v8Ap11 Mc3v1p57 R10p109
LADY MARY LINDSAY	3H1H1H1H	2266	C	2/2 R	G6v1p10
LADY MARY MENZIES	5351H	5362	F	2/2 R	R10p245
LADY MARY MONTAGUE	51H53	6542	D	2/2 R	G6v1p29
LADY MARY MURRAY	5L153	2427L	G	4/4 S	R10p176
LADY MARY PRIMROSE	5L3L5L3L	16L2L2L	Bb	4/4 SS	S8v8p18/19
LADY MARY RAMSAY	1153	5653	D (Eb)	4/4 S	K2v1p10 L8v1p7 L8v8Ap10
					Mc3v1p34 R10p88 R10p268
					S8v8p88 S17p26
LADY MARY STOPFORD	51H53	6542	D	4/4*R	K2v3p4 L8v3p4 Mc3v1p41
					R10p104 S17p39
LADY MCKENZIE OF COUL	5564	751H5H	C	4/4 S	K2v2p13 L8v5p14
LADY MONTGOMERY	113L5L	114L2	Bb	4/4*R	K2v1p17 L8v3p17 L8v8Ap30
					Mc3v1p125 R10p278 S17p5
LADY MUIR MACKENZIE	11H31	27b27bL	C	2/2 R	Mc3v1p109
LADY NELLIE WEMYSS	3535	3524	A	6/8 J	K2v2p35 L8v2p3 Mc3v1p177
[LADY NELLY WEMYSS('S JIG)]					R10p134
LADY OF THE LAKE	316L1	3125	G	6/8	K2v1p32 R10p146
LADY RADCLIFFE'S REEL	1331H	137L2	F	2/2	W1p50
LADY ROSS	3135	27bL24	D	4/4 S	S8v3p3
LADY SHAFTESBURY	13L13	527L2	Eb	2/4*S	Mc3v1p131 R10p271 S17p14
LADY SPENCER CHICHESTER	116L1	136L2	F	4/4 S	K2v2p22 R10p229
LADY SUSAN GORDON	1353	6L5L4L2L	Bb	2/2 R	G6v1p17 R10p294
LADY TERFICHEN [LADY TORPHICHEN]	13b45	13b6b6b	E	2/2 R	K2v4p15
LADY WALLACE	1H513	2466	F	4/4 R	G6v1p13
LADY WALLACE	1H3bH75	7b43b5	C	4/4	S8v8p160
LADYHILL, ELGIN	511H6	5522	D	4/4 S	S8v5p20
LAGER BEER	13b55	7b427bL	B	4/4 S	K2v4p12
LAIRD O' AUCHLUNCART, THE	1H655	1H652	D	4/4 QS	S8v8p29
LAIRD O' BEMERSYDE, THE	1L5L3L1	4L27L5	A	4/4 A	S8v9/4
LAIRD O' DRUMBLAIR, THE	135L3	1H765	A	4/4 S	S8v7p10 S8v8p93
LAIRD O' HAUGHS, THE	125L1H	4525L	Bb	2/4 HP	S8v9/1
LAIRD OF COCKPEN, THE	13b27bL	11H7b5	E	6/8	K2v2p34
LAIRD OF MACINTOSH, THE	5353	7L27L2	G	2/2 R	R10p175
LAIRD'S KILT, THE	1L3L5L1L	4L3L2L2	A	4/4	S8v6p97
LALLA SINCE THE QUEEN'S COME or ELGIN	3565	3565	D	4/4 S	S8v3p7 Mc3v1p52
LAMBERTON RACES	153H2H	1H542	F	4/4*R	Mc3v1p139 R10p232 S17p101
[COL. RENTON'S FAVOURITE]					
LAMENT FOR MR. THOMAS GRANT	13b27bL	13b7bL1	A	4/4	G14p4
OF GLEN ELGIN (AUSTRALIA)					
LAMENT FOR THE AULD GEAN TREE	115L3bL	5L7bL7bL3b	A	4/4	G14p21
OF WESTER ELCHIES					
LAMENT FOR THE LATE MR Wm. CHRISTIE	115L4L	3bL3bL3bL3b	A	4/4	P3p7
LAMENT SIR JOHN MACPHERSON GRANT	13b55	127L0	D	4/4	G14p9
LANG, LANG SYNE, THE	3221	1355	G	4/4	S8v6p25
LANG SYNE	1122	1366	G	4/4 R	K2v3p9
LANGMAN KNAP, THE	1H132	1H11H6	C	4/4	P3p2
LAOIDH AN AMADAIN MHOIR	3H2H1H1H	561H2H	E	2/4	M10v2p23
LARGO BAY	3563	7L233	A	4/4 S	K2v3p12
LARGO LAW	15L13	6522	A	4/4 S	K2v2p6 R10p28
LARGO LAW	3113	61H61H	A	4/4 R	K2v3p12
LARGO'S FAIRY DANCE	3H3H3H3H	3H3H72H	D	4/4 R	L8v5p7
LARGO'S FAIRY DANCE	3H3H3H7	3H4H71H	D	2/4 R	S8v8p88/9
LASS I NEVER SAW, THE	15L55	4255	G	4/4	P3p11
LASS O' CORRIE MILL, THE	137L1	3535	F	4/4 S	K2v1p17
LASS O' GOWRIE	351H1H	662H2H	F	2/4	S9p15
LASS O' PATIES MILL, THE	431H3H	6632	D	2/4 CD	K2v1p21
LASS WI' THE TARTAN PLAIDIE, O!, THE	3L16L1	5236L	A	4/4	S8v6p35
LASS WI' THE TARTAN PLAIDIE, O, THE	3L5L11	6L3L11	A	4/4 A	S8v5p16

Title			Key	Time	References
LASSES FASHION, THE	3b13b7bL	3b154	F#	4/4 R	K2v2p8
LASSES' FASHION, THE	16L15L	16L32	A	2/2 R	R10p35
LASSES LIKE NAE BRANDY	51H65	27b46	A	4/4 R	L8v6p5 Mc3v1p21
LASSES LIKE NAE BRANDY	51H65	27b44	A	4/4*R	K2v2p5 R10p21
LASSES LOOK BEFORE YOU	1313	27b27bL	D	4/4 S	K2v1p8 L8v1p6 L8v8Bp6
[LASSIE LOOK BEFORE YOU or MISS ROSS]					Mc3v1p39 R10p94
LASS(ES) O' BALLANTRAE, THE	5367	5326L	F	4/4 R	Mc3v1p189 S17p52
LASSES OF FOCHABERS, THE	1565	1522	G	2/2	W1p63
LASSES OF STEWARTON, THE	3H2H1H1H	3155	D	4/4*R	K2v3p5 L8v5p6 L8v8Bp10
					Mc3v1p37 R10p94
LASSIE LOOK BEHIND YE	5326L	531H1H	D	2/2 R	R10p87
LASSIE OF THE GLEN, THE	3432	3452	D	4/4	W1p28
LASSIE WI' THE YELLOW COATIE	1151H	61H66	G	4/4*R	L8v4p13 R10p72
LASSINTULLICH OR STEER THE GILL	1H553	1H553H	D	2/2 R	R10p92
LAUGH AT FATE	3111H	6446	D	4/4	S8v6p40
LEA RIG, THE	15L11	1226L	A	4/4 R	K2v2p7 K2v3p12 L8v1p2
					Mc3v1p28
LEBURN'S HIGHLAND BAGPIPE	1H1H53	2466	A	4/4 S	S8v8p98
LEES OF LUNCARTIE, THE	5L343	2347bL	G	4/4 S	L8v3p9 R10p171
[LEES OF LUNCARTY, THE]					
LEFT HANDED FIDDLER, THE	31H37L	31H53	A	2/4 R	S8v7p5 S8v8p95
LEGGET'S IRISH REEL	1H663	6633	G	4/4 HP	M7p9
LEITH HALL	5L133	5L146L	F	4/4 S	R10p239
LENNOX LOVE TO BLANTYRE	1131	2466	F	4/4 R	K2v3p18 L8v4p23 Mc3v1p140
					R10p204 S17p2
LESLIE	1H3H2H5	61H51	D	2/2	Mc3v1p46 R10p85
LESLIE'S MARCH	1H1H1H5	1H51H2H	D	6/8	K2v4p27
LET THAT STAND THERE	1555	62H2H2H	G	4/4 R	L8v6p15
LICK THE LADLE SANDY	5353	7bL7b44	A	2/2 R	R10p21
LIEUT. A. STEWART	3127bL	3146	A	2/2 R	R10p30
LIEUT. ABERCROMBY	1565	4327L	Bb	2/2 R	G6v2p28
LIEUT. COL. BAILLIE OF LEYS	131H3	227L7L	D	4/4 S	Mc3v1p26 S17p162
LIEUT. COL. LUMSDEN	13bL13b	227b2	G	2/2 R	G6v2p36
LIGHT AND AIRY	5311H	5324	F	6/8 J	L8v5p18
LIMERICK LASSES	1H511	4462	D	2/2 R	R10p112
LINK HIM DODDIE	1533	351H3	A	4/4 S	L8v1p5
LINK HIM DODDIE	1533	27b22	A	4/4 S	K2v1p18 Mc3v1p15 R10p17
LINK HIM DODDIE	153b3b	27b22	A	4/4 S	K2v3p18
LITTLE PICKLE	135L3	462H5	A	6/8 J	L8v4p2
LITTLEJOHN'S HAME	15L35	1H765	D	4/4 SS	S8v7p17
LIVERPOOL(HORNPIPE)	331H5H	4H2H1H6	D F	2/2*HP	R10p297 Mc3v1p172 S9p29
LOCH AVON	1353	1342	F	2/2	W1p51
LOCH BUILG	536L5L	6L5L32	Eb	2/2	W1p37
LOCH DERCULICH	13b54	247b4	E	2/2 R	R10p253
LOCH DUICH	331H6	631H3	A	2/4	M10v1p12
LOCH EARN [or TILT SIDE]	1H513	6L27L5L	G	4/4*R	G6v2p15 K2v1p8 L8v1p11
					L8v8Bp13 Mc3v1p94 R10p160
					S17p24
LOCH ERICHT SIDE [LOCH ERROCH SIDE]	351H1H	662H2H	C	4/4 S	K2v2p11 L8v8Bp18 Mc3v1p159
					R10p60
LOCH FYNE	5353	61H51	G	4/4 R	K2v3p8
LOCH GLASSIE	1H555	1H3H1H5	D	4/4*R	K2v1p17 R10p93
LOCH LEVEN CASTLE	1115L	113b3b	A	4/4 R	K2v1p11
LOCH LONG	5L521	5L6L5L6L	A	4/4 S	K2v4p5
LOCH MAREE	5L13b5	3b127bL	A	4/4	S8v6p82
LOCH MUICK	1H511	2266	D	4/4	B9p7
LOCH MUICK	1111	7bL7bL7bL7bL	F	4/4	W1p54
LOCH NESS	11H7b4	3b7bL7bL3b	A	2/2 R	G6v1p24
LOCH O' DRUMMUIR, THE	51H7b3b	57b44	D	4/4 S	S8v5p11
LOCH O' FORFAR, THE or	15L3L5L	15L13	A	4/4 S	S8v8p104
BLAIR'S FAVOURITE					
LOCH OF FORFAR, THE	15L3L5L	15L33	A	4/4 S	G6v2p6
LOCH RUTHVEN	3bH1H53b	7b424	C	4/4 S	R10p266
LOCH RYNACH	1347L	1344	G	4/4 R	L8v2p12
LOCHABER NO MORE	333	323	G	3/4	K2v3p47
LOCHAN A' CHAIT	5L13b5	7b427bL	E	2/2 R	R10p250
LOCHEND SIDE	5L111	3b53b7bL	G	2/2 R	R10p196
LOCHIEL'S MARCH	5112	557b4	A	4/4	K2v1p47
LOCHIEL'S RANT	5154	27bL24	A E	4/4*R	K2v1p9 L8v6p17 Mc3v1p49
[LOCHIEL'S AWA' TO/TAE FRANCE]					R10p254
LOCHLEVEN CASTLE	1115L	113b3b	A	4/4 CD	M7p30
LOCHNABO	1225	1226L	A	4/4 S	S8v3p31
LOCHNAGAR	1155	1H3H2H1H	D	4/4 SC	K2v2p24
LOCHNAGAR WHISKY	1426L	1555	G	4/4	B9p4
LOCHRYNACH	1347L	1344	G	4/4*R	K2v2p16 R10p184
LOCOMOTIVE, THE	3H1H1H3	3H1H1H3	F	4/4	S9p29
LODGE OF GLEN TANA, THE	53bH2H1H	7b427bL	F#	4/4 S	S8v5p15
LOGAN WATER	3b113b	7bL37bL5	B	4/4	K2v3p47
LOGIE O BUCHAN	335	53H2H	D	3/4 W	K2v1p25
"LONACH" COUNTRY DANCE, THE	1H1H1H5	5362	E	2/4	W1p43
LONACH GATHERING, THE	16L3L5L	1522	A	4/4 M	S8v8p33
LONACH HALL	51H26L	51H66	C	4/4	W1p23

LONACH HIGHLANDERS MARCH, THE	15L31	531H1H	F	4/4	W1p52
LONDON BRIDGE	1H11H2H	3H63H1H	C	2/4	S9p29
LONDON SCOTTISH, THE	3456	357b4	A	2/4 PM	S8v8p47
LONG LIFE TO GOOD EARL FIFE	1H1H3H6	5H3H6H0	D	2/4	P3p3
LONGAIR'S PIPES	5431	47bL46	A	2/2	S8v6p75
LOOK BEHIND YOU	5326L	531H1H	D	4/4 R	L8v2p8
(=HOUSE OF LETTERFOURIE, THE)					
LORD AIRLIE	537L2	5353	F	2/2 R	R10p235
LORD ALEXANDER GORDON	1153	5642	A	4/4 S	S17p116
LORD ALEXANDER GORDON	1L153	5642	A	4/4 S	K2v2p5 L8v2p4 R10p26
LORD ALEXANDER GORDON	1L133	5642	A	4/4 S	Mc3v1p25
LORD ARTHUR'S CAIRN	11L5L3L	5L3L6L4L	G	2/2	W1p57
LORD BLANTYRE('S)	3131H	67b27bL	A	4/4 S	K2v2p7 L8v5p1 Mc3v1p19
					R10p34
LORD BREADALBANE'S MARCH	53H61H	53H52H	D	6/8	K2v1p48
LORD BYRON	1356	1H776	D	4/4	S8v6p67
LORD DALHOUSIE	1H3H2H3H	2H3H1H6	D	4/4 R	S17p12
LORD DALHOUSIE	1H3H53H	2H3H1H6	D	4/4*R	K2v2p17 L8v3p5 Mc3v1p48
					R10p94
LORD DOUNE	547bL2	5557b	G	4/4 S	S17p104
LORD DOWN	1565	47L43	G	4/4 S	K2v4p16
LORD DOWN	1551	7bL447bL	G	4/4 S	G6v2p39 R10p201
LORD DREGHORN'S QUICKSTEP	1H51H3	1H62H7	D	6/8	Mc3v1p174
LORD DRUMMOND	51H65	662H2H	D	4/4 R	K2v3p6
LORD DUDLEY'S MARCH	5114	25L5L5	Bb	4/4	W1p18
LORD EGLINTOUNE	5L35L3L	5L322L	Bb	2/2 R	G6v1p15
LORD EGLINTOUN'S AULD MAN	5451	5455	D	4/4 S	K2v2p18 L8v3p6 R10p108
LORD ELCHO	1H546	3547L	G	2/2 R	G6v2p14
LORD ELPHINSTONE	1355	1351H	F	4/4 S	G6v2p25
LORD FIFE'S MARCH	1113	5542	G	4/4	W1p64
LORD GEORGE GORDON LENNOX'S REEL	13b13b	5427bL	G	2/2	W1p65
LORD GLENORCHY	1H3H1H6	51H22	F	4/4 S	R10p208
LORD HAY	5627bL	5655	D	4/4 S	R10p183
LORD HUNTLY'S CAVE	3H4H3H1H	2H5H1H2H	D	4/4 M	S8v7p34 S8v8p25
LORD JAMES MURRAY	1H51H3	22H76	D	4/4*R	L8v6p9 R10p121
LORD JOHN CAMPBELL	137L2	1353	D	4/4 S	K2v2p19 M7p14 R10p115
					S8v8p82
LORD JOHN CAMPBELL	131H1H	2H2H2H2	F	2/2 R	G6v2p23
LORD KELLY	5L3b53b	4L27bL3b	Gm	4/4 S	L8v3p20
LORD KELLY	5L3b53b	7bL47bL1	G	4/4 R	S17p146
LORD KELLY	5L3b53b	4L27bL2	G	4/4 S	K2v3p22 R10p187
LORD KILMAURS	117bL2	113b5	E	2/2 R	R10p256
LORD KINGARTH	5152	517bL2	A	2/2 R	K2v4p17
LORD KINNAIRD	1H1H1H2	1H565	D	4/4 R	L8v2p7
LORD KINNAIRD [LORD KINNEARD]	1H1H1H3	1H565	D	2/2 R	Mc3v1p47 R10p101
LORD LOVAT'S WELCOME	3121	5L151H	F	4/4 SS	R10p221
LORD LOVAT'S WELCOME or MOIREAR SHEIM	3127L	5L151H	G	4/4 S	Mc3v1p91
LORD LYNDOCH [LORD LYNEDOCH]	1H1H51	3636	D	4/4 S	L8v5p8 Mc3v1p66
LORD LYNDOCH [LORD LYNEDOCH]	1H1H51	4646	D	4/4 SC	K2v1p19 M7p16
LORD LYNDOCH [LORD LYNEDOCH]	1H1H51	2646	D	4/4 S	R10p113
LORD LYNDOCH'S WELCOME	1333L	1135	A	4/4 S	R10p154
LORD MACDONALD	5551H	51H2H2	G	4/4*R	K2v1p10 Mc3v1p33 R10p164
					S17p84
LORD MACDONALD	5552H	5523	G	2/4 R	S8v8p58
LORD MACDONALD	1H3H1H5	662H2H	D	4/4 S	Mc3v1p180
LORD McDONALD [LORD MACDONALD]	355H2H	4H2H66	D	4/4 S	K2v4p11 Mc3v1p33 R10p105
					S17p116
LORD McDUFF'S STRATHSPEY	5L126L	5L16L2L	A	4/4	W1p5
LORD MOIRA('S WELCOME)	1135	4327L	F	4/4 S	K2v2p21 K2v3p19 L8v3p13
					L8v8Bp26 Mc3v1p166 R10p210
LORD OF THE ISLES	1H511	6L27L5L	G	4/4 S	K2v4p14
LORD PRESIDENT FORBES	3L15L1L	3L133	A	4/4 S	K2v3p13
LORD RAMSAY	331H5	3342	G	4/4 R	L8v3p8 Mc3v1p84
LORD RAMSAY	3555	31H52	Bb	4/4 S	K2v1p13 R10p286 S17p56
LORD RAMSAY	5315L	6L47L2	G	4/4 S	K2v3p7 L8v3p8 Mc3v1p84
LORD REDHAVEN'S REEL	5L315L	1L322L	A	2/2	W1p7
LORD REIDHAVEN	3L5L5L1	5L12L2L	A	4/4 SS	S8v5p12 S8v6p101
LORD SALTOUN('S REEL)	572H7	5764	A	4/4*R	K2v1p16 L8v6p2 R10p28
LORD SEAFORTH	15L13	436L6L	G A	4/4 S	K2v1p8 L8v5p10 Mc3v1p78
					R10p162 S17p80
LORD STRATHAVEN	1365	1364	F	4/4 S	R10p222
LORN STRATHSPEY, THE	3H2H1H1	27bL44	D	4/4 S	Mc3v1p60
LOTHIAN LASSES	5L13b5	247b4	E	2/2 R	Mc3v1p101
LOUDONS BONNIE WOODS	1135	4327L	G	4/4 SC	K2v1p19
LOVAT'S RESTORATION	1H3H2H3H	62H72H	D	4/4 S	R10p116
LOVE'S YOUNG DREAM	3215L	2222	G	6/8	S9p24
LOW DOWN IN THE BROOM	121H6	662H1H	D	4/4 S	K2v2p17
LOW-BACKED CAR, THE	1352	1555	F	6/8	S9p23
LOWE'S REEL	1115	4246	A	4/4 R	K2v3p12 L8v5p4
LOWLAND RANT	116L1	526L6L	G	4/4 S	K2v4p15
LOWLANDS OF SCOTLAND, THE	3b3b51	56b51	E	2/2 R	K2v4p14
LUNDIN LINKS	3563	6L5L6L5L	F	4/4 S	K2v3p20

Title			Key	Time	Source
LUSS ROAD	17L25L	3L2L3L1L	G	4/4 S	K2v4p14
LYNN BURN	1L7bL5L1L	2L7bL2L7bF	A	4/4 S	G14p20
LYNN OF RUTHRIE	1L3bL1L1	6bL4L3bL3bL	A	4/4 S	G14p26
MABEL BRIGGS	3575	7L232	A	4/4	S8v9/5
MAC GRIOGAIR A RUARO [LAMENTATION FOR MACGREGOR OF RORO]	112	35L5L	A	3/4	Mc3v1p153
MACALLAN	EGH2H2H	31H1H2	G	4/4 S	G14p13
MACALLAN	3L131	4647L	A	4/4 S	S8v7p10
MACCRIMMON'S LAMENT [CHA TILL MI TUILLE]	1545	1655	A	4/4 A	Mc3v1p182
MACDONALD'S KILT	561H3H	2H3H2H6	D	4/4 S	S8v9/9
MACDONALD'S MARCH, THE	3131H	7b7b7b7bL	A	2/4	K2v3p47
MACDOUGALL GILLIES' PIPES	1331H	37b27bL	A	4/4	S8v8p182
MACDUFF	1351H	1522	G	4/4	P3p13
MACFARLANE'S RANT	3H52H6	3H52H1H	D	2/2 R	R10p105
MACGREGOR A RUARI [MACGREGOR OF RORO, ETC]	112	35L5L	A	3/4	M10v2p14
MACGREGOR'S GATHERING	1H2H2H7	5556	D	2/2 R	K2v4p9
MACGREGOR'S MARCH	1H2H55	1H1H4H2H	D	2/4	K2v3p46
MACINTOSH OF MACINTOSH	15L3L1L	4L2L3L5L	Bb	4/4 R	Mc3v1p129
MACIVAR'S	5353	51H22	C	4/4 S	K2v2p12
MACKENZIE FRASER	131H7	62H75	D	2/2 R	S8v10p4
MACKENZIE MURDOCH	1541H	51H22	Bb	2/4 HP	S8v9/5
MACKENZIE'S FAREWELL	1656	1652	A	6/8	K2v1p47
MACKENZIE'S RANT	1553b	7bL27bL7bL	A	4/4 S	K2v2p9
MACKENZIE'S RANT	13b53b	7bL27bL7bL	A	4/4 S	R10p47
MACLACHLAN'S REEL	3551H	1H3H2H2	C	4/4 S	G6v1p11
MACLAGGAN'S JIG	5527bL	5515	A	6/8	M7p38
MACLAUCHLANE'S SCOTCH MEASURE	1122	5223	D	2/2 CD	R10p152
MACLEOD AND MACKAY	35L6L4	46L7L5	G	2/4	S8v6p86
MACLEOD'S QUICKSTEP	11H65	657b2	A	2/4 QS	S8v8p45
MACPHERSON'S BLADE [MACPHERSON'S CAVE]	1H151	6b427L	E F#	4/4 A	S8v7p41 S8v8p17
MACPHERSON'S LAMENT [MACPHERSON'S RANT]	1122	136L6L	G	2/4*	S8v7p40 S8v8p149
MACVICAR'S	5353	51H22	C	4/4 S	R10p68
MAD CAP	135L3L	247L5L	Bb	2/2 R	R10p285
MADAM FREDERICK	1L3L5L5L	1L5L5L1	A	4/4 S	Mc3v1p29
MADAM NERUDA	14#1H4	3L4L4#L5L	Eb	2/4	S8v6p106
MADAM SYLVAIN	53L53L	5576	Eb	2/4 HP	S8v7p43
MADAME DE LENGLEE	1564	547L2	E	4/4 A	S8v8p28
MADAME VANONI	134#1H	5L7L25	Bb	2/4 HP	S8v7p45 S8v8p137
MADGE [AIR:FAREWELL TO SCOTLAND]	15L3L5L	1522	A	6/8	S8v6p38
MADGE, OR FAREWELL TO SCOTLAND	1H535	1H5H2H2H	A	6/8	S8v7p35
MAGDEBURGH WALTZ	655	433	Bb	3/4	S15p2
MAGGIE CAMERON	5333	5156	A	4/4 PS	S8v8p115
MAGGIE LAUDER	1H1H1H1H	2H2H72H	A	4/4 SC	K2v3p23
MAGGIE'S APRON	53b51	53b51	G	4/4 R	K2v3p22
MAGNUS	13b54	5222	E	4/4	M10v2p9
MAID OF ISLAY(, THE) [MAIDS OF ISLAY(, THE)	1555	1563	F	4/4 S	K2v2p5,22 L8v5p17 R10p22,225
MAID OF LOGIE, THE [MAID O' LOGIE, THE]	1221	6L16L2	A G	4/4*	S8v6p9 S9p14
MAIDEN BY THE SILVER DEE	3545	2527L	F	4/4	S8v6p27
MAIDS OF ARROCHAR, THE	3335	3H3H2H6	D	6/8	Mc3v1p182
MAINS OF GARTLY	3bH1H1H2H	3bH1H2H1H	E	2/4 R	S8v8p66
MAINS OF GARTLY('S REEL)	3bH1H1H5	1H3bH2H7b	E	2/2 R	S8v5p6 S8v6p84 S8v7p23
MAIR ROSIT	1524	3b3bH43b	E	2/4 R	S8v8p65
MAIRI BHAN OG	5L121	217bL1	E	3/8	M10v2p8
MAIRI BHOIDHEACH	3542	331H1H	F	4/4 S	R10p207
MAIRI BHOIDHEACH [BEAUTIFUL MARY]	333	16L1	F	3/4	M10v1p5
MAIRI DHONN [BROWN HAIRED MARY]	11H2H5	61H76	D	2/4	M10v1p7
MAIRI MHIN MHEAL-SHUILEACH DHU [MARY GENTLE AND DARK EYED]	6L333	3312	A	4/4*	M10v1p1
MAIR'S HORNPIPE	5H4H1H2H	7L255	D	4/4	M7p35
MAIS' A TAOBH TUATH [BEAUTY OF THE NORTH, THE]	3L135	6L27L5L	Eb	4/4 S	Mc3v1p195
MAJOR GRAHAM	5L111H	5222	D	4/4 S	K2v1p13 K2v3p5
MAJOR JAMES MUNRO	3b5L3b5	2425	D	4/4 S	G6v2p41
MAJOR MACKIE	5L16L2	7L531	A	6/8	K2v4p28
MAJOR McBEAN	1353	662H2	A	4/4 S	R10p24
MAJOR MOLE [MAJOR MOLLE]	153b2	153b2	A	4/4 SC	K2v1p19
MAJOR MOLLE [MAJOR MOLE]	153b1	153b2	B A	2/2*R	G6v2p50 K2v2p9 L8v2p18 R10p47
MAJOR STEWART	11H2H1H	5353	G	4/4 R	K2v3p8
MANCHESTER	1H1H31H	2H754H	D	4/4	S9p30
MANDERSTON HOUSE	1115	127L5	G	4/4 S	G6v1p33
MANSON'S SCHOTTISCHE	1122	357L2	D	2/4	S8v6p87
MAOILE NAN CROGAICHEAN, OR ORKNEY	1311	5L5L22	D	2/2 R	R10p122
MAR CASTLE	5L351H	6562	E	4/4 A	S8v8p10
MAR CASTLE	5L351H	6662	E	4/4 A	S8v7p36
MAR CASTLE	3551H	2326L	D	4/4	B9p5
MAR CASTLE	5315L	3562	E	4/4	W1p38
MARCH	1115L	3b545	A	4/4	K2v1p49

Title					
MARCH TO THE RENDEZVOUS	13L5L3L	5L15L6L	G	4/4	W1p63
MARCHIONESS OF HUNTLY (2nd. Setting)	11H55	11H22	C	4/4 S	K2v2p13 Mc3v1p108 R10p77
MARCHIONESS OF HUNTLY, THE	1L5L4L5L	6L247L	A	4/4 S	L8v4p1 Mc3v1p22 R10p19
MARCHIONESS OF HUNTLY, THE	3545	62H4H7	C	4/4	S9p9
MARCHIONESS OF HUNTLY, THE	1L3L5L1L	4425L	A	4/4 S	M7p21
MARCHIONESS OF HUNTLY'S REEL	113L5L	4L27L6L	A	2/2 R	S15p19
MARCHIONESS OF HUNTLY('S STRATHSPEY)	3L5L4L5L	6L247L	A	4/4*S	K2v2p7 S15p19
MARCHIONESS OF TOWNSHEND'S STRATHSPEY	5L3b53b	24L2L2L	A	4/4	W1p12
MARCHIONESS OF TULLIBARDINE, THE	3135	7b427b	A	2/4*	Mc3v1p178 M10v2p24 S8v8p41
MARCHIONESS SALUTE, THE	13L5L3L	5L3L24L	F	4/4 S	R10p230
MARKET CHORUS	53H2H1H	763H5	D	2/4 CD	K2v1p22
MARMEEL RANT [MARMEEL REEL]	3b13b1	27bL27bL	E	4/4 S	Mc3v1p80 M7p10
MARNOCK'S STRATHSPEY [MARNOCH'S]	3bL1L3bL1L	2L7bF2L7bF	A E	4/4 S	Mc3v1p104 R10p58
MARQUESS OF LORN	3H2H1H1	27bL44	D	4/4 S	R10p120
MARQUIS OF BEAUMONT, THE	1356	5142	A	4/4 R	S17p80
MARQUIS OF HASTINGS, THE [LORD MOIRA]	1135	4327L	F	4/4 S	S17p164
MARQUIS OF HUNTLY	151H6	1522H	F	4/4 S	R10p227
MARQUIS OF HUNTLY'S FAREWELL(, THE)	1L1L5L5L	1311	A	4/4 S	K2v1p8 L8v2p1 Mc3v1p1 R10p12 S9p7 S17p48
MARQUIS OF HUNTLY'S FAREWELL, THE	1L1L3L5L	1311	A	4/4 S	S8v7p16 S8v8p105
MARQUIS OF HUNTLY('S HIGHLAND FLING)	1H3H4H3H	62H75	D	4/4 S	K2v1p6 L8v1p7 L8v8Ap9 Mc3v1p74 R10p97 S9p8 S17p10
MARQUIS OF HUNTLY'S REEL(, THE)	5L15L1	7bL247bL	G	4/4 S	G6v1p19 K2v1p13 L8v5p22 Mc3v1p123 R10p189 S17p36
MARQUIS OF HUNTLY'S REEL, THE	1L3L11	4327L	A	2/2 R	M7p22
MARQUIS OF HUNTLY'S SNUFF MULL	5L126L	5L151H	F	4/4 SS	R10p234
MARQUIS OF HUNTLY'S WELCOME TO THE ROYAL HIGHLANDERS, THE	3155	3542	F	4/4 S	R10p304
MARQUIS OF LORN	5353	4542	G	4/4 S	K2v4p13
MARQUIS OF QUEENSBERRY(, THE)	3H1H1H3H	4H2H75H	C	4/4*R	K2v2p11 L8v4p18 L8v8Bp19 R10p63
MARQUIS OF TULLYBARDINE(, THE) [TULLYBARDINE'S REEL]	1351	5164	A	4/4*R	K2v1p12 L8v2p1 Mc3v1p1 M7p25 R10p12 S8v7p9 S17p115
MARQUIS OF TULLYBARDINE'S REEL, THE	1556	261H6	A	2/4 R	S8v8p106
MARR LODGE	5326L	5322	A	2/2	W1p5
MARRY KETTY	1133	1132	G	4/4 S	S17p118
MARRY ME NOW	5L13b3b	427bL2	A	4/4*R	K2v1p7 R10p55
MARY GRAY	5342	531H3	G	4/4*R	L8v2p12 R10p162 S17p122
MARY JANE DAVIE	531H3	642H4	D	4/4	S8v6p93
MARY KITTY	5L133	1326L	G	4/4 R	Mc3v1p91
MARY OF CASTLECARY	5L112	2124	A	4/4 R	K2v1p18
MARY SCOTT	3521	467L2	A	4/4	S8v6p102
MARY WALKER	1347L	131H3	Bb	2/2 R	S8v7p15
MARY YOUNG AND FAIR	13b54	517L0	A	6/8	K2v1p49
MASON'S APRON	1H111	5L132	A	4/4*R	Mc3v1p2 R10p5
MASON'S APRON, THE	3111	5L142	A	4/4*R	K2v1p23 S17p22
MASTER ANDREW GRANT (BALMORAL)	315L1	311H5	A	2/2 R	Mc3v1p24 S8v3p37
MASTER FRANCIS SITWELL	5364	54H72H	C	4/4 S	S17p16
MASTER JOHN GATHERER'S STRATHSPEY	136L6L	351H3H	D	4/4	W1p31
MASTER PINTO	3L6L16L	3L6L15L	Bb	2/4	Mc3v1p161
MASTER REGINALD MACDONALD	151H5	61H62	A	4/4 S	Mc3v1p3
MATHEMATICIAN, THE	33H44H	73H1H5	D	2/4 HP	S8v7p45 S8v8p130
MAY DAY	5H5H5H5H	5H5H4H2H	D	4/4 S	K2v4p7
MAYEN HOUSE	5L115	3b47bL7bL	G	6/8	W1p66
McDOUGALL'S MARCH	551H1H	3H1H2H1H	D	6/8	K2v4p27
MCFARLANE RANT, THE	3H52H6	3H52H1H	D	4/4 R	S17p43
McGILLAN'S STRATHSPEY	3L5L5L1	3211	A	4/4 S	M7p25
MCINROY OF LUDE	5L13b3b	427b2	Bm	4/4 R	L8v6p11
MCINTOSH OF MCINTOSH	15L3L1L	4L2L3L5L	Bb	4/4 R	L8v5p20
McLARIN'S REEL	5L13b1	2427bL	A	4/4 R	L8v8Bp22
McLEAN'S PIPES	3H1H3H5H	3H1H4H2H	D	6/8	K2v4p27
MEARNS	3565	351H5	A	4/4 J	S8v9/6
MEG MERRILEES	5357	6553	A	4/4*R	K2v1p23 L8v3p21 R10p142
MEG MHOR NA LURACHAN	3b13b5	7b53b5	E	4/4 S	R10p262
MEIKLEOUR BEECHES, THE	117L6L	6L7L12	A	4/4	S8v8p155
MENZIES RANT	11H51	11H62	D	2/2 R	R10p125
MEPHISTOPHELES	1231	3453	D	2/4	S8v6p118
MERRILY DANCED THE QUAKER'S WIFE	1H54H2H	1H561H	D	6/8	K2v1p32
MERRY HARRIERS, THE	1515	7b7b47bL	Em	6/8 J	L8v5p12
MERRY KITTY or HIGHLAND DONALD	3143	3132	G	4/4 S	S8v8p57
MERRY LADS AND BONNY LASSES	37L5L3L	4L2L4L6L	F	2/2 R	R10p231
MERRY LADS OF AYR, THE	3H1H1H5	3H1H4H4H	C	4/4*R	L8v2p16 L8v8Bp15 M7p5 R10p61 S17p7
MERRY LADS OF AYR, THE	3H1H1H1H	3H1H4H5H	C	4/4 R	K2v2p11
MERRY LADS OF FOSS, THE	3565	1H342	D	4/4 R	S17p152
MERRY LADS OF NEW PITSLIGO, THE	1L5L5L5L	1L5L42	A	4/4	W1p4
MERRY MAY THE PAIR BE	1135	1135	A	4/4*R	K2v3p13 R10p26
MERRY MONTH OF MAY, THE	1124	6512	A	6/8	K2v1p29
MESSE, LE	5565	5522	A	2/4	S8v7p47 S8v8p180/1
METHVEN CASTLE	1L5L5L1L	2L4L6L6L	A	2/2	W1p11
MILL BURN, THE	137L2	427L5L	A	4/4 R	K2v3p11 L8v2p4
MILL O' BOYNDIE	1H531	2H642	G	2/2 R	S8v5p2

MILL OF LAGGAN, THE	151H7	2H4H2H2	F	2/2 R	R10p207
MILL OF NEWE	5L3b53b	4L242	E	4/4	W1p47
MILL OF TYNETT	1H521	1H3H2H3	E	4/4	W1p42
MILLADEN	13b53b	7bL47b4	B	4/4 S	S8v7p6 S8v8p76
MILLER LADS	1313	2366	F	4/4 S	R10p212
MILLER O' DERVIL, THE	131H1H	1326L	D	4/4 S	S8v7p11
MILLER O' DRONE, THE	16L5L5L	1L1L23	A	4/4 S	S8v8p108
MILLER O' DRONE, THE	5322	5L1H66	D	4/4 S	L8v8Ap4
MILLER O' HIRN, THE	1351	647L5L	D	4/4 S	S8v3p1
MILLER O' HIRN, THE	1351	6L47L5L	D	4/4 S	Mc3v1p67 S8v7p2 S8v8p71
MILLER O' HIRN'S SON, THE	531H6	5352	D	4/4 S	S8v3p3
MILLER O' HIRN'S WIFE, THE	1353	5642	F	4/4 S	S8v3p53
MILLER OF CASERNEY, THE	13L6L5L	13L22	A	4/4 S	R10p40
MILLER OF DRON(E), THE	16L5L5L	1L422	A	4/4 S	L8v3p1 Mc3v1p2 R10p10
MILLER OF DRONE, THE	16L5L5L	1L1L22	A	4/4 S	S17p50
MILLER OF DRONE, THE	16L5L5L	1L432	A	4/4 S	K2v1p18
MILLER'S DAUGHTER, THE	6L122	5L6L17L	D	4/4 S	Mc3v1p51 R10p126
MILLER'S MAN, THE	1323	5L5L22	D	4/4 S	Mc3v1p71 R10p111
MILLER'S RANT, THE	5L353	6L464	D	4/4	S8v6p91 S8v7p2
MILLHILLS	1L1L3L5L	4L4L6L1	A	4/4 A	S8v9/5
MILLICENT'S FAVOURITE	3H1H53	153H2H	D	4/4	S9p30
MILTON DUFF	151H5	7bL47b4	D	4/4 S	S8v5p17 S8v6p111
MINICAN, THE	513b5	7b7b27bL	Bm	4/4 R	L8v6p11
MINISTER'S RANT, THE	5651H	7b424	A	4/4	S8v6p79
MINSTREL TO HIS SOUL, THE	113b4	26b55	F#	4/4	S8v8p157
MISS ABERCROMBY	3b13b5	43b24	C	2/2 R	R10p273
MISS AGNESS LOUDON	5533	115L5L	Bb	4/4 S	L8v5p19
MISS AMELIA OLIPHANT[,] GASK	5326L	5361H	D	4/4 S	K2v3p5
MISS ANN AMELIA STEWART'S STRATHSPEY [MISS ANN AMELIA MURRAY]	1353	3H1H32	F	4/4 S	L8v8Ap25 R10p211
MISS ANN GORDON, HEATH COTTAGE	13b7bL2	13b53b	E	6/8	G14p8
MISS ANN MONRO	1543b	7bL47b2	B	6/8	G6v2p50
MISS ANN STEWART	5L15L1L	6L5L2L2L	Bb	4/4 S	G6v1p16
MISS ANN STEWART [MISS ANN STEWART, EAST CRAIGS]	5L13b5	247bL2	G	4/4*R	Mc3v1p147 R10p202 S17p110
MISS ANN STEWART, EAST CRAIGS	11H1H3bH	7b43b7bL	G	4/4 S	Mc3v1p189
MISS ANN SYMON'S REEL	331H6	427L2	G	4/4	B9p4
MISS ANNIE MACKINNON	1535	647bL4	A	4/4 R	Mc3v1p181
MISS ANNY STEWART, BOHALLY	1535	47b27bL	A	2/2 R	G6v1p26
MISS AUSTIN	1H53b1	3b525L	G	4/4 S	R10p302
MISS BAIRD OF SAUGHTON(HALL)	5553	5655	F	4/4*R	K2v2p22 L8v6p21 R10p228 S17p102
MISS BARBARA CUNNINGHAM	1513	6L27L5L	G	4/4 S	G6v2p15
MISS BARTLET	37L6L5L	37L42	F	2/2 R	G6v2p22
MISS BETSEY ROBERTSON	5535	22H75	G	2/2 S	R10p166
MISS BETSY ROBERTSON	5535	22H76	G	4/4*R	K2v2p15 Mc3v1p100
MISS BETTY HUNTER	3H1H1H5	6532	C	4/4*R	K2v2p13 R10p77
MISS BISSET, LOGIERAIT	1H2H1H5	7b422	E	2/2 R	G6v2p45
MISS BRANDER	121H2H	5427bL	D	2/2 R	K2v4p18
MISS BROOKE	1175	1H1H47L	A	2/4	S8v3p33
MISS BRUCE	1H555	1H642	G	4/4 R	K2v3p7
MISS BUCHANAN OF CAMBUSMORE	3b111	3b6b54	E	6/8	G6v2p46
MISS C. ELPHINSTONE	15L11	4L5L2L2L	A	4/4 S	G6v2p1
MISS CAMPBELL, LOCHEND	551H1H	2H2H2H6	C	2/2 R	G6v1p36
MISS CAMPBELL, MONZIE [MISS SUSAN CAMPBELL, MONZIES]	5551H	3H2H2H2	C D	4/4 S	G6v1p33 K2v3p3
MISS CAMPBELL OF MONZIE	3L5L4L6L	4L3L2L2	Bb	6/8	G6v2p29
MISS CAMPBELL OF MONZIE(S)	1H53H5	432H2	C	4/4*R	G6v2p19 L8v4p20 Mc3v1p121
MISS CAMPBELL (OF SADDELL)	1311	6L27L5L	Bb	4/4 S	G6v2p26
MISS CAMPBELL OF SADDELL	3b1H3b5	27b24	D	2/2 R	G6v2p40
MISS CAMPBELL'S REEL	536L5L	4L3L22L	F	4/4 R	Mc3v1p196
MISS CAROLINE CAMPBELL	1315L	6L5L4L2L	Bb	2/2 R	R10p291
MISS CAROLINE CAMPBELL	5531	447L2	Bb	4/4 S	R10p291
MISS CATHRINE CHALMERS	3445	327L6L	G	4/4 R	G6v2p15
MISS CHARLOTTE ANN LOWE('S)	3142	317L7L	F	4/4 R	K2v2p22 L8v4p22
MISS CHARLOTTE CAMPBELL	1315L	6L5L4L2L	Bb	4/4 S	K2v2p23
MISS CHARLOTTE DUNDAS	1L47L2	1L353	Bb	4/4 S	G6v2p30
MISS CHARLOTTE ROSS	6424	5353	D	4/4 R	S17p93
MISS CHARLOTTE STEWART	13b55	7b422	D	4/4 R	S17p78
MISS CHARTERS	1H3bH1H7b	47b2H7b	G	4/4*R	L8v5p21 R10p193
MISS CHARTERS	1H3bH1H7b	27b27b	G	2/2 R	Mc3v1p134
MISS CHIRSTY STEWART	2H565	3522H	C	2/2 R	G6v1p35
MISS CHRISTIE OF DURRIE	1H757	2H4H1H6	C	2/2 R	G6v2p21
MISS CLEMENTINA(SARAH) DRUMMOND (OF PERTH)	3125L	3142	A	4/4 S	G6v1p26 K2v3p13
MISS CLEMENTINA STEWART	131H3	337L7L	G	2/2 R	G6v1p31
MISS CLEMENTINA STEWART	1351H	6652	Bb	2/2 R	G6v1p43 R10p201
MISS COLSTON	3131H	7b527bL	A	4/4 S	R10p36
MISS COLSTON	3b13b1H	7b527bL	G	4/4 S	R10p187
MISS COX	1H6L5L3L	5L47L2	Eb	4/4 S	R10p270
MISS CRAWFORD'S REEL	1L7L6L5L	6L5L36	A	4/4 R	K2v1p15
MISS CRAWFORD'S STRATHSPEY	1355	1347L	A	4/4 S	K2v1p15

MISS DALE	3516L	5L144	A	4/4 S	Mc3v1p180
MISS DALLAS	5L126L	5L122	G	4/4 S	G6v1p8
MISS DALRYMPLE	15L15L	2427L	Bb	6/8	G6v1p15
MISS DAVIDSON	1H3H1H3H	1H3H2H6	F	2/2 R	R10p219
MISS DOUGLAS	1H51H5	72H4H4H	D	4/4 R	S17p119
MISS DOUGLAS	5353	6L27L5L	G	4/4 S	R10p182
MISS DOUGLAS OF BRIG(H)TON or BRECHIN CASTLE	1115	1127L	Bb	4/4 S	S8v8p126
MISS DOUGLAS OF SPRINGWOOD PARK	5L131	5L133	D	4/4 S	R10128
MISS DRUMMOND OF KELTIE	15L5L3	15L6L2L	Bb	2/2 R	G6v1p39
MISS DRUMMOND OF LOGIEALMOND	3b3b15	3b7b24	E	4/4 S	G6v2p47
MISS DRUMMOND OF MEGGINCH	1H61H6	31H22H	C	4/4 S	R10p155
MISS DRUMMOND OF PERTH	1525	4242	A	4/4 S	K2v1p6 L8v2p19 L8v8Bp20 Mc3v1p115 R10p44 S9p8 S17p28
MISS DUMBRECK	4213	6361H	Bb A	4/4*R	K2v1p13 Mc3v1p16,127 R10p287 S17p49
MISS DUNDAS OF ARNISTON	3527bL	3565	D	2/2 R	R10p119
MISS DUNDAS'S REEL	1555	7b47bL2	G	4/4 R	G6v1p18
MISS E. ELDER	1L16L5L	4L5L2L2	Bb	2/2 R	G6v1p40
MISS EDMONDSTON	11H52	7L232	Bb	2/2 R	G6v1p15
MISS EDMONDSTONE OF NEWTON	151H5	54H72H	D	4/4 S	G6v2p11
MISS ELDER	153b5	3b527bL	E	2/2 R	G6v1p48
MISS ELENORA ROBERTSON	137L7L	137L5	Bb	2/2 R	R10p285
MISS ELIZA FORSYTH	5122	4513	G	4/4 S	G6v2p14
MISS ELPHINSTONE	1H1H31H	2H2H72H	D	4/4 R	K2v3p5
MISS ERSKINE OF ALVA	5135	67b27bL	A	2/2 R	R10p32
MISS ERSKINE OF TORRY	3b13b1	2427bL	A	4/4 S	G6v2p43
MISS ERSKINE OF TORRY	315L3L	24L27bL	F	4/4 S	Mc3v1p139 R10p232
MISS FALCONER	113b3b	2454	A	4/4 R	K2v3p18 L8v2p18
MISS FARQUHARSON	5L3b11	3b527L	A	4/4 S	S8v3p40
MISS FARQUHARSON OF BALDOVIE	31H35	31H62	C	4/4 S	G6v1p35
MISS FLEMING OF KILLIECHASSIE	1L1L11	5126L	A	2/2 R	R10p15
MISS FLORA MACDONALD	5L345	5125L	A	4/4 S	S8v3p33
MISS FLORA MCDONALD	1151	117b7bL	E	4/4 R	S17p29
MISS FOGO	3155	3142	G	2/2 R	Mc3v1p90 R10p173
MISS FORBES	3565	3542	C	4/4 R	K2v2p12 R10p69 S17p100
MISS FORBES' FAREWELL TO BANFF	3436	5532	G	2/4	K2v3p45
MISS FORBES' FAREWELL TO BANFF	3342	3561H	G	2/2 CD	R10p147
MISS FORBES' FAREWELL TO BANFF	3542	3561H	G	4/4	Mc3v1p185
MISS FORBES' FAREWELL TO BANFF	3236	5532	A	2/4	M10v1p11
MISS FORBES OF PITSLIGO	5L353	5L362	F	4/4 S	R10p305
MISS FORDYCE, AYTON	1513b	247b2	E	2/2 R	G6v2p47
MISS FORSYTH HUNTLY	5L13b3b	7bL247bL	A	2/2 R	R10p58
MISS GAYTON'S HORNPIPE	31H31H	5757	G	2/4	K2v1p26
MISS GAYTON'S HORNPIPE	31H1H5	31H1H5	G	4/4 HP	Mc3v1p172
MISS GEORGINA SCOTT	1H1H35	42H76	F	4/4 S	S17p151
MISS GIBSON	11H52	7L232	Bb	4/4 R	K2v2p23 L8v6p22 L8v8Bp29 S17p15
MISS GIBSON	13b27bL	13b51H	G	4/4 S	K2v3p22
MISS GORDON OF GIGHT	5L3b1H3bH	7b7b47bL	C	2/2 R	G6v2p34
MISS GORDON OF GLASTIRUM	3b15L3b	27bL24	G	2/2 R	G6v1p19
MISS GORDON OF LESMORE	1351	2626L	F	4/4 S	G6v2p22
MISS GRACE STEWART	5L13b5	247bL7bL	G	4/4 S	G6v2p39
MISS GRAHAM	1353	6552	D	4/4 R	K2v3p5
MISS GRAHAM OF INCHBRAKIE	1315L	1L122L	G	4/4	M10v2p13
MISS GRANT	3113	6532	F	2/2 R	G6v1p13 R10p218
MISS GRANT	5115	47bL7bL2	E	4/4 S	G6v2p45
MISS GRANT OF CULLEN HOUSE	5531H	6424	F	4/4 R	Mc3v1p148
MISS GRANT OF GRANT	1547L	151H1H	G	2/2 S	G6v1p8
MISS GRANT OF KINAIRD	3b3b3b1H	7b524	D	2/2 R	G6v1p45 R10p304
MISS GRANT OF KNOCKANDO	5555	2462	A	4/4 S	G6v1p1
MISS GRAY OF CARSE	5L13b5	2422	G	4/4 S	R10p200
MISS GRIEVE OF HOWDAN	3545	62H75	D	4/4 S	S17p114
MISS H. HUNTER OF BLACKNESS	3H2H1H3H	62H75	Eb	2/2 R	G6v2p32
MISS HALDANE OF GLENEAGLES	3142	3125L	C	4/4 S	G6v2p20
MISS HAMILTON OF BANGOWR(IE)	5555	31H22	F	4/4 S	R10p233 S17p108
MISS HANBURY'S FANCY	5L5L32	7L242	Bb	2/2 R	G6v2p30
MISS HAY(OF YESTER)	1H3H2H4H	3H3H77	D	4/4*R	K2v1p14 R10p120
MISS HENDERSON OF FORDEL	5315	4362	A	2/2 R	G6v1p2
MISS HENNY McKENZIE	1343	27b27bL	A	4/4*R	K2v3p17 Mc3v1p104 R10p59
MISS HENRIETTA ABERNETHIE	1H3H2H1H	5322	C	4/4 S	G6v2p20
MISS HERON(OF HERON)	537L2	31H66	F	4/4*R	L8v5p18 R10p222
MISS HOG, NEWLISTON	3b23b1	3b427bL	G	2/2 R	R10p302
MISS HOPE	1126L	4463	G	4/4 S	S17p82
MISS HOPE	1553	1H3H2H2	D	4/4 S	K2v4p9
MISS HOPKINS	5L144	5226L	Bb	2/2*R	R10p283 S17p53
MISS HUTTON	15L3L5L	3L6L13	Bb	4/4 S	G6v1p44
MISS INNES	111H5	2227bL	E	2/2 R	R10p262
MISS INNES OF EDINGIGHT	1155	1327L	G	4/4 S	G6v2p12
MISS ISABELLA CARLE	15L7L6	15L6L6L	Bb	2/4 R	H5p8
MISS ISOBEL EWAN	5151	47bL47bL	E	6/8 J	S8v3p25
MISS JANE FRASER	5535	22H76	G	4/4 R	L8v6p13 Mc3v1p88

MISS JANE GRANT, LYNMORE	1133	1142	F	2/2 R	R10p241
MISS JANE MACINNES, DANDALEITH	1151H	1126L	D	2/2 R	Mc3v1p68
MISS JANE STEWART	1353	5L37L2	Bb	4/4 R	S17p147
MISS JANE WEDDERBURN	3b1H1H5	27b7b4	A	2/2 R	G6v2p43
MISS JEAN ABERDEIN	3b53b5	27bL24	C	2/2 R	G6v1p42
MISS JEAN STEWART	3L126L	1155	A	4/4 S	G6v2p4
MISS JEAN STEWART OF BOHALLY	137L5L	1353	G	2/2 R	G6v1p32
MISS JEANNIE S. GRANT'S FAVOURITE	1214	3241	A	6/8	G14p9
MISS JEANNY WILLIAMSON	1353	2464	F	4/4 R	G6v1p14
MISS JEANY ABERNETHIE	1H31H3H	2H3H4H2H	C	4/4 S	G6v2p21
MISS JEFFREY	1L5L5L1	5426L	A	4/4 S	R10p39
MISS JENNY GUTHRIE	11L5L5L	5646L	A	4/4 S	K2v2p8 R10p38
MISS JESSIE DALRYMPLE	1353	6L464	Bb	4/4 R	Mc3v1p193
MISS JESSIE SCOTT	3H2H1H5	6542	D	4/4*R	K2v2p18 R10p110
MISS JESSIE SMITH	5314	5366	D	4/4 S	L8v4p8
MISS JESSIE STEWART	5L13b4	2454	G	4/4 R	S17p54
MISS JESSIE WEIR	153b5	153b5	E	4/4 S	S8v3p26
MISS JESSY CUMING [MISS JESSY CUMMING)	5151	5422H	D	4/4 S	G6v2p7 R10p124
MISS JOHNSON, PITWORTH	137L5L	1353	Bb	2/2 R	G6v2p34
MISS JOHNSTON	3553	51H3H1H	G	4/4 R	K2v1p10 S17p65
MISS JOHNSTON	13b53b	7bL242	E	2/2 R	G6v1p47
MISS JOHNSTON	5226L	5266	D	2/2 R	R10p116
MISS JOHNSTON OF HILTON	1H155	7b424	E	2/2 R	G6v2p48 R10p260
MISS JOHNSTON OF HILTON	11H7b2	11H3bH2H	C	4/4 S	R10p71
MISS JOHNSTON ROBINSON	5115L	7bL17bL5L	A	4/4 R	K2v3p14
MISS JOHNSTONE	3553	51L3L1L	G	2/2 R	R10p169
MISS JOHNSTONE	1535	27b27bL	A	2/2 R	Mc3v1p24 S8v3p35
MISS KATHERINE STEWART FORBES	1124	1151H	F	4/4 S	R10p242
MISS KATTY GORDON OF EARLSTON'S REEL	151H5	6522	D	4/4 S	G6v1p4
MISS KATTY MAXWELL'S REEL	1H3H1H3	1H3H2H2	C	4/4 S	G6v1p10
MISS KATTY TROTTER	335L3	427L2	G	4/4 R	G6v1p9
MISS KINLOCH OF GILMERTON	3565	3542	D	2/2 R	G6v2p12
MISS L. MONTGOMERIE OF SKELMORLIE	1L1L16L	6L6L22L	Bb	4/4 S	R10p284
MISS LAMONT OF LAMONT	1346	3627L	G	4/4 S	G6v2p13
MISS LAURA ANDREW	1H3H1H3	6547L	E	4/4 A	S8v8p22
MISS LAVINIA WALLACE	3131H	4242H	A	4/4	S8v6p99
MISS LIZZIE LEITH	1125L	13b55	A	4/4 S	S8v3p44
MISS LOUDON	11H31	427L5L	Bb	4/4 R	L8v5p19
MISS LOUISA DUFF	3b15L3b	27bL24	G	2/2 R	R10p198
MISS LUCY CAMPBELL	5555	5562	D	4/4 S	K2v3p4 Mc3v1p36
MISS LUCY CAMPBELL	35L35L	5142	A	2/2 S	G6v1p2
MISS LYALL	11L3bL5L	7bL27bL7bL	A	4/4 S	K2v1p5 Mc3v1p103 R10p41
MISS LYALL or MRS GRANT OF LAGGAN	15L3b2	5L4L2L4L	A	4/4*R	Mc3v1p103 R10p42
MISS LYALL [PANMURE HOUSE]	3bL1L3bL5L	7bL27bL7bL	A	4/4 S	L8v8Bp21
MISS M. ROSS	1H13b5	7b524	E	2/2 R	R10p264
MISS MACDONALD CLACHANTURN'S STRATHSPEY	5L353	5L322	D	4/4	B9p3
MISS MACDOWAL GRANT OF ARNDILLY	51H3bH3bH	4H2H7b2H	C	4/4 S	R10p272
MISS MACINNES	5164	2464	F	2/2 R	R10p243
MISS MACKAY	1353	2662	A	4/4 R	Mc3v1p8
MISS MACKENZIE OF GAIRLOCH	1255	7bL27bL4	A	4/4 S	K2v1p7
MISS MACKENZIE OF GAIRLOCH	1255	7bL27b4	A	4/4 S	R10p49
MISS MACLEAN	3b5L3b5	24L24	G	2/2 R	R10p191
MISS MACLEOD OF COLBECK	5555	6662	F	4/4 S	R10p303
MISS MACPHERSON GRANT OF BALLINDALLOCH	5531H	6662H	F	4/4 S	R10p214
MISS MACPHERSON'S REEL	3L1L5L1	3L5L4L2L	Bb	2/2 R	Mc3v1p129
MISS MARGARET CAMPBELL (OF SADDELL'S)	1351H	6542	A	2/2 R	G6v2p2 R10p37
MISS MARGARET GORDON OF LESSMORE	3342	7L27L5L	G	2/2 R	G6v2p16
MISS MARGARET GRAEME OF INCHBRAKIE	5551	4442	G	4/4 S	Mc3v1p134 R10p192
MISS MARGARET MACKERACHER	1353	3546	G	4/4 S	Mc3v1p92
MISS MARGARET MAITLAND'S REEL	135L3	427L7L	Bb	2/2 R	M7p27
MISS MARIA DUNDAS	5153	6753	G F	4/4*R	K2v2p15 R10p168,235
MISS MARIANE OLIPHANT (ROSSIE)	1L5L6L4L	5L231	G	4/4 S	G6v2p13
MISS MARSTON'S STRATHSPEY	1366	51H2H2H	D	4/4 S	M7p14
MISS MARY ANNE ROBERTSON	3133	6542	D	4/4 R	S17p129
MISS MARY CAMPBELL	331H5	752H2	G	2/2 R	S8v3p28
MISS MARY JAMIESON, ELGIN	316L5L	4L5L26L	A	4/4 S	S8v5p7
MISS MARY MACDONALD	13b27bL	13b23b	G	2/2 R	R10p185
MISS MARY MACDONALD OF CLANRANALD	1H53b1	1H527bL	D	2/2 R	G6v2p42
MISS MARY STEWART OF DERCULICH	1H1H2H2H	3H4H2H2	D	2/2 R	R10p101
MISS MARY WALKER	1347L	131H3	Bb	4/4 R	S8v3p54
MISS MATHESON	316L1	317L2	G	4/4	S8v6p85
MISS MAULE(OF PANMURE)	62H53	5353	C	4/4*R	K2v3p16 L8v3p10 R10p75 S17p96
MISS MAULE'S STRATHSPEY	316L5L	316L2	A	4/4 S	Mc3v1p181
MISS MAY HAY	13b51	7b427bL	E	2/2 R	R10p255
MISS McKENZIE OF APPLECROSS	1H52H2	331H5	A	4/4 R	L8v5p2
MISS McKENZIE OF NESS HOUSE	351H6	554H4H	D	4/4 R	L8v4p8
MISS McLAUCHLAN	1531	227L5L	A	2/2 R	G6v1p28
MISS McLEAN(OF INVERSCADLE)	3b5L3b5	24L24	G	2/2*R	G6v2p38 K2v3p21
MISS McLEOD OF COLBECK	5555	6662	F	4/4 S	G6v1p38
MISS McLEOD OF ROSSES	1353	11H1H3H	D	2/2 R	K2v4p9
MISS McMILLAN'S QUADRILLE	1H1H15	1H1H2H7b	C	6/8	G14p17

MISS MENZIES OF CULDARE(S)	1H1H63	1H1H62	A	4/4*R	K2v1p15 R10p1
MISS MENZIES OF CULDER [CULDARES]	5157	1H2H2H2H	D	2/2 R	G6v1p30
MISS MENZIES OF MENZIES	5132	6L5L4L2L	Bb	2/2 R	R10p292
MISS MILLER OF DALSWINTON	1555	1522	D	4/4 S	G6v2p10
MISS MINNIE FRASER, NETHERTON	316L5L	4526L	A	4/4 S	S8v5p8
MISS MONCRIEFF OF PITLOWER	5L5L31	5562	A	2/2 R	G6v2p6
MISS MONEYPENNY OF PITMILLY	113b2	7bL5L7b2	G	2/2 R	R10p201
MISS MONTGOMERIE OF SKELMORLIE	5524	5551H	F	4/4 S	G6v1p37
MISS MONTGOMERY	5557b	4446	A	4/4 S	K2v4p3
MISS MUIR MACKENZIE	1H1H1H1H	2H3H66	E	4/4 S	R10p277
MISS MURRAY OF ABERCARNEY [ABERCAIRNEY]	5L13b1	4L242	G	2/2 R	G6v1p44
MISS MURRAY OF AUCHTERTYRE	31H31H	31H66	F	4/4 S	R10p217
MISS NANCIE LOW	51H51	1355	F	2/2 R	R10p239
MISS NAPIER OF MERCHISTON HALL	1H2H1H3b	17b42	D	6/8	G6v2p42
MISS NEIL	31H2H5	1H47L2	D	4/4 S	S8v3p10
MISS NISBET OF DIRLETON	1527bL	153b5	A	4/4*R	K2v2p10 L8v6p19 Mc3v1p114 R10p53
MISS NISBET OF DIRLETON	1527bL	1535	A	4/4 R	Mc3v1p26 S17p94
MISS OLIPHANT	5322	5366	D	4/4 S	Mc3v1p38
MISS OSWALD OF DUNAKEER	3b3b54	2427bL	G	2/2 R	G6v1p19
MISS PAUL	1353	4321	A	2/4	S8v6p108 S8v7p46
MISS PENSY MACDONALD	3151H	3147bL	C	2/2 R	R10p75
MISS PRESTON FERNTON	5531H	2362	D	4/4 R	K2v3p4
MISS PRIMROSE	1L5L15	1H625L	A	4/4 S	S8v7p4 S8v8p92
MISS PROUD	3531H	5524	G	4/4 R	K2v4p13
MISS RAMSAY	3H1H31	4326L	G	4/4 R	S17p120
MISS RATTRAY	1H531	4231	D	4/4*R	Mc3v1p34 R10p88
MISS RITCHIE	1115	5142	F	4/4 R	S17p125
MISS ROBERTSON	5L3L6L6L	7L7L13	A	2/2 R	G6v2p7
MISS ROBERTSON	5365	432H2	D	2/2 R	G6v2p9
MISS ROBERTSON OF TULLYBELTON('S STR.)	1L1L26L	5L12L2L	Bb	4/4*S	Mc3v1p138 R10p295
MISS ROSE	1345	4542	A	4/4 S	K2v2p6 R10p31
MISS ROSE OF TARLOGIE	3L3L15L	6L5L4L2L	A	4/4 R	K2v2p6 Mc3v1p23 S17p158
MISS ROSS	5L5L5L1	2326L	Bb	4/4 S	K2v2p23
MISS ROSS	351H6	1H1H22	A	4/4 S	R10p37
MISS SALLY HUNTER OF THURSTON'S JIG	11H61H	62H2H7	D	6/8	Mc3v1p177
MISS SARAH DRUMMOND OF PERTH	1525	4242	A	4/4 S	G6v2p43
MISS SARAH DRUMMOND OF PERTH	1111	447bL2	E	4/4 S	R10p260
MISS SCOT	3L3L11	3L122L	Bb	4/4 S	G6v1p16
MISS SCOTT OF BELVUE	3H1H53	3H1H2H4H	C	4/4 R	G6v2p21
MISS SCOTT OF USAN	1551H	1562	F	4/4*R	K2v2p22 R10p238
MISS SCOTT'S FAVOURITE MARCH	1313	1632	F	4/4	G14p13
MISS SHAW'S FAVOURITE	1H3H5H3H	72H2H5	D	2/4	M10v1p17
MISS SHEPHERD	1524	152H3bH	E	2/4 R	S8v8p67
MISS SHEPHERD	1L3bL5L4L	2L6L4L7bF	A	2/2 R	S8v7p27
MISS SITWELL	1L3L6L2L	1L3L5L1	Bb	4/4 SS	Mc3v1p128 R10p288
MISS SOPHIA CAMPBELL	51H53b	47b42	G	6/8	G6v2p37
MISS SOPHIA DUFF STUART'S FAVOURITE	3111	25L5L5L	D	4/4 R	Mc3v1p75
MISS SOPHIA E. GRANT	3115L	2227L	A	2/2 R	G14p2
MISS STEWART	1333	2247L	A	4/4 S	K2v1p15
MISS STEWART	1133	227L7L	Bb	4/4 S	G6v1p41
MISS STEWART	1353	7bL242	A	2/2*R	G6v2p5 Mc3v1p7 R10p3
MISS STEWART OF ALLANBANK	3b13b5	27b27bL	C	4/4 S	G6v2p33
MISS STEWART OF FASNACLOICH'S	1555	6562	A	4/4 R	K2v1p16
MISS STEWART OF GARTH	3333	7b7bL44	A	4/4 R	S17p149
MISS STEWART OF GARTH	113b5	2427bL	D	4/4 R	K2v3p20
MISS STEWART OF GARTH	1131H	2242H	D	2/2 R	G6v2p10
MISS STEWART(OF) GRANTULLY	1333	2247bL	A	4/4 S	Mc3v1p7 R10p2
MISS STEWART ROBERTSON(OF EDRADYNATE)	331H5	6542	F	4/4*R	K2v3p19 Mc3v1p150 R10p206
MISS STEWART'S STRATHSPEY, PITTYVAICH	111L1L	436L2	G	4/4 S	Mc3v1p68
MISS STEWART'S REEL	1H1H31	22H62H	F	4/4 S	G6v1p12 Mc3v1p188
MISS SUSAN CAMPBELL, MONZIES	51H52	2436L	D	4/4 S	K2v3p3
MISS SUSAN ELLIOT	1H3H2H1H	51H2H2	G	2/2 R	G6v2p13
MISS SUSAN GORDON	1135	3H535	F	2/2 R	Mc3v1p149 R10p223
MISS SUSANNA BAIRD	513b5	27bL24	E	2/2 R	G6v1p48
MISS SUTHERLAND GUNN (ELGIN)	5L133	61H22	F	4/4 S	Mc3v1p165 S8v3p47
MISS TAYLOR	1H1H1H3H	5H3H1H6	C	4/4*R	K2v3p15 R10p81
MISS TINKER	1H565	4522H	F	2/2 R	G6v2p23
MISS TROTTER	1L5L6L5L	447L2	A	4/4 S	K2v2p7 L8v3p3
MISS URQUHART OF MELDRUM	1361H	5326L	D	4/4 S	G6v2p8
MISS VEARIE HAY	15L2L2	15L5L3	Bb	4/4*R	L8v1p22 Mc3v1p193 R10p281
MISS W. MACDOWAL OF ARNDILLY	5H6H5H6H	5H3H2H2H	C	2/2 R	R10p79
MISS WARDLAW	1364	1313H	F	4/4 S	R10p305
MISS WATSON	1L113b	27bL47bL	B	4/4 S	G6v2p49
MISS WATT	135L3L	1222L	Bb	2/2 R	R10p292
MISS WATT'S REEL, NETHER CLUNY	1353	6L6L22	Bb	2/2 R	Mc3v1p138
MISS WEDDERBURN	5L5L5L1	2226L	A	4/4*R	K2v1p15 R10p1 S17p76
MISS WELSH	531H1H	5353	F	2/2 R	R10p215
MISS WEMYSS OF DUNDEE	13L4L5L	13L4L2L	Bb	4/4 R	G6v2p28
MISS WHITEFORD	15L5L1	5226L	Bb	4/4*R	K2v3p21 R10p283 S17p55
MISS WILLIAMSON	3146	51H22	D	4/4 S	G6v1p29
MISS WRIGHT	3b111	3b3b1H3b	E	4/4 R	K2v3p10

MISS WRIGHT OF LATON	1H535	2427bL	D	4/4 R	K2v3p3
MISS YOUNG	5555	3H1H2H2H	C	4/4 S	K2v3p15 R10p80
MO GHILLE GUANACH	5L6L22	6L5L6L2	G	4/4	M10v2p4
MO LAOCHAN BHOIDHEACH	3115L	3142	D	4/4 S	R10p96
MO MHAIRI MHIN MHEALL SHUILEACH	1552	7bL427bL	A	4/4 SS	R10p58
MO NIGHEANAG DHONN	1H57bL1	4551H	C	4/4	M10v2p6
MO ROBAIRNEACH GAOLACH	116L5L	5L323	Bb	6/8	M10v2p3
MO RUN BHAN DHILEAS	1H2H6	653	D	3/4	M10v2p2
MOAN OF THE SEA, THE	3565	3552	Eb	6/8	S8v6p41
MOGGY ON THE SHORE	1H126L	1H14H2H	D	2/2 R	K2v4p10
MONALTRIE	331	255	D	3/4	M10v1p3
MONALTRIE'S	11H51	437L2	F	2/2 R	G6v1p38
MONCRIEFFE HOUSE	1316L	5L3L1L6F	Bb	4/4	W1p14
MONEY IN BOTH POCKETS	1H355	1H354H	D	6/8 J	L8v6p7
MONRO'S RANT	1353	2366	D	4/4 S	S17p158
MONTGOMERIE'S	1113	5557	D	2/2 HP	R10p298
MONYMUSK [MONEYMUSK]	5354	5324	A G F	4/4 S	K2v2p14 L8v1p13 L8v8Bp13 Mc3v1p12 R10p158 S8v8p108/9 S9p11 S17p8
MOR NIGHEAN A GHIOBARLAIN	1154	1121	Am	4/4	M10v2p29
MORAG NIGHEAN DOMHNUILL DUINN or LORD MACDONALD'S	5551H	51H2H2	G	4/4 R	Mc3v1p86
MORAY CLUB, THE	131H3	22H75	D	4/4*R	K2v2p19 R10p117
MORAYSHIRE LASSIE, THE	15L3L5L	136L2	Bb	2/4	S8v6p31
MORDINGTON HOUSE	113bL5L	2L4L2L4L	A	4/4 R	G6v1p46
MORPETH RANT	15L3L3L	6L6L7L7L	Bb	2/2 HP	R10p300
MOTHER KILWINNING	1H531	6L27L5L	Eb	4/4 S	K2v3p22
MOUNT HATTOCK	1126L	1155	D	4/4	W1p32
MOUNTCOFFER HOUSE	551H1H	5216L	D	4/4	P3p3
MOURDUN HILL	5L557b	7bL27bL4L	E	2/2	W1p49
MOVING BOG	131H3	1H3H4H2H	D	2/2 R	K2v4p11
MOY HALL	1H3H53	462H6	C	4/4*R	Mc3v1p116 R10p65
MR A. TROUP'S REEL	1H53H5	4H3H77	F	4/4	B9p7
MR ABEL BANKS	31H63	31H53	C	4/4 S	Mc3v1p160
MR A.G. WILKEN'S FAVOURITE	5313	4666	F	4/4 SS	S8v3p50
MR ALEX WALKER'S STRATHSPEY	5L3L11	1122L	A	4/4	W1p9
MR ALEXANDER ADAM	3353H	2H675	D	2/2 R	S8v3p8
MR ALEXANDER LAWSON'S STRATHSPEY	1315L	11H66	E	4/4	W1p40
MR ALEXANDER MUNRO'S FAVOURITE	1343	2347L	A	4/4 PS	Mc3v1p42
MR ALEXANDER MUNRO'S STRATHSPEY	5311	6L12L2L	G	4/4	W1p61
MR ALEXANDER TROUP'S STRATHSPEY	5L13b5	247b4	F	4/4	W1p54
MR ALEXr. CUNNINGHAM'S STRATHSPEY	146L2	1435	D	2/2 S	Mc3v1p67
MR ALEXr SHERRIFF'S STRATHSPEY	1L415L	4L5L7F2L	A	4/4	W1p10
MR BAILLIE OF MELLERSTAIN	557bL2	5513b	E	4/4 S	R10p259
MR BAILLIE OF MELLERSTON	557bL2	5523b	E	4/4 S	G6v2p45
MR BARCLAY'S REEL	113b5	7b7b42	D	2/2	W1p34
MR BERNARD('S REEL)	15L37L	6L5L3L5L	F	4/4*R	L8v5p17 R10p225
MR BEVERIDGE	31H53	4327L	Eb	4/4 SS	S8v3p62
MR C. BEATTIE'S BONNIE BLANCHE	3b1H6b5	3b53b2	E	4/4 S	S8v3p29
MR CAMPBELL CRAIGNISH	3531H	3542	F	2/2 R	R10p210
MR CHARLES GRAHAM	15L3L1L	227L2	A	4/4 S	G6v1p25
MR CHARLES GRANT'S STRATHSPEY	5426L	3451H	D	4/4	W1p30
MR COMPTON OF COMPTON HALL	1351H	1326bL	A	4/4*R	K2v2p5 R10p23
MR C.T. THOMPSON'S FANCY	315L3L	6L17L2	Bb	4/4 SS	S8v3p57
MR DAVID STEWART	5333	2427bL	A	2/2 R	G6v1p27
MR DONALDSON	1L113	15L2L2L	Bb	4/4 S	R10p294
MR DOUGLAS OF BRIGTON	3L3L11	4L6L4L2L	Bb	4/4 S	G6v1p40
MR DOUGLAS OF SPRINGWOOD PARK	5L17L2	1566	G	4/4 S	K2v2p16 R10p176
MR DUNCAN McKERRACHER'S STRATHSPEY	113b5	7b2H47bL	E	4/4	W1p49
MR DUNDAS MACQUEEN	13b3b5	7b422	C	2/2 R	R10p274
MR DUN'S FROLICK	5153	5153	F	2/2 R	R10p233
MR EAGERS(' STRATHSPEY)	35L35	46L46	A	4/4 S	K2v3p12 L8v3p3
MR FORBES MORRISON'S REEL	1H565	4327L	A	2/2	W1p9
MR G. IRONSIDE'S STRATHSPEY	5564	5551H	E	4/4	W1p41
MR GEORGE ANDERSON	5L3b43b	5L3b47bL	G	4/4 S	R10p199
MR GEORGE GORDON	52H1H5	47b54	G	2/2 R	G6v2p35
MR GEORGE MORRISON'S STRATHSPEY	5315L	4362	Bb	4/4	W1p16
MR GIBSON	5L113b	7bL247bL	G	4/4 R	K2v3p22
MR GIBSON	1H1H51H	2H2H75H	C	4/4 S	S8v3p44
MR GORDON GLENNIE'S STRATHSPEY	136L5L	1342	G	4/4	W1p59
MR GORDON OF HALLHEAD	13L13L	137L2	G	4/4 S	Mc3v1p65
MR GRAHAM OF ORCHILLS	5553	5522	F	4/4 S	Mc3v1p188
MR GRANT OF GLENQUAICH	1155	2266	D	4/4 S	G6v1p30 R10p123
MR GRANT OF KINAIRD	5327L	15L4L2L	Bb	2/2 R	G6v1p40
MR GRAY OF CARSE	5H3H2H7	1H542	C	4/4*R	K2v3p15 L8v5p14 R10p72
MR GUN MUNRO OF POYNTZ-FIELD	1353	632H2	C	2/2 R	R10p78
MR HANNAY OF BARGALY	5165	6542	D	2/2 R	G6v1p30
MR HUNTER'S REEL	51H31	227L5L	E	2/2	W1p41
MR J. ROSE	5L321	5L37L2	Bb	4/4 S	G6v2p29
MR JAMES DAVIDSON'S REEL	1H1H2H4	1H1H3bH1H	E	2/2	W1p46
MR JAMES DUFF STUART	13b1H3b	7bL27b2	G	2/2 R	S8v3p61
MR JAMES GEORGE	3131H	6642	C	4/4 S	K2v3p16 R10p77

MR JAMES HAMILTON	3b13b5	243b2	D	4/4 S	R10p245
MR JAMES McGRIGOR'S REEL	5522	1216L	D	2/2	W1p30
MR JAMES MUNRO'S STRATHSPEY	5351	2466	E	4/4	W1p39
MR JAMES RAMSAY	1L343	5L47L2	A	4/4 S	G6v2p3
MR JAMES TAYLOR	5L3b13b	5L3b13b	F#	4/4 S	S8v3p37
MR JAMES TAYLOR'S REEL	5353	1H542	F	2/2	W1p49
MR JAMES TROTTER	427L2	3542	A	4/4 R	K2v2p7 L8v3p3
MR JAMES WATTIE'S STRATHSPEY	13L11	24L22	G	4/4	W1p58
MR JAMIESON'S REEL	1115L	7bL7bL27bL	E	2/2	W1p48
MR JOHN BROWN	5L13b1	7513b	A	2/2 R	S8v3p41
MR JOHN SHAW STEWART'S STRATHSPEY	5L13b4	2454	Bb	4/4 S	Mc3v1p193
MR JOHN SMITH	131H3	2216L	Eb	2/2 R	G6v1p42 R10p270
MR JOHN SMITH	5L1L5L1	3122L	A	4/4 S	S8v5p10
MR JOHN SMITH'S	113L1	5432	G	4/4 R	S8v3p18
MR JOHN STEWART	1135	1132	F	2/2 R	G6v1p38
MR JOHN STEWART OF GRANTULLY	1353	7bL7bL47b	A	2/2 R	R10p39
MR JOHN WALKER'S REEL	3135	4532	G	4/4	W1p61
MR JOHNSON	1351H	6522	A	2/2 R	G6v1p3
MR JOSEPH BANKS	5L3L5L1L	7L125L	A	4/4 R	Mc3v1p29
MR J.S. SKINNER'S STRATHSPEY	115L3L	5L3L6L4L	G	4/4	W1p56
MR LAIRD OF STRATHMARTIN	116L4	51H26L	D	4/4 S	G6v1p28
MR LINDSAY	13b15	247bL2	E	2/2 R	G6v2p44
MR LUMSDEN	5654	547L2	F	4/4 S	K2v2p22 L8v3p15 R10p222
MR MACDONALD OF STAFFA	3b125L	3b13b3b	G	2/2 S	G6v2p36
MR MACDONALD OF STAFFA	3b142	7bL424	G	2/2 R	G6v2p37
MR MARSHALL	345L1	456L2	A	4/4	S8v6p72
MR MARSHALL'S COMPLIMENTS TO NIEL GOW	1111	116L2	A	4/4	Mc3v1p154
MR MARSHALL'S FAVOURITE	1L115L	2L226L	A	4/4 SS	Mc3v1p153
MR MARTIN	315L3L	314L4	Bb	4/4	S8v6p112
MR MARTIN'S COMPLIMENTS TO DR. KEITH MACDONALD	3L16L4L	2L27L5L	F	4/4 S	Mc3v1p165/187
MR McINTYRE OF GLENOE	11H51	4326L	D	4/4 S	G6v2p9
MR MENZIES OF CULDARE(S)	3565	2427bL	D	4/4*R	L8v6p9 Mc3v1p50 R10p102 S17p148
MR MICHIE'S [RENATTON]	1346L	7L253	G	4/4 S	S8v3p18
MR MOLISON OF HILLHEAD	1H133	2H246	G/Em	4/4 R	L8v5p11
MR MOORE('S STRATHSPEY)	513b5	4427bL	C	4/4 S	G6v2p32 Mc3v1p195
MR MORAY OF ABERCAIRNEY [MURRAY OF ABERCAIRNEY]	13b53b	7bL242	G	4/4 S	L8v3p20 R10p190 S17p146
MR MURDOCH'S REEL	1H1H35	6547L	E	2/2	W1p42
MR MURRAY	5L3L5L4	6L15L3	A	4/4 S	Mc3v1p29
MR PETER McGRIGOR'S STRATHSPEY	536L5L	4L3L22L	F	4/4	W1p51
MR ROBERTSON OF LUDE	5651H	5622	D	4/4 S	Mc3v1p43 R10p120 S17p152
MR ROSS'S PIPES	2H3H61H	2H3H62H	D	4/4 S	S8v3p10
MR STEWART OF DALGUISE	51H51H	47b42	D	4/4 S	G6v1p45
MR STEWART OLIPHANT OF ROSSIE	1151	427L7L	F	2/2 R	G6v1p37
MR STEWART ROBERTSON	13b57b	47b47bL	G	4/4 S	G6v1p43
MR THOM	3b13bL1L	247b2	G	4/4 S	R10p196
MR THOMAS A. GRANT OF GLEN ELGIN, AUSTRALIA	5L3L5L1	5326L	A	4/4	G14p29
MR THOMAS BURT	1126L	1157	A	4/4 R	K2v3p13
MR THOMAS FORBES	53b11	3b13b1	G	2/2 S	Mc3v1p132 S8v3p60
MR THOMSON	5335	1H332	D	4/4 S	S8v3p8
MR WEBSTER	5L13b1	5L13b1	B	4/4 S	K2v3p6
MR WILLIAM DAVIDSON	3L16L2	7L531	A	4/4 S	K2v3p12 L8v6p4
MR WILLIAM DONALD'S FAVORITE	1314L	1422L	Bb	4/4	W1p18
MRS A. MACGLASHAN	111L3B	7bL242	G	6/8	G6v2p34
MRS ADIE [MRS. ADYE]	1125L	127L5L	Bb	4/4 S	L8v3p18 Mc3v1p125 R10p279 S17p54
MRS ALEXANDER BRODIE	4H3H2H7	4H3H66	D	4/4 R	S17p162
MRS ANDERSON OF BALGAY	1531H	1H542	C	2/2 R	G6v1p34
MRS ANDREW KIDD	3L16L5L	4L3L22L	Bb	4/4 SS	S8v3p54
MRS BAIRD	3b215L	7bL242	G	2/2 R	R10p187
MRS BAIRD OF NEWBYTH	351H3H	1H562	C	4/4 S	K2v2p12 R10p75 S17p150
MRS BAIRD OF NEWBYTH	5555	7b427bL	E	4/4 S	G6v1p47
MRS BARCLAY'S REEL	126L5L	4L5L6L2L	Bb	2/2	W1p15
MRS BENTON OF AIRLIE	1335	51H1H3H	F	2/2 HP	S8v3p51
MRS BOURKE	137L2	331H5	F	2/2 R	R10p236
MRS BREMNER, THE MANSE, GLENBUCKET	111H5	2227bL	E	2/2 R	G14p11
MRS BRODIE SHERIFF OF BATTLEBLENT'S S.	1466	2H1H2H2H	D	4/4 S	K2v2p20
MRS BRODIE SHERIFF OF BATTLEBLENT'S R.	5L133	61H53	G	4/4 R	K2v2p20
MRS BROWN OF LINKWOOD	13b55	7b424	E	2/2 R	Mc3v1p79 R10p252
MRS CAMPBELL OF LOCHNELL	1H535	1H3H2H2	C	2/2 R	Mc3v1p107 R10p73
MRS CAMPBELL OF MONZIE	1113b	3b422	G	4/4 S	R10p198
MRS CAPTAIN BURGESS	3L16L5L	3L16L2L	A	4/4	S8v6p105
MRS CHISHOLM	1326bL	1353	A	4/4 S	R10p25
MRS CHISHOLM	1326L	1353	A	4/4 S	Mc3v1p18
MRS CHREE	1H1H3H5H	5H2H62H	F	4/4 S	S8v3p50
MRS CHRISTIE	5551	5547bL	A	4/4 S	K2v3p17 R10p55
MRS COL. GORDON OF PARK'S STRATHSPEY	5L133	6642	G	2/2 S	S15p19/20
MRS COLONEL BAIL[L]IE OF RED-CASTLE	157b7b	4427bL	Bm	4/4 R	L8v6p12
MRS COLONEL BAI(L)LIE OF RED-CASTLE	13b7b7b	4427bL	B	4/4 R	McC3v1p33

MRS COLONEL FORBES	1H522H	1H61H1H	C	4/4 S	R10p78
MRS COLONEL NEYNOE	331H1H	532H2	F	2/2 R	R10p305
MRS COMPTON OF CARHAM-HALL	1351H	1326L	G	4/4 R	S17p86
MRS CRAWFORD	3565	1H3H1H6	D	4/4 R	R10p156
MRS CRAWFORD OF DONSIDE	5L13b4	47b47bL	G	4/4 R	Mc3v1p196
MRS CRAWFURD OF DONSIDE	513b4	47b47bL	Bb	2/2 R	G6v1p18
MRS DAVID GLEN	351H5	3542	A	4/4	S8v6p77
MRS DAVID PATRICK'S FAVOURITE	13b3b4	27bL52	G	2/2 R	G6v2p38
MRS DINGWALL OF BROCKLY'S STRATHSPEY	35L3L5L	3342	F	4/4 S	Mc3v1p151
MRS DOUGLAS MONCRIEFF	3531	427L5L	G	4/4*R	K2v3p7 Mc3v1p95 R10p181
MRS DOUGLAS OF EDNAM	31H31H	31H62	A	4/4 R	K2v2p6
MRS DOUGLAS OF EDNAM	31H31H	31H42	A	2/2 R	R10p31
MRS DRUMMOND OF LOGIEALMOND	1H3bH75	7b542	E	4/4 R	S17p155
MRS DRUMMOND OF LOGIEALMOND	1H3bH7b5	7b542	E	2/2 R	R10p260
MRS DUFF, THE MANSE, GRANGE	3151H	7b527bL	D	2/2 R	G14p8
MRS DUNCAN	1H5H3bH5H	3bH5H2H7b	C	2/2 R	R10p269
MRS DUNDAS MCQUEEN	3546	3551H	A	4/4*R	K2v2p8 R10p36
MRS DUNDAS OF ARNISTON	1H1H2H5	6451	C	4/4*R	K2v2p13 L8v1p15 Mc3v1p113 R10p69
MRS DUNDAS OF ARNISTON	1H2H65	4541	C	2/4 R	S8v8p55
MRS E. M. ROSS'S WELCOME TO KILTARLITY COTTAGE	1345	1H532	A	4/4 PM	S8v9/6
MRS FARQUHARSON OF INVEREY	351H1H	352H2	C	4/4 S	G6v1p35
MRS FERGUSON OF RAITH('S STRATHSPEY)	3155	3542	F	4/4 S	G6v1p37 Mc3v1p190
MRS FLEMING OF MONESS	3L3L17L	5L6L4L2L	Bb	4/4 S	G6v2p27
MRS FLEMING OF MONESS	3L3L12	5L6L4L2L	Bb	4/4 S	Mc3v1p141
MRS FORBES	115L5L	1142	A	4/4*R	K2v2p4 R10p9
MRS FORBES LEITH	1L1L5L3	115L1L	Bb	2/2 R	S8v3p59
MRS FORBES OF BOHARM'S STRATHSPEY	1L131	6L5L2L4L	Bb	2/2 S	Mc3v1p129
MRS FORBES OF NEWE'S REEL	3115L	7L246	A	2/2	W1p3
MRS FORSYTH'S PIBROCH, (MANSE OF ABERNETHY)	1515	157bL4	A	6/8	G14p22/23
MRS FRANCIS WEMYSS	331H7	2H753	D	4/4 R	K2v3p3
MRS FRASER('S REEL), CULLEN	1353	7b242	Bb	2/2 R	Mc3v1p122 R10p293
MRS GARDEN OF TROUP	1156	7L5L7L5L	F	4/4 S	G6v2p24 K2v2p21 L8v1p19 L8v8Ap27 Mc3v1p147 R10p205 S8v8p124 S17p18
MRS GARDEN OF TROUP	31H3H1H	6542	F	2/2 R	G6v2p24
MRS GARDEN OF TROUP	31H3H7	6542	F	2/2 R	R10p244
MRS GENERAL CAMPBELL('S REEL)	3b15L1	247b5	A	4/4 S	K2v2p10 Mc3v1p30 R10p56
MRS GENERAL MAXWELL(OF PARKHILL)	1H3H2H7	1H3H2H6	C	2/2*R	G6v2p20 K2v2p13 R10p82
MRS GEORGE JOHNSTONE OF BYKER	13b54	247b4	B	2/2 R	R10p131
MRS GEORGE STEWART'S STRATHSPEY	5L113b	7bL4L2L2	B	2/2 S	G14p3
MRS GILLIES	1L5L32	15L4L2L	Bb	4/4 S	Mc3v1p126 R10p285
MRS GORDON OF ABERDOUR	1562	1155	G	4/4 S	R10p183
MRS GORDON OF BELSIES	51H53b	7b7b44	D	2/2 SS	R10p224
MRS GORDON OF WHITEHILL	5322	526L6L	G	4/4 S	R10p301
MRS GORDON, UVIE	1H575	72H4H7	D	2/2 R	G6v2p8
MRS GRANT or [I HAE A LASS O' MY AIN]	5L21	5L24	E	9/8	G14p12
MRS GRANT DUFF OF EDEN	16L3L3L	137L2	Bb	4/4	P3p1
MRS GRANT OF GLEN GRANT	15L15	427L2	A	2/2 R	G14p15
MRS GRANT OF LAGAN	47bL11L	3bL5L7bL7bL	A	4/4 R	K2v1p16
MRS GRANT OF LAGGAN	47L11L	3bL5L7bL7bL	A	4/4 S	K2v4p17
MRS GRAY OF QUEBEC	1H531	427L2	A	2/2 R	G6v2p4
MRS GREGORY	3551H	3H4H66	D	4/4 S	G6v2p10
MRS GREIG'S REEL	3565	332H2	F	2/2 R	M7p26
MRS GREIG'S STRATHSPEY	3565	354H2H	F	4/4 S	M7p26
MRS HAMILTON OF WISHAW	3115L	2422L	Bb	2/2 R	Mc3v1p128 R10p288
MRS HASWELL	1555	51H55	Eb	4/4 S	Mc3v1p194
MRS HENRY LUMSDEN OF TILLWHILLY'S STR.	1311	6L5L32	Bb	4/4 S	Mc3v1p137
MRS J. FORBES	1551	7bL447bL	E	2/2	W1p47
MRS J. ROSE	3bH1H51H	2H4H2H7b	D	4/4 S	G6v2p40
MRS JAMES CAMPBELL	1H535	6522H	F	2/2 R	G6v2p25 R10p229
MRS JAMES CHRISTIE	115L3L	1566	Bb	4/4	S8v9/3
MRS JAMES DUFF	1L5L35	4322	A	4/4 S	G6v2p2
MRS JAMES ERSKINE OF KIRKWALL	3b55L1	2427bL	G	2/2 R	G6v2p40
MRS JAMIESON'S FAVOURITE	5L36L6L	5L552	A	6/8	G14p6
MRS JOSEPH LOWE'S	331H3	447L2	F	4/4 S	L8v4p22
MRS KEILLOR	3131H	35H62	D	4/4 S	S8v8p79
MRS KEITH MACDONALD'S [STRATHSPEY]	1L3L5L1	246L5L	A	4/4 S	Mc3v1p23
MRS KENNEDY OF GREENAN	1H1H54	7b47b2H	E	2/2 R	R10p258
MRS L. STEWART OF THE ISLAND OF JAVA	1H3H53H	4327L	C	2/2 R	Mc3v1p117
MRS LEITH OF GLENKENDYS	35L5L3	46L6L4	A	2/2 R	G6v2p1
MRS LEITH OF GLENKINDY'S REEL	1353	4532	G	2/2	W1p57
MRS LINLEY	1H515	2H47bL4	C	4/4 R	G6v2p33
MRS LINLEY	1H515	2H57bL4	C	4/4 R	Mc3v1p194
MRS MACDONALD OF CLANRANALD	113b5	7b424	E	2/2 R	R10p254
MRS MACDONALD OF CLANRANALD	3L3L15L	3L16L2L	Bb	4/4 S	R10p281
MRS MACDONALD, SKEABOST	3H2H1H1H	1H541	D	4/4 R	Mc3v1p40
MRS MACDOUGAL GRANT [MRS. MACDOUALL GRANT]	3546	337L2	F	4/4 S	L8v6p21 Mc3v1p166
MRS MACDOWAL GRANT	3546	347L2	F	4/4 S	R10p213

Title					
MRS MACINROY OF LUDE	11H1H5	7b425	B	4/4 S	Mc3v1p61
MRS MACINROY OF LUDE	5L13b3b	427b2	B	4/4 R	Mc3v1p61
MRS MACKENZIE	551H2H	6532	F	4/4 S	K2v2p21
MRS MACKINNON CORRY	5555	6666	G	4/4	M10v2p16
MRS MACKINNON CORRY or	5555	61H66	G	4/4 S	Mc3v1p98
[BONNY TOUN O' KENMORE]					
MRS MACLEOD	3b111	7b424	G	4/4 S	R10p302
MRS MACLEOD OF ELLANREACH	1H3H1H7	51H62	D	4/4 S	Mc3v1p40
MRS MACLEOD OF ELLANREOCH	1H3H1H5	61H62	D	4/4 S	R10p108
MRS MACLEOD OF GESTO	3535	6442	F	4/4 S	R10p304
MRS MACLEOD OF RAASAY	11H66	5333	A	4/4*R	L8v6p1 Mc3v1p8 R10p6 S17p11
[MRS MACLEOD OF RASAY] [MRS MCLEOD]					
MRS MACMILLAN	51H75	3432	F	4/4 SS	S8v3p48
MRS MACPHERSON GIBSTON	1H3bH1H5	7b542	C	2/2 R	R10p272
MRS MADONALD, ORD	5551	6566	D	4/4 R	Mc3v1p45
MRS MARR'S REEL	3bH1H1H1H	7b427bL	C	2/2	W1p26
MRS MATHESON	3413	4524	A	4/4	S8v6p104
MRS McDONALD	3H1H55	3H1H3H2H	D	6/8	K2v1p48
MRS MCDONALD OF CLANRANALD	113b5	7b424	Em	4/4 R	L8v4p16
MRS MCDONALD OF CLANRANALD	113b1	7b7bL24	E	4/4 R	S17p154
MRS McGEE'S REEL	13b51	47bL42	Bb	6/8	G6v1p17
MRS McHARDY, or GARDEN OF ROSES, THE	1L5L11	116L2L	A	4/4 A	S8v10p3
MRS MCINROY OF LUDE	11H1H5	7b425	Bm	4/4 S	L8v6p11
MRS McINTOSH OF RAIGMORE'S STRATHSPEY	3L16L4L	447L2	A	4/4 S	L8v8Ap6
MRS McKENZIE OF APPLECROSS	546L5L	447L2	A	4/4 S	K2v3p11 L8v5p2
MRS McKENZIE OF APPLECROSS	1H52H2	331H5	A	4/4 R	K2v3p12
MRS McLEOD	11H66	3333	A	4/4 R	K2v1p5
MRS McLEOD OF COLBECK	1156	31H2H2	F	2/2 R	G6v2p22
MRS MCLEOD OF ELANREOCH	1H3H1H5	51H62	D	4/4 S	L8v4p7
MRS MCLEOD OF RASAY	11H66	5333	A	4/4 R	L8v6p1
MRS McMILLAN'S QUADRILLE	1153H	663H3H	C	6/8	G14p10
MRS MCPHERSON OF CLUNY	3565	357L2	A	6/8 J	L8v5p3
MRS McPHERSON OF CLUNY	5L3L1L3L	4L3L6L2L	A	4/4 S	L8v8Ap3
MRS MELVILL, DYSART	3b13b5	7b7bL24	E	2/2 R	G6v2p46
MRS MENZIES OF CULDARES	16L11	16L2L2L	Bb	4/4 S	Mc3v1p137 R10p295
MRS MONEYPENNY	3H2H1H5	3572H	C	4/4*R	K2v2p12 R10p74
MRS MORAY OF ABERCAIRN(E)Y	3155	51H22	D	4/4*R	K2v2p19 Mc3v1p60 R10p118
MRS MORAY OF ABERCA(I)RNEY	1353	2422	D	4/4 S	G6v2p11 K2v2p19 Mc3v1p60
					R10p118 S17p134
MRS MORAY OF ABERCAIRNY	13b53b	7bL242	G	4/4 S	Mc3v1p131
MRS MORTHLAND	3H2H51H	4H3H4H3H	C	4/4 R	K2v2p10
MRS MORTHLAND	547bL3b	6b56b5	A	2/2 R	R10p55
MRS MORTHLAND	113b5	2224	G	2/2 R	R10p186
MRS MOSSMAN	11H53	11H22	D	4/4 S	Mc3v1p59
MRS MUIR MACKENZIE	11H31	27b27bL	C	2/2*R	G6v2p18 K2v3p16
MRS MUIR MACKENZIE	11H31	27bL27bL	C	2/2 R	R10p76
MRS MUIR OF CALDWELL	5551H	5555	D	4/4 S	R10p119
MRS MURRAY OF ABERCA(I)RN(E)Y	5L35L3	436L6L	A	4/4 S	G6v1p25
MRS NORMAN LOCKHART	1351H	627L7L	F	2/2 R	R10p237
MRS OLIPHANT OF CONDIE'S	3131	6L27L5L	G	4/4 S	K2v2p14
MRS OSWALD OF AUCHINCRUIVE	1135	7L27L2	G	2/2 R	R10p182
[AUCHENCRUIVE]					
MRS OSWALD (OF AUCHINCRUIVES) NEW	5311	5362	F	4/4 S	G6v2p23
MRS PROFESSOR CHRISTIE'S WALTZ	752H	1H53H	G	3/4	G14p14
MRS R. DONALDSON	35L6L5L	35L42	G	4/4 S	K2v3p8
MRS RACHEL GIBSON	3135	461H6	A	4/4 R	Mc3v1p28 S17p92
MRS RAIT'S STRATHSPEY	136L5L	1353	A	4/4 S	M7p25
MRS RAMSAY(OF BARNTON)	13b51H	7b427bL	E	4/4 S	K2v1p18 R10p258
MRS ROBERTSON GRISHORNISH	5337L	2H756	G	4/4 S	Mc3v1p89
MRS ROBERTSON OF ALEXANDRIA	331H2H	1H542	D	4/4 S	S17p128
MRS RONALD	3H535	3H52H2H	F	2/2 R	G6v1p36 R10p239
MRS ROSE	1151H	51H22	G	2/2 R	R10p182
MRS ROSS	1565	1546	A	4/4 PS	Mc3v1p78
MRS SCOTT MONCRIEFF	5566	4H2H72H	D	4/4 R	S17p123
MRS SCOTT SKINNER	1561H	3H1H22	D	4/4 S	S8v3p2 S8v7p17 Mc3v1p158
MRS SELLER'S FAVOURITE, DUNLEIGH HOUSE	15L1L1	11H1H2	G	6/8	G14p4
MRS SMALL	311H5H	4H3H72H	D	2/2 R	R10p108
MRS STEPHEN BUCHROMB'S WALTZ	577	51H3H	A	3/4	G14p28
MRS STEWART FLEMING OF KILLI(E)CHASSIE	3L3L17L	5L6L4L2L	Bb	4/4 S	Mc3v1p127 R10p287
MRS STEWART, INVERUGIE	131H3	6246	D	4/4 S	R10p107
MRS STEWART NICHOLSON	316L2	15L15	Eb	4/4 S	R10p274
MRS STEWART OF GARTH	113b5	2427bL	D	2/2 R	R10p245
MRS TULLOCH, EARNHILL	15L3L1L	4L27L6L	Bb	2/2 R	R10p295 S15p25
[MRS TULLOCH'S REEL]					
MRS TULLOCH OF EARNHILLS STRATHSPEY	3L16L4	3147L	Bb	2/2 S	S15p24
MRS WALTER BIGGAR	53b53b	2427bL	G	4/4 S	G6v2p38
MRS WEBSTER	3b53b1	2427bL	B	4/4 S	K2v3p6
MRS WEMYSS OF CUTTLE HILL	3b15L1	3b155	G	2/4 R	Mc3v1p132
MRS WIGHTON OF DUNDEE	5L5L5L2L	5L6L13	A	4/4	P3p16
MRS WILL	1H1H35	6542	D	4/4 S	S8v8p77
MRS WILLS	3H1H3H5H	4H5H4H2H	C	4/4 S	G6v2p18
MRS WILSON	15L3L5L	16L4L2L	Bb	4/4 R	Mc3v1p136 S17p140

MRS WISEMAN	3215	4326	G	2/2 R	S8v3p28	
MRS WRIGHT	5555	7b57b5	E	4/4 S	K2v3p10 L8v6p17 Mc3v1p83	
					R10p253	
MRS WRIGHT OF LAWTON	5555	7b47b4	E	4/4 S	G6v2p44	
[MRS WRIGHT OF LATON]						
MRS YOUNG OF CORNHILLS	1H3H75	1H3H4H2H	F	2/2 R	R10p244	
MUCH ADMIRED GERMAN WALTZ, A	3H54	633	Bb	3/4	S15p12/13	
MUCH ADMIRED NEW OPERA DANCE, A	1H1H1H	2H2H4H	D	3/4	S15p21/2	
MUCH ADMIRED WALTZ, A	5L31	6L42	Bb	3/4	S15p6	
MUILLEANN DUBH [MULIN DHU, THE)	557b6	4444	A	2/2*R	K2v1p7 Mc3v1p114 R10p44	
MUIR O' LOGIE, THE	1L5L5L1	15L2L2L	A	4/4	S8v6p98	
MULL RANT, THE	5L122	5L144	D	4/4 S	R10p128	
MULLIN DHU(, THE)	557b6	4447bL	A	4/4 R	L8v6p4 S17p138	
MUR OSSIAN (OSSIAN'S HALL)	3565	227b2	A	4/4 R	Mc3v1p18	
MURPHY DELANEY	1113	116L7L	Bb	6/8 J	L8v5p20	
MURTHLY CASTLE	3133	2466	D	2/2	W1p33	
MUSCHATS CAIRN	1L5L3L1	5L35L3L	G	2/2 R	Mc3v1p102	
MUSIC O' SPEY, THE	3H2H55	6656	C	4/4 A	S8v3p41	
MUSIC O' SPEY, THE	325L5L	6L6L5L6L	A	4/4 A	S8v7p35	
MY AIN LASSIE	354H2H	6562	D	4/4 S	K2v4p7	
MY BOY TAMMIE	13b57b	4427bL	E	4/4 SC	K2v3p24	
MY BOY TAMMIE	1L3bL5L5L	7bL4L2L7bF	A	4/4 S	S8v3p46	
MY BRAW HIGHLAND LADDIE	1154	17bL21	A	4/4	K2v1p47	
MY HEART IS SAIR	1H1H3H	5H5H3H	D	3/4 W	K2v1p25	
MY HEATHER HILLS	3H3H1H1H	5333	D	4/4 R	K2v1p26	
MY LAME LEG	1565	157b4	A	6/8	K2v1p48	
MY LOVE IS BUT A LASSIE YET	1H31H1	1H32H2	D	2/4 CD	K2v1p22 S9p18	
MY LOVE IS LIKE A RED RED ROSE	111	223	D	3/4 W	K2v1p25	
MY LOVE IS ON THE OCEAN	2H566	2H3H2H1H	D	2/2 R	K2v4p11	
MY OLD KENTUCKY HOME	3312	4453	G	4/4	S9p23	
MY WEE CRIPPLE WEAN	3b1H6b6b	3b53b2	E	6/8 A	S8v3p26	
MY WEE FIDDLE	3H1H1H5	3211H	D	2/2 R	K2v4p7	
MY WIFE'S A WANTON WEE THING	1H1H1H5	7b7b7b2	D	6/8	K2v2p35 L8v6p8 R10p135	
MY WIFE'S A WANTON WEE THING	1H3H1H5	6522	D	4/4 S	Mc3v1p72	
NATHANIEL GOW	1L3L5L3L	1L3L6L2L	Bb	4/4 S	L8v5p20 Mc3v1p163	
NEGRO BREAKDOWN	5L343	5L321	A	2/4 CD	K2v1p22	
NEGRO MELODY	1515	7b5b31	B	2/4 CD	K2v1p21	
NEIL GOW'S COMPLIMENTS TO MR. MARSHALL	1L353	1L47L2	A	4/4 SS	Mc3v1p153	
NEIL GOW'S FAREWELL TO WHISKY	1L326L	5L353	G	2/2 CD	R10p153	
NEIL GOW'S HOUSE	136L7L	1566	D	4/4	W1p28	
NEIL GOW'S STRATHSPEY [NIEL GOW'S]	51H62	51H66	A	4/4 S	Mc3v1p5	
NEIL GOW'S WIFE [NIEL GOW'S WIFE]	3b127bL	3b13b3b	G	4/4 S	K2v1p13 L8v3p19 Mc3v1p123	
					M7p27 R10p186 S17p34	
NEIL ROY	13b54	2454	G	4/4*R	Mc3v1p133 R10p192	
NESS HOUSE	1H542	331H5	G	4/4 R	L8v4p14	
NETHER CLUNY	1353	6L6L22	Bb	2/2 R	R10p289	
NETTA, MISS BRUCE, FOCHABERS	5566	553H3H	A	4/4 SC	S8v5p9	
NEW BOB, THE or [BOGANUADH]	13b54	247b4	Bm	4/4 R	L8v4p10	
NEW BRIDGE DUMFRIES, THE	13b53b	7bL242	G	2/2 R	G6v2p39	
NEW BRIG O' AYR, THE	131H5	5555	F	4/4 R	K2v3p18	
NEW CHRISTMAS	1564	1H3H2H2	G	4/4 R	S17p26	
NEW CHRISTMAS or BASS REEL, THE	3155	1H3H2H2	G	4/4 R	Mc3v1p82	
NEW CLARET	133	133	G	9/8	Mc3v1p185	
NEW FOREST	11H1H3bH	5H5H2H2H	D	2/2	W1p35	
NEW MILL AT LOGIERAIT, THE	1521	7bL244	A	4/4 S	R10p56	
NEW RIGG'D SHIP, THE	1H1H1H1H	2H52H5	C	6/8 J	L8v2p15 Mc3v1p176	
NEW STRATHSPEY, A	1351H	547L2	G	2/2 S	S15p18	
NEW YEAR'S DAY	557b2H	3H4H3H4H	A	4/4 S	R10p50	
NEWBYTH HOUSE	513b5	27bL7b4	E	2/2 R	R10p259	
NEWCASTLE, THE	11L37L	4L665	Bb	4/4	S9p30	
NEWS FROM CADIZ	5131H	6664	F	4/4 S	L8v4p21	
NIEL GOW [NEIL GOW]	51H62	51H66	A G	4/4 S	K2v2p4 L8v1p2 L8v8Bp1 R10p15	
					S9p8 S17p20	
NIEL GOW'S LAMENTATION	1L5L6L5L	246L6L	G	4/4	Mc3v1p157 R10p184	
FOR(JAMES MORAY OF) ABERCAIRN(E)Y						
NIEL GOW'S RECOVERY	3L5L31	6L5L4L2L	Bb	4/4 S	S17p110	
NIEL GOW'S RECOVERY	353H1H	6542	C	4/4 S	K2v2p13	
NIGHEAN DUBH ALASDAIR	117bL2	5147bL	A	4/4 S	R10p29	
NIGHEAN DUBH NAN GEALA CHAS	1H531	5633	G	2/2 R	Mc3v1p87 R10p175	
NINE PINT COGGIE	5L117bL	4224	E	2/2 R	R10p249	
NINE PINT COGGIE, THE	1117bL	4124	Em	4/4 R	L8v4p17 Mc3v1p184 S17p132	
NINE PINT COGGIE, THE	3115L	7bL424	G	4/4*R	K2v3p9 S8v7p27	
NINETY-THIRD'S FAREWELL TO GIBRALTAR	5511	6532	A	2/4 QS	K2v1p49	
NIONAG A CHUIL DUINN NACH FHAN THU	121H6	6136L	G	4/4	M10v1p8	
NORA CREINA	1H135	1H124	F	6/8	S9p25	
NORTH BRIDGE OF EDINBURGH(, THE)	5L113b	27bL47bL	B A	4/4 S	K2v3p6 Mc3v1p61 R10p130	
					S17p70	
NORTH HUNT, THE	5547L	5515	G	4/4 R	R10p178	
NORTH OF THE GRAMPIANS	3551H	351H2H	C	4/4 S	K2v2p11 R10p61	
NORTH OF THE GRAMPIANS(, THE)	3553	351H2H	C	4/4 S	L8v3p12 L8v8Ap19 Mc3v1p109	
[NORTH SIDE OF THE GRAMPIANS, THE]					S8v8p55	
NORTH OF THE TAY	3b115L	3b427bL	E	2/2 R	Mc3v1p82 R10p265	

NORTH OF THE TWEED	15L3b5	247b3b	E	4/4 S	R10p264
NORTH PORT	5653	5662	F	4/4 S	L8v8Bp25
NORTH SIDE OF SPEY, THE	1L1L2L7bF	1L5L11	A	4/4 S	G14p19
NORTHERN MEETING, THE	5653	5653	Bm	4/4 S	L8v6p12
NUAGHALACHD [NOVELTY, THE]	5L3L5L3L	5L5L33	Eb	4/4*R	Mc3v1p195 R10p267
NUAIR BHA MI FEIN 'NAM MHADUIN	5353	6262	A	4/4 PR	Mc3v1p12
(WHEN I WAS A MAIDEN)					
'NULL AIR NA H'EILEANAN	3325L	25L22	G	4/4	M10v2p10
DH'AMERICA GUN TEID SINN					
NULL THAR NAN EILEANAN, OR AMERICA	6451	5155	A	2/2 R	R10p10
NULL THAR NAN EILEANUN or	3H1H2H5	5H52H2H	D	4/4 R	Mc3v1p69
OVER THE ISLES TO AMERICA					
NUT, THE	1131	6332	A	6/8	K2v1p27
O AS I WAS KISS'D YESTREEN	1151	27bL27bL	Am	6/8 J	L8v2p19
O BUT YE BE MERRY [O SHE'S COMICAL]	5564	5531	A	4/4 R	S17p77
O DEAR! WHAT CAN THE MATTER BE?	5555	4444	G	6/8	S9p26
O GIN I WERE A BARON'S HEIR	1H1H2H	3H3H6H	D	3/4 W	K2v1p25
O GIN YE WERE DEAD GUDEMAN	1151	3223	F	2/2 CD	R10p151
O LASSIE ART THOU SLEEPING YET	551H1H	4H3H2H6	D	6/8	K2v2p34
O SHE'S COMICAL	5566	4431	A	2/2 R	R10p8
O SHE'S COMING [O SHE'S COMICAL]	5566	5531	A	4/4 R	K2v2p4 L8v4p2 Mc3v1p22
O THIS IS NO MY AIN LASSIE	354H2H	6562	D	4/4 R	L8v5p8
O WELCOME TO MY DEARIE O	131H1H	6326L	G	2/2 R	R10p178
O WHISTLE AND I'LL COME TO YOU MY LOVE	3H522H	3H561H	D	6/8	K2v1p33
[...LAD]					
OCH MAR THA MI [HOW SAD AM I]	5L11	265	F	3/4	M10v1p3
ODDFELLOWS, THE	3L121	3L632	A	2/4	S8v6p117
O'ER BOGIE [O'ER BOGGIE WI' MY LOVE]	1H1H1H5	1H1H55	C	4/4*R	K2v2p11 L8v1p17 R10p64
O'ER THE HILLS AND FAR AWA'	1H1H1H6	1H1H3H2H	D	2/4	K2v3p47
O'ER THE HILLS AND FAR AWAY	1H1H1H6	1H1H4H2H	D	2/4	K2v1p26
O'ER THE MUIR AMANG THE HEATHER	5L111	6L242	G	4/4 R	K2v2p14 L8v4p12
OFF SHE GOES	3451H	3452	D	6/8 J	L8v4p7 Mc3v1p175 R10p137
					S9p18
OISEAN AN DEIGH NA FEINNE	7bL7bL5L	5L11	A	3/4	M10v2p4
OLD BOG HOLE	1113L	6L5L5L1	A	4/4 CD	K2v1p23
OLD DUMBARTON DRUMS	3332	1554	F	2/2 CD	R10p151
OLD FOLKS AT HOME	3323	11H61H	G	4/4	S9p21
OLD HIGHLAND WEDDING (WITH VARIATIONS)	5551	5527bL	A	6/8	G14p24/25
OLD MAN WILL NEVER DIE, THE	1566	5122	G	2/2*R	R10p301 S17p72
[OLD MAN, THE]					
OLD ROSEN THE BEAU	1356	516L6L	A	6/8	K2v1p29
OLD STRATHSPEY	1H1H1H1H	1H2H75	F	4/4 S	K2v3p19
OOR GUID WIFE	51H1H1H	2H2H2H6	C	4/4 R	K2v3p16
OOR GUIDWIFE	1L5L42	1L5L53	A	2/4	S8v6p97
OPERA HORNPIPE	1H1H2H5	1H1H2H5	D	4/4	M7p35
OPERA REEL	1133	1122	D	2/2 R	K2v4p9
ORACLE, THE	13b53b	47b47bL	F#	4/4 S	S8v10p5
ORANGE AND BLUE	3H1H53	3H3H1H1H	C A	6/8 J	L8v4p20 Mc3v1p121
ORANGE AND BLUE	3H1H51H	3H5H1H1H	D	4/4 SC	K2v1p20
ORANGE AND BLUE	315L3L	3311	A	6/8	K2v2p35
ORANGE AND BLUE	315L1	3511	A	4/4 SC	M7p19 S8v7p20/21
ORCHILL HOUSE	7bL5L4L7bF	7bL5L7bL1L	A	4/4 R	Mc3v1p59
O'REILLY'S JIG	5651H	5627b	A	6/8	M7p38
ORKNEY	1311	5L5L22	D	4/4*R	Mc3v1p51 R10p124
OSSIAN	3b513b	57b3b5	F#	4/4 A	S8v7p36 S8v8p7
OSSIAN'S HALL	3565	227b2	A	2/2*R	R10p25 S17p134
OUR HIGHLAND QUEEN	1313	3H755	D	4/4 A	Mc3v1p156 S8v3p14 S8v7p37
					S8v8p14
OVER THE BORDER	1111	16L62	G	6/8	K2v1p32
OVER THE WATER	1563	1561H	G	6/8	K2v1p31
OYSTER WIVES' RANT, THE	5551	447bL2	A	4/4*R	K2v2p10 Mc3v1p110 R10p53
PADDY CAREY	1H1H65	51H4H7	D	6/8	K2v1p27
PADDY O' CARROL	3333	51H22	D G	6/8	Mc3v1p175 S9p20
PADDY WHACK	11H64	1675	G	6/8	S9p24
PADDY'S DELIGHT	13b21	3b543b	G	2/4 HP	S8v8p144/5
PANMURE HOUSE [MISS LYAL(L)]	11L3bL5L	7bL27bL7bL	A	4/4 S	S17p138
PARAZOTTI	3H3H2H1H	1H1H76	D	2/4	S8v8p175
PARCEL POST, THE	5H5H1H4	7L41H5H	D	2/4 HP	S8v5p1
PARISH OF DALMAILING	1152	7L27L2	Eb	4/4 S	Mc3v1p130
PARKS OF KILBURNIE, THE	353H1H	5642	F	2/2*R	G6v1p12 R10p227 S17p44
[PARKS OF FOCHABERS, THE]					
PARLOUR REEL	1H763	1326L	D	2/2 R	K2v4p10
PASS ABOUT THE FLAGON	5L17bL6L	5L3b42	G	4/4 SS	R10p197
PASS OF BALLATER, THE	13b51H	3bH2H7b2	C	4/4	W1p26
PATE BAILLIE'S JIG	1155	47bL47bL	E	6/8	K2v1p33
PATRICK GLENNNIE'S REEL	131H3	5L37L2	Bb	2/2	W1p19
PATRIOT, THE	1355	2461H	Dm	6/8 J	L8v2p22
PATRONELLA [PETRONELLA]	3211	1H2H75	D	2/4 CD	K2v1p22
PAUL WALLACE	15L37L	6L27L2	F	4/4 R	L8v8Bp25
PAY AS YOU GO	5L13b1	5L124	A	4/4 S	K2v2p9 L8v2p20 R10p49
PEASE BRIDGE	1H3b1H3bH	7b542	D	4/4 S	G6v1p45
PEASE STRAE [CLEAN PEASE STRAE]	1H3H4H3H	2H57b7b	D	4/4 R	L8v1p7 Mc3v1p72 S17p117

PEASE STRAE	1H3H4H3H	2H577	D	2/2 R	R10p86
PEAT BOG, THE	3H2H2H6	5555	D	2/2 R	K2v4p8
PEGGIE'S DUMPLING	3564	5342	A	2/2 R	K2v4p4
PEGGIE'S WEDDING [LADY'S FANCY]	1H1H1H5H	1H1H72H	C	6/8 J	R10p140
PEGGY MENZIES	1H535	1H522	G	2/2 R	Mc3v1p97 R10p157
PERRIE WERRIE, THE	3111	311H6	G	2/2 R	MC3v1p101 R10p167
PERRIE WHERRIE, THE	3111	311H1H	G	4/4 R	K2v2p15
PERSIAN DANCE	3211	4622	G	2/4	M7p29
PERTH ASSEMBLY	3546	3542	F	4/4 R	K2v2p22
PERTH ASSEMBLY, THE	3546	5342	F	4/4*S	L8v1p18 Mc3v1p150 R10p208
PERTH HUNT	5513	1362	C	4/4	S9p3
PERTH-SHIRE HUNT(, THE)	5L3L1L3L	1L3L6L2L	A	4/4*R	G6v2p5 K2v1p8 L8v5p1 L8v8Bp3
[PERTH HUNT(, THE]					Mc3v1p19 R10p4 S8v7p29
					S17p62
PERTHSHIRE HUNT, THE	5L1L1L6L	5L1L33	A	2/4 R	S8v8p104
PERTHSHIRE LASSES, THE	5351H	5326L	Bb	2/2	W1p15
PERTHSHIRE VOLUNTEERS	5L331	447L2	A	4/4 S	G6v2p6 K2v2p3 K2v3p23 L8v1p3
					L8v8Bp3 Mc3v1p16 M7p23
					R10p4 S8v8p91
PETER BAIL[L]IE	3L16L1	3L5L46L	A	4/4 S	M7p25
PETER BAILIE [PETER BAILLIE]	5555	27bL7b5	E	4/4 S	K2v1p18 Mc3v1p30 M7p9
					R10p251
PETER BAILLIE or	5555	7b424	E	4/4 S	S8v7p12 S8v8p66
[LONACH HIGHLAND FLING, THE]					
PETER BAIL[L]IE'S WIFE	5L5L5L1	5236L	A	6/8	K2v1p49
PETER GRAY	13L6L7L	36L4L1	G	2/4 R	S8v7p14
PETER LAING	3345	1H4#47L	F	4/4 S	S8v7p15 S8v8p124
PETER MACLAGAN Esq.	5154	534H2H	E	2/2	W1p39
PETER MILNE	3L3L6L5L	3432	A	4/4	S8v6p104
PETER REID	1H515	1H566	D	4/4 S	R10p86
PETERCAN MCOMISH	3331	2427bL	A	4/4 R	L8v2p2
[BIODAG AIR MAC THOMAIS]					
PETRONELLA	3211	127L5L	F	2/4 CD	R10p150
PETTICOAT'S LOOSE, THE	3b23b2	7bL7bL7bL7bL	Gm	6/8 J	L8v6p23
PHILABEG	5421	27bL24	A	4/4 SC	K2v3p24
PIBROCH O' DONALD DHU	5653	5652	A	6/8	K2v1p31
PIG HUNT, THE	1H5H3H1H	52H75	C	2/4	S8v6p83
PIG TOWN, THE	1516	1546L	A	2/4 R	S8v8p143
PIGEON ON THE GALE	1113	1316L	G	2/2 R	K2v4p14
PIPE MAJOR, THE	1531	3165	A	4/4 PM	S8v8p38
PIPE SLANG, THE	3b111	3b57b3b	A	4/4 R	K2v2p9 R10p46
PIPER KING, THE	3565	3562	A	2/4 PM	S8v8p42
PIPER'S MARCH	1H61H6	7575	D	6/8	K2v4p27
PIPER'S WEIRD, THE or	1123	6532	A	6/8	S8v7p28 S8v8p150
MACRIMMON'S FAREWELL					
PIRRIWIG, THE [AN FHIR GHRUAIG]	1H1H2H7	1H653	E G	2/2*R	R10p261 S17p121
PITNACREE FERRYMAN, THE	1H164	6542	A	4/4 S	K2v1p11
PITNACREE FERRYMAN, THE	5H53H1H	3H2H1H6	D	2/2 R	R10p91
PITTENGARDENER'S RANT	5L136	627L2	D	4/4 S	S8v7p2 S8v8p75
PLOUGHMAN LADDIE, THE	5316L	5L3L24	F	2/2	W1p51
POETS GAVOTTE, THE	5245L	4131	A	2/4	S8v6p122
POLD(Q)WILLY BRIDGE [POLDWILLY BRIDGE]	1H515	1H527	D	4/4 R	K2v1p24 S9p5
POLDUILLY BRIDGE	15L5L5L	15L2L7L	A	2/2	W1p3
POLICEMAN'S CAP	1H1H63	6363	D	4/4 R	K2v3p4
POLL AN DROIGHIONN	315L1	4426L	A	4/4 S	R10p22
POOL REEL, THE	513b5	7b424	Em	4/4 R	L8v5p11
POOLACHRIE	3b5L3b1	3b5L27bL	G	2/4	G14p30
POOR FREDDY'S GONE TO BALMACAAN	153b1	7b547bL	F#	4/4 S	S8v3p30
POP GOES THE WEASEL	1231	1231	G	6/8	S9p17
PORST MOHR IAIN IC EACHINN (JOHN	1531	4327bL	A	4/4 R	Mc3v1p42
MACEACHINN'S BIG TUNE)					
PORT MOR NA LURGANN	5551H	5524	F	4/4 S	R10p206
PORT NA CAILLICHE	3b13b1	27bL27bL	E	4/4 S	R10p262
PORT NAN CON, or BOB O' DOOLY, THE	1553	1544	A	2/2 R	R10p14
PRESIDENT, THE	553H2H	5572H	A	2/4	S8v7p18/19 S8v8p76-9
PRESTON PANS	5213	6L5L6L5L	A	2/2 R	K2v4p6
PRETTY PEG [PRETTY PEGG] [PRETTY PEGGY]	1H3H51	1H3H2H3H	D	4/4*R	K2v2p17 L8v2p8 L8v8Bp9
					Mc3v1p76 R10p90 S17p87
PRETTY PEGGY	1H51H2H	1H547L	D	2/4	S8v8p78
PRINCE ALBERT'S STRATHSPEY	3313	4453	A	4/4 S	M7p21
PRINCE ALFRED'S REEL	15L3b1	2427bL	G	4/4 R	L8v8Bp28
PRINCE ARTHUR'S HIGHLAND FLING	531H3	6542	D	4/4 S	L8v8Ap7
PRINCE CHARLIE [PRINCE CHARLES]	1155	7b427bL	E	4/4*R	K2v1p6 L8v6p16 R10p251
PRINCE CHARLIE'S MEDLEY	5L5L4L4L	5L5L7bL1	A	6/8	R10p265
PRINCE CHARLIE'S WELCOME	5142	5142	G D	4/4 QS	K2v3p45 Mc3v1p155
TO THE ISLE OF SKYE					
PRINCE CONSORT'S REEL, THE	5L13b5	2427bL	A	4/4 R	L8v8Ap1
PRINCE OF WALES, THE	3H1H5L6	3H1H41H	D	2/4 R	S8v8p74
PRINCE OF WALES, THE	3b124	3b13b5	G	4/4 R	L8v8Ap2
PRINCESS ROYAL, THE	3b13b1	6b453b	D	2/4 HP	S8v8p134
PROFESSOR BLACKIE	1331	1H765	D	4/4 A	S8v7p48
PROFESSOR SCOTT	113b3b	24L2L4L	G	2/2 R	S8v3p58

Title					
PULL THE BEASTIE'S FIT	5165	47L12	D	4/4	S8v6p89
PUNKIE WILLIE	53b11	3b3b51H	A	4/4 S	K2v4p17
PUSH ABOUT THE JORUM	537L2	331H7	G	4/4*R	K2v2p14 K2v3p9 L8v6p13
					L8v8Bp11 R10p165
PUT ON THE STEAM	5L13b2	24L2L7bF	Am	4/4 R	L8v2p20
QUAY SIDE, THE	1H155L	11L5L1	A	4/4 HP	Mc3v1p174
QUEENIE	5L131	6L242	A	4/4	S8v6p103
QUEEN'S COMMISSIONER, THE	3542H	751H5H	E	4/4 A	S8v8p12
QUEEN'S DRIVE, THE	3352	3322	Bb	2/4	P3p20
QUEEN'S FIDDLER'S COMPts TO MR TROUP	3H1H53	5532	F	4/4	B9p8
QUEEN'S JUBILEE, THE	1H347L	1H343	A	2/4	S8v6p106
QUEEN'S LANDING, THE	5L13b1	5L13b1	Bm	4/4 S	L8v4p10
QUEEN'S WELCOME TO DEE SIDE, THE	551H5	227b2	A	4/4 S	L8v8Ap1
QUEEN'S WELCOME TO INVERCAULD, THE	3456	3147bL	A	4/4*M	S8v7p31 S8v8p42
QUICKSTEP	5531	5561H	D	6/8	K2v1p47
QUICK-STEP	5414	5422	A	6/8	K2v1p48
QUICKSTEP	5353	5316L	G	2/4	K2v1p49
QUICKSTEP (NAME NOT KNOWN) [UNTITLED]	11H1H1H	7bL7b57bL	A	2/4	M10v1p14
QUICKSTEP	5547bL	5521	A	2/4	M10v1p14
QUICKSTEP, A	1545	4322	G	2/4	M10v2p18
RABBIE BURNS	1532	1535	G	4/4 S	K2v4p12
RACHAEL RAE [RACHEL RAE]	131H5	1H3H2H7	D	4/4 R	K2v1p4 L8v1p6 L8v8Bp6
					S17p145
RACHAEL RAE'S MOTHER	1363	1H522	D	4/4 R	Mc3v1p64
RACHEL RAE	131H5	1H3H3H1H	D	4/4*R	Mc3v1p32 R10p89
RAIGMORE HOUSE	3115L	31H64	A	4/4 R	L8v8Ap6
RAILWAY HORNPIPE	1564	3H2H1H5	D	2/2	G14p7
RANNOCH LODGE	3565	3562	A	4/4 S	K2v2p5 R10p21
RANTIN(G) HIGHLANDMAN, THE	1535	47bL7b2	A	4/4 R	K2v2p7 L8v4p3
RATHA FAIR	5H5H2H4H	5H5H5H5H	D	4/4 R	S17p4
RAVEN, THE or HOOKEYBEAK	51H53	61H75	D	4/4 R	S8v3p5
RECOVERY, THE	1355	1551H	D	4/4 S	K2v1p11
RECRUIT, THE	5551	51H51	D	4/4	S9p31
RED COAT, THE	3366	1311	G	4/4 PS	Mc3v1p48
RED HAIRED GIRL OF TULLOCH, THE	13b55	7bL27bL4	B	4/4 PS	Mc3v1p69
RED HECKLE, THE	57b55	7b424	A	4/4 PM	S8v9/4
RED PLAID, THE	5L13b3b	427bL2	A	4/4 S	K2v4p17
RED RED ROSE	121H6	662H1H	D	6/8*	K2v2p34 K2v3p6
[MY LOVE IS LIKE A RED RED ROSE]					
RED ROB	15L3L1L	4L27L5L	Bb	4/4	S8v6p111
REEL, A	1H3bH3bH1H	7bH7b2H7b	C	2/2	G14p18
REEL, A	31H1H5	427L2	A	2/2	G14p27
REEL, A	1353	1H37L2	F	2/2	G14p3
REEL O' CORSE	5313	6647bL	D	4/4 R	M7p15
REEL O' THUILLEACHAN, THE	5554	5524	A	2/4 R	S8v8p118
REEL O' TULLOCH [REEL O' THUILLEACHAN]	5151	5147bL	A	4/4*R	K2v1p5 L8v1p1 L8v8Bp1
					Mc3v1p3 R10p6 S8v7p24/5
					S8v8p116/7 S17p90
REEL OF BOGIE, THE	1H1H1H5	1H1H55	C	4/4 R	S17p47
REEL OF CLUNY, THE	131H3	1H362	A	4/4 R	K2v3p11 L8v5p3 L8v8Bp2
REEL OF GAMRIE, THE	116L4L	1124	G	4/4	P3p4
REITH'S CLARINET	315L3	426L4	G	4/4 S	S8v3p29
RENATTON'S FANCY	5L346L	7L262	G	4/4 S/	S8v10p16
RENDEZVOUS, THE	113L1	6L27L2	G	4/4*R	K2v2p16 R10p177
RETICULE, THE or [RIDICULE, THE]	3131	3331	F	4/4 R	L8v3p14 S17p59
RETURN FROM INDIA, THE	4233	427L5L	A	4/4 R	K2v1p8
RICHARD'S	5H4H1H5	6542	D	2/2 R	S8v3p11
RIDDRIE	5346	536L7L	A	4/4 S	K2v4p6
RIEFIELD LODGE	3b53b3b	2247bL	G	4/4 S	R10p303
RIGHT OFF THE REEL	13L13L	1532	G	4/4 S	S8v3p28
RIGHTS OF MAN, THE	316L3	1H642	G	2/4 HP	S8v8p145
RIGHTS OF MAN, THE	3217L	6L136	G	4/4 HP	M7p34
RINETTAN'S DAUGHTER	5L3b11	3b13b5L	A	4/4 S	K2v2p9 R10p46
RISE LAZY LUBBER	117bL7bL	3b511	A	4/4 S	G6v1p24
RISE (YE) LAZY LUBBER	117bL7bL	3b511L	A	4/4*R	K2v2p10 R10p49
[RISE YOU LAZY FELLOW]					
R.O. FARQUHARSON ESQ. OF HAUGHTON'S R.	1353	1327L	G	2/2	W1p58
ROAD TO BERWICK, THE	3565	11H2H2	D	2/2 R	G6v2p11
ROARING JELLY	131H2H	4324	D	6/8 J	L8v2p7 R10p137
ROARING RIVIE	5515	1562	D	4/4 S	R10p112
ROB AN LUGI	1353	1342	A	4/4 S	K2v2p8 R10p36
ROB RALSTON'S STRATHSPEY	11H63	7L5L44	D	4/4 S	K2v2p20
ROB ROY MACGREGOR	3b115L	13b53b	E	4/4 S	R10p255
ROBERT CARMACK	13L6L2L	7L41H1H	F	4/4 SS	H5p1
ROBERT MENZIES	5333	5336	A	4/4 S	K2v2p6 R10p32
ROBERT RUSSELL ESQ. OF PILMUIR'S REEL	1H3bH1H5	7b2H7b4	E	2/2	W1p45
ROBERTSON'S	3113	25L5L1	Bb	2/2 HP	R10p300
ROBIN'S NEST	5H3H53	3H5H72H	C	4/4 S	L8v8Bp16
ROBSLEY COTTAGE	521H4	526L2	Eb	4/4 SS	S8v3p61
ROCKIN' STEP, THE or	3131	3111H	A	4/4	S8v8p114
MANSON'S HIGHLAND FLING					
ROCKS OF CASHEL, THE	1565	1542	D	4/4 S	L8v5p7

ROE HUNT, THE	5351H	5362	E	2/2		W1p38
ROLL HER ON THE HILL	5555	6661H	D	4/4 R		K2v1p3
ROLLING SPEY, THE	15L3L1L	1551	G	4/4 S		S8v7p48
ROLLOCKING IRISHMAN, THE	1H11H7	1H2H3H7	D	6/8		S9p21
ROMANCE	3H3H3H6	2H1H1H1H	D	4/4		H5p1
ROMP AMONG THE WHINS	5451	5462	A	2/2 R		R10p37
ROMP AMONG THE WHINS	5451	5362	A	4/4 R		Mc3v1p20
RONALD'S WELCOME	5L123	6526L	G	4/4 S		S8v5p17
RORY McNAB	5151	47bL7b7bL	E	4/4*R		K2v1p12 L8v6p17 R10p257
						S17p143
RORY O' MORE	5351	537L2	A G	6/8 CD		Mc3v1p167 M7p30 R10p144
						S9p22
ROSE AMONG THE HEATHER, THE	3546	3122	A D	4/4 SC		K2v1p20 M7p13
ROSE TREE, THE	1H555	1H2H3H2H	D	2/4 CD		K2v1p21
ROSE TREE, THE	1H555	1H3H3H2H	C	2/4		S9p19
ROSE WOOD	1H51H3	1H362	A	4/4 J		S8v9/8
ROSE WOOD'S DIRK	1353	4527L	A	4/4 S		S8v8p101
ROSE-ACRE	36L5L1L	36L2L2L	A	4/4		S8v6p69
ROSE-ACRE, FAREWELL	3221	5432	A	4/4		S8v6p69
ROSEBUD OF ALLANVALE, THE	3211	4522	A	6/8 A		S8v9/9
ROSIE'S SCHOTTISCHE	5364	531H1H	F	4/4 SC		S8v5p22
ROTHIEMURCHUS RANT	3335	1H61H6	C	4/4 S		G6v1p10 K2v1p11 L8v4p18
[ROTHIEMURCHIE'S RANT]						Mc3v1p105 R10p70 S8v8p21
						S9p11
ROUALEYN'S PLAID	6L5L13	4526L	A	4/4		S8v6p61
ROVER	3115	27L7L5	G	2/2 R		K2v4p15
ROVER, THE	1511	157bL7bL	E	4/4 S		R10p254
ROVER, THE	1H13b4	2512	C	4/4		S8v6p23
ROW, THE	1H1H65	22H76	D	2/2 R		R10p155
ROWAN TREE	3335	6665	A	4/4 SC		K2v3p23
ROXBURGH CASTLE HORNPIPE	1155	4452	A	4/4		M7p34
ROYAL ABERDEENSHIRE HIGHLANDERS' MARCH	1553	51H55	C	4/4		W1p24
ROYAL RECOVERY, THE	1355	1551H	C	4/4 S		L8v5p13
ROYAL RECOVERY, THE	1L3L5L5L	1L5L5L1	Bb	4/4 S		S17p32
ROYAL VISIT TO NEWE 1859, THE	13b55	7b522	F	2/2		W1p53
ROY'S WIFE	5333	5322	G	4/4		S9p8
RU'GLEN LUMS	5521	5L136	F	4/4 S		K2v3p19
RUIDHLE NA MARAGAN DUBH	5362	531H3H	D	2/2 R		R10p95
RUTHRIE	1L3bL5L3bL	6L4L2L7bL	A	2/2 R		G14p27
RYAN'S RANT	151H5	1547bL	A	2/2 R		K2v4p17
'S FHEUDAR DHOMH FHEIN A BHI FALBH	1322	1316L	A	2/4		M10v1p12
['TIS TIME TO GO HOME]						
SADNESS OF LIFE, THE	11H6b5	153b2	C	4/4 A		S8v8p11
SAIGHDEAR RUADH	1H133	2466	G	2/2 R		R10 160
SAILOR'S HORNPIPE	1H1H31H	2H754H	D	4/4 HP		Mc3v1p171 M7p36
SAILOR'S HORNPIPE, THE	1H434	3432	G	2/4		S9p27
SAILOR'S WIFE, THE	13b1H3bH	5H2H54	E	6/8		K2v1p33
SAILOR'S WIFE, THE	121H3bH	5H2H54	F	6/8		G6v1p20
SALAMANCA, THE	5353	173H7	D	2/2 R		K2v4p8
SALLY KELLY	11H1H1H	2H7b2H4H	Dm Em	4/4 R		L8v1p20 S17p21
SALLY KELLY	11H1H1H	2H7b24	F	2/2 R		R10p209
SALMON TAILS UP THE WATER	1553	1524	A	4/4 S		K2v2p7 L8v5p4
SAND JIG	1H51H3	461H4	C	6/8		S9p20
SANDERS BRANE	3b13b1	427bL2	Dm	4/4 S		L8v1p21 R10p219 S17p78
SANDERS BRANE	16L16L	27L5L7L	F	4/4 S		K2v1p14
SANDIE OWER THE SEA	5321	216L5L	F	4/4 A		S8v6p10 S8v7p35
SANDIE'S GOAT	5H5H5H1H	4H6H2H5H	D	2/4 HP		S8v5p19
SANDLAW'S WELCOME	1564	27L32	A	4/4		S8v7p37 S8v8p30/31
SANDY BUCHANAN	5L15L7bL	3b53b1	A	4/4 SC		K2v2p24
SANDY GRANT(O' BATTANGORM)	31H62	31H53	D E	2/4 R		S8v7p3 S8v8p120/1
SANDY IS MY DARLING	11H7b4	3b7bL7bL3	Am	4/4 R		L8v2p19
SANDY IS MY DARLING	11H7b4	3b7bL7bL3b	A	4/4*R		K2v3p18 R10p47
SANDY IS MY DARLING	11H7b4	3b7bL7bL2	A	4/4 R		L8v8Bp20
SANDY KING	371H7	371H6	A	4/4 S		Mc3v1p180
SANDY MACDONALD'S	51H53	11H22	D	4/4 R		Mc3v1p44
SANDY MACDONALD'S FAVOURITE	51H53	11H32	D	4/4 R		Mc3v1p44
SANDY O'ER THE LEA	1353	5222	D	4/4*R		L8v6p6 L8v8Ap8 R10p98 S17p88
SANDY O'ER THE LEA	1353	5322	D	4/4 R		K2v1p9
SANDY SKINNER	1H1H1H6	1H1H1H3	D	2/4		S8v6p88
SANDY TROUP	1235	4532	A	4/4		S8v6p108
SANNY SPEIRS	1151	5764	G	4/4 S		K2v4p12
SARONA	3313	5535	D	4/4 A		S8v7p49 S8v8p162/3
SCHICHALLION	5L13b2	27bL27bL	A	4/4 S		K2v2p9
SCOLDING WIVES OF ABERTARFF, THE	53b3b7b	4226	Gm	4/4*R		L8v5p21 R10p193
S'COMA LEAM FHEIN COGADH NO SITH	13b7b7b	1H1H43b	D	6/8		M10v2p2
SCONE PALACE	153b5	7bL424	F	2/2		W1p56
SCOTCH MIST	3H2H3H5H	3H2H3H4H	C	4/4 S		K2v3p16
SCOTCH MIST	5566	72H1H3H	D	4/4 S		K2v4p10
SCOTCHMAN IN AMERICA, THE	1133H	1H653	G	4/4 SC		K2v2p24
SCOTLAND YET	351H4	5322	D	4/4 S		K2v4p7
SCOTS BONNET	1355	2466	G	2/2 R		G6v1p7
SCOTS WHA HAE	5551H	6661H	D	4/4 SC		K2v3p24

Title			Key	Type	References
SCOTT SKINNER	1H55L3	1H553	A	2/4 R	S8v7p9
SCOTT SKINNER'S COMPLIMENTS TO DR. MACDONALD	11H51	4532	A	4/4 M	S8v7p31
SCOTT SKINNER'S "GHILLIE CALLUM"	137bL4	131H5	A	4/4	S8v6p102
SCOTT SKINNER'S ROCKIN' STEP	3131	3111H	A	4/4 S	S8v7p13
SCURRAN A MORANGE	1L111	7bL2L2L7bL	A	4/4 S	G14p14
SCURRAN A WELLS	15L3bL7bF	15L3bL5L	A	2/2 S	G14p2
SE MO CHAS CHRUBACH	1565	157b4	A	3/8	M10v1p10
SEAFORTH HIGHLANDERS, THE	5431H	7b427b	A	2/4	S8v6p80
SEAFORTH HIGHLANDERS, THE	11H15	11H31	A	4/4 S	Mc3v1p17
SEAN CHAISTEAL GHART	3565	3542	A	2/2 R	R10p14
SEAN PHORT MAITH	3H2H1H3H	62H75	D	2/2 R	R10p92
SEAN RONG MOR	3551	4322	D	2/2 R	R10p91
SEUMAS MOR A' GHLINNE	1361H	527L2	F	2/2 R	R10p207
SGIAN DUBH	1L17bL4L	1L112	B	6/8	K2v2p35
SGIANDUBH	11H7b4	11H1H2H	C	6/8 J	R10p141
SHAKINS O' THE POCKY, THE	1L5L5L1L	16L33	Bb	4/4 S	Mc3v1p164 S8v3p55
SHEEP SHANKS	1H535	2462H	A	4/4*R	K2v3p12 L8v6p2 R10p27
SHERWOOD RANGERS, THE	553H1H	6542	D	2/4	S9p31
SHE'S BONNIE AN' BRAW[AN' THAT'S A']	315L1	6L27L7L	A	6/8	S8v6p14 S8v7p46
SHE'S SWEETEST WHEN SHE SMILES	1526L	1511H	F	4/4 R	K2v2p22 L8v3p16
SHILLELAH, THE	1H663	1362	G	2/4 R	S8v8p142
SIC' A WIFE AS I HAE GOTTEN	5L13b2	4L7bL21	Em	4/4 R	L8v6p16
SICK BOY, THE	13b15	427bL6bL	A	4/4	S8v8p157
SIDH-CHAILLIONN	5L13b2	27bL27bL	A	4/4 S	R10p46
SILLAR'S AWA', THE	6L3L1L3L	6L3L5L3L	Bb	6/8	P3p9
SILVER TASSY, THE	1551H	3H1H53	D	4/4 S	S8v5p6
SILVERWELLS	3113	5422	F	4/4 SS	S8v3p53
SIMON BRODIE	13b42	13b53b	Em	4/4 S	L8v5p11
SIMON BRODIE	1522	3b51H5	E	4/4 S	R10p256
SIR ALEXANDER ANDERSON OF BLELACK	3457	5127L	D	4/4 S	S8v3p7
SIR ALEXANDER DON	3b13bL1L	247b2	G	4/4 S	G6v2p35
SIR ALEXANDER DON	3146	3542	F	4/4 S	Mc3v1p144 S17p100
SIR ALEXr. G.P. CUMMING BARt. OF ALTYRE'S REEL	1H1H2H6	5332	G	2/2	W1p62
SIR ARCHD. DUNBAR [SIR ARCHIBALD DUNBAR]	1347bL	1353	D	4/4 S	K2v2p18 Mc3v1p41 R10p107
SIR ARCHd. GRANT OF MONEY MUSK	5354	5324	G	4/4 S	Mc3v1p97
SIR CHAs. FORBES BARt. OF NEWE'S STR.	5L15L5L	5L12L2	A	4/4	W1p1
SIR DAVID DAVIDSON OF CANTRAY	1H3H76	5367	D	4/4 R	L8v4p6
SIR DAVID DAVIDSON OF CANTRAY	1H3H76	5327	D	4/4 R	K2v3p4
SIR DAVID HUNTER BLAIR	1H555	53H53H	F C G	4/4*R	K2v1p17 L8v3p13 L8v8Bp23 R10p237 S9p6 S17p8
SIR GEORGE ABERCROMBIE BARt OF BIRKENBOG & FORGLEN'S STRATHSPEY	1353	1562	A	4/4	W1p6
SIR GEORGE MACKENZIE	1H515	1H527	D	2/2 R	R10p92
SIR GEORGE MACKENZIE OF COUL	5346	5342	A	4/4 R	S17p137
SIR JAMES BAIRD	15L5L5L	16L6L6L	A	4/4 S	K2v1p16
SIR JAMES DOUGLAS	5351	5336	D	4/4 S	K2v3p4
SIR JAMES GRANT	35L3L5L	35L7L2	Eb	4/4 S	G6v2p31
SIR JAMES M. INNES BARt. OF EDINGIGHT	13b53b	7bL242	E	4/4	W1p44
SIR JAS. G. BAIRD BART.	1111	6L27L2	G	4/4 S	G6v2p14
SIR JOHN LOCKHART ROSS	13b3b4	2424	G	2/2 R	R10p197
SIR JOHN MALCOLM	51H3H2H	5555	D	4/4 S	K2v4p8
SIR JOHN STEWART OF GRANTULLY	3131	1H342	F	4/4 S	R10p245
SIR JOHN STUART FORBES BARt. OF FETTERCAIRN	15L3L5L	6L5L4L2L	Bb	4/4	W1p15
SIR REGINALD MACDONALD	5311	2246	A	2/2 R	R10p14
SIR ROBERT PEEL	15L3L5L	2L27L2	Bb	4/4*R	K2v2p23 R10p290
SIR ROBt G. GORDON BARt. OF LETTERFOURIE'S REEL	1H535	1H362	A	2/2	W1p5
SIR ROGER DE COVERLEY	115	227L	G	9/8 CD	K2v1p27 Mc3v1p169 M7p33 S9p12
SIR RONALD McDONALD [SIR RONALD MACDONALD]	1555	7b47bL2	G	4/4*R	K2v3p22 R10p191 S17p130
SIR WILLIAM WALLACE	1L1L5L1	16L13	A	4/4 A	S8v7p38
SIRDAR'S MARCH, THE [SIRDAR, LORD KITCHENER, THE]	5313	427bL4	A	4/4 QS	S8v7p33 S8v8p52
SIX-MEN LIFT, THE	5361H	56L22	F	4/4	P3p15
SIXTEEN AND SAUCY	551H5	551H1H	C	6/8	S8v6p15
SKATE, THE	5H1H3H5H	2H572H	D	4/4 S	S8v3p12
SKENE OF SKENE	5L143	137L2	G	4/4 S	G6v1p32
SKINNER'S "THE 45"	3451	217L5L	A	2/2 R	S8v5p10 S8v6p105
SKIRDUSTAN	1L15L3bL	5L2L2L7bF	A	4/4 S	G14p18
SKYE AIR, A	5336	1H631	G	4/4	Mc3v1p159
SKYE BOAT SONG	5L125	36L5L5L	G	6/8	K2v3p45
SLEEPING MAGGIE [SLEEPY MAGGIE] [SLEEPY MAGGY]	5153b	5142	B	4/4*R	K2v3p6 L8v4p10 Mc3v1p62 R10p130 S17p63
SLUMBERING MINSTREL, THE	3542	1327L	A	4/4	S8v8p156
SMA' COALS FOR NAILERS	113b3b	4427bL	E	2/2 R	K2v4p13
'SMAIRG A CHIURRADH SPIOCAIRE [MISER, THE]	315L3	3144	F	4/4 R	Mc3v1p188

SMALL COALS FOR NAILERS	113b3b	4427bL	E	4/4 R	M7p10
SMITH OF KILLIECHASSIE, THE	1155	4422	A	2/2 R	R10p41
SMITH OF KILLIECHASSIE, THE	1111	57bL42	A	4/4 PR	Mc3v1p81
SMITH'S A GALLANT FIREMAN	1155	51H42	D	4/4 S	M7p11
SMITH'S A GALLANT FIREMAN(, THE)	1155	51H33	D	4/4 S	K2v1p4 L8v6p10 Mc3v1p44
SMITH'S A GALLANT FIREMAN, THE	1135	51H31	D	4/4 S	S8v7p16
SMOLANACH	5353	6462	A	4/4 R	K2v3p14
SMOLANACH	5353	6262	A	2/2 R	R10p25
SO I'M OFF WITH THE GOOD ST. NICHOLAS BOAT	1565	4233	A	6/8 A	S8v3p30 S8v7p46
SODGER LADDIE [SODGER LAD]	3122	6113	G	6/8 J	L8v2p12 R10p139
SOLDIER'S JOY	5151	51H1H7	D	4/4*R	K2v1p3 Mc3v1p38 M7p11 R10p150
SOLDIER'S JOY, THE	5151	51H1H3	D	4/4	S9p3
SOLDIER'S RETURN	3H562H	3H4H66	D	2/4	M10v2p20
SOLDIER'S RETURN	3H551H	662H1H	D	2/2 R	K2v4p7
SOMEBODY	1H5H2H2H	1H3H6H5H	D	4/4 S	K2v4p7
SOURCE OF SPEY, THE	3b13b5	7b53b5	E	4/4 S	K2v3p9 Mc3v1p100 R10p169
SOUTER JOHNNY	1H565	437L2	D	4/4 R	M7p14
SOUTH OF THE GRAMPIANS	1L3L5L5L	16L11	A	4/4 S	K2v1p12
SOUTH OF THE GRAMPIANS	1L3L5L6L	5L6L5L3L	A	4/4 S	M7p21 S8v8p103
SOUTH SIDE OF SPEY, THE	1L12L7bF	1L13bL1	A	2/2 R	G14p16
SPEED THE PLOUGH	1155	5555	A	4/4*R	K2v1p24 L8v1p2 Mc3v1p5 R10p15 S9p3
SPEED THE PLOUGH or NAVAL PILLAR, THE	1555	436L7L	A	2/4 R	S8v8p96/7
SPINNING WHEEL, THE	3135	7562	D	2/2	S8v6p92 S8v7p3
SPORRAN MULLACH, THE	1L3bL5L1	227bL7bL	A	4/4	W1p12
SPORTING JAMIE	3H2H3H5H	4H3H2H7	D	4/4 S	K2v4p10
SPORTING PEGGY	1H3H2H1	1H3H2H3H	D	2/2 R	K2v4p10
SPORTSMAN'S HAUNT, THE	3bL1L15L	7bL4L2L7bF	B	4/4 S	R10p131
SPRIG OF SHILLELAH, THE	5L122	1522	Bb	6/8	S9p21
SPRING FIELD	3b15L1	47bL44	G	4/4 S	G6v1p43
SPRING SONG	3451H	3H1H76	C	4/4	S8v6p44
SPRITE, THE	51H75	4532	D	6/8	S8v5p8
SQUARE AND COMPASS, THE	131H3	422H3H	C	4/4*R	K2v2p12 R10p68
SQUIRREL, THE	1H133	1H16L7L	A	6/8 J	L8v4p4
ST. CATHERINE'S	11H53	4216L	G	4/4 R	K2v3p9
ST. KILDA WEDDING, THE	1115	236L5L	A	4/4*R/	K2v2p7 Mc3v1p52 R10p16
ST. MUNGO'S WELCOME TO SCOTT SKINNER	5L3L6L1	427L6L	A	4/4 QS	S8v8p24
ST. PATRICK'S DAY	1155	236L6L	G	6/8	S9p22
STACCATO	1526b	51H6b2	D	2/4	S8v6p110
STAR DUST	5655	4765	F	2/4	S8v5p23
STATEN ISLAND	351H1H	6542	D	2/4 CD	K2v1p21
STATEN ISLAND or BURN'S HORNPIPE	3355	1H2H75	D	4/4 HP	M7p36
STEAM BOAT, THE	1H531	427L4	G	2/4 H	K2v1p26
STEAM-BOAT, THE	51H35	135L1	A	4/4 HP	Mc3v1p174
STEER KIMMER	3333	3333	G	2/2 R	K2v4p16
STEER THE GILL	1H1H1H4	1H1H2H3H	D	4/4 R	L8v5p8 Mc3v1p65
STEWART TARTAN	326L5L	5L325	A	4/4 SC	K2v3p24
STEWART'S LASSIE	1541H	5332	G	4/4 S	K2v3p9
STEWART'S RANT, THE	3653	465L6	A	4/4 R	S17p60
STEWART'S RANT, THE	3653	462H6	A	4/4*R	K2v1p15 Mc3v1p3 R10p17
STILLY NIGHT, THE	3316L	5L123	A	4/4 S	K2v3p12
STIRLING CASTLE	1313	5L7L5L7L	D	4/4 S	K2v1p4
STIRLING CASTLE	1353	5L7L27L	D	4/4 S	Mc3v1p55 M7p16 S8v8p78
STIRLINGSHIRE MILITIA	1315	1532	A	2/4 M	Mc3v1p179
STONEBYRES	5L13b2	427bL2	A	4/4 R	K2v3p17
STOOL OF REPENTANCE(, THE)	1H31H5	1H666	A	6/8 J	K2v1p31 L8v4p5 Mc3v1p8 R10p134
STORM KING, THE	1111	115L5L	D	12/8	S8v6p123
STORMONT LADS, THE	1515	6661H	G	4/4 R	K2v1p10 R10p166
STRACHUR	5651	5653	G	4/4 R	K2v3p8
STRATHBOGIE EDITOR, THE	1H1H62	1H1H51	A	2/4 R	S8v8p100
STRATHBOGIE TOAST, THE or BOBERS OF BRECHIN, THE	51H1H5	47b54	G	2/2 R	R10p188
STRATHEARN	1551H	7b542	G	4/4 S	R10p194
STRATHERICK	5L5L3L2L	5L5L5L2	Bb	4/4 S	R10p280
STRATHGLASS HOUSE	1135	51H22	D	4/4 S	Mc3v1p158
STRATHMASHY	7b53b1	7bL3b7bL7bL	C	4/4 S	R10p268
STRATHSPEY, A	1L16L5L	6L5L22	Bb	4/4	G14p20
STRATHSPEY, A	131H3	2742	D	4/4	G14p26
STRATHSPEY COMPOSED BY PETER BAILIE	1H564	547L2	A	4/4 S	K2v3p11
STRONG MAN O' DRUM, THE	3535	351H1H	D	4/4	S8v6p88
STRUAN ROBERTSON'S RANT	13b55	7bL27bL4	E	4/4 S	K2v1p5 L8v2p14 Mc3v1p79 R10p248 S17p62
STUART'S RANT, THE	3654	47b1H7b	A	4/4 R	G6v1p1
STUMPIE	31H1H1H	31H2H2	A	4/4 S	K2v1p6 L8v1p1 L8v8Bp2 Mc3v1p4 R10p13 S17p88
STUMPIE	31H2H1H	31H2H2	A	4/4 S	M7p22
SUCKY BIDS ME	15L16	5126L	G	4/4*R	K2v2p15 R10p174
SUD MAR CHUIR MI'N GEAMHRADH THARUM [THAT'S HOW I SPENT THE WINTER]	3H555	3H52H6	D	4/4 S	Mc3v1p183

Name						
SUMMER DAYS	17L5L1	3455	A	4/4 S	K2v4p6	
SUNDRUM HOUSE	1553	1342	A	4/4 R	K2v3p10	
SUSIE BRODIE	5342	5353	G	4/4 S	K2v2p16	L8v6p13 R10p177
SUTHERLAND	51H51H	51H51H	A	4/4 R	K2v4p4	
SUTHERLAND HIGHLANDERS, THE	5631H	57b47b	A	2/4	S8v6p76	
SWALLOW, THE	331H1H	3H1H2H2	D	4/4*R	L8v1p8 Mc3v1p63 R10p84	
SWEET MEMORIES OF ARDLER	5315L	6L113	G	4/4	S8v6p52	
SWEET MOLLY [cf: HOPETO(U)N HOUSE]	157b5	7b47bL2	E	4/4*R	K2v1p6 L8v2p13 Mc3v1p91	
					R10p248	
SWEET MOLLY	11H1H7b	7b2H1H7b	E	4/4 S	K2v4p15	
SWISS COTTAGE (BALLINDALLOCH)	7L7L6L5L	6L5L7L2	A	2/2 R	G14p7	
SWORD DANCE	1342	1353	A	4/4	S8v7p21	
TAIGEIS AGUS DEALG INNTE [HAGGIS, THE]	3553	351H1H	C	2/2 R	R10p62	
TAIGHEAN GEALA SHIELDAIG or	6451	4427bL	A	4/4 PR Mc3v1p70		
WHITE HOUSES OF SHIELDAIG, THE						
TAIL TODDLE	1H3H4H3H	1H3H2H7	D	2/2 R	K2v4p10	
TAILOR TARTAN	3551H	6753	G	2/2 R	K2v4p12	
TAKIN' ITHER BY THE HAN'	1133	116L5L	Bb	4/4	P3p18	
TALISKER	1153	51H62	A	4/4 S	Mc3v1p31 S8v5p13 S8v6p81	
					S8v7p8	
TALISKER	1H3H54	61H76	D	2/2 R	Mc3v1p36 S8v3p15	
TALISKER	1153	51H62	A	4/4 S	S8v5p13	
TAM O' SHANTER	35L35	47L46	D	4/4 S	M7p14	
TAMMY O' THE MOSS	551H5	662H2H	D	4/4 S	S8v5p20	
TAM'S GREY MARE	153b3b	517b5	Em	4/4 R	L8v4p15	
TANK, THE	11H6L6	2531	Bb	2/4 CD	S15p23/4	
TAP O' NOTH	136L7L	1353	Eb	4/4	W1p36	
TAPPIT HEN, THE	1346	1342	A	6/8	K2v4p28	
TARBOLTON LODGE	11H1H5	3b43b1	E	4/4*R	K2v1p12 R10p246	
TAY BRIG, THE	3344	336L1	A	2/4	S8v6p89	
TAYMOUTH CASTLE	3565	6562	A	4/4 R	S17p91	
TEMPLE HOUSE	13b53b	7bL242	E	6/8	K2v1p33	
TEN POUND FIDDLE, THE	15L3L1	567L2	A	2/2 R	S8v7p5	
TEVIOT BRIDGE [TEVIOT BRIG]	55L6L5L	5L5L42	A G	6/8 J	K2v1p31 Mc3v1p176 R10p134	
THA MI SGITH [I AM WEARY]	11H7b7b	527bL2	A	2/4	M10v1p10	
THA MISE CHO MULADACH	1325	7L113	F	6/8	M10v2p7	
THA MO BHREACAN FLUICH FO'N DILE	3125	1H653	Eb	4/4	M10v2p5	
THA TIGHIUN FODHAM EIRIDH	5L111	6L232	G	4/4	M10v2p8	
THACK COTTAGE, THE	1H53b1	2427bL	G	4/4 S	K2v3p22	
THANE'S	1215	6b547L	G	2/4	S8v6p112	
THANIG ON(AN) GILLE DUBH	116L1	5563	F	6/8	M10v1p5	
AN RAOIR NA BHAILE SO						
THEARLAICH, NAN TIGEADH TU or	1151	157b4	E	2/2 R	Mc3v1p84 R10p247	
FLORA MACDONALD						
THEID MI DHACHAIDH A CHRO CHEANNTAILLE	256b5	257b2	A	2/4	M10v1p11	
THEID MI LEAM FHEIN	11H2H1H	5353	D	2/4	M10v2p20	
THEODORE NAPIER	357L1	6L5L7L2	A	4/4	S8v8p32	
THERE CAM' A YOUNG MAN	13b52	7bL244	A	6/8	K2v1p31	
THERE GROWS A BONNIE BRIER	5L5L5L1	6L221	A	4/4 SC	K2v3p24	
THERE'S MONY A BONNIE LASSIE	552	121H	D	3/4	P3p15	
THERE'S NAETHING LIKE THE TALISKER	5L351H	6427bL	A	4/4 S	S8v8p50	
THIS IS NO MY AIN HOUSE	353H2H	6562	D	4/4*R	K2v1p9 Mc3v1p63 R10p105	
THIS LIFE IS BUT A VISION	331	531	Bb	3/4	P3p5	
THISTLE, THE	3L5L5L5L	1321	A	4/4 SC	K2v1p19	
THOMSON'S GOT A KIRK	3331	2427bL	A	4/4 R	K2v4p3	
THORN BUSH	136L5L	2L247L	A	4/4 S	K2v2p8 L8v2p5 Mc3v1p20	
					R10p33	
THREE A PENNY	1H3H4H3H	62H72H	D	4/4 S	K2v4p11	
THRO' THE WOOD SHE RAN	1H3H1H6	5322	F	4/4 R	S17p58	
THROUGH THE MUIR SHE RAN	1H3H1H6	3522	F	4/4 R	K2v2p21	
THROUGH THE WOOD OF FYVIE	5324	5353	G	4/4*R	K2v2p14 K2v4p16 L8v5p9	
					S17p64	
THROUGH THE WOOD SHE RAN	1H3H1H6	5522	F	4/4 R	L8v4p21	
TIBBY FOULLER O' THE GLEN	113b5	4455	Bb	4/4 S	G6v1p18	
TIGH EACHAINN	6665	3232	G	4/4 S	K2v2p16	
TIGH EACH(A)INN or	1H1H1H7b	5454	E	4/4 S	Mc3v1p85 R10p179	
[AULD ROAD TO TOWIE, THE]						
TIGH IAIN GHROIT [JOHNNY GROAT'S HOUSE]	51H3H2H	72H72H	C	2/2 R	R10p73	
TIGH 'N DUIN	13b1H5	7b442	E	4/4 S	R10p258	
TILL AN CRODH A'DHONNA CHAID !	1565	1552	C	4/4	M10v2p17	
TIMMER LADLE, THE	531H1H	2H1H62	C	4/4 S	S8v5p14	
TIMOUR THE TARTAR	1557	1523	A	2/4 R	S8v8p111	
TIMOUR THE TARTER [TIMOUR THE TARTAR]	1353	51H76	A	4/4*R	K2v1p18 L8v1p3 Mc3v1p6	
					R10p40	
TINK A TINK	1142	1141	A	2/4	S9p19	
TIPPERTY'S JEAN	551H5	662H2H	D	6/8 J	S8v3p13	
TO ANE FAR AWA'	1H1H53	4520	D	4/4	S8v8p172	
TO DAUNTON ME	5114	217bL7b	E	4/4 SC	K2v2p24	
TO THE HIGHLANDS AGAIN	5157b	557b6	A	4/4	P3p21	
TOBAR MO BHEATHA	1H515	1H562	D	4/4 S	R10p96	
TOBERMORY	51H53	4327L	A	4/4 S	S8v8p90	
TOM DEY	5631	326L5L	A	4/4 S	S8v10p14	

TOM DOUGLAS	1H2H54	452H2H	F	2/4	S8v6p102
TOM THUMB	1H51H5	1H2H1H6	C	4/4	S9p5
TOM'S HIGHLAND FLING	11H66	11H62	F	4/4 S	L8v3p15
TOM'S NUGGET	3b11H5	3b127bL	E	4/4 S	S8v5p10
TONAL MACKINLAY	51H53	62H64	D	6/8	S9p13
TONAL MACKINLAY	5553	6664	D	6/8	S8v6p30
TOP O' THE GRAMPIANS, THE	5521	2666	G	4/4 S	S8v8p57
TORRYBURN LASSES [TORRY BURN]	1335	4661H	G	4/4*CD	K2v1p23 L8v8Ap13 Mc3v1p98
					R10p159 S17p30
TOWIE CASTLE	5L3b5L1	447bL7bL	F	2/4	W1p55
TOWN CRIER, THE	5551	4447bL	A	2/2 R	K2v4p17
TRIP TO SKYE	3562	351H3	G	4/4 R	L8v5p9
TRIPLET, THE	3L1L7L5L	31H27L	A	2/4 HP	S8v8p133
TRIPPERS, THE	52H3H2H	52H4H1H	D	6/8	K2v4p27
TRIUMPH	5416	5411	G	2/4	S9p12
TRIUMPH	5342	11H66	A	4/4 CD	M7p32
TRIUMPH, THE	5342	1761H	A	4/4 CD	K2v1p21
TRIUMPH, THE	5342	11H76	A	4/4*CD	Mc3v1p167 R10p142
TROIS GRANDS LUTHIERS, LES	5L111	5L137L	A	4/4 A	S8v7p47 S8v8p158
TRUMPET, THE	1131H	5L5L7L4	Eb	2/4 HP	S8v8p139
TULCHAN LODGE	3L131	6L242	A	4/4	S8v6p103
TULCHAN LODGE	3L131	4L242	A	4/4 S	S8v7p4
TULLOCH CASTLE	3bH1H1H7b	5555	C	4/4 A	S8v8p16
TULLOCHGORUM [CORN BUNTING, THE]	3542	3535	G	4/4 S	K2v1p10 L8v1p14 L8v8Ap14
					Mc3v1p87 R10p158 S8v7p26/7
					S8v8p68/9 S9p7 S17p6
TULLYMET HALL	3b554	2424	A	4/4*R	K2v2p10 R10p56
TULLYVEOLAN MARCH	51H76	561H2H	D	4/4 M	S8v8p35
TUNE YOUR FIDDLES	51H65	51H62H	D	4/4 S	S8v3p4
TURNING LATHE, THE	1353	1H3b55	Am	4/4 R	L8v5p15
TWA TRAMPS, THE	3551	3535	F	4/4	S8v6p109
TWEEDDALE CLUB, THE	51H63	51H2H2	C	4/4 S	G6v2p18 K2v1p17 L8v1p16
					L8v8B17 Mc3v1p113 R10p69
TWEEDSIDE LASSES, THE	116L5L	1562	D	4/4	W1p22
TWIST YE, TWINE YE	5L113b	2555	E	4/4	S8v8p174
TWIST YE TWINE YE EVEN SO	5L125	43b17L	F#	4/4 A	S8v7p21
TWO SISTERS, THE	351H1H	7753	Eb	4/4	S8v6p53
UIST LASSES' DARLING, THE	5331H	3H526	D	4/4* R	K2v2p19 R10p116
UNION BRIG	153b5	7b524	E	2/2 R	S8v3p17
UNION STREET BRIDGE	5L3b53b	4L242	F#	4/4	W1p56
UNTITLED	555	462	Bb	3/4	S15p25/6
UP AN' WA(U)R THEM A' WULLIE	1344	1322	G	4/4*S	K2v3p8 L8v4p1 R10p20
UP AN' WAUR THEM A' WULLIE	1344	1327L	G	4/4 R	K2v3p8
URQUHART CASTLE	1L3L5L3L	47L5L3L	G Bb	4/4 S	L8v5p21 Mc3v1p192
URQUHART CASTLE	1L3L5L3L	37L5L3L	Bb	4/4 S	R10p279
URQUHART'S STRATHSPEY	53b13b	4422	E	4/4 S	M7p9
VALE OF LEVEN	1113	5557	A	4/4 R	K2v4p3
VALLEY OF SILENCE, THE	5L121L	2175	C	4/4 A	S8v8p8/9
VALLEY OF SILENCE, THE	5L121	2175	C	4/4 A	S8v7p39
VICTORIA HORNPIPE	1H542	1H542	A	4/4 HP	Mc3v1p171 M7p35
VIOLET DAVIDSON	1133	531H1H	D	2/2 HP	S8v10p2
VISCOUNTESS DUNCAN	5622	5651H	D	4/4 S	R10p122
VOULEZ VOUS DANSER	3H3H2H1H	72H1H3H	D	6/8	K2v1p27
W. SCOTT COLLINS	3663H	72#6H3T	C	2/4 HP	S8v8p128
WAKING OF THE FAULD, THE	5L117b	415L4L	A	4/4 SS	R10p164
WALKING OF THE PLAIDING, THE	15L15L	15L22	F	4/4 S	R10p243
WALLACE	1L1L5L1	16L13	A	4/4 A	S8v8p4
WALLACE TOWER	1114L	2226L	E	2/2	W1p43
WALLACE TOWER, ABERDEEN	3215	6522	F	4/4 SS	S8v5p17
WALTZ COUNTRY DANCE	1H35	1H1H7	G	3/4	M7p32
WANDERING TINKER(THE)	1H3H3H3H	72H72H	D	4/4*R	K2v1p13 K2v2p12 L8v5p13
					R10p71
WAPPINSHAW, THE	13b3b3b	427bL2	D	2/2 R	R10p218
WARD'S(HORNPIPE)	5755	4325	A	2/4 HP	S8v7p43 S8v8p132/3
WARLOCKS, THE	53b11	447bL7bL	Em	4/4 S	L8v4p15
WARRIOR O' PERSIE, THE	135L3	41H7L2	D Bb	4/4 S	S8v7p11 S8v8p18
WARRIOR'S GRAVE, THE	1H53b1	6bL5L7L5	D	4/4 A	S8v8p10
WARRIOR'S GRAVE, THE	1H53b1	6bL5L7L1	D	4/4 A	S8v7p42
WARRIOR'S RETURN, THE	5356	1H653	D	4/4	S8v6p55
WASHING DAY, THE	13b11	7bL27bL7bL	B	4/4 S	S8v3p6
WASHINGTON	1357L	671H7L	Bb	4/4	S9p31
WATERLOO(REEL)	1H1H35	1113	D/Bm	4/4*R	L8v3p23 R10p149
WA(U)KING O' THE FAULD, THE	5L117b	415L4L	A	4/4 S	K2v1p7
WAVERLEY BALL, THE	331H5	462H6	A	4/4 R	L8v1p4 L8v8Bp5
WAVERLEY BALL, THE	1H516	1H555	A	4/4 S	L8v1p4
WE WON'T GO HOME TILL MORNING	3343	2231	G	6/8	S9p16
WEAVER HAS A DOCHTER, THE	16L15L	16L44	Bb	4/4 S	K2v3p21
WEAVER, THE	1337b	7bL242	A	6/8	K2v4p28
WEAVER'S DAUGHTER, THE	3b13b7b	3b16b6b	G	4/4 S	R10p292
WEDDERBURN HOUSE	1H1H3b1	27b27bL	D	4/4 R	G6v1p46
WEDDING RING, THE	1313	157L5L	Bb	4/4*R	K2v3p21 R10p198
WEE AULD WIFIE	1H1H1H1H	3555	D	4/4	S8v6p47

WEE BIT COGGIE	5356	5324	A	2/2 R	K2v4p4
WEE CUP OF TEA, A	5L13b1	27bL47bL	A	4/4 R	K2v3p17
WEE JAMIE	6532	226L6	G	4/4	S8v6p33
WEE NANNIE	5752	3523	D	4/4 S	K2v4p10
WEE PICKLE TOW, THE	5L152	3331	A	6/8	K2v1p31
WEE PUG, THE	1353	51H55	G	4/4 S	K2v4p12
WEE RORIE'S HIELAN' FLING	5653	4527L	A	4/4	S8v6p100
WEE SAMMY	1L5L4L1	5L37L2	A	4/4 S	K2v4p5
WEE WEE MAN, THE	1H61H1	1H662	G	6/8	K2v1p32
WEE WILLIE'S STRATHSPEY	5L131	6L27L6L	G	4/4	Mc3v1p102
WEEPING BIRCHES OF KILMORACK, THE	3L14#1H	5316L	Eb	4/4	S8v9/2
WELCOME BACK	5L122	5L326L	A	4/4	P3p17
WELCOME, CHARLIE STEWART	5244	4222	D	2/2 R	Mc3v1p45
WELCOME, MR. MARTIN	3155	6455	D	4/4	S8v6p87
WELCOME ROYAL CHARLIE	427L2	4211H	A	2/2 R	K2v4p5
WELCOME TO THE HIGHLANDS	13L5L1	37L22L	A	4/4	S8v6p114
WELCOME TO YOUR FEET AGAIN	151H2	151H6	D C	4/4 S	G6v1p9 K2v1p13 L8v2p17
[YOU'RE WELCOME TO YOUR FEET AGAIN]					L8v8Ap21 R10p61
WELCOME WHISKY BACK AGAIN	5L122	16L5L2L	A	4/4 S	S8v8p96
WELCOME WHISKY BACK AGAIN	1L122	16L5L2L	Bb	4/4 S	Mc3v1p136
WE'LL A' MEET ABOON	5526L	1363	F	6/8	P3p24
WE'LL AYE BE FOND O' INGRAM	5L16L1	6L27L5	A	4/4	S8v6p66
WE'LL AYE GANG BACK TO YON TOON	361H7	5215L	A	2/2 R	S8v3p32
WE'LL AYE GANG BACK TO YON TOWN	5L115	447bL7bL	G	2/2	W1p66
WEMYSS CASTLE	116L4L	4L426L	Bb	4/4 S	G6v1p39
WE'RE A' AE FATHERS BAIRNS	3365	346L6L	G	2/4	P3p1
WEST ADAM ST. CLUB	11H55	11H52	D	4/4 SC	K2v2p24
WEST KILBRIDE	1H112	7L246	A	4/4 R	K2v3p11
WEST WINDS	31H31	427L5	G	2/2 R	K2v4p12
WESTER ELCHIES	3564	532H2	C	2/2 R	G14p12
WEST'S(HORNPIPE)	1H355	1H355	D	4/4*HP	Mc3v1p173 R10p296
WHA' WIDNA FECHT FOR CHARLIE	1133	1132	G	4/4*S	K2v2p15&34 R10p167
WHA'LL BE KING BUT CHARLIE	1H1H3H3H	1H1H3H5	D	6/8	K2v1p32
WHATS A' THE STEER	3333	3333	G	4/4 SC	K2v1p20 Mc3v1p169
WHAT'S A' THE STEER	3H3H3H3H	3H3H3HO	C	2/4 CD	R10p153
WHEN YOU'VE HOOKED HIM HOLD HIM FAST	5357b	4246	A	4/4 R	L8v5p4
WHERE GADIE RINS or	51H3H3H	3H3H2H2H	D	4/4 M	S8v8p26
HESSIANS' MARCH, THE					
WHERE THE ROSES BLUSH AND BLOOM	51H42	4751	D	4/4	S8v6p34
WHIGS OF FIFE, THE	5132	511H3H	F	4/4*R	K2v2p21 L8v1p19 L8v8Ap23
					R10p205 S17p126
WHIPMAN'S RANT	1552	1555	D	4/4 S	R10p100
WHISKY WELCOME BACK AGAIN	1L122	16L5L2L	Bb	4/4 S	K2v2p23 R10p291
WHISTLE O'ER THE LAVE O'T	16L33	5326L	G	4/4 S	G6v1p6 K2v1p11 L8v6p14
					R10p172
WHISTLE O'ER THE LAVE O'T	16L33	51H26L	G	4/4 S	S8v8p59
WHITE COCKADE	3332	3331H	G	4/4 CD	K2v1p23
WHITE COCKADE	3333	5432	G	2/4	S9p12
WHITE COCKADE, THE	3332	1331H	G	4/4*CD	Mc3v1p170 R10p147
WHITE HEATHER	5346	5322	F	4/4 S	K2v4p18
WILD ROSES	536L1	5L6L5L6L	G	4/4 S	K2v4p14
WILL O' THE WISP	1H3b1H3b	7L6b6b5	C	12/8	S8v6p124
WILL YOU RUN AWAY WITH ME	3b3b54	2424	A	4/4*R	K2v1p18 R10p49
[WILL YE RUN AWA' WI' ME]					
WILLIE BLAIR	1353	5122	D	4/4	S8v3p14
WILLIE BLAIR	3131	4246	F	4/4	L8v8Ap24
WILLIE COOK	351H3	6L27L5	A	4/4 S	K2v2p5
WILLIE DAVIE	5553	5557	A	4/4*R	K2v1p24 L8v3p21 R10p143
WILLIE DAVIE	5551	5557	A	4/4 R/	M7p24
WILLIE DOW	11L3L1	5647L	A	4/4 S	S8v10p7
WILLIE DUNCAN	1133	22H62H	C	4/4 S	K2v2p12 L8v4p19 R10p72
WILLIE MACLENNAN	1355	5544	A	4/4 M	S8v7p30
WILLIE SHAW	3H653	31H4H2H	D	4/4 S	K2v1p3
WILLIE WAS A WANTON WAG	351H1H	352H6	D	4/4 S	K2v4p9
WILLIE WINKIE	5351	5326L	F	4/4 S	L8v4p22 S17p66
WILLIE WINKIE	5451	5326L	F	4/4 S	K2v2p22
WILLOW HORNPIPE, THE	31H2H1H	5335	D	4/4	W1p28
WILL'S REEL	13b24	3b523b	F#	2/4 R	S8v7p12
WIND THAT SHAKES THE BARLEY	5552	6661H	D	4/4 R	K2v1p4
WIND THAT SHAKES THE BARLEY, THE	3552	6661H	D	4/4*R	L8v1p6 L8v8Bp8 Mc3v1p35
					R10p89 S17p41
WINTER HOLIE, THE	3211	3255	G	4/4	S8v6p60
WISE MAID, THE	1353	1323	D	2/2 R	K2v4p11
WITCH OF THE WAVE	1355	461H1H	G	4/4 R	K2v3p8
WITCHES, THE	1527bl	153b5	Em	4/4 R	L8v4p15
WITHIN A MILE [OF EDINBURGH TOUN]	5213	6L5L5L1	A	4/4 SC	K2v2p24
WITHIN A MILE OF EDINBURGH TOWN	5H2H1H3H	6551H	G	4/4	S9p11
WIVES AND MAIDS AT HOME	3321	2116L	A	4/4	S8v6p48
Wm. MACHARDY'S STRATHSPEY	15L15	4327L	A	4/4 S	S8v8p100
(WM.) MARSHALL'S STYLE	345L1	456L2	A	4/4 SS	S8v5p1
WOLF O' BADENOCH, THE	1351H	5L7L25	D	4/4	S8v6p65
WONDER, THE	137L2	135L1	Bb	4/4	S9p31

WOO'D AN' MARRIED AN' A'	531	555	F	9/8		G6v1p20
WOOIN' O'T, THE	5571H	2H3H76	D	2/2	R	K2v4p7
WOUNDED HUSSAR, THE	5L12	3b3b2	E	3/4		S8v8p161
YANKEE DOODLE	1H2H1H7	1H2H1H7	D	2/4		S9p17
YE BANKS AND BRAES	1H1H1H	2H2H2H	D	3/4	W	K2v1p25
YE'LL BETTER TAK' IT	1115L	13b15L	A	4/4		P3p10
YESTER HOUSE	5522	5557b	Am	4/4	S	L8v2p19
YESTER HOUSE	5542	5557b	A	4/4	S	R10p29
YETTS OF MUCKART, THE	5553	5522	F	4/4	S	S17p126
YETTS OF MUCKART, THE	1311	6562	A	4/4*R		K2v2p8 K2v3p13 Mc3v1p13
						R10p40
YOE, THE	5L15L1	7L252	G	4/4	S	K2v4p13
YOUNG KING, THE	1H5H72#	6L4L4#L5L	Eb	2/4	HP	S8v8p140
YOUNG MAY MOON, THE	1H1H65	1H2H3H1H	C	6/8		S9p26
YOU'R(E) WELCOME CHARLIE STEWART	5244	5222	D	4/4	R	K2v1p6

6

THEME CODE INDEX

Follow the quite simple
instructions for use of
this numerically ordered
index and you can
construct your own musical
theme code, trace the
tune's title and find a
library where the music
can be seen and copied.
Equally, you can use it in
connection with the A-Z
listings to discover if a
tune has more than one
title, or was reprinted in
the 19th century.

CODE A	CODE B	A-Z SECTION (I) or (II)	TITLE

The PROGRESSION is a numerical sequence from the lowest CODE A coding (1L1L1L1L) to the highest (1T1T3T1T) reading down the first (left-hand) column on each page.

There are no sub-divisions in this section.

Refer to the appropriate section of the A-Z INDEX, (I) or (II) for further information about the tune and where to locate it.

```
1L1L1L1L    7bL4L7bF7bF  (II) HIGHLANDERS FAREWELL TO IRELAND, THE
1L1L1L1L    7bL4L7bF7bF  (I)  HIGHLAND WATCH, THE
                              [HIGHLANDER'S FAREWELL TO IRELAND, THE]
1L1L1L1L    7bL4L7bF7bF  (I)  HIGHLAND REEL
1L1L1L1L    7bL4L7bL7bL  (II) HIGHLAND WATCH'S FAREWELL TO IRELAND
1L1L1L1L    246L2        (I)  MISS GOULDING'S STRATHSPEY
1L1L1L5L    1315         (I)  DUCKS AND GREEN PEASE
1L1L2L7bF   1L5L11       (II) NORTH SIDE OF SPEY, THE
1L1L2L1L    7bL17bL7bF   (I)  HONOURABLE MRS MAULE'S MEDLEY, THE
1L1L3bL1L   1L1L2L7bF    (II) GEORGE THE FOURTH
1L1L3bL1L   1L1L2L7bF    (II) KING GEORGE THE IVth
1L1L3bL3bL  5L5L1L1L     (I)  LORD RAE'S SALUTATION
1L1L3bL3bL  5L3b11       (II) BETTY'S APRON
1L1L3bL5L   1L1L2L7bF    (II) KING GEORGE IV'S WELCOME
1L1L3bL5L   1L1L2L7bF    (I)  HIS MAJESTY'S WELCOME TO SCOTLAND
1L1L3bL5L   7bL4L2L7bF   (I)  MISS MENZIES OF CULDARES' REEL
1L1L3bL5L   7bL5L2L2L    (II) KELO HOUSE
1L1L3bL5L   7bL5L2L2L    (I)  KELO HOUSE
1L1L3L1L    1L5L4L2L     (I)  MISS AUGUSTA MURRAY'S REEL
1L1L3L3L    7L47L2       (I)  MRS DALRYMPLE'S REEL
1L1L3L5L    4L4L6L1      (II) MILLHILLS
1L1L3L      5L17L        (I)  BOUROUGH FAIR
1L1L3L5L    1315L        (II) BRAES O' AUCHTERTYRE, THE
1L1L3L5L    1311         (II) MARQUIS OF HUNTLY'S FAREWELL, THE
1L1L16L     6L6L22L      (I)  MISS L. MONTGOMERIE OF SKERMORLIE
1L1L5L1L    4326L        (I)  COLONEL SMALL'S STRATHSPEY
1L1L5L1L    4327L        (I)  LADY FORD'S STRATHSPEY
1L1L5L5L    7bL3bL4L7bF  (II) GLENLIVAT
1L1L5L5L    1111         (I)  MARQUIS OF HUNTLY'S FAREWELL, THE
1L1L5L5L    1311         (II) MARQUIS OF HUNTLY'S FAREWELL(, THE)
1L1L5L5L    1311         (I)  MARQUIS OF HUNTLY'S FAREWELL, (THE)
1L1L5L5L    1321         (I)  MARQUIS OF HUNTLY'S FAREWELL, THE
1L1L5L5L    1542         (I)  MISS MAXWELL OF MORRESTON'S REEL
1L1L5L6L    2L26L2       (II) FRANK WALKER
1L1L5L6L    2L26L2       (I)  (MR) FRANK WALKER('S) STRATHSPEY
1L1L5L1     6L6L22       (II) LADY GEORGINA( RUSSELL'S REEL)
1L1L5L1     6L6L22       (I)  CAPT PATRICK McKENZIE'S STRATHSPEY
1L1L5L1     6L6L22       (I)  LADY GEORGINA RUSSELL'S REEL
1L1L5L1     6L221        (I)  FOR (LAKE/SAKE/LACK) OF GOLD
1L1L5L1     16L13        (II) WALLACE
1L1L5L1     16L13        (II) SIR WILLIAM WALLACE
1L1L5L3b    4427bL       (I)  ALENBANK HOUSE
1L1L5L3     115L1L       (II) MRS FORBES LEITH
1L1L6L5L    1L1L57L      (I)  EXTRAORDINARY GAZETTE, THE
1L1L16L     6L6L22L      (II) MISS L. MONTGOMERIE OF SKELMORLIE
1L1L11      16L62        (II) BLUE BONNETS OVER THE BORDER
1L1L11      16L62        (I)  BLUE BONNETS OVER THE BORDER
1L1L11      16L62        (I)  DUPLIN HOUSE
1L1L11      5126L        (II) MISS FLEMING OF KILLIECHASSIE
1L1L11      5216L        (I)  MISS FLEMYNG'S REEL
                              [MISS FLEMING OF KILLIECHASSIE]
1L1L26L     5L12L2L      (II) MISS ROBERTSON OF TULLYBELTON('S STR.)
1L1L26L     5L12L2L      (I)  MISS ROBERTSON OF TULLYBELTON'S
                              (REEL/STRATHSPEY)
1L1L35L     5L12L2L      (I)  CLARK'S REEL
1L1L35L     6L12L2L      (I)  MRS LOCKHARTS STRATHSPEY
1L2L3bL4L   5L6bL4L7bF   (II) A. F. IRVINE ESQ.
1L2L3L4L    5L6L7L1      (II) JOHN McNEIL
1L2L3L4L    5L47L2       (II) HOWE O' ECHT, THE
1L3bL1L1    6bL4L3bL3bL  (II) LYNN OF RUTHRIE
1L3bL5L3bL  6L4L2L7bL    (II) RUTHRIE
1L3bL5L4L   2L6L4L7bF    (II) MISS SHEPHERD
1L3bL5L5L   5L5L3bL7bF   (II) DUKE OF ATHOLE'S STRATHSPEY, THE
1L3bL5L5L   7bL4L2L7bF   (II) MY BOY TAMMIE
1L3bL5L1    227bL7bL     (II) SPORRAN MULLACH, THE
1L3bL5L1    2425         (I)  BELINDA
1L3L1L3L    1L116L       (I)  KING'S PARK, THE
1L3L1L1     137L2        (I)  MR RAE'S JIGG
1L3L1L1     547L2        (I)  HOUSE OF CANDACRAIG, THE
1L3L1L1     5426L        (I)  MRS BRODIE OF BRODIE'S STRATHSPEY
1L3L1L1     6516L        (I)  NORTHFIELD HOUSE, DUFFUS
1L3L1L3     2L242        (I)  FAIR METHODIST, THE
1L3L1L3     16L5L4L      (II) AULD STYLE'S AWA', THE
1L3L2L4L    1L3L5L1      (I)  MISS JOAS'S STRATHSPEY
1L3L3L      3L5L5L       (I)  MISS DUNDAS'S MINUET
1L3L3L      6L11         (I)  PLEASURES OF MEMORY
1L3L5L1L    4L3L2L2      (II) LAIRD'S KILT, THE
1L3L5L1L    4425L        (II) MARCHIONESS OF HUNTLY, THE
1L3L5L3L    1L3L2L2      (I)  LOVE MAKES A MAN
1L3L5L3L    1L3L6L2L     (II) NATHANIEL GOW
1L3L5L3L    1L3L6L2L     (I)  MARQUISS OF LORN'S STRATHSPEY
```

1L3L5L3L	1L3L6L2L	(I)	NATHANIEL GOW
1L3L5L3L	1L5L31	(I)	GEOFFREY CRAYON
1L3L5L3L	5L15L2L	(II)	GLENDUACHIE
1L3L5L3L	5L46L2	(II)	CHARLES JOHN FORBES OF NEWE'S STR.
1L3L5L3L	6L15L1	(II)	AMONG THE HEATHER
1L3L5L3L	37L5L3L	(II)	URQUHART CASTLE
1L3L5L3L	37L5L3L	(I)	CAISTAL URCHUDAIN [CAISTEAL URCHUDAINN]
1L3L5L3L	47L5L3L	(II)	URQUHART CASTLE
1L3L5L5L	1L5L5L1	(II)	ROYAL RECOVERY, THE
1L3L5L5L	1L5L5L1	(II)	MADAM FREDERICK
1L3L5L5L	1L5L5L1	(I)	MISS ROSE BLACKHALL'S STRATHSPEY
1L3L5L5L	1L5L5L1	(I)	MADlle HILLISBERG'S FAVORITE SCOTCH DANCE
1L3L5L5L	1L5L5L1	(I)	MADAM FREDRICK('S DANCE)
1L3L5L5L	1L5L5L1	(I)	(ROYAL) RECOVERY, THE
1L3L5L5L	16L11	(II)	SOUTH OF THE GRAMPIANS
1L3L5L5L	16L11	(I)	BALANCE OF COMFORT, THE
1L3L5L5L	1322L	(I)	LADY JARDINE'S STRATHSPEY
1L3L5L6L	5L3L6L6L	(I)	MISS E. CAMPBELL'S STRATHSPEY
1L3L5L6L	5L6L5L3L	(II)	SOUTH OF THE GRAMPIANS
1L3L5L7L	1L3L6L2L	(I)	MR McINNES'S STRATHSPEY
1L3L5L1	246L5L	(II)	MRS KEITH MACDONALD'S [STRATHSPEY]
1L3L5L1	5426L	(I)	MR CHARLES MONTGOMERY'S STRATHSPEY
1L3L6L2L	1L3L5L1	(II)	MISS SITWELL
1L3L6L2L	1L3L11	(I)	LADY BOSWELL OF AUCHENLECK
1L3L6L2L	1L3L11	(I)	MISS SITWELL('S STRATHSPEY)
1L3L6L3L	6L216L	(II)	DR. MACDONALD'S COMPLIMENTS TO MR. JAMES SCOTT SKINNER
1L3L6L3L	13L6L3L	(II)	JOHN McNEIL'S REEL
1L3L6L3L	126L5L	(II)	BALLOCHMYLE BRIG
1L3L6L5L	1L3L22L	(I)	DEPARTED WORTH
1L3L13L	15L2L2L	(I)	MRS FULLARTON OF FULLARTON'S STRATHSPEY
1L3L13L	1522	(I)	MISS CUMMING'S REEL [MISS CUMING]
1L3L16L	3311	(I)	LADY BRUCE'S HORNPIPE
1L3L11	1125L	(I)	LADY CLEMENTINA
1L3L11	3427L	(II)	MARQUIS OF HUNTLY'S REEL, THE
1L3L11	526L6L	(I)	INVERESHIE
1L3L13	6L526L	(I)	MR CUMING'S STRATHSPEY
1L3L13	15L2L2L	(I)	TYNE SIDE STRATHSPEY
1L3L13	16L5L3L	(I)	COL. MacLEOD OF RASAY'S STRATHSPEY
1L3L13	2422	(I)	MISS LOGAN'S STRATHSPEY
1L3L13	4113L	(I)	LADIES REGIMENTALS, THE
1L3L13	437L7L	(I)	CAPTAIN LEITH HAYS REEL
1L3L31	27L5L3L	(II)	BEAUFORT CASTLE
1L3L31	27L5L3L	(I)	CAISTEAL DUNAIDH
1L3L46L	4347L	(I)	SIR NEIL MENZIES BART'S STRATHSPEY
1L4L4L2L	1L4L3L1	(I)	LADY JANE MONTAGUE'S STRATHSPEY
1L11L1	1L144	(I)	MISS McINNES' FANCY
1L11L1	2L26L6L	(I)	KILRACKS REEL
1L5L1L1	137L2	(I)	MISS PRESTON OF FERNTON'S STRATHSPEY
1L5L2L2	7L235	(I)	MISS GRAHAM (OF GARTMORE'S) STRATHSPEY
1L5L3bL3bL	2L4L5L4L	(II)	COLONEL THORNTON
1L5L3bL3bL	2L4L5L4L	(!)	COLONEL THORNTON('S STRATHSPEY)
1L5L3bL5L	7bL4L2L7bF	(I)	HONOURABLE MRS MAULE, THE
1L5L3L1	4L27L5	(II)	LAIRD O' BEMERSYDE, THE
1L5L3L1	5L35L3L	(II)	MUSCHATS CAIRN
1L5L3L1	5L35L3L	(I)	MUSHATT'S CAIRN
1L5L4L2L	1L5L6L1	(I)	ELGIN TRINITY LODGE'S STRATHSPEY, THE
1L5L4L5L	6L247L	(II)	MARCHIONESS OF HUNTLY, THE
1L5L4L5L	6L247L	(II)	DUCHESS OF GORDON, THE
1L5L4L5L	6L247L	(I)	MARCHIONESS OF HUNTLY('S STRATHSPEY)
1L5L4L1	5L37L2	(II)	WEE SAMMY
1L5L4L1	5L422L	(II)	GLENLIVET (WHISKY) [GLENLIVET, THE]
1L5L5L1L	2L4L6L6L	(II)	METHVEN CASTLE
1L5L5L1L	16L33	(II)	SHAKINS O' THE POCKY, THE
1L5L5L3L	1342	(II)	BRIG O' KYLE, THE
1L5L5L5L	1L5L42	(II)	MERRY LADS OF NEW PITSLIGO, THE
1L5L5L5L	1L422L	(I)	RIPE THE RIBS
1L5L5L5L	2L16L6L	(I)	PRINCESS OF WALES'S STRATHSPEY, THE
1L5L5L5L	5L15L5L	(II)	CLUNY'S GOLDEN WEDDING
1L5L5L5L	4322L	(II)	COUNTESS OF SEAFIELD'S STRATHSPEY
1L5L5L1	1L5L6L2L	(I)	HIS GRACE THE DUKE OF GORDON'S RECOVERY
1L5L5L1	15L2L2L	(II)	MUIR O' LOGIE, THE
1L5L5L1	147L2	(I)	MISS FERGUSON OF RATH'S DELIGHT
1L5L5L1	1422	(I)	MRS FERGUSSON OF RAITH'S DELIGHT
1L5L5L1	2326L	(I)	NATH. GOW'S COMPLIMENTS TO HIS BROTHER
1L5L5L1	4526L	(I)	HONble MISS CATHRINE ABERCROMBEY'S STRATHSPEY
1L5L5L1	5426L	(II)	MISS JEFFREY
1L5L6bL5L	1L5L3bL1L	(II)	KING'S, THE
1L5L6bL5L	1L5L4L7bF	(I)	GUR BOIDHEACH NIGHEAN DONN MO CHRIDHE
1L5L6bL5L	1L5L4L7bF	(I)	FAIR IS THE BROWN MAID OF MY HEART
1L5L6L4L	5L231	(II)	MISS MARIANE OLIPHANT (ROSSIE)

```
1L5L6L4L     5L231       ( I )  MISS MARIANE OLIPHANT (ROSSIE'S) STRATHSPEY
1L5L6L5L     1L5L3bL1L   (II)   GEORGE THE FOURTH REEL
1L5L6L5L     1L5L3bL1L   (II)   KING'S REEL, THE
1L5L6L5L     1L5L4L2L    (II)   FAREWELL TO GARTLY
1L5L6L5L     1L5L47L     (II)   CORGARFF CASTLE
1L5L6L5L     6L5L2L2     ( I )  MAID OF THE MILL, THE
1L5L6L5L     6L5L6L5L    ( I )  SANDS OF PORTOBELLO, THE
1L5L6L5L     246L6L      (II)   NIEL GOW'S LAMENTATION
                                FOR( JAMES MORAY OF) ABERCAIRN(E)Y
1L5L6L5L     246L6L      ( I )  (NEIL) NIEL GOW'S LAMENTATION
                                FOR (JAS MORAY ESQr OF) ABERCARNEY
1L5L6L5L     447L2       (II)   MISS TROTTER
1L5L6L6L     5L5L2L2L    (II)   CRAIG ELLACHIE BRIDGE
1L5L6L1      3422L       ( I )  WHA CAN HELP IT
1L5L7bL7bF   1L5L7bL7bL  ( I )  MRS FORSYTH'S STRATHSPEY
1L5L7L       1L5L6L      ( I )  COLONEL HAMILTON OF PENCAITLAND'S
                                WELCOME HOME
1L5L7L5L     3L5L2L2L    (II)   AIRCHIE SYMON
1L5L7L2      1231        (II)   BROWN'S REEL
1L5L15L      1L5L6L2L    ( I )  COUNTESS OF SUTHERLAND'S STRATHSPEY, THE
1L5L15L      2L4L2L7bF   (II)   BRIDGE OF BANFF, THE
1L5L15L      3L122L      (II)   HAPPY TOM
1L5L15L      3L122L      ( I )  MISS (BABY) MONTGOMERY('S) REEL
1L5L15L      16L2L4L     ( I )  MR LAUDER DICK'S STRATHSPEY
1L5L15L      357L2       ( I )  MRS GEORGE ROBERTSON'S REEL
1L5L16L      5L5L2L2L    (II)   GRANTULLY BRIDGE
1L5L16L      6L5L4L2L    ( I )  (CAPT) ROBERTSON OF BALGARVIE'S REEL
1L5L11       1L5L22L     ( I )  MRS WALLACE'S REEL
1L5L11       3L122L      ( I )  LADY HOPE'S STRATHSPEY
1L5L11       116L2L      (II)   MRS McHARDY, or GARDEN OF ROSES, THE
15L11        2416L       ( I )  MY AIN KIND DEARIE O
1L5L13       6L222       ( I )  MISS FANNY STEWART'S STRATHSPEY
1L5L13       16L6L2L     (II)   BISHOP'S MITRE, THE
1L5L13       16L22L      (II)   DOD HOUSE
1L5L13       16L22L      ( I )  DOD HOUSE
1L5L13       16L22L      ( I )  LORD ELPHINSTON'S STRATHSPEY
1L5L15       1H625L      (II)   MISS PRIMROSE
1L5L35L      2L6L46L     ( I )  ALDRIDGE'S HORNPIPE
1L5L31       3L142       ( I )  MISS GRACE CAMPBELL'S STRATHSPEY
1L5L31       6L5L4L3L    ( I )  CAPTAIN MACKDONALD
1L5L32       15L4L2L     (II)   MRS GILLIES
1L5L32       15L4L2L     ( I )  MRS GILLIES('S STRATHSPEY)
1L5L32       15L22L      ( I )  DUMBARTON CASTLE
1L5L33       427L2       ( I )  SCONE PALACE
1L5L33       5453        ( I )  SIR Wm JARDINE'S STRATHSPEY
1L5L35       4322        (II)   MRS JAMES DUFF
1L5L35       4322        ( I )  MRS JAMES DUFF(S') (STRATHSPEY/REEL)
1L5L36       1H642       ( I )  DUNKELD STEEPLE
1L5L36       1H642       ( I )  HORNPIPE
1L5L31H      3H526L      ( I )  GARRET FIELD
1L5L42       1L5L53      (II)   OOR GUIDWIFE
1L6L2L4L     1L6L5L1     (II)   LADY ANN WHARTON DUFF'S STRATHSPEY
1L6L2L4L     1L6L5L1     ( I )  LADY ANN WHARTON DUFF'S STRATHSPEY
1L7bL5L1L    2L7bL2L7bF  (II)   LYNN BURN
1L7L5L3      1L7L22L     ( I )  MISS BLAIRS REEL
1L7L6L5L     6L5L36      (II)   MISS CRAWFORD'S REEL
1L7L35       647L1       ( I )  LA SECULERE
1L11L1       2L26L6L     ( I )  KELRAVOCK'S STRATHSPEY
1L11L1       227L6L      (II)   ECLIPSE
1L12L7bF     1L13bL1     (II)   SOUTH SIDE OF SPEY, THE
1L12L2       1L16L7L     ( I )  MISS JOHNSTON (LATHRISK'S) STRATHSPEY
1L12L2       537L7L      ( I )  MISS WILLIAMSON'S JIGG
1L13bL6bL    2L7bL2L7bF  ( I )  MISS DUNDAS OF MELVILLE'S STRATHSPEY
1L13L1L      1L111       (II)   HENRY A. GRANT ESQ., OF ELCHIES
1L13L3L      2L225L      ( I )  BONNY BANKS OF UGIE, THE
1L13L1       2L27L6L     ( I )  MISS FIELD'S STRATHSPEY
1L15L3bL     2L7bL4L2L   ( I )  MISS GEORGINA MACKAY'S REEL
1L15L3bL     5L2L2L7bF   (II)   SKIRDUSTAN
1L15L3L      2L26L4L     (II)   GEORGE S. FORBES OF ASLOWN'S HORNPIPE
1L15L5L      4L2L2L7bF   (II)   GLENRINNES
1L15L1       2L26L6L     ( I )  KILRAVOCK'S STRATHSPEY
1L15L1       2L222       ( I )  KILRACK'S STRATHSPEY
1L15L1       6L226L      ( I )  RYE-HEAD'S
1L15L2       35L31       ( I )  MR ADm SHIRREFF'S VALTZ
1L16L3L      5L247L      (II)   GLEN GRANT
1L16L5L      4L5L2L2     (II)   MISS E. ELDER
1L16L5L      4L5L2L2     ( I )  MISS E. ELDER(S REEL)
1L16L5L      6L5L22      (II)   STRATHSPEY, A
1L17bL2L     1L113b      (II)   ISLA SIDE LASSES
1L17bL4L     1L112       (II)   SGIAN DUBH
1L17L6L      1L16L7L     ( I )  MRS STENNET'S QUICKSTEP
1L17L7L      6L6L5L5L    ( I )  MRS INGLIS'S STRATHSPEY
```

```
1L17L2      1355        (1)   DUKE OF BUCCLEUGH, THE
1L113L      2L27L6L     (1)   MRS FORDYCE'S (OF AYTON'S) STRATHSPEY
1L115L      1L112L      (1)   KINRARA COTTAGE
1L115L      1L122L      (1)   KINRARA
1L115L      1L322L      (1)   KINRARA
1L115L      2L226L      (11)  MR MARSHALL'S FAVOURITE
1L115L      2L226L      (1)   NEWFIELD COTTAGE
1L115L      2L226L      (1)   (MR) MARSHALL'S (FAVORITE/STRATHSPEY)
1L115L      7bL4L2L7bF  (11)  CORHABBIE
1L115L      2245L       (11)  DUCHESS OF BEDFORD'S STRATHSPEY, THE
1L115L      2245L       (1)   DU(T)CHESS OF BEDFORD'S STRATHSPEY, THE
1L111       7bF7bL7L7bL (1)   MRS A. GRANT'S STRATHSPEY
1L111       1L16L2      (1)   MISS GRANT'S JIG
1L111       7bL2L2L7bL  (11)  SCURRAN A MORANGE
1L111       7bL7bL2L1L  (11)  JAMES LUMSDEN ESQr
1L111       15L2L2L     (1)   MRS DONALDSON'S STRATHSPEY
1L113b      7bL7bF2L7bL (11)  EDINVILLIE
1L113b      24L2L2L     (1)   MONTROSE ASSEMBLY
1L113b      27bL47bL    (11)  MISS WATSON
1L113b      27bL47bL    (1)   MISS WATSON'S REEL
1L113       1L326L      (1)   MAJOR LOGAN'S FAVORITE
1L113       15L2L2L     (11)  MR DONALDSON
1L113       15L2L2L     (1)   MRS DONALDSON('S STRATHSPEY)
1L11        311         (1)   DEATH OF THE FOX, THE
1L115       27L5L3L     (1)   MISS ANGUS, BOTRIPHNIE'S REEL
1L126L      1L125       (1)   DOCTOR GORDON'S COMPLIMENTS TO JOHN MORISON
1L126L      1L253       (1)   FAREWELL TO WHISKY
1L126L      5L253       (11)  FAREWELL TO WHISKY
1L127bL     3b15L4L     (11)  DUNCAN MACPHERSON
1L121       5326L       (1)   MISS SERVICE'S STRATHSPEY
1L122       16L5L2L     (11)  WHISKY WELCOME BACK AGAIN
1L122       16L5L2L     (11)  WELCOME WHISKY BACK AGAIN
1L122       16L5L2L     (1)   WHISKY WELCOME BACK( AGAIN)
1L122       337L2       (1)   ROYAL JOAK
1L124       1L135       (1)   SOUTHESK RIVER
1L124       5125L       (1)   MRS KINLOCH OF GOURDIE'S DELIGHT
1L124       5232        (1)   CULLODEN MUIR
1L13b7bL    1L13b3b     (11)  LADY GRACE STEWART
1L13b7bL    1L13b3b     (11)  LADY GRACE STEWART('S STRATHSPEY)
1L13b1      7bL7bL43b   (1)   LADY DALRYMPLE
                              (OF NORTH BERWICK'S FAVOURITE)
1L13b3b     2L7bL43b    (1)   MISS GEDDES'S STRATHSPEY
1L13b3b     6bL243b     (1)   MISS McLEOD OF DELVEY'S REEL
1L13b5      53b27bL     (1)   MR McGHIE'S STRATHSPEY
1L131       2L242       (1)   MISS GRANT OF ELCHIES
1L131       6L2L6L2L    (1)   JOHNSON'S MUSIC SHOP
1L131       6L4L4L2L    (11)  EDINBURGH CASTLE
1L131       6L5L2L4L    (11)  MRS FORBES OF BOHARM'S STRATHSPEY
1L131       6L5L2L4L    (1)   MRS FORBES OF BOHARM'S STRATHSPEY
1L131       6L5L3L1L    (1)   MR MASSON, MANSE OF BOTRIPHNIE
1L132       1L122L      (1)   LORD ROBt MURRAY'S STRATHSPEY
1L132       1L14H3      (11)  BURNIE, THE
1L132       5522        (1)   MISS CAMPBELL FAIRFIELD'S STRATHSPEY
1L133       2L247L      (1)   SIR DAVID CARNEGIE
                              OF SOUTHESK BARt's STRATHSPEY
1L133       5122        (1)   MISS MARY BANNERMAN'S REEL
1L133       5642        (11)  LORD ALEXANDER GORDON
1L133       6532        (1)   COUNTESS OF FITZWILIAM'S STRATHSPEY
1L13        432         (1)   PAT IN THE CORNER
1L135       17L24       (1)   MISS NELLY BELL'S DOUBLE JIG
1L135       2252        (1)   MISS STEWART OF EDERADEYNAT'S JIGG
1L147L      2322L       (1)   MRS STEWART OF ALLENBANK('S STRATHSPEY)
1L147L      3322L       (1)   NEW TOWN OF EDINBURGH, THE
1L147L      3422L       (1)   NEW TOWN OF EDINBURGH, THE
1L147L      3422L       (1)   LADY CHARLOTTE LEVESON GOWER'S REEL
1L147L      3622L       (1)   NEW TOWN OF EDINBURGH, THE
1L151       6L5L2L2     (1)   MRS BALLANTINE'S REEL
1L153       2L226L      (11)  LADY HAMPDEN
1L153       2L226L      (1)   LADY HAMPDEN'S STRATHSPEY
1L153       2L246L      (1)   INVEREY'S STRATHSPEY
1L153       5642        (11)  LORD ALEXANDER GORDON
1L153       5642        (11)  GLENKINDIE
1L153       5642        (1)   LORD ALEXANDER GORDON'S (REEL/STRATHSPEY)
1L155       6L242       (1)   HONble MRS DRUMMOND OF PERTH'S DELIGHT, THE
1L155       2427bL      (1)   DUNNSTER CASTLE
1L3b7bL2    1115        (1)   CULLEN HOUSE
1L3b15L     7bL4L4L7bF  (1)   MISS LOUISA DRUMMOND LOGIEALMOND'S DELIGHT
1L3b53b     7bL242      (1)   MISS KIRKWOOD'S STRATHSPEY
1L32L4      1L363       (1)   OLD SPEDLING CASTLE'S GHOST'S DANCE
1L36L5L     1L36L2      (1)   MISS MARY DOUGLAS'S STRATHSPEY
1L37bL2     1115        (1)   MISS HACKHART'S (STRATHSPEY/REEL)
1L37L2      1L353       (1)   MISS STEWART FLEMYING
```

```
                                    OF KILLIEHASSY'S STRATHSPEY
1L313L      4L4L4L2L      ( I )  BRITISH BOYS
1L315L      7bL4L4L7bF    ( I )  MISS GORDON OF LASMORES FAVORITE
1L326L      5L353         (II)   NEIL GOW'S FAREWELL TO WHISKY
1L331       447L2         ( I )  PERTHSHIRE VOLUNTEERS (STRATHSPEY, THE)
1L332       5L323         ( I )  MERN'S STRATHSPEY, THE
1L343       5L47L2        (II)   MR JAMES RAMSAY
1L353       1L47L2        (II)   NEIL GOW'S COMPLIMENTS TO MR. MARSHALL
1L353       1L47L2        ( I )  NIEL GOW'S COMPLIMENTS
                                    RETURNED TO MR MARSHALL
1L353       47bL7b7b      ( I )  NETHER BOW HAS VANISHED, THE
1L353       4327bL        ( I )  CAPT SINCLEAR'S STRATHSPEY
1L354       5622          ( I )  LADY FORD'S STRATHSPEY
1L47L6L     5L47L2        ( I )  W. MORRISON OF CULODEN'S COMPLIMENTS
                                    TO JOHN MCGREGOR
1L47L2      1L353         (II)   MISS CHARLOTTE DUNDAS
1L47L2      1L353         ( I )  MISS CHARLOTTE DUNDAS('S STRATHSPEY)
1L415L      4L5L7F2L      (II)   MR ALEXr SHERRIFF'S STRATHSPEY
1L527L      6L6L5L3L      (II)   HILL OF DOUNE, THE
1L553       26L7L5L       (II)   BRIDGE OF BAMORE
1L1H63      6L27L4L       (II)   GALLATON
2L5L7bL7bL  7bF4L2L7bF    (II)   HIGH ROAD TO FORT AUGUSTUS
2L5L7bL7bL  7bF4L2L7bF    ( I )  COIR' A GHEARRAIG
3bL1L1L5    553b5         ( I )  ARGYLESHIRE DANCE
3bL1L2L7bF  3bL5L3bL5L    ( I )  MISS CHISHOLM'S STRATHSPEY
3bL1L3bL1L  2L7bF2L7bF    (II)   MARNOCK'S STRATHSPEY  [MARNOCH'S]
3bL1L3bL5L  7bL5L3bL7bF   (II)   CAOIDH NA H-ALB AIRSON NEILL GHOBHA
                                    [CALEDONIA'S WAIL FOR NEIL GOW]
3bL1L3bL5L  7bL5L3bL7bF   ( I )  CAOIDH NA H'ALBA AIRSON NIAL GHOBHA
                                    [CALEDONIA'S WAIL...]
3bL1L3bL5L  7bL27bL7bL    (II)   MISS LYALL [PANMURE HOUSE]
3bL1L15L    7bL4L2L7bF    (II)   SPORTSMAN'S HAUNT, THE
3bL1L15L    7bL4L2L7bF    ( I )  AM MONADH LIADH [AM MONADH LIATH]
3bL3bL1L3b  115L3b        ( I )  ETTRICK BANKS
3bL3bL2L2L  1L11HO        (II)   CLOG DANCE
3bL5L3bL5L  15L3bL1L      (II)   HEIRESS, THE
3bL5L5L1    7bL4L2L7bF    (II)   KILDRUMMY CASTLE
3bL13bL5    7bL53bL7bL    (II)   CALEDONIA'S WAIL FOR NIEL GOW
3L1L3L1L    5L1L4L2L      ( I )  MISS CAMPBELL'S FANCY
3L1L3L5L    6L5L2L7L      ( I )  COTILLION
3L1L3L5L    6L5L2L7L      ( I )  KISS UNDER THE STAIRS
3L1L3L5L    15L6L2L       ( I )  MISS MACKWORTH'S STRATHSPEY
3L1L3L1     3L1L2L2L      ( I )  HONORABLE MRS DUFF OF ECHT'S REEL, THE
3L1L5L1     3L5L4L2L      (II)   MISS MACPHERSON'S REEL
3L1L5L1     3L5L4L2L      ( I )  MISS GORDON OF CAIRNFIELD'S REEL
3L1L5L1     3L5L4L2L      ( I )  MISS McPHERSON'S REEL
3L1L6L2     4426L         ( I )  SQUITAL BRIDGE
3L1L7L5L    31H27L        (II)   TRIPLET, THE
3L1L42      5L6L11        ( I )  LADY JARDINE OF APPLEGIRTH'S NEW STRATHSPEY
3L1L43      6L27L5L       ( I )  MISS LOWIS'S REEL
3L3L5L1L    1351          ( I )  OSMOND'S RECOVERY
3L3L5L4L    3L3L5L3       (II)   FRASER ARMS, THE
3L3L5L4L    3L3L5L3       ( I )  CEANN AN FHEIDH
3L3L5L5     423L3L        ( I )  MISS JESSY BELL'S JIG
3L3L6L5L    3432          (II)   PETER MILNE
3L3L15L     3L16L2L       (II)   MRS MACDONALD OF CLANRANALD
3L3L15L     3L16L2L       ( I )  MRS McDONALD OF CLANRANALD('S STR.)
3L3L15L     5L6L4L2L      ( I )  MISS SWINTON'S REEL
3L3L15L     6L5L4L2L      (II)   MISS ROSE OF TARLOGIE
3L3L15L     6L6L4L2L      ( I )  MISS ROSE OF TARLOGIE('S REEL)
3L3L15L     6L6L4L2L      ( I )  MISS SWINTON'S STRATHSPEY
3L3L17L     5L6L4L2L      (II)   MRS FLEMING OF MONESS
3L3L17L     5L6L4L2L      (II)   MRS STEWART FLEMING OF KILLI(E)CHASSIE
3L3L17L     5L6L4L2L      ( I )  MRS FLEMING OF MONESS( STRATHSPEY)
3L3L11      3L3L22L       ( I )  MISS PEARSON OF KIPPENROSS'S STRATHSPEY
3L3L11      3L6L4L2L      ( I )  MR ARCHd CAMPBELL BALMARTIN
3L3L11      3L122L        (II)   MISS SCOT
3L3L11      3L122L        ( I )  LADY AUCKLANDS REEL
3L3L11      3L122L        ( I )  MISS (JEAN) SCOTT'S REEL
3L3L11      4L6L4L2L      (II)   MR DOUGLAS OF BRIGTON
3L3L11      4L6L4L2L      ( I )  MR DOUGLAS(S) OF BRIGTON('S STRATHSPEY)
3L3L11      5L5L4L2L      ( I )  SIMPSONS REEL
3L3L11      5L6L4L2L      ( I )  MRS FLEMING STRATHSPEY
3L3L12      5L6L4L2L      (II)   MRS FLEMING OF MONESS
3L3L12      5L6L4L2L      ( I )  MRS FLEMING OF MONESS
3L4L3L6     4L3L1#1       (II)   EXCELSIOR
3L4L5L1     7L5L7L5L      ( I )  PHEBILLIA
3L4L5L3     4L23L1        ( I )  JENNY LIND POLKA
3L4L7L1     4631          (II)   COMPOSER'S FAREWELL
3L4L7L1     656L7L        ( I )  MISS DEANS'S FAVORITE
3L4L11      3L6L41        ( I )  MISS WELLESLEY'S FAVORITE
3L5L3L5L    3L5L6L2L      ( I )  MRS GORDON OF CAIRNESS' STRATHSPEY
```

3L5L3L5L	4L6L7L5L	(I)	MISS MARGt BLAIR'S STRATHSPEY
3L5L3L5L	7L4#L7L5L	(II)	EARL OF FIFE, THE
3L5L3L1	3L5L7F2	(II)	BOTHWELL CASTLE
3L5L3L1	3L5L7F2	(I)	BOTHWELL CASTLE
3L5L4L5L	6L247L	(II)	MARCHIONESS OF HUNTLY('S STRATHSPEY)
3L5L4L6L	4L3L2L2	(II)	MISS CAMPBELL OF MONZIE
3L5L4L6L	7L213	(II)	EDITOR'S FAREWELL, THE
3L5L4L6L	7L235	(I)	MISS CAMPBELL (OF MONZIE'S) REEL
3L5L4L6L	7L531	(II)	LADY CHARLOTTE CAMPBELL
3L5L4L6L	7L531	(I)	LADY CHARLOTTE CAMPBELL'S ([NEW]STRATHSPEY/MEDLEY)
3L5L4L1	3L5L3L2L	(I)	MISS SMYTH (OF METHVEN'S) FAVOURITE
3L5L5L5L	3L5L12L	(I)	MRS GORDON OF PARK
3L5L5L5L	4L5L7L2	(I)	MRS ROBERTSONS STRATHSPEY
3L5L5L5L	6L6L66	(I)	COSEN COLE'S DELIGHT
3L5L5L5L	15L5L5L	(I)	HIGH WAY TO EDINBURGH, THE
3L5L5L5L	1321	(II)	THISTLE, THE
3L5L5L5L	147L2	(I)	LORD ELGIN'S STRATHSPEY
3L5L5L1	4L6L6L4	(I)	MISS BURNETS OF MONBODO'S STRATHSPEY
3L5L5L1	5L12L2L	(II)	LORD REIDHAVEN
3L5L5L1	6L166	(I)	PIQUE'S SCOTS MEASURE
3L5L5L1	3211	(II)	McGILLAN'S STRATHSPEY
3L5L5L1	3211	(I)	MR GILLAN'S STRATHSPEY
3L5L5L1	5216L	(I)	SWEET IS THE LASS THAT DWELLS AMONG (THE) HEATHER
3L5L5L1	5211	(I)	SWEET IS THE LASS THAT DWELLS AMONG THE HEATHE
3L5L6L3L	6L126L	(II)	JAMIE AND HIS BONNIE CATTIE
3L5L6L5L	3L5L13	(II)	CAMPSIE GLEN
3L5L6L5L	3L5L26L	(I)	DUKE OF WELLINGTON'S STRATHSPEY
3L5L6L5L	3L5L24	(I)	WAGGLE CAIRN, THE
3L5L6L5L	3L5L32	(I)	(MISS/LADY) MARY DOUGLAS('S FAVORITE)
3L5L6L5L	3L16L2	(I)	MISS E. GRANT, LOSSYMOUTH'S REEL
3L5L6L5L	3L122L	(I)	MR STIRLING'S JIG
3L5L6L6L	5L135	(II)	I HA'E LAID A HERRIN' IN SA'T
3L5L6L6L	5L135	(I)	I HA'E LAID A HERRING IN SA'T
3L5L6L2	4326L	(I)	MISS MARY URQUHART'S REEL
3L5L7L2	437L2	(I)	LADY CARMICHAEL'S STRATHSPEY
3L5L13L	3L522L	(II)	CARNEGIE'S WELCOME TO SCOTLAND
3L5L13L	5L56L5L	(I)	MARCHIONESS (OF) CORNWALLIS'S STRATHSPEY
3L5L15L	3L5L22L	(I)	ATHOLIAN HILLS
3L5L15L	3L5L33	(I)	MILE TAING' AN U(GH)DAIR
3L5L15L	5L325L	(I)	KIND ROBIE COME AGAIN
3L5L15L	5L532	(I)	MARCHIONESS CORNWALLIS'S STRATHSPEY, THE
3L5L15L	6L5L7L2	(I)	DUCHESS OF YORK'S REEL
3L5L15L	6L5L7L2	(I)	HONble MRS JOHN RAMSAY'S REEL, THE
3L5L15L	6L6L27L	(I)	MISS WHITE'S JIG
3L5L15L	16L15L	(II)	GREIG'S STRATHSPEY
3L5L15L	16L15L	(I)	GRIEG'S STRATHSPEY
3L5L16L	3L5L31	(I)	LOGIE O' BUCHAN
3L5L17L	2444	(I)	HORNPIPE
3L5L11	6L3L11	(II)	LASS WI' THE TARTAN PLAIDIE, O, THE
3L5L11	6L6L22	(I)	LASS O' GOWRIE, THE
3L5L11	2222	(I)	PAS SEUL MISS ISABELLA SIMPSON
3L5L11	3432	(I)	MRS CUMMING BRUCE'S STRATHSPEY
3L5L11	1H532	(I)	MRS ALEXANDER OF BALLAMILES STRATHSPEY
3L5L13	115L2L	(I)	MADAM DIDELOTS REEL
3L5L13	2422	(I)	MAJOR ARCHd CAMPBELL OF ASKOMELL'S STRATHSPEY
3L5L22	1422L	(II)	COUNTESS OF FIFE'S STRATHSPEY, THE
3L5L23	3L5L26L	(I)	COUNTESS OF EGLINTOUN'S DELIGHT
3L5L31	6L5L4L2L	(II)	NIEL GOW'S RECOVERY
3L5L31	6L5L4L2L	(I)	NIEL GOW'S RECOVERY
3L5L33	246L7L	(I)	LADY BERKLEY'S WHIM
3L5L34	447L2	(I)	MR JAMES HECTOR MACKENZIE'S STRATHSPEY
3L5L35	1H765	(I)	JENNY'S HORNPIPE
3L6L5L5L	3L6L2L2L	(II)	HECTOR THE HERO
3L6L16L	3L6L15L	(II)	MASTER PINTO
3L6L16L	3L6L15L	(I)	MASTER PINTO
3L6L17L	3L6L15L	(I)	MISS MARGARET NICOLS HIGH DANCE
3L6L11	326L6L	(II)	FORTY TWA, THE
3L6L36	7563H	(I)	LAMOTT'S JIG
3L7L14	5416L	(I)	HONOURABLE GEORGE MURRAY, THE
3L13L1L	4L5L4L2L	(I)	CAPT PARK OF PARKHALL'S JIGG
3L13L3L	3L122L	(II)	HOGMANAY, OR ADIEU TO THE AULD YEAR
3L13L3L	3L122L	(I)	SORAIDH LEIS AN T'SEANA BHLIADHNA
3L13L	3L4L2L	(II)	DROWN DROUTH
3L13L	3L4L2L	(I)	DROWN DROUTH
3L13L3L	4L2L3L1	(I)	DROWN DROUTH
3L13L5L	4L3L4L2L	(I)	LORD HINCHINBROOKS REEL
3L13L5L	4L3L4L2L	(I)	LADY (H)ELENORA HOME'S REEL
3L13L5L	4L5L4L2L	(I)	GLASGOW COLLEGE

3L13L5L	4L6L4L2L	(I)	CAPT PARK OF PARKHALL'S STRATHSPEY
3L13L5L	4L24L6L	(I)	MISS MARY ANN JOHNSTON'S REEL
3L13L1	3L12L2L	(I)	MISS JANE DUNBAR'S REEL
3L13L1	6L5L2L2	(II)	COUNTESS OF HADDINGTON, THE
3L13L1	6L5L2L2	(I)	COUNTESS OF HADDINGTON('S STRATHSPEY)
3L13L1	6L47L5	(I)	LADY ELIZABETH MARGARET CARNEGIE
3L13L1	7L447L	(I)	LABORIE'S DANCE
3L13L1	15L2L2L	(I)	ANTHONY MURRAY'S REEL
3L13L1	15L2L2L	(I)	MISS MURRAY'S REEL
3L13L1	247L7L	(I)	BRAES OF MAR, THE
3L13L1	247L7L	(I)	MISS ALSTON'S STRATHSPEY
3L13L1	3122L	(I)	AUCHINCRUIVE
3L13L3	3L14L2L	(I)	MISS CAMPBELL SUNDERLAND'S STRATHSPEY
3L15L1L	3L133	(II)	LORD PRESIDENT FORBES
3L15L2	1324	(I)	STEAM BOAT, THE
3L16L3L	3L146L	(II)	GLEN GRANT
3L16L4L	2L27L5L	(II)	MR MARTIN'S COMPLIMENTS
			TO DR. KEITH MACDONALD
3L16L4L	3L112L	(I)	MR Wm ETTLES FAVORITE
3L16L4L	447L2	(II)	MRS McINTOSH OF RAIGMORE'S STRATHSPEY
3L16L5L	7F2L3L1	(I)	SINGLE JIG
3L16L5L	3L2L3L1	(I)	MISS GIBSON'S JIG
3L16L5L	3L16L2L	(II)	MRS CAPTAIN BURGESS
3L16L5L	4L3L22L	(II)	MRS ANDREW KIDD
3L16L1	3L5L46L	(II)	PETER BAIL[L]IE
3L16L1	3L12L6L	(I)	MRS YOUNG'S STRATHSPEY
3L16L1	3L16L2L	(I)	MISS PENUEL GRANT OF GRANT'S STRATHSPEY
3L16L1	5236L	(II)	LASS WI' THE TARTAN PLAIDIE, O!, THE
3L16L2	7L531	(II)	MR WILLIAM DAVIDSON
3L16L4	3147L	(II)	MRS TULLOCH OF EARNHILLS STRATHSPEY
3L111	6L5L4L2L	(I)	SUGAR BANKS
3L111	427L2	(I)	FANCY, THE
3L112	6L26L2	(I)	MR CHURCHILLS REEL
3L126L	1155	(II)	MISS JEAN STEWART
3L126L	1155	(I)	MISS JEAN STEWART('S REEL)
3L121	3L632	(II)	ODDFELLOWS, THE
3L122	1126L	(I)	MRS RAMSAY OF BARNTON'S STRATHSPEY
3L136L	5L3L6L2L	(II)	GEORGE WRIGHT
3L131	3L5L3L2L	(I)	LOCH LOMOND
3L131	3L14L2L	(I)	VILLAGE REEL, THE
3L131	4L242	(II)	TULCHAN LODGE
3L131	6L242	(II)	TULCHAN LODGE
3L131	4647L	(II)	MACALLAN
3L133	1153	(II)	H. MACKWORTH
3L135	3L16L2L	(I)	MRS FOLJAMBE, ELGIN
3L135	6L27L5L	(II)	BEAUTY OF THE NORTH, THE
3L135	6L27L5L	(II)	MAIS' A TAOBH TUATH
			[BEAUTY OF THE NORTH, THE]
3L135	6L27L5L	(I)	MAIS' AN TOABH TUADH
3L135	427L5L	(II)	BURN O' FORGUE, THE
3L135	6216L	(I)	I'LL TELL YOU WHAT
3L143	2532	(I)	AIR
3L14#1H	5316L	(II)	WEEPING BIRCHES OF KILMORACK, THE
3L153	7L5L7L2	(I)	MISS OLIPHANT (ROSSIE'S) STRATHSPEY
3L37L6L	3L35L1	(I)	HIGH-WAY TO LONDON, THE
3L37L6L	3L35L1	(I)	TRIP TO LONDON, A
3L37L3	3L37L1	(I)	NEW RUSSIAN WALTZ, THE
3L411H	4347L	(II)	HAPPY FRANK
3L411H	4347L	(II)	FRANK GILRUTH
3L4L7L1	41H22	(II)	KNOWLES'
4L1L3bL1L	4L1L7bL7bL	(II)	CULLEN OF BUCHAN
4L1L3L1	3L6L4L2L	(I)	MR ROBERT STEWART REEL
4L2L3L1	6L5L32	(I)	ROMP, THE
4L3L3L1L	116L2	(I)	MARRIAGE KNOT, THE
4L5L1L3bL	4L5L7bF1L	(I)	THA FONN GUN BHI TROM
4L5L1L3bL	4L5L7bF1L	(I)	I AM DISPOSED TO MIRTH
4L5L15L	5L6L3b3b	(I)	INVERCAULD'S STRATHSPEY
4L5L15L	45L3b3b	(II)	INVERCAULD
4L7bL11	3b13b5L	(I)	(LASS AMONG) THE ETNOCH'S, (THE)
4L17bL7bL	5L3bL24	(I)	CA' THE EWES
4L13b1	4L7bL7bL4L	(I)	MAJOR McLEAN
4#L35#4	7L2#25	(II)	CLARENCE TOUGH
5L1L1L6L	5L1L33	(II)	PERTHSHIRE HUNT, THE
5L1L3bL1L	5L1L2L7bF	(II)	GEORGE THE IV
5L1L5L1L	5L322L	(I)	LADY SUSAN GORDON'S STRATHSPEY
5L1L5L5L	5L1L4L7bF	(I)	SONNAN MO GHAOIL
5L1L5L5L	1322L	(II)	COUNTESS OF CASSILLIS
5L1L5L5L	1322L	(I)	COUNTESS OF CASSILLI'S REEL
5L1L5L5L	1322L	(I)	MISS MOLLY DAKER'S REEL
5L1L5L1	5L132	(I)	MISS LYLLE OF GARDYNE'S STRATHSPEY
5L1L5L1	3122L	(II)	MR JOHN SMITH
5L2L5L5L	6L6L6L5L	(I)	WOE'S MY HEART THAT WE SHOULD SUNDER

5L2L5L6L	5L2L3L6L	(I)	IAN AN CIOBAIR [IAIN AN CIBEIR]
5L3bL5L3b	4242	(I)	MISS MARGt McDOUGAL OF ARDBEG STRATHSPEY
5L3L7F2L	5L3L5L3	(I)	COLONEL ROBERTSON'S STRATHSPEY
5L3L1L3L	1L3L4L2L	(I)	PERTH HUNT
5L3L1L3L	1L3L6L2L	(II)	PERTH-SHIRE HUNT(, THE) [PERTH HUNT(, THE]
5L3L1L3L	1L3L6L2L	(I)	PERTHSHIRE HUNT, (THE)
5L3L1L3L	1L3L6L2L	(I)	LADY JERSEY'S REEL
5L3L1L3L	4L3L6L2L	(II)	MRS McPHERSON OF CLUNY
5L3L1L3L	5L3L2L2L	(I)	MISS LUCY GORDON'S STRATHSPEY
5L3L1L3L	5L3L6L3L	(II)	CORRIMONY
5L3L1L3L	5L3L6L3L	(I)	COIR A MHONI [COIRE MHONAIDH]
5L3L1L3L	5L35L3L	(II)	D. MORISON'S SEVEN THISTLES
5L3L1L5L	5L3L26L	(II)	GLENGARRY'S DIRK
5L3L1L5L	5L3L26L	(II)	BIODAG DHO'ILL 'IC ALASDAIR, OR GLENGARRY'S DIRK
5L3L1L5L	5L3L26L	(I)	MAC (MH)'IC ALASTAIR
5L3L1L1	322L2	(I)	ALDRIDGE'S JIGG
5L3L1L1	352L2	(I)	UNTITLED
5L3L1L1	516L2	(I)	MRS MAJOR L. STEWART OF THE ISLAND OF JAVA
5L3L1L1	1H527L	(I)	MISS PURSE'S JIG
5L3L1L3	437L2	(I)	INVERNESS or [NORTHERN MEETING, THE]
5L3L1L3	447L2	(I)	MISS MACKENZIE OF AVOCH'S STRATHSPEY
5L3L4L2L	427L5L	(I)	CLACH NA CUDAIN [CLACHNACUDAINN]
5L3L5L1L	4L5L4L2L	(I)	GARSCUBE HOUSE
5L3L5L1L	7L125L	(II)	MR JOSEPH BANKS
5L3L5L3L	1L426L	(I)	PROPHECY OF DANTE, THE
5L3L5L3L	5L5L33	(II)	NUAGHALACHD [NOVELTY, THE]
5L3L5L3L	5L5L33	(I)	NUAGHALACHD [NUADHALACHD]
5L3L5L3L	16L2L2L	(II)	LADY MARY PRIMROSE
5L3L5L3L	227L2	(I)	EARL MOIRA'S RETURN TO ENGLAND
5L3L5L3L	227L2	(I)	LIEUt COLONEL DAVID STEWART'S STRATHSPEY
5L3L5L3L	2226L	(I)	MR W.F. THOMSON'S REEL
5L3L5L3L	547L2	(I)	LADY SUSAN HAMILTON
5L3L5L5L	227L2	(I)	MAJOR DAVID STEWART'S STRATHSPEY
5L3L5L1	5L5L6L2L	(II)	DONSIDE LASSES, THE
5L3L5L1	15L3L2L	(I)	MISS JOAN KIERS STRATHSPEY
5L3L5L1	15L3L2L	(I)	SIR HENDRY'S STRATHSPEY
5L3L5L1	16L2L2L	(I)	LADY MARY PRIMROSE('S FAVORITE)
5L3L5L1	5326L	(II)	MR THOMAS A. GRANT OF GLEN ELGIN, AUSTRALIA
5L3L5L3	6L5L4L2L	(I)	MISS DOUGLASS'S REEL
5L3L5L3	15L4L2L	(I)	MISS SEYMOUR'S REEL
5L3L5L3	16L6L2L	(I)	MISS BROWN'S STRATHSPEY
5L3L5L3	3136L	(I)	BARAIN CHULRABHAIG [BARAIN CHILL-REATHAIG]
5L3L5L4	6L15L3	(II)	MR MURRAY
5L3L5L1H	57L6L2	(I)	ATHOLE VOLUNTEER'S QUICK STEP, THE
5L3L6L2L	5L3L5L3	(I)	MISS BOWIS OF INVERNESS
5L3L6L2L	5L3L6L5L	(II)	DUKE OF SUTHERLAND(, THE)
5L3L6L4L	5L47L2	(II)	FRANCIS SITWELL [MASTER F. SITWELL]
5L3L6L4L	5L47L2	(I)	MASTER F(RANCIS) SITWELL('S STRATHSPEY)
5L3L6L4L	427L5L	(II)	CROSS OF INVERNESS, THE
5L3L6L5L	4347L	(I)	MRS BUTTER OF FASKALLY'S MEDLEY
5L3L6L6L	7L7L13	(II)	MISS ROBERTSON
5L3L6L6L	7L7L13	(I)	MISS ROBERTSON('S REEL)
5L3L6L1	427L6L	(II)	ST. MUNGO'S WELCOME TO SCOTT SKINNER
5L3L11	6L5L4L3L	(I)	MISS ELIZABETH FLEMYNG'S STRATHSPEY
5L3L11	6L15L5L	(II)	HAUGHS O' SPEY, THE
5L3L11	1122L	(II)	MR ALEX WALKER'S STRATHSPEY
5L3L11	2211H	(I)	MRS SMOLETS FAVORITE
5L3L31	5L3L5L3L	(I)	MRS STEWART OF FOSS' STRATHSPEY
5L4L3L5L	3L422L	(I)	MARQUIS OF BOWMONT'S REEL
5L5L1L3L	5L5L4L2L	(II)	DUNDEE
5L5L1L5L	2L1L2L4L	(I)	MR DOUGAL CAMPBELL OF BALLINABY'S STRATHSPEY
5L5L1L5L	5L5L6L2L	(II)	GARTHLAND HOUSE
5L5L1L5L	5L5L6L2L	(I)	GARTHLAND HOUSE (STRATHSPEY)
5L5L1L5L	5L5L6L2L	(I)	PRINCE OF WALES('S) STRATHSPEY, (THE)
5L5L1L5L	147L5L	(I)	HONble MISS ELIZA MURR(A)Y ELIBANK'S STRATHSPEY
5L5L3L2L	5L5L5L2	(II)	STRATHERICK
5L5L3L2L	5L5L5L2	(I)	STRADH FARGAIC [S(T)RATH FHARAGAIC]
5L5L4L4L	5L5L7bL1	(II)	PRINCE CHARLIE'S MEDLEY
5L5L4L	113	(I)	MISS FERRIER'S MINUET
5L5L4L2	15L4L2L	(I)	MISS CRUDENS REEL
5L5L5L1L	2L5L4L7bF	(II)	HONble. MRS. FRASER OF LOVAT, THE
5L5L5L1L	2L5L4L7bF	(I)	COLONEL MACDOWALL OF LOGANS STRATHSPEY
5L5L5L1L	2L5L4L7bF	(I)	MRS STEWART'S STRATHSPEY
5L5L5L1L	2L5L4L7bF	(I)	MRS FRASER OF LOVAT'S STRATHSPEY
5L5L5L1L	2L226L	(I)	MR STEUART'S JUNr STRATHSPEY
5L5L5L1L	5L5L26L	(II)	BRIDGE OF BUCKET
5L5L5L1L	316L3L	(I)	MISS CHARLOTTE CARRUTHERS'S FAVORITE
5L5L5L2L	5L5L13	(II)	FLAGSTAFF, THE
5L5L5L2L	5L6L13	(II)	MRS WIGHTON OF DUNDEE

```
5L5L5L3L    5L5L11      ( I )   LADY MENZIES OF CASTLE MENZIES' STR./MEDLEY
5L5L5L      3L5L1       ( I )   LOVE WILL FIND OUT THE WAY
5L5L5L3L    126L5L      (II)    BALLOCHMYLE BRIG
5L5L5L4L    4L2L6L6L    ( I )   NANCY'S TO THE GREEN-WOOD GANE
5L5L5L4L    337L7L      ( I )   CAT IN PATTENS, THE
5L5L5L5L    5L1L5L5L    ( I )   (BONNIE) BLACK EAGLE, (THE)
5L5L5L5L    5L1L26L     ( I )   LOCH ALOIE
5L5L5L5L    5L1L26L     ( I )   MARQUESS OF TWEEDDALE'S STRATHSPEY, THE
5L5L5L5L    5L1L26L     ( I )   LADY MONTGOMERIES STRATHSPEY
5L5L5L5L    5L1L26L     ( I )   MRS LEITCH'S STRATHSPEY
5L5L5L5L    6L6L6L5L    ( I )   GENTLE SHEPHERD, THE
5L5L5L5L    6L6L13      (II)    IRISH GIRL, THE
5L5L5L5L    6L6L13      ( I )   IRISH AIR, AN [IRISH GIRL, THE]
5L5L5L5L    6L6L13      ( I )   CAIRNGORAM MOUNTAIN
5L5L5L5L    6L6L13      ( I )   'N CARN GORM
5L5L5L5L    6L213       ( I )   SHORT LIFE TO (ALL) STEPMOTHERS
5L5L5L5L    2125L       ( I )   MERRY GIRLS OF (EPSOM/YORK), THE
5L5L5L5L    2226L       ( I )   MISS AUGUSTA MURRAY
5L5L5L5L    236L6L      ( I )   VALE OF KEAPPOCH
5L5L5L7L    3422L       ( I )   CAPT WALTON CAMPBELL'S STRATHSPEY
5L5L5L1     5L5L2L2L    (II)    DUNCAN R. DAWSON'S STRATHSPEY
5L5L5L1     5L5L5L1     (II)    FAIR HAIRED LASSIE
5L5L5L1     5L5L21      ( I )   MISS ZOFFANY WEIPPERT WALTZ
5L5L5L1     6L6L6L1     ( I )   WEEL MAY YE A' BE
5L5L5L1     6L6L6L1     ( I )   HEY TUTTIE TETTIE
5L5L5L1     6L221       (II)    THERE GROWS A BONNIE BRIER
5L5L5L      111         ( I )   UAIGH A' BHAIRD
5L5L5L1     1346L       ( I )   MRS CHARLES GRAHAME'S STRATHSPEY
5L5L5L      114         ( I )   CAROLAN'S LAMENT
5L5L5L1     2216L       ( I )   MISS WEDDERBURN'S REEL
5L5L5L1     2226L       (II)    MISS WEDDERBURN
5L5L5L1     2226L       (II)    BURN O' CAIRNIE or MISS WEDDERBURN*
5L5L5L1     2226L       ( I )   MISS WEDDERBURN('S REEL)
5L5L5L1     2226L       ( I )   BURN OF CARNIE, THE
5L5L5L1     2231        ( I )   [MISS WEDDERBURN'S] JIGG
5L5L5L1     2326L       (II)    MISS ROSS
5L5L5L1     2326L       ( I )   MISS ROSS('S STRATHSPEY)
5L5L5L1     326L6L      ( ! )   FLOWERS OF THE FOREST, THE
5L5L5L1     3211        (II)    CAPTAIN GILLANS
5L5L5L1     3426L       (II)    CORRIEGILLS
5L5L5L1     3427L       ( I )   MR GILLAN'S REEL
5L5L5L1     426L5L      ( I )   FLOWERS OF THE FOREST, THE
5L5L5L1     426L6L      ( I )   FLOWERS OF THE FOREST, THE
5L5L5L1     427L2       ( I )   HIGHLAND (LASSES) FAIR, THE
5L5L5L1     5236L       (II)    PETER BAIL[L]IE'S WIFE
5L5L5L2     3L6L46L     ( I )   I'VE MADE A VOW
5L5L5L2     5L5L11      ( I )   PADDY O' RAFFERTY
5L5L5L2     5L5L21      ( I )   GEORGINA, THE
5L5L5L2     326L6L      ( I )   FLOWERS OF THE FOREST, THE
5L5L5L3     6L6L23      ( I )   MRS BAIRD OF NEWBYTH'S JIGG
5L5L5L3     2215        ( I )   L'ETE
5L5L5L      331         ( I )   MISS JEAN DOUGLAS'S VALTZ
5L5L6L6L    7L533       ( I )   MR JOHN SMYTH'S REEL
5L5L6L1     5L13L2L     ( I )   LADY ABERCROMBY'S STRATHSPEY
5L5L6L      111         ( I )   BLACK JOCK
5L5L7bL7bL  1151        ( I )   MISS JANE McINNES
5L5L7L      113b        ( I )   BRAIGHE LOCHIALL
5L5L7L      113         ( I )   O BONNY LASS
5L5L15L     5L5L12L     (II)    APPIN HOUSE
5L5L15L     113b4L      ( I )   A' BHLIADHNA GUS AN AIMSIR SO
5L5L15L     1232        ( I )   ALAMODE BEEF HOUSE, THE
5L5L15L     1311        ( I )   KEITH-HALL
5L5L17bL    2144        ( I )   CARLAND'S DEVOTION
5L5L11      5L5L55      ( I )   MISS ANN DEWAR FRAZER OF TORBRECK'S REEL
5L5L11      117L7L      ( I )   AUTHORS LAMENT FOR LORD MC.D-, THE
5L5L11      225L5L      ( I )   I'VE SEEN MID-WINTERS DREARY HOURS
5L5L11      226L5L      ( I )   YEAR OWER YOUNG, A
5L5L11      2226L       (II)    HUNDRED YEARS SINCE, A
5L5L11      2226L       ( I )   HUNDRED YEARS SINCE, A
5L5L11      315L3L      (II)    HIGHLAND EMIGRANTS, THE
5L5L11      326L5L      (II)    AULD BRIG O' AYR, THE
5L5L11      3216L       ( I )   MAIRI GHREANNAR
5L5L11      3211H       ( I )   DOWN THE BURN DAVIE
5L5L1       133         ( I )   FIELDS OF ODIN, THE
5L5L11      3332        ( I )   MY LOVE'S BONNY WHEN SHE SMILES ON ME
5L5L11      3332        ( I )   FLOWER OF EDINBURGH, (THE)
5L5L11      3342        (II)    FLOWERS OF EDINBURGH, THE
5L5L11      3342        (II)    EARL OF HOPETOUN'S REEL
5L5L11      3532        ( I )   FLOWERS OF EDINBURGH, THE
5L5L11      3542        ( I )   FLOWERS OF EDINBURGH, THE
5L5L1       322         ( I )   LADY BERNARD'S LAMENT
5L5L13      226L6L      ( I )   AN' THOU WERE MY AIN THING
```

```
5L5L13        226L3      ( I )  AND THOU WERE MY AIN THING
5L5L13        226L3      ( I )  AN THOU WERE MY AIN THING
5L5L13        326L3      ( I )  AN THOU WERE MINE AIN THING
5L5L13        436L6L     ( I )  MRS GEO. ABERCROMBY'S REEL
5L5L13        6316L      ( I )  McNIEL'S STRATHSPEY [McNEILL'S RANT]
5L5L26L       1353       (II)   CAPTAIN ROSS
5L5L26L       1353       ( I )  EARL OF SEAFORTH'S REEL, THE
5L5L26L       1353       ( I )  CAPTAIN ROSS('S REEL)
5L5L22        5L6L11     (II)   COMIN' THRO' THE RYE
5L5L22        5L6L11     ( I )  GIN A BODY MEET A BODY
5L5L22        5L6L11     ( I )  COMIN' THRO' THE RYE
5L5L22        5L6L12     ( I )  CALEDONIAN QUADRILLES (SECOND SET)
5L5L22        347L7L     ( I )  DANCED BY THE MISSES JOBSON
5L5L22        5211       ( I )  RECOVERY, THE
5L5L31        5L5L2L2L   ( I )  GREAT NEWS FROM CAMPERDOWN
5L5L31        6L420      ( I )  MISS MARGRET RANKINE'S REEL
5L5L31        5562       (II)   MISS MONCRIEFF OF PITLOWER
5L5L31        5562       ( I )  MISS MONCRIEFF OF PITLOWER'S REEL
5L5L32        7L242      (II)   MISS HANBURY'S FANCY
5L5L32        7L242      ( I )  MISS HANBURY'S FANCY
5L5L52        36L7L5L    ( I )  BATH RACES
5L6L1L3L      4L622L     ( I )  MISS SARAH GEORGIANA DUFF
                                OF MUIRTOWN'S STRATHSPEY
5L6L5L3L      2L4L6L4L   ( I )  LADY DUFF OF DELGATY
5L6L5L3L      5L15L5L    (II)   DUCHESS OF BUCCLEUCH, THE
5L6L5L3L      5L15L5L    ( I )  DUCHESS OF BUCCLEUGH('S FAVORITE), THE
5L6L5L5L      426L6L     ( I )  BUSK YE, BUSK YE
5L6L5L1       2135       (II)   JOHNNIE SMITH MY FALLA FINE
5L6L5L1       426L0      ( I )  BRAES OF YARROW, THE
5L6L5L2       1H653      ( I )  TRIP TO SLIGO, A
5L6L7L        113        ( I )  ROBIN ADAIR
5L6L10        4210       ( I )  BUSK YE, BUSK YE
5L6L1         111        ( I )  PAST ONE O'CLOCK
5L6L1         111        ( I )  BANKS OF TAY, (THE)
5L6L1         111        ( I )  KITTY TYRREL
5L6L1         111        ( I )  BURLESQUE ON BLACK JOAK
5L6L1         221        ( I )  AILEEN A ROON
5L6L1         335        ( I )  SPINNING O'T, THE
5L6L26L       5L6L44     (II)   INVERCAULD
5L6L26L       5L6L44     ( I )  INVERCAULD'S(REEL/RANT/STRATHSPEY)
5L6L22        6L5L6L2    (II)   MO GHILLE GUANACH
5L7bL7bL7bL   111H1H     ( I )  SWEET'S THE LASS THAT LOVES ME
5L7bL7bL7bL   3b111      ( I )  DONALD McQUEEN
5L7bL15L      5L7bL11    (II)   I THOUGHT THAT SHE WAS MINE
5L7bL11       3b53b7bL   ( I )  LOCHNESS SIDE
5L7L12        3111       ( I )  CALL A DANCE
5L7L13        51H52      ( I )  PLOUGHMAN'S DANCE, THE
5L7L27L       1231       ( I )  DUNCAN GRAY
5L7L21        1231       ( I )  DUNCAN GRAY CAM' HERE TOO WOO
5L7L41H       5221       ( I )  GATES OF EDINBURGH, THE
5L7L43        6L6L21     (II)   HAUNT OF THE GNOMES, THE
5L14L6L       4L326L     ( I )  MISS ANN MURRAY'S STRATHSPEY
5L15L1L       6L5L2L2L   (II)   MISS ANN STEWART
5L15L2L       4L5L6L2L   ( I )  LESLEY HOUSE [LESSLEY HOUSE]
5L15L3L       1L132      (II)   GLENMORISTON
5L15L3L       1L132      ( I )  TIGHEARNA GLINNAMORISTOIN
                                [...GHLINNE MOIREASTUINN]
5L15L4L       2L27L2     ( I )  Dr ROSS OF DORNOCH
5L15L5L       5L12L2     (II)   SIR CHAs. FORBES BARt. OF NEWE'S STR.
5L15L5L       1426L      ( I )  GAVISIDE
5L15L7bL      3b53b1     (II)   SANDY BUCHANAN
5L15L1        2L27L6L    ( I )  LADY HAMILTON
5L15L1        5L5L15     ( I )  GUSTAVUS GALOP, THE
5L15L1        5L13b5     (II)   HEATHER BELL
5L15L1        6L5L2L2L   ( I )  MISS ANN STEWART'S REEL
5L15L1        7bL7bL22   ( I )  MISS JEANY CAMERON'S STRATHSPEY
5L15L1        7bL247bL   (II)   MARQUIS OF HUNTLY'S REEL(, THE)
5L15L1        7bL247bL   ( I )  MARQUIS OF HUNTLY'S (STRATHSPEY/REEL)
5L15L1        7L252      (II)   YOE, THE
5L15L1        427L7L     ( I )  MISS JANE STIRLING'S STRATHSPEY
5L15L1        5122       (II)   BRODIE OF BRODIE
5L15L1        5122       ( I )  MR BRODIE OF BRODIE'S STRATHSPEY
5L15L3b       5L13b5     (II)   INVERARY CASTLE [INVERARAY CASTLE]
5L15L3b       5L13b5     ( I )  CAISTAL INN'RARA [CAISTEAL INBHER-AORA]
5L15L3        3637L      ( I )  HERBERTS DELIGHT
5L16L5L       4367L      ( I )  MISS KINLOCH OF GOURDIE'S DOUBLE JIG
5L16L6L6L     1342       ( I )  CREWE HALL
5L16L1        6L27L5     (II)   WE'LL AYE BE FOND O' INGRAM
5L16L1        6L27L5     (II)   I'LL/WE'LL AYE BE FOND O' INGRAM
5L16L1        327L5L     ( I )  DUKE OF MANCHESTER'S FANCY, THE
5L16L2        5L16L7L    ( I )  STRATHSPEY
5L16L2        5L153      ( I )  MRS FULLARTON OF FULLARTON
```

```
5L16L2      7L531       (II) MAJOR MACKIE
5L16L2      1316L       (I)  MISS BALFOUR'S STRATHSPEY
5L16L2      5346L       (I)  MISS A. HEDDERWICK'S STRATHSPEY
5L17bL6L    5L3b42      (II) PASS ABOUT THE FLAGON
5L17bL6L    5L3b42      (I)  HO CUIR A NALL AM BODACH
5L17bL      13b5        (I)  SHEPHERD ADONIS, THE
5L17bL2     5L13b2      (II) EWIE WI' THE CROOKED HORN
5L17bL2     5L13b2      (I)  CHOARA CHROM [A' CHAORAN CHROM]
5L17bL2     5L143b      (II) EWIE WI' THE CROOKIT HORN, THE
5L17bL2     5L143b      (I)  EW(I)E WI' THE CROOKE'D HORN, THE
5L17bL2     5L143       (I)  CARRON'S REELL
5L17bL2     5L143       (I)  CROOKED HORN EWE, THE
5L17bL2     5L343       (I)  CROOKED HORN'D EWE, THE
5L17bL2     3b7bL5L3bL  (II) HIGHLAND QUEEN, THE
5L17bL2     3b17bL5L    (I)  GENTY TIBBY
5L17bL2     3b3b47bL    (I)  MISS RUTHERFORD KINGHORN'S STRATHSPEY
5L17bL2     517bL7bL    (I)  TIBBY FOWLER IN THE GLEN
5L17bL2     5125L       (II) GAIR'S RANT
5L17bL2     5551        (II) FAREWELL TO DUNDEE
5L17L1      526L6L      (I)  BOAT OF BOG, THE [BRIDGE OF SPEY, THE]
5L17L1      526L6L      (I)  BRIDGE OF SPEY, THE
5L17L2      5L143b      (I)  EWIE WI' THE CROOKED HORN, THE
5L17L2      5L143       (I)  EWIE WI' THE CROOKED HORN, THE
5L17L2      5L145       (I)  MISS HELEN McINNES
5L17L2      1324        (I)  SWEET RICHARD
5L17L2      1566        (II) MR DOUGLAS OF SPRINGWOOD PARK
5L17L2      1566        (II) CROPIE'S STRATHSPEY
5L17L2      3125L       (I)  MISS McPHERSON GRANT'S JIG
5L17L2      3561H       (I)  EARL OF DALHOUSIE'S WELCOME
                             FROM THE PYRENEES, THE
5L115L      4L5L2L4L    (II) BRAES OF MORVEN, THE
5L115L      1140        (I)  JOCK O' THE SIDE
5L11        5L22        (I)  MINUET
5L115L      3522        (I)  MRS SPENCE'S STRATHSPEY
5L116L      225L5L      (I)  BAY OF BISCAY, THE
5L117bL     5L3b3b3b    (I)  ANNIE'S SCOTS MEASURE
5L117bL     1255        (I)  COMING THRO THE BROOM MY JO
5L117bL     2112        (I)  KATH'RINE OGGIE
5L117bL     2112        (I)  KATRIN HOGGIE
5L11        7bL22       (I)  GALLANT GRAHAM(S), (THE)
5L117bL     2214        (I)  MORE N'INGHEAN GHIBERLAN
5L117bL     3b443b      (I)  I LOVE THE YOUTH
5L117bL     4224        (II) NINE PINT COGGIE
5L117bL     53b3b3b     (I)  OLD WITCH OF OCHILTREE, THE
5L117b      415L4L      (I)  MY PEGGY IS A YOUNG THING
5L117b      415L4L      (I)  WAAKING OF THE FAULD, THE
5L117b      417bL2      (I)  AULD MAN'S MARE'S DEAD, THE
5L110       3b212       (I)  KATHERINE OGIE
5L111       5L111       (II) DONALD TO YOUR SOALS
5L111       5L137L      (II) TROIS GRANDS LUTHIERS, LES
5L111       5L222       (I)  MRS MACKINZIE OF CROMARTY'S STRATHSPEY
5L111       6L222       (I)  ALDAVALIGH
5L111       6L222       (I)  RISE AND FOLLOW CHARLIE
5L111       6L222       (I)  O'ER THE MOOR AMANG THE HEATHER
5L111       6L232       (II) THA TIGHIUN FODHAM EIRIDH
5L111       6L242       (II) O'ER THE MUIR AMANG THE HEATHER
5L111       6L242       (II) ALDIVALLOCH or
                             O'ER THE MUIR AMANG THE HEATHER
5L111       6L242       (I)  ALDAVALOCH
5L111       6L242       (I)  THA TIGH'N FODHAM EIRIDH
5L111       6L242       (I)  O'ER THE MOOR, AMONG THE HEATHER
5L111       7bL541      (I)  MISS BAINE'S STRATHSPEY
5L11        17L2        (I)  SINGLE HORNPIPE
5L11        17L2        (I)  MISS MARY LUMSDEN'S FAVOURITE
5L11        115L        (I)  DA MIHI MANUM
5L11        117bL       (I)  BONNY DUNDEE
5L11        117bL       (I)  GABERLUNZIE MAN, THE
5L11        111         (I)  COLD FROSTY MORNING, (A)
5L111       115L4L      (I)  MRS GENERAL STEWART'S STRATHSPEY
5L11        113b        (I)  BONNIE DUNDEE
5L11        113         (I)  THA MI MO CHADAL
5L11        113         (I)  JOHN HAY'S BONNIE LASSIE
5L111       215L6L      (I)  BLACK AT THE BONE
5L111       216L6L      (I)  HARD TO THE BONE
5L111       216L6L      (I)  BLACK AT THE (BANE) BONE
5L111       2231        (I)  PUT THE GOWN UPON THE BISHOP
5L111       2247bL      (I)  SHORT LIFE TO ALL STEPMOTHERS
5L111       2244        (I)  SHEPHERD'S SON, THE
5L111       237L6L      (I)  DUBH AIG CHREABH
5L111       3b217bL     (I)  KATHERINE OGIE
5L111       3b212       (I)  HIGHLAND MARY
5L111       3b212       (I)  KAT(HRINE) OG(G)IE
```

5L111	3b3b3b4	(I)	JOHN ANDERSON MY JO
5L111	3b3b54	(I)	BONNY JEAN OF St. ANDREWS
5L111	3b3b54	(I)	SCOTCH MEASURE, A
5L111	3b3b54	(I)	JOHN ANDERSON MY JO
5L111	3b53b7bL	(II)	LOCHEND SIDE
5L111	3b53b7bL	(I)	LOCHNESS SIDE
5L111	3253	(I)	HONble EDWARD SPENCER COWPERS
5L111	3366	(I)	MONTROSE SCOTS MEASURE
5L111	436L1	(I)	WHY LEFT I MY HAME?
5L111	443b7bL	(I)	MR MORTHLAND'S FAVORITE(STRATHSPEY)
5L111	526L6L	(II)	GLEN COTTAGE
5L111	543b7bL	(II)	DUNCAN McQUEEN
5L111	543b7bL	(I)	DONNACHA MAC SHUINE
5L111	5542	(I)	LOVE AND FICKLE FORTUNE
5L112	4L7bL7bL1	(I)	Sr ADAM FERGUSON'S REEL
5L11	25L5L	(I)	CHEVY CHASE
5L11	25L0	(I)	WILLIAM AND MARGARET
5L112	7bL222	(I)	FIFE DOCKS
5L112	2124	(II)	MARY OF CASTLECARY
5L11	222	(I)	MODERATE
5L11	222	(I)	'S NEONACH LE CLANN DONAIL MI
5L122	3b3b3b4	(I)	JOHN ANDERSON, MY JO
5L112	3b3b3b4	(I)	JOHN ANDERSON MY JOE
5L112	5552	(I)	ST. PATRICK'S DAY
5L11	265	(II)	OCH MAR THA MI [HOW SAD AM I]
5L113b	5L111	(II)	AN GABH THU BEAN DHO'ILL BHIG?
			[LITTLE DONALD'S WIFE]
5L113b	5L111	(I)	CAPT SIMON FRASER OF KNOCKY'S FAV.
5L113b	5L111	(I)	LADY WALLACE
5L113b	7bL4L2L2	(II)	MRS GEORGE STEWART'S STRATHSPEY
5L113b	7bL247bL	(II)	MR GIBSON
5L113b	27bL24	(I)	COLLIE CAN
5L113b	27bL47bL	(II)	NORTH BRIDGE OF EDINBURGH(, THE)
5L113b	27bL47bL	(I)	NORTH BRIDGE OF EDINBURGH, THE
5L113b	2455	(I)	HIGHLAND PRESIDENT, THE
5L113b	2555	(II)	TWIST YE, TWINE YE
5L113b	427bL1	(I)	KEAPPOCH'S FAREWELL
5L113b	427bL1	(I)	O I HAE SEEN THE WILD FLOWERS BLA'
5L113b	51H1H1H	(I)	MR CREAGH'S IRISH TUNE
5L11	312	(II)	FIR A BHATA [2ND.TUNE]
5L113	6422	(I)	BESSY HAGGICE
5L115	3b47bL7bL	(II)	MAYEN HOUSE
5L11	53b6b	(I)	TAM GLEN
5L11	531	(I)	SMITH HE'S BLACK AN' BRUCKET, THE
5L115	447bL7bL	(II)	WE'LL AYE GANG BACK TO YON TOWN
5L115	53b3b7bL	(I)	LORD ELCHO'S FAVOURITE
5L115	53b3b7bL	(I)	MY TOCHER'S THE JEWEL
5L115	553b7bL	(I)	LORD ELCHO
5L115	7b3b3b7bL	(I)	HIGHWAY TO EDINBURGH
5L117b	415L4L	(II)	WA(U)KING O' THE FAULD, THE
5L117b	415L4L	(II)	WAKING OF THE FAULD, THE
5L111H	526L5L	(I)	WAWKING OF THE FAULDS, THE
5L111H	5222	(II)	MAJOR GRAHAM
5L111H	5222	(I)	MAJOR GRAHAM (OF INCHBRAKIE)
5L111H	6416L	(I)	LADY MUIR McKENZIE'S FAVORITE
5L111H	6422	(I)	MAJOR GRAHAM'S STRATHSPEY
5L121L	2175	(II)	VALLEY OF SILENCE, THE
5L125L	5L251	(I)	CHAPTER OF KING'S, THE
5L125L	2465	(I)	OPERA POLKA, THE
5L125L	3b227bL	(I)	SEAN TRUIDH'S UILLACHAN
			[SEANN TRIUBHAIS UILLEACHAIN]
5L125L	3b247bL	(II)	GIN YE KISS MY WIFE, I'LL TELL THE MINISTER
5L126L	5L16L2L	(II)	LORD McDUFF'S STRATHSPEY
5L126L	5L122	(II)	MISS DALLAS
5L126L	5L122	(I)	MISS DALLAS('S REEL)
5L126L	5L143	(I)	NESS SIDE
5L126L	5L151H	(II)	MARQUIS OF HUNTLY'S SNUFF MULL
5L126L	5L151H	(I)	HO CHA N'EIL MULAD OIRNN'
5L126L	5L151H	(I)	MARQUIS OF HUNTLY'S SNUFF MILL, THE
5L126L	5L161H	(I)	MISS BRODIE OF BRODIE'S REEL
5L126L	5L57L2	(II)	J. SCOTT SKINNER'S COMPLIMENTS
			TO MR. PETER DAVIDSON
5L126L	4453	(II)	LADY ANN HOPE
5L127bL	5L121H	(II)	COILANTOGLE [COILLE AN TOGAIL OR
			CHEAP MUTTON]
5L127bL	5L121H	(I)	CHEAP MUTTON
5L127bL	5L143b	(I)	CROOKED HORN
5L127bL	7bL7bL7bL5L	(I)	JACKSON'S COG IN THE MORNING
5L127bL	3b27bL5L	(I)	SALLY MCGIE
5L127bL	5127b	(I)	HUMOURS OF LISTIVAIN, THE
5L12	7bL7b4H	(I)	MRS CHARLES MENTEATH OF CLOSE-BURN'S JIG
5L121	4L6L2L2	(I)	DUCHESS OF ARGYLE, THE

12

5L121	5L16L5L	(I)	PERTHSHIRE DANCING MEASURES & C No. 11
5L121	5L121	(I)	PRINCESS AMELIA'S FANCY
5L121	5L121	(I)	MAZURKA
5L121	5L154	(I)	N' TROOPA GHAELACH ['N TRUPA GHAIDHEALACHD]
5L121	5L333	(I)	MURT GHLINN-COMHAIN [MORT GHLINNE COMHAINN]
5L121	6L27L5L	(II)	DEVERONSIDE
5L121	7bL7bL23b	(I)	CAMERON HOUSE, A STRATHSPEY
5L121	7bL7bL47bL	(I)	MRS FERGUSON OF REATH('S STRATHSPEY)
5L121	7b47bLO	(I)	BANKS OF NORTH ESK
5L121	1321	(I)	DUKE OF ARGYLE('S STRATHSPEY)
5L121	217bL1	(II)	MAIRI BHAN OG
5L121	2175	(II)	VALLEY OF SILENCE, THE
5L121	447bL7bL	(I)	MR(S) SHEARER (OF BUCHROMB'S) STR.
5L121	4427bL	(I)	MR CHAs GRAHAM'S WELCOME HOME
5L121	4427bL	(I)	MR CHAS GRAHAM'S WELCOME HOME
5L121	4527L	(II)	I DAURNA SAY NO
5L121	4552	(II)	DUKE OF FIFE'S WELCOME TO DEESIDE, THE
5L121	5326L	(I)	QUICK STEP
5L121	51H62	(I)	DUCHESS OF YORK'S WELCOME TO LONDON
5L122	5L111	(I)	PUT THE GOWN UPON THE BISHOP
5L122	5L111	(I)	BONNY LASS WILL YOU LYE IN A BARRACK
5L122	5L123	(I)	MORMOND
5L122	5L126	(I)	MRS CARMICHAEL OF SKIRLING'S STRATHSPEY
5L122	5L144	(II)	MULL RANT, THE
5L122	5L144	(I)	WILL YOU GO TO SHERIFF MOOR
5L122	5L152	(I)	LADY ELIZABETH STANLEY'S JIG
5L122	5L326L	(II)	WELCOME BACK
5L122	7bL5L7bL4L	(I)	DUGI CAMPBELL ESQr. OF BALLINABY'S JIG
5L122	16L5L2L	(II)	WELCOME WHISKY BACK AGAIN
5L122	16L17L	(I)	DUKE OF YORK'S COTILLION
5L122	1522	(II)	SPRIG OF SHILLELAH, THE
5L122	1522	(I)	SPRIG OF SHILLELAH, THE
5L122	151H5	(I)	DUCHESS OF GORDON'S REEL
5L122	3125L	(I)	SANDFORD LODGE
5L122	3231	(I)	BLACK MARY
5L122	3222	(I)	BLACK JOCK
5L122	3322	(I)	BLACK JOCK
5L122	326L2	(I)	ROB ROY'S RANT
5L122	47b47bL	(I)	YOUTH THAT I LOVE, THE
5L122	5451	(I)	BONNIE DUNDEE
5L122	5522	(II)	BONNY LASS O' ROTHIEMAY, THE
5L122	5551H	(I)	MISS FARQUHARSON OF INVERCAULD'S STR.
5L122	51H2H6	(II)	DR. MANSON
5L12	3b3b2	(II)	WOUNDED HUSSAR, THE
5L12	3b3b2	(I)	CAPTAIN O' KAIN(E)
5L12	3b3b2	(I)	ALLOA HOUSE
5L123	5L6L6L5L	(I)	MORDELIA
5L123	5L133	(I)	MORGIANA IN IRELAND
5L12	310	(I)	ROSA WALTZ, THE
5L123	1461H	(II)	GATHERIN' O' THE GUNNS, THE
5L12	332	(I)	WHERE HELEN LIES
5L123	6526L	(II)	RONALD'S WELCOME
5L125	36L5L5L	(II)	SKYE BOAT SONG
5L125	43b17L	(II)	TWIST YE TWINE YE EVEN SO
5L126	5236L	(I)	NIEL GOW'S LAMENT
			FOR THE DEATH OF HIS 2d. WIFE
5L127b	47b47bL	(I)	(NEIL) NIEL GOW'S LAMENTATION
			FOR THE DEATH OF HIS BROTHER (DONALD)
5L121H	5562	(I)	MRS HAMILTON OF SUNDRUM
5L13b4L	5L3b22	(I)	MAID THAT TENDS THE GOATS, THE
5L13b4L	5L3b22	(I)	NIGHEAN DONN NAN GABHAR
5L13b1	4L7bL27bL	(II)	CARRON
5L13b1	4L7bL22	(I)	DUTCHESS OF DEVONSHIRE'S REEL
5L13b1	4L7bL23b	(I)	BRAES OF BUSHBIE, (THE)
5L13b1	4L242	(II)	MISS MURRAY OF ABERCARNEY [ABERCAIRNEY]
5L13b1	4L242	(I)	MISS MURRAY OF ABERCARNEY('S REEL)
5L13b1	5L14L7bL	(I)	MRS McQUHAE'S STRATHSPEY
5L13b1	5L124	(II)	PAY AS YOU GO
5L13b1	5L124	(I)	MRS SHEARER OF BUCHROMB
5L13b1	5L13b1	(II)	QUEEN'S LANDING, THE
5L13b1	5L13b1	(II)	MR WEBSTER
5L13b1	5L13b1	(II)	CAPTAIN GEORGE HUNTER
5L13b1	7bL7bL43b	(I)	GENERAL ELLIOT
5L13b1	7bl27bL4L	(I)	LOVE IN A VILLAGE
5L13b1	27bL47bL	(II)	WEE CUP OF TEA, A
5L13b1	2427bL	(II)	McLARIN'S REEL
5L13b1	2454	(II)	CRAIG COYNACH
5L13b1	247b2	(II)	EARL OF SEAFIELD'S REEL, THE
5L13b1	247b2	(II)	BLAIR ATHOLE
5L13b1	3b7bL3b7bL	(I)	AN SEANN STAOILEADH [AN SEANN STOILE]
5L13b1	3b6b24	(I)	MARY'S LAMENT
5L13b1	415L6bL	(I)	CLUB, THE

5L13b1	417bL2	(I)	YE'RE WELCOME CHARMING CHARLIE
5L13b1	427b2	(II)	DESKRYSHIEL
5L13b1	53b53b	(I)	BRAES OF BRAEDALBANE
5L13b1	5417bL	(I)	DUNCAN McQUEEN
5L13b1	543b7bL	(I)	DUNCAN MACQUEEN('S STRATHSPEY)
5L13b1	7513b	(II)	MR JOHN BROWN
5L13b2	4L7bL21	(II)	SIC' A WIFE AS I HAE GOTTEN
5L13b2	4L7bL21	(II)	LADS OF LEITH
5L13b2	4L7bL23b	(II)	CAPT[AIN] CAMPBELL
5L13b2	4L7bL23b	(II)	CAPT. CAMPBELL
5L13b2	5L13b5	(I)	MISS LINDSAY'S STRATHSPEY
5L13b2	7bL7bL43b	(I)	McGILPIN'S STRATHSPEY
5L13b2	7bL27bL2	(I)	OVER THE WATER
5L13b2	7bL43b5	(I)	ABERDEEN RACES, THE
5L13b2	24L2L7bF	(II)	PUT ON THE STEAM
5L13b2	27bL27bL	(II)	SIDH-CHAILLIONN [SHICHALLION]
5L13b2	2247bL	(II)	COIRECHOILLE
5L13b2	427bL2	(II)	STONEBYRES
5L13b3b	7bL247bL	(II)	MISS FORSYTH HUNTLY
5L13b3b	7bL247bL	(I)	MISS FORSYTH'S REEL
5L13b3b	123b2	(I)	CATHARINE OGGIE
5L13b3b	27bL7bL7bL	(I)	JOHN ANDERSON, MY JO, JOHN
5L13b3b	217bL5L	(I)	WHISKY, THE
5L13b3b	427bL1	(I)	KING'S WELCOME TO SCOTLAND, THE
5L13b3b	427bL2	(II)	MARRY ME NOW
5L13b3b	427bL2	(II)	RED PLAID, THE
5L13b3b	427bL2	(II)	I WISH YOU WOULD MARRY ME NOW
5L13b3b	427bL2	(I)	MISS McDONALD St. MARTINS STRATHSPEY
5L13b3b	427bL2	(I)	TENTH OF JUNE, THE
5L13b3b	427bL2	(I)	I WISH YOU WOULD MARRY ME NOW
5L13b3b	427b2	(II)	MCINROY OF LUDE
5L13b3b	427b2	(II)	MRS MACINROY OF LUDE
5L13b3b	4422	(II)	HOUSE OF EDINGLASSIE, THE
5L13b3b	553b1	(I)	MISS PLASKETT'S REEL
5L13b4	2422	(I)	LADY CAMPBELL ARDKINLASS'S STRATHSPEY
5L13b4	2454	(II)	MISS JESSIE STEWART
5L13b4	2454	(II)	MR JOHN SHAW STEWART'S STRATHSPEY
5L13b4	2454	(I)	MISS HAY'S REEL
5L13b4	2454	(I)	(MR JOHN) SHAW STEWART('S STRATHSPEY) [SIR JOHN SHAW STEWART'S]
5L13b4	2454	(I)	MISS JESS(Y) STEWART'S REEL [MISS JESSIE STEWART]
5L13b4	47b47bL	(I)	MRS CRAWFURD OF DONSIDES REEL [MRS CRAWFORD OF DONSIDE]
5L13b4	47b47bL	(I)	BONNY LASS OF LUSS, THE
5L13b4	47b47bL	(II)	MRS CRAWFORD OF DONSIDE
5L13b4	5522	(I)	MODERATE
5L13b5	4L7bL27bL	(I)	MISS DOROTHEA S. CHEYNE OF EDINr
5L13b5	5L7bL24	(I)	COL. FARQUHARSON'S STRATHSPEY
5L13b5	7bL7bL7bL7bL	(I)	BRUACHAN LOCH NEISH [BRUACHAN LOCH NIS]
5L13b5	7bL7bL7bL2	(I)	MRS CAMPBELL OF ORMIDALE'S STRATHSPEY
5L13b5	7bL7b2H3bH	(I)	MISS DALRYMPLE OF FORDEL'S STRATHSPEY
5L13b5	27bL7bL4	(I)	CAPT DOUGLAS'S STRATHSPEY
5L13b5	27bL27bL	(I)	MISS HAIG OF DOLLARFIELD'S STRATHSPEY
5L13b5	247bL7bL	(II)	MISS GRACE STEWART
5L13b5	247bL7bL	(I)	MISS GRACE STEWART('S STRATHSPEY)
5L13b5	247bL2	(II)	MISS ANN STEWART [MISS ANN STEWART, EAST CRAIGS]
5L13b5	247bL2	(I)	MISS (ANN) STEWART, EAST CRAIGS REEL
5L13b5	247bL4	(I)	MISS GRACE ABERCROMBY OF BIRKENBOG'S STRATHSPEY
5L13b5	2427bL	(II)	PRINCE CONSORT'S REEL, THE
5L13b5	2427bL	(I)	DEE WATER
5L13b5	2422	(II)	MISS GRAY OF CARSE
5L13b5	2422	(II)	BALMORAL BRIDGE
5L13b5	2424	(I)	MISS CLEMENTINA STEWART'S STRATHSPEY
5L13b5	2425	(I)	MISS MARY DUFF OF HATHORN'S JIG
5L13b5	2454	(I)	MARGATE CLIFFS
5L13b5	2454	(I)	MISS JESSY STEWART'S STRATHSPEY
5L13b5	247b4	(II)	LOTHIAN LASSES
5L13b5	247b4	(II)	MR ALEXANDER TROUP'S STRATHSPEY
5L13b5	247b4	(I)	LOTHIAN LASSES
5L13b5	247b4	(I)	LORD MAUCHLINE'S REEL
5L13b5	247b4	(I)	MR ROBINSON'S JIG
5L13b5	247b4	(I)	LADY LOUGHBOROUGH'S REEL
5L13b5	2527bL	(I)	MISS BARBARA STEWART
5L13b5	3b127bL	(II)	LOCH MAREE
5L13b5	4243b	(II)	DUNCAN'S RANT
5L13b5	5427bL	(I)	MISS LAURENSON OF INVEREIGHTY'S STRATHSPEY
5L13b5	7b427bL	(II)	LOCHAN A' CHAIT
5L13b5	7b427bL	(II)	DALWHINNIE
5L13b5	7b427bL	(II)	GEORGE GORDON ESQr.'s STRATHSPEY

```
5L13b5    7b427bL     (II) GORDON STEWART FORBES' (H.E.I.C.S.) JIG
5L13b5    7b422       (II) ABERDEEN HUNT
5L13b5    7b422       (I)  MISS MARY OGSTON'S STRATHSPEY
5L13b5    7b422       (I)  ABERDEEN HUNT
5L13b5    7b2H7b7bL   (I)  MISS C. McDUFFIE'S STRATHSPEY
5L13b5    3bH2H23b    (II) HAUGHS OF DELBAGIE, THE
5L131     5L5L3L1L    (II) CATHKIN BRAES
5L131     5L132       (II) BOGNIEBRAE
5L131     5L133       (II) MISS DOUGLAS OF SPRINGWOOD PARK
5L131     5L153       (I)  DICK O' THE COW
5L131     5L242       (I)  ENGLAND'S GLORY
5L131     6L27L6L     (II) WEE WILLIE'S STRATHSPEY
5L131     6L27L6L     (I)  WEE WILLIE'S STRATHSPEY
5L131     6L242       (II) QUEENIE
5L131     6L243       (I)  MRS MONCRIEFF OF REEDIE'S DELIGHT
5L131     6L244       (II) AULD BIRK TREE, THE (BANCHORY)
5L13      17L2        (I)  MISS BAIRD OF SAUGHTONHALL'S HORNPIPE
5L131     2242        (I)  COUNTESS OF LOUDEN
5L131     3126L       (II) BURNIE O' AUCHRASK, THE
5L131     3342        (I)  ASSEMBLIES, THE
5L131     3555        (II) DUMBARTON CASTLE
5L131     47bL7bL4    (II) FERRINTOSH [FERINTOSH]
5L131     47L7bL4     (I)  AN TOISEACHD
5L131     47L7L4      (II) FERNTOSH WHISKY
5L131     4242        (I)  (NEW) HIGHLAND LADDIE, (THE)
5L131     436L6L      (II) CIRCUS, THE
5L131     4326L       (I)  MR J. AITKEN'S FAVOURITE
5L131     4327L       (II) BANKS OF BOGGIE, THE
5L131     5426L       (I)  HONble MISS PETRIE'S STRATHSPEY
5L131     5542        (I)  JULIANA
5L132     5L131       (I)  LADY LUCY LESSLIE MELVILLE'S WALTZ
5L132     5L135       (I)  MR McINTOSH'S STRATHSPEY
5L132     5L146       (I)  WAGER, THE
5L132     335L1       (I)  ARGYLL IS MY NAME
5L132     4242        (I)  SPANISH BARBER
5L132     5216L       (I)  HOUSE OF CRAIG, THE
5L132     3H1H32      (I)  TRAFALGAR
5L133     5L133       (I)  MISS JANE CAMPBELL'S STRATHSPEY
5L133     5L146L      (II) LEITH HALL
5L133     5L146L      (I)  LEITH-HALL
5L133     6L27L5L     (II) JOHNNIE'S HIGHLAND FLING
5L133     6L242       (I)  MISS MARY ANN WHITEFOORD'S STRATHSPEY
5L133     6L243       (I)  MISS FARQUHARSON OF INVERCAULD (STR.)
5L133     6L244       (II) LADY LOUISA GORDON
5L133     6L244       (I)  LADY LOUISA GORDON('S REEL)
5L133     6L244       (I)  MISS McLEOD (OF COLBECK)'S
                            (FAVORITE/STRATHSPEY)
5L133     6L244       (I)  MISS FARQUHARSON (OF INVERCAULD)'S STR.
5L133     6L244       (I)  LITTLE PEGGY'S LOVE
5L133     1326L       (II) MARY KITTY
5L133     2221        (I)  PUT THE GOWN UPON THE BISHOP
5L133     3322        (I)  CHRISTMAS DAY IN THE MORNING
5L133     3323        (II) IRISH GIRL, THE
5L133     3323        (I)  IRISH GIRL, (THE)
5L133     4336L       (I)  IRISH HAUTBOY, THE
5L133     4426L       (I)  MISS MARGRET STEUART
                            OF STEUART LODGE'S REEL
5L133     4437L       (I)  IRISH HOBOY
5L133     5133        (II) CHALLENGE BREAKDOWN
5L133     5222        (I)  MISS FORDYCE OF CULSH REEL
5L133     5233        (I)  MISS BALFOUR'S JIG
5L133     536L6L      (I)  DRUMLANRIG CASTLE
5L133     536L6L      (I)  SPARK'S RANT
5L133     5353        (II) JAMIE MACKINTOSH
5L133     546L6L      (I)  PRINCE OF WALES STRATHSPEY, THE
5L133     5522        (I)  MISS WILLY ALEXANDER
5L133     6562        (I)  MISS DICKINSON'S REEL
5L133     6632        (I)  SIR JOHN MAXWELL'S STRATHSPEY
5L133     6642        (II) MRS COL. GORDON OF PARK'S STRATHSPEY
5L133     6642        (I)  McBEAT
5L133     61H22       (II) MISS SUTHERLAND GUNN (ELGIN)
5L133     61H53       (II) MRS BRODIE SHERIFF OF BATTLEBLENT'S R.
5L134     7L5L26L     (I)  FLOWERS OF EDINBURGH, THE
5L134     3427L       (II) BRECHIN LASSES
5L134     3427L       (I)  BREECHAN LASSES [BRECHIN LASSES]
5L135     5L326L      (II) FISHERS' REEL O' BUCKIE, THE
5L135     5L322       (I)  MR JAMES JENKINS FAVORITE
5L135     6L5L62      (I)  BRAES OF ALDCLUNE, THE
5L135     6L246       (II) HONble SEYMOUR EGERTON'S REEL, THE
5L135     526L1       (I)  MR DUFF (OF FETTERESSO'S) STRATHSPEY
5L135     51H46L      (II) CAPTAIN ROBERTSON, LUDE[S]
5L135     51H46L      (I)  CAPTAIN ROBERTSON LUDES STRATHSPEY
```

5L135	6216L	(I)	I'LL TELL YOU WHAT
5L135	1H652	(I)	EDINBURGH JIGG
5L136	5136L	(I)	MISS GRAHAM'S DELIGHT
5L136	627L2	(II)	PITTENGARDENER'S RANT
5L136	2H2H1H6	(I)	MISS LESLIES FANCY
5L131H	5122	(I)	WIDOW'S LILT, THE
5L147L	5L145	(I)	SKENE'S QUICK STEP, THE
5L143	137L2	(II)	SKENE OF SKENE
5L143	137L2	(I)	SKENE OF SKENE('S STRATHSPEY)
5L144	35L31	(I)	LANGO LEE
5L144	35L31	(I)	BANKS OF THE DEE, THE
5L144	35L31	(I)	NEW LANGO LEE
5L144	5226L	(II)	MISS HOPKINS
5L144	5226L	(II)	CUIR SA CHISTE MHOIR MI or
			MISS CRUIKSHANK'S REEL
5L144	5226L	(I)	MISS CRUICKSHANK'S REEL
5L144	5226L	(I)	MISS HOPKINS(REEL)
5L151	2427L	(I)	MISS FRASER OF FRASERFIELD'S REEL
5L152	4L7bL42	(I)	MR DUNCAN OF GARMOUTH'S STRATHSPEY
5L152	3331	(II)	WEE PICKLE TOW, THE
5L153b	4L7bL42	(I)	MASTER McDONALD St MARTIN'S STRATHSPEY
5L153b	53b42	(II)	GEORGE REID ESQ.
5L153	5L153	(II)	JOHNNY PRINGLE [JOHNNIE PRINGLE]
5L153	5L153	(I)	MISS BURNET'S REEL
5L153	5L153	(I)	JOHNNY PRINGLE
5L153	5L153	(I)	TOMMY PRINGLE
5L153	6L31H6	(II)	CALUM A GHLINNE
5L153	6L41H6	(I)	CALUM A GHLINNE
5L153	2427L	(II)	LADY MARY MURRAY
5L153	2427L	(I)	LADY MARY MURRAY'S STRATHSPEY
5L153	3226L	(II)	ANNIE O' FIDDOCHSIDE
5L153	447L2	(I)	ARNDILLY HOUSE
5L153	5555	(I)	LA FINALE
5L153	61H65	(I)	MR WILLIAM FERGUSON'S REEL
5L155	2L242	(I)	MISS RUTHERFOORD'S JIGG
5L155	5L132	(I)	RUTHVEN'S RANT
5L155	5L1H3H6	(I)	SHAKE YOURSELF
5L155	6L242	(I)	HONle MRS DRUMMOND OF PERTH'S FAVORITE, THE
5L155	236L6L	(I)	SIR ARCHIBALD CAMPBELL'S FAVORITE
5L155	236L6L	(I)	ST. PATRICK'S DAY IN THE MORNING
5L155	47bL54	(I)	HUMOURS OF CULLEN, THE
5L155	4222	(I)	I STOOD UPON THE PIER OF LEITH
5L155	437L6L	(II)	COLONEL JACKSON
5L155	51H22	(II)	DUNCAN BAIN'S BARGAIN
5L23L2L	5L23L1L	(I)	LADY DOWNE'S FANCY
5L27L	5L21	(I)	PAS SEUL MISS SOPHIA GRANT
5L215L	1433	(I)	FOR OUR LANG BIDING HERE
5L21	5L24	(II)	I HAE A LASS O' MY AIN OR MRS GRANT
5L21	5L24	(II)	MRS GRANT or [I HAE A LASS O' MY AIN]
5L223	16L16L	(I)	MY DAD WAS AN IRISH BLADE
5L236L	5L144	(I)	MISS CUMMINGS FANCY
5L247bL	5L251	(I)	MR CREECH'S STRATHSPEY
5L3b5L1	447bL7bL	(II)	TOWIE CASTLE
5L3b5L3b	247b3b	(I)	SUNDRUM HOUSE
5L3b7bL3bL	5L3b55	(I)	TIGHEARNA CHULODAIR [...CHUIL FHODAIR]
5L3b7bL5L	5L3b53b	(I)	MRS ROSE'S STRATHSPEY
5L3b17bL	4L424	(I)	RT HON LADY SALTOUN'S STRATHSPEY, THE
5L3b11	27bL4L7bL	(I)	RT HON LADY SALTOUN'S REEL, THE
5L3b11	3b13b5L	(II)	RINETTAN'S DAUGHTER
5L3b11	3b527L	(II)	MISS FARQUHARSON
5L3b11	427b2	(II)	HOUSE OF INVERERNAN, THE
5L3b11	53b42	(II)	CLANSMEN'S QUICK STEP, THE
5L3b13b	5L3b13b	(II)	MR JAMES TAYLOR
5L3b27bL	3b45L1	(I)	CAPTAIN OAKHAIN
5L3b27bL	3b55L1	(I)	WOUNDED HUSSAR
5L3b27bL	3b55L1	(I)	CAPTAIN O KAIN
5L3b3b1H	7b422	(II)	DAWTED MARY
5L3b3b1H	7b422	(I)	MAIRI BHEADARACH
5L3b47bL	3b51H5	(I)	MISS CLAVERING'S FANCY
5L3b43b	5L3b47bL	(II)	MR GEORGE ANDERSON
5L3b53b	4L27bL2	(II)	LORD KELLY
5L3b53b	4L27bL2	(I)	LORD KELLY'S (REEL/STRATHSPEY)
5L3b53b	4L27bL3b	(II)	LORD KELLY
5L3b53b	4L27bL3b	(I)	LORD KELLY'S REEL
5L3b53b	4L242	(II)	UNION STREET BRIDGE
5L3b53b	4L242	(II)	MILL OF NEWE
5L3b53b	4L242	(I)	LADY SUSAN GORDON'S STRATHSPEY
5L3b53b	5L3b53b	(II)	COL. FARQUHARSON OF INVERCAULD'S STR.
5L3b53b	7bL27bL3b	(I)	LORD KELLY'S REEL
5L3b53b	7bL242	(I)	MR GARDEN (OF TROUP'S) STRATHSPEY
5L3b53b	7bL47bL1	(II)	LORD KELLY
5L3b53b	7bL7b7bL3b	(I)	(LORD/EARL) OF KELLY'S REEL, (THE)

```
5L3b53b      027bL2      (I)   LORD KELLY'S REEL
5L3b53b      24L2L2L     (II)  MARCHIONESS OF TOWNSHEND'S STRATHSPEY
5L3b53b      227bL2      (I)   LORD KELLY'S REEL
5L3b53b      247b2       (II)  DUPPLIN CASTLE
5L3b53b      4542        (I)   MISS HENRIETTA DUFF'S FAVORITE
5L3b51H      7b427bL     (II)  JOHN MARSHALL
5L3b1H3bH    7b7b47bL    (II)  MISS GORDON OF GIGHT
5L3b1H3bH    7b7b47bL    (I)   MISS GORDON OF GIGHT('S REEL)
5L35L3L      5L322L      (II)  LORD EGLINTOUNE
5L35L3L      5L322L      (II)  EARL OF EGLINTON, THE
5L35L3L      5L322L      (I)   LORD EGLINTON'S REEL
5L35L2       331H3       (I)   MISS GARDEN OF TROUP'S REEL
5L35L3       436L6L      (II)  MRS MURRAY OF ABERCA(I)RN(E)Y
5L35L3       436L6L      (I)   MRS MURRAY OF ABERCARNY
5L35L4       5L37L7L     (II)  LADY MADALINA GORDON
5L35L4       5L37L7L     (I)   LADY MADELINA GORDON'S REEL
5L35L4       5L37L7L     (I)   CAPT McDONALD'S FANCY
5L36L5L      4L3L5L3L    (I)   REEL OF TYRIE, THE
5L36L5L      4L5L22L     (I)   MISS MARTINE'S REEL
5L36L5L      247L2       (I)   MR McLAE'S FAREWELL
5L36L5L      247L2       (I)   MRS McLEA'S FAREWELL
5L36L6L      5L552       (II)  MRS JAMIESON'S FAVOURITE
5L36L1       5L321       (I)   (HOW SWEET THIS) LONE VALE, (THE)
5L36L2       5L36L1      (I)   COL. BOYLE OF SHEWALTON
5L37bL2      1115        (I)   MISS HACKHARTS STRATHSPEY
5L37L6L      6L332       (II)  FAREWEEL TO WHISKY, O
5L37L2       5L365       (II)  HOWARD'S
5L37L2       221H5       (I)   MRS MENZIES OF COUFARES REEL
5L315L       1L322L      (II)  LORD REDHAVEN'S REEL
5L315L       6L426L      (II)  CALTON HILL
5L31         5L21        (I)   MAD OR POOR BOY, THE
5L31         6L42        (II)  MUCH ADMIRED WALTZ, A
5L311        51H2H2H     (I)   PASS OF GLEN TILT, THE
5L314        4512        (I)   BARBARA, THE
5L315        5225        (I)   DUKE OF BUCCLEUGH'S MARCH, THE
5L326L       5L321       (I)   DEAR LAMB, THE
5L326L       5L353       (II)  DUCHESS OF ATHOLE
5L326L       5L353       (I)   MISS MARY GILESPIE'S STRATHSPEY
5L326L       5L353       (I)   DUTCHESS OF ATHOLL ('S STRATHSPEY), (THE)
5L326L       5L526L      (I)   MISS CAMPBELL'S STRATHSPEY
5L327L       5L321       (I)   MAD (OR POOR) BOY, THE
5L321        5L37L2      (II)  MR J. ROSE
5L321        5L37L2      (I)   MR I. ROSE'S STRATHSPEY [MR J ROSE]
5L321        6L5L6L2L    (I)   MISS GARDEN OF TROUPS FAVORITE
5L321        6L244       (II)  ELLON CASTLE
5L322        5L326L      (I)   LADY MUNRO'S REEL
5L323        5L316L      (II)  GARRY HILLS
5L321H       5236L       (II)  AMERICAN, THE
5L331        447L2       (II)  PERTHSHIRE VOLUNTEERS
5L331        447L2       (I)   PERTHSHIRE VOLUNTEERS (STRATHSPEY)
5L33         26L1        (I)   O WHAT WILL I DO
5L333        5L344       (I)   EARL OF BUCHAN'S STRATHSPEY, THE
5L33         552         (I)   MISS WEMYSS OF WEMYSS FAVORITE
5L346L       7L262       (II)  RENATTON'S FANCY
5L347L       5L342       (I)   GENERAL SIR HECTOR MUNRO'S REEL
5L342        5L353       (I)   READY PENNY, THE
5L342        7L244       (II)  GRAHAM'S RANT
5L343        5L321       (II)  NEGRO BREAKDOWN
5L343        5L347L      (I)   MR GEORGE ANDERSON'S STRATHSPEY
5L343        5L47L2      (I)   MR JAMES RAMSY'S STRATHSPEY
                                 [MR JAMES RAMSAY]
5L343        2347bL      (II)  LEES OF LUNCARTIE, THE
                                 [LEES OF LUNCARTY, THE]
5L343        2347bL      (I)   WHEN YOU GO TO THE HILL TAKE YOUR GUN
5L343        2347bL      (I)   LEES OF LUNCARTIE, THE
5L343        2347bL      (I)   LADY BAIRD'S DELIGHT
5L343        2427L       (I)   BRIDGE OF LYON, THE
5L343        2427L       (I)   LEES OF LUNCARTIES STRATHSPEY, THE
5L343        4322L       (I)   MRS JAMES McINNES' STRATHSPEY
5L343        3H5H52      (II)  DONALD DINNIE
5L344        537L7L      (I)   VICTORY, THE
5L345        5125L       (II)  MISS FLORA MACDONALD
5L352        3331        (I)   ROCK AND A WEE PICKL(E) TOW, (THE)
5L353        5L252       (II)  HEATHERY BREEZE, THE
5L353        5L36L2      (II)  DUCHESS OF ATHOLE('S SLIPPER, THE)
                                 [DUCHESS'(S) SLIPPER, THE]
5L353        5L36L2      (II)  DUTCHESS OF ATHOLE'S SLIPPER, THE
5L353        5L36L2      (I)   CROSS OF BOWMORE, THE
5L353        5L36L2      (I)   DUTCHESS (OF ATHOLE)'S SLIPPER, (THE)
5L353        5L326L      (I)   TRIP TO EDINBURGH
5L353        5L322       (II)  MISS MACDONALD CLACHANTURN'S STRATHSPEY
5L353        5L332       (I)   ARTHUR SEAT
```

5L353	5L362	(II)	MISS FORBES OF PITSLIGO
5L353	5L362	(I)	COLONEL McLEOD'S STRATHSPEY
5L353	5L362	(I)	MISS FORBES OF PITSLIGO'S STRATHSPEY
5L353	5L426L	(I)	MISS CAMPBELL OF SMIDDY GREEN'S STR.
5L353	5L526L	(I)	BORDER CHIEFTAINS, THE
5L353	6L464	(II)	MILLER'S RANT, THE
5L353	47L7L6L	(I)	LADY LOUDOUN'S REEL
5L353	4326L	(I)	MY HEARTY WANTON CARLIE
5L353	4322	(I)	HONble MISS COURTENAY'S REEL
5L353	4362	(I)	ONE CHOPPIN MAIR
5L353	4542	(I)	MRS MACKAY'S STRATHSPEY
5L353	5247L	(I)	HONble MISS RUTHVEN'S REEL
5L353	6522	(I)	MRS A. ROSE OF KILLRAVOCK'S STRATHSPEY
5L354	51H62	(I)	MR R. DOWNIES FANCY
5L351H	537L2	(II)	GAVIN J. HAMILTON'S STRATHSPEY
5L351H	537L2	(II)	HAMILTON'S
5L351H	547L2	(II)	BRIDGE OF BRECHIN, THE
5L351H	5642	(I)	MISS FOTHERINGHAM'S STRATHSPEY
5L351H	5642	(I)	MR DAVID DUN'S STRATHSPEY
5L351H	51H53	(I)	GREEN PARK PALLISADES, THE
5L351H	6427bL	(II)	THERE'S NAETHING LIKE THE TALISKER
5L351H	6562	(II)	MAR CASTLE
5L351H	6662	(II)	MAR CASTLE
5L365	437L5L	(I)	MR MACKENZIE MILLBANK'S REEL
5L31H3	5522	(I)	MR GEORGE GORDON'S STRATHSPEY
5L31H3	51H4H6	(I)	MRS COL: SINCLAIR OF FORSS'S STRATHSPEY
5L31H5	3142	(III)	HUGH DUNLOP
5L31H5	657L2	(I)	LADY MARY MONTGOMERY'S REEL
5L31H5	657L2	(I)	LADY BETTY COCHRAN'S REEL
5L31H1H	5556L	(I)	SIR WALTER SCOTT
5L31H3H	2H2H2H6	(I)	MISS REDDIES REEL
5L47L6L	5L47L2	(II)	CARRON WATER
5L457L	37L31	(I)	HONble MISS JESSIE A. RUTHVEN'S FAVOURITE
5L455	6L1H22	(I)	COMING THROUGH THE HEATHER
5L521	5L6L5L6L	(II)	LOCH LONG
5L53b1	22H27bL	(I)	MAID OF CRAIGMADHE, THE
5L53b1	3b53b7bL	(I)	NIAN NAN COARACH [NIGHEAN...]
5L531	6L642	(I)	MR McINTOSH'S REEL
5L547bL	3b515L	(I)	BOYNE WATER
5L552	3417L	(I)	LORD CATHCART('S WELCOME HOME)
5L557b	7bL27bL4L	(II)	MOURDUN HILL
5L565	1532	(II)	JEFFREY'S QUICKSTEP
6bL3b27bL	3b55L1	(I)	CAPTAIN OAKHAIN
6L3L1L3L	6L3L5L3L	(II)	SILLAR'S AWA', THE
6L3L6L3L	115L5L	(II)	JOHN OF BADENYON
6L4L5L1	3327L	(I)	MR GEORGE JENKIN'S SCOTISH MEASURE
6L5L6L5L	5L332	(I)	MISS E. BAILLIE'S STRATHSPEY
6L5L13	4526L	(II)	ROUALEYN'S PLAID
6L5L13	4526L	(II)	BOVAGLIE'S PLAID
6L5L4	351H	(I)	CREACH NA CIADAINN
6L6L5L1	4522	(II)	LADY HARRIET SUSAN KER
6L6L6L5L	1113	(I)	WALLI'S HUMOUR IN TAPPING THE ALE
6L15L1	327L2	(I)	NON MUNTON HUNT
6L16L5L	6L47L2	(I)	DUCHESS OF BUCCLEUCH'S WELCOME TO SCOTLAND, THE
6L11	111	(I)	COLD FROSTY MORNING, THE
6L11	111	(I)	CHAMI MA CHATTLE
6L111	226L5L	(I)	PEGGIE I MUST LOVE THEE
6L111	226L6L	(I)	PEGGY, I MUST LOVE THEE
6L111	426L6L	(I)	PEGGY I MUST LOVE THEE
6L11	337	(I)	OCH IS OCH MAR ATA MI
6L11	331H	(I)	OCH IS OCH MAR ATA MI
6L111H	5451	(I)	FIFE AND ALL ABOUT IT
6L111L	5551	(I)	FIFE AND ALL THE LANDS ABOUT IT
6L125L	6L123	(II)	AN NOCHD GUR FAOIN MO CHODAL DHOMH
6L122	5L6L17L	(II)	MILLER'S DAUGHTER, THE
6L122	5L6L11	(I)	MILLER'S DAUGHTER('S STRATHSPEY), THE
6L122	37L11	(I)	COUNTRY FARMER
6L122	3322	(I)	BLACK JOCK
6L12	335	(I)	ROCK AND A WI PICKLE TOW, A
6L12	331H	(I)	THRO' THE WOOD LADDIE
6L133	3321	(I)	SEA MEW, THE
6L15	7L27L	(I)	MALT MAN (COMES ON MONDAY), (THE)
6L155	4222	(I)	(I SATE UPON) THE PEER OF LEITH
6L165	4662	(I)	ELLECTION REEL, THE
6L236L	315L5L	(I)	SONG OF DEATH, THE
6L232	6L236L	(I)	HO CHA CHEILLIN NACH TU B'FHEARR LEAM
6L326L	6L331	(I)	HIGHLAND RANT, THE
6L333	3312	(II)	MAIRI MHIN MHEAL-SHUILEACH DHU [MARY GENTLE AND DARK EYED]
6L351	6L353	(I)	WERE NA MY HEART(S) LIGHT I WAD DIE
6L362	3331	(I)	ROCK AND A WEE PICKLE TOW, A

```
6L47L5L      1533        ( I ) BOLD ROBIN HOOD
6L522        315L5L      ( I ) DAN FHRAOICH
6L642        6L641       ( I ) TAYLOR'S MARCH, THE
6L66         511         ( I ) YOUNG LADY'S PANEGYRICK ON HER LOVER, A
7bL5L4L7bF   7bL5L7bL1L  ( II) ORCHILL HOUSE
7bL5L4L7bF   7bL5L7bL1L  ( I ) ORCHILL HOUSE
7bL5L4L7bL   153b5       ( II) CALUM BREUGACH [CALLUM BROUGACH]
7bL5L4L7bL   153b5       ( I ) COL. McDONALD'S STRATHSPEY
7bL5L4L7bL   153b5       ( I ) CALLAM BROUGACH [CALUM BREUGACH]
7bL5L4L7bL   1535        ( I ) COLONEL MACDONELL'S STRATHSPEY
7bL5L4L7bL   1535        ( I ) COLONEL MACDONALD'S STRATHSPEY
7bL5L4L7bL   3b212       ( I ) CALLAM BROGACH
7bL5L13b     5554        ( I ) GUR MULADACH A THA MI
7bL7bL5L     5L11        ( II) OISEAN AN DEIGH NA FEINNE
7bL7bL6L     6L5L1       ( I ) WHY DOES LADY LINLEY WEEP
7bL7bL1      3b10        ( I ) COL. GARDINER'S LAMENT
7bL111       1417bL      ( I ) B'FHEARRLEAMSA NA BREACAN
7bL3b11      3b3b15L     ( I ) LASS AMONGST THE ACTENOCH, THE
7bL3b3b      3b51        ( I ) LEAM IS AITHEARR AN T SUAIN
7L5L11       5L311       ( I ) LA MONACA
7L5L32       1353        ( I ) INVERNESSHIRE HUNT
7L7L6L5L     6L5L7L2     ( II) SWISS COTTAGE (BALLINDALLOCH)
7L12         523         ( I ) JACK OF THE GREEN
7L152        7bL13b1     ( I ) BARBARA NI' MHIC PHERSON
                               [BARBARA NIC A' PHEARSAIN]
7L222        1313        ( I ) WELSH JIG, THE
7L243        7L241       ( I ) DEAD AN' YE SHANT
7L257        5332        ( I ) BEWARE OF THE RIPPLES
0055         1H1H2H4H    ( I ) KING SHALL ENJOY, THE
005          1H72H       ( I ) SALLY IN OUR ALLEY
01H1H1H      2H2H3H3H    ( I ) OLIVER CROMWELL'S MARCH
03H1HO       4H2H75      ( I ) MISS HOPE
03H1H6       53H1H6      ( I ) HERE'S A HEALTH TO THEM THAT'S AWA'
11H2H1H      3H4H3H2H    ( II) BRIDGE OF LODI, THE
11L1L2L      3L4L5L7L    ( I ) CUMBERLAND RANT, THE
11L1L3L      5L6L11      ( I ) MR LAWRENCE AINSWORTH'S MARCH
11L1L5L      3L113       ( II) COLLEGE (HORNPIPE), (THE)
11L1L5L      3L113       ( I ) COLLEGE HORNPIPE, THE
11L2L2L      5L123       ( I ) MRS BIRCH'S REEL
11L3bL1L     27bF2L7bF   ( I ) MRS FRASER'S STRATHSPEY
11L3bL5L     4L27bL7bL   ( I ) MISS LYLE'S STRATHSPEY [MISS LYALL]
11L3bL5L     7bL27bL7bL  ( II) PANMURE HOUSE  [MISS LYAL(L)]
11L3bL5L     7bL27bL7bL  ( II) MISS LYALL
11L3bL5L     7bL27bL7bL  ( I ) PANMURE HOUSE [MISS LYALL]
11L3L5L      6L123       ( I ) EARL OF WIGTON'S LAMENT
11L3L5L      1135        ( II) DR. BAIRD
11L3L5L      1366        ( I ) BANQUO'S GHOST
11L3L1       47L43       ( I ) MR OFFICER'S STRATHSPEY
11L3L1       5647L       ( II) WILLIE DOW
11L5L1L      11L5L5L     ( II) HONEST DUNCAN
11L5L1L      11L5L5L     ( I ) MISS DOWNIE'S STRATHSPEY
11L5L1L      11L5L5L     ( I ) GARDEN SHIEL
11L5L1L      11L5L5L     ( I ) HONEST DUNCAN
11L5L3L      5L3L6L4L    ( II) LORD ARTHUR'S CAIRN
11L5L3L      13L21       ( II) COCK OF THE NORTH, THE
11L5L3L      13L21       ( I ) COILEACH AN TOABH TUADH
11L5L5L      237L2       ( I ) LADY CUNNINGHAM (OF LIVINGSTONE)
                               ('S STRATHSPEY)
11L5L5L      247L2       ( I ) LORD ELCHO'S STRATHSPEY
11L5L5L      247L2       ( I ) LADY ELPHISTON'S STRATHSPEY
11L5L5L      247L2       ( I ) LADY CUNNINGHAM'S STRATHSPEY
11L5L5L      5646L       ( II) MISS JENNY GUTHRIE
11L5L5L      5646L       ( I ) MISS JENNY GUTHRIE'S (STRATHSPEY)
11L5L1       6L6L22      ( I ) SAMSON DUNCAN'S COMPts TO CHAs DUFF
11L5L1       15L6L7L     ( I ) MISS E. MacLEOD'S REEL
11L5L1       22L7L5L     ( II) DORSINCILLY
11L17L       25L43       ( I ) SECOND BATTn SCOTCH BRIGADE, THE
11L1         112         ( I ) LADY MARGt STEWART'S MINUET
11L12        22L23       ( I ) LA DOUBLE INCONSTANCE
11L13b       27bL24      ( I ) BAUK, THE
11L13        11L2L2      ( II) DUCHESS OF ATHOLE'S FAVOURITE, THE
11L13        11L2L2      ( I ) DUCHESS OF ATHOL(L)'S
                               (DELIGHT/FAVORITE), THE
11L11H       1H542       ( I ) ROTHIEMAY
11L27F       3522        ( I ) UNDER THE ROSE
11L3b1       157bL4      ( I ) DUC D'ANGOULEME'S STRATHSPEY, LE
11L37L       4L665       ( II) NEWCASTLE, THE
12L12L       1114        ( I ) EIGHTY THIRD REGts MARCH, THE
13bL5L5L     17bL5L4L    ( I ) BRAES OF BALQUHIDDER, THE
13bL11       3b147bL     ( I ) TAKE CARE OF MY CAP
13bL13b      7bL27bL7bL  ( II) BRIDGE OF ALFORD, THE
13bL13b      227b2       ( II) LIEUT. COL. LUMSDEN
```

13bL13b	227b2	(I)	LIEUT: COL: LUMSDEN'S REEL
13bL13b	53b24	(II)	BRIG O' FEUGH, THE
13bL15	63b3b7bL	(I)	Jn. GOW'S COMPLIMENTS
			TO THE MINSTRELS OF SCOTLAND
13L1L3L	2L47L2	(I)	COLONEL CAMPBELL OF SHAWFIELD'S STRATHSPEY
13L1L3L	5L6L2L2	(I)	COUNTESS OF BUCHAN'S STRATHSPEY
13L1L3L	16L2L2	(I)	DUKE OF RICHMOND'S WELCOME
			TO GORDON CASTLE, THE
13L1L3L	16L2L2	(I)	MISS JEAN ROBERTSON'S STRATHSPEY
13L1L3L	136L2	(I)	MISS HUNTER BLAIR'S STRATHSPEY
13L1L5L	1322L	(I)	MISS ELIZA M. TOD'S HORNPIPE
13L1L5L	2215	(I)	TOW'RING TINTO
13L1L1	13L7F2L	(I)	CALTON HILL, THE
13L4L3L	47L42	(I)	MISS MARY ANN HUNTER OF BURNSIDE'S HORNPIPE
13L3L1	6L7L16L	(II)	FISHER'S RANT, THE or DRUMNAGARRY
13L3L1	6L7L16L	(II)	DRUMNAGARRY [cf: FISHER'S RANT]
13L3L1	13L7F2L	(I)	SHE STOOPS TO CONQUER
13L3L1	437L5L	(I)	TO MARRY OR NOT TO MARRY
13L4L2L	13L15	(I)	POTTER HILL HOUSE
13L4L3L	1L113	(I)	COLONEL SIR ROBERT H. DICK'S MARCH
13L4L3L	4L3L2L2	(II)	FAIRBAIRN'S(STRATHSPEY)
13L4L5L	13L4L2L	(II)	MISS WEMYSS OF DUNDEE
13L4L5L	13L4L2L	(I)	MISS WEMYSS OF DUNDEE('S REEL)
13L4L5L	157L2	(II)	LADY BETTY BOYLE
13L4L5L	157L2	(I)	LADY MADELINA SINCLAIR'S REEL
13L4L5L	157L2	(I)	LADY BETTY BOYLE('S REEL)
13L5L3L	2L47L2	(I)	WHAT A BLUNDER
13L5L3L	5L3L24L	(II)	MARCHIONESS SALUTE, THE
13L5L3L	5L3L24L	(I)	FAILTE NA BAN MHARC
13L5L3L	5L15L6L	(II)	MARCH TO THE RENDEZVOUS
13L5L5L	1532	(II)	DUMBARTON CASTLE
13L5L1	37L22L	(II)	WELCOME TO THE HIGHLANDS
13L5L1	37L22L	(II)	FAREWELL TO THE HIGHLANDS
13L5L6	13L53	(II)	DOCTOR, THE
13L6L2L	7L41H1H	(II)	ROBERT CARMACK
13L6L5L	4L3L2L2L	(II)	HON. CHAS. BRUCE, THE
13L6L5L	4L3L2L2L	(I)	HONble CHARLES BRUCE'S REEL, THE
13L6L5L	13L22	(II)	MILLER OF CASERNEY, THE
13L6L6L	1446L	(I)	MR E. MARJORIBANKS'S QUICKSTEP
13L6L7L	36L4L1	(II)	PETER GRAY
13L6L7L	357L2	(I)	MORPETH RANT, THE
13L6L1	2343	(I)	MRS CONDIE'S REEL
13L13L	2L27L6L	(I)	MRS HARDIE'S STRATHSPEY
13L13L	4L2L26L	(II)	ISLE OF SKYE(, THE)
13L13L	4L2L26L	(I)	ISLE OF SKY, (THE)
13L13L	6L47L2	(I)	MISS CHARLOTTE HALL'S STRATHSPEY
13L13L	16L2L2L	(I)	WILLIE'S AWA'
13L13L	16L2L2L	(I)	LORD SPENCER'S STRATHSPEY
13L13L	1233	(I)	COTILLION
13L13L	137L2	(I)	MR GORDON OF HALLHEAD'S STRATHSPEY
13L13L	1532	(II)	RIGHT OFF THE REEL
13L13L	2426L	(II)	COLONEL CRAWFURD'S REEL
13L15L	4L2L22	(I)	DONALD SIMON
13L13L	137L2	(II)	MR GORDON OF HALLHEAD
13L17L	25L21	(I)	MASTER THOs BUCHAN'S
13L10	2423	(I)	MISS STEPHENS DELIGHT
13L11	6L242	(I)	LADY KEITH'S STRATHSPEY
13L11	24L22	(II)	MR JAMES WATTIE'S STRATHSPEY
13L11	546L2	(I)	PITLOWER HARMITAGE
13L12	13L4L2L	(I)	LADY PENUEL GRANT'S STRATHSPEY
13L12	3333	(I)	(MASTER WILLIAM DUGUID'S) HORNPIPE
13L13	7L27L5L	(I)	MISS CLAVERING'S STRATHSPEY
13L13	13L26L	(I)	MISS DUNLOP'S REEL
13L13	1214	(I)	MR PIRIE OF WATERTON'S HORNPIPE
13L13	25L24	(I)	MISS MURRAY'S HORNPIPE
13L13	2426L	(II)	EARL OF DALKEITH(, THE)
13L13	2426L	(I)	EARL OF DALKEITH'S REEL
13L13	2426L	(I)	COLONEL CRAWFORD'S (STRATHSPEY/REEL)
13L13	427L5L	(I)	MRS SMITON'S STRATHSPEY
13L13	427L2	(II)	BOB MORRIS
13L13	436L2	(I)	MISS JEAN CAMPBELL ARDMORE'S REEL
13L13	4522	(I)	MRS ROSS'S REEL
13L13	4522	(I)	MRS COLONEL GORDON OF LEITCHIESTON'S REEL
13L13	527L2	(II)	GREENEND PARK
13L13	527L2	(II)	LADY SHAFTESBURY
13L13	527L2	(I)	GREENEND PARK
13L13	527L2	(I)	LADY SHAFTSBURY('S STRATHSPEY)
13L13	527L2	(I)	NORTH HUNT, THE
13L13	5216L	(I)	HEATHER BRAES
13L13	547L2	(I)	LADY SHAFTSBURY'S STRATHSPEY
13L15	7L432	(II)	GLORIES OF "THE STAR", THE
13L25L	47L13L	(I)	DANCED BY ALDRIDGE

13L25L	47L27L	(I)	MR ALDRIGES FAVORITE HORNPIPE
13L35L	447L2	(I)	BUCKINGHAM HOUSE
13L32	13L5L5L	(I)	BECKFORD'S ELECTION
13L51	25L7L4	(II)	HIGH LEVEL, THE
14L3L5L	6L7L17L	(II)	FISHERS RANT, THE
14L3L2	347L5L	(I)	SIR CHAs ROSS OF BALNAGOWAN'S HORNPIPE
15L1L5L	2L27L2	(I)	MRS LOUGHNAN'S STRATHSPEY
15L1L5L	4L27L5L	(II)	EMSLIE'S FIDDLE
15L1L5L	15L6L2L	(I)	LADY GRANTLEY'S STRATHSPEY
15L1L1	11H1H2	(II)	MRS SELLER'S FAVOURITE, DUNLEIGH HOUSE
15L1L4	27L2L1	(I)	MR ALEXr. THOM'S HORNPIPE
15L2L2	15L1L5L	(I)	ISLAY BACHELOR'S STRATHSPEY
15L2L2	15L5L3	(II)	MISS VEARIE HAY
15L2L2	15L5L3	(I)	MISS LLOYD'S FAVORITE REEL
15L2L2	15L5L3	(I)	MISS VEARIE HAY('S REEL)
15L3bL7bF	15L3bL5L	(II)	SCURRAN A WELLS
15L3bL1L	7bL4L2L2	(II)	CORGARFF CASTLE
15L3bL1L	7bL27bL4L	(I)	MRS Dr STEWART'S REEL
15L3bL1L	7b527L	(II)	LADY AUGUSTA GORDON LENNOX'S STRATHSPEY
15L3bL5L	15L11	(I)	MR ALEXr LESLIE'S STRATHSPEY
15L3L1L	2L27L6L	(I)	MISS OATS'S STRATHSPEY
15L3L1L	2L27L2	(II)	KITTLE CATTLE
15L3L1L	2L226L	(I)	MISS DEFFELL'S STRATHSPEY
15L3L1L	4L2L3L5L	(II)	MCINTOSH OF MCINTOSH
15L3L1L	4L2L3L5L	(II)	MACINTOSH OF MACINTOSH
15L3L1L	4L5L6L7L	(II)	CAIRNTOUL
15L3L1L	4L27L5L	(II)	RED ROB
15L3L1L	4L27L6L	(II)	MRS TULLOCH, EARNHILL [MRS TULLOCH'S REEL]
15L3L1L	4L242	(I)	DUTCHESS OF ARGYLE, THE
			[DUCHESS OF ARGYLL, THE]
15L3L1L	4L2L3L5L	(II)	BRIDGE OF INVER, THE
15L3L1L	15L13	(II)	GLENAVON FOREST
15L3L1L	1432	(I)	LADY CARMICHAEL
15L3L1L	1551	(II)	ROLLING SPEY, THE
15L3L1L	227L2	(II)	MR CHARLES GRAHAM
15L3L1L	227L2	(I)	MR CHARLES GRAHAM(S STRATHSPEY)
15L3L1L	427L5L	(II)	GARELOCH, THE
15L3L1L	427L2	(I)	MISS ISABELLA McKENZIE'S STRATHSPEY
15L3L1L	4522	(II)	GOLLOCHY'S FAREWELL
15L3L1L	4522	(II)	DOCTOR, THE [MISS JANE STEWART]
15L3L1L	4522	(I)	BALVENIE CASTLE
15L3L1L	4522	(I)	DOCTOR, THE
15L3L1L	4522	(I)	GOLLOCHY'S FAREWEL
15L3L1L	4562	(I)	MISS JEAN MILLERS REEL
15L3L2L	15L13	(II)	AMONG THE OCHILS
15L3L2L	4637L	(I)	DUKE OF GORDON'S FAVORITE, THE
15L3L3L	6L6L7L7L	(II)	MORPETH RANT
15L3L3L	6L6L7L7L	(I)	MORPETH RANT
15L3L4L	2L242	(II)	LADY MADELINA SINCLAIR
15L3L4L	2L242	(I)	LADY MADELINA SINCLAIR'S REEL
15L3L5L	2L4L6L4L	(I)	HONble MISS HAMILTON'S REEL, THE
15L3L5L	2L6L26L	(II)	ATHOLE'S BONNY LASSES
15L3L5L	2L27L2	(II)	SIR ROBERT PEEL
15L3L5L	2L27L2	(I)	MISS BRANDER'S REEL
15L3L5L	2L27L2	(I)	SIR ROBERT PEEL
15L3L5L	2L27L2	(I)	MRS. COL. CAMPBELL'S OF BALLOCHYLL REEL
15L3L5L	3L6L13	(II)	MISS HUTTON
15L3L5L	3L6L13	(I)	MISS HUTTON'S STRATHSPEY
15L3L	5L4L2L	(I)	MR W. THOM'S HORNPIPE
15L3L5L	4L3L2L6F	(II)	ARDCLACH
15L3L5L	4L3L2L2	(I)	MR JAMES MONTGOMERY'S JIG
15L3L5L	4L436L	(I)	MISS MACLACHLAN'S REEL
15L3L5L	5L2L7L2	(I)	MAJOR MACDONALD'S RANT
15L3L5L	6L2L7L2	(I)	MR ARCHd CAMPBELL ARDMORE'S REEL
15L3L5L	6L5L2L2	(I)	LORD NELSON
15L3L5L	6L5L4L2L	(II)	SIR JOHN STUART FORBES BARt. OF FETTERCAIRN
15L3L5L	6L5L4L2L	(I)	MR JAMES MONTGOMERY'S REEL
15L3L5L	6L6L6L2L	(II)	LADY FORBES OF NEWE'S REEL
15L3L5L	6L15L2	(I)	MRS MACKENZIE
15L3L5L	6L27L6L	(I)	MISS BARSTOW'S REEL
15L3L5L	6L47L2	(I)	MISS JESSY ROBERTSON'S REEL
15L3L5L	15L13	(II)	LOCH O' FORFAR, THE or BLAIR'S FAVOURITE
15L3L5L	15L13	(I)	LOCH OF FORFAR, THE
15L3L5L	15L33	(II)	LOCH OF FORFAR, THE
15L3L5L	16L4L2L	(II)	MRS WILSON
15L3L5L	16L4L2L	(I)	MRS WILSON('S REEL)
15L3L5L	1112	(I)	SEVENTY THIRD (REGt's) MARCH, THE
15L3L5L	136L2	(II)	MORAYSHIRE LASSIE, THE
15L3L5L	137L2	(II)	LADY MADELINA SINCLAIR'S BIRTHDAY
15L3L5L	137L2	(I)	MISS CALL'S REEL
15L3L5L	137L2	(I)	LADY MADELINA SINCLAIR'S BIRTH DAY
15L3L5L	137L2	(I)	LADY BURDIT'S REEL

```
15L3L5L      1522         (II)  MADGE [AIR:FAREWELL TO SCOTLAND]
15L3L5L      25L7L5L      (I)   MISS G. GORDON
15L3L5L      26L4L6L      (I)   MISS MARGARET OSWALD (OF SCOTSTOWN'S) REEL
15L3L5L      5122         (I)   MISS GEORGINA B. STEWART
15L3L1       127L5L       (I)   JOLLITY
15L3L1       1522         (I)   DRURY LANE HORNPIPE
15L3L1       2637L        (I)   MISS JANET McKERRELL'S REEL
15L3L1       567L2        (II)  TEN POUND FIDDLE, THE
15L3L1       6522         (II)  KATIE'S BIRTHDAY
15L3L3       4522         (I)   GLASGOW TONTINE
15L4L5L      7L431        (I)   MISS MACKENZIE OF AVOCH'S REEL
15L5L1L      2L226L       (I)   MISS HUME'S REEL
15L5L1L      2L226L       (I)   MISS SMYTH OF METHVEN'S REEL
15L5L1L      2426L        (I)   CAPTAIN BISSET'S STRATHSPEY
15L5L3L      2L4L6L4L     (II)  ATHOLE'S HONEST MEN
15L5L5L      3L4L5L5L     (I)   MR SMITON'S HORNPIPE
15L5L5L      5L5L5L3      (I)   MY DEARIE IF THOU DIE
15L5L5L      5L134        (I)   THA BHUAIDH AIG AN FHIODHDAIR
15L5L5L      6L6L21       (I)   MILL, MILL O, THE
15L5L5L      7L245        (I)   JIG
15L5L5L      15L2L2L      (I)   N'COMUN RIOGHAIL GAELACH
                                ['N COMUNN RIOGHAIL GAIDHEALACHD]
15L5L5L      15L2L7L      (II)  POLDUILLY BRIDGE
15L5L5L      15L6L2L      (I)   ABERDEEN RACES
15L5L5L      16L6L6L      (II)  SIR JAMES BAIRD
15L5L5L      16L6L6L      (I)   MISS McLAINE OF TARLOISK'S STRATHSPEY
15L5L5L      16L6L6L      (I)   SIR JAMES BAIRD'S (FAVORITE/STRATHSPEY)
15L5L5L      16L22L       (I)   MR DUN'S FAVOURITE
15L5L5L      1111         (I)   MY DEARIE AND THOU DIE
15L5L5L      1332         (I)   ROSE TREE, THE
15L5L5L      4332         (I)   ALLEGRETTO
15L5L5L      4332         (I)   TARRY A WHILE
15L5L6L      1113         (I)   LEE RIGG, THE
15L5L6L      314L6L       (II)  AN(N) GILLE DUBH CIAR DUBH
15L5L1       5L5L5L1      (I)   MY DEARIE AN YE DIE
15L5L1       5L5L5L1      (I)   MY DEARIE, IF THOU DIE
15L5L1       227L2        (II)  DR. WHYTE
15L5L        13b4         (I)   WHO'D HAVE THOUGHT IT
15L5L1       3356         (I)   COL. FERRIER OF THE SCOTS BRIGADE'S MARCH
15L5L1       4322         (I)   MISS FERGUSSON OF REITH'S STRATHSPEY
15L5L1       5226L        (II)  MISS WHITEFORD
15L5L1       5226L        (I)   MISS CALL'S REEL
15L5L1       5226L        (I)   MRS JOHNSTON OF WOODHILLS REEL
15L5L1       5226L        (I)   MRS WHITEFOORD'S REEL
15L5L2       15L11        (I)   PADDEEN O RAFARDIE
15L5L2       15L11        (I)   GIGG
15L5L2       15L11        (I)   PADDY O' RAFFERTY
15L5L3b      27bL7bL4     (I)   MR ANDREW THOMSONS REEL
15L5L3       15L2L2       (I)   MISS MACLEAN OF DUART'S REEL
15L5L3       15L6L2L      (II)  MISS DRUMMOND OF KELTIE
15L5L3       15L6L2L      (I)   MISS DRUMMOND OF KELTIE'S REEL
15L5L3       5422         (I)   WILLIAM GIBSON CRAIG, M.P.
15L5L3       5432         (I)   LEWIS RICARDO, M.P.
15L6L2L      16L11        (I)   EGLINTON CASTLE
15L6L3L      1552         (II)  FAREWELL! I MAUN CROSS THE SEAS
15L6L4L      5L5L5L3      (I)   EARL OF DALHOUSIE'S MARCH
15L6L5L      4L3L2L2      (II)  COUNTESS OF SUTHERLAND, (THE)
                                [LADY HAMILTON]
15L6L5L      4L3L2L2      (II)  LADY HAMILTON
15L6L5L      4L3L2L2      (I)   LADY HAMILTON'S REEL
15L6L5L      4L3L2L2      (I)   COUNTESS OF SUTHERLAND'S REEL, THE
15L6L5L      4L3L22L      (I)   GLASGOW LADIES (REEL)
15L6L5L      6L27L2       (I)   EARL OF ELGIN'S FAVOURITE
15L6L5L      1135         (I)   JOCKEY'S RETURN FROM DOVER
15L6L5L      1232         (II)  AULD INN, THE
15L6L5L      1322L        (I)   DUKE OF GORDON AND HIS VOLUNTEERS, THE
15L6L6L      1123         (I)   FIDLERS' CONTEMPT
15L6L6L      1123         (I)   FUADH NA MFILAIRAN
15L6L7L      1547L        (I)   MISS BURBRIDGE'S FANCY
15L6L0       7L5L10       (I)   RAITH HOUSE
15L6L1       5L6L4L2L     (I)   HORNPIPE, A
15L6L1       5L6L4L2L     (I)   LADY McNEIL
15L6L1       7L531        (I)   MR STEWART JUNR OF CARNOCK'S REEL
15L6L1       15L6L2       (I)   MISS HORN'S STRATHSPEY
15L6L1       15L6L2       (I)   COUNTESS OF MANSEFIELD'S STRATHSPEY, THE
15L6L        111          (I)   TWEED SIDE
15L6L        111          (I)   CALLUM A GHLINNE
15L6L        113          (I)   TWEED SIDE [MEDLEY OVERTURE (8)]
15L6L1       426L5L       (I)   BONNIEST LASS IN A' THE WORLD, THE
15L6L1       457L2        (I)   MISS BROWN'S JIG
15L6L1       4531H        (I)   MRS BLAIR OF BLAIR'S STRATHSPEY
15L6L2       15L2L6F      (I)   LADY BATH'S STRATHSPEY
```

22

```
15L6L2      15L17L       (I)   PADEEN O BASARDEE
15L6L       522          (I)   RINN M'EUDAIL MO MHEALLADH
15L7bL4L    3bL5L15L     (I)   CALLAM'S FROLLOCK
15L7bL2     15L11H       (I)   WE'RE A' KISS'D SLEEPING
15L7L6      15L6L6L      (II)  MISS ISABELLA CARLE
15L13L      1322         (I)   MISS BETTY McDONALD'S REEL
15L15L      2L5L42       (I)   GLASGOW BELLS
15L15L      3L122L       (II)  DAVIE TAYLOR
15L15L      6L211L       (I)   MARK IN THE DUMPS
15L15L      7L322L       (II)  BRUCE'S LETTER BOX, HUNTLY
15L15L      15L1L5L      (I)   CAISTAL DUNROBHAIN [CAISTEAL DHUNROBAINN]
15L15L      15L22        (II)  WALKING OF THE PLAIDING, THE
15L15L      15L22        (I)   WAUKING OF THE PLAIDEN, THE
15L15L      117bL7bL     (I)   UNTITLED (No.35)
15L15L      131H2        (I)   LADY LOUISA PAGET'S STRATHSPEY
15L15L      1525L        (I)   LES PIEDMONTESE [LES PIADMONTESE]
15L15L      11H52        (I)   BETSY HOWISON'S FAVORITE
15L15L      2427L        (II)  MISS DALRYMPLE
15L15L      2427L        (I)   DOUBLE JIG
15L15L      2427L        (I)   MISS DALRYMPLE'S JIG
15L15L      2427L        (I)   CARLETON HOUSE
15L15L      3b3b7bL7bL   (I)   JOHN O' BADENYON(D)
15L15L      3b417bL      (I)   JOHN OF BADENYON
15L15L      35L1L5L      (II)  DUNROBIN CASTLE
15L15L      427L2        (II)  JAMES McINNES, ESQ., DANDALEITH
15L16L      2L27L2       (I)   LORD MACDONALD'S STRATHSPEY
15L16L      2L47L2       (I)   LONDON HIGHLAND SOCIETY, THE
15L16L      4L5L2L2      (I)   MISS ELPHINSTONE'S STRATHSPEY
15L16L      27L15        (I)   MRS DUFF'S REEL
15L16L      27L36        (I)   MISS GRACE HAY'S REEL
15L11       4L5L2L2L     (II)  MISS C. ELPHINSTONE
15L11       4L5L2L2L     (I)   MISS C. ELPHINSTONE('S STRATHSPEY)
15L1        15L1         (I)   JULIANA'S WALTZ
15L11       5L122        (I)   MISS SHAND'S STRATHSPEY
15L11       1226L        (II)  LEA RIG, THE
15L11       1226L        (II)  AN OIDHCHE A BHA BHANAIS ANN [LEA RIG, THE]
15L11       1226L        (I)   (MY) AIN KIND DEARIE
15L11       1227L        (I)   LEE RIGG, THE
15L11       2223         (I)   UNTITLED
15L11       2242         (I)   EARL OF DUNMORE'S REEL, THE
15L11       2326L        (I)   WEDDING, THE
15L11       2326L        (I)   MY AIN KIND DEARIE
15L11       3426L        (I)   LEE RIGG, THE
15L11       436L2        (I)   LADY SUSAN STEWART'S STRATHSPEY
15L11       4326L        (I)   MRS GILLESPIE'S REEL
15L11       4542         (I)   MISS OGILVY OF ISLABANK'S JIGG
15L11       5126L        (I)   SUCKIE BIDS ME
15L11       5326L        (I)   LORD BANFF
15L11       5352         (II)  LADY GEORGINA CAMPBELL
15L11       5352         (I)   MISS MARRION CAMPBELL ARDMORE'S REEL
15L11       5622         (I)   CAPTAIN FLETCHER'S FAVORITE
15L1        26L2         (I)   MISS SCOTT
15L12       15L6L1       (I)   GROVE, THE
15L12       1226L        (I)   MY AIN KIND DEARY
15L12       3125L        (I)   MISS MARY MURRAY'S JIG
15L1        3b3b2        (I)   ALLOA HOUSE
15L13b      5222         (I)   MRS RUTHERFORD'S JIG
15L13       2L242        (I)   SIR DAVID HUNTER BLAIR'S NEW REEL
15L13       15L11        (I)   PERTHSHIRE DANCING MEASURES & C No. 10
15L13       15L22L       (II)  KIRKMICHAEL PLOUGHS
15L13       15L22L       (I)   KIRKMICHAEL PLOUGHS
15L13       157L2        (I)   SWEET BELLS OF GLASGOW, THE
15L13       25L24        (I)   CAPT JAS ROBERTSON 76th REGt's REEL
15L13       26L24        (I)   MISS THOMSON OF LECKYBANK'S STRATHSPEY
15L13       2226L        (I)   MISS JENNY GORDON'S STRATHSPEY
15L13       2226L        (I)   MISS MACKENZIES REEL
15L13       2242         (I)   MISS CHARTERE'S REEL
15L13       246L6L       (I)   MISS WALKER'S STRATHSPEY
15L13       2426L        (I)   COLONEL CRAWFORD'S STRATHSPEY
15L13       436L6L       (II)  LORD SEAFORTH
15L13       436L6L       (II)  HIGHLAND PLAID, THE
15L13       436L6L       (I)   HIGHLAND PLAID, THE
15L13       436L6L       (I)   LORD SEAFORTH('S STRATHSPEY/REELL)
15L13       437L2        (II)  DUNROBIN CASTLE
15L13       437L2        (I)   MISS ROSE OF DRANIE'S REEL
15L13       437L2        (I)   MISS JEANY SANDEMAN'S REEL
15L13       4326L        (I)   MISS I. McLEOD'S REEL
15L13       4332         (I)   LORD MACDONALD'S FAVOURITE
15L13       447bL2       (I)   WATERMEN'S RANT, THE
15L13       4542         (I)   MR C. CAMPBELL'S REEL
15L13       5142         (I)   WEYMOUTH FETE
15L13       5326L        (I)   LORD BANFF'S STRATHSPEY
```

15L13	547L2	(I)	LADY SHAFT(E)SBURY
15L13	5426L	(I)	LORD BANFF'S (STRATHSPEY/REEL)
15L13	5426L	(I)	LADY CHARLOTTE LEVESON GOWER'S STRATHSPEY
15L13	5422	(I)	LORD BANFF'S STRATHSPEY
15L13	5531	(I)	WHILST I FONDLY VIEW YE CHARMER
15L13	5555	(I)	LOVE SICK JOCKY
15L13	51H62	(I)	COCK OF THE NORTH, THE
15L13	6426L	(I)	LORD BANFF'S STRATHSPEY
15L13	657L2	(I)	TWINKLING STAR, THE
15L13	6522	(II)	LARGO LAW
15L13	6522	(I)	MR CONNEL'S STRATHSPEY
15L13	6522	(I)	LARGO LAW
15L13	6523	(I)	DUMFRIES-SHIRE HUNT, THE
15L13	6562	(I)	HONble MISS GEORGINA ELPHINSTON'S STRATHSPEY
15L1	366	(I)	LASS OF HUMBER SIDE, THE
15L13	6622	(I)	LURG'S REELL
15L14	5432	(I)	MRS JOHN CLARK'S DELIGHT
15L15	426L5L	(I)	WHEN WILL YE WED ME WITH A RING
15L15	427L2	(II)	MRS GRANT OF GLEN GRANT
15L15	4327L	(II)	Wm. MACHARDY'S STRATHSPEY
15L15	6521	(I)	THEATER, THE
15L16	5126L	(II)	SUCKY BIDS ME
15L16	5126L	(I)	SUCKY BIDS ME
15L16	5162	(I)	MISS JEAN WATERSON'S FANCY
15L16	5226L	(I)	SUKEY BIDS ME
15L16	6326L	(I)	PAD(D)IE'S RESOURCE
15L16	6326L	(I)	LADY CARLISLE'S REEL
15L1	666	(I)	IRISH SHANTRUSE
15L11H	157L2	(I)	GIGG
15L11H	5322	(I)	MR WILLIAM KILMAN'S STRATHSPEY
15L25L	1231	(I)	Dr. JAMES HAMILTON'S QUICK STEP
15L25L	37L25L	(I)	GAVOTTA
15L25L	3332	(I)	ADESTE FIDELES
15L26L	15L6L1	(I)	MERRILY DANCE(D) THE QUAKER('S WIFE)
15L27L	16L2L4	(I)	LADY DUNBAR OF NORTHFIELD'S STRATHSPEY
15L27L	1H4#6L3	(II)	DR. SHAW
15L21	15L23	(I)	MONYFIETH RANGERS REEL
15L21	5216L	(I)	EDINBURGH THEATRE ROYAL
15L22	3637L	(I)	WOOBURN ABBEY
15L3b	7bL4L4	(I)	(THERE'S) THREE GOOD FELLOWS (DOWN IN YON GLEN)
15L3b1	2427bL	(II)	PRINCE ALFRED'S REEL
15L3b1	3b543b	(II)	BRITISH PRESS, THE
15L3b2	5L4L2L4L	(II)	MISS LYALL or MRS GRANT OF LAGGAN
15L3b2	5L4L2L4L	(I)	MISS LYLE'S REEL [MISS LYALL] [MRS GRANT OF LAGGAN]
15L3b2	5L5L2L4L	(I)	MISS STEWART'S REEL
15L3b2	27bL53b	(I)	MISS HAMILTON'S REEL, THE
15L3b2	27bL53b	(I)	MRS PARKER'S REEL
15L3b3b	2453b	(II)	ARTHUR'S SEAT
15L3b5	247b3b	(II)	NORTH OF THE TWEED
15L31L	247L2	(I)	NEW MAGGIE LAUDER
15L35L	4L5L4L4	(I)	MISS JESSY MILLERS REEL
15L35L	15L35L	(I)	RUSSIAN AIR
15L35L	3352	(I)	HIS GRACE THE DUKE OF ATHOLE'S MARCH
15L35L	346L1	(I)	MISS DIANA SINCLAIR'S STRATHSPEY
15L37L	6L5L3L5L	(II)	MR BERNARD('S REEL)
15L37L	6L5L3L5L	(I)	MR BERNARD'S REEL
15L37L	6L27L2	(II)	PAUL WALLACE
15L37L	361H3	(II)	ARCHIE MENZIES
15L31	357L2	(II)	DR. PROFEIT
15L31	46L7L5L	(I)	KING OF CORSICA, THE
15L31	4115L	(I)	MISS C. RAMSAY'S FANCY
15L31	5333	(I)	LORD ELCHO'S MARCH
15L31	531H1H	(II)	LONACH HIGHLANDERS MARCH, THE
15L31	6522	(II)	JOCKS RAP
15L32	16L5L3L	(I)	MR MATTHEW'S REEL
15L33	25L7L7L	(I)	QUICK STEP SOUTH FENCIBLES
15L33	5326L	(I)	WHISTLE O'ER THE LEAVE O'T
15L33	62H54	(I)	LORD DUNCAN
15L34	15L13	(I)	MARCH FOR THE CLANS, A
15L3	427L	(I)	PRINCE HOHENZOLLERN'S WALTZ
15L35	26L7L7L	(I)	MRS FARQUHAR'S REEL
15L35	1H522	(I)	GORDON OF LESSMOR'S STRATHSPEY
15L35	1H765	(II)	LITTLEJOHN'S HAME
15L31H	7532	(I)	MISS KATHARINE MILLER'S BIRTH DAY
15L41	15L41	(I)	CHRISTMAS EVE
15L42	15L6L1	(I)	QUAKER'S WIFE
15L43	15L6L1	(I)	MERRILIE DANC'D THE QUAKER'S WIFE
15L53	15L6L1	(I)	QUAKER'S WIFE, THE
15L55	4255	(II)	LASS I NEVER SAW, THE

15L5ö	5126L	(I)	SUCKY BIDS ME
15L1H6	4325L	(II)	ANGUS CAMPBELL
15L1H6	4327L	(II)	ANGUS CAMPBELL
16bL3b	3b13b	(I)	MY LOVE HAS FORSAKEN ME KEN YE FOR WHY
16L1L3	3342	(I)	STORMONT'S GHOST
16L3L1L	2L232	(I)	MISS BURNETT FASQUE'S STRATHSPEY
16L3L3L	137L2	(II)	MRS GRANT DUFF OF EDEN
16L3L5L	6L6L42	(I)	PRINCESS ROYAL, THE
16L3L5L	1522	(II)	LONACH GATHERING, THE
16L3L1	567L2	(II)	JAMES D. LAW'S REEL
16L5L3L	4L3L2L6F	(II)	LADDIE WI' THE BONNET BLUE, THE
16L5L3L	5L3L6L2L	(I)	MRS SKINNER OF DRUMINS' STRATHSPEY
16L5L3L	5L6L5L3L	(I)	MRS McCOMBIE OF TILLIFOUR'S STRATHSPEY
16L5L3L	5L37L4	(I)	HONble MRS MURRAY ELLIBANK'S STRATHSPEY
16L5L3L	16L22	(II)	FAIRLIE CASTLE
16L5L3L	547L2	(I)	W.F. CAMPBELL ESQr. OF ISLAY AND SHAWFIELD'S STRATHSPEY
16L5L4L	4L3L2L2	(I)	MEMORY OF JOYS THAT ARE PAST, THE
16L5L5L	1L1L22	(II)	MILLER OF DRONE, THE
16L5L5L	1L1L22	(I)	MILLER OF DRONE, THE
16L5L5.	1L1L23	(II)	MILLER O' DRONE, THE
16L5L5L	1L422	(II)	MILLER OF DRON(E), THE
16L5L5L	1L423	(I)	MILLER OF DRON(E)
16L5L5L	1L432	(II)	MILLER OF DRONE, THE
16L5L5L	2L422	(I)	MILLER OF DRONE, THE
16L5L5L	5L5L34	(I)	ANDROMEDA, THE
16L5L5L	5L36L6L	(I)	MRS MUIR MACKINZIES DELIGHT
16L5L5L	1532	(I)	MR DAVIDSON OF CANTRAY'S STRATHSPEY
16L5L6L	16L2L2	(I)	MISS OGILVY OF CLOVA'S FAVOURITE
16L5L1	7L213	(II)	DUKE OF BUCCLEUCH, THE
16L5L1	2326L	(II)	ARKANSAS TRAVELLER
16L5L1	3432	(I)	MISS MARY LEE'S DELIGHT
16L5L3	16L4L2L	(I)	MR BRANDER OF SPRINGFIELD'S STRATHSPEY
16L6L5L	4L5L2L2	(II)	FAREWELL TO HUNTLY
16L6L6L	3L5L5L3	(II)	ACROSS THE MEADOWS
16L6L	113	(I)	TWEED SIDE
16L6L1	5552	(I)	ANDANTE
16L6L3	1126L	(I)	FRANCIS GARDEN ESQr. JUNr's FAVORITE
16L7L5L	1753	(I)	MR Wm. CAMPBELL ARDMORE'S REEL
16L7L67L	5L123	(I)	BRAES OF BROTHERTOWN, THE
16L7L1	2432	(I)	WIT WITHOUT MONEY
16L1	5L5L3	(I)	UNTITLED
16L15L	16L13	(i)	MRS DUFF (OF FETTERESSO'S) BIRTHDAY
16L15L	16L32	(II)	LASSES' FASHION, THE
16L15L	16L44	(II)	WEAVER HAS A DOCHTER, THE
16L15L	1310	(I)	O HE DE NO'S [AR HYD Y NOS]
16L15L	1332	(I)	SUTTOR'S DAUGHTER, THE [SUTOR'S DOCHTER, THE]
16L15L	1332	(I)	NITHIAN A GHREISICH
16L15L	1332	(I)	WILT THOU BE MY DEARIE
16L15L	147L2	(I)	LADY SCOTT'S STRATHSPEY
16L15L	1432	(I)	WILT THOU BE MY DEARIE
16L15L	26L11	(I)	SPRING FOR ME REVIVES IN VAIN, THE
16L15L	26L11	(I)	SORAIDH SLAN DO'N AILLEAGAN
16L15L	2426L	(I)	MARQUIS OF HUNTLEY'S WELCOME TO THE CHAIR
16L15L	36L11	(I)	CEUD SORAIDH UAM D'ON AILLEAGAN
16L15L	3423	(II)	HO!RO! MO NIGHEAN DONN BHOIDHEACH
16L15L	436L6L	(I)	DUKE OF GORDON'S (FAVORITE/STRATHSPEY)
16L16L	27L5L7L	(II)	SANDERS BRANE
16L11	16L2L2L	(II)	MRS MENZIES OF CULDARES
16L11	16L2L2L	(I)	MRS MINZIES OF CULDARE'S STRATHSPEY
16L11	16L11	(I)	MISS GEORGINE SCOTT OF SEA BANK'S WALTZ
16L11	5632	(I)	MISS ADAMINA DUNCAN'S STRATHSPEY
16L13	16L22	(I)	MISS McDOUGAL'S STRATHSPEY
16L13	27L24	(I)	LADY ELINOR CAMPBELL'S REEL
16L25L	16L25L	(I)	MERRY WIVES OF WINDSOR, THE
16L27L	16L36	(I)	MISS GRANT OF GRANT'S FAVORITE
16L21	35L31	(I)	LAMENT OF FLORA McDONALD
16L23	3451H	(I)	TANK, THE
16L23	4326L	(I)	WHISTLE O'ER THE LAVE O'T
16L23	5326L	(I)	WHISTLE O'ER THE LAVE O'T
16L24	1636	(I)	I CANNOT WIN AT HER FOR HER BIG BELLY
16L33	5126L	(I)	WHISTLE O'ER THE LEAVE O'T
16L33	5326L	(II)	WHISTLE O'ER THE LAVE O'T
16L33	5326L	(I)	WHISTLE O'ER THE LAVE O'T
16L33	51H26L	(I)	WHISTLE O'ER THE LAVE O'T
17bL3bL7bL	17bL3bL5	(I)	BANKS OF THE DEVERON, THE
17bL6bL7bL	17bL3b5L	(I)	PERTHSHIRE DANCING MEASURES & C No. 7
17bL7bL	23b2	(I)	MODERATE
17bL1	3b3b3b	(I)	COIR A' CHEATHAICH
17bL3b4L	17bL3b5	(I)	EARL OF GALLOWAY'S REEL
17bL3b2	547b5	(I)	MY MOTHER'S AYE GLOWRING O'ER ME

17bL3b5	3b547bL	(I)	MISS ELEANORA HAMILTON'S REEL
17L3L5L	5L7L13	(I)	MARCHIONESS OF TWEEDDALE, THE
17L5L1L	17L6L2	(I)	LADY SCOTT'S REEL
17L5L3L	5L132	(I)	TYRISH RUIN, THE
17L5L6L	6L211	(I)	TURN IN THE PARK, A
17L5L	122	(I)	FOR THE LOVE OF GEAN
17L5L1	3455	(II)	SUMMER DAYS
17L6L5L	4L3L2L5L	(II)	GARDEN'S STRATHSPEY
17L6L5L	13L6L2L	(II)	HOUSE OF CLOVA, THE
17L6L5L	347L2	(I)	HENRY McLIESH'S COMPLEMENTS TO A. LEBURN
17L6L1	3434	(II)	BELFAST ALMANAC, THE
17L6L1	3434	(I)	BELFAST ALMANACK, THE
17L6L1	3434	(I)	IRISH AIR
17L6L1	3434	(I)	BOB IN THE BED
17L6L1	3434	(I)	POOR SOLDIER, THE
17L6L3	661H5	(I)	WILL YE LEND ME YOUR LOOM LASS
17L6L6	2H71H6	(I)	MR GEORGE HOGARTH'S FAVORITE
17L15L	17L5L6L	(I)	SIBYL
17L15L	1211	(I)	SKY AIR
17L15L	5333	(I)	MOORLAND BALLAD
17L17L	17L42	(I)	TRIP TO LIVERPOOL
17L17L	5327L	(I)	NEW POLONES, THE [POLONESE DANCE]
17L17L	5421	(I)	LA POLONESE
17L11	3434	(I)	MRS MUIR MACKENZIE'S DELIGHT
17L11	3434	(I)	SCOTCH COLLOPS
17L1	201	(I)	LARK MINUET, BY HAYDN
17L12	17L6L5L	(I)	AULD GOODMAN, THE
17L12	17L32	(I)	TWO MISERS
17L12	3327L	(I)	VERTIGO
17L12	4212	(I)	LE VERTIGO
17L12	4312	(I)	NEW FANDANGE, THE
17L1	3b21	(I)	OLD COLLIN'S COMPLAINT
17L13b	243b1	(I)	MOLLY'S DELIGHT
17L13	15L22	(I)	MRS BAILLIE OF DUNAIN'S STRATHSPEY
17L26L	1151	(I)	MISS MOLLY SCOT'S RANT
17L3b2	547b5	(I)	HEALTH TO BETTY, A
17L3b2	547b5	(I)	MY MOTHER'S AY GLOWRIN' O'ER ME
17L31	1H641H	(I)	COUNTESS OF BREADALBANE'S JIG, THE
17L32	6L232	(I)	PUBLICK UTILITY
17L32	3522	(I)	MISS MACLEOD OF GEANIES
17L47L	1253	(II)	DAVID ADAMS
17L47L	1H643	(II)	DAVIE WORK
17L43	2115L	(I)	COTILLON
100	665	(I)	CUMHA ROTHA
1021	3043	(I)	ALLEGRO
111L1L	436L2	(II)	MISS STEWART'S STRATHSPEY, PITTYVAICH
111L1L	436L2	(I)	LADY ANNE HOPE'S REEL
111L1L	436L2	(I)	MISS STEWART'S STRATHSPEY
111L1L	436L2	(I)	EARL OF GLENCAIRN'S STRATHSPEY, (THE)
111L1L	446L2	(I)	LADY ANN HOPS STRATHSPEY
111L1	4327L	(I)	HIGHLAND CHIEFTAIN, THE
111L3b	7bL242	(II)	MRS A. MACGLASHAN
111L3b	7bL242	(I)	MRS A. MACGLASHAN('S JIGG)
111L5	437L2	(I)	MISS NAPIER'S REEL
113bL5L	2L4L2L4L	(II)	MORDINGTON HOUSE
113bL5L	2L4L2L4L	(I)	MORDINGTON HOUSE
113bL5	7bL27bL7bL	(I)	MISS KELMAN'S STRATHSPEY
113L1L	2L27L5L	(I)	MRS McKENZIE'S STRATHSPEY
113L1L	4L6L4L2	(II)	COUNTESS OF BREADALBANE
113L1L	1554	(I)	MISS RUNNINGTON'S REEL
113L1L	427L2	(I)	MR JOHN CAMPBELL ARDMORE'S STRATHSPEY
113L3L	1531	(I)	HORNPIPE
113L5L	4L2L4L2	(I)	MISS McNIELLS REEL
113L5L	4L5L2L2	(I)	MISS MILLER'S REEL
113L5L	4L6L22	(I)	DIBDINS FANCY
113L5L	4L6L42	(I)	PRINCES FAVORITE, THE
113L5L	4L6L43	(I)	PRINCE(OF WALES)'S (FAVORITE/FANCY)
113L5L	4L24L6L	(I)	MR MALCOLMS REEL
113L5L	4L27L6L	(II)	MARCHIONESS OF HUNTLY'S REEL
113L5L	4L226L	(II)	COUNTESS OF BREADALBANE
113L5L	4L226L	(I)	COUNTESS OF BREADALBANE'S REEL
113L5L	6L133	(II)	KINRARA
113L5L	6L133	(I)	CEANRARA [CEANN RARA]
113L5L	6L26L2	(I)	DUCHESS OF GORDON'S NEW STRATHSPEY, THE
113L5L	112L2L	(I)	DUTCHESS OF MANCHESTER'S FAREWELL TO THE HIGHLANDS OF SCOTLAND, THE
113L5L	112L2L	(I)	HONEST MEN AND BONNY LASSES
113L5L	114L2	(II)	LADY MONTGOMERY
113L5L	117L2	(I)	LADY MONTGOMERIE('S REEL) [LADY MONTGOMERY]
113L5L	1111	(I)	MISS CAROLINE GRANT'S STRATHSPEY
113L5L	1322L	(I)	HIE OVER HUNT (STRATHSPEY)
113L1	4L6L4L2	(I)	COUNTESS OF BREADALBANE'S

			FAVORITE STRATHSPEY
113L1	6L5L3L2L	(I)	MRS MONTGOMRIE OF STAIR'S STRATHSPEY
113L1	6L27L2	(II)	RENDEZVOUS, THE
113L1	6L27L2	(I)	AN COISIR [AN CHOISIR]
113L1	6L216L	(I)	MR CAMPBELL'S HORNPIPE
113L	114	(I)	LADYKIRK HOUSE
113L1	27L5L2	(I)	TREEBLE HORNPIPE, No. 4
113L1	27L5L2	(I)	ALDRIGE FAVORITE HORNPIPE
113L1	226L2	(I)	DRUCHEN LAIRD'S STRATHSPEY, THE
113L1	3216L	(II)	DARLING ANNIE
113L1	3216L	(II)	ANNA IS MY DARLING
113L1	3216L	(II)	ANNIE IS MY DARLING
113L1	3216L	(I)	ANNA THUG MI GRADH DHUIT
113L1	4522	(I)	LADY GLASGOW'S FAVORITE
113L1	5226L	(I)	GLASGOW FLOURISH
113L1	5432	(II)	MR JOHN SMITH'S
113L3	657L2	(I)	MRS SMALL OF DIRNANEAN DELIGHT
113L3	1H67L2	(I)	MISS ANN DAVIDSON'S JIG
114L1	7bL55L7bL	(I)	(DUNKELD) HERMITAGE BRIDGE, (THE)
114L5	3L4L3L2L	(I)	MRS BLAIR OF MERCHISTON
115L3bL	7bF1L7bL7bF	(I)	GUR MISE THA SO MHULAD E O UIM O
115L3bL	5L7bL7bL3b	(II)	LAMENT FOR THE AULD GEAN TREE
			OF WESTER ELCHIES
115L3L	1L3L6L3	(I)	MISS BURNS STRATHSPEY
115L3L	5L3L6L4L	(II)	MR J.S. SKINNER'S STRATHSPEY
115L3L	5L5L5L5L	(II)	DUNCAN QUADRILLE, THE
115L3L	1142	(I)	TORE OF TROUP, THE
115L3L	1142	(I)	LADY MARY LINDSAY'S STRATHSPEY
115L3L	1566	(II)	MRS JAMES CHRISTIE
115L4L	3bL3bL3bL3b	(II)	LAMENT FOR THE LATE MR Wm. CHRISTIE
115L4L	7bL4L4L5L	(I)	AULD ROBIN GRAY
115L4L	7bL7bL7bL3b	(I)	I'LL BID MY HEART BE STILL
115L5L	2L236L	(I)	MR AND: LAUGHLAN'S WELCOME TO BANFF
115L5L	2L426L	(I)	MISS TAYLOR'S FAVORITE, THE
115L	5L3L5L	(I)	O' KELLY'S RANT
115L	5L3L5L	(I)	DRUNK AT NIGHT AND DRY IN THE MORNING
115L5L	3L5L3L1L	(I)	COTTILLION 8th
115L5L	3L5L3L3L	(I)	COTTILLION 2nd
115L5L	6L5L6L5L	(I)	LADY MENZIES OF CASTLE MENZIES(REEL)
115L5L	7bL47L7bL	(I)	MRS McLEOD OF COLBECKS STRATHSPEY
115L5L	7bL47bL7bL	(I)	ILLUMINATION (NOVEMBER THE 5th, 1788), THE
115L5L	15L22	(I)	HONble MR BAILLIES STRATHSPEY
115L5L	115L5L	(I)	ALLEGRO
115L5L	115L5L	(I)	FINE FLOWERS IN THE VALLEY
115L5L	116L6L	(I)	MISS JEAN DOUGLAS'S FAVORITE
115L5L	1122L	(II)	LADS OF TARLAND, THE
115L5L	1131	(I)	BONNY JEAN
115L5L	1132	(II)	HAUD AWA' FRAE ME DONALD
115L5L	1132	(I)	BONNY JANE
115L5L	1132	(I)	BONNY JEAN (OF ABERDEEN)
115L5L	1142	(II)	MRS FORBES
115L5L	1142	(I)	MRS Dr. FORBES' REEL
115L5L	1142	(I)	BONNY JEAN OF ABERDEEN
115L5L	1162	(I)	MISS JENNER'S FAVORITE
115L5L	1321	(I)	COVENTRY DANCE, THE or FEATHERS, THE
115L5L	247bL7bL	(I)	MISS SARJENT LIVINGTON'S REEL
115L5L	247L2	(I)	COLLEGE OF St. ANDREWS, THE
115L5L	3321	(I)	FEATHERS, THE
115L5L	5555	(I)	ADI. MITCHEL'S WALTZ
115L6L	1122L	(II)	KINRARA
115L6L	1122L	(I)	KINRARA(STRATHSPEY)
115L6L	1122L	(I)	COUNTESS OF DALKEITH'S STR., (THE)
115L6L	1322	(I)	St. KILDA (SONG/AIR), (A)
115L	6L11H	(I)	AULD ROB MORRIS, (THERE'S)
115L	7bL7bL2	(I)	WE'LL PUT THE SHEEP-HEAD IN THE PAT
115L7bL	113b5	(II)	BONNIE ANNIE
115L7bL	113b5	(I)	ABERCROMBIE PLACE
115L7bL	113b5	(I)	BONNY MARY
115L7bL	113b5	(I)	LETHEN'S REEL(L)
115L7bL	113b5	(I)	LADY ELIBANK'S FAVO(U)RITE
115L7bL	113b5	(I)	BONNY ANNIE
115L1	6L5L6L5L	(I)	MISS STEWART'S REEL
115L	115L	(I)	FAIRY QUEEN, THE
115L	115L	(I)	MAY IS MY LOVE
115L1	116L2	(I)	MISS THOMSON'S FAVORITE
115L	113b	(I)	MAY IS MY LOVE
115L	123	(II)	COTTAGE HYMN, A
115L	133	(I)	LADY GRACE STEWART'S MINUET
115L1	3331	(I)	SQr PARSONS MARCH
115L1	3553	(II)	LADY HALL
115L1	1H12L2L	(I)	BALL ROOM, THE
115L2	436L2	(I)	LORD GLENCAIRN'S STRATHSPEY

115L3b	115L1	(I)	HUMOURS OF [THE] GLEN
115L	331	(I)	MISS JOHNSTON'S MINUET
115L5	437L2	(I)	MISS NAPIER'S (REEL/FANCY)
115L	553	(I)	LADY MARY HAY'S MINUET
115L	553	(I)	MISS HENDERSON'S MINUET
115L3b	114L1	(I)	HUMOURS OF GLEN, THE
116L2L	111L3L	(I)	MRS T. BENSON'S REEL
116L3L	1L37L2	(I)	Dr IRVINE'S STRATHSPEY
116L	3L3L1	(I)	MISS KENNEDY'S MINUET
116L4L	2L47L5L	(I)	MISS ROLLO'S STRATHSPEY
116L4L	4L426L	(II)	WEMYSS CASTLE
116L4L	4L426L	(I)	WEMYSS CASTLE(STRATHSPEY)
116L4L	1124	(II)	REEL OF GAMRIE, THE
116L5L	4L4L7F2L	(I)	MISS MATILDA GRANT'S STRATHSPEY
116L5L	4L5L4L2L	(I)	MRS STEWART ALLEAN'S REEL
116L5L	4L5L6L2L	(II)	COMIN' THRO' KILBLEEN
116L5L	5L5L12	(I)	LADY HEATHCOT'S FANCY
116L5L	5L142	(I)	FRASER'S QUICK STEP, THE
116L5L	5L323	(II)	MO ROBAIRNEACH GAOLACH
116L5L	5L332	(I)	LADY DICK LAUDER'S STRATHSPEY
116L5L	6L5L22	(I)	MISS NORRIS'S FANCY
116L5L	117L2	(I)	MR WHITE'S STRATHSPEY
116L5L	1132	(I)	LADY MINTO'S FAVOURITE
116L5L	1136	(I)	COl. NICHOLSON
116L5L	1136	(I)	SNAW FOURTEEN
116L5L	1315L	(I)	SIR (JOHN/GEORGE) STEWART
			OF GRAN(D)T(UL)LY'S (STRATHSPEY/REEL)
116L5L	1562	(II)	TWEEDSIDE LASSES, THE
116L5L	3521	(I)	BONAR BRIDGE, THE
116L5L	3521	(I)	MI M'SHUIDH 'N EIREADH BATA
116L5L	447L2	(II)	EARL GREY
116L5L	5562	(I)	MISS DALZELL'S STRATHSPEY
116L5L	51L34	(I)	DAWNING OF THE DAY, THE
116L6L	116L2	(II)	COME AGAIN
116L6L	1113L	(I)	MISS WARDLAW'S STRATHSPEY
116L6L	2232	(I)	MISS STEWART OF BALLECHEN'S FAVOURITE
116L	7L7L6L	(I)	THERE CAME A GHAIST TO MARGRET'S DOOR
116L1	116L1	(I)	LONG LIFE TO STEPMOTHERS
116L1	116L1	(I)	FEUDAL TIMES
116L1	116L2	(I)	LORD SPENCERS STRATHSPEY
116L1	136L2	(II)	LADY SPENCER CHICHESTER
116L1	136L2	(I)	LORD SPENCER CHICHESTER'S STRATHSPEY
116L1	247L2	(I)	LADY CATHCART'S STRATHSPEY
116L1	3211	(I)	DOUN THE BURN DAVIE
116L1	3213	(I)	DOWN THE BURN DAVIE
116L1	3313	(I)	DOWN THE BURN DAVIE
116L1	3632	(II)	CAT'S BACK, THE (STRATHPEFFER)
116L1	526L6L	(II)	LOWLAND RANT
116L1	526L6L	(I)	SIR JOHN WHITEFOORD('S STRATHSPEY)
116L1	5232	(I)	MISS SHANK'S STRATHSPEY
116L1	5563	(II)	DARK HAIRED YOUTH, THE
116L1	5563	(II)	THANIG ON(AN) GILLE DUBH
			AN RAOIR NA BHAILE SO
116L2	7L6L11	(I)	MISS ROBERTSON'S FANCY
116L2	7L6L11	(I)	DUKE OF BRUNSWICK'S MARCH
116L2	1115	(I)	MISS JESS(IE) HUNTER'S STRATHSPEY
116L2	1351H	(I)	LADY PEEL
116L2	1351H	(I)	MISS GIBSON CRAIG
116L2	316L6L	(I)	THERE'S NAE LUCK ABOUT THE HOUSE
116L2	4433	(I)	MR WILLm FERGUSON OF REATHS REEL
116L3	116L1	(I)	SHORT LIFE TO STEPMOTHERS
116L	352	(I)	DI-MOLADH AN UISGE-BHEATHA
116L4	5126L	(I)	COUNTESS OF MOIRA, THE
116L4	527L2	(I)	MRS BROWN OF KELLY-BANK'S STRATHSPEY
116L4	5326L	(I)	MRS ROBERTSON OF LAWERS STRATHSPEY
116L4	51H26L	(II)	MR LAIRD OF STRATHMARTIN
116L4	51H26L	(I)	LADY GOWERS STRATHSPEY
116L4	51H26L	(I)	MRS LAIRD OF STRATHMARTINS STRATHSPEY
116L6	5222	(I)	MRS FERGUSON'S STRATHSPEY
117bL5L	1115	(I)	GENERAL GORDON CUMING SKENE'S STRATHSPEY
117bL5L	3b3b27bL	(I)	CORDWAINER'S MARCH, THE
117bL7bL	117bL5L	(I)	TIBBIE FOWLER OF THE GLEN
117bL7bL	117bL5L	(I)	FOULLER'S RANT, THE
117bL7bL	117bL5L	(I)	SEME RUNE TALLANACH
117bL7bL	113b4	(I)	ROYALTY
117bL7bL	113b5	(I)	THROID MO BHEAN IS THROID I RIUM
117bL7bL	113b5	(I)	MISS OSWALD OF AUCHINCRUIVE
117bL7bL	3b511L	(II)	RISE (YE) LAZY LUBBER
			[RISE YOU LAZY FELLOW]
117bL7bL	3b511L	(I)	RISE (YE) LAZY LUBBER
117bL7bL	3b511	(II)	RISE LAZY LUBBER
117bL7bL	3b511	(I)	RISE LAZY LUBBER

117bL	7bL7bL55L	(I)	AN TUR A BHITHINN URAD
117bL	117bL	(I)	PADDYS FANCY
117bL1	3b3b50	(I)	ALLAN LOGANS CANT
117bL2	113b5	(II)	LORD KILMAURS
117bL2	113b5	(I)	WAY TO AIR, THE
117bL2	113b5	(I)	LORD KILMAUR'S (REEL)
117bL2	5147bL	(II)	DARK HAIR'D MARY
117bL2	5147bL	(II)	NIGHEAN DUBH ALASDAIR
117bL2	5147bL	(I)	TIBBY FOWLER (O' THE GLEN)('S RANT)
117bL2	557b2H	(I)	COMMIN' THRO' KILBLEEN
117bL3b	113b5	(I)	SOCIETY'S FAVOURITE, THE
117bL3b	3b43b3b	(I)	GREEN GROWES THE RASHES
117bL3b	43b7bL7bL	(I)	DRUIMIONN DUBH
117bL3b	543b3b	(I)	EVAN BANKS
117L5L	5L131	(I)	ANGEL'S WHISPER, THE
117L5L	1111	(I)	SOW'S TAIL, THE
117L5L	1122	(I)	MISS ELIZABETH MAGd FORDYCE STRATHSPEY
117L5L	1153	(I)	COUNTESS OF DALHOUSIE'S FAVORITE, THE
117L5L	1155	(I)	CAPTAIN MAC(K)INTOSH('S FAVOURITE)
117L5L	3b3b42	(I)	AN CRONAN MUILLACH [AN CRONAN MUILEACH]
117L5L	3432	(I)	HAYDN, THE
117L6L	6L7L12	(II)	MEIKLEOUR BEECHES, THE
117L6L	4435	(II)	FLOWER O' THE QUERN, THE
117L7L	6L6L5L3L	(I)	WELSH DANCE, A
117L7L	1123	(II)	JENNY GEDDES
117L7L	1133	(I)	CAPT CHARLES GORDON, R.N. HUNTLY
117L	124	(I)	SLAUNT RI PLULIB
117L1	327L6L	(II)	CALLER HERRING
117L1	327L6L	(I)	PAS SEUL MISS JANE FORBES
117L1	327L6L	(I)	CALLER HERRING'
117L2	1110	(I)	DING DONG, DING DONG
117L2	1313	(I)	MISS ANN GRAHAM OF FINTRY'S STRATHSPEY
117L2	317L2	(I)	MISS ROBERTSON
117L4	117L1	(I)	DUCHESS OF BEDFORD'S WALTZ, THE
117L4	6425	(I)	LA TAISON DOR
110	27L0	(I)	TAK' YOUR AULD CLOAK ABOUT YE
1111L	2L7bL4L2L	(I)	LORD MONTGOMIRIE'S STRATHSPEY
1111L	3L5L11	(II)	DOCTOR PROFEIT'S STRATHSPEY
1113L	6L5L5L1	(II)	OLD BOG HOLE
1113L	1322	(I)	CAPTAIN JOHNSTON'S MARCH
1113L	1516L	(I)	NIAL BROCDHAIR [NIALL BROCHDAIR]
1114L	2226L	(II)	WALLACE TOWER
1115L	3bL5L7bL7bL	(I)	STRADH SPEA [SRATH SPE]
1115L	5L5L10	(I)	CIA IAD NA DEE 'SNA DUILE TREUN
1115L	5L5L11	(I)	CIA IAD NA DEE 'SNA DUILE TREUN
1115L	5L13b2	(II)	CASHMERE SHAWL, THE
111	5L5L3	(II)	FRENCH WALTZ, A
1115L	7bL3bL4L1L	(II)	AUCHINDOUN CASTLE
1115L	7bL7bL27bL	(II)	MR JAMIESON'S REEL
1115L	113b3b	(II)	LOCH LEVEN CASTLE
1115L	1155	(I)	CAPT MACINTOSH
1115L	13b15L	(II)	YE'LL BETTER TAK' IT
1115L	13b53b	(II)	BLAIR ATHOLE
1115L	1355	(I)	CAPTAIN MACINTOSH'S STRATHSPEY
1115L	225L2	(I)	HONOURABLE COLONEL HAMILTON'S MARCH
1115L	3b3b42	(II)	GLOOMY WINTER
1115L	3b3b42	(I)	MR NAIRNE'S STRATHSPEY
1115L	3b3b42	(I)	COME MY BRIDE, HASTE, HASTE AWAY
1115L	3b3b42	(I)	LORD BALGONIE'S FAVORITE
1115L	3b3b42	(I)	GLOOMY WINTER'S NOW AWA'
1115L	3b3b42	(I)	REVd PATRICK McDONALD OF KILMORE
1115L	3b545	(II)	MARCH
1115L	446L2	(I)	LADY ANN HOP'S STRATHSPEY
1115L	4422	(I)	RT HON LORD TORPHICHEN'S MARCH
1115L	526L6L	(I)	LADY ADMIRAL GORDON'S
111	6L5L5L	(I)	MR ALEXr. HUNTER OF BLACKNESS'S FAVORITE MINUET
1116L	5L6L4L2L	(I)	MiSS HUNTER (BLACKNESS) 'S STRATHSPEY
1116L	5L213	(I)	MORNING SERENADE
111	7bL7bL5L	(I)	MY MOTHER'S AY GLOWRING O'ER ME
111	7bL7bL2	(I)	RORIE DALL'S SISTER'S LAMENT
1117bL	7bL27bL5L	(I)	LORD ANTRIM'S DELIGHT
1117bL	117bL5L	(I)	TIBBY FOWLER
1117bL	217bL5L	(I)	TIBBY FOWLER O' THE GLEN
1117bL	3b3b7b2	(I)	LEWIS AIR, A
1117bL	3b554	(I)	DEAD MARCH, THE
1117bL	4124	(II)	NINE PINT COGGIE, THE
1117L	5L5L3L5L	(II)	FIRESIDE AT HAME, THE
1117L	5L5L5L3	(I)	SLOW
111	7L5L1	(I)	SCOTCH MEASURE, A
111	7L5L2	(I)	MINUETTO
111	7L6L5L	(I)	MOLE CATCHER'S DAUGHTER, THE

111	7L7L5L	(I)	IRISH AIR
111	7L7L5L	(I)	MY MOTHER'S AY GLOWRING O'ER ME
111	7L7L5L	(I)	HARLEQUINS LAMENT FOR THE LOSS OF COLOMBINE
1111	3L111	(I)	MISS MAXWELL OF MONRIETH'S FAREWELL TO THE W.L. FENCIBLES
111	14L4L	(I)	THA GRUAGACH SAN AODAN
111	14L4L	(I)	MAID OF EDIN, THE
1111	5L5L5L3	(I)	THOU ART GONE AWA' (MARY/,NEW SETT)
1111	6L6L22	(I)	TIVIOT BANKS
1111	6L6L63	(II)	BLUE BONNETS
1111	6L27L6L	(I)	MR MENZIES (OF CULDAIR'S) STRATHSPEY
1111	6L27L2	(II)	SIR JAS. G. BAIRD BART.
1111	6L27L2	(I)	SIR JAMES G. BAIRD BART('s STRATHSPEY)
1111	6L213	(I)	LANG LIFE TO NEIL GOW
1111	6L432	(I)	FAVORITE QUICK STEP, A
111	17bL7bL	(I)	RATHER SLOW
1111	7bL7bL7bL7bL	(II)	LOCH MUICK
1111	7bL7bL47bL	(II)	DUKE OF ATHOLE(, THE)
1111	7bL7bL47bL	(I)	DUKE OF ATHOLL ('S STRATHSPEY), THE
111	17bL1	(I)	SHEPHERD ADONIS, THE
1111	7bL13b2	(I)	HA DA LOLAL O
1111	7bL247bL	(II)	GLENBURNIE RANT(, THE)
1111	7bL247bL	(I)	GLENBURNIE RANT, THE
1111	7bL3b7bL5L	(I)	IRISH AIR, AN
1111	14L2L2	(I)	EDIN CASTLE
111	115L	(I)	LORD JOHN
1111	16L62	(II)	OVER THE BORDER
1111	16L62	(I)	BLUE BONNETS OVER THE BORDER
1111	16L63	(I)	MARCH, MARCH, ETTRICK AND TEVIOTDALE
1111	16L64	(I)	BLUE BONNETS
111	111	(I)	CELEBRATED STORM WALTZ, THE
111	111	(I)	GOOD NIGHT AND JOY BE WI' YOU A'
1111	115L5L	(II)	STORM KING, THE
1111	116L2	(II)	MR MARSHALL'S COMPLIMENTS TO NIEL GOW
1111	116L2	(I)	(MR) MARSHALL'S COMPLIMENTS TO NIEL GOW
1111	117bL3b	(I)	MISS MARY BALFOUR'S STRATHSPEY
1111	1111	(I)	NEW WAY TO EDINr, THE
1111	1111	(I)	CEANN NA DROCHAID BIG
1111	1111	(I)	CLAN'S GATHERING, THE
1111	1111	(I)	JOHN TOD
1111	1111	(I)	RIVAL CANDIDATES
1111	1127L	(I)	MISS MURRAY OCHTERTYRE
1111	1155	(I)	CRUIMEACHADH CHLAUN RAONUILL
1111	1155	(I)	DARTFORD LODGE
1111	1164	(I)	MISS FIELDING'S REEL, THE
111	112	(I)	MISS MONTGOMERY'S MINUET
111	112	(I)	MARQUIS OF HUNTLY'S FAVORITE, THE
111	113b	(I)	SHEPHERDS OF YARROW, THE
111	113	(I)	MINUET
111	113	(I)	SWEET LITTLE BARBARA
1111	1325L	(I)	LODOISKA
111	115	(I)	MISS BABIE GRAY'S MINUET
111	115	(I)	RANGERS FROLICK
1111	1627b	(II)	FLAP OF THE EAGLE'S WING, THE
1111	11H52	(I)	STRATHSPEY, A
1111	11H65	(I)	BARRING OF THE DOOR, THE
1111	11H5H1H	(I)	LORD NELSON'S WALTZ
1111	15H4H2H	(I)	LE DEROUTTE DE PALATINE or MISS BENTINCK'S FANCY
1111	27L7L2	(I)	SIR PATRICK SPENS
1111	27L11	(I)	CAPTAIN FLEMING
1111	27L24	(I)	ALLY CROAKER
111	122	(I)	WEARY PUND O' TOW, THE
1111	226L5L	(I)	ROBIN CUSHIE
1111	226L5L	(I)	KIND ROBIN LO'ES ME
1111	226L6L	(I)	KIND ROBIN LO'ES ME
1111	2227L	(II)	CIRCASSIAN CIRCLE
1111	2221	(I)	SFHADDE MAR SEO THA SINN
1111	2221	(I)	TOO LONG IN THIS CONDITION
1111	2222	(I)	O'ER THE MOOR AMANG THE HEATHER
1111	2222	(I)	MISS MARGRET HAMILTON SUNDRUM'S STRATHSPEY
1111	2222	(I)	NEW MARCH, A
1111	2222	(I)	PORT LENOX
1111	2222	(I)	VENERABLE, THE
1111	2222	(I)	GERMAN DANCE
1111	2235L	(I)	WOOD CUTTERS, THE
1111	2237L	(I)	MISS RAMSAY OF BARNTON
1111	2231	(I)	DESERTER, THE
1111	2231	(I)	ROSETTE QUICK STEP
1111	2235	(I)	COLONEL ROBERTSON OF LAWERS STRATHSPEY
1111	2242	(I)	PRINCESS ELIZABETH'S FANCY
1111	2255	(I)	MISS DIROM'S (STRATHSPEY/REEL)

111	123	(I)	SKYE AIR
1111	236L6L	(I)	MR ALLAN GRANT'S STRATHSPEY
1111	2316L	(I)	LADY LOUDON'S FAVORITE
1111	2313	(I)	UNTITLED
1111	247L2	(I)	MAGGY LAUDER
1111	2431	(I)	PRINCE WILLIAM
1111	2662	(II)	BRAES OF MARR
111	13b3b	(I)	DEOCH SLAINT' AN RIGH
111	13b4	(I)	THA MULAD, THA SGIOS ORM
111	131	(I)	MISS DR. GRANT'S MINUET
111	131	(I)	SINGLE HORNPIPE, A
1111	3122L	(I)	MRS BUCHAN OF AUCHMACOY
1111	3210	(I)	ALL'S WELL
1111	3232	(I)	MISS BUCHANAN OF DULLATER'S STRATHSPEY
111	133	(I)	LADY HERRIOT CUNNINGHAM'S MINUET
1111	3311	(I)	A (SUPPOSED) CONFAB
			BETWEEN A QUAKER AND A SECEEDER
1111	3333	(I)	OXONIAN BALL, THE
1111	3333	(I)	PRINCE ERNEST'S VALTZ
1111	3352	(I)	MR FAIRBANKS RIGADOON
1111	3356	(I)	KELSO VOLUNTEERS MARCH, THE
111	135	(I)	MISS NANCY GIBSON'S MINUET
1111	427L2	(I)	SPEY RIVER
1111	4227bL	(I)	MR J R COUTTS'S STRATHSPEY
1111	436L2	(I)	GLENCAIRN'S STRATHSPEY
1111	4326L	(I)	MISS ELISA SKENE'S REEL
1111	447bL2	(II)	MISS SARAH DRUMMOND OF PERTH
1111	447bL2	(I)	HONOURABLE MR DRUMMOND BURREL, THE
1111	447bL2	(I)	MISS SARAH DRUMMOND OF PERTH
			('S STRATHSPEY)
1111	4415	(I)	MOLLY APPLE PYE
1111	4425L	(I)	MISS ELIZABETH CARNEGIE'S HORNPIPE
1111	4466	(I)	ST ANDREWS ASSEMBLY, THE
1111	57bL42	(II)	SMITH OF KILLIECHASSIE, THE
1111	516L6L	(II)	A BHEAN AN TAIGH NACH LEIG THU STEACH AM FEA
			R A THA AIR FOGAIRT [GOOD WIFE, ADMIT THE WA
1111	516L6L	(I)	A BHEAN AN TAIGH NACH LEIG U STEACH
			AM FEAR A THA AIR FOGAIRT
1111	5151	(I)	SHE GRIPED AT YE GREATEST ON'T
1111	526L6L	(I)	OF A' THE AIRTS THE WIN' CAN BLAW
1111	526L6L	(I)	MISS ADMIRAL GORDON'S (STRATHSPEY/REEL)
1111	5314L	(I)	CAPTAIN CAMERON'S VOLUNTEERS MARCH
1111	531H1H	(I)	PUMP ROOME, THE
1111	5416L	(I)	MISS ADMIRALL GORDON'S STRATHSPEY
1111	5433	(I)	PATTY'S DELIGHT
1111	5531	(I)	AH! CA! IRA
1111	5555	(I)	DENMARK DANCE
1111	5562	(I)	PROMENADE, THE
1111	5565	(I)	MRS MITFORD'S FANCY
1111	5632	(I)	SCOTT OF YARROW, THE
1111	5632	(I)	DONALD BUTCHER'S BRIDAL
1111	5642	(I)	DONALD BUTCHER'S BRIDAL
1111	51H22	(II)	DUKE OF GORDON('S BIRTHDAY, THE)
1111	51H22	(I)	DUKE OF GORDON('S BIRTH DAY), (THE)
1111	51H32	(I)	DUKE OF GORDON, THE
1111	51H52	(I)	MISS THOMPSONS REEL, THE
1111	7b47bL7bL	(I)	HIGHLANDERS FAREWELL TO IRELAND
1111	72H4H7	(I)	MISS FRASER OF BROOMHILL'S REEL
1111	1H525L	(I)	COTILLION
1111	1H51H5	(I)	FOLKSTONE CAMP
111	27L7L	(I)	'S TU MO LUAIDH NA'M FAIGHINN THU
111	27L7L	(I)	TAK' YOUR AULD CLOAK ABOUT YE
1112	7L7L7L1	(I)	LADY CHARLOTTE CAMPBELL'S VALTZ
1112	7L556	(I)	MASTER THOMAS BEST'S HORNPIPE
1112	16L7L2	(I)	COLIN'S REQUEST
1112	1117L	(I)	ASH WEDNESDAY
1112	1112	(I)	MISS E. CARNEGIE'S HORNPIPE
1112	1112	(I)	WALTZ DANCED BY MISS SCRYEMSURE
			AND MISS LINDSAY
1112	147b1	(I)	GUR BOIDHEACH, BOIDHEACH AN CNOCAN
111	222	(I)	MR DUFF'S FAVOURITE MINUET
111	222	(I)	MR MARSHALL'S GRAND MINUET
111	222	(I)	MARSHAL SAX(E)'S MINUET
111	222	(I)	SMEORACH CLANN DONAILL
			[SMEORACH CHLAINN DOMHNUILL]
111	222	(I)	MISS CHARLOTE KER'S MINUET
111	222	(I)	LOVELY NANCY
111	222	(I)	HONBLE MISS DRUMMOND OF PERTH'S MINUET
1112	2223	(I)	DYSART HOUSE STRATHSPEY
111	223	(II)	MY LOVE IS LIKE A RED RED ROSE
111	23b1	(I)	AIR
1112	3b525	(I)	SHARP AND FLAT

1112	36L4L1	(II)	BONNYGATE FIDDLER, THE
1112	37L15L	(!)	ROYAL PAISLEY VOLUNTEER'S MARCH, THE
1112	3332	(I)	DUKE WILLIAM'S MARCH
1112	3334	(II)	COLOSSEUM, THE
1112	3334	(II)	KAY'S HORNPIPE
1112	3334	(I)	SIXTEEN REGts MARCH, THE
1112	3334	(I)	LORD ROLLO'S MARCH
1112	3334	(I)	GRAND MARCH, THE
111	234	(I)	SIR JAMES [B]ASON
1112	4231	(I)	BONNY TOWN OF EDINBURGH, THE
1112	4443	(I)	JOHN COME KISS ME NOW
1112	5117bL	(I)	JOHNNY COPE
1112	5412	(II)	FAILLIRINN 'ILLIRINN
111	3b17bL	(I)	KEAPACH 'NA FASACH
111	3b3b5L	(I)	DEAL STICK THE MIN(I)STER, THE
111	3b3b2	(I)	WHEN SHE CAM BEN SHE BOBED
111	3b3b3b	(I)	WHEN SHE CAME BEN SHE BOBED
111	3b3b4	(I)	COLD AND RAW
111	3b3b4	(I)	WHEN SHE CAM BEN SHE BOBBIT
1113b	3b422	(II)	MRS CAMPBELL OF MONZIE
1113b	3b422	(I)	MISS CAMPBELL OF MONZIE'S STRATHSPEY
111	3b3b5	(I)	WHEN SHE CAME BEN SHE BOBBED
111	3b3b5	(I)	UP IN THE MORNING EARLY
1113b	427bL7bL	(I)	BANKS OF SPEY, THE
1113b	427L2	(I)	LA TRENISE
1113b	5117bL	(I)	JOHNNY COPE
1113	2L6L6L2L	(I)	BRAES OF MARR
1113	16L6L4L	(I)	MISS CRICHTON'S SCOTT'S MEASURE
1113	6L6L6L1	(I)	LORD CORNWALLIS OR RODNEYS MARCH
1113	7L7L7L2	(I)	MISS ROBERTSON KILTEARN'S REEL
1113	15L13L	(I)	HON: MISS CHARLOTTE McKINZIE'S FAVORITE, THE
1113	15L12	(I)	FEMALE LOVER'S CHALLENGE, THE
1113	16L6L5L	(I)	O'ER THE HILLS AND FAR AWAY
1113	112L2	(I)	COUNTESS OF CASSILLI'S STRATHSPEY
1113	115L7L	(I)	MURPHY DELANEY
1113	116L7L	(II)	MURPHY DELANEY
1113	116L7L	(I)	MURPH(E)Y DELANEY
1113	117L2	(I)	MISER, THE
1113	1111	(I)	MISS MACLEOD OF DALVEY'S WALTZ
1113	1113	(II)	ECLIPSE
1113	1127L	(I)	MURPHY DELANEY
1113	1124	(I)	WHIP HER AND GIRD HER
1113	1142	(I)	NORTH HIGHLAND 4
1113	1162	(I)	COLONEL MONTGOMERIE'S COMPLEMENTS TO ORANGFIELD
111	313	(I)	GIN YE WONNE TAKE ME
111	313	(I)	JOCKY SAID TO JENNY
1113	1316L	(II)	PIGEON ON THE GALE
1113	1342	(I)	NORTH HIGHLAND REEL, A
111	315	(I)	JOCKY SAID TO JENNY
1113	25L5L7L	(I)	INDIANS MARCH
1113	27L5L3L	(I)	HORNPIPE
111	321	(I)	LADY COVENTRY'S MINUET
1113	2121	(I)	ENCE CROUDIE TWICE CROUDIE, &C.
1113	2121	(I)	ALE WIFE AND HER BARREL, THE
1113	226L5L	(II)	BONNIE BANKS O' LOCH LOMOND
1113	2211	(I)	HOLLOW DRUM, THE
1113	2211	(I)	WHEN THE HOLLOW DRUM
1113	2221	(I)	MACPHERSON'S LAMENT
1113	2223	(I)	BLENHEIM HOUSE
1113	2224	(I)	SCOTS THISTLE, THE
1113	2246	(II)	HIGHLAND WHISKEY [HIGHLAND WHISKY]
1113	2246	(I)	HIGHLAND WHISKY [HIGHLAND WHISKEY]
1113	2333	(I)	NORTH REEL, THE
111	331	(I)	THEODORE MINUET, THE
111	331	(I)	MISS CHARTER'S MINUET OF AIMSFIELD
1113	3113	(I)	LOYAL EDINBURGH SPEARMEN'S MARCH, THE
1113	3113	(I)	MORISON'S FANCY
111	333	(I)	BATTLE OF FALKIRK, THE
111	334	(I)	MISS HUNTER'S MINUET
111	335	(I)	DUCHESS OF GORDON, THE
1113	31H1H5	(I)	BOUNDING ROE, THE
111	345	(I)	HOOLY AND FAIRLY
1113	5114	(I)	FOURTH DRAGOON'S SLOW MARCH, THE
1113	5151	(II)	EAST NEUK OF FIFE(, THE)
1113	5151	(I)	EAST NEUK OF FIFE (No. 5), THE
1113	526L6L	(I)	MISS MILLIKEN'S REEL
1113	526L6L	(I)	VISCOUNT HAMILTON
1113	5312	(I)	CAPT MARSHALL'S FANCY
1113	5322	(I)	MRS BISSET'S STRATHSPEY
1113	5542	(II)	LORD FIFE'S MARCH

1113	5552	(I)	WOOD'S HORNPIPE
1113	5555	(I I)	CAPTAIN BARCLAY
1113	5557	(I I)	VALE OF LEVEN
1113	5557	(I I)	MONTGOMERIE'S
1113	5551H	(I)	WESTBURN
111	356	(I)	AN THE KIRK WAD LET ME BE
111	356	(I)	O (DEAR) MOTHER (WHAT SHALL I DO)
111	356	(I)	BLYTHSOME BRIDAL, THE
111	356	(I)	AND THE KIRK WOULD LET ME BE
1113	5751	(I I)	GEORGE TAYLOR
1113	5753	(I)	MUIRTOWN HOUSE
111	351H	(I)	AND THE KIRK WOULD LET ME BE
1113	51H52	(I)	MISS WOODCOCK'S REEL
1113	6361H	(I)	JOHNNY IN THE NETHER MAINS
1113	6361H	(I)	JAMAICA
1113	6361H	(I)	ORCHILL'S DELIGHT
111	364	(I)	PARKES OF GLAMES SINGLE HORNPIPE, THE
1113	6522	(I)	MRS CAPT REID'S STRATHSPEY
1113	6522	(I)	MISS ANNY FORBES REEL
1114	7bL27bL4	(I)	MISS COLT OF SEACLIFF'S STRATHSPEY
1114	7L224	(I)	MISS MARY ANN JOHNSTON'S FAVOURITE
1114	1112	(I)	MUCH TO DO ABOUT NOTHING
111	425L	(I)	'SMI GABHAIL AN RATHAID
1114	217bL4	(I)	BOGEN LOCHAN
1114	356L6L	(I)	MR MORISON OF BOGNIE
1115	7bL4b72	(I)	MRS FARQUHARSON OF MONALTRIE'S DELIGHT
1115	7L7L7L4	(I)	RAKES OF LONDON, THE
1115	7L7L7L5	(I)	RAKES OF MALLO, THE
1115	117bL4	(I)	ATHOLE CUMMERS, (THE)
1115	117bL4	(I)	FAIRLY SHOT OF HER
1115	117L7L	(I I)	BRECHIN CASTLE
1115	117L7L	(I)	MISS DOUGLAS OF BRIGTON'S STRATHSPEY
1115	117L7L	(I)	LADY HARRIOT HAY'S STRATHSPEY
1115	117L7L	(I)	BRECHIN CASTLE
1115	1110	(I)	PAS SEUL MISS HELEN HADDEN
1115	1115	(I)	DENNY'S HORNPIPE
1115	1116	(I)	SIR JOHN STEWART'S FAVOURITE
1115	1116	(I)	DELVEN HOUSE
1115	1126L	(I)	MISS ANN MOIR'S BIRTHDAY
1115	1127L	(I I)	BRECHIN CASTLE
1115	1127L	(I I)	MISS DOUGLAS OF BRIG(H)TON or BRECHIN CASTLE
1115	1124	(I I)	BOG AN LOCHAN, or ATHOLE CUMMERS
1115	1124	(I I)	ATHOLE CUMMERS, (THE)
1115	1124	(I)	BOG AN LOCHAN
1115	1124	(I)	LADY GRANT OF GRANT'S REELL
1115	1124	(I)	ATHOL CUMMERS, THE
1115	1126	(I)	LORD BREADALBANE'S DELIGHT
1115	1126	(I)	MR BINDEN'S FANCY
1115	1136	(I)	LORD COLLINGWOOD
1115	1166L	(I I)	CHISHOLM, THE, OR 'S TOIGH LEAM FHEIN AN T-SIOSALACH
1115	1166L	(I)	S'TOIL LEAM FEIN AN SIOSALACH ['STOIGH LEAM...]
1115	127L5	(I I)	MANDERSTON HOUSE
1115	127L5	(I)	MANDERSTON HOUSE
1115	11H66	(I)	MOONLIGHT ON THE GREEN
111	521	(I)	PAS SEUL MISS MARGARE(T) RUSSEL OF ADEN
111	521	(I)	VIOTTI'S POLLACCA
1115	227L7L	(I)	INSTALLATION, THE
1115	2221	(I)	GENERAL WASHINGTON'S MARCH
1115	2226	(I)	CALIMBO
1115	2226	(I)	GO WHERE YOU WILL I WILL FOLLOW
1115	2247L	(I I)	H.R.H. THE PRINCE OF WALES' WELCOME TO DEESIDE
1115	2243	(I)	RULE BRITANIA
1115	2246	(I)	MR FERGUSON OF RAITH'S STRATHSPEY
1115	236L5L	(I I)	ST. KILDA WEDDING, THE
1115	236L5L	(I)	A BHANAIS IORTACH [A'BHANAIS IRTEACH]
1115	2665	(I)	NOREA'S SCOTS MEASURE
1115	27b27bL	(I)	MR GEORGE JENKIN'S REEL
111	535	(I)	HOOLY AND FAIRLY
1115	31H42	(I)	HIGHLAND COTT, THE
1115	33H1H5	(I)	EARL CORNWALLISE'S MARCH
1115	4111	(I)	MOUNT YOUR HORSES
1115	4246	(I I)	LOWE'S REEL
1115	47b15L	(I)	NOW WAT YE WHA I MET YESTREEN
1115	41H64	(I)	VILLAGE BELLS, THE
1115	5142	(I I)	MISS RITCHIE
1115	5142	(I)	MISS RITCHIE('S REEL)
1115	5211	(I)	MISS TOD'S (GEORGES SQUARE) ALLAMADE
111	555	(I)	DRUNKEN WIFE OF GALLOWAY, THE

1115	5#1#51	(I)	RUSSIAN DANCE, THE
1115	642H5	(I)	HEROES OF CIUDAD RODERIGO, THE
1115	7531	(I)	MR FISHER'S HORNPIPE
1115	1H562	(I)	MISS LAKE'S REEL
111	633	(I)	'SLIONAR EUBH' AGUS IOLACH
1116	51H4H7	(I)	IRISH BLANKET, THE
1111H	356L2	(I)	KILDRUMMIE CASTLE
1111H	5125L	(I)	MISS HELEN CAMPBELL ARDMORE'S JIG
111	3H51	(I)	MISS STEWART'S MINUET
1125L	6L5L3L2L	(I)	MRS JOHN STIRLING'S JIGG
1125L	6L5L4L2L	(I)	LADY SOPHIA CECIL'S FANCY
1125L	1126L	(I)	BELL'S WELL
1125L	127L5L	(II)	MRS ADIE [MRS. ADYE]
1125L	127L5L	(I)	MRS ADYE('S STRATHSPEY) [MRS ADIE]
1125L	13b55	(II)	MISS LIZZIE LEITH
1125L	1322	(I)	MRS HAMILTON (OF WISHAW) 'S STRATHSPEY
1125L	1322	(I)	LADY BELHAVEN'S DELIGHT
1125L	1322	(I)	(MR) JENKINS SHAN TRUISH
1125L	1354	(I)	MISS ANDERSON'S FAVORITE
1125L	3b227bL	(I)	DEIL STICK THE MINISTER
1125L	3b247bL	(I)	DR Wm GRANT'S REELL
1125L	3543	(I)	ROYAL VICTORY, THE
1125L	427L2	(I)	LADY CHARLOTTE FLETCHER OF SALTON
1126L	5L3L3L2L	(II)	KILDRUMMIE LODGE
112	6L6L5L	(I)	WAL(L)ACE'S LAMENT
1126L	1111	(II)	DUNT THE GRUND AT LEISURE
1126L	1111	(I)	SHENVALL, THE
1126L	1111	(I)	LADY GRANT OF MONYMUSK'S REELL
1126L	1111	(I)	LOCHGERY'S RANT
1126L	1143	(I)	MISS COLQUHOUN'S REEL
1126L	1151	(I)	DELACHAPLE'S REEL
1126L	1151	(I)	LADY ELGIN'S REEL
1126L	1154	(I)	LORD ELGIN'S REEL
1126L	1155	(II)	BANKS OF SPEY, THE
1126L	1155	(II)	MOUNT HATTOCK
1126L	1155	(I)	BANKS OF SPEY, THE
1126L	1155	(I)	LAST PINT, THE
1126L	1157	(II)	MR THOMAS BURT
1126L	1151H	(I)	JOHN MORISON'S COMPts TO MR NATHI. GOW
1126L	111H6	(I)	SIR ARCHd DUNBAR OF NORTHFIELD'S STRATHSPEY
1126L	1565	(II)	CLOG DANCE, A
1126L	1561H	(I)	MRS CAPTn STEWART OF FINCASTLE'S STR.
1126L	11H53	(I)	EPPIE McNAB
1126L	4453	(II)	LADY ANN HOPE
1126L	4453	(I)	LORD MURRAY
1126L	4463	(II)	MISS HOPE
1126L	4463	(I)	MISS HOPE('S STRATHSPEY)
1127bL	113b5	(II)	HIGHLANDERS IN PARIS, THE
1127bL	3b247bL	(I)	DILL STICK THE MINISTER
1127bL	3b247bL	(I)	SHANTRUISH
112	7bL7b4	(I)	JACK O' THE GREEN
1127L	5L3L1L5L	(I)	HORNPIPE
1127L	1127L	(I)	SHORT FOLLY, THE
1127L	1121	(I)	MISSES FORBES' WALTZ, THE
1127L	1144	(I)	EARL OF KINTORE, THE
112	7L64	(I)	MR McPHADDEN'S FAVORITE
1120	3210	(I)	THA LOINGEAS FO BREIDE
1120	3210	(I)	NURSE'S LAMENTATION FOR THE LOSS OF HER FOSTER CHILD, A
1121	5L235	(II)	HARK! HOW SKINNER'S FIDDLE RINGS
1121	7bL446	(I)	'S MATH AN LA FHUAIR M'EUDAIL
1121	16L22	(I)	MR MALCOLM'S STRATHSPEY
112	110	(I)	OCH O RO U
1121	1111	(I)	DUKE OF ATHOLES DELIGHT, THE
1121	1151H	(I)	DUNT THE GRUND AT LEISURE
112	112	(I)	LADY ELIZA LINDSAY'S MINUET
1121	2154	(I)	WAY TO GROW RICH, THE
1121	2243	(I)	HUNTLY LODGE
112	123	(I)	MR HARRY ANGELO JUNrs FAVORITE
1121	3223	(I)	MAC MO RIGH S'DOL NA EIDEADH
1121	3343	(I)	VILLAGE MAID, THE
1121	3343	(I)	DYSART MASSON LODGE HARMONY
1121	4365	(I)	YORK HOUSE
112	154	(I)	FETE CHAMPETRE MINUET, THE
112	156	(I)	MISS MACWHINNIE'S FAVOURITE
1121	1H532	(I)	MISS POLE'S REEL
1121	1H1H2H1H	(I)	SIEGE OF MANHEIM
1122	5L6L11	(I)	MILLERS WEDDING, THE
1122	5L6L11	(I)	MILLER'S DAUGHTER, THE
112	26L5L	(I)	MACGREGOR OF RUARU/RORO, ETC.
1122	15L22	(II)	HOCH HEY JOHNNIE LAD
1122	15L22	(I)	HEY HOW JOHNNIE LAD

1122	15L22	(I)	LASSES OF THE FERRY, THE
1122	15L22	(I)	HEY HO JOHNIE LAD
1122	15L22	(I)	REEL, THE
1122	17L6L5L	(I)	MACPHERSON'S LAMENT
1122	17L6L6L	(I)	MCPHERSON'S FAREWELL
1122	116L5L	(I)	MAC FOSET'S FAREWELL
1122	116L5L	(I)	MACPHERSON'S FAREWELL
1122	117bL4	(II)	GINNIE PIN YOUR BONNET ON
1122	1112L	(I)	MRS MUIR OF WARRISTON'S STRATHSPEY
1122	1115L	(I)	COLONEL MCDOWALL'S MARCH
1122	1111	(I)	SIR ALLAN MCLEAN'S REEL
1122	1113	(I)	MAJOR MACBEAN 6TH REGt's MARCH
1122	1113	(I)	EARL OF FIFE'S STRATHSPEY, THE
1122	1121	(I)	DEVONSHIRE HOUSE
1122	1122	(II)	KATE DALRYMPLE
1122	1122	(II)	JINGLIN JOHNNIE
1122	1122	(I)	(OLD) HIGHLAND LADDIE, THE
1122	1122	(I)	JINGLIN' JOHNNY
1122	1122	(I)	MEDLEY OVERTURE (5)
1122	1122	(I)	NEW YEAR'S GIFT
1122	1125	(I)	BEAUX STRATAGEM, THE
1122	1125	(I)	CALL IT WHAT YOU PLEASE
1122	1132	(I)	NEW HIGHLAND LADDIE, THE
1122	1153	(I)	ROYAL GLASGOW VOLUNTEERS FAREWELL
1122	1154	(I)	SHREWSBURY RAKES
1122	1155	(II)	GRANT LODGE
1122	1155	(I)	COMING THROUGH THE RAYE
1122	1155	(I)	ROGER'S FAREWELL
1122	1155	(I)	GRANT LODGE
1122	1155	(I)	SIR ALEXr DON'S STRATHSPEY
1122	1155	(I)	ALE WIFE AND HER BARREL, THE
1122	1155	(I)	SIR ALEX DONS STRATHSPEY
1122	1151H	(I)	MISS J. SOMERVELL'S FAVOURITE STRATHSPEY
1122	1151H	(I)	LORD LOVAT'S STRATHSPEY
1122	1151H	(I)	BRECHIN LILT, THE
1122	1166	(II)	AULD LANG SYNE
1122	111H6	(II)	GAELIC AIR, A
1122	111H6	(I)	HE NA BODDACHIN
1122	125L5L	(I)	McPHERSON'S FAREWELL
1122	1253	(I)	MISS MARGRET ROBERTSON'S JIG
1122	136L6L	(II)	MACPHERSON'S LAMENT [MACPHERSON'S RANT]
1122	1311H	(I)	WILLIE CAMERON
1122	1322	(I)	HIGHLAND LADIE
1122	1322	(I)	HIGHLAND LASSIE
1122	1366	(II)	LANG SYNE
1122	1366	(II)	AULD LANG SYNE
1122	1366	(I)	AULD LANGSYNE
			(SHOULD AULD ACQUAINTANCE BE FORGOT?)
1122	1542	(I)	COLONEL MONTGOMRIE'S MARQUIE
1122	161H5	(I)	MERRY LADS OF KILLAROW, THE
1122	2122	(I)	BONNY LASSI TAKE A MAN
112	222	(I)	SLOW
1122	36L7L5L	(I)	ST PIERRES HORNPIPE
1122	315L3L	(I)	MR MORISON'S JIGG
1122	3125L	(I)	COTILLION
1122	3125L	(I)	CAPE TRAFALGAR
1122	3125L	(I)	QUICK STEP
1122	3125L	(I)	ANDANTINO
1122	3131	(I)	FLOW THOU REGAL PURPLE STREAM
1122	327L5	(I)	WELCH AIR, A
1122	3211	(I)	DUTCH LADY, THE
1122	3326L	(I)	KELSO VOLUNTEERS QUICK STEP, THE
1122	3321	(I)	TWEED SIDE
1122	3322	(I)	KINMONT WILLIE
1122	3332	(I)	ALLEGRO
1122	3334	(I)	DUNDEE VOLUNTEERS MARCH, THE
1122	3334	(I)	DUNDEE VOLUNTEERS MARCH
1122	3347L	(I)	MISS BETTY FORBES' REEL
1122	3344	(I)	MRS LAIRD'S HORNPIPE
1122	3366	(I)	SIR JAMES ST CLAIR ERSKINE
1122	347L5L	(I)	MRS HEPBURN BELCHES
1122	347L2	(I)	MRS COLQUHOUN GRANTS STRATHSPEY
1122	347L2	(I)	MRS GRANT
1122	3413L	(I)	LITTLE LEAPER, THE
1122	3413	(I)	LA PAPILLON
1122	357L2	(II)	MANSON'S SCHOTTISCHE
1122	3527L	(I)	MISS ROSE'S FANCY OF JAMAICA
1122	3547L	(I)	LAUDER LILT, THE
1122	351H1H	(I)	MRS SMALL OF DIRNANEAN'S JIGG
1122	31H52	(I)	HAND ORGAN, THE
1122	31H55	(I)	BELLEISLE MARCH, (THE)
1122	31H2H2H	(I)	LE GARCON VOLAGE

1122	4125L	(I)	MISS BARBARA ARGO'S JIG
1122	4524	(I)	MISS BROWN OF KELLY-BANK'S REEL
1122	5226L	(I)	BANKS OF SPEY, THE
1122	5226L	(I)	BALLOON, THE
1122	5226L	(I)	LADY JOHN SCOTT
1122	5223	(II)	MACLAUCHLANE'S SCOTCH MEASURE
1122	5223	(I)	HIGHLAND LASSIE O, THE
1122	5223	(I)	INVERNESS SCOTS MEASURE, THE
1122	5223	(I)	MR McLAINE'S SCOTCH MEASURE
1122	5223	(I)	MCLACHLAN'S SCOTTISH MEASURE
1122	5223	(I)	MACHLACHLANE'S SCOTS MEASURE
1122	5511	(I)	MARSEILLOIS, THE
1122	5511	(I)	YE SONS OF FREEDOM
1122	5522	(I)	HIGHLAND LADDIE, THE
1122	5543	(I)	MISS EVERILDA FRASER
1122	6223	(I)	INVERNESS SCOTS MEASURE, THE
1122	6527bL	(I)	LAST PINT OF ALE, THE
1122	6522	(I)	LAST PINT OF ALE, THE
1122	6547bL	(I)	LAST PINT ALE, THE
1122	71H26	(I)	LUG OF THE SPADE, THE
1122	1H151H	(I)	MISS JANE WEDDERBURN'S STRATHSPEY
1123b	5L5L5L3bL	(I)	DEAR TO ME IS MY HERO
1123b	5L5L5L3bL	(I)	'S TOIGH LEAM FEIN MO LAOCHAN
			(DEAR TO ME IS MY LITTLE HERO)
112	3b13b	(I)	BRITANGUE
112	3b15	(I)	MR HAMILTON OF BARGENNY'S MINUET
112	3b3b2	(I)	LADY OF THE FLOW'RY FIELD, THE
112	3b3b3b	(I)	TROON HOUSE, THE
112	3b3b4	(I)	MOOR LAND WILLIE
112	3b3b4	(I)	UP IN THE MORNING EARLY
112	3b3b5	(I)	BONNY LAD LAY YOUR PIPES DOWN
1123b	3b57b2	(II)	CAPTAIN MENZIES
112	35L5L	(II)	MACGREGOR A RUARI [MACGREGOR OF RORO, ETC]
112	35L5L	(II)	MAC GRIOGAIR A RUARO
			[LAMENTATION FOR MACGREGOR OF RORO]
112	35L5L	(I)	MACGRIOGAIR A RUARO
112	35L5L	(I)	LAMENTATION FOR MCGRIGOR (OF RORO)
1123	5L162	(I)	HUMOURS OF LIMERICK, THE
1123	5L166	(I)	MRS ROBERTSON OF LAWERS DELIGHT
112	37L1	(I)	MISS SWINTON'S MINUET
112	315L	(I)	IT WAS O'ER IN YON SOA
112	315L	(I)	LADY ELIZABETH CRICHTON'S MINUET
1123	16L7L5L	(I)	FAVORITE TUNE FROM MOTHER GOOSE, A
1123	1121	(I)	SWISS WALTZ
1123	1121	(I)	MISS ADAMS FAVORITE WALTZ
1123	1121	(I)	SPANISH FANDANGO
1123	1166	(I)	DUNGARVEN
112	321	(I)	MRS RIDDELL'S MINUET
112	321	(I)	MISS WOOD'S MINUET
1123	247L7L	(I)	MISS NISBET'S STRATHSPEY
112	331	(I)	FAVORITE MINUET, A
112	331	(I)	SHEPHERD'S PIPE, THE
1123	427L5L	(I)	LA COUNTERFAITTE
112	343	(I)	WATER PARTED FROM THE SEA
112	351	(I)	LORD BALGOWNIES MINUET
112	351	(I)	MASTER MASON'S MUSICK, THE
112	353	(I)	JACK ON THE GREEN
112	351H	(I)	LADY JEAN LINDSAY('S MINUET)
1123	6532	(II)	PIPER'S WEIRD, THE or MACRIMMON'S FAREWELL
1123	1H233	(I)	COTILLON
1124	1127L	(I)	KINNAIRD CASTLE
1124	1151H	(II)	MISS KATHERINE STEWART FORBES
1124	1151H	(I)	MISS KATHARINE STEWART FORBES
			(' STRATHSPEY)
1124	1232	(I)	DEVONSHIRE, THE
1134	1423	(I)	KING STREET FESTINO
1124	153b1	(I)	TIBBY FOWLER'S GRAND DAUGHTER
1124	27L25L	(I)	MISS MARY ANN URQUHART'S HIGH DANCE
1124	27L25L	(I)	GAVOT LA ROSE
1124	6512	(II)	MERRY MONTH OF MAY, THE
1124	6521	(I)	MR CROOK'S FAVOURITE
1125	1125	(II)	BLACKBIRDS, THE
1125	147L7L	(I)	MUSETTE
1125	317L5L	(I)	MARCHIONESS, THE
1125	317L5L	(I)	SOLDIER'S DANCE
112	553	(I)	LASSIE LOST HER SILKEN SNOOD, THE
112	555	(I)	FRENET HA'
112	556	(II)	FIR A BHATA [1ST.TUNE]
112	556	(I)	MISS MACDONALD KINLOCHMOIDART'S FAVOURITE
112	565	(I)	MARI NIGHEAN DEORSA
112	565	(I)	MARY THE DAUGHTER OF GEORGE
1126	5211	(I)	MISS DOUGLAS'S FANCY

112	665	(I)	LADY RAMSAY OF BALMAINS MINUET
1121H	5326L	(I)	MISS AMELIA CLARKE'S STRATHSPEY
112	1H1H5	(I)	THEID, SGUN D'THEID MI THAIRIS
113b	5L5L5	(I)	TIGH AN DROM [TAIGH AN DROMA]
113b	7bL7bL4	(I)	JACK IN THE WEST
113b	7bL7b4	(I)	THRO' THE MUIR AT NIGHT
113b1	27bL42	(I)	MR LIVINGSTON OF PARK HALL'S STRATHSPEY
113b1	27bL44	(I)	MR GEORGE NEWTON'S JIG
113b1	3b17bL5L	(I)	MAC CAOIDH CHONASAIN
113b1	3b3b7b7b	(I)	BRAYS OF ANGUS, THE
113b1	7b7bL24	(II)	MRS MCDONALD OF CLANRANALD
113b1	7b7bL24	(II)	CLANRANALD
113b1	7b7bL24	(I)	CLANRANNALD'S REEL
113b2	7bL5L7b2	(II)	MISS MONEYPENNY OF PITMILLY
113b2	7bL5L7b2	(I)	MISS MONEYPENNY OF PITMI(L)LY'S REEL
113b2	7bL7bL42	(II)	CAPT. CAMPBELL OF CARPHEN
113b2	7bL7bL42	(I)	CAPT CAMPBELL OF CARPHEN'S STRATHSPEY
113b2	127L7L	(I)	DAWNING OF DAY, THE
113b2	227b2	(I)	MR GEORGE FORBES Yr OF NEW AND EDINGLASSIE
113b2	247b5	(I)	CAROLAN'S FAREWELL TO MUSIC
113b2	27b27bL	(II)	LADY ERSKINE
113b2	27b27bL	(I)	LADY ERSKINE'S REEL
113b2	423b1	(I)	WHEN THE KINE HAD GIVEN A PAIL FULL
113b2	547b5	(I)	MY MOTHER'S AY GLOWRING O'ER ME
113b3b	7bL242	(I)	MRS STEWART OF BINCHILL'S REEL
113b3b	114L1	(I)	HUMOURS OF GLEN
113b3b	24L2L4L	(II)	PROFESSOR SCOTT
113b3b	27bL27bL	(I)	MRS McLEOD OF DELVEY'S STRATHSPEY
113b3b	27bL24	(I)	SYMON BRODIE
113b3b	27bL53b	(II)	FORFAR HUNT
113b3b	2454	(II)	MISS FALCONER
113b3b	247b2	(II)	FORFAR HUNT, THE
113b3b	3b7bL24	(I)	MISS CLEMENTINA STEWART'S JIGG
113b	3b3b3b	(I)	AND WHEN SHE CAME BEN SHE BOBED
113b3b	3b443b	(I)	GILDEROY
113b3b	4227bL	(I)	BOBBY'S FANCY
113b3b	4427bL	(II)	SMALL COALS FOR NAILERS
113b3b	4427bL	(I)	MISS MILLER'S REEL
113b3b	443b3b	(I)	UP IN THE AIR
113b3b	47b47bL	(I)	FOSS' RECOVERY
113b	3b54	(I)	AULD EAGE AND YOUNG NEVER GREES THE GITHER
113b3b	543b2	(I)	MISS MOREHEAD'S REEL
113b3b	543b4	(I)	BONNY CHARLIE
113b3b	5443b	(I)	GILDEROY
113b3b	553b3b	(I)	BONNY CHARLIE
113b3b	557b5	(II)	I LOST MY LOVE
113b3b	557b5	(I)	I LOST MY LOVE AND I (DINNA KEN HOW/CARE NOT)
113b3b	551H1H	(I)	LUCKY MINUTE, THE
113b3b	56b55	(I)	MR JOHNSTON GRANT'S STRATHSPEY
113b3b	51H1H1H	(I)	PORT ATHOL
113b3b	61H2H6	(I)	NACH BEIR THU AIR A' BHAN' MHEARLACH
113b	3b77bL	(I)	McDONALD OF KEPPACH'S LAMENTATION
113b	422	(I)	MO GHAOL AN COLGAIRNEACH SPRAICEIL
113b4	2427bL	(I)	MRS KEIR OF MILLBANK'S REEL
113b4	26b55	(II)	MINSTREL TO HIS SOUL, THE
113b	43b4	(I)	OLD AGE AND YOUNG
113b	443b	(I)	AN OLD WELSH TUNE
113b	443b	(I)	MORFA RHUDDLAN
113b	444	(I)	BISHOP OF ARGYLE'S LAMENT
113b4	5247bL	(I)	MISS ELEANORA KER'S REEL
113b4	553b7bL	(I)	HABBIE'S HOW
113b5	7bL7bL7bL2	(I)	MR F-----'S BIRTH-DAY
113b5	7bL242	(I)	WELCOME TO YOUR AIN HOUSE
113b5	7bL424	(II)	BELLADRUM
113b5	7bL424	(I)	MISS BAIN'S STRATHSPEY
113b5	7bL424	(I)	BELLADRUM('S STRATHSPEY)
113b5	1124	(I)	NOORAH CREENAH
113b	514	(I)	MISS EVERILDA FRASER
113b5	2227bL	(I)	HENRY B. STEWART, Esqr. OF BALNAKELLIE'S REEL
113b5	2224	(II)	MRS MORTHLAND
113b5	2224	(I)	MR MORTHLAND ('S REEL) [MORTLAND'S REEL]
113b5	2224	(I)	MR MORTHLAND'S REEL
113b5	2427bL	(II)	MISS STEWART OF GARTH
113b5	2427bL	(II)	MRS STEWART OF GARTH
113b5	2427bL	(I)	MISS POLLY WELSH ('S REEL)
113b5	2427bL	(I)	MISS BURNET OF MONBODDO'S REEL
113b5	2427bL	(I)	DUTCHESS OF DORSET'S REEL, THE
113b5	2422	(I)	BROUGHTY CASTLE
113b5	2454	(I)	NEW BRIDGE OF RUTHERGLEN, THE
113b5	247b5	(I)	MR LEID'S STRATHSPEY

113b5	27b47bL	(I)	LORD GLENLYON'S REEL
113b	53b7bL	(I)	CHEAPUICH NA FASOCH
			[(A') CHEAPACH NA FASACH]
113b5	47bL37b	(I)	LADY LAWRIES REEL
113b5	427bL2	(I)	MRS R. JOHNSTON'S REEL
113b5	4247bL	(I)	MRS KEIR OF MILLBANK'S STRATHSPEY
113b5	4444	(I)	MISS AINSLIE'S STRATHSPEY
113b5	4455	(II)	TIBBY FOULLER O' THE GLEN
113b5	4455	(I)	DUNROBIN CASTLE
113b5	4455	(I)	TIBBY FOULLER O' THE GLEN
113b5	446b5	(II)	DRUNKEN WIVES OF FOCHABERS
113b5	446b5	(I)	DRUNKEN WIVES OF FOCHABERS, THE
113b5	5427bL	(I)	MISS SCOTT OF BALWILLIE'S REEL
113b	557b	(I)	I HAVE A WIFE OF MY AIN
113b	551H	(I)	MY TIME O YE MUSES
113b	551H	(I)	PHEBE
113b	551H	(I)	YON WILD MOSSY MOUNTAINS
113b5	67b67b	(I)	BHLIAN UR ['BHLIADHNA' UR]
113b5	7b7bL24	(I)	MISS McKENZIE OF COULS REEL
113b5	7b7bL24	(I)	MISS BRUCE OF KINROSS'S REEL
113b5	7b4b7L4	(I)	MISS GRAHAM OF AIRTH'S STRATHSPEY
113b	57b4	(I)	HARDY KNUTE
113b5	7b47bL2	(I)	MRS FULLARTON OF ROSEMOUNT'S REEL
113b5	7b427bL	(II)	CAPTAIN FRANCIS WEMYSS DELIGHT
113b5	7b427bL	(I)	CAPTAIN FRANCIS WEMYSS DELIGHT
113b5	7b427bL	(I)	EARL OF FIFE'S BIRTH DAY, THE
113b5	7b422	(I)	CARLE HE CAME O'ER THE CRAFT, THE
113b5	7b424	(II)	MRS MCDONALD OF CLANRANALD
			[MRS MACDONALD OF CLANRANALD]
113b5	7b547bL	(I)	MRS ABERCROMBY (OF GLASSA)
			'S (STRATHSPEY/REEL)
113b5	7b547bL	(I)	MRS GORDON OF ABERDOURS'S STRATHSPEY
113b5	7b644	(I)	DALKEITH HOUSE
113b5	7b7b24	(I)	LOCH CATHRINE
113b5	7b7b42	(II)	MR BARCLAY'S REEL
113b5	7b7b7b7b	(I)	PRIOR'S OR MR MALIE'S STRATHSPEY
113b5	7b2H47bL	(II)	MR DUNCAN McKERRACHER'S STRATHSPEY
113b5	1H7b27bL	(I)	MR BERRY'S REEL
1135L	1332	(I)	I STILL MAY BOAST MY WILL IS FREE
113	6L4L4	(I)	MINUET
1130	2240	(I)	CUBE MARCH
113	15L6L	(I)	MY APRON DEARIE
113	15L5	(I)	BONNY EARL OF MURRAY, THE
113	16L5L	(I)	IRISH AIR
1131	6L27L5L	(II)	JAMES McINNES, ESQ., DANDALEITH
1131	6L27L7L	(I)	STRATHSPEY
1131	7L7L25L	(I)	CORN RIGGS
1131	7L7L27L	(I)	JINKING OF THE LOOM, THE
1131	1115L	(I)	HORNPIPE
1131	1126L	(I)	MRS HAMILTON OF BARGENNY'S REEL
1131	1122	(I)	LADY DUNBAR OF NORTHFIELD'S STRATHSPEY
1131	1136L	(II)	JOSEPH HUME
1131	1132	(I)	CAPTAIN MacDONALD'S STRATHSPEY
1131	1132	(I)	BALLENDALLOCH CASTLE
113	112	(I)	LONG ROOM OF SCARBROUGH, THE
113	115	(I)	RAKES OF KILKENNY, (THE)
1131	1511	(I)	RAKES OF KILKENNY
113	116	(I)	SULLIVANS FANCY
113	116	(I)	JACKSON'S RAKES OF KILKENNY
1131	11H7L2	(I)	EARL OF ERROL'S STRATHSPEY
1131	25L11	(I)	SAVAGE DANCE, THE
1131	26L7L5L	(I)	TRIP TO THE CAMP, A
1131	27L5L5L	(I)	MRS R. CATTO'S HORNPIPE
1131	2246	(I)	ELGIN ACADEMY, THE
1131	2266	(I)	LENOX LOVE TO BLANTYRE
1131	2266	(I)	HOW CAN I &C
1131	2366	(I)	LENNOX'S LOVE TO BLANTYRE
1131	247L2	(I)	HONble MISS ELPHINSTON'S STRATHSPEY
1131	2462	(I)	MR FRANCISCO D'SOUZA'S FAVORITE
1131	2466	(II)	LENNOX LOVE TO BLANTYRE
1131	2461H	(I)	MISS CHRISTINA STEWART'S REEL
1131	2662	(I)	GREEN GROW THE RASHES O'
1131	2664	(I)	DAN OSSIAN [DAN OISEIN]
1131	22H66	(I)	LENNOX LOVE TO BLANTYRE
1131	3331	(I)	RUAIG GHLENNE FRUIN
1131	3353	(I)	TOO OLD TO MARRY
1131	3433	(I)	SAM JONES
113	135	(I)	MR ROCHEAD'S MINUET
1131	3555	(I)	MR PATRICK DUFF JUNr's STRATHSPEY
1131	4325L	(I)	ADMIRAL RODNEY'S TRIUMPH
1131	447L5L	(II)	CEASE YOUR FUNNING
1131	4427L	(I)	CITTY SPOON AND TREEN LADLE

1131	4650	(I)	MONMOUTH STREET
113	154	(I)	LADY MARY POWIS'S MINUET
1131	5535	(I)	COLONEL ROBERTSON OF STROWAN'S MARCH
1131	6252	(I)	DUTCHESS OF BEDFORD'S FANCY, THE
1131	6332	(II)	NUT, THE
1131	6447L	(I)	LADY STORMONT'S STRATHSPEY
1131	657L2	(I)	DRAWING ROOM, THE
1131	1H5H4H2H	(I)	MISS BENTINCK'S FANCY
1131	1H5H4H2H	(I)	LADY MARY BENTINCK'S FANCY
1132	6L6L22	(I)	TARRY WOO
1132	7L7L25L	(I)	CORN RIGGS
1132	7L7L25L	(I)	MISS BOW'S DANCE
1132	7L7L25L	(I)	CORN RIGGS (ARE BONNY)
1132	7L223	(I)	DUPLIN CASTLE
113	215L	(I)	VAUHALL'S MINUET
1132	131H6	(II)	HUNTINGTOWER
1132	2243	(I)	WAEFU' HEART, THE
1132	2255	(I)	DALKEITH MAIDEN BRIDGE
1132	227b6	(I)	SIC A WIFE AS WILLIE HAD
113	223	(I)	JOHNNY AND NELLY
113	223	(I)	THERE WAS A LAD AND A LASS IN A KILOGIE
113	223	(I)	MARY SCOT
113	223	(I)	BANNOCKS O' BARLEY MEAL
1132	236L5L	(II)	BANKS OF LOMOND, THE
1132	2353	(I)	PORT GORDON
1132	2356	(I)	PORT GORDON
1132	231H1H	(I)	MISS OLIPHANT OF GASK'S DELIGHT
113	224	(I)	THO' FOR SEVEN LONG YEARS
113	224	(I)	MISS BURNETT'S MINUET
113	226	(I)	BANOKS OF BEAR MEAL
1132	2666	(I)	SCOTS MEASURE, (THE GLASGOW)
1132	3232	(I)	BEAM OF JOY, THE
1132	3366	(I)	MISS BARTRAM'S STRATHSPEY
1132	3555	(I)	BONNY GREY-EY'D MORN, THE
1132	4433	(I)	HIGHLAND LADDY
1132	4443	(I)	JOHN COME KISS ME NOW
1132	5531	(I)	MR DAVID DUN'S HORNPIPE
1132	51H1H7	(I)	MERRY SCOT, THE
1132	6532	(I)	NORTHLAND JOCKEY
1133	5L133	(I)	MISS JANE STEWART'S STRATHSPEY
1133	7L27L2	(I)	SIR HEW DALRYMPLE Bt.(N BERWICK'S) REEL
1133	115L5L	(II)	BELLS O' LOCH LOMON
1133	116L5L	(II)	TAKIN' ITHER BY THE HAN'
1133	117L7L	(II)	GATHERING, THE
1133	117L7L	(I)	LOVE IN A VILLAGE, (A REEL IN)
1133	117L7L	(I)	MISS HAY OF DRUMELZIER'S MEDLEY
1133	1122	(II)	OPERA REEL
1133	1122	(I)	OPERA REEL, THE
1133	1132	(II)	MARRY KETTY
1133	1132	(II)	WHA' WIDNA FECHT FOR CHARLIE
1133	1132	(II)	HIGHLAND DONALD
1133	1132	(I)	LADY CHARLOTTE LENOX'S REEL
1133	1132	(I)	WHA WADNA' FIGHT FOR CHARLIE?
1133	1132	(I)	MARRY KETTY, (WILL YOU GO AND)
1133	1132	(I)	MARY KETTY
1133	1142	(II)	MISS JANE GRANT, LYNMORE
1133	1142	(I)	MISS JANE GRANT('S REEL)(,LYNMORE)
1133	136L2	(I)	PARSON IN BOOTS, THE
1133	136L3	(I)	PARSON AND HIS BOOTS, THE
1133	146L2	(I)	MRS CAMPBELL ARDMORE'S JIG
1133	227L7L	(II)	MISS STEWART
1133	227L7L	(I)	MISS STEWART('S STRATHSPEY)
1133	227L7L	(I)	MISS BIGG'S (OF NEWCASTLE'S) DELIGHT
1133	2215L	(I)	CIOD E BHIODH TU 'GIARRAIDH
			[St. KILDA SONG AND DANCE, A]
1133	2211	(I)	FITZ WILLIAM, THE
1133	2221	(I)	PUT THE GOWN UPON THE BISHOP
1133	2247L	(I)	FOURTEENTH REGt's NEW QUICK STEP
1133	2244	(I)	DANCED BY MASTER D. ALISON
1133	2244	(I)	MISS WILLIAMSON OF POLMONT'S REEL
1133	2244	(I)	PEACE UPON A TRENCHER
1133	227b7b	(I)	LADY JANE MURRAY'S RANT
1133	227b7b	(I)	CAILLEACH OUER
1133	2277	(I)	LADY JEAN MURRAY'S RANT
113	323	(I)	I'LL HAE HER AWA' IN SPITE O' HER MINNIE
1133	236L2	(I)	PARSON AND HIS BOOTS, THE
1133	2466	(I)	FAIRY KING
1133	22H22H	(I)	WILLIE DUNCAN
1133	22H62H	(II)	WILLIE DUNCAN
1133	3221	(I)	WIDOW GIN THOU BE WAKING
113	333	(I)	LOVE IS THE CAUSE OF MY MOURNING
1133	3316L	(II)	JOHNNIE'S FRIENDS ARE NE'ER PLEASED

1133	3316L	(I)	JOHNNY'S FRIENDS ARE NE'ER PLEASED
1133	3332	(II)	DAYS THAT WE HA'E SEEN, THE
1133	3343	(II)	FAREWELL TO THE GLEN
113	335	(I)	MISS BETSEY CAMPBELL OF SHAWFIELD'S MINUET
1133	4212	(I)	BONNY LASSIE TAKE A MAN
1133	4233	(I)	OLD HIGHLAND LADDIE, THE
1133	5121	(I)	MARCH OF THE 25th REGt.
1133	5326L	(I)	WHISTLE O'ER THE LAVE O'T
1133	5322	(I)	MISS BULLOCK'S FANCY
1133	5331H	(I)	HONBle COLONEL HAMILTON'S QUICK STEP
1133	5342	(I)	MR BROWN OF KELLYBANK'S MARCH
1133	531H1H	(II)	VIOLET DAVIDSON
1133	5411	(I)	LA SCIMBALLE
1133	5432	(I)	WONDER, THE
1133	5515	(I)	DUKE OF YORK'S MARCH
1133	5521	(I)	CAPTAIN JOHNSTON'S QUICK STEP
1133	5522	(I)	MRS BLAIR OF BLAIR'S FAVORITE
1133	5532	(I)	COLLEGIAN, THE
1133	5552	(I)	(BONNY) LASS OF LIVINGSTON, THE
1133	5552	(I)	SALT FISH AND DUMPLINS
1133	5552	(I)	LASS OF LEVINGSTONE, THE
1133	5552	(I)	LASS OF LIVINGSTON, THE
1133	5553	(I)	MARY'S DREAM
1133	5561H	(I)	PUBLIC THANKS
1133	551H1H	(I)	AUCHTERTOOL VOLUNTEERS MARCH
1133	561H1H	(I)	MR MUNRO OF POINTSFIELD'S REEL
1133	51H33	(I)	RALPH'S FROLICK
1133	51H51	(II)	CAIRDING O'T, THE
1133	51H52	(I)	CARDING O'T, THE
1133	51H52	(I)	MY LORD SEFOTH'S SCOTCH-MEASURE
1133	51H54	(I)	ALEXr. CHIVAS ESQr's HORNPIPE
1133	6221	(I)	WIDOW ARE YE WAUKIN'
1133	6222	(I)	PRINCE OF TUNIS, THE
1133	6231	(I)	WIDOW ARE YE WAKING
1133	6361H	(I)	WILL YE GO TO THE FOREST MY BONNIE LASS
1133	6423	(II)	DUNCAN QUADRILLE, THE
1133	6522	(II)	DUCHESS OF BEDFORD
1133	6522	(II)	DUCHESS OF MANCHESTER, THE [LADY GEORGINA GORDON]
1133	6522	(II)	LADY GEORGINA GORDON'S STRATHSPEY
1133	6522	(I)	LADY GEORGINA GORDON'S (REEL/STRATHSPEY)
1133	6522	(I)	LORD FINCASTLE'S REEL
1133	6522	(I)	DUCHESS OF MANCHESTER'S STRATHSPEY, (THE)
1133	6542	(I)	MISS ADAM'S REEL
1133	6623	(I)	ALLAN WATER
1133	7b422	(II)	CARLE HE CAM(E) O'ER THE CRAFT, THE
1133	7b422	(I)	CARLE HE CAME O'ER THE CRAFT (WI' HIS BEARD NEW SHAVEN), THE
1133	7422	(I)	CARLE HE CAME O'ER THE CRAFT, THE
1133	1H51H5	(II)	DELVIN SIDE
1134	1124	(I)	RANGER'S FROLICK
113	423	(I)	MISS HEDGE'S MINUET
113	465	(I)	IRISH AIR
1135	7L27L2	(II)	MRS OSWALD OF AUCHINCRUIVE [AUCHENCRUIVE]
1135	7L27L2	(I)	MRS OSWALD (OF AUCHINCRUIVE'S) NEW REEL
1135	1125L	(I)	MISS MURRAY OF POLMAIZE'S REEL
1135	1122	(I)	LINLITHGOW LOCH
1135	1122	(I)	DUTCHESS OF GORDON'S REEL
1135	1132	(II)	MR JOHN STEWART
1135	1132	(I)	MR JOHN STEWART('S REEL)
1135	1135	(II)	MERRY MAY THE PAIR BE
1135	1135	(I)	GU MO MEAR A CHARAID
1135	27L5L7L	(I)	MISS McQUEIR'S REEL
1135	2210	(I)	OH NO WE NEVER MENTION HER
1135	2227bL	(I)	EIGHT MEN OF MOIDART, (THE)
1135	2246	(II)	ALBERT
1135	2246	(I)	MISS DAWSON'S JIG
1135	2255	(I)	MRS DUFF'S RECOVERY
1135	2431	(I)	MEASON'S OF YORK
1135	3122	(I)	MERRY SHERWOOD or STRAW BONNET, THE
1135	3311	(I)	NEW WAY OF WOOING, THE
1135	3313	(I)	TORPHICHEN'S RANT
1135	3531	(I)	WAY TO ELGIN, THE
1135	3631H	(I)	SMITH'S MAGGOT, THE
113	531H	(I)	PANGS OF LOVE, THE
1135	4131	(I)	CASTLE GRANT
1135	4131	(I)	MISS BURGOYNE'S FANCY
1135	427L1	(II)	LADY CHARLOTTE CAMPBELL'S REEL
1135	427L2	(II)	LADY CHARLOTTE CAMPBELL
1135	427L2	(I)	LADY CHARLOTTE CAMPBELL'S (REEL/MEDLEY/NEW REEL) REEL, (THE)
1135	4246	(II)	DUKE OF KENT, THE

1135	437L7L	(I)	EARL MOIRA
1135	4327L	(II)	LOUDONS BONNIE WOODS
1135	4327L	(II)	LORD MOIRA('S WELCOME)
1135	4327L	(I)	LORD MOIRA ('S WELCOME TO SCOTLAND)
1135	4327L	(I)	MARQUIS OF HASTINGS, THE
1135	4327L	(I)	EARL MOIRA ('S STRATHSPEY)
1135	4327L	(I)	EARL OF MOIRA'S WELCOME TO SCOTLAND
1135	447L7L	(I)	MISS GRIERSON'S STRATHSPEY
1135	4427L	(I)	LORD JOHN CAMPBELL'S NEW STRATHSPEY
1135	4427L	(I)	LORD MOIRA'S WELCOME (TO SCOTLAND/HOME)
1135	4327L	(II)	MARQUIS OF HASTINGS, THE [LORD MOIRA]
1135	4652	(I)	MISS LESLIE OF BERRYDEN'S STRATHSPEY
1135	5126L	(II)	A DHOMHNUILL, A DHOMHNUILL
113	553	(I)	LADY MARY KEITH'S MINUET
1135	5326L	(I)	SKYE AIR (No.168)
113	554	(I)	MINUET
1135	54#31	(I)	MISS JANE CARNEGIE'S ALLAMANDE
113	555	(I)	SCOTCH TUNE
113	555	(I)	MARY SCOT(TS THE FLOWER OF YEARON)
113	556	(I)	MARY SCOT(T)
113	556	(I)	YE'LL AY BE WELCOME BACK AGAIN
113	557	(I)	LADY BINNIE'S MINUET
113	557	(I)	MISS WADE'S MINUET
1135	572H7	(I)	FLY NOT YET
113	551h	(I)	MR ROBERT HENDERSON'S WALTZ
113	551H	(I)	BONNY BELL
1135	51H22	(II)	STRATHGLASS HOUSE
1135	51H22	(I)	STRATHGLASS HOUSE
1135	51H31	(II)	CARRICK'S RANT or
			SMITH'S A GALLANT FIREMAN, THE
1135	51H57	(I)	PRIZE OR 325, THE
1135	6561H	(I)	HONble MISS STUART, BLANTYRE'S
			STRATHSPEY, THE
1135	662H1H	(I)	COUNTESS OF BUCHAN'S STRATHSPEY, THE
1135	671H1H	(I)	GRACES, THE
1135	7b422	(I)	CARLE HE CAME O'ER THE CROFT, THE
1135	7b2H24	(I)	MRS GORDON OF KNOCKESPOCH
1135	7424	(I)	MISS LESLIE OF ROTHY'S REEL
1135	1H41H4	(I)	WHIP THE CAT
113	51H5	(I)	LEEZIE LINDSAY
1135	1H642	(I)	MISS RABINA BOSWELL'S REEL
1135	1H642	(I)	AYR RACES
1135	1H642	(I)	LADY DUNCANNON'S REEL
1135	1H1H62H	(I)	STRATH EARN SIDE
1135	1H1H76	(I)	BERKS OF ABERGELDE, THE
1135	1H1H1H6	(I)	MISS MCLEAN OF LOCHBOWIE'S STRATHSPEY
1135	1H3H1H5	(II)	BRAES OF AUCHTERTYRE, THE
1135	1H3H1H5	(I)	BRAES OF AUCHTERTYRE, THE
1135	1H4H62H	(I)	COLLr. Wm. SIMSON'S STRATHSPEY
1135	3H535	(II)	MISS SUSAN GORDON
1135	3H535	(I)	MISS SUSAN GORDON('S REEL)
1136	5552	(I)	LASS OF LIVINGSTONE, THE
1136	5622	(I)	FALCONER'S LAMENT, THE
1136	53H22	(I)	MRS ROSE OF KILRAVOCK'S STRATHSPEY
113	667	(I)	JAMY COME TRY ME
113	661H	(I)	JAMIE COME TRY ME
1131H	5L5L7L4	(II)	TRUMPET, THE
1131H	5L5L7L4	(I)	HORNPIPE
1131H	2242H	(II)	MISS STEWART OF GARTH
1131H	2242H	(I)	MISS STEWART OF GARTH('S REEL)
1131H	224#2H	(I)	MRS GLENNIE'S REEL
1131H	224#2H	(I)	THERE'S NAE HARM DONE GOODWIFE
1131H	5216L	(I)	CAPT CHARLES STEWART'S JIGG
1131H	5221	(I)	ALLAN WATER
1131H	5221	(I)	MY LOVE ANNIE'S VERY BONNY
113	1H53	(I)	FAITH I DEFIE THEE
113	1H55	(I)	MISS GRACE STEWART'S MINUET
1131H	5552	(I)	LASS OF LIVINGSTON, THE
1131H	637L2	(I)	MISS MARY CAMPBELL ARDMORE'S JIG
113	1H61H	(I)	GRACE'S FAREWELL
1131H	7351	(I)	MISS MOODIE'S HORNPIPE
1131H	2H4H2H5	(I)	MISS JAMIESON'S JIG
1133H	1H653	(II)	SCOTCHMAN IN AMERICA, THE
1147bL	112H2H	(II)	BARGENNY'S BOWLING GREEN
1147bL	112H2H	(I)	BARGENNY'S BOWLING GREEN
1147bL	113bH2H	(I)	BARGENNY BOWLING GREEN
1147bL	2545	(I)	HO RO GU'M B'AOBHUIN LEAM,etc.
1147L	1115	(I)	COUNTESS OF ANCRAM'S
			(STRATHSPEY/BIRTHDAY), THE
1147L	1154	(I)	HODDOM CASTLE
1147L	1165	(I)	MRS MONRO BINNING'S FAVORITE
114	7L14	(I)	MINUET

1141	1141	(I)	MISS SIBBALDS WALTZ
1141	1145	(I)	MRS Dr. STEWART'S STRATHSPEY
1141	1152	(I)	CHA D'THEID MI GU LOCH BHRAOIN NO GHEARRLOCH
1141	1152	(I)	NEITHER SHALL I GO TO LOCH BROOM NOR GAIRLOCH
1141	1154	(I)	A PHIURAG GHAOLACH
1142	7L7L25L	(II)	CORN RIGS
1142	1125L	(I)	O.P. DANCE, THE
1142	1141	(II)	TINK A TINK
1142	1141H	(I)	EARL OF ELGIN'S STRATHSPEY, (THE)
1142	2253	(I)	GIN LIVING WORTH
1142	2253	(I)	WAE'FUL HEART, THE
1142	227b6	(I)	SIC A WIFE AS WILLIE HAD
1142	3364	(I)	LES FEUX D'ARTIFICE
1142	3364	(I)	MISS SANDWICH COTILLON
1142	3442	(I)	MISS MACDOWALL GRANT'S REEL
1142	3556	(I)	LADY CHARLOTTE PERCY'S SCOTCH MEASURE
1142	57bL7bL4	(I)	STEWARTS MARCH, THE
1142	57bL7bL4	(I)	ISOBAIL NI CAOIDH
1142	5122	(I)	JOCKY FOU AND JENNY FAIN
1142	6750	(I)	BERWICK BRIDGE
1142	1H633	(I)	STOLEN KISS, THE
1143b	5L16b5	(I)	MRS DUNDAS OF ARNISTON'S STRATHSPEY
1143	447bL4	(I)	WHEN I WAS A WEE THING
1143	56L17L	(I)	QUICK STEP 45th REGt
1143	56L11	(I)	LINCOLN RACES
1144	7bL7bL47b	(I)	NEW JOHNNY COPE
1144	2255	(I)	JOHNNIE FAA
1144	3347L	(I)	HIS GRACE THE DUKE OF BUCCLEUCH'S STRATHSPEY
1144	5527L	(I)	MISS CHALMER'S JIGG
1144	5527L	(I)	COW KEEPER
1145	1125L	(I)	(GERMAN) WALTZ
114	551	(I)	MARSAIL LOCHINALIE
114	551H	(I)	MRS RENNY TAILYOUR'S MINUET
1145	1H532	(I)	STONEHAVEN ASSEMBLY
1146	5421	(I)	DUKE OF WELLINGTON'S NEW WALTZ
1146	557L2	(II)	CANTY AULD MAN, THE
1141H	5230	(I)	MY LODGING IS ON THE COLD GROUND
1141H	5233	(I)	MY LODGING IS ON THE COLD GROUND
115	2L24	(I)	COUNTESS OF SEAFIELD, THE
115	6L27L	(I)	SIR ROGER DE COVERLEY
115	7L27L	(I)	MISS GORDON, (LIVERPOOL)
1151	7bL7bL47bL	(I)	O AS I WAS KISS'D YE'STREEN
115	115L	(I)	MISS SALLY McDONALD'S MINUET
1151	1137bL	(I)	LADY FLORA MACDONALD
1151	117b7bL	(II)	MISS FLORA MCDONALD
1151	117b7bL	(II)	FLORA MACDONALD [FLORA McDONALD]
1151	117b7bL	(I)	MISS (FLORA) MACDONALD'S (REEL/RANT/QUICK-STEP)
1151	1354	(I)	LADY MILNER'S REEL
1151	157b4	(II)	THEARLAICH, NAN TIGEADH TU or FLORA MACDONALD
1151	27bL27bL	(II)	O AS I WAS KISS'D YESTREEN
1151	27bL27bL	(II)	KISSED YESTREEN
1151	27bL27bL	(I)	(O AS/SAE WEEL AS/SAE BRALEY AS) (I WAS) KISS'D YESTREEN
1151	27bL47bL	(I)	O AS I WAS KISS'D TH'STREEN
1151	2227L	(I)	NANCY DAWSON
1151	2236L	(I)	MISS READ'S REEL
1151	2462	(I)	DROPS OF DRINK
1151	3225L	(I)	WATSON'S SCOTCH MEASURE
1151	3225L	(I)	O GIN YE WERE DEAD GUDEMAN
1151	3221	(I)	WATSON'S SCOTS MEASURE
1151	3222	(I)	O GIN YE WERE DEAD GUDE MAN
1151	3223	(II)	O GIN YE WERE DEAD GUDEMAN
1151	3223	(I)	O GIN YE WERE DEAD GUDEMAN
1151	46L25L	(II)	DUMFRIES HOUSE
1151	46L25L	(I)	DUMFRIES HOUSE
1151	47L7L6L	(I)	MASQUERADE DANCE
1151	47L31	(I)	W. MORRISON'S COMPLIMENTS TO MR SCOTT 78th REGt. BAND
1151	427L5L	(I)	MISS JANE GORDON'S REEL
1151	427L7L	(II)	MR STEWART OLIPHANT OF ROSSIE
1151	427L7L	(I)	MR STEWART (OLIPHANT) OF ROSSIE(S REEL)
1151	427L2	(I)	LADY ANSTRUTHER'S REEL
1151	437L2	(I)	MRS OSWALD OF AUCHENCRUIVE'S JIG
1151	4525L	(II)	DUMFRIES HOUSE
1151	4525L	(I)	DUMFRIES HOUSE
1151	4642	(I)	MRS CUMINE OF AUCHRY'S STRATHSPEY
1151	4642	(I)	CLYDE RIVER

1151	516L2	(II)	ALEXANDER TROUP
115	153	(I)	MRS OSWALD OF DUNNIKEERS MINUET
1151	5764	(II)	SANNY SPEIRS
1151	4H3H2H6	(I)	MISS CRAUFURD'S REEL
1152	6L5L7L2	(II)	CROQUET GREEN, THE
1152	7bL7bL42	(I)	JOHNNY COPE
1152	7bL47b4	(I)	MISS ANN ROSS'S REEL
1152	7L5L11	(I)	SECOND MEDLEY DANCE
1152	7L27L2	(II)	PARISH OF DALMAILING
1152	7L27L2	(I)	PARISH OF DALMAILING
1152	1153H	(II)	EASTER ELCHIES
1152	1153H	(I)	EASTER ELCHIES
115	215	(I)	FRIENDSHIP
115	227L	(II)	SIR ROGER DE COVERLEY
115	226	(I)	FYE LET US AW' TO THE BRIDAL
1152	3122	(I)	GRACES, THE
1152	3211	(I)	AIR DE CHASSE
1152	517bL5L	(I)	MRS GORDON'S FAVORITE
1152	5427bL	(I)	AULD MAID OF FIFE, THE
1152	7b427bL	(I)	MR CHARLES GIBSON, PITLOCHRY'S STRATHSPEY
1153	5L5L47L	(II)	CROWHILLOCK
1153	5L5L47L	(I)	CROWHILLOCK'S STRATHSPEY
1153	117L5L	(I)	WESTERN ISLE DANCE
1153	1126L	(I)	UNTITLED
1153	1136L	(I)	MISS ANNE GORDON
1153	1142	(II)	GLASGOW LASSES(, THE)
1153	1142	(I)	CIRCUS REEL, THE
1153	1142	(I)	MR JAs. CAMPBELL BALMARTIN
1153	1142	(I)	GLASGOW LASSES, THE
1153	112H7	(I)	MR EDWARD SIMPSON'S FANCY
1153	1255	(I)	SHE ROW'D HIM IN HER APRON
1153	1255	(I)	THA MO GHAOLS' AIG DONAL
1153	26L7L5L	(I)	MARCHIONESS OF TWEEDDALE
1153	26L7L5L	(I)	MISS M. McL. MENZIES' REEL
1153	26L15L	(I)	BRIDGE OF KILLAROW, THE
1153	27L27L	(I)	CARYSFORT, THE
1153	2462	(I)	MRS STEWART'S REEL
115	326	(I)	FYE LET US A' TO THE BRIDAL
115	331	(I)	LADY HELENORA HOME'S MINUET
1153	3153	(II)	EARL MARISCHAL
1153	3153	(I)	EARL (OF) MARSHALL ('S REEL)
			[EARL MARISCHAL'S REEL]
115	331H	(I)	(BATTLE OF) PENTLAND HILL(S)
1153	4253	(II)	CIORSDAN MHOR [MISS STEWART BUNRANNOCH]
1153	4253	(II)	COIRSDAN MHOR or MISS STEWART BUN RANNOCH
1153	4253	(I)	MRS STEWART, BUN RANNOCH'S REEL
1153	5322	(I)	JACKSON'S DREAM
1153	5355	(I)	MA HURRAMAN
1153	5642	(II)	LORD ALEXANDER GORDON
1153	5653	(II)	LADY MARY RAMSAY
1153	5653	(I)	LADY MARY RAMSAY ('S STRATHSPEY)
1153	51H46L	(I)	MR JAs. McLACHLAN'S RANT
1153	51H53	(I)	AULD TOON O' EDINBURGH, THE
1153	51H62	(II)	TALISKER
1153	51H2H2	(I)	YES OR NO
1153	51H3H2H	(I)	ROYAL TERRACE, THE
1153	657L2	(I)	BURLESQUE, THE
1153	6526L	(I)	MISS CAMPBELL'S STRATHSPEY
1153	6526L	(I)	MISS CAMPBELL OF KILBRIDE'S STRATHSPEY
1153	1H531	(I)	SOFT MAY MORN
1153	1H531	(I)	MADAINN CHIUIN CHEITEIN
1153	1H631	(I)	MADAINN CHIUN CHEITEIN
1154	17bL25L	(I)	MOR NIAN A GHIBARLAN
			[MOR NIGHEAN A GHIOBARLAIN]
1154	17bL21	(II)	MY BRAW HIGHLAND LADDIE
1154	1121	(II)	MOR NIGHEAN A GHIOBARLAIN
1154	1121	(I)	MOR NIAN A GHIOBALAIN
1154	1121	(I)	DEAR HIGHLAND LADDIE, THE
1154	1154	(I)	BOATMEN'S SONG, THE
1154	1154	(I)	LUINNAG FERRAMH BATA
1154	1154	(I)	AS YOU LIKE IT
1154	1425L	(I)	MOAR NEIN I GIBERLAN
1154	2461H	(I)	THERE'S MY THUMB
115	431H	(I)	PENTLAND HILLS
1154	4321	(I)	MISS HAY MACKENZIE'S FAVORITE
1155	6L427L	(I)	NEW ROYAL QUICK STEP, THE
1155	7bL6L7bL1	(I)	AN CRONAN MUILEACH
1155	7bL7bL7bL4	(II)	BALMORAL HIGHLANDERS, THE
1155	7L5L7L5L	(I)	MRS GARDEN OF TROUP'S STRATHSPEY
1155	1125L	(I)	DUFF HOUSE
1155	1126L	(I)	THERE'S NOUGHT SAE SWEET AS LOVE
1155	1147bL	(II)	JENNY SUTTON

1155	1147L	(I)	JENNY SUTTON
1155	1137L	(I)	JENNY SUTTON
1155	1142	(I)	PERTH REEL
1155	1142	(I)	GLASGOW LASSES
1155	1142	(I)	LADY LOUISA MACDONALD STRATHSPEY
1155	1152	(II)	BEN NEVIS
1155	1152	(II)	KNOCKANDO HOUSE
1155	1152	(I)	DUNCAN DAVIDSON
1155	1152	(I)	KNOCKANDO ('S REEL/HOUSE)
1155	1152	(I)	BENNEVIS
1155	1154	(I)	GENTLE ANN
1155	1155	(I)	MASTER JAMES ROSE'S HORNPIPE
1155	1162	(I)	DUNCAN DAVIDSON
1155	136L1	(I)	CIA MAR IS URRA' SINN FUIREACH O'N DRAM
1155	136L1	(I)	LEGACY, THE
1155	1327L	(II)	MISS INNES OF EDINGIGHT
1155	1327L	(I)	MISS INNES OF EDINGIGHT('S REEL)
115	515	(I)	MOUNT YOUR BAGGAGE
1155	151H3bH	(I)	LADY MARY HAY'S SCOTCH MEASURE
1155	2223	(I)	MY HEART IS SAIR FOR SOMEBODY
1155	2243	(I)	MISS WEDDERBURN COLVILL'S FAVORITE
1155	2266	(II)	MR GRANT OF GLENQUAICH
1155	2266	(I)	MR GRANT OF GLENQUICH'S STRATHSPEY [MR GRANT OF GLENQUAICH]
1155	2266	(I)	MRS KELTY AUCHTERMUCHTY'S FAVOURITE
1155	2266	(I)	EAST NOOK OF FIFE, THE
1155	2266	(I)	SANDY O'ER THE LEE
1155	2261H	(II)	EAST NEUK O' FIFE, THE
1155	236L6L	(II)	ST. PATRICK'S DAY
1155	236L6L	(I)	St. PATRICK'S DAY(IN THE MORNING)
1155	2416L	(I)	HON: MR MAULE OF PANMURE'S MARCH, THE
1155	2445L	(I)	GALLOWAY'S HORNPIPE
1155	2466	(I)	THERE'S MY THUMB I'LL NE'ER BEGUILE YOU
1155	3b3b55	(I)	YOUNG MAIDENS I TO YOU CONSIGN
115	53b5	(I)	SHE'S SWEETEST WHEN SHE'S NAKED
1155	316L6L	(I)	St. PATRICK'S DAY
1155	326L6L	(I)	St. PATRICK'S DAY IN THE MORNING
1155	336L6L	(I)	St. PATRICK'S DAY
115	536	(I)	COME O'ER THE STREAM, CHARLIE
1155	47bL27bL	(I)	MR RENTON'S JIG
1155	47bL47bL	(II)	PATE BAILLIE'S JIG
1155	427L5L	(I)	PERTH BARRACKS
1155	4326L	(II)	CAPT. FIFE
1155	4326L	(II)	CAPTAIN FIFE
1155	4326L	(I)	MR G. PATERSON'S REEL
1155	4326L	(I)	CAPTAIN FIFE'S STRATHSPEY
1155	4415L	(I)	MISS STENHOUSE'S FAVORITE
1155	4422	(II)	SMITH OF KILLIECHASSIE, THE
1155	4422	(I)	SMITH OF KILLECHASSIE, THE
1155	4452	(II)	ROXBURGH CASTLE HORNPIPE
1155	4452	(I)	ROXBURGH CASTLE(HORNPIPE)
1155	42H2H6	(I)	LADY BETTY COCHRAN'S REEL
1155	42H2H6	(I)	DUCHESSES OF RUTLAND'S REEL, THE
1155	42H2H6	(I)	LADY ELIZABETH HERONS REEL
1155	5126L	(I)	THUG A' MULT A MONNADH AIR
1155	5126L	(I)	CAW THE WITHER TO THE HILL
1155	5151H	(I)	MISS MACDONALD OF BARRODALES FAVORITE
1155	5162	(I)	LADY JEAN DUNDASS'S STRATHSPEY
1155	5211H	(I)	BROOM (OF) (COWDENKNOWES), THE
1155	5522	(I)	MISS DORSET
1155	5522	(I)	LADY CATHCART OF EARLSTON'S REEL
1155	5542	(I)	LORD FRANCIS RUSSELL
1155	5555	(II)	SPEED THE PLOUGH
1155	5555	(I)	SPEED THE PLOUGH
1155	51H22	(I)	MISS BELL'S REEL
1155	51H22	(I)	MY FRIEND AND PITCHER
1155	51H32	(I)	CARRICK'S REEL
1155	51H32	(I)	SMITH'S A GALANT FIREMAN, THE
1155	51H33	(II)	SMITH'S A GALLANT FIREMAN(, THE)
1155	51H33	(II)	CARRICK'S RANT
1155	51H33	(I)	CLURIE'S REELL
1155	51H33	(I)	CARRICK'S (RANT/REEL)
1155	51H42	(II)	SMITH'S A GALLANT FIREMAN
1155	51H42	(I)	SMITH'S A GALANT FIREMAN, THE
1155	51H1H1H	(I)	MAJOR MONTGOMERIE'S QUICK STEP
1155	51H1H1H	(I)	O'ER THE MUIR TO KETTY
1155	51H1H1H	(I)	OSWALD'S SCOTS MEASURE [McKEENY'S...]
1155	6355	(I)	MISS SCAFFE
1155	6542	(I)	CARLE HE CAME O'ER THE CRAFT, THE
1155	6642	(I)	GENERAL GRANT'S STRATHSPEY
1155	6643	(I)	BRIDGE OF DYE, THE
1155	6661H	(I)	MISS CHURCHILL'S STRATHSPEY

```
1155       6677        ( I ) SMASH THE WINDOWS
1155       661H3H      ( I ) EDINBURGH VOLUNTEER'S MARCH
1155       661H3H      ( I ) EDINr VOLUNTEER'S MARCH
1155       671H1H      ( I ) MITTINS DANCE, THE
1155       61H55       ( I ) AIRE DE L'OPERA FRANCOISE
1155       7b427bL     ( II ) PRINCE CHARLIE  [PRINCE CHARLES]
1155       7b427bL     ( I ) PRIONNS' TEARLACH [PRINCE CHARLES]
1155       7b424       ( II ) EARL OF BREADALBANE('S HERMITAGE) (THE)
1155       7b424       ( I ) EARL OF BREADALBANE'S (HERMITAGE/REEL)
1155       7b547bL     ( I ) JIGG, A
1155       7b654       ( I ) HEBRIDEAN DANCING MEASURES & C NO. 5
1155       1H522       ( I ) PRINCESS SOPHIA'S REEL
1155       1H562       ( II ) DASHING WHITE SERGEANT
1155       1H642       ( I ) FAIRWELL, THE
1155       1H662       ( I ) DASHING SERJEANT  [DASHING WHITE SERJEANT]
1155       1H1H1H1H    ( I ) MARQUIS OF HUNTLY'S FAREWELL, THE
1155       1H2H75      ( I ) ATHOLE VOLUNTEER'S MARCH, THE
1155       1H3H1H1H    ( I ) LOCHNAGAR
1155       1H3H2H1H    ( II ) LOCHNAGAR
1155       2H2H4H2H    ( I ) MR ALEXANDER OSWALD'S REEL
1156       7L5L7L5L    ( II ) MRS GARDEN OF TROUP
1156       7L5L7L5L    ( I ) MRS GARDEN (OF TROUP/E)( 'S STRATHSPEY)
1156       1156        ( I ) BRIDE, THE
1156       22H62H      ( I ) FRANK WALKER'S STRATHSPEY
1156       31H2H2      ( II ) MRS McLEOD OF COLBECK
1156       31H2H2      ( I ) MRS MCLEOD OF COLBECK('S REEL)
115        642         ( I ) BEDFORD JIG, THE
1156       1H411       ( I ) MISS SAUNDER'S FANCY
1157b      61H66       ( I ) LASSIE IN THE YELLOW COATIE, THE
1151H      1126L       ( II ) MISS JANE MACINNES, DANDALEITH
1151H      1126L       ( I ) MISS JANE MCINNES( ,DANDALEITH)
1151H      1165        ( I ) MISS FERGUSON OF KILKERRAN'S REEL
1151H      137L2       ( I ) HARLEQUIN
1151H      2246        ( I ) LADY RACHAEL RUSSELL
1151H      436L2       ( I ) COUNTESS OF UXBRIDGE'S STRATHSPEY, THE
1151H      5142        ( I ) MISS HUME'S REEL
1151H      5542        ( I ) I'LL NEVER GO TO FRANCE
1151H      5551H       ( I ) CALEDONIAN MARCH, THE
1151H      5551H       ( I ) SCOTCH MARCH
1151H      51H22       ( II ) CADGERS IN/(OF) THE CANONGATE, (THE)
1151H      51H22       ( II ) MRS ROSE
1151H      51H22       ( I ) MRS ROSE('S REEL)
1151H      51H22       ( I ) CADGERS OF (THE) CANNONGATE, (THE)
1151H      51H3H1H     ( II ) GORDON HIGHLANDERS, THE
1151H      637L7L      ( I ) LADY BARBARA ASHLEY COOPERS STRATHSPEY
1151H      6326L       ( i ) MRS CUNNINGHAM OF BONNINGTONE'S STR.
1151H      647L5L      ( I ) MISS BETTSY ROBINSON'S REEL
1151H      656L2       ( I ) FORFAR ASSEMBLY
1151H      6651H       ( I ) FAVOURITE HIGHLAND AIR, A
1151H      662H2H      ( I ) MISS JEANY GRANT'S REEL
1151H      662H2H      ( I ) LASSIE WITH THE YELLOW COATY, THE
1151H      61H66       ( II ) LASSIE WI' THE YELLOW COATIE
1151H      61H66       ( I ) LASSIE WI' THE YELLOW COATIE, (THE)
1151H      62H2H1H     ( I ) FOR (THE) LACK/SAKE OF GOLD
                             (SHE LEFT ME/I LOST HER)
1151H      7b7b66      ( I ) LASSIE WITH THE YELLOW COATIE, THE
115        1H1H3       ( I ) MISS C. GEDDES'S WALTZ
1151H      3H4H2H2     ( I ) MISS BOYCE'S REEL
1152H      1151H       ( I ) WALTZ
1153H      663H3H      ( II ) MRS McMILLAN'S QUADRILLE
1153H      1H522       ( II ) LADY DUMFRIES
1153H      1H522       ( I ) LADY DUMFRIES'S REEL
1166L      1155        ( I ) MISS ADMIRAL GORDON'S WALTZ
1160       5230        ( I ) I LO'E NE'ER A LADDIE BUT ANE
1162       1127L       ( I ) 'SOLC A FHUAIR MI TUS A GHEAMHRAIDH
1162       1162        ( I ) MISS POINTZRICKET'S FANCY
1162       1165        ( I ) MISS MALCOMB'S REEL
1162       35L13L      ( I ) L'AMOUR DE VILLAGE
1164       7L7L6L2     ( I ) MISS OGLEVES FANCY
1165       1132        ( II ) CAMERON HIGHLANDERS, THE
1165       456L2       ( I ) MAJOR JOHN BRUCE'S QUICK STEP
116        551         ( I ) HERO AND LEANDER
116        551         ( I ) LEANDER ON THE BAY
1165       1H4H72H     ( I ) MR WILLIAM JARDINE'S STRATHSPEY
1166       5122        ( II ) I LO'E NAE A LADDIE BUT ANE
1166       5122        ( I ) I LO'E NA A LADDIE BUT ANE
1166       51H2H5      ( i ) COTTILION
1161H      5122        ( I ) MY LODGING IS ON THE COLD GROUND
116        1H71H       ( I ) LADY MARGRET CARNEGIE'S MINUET
117b1      7bL7bL42    ( I ) BALOO MY BOY MY WEE BIT LADDIE
117b       511         ( I ) A BHANARACH DHONN A' CHRUIDH
117b       511         ( I ) BROWN MILKMAID, THE
```

117b	552	(I)	AUBURN-HAIR'D BONNY DEY, THE
117b5	1H3b55	(I)	RISING BREEZE, THE
117b7b	117b7b	(I)	UNTITLED
1175	1H1H47L	(II)	MISS BROOKE
117	762H	(I)	PEOPLE'S JIG, THE
1171H	1H16L7L	(I)	MISS EUPHEMIA LOWE'S JIG
111H1	6L217L	(I)	MRS BOSWELL OF AUCHINLEEK'S FAVORITE
111H	335	(I)	HAWK WHOOPS ON HIGH, THE
111H3	422H4H	(I)	SPACE AND COMPASS
111H3	422H4H	(I)	GUTHRIE CASTLE
111H3	7b7bL7bL3	(I)	FURTHER BENN THE WILCOMER, THE
111H	447L	(I)	LADY BAIRD'S MINUET
111H5	1125L	(I)	TRIP TO St. ANDREWS, A
111H	522	(I)	I HAD A HORSE AND I HAD NAE MAIR
111H5	2227bL	(II)	MRS BREMNER, THE MANSE, GLENBUCKET
111H5	2227bL	(II)	MISS INNES
111H5	427L5L	(I)	FEATHERS, THE
111H5	5642	(I)	AM BOTAL DUDH S'AN SLEIGA CHREACHUN [AM BOTAL DUBH...]
111H5	6531	(I)	QUICK STEP, A
111H	655	(I)	(MISS CLEMIE STEWART'S) MINUET
111H6	662H2	(I)	MISS L. MONTGOMERY OF SKERMORLIE'S STRATHSPEY
111H1H	357L5L	(I)	MAJOR KER'S QUICK STEP
111H1H	4522	(I)	TRIP TO YORK, A
111H1H	5236	(I)	MADAM SEFOTH'S SCOTCH-MEASURE
111H1H	51H51	(I)	MISS HELLEN RENNY'S SCOTCH MEASURE
111H1H	632H2	(I)	LADY EGLINTON'S REEL [LADY EGLINTOUNE'S REEL]
111H1H	1H135	(II)	BOTTOM OF THE PUNCH BOWL, THE
111H1H	1H135	(I)	BOTTOM OF THE PUNCH BOWL, THE
111H1H	1H542	(I)	MISS ELIZA BRODIE'S STRATHSPEY
111H1H	1H542	(I)	JIGG, A
111H1H	1H66H2H	(I)	DUPLIN HOUSE
111H1H	1H66H2H	(I)	BLUE BONNETS OVER THE BORDER
111H1H	1H66H3H	(I)	BLUE BONNETS
111H1H	1H3H1H5	(I)	O'ER THE MOOR AMANG THE HEATHER
111H1H	2H7b2H1H	(I)	SLOW
111H1H	2H755	(I)	LADY ELIZA LINDSAY'S HORNPIPE
111H1H	2H3H1H1H	(I)	BONNY PEGGY KISS'D ME
111H1H	2H4H2H5	(II)	HARVEST HOME
111H1H	3H1H71H	(I)	A.F. GRAY ESQr's HORNPIPE
112H1H	31H42	(I)	LADY ANN ERSKIN'S REEL
11#35	11#31	(I)	WALTZ
125L1L	5L122L	(I)	MRS HUGH LUMSDEN'S STRATHSPEY
125L3L	1L3L5L5L	(II)	COUNTESS OF CRAWFORD, THE
125L4L	1236L	(I)	MISS MARGARET DRYSDALE'S STRATHSPEY
125L5L	1236L	(I)	MRS COUTS TROTTER'S FAVORITE
125L6L	6L211	(I)	PERTHSHIRE DANCING MEASURES & C
125L6L	2231	(I)	LIKE LIGHTNING GLEAMS
125L1H	4525L	(II)	LAIRD O' HAUGHS, THE
126L5L	4L5L6L2L	(II)	MRS BARCLAY'S REEL
126L5L	4L3L2L7L	(I)	MUFFIN, THE
126L5L	4L3L2L7L	(I)	BULL'S HEAD, THE
126L5L	1155	(II)	GANE IS MY JEAN
126L	124	(I)	SIR JOHN SCOTT'S FAVOURITE
126L1	3422	(I)	MISS MURRAY OF ELLIBANK'S FAVORITE
127bL5L	7bL5L7bL5L	(I)	MISS MAULE OF PANMURE'S REEL
127L7L	1515	(I)	UNTITLED
127L0	1240	(II)	BRITANNIA THE PRIDE OF THE SEAS
127L1	127L1	(I)	MISS HONYMAN OF ARMADALE'S WALTZ
127L1	237L7L	(I)	DUNCAN GRAY
1213L	17L22L	(I)	MISS CATHERINE FORSYTH'S REEL
1215L	5L5L11	(II)	BELTED PLAID, THE
1215L	5L37L2	(I)	WEYMOUTH FETE, THE
1215L	6L7L13	(I)	BUCKLAND DOWNS
1215L	16L22	(II)	BALLETERACH STRATHSPEY
1215L	1232	(I)	PAS SEUL MISS ELIZA ROBERTSON
1215L	2437L	(I)	LADY SUSAN GORDON'S QUICK STEP
1216L	1232	(I)	LOVELY FANCY
1217L	6L237L	(I)	DUTCHESS OF MANCHESTER'S FAVORITE
1211	7bL7b47bL	(II)	CASAG LACHDUNN RUAIRDH RUAIDH [RED RODERICK'S DUN COAT]
1211	4522	(II)	CLAN CHATTAN
1212	1231	(II)	HAYMAKERS' JIG
1212	1234	(I)	MISS FRANCES RUSSELL
1212	1234	(I)	SINGLETON HALL
1212	1535	(I)	GET UP AND BAR THE DOOR
1212	1535	(I)	I'LL DRINK A HEALTH TO CHARLIE
1212	1535	(I)	JOHNIE BLUNT
1212	1623	(I)	HIGHLAND LADDIE, THE
1212	11H52	(I)	MAN'S GANE GYTE, THE

1212	11H65	(I)	MISS IN HER OWN HAIR
1212	11H4H1H	(I)	LORD NELSON'S WALTZ
1212	3215	(I)	FAITHFULL SHEPHERD, THE
1212	4522	(I)	MISS CRAWFORD'S FAVORITE
121	3b3b4	(I)	LAOIDH GHARA 'SNAM BAN
1214	3241	(II)	MISS JEANNIE S. GRANT'S FAVOURITE
1214	3431	(I)	REPLEYS DELIGHT
1214	3431	(I)	SHILLING O' GAIREY
121	57L1	(I)	FREEMASON'S ANTHEM, THE
1215	1256L	(I)	ROTTERDAM FAVORITE WALTZ
1215	1256L	(I)	MINUET IN PORUS
1215	1256L	(I)	ELBA WALTZ, THE
1215	427L5L	(I)	MISS CHARLOTTE MONRO'S ALLAMANDE
1215	436L7L	(I)	HONble CAPTAIN ELLIOT'S QUICK STEP
121	554	(I)	WHERE IS MY LOVE
1215	5431	(I)	MONTRILE
1215	5555	(I)	AN GROATHA
1215	6b547L	(II)	THANE'S
1215	61H3H2H	(I)	JACKSON'S MORNING BRUSH
1215	61H4H2H	(I)	JACKSON'S MORNING BRUSH
1215	2H652	(II)	FLORA'S FROLICS
121	6b7L1	(I)	FREE MASONS ANTHEM, THE
1226L	1211H	(I)	DUTCHESS OF GORDON'S REEL, THE
1226L	1211H	(I)	MISS HAY'S REEL
1227bL	11H7b5	(I)	WHEN SHE CAME BEN SHE BOBED
1221	6L16L2	(II)	MAID OF LOGIE, THE [MAID O' LOGIE, THE]
1221	1247bL	(I)	QUICK STEP, 22nd REGT
1221	2547bL	(II)	FINGAL'S CAVE
1221	5522	(II)	ISLA SIDE
122	332	(I)	WHERE HELEN LIES
1223	3322	(I)	LONDON NEW MARCH
1225	1226L	(II)	LOCHNABO
122	541	(I)	KATE OF KINROSS
1225	4215L	(II)	CA' THE STIRKS (FRAE OUT THE CORN)
1225	47b15L	(I)	WAT YE WHO YOU MET THE STREEN
1225	47b25L	(I)	WAT YE WHA I MET THE STREEN
1225	47b3b5L	(I)	WAT YE WHA I MET YESTREEN
1225	47b3b5L	(I)	LORD HADDO'S (FAVOURITE) STRATHSPEY
122	554	(I)	SLOW
1225	7b547bL	(I)	MRS GRAHAM OF ORCHILL'S STRATHSPEY
123b7L	1H6b21	(I)	COTTILON
123b2	123b1	(I)	MISS SUTTON'S FAVORITE
123b2	1255	(I)	MR SAMl. HEPBURN'S FAREWELL
123b2	1755	(I)	SHAWL DANCE DANCED BY THE MISSES KIRKALDY
123b	221	(I)	NEW SHIELDS
123b4	4217bL	(I)	DALSWINTON HOUSE
123b5	47b15L	(II)	COMING THROW THE BROOM MY JO
123b5	47b15L	(I)	COMING THROW THE BROOM MY JO
123b6b	527bL4	(I)	MISS BELL KENNEDY'S REEL
1235L	4L211	(I)	PONEY RACES
1235L	1236	(I)	MRS GUN MONRO OF POYNTZFIELD'S FANCY
1237L	4L3L2L3	(I)	MISS WHARTON DUFF
1237L	1255L	(I)	QUICK STEP 17th REGt
1230	1H67O	(I)	CAMPBEL'S FROLICK
1231	6L27L2	(I)	COTILLION
1231	6L215L	(I)	LA PETITE PARISIANE
1231	1237L	(I)	MR MATTHEW'S STRATHSPEY
1231	1231	(II)	POP GOES THE WEASEL
1231	1231	(I)	POP GOES THE WEASEL
1231	25L4#2	(I)	QUIET AND SNUG
1231	27L15	(I)	JUNTA OF SEVILLE, THE
123	123	(I)	DANCE, A
1231	3453	(II)	MEPHISTOPHELES
1231	427L5L	(I)	LADY CAROLINE DOUGLAS'S FAVORITE
1231	4321	(I)	QUICK STEP 25th. REGt
1231	4322	(I)	LADY SOPHIA KEPPEL
1231	457L2	(I)	HONble MRS BUCHANAN'S FAVORITE, THE
1231	4525L	(I)	HONble HENRY ERSKINE'S FAVORITE, THE
1231	1H642	(I)	COTILLON
1232	1231	(II)	HAY-MAKERS, THE
1232	1231	(I)	HAY MAKERS, THE
1232	315L2	(II)	BONNIE DOON
1232	315L2	(I)	LAMBERTON RACES
1232	315L2	(I)	(YE) BANKS (AND BRAES) O' (BONNIE) DOON
1232	315L2	(I)	(ROYAL) CALEDONIAN HUNT'S DELIGHT
1232	315L2	(I)	CALEDONIAN HUNT'S DELIGHT, THE
1232	3511	(I)	MISS BLAND'S ALLEMAND
1232	47L42	(I)	TRIP TO THE LAWNDRY, A
1233	3455	(I)	GAVOTT
1233	4111	(I)	FRENCH LIBERTY
1233	427L5L	(II)	LADY BINNING
1233	427L5L	(I)	LADY BINNING('S STRATHSPEY)

1233	4453	(I)	CAMBRIDGE LIGHT DRAGOONS, THE
1233	5555	(I)	MARY'S DREAM, (NEW SET OF)
1233	5755	(I)	LADY DOWNE'S ALLAMANDE
1233	6537L	(I)	DOUBLE JIG
1234	3542	(I)	LOCAL ATTACHMENT
1234	3642	(I)	MISS GEORGIANA FORBES'S FAVORITE
1234	56L27L	(I)	DOUBLE JIG
1234	527L5L	(I)	NANCY'S CHOICE
1234	5235L	(I)	LOCHLEVEN SIDE
1234	5431	(II)	DRUNKEN PARSON, THE
1234	5556	(I)	GAVOT BY MR MACLEAN
1234	5644	(I)	GARDENER'S MARCH, THE
1234	52H1H1H	(I)	LA NEVELL HOLLANDOIS
1235	6L427L	(I)	LILLING HALL
1235	6L427L	(I)	LINNEN HALL
1235	1620	(I)	DUNNIKEER HOUSE
1235	37L5L5L	(I)	WELCH HARPER, THE
1235	4532	(II)	SANDY TROUP
1235	1H532	(I)	MR NEIL MACBRAYNS JIGG
1236	1236L	(I)	MRS SPENS MONRO'S JIG(G)
1231H	6413	(I)	ALLEGRO
1231H	6621	(I)	TIMES, THE
1231H	3H72H5	(I)	HUM DRUM, THE
1232H	2H2H3H2	(I)	VAGA'RY, THE
1240	5620	(I)	MARRIAGE OF FIGARO
1242	3415L	(I)	TO BIDE MY LANE FULL LOATH AM I
1242	6b425L	(I)	SECRET STREAM, THE
1242	1H522	(I)	OPERA DANCE
1243	1231	(I)	Sra MARANERI E Sr BUGIENI PAS DE DEUX
1244	2215	(I)	BONNY HOUSE O' AIRLY, THE
1244	4221	(I)	SI' NAILL SO DHUISG MI
124	452	(I)	B'E SUD IORRAM NA TRUAIGH
1245	1241	(I)	DRUB THE ROGUES
1245	3244	(I)	BONNIE HOUSE OF AIRLY, THE
1245	4245	(I)	GRAIDHEAN DONN
1256L	5L121	(II)	LADY ISABELLA WEMYSS' STRATHSPEY
1256L	5L121	(I)	LADY ISABELLA WEMYSS'S STRATHSPEY
1251	6L5L0L	(I)	EW-BUGHTS MARION
1251	127L5L	(I)	BERWICKSHIRE MILITIA'S QUICK STEP, THE
125	127L	(I)	MISS SCOT OF HARDEN
1251	46L25L	(I)	QUICK STEP
1252	5652	(I)	RANELAGH GARDEN
1253	6L7L27L	(I)	MISS M. WHITE OF BRACHLOCH
1253	1240	(I)	SAW YE JOHNNY COMING CO SHE
1253	1250	(I)	SAW YE JOHNNY COMING?
1253	1250	(I)	FEE HIM FATHER FEE HIM
1253	1251	(I)	BLACK DANCE, THE
1253	1253	(I)	SAW YE JOHNNY COMING (QUO SHE)
1253	1253	(I)	BLACK DANCE, (THE)
1253	1266	(I)	NA COMPUICH A'G'OL [NA COMPAICH AG OL]
1253	1666	(I)	COLONEL CUMMING OF ALTYRE
1253	6221	(I)	O WHAT NEEDS I MY APRON WASH
1253	6422	(I)	FRENCH TAPTOO
1254	2121	(II)	GORDON, THE [GORDONS THE]
125	465	(I)	GO WHERE GLORY WAITS THEE
1255	6L7L33	(II)	BONNIE GLENFARG
1255	7bL27bL4	(II)	MISS MACKENZIE OF GAIRLOCH
1255	7bL27b4	(II)	MISS MACKENZIE OF GAIRLOCH
1255	4411	(I)	FOR OUR LANG BIDING HERE
1255	457L2	(I)	SPLASH'D PETTICOAT
1255	5255	(I)	OMNIA VINCIT AMOR
1255	7b542	(I)	COLONEL CAMPBELL OF KINGSBURGH'S STRATHSPEY
1256	5530	(II)	CRADLE SONG, THE
1256	52H65	(I)	THA MISE FO MHULAD
1256	52H65	(I)	MOURNFUL AM I
1256	2H52H1H	(I)	GE DO THA MI M'AONAR SNA GLEANNAIBH
1256	2H52H1H	(I)	THOUGH I AM ALONE IN THE VALE
1262	1266L	(I)	MEDLEY OVERTURE (13)
1262	1266L	(I)	HEY JENNY COME DOWN TO JOCK
1262	3331	(I)	A ROCK AND A WEE PICKLE TOW
1265	36L10	(I)	GU MO SLAN A CHI MI MO CHAILINN DILEAS DONN
1265	36L11	(II)	GU MA SLAN A CHI MI [MAY I SEE YOU HAPPY]
1265	3110	(I)	BLYTHSOME MAY I SEE THEE
1261H	1H61H6	(I)	LOCH BHRAOIN
121H5	222H2H	(I)	MY LOVE'S IN THE BROOM
121H6	6136L	(II)	NIONAG A CHUIL DUINN NACH FHAN THU
121H6	662H1H	(II)	LOW DOWN IN THE BROOM
121H6	662H1H	(II)	RED RED ROSE
			[MY LOVE IS LIKE A RED RED ROSE]
121H6	662H1H	(I)	MY LOVE IS LIKE A RED RED ROSE
121H7	66L12	(I)	WILL YE GO (TO) (THE) (EWE-BUGHTS)
			(MARION?)

```
121H7        662H1H      ( I )  MY LOVE IS LIKE THE RED, RED ROSE
121H2H       5427bL      ( II ) MISS BRANDER
121H2H       7b427bL     ( II ) IT WINNA DO
121H2H       7b427bL     ( I )  IT WINNA DO
121H3bH      5H2H54      ( II ) SAILOR'S WIFE, THE
121H3bH      5H2H54      ( I )  MISS DUFF OF MUIRTON'S JIG
121H3bH      5H2H54      ( I )  SAILOR'S WIFE, (THE)
121H3bH      5H2H7b4     ( I )  SAILOR'S WIFE, THE
121H3bH      5H2H1H5     ( I )  SAILOR'S WIFE, THE
13b4L4L      3b3b7bL6bL  ( I )  HEATHER HOUSE, THE
13b5L5L      5L111       ( II ) DRUMMER, THE
13b5L5L      7bL7bL24    ( I )  DRUMMER, THE
13b5L5L      7bL7bL47bL  ( I )  DRUMMER, THE
13b5L5L      7bL247bL    ( II ) DRUMMER(S), THE
13b5L5L      7bL247bL    ( I )  DRUMMER, THE
13b5L5L      7bL243b     ( I )  GOOD MORROW TO YOUR NIGHT-CAP
13b5L1       27bL27bL    ( II ) HONble. GEORGE CARNEGIE, THE
13b5L1       27bL27bL    ( I )  HONble GEORGE CARNEGIE'S STRATHSPEY, THE
13b5L3b      7bL24L2     ( I )  MISS KELMAN'S REEL
13b5L3b      247bL2      ( I )  HONOURABLE MISS FRANCESS HAY'S REEL
13b7bL7bL    13b57b      ( I )  MR JAFFREY'S (JUNr) STRATHSPEY
13b7bL2      13b53b      ( II ) MISS ANN GORDON, HEATH COTTAGE
13b7L2       13b7b6b     ( I )  MISS SMOLLET'S STRATHSPEY
13b7bL3b     13b41       ( I )  MISS MCDONALD OF LEYNDALE'S REEL
13b7bL4      13b15       ( I )  UP IN THE MORNING EARLY
13b7bL4      1515        ( I )  UP IN THE MORNING EARLY
13b7bL7b     13b11H      ( I )  MRS RIGG JUNr
13b7L        124         ( I )  MERRY BEGGARS, THE
13b14L       13b14L      ( I )  DAN DHEIRG DARGO
13b15L       7bL2L7bL2   ( I )  WITCHES HILL, THE
13b15L       7bL4L7bL2   ( II ) BALMORAL CASTLE
13b15L       7bL5L4L7bF  ( I )  MR STEWART OF BALLECHEN'S WELCOME HOME
13b15L       7bL5L4L7bF  ( I )  FAVORITE SLOW TUNE, A
13b15L       7bL7b47bL   ( I )  MISS RUSSELL OF BLACKHALL('S REEL)
13b15L       13b11       ( II ) CLAN FRASER
13b15L       13b55       ( I )  AYR HARBOUR
13b17bL      3b53b7bL    ( I )  ROBIN FILL THE DRINK ABOUT
13b11        7bL7bL42    ( I )  LADY MONTAGUE'S STRATHSPEY
13b11        7bL27bL7bL  ( II ) WASHING DAY, THE
13b11        27bL42      ( I )  MONTROSE BRIDGE
13b11        3b15L7bL    ( I )  UGI NAN GU 'SMO THRIALL DACHAIDH
13b13b       7bL27bL2    ( I )  MISS DINNING OF NEWLAND'S STRATHSPEY
13b13b       13b47bL     ( I )  MOLL IN THE WADD
13b13b       2427b       ( I )  LADY MARY LINDSAY'S STRATHSPEY
13b13b       2427b       ( I )  LADY MARY MURRAY'S STRATHSPEY
13b13b       427L2       ( I )  JUST SO
13b13b       53b22       ( II ) BANKS O' LOSSIE, THE
13b13b       5427bL      ( II ) LORD GEORGE GORDON LENNOX'S REEL
13b14        13b6b4      ( I )  DONALD COUPER AND HIS MAN
13b15        13b7bL4     ( I )  BRECHIN CASTLE
13b15        247bL2      ( II ) MR LINDSAY
13b15        247bL2      ( I )  MR LINDSAY('S REEL)
13b15        427bL6bL    ( II ) SICK BOY, THE
13b1         51H1H       ( I )  SOLITUDE, THE
13b1         51H3bH      ( I )  SOLITUDE, (THE)
13b11H       7b43b7bL    ( I )  WATSON'S CLASS
13b27bL      123b1       ( I )  DUNSKY
13b27bL      13b7bL1     ( II ) LAMENT FOR MR. THOMAS GRANT OF GLEN ELGIN
                                (AUSTRALIA)
13b27bL      13b13b      ( I )  MISS JEAN MAXWELL OF MONREITH'S REEL
13b27bL      13b23b      ( II ) MISS MARY MACDONALD
13b27bL      13b53b      ( I )  MRS FRASER OF CULDUTHEL'S STRATHSPEY
13b27bL      13b55       ( I )  MRS DONALDSON'S STRATHSPEY
13b27bL      13b55       ( I )  LAIRD OF GLENBUCKIE'S HIGHLAND FLING, THE
13b27bL      13b51H      ( II ) MISS GIBSON
13b27bL      13b51H      ( I )  YOUNG INVERCAULD'S STRATHSPEY
13b27bL      13b1H5      ( I )  LASS IF I COME NEAR YOU
13b27bL      11H7b5      ( II ) LAIRD OF COCKPEN, THE
13b27bL      11H7b5      ( I )  LAIRD O' COCKPEN, THE
13b27bL      11H75       ( I )  LAIRD O' COCKPEN(, NO.3), THE
13b27bL      11H75       ( I )  WHEN SHE CAM BEN SHE BOBBED
13b27bL      11H1H5      ( I )  LASSIE I'LL COME NEAR YOU
13b27bL      7b422       ( I )  MOCH MADAINN CHEITEIN
13b2         15L1L       ( I )  MISS HENDERSON'S MINUET
13b2         13b2        ( I )  CHA BHAS THIG AIR LOACH ACH CADAL
13b21        3b543b      ( II ) PADDY'S DELIGHT
13b21        427LO       ( I )  DO CHINNEADH BHI GUN CHEANN
13b22        5L3b1H3bH   ( I )  MRS SAMUEL ANDERSON'S STRATHSPEY
13b2         211         ( I )  HOLIN GREEN HOLIN
13b22        13b13b      ( I )  LORD CHARLES MURRAY'S STRATHSPEY
13b22        13b53b      ( I )  (OLD) SIMON BRODIE
13b22        156b5       ( I )  IOMRADH EADAR ILA 'S UIST
```

13b22	156b5	(I)	UNTITLED
13b23b	5L7bL7bL5	(I)	THA MO GHOAL AIR A NIGHEAN
13b24	1251	(I)	MISS GRANT'S FAVOURITE
13b24	13b51H	(I)	COLONEL ROBERTSON OF STREWAN'S WELCOME HOME
13b24	3b523b	(II)	WILL'S REEL
13b24	6b57bL1	(I)	UNTITLED
13b27b	427bL2	(I)	BRIDGE OF ANAS, THE
13b27b	427bL2	(I)	BRAES OF ANGUS, THE
13b3b	7bL7bL4	(I)	WHY SHOULD I NOT LIKE MY LOVE
13b3b	7bL7bL4	(I)	I LOVE MY LOVE FOR SHE LOVES ME
13b3b1	27bL7bL2	(I)	BRAES OF LAINE, THE
13b3b1	247b2	(I)	MR ALEXr MONTGOMERIE'S REEL
13b3b	13b6b	(I)	OLD SIR SIMON THE KING
13b3b3b	7bL222	(I)	GARTH'S FIRE-SIDE
13b3b3b	427bL2	(II)	WAPPINSHAW, THE
13b3b3b	427bL2	(I)	WEAPON SHAW, THE [WAPPINSHAW, THE]
13b3b3b	427bL2	(I)	MISS JESSIE STEWART GARTH'S REEL
13b3b4	27bL52	(II)	MRS DAVID PATRICK'S FAVOURITE
13b3b4	27bL52	(I)	MRS DAVID PATRICK'S FAVORITE
13b3b	422	(I)	TAK YOUR AULD CLOAK ABOUT YOU
13b3b4	2424	(II)	SIR JOHN LOCKHART ROSS
13b3b4	2424	(I)	SIR JOHN LOCKHART ROSS('S STR./REEL)
13b3b4	2424	(I)	SIR JAMES CAMPBELL'S STR.(AND GIGG)
13b3b4	2424	(I)	LADS OF THE SHAWS, THE
13b3b5	13b22	(II)	BLAIR DRUMMOND
13b3b5	13b55	(I)	SIR CHARLES FORBES OF NEW AND EDINGLASSIE
13b3b5	23b12	(I)	JIGG, A
13b3b5	47b15L	(I)	WAT YE WHA I MET YESTREEN
13b3b5	7b427bL	(I)	LEVEN HOUSE
13b3b5	7b422	(II)	MR DUNDAS MACQUEEN
13b3b5	7b422	(I)	MR DUNDAS MCQUEEN('S REEL)
13b47bL	13b55	(I)	CAPTAIN RIDDELL'S STRATHSPEY
13b47bL	13b55	(I)	MISS JEAN JOHNSTON'S STRATHSPEY
13b47bL	13b57b	(I)	CAPT CHARLES CRAWFORD'S FAREWELL
13b42	13b53b	(II)	SIMON BRODIE
13b42	13b53b	(I)	TAM NA HURITH STRATHSPEY
13b42	13b55	(I)	COUNTESS OF SELKIRK'S FAVORITE, THE
13b42	13b1H1H	(I)	FOYER'S STRATHSPEY
13b42	11H3bH1H	(I)	MR DAVID BLACK'S FAVOURITE
13b43b	7bL27bL7bL	(II)	CAPTAIN McKENZIE
13b43b	13b53b	(I)	CUDDIE'S WEDDING
13b43b	13b55	(I)	HE MAN DU I O RO U
13b43b	2427bL	(II)	COUNTY HALL
13b44	13b55	(II)	HOUSE OF GRAY, THE
13b44	13b55	(I)	HOUSE OF GRAY, THE
13b44	13b6b6b	(I)	LADY TERFICHEN'S RANT [LADY TORPHICHEN]
13b44	5527bL	(I)	MISS LOGAN'S JIG
13b4	456b	(I)	BLAR LEINE
13b45	13b6b6b	(II)	LADY TERFICHEN [LADY TORPHICHEN]
13b4	556	(I)	FERNY BED, THE
13b45	6b554	(I)	AIR BY MR ARNE
13b45	1H1H3b3b	(I)	LOTS OF KISSES
13b46b	5217L	(II)	BACK TO THE HILLS
13b55L	13b11	(I)	MISS FALCONER'S STRATHSPEY
13b57bL	7bL4L7bL7bL	(I)	SWEET DAWNS THE DAY
13b57bL	13b54	(I)	HO RIN O I RI O HO NIGHEAN AN AIRICH
13b57bL	13b55	(I)	HOIRRIONN O(!) AIR NIGHEAN AN AIRICH
13b57bL	1515	(I)	UP IN THE MORNING EARLY
13b5	7bL24	(I)	MARQUIS OF TULLIBARDINE('S GIGG), (THE)
13b57b	4427bL	(II)	MY BOY TAMMIE
13b50	6b450	(II)	CHAMPION HORNPIPE
13b51	7bL4L7bL7bL	(I)	IN YOUTH WHEN THE HEART IS WARM
13b51	13b47bL	(I)	CASTLE POOL, THE
13b51	247b2	(I)	MR BOSWELL OF AUCHINLECK'S REEL
13b51	27b27bL	(I)	LADY EMELLIA KER'S REEL
13b51	27b47b	(I)	MISS RICHARDSON'S STRATHSPEY
13b5	13b5	(II)	I HA'E A WIFE O' MY AIN
13b5	13b5	(I)	I HA(V)E A (WIFE/HOUSE) O' MY AIN
13b51	47bL42	(II)	MRS McGEE'S REEL
13b51	47bL42	(I)	MAGIC MIRROR, THE
13b51	47bL42	(I)	MRS McGHIES REEL
13b5	151	(I)	MISS PEGGY MONTGOMERIE'S HORNPIPE
13b5	151	(I)	CLARK'S HORNPIPE
13b51	53b51	(I)	MISS MACRAE OF INVERINAT'S REEL
13b51	5427bL	(II)	DALKEITH'S LAMENT
13b51	7b427bL	(II)	MISS MAY HAY
13b51	7b427bL	(I)	MISS MAY HAY('S REEL)
13b51	7b427bL	(I)	LORD BINNING'S REEL
13b51	7b427bL	(I)	MISS GORDON (OF LESMORE) 'S REEL
13b52	7bL244	(II)	THERE CAM' A YOUNG MAN
13b52	7bL244	(I)	BRISK YOUNG LAD, THE
13b52	7bL244	(I)	BUNG YOUR EYE

13b52	7bL244	(I)	LADY BEWMONT'S GIG
13b52	7bL27b2	(I)	MRS HAMILTON OF SUNDRUM'S (JUNr) REEL
13b52	13b55	(I)	IRISH BILLY
13b52	13b55	(I)	IRISH FOOTMAN, THE
13b52	13b55	(I)	POT STICK, THE
13b52	13b57b	(I)	HUNTINGTONE CASTLE
13b52	4427b	(I)	MISS DUNDASS OF DUNDASS'S STRATHSPEY
13b52	5244	(I)	PORT GLASGOW ASSEMBLY, THE
13b53b	5L3b27bL	(II)	CORTES GARDENS
13b53b	7bL27bL7bL	(II)	MACKENZIE'S RANT
13b53b	7bL27bL7bL	(I)	MILLER'S FAVOURITE, THE
13b53b	7bL27bL7bL	(I)	ABERCARNEY'S REEL
13b53b	7bL27bL7bL	(I)	INVEREY'S OR CAPTAIN MCKENZIE'S (REEL/STRATHSPEY)
13b53b	7bL27bL2	(I)	MISS MARGARET BUCHAN'S STRATHSPEY
13b53b	7bL27bL5	(I)	MISS HAIG OF BEMMERSIDE
13b53b	7bL224	(I)	MR ADAM FERGUSON'S FAVORITE REEL
13b53b	7bL242	(II)	TEMPLE HOUSE
13b53b	7bL242	(II)	MISS JOHNSTON
13b53b	7bL242	(II)	NEW BRIDGE DUMFRIES, THE
13b53b	7bL242	(II)	MR MORAY OF ABERCAIRNEY [MURRAY OF ABERCAIRNEY]
13b53b	7bL242	(II)	DOMINIE'S DELIGHT, THE
13b53b	7bL242	(II)	MRS MORAY OF ABERCAIRNY
13b53b	7bL242	(II)	SIR JAMES M. INNES BARt. OF EDINGIGHT
13b53b	7bL242	(I)	MR MURRAY (OF ABERCAIRNEY)('S STR.)
13b53b	7bL242	(I)	MISS MARY G: ABERNETHIE'S STRATHSPEY
13b53b	7bL242	(I)	MISS LAY'S REEL
13b53b	7bL242	(I)	MISS JOHNSTON('S REEL)
13b53b	7bL242	(I)	NEW BRIDGE (OF) DUMFRIES, THE
13b53b	7bL242	(I)	DUNKELD HOUSE
13b53b	7bL27b2	(I)	MISS CAMPBELL OF SHAWFIELD'S STRATHSPEY
13b53b	7bL47b4	(II)	MILLADEN
13b53b	13b52	(I)	MISS CATHRINE CAMPBELL ARDMORE'S STRATHSPEY
13b53b	13b53b	(II)	COUTIE'S WEDDING [CUTTIE'S WEDDING]
13b53b	13b53b	(I)	CUTTY'S (COUTIES) WEDDING
13b53b	13b53b	(I)	SHOGALLIE'S REELL
13b53b	1353	(I)	MRS MORAY OF ABERCAIRNEYS STRATHSPEY
13b53b	25L7bL2	(II)	LADS O' ELGIN, THE
13b53b	2452	(II)	BANKS OF EARN
13b53b	247b2	(I)	DELVIN CAMP
13b53b	247b4	(I)	HURLY BURLY, THE
13b53b	247b4	(I)	DUNKELD HOUSE
13b53b	27b47bL	(I)	MISS CAMERON OF GLENEVIS STRATHSPEY
13b53b	47bL27bL	(I)	MR JOHN SMITH'S STRATHSPEY
13b53b	4242	(I)	MISS ANN DRYSDALE'S KIRKALDY REEL
13b53b	43b27bL	(II)	DELNABO
13b53b	47b47bL	(II)	ORACLE, THE
13b53b	57bL5L4L	(I)	UNTITLED
13b53b	53b42	(II)	Dr. CAMERON'S STRATHSPEY
13b53b	56b47bL	(I)	FORFAR INSTRUMENTAL BAND'S LAMENT FOR THE DEATH OF WILLIAM PEART, THE
13b53b	7b422	(II)	GENERAL MACDONALD
13b53b	7b422	(I)	GENERAL MACDONALD'S STRATHSPEY
13b53b	7b527bL	(I)	FIFE NESS
13b53b	1H3b1H3b	(I)	BRIDE'S GARTER, THE
13b54	2442	(I)	MRS DARLEY OF TIBERMORAY'S REEL
13b54	2454	(II)	NEIL ROY
13b54	246b5	(I)	DAVID HUME'S LAMENTATION
13b54	247b4	(II)	NEW BOB, THE or [BOGANUADH]
13b54	247b4	(II)	MRS GEORGE JOHNSTONE OF BYKER
13b54	247b4	(II)	LOCH DERCULICH
13b54	247b4	(II)	BOGANNACH, THE
13b54	247b4	(I)	BOGANUADH, THE (NEW BOB, THE)
13b54	247b4	(I)	LORD BINNY'S REEL
13b54	247b4	(I)	MRS GEORGE JOHNS(T)ON (OF BYKER) 'S REEL
13b54	247b4	(I)	LORD BINNY'S REEL
13b54	3b3b13b	(I)	SCOTCH MINISTER, A
13b54	427bLO	(I)	THERE'S GRACE IN YOUR GRAY LOCKS
13b54	427bLO	(I)	MARAIDH BHAN OG
13b54	43b11	(I)	('TWAS) WITHIN A FURLONG TO EDINBURGH
13b54	517LO	(I)	MAIRI BHAN OG
13b54	517LO	(II)	MARY YOUNG AND FAIR
13b54	5222	(II)	MAGNUS
13b54	5222	(I)	MANUS
13b54	5424	(I)	BOGANUADK
13b55	7bL27bL4	(II)	STRUAN ROBERTSON'S RANT
13b55	7bL27bL4	(II)	RED HAIRED GIRL OF TULLOCH, THE
13b55	7bL27bL4	(I)	(STRUAN)ROBERTSON'S RANT
13b55	7bL244	(I)	HUMORS OF HILLSBROUGH, THE
13b55	7bL7b7bL4	(I)	DAVIE RAE
13b55	127LO	(II)	LAMENT SIR JOHN MACPHERSON GRANT

13b55	13b3b3b	(I)	MAIDS IN THE MORNING, THE
13b55	27bL7b2	(I)	MR ADAM ROBERTSON'S FAVORITE
13b55	27b42	(I)	MOORLAND WILLY
13b55	3b115L	(I)	MISS WHITELOCK'S DELIGHT
13b55	3b111	(I)	MR NISBET OF DIRLETON'S FAVORITE
13b55	3b7b47bL	(II)	KILTY LADS, THE
13b55	427bL2	(I)	MR OSWALD'S REEL
13b55	4427bL	(I)	GEORDY AGAM
13b55	47b43b	(I)	POLTALLOCH or MALCOLM'S MANSION
13b55	523b1	(I)	SWEET ANNIE (FRAE THE SEA BEACH CAME)
13b55	5255	(I)	WANTONESS FOR EVER MORE
13b55	7b427bL	(II)	LAGER BEER
13b55	7b427bL	(I)	COUNTESS OF DUNMORE'S STRATHSPEY, THE
13b55	7b422	(III)	MISS CHARLOTTE STEWART
13b55	7b422	(I)	LADIES OF ARGYLE, THE
13b55	7b422	(I)	MISS CHAt STEWART'S REEL [MISS CHARLOTTE STEWART]
13b55	7b424	(II)	MRS BROWN OF LINKWOOD
13b55	7b424	(I)	MRS BROWN (OF LINKWOOD'S) (REEL)
13b55	7b522	(II)	ROYAL VISIT TO NEWE 1859, THE
13b55	7b7b27bL	(I)	MY PEGGY'S FACE (,MY PEGGY'S FORM)
13b55	7b7b27bL	(I)	GLAMMIS CASTLE
13b55	7b7b27bL	(I)	ANDERSON'S (FAREWELL/RANT)
13b55	7b7b42	(I)	COUNTESS OF DALKEITH'S FAVORITE, THE
13b55	7b2H7b5	(I)	LONDON NAIRNSHIRE MEETING, THE
13b57b	7bL246b	(I)	MRS COLL:FARQUHARSON'S FAVOURITE
13b57b	3b7b47bL	(I)	MUIRLAND WILLIE
13b57b	3b7b42	(I)	MUIRLAND WILLIE
13b47b	3b1H47bL	(I)	MUIRLAND WILLIE
13b57b	427bL2	(I)	CHARLIE, HE'S MY DARLING, ORIGINAL SET
13b57b	427bL2	(I)	DUKE OF BUCCLEUGH AND HIS FENCIBLES, THE
13b57b	4420	(I)	MY BOY TAMMY
13b57b	46b52	(I)	DRIBBLES OF BRANDY
13b57b	47b47bL	(II)	MR STEWART ROBERTSON
13b57b	47b47bL	(II)	DR. MANSON OF SPYNIE
13b57b	47b47bL	(I)	STEWART ROBERTSON'S STRATHSPEY
13b57b	47b47bL	(I)	MUIRLAND WILLIE
13b57b	47b47L	(I)	MUIRLAND WILLIE
13b57b	47b42	(I)	MUIRLAND WILLIE
13b57b	552H1H	(I)	MISS JESSIE ROSE'S STRATHSPEY
13b57b	7b427bL	(I)	MRS Dr. GORDON, ELGIN
13b57b	7b423b	(I)	CHARLIE STEWART TEARLACH STIUBHARD
13b51H	27b15L	(I)	POTATOE DIGGER, THE
13b51H	523b1	(II)	CROALL'S
13b51H	6b1H53b	(II)	CURRANT BUSH, THE
13b51H	6b1H51H	(I)	CHARLIE IS MY DARLING, (OH!),MODERN SET
13b51H	7b427bL	(II)	MRS RAMSAY(OF BARNTON)
13b51H	7b427bL	(I)	MRS RAMSAY OF BARNTON('S STRATHSPEY)
13b51H	7b7b22	(I)	MISS BAIRD'S STRATHSPEY
13b5	1H1H7b	(I)	JOCKIE AND SANDIE
13b51H	3bH7b42	(I)	EARL OF DUNMORE, THE
13b51H	3bH7b45	(I)	I'LL TOUZLE YOUR KURCHY
13b51H	3bH1H2H5	(II)	KAIL POT, THE
13b5	1H3bH2H	(I)	TEARS OF SCOTLAND, THE
13b51H	3bH2H7b2	(II)	PASS OF BALLATER, THE
13b52H	1H1H1H5	(I)	GREEN LEAVES WERE US BETWEEN
13b53bH	7b542	(I)	MISS AUGUSTA CHARTEIR'S STRATHSPEY
13b6b3b	11H6b4	(I)	STEUART LODGE
13b6b4	47bL24	(I)	MY LADDIE IS A SAILOR
13b7b7b	4427bL	(II)	MRS COLONEL BAI(L)LIE OF RED-CASTLE
13b7b7b	1H1H43b	(II)	S'COMA LEAM FHEIN COGADH NO SITH
13b1H3b	7bL27b2	(II)	MR JAMES DUFF STUART
13b1H5	7b442	(II)	TIGH 'N DUIN
13b1H1H	4522	(I)	SIR JAMES CAMPBELL'S JIGG
13b1H1H	7b424	(I)	LADY MARY LINDSAY'S JIG
13b1H1H	3bH1H45	(I)	MISS DRUMMOND'S FAVORITE
13b1H2H	7b427bL	(I)	LADY SUSAN STEWART'S STRATHSPEY
13b1H2H	7b443b	(I)	BENNY SIDE
13b1H3bH	7b427bL	(II)	EARL OF HYNDFORD('S REEL)
13b1H3bH	7b427bL	(I)	EARL OF HYNDFORD'S REEL
13b1H3bH	7b443b	(I)	NAE FAIRER BLOOMS THE DAISY
13b1H3bH	7b443b	(I)	BENNY SIDE
13b1H3bH	5H2H54	(II)	SAILOR'S WIFE, THE
135L3L	4L216L	(II)	BALMORAL CASTLE
135L3L	6L275L	(II)	CATTERTHUN
135L3L	13L55	(II)	AULD KIRK OF MACALLAN, THE
135L3L	1222L	(II)	MISS WATT
135L3L	1225L	(I)	MISS WATT('S REEL)
135L3L	137L2	(I)	MISS BARBARA CAMPBELL'S STRATHSPEY
135L3L	247L5L	(II)	MAD CAP
135L3L	247L6L	(I)	MAD CAP
135L5L	7bL7bL24	(I)	DRUMMER, THE

135L5L	1132	(I)	BONNY JEAN
135L5L	1522	(I)	HURRAH! FOR THE BONNETS OF BLUE
135L1	4L3L2L2	(I)	MRS GORDON OF CAIRNESS' REEL
137L2	331H5	(I)	LADY CHARLOTTE CAMPBELL
135L3	137L2	(I)	GARTHLAND'S STRATHSPEY
135L3	2466	(I)	BANFF CASTLE
135L3	427L7L	(II)	MISS MARGARET MAITLAND'S REEL
135L3	4522	(II)	BRIDGE OF DEE
135L3	462H5	(II)	LITTLE PICKLE
135L3	41H7L2	(II)	WARRIOR O' PERSIE, THE
135L3	1H765	(II)	LAIRD O' DRUMBLAIR, THE
135L4	1356	(I)	JACKSON'S ROLLER
136L5L	2L247L	(II)	THORN BUSH
136L5L	2L247L	(I)	GEORGE ROBERTSON, ESQr's STRATHSPEY
136L5L	4L3L2L2	(I)	MISS STANHOPE'S REEL
136L5L	4L3L2L4	(I)	BRAHAN CASTLE
136L5L	4L5L2L2L	(I)	MISS BETTY SCOTT'S FAVORITE
136L5L	5L322	(I)	LADY GEORGE MURRAY
136L5L	5L432	(I)	GENERAL CAMPBELL (OF MONZIES') STRATHSPEY
136L5L	7L223	(I)	CAPTAIN SHALL NOT GET THEE, THE
136L5L	136L2	(II)	BRAES OF NEWE, THE
136L5L	1322L	(II)	EASTER SKENE
136L5L	1342	(II)	MR GORDON GLENNIE'S STRATHSPEY
136L5L	1353	(II)	MRS RAIT'S STRATHSPEY
136L5L	1356	(II)	HOUSE OF CRAIG, THE
136L5L	1366	(I)	MISS JANE WOOD McKINZI'S STRATHSPEY
136L5L	147L5	(I)	MISS CRAGIE OF DUMBARNIE'S STRATHSPEY
136L5L	1462	(I)	LADY MONTGOMERY'S STRATHSPEY
136L5L	447L2	(I)	MRS ANN SUTHERLAND'S STRATHSPEY
136L5L	5532	(II)	BONNIE CHARLIE
136L6L	1166	(I)	LADY TEMPLE'S STRATHSPEY
136L6L	1323	(I)	STRATHSPEY REEL, A
136L6L	351H3H	(II)	MASTER JOHN GATHERER'S STRATHSPEY
136L7L	5L31H3	(II)	JOHN LAMONT'S REEL
136L7L	136L1	(I)	MISS B. CAMPBELL OF SHAWFIELD'S WALTZ
136L7L	1353	(II)	TAP O' NOTH
136L7L	1353	(II)	HOUSE OF GLENKINDY, THE
136L7L	131H3	(I)	MORAY-SHIRE FARMER'S CLUB, THE
136L7L	1566	(II)	NEIL GOW'S HOUSE
136L7L	1673	(I)	MISS ERSKINE WADE'S JIGG
136L1	5L5L3L2L	(I)	MISS JESSIE SCALES HORNPIPE
136L1	1355	(I)	MR ALEXr. CAMPBELL'S STRATHSPEY
136L1	37L42	(I)	GLENGARRY'S STRATHSPEY
136L2	7L5L15	(I)	ALEGRO [ALLEGRO]
136L2	7L531	(I)	CARO DOLCE
136L2	1353	(I)	MISS METHUEN'S REEL, THE
136L2	1353	(I)	CUMNOCK FAIR
136L2	1353	(I)	MISS BLAKE'S STRATHSPEY
136L3	136L7L	(I)	BALLEMONNY RACES
136L4	527L6L	(I)	JOLLY BOAT
137bL4	131H5	(II)	SCOTT SKINNER'S "GHILLIE CALLUM"
137L5L	4L3L2L7L	(I)	PEMBROKE'S MAGGOTS
137L5L	6L4L5L1L	(I)	LADY ELIZABETH CRICHTONS REEL
137L5L	6L4L5L3L	(I)	MRS BOSWELL OF AUCHINLECK'S REEL
137L5L	1333	(I)	MISS ELIZABETH CAMPBELL'S REEL
137L5L	1343	(I)	MISS NORTON'S REEL
137L5L	1353	(II)	MISS JEAN STEWART OF BOHALLY
137L5L	1353	(II)	MISS JOHNSON, PITWORTH
137L5L	1353	(I)	MISS JOHNSON(,PITWORTH)
137L5L	1353	(I)	MISS JEAN STEWART OF BOHALLY('S REEL)
137L5L	3637L	(I)	MISS BALFOUR'S REEL
137L6L	5L7L3L2L	(I)	McLEOD'S LESS SALUTATION
137L6L	5L7L3L2L	(I)	FAILTE BHEAG MHIC LEOID
137L6L	5L343	(I)	SIR HENRY TROLLOPE'S FANCY
137L6L	5L432	(II)	CLUNY CASTLE
137L6L	6L47L0	(I)	LET ME ALONE
137L7L	137L7L	(I)	CUDDY CLAWED HER
137L7L	137L1	(I)	CUDDY CLAW'D HER
137L7L	137L5	(II)	MISS ELENORA ROBERTSON
137L7L	137L5	(I)	MISS ELEONORA ROBERTSON'S REEL [MISS ELENORA ROBERTSON]
137L7L	11H65	(I)	COUNTESS OF KINNOUL'S DELIGHT, THE
137L0	3210	(I)	MAID OF LODI, THE
137L0	3220	(I)	PAS SEUL
137L1	4L3L25L	(II)	AULD BRIG O' DON, THE
137L1	6L6L5L1	(I)	SHIUBHAIL MI iLE'S CEANN-TIRE
137L	127L	(I)	CALEB QUOTEM'S FREAK
137L1	3535	(II)	LASS O' CORRIE MILL, THE
137L1	3535	(II)	CARLISLE LASSES
137L2	4L64#4	(II)	BANKS
137L2	135L1	(II)	WONDER, THE
137L2	1315	(I)	CORN RIGGS

137L2	1332	(I)	MR BINDON'S QUICK STEP
137L2	1335	(I)	MISS BUCHAN OF KELLY'S STRATHSPEY
137L2	1335	(I)	FREE MASON'S MARCH, THE
137L2	1353	(II)	LORD JOHN CAMPBELL
137L2	1353	(I)	LORD JOHN CAMPBELL'S STRATHSPEY
137L2	1515	(I)	MISS ESTER OSWALD (OF AUCHINCRUIVE'S) STRATHSPEY
137L2	3365	(I)	LADY BAIRD'S NEW REEL
137L2	331H5	(II)	MRS BOURKE
137L2	331H5	(I)	LADY AUGUSTA MURRAY'S REEL
137L2	331H5	(I)	MRS J.W. BOURKE'S REEL
137L2	3422	(I)	CAPTAIN MACDUFF ('S DELIGHT)
137L2	3456	(I)	MRS JOHN ANDERSON'S FAVOURITE
137L2	427L5L	(II)	MILL BURN, THE
137L4	131H3	(I)	MISS MARY BUCHANAN'S STRATHSPEY
137L4	37L6L7L	(I)	MRS McKINLAY'S FAVOURITE
137L4	37L13L	(I)	LA MARQUISE DOUBLE JIG
137L4	46L11	(I)	JOHN KNOX
1313L	1522	(II)	BONNIE LASS O' BONACCORD, THE
1314L	1422L	(II)	MR WILLIAM DONALD'S FAVORITE
1315L	1L122L	(II)	MISS GRAHAM OF INCHBRAKIE
1315L	1L122L	(I)	McINTOSH'S MAGGOT
1315L	1L122L	(I)	MISS GRAHAM OF INCHBRAKIE'S STRATHSPEY
1315L	1L222L	(I)	MISS GRAHAM OF INCHBRAKIE'S STRATHSPEY FOR THE HARPSICHORD
1315L	5L335	(I)	MY FAIR YOUNG LOVE
1315L	5L335	(I)	MO RUN GEAL OG
1315L	6L5L4L2L	(II)	MISS CHARLOTTE CAMPBELL
1315L	6L5L4L2L	(II)	MISS CAROLINE CAMPBELL
1315L	6L6L4L2L	(I)	COLONEL McLEOD'S REEL
1315L	6L133	(II)	INVER FIDDOCH
1315L	7bL220	(I)	LASS THAT STOLE MY HEART AWA, THE
1315L	7bL222	(I)	DEIL TAKE THE GAIR AND THE BRAGRIE O'IT
1315L	1210	(I)	LAOIDH AN T'SLANUIGHEAR
1315L	1311	(I)	MRS MAJOR MITCHELL'S STRATHSPEY
1315L	1353	(II)	CUTTY SARK
1315L	1353	(II)	CLACH-NA-CUDDIN
1315L	1363	(II)	CLACH NA CUDAIN
1315L	11H66	(II)	MR ALEXANDER LAWSON'S STRATHSPEY
131	5L33	(I)	MO RUN GEAL OG
1316L	5L3L1L6F	(II)	MONCRIEFFE HOUSE
1316L	5L3L6L6L	(I)	MR WILLm. SKENE QM ABERDEENSHIRE REGT.'S FAVOURITE
1316L	5L5L3L1L	(I)	MISS BEATON'S REEL
1316L	5L6L3L2L	(I)	MISS GRANT OF GRANT'S STRATHSPEY
1316L	5L6L4L2L	(I)	MISS BARBARA MUNRO'S REEL
1316L	512L2L	(II)	COL. CALL'S STRATHSPEY
1316L	5L132	(I)	SIR ALEXr. MUNRO'S REEL
1316L	5L352	(I)	CHARLES DUFF'S COMPLEMENTS
1316L	5L462	(I)	MRS FARQUHARSON (OF MONALTRIE'S) STR.
1316L	6L431	(I)	LADY DUNBAR OF NORTHFIELD'S REEL
1316L	7L27L5L	(I)	GO TO THE DEVIL AND SHAKE YOURSELF
1316L	1314	(I)	JUBILEE, THE
1316L	151H2	(I)	NANCY STUART
1316L	1632	(II)	DUNCAN QUADRILLE, THE
1311	2L2L6L5L	(I)	I WISH MY LOVE WERE IN A MIRE
1311	5L3L3L5L	(II)	FANCY HORNPIPE
1311	5L5L22	(II)	ORKNEY
1311	5L5L22	(I)	MAOL NAN CROGAN
1311	5L5L22	(I)	PERTHSHIRE DANCING MEASURES & C No. 17
1311	5L5L22	(I)	ORKNEY(REEL)
1311	6L5L32	(II)	MRS HENRY LUMSDEN OF TILLWHILLY'S STR.
1311	6L5L32	(I)	MRS HENRY LUMSDEN OF TILLWHILLY'S STR.
1311	6L27L5L	(II)	MISS CAMPBELL (OF SADDELL)
1311	6L27L5L	(I)	MISS CAMPBELL (OF SADDELL'S) STRATHSPEY
1311	6L36L2	(I)	MISS BELL CAMPBELL OF KINGSBURGH'S SCOTS MEASURE
1311	1353	(II)	CLACHNACUDDIN
1311	1363	(II)	CLACH NA CUDAIN
1311	1521	(I)	TIGHEARNA BHRODHI
1311	6562	(II)	YETTS OF MUCKART, THE
1312	1336	(I)	LEWIS GORDON
1312	1351H	(I)	LEWIS GORDON
1312	1361H	(I)	LEWIS GORDON
1312	1361H	(I)	LEWIE GORDON
131	267L	(I)	DOUBLE HORNPIPE
1313	5L7L5L7L	(II)	STIRLING CASTLE
1313	5L7L45	(I)	TOP OF BALVENIE, THE
1313	6L27L5L	(I)	MR COLIN CAMPBELL'S STRATHSPEY
1313	7bL7bL47bL	(I)	HAMILTON HOUSE
1313	7bL247bL	(I)	HAMILTON HOUSE
1313	1124	(I)	HOOP HER AND GIRD HER

131	313	(I)	GIN YE WONNE TAKE ME YE MAY LET ME BE
131	313	(I)	JOCKY SAID TO JEANY
1313	136L2	(I)	DR HAYDN'S STRATHSPEY
1313	136L2	(I)	LADY CHARLOTTE CAMPBELL'S STRATHSPEY
1313	1312	(I)	PANDOURS DANCE, THE
1313	1313	(II)	CIRCASSIAN CIRCLE
1313	1313	(I)	CIRCASSIAN CIRCLE
1313	1322	(!)	NO CATCHEE NO HAVEE
1313	1324	(I)	NORTH HIGHLAND 2
1313	1347L	(I)	BOGNOR ROCK
1313	1357	(I)	BACK OF THE CASTLE, THE
1313	1362	(I)	SIR WILLIAM DICK'S REEL
1313	157L5L	(II)	WEDDING RING, THE
1313	157L5L	(I)	PORT NA FAINNE
1313	1632	(II)	MISS SCOTT'S FAVOURITE MARCH
1313	1632	(I)	MRS RAMSAY OF BARNTON'S FAVORITE
1313	11H64	(I)	Dr RUTHERFORD OF CRAIGOW'S STRATHSPEY
1313	26L4L2	(I)	MRS DUFF OF CARNUCIE'S STRATHSPEY
1313	27L11	(I)	STORACE
1313	2216L	(I)	LADY BAIRD'S REELL
1313	2366	(II)	MILLER LADS
1313	2366	(I)	GILLEAN BAN A MHUILFHEAR [...A' MHUILLEIR]
1313	247L2	(I)	MOWBRAY CASTLE
1313	2662	(I)	MRS KELSO OF DANHEITH'S REEL
1313	27b27bL	(II)	LASSES LOOK BEFORE YOU
			[LASSIE LOOK BEFORE YOU or MISS ROSS]
1313	27b27bL	(I)	LOOK BEFORE YOU
1313	27b27bL	(I)	MISS (AGNES) ROSS('S REEL/STRATHSPEY)
1313	22H75	(I)	MISS HANNAH'S JIG
1313	31H22	(I)	MISS LOUISA RUSH'S REEL
1313	5226L	(I)	QUICK STEP, 42nd REGt
1313	5252	(I)	MISS BAIRD OF SAUGHTON HALL'S ALLAMANDE
1313	5252	(I)	LA BELLE ISABELL
1313	5252	(I)	MISS NANCY RAMSAY'S FAVORITE
1313	5252	(I)	CONVENTION, THE
1313	5655	(II)	HEATHER BELLS
1313	6342	(I)	MISS DUNBAR OF NORTHFIELD'S FAVORITE
1313	1H661H	(I)	MISS SHERRIFF'S STRATHSPEY
1313	1H2H75	(I)	JOHN GULLIVER'S REEL
1313	1H2H1H6	(II)	HARVEST HOME
1313	1H3H1H6	(II)	HARVEST HOME
1313	3H755	(II)	OUR HIGHLAND QUEEN
1314	156L7L	(I)	FOX OUTWITED, THE
1314	1632	(I)	TROUP HOUSE
1314	527L5L	(I)	CAMPBELL'S ALLEMAND
1315	1316L	(I)	MISS MELVEL DYSART
1315	1322	(II)	BLAIR DRUMMOND
1315	1322	(I)	BLAIR DRUMMOND
1315	1532	(II)	STIRLINGSHIRE MILITIA
1315	2266	(I)	MISS WILLIAMS
1315	2422	(I)	MRS P. CAMPBELL'S STRATHSPEY
1315	3647L	(I)	TURK'S HEAD
1315	5511	(I)	CARLTON HOUSE
1315	6420	(I)	BESSY'S HAGGIES
1315	6422	(I)	BONNY BESSY
1315	6422	(I)	BESSIES HAGGIES
1315	3H562	(I)	KIRN, THE
1316	1342	(I)	MISS PARKINSON'S STRATHSPEY
1316	2422H	(I)	MISS MILLER OF DALSWINTON'S FANCY
1316	2422H	(I)	BESSIE'S HAGGIES
1316	5536L	(I)	PAS SEUL
1317	4742	(I)	CAPT GORDON, SCOTS GREY'S JIG
1311H	5326L	(II)	HONble. MISS DRUMMOND OF PERTH, THE
1311H	5326L	(II)	HONOURABLE MRS. DRUMMOND OF PERTH, THE
1311H	5326L	(II)	LADY GWYDER
1311H	5326L	(I)	LADY GWYDIR
1311H	5326L	(I)	HONble MRS DRUMMOND OF PERTH'S STRATHSPEY
1311H	5326L	(I)	MISS PEGGY CAMPBELL'S STRATHSPEY
1311H	557L2	(I)	MISS ISAAC FORSYTH, (ELGIN)
1311H	662H2	(I)	MRS McLEOD OF COLBECK'S STRATHSPEY
1311H	64H72H	(I)	MISS CATHRINE ABERCROMBY'S DELIGHT
1311H	1H3H72H	(I)	MISS RAE'S JIG
1311H	3H652	(I)	HIGH WAY TO NEWFIELD, THE
1311H	5H2H2H6	(II)	JOHN ANGUS
1311H	5H2H2H6	(I)	JOHNSTON'S REEL
1311H	5H2H2H6	(I)	MR JOHN ANGUS' REEL
1311H	5H2H2H6	(I)	MARSHALL'S STRATHSPEY
1313H	1H522	(I)	MISS JESSY STEWART'S JIGG
131	6H1H3	(I)	MISS BAIRD'S MINUET
1325L	1312	(I)	MISS GRAHAM OF MOSSKNOW'S FAVORITE
1325L	1322	(I)	MARSHALL FANCY
1325L	1353	(I)	MR PETER ANDERSON'S REEL

1326bL	1353	(II)	MRS CHISHOLM
132	6L5L5L	(I)	LAMENT FOR LORD BALLENDEN, A
1326L	1323	(II)	DON SIDE
1326L	1323	(I)	DON SIDE
1326L	1323	(I)	BOAT OF LOGY, THE
1326L	1344	(I)	MR STEWART OF BALLAICHIN'S STRATHSPEY
1326L	1346	(I)	MISS BLAGROVE'S STRATHSPEY, THE
1326L	1353	(II)	MRS CHISHOLM
1326L	1353	(I)	ORCHILL HOUSE
1326L	1353	(I)	MRS CHISHOLM(OF CHISHOLM'S STRATHSPEY)
1326L	1355	(I)	MISS JANE CARNEGIE OF SOUTHESK'S STRATHSPEY
1326L	1361H	(I)	MRS C.K. JOHNSTON'S REEL
1326L	131H6	(I)	NATH. GOW'S LAMENT FOR (HUGH) EARL OF EGLINTOUN
1326L	1535	(I)	MIRRY NIGHT AT TUMBLE BRIDGE, THE
1326L	4463	(I)	MISS HOPE'S (REEL/STRATHSPEY)
1327bL	1313	(I)	MISS HAY OF LEY'S STRATHSPEY
1327bL	1323	(I)	MISS MARY MacDONALD'S REEL
1327L	1153	(II)	BRAES OF RHYNIE, THE
1327L	1323	(I)	FORBES'S RANT, THE
1327L	1331H	(I)	LADY LUCY RAMSAY'S REEL
1327L	1344	(I)	QUICK STEP, FENCIBLES
1327L	1353	(I)	MISS ANN AMELIA STEWART'S STRATHSPEY
1327L	1355	(I)	MR FLETCHER'S REEL
1321	5L122L	(I)	LADY ARCHd CAMPBELL'S REEL
1321	6L5L2L2	(I)	LORD OGILVY
1321	6L131	(I)	FULL MOON, THE
1321	7L27L2	(II)	ITALIAN OPERA DANCE
1321	7L221	(I)	ITALIAN MONFRINA
1321	7L221	(I)	GRACES, THE
1321	1326L	(I)	UNTITLED
1321	1321	(I)	SANTO CARLO DI NAPOLI
1321	1321	(I)	ALBINIA
1321	1362	(I)	MISS GUTHRIE OF GUTHRIE'S STRATHSPEY
1321	1362	(I)	FINGAL'S CAVE
132	115	(I)	MISS NAPIER'S MINUET
1321	11H65	(II)	BREACAN MAIRI HUISTEAN [MARY HUISTEAN'S PLAID]
1321	3165	(I)	GUDE FORGIE ME FOR LIEIN
1321	3165	(I)	LOTHIAN LASSIE, THE
1321	3165	(I)	LAST MAY A BRAW WOOER, &c. [LOTHIAN LASSES]
132	134	(I)	OPEN THE DOOR TO THREE
1321	3535	(I)	MISS RUSSELL OF BLACK HALL'S FAVORITE DANCE
1321	57L21	(II)	ITALIAN MONFRINA
1321	6161	(I)	'S E COINNEACH OG A FHUAIR AN TOGAIL
132	11H6	(I)	BIRKS OF BALNABOATH
1321	1H632	(II)	BRUCE'S MARCH
1321	1H632	(II)	KING ROBERT THE BRUCE
1322	115L1	(I)	MRS LAIRD OF STRICKMERTENS FAVORITE
1322	115L1	(I)	FAVOURITE WELCH AIR, A
1322	136L6L	(II)	DELRACHNIE'S RANT
1322	136L6L	(I)	PRINCE'S WELCOME TO INVERNESS, THE
1322	136L6L	(I)	DELRACHNAY'S RANT
1322	1316L	(II)	'S FHEUDAR DHOMH FHEIN A BHI FALBH ['TIS TIME TO GO HOME]
1322	1313	(I)	WATTIE LANG
1322	1313	(I)	MISS (M./POLLY) SKINNER'S REEL
1322	1343	(I)	DUKE'S REEL, THE
1322	3325L	(I)	MILK MAID'S HORNPIPE, THE
132	243	(I)	DAUPHIN MINUET, THE
132	243	(I)	AFTON WATER
1322	537L7L	(I)	MISS McKINNON OF LIVERIES REEL
1322	51H26L	(I)	MRS BEARD'S STRATHSPEY
1322	51H26L	(I)	MRS GORDON OF ABERGELDIE'S STRATHSPEY
1322	6651	(I)	MAID OF BATH, THE
1323	5L5L22	(II)	MILLER'S MAN, THE
1323	5L5L22	(II)	FANNY FARQUHARSON
1323	5L5L52	(I)	PATRICK SARFFIELD or NEW LANGO LEE
1323	5L152	(I)	JUDY OF FLANIGAN
1323	5L152	(I)	ORIGINAL LANGO LEE, (THE)
1323	5L152	(I)	LANGOLIL [LANGO LEE]
1323	5L326L	(I)	BONNY LASS TO MARRY ME, A
1323	5L335	(I)	MISS JANE CAMPBELL (OF MONZIE'S) STRATHSPEY
1323	1326L	(I)	STRATH-NITH
1323	1321	(I)	MOUNTING OF THE AIR BALLOON, THE
1323	1336L	(I)	KELSO RACES
1323	11H1H1H	(I)	CUMH PHARIC MOR MHIC CRUIMMEN
1323	11H1H1H	(I)	LAMENT ON THE DEATH OF PATRICK MORE McCRUIMMEN
1323	6355	(I)	CUMH CHLAIBH
1324	137L7L	(I)	MR JOHN GEORGE CAMPBELL'S REEL
1324	1313	(I)	PERTHSHIRE DANCING MEASURES & C No. 5

1324	1313	(I)	KISS ME FAST (MY MOTHER'S COMING)
1324	1315	(II)	KISS ME FAST(MY MINNIE'S COMING)
1324	1315	(I)	KISS ME FAST MY MINNIE'S COMING
1324	1353	(I)	REEL
1324	1353	(I)	KEEP THE COUNTRY BONNY LASSIE
1324	131H5	(I)	CAPT BLAIR (OF THE ROYALS') QUICKSTEP
1324	151H5	(I)	HOOLY AND FAIRLY
1324	151H5	(I)	MEDLEY OVERTURE (7)
1324	11H52	(I)	MISS MARGRETT DALRYMPLE'S JIG
1324	11H52	(I)	PARKHILL HOUSE
1324	37L11L	(I)	AURETT'S DUCH SKIPPER
1324	3421	(I)	FAUSAN'S MAGGOT
1324	3421	(I)	LILLIE BULERA
1324	3432	(I)	JACK'S ALIVE
1324	3513	(I)	MARCH
1324	3525L	(I)	LA NOWELLA BALLANDOISE
1324	3527L	(I)	MISS B. CAMPBELL'S BUMPKIN
1324	3544	(I)	MR BARCLAY DUN'S HORNPIPE
1324	3642	(II)	EARL OF EGLINTON'S BIRTHDAY
1324	31H54	(I)	MISS MACDONALD KENLOCHMOIDART
1324	51H52	(I)	CLOAK BAG
1325	7L113	(II)	THA MISE CHO MULADACH
132	551	(I)	FHUAIR MI LITIR O'N GHOBHADH
1326	1321	(I)	JOHN SMALL'S MINUET
1326	1353H	(I)	BATTLE, THE
1326	1353H	(I)	HIGHLAND BATTLE, A
1333L	1135	(II)	LORD LYNDOCH'S WELCOME
1336L	1362	(II)	ABOYNE CASTLE
1337L	3553	(I)	STRASBURGH DANCE, THE
1311	5L5L22	(II)	MAOILE NAN CROGAICHEAN, OR ORKNEY
1331	5L5L22	(I)	HONble MISS K. ELPHINSTON'S
1331	7L227L	(II)	HOUSE OF CLUNY, THE
1331	7L227L	(I)	HOUSE OF CLUNY, THE
133	113	(I)	JOHN HAY'S BONNY LASSIE
1331	1327bL	(I)	MOOR SO WETT, THE
1331	1321	(I)	ROYAL EXCHANGE
1331	27bL27bL	(I)	DUKE OF HAMILTON'S REEL
1331	2462	(I)	FOOTS VAGARIES
1331	2662	(II)	GREEN GROW THE RASHES(O!)
1331	2662	(I)	GRANT'S (RANT/OF STRATHSPEY), THE
1331	2662	(I)	GREEN GROW THE RASHES (O!)
133	132	(I)	NEW LONG ROOM AT SCARBOROUGH, THE
133	132	(I)	NEW CLARET
133	133	(II)	NEW CLARET
133	133	(I)	ANTIGUA BILLEY
133	133	(I)	NEW CLARET
133	135	(I)	CO A NI MIREADH RI MAIRI
133	136	(I)	SCOTS WRIGGLE, THE
133	144	(I)	CHILING O GUIRY
1331	5522	(I)	COUNTESS OF EGLINTON'S STRATHSPEY, THE
1331	5632	(I)	HIGHLAND CHEESE IS RARE LASSES
1331	5632	(I)	DELGATY ICE HOUSE
1331	5662	(I)	DUCHESS OF GORDON'S BANQUET, THE
133	11H5	(I)	DROPS OF BRANDY
1331	1H765	(II)	PROFESSOR BLACKIE
133	211	(I)	MINUET
1332	135L3	(I)	SOUTH AND NORTH
1332	135L3	(I)	BOTH SIDES OF THE TWEED
1332	1323	(I)	PITKERIE'S REEL
1332	1323	(I)	REEL OF THE MEARN'S, THE
1332	1323	(I)	CORRIMONIES REEL
1332	1333	(II)	GILLIE CALLUM [GILLIE CALUM]
1332	1333	(I)	GILLIE CALLUM DA PHEITHEIN
1332	551H1H	(I)	MILK MAID, THE
1333	5L27L2	(I)	MR MORRISON SUPERVISOR DINGWALL
133	36L6L	(I)	FAIR HELEN
1333	7L27L7L	(I)	CAPTAIN DASH'S REEL
1333	7L222	(I)	ARNE'S GIGG
1333	137L7L	(I)	MISS STEUART OF STEUART LODGE'S REEL
1333	1331H	(I)	QUICKSTEP 13th REGt.
1333	1342	(I)	I'LL HAE HER AWA' IN SPITE O' HER MOTHER
1333	1376	(I)	FHEARAIBH MO RUIN NA DIULTAIBH IOMART
133	321	(I)	IF LOVE IS THE CAUSE OF MY MOURNING
1333	227L2	(I)	MR E. CAMPBELL ARDMORE'S REEL
1333	2247bL	(II)	MISS STEWART(OF) GRANTULLY
1333	2247bL	(I)	MISS STEWART (OF) GRANDTULLY ('S STRATHSPEY)
1333	2247L	(II)	MISS STEWART
1355	2355	(I)	CEANN NA DROCHAID MHORIDH
1355	2355	(I)	END OF THE GREAT BRIDGE, THE
133	333	(I)	PORT ATHOLL
133	333	(I)	LOVE IS THE CAUSE OF MY MOURNING

133	333	(I)	I'LL NEVER LEAVE THEE
1333	527L2	(I)	MR OSWALD'S (OF AUCHINCRUIVE'S) STR.
1333	62H66	(I)	MISS BELSCHES'S STRATHSPEY
1334	2466	(I)	THERE'S MY THUMB
1335	7L5L3L1	(I)	DUKE OF CLARENCE'S FANCY, THE
1335	137L7L	(I)	MISS WARDLAW'S REEL
1335	1322	(I)	QUEEN MAB
1335	1322	(I)	BLAIR DRUMMOND'S REEL
1335	1337L	(I)	MISS CAY'S JIGG
1335	1347bL	(II)	CELTIC SOCIETY'S QUICKSTEP, THE
1335	1362	(I)	LADY MARY HAY'S FAVOURITE
133	522	(I)	DIVISION ON AN OLD GROUND BASS FOR VIOLINS, A
1335	2461H	(I)	WILTON LODGE, A STRATHSPEY
1335	357L2	(II)	HONble. COLONEL WEMYSS, THE
1335	357L2	(II)	GENERAL WEMYSS OF WEMYSS
1335	357L2	(I)	HONble COLONEL (Wm) WEMYSS
1335	357L2	(I)	WEMYSS CASTLE
1335	357L2	(I)	(GENERAL/COLONEL) WEMYSS (OF WEMYSS)'S REEL
1335	357L2	(II)	COLONEL WEMYSS
1335	427L5L	(I)	ROCKET, THE
1335	4461H	(I)	TADIE'S WATTLE
1335	4651H	(I)	LORD SEYMOUR'S REEL
1335	4661H	(II)	TORRYBURN LASSES [TORRY BURN]
1335	4661H	(I)	BUTTLER'S REEL, THE
1335	4661H	(I)	TORRY BURN
133	555	(I)	PADDY'S FLIGHT
133	556	(I)	PEGEY'S LAMENT
1335	5662	(I)	HONble MISS BAGOT'S STRATHSPEY
1335	5662	(I)	PRINCESS MARY'S FANCY
133	551H	(I)	MISS D. COOPER'S MINUET
1335	51H1H3H	(II)	MRS BENTON OF AIRLIE
1335	627L5L	(I)	DUKE OF CLARENCES FANCY, THE
1335	637L5L	(I)	DUKE OF CLARENCE'S FANCY, THE
1335	6521	(I)	MAIRI NIGHEAN DHEORSA
1335	6662	(I)	LADY LOUISA GORDON'S FANCY
1335	662H2	(I)	MISS PRATT'S REEL
1335	671H3H	(I)	MISS LAIRD'S ALAMANDE
1335	61H31	(I)	BEVERLY SCHOLL BOYS
1335	61H55	(I)	CHELSEA STAGE
1336	1H37L2	(I)	WILLm SWANSON, ESQr's REEL
1337b	7bL242	(II)	WEAVER, THE
1331H	137L2	(II)	CREAG NA POLLAICH
1331H	137L2	(II)	GARTHLANDS
1331H	137L2	(II)	LADY RADCLIFFE'S REEL
1331H	137L2	(I)	GARTHLAND ('S STRATHSPEY)
1331H	147L2	(II)	GARTHLAND'S
1331H	147L2	(I)	GARTHLAND'S STRATHSPEY
1331H	37b27bL	(II)	MACDOUGALL GILLIES' PIPES
1331H	6366L	(II)	FEASGAR CIUIN [LOVELY EVENING]
1331H	6633	(I)	LORD SALTON'S GAVOTT
1331H	7b424	(I)	MAJOR McLEAN(OF 60th. REGt.) 'S REEL
1331H	2H1H52	(I)	('S) ANN AGAM THA BHEANAG IS MAISICHE SUILE
1332H	1331H	(I)	MISS HERRAN OF INGLISTON'S FAVOURITE WALTZ
1333H	1H652	(II)	BILLY'S REVERIE
1346L	7L253	(II)	MR MICHIE'S [RENATTON]
1347bL	1353	(II)	SIR ARCHD. DUNBAR [SIR ARCHIBALD DUNBAR]
1347bL	1353	(I)	SIR ALEXr DUNBAR'S STRATHSPEY
1347bL	1353	(I)	SIR ARCHd DUNBAR
1347L	6L5L4L2L	(I)	AITKEN'S REEL
1347L	6L7L13L	(I)	SUMMERS AMUSEMENT
1347L	6L17L2	(I)	GAVOTTA
1347L	127L5L	(I)	GUARDIAN ANGELS
1347L	137L3	(II)	LADY CHARLOTTE CAMPBELL
1347L	1342	(II)	BHA MI'N DUIL
1347L	1344	(II)	LOCHRYNACH [LOCH RYNACH]
1347L	1344	(I)	LOCHRYNACH
1347L	1351	(I)	THREE CAPTAINS, THE
1347L	1351	(I)	MR Wm. CLARK'S FAVOURITE
1347L	1353	(II)	HON. CAPT. MAITLAND
1347L	1353	(II)	CAPTAIN MAITLAND
1347L	1353	(I)	HONble CAPTn MAITLAND'S STRATHSPEY
1347L	1353	(I)	NORTH HIGHLAND REEL, A
1347L	131H3	(II)	(MISS)MARY WALKER
1347L	131H5	(I)	MISS KITTY CAMPBELL OF SHAWFIELDS REEL
1347L	1554	(II)	EARL OF LAUDERDALE, THE
1347L	1554	(I)	EARL OF LAUDERDALE ('S REEL)
1347L	153H5	(I)	LA DORIVAL
1341	1327L	(I)	TAIL TODDLE
1341	1341	(I)	LOVER'S STREAM
1341	1553	(I)	FAREWELL BUT REMEMBER THE HOUR

134	134	(I)	OPEN THE DOOR TO THREE
1342	5L342	(I)	EDINBURGH CASTLE
1342	7bL47b7b	(I)	MISS PATERSON'S REEL
1342	7L226L	(I)	TRIP TO THE PANTHEON
1342	7L242	(I)	LADY PENNYMAN'S ALLEMAND
1342	16L6L5L	(I)	SHOE MAKERS DAUGHTER
1342	16L6L5L	(I)	DUTCHESS OF BUCCLEUCH'S REELL
1342	135L3	(I)	TUATH IS DEAS
1342	1343	(II)	GILLIE CALUM [GILLE CALUIM]
1342	1343	(I)	GILLE CALLUM [GILLE CALUIM]
1342	1343	(I)	MISS STUART OF ALLANBANK'S STRATHSPEY
1342	1353	(II)	GILLIE CALLUM [GHILLIE CALLUM or SWORD DANCE]
1342	1353	(II)	SWORD DANCE
1342	1353	(I)	TAIL TODDLE
1342	1353	(I)	KHEELLUM KHALLUM TAA FEIN
1342	26L16L	(I)	(MR E. MARJORIBANKS'S) HORNPIPE
134	223	(I)	FY ON THE WARS
1342	37L25L	(I)	NINETEENTH OF MAY
1342	37L22	(I)	ALLAMAND
1342	3210	(I)	AIR ESPAGNOL
1342	3211	(I)	MADAM PARRISOT'S HORNPIPE
1342	3550	(I)	TO RODNEY WE WILL GO
1342	3555	(I)	TO RODNEY WE WILL GO
1342	31H64	(II)	HOWARD'S
1342	5313	(I)	LA BELLE JEANNETTE
1342	547L5L	(I)	NEW ACADEMY, THE
1342	671H6	(I)	MERRY MEETING, THE
1343	5L6L4L2L	(I)	BARSKEMMING BRIDGE
1343	5L142	(I)	MISS SANDFORD'S JIGG
1343	6L27L5L	(I)	MISS MACNEIL'S FAVORITE
1343	7L225L	(I)	LE PETIT BOSSU
1343	1322	(I)	MISS ABERNETHIE OF MAYHEN'S REEL
1343	1356	(I)	JACKSON'S FOLLY
1343	1362	(I)	MRS FARQUHAR'S STRATHSPEY
1343	25L7bL2	(I)	MILKMAIDS OF BLANTYRE, THE
1343	237L5L	(I)	BROTHERS, THE
1343	2347L	(II)	MR ALEXANDER MUNRO'S FAVOURITE
1343	2427bL	(I)	COUNTY HALL REEL
1343	2427bL	(I)	KING OF FRANCE HE RUN A RACE, THE
1343	27b27bL	(II)	MISS HENNY McKENZIE
1343	27b27bL	(I)	KING OF FRANCE, THE
1343	27b27bL	(I)	LADY DOLL SINCLAIR'S REEL
1343	27b47bL	(I)	LAY'S OF LUNKERTY, THE
1343	326L6L	(I)	CASTLE DOWN
1343	3232	(II)	HIGHLAND LADDIE
1343	3232	(I)	(ORIGINAL) HIGHLAND LADDIE, THE
1343	3232	(I)	BONNIE LADDIE, HIELAND LADDIE
1343	3313L	(I)	MERRY SHEPHERD, THE
1343	3411	(I)	DYSART VOLUNTEERS MARCH
1343	427L7L	(I)	MRS MUIR OF CALDWELL'S REEL
1343	436L7L	(I)	COL. GARDEN'S BIRTH DAY
1344	1327L	(II)	UP AN' WAUR THEM A' WULLIE
1344	1322	(II)	UP AN' WA(U)R THEM A' WULLIE
1344	1322	(I)	UP AND WAR THEM A' WILLIE (/WULLIE)
1344	1322	(I)	CUIR AIR DO SHON FHEIN UILLIAM
1344	1322	(I)	THERE IS NO LUCK ABOUT THE HOUSE
1344	1341	(I)	UNTITLED
134	512	(I)	IRISH HEROES, THE
1345	137L2	(I)	MRS MOSMAN'S STRATHSPEY
1345	1327L	(I)	MISS MARY McDONALD'S REEL
1345	1341	(I)	LADY MARY RAMSAY'S VALTZ
1345	1352	(I)	LITTLE ASSEMBLY, THE
1345	1642	(I)	MISS MONTGOMRIE OF ANNICK LODGE
1345	4542	(II)	MISS ROSE
1345	4542	(I)	MISS ROSE('S STRATHSPEY)
1345	1H532	(II)	MRS E. M. ROSS'S WELCOME TO KILTARLITY COTTAGE
1346	1342	(II)	TAPPIT HEN, THE
1346	3316L	(I)	GLASGOW THEATRE HORNPIPE
1346	3432	(I)	FETTERESSO HOUSE
1346	3627L	(II)	MISS LAMONT OF LAMONT
1346	3627L	(I)	MISS LAMONT OF LAMONT('S STRATHSPEY)
1346	5125	(II)	HEY THE BONNIE BREAST KNOTS
1346	5211	(I)	FRIENDSHIP IS ALWAYS THE ENTRY TO LOVE
1346	5327L	(I)	MISS STEWART MENZIES OF CULDAR'S FAVORITE
1346	5327L	(I)	MISS SOPHIA DIROM'S REEL
1346	51H46L	(I)	MR BLACK'S STRATHSPEY
134#1H	5L7L25	(II)	MADAME VANONI
1357L	671H7L	(II)	JENKINS
1357L	671H7L	(II)	WASHINGTON
1357L	671H7L	(I)	JENKINS(' HORNPIPE)

1351	6L27L5#L	(II)	KILDRUMMY CASTLE
1351	6L47L5L	(II)	MILLER O' HIRN, THE
1351	6L47L2	(II)	LADY CHARLOTTE BRUCE
1351	6L47L2	(I)	LADY CHARLOTTE BRUCE'S STRATHSPEY
1351	1342	(I)	MISS RIGG OF MORTON'S JIGG
1351	1355	(I)	CRAIG ELACHIE
1351	11H66	(I)	BEGGARS' MEAL POKES, THE
1351	11H76	(I)	JOLLY BEGGAR, THE
1351	27L47L	(I)	BONNY LASSES OF ABERDEEN
1351	2252	(I)	MR GIBB'S JIG
1351	247L5L	(I)	HONble MISS ELLIOT'S STRATHSPEY
1351	2461H	(I)	THERE'S MY THUMB I'LL NE'ER BEGUILE THEE
1351	2626L	(II)	MISS GORDON OF LESMORE
1351	2626L	(I)	MISS GORDON OF LESMORE('S STRATHSPEY)
135	142	(I)	BLACK STOOL, THE
1351	427L5L	(I)	MISS HERRIES FORBES REEL
1351	4323	(I)	MISS PEGGY McKENZIE'S REEL
1351	5164	(II)	MARQUIS OF TULLYBARDINE(, THE) [TULLYBARDINE'S REEL]
1351	5164	(I)	MARQUIS OF TULLYBARDINE('S REEL)
135	155	(I)	YOU'VE BEEN LONG AWAY
1351	5532	(I)	LADY BETTY RAMSAY'S REEL
135	156	(I)	CASTLE BAR
1351	6252	(I)	QUICK STEP, (A)
1351	647L5L	(II)	MILLER O' HIRN, THE
135	11H5	(I)	SUPPER'S READY
1351	1H1H51	(II)	FAY HORNPIPE
1352	5L6L11	(I)	TRIP TO SPA(, A)
1352	5L7L25	(I)	SNAKES LANE
1352	7L5L7L5L	(I)	MISS ANN BAIN'S FANCY
1352	7L213L	(I)	LADY SHAFTSBURY'S STRATHSPEY
1352	135L2L	(I)	HIGHLAND PORT. BY RORY DALL, A
1352	137L2	(I)	CULLODEN FIGHT
1352	1352	(I)	HIGHLAND SOLO
1352	1352	(I)	RORY DALL'S PORT
1352	1353	(I)	HONble MRS LESLIE CUMING, THE
1352	131H5	(I)	JOCKIE'S FOU & JANNIE'S FAINE
1352	1555	(II)	LOW-BACKED CAR, THE
1352	11H76	(II)	JOLLY BEGGAR, THE
1352	11H1H6	(II)	CRAIL
135	226	(I)	FY LET US A' TO THE WEDDING
1352	3234	(I)	COL. E. WILDMAN'S QUICK STEP
1352	437L5L	(I)	BLENHEIM HOUSE
1352	6527L	(I)	BLUE JOAK
1352	61H52	(I)	TRIP TO RICHMOND
1353	5L7L27L	(II)	KIRN, THE (HARVEST HOME)
1353	5L7L27L	(II)	STIRLING CASTLE
1353	5L7L27L	(II)	HARVEST HOME
1353	5L7L27L	(I)	MR BRUCE'S REEL
1353	5L135	(I)	DUNDARY
1353	5L242	(I)	MACARONI FOP, THE
1353	5L37L2	(II)	MISS JANE STEWART
1353	5L37L2	(I)	MISS JANE STEWART('S REEL)
1353	5L37L2	(I)	HONble MISS ELPHINSTONE'S REEL, THE
1353	5L37L2	(I)	LADY CHARLOTTE CAMPBELL'S REEL
1353	5L322	(II)	GLENFIDDICH
1353	5L322	(II)	BALMORAL STRATHSPEY, THE
1353	5L322	(I)	GLENFIDDICH (STRATHSPEY)
1353	5L347L	(I)	MISS OGILVIE'S REEL
1353	6L5L4L2L	(II)	LADY SUSAN GORDON
1353	6L5L4L2L	(I)	LADY SUSAN GORDON('S REEL)
1353	6L5L4L2L	(I)	MISS JOHNSTON'S REEL
1353	6L5L4L3L	(I)	MISS EASTWOOD'S FANCY
1353	6L5L5L5L	(I)	ARDROSSAN CANAL, THE
1353	6L6L22	(II)	NETHER CLUNY
1353	6L6L22	(II)	MISS WATT'S REEL, NETHER CLUNY
1353	6L6L22	(I)	RUN DOWN THE TOWN IN HASTE
1353	6L6L22	(I)	MISS WATT'S REEL (NETHER CLUNY)
1353	6L6L22	(I)	HIGHLAND WEDDING, THE
1353	6L27L6L	(I)	TRIP TO STRATHBOGIE, A
1353	6L427L	(I)	MR CHARLES STEWART (PETTYVAICH)
1353	6L464	(II)	MISS JESSIE DALRYMPLE
1353	6L464	(I)	MISS STEVENSON'S REEL
1353	6L464	(I)	MISS (JESSY) DALRYMPLE'S REEL [[MISS JESSIE DALRYMPLE]
1353	6L464	(I)	MISS DALRYMPLE'S REEL
1353	7bL7bL47b	(II)	MR JOHN STEWART OF GRANTULLY
1353	7bL7bL47b	(I)	MR JOHN STEWART OF GRANTUL(L)Y('S REEL)
1353	7bL27bL7bL	(I)	MACKENZIE'S RANT
1353	7bL247bL	(II)	CARN DUBH
1353	7bL242	(II)	MISS STEWART
1353	7bL242	(I)	MISS STEWART (OF GRANTULLY) 'S REEL

1353	7L5L47L	(I)	MRS CARTER'S STRATHSPEY
1353	7L6L3L2	(I)	GLASGOW FLOURISH
1353	7L225L	(I)	MISS KITTY CAMPBELL'S STRATHSPEY
1353	7L242	(I)	MRS FRASER'S REEL
1353	7L727L	(I)	MR MARSHALL'S STRATHSPEY, EDINr
1353	15L4L2L	(I)	MISS SYME'S REEL
1353	137L1	(I)	MISS MARGARET GRAHAM
			OF GARTMORE'S STRATHSPEY
1353	1327L	(II)	R.O. FARQUHARSON ESQ. OF HAUGHTON'S R.
1353	1327L	(I)	ROAD TO CLERK-SEAT, THE
1353	1323	(II)	WISE MAID, THE
1353	1324	(I)	MONALTRIE'S WELCOME HOME TO BALLATERS
1353	1322H	(I)	MISS ELLIOTT'S STRATHSPEY
1353	1332	(I)	LADY GORDON CUMMING'S STRATHSPEY
1353	1342	(II)	ROB AN LUGI
1353	1342	(II)	LOCH AVON
1353	1342	(I)	ROB ON LUGY [ROB AN LUGI]
1353	1355	(I)	DUTCHESS OF MONTROSE'S REEL
1353	1362	(I)	UDNY ACADEMY
1353	1455	(II)	GERTIE GIBB
1353	1511	(I)	MARCH DES GENS D'ARMES
1353	1562	(II)	SIR GEORGE ABERCROMBIE BARt
			OF BIRKENBOG & FORGLEN'S STRATHSPEY
1353	1653	(I)	CORONATION STRATHSPEY, THE
1353	1761H	(II)	CHARLESTOWN BREAKDOWN
1353	11H22	(I)	CHARLES LILT
1353	11H1H3H	(II)	MISS McLEOD OF ROSSES
1353	26L7bL2	(I)	LADS OF ELGIN, THE
1353	27bL47bL	(I)	MRS ABERNETHY'S STRATHSPEY
1353	27L7L7L	(I)	MISS GARDEN OF TROOP'S STRATHSPEY
1353	227bL7bL	(I)	GREY DAY LIGHT [GRAY DAY LIGHT]
1353	2226L	(I)	MR ROBERT HUNTER'S STRATHSPEY
1353	2223	(II)	CERES GREEN
1353	2247bL	(I)	MRS DOCTOR ABERNETHIE'S REEL
1353	227b7b	(I)	GREY DAY LIGHT
1353	237L7L	(I)	LADY LUCY RAMSAY'S STRATHSPEY
1353	2326L	(I)	NEW BRIDGE OF SPEY, THE
1353	2366	(II)	MONRO'S RANT
1353	2366	(II)	AM BODACH LUIDEACH ODHAR
1353	2366	(I)	LARICKILLE
1353	2366	(I)	DUTCHESS OF ATHOLE'S REEL
1353	2366	(I)	MISS CUMMYN'S REEL
1353	2366	(I)	PEEP (A/OF) DAY,(THE)
1353	2366	(I)	MUNRO'S RANT, (THE)
1353	2366	(I)	MISS MONRO'S STRATHSPEY
1353	2361H	(I)	PEEP OF DAY
1353	2416L	(I)	JAMES B. DUNBAR'S STRATHSPEY
1353	2427bL	(I)	CAPT CAMPBELL OF ORMIDALE'S REEL
1353	2427bL	(I)	MISS CORBETT'S REEL
1353	2422	(II)	MRS MORAY OF ABERCA(I)RNEY
1353	2422	(I)	MRS MORAY (MURRAY) OF ABERCAIRNEY
			('S STRATHSPEY)
1353	2422	(I)	MISS STEWART OF GARTH'S STRATHSPEY
1353	2427b	(I)	MISS CORBET'S REEL
1353	2427	(I)	MISS CORBET'S REEL
1353	2464	(II)	MISS JEANNY WILLIAMSON
1353	2464	(I)	MISS DARRELL'S FANCY
1353	2464	(I)	MISS MARY ANN HAIG'S STRATHSPEY
1353	2464	(I)	MISS MALCOLM'S HORNPIPE
1353	2464	(I)	MISS JEANNY WILLIAMSON('S REEL)
1353	2464	(I)	MORTLACH REEL, THE
1353	2464	(I)	TRIP TO KELSO
1353	2466	(I)	COL. CAMPBELL'S REEL
1353	2466	(I)	MISS ANN GREIG'S REEL
1353	2466	(I)	LADS OF THE PRINTFIELD, THE
1353	2466	(I)	PERTH HUNT, THE
1353	2561H	(I)	MR STIRLING OF KEIRS REEL
1353	242H4H	(I)	MISS DINWIDDIE'S REEL
1353	2662	(II)	MISS MACKAY
1353	27b27bL	(I)	FOUR AND TWENTY HIGHLANDMEN
135	331	(I)	ONE DAY I HEARD MARY SAY
135	331	(I)	I'LL NEVER LEAVE THEE
135	331	(I)	LOVE IS THE CAUSE OF MY MOURNING
135	333	(I)	LOCHABER
135	333	(I)	LOVE IS THE CAUSE OF MY MOURNING
135	333	(I)	I'LL NEVER LEAVE THEE
1353	3546	(II)	MISS MARGARET MACKERACHER
1353	427L5L	(II)	HIRN DEVIL, THE
1353	427L5L	(I)	HAYDEN'S SURPRISE
1353	427L5L	(I)	PORTEOUS MOB, THE
1353	427L1	(I)	RING DOVE, THE
1353	427L2	(II)	GRANITE CITY, THE

1353	427L2	(I)	VICTORY, THE
1353	4211	(I)	PARLALAW
1353	4242H	(I)	LADY CATHERINE BLYTH
1353	437L7L	(I)	MISS MARY BOWER OF KINCALDRUM'S REEL
1353	4325L	(I)	PAS SEUL MISS JANE HECTOR
1353	4327bL	(II)	JOHN McCOLL'S REEL
1353	4321	(II)	MISS PAUL
1353	4362	(I)	THREE SIFTERS REEL, THE
1353	432H2	(I)	ORTON HOUSE
1353	432H2	(I)	MRS DUFF (OF FETTERESSO'S) STRATHSPEY
1353	4437L	(II)	ABERLOUR RIFLE VOLUNTEER MARCH
1353	4527L	(II)	ROSE WOOD'S DIRK
1353	4522	(II)	BRIG O' DEE
1353	4532	(II)	MRS LEITH OF GLENKINDY'S REEL
1353	4542	(II)	GLENBUCKET LODGE
1353	461H6	(I)	FOR THE SAKE OF SOME-BODY
1353	5122	(II)	WILLIE BLAIR
1353	5222	(II)	SANDY O'ER THE LEA
1353	5222	(I)	SANDY O'ER THE LEE
1353	5322	(II)	SANDY O'ER THE LEA
1353	5322	(II)	BELLADRUM HOUSE [TIGH BHEALLADRUM]
1353	5322	(I)	TIGH BHEALLADRUM [TAIGH BHEALLADRUM]
1353	5353	(II)	CHARLES LESLIE
1353	5353	(I)	HIGHLAND REEL, THE
1353	5353	(I)	JACKEY LAITEN [JACK LATTIN]
1353	5353	(I)	CHARLES LESLIE (OF FINDRASSIE'S STRATHSPEY)
1353	5354	(II)	JACK LATTIN
1353	532H2	(I)	MR GUN MONRO POYNTZFIELD('S REEL)
1353	5433	(I)	DALNAGLARE'S RANT
1353	5622	(I)	MISS ELTON'S STRATHSPEY
1353	5642	(II)	MILLER O' HIRN'S WIFE, THE
1353	51H52	(II)	CHARLIE
1353	51H53	(II)	COLQUHALZIE FIR TREES
1353	51H55	(II)	WEE PUG, THE
1353	51H76	(II)	TIMOUR THE TARTER [TIMOUR THE TARTAR]
1353	51H76	(I)	PETER STREET
1353	51H76	(I)	TIMOUR THE TARTAR
1353	51H3H5	(II)	FARNIE HOUSE
1353	632H2	(II)	MR GUN MUNRO OF POYNTZ-FIELD
1353	6432	(I)	MISS ELDERS
1353	6543	(I)	TRIP TO SHORTS, A
1353	6552	(II)	MISS GRAHAM
1353	6553	(I)	ATHOL HIGHLANDERS MARCH, THE
1353	6647L	(II)	ABERDEENSHIRE VOLUNTEERS
1353	662H2	(II)	MAJOR McBEAN
1353	662H2	(I)	MAJOR MACBEAN'S 14th REGT's STRATHSPEY
1353	671H3	(II)	BALMORAL REEL, THE
1353	671H3	(I)	MRS McINNES OF DANALIETH'S REEL
1353	671H1H	(II)	CURRIE'S RAMBLES
1353	61H53	(II)	DUNBLANE
1353	61H53	(I)	MR JOHN CUNNINGHAM'S STRATHSPEY
1353	7b242	(II)	MRS FRASER('S REEL), CULLEN
1353	7651H	(I)	TIMOUR THE TARTAR
1353	1H3b55	(II)	TURNING LATHE, THE
1353	1H37L2	(II)	REEL, A
1353	1H353	(II)	KILCOY CASTLE
1353	1H353	(I)	CALLUM FIDHDAIR
135	31H6	(I)	EMON O KNUCK
1353	1H622	(I)	LORD McDONALD'S STRATHSPEY
1353	1H1H64	(II)	Dr. MARSHALL'S HORNPIPE
1353	3H3H65	(I)	OSWALD'S DREAM
1353	3H1H32	(II)	MISS ANN AMELIA STEWART'S STRATHSPEY [MISS ANN AMELIA MURRAY]
1353	3H1H32	(I)	MRS MACINTYRE ('S STRATHSPEY)
1353	3H1H32	(I)	MISS (ANN) (AMELIA) STEWART ('S) (STRATHSPEY)
1353	3H1H32	(I)	MRS McINTYRE
1353	3H3H65	(I)	BLYTHE HAE I BEEN WHEN I STRAY'D WI' MY LOVE
1354	5L47L2	(I)	DOCTOR LAING
1354	1325L	(I)	RIDICULE, (THE/LA)
1354	1326L	(I)	MISS CATHERINE ANSON'S STRATHSPEY
1354	1362	(I)	HIGHWAY TO EDINBURGH, THE
1354	2466	(I)	SCOTS BONNET
1354	2466	(I)	THERE'S MY THUMB
1354	2461H	(I)	THERE'S MY THUMB (I'LL NE'ER BEGUILE THEE)
1354	3522	(I)	TRUMPET AIR, A
1354	4352	(I)	THREE SHEEP SKINS
1354	4431	(I)	MISS DRAK'S DELIGHT
1354	4653	(II)	BIRKS OF DELHANDY, THE
1354	6440	(I)	ROXBURGHSHIRE CAVALRY'S MARCH, THE
1355	6L237L	(I)	MERRY TODAY

1355	6L237L	(I)	MISS HAY'S DOUBLE JIGG
1355	7L245	(I)	QUICK MARCH, 19th REGt
1355	1241	(I)	DUKE OF YORK IN BERLIN, THE
1355	1322	(I)	BLAIR DRUMMOND'S REEL
1355	1347L	(II)	MISS CRAWFORD'S STRATHSPEY
1355	1342	(I)	MISS JESSIE REID'S STRATHSPEY
1355	1351	(I)	RUSSIAN WALTZ, THE
1355	1355	(II)	DUKE OF ROXBURGHE, THE
1355	1351H	(II)	LORD ELPHINSTONE
1355	1351H	(I)	LORD ELPHINSTONE('S STRATHSPEY)
1355	1522H	(I)	RECOVERY, THE
1355	1551H	(II)	ROYAL RECOVERY, THE
1355	1551H	(II)	RECOVERY, THE
1355	1551H	(I)	RECOVERY, THE
1355	1551H	(I)	LITTLE PEGGY'S LOVE
1355	1564	(I)	CAPTAIN'S LADY, THE
1355	1564	(I)	MOUNT YOUR BAGGAGE
1355	11H62	(I)	MRS JOHN WELLING'S STRATHSPEY
1355	26L27	(I)	MONTROSE ASSEMBLY
1355	2466	(II)	SCOTS BONNET
1355	2466	(II)	BLUE BONNETS OVER THE BORDER
1355	2466	(I)	SCOTS BONNET, (THE)
1355	2466	(I)	LA BELLA ROSA
1355	2466	(I)	BLUE BONNETS OVER THE BORDER
1355	2461H	(II)	PATRIOT, THE
1355	2461H	(I)	SPANISH PATRIOT
135	531	(I)	FAVOURITE GERMAN AIR, A
135	531	(I)	DEATH OF ADMIRAL BENBOW
1355	3122	(I)	JOCKY TO THE FAIR
1355	3122	(I)	GENERAL ACTION
1355	3122	(I)	JOCKEY TO THE FAIR
1355	4237L	(I)	MISS GUTHRIE OF CRAIGIE'S JIGG
1355	4326L	(I)	MISS CATHERINE STEWART OF DESKY'S REEL
1355	4327L	(I)	HEY TO C(O)UPER
1355	4327L	(I)	WARKWORTH CASTLE
1355	4357L	(I)	I SAW AN EEL CHASE THE DEEL
1355	4366	(I)	BRIDGE OF FOCHABERS, THE
1355	4423	(I)	J. LEE ALLAN ESQ OF ERROL'S STR.
1355	4432	(I)	TREBAN MORGANOUGH
1355	4452	(I)	THREE SHEEP SKIN'S, THE
1355	457L2	(I)	PERTH RACES
1355	457L2	(I)	MISS COLQUHOUN('S REEL)
1355	4527L	(I)	MRS DRYSDALE'S JIG
1355	4642	(I)	MR RITCHIE'S STRATHSPEY
1355	4655	(I)	HISTORICAL WAR SONG
1355	461H1H	(II)	WITCH OF THE WAVE
1355	5226L	(I)	COME SWEET LASS
1355	5362	(I)	CAPTAIN SINCLAIR'S REEL
1355	5531	(I)	LA MIGNONETTE FRANCOISE
1355	5532	(I)	LADIES OF ABERDEEN
1355	5544	(II)	CHAMPION MARCH, THE [WILLIE MACLENNAN]
1355	5544	(II)	WILLIE MACLENNAN
1355	5555	(I)	MORNING THOUGHT, THE
135	556	(I)	IF E'ER YE DO WELL IT'S A WONDER
1355	5755	(I)	MISS S. CAMPBELL OF SADDLE'S ALLAMANDE
1355	6653	(I)	MR HOBHOUSE'S FAVORITE
1355	661H1H	(I)	ALLEGRO
1355	6753	(I)	LIEUt MORISON'S (DUMFRIES MILITIA) REEL
1355	6776	(I)	WILLIAM'S GHOST
1355	671H1H	(I)	SHIVAS HOUSE
1355	61H53	(I)	BLEAK WAS THE MORN
1355	61H1H6	(I)	BANKS O' TWEED, THE
1355	62H76	(I)	O SAW YE MY FATHER/(MOTHER)
1355	62H1H6	(I)	SAW YE MY FATHER?
1355	64H1H6	(I)	SAW YE MY FATHER
1355	64H1H6	(I)	SAW YOU MY FATHER
1355	7231	(I)	WEAZLE, THE
1355	7531	(I)	HAPPY CLOWN, (THE)
1355	7531	(I)	ONE EVENING AS I LOST MY WAY
1355	7542	(I)	HAPPY CLOWN
1355	72H1H1H	(I)	L'ALSACIENNE
135	51H3	(I)	TIROLIEN AIR
1355	1H316L	(I)	MISS GRAHAM'S HORNPIPE
1355	1H453	(I)	LAWLAND LADS THINK THEY'RE FINE, THE
1355	1H522	(I)	MR GRANT OF KINNEARD'S REEL
1355	1H633	(I)	SECRET KISS, THE
135	51H1H	(II)	CELEBRATED TYROLESE WALTZ, THE
1355	1H2H53	(I)	MISS St CLAIR ERSKINE OF SINCLAIR
1355	1H2H65	(I)	MUSICAL SOCIETY OF FORFAR'S MARCH, THE
1356	1221	(I)	NOW WINTER'S WIND
1356	1347L	(I)	PENTONVILLE ASSEMBLY, THE
1356	1352	(I)	MISS GRACE HAY'S DELIGHT

1356	1352	(I)	CREAM POT, (THE)
1356	2467	(I)	SIR JOHN MCGREGOR MURRAY'S STRATHSPEY
1356	4347L	(I)	LADY HOOD'S FAVORITE
1356	4635	(I)	NEW TURRIFF HUNT, THE
1356	516L6L	(II)	OLD ROSEN THE BEAU
1356	5125L	(I)	GALLOP TO KINROSS, A
1356	5142	(II)	MARQUIS OF BEAUMONT, THE
1356	5432	(I)	MISS ANN DRUMMOND SMYTH'S REEL
1356	5642	(I)	CHARLES GRAY ESQr OF CARSE'S STRATHSPEY
1356	636L2	(I)	INNES'S JIG
135	664	(I)	DANCED BY MISS NEISH AND MISS HACKNEY
1356	7b7bL45	(I)	FASKALLY HOUSE
1356	1H113	(I)	GEORGIA GRENADIER'S MARCH, THE
1356	1H521	(I)	WERTEMBURG WALTZ, THE
1356	1H633	(I)	MY BONNY MARY
1356	1H642	(I)	MISS JESSY CAMPBELL'S REEL
1356	1H776	(II)	LORD BYRON
1356	1H2H1H7	(II)	FILL YOUR GLASSES
1357	1525L	(I)	REJOICING NIGHT, THE
1357	5315L	(I)	MISS FOWLER'S DELIGHT
1357	6527L	(I)	SHIPPARD'S WIFE, THE
1357	6562	(II)	EDGE OF THE EVENING, THE
1357	7750	(I)	LORD HARRINGTON'S VOLUNTEERS
1357	1H355L	(I)	GARLAND, THE
1357	1H1H77	(I)	AUSTRIAN REVEILE, THE
1357	1H1H1H2H	(I)	ADMIRAL HOWE'S MARCH
1351H	5L7L25	(II)	WOLF O' BADENOCH, THE
1351H	117L2	(I)	CAPT KELLER'S REEL [CAPt. KEELER]
1351H	137L2	(II)	CAPTAIN KEELER
1351H	137L2	(I)	CAPTAIN KELLER'S REEL
1351H	137L4	(I)	CAPTAIN KEELER'S REEL
1351H	1325L	(I)	DUKE OF HAMILTON AND HIS VOLUNTEERS
1351H	1325L	(I)	SIR ARCHd CAMPBELL'S JIGG
1351H	1326bL	(II)	MR COMPTON OF COMPTON HALL
1351H	1326L	(II)	MRS COMPTON OF CARHAM-HALL
1351H	1326L	(I)	MR COMPTON OF CARHAM-HALL'S REEL [MR COMPTON OF COMPTON HALL]
1351H	1321	(I)	CAPT CAMPBELL OF BLYTHSWOOD'S FAV.
1351H	1362	(II)	EARL OF FIFE'S WELCOME TO BANFF, THE
1351H	147L5L	(I)	MISS CORBETT'S STRATHSPEY
1351H	157L7L	(I)	MR RONALD CRAWFORD OF FRESKIEHALL'S STRATHSPEY
1351H	1522	(II)	MACDUFF
1351H	246L2	(I)	LADY CLINTON'S FANCY
1351H	2H1H65	(II)	EARL O' DEAN, THE
1351H	46L16L	(I)	DUKE OF CLARENCES HORNPIPE
1351H	4246	(I)	DUKE OF KENT'S REEL
1351H	57L22	(I)	PATRICK GEORGE MONCRIEFF ESQr OF REEDIE'S JIGG
1351H	5122	(I)	EBDEN'S QUICK STEP
1351H	5226L	(I)	MILK POT, THE
1351H	5222	(I)	MISS GORDON OF CLUNY
1351H	5231	(I)	COTILLON
135	1H53	(I)	STADHOLDERS, THE
1351H	537L7L	(I)	MISS CAMPBELL'S REEL
1351H	537L7L	(I)	MISS (JESSY) CAMPBELL'S REEL
1351H	537L2	(II)	DEVIL AND THE DIRK, THE
1351H	5326L	(I)	MISS MOYSEY'S REEL
1351H	5322	(I)	WEMYS CASTLE
1351H	547L2	(II)	NEW STRATHSPEY, A
1351H	547L2	(I)	LADY ARBUTHNOTT'S FAVORITE
1351H	547L2	(I)	DUKE OF YORK'S BIRTHDAY
1351H	547L2	(I)	MARQUIS OF HUNTLY'S WELCOME HOME, THE
1351H	5426L	(I)	PEARL, THE
1351H	5442	(I)	MISS WATSON'S FAVORITE
1351H	557L2	(I)	MR J.R. COUTTS
1351H	5527L	(I)	MIDNIGHT HOUR, THE
1351H	5533	(I)	PEGGY IN DEVOTION
1351H	5542	(I)	TWA CORBIES, THE
1351H	5542	(I)	MISS MARY GORDON OF BRAID
1351H	5544	(I)	QUICK STEP
1351H	5555	(I)	MUSICAL SOCIETY'S MARCH
1351H	51H3H2H	(I)	MR PATRICK DUFF'S STRATHSPEY
1351H	627L7L	(II)	MRS NORMAN LOCKHART
1351H	627L7L	(I)	MRS NORMAN(D) LOCKHART('S REEL)
1351H	6442	(I)	MRS RIDDELL'S HORNPIPE
1351H	6527L	(I)	ROSEBUD BY MY EARLY WALK, A
1351H	6527L	(I)	SHEPHERD'S WIFE, THE
1351H	6521	(I)	SHEPHERD'S WIFE, THE
1351H	6522	(II)	MR JOHNSON
1351H	6522	(I)	MR JOHNSON('S REEL)
1351H	6542	(II)	MISS MARGARET CAMPBELL (OF SADDELL'S)

1351H	6542	(I)	MISS MARGARET CAMPBELL (OF SADDELL'S) REEL
1351H	6553	(I)	MARCH OF THE 17 REGt
1351H	6652	(II)	MISS CLEMENTINA STEWART
1351H	6652	(I)	MISS CLEMENTINA STEWART'S REEL
1351H	61H32	(I)	MR J. J. HENRY'S STRATHSPEY
1351H	61H55	(I)	SIR RICHARD STRACHAN
1351H	61H51H	(I)	CHARLIE, YE ARE WELCOME
1351H	7b427bL	(II)	DR. SHAW
135	1H75	(I)	MISS KATTY MONTGOMERIE'S MINUET
1351H	7756	(I)	TRIP TO PANCRASS, A
1351H	1H452	(I)	AH SURE A PAIR
135	1H1H5H	(I)	MISS JANE FRAZER'S MINUET
1351H	3H1H1H1H	(I)	ST JAMES'S
1351H	3H3H66	(I)	BANKS OF FORTH, (THE)
1352H	1353	(II)	BEAN NA GABHAR
1353H	1H422	(I)	MR GARDEN (OF TROUP'S) FAREWELL TO FRANCE
1353H	1H453	(I)	(NEW) HIGHLAND LADDIE, (THE)
1353H	1H453	(I)	HIGHLAND LADDIE [cf: WAVERLEY]
135	3H1H1H	(I)	TYROLESE SONG OF LIBERTY
1366L	1133	(I)	NOCHD FUR FAOIN (MO CHADAL DOMH)
1361	3562	(I)	DRUMNAGOUR
136	152	(I)	KISS FOR NOTHING, A
1362	1351H	(I)	MISS SITWELL'S STRATHSPEY
1362	1366L	(I)	MISS MACDONALD BUCHANAN'S STRATHSPEY
1362	1366	(I)	MISS MITCHEL'S STRATHSPEY
1362	1361H	(I)	MISS MAC INTOSH'S REEL
1362	317L5L	(I)	MRS WILLm MARSHALL'S REEL
1363	6L247L	(II)	FYVIE SENSATION
1363	7L127L	(I)	DOUBLE JIG
1363	1366	(II)	DEAN BRIG REEL
1363	1366	(I)	GIULLAN NAM BO
1363	1547L	(II)	DUNECHT HOUSE
1363	237L5L	(I)	COTILLION
1363	5632	(II)	FISHER'S WEDDING
1363	6532	(II)	FISHER'S WEDDING, THE
1363	6564	(I)	COTTAGE BOY, THE
1363	662H2	(I)	CAPT DOUGAL CAMPBELL KILMARTIN'S STR.
1363	1H522	(II)	RACHAEL RAE'S MOTHER
1364	1313H	(II)	MISS WARDLAW
1364	1313H	(I)	MISS MAC INTOSH'S FAVOURITE
1364	1313H	(I)	MISS WARDLAW('S STRATHSPEY)
1364	5543	(I)	DRUM HOUSE
1364	2H755	(I)	ASTLEY'S HORNPIPE
1364	2H765	(I)	JINKINSON'S HORNPIPE
1365	6L225L	(I)	MISS HALDANE'S JIGG
1365	1362	(I)	FAVORITE TUNE FROM MOTHER GOOSE, A
1365	1362	(I)	GRIMALDIE
1365	1364	(II)	LORD STRATHAVEN
1365	1364	(I)	LORD STRATHAVEN'S STRATHSPEY
1365	2424	(I)	BRAES OF YARROW, THE
1365	552H2H	(I)	DUTCHESS OF MANCHESTER'S NEW STRATHSPEY
1365	6527L	(I)	MISS M. TAIT'S JIGG
1366	137L5L	(II)	JAMIE'S PAPER
1366	1325L	(I)	MISS BETTY MUNRO'S REEL
1366	1663	(I)	MISS ISABELLA HUTCHISON'S JIG
1366	5353	(II)	DUNFERMLINE ABBEY
1366	5353	(I)	MISS CUMINE OF AUCHRY'S STRATHSPEY
1366	51H2H2H	(II)	MISS MARSTON'S STRATHSPEY
1366	51H2H2H	(I)	LITTLE PEGGY'S LOVE
1366	51H2H2H	(I)	MISS NORTON OF NORTON'S STRATHSPEY
136G	53H2H6	(I)	MISS HELAN WILLIAMSON'S REEL
1361H	3532	(I)	NEW LONDON, THE
1361H	527L2	(II)	SEUMAS MOR A' GHLINNE
1361H	5326L	(II)	MISS URQUHART OF MELDRUM
1361H	5327L	(I)	MISS GORDON OF NETHERMUIR'S STRATHSPEY
1361H	5327L	(I)	MISS URQUHART OF MELDRUM('S REEL)
1361H	51H32	(I)	LADY GILFORD'S REEL
1361H	3H316L	(I)	BUTCHER BOY, THE
1363H	1H542	(I)	MISS ADAMS STRATHSPEY
1375	1622	(II)	CLUNY CASTLE, INVERNESS-SHIRE
1375	637L7L	(I)	ELTHAM ASSEMBLY
1374H	3H2H34	(I)	WHEN FAIRIES DANCE ROUND
131H1	132H2	(I)	MAVIS BANK
131H1	27L27L	(I)	IN THE STYLE OF AN OPERA DANCE
131H1	41H2H2	(I)	MISS JENNY DUFF'S REEL
131H1	2H2H75	(I)	COTTILION
131H3	5L7L44	(II)	EDRADYNATE HOUSE
131H3	5L37L2	(II)	PATRICK GLENNNIE'S REEL
131H3	7bL27bL7bL	(I)	MR ANDERSON'S STRATHSPEY
131H3	7L272	(I)	MRS. ROBERT CAMPBELL OF SKIPNESS STR.
131H3	1347L	(I)	SPELL, THE
131H3	1342	(I)	MISS JEAN ROBERTSON'S REEL

131H3	27bL27bL	(I)	LADY WHITEFOORD'S REEL
131H3	227L7L	(II)	LIEUT. COL. BAILLIE OF LEYS
131H3	227L7L	(I)	LEIUt COL: BAILLIE OF LEYS STRATHSPEY
131H3	2216L	(II)	MR JOHN SMITH
131H3	2216L	(I)	MR JOHN SMITH'S REEL [MR JOHN SMITH]
131H3	2464	(I)	MR MARSHALL'S REEL
131H3	27b44	(II)	CRAIGELLACHIE BRIDGE
131H3	27b44	(I)	CRAIGELLACHIE BRIDGE
131H3	2742	(II)	STRATHSPEY, A
131H3	22H75	(II)	MORAY CLUB, THE
131H3	337L7L	(II)	MISS CLEMENTINA STEWART
131H3	337L7L	(I)	MISS CLEMENTINA STEWART'S REEL
131H3	337L7L	(I)	PRINCE OF WALES, THE
131H3	46L7L5L	(I)	MISS FORBES OF EDINGLASSIE'S STRATHSPEY
131H3	427L5L	(I)	MISS MACKINTOSH'S REEL
131H3	427L7L	(I)	MRS MARSHALL'S REEL, EDINr
131H3	422H3H	(II)	SQUARE AND COMPASS, THE
131H3	422H3H	(I)	SQUARE AND COMPASS, THE
131H3	4362	(I)	HONble MISS HAMILTON'S REEL, THE
131H3	4362	(I)	MISS STEWART MITCHELL'S REEL
131H3	4362	(I)	MISS EYRE'S REEL, THE
131H3	6246	(II)	MRS STEWART, INVERUGIE
131H3	6246	(I)	MRS STEWART'S STRATHSPEY
131H3	61H51	(II)	COUNTRY LASSES
131H3	1H345	(I)	NOVAR HOUSE
131H3	1H362	(II)	REEL OF CLUNY, THE
131H3	1H642	(II)	DONALD THE PIPER*
131H3	1H2H1H6	(I)	MR REID'S REEL
131H3	1H3H4H2H	(II)	MOVING BOG
131H5	1347L	(I)	SPELL, THE
131H5	227L5L	(II)	DAVIE COURAGE
131H5	2366	(I)	MISS CUMMING BRUCE
131H5	4562	(I)	MR ROBERT GORDON'S REEL
131H5	5555	(II)	NEW BRIG O' AYR, THE
131H5	1H3H2H5	(I)	RACHEL RAE
131H5	1H3H2H7	(II)	RACHAEL RAE [RACHEL RAE]
131H5	1H3H2H7	(I)	RAECHEAL REA'S RANT [RACHEL RAE]
131H5	1H3H3H1H	(II)	RACHEL RAE
131H6	22H75	(II)	BIRTHDAY 1790, THE
131H6	3347L	(I)	MRS BUTTERS' REEL
131H6	436L2	(I)	MISS STEWARTS
131H6	51H4H2H	(II)	JOHNNY GALBRAITH
131H6	6427L	(I)	ARTILLERY ROUT, THE
131H6	6522	(II)	GARIBALDI
131H6	6542	(I)	MR SHEPHERD'S STRATHSPEY
131H6	662H2H	(I)	LOW DOWN IN THE BROOM
131H6	672H2	(I)	MISS MARY MURRAY'S REEL
131H6	1H422	(I)	MISS JANET McKERRELL'S STRATHSPEY
131H6	1H661H	(I)	O'ER THE DYKE
131H6	1H4H72H	(I)	MR TAIT'S STRATHSPEY
131H7	532H2	(II)	GREEN SHADES OF GASK, THE
131H7	532H2	(I)	GREEN SHADES OF GASK, THE
131H7	62H75	(II)	MACKENZIE FRASER
131H7	1H771H	(I)	BIRKS OF ABERGELDY
			[BERKS OF ABERGELDE, THE]
131H1H	1326L	(II)	JOHN[N]IE STEELE
131H1H	1326L	(II)	MILLER O' DERVIL, THE
131H1H	1352	(I)	HUMOURS OF BURROW, THE
131H1H	1352	(I)	FOR(R)EST(, THE)
131H1H	5232	(I)	MISS THOM'S REEL
131H1H	5542	(I)	LADY ELISABETH MONCREIFFE'S REEL
131H1H	6326L	(II)	O WELCOME TO MY DEARIE O
131H1H	663H6	(I)	SCOTS CAME O'ER THE BORDER, THE
131H1H	61H53	(II)	AULD TOUN O' AYR, THE
131H1H	71H66	(I)	THA MI TINN LEIS A GHOAL
131H1H	1H1H71H	(II)	BIRKS OF ABERFELDIE, (THE)
			[BIRKS OF ABERGELDIE, THE]
131H1H	1H1H71H	(I)	BIRKS OF ABERFELDY, (THE)
131H1H	1H1H71H	(I)	BIRKS OF ABERGELDY, (THE)
131H1H	1H1H1H1H	(I)	BIRKS OF ABERGELDIE
131H1H	1H1H2H2H	(II)	BIRKS OF ABERFELDY
131H1H	1H1H2H2H	(I)	BIRKS OF ABERGELDIE [BIRKS OF ABERFELDIE]
131H1H	2H2H2H2	(II)	LORD JOHN CAMPBELL
131H1H	2H2H2H2	(I)	LORD JOHN CAMPBELL'S REEL
131H1H	2H2H2H2	(I)	MRS Wm. MURRAY OF POLONAISE
131H1H	2H4H62H	(I)	MISS CATHERINE BISSET'S STRATHSPEY
131H1H	3H2H1H5	(I)	GREEN PURSE, THE
131H1H	3H3H5H2H	(I)	LADY KINLOCH OF GILMERTON'S STRATHSPEY
131H2H	4324	(II)	ROARING JELLY
131H2H	4324	(I)	SMASH THE WINDOWS
131H2H	4324	(I)	GRAY'S FAVORITE JIG
131H2H	4324	(I)	ROARING JELLY

131H3H	1H47L7L	(II)	DUNNOTTAR CASTLE
131H3H	1H526L	(I)	DUKE OF BUCCLEUCH, THE
131H3H	1H532	(I)	WEST LOWLANDS STRATHSPEY
131H3H	2H1H26L	(II)	DUKE OF RICHMOND'S BIRTHDAY, THE
131H3H	6H3H2H6	(II)	AULD STEWARTS OF FOTHERGILL
133H6	1H66L2	(I)	BUXOM JOAN
145L1	145L1	(I)	GERMAN VALTZ
146L7L	1435	(I)	MISS ABERCROMBY
146L2	1415	(I)	MRS McDOWAL GRANT OF ARNDILLY'S STR.
146L2	1423	(I)	MR DAVIDSON'S STRATHSPEY
146L2	1435	(II)	MR ALEXR. CUNNINGHAM'S STRATHSPEY
146L2	1435	(I)	MR ALEXr CUNNINGHAM('S STRATHSPEY)
147L5L	141H5	(I)	EARL OF DALHOUSIE'S HAPPY RETURN
			TO SCOTLAND, THE
147L7L	147L2	(I)	MISS COCKBURN HOPE PARK'S STRATHSPEY
147L2	1315	(II)	CORN RIGS
147L2	1453	(I)	BRAES OF BALLINDALLOCH, THE
147L2	5551H	(I)	MISS DICKSON'S STRATHSPEY
1411	3625	(I)	GENERAL TEST, THE
1412	32H1H1H	(I)	GIDEN HALL
1414	16L23	(I)	MR SAMUEL MACKNIGHT'S FAVOURITE
1415	4321	(I)	LA NOUVELLE ANGLOISE
1415	4321	(I)	HEREFORDSHIRE LASSES, THE
1411H	1411	(I)	CHINESE DANCE
1426L	1555	(II)	LOCHNAGAR WHISKY
1426L	1553H	(I)	MISS CHRISTIE'S STRATHSPEY
1427bL	17b55	(I)	GHILLEADH DHUINN S'TOIL LEAM U
			[A' GHILLE DHUINN IS TOIGH LEAM THU]
1427L	145L5L	(I)	BUCHAN MAIDS ARE BRAW AN' BONNY
142	134	(I)	OPEN THE DOOR TO THREE
1423	127L3	(I)	LA NINA
1423	146L2	(I)	MR DAVIDSON'S STRATHSPEY
1425	1452	(II)	CHUIR I GLUN AIR A' BHODACH
1425	1452	(II)	CUIR I GLUN AIR A BHODACH
1425	437L2	(I)	CHARLES SHARPE ESQr. OF HODDOM'S FAVORITE
143b7bL	147bL4	(I)	GLENKELRY STRATHSPEY
143b5	7b53b1	(I)	HORUINN O U ORO
1437L	1451	(I)	WALTZ
1432	1432	(I)	RAINBOW, THE
1432	1432	(I)	LA BAGATELLIER
1433	6L6L21	(I)	CALEDONIAN SPAW
1433	2222	(I)	SPAIDSEARACHD DHONUILL CHRUAMAICH
1434	1422	(I)	NORTH HIGHLAND 20
1434	5422	(I)	C'UIN A THIG THU ARS AM BODACH
1434	5422	(I)	AMOROUS LOVER, THE
1435	2425L	(I)	LAMMERMUIR LILT
1431H	147L2	(I)	GARTHLANDS (STRATHSPEY)
1431H	5426L	(I)	MRS REID OF KILCALMKILL'S STRATHSPEY
1447bL	5511	(I)	OCH IS OCHAN MO CHARADH
1451	53b7bL7bL	(I)	ORAN AN AOIG
1452	4331	(I)	HIGHLANDERS' MARCH, THE
1452	4351	(I)	RETREAT, THE
1453b	1453b	(I)	O HI EILE, O HO HI RI
1453	6L247L	(II)	LADY LOUISA CORNWALLIS' STRATHSPEY
1453	6L247L	(I)	LADY LOUISA CORNWALLIS' STRATHSPEY
1453	5322	(II)	BELLADRUM HOUSE
1454	1457b	(I)	HUMOURS OF PANTEEN, THE
1455	5122	(II)	CHARLOTTE'S REVERIE
1456	5652	(II)	COLONEL SMITH'S LAMENT
1456	1H522	(I)	MISS McQUEEN'S REEL [McQUEEN'S REEL]
1456	1H522	(I)	MISS GRANT'S STRATHSPEY
1451H	3bH6b55	(II)	FYVIE CASTLE
1451H	5H1H2H2H	(I)	STORMONT BRAES, THE
1466	5126L	(II)	CRAIG-ROY
1466	2H1H2H2H	(II)	MRS BRODIE SHERIFF OF BATTLEBLENT'S S.
1461H	1362	(I)	HONble MISS MACKINZIE ELPHINSTONE'S
			FAVOURITE, THE
1473H	144H1H	(I)	DUKE'S BIRTH DAY, THE
14#27L	6L15L3L	(II)	BOB WILLIAMSON
14#1H4	3L4L4#L5L	(II)	MADAM NERUDA
155L	151H	(I)	MISS OSWALD'S BASS MINUET
155L3	15L3L1L	(I)	HAMPSTEAD ASSEMBLY
135L3	4542	(I)	ROSE BUDD, THE
156L5L	5L432	(II)	COUNTRY DANCE
156L5L	1543	(I)	TRIP TO FORNETH, A
156L7L	16L21	(I)	MISS MARY DOUGLAS'S WALTZ
156L1	1513H	(I)	DUCHESS OF ROXBURGHE'S STRATHSPEY, THE
156L1	1H57L2	(I)	SLAN GUN TIG MO RUN A NALL
156L2	1533	(I)	FOX CHASSE, THE
156L2	1531H	(I)	SAILOR LADDIE, THE
156L2	1565	(I)	MISS ROSS'S STRATHSPEY
157bL4	153b1H	(I)	WHEN I PARTED

157bL4	151H5	(I)	MR A. OSWALD'S JIG
157b4	11H54	(I)	HOOPERS JIGG
151	4L7bL4	(I)	MARY OF GLENFYNE
1515L	6L542	(I)	ROYAL BOARDING SCHOOL , THE
1515L	6L542	(I)	FIFTH OF DECEMBER
1515L	7bL247bL	(II)	HONOURABLE PEACE, AN
1515L	7bL247bL	(I)	HONOURABLE PEACE(, THE/AN)
1515L	7bL247bL	(I)	MRS STEWART (KIRKMICHAEL'S) REEL
1515L	7bL427bL	(I)	HO RO HOI HUG ORIONNAN, EC
1515L	7bL427bL	(I)	WIND BOUND SAILOR, THE
1515L	1153b	(II)	CAPTAIN ELPHINSTON
1515L	1153b	(I)	HONble CAPTN ELPHINSTON ('S STRATHSPEY)
1316L	4L6L2L2	(I)	MRS CUTHIL OF JOCK'S LODGE FAVORITE
1511	157bL7bL	(II)	ROVER, THE
1511	157bL7bL	(I)	OH 'SE MO RUN AN T-OIGEAR
1511	1522	(I)	KELSO BOWLINGREEN
1511	1535	(I)	DEOCH SLAINNTE DO'N AIRMAILT
			THA FLANNRIOSE SA CEANNAS
1512	1512	(I)	MR WILLS'S STRATHSPEY
1512	1551	(I)	MRS BILLINGCROFT'S WALTZ
1513b	7bL27b2	(I)	MISS NISBET OF DIRLETON'S STRATHSPEY
1513b	7L47L2	(I)	MISS YORK'S HORNPIPE
1513b	1522	(I)	MR EDMONDSTONE OF NEWTON'S STRATHSPEY
1513b	247b2	(II)	MISS FORDYCE, AYTON
1513b	247b2	(I)	MISS FORDYCE'S (OF AYTON'S) REEL
1513	6L27L5L	(II)	MISS BARBARA CUNNINGHAM
1513	6L27L5L	(I)	MISS BARBARA CUNNINGHAM('S STRATHSPEY)
1513	6L237L	(I)	MRS MAITLAND (OF RANKEILLOR'S) REEL
151	417bL	(I)	MY BONNY LADDIE HAS MY HEART
1515	7L247L	(I)	QUICK
1515	1427bL	(I)	DONALD CAIRD'S COME AGAIN
1515	156L2	(I)	MRS LAING'S STRATHSPEY
1515	157bL4	(II)	MRS FORSYTH'S PIBROCH, (MANSE OF ABERNETHY)
1515	157L2	(I)	WELCOME FROM VIGO
1515	1524	(I)	MISS HONEYMAN'S STRATHSPEY
1515	1524	(I)	COL. MONTGOMERY'S QUICK STEP
1515	1562	(I)	MR McDONALD
1515	1562	(I)	TAYNADALOCH HOUSE
1515	1616	(I)	LADIES OF EDINBURGH, THE
1515	357L2	(I)	WELLCOME FROM VIGO
1515	47bL37bL	(I)	MRS BLAIR OF BLAIR'S REEL
1515	427L2	(I)	LASSES OF THE BARN, THE
1515	427L4	(I)	MR Wm HAIG'S STRATHSPEY
1515	4327L	(I)	MACHINE WITHOUT HORSES, THE
1515	4342	(I)	BLACK EYED MILKMAID, THE
1515	432H2	(I)	LORD CHICHESTER SPENCER'S REEL
1515	4427L	(I)	QUICK
1515	4427L	(I)	TINK A TINK
1515	54H2H2	(I)	MR DRUMMOND OF PERTH'S STRATHSPEY
1515	6633	(I)	MISS CAMPBELL JURA'S REEL
1515	6661H	(II)	STORMONT LADS, THE
1515	6661H	(I)	STORMO(U)NT LADS(IS WALKING), THE
1515	7b5b31	(II)	NEGRO MELODY
1515	7b7b47bL	(II)	MERRY HARRIERS, THE
1515	1H526L	(I)	DUNKELD HOUSE
1516	1546L	(II)	PIG TOWN, THE
1516	1542	(I)	FLINTO
1516	3215	(I)	MOUNT YOUR BAGGAGE [MOUNT MY BAGGAGE]
1516	3322	(I)	ROAD TO DOWN, THE
1516	3525L	(I)	ONE BOTTLE MORE
1516	31H42	(I)	GALSHILS GRAY
1516	4215	(I)	MOUNT YOUR BAGGAGE
1516	5125L	(I)	MISS MAXWELL'S FANCY
1516	5125L	(I)	MISS ROBERTS FANCY
1516	5125L	(I)	MISS GORDON OF PARK
1516	5125L	(I)	MAC'S FANCY
1516	521H1H	(I)	BLIND LOVER, THE
1516	5311	(I)	MISS CHARLOTE STIRLING
1516	5542	(II)	DRUMINS
1516	5542	(I)	STRATHDOWN
1516	5542	(I)	DRUMIN'S STRATHSPEY
1516	51H3H5	(II)	CLIFF HORNPIPE, THE
1511H	1527bL	(II)	FANG THE FIDDLERS
1511H	1542	(I)	SKENE'S ELECTION
1511H	53H2H2H	(I)	DUKE OF GORDON'S STRATHSPEY
1513H	1H522	(I)	MRS GRANT'S STRATHSPEY
1513H	1H522	(I)	MRS GRANT'S FANCY
1513H	1H562	(I)	EARL OF EGLINTON'S STRATHSPEY
1526L	1511H	(II)	SHE'S SWEETEST WHEN SHE SMILES
1526L	1511H	(I)	SHE'S SWEETEST WHEN SHE('S NAKED/SMILES)
1526L	1551H	(II)	ALLOWA' KIRK [ALLOA KIRK]
1527bL	153b5	(II)	WITCHES, THE

1527bL	153b5	(II)	MISS NISBET OF DIRLETON
1527bL	1535	(II)	MISS NISBET OF DIRLETON
1527bL	1535	(I)	MISS NISBET OF DIRLETON ('S REEL)
1527bL	1551	(I)	I WAS NOT-SINCE MARTINMASS
1527bL	1565	(I)	BOB'S WHIM
1527bL	157b1	(I)	MRS MCLEOD OF DUNVIGGEN CASTLE'S REEL
1527bL	157b5	(I)	CLANRONALD HOUSE
1527L	6L136L	(I)	MISS AMELIA MARY DUFF
			OF MUIRTOWN'S STRATHSPEY
1527L	137L2	(I)	MISS MAULES WALTZ OR COUNTRY DANCE
1527L	1555	(I)	TOP OF THE LAW, THE
1527L	1551H	(I)	MISS CATHERINE STEWART
1527L	6547L	(I)	BONNIEST LASS IN A' THE AULD TOWN
1521	7bL244	(II)	NEW MILL AT LOGIERAIT, THE
152	151	(I)	AM BODACH A CHIANAMH
152	155	(I)	MISS ANN CAMERON'S JIG
1522	16L15L	(I)	PAS REDOUBLE
1522	1365	(I)	(MY HEART IS SAIR FOR) SOMEBODY
1522	153b5	(I)	LADY CHARLOTTE RAWDONS STRATHSPEY
1522	1551L	(II)	FIVE-MILE CHASE, THE
1522	151H5	(I)	MISS MADELINA MAXWELL OF MONRIETH
1522	3b51H5	(II)	SIMON BRODIE
1522	3b51H5	(I)	SYMON BRODIE [SIMON BRODIE]
1522	5426L	(I)	LADY GRANT OF DALVEY'S REEL
1523	1523	(I)	BOTTLE OF PUNCH, THE
1523	1523	(I)	HIGHWAY TO DUBLIN, THE
1523	151H5	(I)	NEW MILLS HOUSE
1524	1515	(I)	WATIE LAING
1524	1515	(I)	BEDDING OF THE BRIDE, THE
1524	1523	(I)	BOTTLE OF PUNCH
1524	1551	(II)	LADAR MOR A' GHOGAIN
1524	1551H	(I)	PENNY WEDDING REEL, THE
1524	151H5	(I)	JOHN BARLYCORN
1524	152H3bH	(II)	MISS SHEPHERD
1524	17b47L	(I)	MRS FRASER OF GORTULEG'S FAVOURITE
1524	17b41	(!)	LAIRD OF McNAB'S FAVORITE, THE
1524	12H3H2H	(I)	MONKTON LASSES, THE
1524	3b3bH43b	(II)	MAIR ROSIT
1524	511H5	(I)	CHESTHILL HOUSE
1525	1523	(I)	MR FRASER'S FANCY
1525	1555	(I)	SPORT, THE
1525	1555	(I)	YELL YELL
1525	1666	(I)	MISS McCLOUD'S FANCY
1525	2422	(I)	LADY PERTH'S STRATHSPEY
1525	2424	(!)	ISLE OF MAN
1525	243b2	(I)	LORD STRATHMOR'S STRATHSPEY
1525	4242	(II)	MISS DRUMMOND OF PERTH
1525	4242	(II)	MISS SARAH DRUMMOND OF PERTH
1525	4242	(I)	MISS (SARAH) DRUMMOND OF PERTH
			('S STRATHSPEY)
1525	4242	(I)	CALAM CRUBACH ANN'S A GHLENN
1525	4242	(I)	CRIPPLE MALCOM IN THE GLEN
1525	7b542	(I)	TURRIFF HUNT
1526b	51H6b2	(II)	STACCATO
1526	151H3	(I)	BORLUM'S REEL
1526	3521	(I)	LAST PINT ALE, THE
1526	3542	(I)	MISS LYNOTT'S REEL
1526	4257L	(I)	ROYAL NAVY, THE
1522H	1565	(I)	DUCHESS OF YORK'S FANCY, THE
153b5L	3b3b7bL4	(I)	LADY HARRIET SUTTIE'S STRATHSPEY
153b7bL	153b5	(I)	MRS MACDONALD OF CLANRANALD'S REEL
153b1	17bL6bL4	(II)	JAMES DOCKAR
153b1	153b2	(II)	MAJOR MOLLE [MAJOR MOLE]
153b1	153b2	(I)	MAJOR MOLLE'S (OF THE 9th REGt
			OF FOOT) REEL
153b1	27bL27bL	(I)	RAKISH HIGHLAND MAN, THE
153b1	27bL47bL	(I)	MR ROBERTSON'S STRATHSPEY
153b1	27bL47bL	(I)	MISS SMITH
153b1	2427bL	(I)	MISS HENNY MITCHELSON REEL
153b1	2427bL	(I)	PERSIE HOUSE REEL
153b1	2424	(I)	MRS BOYD OF PINKIE'S STRATHSPEY
153b1	27b24	(I)	LADY BARONESS KEITH
153b1	5424	(II)	FORTINGALL FAIRS
153b1	5424	(I)	FORTINGALL FAIRS
153b1	7b547bL	(II)	POOR FREDDY'S GONE TO BALMACAAN
153b1	1H2H7b7bL	(I)	MR GEORGE JENKIN'S STRATHSPEY
153b2	153b2	(II)	MAJOR MOLE [MAJOR MOLLE]
153b3b	1527bL	(II)	JOHN CHEAP THE CHAPMAN
153b3b	1527bL	(I)	JOHN CHEAP THE CHAPMAN
153b3b	27b22	(II)	LINK HIM DODDIE
153b3b	47b27bL	(I)	MISS HENDERSON, TRINITY'S FAVORITE
153b3b	517b5	(II)	TAM'S GREY MARE

153b4	153b5	(I)	LINKY LANKY
153b5	7bL424	(II)	SCONE PALACE
153b5	7bL424	(I)	MISS BOTHWICK'S REEL
153b5	1524	(I)	RT HON LORD ELCHO, THE
153b5	153b5	(II)	MISS JESSIE WEIR
153b5	1544	(I)	BEAUFORT CASTLE
153b5	2424	(II)	DUNKELD HERMITAGE
153b5	2424	(I)	DUNKELD HERMITAGE
153b5	3b527bL	(II)	MISS ELDER
153b5	3b527bL	(I)	MISS ELDER(S REEL)
153b5	4427bL	(II)	GLENBURNEY RANT, THE
153b5	7b47bL4	(I)	HILLAND TUNE
153b5	7b524	(II)	UNION BRIG
1531	1L2L4L3L	(I)	MISS HAY OF DRUMELZIER'S MEDLEY
1531	1L2L4L3L	(I)	HARLEQUIN TUNE
1531	5L5L14	(I)	PATIE & PEGGY
1531	5L11L1L	(II)	JOHNNIE GIBB O' GUSHETNEUK
1531	5L221	(I)	MRS McLEOD OF COLBECKS VALTS
1531	7bL427bL	(I)	MISS DUFF OF FETTERESSO'S STRATHSPEY
1531	1527bL	(I)	CLODUN REEL
1531	1542	(I)	PORT A BHODICH
1531	1542	(I)	CARLES RANT, THE
1531	227L5L	(II)	MISS McLAUCHLAN
1531	227L5L	(I)	MISS McLAUCHLAN('S REEL)
1531	2226L	(I)	CRICHTON CASTLE
1531	2326L	(I)	SEAFORTH'S SALUTATION
1531	2326L	(I)	FAILTE MHIC CAONNICH
1531	247L5L	(I)	HANDSOME JEWESS, THE
1531	247L5L	(I)	MISS ABERCROMBY'S REEL
1531	2427bL	(II)	INVEREY'S RANT
1531	2427bL	(I)	MR MACKAY'S REEL
1531	2427bL	(I)	INVEREYS RANT
1531	27b22	(I)	LINK HIM DODIE
1531	3165	(II)	PIPE MAJOR, THE
153	135	(I)	MOLADGH MARI
153	135	(I)	MARY'S PRAISE FOR HER GIFT
1531	427L5L	(I)	LA NOVELLE HOLENDOISE
1531	427L6L	(I)	EARL OF ANGUS AND ARRAN, THE
1531	4327bL	(II)	PORST MOHR IAIN IC EACHINN (JOHN MACEACHINN'S BIG TUNE)
1531	4327bL	(I)	HIGHLAND DANCE, A
1531	4327bL	(I)	NORTH HIGHLAND 15
1531	4347L	(I)	MRS PENDER'S STRATHSPEY
1531	7b427bL	(I)	THUSSEL LODGE, THE
1531	7b442	(II)	GORTHLECK'S HIGHLAND PLAID
1531	7b442	(I)	BREACHDAN UR FHIR GHORTALEIC [BREACAN UR FHIR GHORTUILEIC]
1531	7b527bL	(II)	HIGHLAND SOCIETY OF LONDON, THE
1532	6L5L4L3	(I)	JOHN CUMINE ESQr OF AUCHRY'S STRATHSPEY
1532	1532	(I)	TRIP TO THE JUBILEE
1532	1535	(II)	RABBIE BURNS
1532	1535	(I)	O GIN YE WERE DEAD GUDEMAN
1532	2246	(I)	SKYE DANCE, (A)
1533	1522	(II)	CAMPBELLS ARE COMING, THE
1533	1522	(I)	HOB OR NOB
1533	1542	(I)	CARLIN IS YOUR DAUGHTER READY
1533	1542	(I)	BOB O' DOOLY, THE
1533	27b22	(II)	LINK HIM DODDIE
1533	27b22	(I)	BLUE BRITCHES
1533	27b22	(I)	LINK HIM DODDIE
1533	351H3	(II)	LINK HIM DODDIE
1533	5226L	(I)	COME SWEET LASS
1534	3147L	(I)	REABART MORE
1535	5L27L2	(II)	BEN-A'CHIE
1353	7bL7bL24	(I)	LORD ALBREMARLE (REEL/'S DELIGHT)
1535	7bL7bL24	(I)	DUKE OF ROXBURGH'S REEL
1535	1527bL	(II)	BEDDING OF THE BRIDE, THE
1535	1527bL	(I)	BEAN NA BAINNSE
1535	1535	(I)	COCK IN THE AIR, THE
1535	27bL7b4	(I)	DUTCHESS OF HAMILTON'S REEL, THE
1535	2422	(I)	DUKE OF ATHOLE'S FORREST, THE
1535	2424	(I)	MR BAIRD OF NEWBYTH'S REEL
1535	2662	(II)	BRIDGE OF GARRY, THE
1535	2662	(I)	BIRKS OF INVERGARY, THE
1535	2662	(I)	BRIDGE OF GARRY, THE
1535	27b27bL	(II)	MISS JOHNSTONE
1535	35L11	(I)	LA BELL GUIMORE
1535	3527L	(I)	MISS ELDERS REEL
1535	3527	(I)	MISS ELDERS REEL
1535	351H3	(II)	BRIDGE OF PERTH, (THE)
1535	47bL7b2	(II)	RANTIN(G) HIGHLANDMAN, THE
1535	47bL7b2	(I)	RANTING (ROARING) HIGHLANDMAN, THE

1535	47b27bL	(II)	MISS ANNY STEWART, BOHALLY
1535	47b27bL	(I)	BRIDGE OF CRAIGE, THE
1535	47b27bL	(I)	MISS ANNY STEWART BOHALLY'S REEL
1535	627L2	(I)	HON: MR McKINZIE OF SEAFORTH'S BIRTH DAY, THE
1535	647bL4	(II)	MISS ANNIE MACKINNON
1535	6542	(II)	DALRY HOUSE
1535	6542	(I)	DALRY HOUSE
1535	1H522	(I)	LOCH TAY
1536	351H3	(II)	BRIDGE OF PERTH, THE
1536	4225	(I)	YEO YEO
1531H	7L527	(I)	CAPRICIOUS LOVERS, THE
1531H	2525	(I)	STRATHSPEY, A
1531H	2646	(II)	COUNTESS OF ROTHES, (THE)
1531H	2646	(I)	COUNTESS OF ROTHES'S STRATHSPEY, THE
1531H	5126L	(I)	MR SLOAN'S REEL
1531H	5132	(I)	CATCH AS CATCH CAN
1531H	5622	(I)	ANDANTE
1531H	53H1H5H	(I)	BRAES OF WAUGHOPE, THE
1531H	1H542	(II)	MRS ANDERSON OF BALGAY
1531H	1H542	(I)	MRS ANDERSON OF BALGAY('S REEL)
1531H	2H71H1H	(I)	NEW ALLEMAND
1547bL	153b5	(I)	DUNCAN McDUFF
1547L	1574	(I)	MANAGERS LAST KICK, THE
1547L	151H3	(I)	MISS WALKER'S STRATHSPEY
1547L	151H1H	(II)	MISS GRANT OF GRANT
1547L	151H1H	(I)	MISS GRANT OF (GRANT/MONYMUSK) ('S REEL)
1547L	152H5	(I)	GERMAN AIR
154	17L1	(I)	MISS AGNES GORDON'S MINUET
1541	2427L	(I)	BOCHD LIATH NA'N GOBHAR
1541	3452	(I)	LADS AND THE LASSES, THE
1541	47b66	(I)	FOR OUR LANG BIDING HERE
1542	7bL7bL7bL4	(I)	FAILTE PHROINSA
1542	7bL7bL7bL4	(I)	PRINCE'S SALUTE, THE
1542	7bL7bL27bL	(I)	BISHOP, THE
1542	7bL427bL	(II)	BISHOP, THE
1542	1357	(I)	MISS ELIZA ROBINSON'S REEL
1542	1511H	(I)	EMPTY (PURSE/POCKETS), (THE)
1542	1525L	(I)	ROYAL ARTILLERY WHIM, THE
1542	1541	(I)	BLACK MARE, THE
1542	1565	(I)	STORNWAY LASSIES
1542	151H5	(I)	MISS JESSY HUME'S REEL
1542	3132	(I)	HAUNTED TOWER, THE
1542	356L7L	(I)	MISS DOUGLAS'S JIG
1542	3532	(I)	LA PLASIR L'ETE
1542	3535	(I)	TULLOCHGORUM
154	242	(II)	A CHO-DHALTA MO RUIN! SEACAINN AN DUN!
1542	4527L	(I)	MISS STEWART'S FAVORITE
1542	5135	(I)	HEMP DRESSERS
1542	5135	(I)	WHEN SOL HAD LOOS'D
1543b	7bL47b2	(II)	MISS ANN MONRO
1543b	7bL47b2	(I)	MISS ANN MONRO('S QUICK STEP)
1543	1543	(I)	CELEBRATED SWISS WALTZ, THE
1543	2532	(I)	DUKE OF ATHOLL'S MARCH
1544	1521	(II)	ARRAN BOAT, THE
1544	27bL61H	(I)	CA' THE EWES TO THE KNOWES
1544	51H51	(II)	DHU HILL, THE
154	465	(I)	YEMON O NOCK
1545	1452	(II)	BALLINDALLOCH CASTLE
1545	1655	(II)	MACCRIMMON'S LAMENT [CHA TILL MI TUILLE]
1545	2411	(I)	NEW GYPSIE, THE
1545	22H76	(I)	HARROGATE ASSEMBLY
1545	4322	(II)	QUICKSTEP, A
1545	4362	(I)	DUTCHESS OF GORDON, THE
1545	47b27bL	(I)	MISS MASTERTON'S FAVORITE
1546	7L122	(II)	ISLA BANK
1546	1542	(I)	MR BRODIE'S REEL
1546	3542	(I)	ROYAL SALUTE, THE
1546	351H3	(I)	BRIDGE OF PERTH, (THE)
1546	5321	(I)	BOATIE ROWS, THE
1546	531H3	(II)	BRIDGE OF PERTH, THE
1546	5411	(I)	TRIP TO HINKSTON
1546	5521	(I)	LIFE WE LOVE, THE
1541H	5332	(II)	STEWART'S LASSIE
1541H	547L2	(I)	IRON TOWER
1541H	51H22	(II)	MACKENZIE MURDOCH
1555L	6L5L44	(I)	ALEXr McGLASHAN'S FAREWELL
155	5L44	(I)	COMPOSED AND DANCED BY MR McDONALD
1557L	1553	(II)	DEVIL AND THE DIRK, THE
1551	7bL447bL	(II)	LORD DOWN
1551	7bL447bL	(II)	MRS J. FORBES
1551	7bL447bL	(I)	LORD DOWN'S STRATHSPEY

1551	7L425L	(I)	DUKE OF YORK'S FAVOURITE
1551	7L4#25L	(I)	DUKE OF YORK'S FAVOURITE
1551	1562	(II)	GLENQUEY
1551	1562	(I)	PUDDING MAGGIE
1551	1562	(I)	MR ALEXr McDOUGALL ARDBEG'S REEL
1551	2662	(I)	HA'D THE CRADLE ROCKIN'
1551	2662	(I)	IRISH WHISKY
1551	22H4H7	(II)	LADY DAVIDSON OF CANTRAY
1551	427bL5L	(II)	FUTTERAT WI' THE GREY TAIL, THE
1551	427bL5L	(I)	HILLS OF CROMDALE, THE
1551	427bL5L	(I)	FUTTERAT WI' THE GRAY TAIL, THE
155	154	(I)	MEDLEY OVERTURE
155	154	(I)	MISS LUNDIE'S JIG
155	154	(I)	UP WI 'T AILLY NOW
155	154	(I)	DEVIL IN DENMARK
1551	7b47bL3b	(I)	HOPETOUN HOUSE
1552	7bL427bL	(II)	MO MHAIRI MHIN MHEALL SHUILEACH
1552	7bL427bL	(I)	PERTHSHIRE DANCING MEASURES & C No. 15
1552	1127bL	(II)	DUCHESS OF GORDON, THE
1552	1127bL	(I)	DUCHESS OF GORDON, THE
1552	1127bL	(I)	BLACK LASSIE'S NO CANTY, THE
1552	1127bL	(I)	BLACK GIRL IS NOT CHEERFULL, THE
1552	1127bL	(I)	CHA N EIL FONN AIRA NIGHEAN DUIBH
1552	1127bL	(I)	DUTCHES OF GORDON'S STRATHSPEY, THE
1552	1551	(I)	SHELAH O' NEAL
1552	1555	(II)	WHIPMAN'S RANT
1552	1555	(I)	ALWAYS IN HUMOUR (/NEVER OUT OF HUMOUR)
1552	1555	(I)	IS YOUR GRAITH IN ORDER
1552	1555	(I)	WHIPMAN'S RANT, THE
1552	1555	(I)	LAWLAND LADS WI' HIGHAND KILTS, THE
1552	1555	(I)	ANDANTE
1552	1551H	(I)	BRAES OF LITTLE MILL, THE
1552	46L11	(I)	MISS ANN CARNEGIE'S FAVOURITE VALTZ
1552	47L17L	(I)	NYMPH OF THE DANUBE, THE
155	244	(I)	FIG FOR A KISS, A
1552	5135	(I)	DIEL'S AWA' WI THE EXCISEMAN
155	22H7	(I)	MISS STAGS FANCY
1553b	7bL27bL7bL	(II)	MACKENZIE'S RANT
1553	1212	(I)	HUNT THE SQUIRREL
1553	1342	(II)	SUNDRUM HOUSE
1553	1524	(II)	SALMON TAILS UP THE WATER
1553	1524#	(I)	NORTH HIGHLAND 9
1553	1544	(II)	PORT NAN CON, or BOB O' DOOLY, THE
1553	1553	(I)	KEITHMORE
1553	27bL24	(I)	CARLEN IS YOUR DAUGHTER READY
1553	2542	(I)	LADY CHARLOTTE HAMILTON'S REEL
1553	5353	(II)	JOCKEY LATIN
1553	5353	(I)	JACKIE LATIN
1553	5354	(I)	JOCKEY LATIN [JACK LATIN] [JACKIE LATIN]
155	354	(I)	QUICK
1553	547L2	(I)	MISS ELEXA SCOTT'S STRATHSPEY
1553	51H55	(II)	ROYAL ABERDEENSHIRE HIGHLANDERS' MARCH
1553	6523	(I)	FAOILEAGAN SGARBA
1553	1H3H2H2	(II)	MISS HOPE
1554	7bL442	(I)	NORTH HIGHLAND 1
1554	7bL442	(I)	HIGHLAND DANCE
1554	1551	(I)	CASSAC
1554	2665	(I)	BELL OF CRAIGFOODIE, THE
1554	2665	(I)	LEITH SCOTS MEASURE, THE
1554	3315	(I)	BANKS OF HELICON, THE
1554	3525L	(I)	FORTY-SECOND Regt. 2ND QUICKSTEP
1554	4663	(I)	TIDE CAME IN, THE
1554	5454	(II)	A CHO-DHALTA MO RUIN
1554	6b423b	(I)	HOUSE OF GLAMS
1554	6b423b	(I)	MEDLEY OVERTURE (12)
1554	6b423b	(I)	ROSLIN CASTLE
1554	6b43b3b	(I)	ROSLIN CASTLE
1554	1H2H2H2	(I)	LADY HARRIOT HOPE'S REEL
1554	1H3H2H2	(I)	LADY HARRIOT HOPE ('S REEL)
1555	7bL7bL7bL7b	(I)	COLI MERCER OF ALDIE'S STRATHSPEY
1555	1525L	(I)	HIGHLAND-MAN KISS'D HIS MOTHER, THE
1555	1522	(II)	BRAES ABOON BONAW
1555	1522	(II)	MISS MILLER OF DALSWINTON
1555	1522	(I)	MISS JEAN DALRYMPLE'S STRATHSPEY
1555	1522	(I)	MISS MILLER OF DALSWINTON'S STRATHSPEY
1555	1524	(I)	PRINCE CHARLIE'S FAREWELL TO SCOTLAND
1555	1532	(I)	BRAES ABOON BONAW, THE
1555	1551	(I)	COSSACK'S DANCE, THE
1555	1551	(I)	DUNCAN DAVIDSON
1555	1552	(I)	DUNCAN DAVIDSON
1555	1552	(I)	GORDIAN KNOT, THE
1555	1552	(I)	MRS GORDONS FANCY

1555	1553	(I)	MARR HILLS
1555	1555	(I)	DANSE BASSE
1555	1562	(I)	MR DRUMMOND YOUNGER OF PERTH'S STRATHSPEY
1555	1562	(I)	DUNCAN DAVIE
1555	1563	(II)	MAID OF ISLAY(, THE) [MAIDS OF ISLAY(, THE)
1555	1563	(I)	FEAR CHUL CHARN
1555	1563	(I)	CULCAIRN'S STRATHSPEY
1555	1563	(I)	(MAID[S]/LASS) OF ISLA, THE
1555	157b5	(I)	DELVIN SIDE
1555	151H3	(I)	MAID OF ISLA
1555	152H2	(I)	FORT GEORGE ASSEMBLY
1555	152H5	(I)	TEMPEST, THE
1555	1632	(I)	MRS RAMSAY
			(OF INVERNETTIE LODGE'S) STRATHSPEY
1555	11H52	(II)	DUNCAN DAVIDSON
1555	11H52	(I)	YE'LL AYE BE WELCOME BACK AGAIN
1555	11H52	(I)	DUNCAN DAVIDSON
1555	11H62	(I)	DUNCAN DAVIDSON
1555	2454	(II)	BRAES OF TULIMET [BRAES OF TULLYMET]
1555	27b67b	(I)	PLSH LE FAWNA
1555	3666	(I)	LET THAT STAND THERE
155	542	(I)	McGRIGOR'S SEARCH
1555	436L7L	(II)	SPEED THE PLOUGH or NAVAL PILLAR, THE
1555	4666	(I)	MARQUIS OF HUNTLY'S MARCH, THE
1555	553b4	(II)	GENTLE DARK EYED MARY
1555	5542	(I)	GIGA
1555	51H55	(II)	MRS HASWELL
1555	51H55	(I)	MRS HASWALL(INVERARAY'S STRATHSPEY)
1555	51H2H5	(I)	KINGS ARMS, THE
1555	54H2H2	(I)	EARL OF ELGIN'S (FAVORITE/STRATHSPEY)
1555	54H2H2	(I)	DUCHESS D. OF RICHMOND'S STRATHSPEY THE
1555	6525L	(I)	COLONEL H.F. CAMPBELL'S STRATHSPEY
1555	6562	(II)	MISS STEWART OF FASNACLOICH'S
1555	6562	(I)	MISS STEWART OF FASNACLOICH'S(REEL)
1555	61H55	(I)	CIRCUS WALTZ
1555	62H2H2H	(II)	LET THAT STAND THERE
1555	7b47bL2	(II)	SIR RONALD McDONALD [SIR RONALD MACDONALD]
1555	7b47bL2	(II)	MISS DUNDAS'S REEL
1555	7b47bL2	(I)	LADY BETTY HAY'S REEL
1555	7b47bL2	(I)	MISS DUNDAS(S REEL)
1555	7b47bL2	(I)	SIR RONALD McDONALD'S REEL
1555	7b542	(II)	GLENBUCKET CASTLE
1555	7b7b7bL2	(I)	HOPETOUN HOUSE
1555	1H532	(I)	BRAES ABOON BONAW, THE
1555	1H57b1	(I)	MACDONELL SONG, A
1556	261H6	(II)	MARQUIS OF TULLYBARDINE'S REEL, THE
1557b	427bL1	(I)	BOYNE WATER
1557b	4242	(I)	KNITT THE POCKEY
1557	1523	(II)	TIMOUR THE TARTAR
1557	5523	(II)	BABES IN THE WOOD
1557	5524	(I)	TIMOUR THE TARTAR
1551H	1562	(II)	MISS SCOTT OF USAN
1551H	1562	(I)	MISS SCOTT OF USAN('S REEL)
1551H	152H2	(I)	INVERCAULD'S STRATHSPEY
1551H	5326L	(I)	MRS BAILLIE COOPER'S STRATHSPEY
1551H	57b27bL	(II)	COTTAR'S WIFE, THE
1551H	57b27bL	(I)	COATTER WIFE, THE
1551H	6522	(I)	MR WILLIAM STEWART'S STRATHSPEY
1551H	7b547bL	(I)	SMILIN' KATIE
1551H	7b542	(II)	STRATHEARN
1551H	7b542	(I)	STRATHEARN
1551H	7754	(I)	SHE ROSE AND LET ME IN
1551H	7756b	(I)	SHE ROSE AND LET ME IN
1551H	7756	(I)	SHE ROSE AND LET ME IN
1551H	1H522	(I)	MR RITCHIE'S REEL
1551H	3H750	(I)	HAWTHORN (THATS BLOOMS), THE
1551H	3H1H52	(I)	MARLY HOUSE
1551H	3H1H53	(II)	SILVER TASSY, THE
1551H	3H5H3H2H	(I)	MR MACLEOD OF GEANIES' STRATHSPEY
1553bH	1H7b54	(I)	LOVE SONG, A
156b2	3b3b7L7L	(I)	MISS MOLLY GRANT'S REEL
1562	1155	(II)	MRS GORDON OF ABERDOUR
1562	1155	(I)	MRS GORDON OF ABERDOUR('S REEL)
1562	1155	(I)	MISS GRACE GRANT'S REEL
1562	1511H	(I)	MISS MACINTOSH'S JIGG
1562	1561H	(I)	DANCING SETT
1562	1561H	(I)	MARQUIS OF GRANBY
1562	1561H	(I)	O'ER THE WATER TO CHARLIE
1562	1561H	(I)	LADS OF NAIRN, THE
1562	151H5	(I)	LADY CHARLOTTE MURRAY'S STRATHSPEY
1562	3125L	(I)	MISS CATHERINE HALES JIG
1562	3431	(I)	MR DAVID MAXWELL'S FAVOURITE

1563	1326L	(I)	STRATHSPEY WRIGGLE, THE
1563	1322	(II)	JOHN BEGG ESQ
1563	1563	(II)	HATTONBURN
1563	1561H	(II)	OVER THE WATER
1563	436L2	(I)	ARTHUR'S SEAT
1564	1H3H2H2	(I)	LADY HARRIOT HOPE'S REEL
1564	27L32	(II)	SANDLAW'S WELCOME
1564	5322	(II)	GOOD MORNING, MRS. BARCLAY
1564	547L2	(II)	MADAME DE LENGLEE
1564	5532	(I)	NEW YEAR'S DAY
1564	1H2H2H2	(I)	LADY HARIOT HOPE'S REEL
1564	1H3H2H2	(II)	NEW CHRISTMAS
1564	1H3H2H2	(II)	LADY HARRIET HOPE
1564	3H2H1H5	(II)	RAILWAY HORNPIPE
1565	6L6L7L1	(I)	MISS BUTT'S FAVORITE
1565	7bL47b4	(II)	CHAILLEACH OIDHCHE [CAILLACH OIDHCHE]
1565	1366	(I)	JOHN McGREGOR'S STRATHSPEY
1565	157L2	(I)	LADY JANE DUNDAS'S REEL
1565	157L2	(I)	LADY CHARLOTE'S DELIGHT
1565	1527L	(I)	PRESTO
1565	1527L	(I)	MISS THOMSON
1565	1522	(II)	LASSES OF FOCHABERS, THE
1565	1522	(I)	WIDOW'S RANT, THE
1565	1535	(II)	LADY GLASGOW
1565	1535	(I)	LADY GLASGOW('S STRATHSPEY)
1565	1547L	(I)	MISS PEGGY GORDON'S REEL
1565	1541	(I)	MISS COOPER'S FANCY
1565	1542	(II)	ROCKS OF CASHEL, THE
1565	1542	(I)	MRS GIBBON'S STRATHSPEY
1565	1542	(I)	ROCKS OF CASHEL, THE
1565	1542	(I)	(CASSEL/CASTLE) REEL, (THE)
1565	1544	(II)	HAUD THE LASS TILL I COME AT HER
1565	1544	(I)	HAD THE LASS TILL I WINN AT HER
1565	1544	(I)	LASS WI' A LUMP O' LAND, THE
1565	1546	(II)	MRS ROSS
1565	1552	(II)	TILL AN CRODH A'DHONNA CHAID !
1565	1553	(II)	GRACEFUL MOVE, THE
1565	1562	(I)	MARR HILL'S STRATHSPEY*
1565	1562	(I)	ROCKS OF CASHELL
1565	1562	(I)	MISS MONCRIEFF OF REEDIE'S STRATHSPEY
1565	1562	(I)	PETERHEAD BATH
1565	1565	(I)	KIND KIMMER
1565	1565	(I)	BATH WALTZ, THE
1565	1561H	(I)	SHANBUIE
1565	157b2	(I)	LADS OF BOOT, THE
1565	157b2	(I)	HA'D THE LASS TILL I WIN AT HER
1565	157b4	(II)	MY LAME LEG
1565	157b4	(II)	SE MO CHAS CHRUBACH
1565	157b4	(I)	GI'E ME A LASS WI' A LUMP O' LAND
1565	151H3	(II)	BRIG O' PERTH, THE
1565	151H1H	(II)	JENNY LATIN
1565	151H1H	(I)	JEANY LATIN
1565	331H3	(II)	BRIG O' PERTH, THE
1565	3512	(I)	SIR RICHARD STRACHAN
1565	351H3	(I)	BRIDGE OF PERTH
1565	47L43	(II)	LORD DOWN
1565	4225L	(I)	COTILLON
1565	4225L	(I)	JACK IN THE BOX
1565	4233	(II)	SO I'M OFF WITH THE GOOD ST. NICHOLAS BOAT
1565	437L4	(I)	WHIM, THE
1565	4327L	(II)	LIEUT. ABERCROMBY
1565	4327L	(I)	LIEUt ABERCROMBY('S REEL)
1565	4321	(I)	RURAL ASSEMBLY, THE
1565	4321	(I)	RAINBOW, THE
1565	4321	(I)	MARIONETS
1565	4362	(I)	MR MONRO BINNING'S STRATHSPEY
1565	4622H	(I)	MISS CARSINA GORDON GRAY'S FAVOURITE
1565	51H3H2H	(I)	BATTLE OF BOTHWELL BRIG
1565	6225	(I)	MO CHAILIN DONN OG
1565	6225	(I)	YOUNG MAID WITH THE GOLDEN LOCKS
1565	6527L	(I)	MRS MUIR McKENZIES FANCIE
1565	6653	(I)	MNATHAN CHROSPUIL IS BHAILE MHUIRICH
1565	671H5	(II)	BANKS O' CLYDE, THE
1565	61H32	(I)	MISS MCDONALD OF BOROUGHDALE'S JIG
1565	1H47L2	(I)	MAJOR BROOKS'S STRATHSPEY
1565	1H542	(II)	CAPTAIN KENNEDY
1565	1H542	(I)	(CAPTAIN/MR ROBERT) KENNEDY'S REEL
1565	1H542	(I)	SHANE'S CASTLE
1565	2H4H66	(I)	(NEIL) GOW'S LAMENT(ATION) FOR ABERCA(I)RNEY
1565	3H542	(I)	MISS WALLACE'S REEL
1565	4H642	(I)	MISS WALLACE'S REEL

1566	1525L	(I)	COUPAR ANGUS JIGG
1566	1542	(I)	MISS CHRICHTON'S REEL
1566	1562	(I)	GUR LIONAR GOBHLAN DUBH FRAOICH ANN
1566	11H51	(I)	GOLDEN ISLAND, THE
1566	11H51	(I)	TO HIS CRUTCH
1566	5125L	(I)	MISS MAJOR MACLEOD
1566	5122	(II)	OLD MAN WILL NEVER DIE, THE [OLD MAN, THE]
1566	5122	(I)	SIGr FIDDLIDEE
1566	5122	(I)	PERTHSHIRE DANCING MEASURES & C No. 2
1566	5122	(I)	(BRIDGE/BANKS) OF NAIRN, THE
1566	5122	(I)	OLD MAN WILL NEVER DIE, THE
1566	7623	(I)	CHESTHILL'S FAVORITE AIR
1567	1H532	(I)	WASP, THE
1561H	1561H	(I)	CLIFTON HOUSE
1561H	1561H	(I)	GUESS AGAIN
1561H	5211	(I)	WILL YOU TO FLANDERS
1561H	5222	(I)	KEITH MORE
156	1H1H1H	(I)	YELLOW HAIR'D LADDIE, THE
1561H	3H1H22	(II)	MRS SCOTT SKINNER
1561H	3H3H2H2	(I)	WHO CAN HELP IT
157b1	7b47bL2	(I)	SWEET MOLLY
157b1	7b47bL2	(I)	HOPETOUN HOUSE
157b2	1535	(I)	TULLOCH GOIRM
157b2	1551	(I)	BHANARACH DHONN A CHRUIDH
157b5	7b47bL2	(II)	SWEET MOLLY [cf: HOPETO(U)N HOUSE]
157b5	7b47bL2	(I)	SWEET MOLLY
157b5	7b47bL2	(I)	HOPETOUN HOUSE
157b	652	(I)	FEIDAG GHORACH AN T'SLEIDH
157b	654	(I)	BODHAN ARIDH M'BRAIGH RANNOCH
			[BOTHAN AIRIDH 'M BRAIGHE RAINEACH]
157b7b	4427bL	(II)	MRS COLONEL BAIL[L]IE OF RED-CASTLE
1575	4332	(I)	MISS DAVIE'S WALTZ
1575	5335	(I)	MISS CHRISTINA ABERCROMBY'S HIGH DANCE
1575	5335	(I)	MADAM DEL CARO'S REEL
1575	52H3H1H	(I)	GODDESSES, THE
1577	337L7L	(I)	MRS REID OF ADAMTON'S FAVOURITE
151H2	151H6	(II)	WELCOME TO YOUR FEET AGAIN
			[YOU'RE WELCOME TO YOUR FEET AGAIN]
151H2	151H6	(I)	BONNY LASS WI' THE TOCHER, THE
151H2	151H6	(I)	WELCOME TO YOUR FEET AGAIN, (YOU'RE)
151H2	151H1H	(I)	YOU'RE WELCOME TO YOUR FOOT
151H2	151H3H	(I)	COL. GRANT OF GRANT'S STRATHSPEY
151H3b	5424	(I)	BARLEY BROTH
151H3	5L257L	(II)	GENERAL BAILLIE
151H3	156L2	(I)	HONble MISS RUTHVEN'S STRATHSPEY
151H3	26L16L	(I)	EXPRESS, THE
151H3	247L2	(I)	SIR HARRY INNES'S REELL
151H3	351H1H	(II)	DUNS DINGS A'!
151H3	427L5L	(I)	MISS GORDON OF SHIELDAGREEN'S REEL
151H3	427L2	(I)	VIRGINS FROLICK, THE
151H3	4542	(I)	MR HUNTER'S REEL
151H3	6532	(I)	MR GARDEN JUNr (OF TROUP'S) STRATHSPEY
151H4	22H76	(I)	MAJOR CHURCHILL'S DANCE
151H5	6L237L	(I)	MORNING WALK TO BERRY-DEN, A
151H5	7bL47b4	(II)	MILTON DUFF
151H5	1524	(II)	CORIMONIE'S RANT [CORIEMONIE'S RANT]
151H5	1524	(I)	CORIMONIE'S (STRATHSPEY/RANT)
151H5	1525	(I)	GENERAL CAMPBELL'S STRATHSPEY
151H5	1547bL	(II)	RYAN'S RANT
151H5	1542	(I)	MR STIRLING OF KEIR'S REEL
151H5	1542	(I)	LADY ELIZABETH PERCY'S FANCY
151H5	1542	(I)	PUTNEY BOWLING GREEN
151H5	1562	(I)	RAB THE RANTER
151H5	1564	(I)	LADY BEATRICE HAMILTON
151H5	1566	(I)	BATTLE OF LANGSIDE, THE
151H5	1566	(I)	MISS ELPHINSTONE'S STRATHSPEY
151H5	151H1	(I)	CASTLE GRANT
151H5	151H1H	(I)	MISS GRACE SPEIRS STRATHSPEY
151H5	11H24	(I)	GENERAL CAMPBELL'S JIGG
151H5	11H62	(I)	PAINTERS' RANT, THE
151H5	13H2H2	(I)	MISS FAIRFAX'S STRATHSPEY
151H5	2424	(I)	COL. CATHCART'S REEL
151H5	4321	(I)	MISS FLOCKHARTS GERMAN VALTZ
151H5	4341	(I)	GOLF CLUB, THE
151H5	4344	(I)	ABOUT SHE GOES
151H5	443b1	(I)	SCOTCH SCOLLOPS
151H5	4622	(I)	SCONE PALACE
151H5	4632	(I)	MISS JULIET MORISON
			(OF FETTERESSO'S) STRATHSPEY
151H5	461H6	(I)	MRS CHARLES FERGUSSON'S REEL
151H	552	(I)	CAPUCHIN, THE
151H5	52H3H1H	(I)	HOUSE OF CAIRNFIELD, THE

151H5	52H4H1H	(I)	ALLEGRETTO
151H5	54H72H	(II)	MISS EDMONDSTONE OF NEWTON
151H5	54H72H	(I)	MISS EDMONDSTONE OF NEWTON'S STRATHSPEY
151H5	657L2	(I)	OXFORD CASTLE
151H5	6522	(II)	MISS KATTY GORDON OF EARLSTON'S REEL
151H5	6522	(I)	MISS (KATTY) GORDON (OF EARLSTON) 'S REEL
151H5	6522	(I)	LASSES OF THE BORDER, THE
151H5	6542	(I)	MISS HELEN McCALL'S STRATHSPEY
151H5	61H62	(II)	MASTER REGINALD MACDONALD
151H5	64H1H6	(I)	NEW THEATRE, THE
151H5	1H52H2	(II)	DUKE OF PERTH
151H5	1H52H2	(I)	DRUNKEN WIVES OF ABERDEEN, THE
151H5	1H52H2	(I)	DUKE OF PERTH'S REEL (THE)
151H5	1H1H22	(II)	GLEN ELG
151H5	1H1H22	(II)	GLENELG
151H5	2H1H22	(I)	FAVOURITE HIGHLAND STRATHSPEY, A
151H6	1522H	(II)	MARQUIS OF HUNTLY
151H6	1522H	(I)	MARQUIS OF HUNTLY (NEW STRATHSPEY)
151H6	1542	(I)	MISS WILLIS'S STRATHSPEY
151H6	3557	(I)	WILLIAM'S LOVE
151H6	432H2	(I)	GRANT'S REEL
151H6	4522	(I)	CLEEK HIM INN
151H6	53H4H2H	(I)	LA TRENISE
151H6	6555	(I)	YORK HORNPIPE, THE
151H6	662H2H	(I)	MARCHIONESS OF HUNTLY'S STRATHSPEY, THE
151H6	5H5H2H2H	(II)	BRIG O' BALLATER, THE
			[BRIDGE OF BALLATER, THE]
151H6	5H5H2H2H	(I)	BRIGG OF BALATER, THE
			[BRIG O' BALLATER, THE]
151H7	5351H	(I)	LADY ELCHO'S
151H7	6543	(I)	NUMBER THREE
151H	776	(I)	MISS (FLORA) McLEOD (OF COLBECK)'S MINUET
151H7	2H4H2H2	(II)	MILL OF LAGGAN, THE
151H7	2H4H2H2	(I)	MILL OF LAGGAN(, THE)
151H1H	5122	(II)	ANDERSON'S RANT
151H1H	5122	(I)	ANDERSON'S RANT
151H1H	51H22	(I)	KIRKALDY MERCHANT'S HALL
151H1H	6542	(I)	MR GRAHAM STIRLING OF AIRTH'S STRATHSPEY
151H1H	64H72H	(I)	MISS MAXWELL'S STRATHSPEY
151H1H	2H1H22	(I)	MISS GRAHAM OF ORCHILL'S REEL
151H1H	2H2H4H2H	(I)	MERRY FIDLER, THE
151H2H	151H2H	(I)	MISS STEVENS OF BROADLAND'S REEL
151H2H	4531	(I)	DUBLIN VOLUNTEERS QUICK MARCH
151H3H	6642	(I)	CAPT ARCHd. DOUGLASS' STRATHSPEY
151H3H	11H2H2	(II)	GLENGAIRN
152H6	61H22	(I)	MISS BELL'S FAVOURITE
153bH1H	6b427L	(II)	G.S. MACKAY
153bH1H	6b547L	(II)	ALICK YOUNG
153H	152H	(I)	GENERAL ATTACK
153H1H	1H642	(I)	MR JOHN STEWART'S REEL
153H1H	2H4H2H2H	(I)	ARTHUR'S SEAT
153H2H	1H542	(II)	LAMBERTON RACES [COL. RENTON'S FAVOURITE]
153H2H	1H542	(I)	LAMBERTON RACES
153H2H	1H542	(I)	O WHAT A BEAW MY GRANNY WAS
153H2H	1H552	(I)	MISS NANCY ROBINSON'S REEL
153H2H	1H7b27bL	(I)	MISS CUMMINGS FANCY
153H2H	1H7b27bL	(I)	MRS GOW'S STRATHSPEY
153H3H	4H3H72H	(I)	MISS NANCY WATERSTON'S FANCY
16b13b	2454	(II)	DRIVE HOME THE MAINLANDERS
16b5	43b7bL	(I)	SAILOR'S DELIGHT, THE
1611	1632	(I)	COMELY, THO' BLACK-O'-BLEE
1613	1627L	(I)	SIR ARCHd DUNBAR OF NORTHFIELD'S STRATHSPEY
1627L	15L6L2L	(I)	MR DUNCAN FORBES DUFF OF MUIRTOWN'S R.
1621	4445	(I)	RATHER SLOW
1624	1615	(I)	LORD BRADALBAN'S MARCH
1624	1655	(I)	BODAICH NA 'M BRIGIS
1632	1313	(I)	MISS MARGARET DUNBAR'S STRATHSPEY
1632	1321	(I)	RT HON LORD TORPHICHEN'S QUICK STEP
1635	47b27bL	(I)	MISS JESSY WALLACE REEL
1631H	3125L	(I)	BOWMEN OF THE BORDERS REEL, THE
165	6L11	(I)	FHIR A BHATA [FEAR A' BHATA]
1652	5L5L13	(I)	PATIE AND PEGGY
1653	5322	(I)	MISS CARNEGY OF LOWER'S STRATHSPEY
1653	1H642	(I)	GAELIC SOCIETY OF PERTH, THE
1653	1H642	(I)	JOHN STEWART ESQr. OF GARTH'S
			FAVORITE STRATHSPEY
1655	1642	(I)	LORD DUNCAN'S VICTORY
1655	1642	(I)	DALMORE PARK
1655	27b7bL2	(I)	DR FOWLER'S CLOCKBAG
1655	27b27bL	(I)	GLENGARRIE'S REELL
1655	27b27bL	(I)	DUKE OF CUMBERLAND'S REEL, THE
1655	27b27bL	(I)	CLOAK BAGG, THE

```
1655       47b27bL     (II)  DUKE OF CUMBERLAND
1655       47b27bL     ( I)  DUKE OF CUMBERLAND('S STRATHSPEY, THE)
1656       1652        (II)  MACKENZIE'S FAREWELL
1663       6522        ( I)  UNA OF ULVA
17b17bL    4445        ( I)  MOTHER'S LAMENT
                             ON THE DEATH OF HER CHILD, A
17b55      17b7b4      (II)  DELVIN SIDE
17b55      17b7b4      ( I)  DELVIN SIDE
17b55      57b7b4      (II)  DELVINE SIDE
176b5      3b125L      (II)  HUNTLY CASTLE
17b7b4     1555        ( I)  YEAL YEAL
17b7b5     17b7b4      ( I)  DELVIN SIDE
17b7b5     7b7b7b4     (II)  DELVIN SIDE
17b7b5     7b7b7b4     ( I)  DELVEN SIDE [DELVIN SIDE]
17b1H5     7b1H64      (II)  CAILLACH LIATH RASAR
                             [GREY OLD LADY OF RAASAY, THE]
1751       4215L       ( I)  QUICK STEP
1753       37L25L      ( I)  HAMBURG DANCE
1754       36L16L      ( I)  ADMIRAL McBRIDE'S HORNPIPE
1764       47L16L      ( I)  HORNPIPE, A
1765       657L2       ( I)  BATH MEDLEY, THE
171H       513         ( I)  HIGH WAY TO WARINGTON, THE
173bH1H    2H7b2H4H    ( I)  CULLODEN WELL
11H6L6     2531        (II)  TANK, THE
11H1       7bL7b7bL    ( I)  MRS FOGG'S FANCY
11H1       111         ( I)  ASIOLTA FIGLIO
11H11      526L6L      ( I)  SCOTCH MEASURE, A
11H12      11H33       (II)  JAMIE HARDIE
11H15      11H31       ( I)  SEAFORTH HIGHLANDERS, THE
11H11H     22H66       ( I)  KEY OF KINDNESS, THE
11H11H     657L2       ( I)  MISTAKE, THE
11H11H     7b524       ( I)  MRS GEORGE ROBERTSON GREENOCK'S STR.
11H13H     5L2H11H     ( I)  ALLEMAND DE GRACS
11H15      11H31       (II)  SEAFORTH HIGHLANDERS, THE
11H22H     3H4H74      ( I)  TRIP TO BRISTOL
11H3b1     27bL7b2     (II)  GLENLIVET
11H3b5     7bL7b27bL   ( I)  MISS ELIZABETH MYLNE'S STRATHSPEY
11H3b5     7bL7b22     (II)  HONble. MISS JESSIE A. RUTHVEN
11H3b5     7bL7b22     ( I)  HONble MISS JESSIE A. RUTHVEN'S STRATHSPEY
11H3b5     1524        ( I)  GENERAL STEWART OF GARTH'S REEL
11H3b5     2427bL      ( I)  MR STRANG OF LOPNESS'S REEL
11H3b5     27b22       ( I)  MISS ELEANORA ROBERTSON'S FAVOURITE
11H3b1H    7b424       ( I)  MR REID'S REEL
11H31      11H44       ( I)  BACHELERS MISERIES
11H31      27bL27bL    (II)  MRS MUIR MACKENZIE
11H31      27b27bL     (II)  MRS MUIR MACKENZIE
11H31      27b27bL     (II)  LADY MUIR MACKENZIE
11H31      27b27bL     ( I)  MRS/LADY) MUIR MACKENZIE'S REEL
11H31      3131        ( I)  PRINCE REGENT'S FAVORITE
11H31      3131        ( I)  I'LL GANG NA MAIR TO YON TOWN
11H31      3131        ( I)  PRINCE REGENT'S FAVORITE
11H31      3132        (II)  I'LL GANG NAE MAIR TO YON TOWN
11H31      3132        ( I)  I'LL GANG NAE MAIR TO YON TOWN
11H31      3132        ( I)  WELLCOME TO THE COUNTRY
11H31      3142        (II)  I'LL GANG NAE MAIR TO YON TOUN
11H31      3142        ( I)  WE'LL GANG NAE MAIR TO YON TOUNE
11H31      3542        (II)  I'LL GANG NAE MAIR TO YON TOUN
11H31      427L5L      (II)  MISS LOUDON
11H3       11H4        ( I)  CUDGELL, THE
11H35      11H2H2      ( I)  MRS WATT'S STRATHSPEY
11H35      27b22       ( I)  CAPT DAVID STEWART,
                             42nd ROYAL HIGHLANDER'S REEL
11H35      27b22       (II)  CAPTAIN DAVID STEWART 42nd. R. HLRS.
11H35      427L2       ( I)  MISS WEMYSS OF WEMYSS'S REEL
11H35      44H4H2H     ( I)  COLDSTREAM MARCH
11H35      652H2H      ( I)  LADY ALEXr RUSSELL
11H36      3527L       ( I)  JIGG
11H3       652         ( I)  BANKS OF THE SHANNON, THE
11H31H     51H72H      (II)  HOUSE OF NEW, THE
11H31H     51H72H      ( I)  HOUSE OF NEW, THE
11H33H     3H2H2H1H    ( I)  LA TRENISE
11H45L     351H4       ( I)  MISS HALLIFAX'S FAVOURITE
11H46L     5L136       ( I)  MARQUISS OF LORN'S STRATHSPEY, THE
11H45      2642        ( I)  SUNDRUM HOUSE
11H51      11H55       ( I)  CAN YE SEW CUSHIONS
11H51      11H62       (II)  MENZIES RANT
11H51      2462        ( I)  MR ROSS'S STRATHSPEY
11H51      427L5L      ( I)  MISS BARBARA HAY'S FAVORITE
11H51      437L2       (II)  MONALTRIE'S
11H51      437L2       ( I)  MONALTRIES( REEL)
11H51      4326L       (II)  MR McINTYRE OF GLENOE
11H51      4326L       ( I)  MR MACINTYRE OF GLENOE('S STRATHSPEY)
```

11H51	4532	(II)	DR. MACDONALD
11H51	4532	(II)	SCOTT SKINNER'S COMPLIMENTS TO DR. MACDONALD
11H51	4647L	(II)	DRUMIN
11H52	7bL7b41	(I)	MISS ISABELLA ROBERTSON'S REEL
11H52	7L232	(II)	MISS GIBSON
11H52	7L232	(II)	MISS EDMONDSTON
11H52	7L232	(II)	CUMBERLAND, THE OR MISS GIBSON
11H52	7L232	(I)	MRS ROBERTSON'S REEL
11H52	7L232	(I)	MISS EDMOND(STON)'S REEL [MISS EDMONDSTON]
11H52	7L232	(I)	MISS (NANCY) GIBSON'S REEL (OR THE CUMBERLAND REEL)
11H52	7L232	(I)	CUMBERLAND REEL, THE OR UNAS LOCH [CUMBERNAULD REEL]
11H52	16L6L2	(I)	MRS CAPt SKENE'S STRATHSPEY
11H52	1116L	(I)	MISS WEMYSS OF WEMYSS
11H52	1234	(I)	DANCED BY 14
11H52	11H1H1	(I)	SPINNING WHEEL, THE
11H52	13bH1H1H	(I)	FIENT A CRUM O' THEE SHE FA'S, THE
11H52	31H52	(I)	KING OF PRUSSIA'S REEL
11H52	31H52	(I)	LOVELY MALLY
11H5	262	(I)	RAGGED SAILOR, THE
11H52	6211H	(I)	RAGGED SAILOR, THE
11H53b	7bL7b27bL	(I)	MR GEORGE MUNRO'S REEL
11H53b	46b7b5	(I)	BRITISH TARS CAN DO IT
11H53	115L5L	(I)	WALLACE('S) MARCH
11H53	1327L	(I)	JIG
11H53	11H22	(II)	MRS MOSSMAN
11H53	11H22	(I)	MRS MOSMAN'S STRATHSPEY
11H53	11H55	(I)	CAN YE SEW CUSHIONS
11H53	11H75	(I)	NEWGATE BROTH
11H53	27b42	(I)	WHERE WAD BONIE ANNIE LY
11H53	21H42	(I)	WHERE WILL OUR GOODMAN LIE
11H53	4216L	(II)	ST. CATHERINE'S
11H53	51H3H1H	(II)	BALMORAL CASTLE
11H53	51H3H1H	(I)	LADY ELCHO'S MEDLEY
11H53	51H3H2H	(I)	RT HON EARL(E) OF BR(E)ADALBINE'S STR.
11H53	51H3H2H	(I)	HONBIe EARL OF BREADALBINE'S STRATHSPEY
11H54	11H22	(I)	KENMURE'S ON AN' AWA (WILLIE)
11H55	11H22	(II)	KENMURE'S ON AN' AWA WILLIE [KENMORE LADS]
11H55	11H22	(II)	MARCHIONESS OF HUNTLY (2nd. Setting)
11H55	11H22	(I)	(MRS YOUNG'S) STRATHSPEY
11H55	11H22	(I)	KENMURE'S ON AND AWA' (WILLIE)
11H55	11H52	(II)	WEST ADAM ST. CLUB
11H55	11H66	(I)	JUST SO IN THE NORTH
11H55	11H2H2	(I)	MISS GRAHAM OF ORCHILLS STRATHSPEY
11H55	3623	(I)	COTTILLION 1st
11H55	4323	(I)	WEMYSS CASTLE REEL
11H55	4542	(I)	DRUMBAIN'S REEL
11H55	4542	(I)	MISS ROSS'S REEL
11H55	6547bL	(II)	GLENLYON [GLEN LYON]
11H55	6547bL	(I)	GLEN LYON'S (STRATHSPEY/REEL/RANT)
11H55	6547bL	(I)	MISS ROBERTSON OF BODDOM'S STRATHSEPEY
11H51H	7bL7b47bL	(I)	LIEUt. HOWARD DOUGLAS'S STRATHSPEY
11H51H	22H66	(I)	INVERCALLDS REEL [INVERCAULD'S REEL]
11H51H	7b525	(II)	CULLODEN HOUSE
11H51H	7b525	(I)	CULLODON HOUSE
11H53bH	7bL7b7b5H	(I)	MAJOR BAILLIE OF DUNAIN'S STRATHSPEY
11H53bH	27b42	(I)	MISS J. DALRYMPLE'S STRATHSPEY
11H6b5	153b2	(II)	SADNESS OF LIFE, THE
11H67L	3L4L32	(I)	COTILLION
11H62	11H3H6	(I)	SIR WALTER SCOTT BART.
11H62	3H643	(II)	DR. GORDON STABLES(' REEL)
11H63	7L5L44	(II)	ROB RALSTON'S STRATHSPEY
11H63	11H62	(II)	BRIG O' BALGOWNIE, THE
11H63	11H65	(I)	GENERAL TOAST, THE
11H63	11H75	(I)	PADDY WHACK
11H63	237L7L	(I)	WILL THE WEAVER
11H63	637L2	(I)	LASSES OF BERWICK
11H63	637L2	(I)	MRS ROSE OF KILRAVOCK'S JIGG
11H64	1675	(II)	PADDY WHACK
11H64	1675	(I)	PADDY WHACK
11H64	1764	(II)	APPLE TREE, THE
11H65	11H52	(II)	DUNTULM QUICKSTEP
11H65	216L2	(I)	MRS MONTGOMERY'S JIG
11H65	3532	(I)	MISS BUNBURY'S JIG
11H65	437L2	(I)	CAPTAIN JAMES BLACK OF THE 98th QUICKSTEP
11H65	4527L	(II)	KINLOCHEWE
11H65	57b42	(II)	BLACK SHEPHERDESS, THE
11H65	657b2	(II)	MACLEOD'S QUICKSTEP
11H66	11H53	(I)	MISS MUNRO'S REEL
11H66	11H62	(II)	TOM'S HIGHLAND FLING

```
11H66       3333        (II)  MRS McLEOD
11H66       5333        (II)  MRS MACLEOD OF RAASAY
                              [MRS MACLEOD OF RASAY]   [MRS MCLEOD]
11H66       6322        (I)   MISS POURIE OF RESWALLIE'S FAVOURITE
11H61H      11H24       (II)  CA' THE WETHERS TO THE HILL
11H61H      11H24       (II)  GLENTILT
11H61H      11H31       (II)  KING'S GUN, THE
11H61H      6562        (I)   MISS MARGARET EWING'S STRATHSPEY
11H61H      61H24       (II)  GLEN TILT LODGE
11H61H  ,   62H2H7      (II)  MISS SALLY HUNTER OF THURSTON'S JIG
11H61H      62H2H7      (I)   MISS SALLY HUNTER OF THURSTON('S JIGG)
11H7b2      11H57b      (I)   HATTON OF BUCHROMB'S REEL
11H7b2      11H3bH2H    (II)  MISS JOHNSTON OF HILTON
11H7b4      11H1H1H     (I)   MISS ROSE'S JIG
11H7b4      11H1H2H     (II)  SGIANDUBH
11H7b4      11H1H3bH    (I)   ARNISTON HOUSE
11H7b4      11H1H3bH    (I)   MISS FARQUHARSON OF INVERCAULD'S JIGG
11H7b4      3b7bL7bL7bL (I)   LOCHNESS
11H7b4      3b7bL7bL2   (II)  SANDY IS MY DARLING
11H7b4      3b7bL7bL2   (I)   LORD CHIEF BARON'S FAVORITE
11H7b4      3b7bL7bL3b  (II)  SANDY IS MY DARLING
11H7b4      3b7bL7bL3b  (II)  LOCH NESS
11H7b4      3b7bL7bL3   (II)  SANDY IS MY DARLING
11H7b4      3b112       (II)  CAULD KAIL
11H7b       541         (I)   YOUNG BENJIE
11H7b6      7b47bL4     (II)  BLACK HAIR'D LAD, THE
11H7b7b     11H7b4      (I)   TODLEN BUTT AND TODLEN BEN
11H7b7b     3b524       (I)   MATTHEW BRIGGS
11H7b7b     527bL2      (II)  CUTTING FERNS
11H7b7b     527bL2      (II)  THA MI SGITH [I AM WEARY]
11H7b7b     527bL2      (I)   CUTTING FERNS
11H7b7b     53b7bL2     (I)   WHY SHOULD I SIT AND SIGH
11H7b1H     7b47b7bL    (I)   MR D. STEWART OF GARTH'S JIGG
11H74       157L2       (I)   MRS TROTTER (OF CASTLELAW'S) QUICK STEP
11H76       5127L       (I)   LADY MADALINA SINCLAIR'S REEL
11H76       5222        (II)  ANNIE LAURIE
11H76       6231        (I)   SACK POSSETT
11H76       6231        (I)   (O/HAY) JENNY COME DOWN TO JOCK
11H7        671H        (I)   MINUET
11H76       5H1H2H2H    (I)   LADY HELONORA HOME'S REEL
11H76       5H1H2H2H    (I)   P. BAILLIE'S STRATHSPEY
11H76       5H1H2H2H    (I)   LADY ELEANORA DUNDASS'S REEL
11H76       5H1H2H2H    (I)   MISS MEYNELL'S REEL
11H71H      6522        (I)   RAKES OF ADAIR, THE
11H71H      6524        (I)   WE'LL A' TO KELSO GO
11H72H      3H761H      (I)   MISS JENNY ELLIOT'S STRATHSPEY
11H72H      3H1H4H7     (I)   MISS GARDNERS FANCY
11H74H      3H4H2H5     (I)   MRS GRANT'S STRATHSPEY
11H1H1      2L23bH4     (I)   MISS RANDON'S DANCE
11H1H1      11H2H2      (I)   MRS MONTGOMERY OF COILSFIELD'S REEL
11H1H1      11H2H2      (I)   MISS RAE (OF ESKGROVE)'S JIG(G)
11H1H1      11H2H2      (I)   NEW YEARS DAY
11H1H3      6L112       (I)   KENTISH MARCH
11H1H3      116L6L      (II)  LADY CHARLOTTE DURHAM
11H1H3      137L2       (I)   MISS WHITE OF BRACHLOCH'S STRATHSPEY
11H1H3      22H2H5      (II)  BOTTOM OF THE PUNCHBOWL
11H1H4      22H2H6      (II)  CUT AND COME AGAIN
11H1H       513         (I)   MAGY'S TOCHER
11H1H5      11H1H2      (I)   KINRARA
11H1H5      11H1H2      (I)   GRACE'S FAREWELL
11H1H5      22H2H6      (I)   MARSHALL'S STRATHSPEY
11H1H5      3b43b1      (II)  TARBOLTON LODGE
11H1H5      3b43b1      (II)  HATTON BURN [TARBOLTON LODGE]
11H1H5      432H1H      (I)   QUICK STEP, 15th REGt
11H1H5      7b427bL     (I)   LADY GORDON OF GORDONSTOWN'S STRATHSPEY
11H1H5      7b425       (II)  MRS MACINROY OF LUDE [MRS MCINROY OF LUDE]
11H1H5      7b7b47bL    (I)   McKINNON'S REEL
11H1H6      3532        (I)   MRS J. BISHOP'S STRATHSPEY
11H1H7b     3b524       (I)   DRUMMOND CASTLE
11H1H7b     3b544       (I)   DRUMMOND CASTLE
11H1H7b     57b7bL4     (II)  DRUMMOND CASTLE
11H1H7b     7b2H1H7b    (II)  SWEET MOLLY
11H1H7b     7b2H1H7b    (I)   SWEET MALLY [SWEET MOLLY]
11H1H7b     7b2H1H7b    (I)   BONNET MAKERS OF DUNDEE, THE
11H1H7      5533        (I)   WHERE WILL (Y)OUR GOODMAN L(A)YE
11H1H7      2H51H1H     (II)  DOUGLAS
11H1H7      2H51H1H     (I)   BRIDGE OF LODI
11H1H7      2H51H1H     (I)   (MASTER JOHN TURNER'S) HORNPIPE
11H1H1H     7bL7b57bL   (II)  QUICKSTEP (NAME NOT KNOWN) [UNTITLED]
11H1H1H     5353        (I)   GILLAN NA DROVER
11H1H       1H55        (I)   HOW LONG AND DREARY IS THE NIGHT
11H1H1H     7b2H7b7bL   (II)  FOREST OF GARTH, THE [FOREST OF GAICK, THE]
```

11H1H1H	7b2H7b7bL	(I)	FOREST OF GA-ICK, THE [FOREST OF GARTH]
11H1H1H	1H364	(II)	LADY JEMIMA CORNWA(L)LIS
11H1H1H	1H364	(I)	LADY JEMIMA CORNWALIS' REEL
11H1H1H	1H522	(I)	MRS DONALDSON'S STRATHSPEY
11H1H1H	1H3bH7b4	(I)	PORT RORIE DALL
11H1H1H	2H7b24	(II)	SALLY KELLY
11H1H1H	2H7b2H4H	(II)	SALLY KELLY
11H1H1H	2H7b2H4H	(I)	SALLY KELLY
11H1H1H	2H72H4H	(I)	HERMET IN LONDON'S REEL, THE
11H1H1H	2H2H4H2H	(I)	PRINCESS ROYAL, THE
11H1H1H	2H3H1H6	(I)	MR W. LESSLIE'S STRATHSPEY
11H1H	2H77	(I)	COUNTRY LASS, (THE)
11H1H3bH	47b7b2H	(I)	MR GARDEN JUNr's RETURN
			AND WELCOME TO TROOP HOUSE
11H1H3bH	57b42	(I)	BRIGIS LACHLAINN
11H1H3bH	7b3b47bL	(I)	MRS HOUSTON OF ROSEHALL ('S FAVOURITE)
11H1H3bH	7b424	(I)	MR JAMES BUCHANAN'S STRATHSPEY
11H1H3bH	7b43b7bL	(II)	MISS ANN STEWART, EAST CRAIGS
11H1H3bH	7b43b7bL	(I)	MISS ANN STEWART (EASTCRAIGS STRATHSPEY)
11H1H3bH	7b53b2	(II)	KNIT THE POCKY
11H1H3bH	7b53b2	(I)	LADY McINTOSHE'S REEL
11H1H3bH	7b53b2	(I)	KNIT THE POCKY
11H1H3bH	7b542	(I)	KNIT THE POCKY
11H1H3bH	7b7b47bL	(II)	ABERCAIRNY HOUSE
11H1H3bH	7b7b47bL	(I)	ABERCAIRNEY HOUSE [ABERCAIRNY HOUSE]
11H1H3bH	7b7b47bL	(I)	MR JOHN SMITH'S STRATHSPEY
11H1H3bH	2H424	(I)	MISS EWING'S REEL
11H1H3bH	2H7b4H7b	(I)	BELHELVIE HOUSE
11H1H3bH	5H5H2H2H	(II)	NEW FOREST
11H1H3H	1H542	(I)	BARBERINI'S MINUET
11H1H3H	1H1H53	(II)	ARGYLE BOWLING GREEN (THE)
			[ARGYLL BOWLING GREEN]
11H1H3H	1H1H53	(I)	ARGYLL('S) BOWLING GREEN, (THE)
11H1H3H	2H223	(I)	DUNCAN'S LILT
11H1H3H	2H1H53	(I)	ARGYLL'S BOULING GREEN
11H1H4H	7b53b3b	(I)	KNECT THE POCKIE
11H1H5H	3H3H1H1H	(I)	(ABERDEEN) SCOTS MEASURE, (A/THE)
11H2H5	31H2H5	(I)	FRIEND TO THE POOR, A
11H2H5	6542	(I)	HAMILTON RACES
11H2H5	61H76	(II)	MAIRI DHONN [BROWN HAIRED MARY]
11H2H6	12H5H3H	(I)	FAREWELL TO WHISKY
11H2H6	5352	(II)	CAPTAIN WHITE
11H2H	7b44	(I)	DOUBLE HORNPIPE NO. 2
11H2H7b	7b2H1H7b	(II)	BURNT LEG, THE
11H2H7	6231	(I)	JIGG
11H2H1H	31H42	(II)	LADY ANN ERSKINE
11H2H1H	5353	(II)	THEID MI LEAM FHEIN
11H2H1H	5353	(II)	GILLAN A DROVER
11H2H1H	5353	(II)	MAJOR STEWART
11H2H1H	5353	(II)	DROVER LADS, THE [GILLEAN AN DROVER]
11H2H1H	5353	(I)	MAJOR(L.) STEWART('S REEL)
11H2H1H	5353	(I)	MISS JEAN CAMPBELL ARDMORE'S JIG
11H2H1H	5353	(I)	PERTHSHIRE DANCING MEASURES & C No. 12
11H2H1H	3H4H5H2H	(II)	HORNPIPE
11H22	31H47L	(I)	PRESTO
11H2H2H	6b554	(I)	IRISH LASSES
11H2H2H	1H755	(I)	MAGGIE('S LAMENTATION)
11H2H2H	3H1H1H2H	(I)	WHISKY BOTTLE, THE
11H2H2H	3H1H1H2H	(I)	BOTTLE OF WHISKY, THE
11H3bH1H	5427bL	(I)	MR GARDEN (OF TROUP'S) REEL
11H3bH1H	57b42	(I)	COL. ALEXr GRANT'S STRATHSPEY
11H3bH1H	51H2H1H	(I)	MR McDONALD OF GORDON CASTLE'S STR.
11H3bH2H	7b7b7b7b	(I)	MRS FRASER OF FOYERS'S STRATHSPEY
11H3bH2H	7b7b7b7b	(I)	CALEDONIAN CANAL, THE
11H3H4	22H4H5	(I)	MARCH OF LORD McDONALD'S HIGHLANDERS
11H3H1H	161H2	(I)	MARCHIONESS OF HUNTLY'S FAVORITE, THE
11H3H1H	161H2	(I)	DUCHESS OF GORDON'S FAVORITE, THE
11H3H1H	5122	(I)	BEARD OF THE THISTLE, THE
			[THISTLE'S BEARD, THE]
11H3H1H	51H3H1H	(I)	RATHER SLOW
11H3H1H	6262	(I)	JOHNSON'S MUSIC SHOP
11H3H1H	61H62	(I)	HON: MRS MAULE'S STRATHSPEY, THE
11H3H1H	1H553	(I)	SIR Wm GORDON CUMMING'S REEL
11H3H	2H54	(I)	MISS McDOUALL'S MINUET
11H3H	2H75	(I)	LADY AMELIA KER'S MINUET
11H3H3H	52H1H1H	(I)	MISS HAY OF YESTER'S ALLAMANDE
11H3H3H	5H5H1H1H	(I)	SPA (DANCE), (THE)
11H3H3H	5H5H1H1H	(I)	SPAW, THE
11H3H5H	2H4H2H6	(I)	MISS MONCREFF OF REEDY'S REEL
11H5H3H	4H2H3H1H	(I)	LADY OF THE MANOR
11H5H3H	5H6H4H2H	(I)	LORD ALEXr GORDON'S REEL
1H2H42	2266	(I)	MISS ISABELLA HEGGIE

12H51H	11H72H	(I)	COL. HAMILTON OF PENCAITLAND
12H61H	11H72H	(I)	MR HAMILTON OF PENCAITLAND'S STRATHSPEY
12H3H5H	2H4H2H1H	(I)	LA NINETTE
13bH7b4	3b53b7bL	(I)	MR JOHN GOW'S DELIGHT
13H62H	13H2H3H	(I)	MR JOHN GRAHAM'S FAVORITE
13H74	3542	(I)	MISS CATHERINE HAYWOOD'S JIG
13H1H3	4442	(I)	BRITISH BOY'S
13H2H3H	2H3H1H6	(I)	LORD DALHOUSIE
13H4H3H	1H3H2H7	(I)	TAIL TODDLE
13H5H3H	14H72H	(I)	NIEL GOW'S COMPLIMENTS
			RETURN'D TO MR MARSHALL
14H2	35H4	(I)	MINUET
15H5H5H	15H47bL	(II)	HIGHLANDMAN KISS'D HIS MOTHER, THE
16H5H2H	551H3H	(I)	PATTIE AND PEGGY
25L1L3L	5L222L	(I)	TRIP TO GLASGOW
25L13L	3L322L	(I)	LADY ELPHINSTONE'S FAVORITE
25H3H5	37L45	(I)	MANLY HEART, THE
26L6L1	5L6L22	(I)	DAFT ROBIN
27bL5L2L	15L22	(I)	LUDE'S SUPER
27L24	16L11	(I)	FRENCH AIR
27L25	27L31	(II)	HOME RULE
215L	211	(I)	THA MO CHION AIR AN UR GHIBHT
215L	212	(I)	MO CHEAN AIR AN UR GHIBHT [MO CHION...]
217bL5L	3b3b42	(II)	HILL O RO, HILL O RO
217bL	7bL5L1L	(I)	OSSIAN 'AN DEIGH NAM FION
2115	27bL7bL2	(I)	ROSEBUD BY MY EARLY WALK, A
2121	7L252	(I)	MISS JESSIE CUMMINGS ALLAMANDE
2121	2532	(II)	CASTLE GRANT
2121	427bL2	(II)	CATHERINE OGIE
2227L	117L2	(I)	PRIEST IN HIS BOOTS, THE
222	113	(I)	RORY DALL'S SISTER'S LAMENT
2221	25L7L5L	(I)	FAVORITE, A
2222	427L1	(I)	LA LESGERE
2233	6666	(I)	'N ANN AIR MHIRE THA SIBH
2235	3336	(I)	CUMH NA PEAHAIR
2235	3336	(I)	SISTERS LAMENT, THE
2255	5211H	(I)	BROOM (OF) COWDENKNOWS, (THE)
236L1	5562	(I)	SKYE AIR, A
2311	2533	(I)	AIR FLAMAND
2353	5523	(I)	LA VILLETTE
2531	4251	(I)	NA LOGAISEAN
2532	317bL2	(II)	BIODAG AIR MAC ALASDAIR
			[MACALISTER WEARS A DIRK]
2533	2522	(I)	CAMPBELLS ARE COMING, THE
2555	7bL242	(I)	BRAES OF TULLIEMET
2555	2454	(II)	BRAES O' TULLYMET or BIRNIEBOOZLE
2555	2454	(I)	BRAES OF TULLYMET, THE [BRAES O' TULLYMET]
2555	4444	(I)	BRAES OF TULLYMET, THE
2556	2563	(I)	MR DUNn CAMPBELL ROCKSIDE'S REEL
256b5	257b2	(II)	THEID MI DHACHAIDH A CHRO CHEANNTAILLE
256	255	(I)	FAILTE FIR BHOISDAIL
2565	2552	(I)	MR HAIGES FAVOURITE
21H1H1	2H1H52	(I)	LORD RONALD
3b1L3bL1L	4527b	(I)	LADY WALLACE
3b1L3bL5L	4524	(I)	LADY WALLACE REEL
3b1L3bL5L	4527b	(I)	LADY WALLACE'S REEL
3b1L3b5	7b427bL	(I)	MISS GEORGINA CARNEGIE
3b5L1L3b	47bL4L2	(I)	MR JO. REID'S REEL
3b5L3bL5	24L2L4	(I)	AN T'AISEADH DO DH'EIREANN
3b5L3bL1L	27bL27bL	(I)	MISS H. WAUCHOPE'S FAVOURITE
3b5L3bL2L	5L7b47bL	(I)	NETHERBY HOUSE
3b5L3bL5L	3b556b	(I)	SIR HUGH MUNRO OF FOWLIS'S FAVOURITE
3b5L5L1	27bL3b7bL	(I)	MISS RAE'S STRATHSPEY
3b5L5L3b	3b53b1	(II)	BALMORAL GILLIES
3b5L6bL5L	4422	(I)	LADY WALLACE'S REEL
3b5L7L5L	7bL644	(I)	INN OF KILLIN, THE
3b5L15	24L7bL4	(II)	JAMES MORRISON
3b5L3b1	3b5L27bL	(II)	POOLACHRIE
3b5L3b5	24L24	(II)	MISS McLEAN(OF INVERSCADLE) [MISS MACLEAN]
3b5L3b5	24L24	(I)	MISS McLEAN OF INVERSCADLE(S REEL)
3b5L3b5	2425	(II)	MAJOR JAMES MUNRO
3b5L3b5	2425	(I)	MAJOR JAMES MONRO('S STRATHSPEY)
3b5L3b5	2454	(I)	MISS ANN McNEE'S REEL
3b5L3b5	247b5	(II)	GLEN TRUIM
3b5L3b6b	24L25	(I)	MONTROSE RACES
3b7bL7bL7bL	3b111	(I)	KNOCKANDOE'S (STRATHSPEY/REEL)
3b7bL3b5	3b127bL	(I)	VAN DIEMEN'S LAND
3b7L1L1	3b155	(I)	LOCHGARY'S STRATHSPEY
3b7L5L7L	3b13b5	(I)	MRS BURN CALLANDER'S REEL
3b7L11L	3b7L15	(I)	DEATH OF NELSON, THE
3b11L1	3b142	(I)	MISS GAUSSEN'S FANCY
3b11L3b	27bL42	(I)	LADY HARRIET HAY'S STRATHSPEY

3b13bL1L	246b2	(I)	MR HORN'S STRATHSPEY
3b13bL1L	247b2	(II)	SIR ALEXANDER DON
3b13bL1L	247b2	(II)	MR THOM
3b13bL1L	247b2	(I)	MR HORN'S STRATHSPEY
3b13bL1L	247b2	(I)	SIR ALEX(ANDE)r DON('S STR.)
3b15L3bL	1L3bL5L1	(II)	BALMORAL CASTLE
3b15L3bL	247b2	(I)	TWO TO ONE
3b15L5L	7bL242	(I)	MISS MARGt STEWART MENZIES REEL
3b15L5L	7bL242	(I)	MRS IRVINE'S REEL
3b15L5L	113b5	(II)	FEARGAN
3b15L1	27bL47bL	(II)	GOBBIE O, THE
3b15L1	27bL47bL	(I)	CAMELEON, THE
3b15L1	27bL47bL	(I)	MISS STEWART DOWALLY'S JIGG
3b15L1	27bL47bL	(I)	GOBY (O), THE
3b15L1	27bL47bL	(I)	ROAD TO DROCHE(R)DAY, THE
3b15L1	2452	(II)	LADY HAMILTON (OF)DALRYMPLE
3b15L1	2452	(I)	LADY (HAMILTON) DALRYMPLE ([OF] NORTH BERWICK)'S STRATHSPEY
3b15L1	247b4	(I)	MISS JEAN ALVES'S REEL
3b15L1	247b5	(II)	MRS GENERAL CAMPBELL('S REEL)
3b15L1	247b5	(I)	MRS GENERAL CAMPBELL'S REEL
3b15L1	3b17bL4	(I)	MISS MARY JEAN HOME'S STRATHSPEY
3b15L1	3b124	(I)	MISS FRANCES DRUMMOND'S JIGG
3b15L1	3b145	(II)	BUCKINGHAM HOUSE or ATHOLE BROSE
3b15L1	3b145	(I)	BUCKINGHAM HOUSE
3b15L1	3b145	(I)	SIR JOHN STEWART'S STRATHSPEY
3b15L1	3b155	(II)	ALISTER MCALISTER
3b15L1	3b155	(II)	ALASDAIR MACALISTER [ALASDAIR MAC ALASDAIR]
3b15L1	3b155	(II)	MRS WEMYSS OF CUTTLE HILL
3b15L1	3b155	(I)	MRS WEMYSS OF CUTTLEHILL('S STRATHSPEY)
3b15L1	3b155	(I)	MISS E. BELL'S FAVORITE STRATHSPEY
3b15L1	3b57bL7bL	(I)	HE'S BONNY, HE'S O'ER THE HILL THIS NIGHT (THAT I LOE WEEL ETC]
3b15L1	3b51H1H	(I)	WEST BARNS BREWERY
3b15L1	47bL44	(II)	SPRING FIELD
3b15L1	47bL44	(I)	SPRING FIELD
3b15L3b	27bL24	(II)	MISS GORDON OF GLASTIRUM
3b15L3b	27bL24	(II)	MISS LOUISA DUFF
3b15L3b	27bL24	(I)	MISS LOUISA DUFF
3b15L3b	27bL24	(I)	MISS GORDON OF GLASTIRUM('S REEL)
3b15L3b	27bL44	(I)	MISS MILNE'S STRATHSPEY
3b15L3b	247b2	(I)	MR (CHARLES) SHARP (OF HODDOM)'S REEL
3b15L3b	47bL24	(I)	HONble MR RAMSAY MAULE'S REEL
3b15L3b	427bL4	(II)	CAPTAIN H. MUNRO
3b15L3b	427bL4	(I)	CAPT H. MUNRO(OF NEWTOWN'S REEL)
3b15L3b	47b27bL	(II)	BRIG O' POTARCH, THE
3b17bL4L	3bL7bL3b7bL	(I)	Dr STEWART'S REEL
3b17bL	4L7bLO	(I)	WILLIE'S DROWN'D AT GAMRY
3b17bL5L	3b13b5	(I)	MRS HAMILTON OF SUNDRUM'S REEL
3b17bL7bL	113b5	(I)	MAJOR FRASER OF CULDUTHIL'S STRATHSPEY
3b17bL7bL	116b5	(I)	MRS CASEY
3b17bL7bL	3b13b5	(I)	MADAM CASSEY
3b17bL2	3b13b5	(I)	MRS GORDON OF MOONMORE'S STRATHSPEY
3b17bL3b	41H6b1H	(I)	COL. McDONALD'S STRATHSPEY
3b17bL4	3b13b5	(I)	DUNCAN SWINE'S WIFE
3b17bL4	3b13b5	(I)	MISS MARGARET GORDON (OF LESSMORE'S) STRATHSPEY
3b17bL4	3b11H5	(I)	NIAN DOUN A BUAIN NAN DEARCAG [NIGHEAN DONN...]
3b17L2	3b15L1	(I)	WELCOME TO ALL STRANGERS
3b115L	7bL7bL7bL7bL	(II)	CAWDOR FAIR
3b115L	7bL7bL7bL7bL	(I)	FRIOMH IS CROAGH TIGH CHALLADAIR [FREUMH A'S CRAOBH TAIGH CHALLADAIR]
3b115L	7bL27bL7bL	(II)	DUCHESS OF ATHOLE'S REEL, THE
3b11	5L11	(I)	KEY OF THE CELLER, THE
3b11	5L11	(I)	MARCHIONESS OF TWEEDDALE'S DELIGHT
3b115L	13b53b	(II)	ROB ROY MACGREGOR
3b115L	13b53b	(I)	ROB RUADH MACGHRIOGAIR
3b115L	13b54	(I)	ROB ROY
3b115L	2424	(I)	MAJOR RAY'S STRATHSPEY
3b115L	3b3b53b	(II)	GLEN GELDER
3b115L	3b427bL	(II)	NORTH OF THE TAY
3b115L	3b53b2	(II)	CLOUD AND THE CHILL, THE
3b117bL	3b115	(I)	LAMENT FOR THE DEATH OF LADY DUNBAR OF NORTHFIELD
3b117bL	3b3b43b	(I)	PEACOCK, THE
3b11	117bL	(I)	MUCKING OF GEORDY'S BYRE, THE
3b11	111	(I)	TAM GLEN
3b11	111	(I)	MUCKING OF GEORDIE'S BYRE, THE
3b111	3b3b1H3b	(II)	MISS WRIGHT
3b111	3b554	(I)	HOW SWEET IT IS LOVE
3b111	3b57b3b	(II)	PIPE SLANG, THE

```
3b111       3b57b3b      ( I )  FEADAN GLAN A PHIOBAIR
3b111       3b6b54       ( II)  MISS BUCHANAN OF CAMBUSMORE
3b111       3b6b54       ( I )  HONble MR RAMSAY MAULE'S FAVORITE
3b111       3b6b54       ( I )  MISS BUCHANAN OF CAMBUSMORE'S JIGG
3b111       7b424        ( II)  MRS MACLEOD
3b111       7b424        ( I )  MRS McLEOD OF RASEY'S STRATHSPEY
3b11        27bL2        ( I )  POOR LAWRIE
3b11        27bL2        ( I )  WHEN PETTIE CAME OVER THE GLEN
3b11        27bL4        ( I )  HOTT MUTTON PYES
3b113b      7bL37bL5     ( II)  LOGAN WATER
3b11        3b12         ( I )  BROSE AND BUTTER
3b11        3b12         ( I )  WILLIE HAS GOTTEN A WIFE
3b11        3b12         ( I )  MARQUIS OF LORN'S FANCY
3b113b      13b45        ( I )  LORD ARBUTHNOT
3b113b      13b1H5       ( II)  FAIRY HILLOCK, THE
3b11        3b14         ( I )  UILLIAM 'S CALUM'S MORAG
3b11        3b14         ( I )  BROSE AND BUTTER
3b113b      27bL7bL4     ( I )  MR S. MONCRIEFF'S STRATHSPEY
3b113b      27bL27bL     ( I )  CRAIGIE HOUSE
3b113b      27bL25       ( I )  LADY LOUISA GORDON'S STRATHSPEY
3b113b      27bL47bL     ( I )  MRS GRANT OF SEABANK'S STRATHSPEY
3b113b      43b15        ( I )  YOUR BONNY FACE WHERE BLOOMS THE ROSE
3b113b      5553b        ( I )  NIVEN'S SCOTS MEASURE
3b113b      56b47bL      ( I )  MEMORY OF DEPARTED WORTH, THE
3b115       3b7bL3b1     ( I )  MY DADDY'S A DELVER OF DYKES
3b115       543b7bL      ( I )  McINTYRE'S FAREWELL
3b116b      27bL25       ( I )  BURNSIDE HOUSE
3b117b      3b13b4       ( I )  PATTSY FROM CORK
3b111H      3bH7b43b     ( I )  BARD STRIKES HIS HARP, THE
3b111H      3bH7b43b     ( I )  JESSAMINE BOWER, THE
3b125L      3b13b3b      ( II)  MR MACDONALD OF STAFFA
3b125L      3b13b3b      ( I )  MR MACDONALD OF STAFFA('S STRATHSPEY)
3b125L      3b13b5       ( I )  MISS JESSY CRAWFORD'S STRATHSPEY
3b125L      3b144        ( I )  LADY ELISABETH MONTAGUE'S JIG
3b127bL     3b13b3b      ( II)  NEIL GOW'S WIFE [NIEL GOW'S WIFE]
3b127bL     3b13b3b      ( I )  NIEL GOW'S WIFE
3b123b      11H10        ( II)  BARN DANCE
3b124       3b13b5       ( II)  PRINCE OF WALES, THE
3b13b7bL    3b154        ( II)  LASSES FASHION, THE
3b13b7bL    3b154        ( I )  AM FASAN AIG NO CAILLEAGAN
                                [AM FASAN AIG NA CAILEAGAN]
3b13b7bL    3b16b6b      ( I )  THA NIGHEAN AIG A BHREABADAIR
3b13b1      2L7bF2L7bF   ( I )  MARNOCH'S STRATHSPEY
3b13b1      7bL427bL     ( I )  MAJOR FRASER OF KNOCKY'S FAREWELL
3b13b1      7bL427bL     ( I )  'SE SO MARBH RANN MO CHARAID
3b13b       113b         ( I )  AN REIR BHRUADAIR MI M'CHADAL
3b13b1      27bL27bL     ( II)  PORT NA CAILLICHE
3b13b1      27bL27bL     ( II)  MARMEEL RANT   [MARMEEL REEL]
3b13b1      2427bL       ( II)  MISS ERSKINE OF TORRY
3b13b1      2427bL       ( I )  MISS ERSKINE OF TORY'S STRATHSPEY
                                [MISS ERSKINE OF TORRY]
3b13b1      2427bL       ( I )  CAPT JAMES ABERCRUMBIE'S REEL
3b13b1      2427bL       ( I )  WARWICK CASTLE
3b13b1      2427bL       ( I )  MISS BLACKWOOD'S FANCY
3b13b1      27b27bL      ( I )  MARION DUNN
3b13b1      3b7bL7bL7bL  ( I )  MR BUSBY MAITLANDS REEL
3b13b1      3b7bL7bL7bL  ( I )  EARL OF GLENCAIRN'S, THE
3b13b1      3b7bL7bL7bL  ( I )  SIR JAMES COLQUHOUN'S REELL
3b13b1      3b7bL7bL7bL  ( I )  HIGHLAND WATCH, THE
3b13b1      3b17bL7bL    ( I )  MY PEGGY THOU ART GANE AWAY
3b13b1      3b17bL7bL    ( I )  HIGHLAND WATCH (NOW THE 42nd REGt
                                or ROYAL HIGHLANDERS), THE
3b13b1      3b47bL7bL    ( II)  FORTY-SECOND HIGHLANDERS' FAREWELL, THE
3b13b1      3b53b7bL     ( I )  MR STEUART'S OF DEVONSHIRE STREET'S
                                FAVORITE
3b13b1      3b7b50       ( I )  JEANIE IS FAUSE AN' UNKIND
3b13b1      427bL2       ( II)  SANDERS BRANE
3b13b1      427bL2       ( I )  SANDERS (BRANE/RANIES) (STRATHSPEY)
3b13b1      543b7bL      ( I )  TAYMOUTH
3b13b1      6b453b       ( II)  PRINCESS ROYAL, THE
3b13b1      7b7b44       ( I )  DONALD ROBERTSON, ESQr's STRATHSPEY
3b13b2      4243b        ( I )  TENANT OF MY OWN, A
3b13b       3b14         ( I )  BROSE AND BUTTER
3b13b3b     3b11H5       ( I )  LADS WITH THE KILTS, THE
3b13b3b     3b11H5       ( I )  GILLIBH NA FELA
3b13b4      51H1H5       ( I )  UNTITLED
3b13b5      7bL27bL2     ( I )  MR RONALD CRAWFORD('S STRATHSPEY)
3b13b5      27bL27bL     ( I )  LADY HAMPDON'S REEL
3b13b5      27bL24       ( II)  COLONEL MCBAIN [COLONEL MACBEAN]
3b13b5      27bL24       ( I )  (COLONEL McBAIN'S) (REEL)
3b13b5      227b2        ( I )  ROSS LODGE
3b13b5      227b2        ( I )  BEAUTIFULL TOWN OF GLASGOW, THE
```

3b13b5	2427bL	(I)	LOCH LOMOND SIDE
3b13b5	2424	(I)	MRS GARDEN OF DALGETY'S REEL
3b13b5	2424	(I)	LADY GORDON OF GORDONSTOWN'S REEL
3b13b5	243b2	(II)	MR JAMES HAMILTON
3b13b5	2454	(I)	COLONEL BELCHES FAVORITE STRATHSPEY
3b13b5	2454	(I)	LADY CARNEGIE OF SOUTHESK'S STRATHSPEY
3b13b5	2454	(I)	GENERAL GORDON CUMING SKENE'S REEL
3b13b5	247b4	(I)	MRS HOGGAN'S STRATHSPEY
3b13b5	27b27bL	(II)	MISS STEWART OF ALLANBANK
3b13b5	27b27bL	(I)	MISS STEWART OF ALLANBANK'S STRATHSPEY
3b13b5	3b124	(I)	MONAGHAN JIG, THE
3b13b5	3b13b1	(II)	JEANIE AND HER LOWLAND LADDIE
3b13b5	3b11H5	(I)	FARE THEE WEEL THOU FIRST AND FAIREST
3b13b5	43b24	(II)	MISS ABERCROMBY
3b13b5	43b24	(I)	MISS ABERCROMBY('S REEL)
3b13b5	4424	(I)	MISS ABERCROMBY'S REEL
3b13b5	46b7b5	(I)	DRUNKEN WIVES OF FOCHABERS, (THE)
3b13b5	46b7b5	(I)	O LET ME IN THIS AE NIGHT
3b13b5	7b7bL24	(II)	MRS MELVILL, DYSART
3b13b5	7b7bL24	(I)	MRS MELVILL DYSART REEL
3b13b5	7b47bL4	(I)	SIR GILBERT STIRLING'S STRATHSPEY
3b13b5	7b53b5	(II)	SOURCE OF SPEY, THE
3b13b5	7b53b5	(II)	MEG MHOR NA LURACHAN
3b13b5	7b53b5	(I)	MADHAIR SPEA [MATHAIR UISGE SPE]
3b13b5	7b7b27bL	(II)	GIN I HAD A BONNY LASS
			(LITTLE SLEEP WAD SAIR ME)
3b13b5	7b7b24	(I)	Dr Wm GRIGOR OF ELGIN'S REEL
3b13b5	7b7b42	(I)	CAPT WILLIAM LOGAN'S REEL
3b13b5	7b7b42	(I)	MISS PARK'S REEL
3b13b5	1H7b52	(I)	PAISLEY LADIES
3b13b5	1H7b52	(I)	MR HUNTER'S REEL
3b13b6b	2423b	(I)	MR ROBERT BISSIT'S STRATHSPEY
3b13b6b	2423b	(I)	MISS STEWART OF GARTH'S STRATHSPEY
3b13b6b	2454	(I)	MISS RAE'S (FAVORITE/STRATHSPEY)
3b13b7b	3b16b6b	(II)	WEAVER'S DAUGHTER, THE
3b13b7b	4247bL	(I)	MRS REAS REEL
3b13b1H	7b527bL	(II)	MISS COLSTON
3b13b1H	7b527bL	(I)	MISS COLSTON'S STRATHSPEY
3b13b1H	7b527bL	(I)	MISS FERGUSON OF RAITH'S STRATHSPEY
3b13b1H	7b522	(I)	MRS CAPTAIN ROSS
3b13b1H	7b522	(I)	MISS (BETTY) CAMPBELL ('S REEL)
3b13b1H	3bH7b44	(I)	MISS MAXWELL OF MORISTON
3b13b1H	3bH7b7b4	(I)	MISS JULIA SINCLAIR'S FAVORITE
3b151	27bL47bL	(II)	BALNAGOWN
3b147bL	3b141	(I)	MR Wm. TENNANT'S FAVORITE
3b142	7bL424	(II)	MR MACDONALD OF STAFFA
3b142	7bL424	(I)	MR MACDONALD'S REEL
			[MR MACDONALD OF STAFFA]
3b142	17L13b	(I)	SURINAM BIRDS, THE
3b145	3b527b	(I)	LADY CHARLOTTE GOOLD'S REEL
3b157bL	7bL5L7bL7bL	(I)	NIAN TORMAID [NIGHEAN THORMAID]
3b15	7bL42	(I)	GLASSERTON HOUSE
3b151	27bL47bL	(I)	LUMPS OF PUDDINGS
3b154	23b11	(I)	O MO CHUID CHUIDEACHDA
3b154	23b11	(I)	O THOU MY CHOICE OF COMPANIONS
3b154	2424	(I)	LADY STORMOUNT'S STRATHSPEY
3b154	3b17b5	(I)	WALTZ, THE
3b151H	27bL7b7bL	(I)	MR JOHN TROTTER'S REEL
3b151H	427L5L	(I)	CONTENDING PARSONS, THE
3b151H	7b7b7bL4	(II)	BALLINDALLOCH'S DREAM
3b16b4	57b42	(I)	LADY ELISABETH MONTAGUE'S REEL
3b175	3b3bH47L	(II)	CAIRNGORM, THE
3b11L1	227b2	(I)	MISS FARQUHAR'S STRATHSPEY
3b11H5	3b127bL	(II)	TOM'S NUGGET
3b11H5	46b7b5	(I)	MISS MARY DOUGLAS'S REEL
3b11H5	46b7b5	(I)	WHAT THE D...L AILS YOU
3b11H1H	7b7b45	(I)	O LET ME IN THIS AE NIGHT
3b11H1H	7b7b45	(I)	MRS KEPLING'S STRATHSPEY
3b11H1H	7b7b55	(I)	LOVE AND OPPORTUNITY or
			LET ME IN THIS AE NIGHT
3b11H1H	7b7b55	(I)	LET ME IN THIS AE NIGHT
3b11H3bH	7b521	(II)	COUNTESS OF SUTHERLAND, THE
3b11H3bH.	7b521	(I)	COUNTESS OF SUTHERLAND'S REEL, THE
3b25L7bL	7bL7bL13b	(I)	JOHN ANDERSON'S (AULDEST) DAUGHTER
3b25L	7bL7bL2	(I)	OLD PLANTATION GIRLS
3b25L1	3b254	(I)	MY LOVE IS LOST TO ME
3b27bL3bL	3b241	(II)	BRAES OF MAYEN, THE
3b27bL5L	3b211	(I)	GUR TROM AN DEIGH MO THURAIS MI
3b215L	3bL4L5L1	(I)	LAMENT FOR THE DEATH OF HUGH ALLAN
3b215L	7bL242	(II)	MRS BAIRD
3b215L	7bL242	(I)	MRS BAIRD(HILL'S REEL)
3b215L	3b214L	(I)	JACKSON'S HOBBY

```
3b215L        3b247bL       ( I )  MISS MAINY BELL'S STRATHSPEY
3b217bL       3b215         ( I )  AN SEALLADH MO DHEIREADH DO THUG TEARLACH
3b211         7bL4L7bL7bL   ( I )  LOGAN WATER
3b211         7bL4L7bL5     ( I )  LOGAN WATER
3b21          111           ( I )  McDONOGH'S LAMENTATION
3b211         27bL47bL      ( I )  MR NcNIEL ELISTER'S FAVORITE
3b211         3b3b54        ( I )  MISS DRUMMOND OF PERTH'S
                                   FAVORITE SCOTS MEASURE
3b211         3b3b54        ( I )  WHEN ABSENT FROM THE NYMPH (I LOVE)
3b211         443b1         ( I )  HUGH GILMOUR'S LAMENT FOR NIEL GOW
3b211         523b1         ( I )  COTILLON
3b212         4L7bL12       ( I )  DUBLIN KEY
3b21          27bL1         ( I )  ALASTAIR OG
3b212         3b3b54        ( I )  O JEAN I LOVE THEE
3b212         4112          ( I )  Wm. SHEPHERD'S LAMENTATION
                                   FOR THE DEATH OF SIR RALPH ABERCROMBY
3b212         5414          ( I )  NIAN DOUN AN T'SUGRIDH
                                   [NIGHEAN DONN AN T-SUGRAIDH]
3b213b        51H1H3bH      ( I )  RODERICH DHU [RUARI DUBH]
3b213b        1H557b        ( II ) CULLODEN DAY
3b215         3b115         ( I )  PRINCESS ROYAL
3b215         3b211         ( I )  PRINCESS ROYAL, THE
3b215         3b215         ( I )  PRINCESS ROYAL, (THE)
3b215         3b27b7b       ( I )  LAWERS HOUSE
3b215         47bL47bL      ( I )  MR FARQUHAR CAMPBELL'S STRATHSPEY
3b21          542           ( I )  (LOVELY) MISS WEIR
3b215         427bL7bL      ( I )  MR MILLER'S STRATHSPEY
3b21          543b          ( I )  HEITHER TOPS, THE
3b215         1H1H1H7b      ( I )  I WOUD HAVE MY GOWN MADE
3b216b        6b554         ( I )  MISS ELIZA BRODIE
3b211H        5547bL        ( I )  JENNY NETTLES
3b211H        57b47bL       ( II ) JENNY NETTLES
3b211H        57b47bL       ( I )  JENNY NETTLES
3b211H        57b42         ( I )  JANNY NETTLES
3b211H        7701H         ( I )  CYPRUS GROVE, THE [CYPRESS GROVE, THE]
3b211H        3bH7b42       ( I )  HONOURABLE MISS FRANCESS HAY'S Q/STEP
3b211H        3bH7b44       ( I )  LADY CAMPBELL OF ARDKINGLASS'S JIGG
3b211H        3bH1H1H7b     ( ! )  O WERE I ON PARNASSUS HILL
3b213bH       2H1H1H1H      ( I )  HIGHLAND KING
3b225L        7bL247bL      ( I )  SHAN DOL GRIGRUGH
3b221         113b3b        ( I )  MY MARY'S SMILE IS LIKE THE MORN
3b221         113b3b        ( I )  JOCKEY'S DREAM
3b221         3b211         ( I )  LA NONIME
3b224         3b56b5        ( I )  EISD MO CHAILEAG EISD
3b23b5L       3b23b5L       ( I )  RATHER SLOW
3b23b7bL      3b43b3b       ( I )  A 'CHEUD LUAN DO'N RAIDH
3b23b1        3b427bL       ( II ) MISS HOG, NEWLISTON
3b23b1        3b427bL       ( I )  MISS HOG (OF NEWLISTON'S) REEL
3b23b1        3b7b27bL      ( I )  BREECHES (BRITCHES) MAKER THE
3b23b1        5550          ( I )  ROB DOUN [ROB DONN]
3b23b1        5550          ( I )  MODERATE
3b23b2        4L7bL4L7bL    ( I )  CAPTAIN'S LADY, (THE)
3b23b2        7bL7bL7bL7bL  ( II ) PETTICOAT'S LOOSE, THE
3b23b2        7bL7bL7bL7bL  ( I )  CAPTAIN'S LADY, THE
3b23b2        7bL7bL7bL7bL  ( I )  PETTICOAT('S) LOOSE, (THE/MY)
3b23b2        47bL47bL      ( I )  LADY WHITEFORD'S REEL
3b23b4        3b217bL       ( I )  PERTHSHIRE DANCE
3b243b        127bL6        ( I )  RIBHINN, ALUINN, AOIBHINN OIG
3b243b        127bL6        ( I )  FAIR, BEAUTIFUL AND CHEARFUL MAID
3b253b        517L6bL       ( I )  RIBHINN ALAINN, AOIBHINN OG [...EIBHINN OG]
3b254         6b422         ( I )  ANTHIA (THE LOVELY)
3b251H        7b555         ( I )  SCOTS QUEEN, THE
3b3b7bL7bL    111H1H        ( I )  GOOD NIGHT AND JOY
3b3b7bL7bL    3b3b54        ( I )  HAD AWA' FRAE ME DONALD
3b3b15L       3b57b7b       ( I )  COUNTESS OF DUNMORE'S FAVORITE, THE
3b3b11        7bL46b4       ( I )  NEW FAIR, THE
3b3b11        3b3b15L       ( I )  LASS AMONG THE EATNOCH, THE
3b3b11        3b53b7bL      ( I )  BANKS OF FORTH, THE
3b3b11        43b27bL       ( I )  FY GAR RUB HER O'ER WI STRAE
3b3b11        4427bL        ( I )  FY GAR RUB HER O'ER WI' STRAE
3b3b1         3b3b4         ( I )  MOORLAND WILLIE [cf: MUIRLAND WILLIE]
3b3b13b       556b4         ( I )  KATE AMANG THE CLOVER
3b3b13b       556b4         ( I )  LOVELY JEANIE
3b3b15        27bL7b2       ( I )  MR RICHd. CAMPBELL'S REEL
3b3b15        3b7b24        ( II ) MISS DRUMMOND OF LOGIEALMOND
3b3b15        3b7b24        ( I )  MISS DRUMMOND OF LOGIEALMOND'S STRATHSPEY
3b3b15        43b21         ( I )  FY GAR RUB HER (O'ER WITH STRAW)
3b3b15        1H51H1H       ( I )  ETRICK BANKS
3b3b15        1H51H3bH      ( I )  ETRICK BANKS
3b3b15        1H1H3bH3bH    ( I )  O LET ME IN THIS AE NIGHT
3b3b11H       53b15L        ( I )  MACARIA
3b3b11H       57b47bL       ( I )  JENNY NETTLES
```

```
3b3b11H      3bH1H1H7      ( I )  GORDON CASTLE
3b3b11H      3bH1H1H1H     ( I )  GORDON CASTLE
3b3b13bH     1H1H53bH      ( I )  ETTRICK BANKS
3b3b27bL     3b3b3b1H      ( II ) DELLAGYLE POOL
3b3b2        15L1          ( I )  DRIMEN DUFF
3b3b2        17bL1         ( I )  DRIMEN DUFF
3b3b2        17L1          ( I )  DRIMINDOO
3b3b2        155           ( I )  NORTH HIGHLAND 13
3b3b24       117bL1        ( II ) GEANIE'S LAMENT
3b3b3b1      7bL27b7b      ( II ) COLLAR GREEN
3b3b3b1      3b227bL       ( II ) BREEKS ARE LOOSE AND THE BUTTONS AWA', THE
3b3b3b1      3b527bL       ( I )  LIEUt COLONEL MONTGOMERY'S REEL
3b3b3b      11H1H         ( I )  CONTENTED WI' LITTLE AND CANTY WI' MAIR
3b3b3b      422           ( I )  TAK' YOUR AULD CLOAK ABOUT YE
3b3b3b      457b          ( I )  HEY JENNY COME DOUN TO JOCK
3b3b3b5      3b3b24        ( I )  (O GIN I WERE) FAIRLY SHOT O' HER
3b3b3b      554           ( I )  ONOCHIE OH
3b3b3b      555           ( I )  SISTER OF LOVES
3b3b3b      555           ( I )  PHIURAG NAN GAOL
3b3b3b1H     7b524         ( II ) MISS GRANT OF KINAIRD
3b3b3b1H     7b524         ( I )  MISS GRANT OF KINAIRD'S REEL
3b3b47bL     3b17bL5L      ( I )  GREEN SLEEVES
3b3b47bL     3b17L5L       ( I )  GREEN SLEEVES
3b3b47bL     3b125L        ( I )  MR FLEMYNG'S REEL
3b3b47bL     3b125L        ( I )  GREEN SLEEVES
3b3b47L      3b125L        ( I )  MR FLEMYNG'S REEL
3b3b41       115L5L        ( I )  (YOUNG) JOCKEY WAS THE BLYTHEST LAD...
3b3b43b      3b3b42        ( I )  LADY WARWICK'S REEL
3b3b44       3b13b5        ( I )  MR DUGALD CAMPBELL ARDMORE'S FAVORITE
3b3b44       3b3b27bL      ( I )  CAW HAWKEY THROUGH THE WATER
3b3b44       5527bL        ( I )  ROUND THE WORLD FOR SPORT
3b3b44       5544          ( I )  JACKSON OVER THE WATER
3b3b44       5551          ( I )  ROUND THE WORLD FOR SPORT
3b3b4#       552           ( I )  A LEANNAIN MO RUIN
3b3b51       56b51         ( II ) LOWLANDS OF SCOTLAND, THE
3b3b5        213b          ( I )  UNTITLED
3b3b53b      41H1H6b       ( I )  ORIGINAL AIR TO WHICH THE POEMS
                                  OF OSSIAN WERE SUNG IN STRATHSPEY TIME
3b3b54       2427bL        ( II ) MISS OSWALD OF DUNAKEER
3b3b54       2427bL        ( I )  MISS OSWALD (OF DUNAKEER) 'S REEL
3b3b54       2424          ( II ) WILL YOU RUN AWAY WITH ME
                                  [WILL YE RUN AWA' WI' ME]
3b3b54       2424          ( I )  'N DEAN THU RUIDH AIR FALBH LEAM
3b3b54       4511          ( I )  I CONNA' BUCKLE TO
3b3b55       3b3b55L       ( I )  SE' N RIGH A' TH'AGAINN IS FEARR LEINN
3b3b55       4213b         ( I )  MRS ROBERTSON OF LADYKIRK'S FAVORITE
3b3b57b      3b7b42        ( I )  QUICKSTEP
3b3b53bH     7b6b51        ( I )  MO NIGHEAN DHUBH NA TREIG MI
3b3b6b7b     557b2         ( II ) DIAMOND, THE
3b3b6b7b     557b2         ( I )  DIAMOND REEL, THE
3b3b6b7b     557b2         ( I )  MISS STEEL OF NORWICH'S REEL
3b3b1H5      7b544         ( I )  MISS MILLER OF GLENLEE'S STRATHSPEY
3b3b1H5H     227b4H        ( II ) ANNIE ALLAN
3b3b3b3bH2H  7b3b6b5       ( I )  COME ASHORE JOLLY TAR AND YOUR TROUSERS ON
3b413b       447bL2        ( I )  DAVID EARL OF CASSIL'S REEL
3b427bL      13b55         ( I )  MR JAMES FAIRLEY'S STRATHSPEY
3b421        4L23b1        ( I )  WEAVER, THE
3b421        4L27b2        ( I )  LADY ELPHINSTON'S REEL
3b421        4L27b2        ( I )  ROYAL EDINBURGH VOLUNTEERS, THE
3b421        4L27b2        ( I )  DUTCHESS OF PORTLAND'S REEL
3b42         23b1          ( I )  THERE'LL NEVER BE PEACE
                                  TILL JAMIE COMES HAME
3b42         23b1          ( I )  THERE ARE FEW GOOD FELLOWS
                                  WHEN JAMIE'S AWA'
3b422        3b456         ( I )  BLACK STRAP
3b423b       127L5L        ( I )  MISS ROSS ANKERVILLE
3b43b7bL     3b3b51        ( I )  NORTH HIGHLAND 24
3b43b        7L27L         ( I )  MAGGIE'S TOCHER
3b43b1       3b427bL       ( I )  BREECHES LOOSE
3b451H       3b455         ( I )  UNTITLED
3b41H2H      1H7b55        ( I )  MORAY'S FROLICK, THE
3b41H2H      1H7b7b4       ( I )  MISS FARQUHARSON BALDOVIE'S DELIGHT
3b51L3b      43b4L2        ( I )  TARTAN BONNET, THE
3b55L1       24L24         ( II ) CASTLE FORBES
3b55L1       2427bL        ( II ) MRS JAMES ERSKINE OF KIRKWALL
3b55L1       2427bL        ( I )  MRS JA(ME)S ERSKINE OF KIRKWALL('S REEL)
3b55L1       3b53b7bL      ( II ) BRISK BOB
3b55L1       3b53b7bL      ( I )  BRISK BOB
3b55L1       3b53b7bL      ( I )  MRS HASWALL'S FAVOURITE
3b55L3b      4544          ( I )  FALL OF FYERS, THE
3b513b       247b2         ( I )  MR GARDEN OF TROUP'S RETURN HOME FROM BATH
3b513b       247b2         ( I )  MRS GUNN'S STRATHSPEY
```

```
3b51        3b43b        ( I )   QUICK DREAM, THE
3b51        3b53b        ( I )   FINGALL'S LAMENTATION
3b513b      57b3b5       (II )   OSSIAN
3b527bL     3b211L       ( I )   SIR WILLIAM BLACK'S LAMENT
3b527bL     3b51H5       ( I )   JAMIE BOICK, A STRATHSPEY
3b524       3b51H5       (II )   DONALD QUAICH
3b524       3b51H5       ( I )   DONALD QUAICH
3b53b7bL    3b541        ( I )   MILLER'S RANT, THE
3b53b1      2427bL       (II )   MRS WEBSTER
3b53b1      2427bL       (II )   JOHNNIE'S MADE A WADDIN' O'T [WEDDIN']
3b53b1      2427bL       ( I )   SIR JAMES BAIRD'S NEW STRATHSPEY
3b53b1      2427bL       ( I )   GO TO THE DEVIL AND SHAKE YOURSELF,
                                 [THE ORIGINAL SET OF]
3b53b1      2427bL       ( I )   UNTITLED
3b53b1      2424         ( I )   LADY CHARLOTTE CADOGAN'S REEL
3b53b1      2424         ( I )   FRITH OF CROMORTIE, THE
3b53b1      27b27bL      ( I )   DUCKERS OF DOWN, THE
3b53b1      3b527bL      ( I )   DUKERS OF DOON, THE
3b53b1      3b527bL      ( I )   YELLOW HAIR'D LASSIE, THE
3b53b1      3b527bL      ( I )   NATHANIEL GOW'S LAMENT
                                 FOR (THE DEATH OF) HIS BROTHER
3b53b1      3b53b7bL     (II )   BRISK BOB
3b53b3b     2247bL       (II )   RIEFIELD LODGE
3b53b3b     2247bL       ( I )   RIEFIELD LODGE
3b53b5      27bL24       (II )   CAPT. McDUFF
3b53b5      27bL24       (II )   MISS JEAN ABERDEIN
3b53b5      27bL24       ( I )   CAPT McDUFF'S REEL
3b53b5      27bL24       ( I )   MISS JEAN ABERDEIN('S REEL)
3b53b5      27bL24       ( I )   MRS GRANT OF VIEWFIELD'S REEL
3b53b5      2427bL       (II )   GIN HAD A BONNY LASSIE
3b53b5      2427bL       ( I )   (GIN/IF I HAD/HE THAT HAS) A BONNY LASS
                                 (LITTLE SLEEP WOU'D SERVE ME)
3b53b5      3b53b1       ( I )   GO TO THE DEVIL AND SHAKE YOURSELF,
                                 [NEW SET OF]
3b53b5      3b7b24       ( I )   MRS Dr NICOL'S REEL
3b53b5      1H2H7b7bL    (II )   LADY HELEN DOUGLAS
3b53b5      1H2H7b7bL    ( I )   LADY HELEN DOUGLAS'S REEL
3b547bL     3b541        ( I )   NORTH HIGHLAND 6 (REEL), (A)
3b551       3b127bL      ( I )   LADY MARY ANN CARNEGIE'S STRATHSPEY
3b554       2424         (II )   TULLYMET HALL
3b554       2424         ( I )   TULLYMET HALL
3b554       3b51H2H      ( I )   MRS MAJOR RAY'S FAVORITE
3b556       1H553bH      ( I )   ON A BANK OF FLOWERS
3b57b5      1H3bH44      ( I )   'N CUALA SIBH MAR THACHAIR DHUIN
3b57b1H     7b53b1       ( I )   BRIGUS MHIC RUARIDH
                                 [BRIOGAIS MHIC RUARAIDH]
3b51H3b     3b51H1H      ( I )   DUNSE DINGS A'
3b51H7b     6b543b       ( I )   FAVORITE JIGG, A
3b51H1H     3b57b2       ( I )   NIRE NORE
3b51H       3bH3b4       ( I )   HARK 'TIS A VOICE FROM THE TOMB
3b6b27bL    3b51H1H      ( I )   YOUNG SIMON STRATHSPEY
3b6b57b     16bL4L1      (II )   DIAMOND, THE
3b1H3b4     3b1H14       ( I )   SEALG IS SUGRADH NAN GLEANN
3b1H3b5     27b24        (II )   MISS CAMPBELL OF SADDELL
3b1H3b5     27b24        ( I )   MISS CAMPBELL (OF SADDELL'S) REEL
3bH1H3bH1H  2H7b27b      (II )   LADY GEORGINA GORDON
3b1H6b5     3b53b2       (II )   MR C. BEATTIE'S BONNIE BLANCHE
3b1H6b6b    3b53b2       (II )   MY WEE CRIPPLE WEAN
3b1H7b5     643b5        ( I )   FIRR TREE, THE
3b1H1H1     22H7b7bL     (II )   LADY BROME'S STRATHSPEY
3b1H1H1     22H7b7bL     ( I )   MR MACKINZIES STRATHSPEY
3b1H1H1     22H7b7bL     ( I )   LADY BROMES STRATHSPEY
3b1H1H5     27b7b4       (II )   MISS JANE WEDDERBURN
3b1H1H5     27b7b4       ( I )   MISS JANE WEDDERBURN('S REEL)
3b1H1H7b    433bH4H      ( I )   THERE'S NOTHING SO FATAL AS WOMAN
3b1H3bH3b   554H2H       ( I )   YOUNG COLIN THE PRIDE OF THE PLAIN
3b3bH1H1H   6b7b53bH     ( I )   PAT RIOT
33L47L      33L43        (II )   BAKER, THE
35L1L3L     5L222L       ( I )   TRIP TO GLASGOW
35L1L5L     351H3        ( I )   MRS RICHARDSON PITFOUR'S REEL
35L1L1      532L2        ( I )   LAMENT FOR SIR HARRY NIVEN LUMSDEN
                                 BARt. OF ACHINDOIR
35L2L2      35L6L1       ( I )   (O) WHISTLE AND I'LL COME TO YOU MY LAD
35L3L1L     4L27L4       (II )   FORBES MORRISON
35L3L1L     4L242        ( I )   CAMPBELL'S REEL
35L3L5L     2L27L6L      ( I )   JACQUETTA AGNETTA MARIANA JENKS
35L3L5L     4L5L2L2      ( I )   DUFF HOUSE
35L3L5L     7L27L2       ( I )   MISS McKINZIE'S REEL
35L3L5L     35L2L2       ( I )   THRE WEEKS AFTER MARRIAGE
35L3L5L     35L7L2       (II )   SIR JAMES GRANT
35L3L5L     3342         (II )   MRS DINGWALL OF BROCKLY'S STRATHSPEY
35L3L5L     3342         ( I )   MRS DINGWALL OF BROCKL(E)Y'S STRATHSPEY
```

35L3L5L	367L2	(I)	MISS SCOTT'S STRATHSPEY
35L3L5L	3642	(I)	UNTITLED
35L3L1	6L27L7L	(II)	BEN ALLIGEN
35L3L1	427L5	(II)	BAKER, THE
35L5L5L	6L6L21	(I)	SOLDIER'S RETURN, THE
35L5L5L	6L6L21	(I)	MILL (MILL) O, THE
35L5L5L	6L16L6L	(I)	I'LL NE'ER RETURN MORE
35L5L1	2L2L5L5L	(I)	MY DEARY IF THOU DIE
35L5L1	6L6L21	(I)	MILL MILL O, THE
35L5L1	6L27L2	(I)	LADY HAMILTON'S REEL
35L5L2	35L11	(I)	PADDY O RAFERTY
35L5L3	3211	(I)	NACH TRUAGH MO CHAS
35L5L3	46L6L4	(II)	MRS LEITH OF GLENKENDYS
35L5L3	46L6L4	(I)	MRS LEITH (OF GLENKENDY)'S(REEL)
35L6L5L	5L125	(II)	EAST KILBRIDE
35L6L5L	6L27L5	(II)	HIGHLAND MINSTREL BOY, THE
35L6L5L	35L1L1	(II)	KERR'S HORNPIPE
35L6L5L	35L6L1	(I)	GEORGE KINLOCH
35L6L5L	35L6L1	(I)	(MRS) KINLOCH (OF KINLOCH)
35L6L5L	35L6L2	(I)	COUNTESS OF LOUDOUN & MOIRA'S STRATHSPEY, THE
35L6L5L	35L26L	(I)	LEE MILLS
35L6L5L	35L23	(I)	PEASANTS, THE
35L6L5L	35L42	(II)	MRS R. DONALDSON
35L6L5L	357L2	(I)	MISS COCHRAN'S JIG
35L6L	106	(I)	GLOAMIN', THE
35L6L	111	(I)	STACK IN VIRGO
35L6L	116	(I)	BE CONSTANT STILL
35L6L	111H	(I)	BE CONSTANT STILL
35L6L1	226L5L	(I)	BONNIEST LASS IN A' THE WARLD, (THE)
35L6L1	35L6L2	(I)	MR JOHN BEGG'S FAVOURITE
35L6L1	426L5L	(I)	BONNIEST LASS IN A' THE WARLD, THE
35L6L1	5332	(II)	HUNDRED PIPERS, THE
35L6L4	46L7L5	(II)	MACLEOD AND MACKAY
35L7bL2	3213	(I)	FAIR AN' LUCKY
35L7L2	3542	(I)	MAJOR WEBSTERS DELIGHT
35L11	2436L	(I)	LEA RIG, THE
35L11	2436L	(I)	MY AIN KIND DEARY (O)
35L12	35L11	(I)	PADDY O' FLANAGAN
35L35L	4325L	(I)	O.P. HAT, THE
35L35L	4325L	(I)	RUSSIAN DANCE, (THE)
35L35L	5142	(II)	MISS LUCY CAMPBELL
35L35L	5142	(I)	PASS OF KELECRANKIE, THE
35L35L	5142	(I)	MISS LUCY CAMPBELL('S REEL)
35L31	6622	(I)	MISS HAMILTON OF BLANDFIELD'S STRATHSPEY
35L32	2465	(II)	BALMORAL HORNPIPE
35L32	35L37L	(I)	LINNA MACHREE
35L32	35L37L	(I)	JACKSON'S RAMBLE
35L33	16L5L3	(I)	BANKS OF NITH, THE
35L33	35L31	(I)	IRISH MILKMAID, THE
35L33	5755	(I)	MISS MARY ANN GORDON
35L35	42L46	(I)	WASHER WOMAN(, THE) [IRISH WASHERWOMAN, THE]
35L35	45L46	(I)	IRISH WASHER WOMAN, THE
35L35	46L46	(II)	IRISH WASHERWOMAN(, THE)
35L35	46L46	(II)	MR EAGERS(' STRATHSPEY)
35L35	46L46	(II)	EAGER'S STRATHSPEY
35L35	46L46	(I)	CORPORAL CASSEY
35L35	46L46	(I)	(IRISH) WASHER WOMAN, (THE)
35L35	47L46	(II)	TAM O' SHANTER
35L35	51H22	(I)	PADDY O'CONNOR
35L36	4646	(I)	MISS MARGt GREIG OF QUEBEC
35L42	35L5L3	(I)	COLONEL HAY'S STRATHSPEY
35L43	15L5L1	(I)	TRAFALGAR HORNPIPE
35L46	547L2	(I)	MISS CRAW'S FAVORITE STRATHSPEY
36L3L1L	35L2L2	(I)	MR JAMES JENKINS'S STRATHSPEY
36L5L1L	36L2L2L	(II)	ROSE-ACRE
36L5L3L	157L2	(I)	HONble MRS JOHN RAMSAY'S STRATHSPEY
36L5L2	36L5L1	(I)	TODLEN HAME
36L6L	36L2	(I)	DRUNKEN GAUGER, THE
37L5L3L	4L2L4L6L	(II)	MERRY LADS AND BONNY LASSES
37L5L3L	4L2L4L6L	(I)	FLEASGAICH OG A'S CAILEAGAN
37L5L7L	227L2	(I)	NORRY'S CAKE
37L6L5L	7F2L4L6L	(I)	MRS PATRICK STERLING OF KIPPENDAVIE'S REEL
37L6L5L	4L3L2L2	(I)	SPEED THE HARROW
37L6L5L	37L6L5L	(I)	NOREA'S WISH
37L6L5L	37L6L1	(I)	LADY ELIZA CALLANDERS FAVOURITE
37L6L5L	37L42	(II)	MISS BARTLET
37L6L5L	37L42	(I)	MISS BARTLET('S REEL)
37L6L5L	326L2	(I)	GUDEWIFE OF PEEBLES
37L6L1	5L3L5L5L	(I)	MISS CUMINE OF LOGIE'S REEL
37L6L1	325L2	(I)	MISS TAIT

```
37L37L     37L31       ( I )  MISS BASS WALTZ
37L35      657L2       ( I )  MISS JANE CARNEGIE'S FAVOURITE VALTZ
37L35      1H365       ( I )  MR F. G. CAMPBELL OF TROUP
                              AND GLENLYON'S REEL
37L45      1H653       ( I )  MISS JESSY DEWAR'S FAVOURITE
37L53      36L2H1H     ( I )  MISS MARGARET SMITH'S WALTZ
37L62      7L152       ( I )  MISS ANDERSON'S FAVOURITE
3035       3035        ( I )  MINIKIN FENCIBLE MARCH, THE
311L1L     437L5L      ( I )  COILSFIELD HOUSE
311L1      3152        ( I )  MISS MURRAY'S REEL
311L1      3156        ( I )  MISS LOUGHNAN'S FAVORITE
313L1L     3L132       ( I )  CLOUDEN BRAES
313L1L     5L7L52      ( I )  LORD FREDERICK AND HIS FENCIBLES
313L2L     5L7L52      ( I )  LORD FREDERICK AND HIS FENCIBLES
313L5L     2L222       ( I )  HIGHLAND DRESS, THE
313L5L     4L422       ( I )  LADY CATHERINE BLIGH'S REEL
313L5L     4L422       ( I )  MRS DUNCAN'S FANCY
313L5L     4L422       ( I )  ISLE OF MULL, THE
313L5L     547L2       ( I )  MISS ALSTON STEWART OF URRARD'S REEL
313L1      4L27L2      ( II ) GLEN LYONS RANT
313L1      4L27L2      ( I )  GLEN LYONS RANT
313L1      157L2       ( I )  LADY CHARLOTTE BENTINCKS REEL
313L1      31L22       ( I )  LEUt COLONEL MONTGOMRIE
                              OF SKERMORLIE'S STRATHSPEY
313L2      3163        ( II ) HURRICANE, THE
314L3L     2L222L      ( I )  CAPT ROSE OF KILRAVOCK'S STRATHSPEY
315L       1L3L1       ( I )  PURIE'S FAREWELL
315L2L     3L5L6L6L    ( I )  EGLINTON CASTLE
315L3L     1L362       ( II ) JUMPERS
315L3L     1L57L2      ( I )  MARCHIONESS OF HUNTLY'S JIG, THE
315L3L     2L226L      ( II ) CASTLE NEWE
315L3L     4L3L5L3L    ( I )  UNION GROVE
315L3L     24L27bL     ( II ) MISS ERSKINE OF TORRY
315L3L     24L27bL     ( I )  MISS ERSKINE OF TORRY('S STRATHSPEY)
315L3L     24L27bL     ( I )  LOCH RANNOCH SIDE
315L3L     314L4       ( II ) MR MARTIN
315L3L     3122        ( I )  MRS GLASS
315L3L     3135        ( II ) FAIR FA' THE MINSTREL
                              [MART DO CHRO A' MHEINANICH]
315L3L     3135        ( I )  MART DO CHRO' A MHEINANICH
                              [MART DHE CRODH A' MHEINEIRICH]
315L3L     3311        ( II ) ORANGE AND BLUE
315L3L     436L2       ( I )  HONble MISS P. ELPHINSTONE'S
                              STRATHSPEY, THE
315L3L     437L2       ( I )  MISS MURRAY OF MURRAYFIELD'S STRATHSPEY
315L5L     1L5L2L2L    ( I )  ABOYNE CASTLE
315L5L     5L122       ( I )  FALLEN HERO (NELSON), THE
315L5L     5L122       ( I )  MISS WELLWOOD'S FANCY
315L5L     7bL235      ( I )  PITLOWER HOUSE
315L5L     1132        ( I )  BONNY JEAN OF ABERDEEN
315L5L     35L34       ( I )  HAD AWA FRAE ME DONALD
315L5L     3132        ( I )  ISLAND OF MULL, THE
315L5L     3522        ( II ) ALVA HOUSE
315L5L     31H22       ( II ) HECKLEBIRNIE
315L5L     5122        ( I )  SIR GEORGE RAMSAY'S LAMENT
315L7bL    7bL427bL    ( II ) HAGGIS OF DUNBAR, THE
315L7bL    7bL427bL    ( I )  HAGGIES O' DUNBAR, THE
315L1      3L5L13L     ( I )  FROLICK, THE
315L1      6L27L7L     ( II ) SHE'S BONNIE AN' BRAW[ AN' THAT'S A']
315L1      227L4       ( I )  MISS CLARK'S STRATHSPEY
315L1      247b2       ( I )  COLONEL CAMPBELL'S REEL
315L1      247b5       ( II ) CALEDONIAN HUNT, THE
315L1      247b5       ( I )  CALEDONIAN HUNT, THE
315L1      247b5       ( I )  MRS GENERAL CAMPBELL'S REEL
315L1      247b5       ( I )  LADY CHARLOTTE MURRAY'S REEL
315L1      2535        ( I )  COBLER OF CASTLEBERY, THE
315L1      316L2       ( II ) HOO DINNA YE PLAY MAIR
315L1      3136L       ( I )  PANTALOONS, THE
315L1      3131        ( II ) DAFT WILLIE DAWSON
315L1      3135        ( I )  LIEUt DUNBAR (22nd REGt's) REEL
315L1      3142        ( I )  MISS ROBINSON OF CLERMESTON'S REEL
315L1      3145        ( II ) ATHOLE BROSE
315L1      3145        ( I )  ATHOL BROSE
315L1      3151H       ( I )  CHISHOLMS FROLICK
315L1      311H5       ( II ) MASTER ANDREW GRANT (BALMORAL)
315L1      311H6       ( II ) BUCKINGHAM HOUSE [ATHOLE BROSE]
315L1      3211        ( I )  DOWN THE BURN DAVIE
315L1      3342        ( II ) EARL OF FIFE'S FIRESIDE, THE
315L1      3342        ( I )  EARL OF FIFE'S FIRESIDE, THE
315L1      357L2       ( I )  GOOD LUCK
315L1      3511        ( II ) ORANGE AND BLUE
315L1      437L2       ( II ) GOODEN WELL
```

315L1	437L2	(I)	GOODEN WELL
315L1	437L2	(I)	MR BUIST'S FROLIC
315L1	437L2	(I)	MRS ROBERTSONS OF LAWERS REEL
315L1	447L2	(I)	MR STEWART OF BALECHIN'S STRATHSPEY
315L1	4426L	(II)	POLL AN DROIGHIONN
315L3L	6L17L2	(II)	MR C.T. THOMPSON'S FANCY
315L3	6L27L5	(I)	MISS MAITLAND (OF FREUGH) REEL
315L3	7L531H	(I)	LIEUT. BARRY'S REEL
315L3	3144	(II)	'SMAIRG A CHIURRADH SPIOCAIRE [MISER, THE]
315L3	422L4	(I)	LADY GEORGINA GORDON'S STRATHSPEY
315L3	426L4	(II)	REITH'S CLARINET
315L3	4642	(I)	MR JOHN GRAHAM
315L3	5347L	(I)	CAPT WHITE 73rd REGt's STRATHSPEY
315L4	547L2	(I)	MRS MAJOR SHAW
316L	5L3L7L	(I)	COBLER OF CASTLEBERRY, THE
316L5L	3L142	(I)	MR A. CAMPBELL'S STRATHSPEY
316L5L	4L2L4L6L	(II)	BOB SIMMS
316L5L	4L5L26L	(II)	MISS MARY JAMIESON, ELGIN
316L5L	5L2L31	(I)	LAMENT, THE
316L5L	5L47L2	(I)	PLOUGH BOY'S REEL, THE
316L5L	6L5L22L	(I)	MR PETER PATTISON'S REEL
316L5L	7L37L5L	(II)	LADY ANN HOPE
316L5L	7L37L5L	(I)	LADY ANN HOPE('S STRATHSPEY)
316L5L	7L425L	(I)	CHARMS OF THE FAIR, THE
316L5L	7L425L	(I)	RAKES OF ROCHESTER, (THE)
316L5L	2462	(I)	MR ANDREW NICOLL'S REEL
316L5L	316L7L	(II)	CANTY JEANIE MUNRO
316L5L	316L2	(II)	MISS MAULE'S STRATHSPEY
316L5L	316L2	(I)	CAPT CAMPBELL OF SUNDERLAND'S REEL
316L5L	316L2	(I)	MISS MAULE'S STRATHSPEY
316L5L	3215	(I)	MISS MURRAY LINTROSE
316L5L	3562	(II)	BRIDGE OF GAIRN, THE
316L5L	4526L	(II)	MISS MINNIE FRASER, NETHERTON
316L5L	5353	(I)	LAMENT FOR MR RAMSAY OF BARNTON
316L6L	315L5L	(I)	PRINCE REGENTS FAVORITE, THE
316L6L	457L2	(I)	MR HOPE'S JIG
316L1	316L2	(I)	LADY OF THE LAKE
316L1	317L2	(II)	MISS MATHESON
316L1	3125L	(I)	MOLL IN THE WAD [MOLL ITH WAD]
316L1	3125	(II)	LADY OF THE LAKE
316L1	3125	(I)	LADY OF THE LAKE, THE
316L2	15L15	(II)	MRS STEWART NICHOLSON
316L2	15L15	(I)	MRS STEWART NICHOLSON('S STRATHSPEY)
316L2	3151H	(I)	MISS COX'S FAVOURITE
316L2	346L6L	(I)	MRS MONTGOMRIE OF SKERMORLIE'S STR.
316L2	3535	(I)	BONNY LASSIE TURN YOU
316L2	331H5	(I)	MISS CHARLOTE ROSS'S REEL
316L3	1H642	(II)	RIGHTS OF MAN, THE
317bL2	313L1L	(II)	DUCHESS OF HAMILTON
317L3L	1L3L11	(I)	MISS CUMINE OF LOGIE'S STRATHSPEY
317L5L	351H6	(I)	MISS MARGARET GRANTS REEL
317L6L	6L211	(I)	FAVORITE AIR, A
317L2	313L1L	(II)	DUCHESS OF HAMILTON, THE
317L2	313L1L	(II)	DUCHESS OF HAMILTON, THE
317L2	313L1L	(I)	DUCHESS OF HAMILTON, THE
317L2	3135	(I)	LANDLADY OF INVER INN, THE
317L2	311H4	(I)	MISS BROWN'S REEL
317L2	311H4	(I)	MISS DUFF OF MUIRTOWN'S REEL
317L2	311H1H	(I)	MISS DALRYMPLE (OF NORTH BERWICK'S) QUICK STEP
317L2	331H7	(I)	PUSH ABOUT THE JORUM
3115L	1L5L35	(II)	HURDLE RACE, THE
311	5L3L3L	(I)	LADY ORMINSTON
311	5L3L3L	(I)	SINGLE HORNPIPE No. 2
3115L	4L3L6L2L	(II)	FALLS OF CORRYMULZIE, THE
3115L	7bL7bL20	(I)	COLLIER'S BONNY (LASSIE/DAUGHTER), THE
3115L	7bL7bL24	(II)	COLLIER'S DAUGHTER, THE
3115L	7bL7bL24	(I)	COALLIER'S DAUGHTER, THE
3115L	7bL424	(II)	NINE PINT COGGIE, THE
3115L	7bL424	(I)	COLLIER'S DAUGHTER, THE
3115L	7bL424	(I)	NINE-PINT COGGIE, THE
3115L	7L246	(II)	MRS FORBES OF NEWE'S REEL
3115L	2227L	(II)	MISS SOPHIA E. GRANT
3115L	2422L	(II)	HAMILTON OF WISHAW [MR.]
3115L	2422L	(II)	MRS HAMILTON OF WISHAW
3115L	2422L	(I)	(MR HAMILTON OF) WISHAW('S) (REEL)
3115L	2426L	(I)	MR HAMILTON OF WISHAW'S REEL
3115L	2462	(I)	MR THOs JARVIS REEL
3115L	3142	(II)	MO LAOCHAN BHOIDHEACH
3115L	3562	(II)	DELNADAMPH LODGE
3115L	31H64	(II)	RAIGMORE HOUSE
3116L	5L26L2	(I)	HEN'S NEST, THE

311	15L5L	(I)	LADY ANN BOTHWEL'S LAMENT
311	15L5L	(I)	BALOU MY BOY [BALOW MY BOY]
3111	5L132	(I)	MASON LADDIE, THE
3111	5L132	(I)	BRAES OF GLENORCHY, THE
3111	5L132	(I)	ISLA REEL, THE
3111	5L132	(I)	MASON'S APRON, THE
3111	5L142	(II)	MASON'S APRON, THE
3111	25L5L5L	(II)	MISS SOPHIA DUFF STUART'S FAVOURITE
3111	2347L	(I)	LADY JARDINE'S REEL
3111	3111	(I)	LA SIMPLICITA
3111	3142	(I)	MISS PILLANS'S STRATHSPEY
3111	3152	(I)	KEETHS REEL
3111	311H5	(II)	BANKS OF CLYDE, THE
3111	311H6	(II)	KISSING IS(THE) BEST OF A'
3111	311H6	(II)	BRIDGE OF TURK, THE
3111	311H6	(II)	PERRIE WERRIE, THE
3111	311H6	(I)	PERRIE WERRIE, THE
3111	311H6	(I)	BREAD AND CHEESE TO ROARY
3111	311H1H	(II)	PERRIE WHERRIE, THE
3111	357L2	(I)	MR OLIPHANT OF CONDIE'S WILLCOME HOME
3111	351H7	(I)	JENNY'S WHIM
3111	465L2	(I)	MISS TYTLER'S STRATHSPEY
3112	7L225	(I)	MRS MONTGOMRIE OF ANNICK LODGE
3112	7L245	(I)	MISS JANE GRANT OF GRANT'S REEL
3112	7L445	(I)	MISS BAKER'S HORNPIPE
3112	7L445	(I)	HORNPIPE, DANC'D BY ALDRIDGE'S
3112	2252	(I)	MISS PARKER'S REEL
3112	3122	(I)	LADY VIRGINIA MURRAY'S FANCY
3112	311H6	(I)	NEW BARRACKS, THE
3112	311H1H	(I)	LADY MARY ANN CARN(E)GIE'S FAVOURITE
3112	331H6	(I)	KISSING'S BEST OF ALL
3112	3542	(I)	MAJOR, THE
3112	4223	(I)	BLYTHE JOCKEY
3112	4225	(I)	SECOND TURKS MARCH
3112	4246	(I)	NOBLE SQUIRE D'ACRE COMES OVER THE BORDER
3112	5225	(I)	MR MURRAY OF SIMPRIMS FAVORITE
3112	5225	(I)	GREEN RIBON, THE
3112	5225	(I)	BLUE RIBBON SCOTTISH MEASURE, THE
311	311	(I)	CHIVEY CHACE
3113	115L1	(I)	CARLE AN' THE KING COME
311	312	(I)	NORTH HIGHLAND 3
311	312	(I)	FARR AWA' WEDDING, THE
311	314	(I)	I DINNA KEN
311	316	(I)	BATA BHARRA
311	316	(I)	HIGH WAY TO GREENVALE, THE
3113	25L5L1	(II)	ROBERTSON'S
3113	25L5L1	(I)	ROBERTSON('S HORNPIPE)
3113	316L6L	(I)	DRUNKEN DRUMMER, THE
3113	5422	(II)	SILVERWELLS
3113	51H25	(I)	QUICK STEP
3113	51H34	(I)	MRS BURNS' REEL
3113	6532	(II)	MISS GRANT
3113	6532	(I)	MISS GRANT (OF GRANT) ('S REEL)
3113	61H61H	(II)	LARGO LAW
3115	27L7L5	(II)	ROVER
3115	3147bL	(II)	BIRK HALL
3115	3142	(I)	SYLPH, THE
3115	3532	(I)	COSSACK DANCE
3115	427L2	(I)	TEMPLE, THE
3115	4224	(I)	MR ALEXr THOM'S HORNPIPE
3115	4226	(I)	GREEN GARTERS, THE
3115	61H52	(I)	SALLY'S WISH
3115	7552H	(I)	DOWNSHIRE (CAMPERDOWN) QUICK STEP, THE
3115	7552H	(I)	MISS (ISABELLA) CAMPBELL'S DELIGHT
3115	1H1H3H3H	(I)	LASS OF LEVING-STONE, THE
3116	3144	(II)	FIELD OF BANNOCKBURN, THE
3116	5114	(I)	COMPLAINING MAID
3111H	317bL7b	(I)	ALEE MARLEY
3111H	317bL7b	(I)	ELSIE MARLY
3111H	6446	(II)	LAUGH AT FATE
3111H	7b524	(I)	NORTH HIGHLAND 17
3111H	2H2H61H	(I)	HALLOW EVEN
3113H	7555	(I)	COL. LESLIE'S MARCH
3115L	7L245	(I)	MISS CAMERON'S REEL
3125L	3L6L37L	(I)	BALGAY HOUSE
3125L	6L3L7L2	(I)	MRS PETERKIN OF GRANGE HALL'S STR.
3125L	6L435	(I)	BUCK'S OF ST. JAMES'S
3125L	3142	(II)	MISS CLEMENTINA(SARAH) DRUMMOND (OF PERTH)
3125L	3142	(I)	MISS CLEMENTINA SARAH DRUMMOND OF PERTH'S STRATHSPEY
3125L	3522	(I)	NEWCASTLE BRIDGE

3125L	31H22	(I)	OAK TREE
3126L	7L5L12	(I)	MISS JANE DOUGLAS'S FAVORITE
3127bL	1356	(I)	MISS CHARLOTTE ALSTON STEWART'S REEL
3127bL	3146	(II)	LIEUT. A. STEWART
3127bL	3146	(I)	LIEUt. A. STEWART(, 94th REGt's REEL)
3127L	5L151H	(II)	LORD LOVAT'S WELCOME or MOIREAR SHEIM
3127L	15L7bL4L	(II)	EIGHT O'CLOCK TRAIN
3127L	1647L	(I)	MR H.R. DUFF'S FAVORITE
3127L	3146	(I)	LIEUT. A. STEWART, 94th REGt's REEL
3127L	3151H	(I)	SHURLEY'S FANCY
3121	5L151H	(II)	LORD LOVAT'S WELCOME
3121	5L151H	(I)	MORFHEAR SHIMM [MORAR SIM]
3121	5555	(I)	MAIDS OF KILEARNEY, THE
3121	6113	(I)	MEDLEY OVERTURE (6)
3121	6531	(I)	MACGREGORS' GATHERING, THE
3122	3113	(I)	SOLDIER LADDIE, THE
3122	3111H	(I)	WAP AT THE WIDOW MY LADDIE
3122	3125L	(I)	BON TON, (THE)
3122	3121H	(I)	WAP AT THE WIDOW
3122	3131H	(I)	(WAP AT) THE WIDOW (MY LADDIE)
3122	3153	(I)	IRISH SHELALEY, THE
3122	3361H	(I)	LORD LOVAT
3122	6113	(II)	SODGER LADDIE [SODGER LAD]
3122	6113	(I)	SODGER LADDIE, (MY/THE)
3122	6113	(I)	SAILOR LADDIE, (THE)
3123	351H4	(I)	MISS CALDWALL'S FAVORITE
3123	4552	(II)	HECTOR MACDONALD
3123	1H61H5	(I)	CASTLE GUTHRIE
3124	3113H	(I)	WIVES OF TORPHICAN, THE
3125	1H653	(II)	THA MO BHREACAN FLUICH FO'N DILE
3135L	1351H	(I)	PRINCESS OF WIRTEMBURG'S DEPARTURE FROM ENGLAND, THE
3135L	5132	(I)	AIRNDALLY HOUSE
3131	6L27L5L	(II)	MRS OLIPHANT OF CONDIE'S
3131	6L27L5L	(I)	MR OLIPHANT OF CONDIE'S STRATHSPEY
3131	6L27L5L	(I)	MISS DOUGLAS
3131	6L237L	(I)	MARCHIONESS OF NORMANBY, THE
3131	7L27L2	(I)	MISS ANNE CAMPBELL BALMARTIN'S REEL
3131	2427bL	(I)	HA! BIDAG ER MAC HOMAISE [THA BIODAG AIR MAC THOMAIS]
3131	2427L	(I)	ALDRIDGE'S DANCE
3131	2427L	(I)	DRURY LANE
3131	2424	(I)	SIR JOHN MOORE'S REEL
3131	2531	(I)	PRINCE DOLGORUCKI
3131	3111H	(II)	ROCKIN' STEP, THE or MANSON'S HIGHLAND FLING
3131	3111H	(II)	SCOTT SKINNER'S ROCKIN' STEP
3131	3124	(I)	WEIPPERT'S FANCY
3131	3134	(I)	PIPE REEL, A
3131	3147bL	(I)	MRS ROSS'S RANT
3131	3162	(I)	DUCHESS OF BUCCLEUCH, THE
3131	3331	(II)	RETICULE, THE or [RIDICULE, THE]
3131	3331	(I)	RIDICULE, THE [RETICULE THE]
3131	3542	(I)	MRS MENZIES OF CULDARE'S REEL
3131	3562	(I)	BADE MALT NE'ER MAKES GOOD ALE
3131	4246	(II)	WILLIE BLAIR
3131	437L5L	(II)	GENERAL GRAHAM
3131	447L5L	(I)	LADY HARRIOT CAVENDISH'S TRIP
3131	5322	(I)	PAS SEUL
3131	627L5L	(I)	MISS MACDONALD OF POWDER HALL'S REEL
3131	72H1H1H	(I)	HARPER'S FANCY
3131	1H342	(II)	SIR JOHN STEWART OF GRANTULLY
3131	1H342	(I)	MISS HAY'S REEL
3131	1H342	(I)	KILWINAN LODGE
3131	1H342	(I)	SIR JOHN STEWART (OF GRANDTULLY) ('S STRATHSPEY)
3131	1H1H1H3	(I)	CAVE OF ENCHANTMENT
3131	1H2H5O	(I)	KISS MY BONNY MOW
3131	1H2H65	(I)	A' BODY'S LIKE TO BE MARRI'D BUT ME
3132	3142	(I)	KIND GOODWIFE OF KETTICH'S MILL, THE
3132	531H1H	(I)	BONNY LASS OF FANNHIVEN, THE
313	314	(I)	HOW SHE'LL NE'ER BE GUIDED
313	314	(I)	REEL OF HARDEN, THE
313	316	(I)	MR DUGALD CAMPBELL ARDMORE'S JIG
3133	26L22	(II)	APPIN HOUSE
3133	26L22	(I)	APPIN HOUSE
3133	27bL44	(I)	MISS NICOL'S STRATHSPEY
3133	2466	(II)	MURTHLY CASTLE
3133	3124	(II)	HIGHLAND DONALD KISSED KITTY
3133	3132	(II)	HIGHLAND DONALD KISS'D KITTY (cf:.WILL YOU GO AND MARRY KETTY)
3133	3132	(II)	BRAES OF BALQUHITHER, THE [BALQUHIDDER]

3133	3132	(I)	MARRY KETTAY
3133	3132	(I)	MULCHARD'S DREAM
3133	3132	(I)	BRAES OF BALQUIDDER, THE
3133	627L2	(I)	LADY AMELIA MURRAY'S REEL
3133	6532	(I)	BRAES OF BALQUHIDER
3133	6532	(I)	BRAES OF BALWHEDAR
3133	6542	(II)	MISS MARY ANNE ROBERTSON
3133	652H2	(I)	CAPT McDUFF'S FAREWELL TO THE PARLIAMENT HOUSE
3134	3136	(II)	BIDE YE YET
3134	311H6	(II)	KISSING IS BEST OF A'
3134	4245	(I)	JOLLY TOPER
3135	7L5L7L2	(I)	MRS MONTGOMERY'S REEL
3135	7L5L7L2	(I)	MRS CHAs DALRYMPLE'S REEL
3135	27bL24	(II)	LADY ROSS
3135	27bL24	(II)	BONNIE NELLIE
3135	227b2	(I)	MR JAMES BOSWELL'S JIG
3135	247bL2	(I)	JOCK'S LODGE
3135	247bL2	(I)	CUT AND DRY
3135	247bL2	(II)	CUT AND DRY
3135	2427bL	(I)	CORPORAL, THE
3135	2424	(I)	STRUAN ROBERTSON'S RANT
3135	317L2	(I)	ABERDEEN ASSEMBLY, THE
3135	3111H	(II)	FLAGGON, THE [FLAGON, THE]
3135	3111H	(I)	NEIL GOW'S FANCY
3135	3111H	(I)	FLAGGON, THE
3135	3154	(I)	CAMERONIAN RANT
3135	3175	(II)	HALE-WHEEL
3135	3535	(I)	MISS JESSIE DUN'S STRATHSPEY
3135	3542	(I)	LADY DOUNE'S REEL
3135	3622	(I)	DUTCHESS OF MANCHESTER, THE
3135	31H2H2	(II)	GENERAL DRUMMOND
3135	31H2H2	(I)	GENI. DRUMMOND'S REEL or HASTINGS CAMP
3135	4246	(I)	MISS SUSANNA RENTON'S REEL
3135	4246	(I)	MR DUNCAN'S DELIGHT
3135	4322L	(II)	CLOCHNABEN*
3135	457L2	(I)	HONble MR W. MELVILLE'S, THE
3135	4532	(II)	MR JOHN WALKER'S REEL
3135	4542	(I)	LADY JANE MONTGOMERY'S REEL
3135	4642	(I)	MR CRAWFURD OF ARDMILLAN'S REEL
3135	461H6	(II)	MRS RACHEL GIBSON
3135	461H6	(I)	MRS RACHAEL GIBSON('S REEL)
3135	42H75	(I)	MR ROBERT AITKEN'S REEL
3135	5153	(II)	CAMERONIAN RANT, THE
313	554	(I)	DRUNKEN MAG YOUNG
313	554	(I)	JENNY COME TYE MY GRAVAT
313	556	(I)	LAST MERRY NIGHT, THE
3135	6542	(II)	ALEXANDER RAMSAY ESQ.'S REEL
3135	6542	(I)	EARL OF FIFE'S REEL
3135	6542	(I)	FOSTER MEADS
3135	671H6	(I)	THREE FINGER'D JACK
3135	7b427b	(II)	MARCHIONESS OF TULLIBARDINE, THE
3135	7b7b22	(II)	DUNCAN ON THE PLAINSTONES (ELGIN)
3135	7562	(II)	SPINNING WHEEL, THE
3135	1H542	(I)	MISS HALKET CRAIGIE'S REEL
3135	1H542	(I)	DUCHESS OF BUCCLEUGH'S REEL, THE
3135	1H622H	(I)	MISS CHARLOTE ROSS'S STRATHSPEY
3135	1H636	(II)	DR. McHARDY
3135	1H3H2H2	(I)	MISS SUSAN BOGG'S STRATHSPEY
3136	1642	(I)	PETERHEAD LADIE'S STRATHSPEY
3136	5122	(II)	ALI BOBO
313	7b44	(I)	RATTLING ROARING WILLIE
3131H	3542	(I)	HAY STACK, THE
3131H	3542	(I)	MISS (ANNE) CARRE'S REEL
3131H	35H62	(II)	MRS KEILLOR
3131H	4242H	(II)	MISS LAVINIA WALLACE
3131H	5342	(I)	MISS ALLISON CHALMERS REEL
3131H	6225	(II)	CRIPPLE BRIGADE, THE
3131H	6642	(II)	MR JAMES GEORGE
3131H	6642	(I)	MR JAMES GEORGE('S STRATHSPEY)
3131H	67b27bL	(II)	LORD BLANTYRE('S)
3131H	67b27bL	(I)	LORD BLANTYRE'S STRATHSPEY
3131H	7b527bL	(II)	MISS COLSTON
3131H	7b7b7b7bL	(II)	MACDONALD'S MARCH, THE
3141	31H51	(I)	LADY CHARLOTTE CHOLMONDELEY'S FANCY
3142	7L5L11	(I)	HERNITE, THE
3142	7L5L13	(I)	HARRIOT, THE
3142	7L5L35L	(I)	MISS F. BAIRD'S JIG
3142	317L7L	(II)	MISS CHARLOTTE ANN LOWE('S)
3142	3125L	(II)	KEEL ROW(, THE)
3142	3125L	(II)	MISS HALDANE OF GLENEAGLES
3142	3125L	(I)	MISS SCOTT'S FAVORITE

3142	3125L	(I)	MISS HALDANE OF GLENEAGLES ('S STRATHSPEY)
3142	3125L	(I)	AMELIA
3142	3125L	(I)	(WEEL MAY) THE KEEL ROW
3142	3125L	(I)	LASSES OF MELROSS, THE
3142	3127L	(I)	WEEL MAY THE KEEL ROW
3142	3147bL	(II)	GAELIC AIR, A
3142	3147bL	(II)	GLENGARRY'S MARCH
3142	3151H	(I)	DRUM HOUSE [or KEEP IT UP]
3142	3151H	(I)	GENERAL CAMPBELL OF MONZIES WELCOME HOME
3142	3152H	(II)	BALLECHIN RANT
3142	327L5L	(I)	WEEL MAY THE KEEL ROW
			[LASSIE'S PETITION TO NEPTUNE, THE]
3142	357L2	(I)	MR ROBt BOWMAN'S FANCY
3142	3512	(I)	BOWMAN'S FANCY
3142	3542	(I)	MISS SPIER'S REEL
3142	361H1H	(II)	JAMES O. FORBES ESQ. OF CORSE
3142	361H1H	(II)	J.O. FORBES ESQ. OF CORSE
3142	31H25L	(I)	BRAES OF CRAIGE, THE
3142	427L5L	(I)	ISLINGTON ASSEMBLY
3142	5352	(I)	NEW YORK GIRLS
3142	5521	(I)	FALMOUTH ASSEMBLY
3142	5622	(I)	BRITISH CONQUESTS
3142	1H531	(I)	IRISH LILT
3142	1H531	(I)	STAR, THE
3142	1H2H4H2H	(I)	RACK OF SILLY, THE
314	324	(I)	BERKES OF PLUNKETTY, THE
3143	3132	(II)	MERRY KITTY or HIGHLAND DONALD
3143	311H6	(I)	MR HENRY ERSKINE'S REEL
3144	3122	(I)	BIG BOW WOW, THE
3144	327L4	(I)	DUMB GLUTTON, THE
3144	327L4	(I)	DUMB WAITER
3144	357L2	(I)	MR GEO. F. MACKENZIE OF ALLANGRANGE'S STR.
3144	57L25L	(I)	MISS PETRIE'S FANCY, THE
3144	5435	(I)	MAIL COACH, THE
3146	6L27L5L	(I)	MRS GARDEN OF TROOP
			AND GLENLYON'S STRATHSPEY
3146	3542	(II)	SIR ALEXANDER DON
3146	3542	(I)	SIR ALEXANDER DON
3146	551H1H	(I)	THEODORE
3146	51H22	(II)	MISS WILLIAMSON
3146	51H22	(I)	MISS WILLIAMSON('S STRATHSPEY)
3146	6531	(I)	NONE LIKE IT
3146	1H37L2	(I)	MISS C. BARTLET'S STRATHSPEY
3146	1H322	(II)	JOLLY BUTCHER, THE
3141H	31H2H2	(I)	MISS FORDYCE OF AYTON'S FAVORITE REEL
3151	25L7bL2	(I)	BLACKHALL HOUSE
3151	25L7L2	(I)	IRISH LASSES, THE
3151	26L7L2	(II)	ABERGELDIE CASTLE
3151	3152	(I)	ATHOLE LADS, THE
3151	3156	(II)	CHORUS JIG, THE
3151	3156	(I)	CHORUS JIG, THE
3151	3H3H2H2	(I)	BUSH AT THE FOOT OF THE GARDEN, THE
3152	7L5L15	(I)	MISS ROBERTSON OF CLAVERSTON'S JIGG
315	217L	(I)	(A)N' EACAIG [AN EUCHDAG]
3152	3142	(I)	MAJOR, THE
3152	3151	(I)	(ARE YOU) ALWAYS PLEASED
3152	311H6	(I)	MISS ANSONS REEL
3152	311H1H	(II)	DOMHNULL CLEIREACH
3152	311H1H	(I)	DONALD CLEIREACH or NEAT SHOE, THE
			[DOMHNULL CLEIREACH]
3152	311H1H	(I)	CARLE CAN YE WHISTLE
3152	311H1H	(I)	LORD LEWIS GORDON'S STRATHSPEY
3152	3532	(I)	GOWAN BANK, THE
3152	351H1H	(I)	BUCHANANS REEL
3152	61H62H	(II)	BALLANGEICH
315	316	(I)	MRS FRASER OF CULBOCKIE'S JIG
315	316	(I)	KICK THE (ROGUES/SCRUBS) OUT
315	316	(I)	KICK THE WORLD BEFORE YOU
3153	25L27L	(I)	MR BRUCE'S STRATHSPEY
3153	2427bL	(I)	LORD ABOYN'S STRATHSPEY
3153	3142	(I)	CAPn COOK
3153	311H5	(I)	NEW GERMAN WALTZ
3153	321H6	(II)	CAM' YE BY ATHOL
3153	321H6	(II)	BONNIE PRINCE CHARLIE
3153	321H6	(I)	BONNIE PRINCE CHARLIE
3153	323H1H	(I)	BONNIE PRINCE CHARLIE
3153	5153	(I)	CAMERONIAN'S RANT, THE
3153	5432	(I)	MR FLETCHER'S STRATHSPEY
3153	5764	(II)	FOX, THE
3153	5764	(I)	FOX (CHAC'D), THE
3153	6532	(I)	HUME CASTLE
3153	6562	(I)	SIR JOHN HENDERSON('S JIGG)

315	31H5	(I)	PIPERS MAGGOT, (THE)
3153	1H543	(I)	QUEEN'S PALACE
3153	1H53H1H	(I)	DORSET:SHIRE MARCH
315	31H6	(I)	PIPERS MAGGOT
3153	1H61H7	(I)	MRS CAPt McBARNET'S STRATHSPEY
3154	15L7L2	(I)	HIE OVER HUNT
315	422H	(I)	IRISH DANCE
315	422H	(I)	LORD GRANTHAM'S WHIM
315	422H	(I)	IRISH QUICK STEP, THE
3155	1322	(I)	MISS MILLER OF GLENLEE'S REEL
3155	12H2H2	(I)	MISS MAXWELL'S REEL
3155	12H2H2	(I)	NEW CHRISTMASS
3155	2227bL	(I)	CORPORAL, THE
3155	3125L	(II)	BONNIE BANCHORY
3155	3142	(II)	DUNNECHAN (REEL) DUNNICHEN HOUSE
3155	3142	(II)	MISS FOGO
3155	3142	(I)	MISS RANKEN'S REEL
3155	3142	(I)	DUNNICHEN HOUSE
3155	3142	(I)	MISS FOGO (KILLORN'S REEL)
3155	3153	(I)	MR JOHN CAMPBELL ARDMORE'S FAVORITE
3155	3161H	(I)	LATHER AWA' WI' YOUR OAK STICK
3155	3161H	(I)	HUMOURS OF KILKENNY, THE
3155	311H5	(I)	NEW GERMAN WALTZ, (THE)
3155	311H5	(I)	MISS MARGt CHRISTIE'S VALTZ
3155	321H6	(I)	LADY ANN CARNEGIE'S FAVORITE
3155	321H6	(I)	CAM' YE BY ATHOL
3155	3532	(I)	MISS HAMILTON OF WISHAW'S STRATHSPEY
3155	3542	(II)	MRS FERGUSON OF RAITH('S STRATHSPEY)
3155	3542	(II)	MARQUIS OF HUNTLY'S WELCOME TO THE ROYAL HIGHLANDERS, THE
3155	3542	(I)	MRS FERGUSON OF RAITH'S STRATHSPEY
3155	3542	(I)	MARQUIS OF HUNTLY'S WELCOME TO THE ROYAL HIGHLANDERS
3155	4211	(I)	DUKE OF YORK'S QUICK STEP, THE
3155	4266	(I)	McDONALD OF THE ISLES SALUTATION
3155	4266	(I)	FAILTE MHIC DHONAIL GHUIRM
3155	437L2	(I)	MRS SEVEWRIGHT'S REEL
3155	437L2	(I)	MRS ANDw SIVEWRIGHT OF EDINr
3155	4324	(I)	MR POPE'S STRATHSPEY
3155	4542	(II)	BRIDGE OF DEE, THE
3155	4542	(I)	BRIDGE OF DEE, THE
3155	42H2H2	(I)	MISS OGILVIE'S REEL
3155	42H2H2	(I)	LADY (BETTY) COCHRAN'S REEL
3155	42H2H6	(I)	LADY BETTY COCHRAN'S REEL
3155	551H2H	(I)	POLWART ON THE GREEN
3155	51H22	(II)	MRS MORAY OF ABERCAIRN(E)Y
3155	51H22	(I)	MRS MURRAY OF ABERCARNEY'S REEL
3155	6455	(II)	WELCOME, MR. MARTIN
3155	1H52H2	(II)	DUBH CHNOCAN
3155	1H2H2H2	(I)	NEW CHRISTMASS
3155	1H3H2H2	(II)	NEW CHRISTMAS or BASS REEL, THE
3155	1H3H2H2	(I)	NEW CHRISTMAS
3155	1H3H2H2	(I)	BASS REEL
3156	4642	(I)	ROY STEWART'S REEL
3151H	27bL44	(I)	MISS FINLAY'S STRATHSPEY
3151H	3126L	(I)	LADY BALCARRAS'S REEL [LADY BALCARRES'S REEL]
3151H	3122	(I)	MISS BROWN'S FAVOURITE
3151H	3147bL	(II)	MISS PENSY MACDONALD
3151H	3147bL	(II)	LADY BELHAVEN
3151H	3147bL	(I)	MISS (PENSY) MACDONALD (NOW LADY BALHAVEN)('S REEL)
3151H	3162	(I)	JAMES FERGUSSON ESQr W.S.'S REEL
3151H	3162	(I)	MR JOHN STEWART OF GARTH'S REEL
3151H	51H22H	(I)	MISS WHITEFORD'S REEL
3151H	662H2H	(I)	MISS BETTY CATHCART'S REEL
3151H	7b527bL	(II)	MRS DUFF, THE MANSE, GRANGE
3151H	7b7b7bL4	(I)	BALENDALLOCH'S DREAM [BALLINDALLOCH'S DREAM]
3151H	1H7b24	(I)	MISS BETTY SHAW'S REEL
3151H	3H4H3H2H	(I)	DALMENY HOUSE
315#6	1642	(I)	PRINCESS OF WALES'S REEL
3162	3125L	(I)	MISS DOBBIE'S STRATHSPEY
3163	3124	(I)	HONble FOX MAULE'S FAVORITE, THE
3164	4225L	(I)	TRISTRAM SHANDY
3165	3522	(I)	SCOTLAND YARD
3165	31H42	(I)	NEW BRIDGE OF BALLATERS
3165	4325	(II)	FRANK'S
3165	4522	(II)	BECAUSE HE WAS A BONNY LAD
3165	4522	(I)	BECAUSE (HE/I) WAS A BONNY LAD
3165	4642	(I)	BECAUSE HE WAS A BONNY LAD
3165	1H332	(II)	FERRY, THE

3165	1H522	(I)	ANOTHER [St KILDA SONG AND DANCE]
3166	513H1H	(I)	PARKS OF DUNLOP, THE
3161H	5330	(I)	BANKS OF CLYDE, THE
3175	327L5L	(I)	TRIP UP THE STAIRS, THE
3175	651H1	(I)	GREEN PEASE
3175	2H62H5	(I)	HARK THE COCK THAT CROW'D
3176	5531	(II)	FHEAR NAN CASUN CAOLA (REJECTED LOVER, THE)
311H1	27bL44	(II)	DUCHESS OF BUCCLEUGH, THE
311H1	27bL44	(I)	DU(T)CHESS OF BUCCLEUCH('S STR., THE)
311H3	422H4	(I)	MISS BULMAN'S FAVORITE
311H3	432H2	(I)	MISS CLEMENTINA STEWART'S REEL
311H3	4542	(II)	LADY GEORGE BEAUCLARK [BEAUCLERK]
311H3	4542	(I)	LADY GEORGE BEAUCLARK'S REEL
311H5	27bL7b7bL	(I)	LADY CHARLOTTE MURRAY ('S FAVORITE) (JIG)
311H5	3127bL	(II)	ACHMONY
311H5	3142	(I)	HIGHLANDER, THE
311H5	3142	(I)	POSADH PEATHAR (IN BHAIN)
311H5	4327L	(I)	SWARD HOUSE
311H5	432H2	(I)	MISS KATHRINE MELVEL'S REEL
311H5	4562	(I)	MISS DOUGLAS BRIGTON'S JIGG
311H5	51H22H	(I)	BONNY BRAES OF SKELMORLY, THE
311H5	637L2	(I)	LA ROSALIA
311H5	7427bL	(I)	MR ROBt ADAMSON JUNr REEL
311H5	1H3H1H2	(I)	PENNYCUICK HOUSE
311H5	4H3H72H	(I)	BEGIN THE DANCE
311H6	27bL7b2	(I)	BECKY MURRAY
311H6	27bL7b2	(I)	FIR TREE, THE
311H6	437L2	(II)	CASTLE GORDON
311H7b	27bL7b2	(II)	FIR TREE, THE
311H7b	27bL7b2	(I)	FIR TREA, THE
311H7	27bL7b2	(I)	UP IN THE AIR
311H7	1H542	(I)	MISS CAMPBELL OF SHAWFIELD'S
311H1H	3126L	(I)	MISS MONTGOMRIE OF SKERMORLIE'S STRATHSPEY
311H1H	3122H	(I)	COUNTESS OF DUMFRIES JUNr's REEL
311H1H	3142	(I)	MISS CATHne SHIRREFF'S FAVORITE
311H1	312H2	(I)	LADY CRAWFURD'S REEL
311H1	312H2	(I)	MARCHMONT HOUSE
311H1H	31H3H6	(I)	WILLIE WAS A WANTON WAG
311H1H	427L2	(I)	MELBOURNE HOUSE
311H1H	545L2	(I)	ALL THE WORLD'S A STAGE
311H1H	2H2H22	(II)	DRUMSHEUGH
311H1H	2H2H22	(I)	DRUMSHUGH [DRUMSHEUGH]
311H1H	2H2H22	(I)	JACK'S DELIGHT
311H5H	4H3H72H	(II)	MRS SMALL
311H5H	4H3H72H	(I)	MISS STEWART OF DERCULUH'S REEL
312H5	6561	(I)	MEDLEY COTTILION
313H1H	2H4H2H2	(I)	MISS LOGAN, AYR
313H2H	6562	(I)	MISS WELSH'S FANCY
313H2H	6562	(I)	THIS IS NOT MY AIN HOUSE
313H2H	6662	(I)	THIS IS NO MY AIN HOUSE
313H2H	2H3H2H2	(I)	MACPHERSON'S RANT
315H3H	2H3H2H2	(I)	MACLACHLAN'S RANT [McLACHLAN'S REEL]
325L5L	6L6L5L6L	(II)	MUSIC O' SPEY, THE
325L7L	4313	(II)	DOLLS' LEVEE, THE
325L1	3236	(II)	GOUROCK BAY
325L1	3236	(II)	HAWTHORN HEDGES
325L2	35L41	(I)	BLACK EY'D SUSAN
325L3	7L55L3	(I)	FERGUSON'S RANT
326L5L	2L47L2	(I)	MISS MARY ABERCROMBY'S STRATHSPEY
326L5L	5L325	(II)	STEWART TARTAN
326L6L	2211	(I)	TARRY WOOL
326L1	5L6L22	(I)	ROBIE DONNA GORACH
326L1	5L6L22	(I)	DAFT ROBIN
326L1	5L422	(I)	CARRON SIDE
326L4	3211H	(II)	AULD WIFE AYONT THE FIRE, THE
326L4	3211H	(I)	AULD WIFE (AYONT THE FIRE), THE
326L4	3311H	(I)	AULD WIFE AYONT THE FIRE, THE
327L5L	3L125L	(I)	MISS GUNNING'S (REEL/DELIGHT)
327L5L	5L5L52	(I)	YOUNG MYRTLE, THE
327L2	3211H	(I)	AULD WIFE AYONT THE FIRE
327L2	3236L	(I)	AULD STUART'S BACK AGAIN, THE
327L2	3246L	(I)	OLD STUARTS BACK AGAIN
327L2	321H5	(I)	AULD WIFE AYONT THE FIRE, THE
327L2	3427L	(I)	NEW COTILLON, THE
327L2	3434	(I)	SAUNY'S DELIGHT
327L4	327L3	(I)	M'EUDAIL, IS M'ULAIDH, IS M'AITHIR
3213L	6L17L7L	(II)	DEIL O' BALDARROCH, THE
3215L	6L432	(I)	BALL, THE
3215L	6L432	(I)	BALL, THE
3215L	6L452	(I)	HONble MISS CATHERINE ELLIOT'S REEL
3215L	7L211	(I)	HANDEL'S HORNPIPE
3215L	7L211	(I)	QUICK MARCH BY MR HANDEL

3215L	2222	(II)	LOVE'S YOUNG DREAM
3215L	2422L	(I)	MRS ARCHd CAMPBELL OF ASKOMELL'S STR.
3215L	3565	(I)	MISS MACKENZIE'S STRATHSPEY
3215L	5620	(I)	PAS DEUX MISSES GRANT OF MONYMUSK
3215L	5622	(I)	HAYDN'S CELEBRATED MOVEMENT
3216L	5L5L12	(I)	WALKER'S FAVOURITE
3216L	6L221	(I)	KELVIN GROVE
321	7L6L1	(III)	LA SIESTA
3217L	6L136	(III)	RIGHTS OF MAN, THE
3217L	6L27L5L	(I)	HESSIAN ALLEMANDE
3217L	6L237L	(I)	CORRILLE REVIV'D
3210	6L7L30	(I)	GIGA
3210	5620	(I)	HOPE TOLD A FLATTERING TALE
3211	6L225	(I)	I LOVE MY LOVE IN SECRET
3211	7bL527bL	(I)	NORTH HIGHLAND 12
3211	7bL7b27bL	(I)	HIGHLAND DANCE, A
3211	115L5L	(I)	CARLE AN' THE KING COME
3211	127L5L	(II)	PETRONELLA
3211	127L5L	(I)	PETRONELLA
3211	2232	(I)	ROYALTY, THE
3211	247L2	(I)	MISS HARDIE'S MEASURE
3211	326L1	(I)	CARRIL'S LAMENT
3211	3211	(I)	NEGROE, THE
3211	3255	(II)	WINTER HOLIE, THE
3211	3522	(I)	MOSS HOUSE, LOGIEALMOND, THE
3211	31H52	(I)	BRAVE LADS OF GALLAWATER
3211	4322	(I)	PERSIANS REVEILLE, THE
3211	4522	(III)	ROSEBUD OF ALLANVALE, THE
3211	4532	(I)	W. MORRISON'S FAVORITE
3211	4622	(III)	PERSIAN DANCE
3211	4622	(I)	PERSIAN DANCE
3211	5532	(I)	MISS C. DALRYMPLE'S JIG
3211	5552	(I)	BRAW, BRAW LADS (OF GALLA WATER)
3211	567L2	(I)	MARQUIS OF LORNE'S STRATHSPEY
3211	5625L	(I)	MR GIBSON'S FAVORITE
3211	5625L	(I)	HAYDN, THE
3211	6542	(I)	IRISH AIR
3211	61H22	(I)	THIRD (CAMPERDOWN) MEDLEY DANCE
3211	1H2H75	(II)	PATRONELLA [PETRONELLA]
3211	1H2H1H5	(I)	PETRONELLA
3212	115L1	(I)	CARLE AN THE KING COME
3212	4323	(I)	MISS MANAGIES HORNPIPE
3212	5367	(I)	STIRLING VALE
3212	5367	(I)	STRILY VALE
3213	115L1	(I)	CARLE AND THE KING COME
3213	27L15	(I)	CRACKENBERG CASTLE
3213	5552	(I)	SILKEN-SNOODED LASSIE, THE
3214	7L232	(I)	ROSS CASTLE
3215	2324	(I)	COMA LEAM, COMA LEAM COGADH NO SITH
3215	3212	(II)	DUNDERAVE
3215	3215	(I)	LA BALLET HOLLANDOISE
3215	4326	(III)	MRS WISEMAN
3215	6422	(I)	RINAWAY BRIDE, THE
3215	6444	(I)	HENRY PATERSON ESQr
3215	6522	(III)	WALLACE TOWER, ABERDEEN
3211H	357L2	(I)	HIS MAJESTY'S RECOVERY
3211H	5231	(I)	OUR AIN COUNTRIE
3211H	2H2H61H	(I)	HOLY EVEN
3211H	3H2H66	(I)	WHY HANGS THAT CLOUD
3211H	3H2H66	(I)	HALLOW E'EN
3211H	4H3H55H	(I)	LA MEGARDE
3226L	5L121	(III)	AULD HOUSE, THE
322	011	(I)	MISS CALEY
3221	1355	(II)	LANG, LANG SYNE, THE
3221	5432	(II)	ROSE-ACRE, FAREWELL
3221	6651	(I)	LAMENT FOR MRS TULLOCH, KIRKMICHAEL, A
3223	3231	(I)	WE'RE A' NODDIN'
3223	6521	(II)	FAREWELL TO GAIRLOCH
3224	3252	(I)	TAKE ME JENNY
3225	1H2H66	(I)	NORTHERN LASS
3225	3H2H66	(I)	NORTHERN LASS, THE
3231	1575	(I)	MISS DRYSDALE'S FAVORITE REEL
3231	3236L	(III)	FALLS OF TARNASH, THE
3231	3255	(III)	FLOWER O' STRATHBOGIE, THE
3231	6543	(I)	WARLEY CAMP
3231	7675	(III)	BIRNAN HALL
3232	7L7L55	(I)	MRS ERNEST LESLIE'S STRATHSPEY
3232	11H1H2	(I)	MISS G. MACKAY'S FAVORITE
3232	3211	(I)	LE FONTAINBLEAU
3232	3434	(I)	UNTITLED
3232	536L6	(I)	DUNROBIN CASTLE
323	321	(I)	O MY LOVE! LEAVE ME NOT

3233	427L5L	(I)	LADY MARIA PARKER
3233	427L2	(I)	LADY MARIA PARKER'S STRATHSPEY
3233	51H22	(I)	PADDY O' CARRAL
3234	5L111	(I)	MY LOVE'S A BONNY NAETHING
3234	226L6L	(I)	LAST CRADLE SONG, THE
3235	5L111	(I)	MY LOVES A BONNY NAITHING
3235	1554	(I)	EDINBURGH SCOTCH MEASURE, THE
3235	2665	(I)	I FIX MY FANCY ON HER
3235	2666	(I)	BRIGHT CYNTHIA'S POWER
3235	2666	(I)	I FIXT MY FANCY ON HER
3235	3122	(I)	BRAES OF ATHOLE, THE
3235	3236L	(II)	DARGAI
323	554	(I)	DRUNKEN MAGG YOUNG
3235	6422	(I)	HIGHLAND LASSIE, THE
3235	6422	(I)	HIGHLAND LADDIE, THE
3235	6422	(I)	(AS I CAME O'ER) THE CAIRNEY MOUNT
3235	1H61H6	(II)	GLEN LEAN
3235	1H1H55	(I)	LASS OF PATIES MILL, THE
3235	1H1H75	(I)	LOSS OF BETTIES MILLS, THE
3235	1H1H1H5	(I)	LASS OF PATIES MILL, THE
3235	1H1H3HO	(I)	LASS OF PATIES MILL, THE
3235	1H1H3H5	(I)	LASS OF PATY'S MILL, THE
3235	4H2H2H2	(I)	MISS SALLY BARTLETT'S REEL
3236	3122	(II)	BRAES OF ATHOLE, THE
3236	3122	(I)	GENERAL GRANT'S REELL
3236	3122	(I)	BRAES OF ATHOLE, (THE)
3236	3122	(I)	ATHOL BRAYS
3236	3222	(I)	GAIRM NA 'N COILEACH
3231H	56L6L2	(I)	SOLDIERS TAKE AWAY THE WOUNDED
3231H	527L2	(I)	MR SAMI ROSES REEL
3243	5523	(I)	LA NEUVENNE
3243	6532	(I)	ROYAL HUNT, THE
3245	3253	(I)	TRIHODYAN
3251	437L7L	(I)	MISS ST. GEORGE'S DOUBLE JIGG
3252	3562	(I)	UNION, THE
3253	3111	(I)	RT HON LORD JOHN SCOTT, THE
3253	551H1H	(I)	POLWART ON THE GREEN
3254	2211	(I)	SCOTTS GAVOT, THE
3254	5501H	(I)	(AT) POLWART (ON THE) GREEN
3254	5551H	(I)	MEDLEY OVERTURE
3254	5551H	(I)	POLWART ON THE GREEN
3254	551H1H	(I)	POLWART ON THE GREEN
3255	3322	(I)	RIVEN RANT, THE
3255	3551H	(I)	LAIRD OF COCKPEN'S SCOTCH-MEASURE, THE
3255	5255	(I)	SCOTCH MEASURE
3255	551H1H	(I)	POLWART(ON THE) GREEN
3255	6252	(I)	LAKES OF KILLARNEY, THE
3255	6262	(I)	LAKES OF KILLARNEY (KELLARNIE) THE
3255	6665	(I)	WOES MY HEART THAT WE SHOULD SUNDER
3255	61H55	(I)	SHE HAD SOMETHING ELSE TO DO
3256	51H27L	(I)	MERRY LADS OF HUNTING TOWER, THE
3251H	1H61H1H	(I)	LORD DUNMORE'S DELIGHT
3263	3261H	(II)	CLOUT THE CAULDRON
3263	1H563	(II)	CHUNNAIC MI ON(AN) DAMH DONN ...
3265	3262	(I)	CADGER WATTY
3265	1H525	(I)	CRAIGIEBURN(WOOD)
3265	3H652	(I)	MR P. P. SHIRREFF'S FAVORITE
321H5	1H61H5	(I)	QUICKSTEP, 43rd REGt.
321H7	5620	(I)	LAY TO THE ROYAL HIGHLANDERS, OR 42 REGt
321H1H	526L5L	(I)	HER ABSENCE WILL NOT ALTER ME
321H1H	526L6L	(I)	WHEN ABSENT FROM THE NYMPH I LOVE
321H1H	5221	(I)	O ONCE I LOV'D (A BONNY LASS)
321H1H	5320	(I)	SIR JOHN SINCLAIR
321H1H	5322	(I)	BY BRAIDS WEE LIMPID STREAM
321H1H	1H2H76	(I)	LAST TIME I CAME O'ER THE MOOR, THE
321H1H	2H2H2H6	(I)	NEW SCOTCH-MEASURE, A
321H1H	3H2H76	(I)	LAST TIME I CAME O'ER THE MOOR, THE
3236	5532	(II)	MISS FORBES' FAREWELL TO BANFF
333L3	427L2	(I)	MISS STRONG'S JIG
335L5L	5553	(I)	MRS STEWART, BENCHILL'S REEL
335L3	427L2	(II)	MISS KATTY TROTTER
335L3	427L2	(I)	MISS (KETTY) TROTTER'S REEL
335L3	1H1H31H	(I)	MR W. JOPP'S HORNPIPE
335L3	1H1H1H6	(I)	DANDY DINMOTTE
336L5L	1221	(I)	BONNY PEGGY
336L2	1515	(I)	HIGHLAND REEL, A
336L2	1515	(I)	B'FHEARR LEAM FHIN NA LAIR IS OIGEACH
337L5L	31H22	(I)	MILLAR OF FIFE, THE
337L7L	1155	(I)	HORNPIPE
3315L	6L422	(I)	MISS MARKBY'S FANCY
3315L	1216L	(II)	HO RO GUM B'AOIBHINN LEAM
3315L	1532	(I)	MAID OF PALAISEAU, THE

3316L	5L123	(II)	STILLY NIGHT, THE
3316L	5L132	(II)	JOHN McALPIN(E)
3316L	5L132	(I)	MR BRANDER OF PITGAVNEY'S STRATHSPEY
3316L	6L5L7bL6L	(II)	BANFFSHIRE VOLUNTEERS, THE
3316L	6L233	(I)	MAC S'HIMI MOR A BASACHA(DH)
331	6L7L1	(I)	POMPEY RAN AWAY
331	6L10	(I)	EARL DOUGLAS'S LAMENT(ATION)
3316L	1353	(I)	MAC MHIC AILLEAN [MAC 'IC AILEIN]
3317L	7L6L5L5L	(II)	AWA' AWA'
3317L	2221	(I)	MISS CAMPBELL OF JURRA'S ALLAMNDE
3310	5530	(I)	MISS MARY DOUGLAS'S ALLAMAND
3310	1H62H5	(I)	JESS McFARLANE
331	15L6L	(I)	SCOTS TUNE
331	15L1	(I)	HORSE-MAN'S PORT
3311	6L5L5LO	(I)	DONALD
3311	7L5L5LO	(I)	DONALD
331	111	(I)	LOUVRE, THE
3311	115L5L	(I)	COLLIER'S (DAUGHTER/LASS), THE
3311	2226L	(I)	MACKINTOSH'S LAMENT
3311	2231	(I)	TURKISH MARCH
3311	2233	(I)	ROUSSEAU'S DREAM
3311	2332	(I)	OSWALD'S WISH
3311	3211	(I)	LA RACROCHEUSE
3311	4422	(I)	CACINA
3311	4522	(I)	CARSE HOUSE
331	155	(I)	WOO'D AN' MARRY'D AN A'
3311	5532	(I)	SKENE HOUSE
3311	5532	(I)	LILLIGNONETH FRANCOISE
3312	227L6L	(I)	NEW MILLER'S DAUGHTER
3312	4453	(II)	MY OLD KENTUCKY HOME
331	255	(II)	MONALTRIE
3312	1H521	(I)	HE'S DEAR TO ME THO' HE'S FAR FRAE ME
331	35L3	(I)	MISS DUNBAR OF NORTHFIELD'S HORNPIPE
3313	27b27bL	(I)	LINKS OF LEITH
331	331	(I)	WE MET
3313	4324	(I)	NORTH HIGHLAND 19
3313	4324	(I)	HIGHLAND REEL, A
3313	4453	(II)	PRINCE ALBERT'S STRATHSPEY
3313	5535	(II)	SARONA
3313	5554	(I)	LOW LANDS OF HOLAND, THE
3313	5555	(I)	CRIEF FAIR
3313	5551H	(II)	CORDUROY, THE
3313	551H1H	(I)	MISS NANCY CAMPBELL'S SCOTS MEASURE
3313	551H1H	(I)	BE KIND TO THE YOUNG THING
3313	551H1H	(I)	POLWART ON THE GREEN
331	356	(I)	O DEAR MOTHER WHAT SHALL I DO
3313	6621	(I)	(LAMENT OF) MARY, QUEEN OF SCOTS (LAMENT)
3313	2H36L6	(I)	BONNY HIGHLAND HILLS, THE
3313	2H36L6	(I)	NEW STRATHSPEY REEL, A
331	432	(I)	LAY BY YOUR WHEEL BETTY
331	432	(I)	LAY BY YOUR WHEEL BETTY
331	445	(II)	CAMPBELL OF DUNTROON'S WELCOME
331	531	(II)	THIS LIFE IS BUT A VISION
3316	527L5	(I)	LA FAFORITTE
331	653	(I)	GIL MORRIS
3311H	335L1	(I)	QUICKSTEP, TURKISH
3311H	5212	(I)	WINTER IT IS PAST, THE
3311H	5222	(I)	WINTER IT IS PAST, THE
3325L	25L22	(II)	'NULL AIR NA H'EILEANAN DH'AMERICA GUN TEID SINN
3325L	3325L	(I)	QUICK STEP, A
3325L	4431	(I)	MARQUIS OF GRANBY'S DELIGHT
3326L	6L231	(II)	AGUS HO "MORAG"
3327L	3333	(I)	AULD GA'D AEVER, THE
332	16L5L	(I)	KENNET'S DREAM
3321	7L212	(II)	FAVORITE FRENCH DANCE, A
3321	7L213	(I)	VOULEZ VOUS DANSER MADEMOISELLE
332	115L	(I)	CHAPEL KEITHACK
3321	16L11	(II)	HYMN OF THE FOOLISH MAN, THE
332	117L	(I)	MINUET BY FELTON
332	113	(I)	PAS SEUL MISS ELSY HADDEN
3321	131HO	(I)	EIRIDH NA FINNEACHA' GAIDHEALACHD
3321	2116L	(II)	WIVES AND MAIDS AT HOME
3321	3361H	(I)	M'BAILE M'BEIL MO LEANNAN FEIN
332	135	(I)	SILLER CROWN, THE
332	143	(I)	CELEBRATED GERMAN MINUET, THE
3321	4432	(II)	BLOOMS OF BON-ACCORD, THE [COCKERS ROSES]
332	165	(I)	PRINCE OF WALES MINUET, THE
3322	16L7L5L	(I)	MISS WALLACE'S FANCY
3322	1113	(I)	CAPTAIN CAMPBELL OF ARGARTER'S MARCH
3322	1126L	(I)	PARTING KISS, THE
3322	1132	(I)	LADY'S PLAY THING, THE

3322	1131H	(I)	CAPT JOHNSTON'S LAMENT
3322	1155	(I)	ARROCAR HOUSE
3322	1332	(I)	MRS BRODIE'S DELIGHT
3322	3211	(I)	WHEN I FOLLOWED A LASS
3322	3211	(I)	JUMPIN(G) JOHN [JUMPING JOAN]
3322	3212	(I)	JUMPIN JOHN
3322	3355	(I)	BEHIND THE BUSH IN THE GARDEN
3322	3356	(I)	PERTHSHIRE DANCING MEASURES & C No. 13
3322	3351H	(I)	BARLEY (SUGAR) (CAKES)
3322	3361H	(II)	JOHNNIE LAD [JOHNNY LAD]
3322	3411	(I)	LAR(R)Y GROGAN
3322	3411	(I)	IRISH
3322	4433	(I)	BETTER LATE THAN NEVER
332	313	(I)	DRUNK AT NIGHT AND DRY IN THE MORNING
3323	11H61H	(II)	OLD FOLKS AT HOME
3323	3324	(I)	MISS DAVIDSON OF TULLOCH'S JIGG
3323	6531	(I)	GIL MORICE
3323	6532	(I)	GILL MORICE
3323	6542	(I)	GILL MORRIS
3324	17L10	(I)	HEAVING OF THE LEAD
3324	3335	(I)	NORTH HIGHLAND 7
3324	3335	(I)	JIGG, A
3324	5655	(I)	GREEN GROWS THE RASHES
3325	1121	(I)	PARODY ON JESSIE OF DUMBLANE
3325	3325	(I)	SPANISH JIG, A
332	554	(I)	BONNY YOUNG LAD IS MY JOCKEY, A
3325	5655	(I)	GREEN GROWS THE RASHES
332	653	(I)	GIL MORICE
3326	5551	(I)	TWINE (YE) WEEL THE PLAIDEN
332	1H1H6	(I)	CUMHADH RAOINUILL MHIC AILEAIN OIG
333	5L5L2	(I)	BLINK O'ER THE BURN SWEET BESSY
333	15L1	(I)	CELEBRATED TRUMPET TUNE, THE
333	15L1	(I)	MISS JUBB'S MINUET
3331	6L6L12	(I)	O MERRY MAY THE MAID BE
333	16L1	(II)	MAIRI BHOIDHEACH [BEAUTIFUL MARY]
3331	7bL27b7b	(I)	COLLAR-GREEN
333	113	(I)	OH LADDIE I MAUN LO'E THEE
3331	2227bL	(II)	HOBBLE JENNY
3331	2227bL	(I)	CANTY BODY
3331	2227bL	(I)	DUKE OF GORDON'S REEL, THE
3331	2227L	(I)	ARNDILLY'S REEL
3331	2245	(I)	JEM OF ABERDEEN
3331	2427bL	(II)	PETERCAN MCOMISH [BIODAG AIR MAC THOMAIS]
3331	2427bL	(II)	THOMSON'S GOT A KIRK
3331	2427bL	(II)	BIODAG AIR MAC THOMAIS [BIODAG AIN M' OMISH]
3331	2427bL	(I)	THA BIODAG AIG MAC THOMAIS [McHOMAS HAS A DIRK]
3331	2427bL	(I)	BIODAG AIR MACTHOMAIS
333	131	(I)	WAPPAT THE WIDOW MY LADY
3331	3335	(II)	DROVER, THE
3331	3347bL	(I)	REEL OF TULLOCH, (THE) (OLD SETT)
3331	3361H	(I)	GAELIC AIR, A
3331	3361H	(I)	BHEIR MI SORAIDH (THUN A' BHAILE)
3331	447L2	(II)	GAREY COTTAGE
3331	4442	(I)	MERRY TAYLORS
3331	5556	(II)	INVERARAY MARCH
3331	6421	(I)	FALCONERS WHIM, THE
333	11H7	(I)	MRS LUNDIE'S MINUET
333	26L6L	(I)	O! 'SMIS THA FO LEON
3332	6L6L23	(I)	(LORD ABOYNE'S WELCOME) or CUMBERNAULD HOUSE
333	211	(I)	UNTITLED
3332	1113	(I)	MARCHE
3332	1115	(I)	EXETER CHANGE
3332	1121	(I)	MISS CARNEGIE'S FAVOURITE VALTZ
3332	1122	(II)	I'LL BREAK YOUR HEAD FOR YOU
3332	1122	(I)	PERTHSHIRE DANCING MEASURES & C NO. 16
3332	1331H	(II)	WHITE COCKADE, THE
3332	1554	(II)	OLD DUMBARTON DRUMS
3332	1554	(I)	(OLD) DUMBARTON DRUMS (BEAT BONNY [O])
3332	1555	(I)	DUMBARTON DRUMS
3332	1565	(I)	MARCH 3d RIGt OF GUARDS
3332	1565	(I)	LONDON MARCH (THE)
3332	1664	(I)	DUMBARTON DRUMS
3332	3323	(I)	LORD LEWIS GORDON'S REEL
3332	3331H	(II)	WHITE COCKADE
3332	3331H	(I)	RANTING HIGHLANDMAN, THE
3332	331H1H	(I)	DUCHESS OF BUCCLEUGH'S REEL, THE
333	235	(I)	DUNCAN'S COMPLAINT
3332	46L6L7L	(II)	DUCHESS TREE, THE
3332	4443	(I)	AIKEN DRUM

3332	5331	(I)	MAZZINGHIS FANCY
3332	5556	(I)	PINKY HOUSE
3332	5556	(I)	CORYDONS COMPLAINT
3332	5551H	(I)	AS SYLVIA IN A FOREST LAY [PINKIE HOUSE]
3332	5551H	(I)	PINKIE HOUSE
3333	15L5L5L	(I)	MR YEAMAN OF MURIE'S MARCH
3333	17L6L5L	(I)	MY NANNY O
3333	1554	(I)	DUMBARTON'S DRUMS
3333	1555	(I)	TO SERVE A GALLANT LADY
3333	27bL44	(I)	MISS STEWART OF GARTH'S REEL
333	321	(I)	McINTOSH'S LAMENT
3333	2144	(I)	MISS NICOL'S STRATHSPEY
3333	2212	(I)	WINE CANNOT CURE
333	323	(II)	LOCHABER NO MORE
333	323	(I)	'S FLUICH AN OIDHCHE NOCHD 'SGUR FUAR I
			[FAREWELL TO LOCHABER]
3333	2322	(I)	A' GHLAS MHEUR
333	324	(I)	LOCHABER NO MORE
333	331	(I)	IRISH LAMENTATION
333	331	(I)	LOCHABER (NO MORE)
3333	3211	(I)	McINTOSH'S LAMENT
3333	3221	(I)	SOUR PLUMBS IN GALLASHIELS
333	333	(I)	LADY LOUISA ANN DOUGLAS, A MEDLEY WALTZ
333	333	(I)	PORT ATHOLL
333	333	(I)	LOCHABER (NO MORE)
3333	3333	(II)	WHATS A' THE STEER
3333	3333	(II)	DOON THE WATER
3333	3333	(II)	STEER KIMMER
3333	3335	(I)	OLD BUFFS MARCH, THE
3333	331H4	(I)	LORD HARDWICK'S MARCH
3333	3655	(I)	MO CHAILIN OG THOIR LE TOIGH AN AIRE DHOMH
3333	362H2	(I)	MR JAMES BELFOUR'S FANCY
3333	31H64	(II)	AURORA
3333	427L6L	(I)	GLEN STEWART
3333	4404	(I)	AWAY WITH MELANCHOLY
3333	5133	(I)	JEANETTE AND JEANNOT
3333	5222	(I)	GALLOW SHIELS
3333	5222	(I)	SOUR PLUMS OF GALLOW-SHIELS
3333	537L2	(I)	WHITE COCKADE, THE
3333	5331	(I)	IRISH TUNE, AN
3333	5332	(I)	HIGHLAND LAD MY LOVE WAS BORN, A
3333	547L2	(I)	WHITE COCKADE, THE
3333	5432	(II)	WHITE COCKADE
3333	5521	(I)	LORD ABOYNE
333	351H	(I)	MR G. KENNEDY'S MINUET
3333	51H22	(II)	PADDY O' CARROL
3333	51H22	(I)	PADDY O' CAR(R)OL
3333	6453	(I)	FALLS OF FOYERS, THE
3333	6531	(I)	GLENARA
3333	6532	(I)	HUME CASTLE
3333	6555	(I)	BARCARO(L)LE FROM MASANIELLO
3333	7b7bL44	(II)	MISS STEWART OF GARTH
3333	7b7bL44	(II)	DUNFERMLINE RACES
3333	7b7bL44	(I)	DUNFERMLINE RACES
3333	1H315	(II)	CUT AND DRY
333	416L	(I)	MERRY DANCERS
333	427L	(I)	DANCE TO YOUR DADDY & C. WITH VARIATIONS
3334	3323	(I)	LA GRANDE MARCHE DU FAMEUX GEN. BUONAPARTE
3334	3356	(I)	PLOUGHMAN SAILOR, A
3334	5430	(I)	ALLEGRO
3335	1122	(I)	FAVORITE MARCH, A
3335	2224	(I)	IRISH DANCE
3335	3324	(I)	LASTRUMPONY
333	542	(I)	LAWREL OF VICTORY, THE
3335	4422	(I)	MISS MACKENZIE OF CROMARTIE'S STR.
3335	4446	(I)	MISS ANNIE ROBERTSON (DINGWALL)
333	553	(I)	MISS ROBERTSON'S MINUET
333	554	(I)	KIRKFORTHER
333	555	(I)	MISS BOSSWELL OF AUCHINLECK'S VALTZ
3335	5655	(I)	GREEN GROWS THE RASHES
3335	656L2	(I)	MRS FRASER'S CULDUTHOL'S FANCY
3335	6565	(II)	BANKS OF THE ALLAN, THE
3335	6565	(I)	BANKS OF ALLAN, THE
3335	6624	(I)	MISS BROWN OF LINKWOOD'S STRATHSPEY
3335	6660	(I)	O ROWAN TREE, THOU'LT AYE BE DEAR
3335	6665	(II)	ROWAN TREE
3335	6665	(I)	KITTIE OF CRILE
3335	1H523	(I)	EDINBURGH WAITS, THE
3335	1H652	(I)	LADY OF THE LAKE
3335	1H653	(I)	LADY OF THE LAKE, THE
3335	1H61H6	(II)	ROTHIEMURCHUS RANT [ROTHIEMURCHIE'S RANT]
3335	1H61H6	(I)	LASSIE WIE THE LINT WHITE LOCKS

3335	1H61H6	(I)	GRANT'S STRATHSPEY
3335	1H61H6	(I)	ROTHEMURCHES (RANT/STRATHSPEY/REEL)
3335	1H1H55	(I)	LASS OF PATIE'S MILL, THE
3335	3H3H2H6	(II)	MAIDS OF ARROCHAR, THE
3335	3H3H2H6	(I)	WALLACE'S LAMENT AFTER THE BATTLE OF FALKIRK
3335	3H3H2H6	(I)	MAIDS OF ARROCHAR, THE
3335	3H3H3H6	(I)	LAMENT OF WALLACE(, AFTER THE BATTLE OF FALKIRK), THE
3336	3316L	(I)	QUICKSTEP OF THE W LOWLAND FENCIBLE REG
3336	3325	(II)	COCK O' THE NORTH, THE
3336	51H22	(I)	McLEAN'S BONNY LASSIE
3336	1H1H72H	(I)	AN CRANN TAIRADH [AN CRANN-TARA]
3331H	2215L	(I)	PRINCE EDWARD'S FANCY
3331H	3336	(I)	COLLA CITEACH
3331H	5221	(I)	A' FOR THE LOVE O' NANNY
3331H	5222	(I)	(SOUR PLUMS [IN]) GALLA SHIELS
3331H	5522	(I)	HACKNEY ASSEMBLY
3331H	3H2H1H6	(I)	CONCERT ROOM
334	15LO	(I)	MINUET
3342	6L6L11	(I)	JOHNNY'S GRAY BREEKS
3342	7L27L5L	(II)	MISS MARGARET GORDON OF LESSMORE
3342	7L27L5L	(I)	MISS MARGARET GORDON OF LESSMORE'S REEL
3342	16L15	(I)	DEPARTURE, THE
3342	1732	(I)	COL. MUNRO'S QUICK STEP
3342	11H3H1H	(I)	IORRAM IOMRUIGH [IORRAM IOMRAIMH]
334	221	(I)	OH ONOCHIE O
3342	37L25L	(I)	MISS COOK'S FANCY
3342	3311H	(I)	MISS STEWART'S JIG
3342	3331H	(I)	WHITE COCKADE, THE
3342	331H1H	(I)	NEAT SHOE, THE
3342	331H3H	(II)	ALLT GHIUSACH
3342	357L2	(I)	LADY CHARLOTTE BRUCE'S (FAVOURITE/STRATHSPEY)
3342	3561H	(II)	MISS FORBES' FAREWELL TO BANFF
3342	3561H	(I)	MISS FORBES' FAREWELL
3342	3621	(I)	MISS WARDLAW'S FAVORITE
3342	31H51H	(I)	ALEXr ARTHUR DUFF ESQr
3342	31H2H6	(II)	DUFF OF MUIRTOWN
3342	4667	(I)	LOYAL KIRKCALDY VOLUNTEERS SLOW & QUICK MARCH, THE
3342	5331H	(I)	MEDLEY OVERTURE (2)
3342	5555	(I)	LADY MARY ANN
3342	5551H	(I)	PINKEY HOUSE [PINKIE HOUSE]
3343	2121	(I)	LADY CHARLOTTE CAMPBELL'S WALTZ
3343	2121	(I)	LADY HOPE'S FAVORITE WALTZ
3343	2217L	(I)	TRIO
3343	2231	(II)	WE WON'T GO HOME TILL MORNING
3343	2231	(I)	MAL BROUKE
334	332	(I)	FOX HUNTERS JIG
3343	3327L	(I)	FEMALE HERO, THE
3343	3321	(I)	MISS TILNEY LONG'S WALTZ
3343	3322	(I)	BRITISH HERO, THE
3343	3322	(I)	SCOTCH HERO'S REEL, THE
3343	1H525L	(I)	SHAM FIGHT, THE
3344	2230	(I)	LABYRINTH
3344	336L1	(II)	TAY BRIG, THE
3344	337L2	(I)	LADY'S FAVOURITE, (THE)
3344	3325L	(I)	MISS LINDSAY STEUART OF STEUART LODGE'S STRATHSPEY
3344	3327bL	(II)	AMULREE [AMBULREE]
3344	3327bL	(I)	CAPT MACKENZIES REEL
3344	3327bL	(I)	AMBELREE [AMBULREE] [AMULREE]
3344	3322	(I)	BUFF AND BLUE
3344	3322	(I)	THERE'S NAE LUCK ABOUT THE HOUSE
3344	331H1H	(I)	MISS BALCETTI'S REEL
3344	5523	(I)	NA'ER A BOTTOM, THE
3344	5544	(I)	JACKSON OVER THE WATER, 1780
3345	427L7L	(I)	LA TROMPE
334	546	(I)	MADAM HYNEL'S MINUET
334	553	(I)	(MR) FAIRVIELLES MINUET
3345	1H4#47L	(II)	PETER LAING
3546	347L2	(I)	MRS McDOWAL GRANT(OF ARNDILLY)
3546	347L2	(I)	BONNY JEAN
3341H	337L7L	(I)	MISS MACKINZIE'S REEL
3350	2240	(I)	ANDANTE
335	111H	(I)	IN WINE THERE IS ALL
3351	2253	(I)	LA NOUVELLE HOLLANDOISE
3351	336L6L	(I)	GANNACHIE BRIDGE
3351	5347bL	(I)	CHA CHEILINN SUGRADH VILEAM
3352	6L6L25L	(I)	IRISH LASSIE, THE
3352	6L6L23	(I)	CUMERNAD HOUSE [CUMBERNAULD HOUSE]

3352	7L222	(I)	BONNY SALLY
3352	7L6L11	(I)	MISS MARY JOHNSTONE HOPE'S BIRTH DAY
335	211	(I)	THA CRODHAIGH MACALLAN
335	211	(I)	ORIGINAL GALLIC AIR, AN
335	212	(I)	WILL YE GO THE BROOM
3352	11H1H1H	(I)	BANKS OF YARROW, THE
3352	35L05L	(I)	LASSIE I LO'E BEST OF A', THE
3352	37L11	(I)	CRITIC, THE
3352	3211	(I)	LE CRITIQUE
3352	3315L	(I)	SARAH WILLIAMSON'S LAMENT
3352	3322	(II)	QUEEN'S DRIVE, THE
3352	3351	(I)	SLEEPY BODY
3352	3552	(I)	FOURTEEN OF OCTOBER, THE
3352	3552	(I)	YE GODS, WAS STREPHON'S PICTURE BLEST
3352	3651	(I)	SLEEPY BODY
3352	5551H	(I)	GENTLE LOVE
3352	1H1H3H2H	(I)	WARS ALARM, THE
335	31L5L	(I)	MISS ISABELLA SCOTT'S SINGLE HORNPIPE
3353	1764	(I)	(HENDRIE'S) HORNPIPE
335	321	(I)	DUSTY MILLER, (THE)
3353	2232	(I)	GARDNER, THE
3353	3315L	(I)	HENRY'S COTTAGE MAID
3353	3322	(I)	SIMON BRODIE
3353	3733	(I)	BALTIOURA
3353	41H53	(II)	JOHN OF PARIS
3353	5764	(I)	DE'IL AMONG THE MANTUA-MAKERS, THE
3353	1H353	(I)	CALLUM FIDHDAIR [CALUM FIGHEADAIR]
335	422	(I)	MISS GARDEN CAMPBELL OF TROUP'S HORNPIPE
3354	2211	(I)	CAPT JIPHSON'S WHIM
3354	2230	(I)	LABYRINTH, THE
3354	2243	(I)	BON TON or NEW YEAR'S GIFT
3354	3351H	(I)	BOHEMIAN WALTZ
3354	6423	(I)	NATH: GOW'S COMPLts TO MR W.K. JENKINS
3355	2244	(I)	FLORINO
3355	3111L	(I)	TRIP TO HANAU, A
3355	3113	(I)	DYSART VOLUNTEER'S MARCH
3355	3211	(I)	SPANISH AIR
335	535	(I)	WHEREFOR CAME YOU HERE ISE WARRANT
3355	3532	(I)	DYSART VOLUNTEERS QUICK STEP
335	531H	(I)	MOMENTS APPROACHING, THE
335	531H	(I)	SIR NORMAN McLEOD'S LAMENT
3355	4244	(I)	STEWART CUMMING
335	543	(I)	MINUET DE LA COUR
3355	4517L	(I)	EARL OF BRADALBANE'S DELIGHT
3355	5433	(I)	QUEEN OF THE MAY, THE
3355	5532	(I)	LA MIGNONETTE
335	556	(II)	HAPPY WE'VE BEEN A' THEGITHER
3355	6421	(I)	ANWICK LODGE [ALNWICK LODGE]
3355	6632	(I)	SUIHEL SHEMES
3355	6632	(I)	LAMENT FOR KING JAMES
3355	6775	(I)	WILLIAM'S GHOST
3355	62H65	(I)	WILLIE ARE YE WAUKIN
3355	1H313H	(I)	LA FRANG
3355	1H57L2	(I)	MISS JOHNSTON OF HILTON'S FANCY
3355	1H522	(I)	PEGGY WITH THE GOWDEN HAIR
3355	1H522	(I)	PETTICOAT, THE
3355	1H1H50	(I)	ANDANTE
3355	1H1H1H3H	(I)	PRINCE EUGENE'S MARCH
3355	1H2H75	(II)	STATEN ISLAND or BURN'S HORNPIPE
3355	1H2H1H7	(I)	ANNA HUME
3355	1H3H75	(I)	STATEN ISLAND HORNPIPE [BURNS HORNPIPE]
335	53H2H	(II)	LOGIE O BUCHAN
335	53H2H	(I)	LOGIE O' BUCHAN
335	53H3H	(I)	LOGIE O' BUCHAN
3356	5555	(I)	AULD ROBIN GRAY
3356	51H1H3	(I)	SPINNING WHEEL, THE
3356	1H765	(I)	BRES OF BIRNAM, THE
3351H	547L2	(II)	FAVORITE DANCE, A
3351H	61H51H	(II)	DRAW THE SWORD [FOR] SCOTLAND
3352H	5322	(II)	BOATIE ROWS, THE
3353H	2H675	(II)	MR ALEXANDER ADAM
3362	35L31	(I)	LADY MAY FROWN, AND BE KIND ENOUGH TOO, A
3362	331H1H	(I)	MISS MARY JARVI'S REEL
3362	6355	(I)	MISS E. ERSKINE
3363	7b7b7bL7bL	(I)	FARTHER BEEIN THE WELLCOMER, THE
3364	7L7L51	(I)	WELLINGTON DANCE, THE
3364	5342	(I)	MR MARSHALL'S REEL
3365	2427L	(II)	AVIMORE [AVIEMORE]
3365	346L6L	(II)	WE'RE A' AE FATHERS BAIRNS
3365	31H66	(I)	EAS NA SMUID
3365	1H542	(I)	MR A. JAFFRAY'S STRATHSPEY
3366	1311	(II)	RED COAT, THE

3366	3311	(I)	BALLNADALLACH
3366	3355	(I)	HUMOURS OF KILDARE, THE
3366	3355	(I)	PITHER IN ENOUGH
3366	5311	(I)	GORDON CASTLE
3366	5311	(I)	BALLENDALLOCH'S REELL
3366	5311	(I)	CAMBDELMORE
3366	5321	(I)	CAMDALE MORE
3366	5532	(I)	AP SHENKIN
3366	6362	(I)	MISS OSWALD
3366	4H2H75	(I)	Lt. RIDDOCH'S QUICK MARCH
3361H	5535L	(I)	QUICK STEP
3361H	61H62	(I)	PETTICOAT TIGHT
3362H	751H3H	(I)	MUSES, THE
3362H	751H5H	(I)	MUSES, THE
337b2	3131H	(I)	RULE A WIFE AND HAVE A WIFE
3374H	361H7	(I)	KNOLE PARK
3374H	361H7	(I)	MISS BOYN
331H	216	(I)	ALASTAIR M'ANSACHD [ALASTAIR M'ANNSACHD]
331H3	27bL24	(I)	MR EDWARD WARDEN'S FAVORITE
331H3	427L2	(II)	FOX CHASE
331H3	447L2	(II)	MRS JOSEPH LOWE'S
331H4	321H3	(I)	DUKE OF QUEENSBURY'S SCOTCH MEASURE, THE
331H4	4542	(I)	MISS CHARLES MURRAY'S REEL
331H5	3342	(II)	LORD RAMSAY
331H5	3342	(II)	BRIG O' TILT, THE [BRIDGE OF TILT]
331H5	4425L	(I)	MISS W. DALRYMPLES FANCY
331H5	4542	(I)	MISS STEWART STENTON'S REEL
331H5	462H6	(II)	WAVERLEY BALL, THE
331H5	6422	(II)	GIBSON'S WHISKY
331H	565	(I)	OVER THE BORDER
331H5	657L2	(I)	LADY BETTY COCHRAN'S REEL
331H5	6542	(II)	MISS STEWART ROBERTSON(OF EDRADYNATE)
331H5	6542	(II)	BONNIE BIRKS OF BALMORAL, THE
331H5	6575	(I)	ARCHd BUTTER, ESQr. OF PITLOCHRIE'S R.
331H5	6622	(I)	LASS OF PETTIE'S MILL, THE
331H5	662H2	(I)	MR Wm CAMPBELL BALMARTIN'S REEL
331H5	67b27bL	(II)	COMELY GARDEN
331H5	67b27bL	(I)	COMELY GARDEN(S)
331H5	6727L	(II)	COMELY GARDEN
331H5	7b447bL	(II)	FORBES' SNEESHIN MULL
331H5	752H2	(II)	MISS MARY CAMPBELL
331H5	2H4H72H	(I)	MR. BRISBANE'S STRATHSPEY
331H5	4H3H72H	(I)	MISS MURE'S REEL
331H6	333H2H	(I)	SIR ARCHd DUNBAR BARt OF NORTHFIELD'S STRATHSPEY
331H6	31H2H2	(I)	MISS (ISABELLA/J.) MURDOCH'S REEL
331H	642	(I)	ROYAL(L) LAMENT, THE
331H6	427L2	(II)	MISS ANN SYMON'S REEL
331H6	432h2	(I)	FONCASTELLE HOUSE
331H6	631H3	(II)	LOCH DUICH
331H7	63H3H7	(I)	THA MI FODH GHRUAIM
331H7	2H753	(II)	MRS FRANCIS WEMYSS
331H1H	337L7L	(I)	KENILWORTH CASTLE
331H1H	3322	(I)	LA TERZA
331H1H	3342	(II)	FORDELL HOUSE
331H1H	3342	(I)	FORDELL HOUSE
331H1H	332H2	(I)	LADY ANN HAMILTON'S REEL
331H1H	532H2	(II)	MRS COLONEL NEYNOE
331H1H	6362	(I)	SCOTCH MILITIA, THE
331H1H	6542	(I)	MISS SHAW STEWART'S STRATHSPEY
331H1H	6542	(I)	MISS BEGBIES REEL
331H1H	6542	(I)	LADY MADELINA SINCLAIR
331H1H	1H3H2H2	(I)	SWALLOW, THE
331H1H	1H3H2H2	(I)	MERRY COBLERS
331H1H	3H1H2H2	(II)	SWALLOW, THE
331H1H	3H1H2H2	(I)	SWALLOW, THE
331H1H	3H1H5H5H	(I)	LIEUt. WHITEFORD BELL'S MARCH
331H2H	1H542	(II)	MRS ROBERTSON OF ALEXANDRIA
331H3H	6522	(I)	MR D. BRIDGES REEL [MR D. BRIDGES JNR'S REEL]
331H5H	4H2H1H6	(II)	LIVERPOOL(HORNPIPE)
331H5H	4H2H1H6	(I)	LIVERPOOL HORNPIPE, THE
332H6	572H1H	(I)	MOON WALTZ
334H7	333H2H	(I)	MISS BROOK'S DANCE
345L1	456L2	(II)	(WM.) MARSHALL'S STYLE
345L1	456L2	(II)	MR MARSHALL
346L5L	5L432	(I)	L'ETE
346L1	3L1L3L5L	(I)	JOHNNY'S GREY BREEKS
346L1	5L121	(I)	BONNIE JEANIE GRAY
347L5L	1L432	(I)	CHARLOTTE AND WERTER
347L5L	1232	(I)	VALLIANT SCOTCHMAN
347L1	347L1	(I)	THREE SISTERS

3411	5L325L	(I)	TELEGRAPH, THE
3411	6L237L	(I)	MRS OSWALD (OF AUCHINCRUIVE'S) FAVOURITE QUICK STEP
3411	345L5L	(I)	MERRY DANCERS, (THE)
3411	3411	(I)	QUICK MARCH EAST YORK MILITIA
3412	3411	(I)	DANCED IN HARLEQUIN HIGHLANDER
3413	4524	(II)	MRS MATHESON
3413	6432	(I)	THO' I AM NOW A VERY LITTLE LAD
3426L	16L15L	(I)	MISS ELLIOT'S FAVOURITE
3427L	5L5L5L1	(I)	KATTY DARLING
3427L	2432	(I)	MR ROBERT FERGUSON OF RAITH'S REEL
3427L	3421	(I)	MR ARTHUR THOMSON'S WALTZ
342	123	(I)	HOSSIER'S GHOST
3421	3421	(I)	MISS CUMIN'S GERMAN WALTZ
3422	1113	(II)	BIT OF HEATHER, A
3422	362H1H	(I)	HIGHLAND AIR
3422	362H1H	(I)	UNTITLED
3423	1131H	(I)	LOGAN BANKS
3423	1211L	(I)	FRISK IT
342	321	(I)	RINN M'EUDAIL MO MHEALLADH
3423	3333	(I)	NO SURE
3423	3421	(I)	MISS CUNNINGHAM'S FANCY
3424	316L7L	(I)	MISS MARGt. BALFOUR'S FANCY
3425	1121	(II)	JESSIE(OF DUNBLANE)
3426	5551	(I)	LASSIE LOST HER SILKEN SNOOD, THE
3426	5651	(I)	TWINE WEEL THE PLAIDEN
342	666	(I)	JOCKIE BLYTH AND GAY
3431	37b27bL	(II)	BLACK WATCH, THE
3431	37b27bL	(II)	FINGAL'S DIRK
3432	6L232	(I)	MISS GRAHAM'S JIGG
3432	3452	(II)	LASSIE OF THE GLEN, THE
3432	5221	(I)	SIXPENCE UNDER MY THUMB, A
3432	5421	(I)	WHEN I'VE GOT SAXPENCE UNDER MY THUMB
3434	37L27L	(I)	MISS WATT'S JIG
3436	5532	(II)	MISS FORBES' FAREWELL TO BANFF
3436	5532	(I)	MISS BUCHAN OF AUCHMACOY'S HIGH DANCE
3436	5532	(I)	MISS (HERRIES) FORBES'S FAREWELL (TO BANFF) [MISS FORBES' FAREWELL]
3431H	647L2	(I)	HODDOM CASTLE
344	515	(I)	LADY GLENCAIRN'S MINUET
3445	327L6L	(II)	MISS CATHRINE CHALMERS
3445	327L6L	(I)	MISS CATHRINE CHALMERS (REEL)
3450	61H65	(I)	LA BISSETTE
3451	117L2	(II)	DOVE COT, THE
3451	217L5L	(II)	SKINNER'S "THE 45"
3451	3420	(I)	OLD UNCLE NED
3451	35#17L	(I)	SALLY ROBINSON'S FAVORITE
3451	5131	(I)	ROSABELL
345	211	(I)	MO GHRADH FODH LEON
3452	1232	(I)	INVERESK HOUSE
3452	5311	(I)	DRINK TO ME ONLY
3452	5543	(I)	GAVOT
3453	6L5L32	(I)	CAPT McDONALD'S REEL
3453	6L5L32	(I)	LADY AGNES PERCY'S REEL
3453	6L17L5L	(I)	MRS MUIR (OF WARRISTON'S) REEL
3453	151H1H	(I)	VOWS OF ENDLESS LOVE, THE
3453	2121	(I)	MARRIAGE MORN, THE
3453	2432	(I)	FLOWERS OF THE FOREST, THE
3453	3110	(I)	SIMPLICITY
3453	351H1H	(II)	HAGGIS, THE
3453	427L5L	(I)	RED FLAG, THE
3453	4430	(I)	HOME, SWEET HOME
3453	4433	(I)	HOME, SWEET HOME
3453	47b27bL	(I)	MR CAMPBELL OF GLENLYON'S REEL
3453	1H751	(II)	HERR ROLOFF'S FAREWELL
3454	7L415	(I)	MISS ANN AMELIA STUARTS ALLAMAND
3455	3211	(II)	DERNCLEUCH
3455	3444	(II)	BARONY O' BRACKLEY, THE
3455	3450	(I)	MISS HAGGART'S ALLAMANDE
3455	4362	(II)	GRAND OLD McINTYRE
345	551H	(I)	BESS BELL
3455	61H65	(I)	LES PLASCER'E DE METZ
3455	61H65	(I)	CHARLOTE COTTILION, THE
3455	64H2H2H	(I)	MOSCOW
3455	1H1H42	(I)	L'ORDNANCE
3455	1H1H53	(I)	ORDINANCE, THE
3456	3147bL	(II)	QUEEN'S WELCOME TO INVERCAULD, THE
3456	3213	(II)	HYND'S WEE CABIN
3456	3562	(I)	MISS McREADY OF PERSTON'S FAVOURITE
3456	357b4	(II)	LONDON SCOTTISH, THE
3456	71H1H2	(I)	SIR JOHN SINCLAIR OF STEVINGSTOUN
3456	1H754	(I)	PARSON OF BRENTFORD, THE

3457	5127L	(II)	SIR ALEXANDER ANDERSON OF BLELACK
3451H	1232	(I)	TASTE LIFE'S GLAD MOMENTS
3451H	1232	(I)	LIFE LET US CHERISH
3451H	3452	(II)	OFF SHE GOES
3451H	3452	(I)	OFF SHE GOES
3451H	5135L	(I)	MRS SPICER'S FANCY
3451H	5432	(I)	MISS MASTERTON'S GIGG
3451H	3H1H76	(II)	SPRING SONG
3453H	42H31H	(I)	JENNY LIND POLKA
3461	7L135L	(I)	ABROAD AND AT HOME
3467	5222	(I)	MAID OF ELGIN, THE
341H7L	3463H	(II)	BLACKSMITH O' BOTRIPHNIE, THE
341H3	4542	(I)	HARE IN THE CORN, THE
342H1H	342H7	(I)	MRS HAMILTON OF PENTCAITLAND
34#5	722	(II)	ADNIL'S MAZURKA
356L6L	5L57L2	(I)	CONTRIVANCE, THE
356L6L	5L67L2	(I)	CONTRIVANCE, THE
357L1	6L5L4L2L	(I)	DOUBLE JIG
357L1	6L5L7L2	(II)	THEODORE NAPIER
357L2	3522	(I)	MISS WILLIAMSON'S REEL
357L2	437L6L	(I)	MISS CUNNINGHAM OF LAINSHAW'S FAVOURITE
3515L	6L7L12	(I)	MISS OLIPHANT'S REEL
3516L	5L144	(II)	MISS DALE
3516L	61H53	(I)	MO RUN AN DIUGH MAR AN DE THU
3517L	2431	(I)	LADY NORTH'S FANCY
3511	27L53	(I)	GEORDIE AFFLICK
3511	27L53	(I)	MISS MAXWELL GORDON'S REEL
3511	2543	(I)	CRONA'S VALE
3511	4327L	(I)	LA BELLE ALLIANCE
3511	4622H	(I)	YOU'RE WELCOME HOME
3511	62H65	(I)	MISS BRODIE'S FANCY, THE
3512	3432	(I)	(NEW) GERMAN SPA (DANCE), THE
3513	6L15L1	(I)	MR HOGERT'S HORNPIPE
3513	6L27L5L	(I)	CAPTAIN PRYCE GORDON or
			GLEN LOCKARTS STRATHSPEY
351	355	(I)	ROB(IN) SHEAR'D IN HER'ST
3513	1H2H55	(I)	MARCH, A
3515	353H5	(I)	EVENING STAR, THE
351	1H51	(I)	HO RO MO BHOBAN AN' DRAM
3511H	72H53H	(II)	KIRK'S HORNPIPE
3525L	351H1H	(I)	MISS SCOTT'S FAVORITE
3526L	13L3L5L	(I)	NACH BOCHD A BHI'M FALACH
3527bL	3565	(II)	MISS DUNDAS OF ARNISTON
3527bL	3565	(I)	MISS DUNDAS(S) OF ARNISTON('S REEL)
3527L	1232	(I)	GIGG
3527L	3551	(I)	BRIGHTON WALTZ, THE
3521	3562	(I)	HAPPY NIGHT, THE
3521	4521	(I)	MISS FORD'S FANCY
3521	467L2	(II)	MARY SCOTT
3522	3533	(I)	CAMPBELLS ARE COMING (O HO), (THE)
3522	3536	(I)	TULLOCH GORUM
3522	3531H	(I)	LOUDOUN CASTLE
3522	3553	(I)	CAMPBELLS ARE COMING, THE
3523	3521	(I)	FRISKY, THE
3523	1H527L	(I)	CLERKENWELL ASSEMBLY
3524	1232	(I)	PAS DI TROIS
3524	3551H	(II)	'CHAILLEACH MHUSGACH [DRUNKEN WIFE]
3524	3551H	(I)	DRUNKEN WIFE, THE
3524	627L5L	(I)	ALLEMAND
3525	1443	(I)	AIR
352	666	(I)	JOCKIE BLYTH AND GAY
3536L	25L36L	(I)	LIDDEL BOWER, THE
3530	2420	(I)	WHA'LL HAE MY DAINTY WHITE PUDDINGS
3531	7L27L5L	(II)	CARDOWNIE
3531	1316L	(I)	BALLEST HEAVERS, THE
3531	1321	(I)	GIVE ME LOVE AND LIBERTY
3531	1332	(I)	JEW, THE
3531	2427bL	(II)	JOHNNIE('S) MADE A WEDDING O'T
3531	2427bL	(I)	JOHNNY'S MADE A WADDING O'T
3531	2422	(I)	MRS CAMPBELL OF BALINABY'S REEL
3531	47bL7b7bL	(I)	BURNSIDE OF TYNET
3531	427L5L	(II)	MRS DOUGLAS MONCRIEFF
3531	427L5L	(I)	MISS DOUGLASS MONCRIEF'S REEL
3531	4326L	(I)	MRS J. GRANTS STRATHSPEY
3531	4642	(II)	JEANIE'S DOLL IS DRESSED AGAIN
3532	1121	(I)	UNTITLED
353	211H	(I)	KINFAUN'S HOUSE
3532	237L2	(I)	MISS MARY DOUGLASS('S REEL)
3532	3132	(I)	CUCKOO, THE
3532	3553	(I)	CAMPBELLS ARE COMING, THE
3533	3522	(II)	CAMPBELLS ARE COMIN(G), THE
3533	3522	(I)	CAMPBELLS ARE COMING, THE

3534	427L5L	(I)	FOLEY HOUSE
3535	7L27L2	(I)	FOLLY AS IT FLIES
3535	227L2	(I)	MISS ONSLOW'S REEL
3535	2427bL	(I)	(IF I HAD/HE THAT HAS) A BONNIE LASSIE
			(LITTLE SLEEP WOU'D SAIR ME)
3535	2427bL	(I)	NORTH LOCH, THE
3535	357L2	(I)	SIR Ja: GRANT'S STRATHSPEY*
3535	3524	(II)	LADY NELLIE WEMYSS
			[LADY NELLY WEMYSS('S JIG)]
3535	3524	(I)	JACK HOLME'S REEL
3535	3524	(I)	LADY NELLY WEMYSS('S (JIG/REEL)
3535	3547L	(I)	MISS MUNRO DINGWALL'S REEL
3535	357b7bL	(II)	BELTED PLAID AND HEALTH TO WEAR IT, THE
3535	357b7bL	(I)	AM BREACDHAN UR GU MEAL U E
			[AM BREACAN UR GUM MEAL THU E]
3535	351H6	(I)	CRO NAN GOBHAR
3535	351H1H	(II)	STRONG MAN O' DRUM, THE
3535	31H35	(II)	BUCK O' THE CABRACH, THE
3535	31H42	(II)	LADY JEMIMA JOHNSTON
3535	31H42	(I)	LADY JEMIMA JOHNSTON'S STRATHSPEY
3535	31H75	(I)	MR GEO. THOMSON JUNr'S HORNPIPE
3535	427L5L	(I)	FOLEY HOUSE
3535	4646	(I)	MISS JOHNSTON (OF HILTON'S) REEL
3535	467b5	(I)	WRIGHT'S RANT, THE
3535	47b1H6	(I)	WRIGHT'S RANT, (THE)
3535	6424	(I)	SICH A GETTIN' UP STAIRS
3535	6442	(II)	MRS MACLEOD OF GESTO
3535	6442	(I)	MRS McLEOD OF GEASTOW'S STRATHSPEY
3535	62H32	(I)	BY JOVE I'LL BE FREE
3535	64H75	(I)	WELLINGTON AND VICTORY
3535	7b47b2	(I)	NORTH HIGHLAND 18
3535	1H325L	(I)	PEEP AT THE JUBELEE, A
3535	1H543	(I)	EPPING CHACE
3536	3542	(I)	GORDON CASTLE
3537	1H537	(I)	MRS ANDREW'S STRATHSPEY
3531H	227b4	(I)	MR JOHN DYKES REEL
3531H	357L2H	(I)	BOTHWELL CASTLE
3531H	3514	(I)	MISS PROUD'S REEL
3531H	3524	(I)	MISS PROUD'S REEL
3531H	3524	(I)	FILE-BEK IS AY READY, THE
3531H	3542	(II)	COLBECK HOUSE
3531H	3542	(II)	MR CAMPBELL CRAIGNISH
3531H	3542	(I)	MR CAMPBELL YOUNGER OF CRAIGNISH'S REEL
3531H	3542	(I)	COLBECK HOUSE
3531H	357b2	(II)	A' CHRIDHEALACHD [MERRY MAKING, THE]
3531H	357b2	(I)	A CHRIODHALACHD [A' CHRIDHEALACHD]
3531H	5524	(II)	MISS PROUD
3531H	5524	(I)	MISS PROUD('S REEL)
3546L	5L5L2L2L	(II)	BRAES OF LETTERFOURIE, THE
3542	7L237L	(I)	MISS DINWIDDIE'S REEL
3542	1327L	(II)	SLUMBERING MINSTREL, THE
3542	36L7L5L	(I)	LORD FIFE'S WELCOME TO ELGIN
3542	331H1H	(II)	MAIRI BHOIDHEACH
3542	3455	(I)	MR GEORGE GRANT'S STRATHSPEY
3542	3531	(I)	PORT A BHODICH
3542	3535	(II)	TULLOCHGORUM [CORN BUNTING, THE]
3542	3535	(I)	TULLOCH GORUM [CORN BUNTING, THE]
3542	3531H	(II)	BRIG O' DEE, THE
3542	3542	(I)	DOUBLE ENTENDRE
3542	3565	(I)	LADY L. RAMSAY'S REEL
3542	3561H	(II)	MISS FORBES' FAREWELL TO BANFF
3542	3561H	(I)	MISS FORBES'S FAREWELL TO BANFF
3542	3561H	(I)	TULLOCH GORUM
3542	351H5	(I)	CAPT FLETCHER'S REEL
3542	351H5	(I)	PLOUGHMAN (JOLLY), THE
			[JOLLY PLOUGHMAN, THE]
3542	4531H	(II)	BRIG O' DEE, THE [BRIDGE OF DEE]
3542	56L7L1	(I)	DANCE IN QUEEN MAB
3543	1213	(I)	ALEXANDER, THE
3543	2427bL	(I)	MR A. MACWHINNIE'S REEL
3543	1H553	(I)	CUPID IN IRELAND
3543	3H1H22	(II)	COLONEL FORBES C.B.
3544	3535	(I)	TULLOCH GORUM
3545	2527L	(II)	MAIDEN BY THE SILVER DEE
3545	3112	(I)	MR JOHN TROTTER OF CASTLELAW'S HORNPIPE
3545	4312	(I)	LA CARMAGNOLE
3545	62H75	(II)	MISS GRIEVE OF HOWDAN
3545	62H4H7	(II)	MARCHIONESS OF HUNTLY, THE
3546	221H6	(I)	DAVID STEWART IRVINE ESQr's REEL
3546	3122	(II)	ROSE AMONG THE HEATHER, THE
3546	337L2	(II)	MRS MACDOUGAL GRANT [MRS. MACDOUALL GRANT]
3546	337L2	(I)	TRIP TO INCHCOMB, A

3546	337L2	(I)	MISS HUNTER (OF BURNSIDE) 'S STRATHSPEY
3546	337L2	(I)	MRS MACDOUALL GRANT ('S STRATHSPEY)
			[MRS MACDOUGAL GRANT]
3546	347L2	(II)	MRS MACDOWAL GRANT
3546	3521	(I)	BOATY ROW'S WELL, THE
3546	3547L	(I)	WILD GOOSE, THE
3546	3542	(II)	PERTH ASSEMBLY
3546	3542	(I)	BUTTER'D PEASE
3546	3542	(I)	ROYAL CIRCUS
3546	3551H	(II)	MRS DUNDAS MCQUEEN
3546	3551H	(I)	DEIL'S DEAD, THE
3546	3551H	(I)	MRS DUNDAS McQUEEN('S REEL)
3546	3561H	(I)	INVERNESS NORTHERN MEETING
3546	3642	(I)	METHVEN CASTLE
3546	5122	(II)	HOUSE OF PARK, THE
3546	5122	(I)	HOUSE OF PARK, THE
3546	5322	(I)	BOATIE ROWS, THE (THIRD SETT)
3546	5342	(II)	PERTH ASSEMBLY, THE
3546	547L2	(I)	MISS DONALDSON'S STRATHSPEY
3546	557L2	(I)	MISS GORDON OF BRAID
3546	51H22	(I)	LORD TORPHICHEN'S STRATHSPEY
3546	51H32	(I)	LORD TORPHICHEN'S FAVORITE
3546	52H1H1H	(I)	DURIE HOUSE
3546	72H1H3H	(I)	EIGHTH OF DECEMBER, THE
3546	72H1H3H	(I)	HONble MISS H. ELLIOT'S REEL
3546	75H3H1H	(II)	LADY CHARLOTTE CAMPBELL
3546	75H3H1H	(I)	LADY CHARLOTTE CAMPBELL'S STRATHSPEY
3547b	3511H	(I)	DRUNKEN WIFIE, THE
3541H	357L2	(I)	SIR DAVID HUNTER OF BLAIR'S NEW REEL
3541H	5541H	(I)	DUKE OF WELLINGTON'S NEW WALTZ
3542H	751H5H	(II)	QUEEN'S COMMISSIONER, THE
3550	61H6O	(I)	AULD ROBIN GRAY
3551	27L11	(I)	LADY BRUCE OF SCOTSTON
3551	3222	(I)	OH! SUSANNAH
3551	3535	(II)	TWA TRAMPS, THE
3551	3552	(II)	ATHOLE LADS
3551	4322	(II)	SEAN RONG MOR
3551	5152	(I)	NEW MARRIED WIFE, THE
3551	5166	(I)	MISS MILLAR'S STRATHSPEY
3551	5451	(I)	FORTRESS, THE
3551	1H33H5	(I)	ORECK'S SCOTCH-MEASURE
3552	3551	(I)	(MERRY) PLOWMAN, THE
3552	3553	(I)	CUDDY CLAW'D HER
3552	6661H	(II)	WIND THAT SHAKES THE BARLEY, THE
3553	2442	(I)	HAWICK, A STRATHSPEY
3553	3532H	(I)	NORTH OF THE GRAMPIANS
3553	3542	(II)	CUTTYMAN AND TRELADLE
			[CUTTYMUN AND TREELADLE]
3553	3551H	(II)	CAMERONIAN, THE
3553	351H1H	(II)	HAGGIS, THE
3553	351H1H	(II)	TAIGEIS AGUS DEALG INNTE [HAGGIS, THE]
3553	351H1H	(I)	TAIGEIS AGUS DEALG INNT' [HAGGIS, THE]
3553	351H2H	(II)	NORTH OF THE GRAMPIANS(, THE)
			[NORTH SIDE OF THE GRAMPIANS, THE]
3553	351H2H	(I)	TAOBH' TUADH NAN GARBH BHEANN
3553	351H2H	(I)	NORTH OF THE GRAMPIANS
3553	352H1H	(I)	SILVER MINERS WALTZ, THE
3553	352H1H	(I)	MRS LESTER
3553	352H1H	(I)	BRUNSWICK WALTZ, THE
3553	5362	(I)	MISS DUNBAR'S STRATHSPEY
355	357b	(I)	GUZZLE TOGETHER
355	357	(I)	SOUTERS OF SELKIRK, THE
355	351H	(I)	NEW IRISH JIG, THE
355	351H	(I)	COMMA LEAM FEIN A MINISTEIR
355	351H	(I)	BLEWITT'S JIG
3553	51H3H1H	(II)	MISS JOHNSTON
3553	51H3H1H	(II)	MISS JOHNSTONE
3553	51H3H1H	(I)	MISS JOHNSTON(E)
			(OF HOUGHTON HALL) ('S REEL)
3553	51H3H2H	(II)	GUN BHRIS MO CHRIDH' ON DH'FHALBH THU
			[MY HEART IS BROKE SINCE THY DEPARTURE)
3553	51H3H2H	(I)	GUN BHRIS MO CHRI O'N DH('FH)ALBH THU
3554	1322	(I)	BEVIS MOUNT
3554	4322	(I)	PERTHSHIRE DANCING MEASURES & C No. 3
3554	4665	(I)	BUTTER'D PEASE
3554	47b47b	(I)	WAS YE AT THE BRIDAL
355	467	(II)	ANDREW CARR
355	467	(I)	ANDREW CARR
355	467	(I)	PARKS OF YESTER, THE
3555	236L6L	(I)	MISS Z. LOUGHNAN ('S STRATHSPEY)
3555	3521	(I)	NARRATOR, THE
3555	3555	(I)	JAMES HADDEN, ESQr's HORNPIPE

3555	3551H	(I)	EARL OF LEVEN'S FAVORITE, THE
3555	3566	(I)	NORTH HIGHLAND 23
3555	3566	(I)	SEAL-FISHER'S SONG, THE
3555	3566	(I)	MAOL DONAIDH
3555	3572	(I)	SHEPHERD, THE
3555	351H1H	(II)	LADY HELEN WEDDERBURN
3555	351H1H	(I)	LADY HELEN WEDDERBURN'S REEL
3555	353H1H	(I)	MISS GORDON'S STRATHSPEY
3555	31H52	(II)	LORD RAMSAY
3555	31H52	(I)	LORD RAMSAY('S STRATHSPEY)
3555	31H2H2	(I)	MISS KNOX'S FANCY
3555	31H3H6	(I)	MO LEANNAN FALAICH
3555	4362	(I)	MISS OMMANNY'S REEL
3555	4362	(I)	MULLONIE'S JIG
3555	4646	(I)	LADY PORTMORE'S FANCY
3555	4666	(I)	TARGET, THE
3555	5322	(I)	GARLAND, THE
3555	5555	(I)	BLACK EAGLE, THE
3555	5564	(I)	DANCED BY MASTER McEWEN AND MASTER DUNCAN
355	556	(I)	BRAES OF BALANDINE, THE
355	551H	(I)	SCOTS LAMENT
3555	6124	(I)	SICILIAN WALTZ
3555	6362	(I)	NEWBYTH HOUSE
3555	6525L	(II)	COL H. F. CAMPBELL
3555	6562	(I)	MOLONIE'S GIG
3555	6633	(I)	PEGGY I MOST LOVE THEE
3555	6665	(I)	A WAYS MY HEART THAT WE MUN SUNDER
3555	666H6H	(I)	SWEET'S THE LASS THE LOE'S ME
3555	61H55	(I)	AULD ROBIN GRAY
3555	61H60	(I)	AULD ROBIN GRAY, (NEW SET OF)
3555	61H66	(I)	CHARLOTTE, THE
3555	1H555	(I)	BLACK EGLE, THE
3555	1H1H75	(I)	A FAVOURITE COTILLON
3555	1H3H1H5	(I)	REGISTER OFFICE, THE
3555	1H3H1H6	(I)	ABBOT'S STRATHSPEY, THE
3555	1H3H1H6	(I)	FORNETH HOUSE
3555	1H3H2H2H	(I)	GLENBUCKET'S BREEKS
3555	4H2H70	(I)	LOVE SLIP, THE
3556	317L2	(I)	MRS MACDOWALL GRANT'S NEW STRATHSPEY
3556	3552	(I)	CATCH HER IF YOU CAN
355	656	(I)	SLOW
355	656	(I)	BRAES OF BALLANDINE
3556	1H133	(I)	WILLY'S THE LAD FOR ME
3556	1H1H1H5	(I)	WILLIE WAS A WANTON WAG
3551H	2326L	(II)	MAR CASTLE
3551H	3551H	(I)	KILLWORTH VOLUNTEERS' QUICK MARCH, THE
3551H	351H2H	(II)	NORTH OF THE GRAMPIANS
3551H	526L2	(I)	DUNIRA LODGE
3551H	53H2H2	(I)	MR McINTOSH OF McINTOSH'S STRATHSPEY
3551H	6531H	(I)	BONNY MARY
3551H	6753	(II)	TAILOR TARTAN
355	1H1H5	(I)	SCOTS JENNY
3551H	1H651	(I)	LORD McLEOD'S STRATHSPEY
3551H	1H3H2H2	(II)	MACLACHLAN'S REEL
3551H	1H3H2H2	(I)	MACLACHLAN'S (STRATHSPEY/REELL)
3551H	1H3H2H2	(I)	CRONSTOUNE
3551H	2H2H66	(II)	BLAIRNANE'S RANT
3551H	3H1H3H1H	(I)	MISS JOHNSTON
3551H	3H3H2H1H	(I)	WHAT WILL I DO GIN MY HOGGIE DIE
3551H	3H3H2H1H	(I)	COCKS LOUNS WALIE HOYN
3551H	3H3H2H1H	(I)	MOSS PLATE
3551H	3H3H2H1H	(I)	NEW WAY OF WOOING
3551H	3H3H2H1H	(I)	BOATIE ROWS, THE
3551H	3H4H66	(II)	MRS GREGORY
3551H	3H4H66	(I)	MRS GREGORY'S STRATHSPEY
3552H	5230	(I)	BOATIE ROWS, THE
3552H	5330	(I)	BOATTIE ROWS, THE
3552H	5332	(I)	WEEL MAY THE BOATIE ROW
355	2H2H2H	(I)	WALY WALY
3560	61H60	(I)	AULD ROBIN GRAY
356	17L7L	(I)	O SWEET IS THE FEELING
3562	351H3	(II)	TRIP TO SKYE
3562	351H3	(I)	TRIP TO SKYE, A
3562	3H5H77	(I)	MISS DUFF'S STRATHSPEY
3563	6L5L6L5L	(II)	LUNDIN LINKS
3563	7L233	(II)	LARGO BAY
3563	4342	(I)	HARE IN THE CORN, THE
356	351H	(I)	PARKS OF YESTER, THE
3564	27L5L3L	(I)	UP THE TOWN IN HASTE
3564	3127bL	(II)	BRIOGAN SEAMBO
3564	3127bL	(I)	SHAMBOE BREECHES
3564	3127bL	(I)	BERNARD'S WELL

3564	3127bL	(I)	LORD ADAM GORDON'S REEL
3564	3127L	(I)	SHAMBO BREECKS
3564	351H3H	(I)	BESSY BELL (AND MARY GRAY)
3564	351H4H	(I)	BESSY BELL AND MARY GRAY
3564	353H4H	(I)	BESSIE BELL (AND MARY GRAY)
3564	462H6	(I)	WAS YOU AT THE WEDDING
3564	527L2	(II)	DUNIQUAICH
3564	5342	(II)	PEGGIE'S DUMPLING
3564	532H2	(II)	WESTER ELCHIES
3564	532H2	(II)	HILL O' NIGG, THE
3564	54H72H	(I)	EARL OF MORAY'S REEL, THE
3564	6327bL	(II)	ALLT A' GHOBHAINN [SMITH'S BURN, THE]
3564	1H542	(I)	BODACHAN A GARIE
3564#	34#1H4	(II)	CARNIE'S CANTER
3565	4L217bL	(I)	CAPTAIN MOUNSEY'S STRATHSPEY
3565	11H2H2	(II)	ROAD TO BERWICK, THE
3565	11H2H2	(II)	BUCK OF THE CABRACH, THE
3565	11H2H2	(I)	ROAD TO BERWICK, THE
3565	11H2H2	(I)	BUCK OF THE CABRACH, THE
3565	25L35	(I)	KING'S JIG, THE
3565	27bL27bL	(I)	CAPT MACKENZIE'S REEL
3565	227b2	(II)	OSSIAN'S HALL
3565	227b2	(II)	MUR OSSIAN (OSSIAN'S HALL)
3565	227b2	(I)	OSSIAN'S HALL
3565	2427bL	(II)	MR MENZIES OF CULDARE(S)
3565	2427bL	(II)	BRAES OF GLENDOCHERT [GLENDOCHART]
3565	2427bL	(I)	MR(S) (STEWART) MENZIES OF CULDARE ('S REEL)
3565	2427bL	(I)	BRAES OF GLENDOCHERT, (THE)
3565	2427L	(I)	BRAES OF GLENDOCHERT'S REEL, THE
3565	22H75	(I)	MARIA'S FROLIC
3565	3125L	(I)	H R H THE PRINCESS CHARLOTTE'S FAVORITE
3565	311H1H	(II)	EDRADYNATE HOUSE
3565	332H2	(II)	MRS GREIG'S REEL
3565	357bL4	(I)	DRUMMORE'S RANT
3565	357L2	(II)	MRS MCPHERSON OF CLUNY
3565	3524	(II)	DRUMMOND'S RANT
3565	3535	(II)	CLYDESDALE LASSES [CLYDE SIDE LASSES]
3565	3535	(I)	CLYDESDALE LASSES, THE
3565	3542	(II)	MISS FORBES
3565	3542	(II)	IN THE GLOAMIN'
3565	3542	(II)	MISS KINLOCH OF GILMERTON
3565	3542	(II)	SEAN CHAISTEAL GHART
3565	3542	(I)	MISS FORBES'S REEL [LADY FORBES'S REEL]
3565	3542	(I)	MISS KINLOCH OF GILMERTON('S REEL)
3565	3542	(I)	MISS MATILDA LOCKHART'S REEL
3565	3542	(I)	MISS FORBES
3565	3552	(II)	MOAN OF THE SEA, THE
3565	3562	(II)	RANNOCH LODGE
3565	3562	(II)	PIPER KING, THE
3565	3565	(II)	LALLA SINCE THE QUEEN'S COME or ELGIN
3565	3565	(I)	BIG BOW-WOW
3565	3566	(I)	CUIRIBH SREANG AIR NA BODAICH
3565	3567	(I)	DEAR DUBLIN
3565	3567	(I)	TRIP TO DUBLIN
3565	357b4	(I)	WEE BOBBIT BLANCH OF MIDDLEBIE
3565	351H5	(II)	MEARNS
3565	351H5	(I)	HADDINGTON ASSEMBLY
3565	352H2	(II)	CARMICHAEL'S FANCY
3565	352H2H	(II)	HOUSE OF BELLABEG, THE
3565	353H2H	(I)	LADY MARY DOUGLAS'S FAVORITE
3565	353H2H	(I)	NEWCASTLE VOLUNTEERS QUICK STEP
3565	354H2H	(II)	MRS GREIG'S STRATHSPEY
3565	3642	(I)	CORNHILL DANCE
356	531H	(I)	SOUTERS OF SELKIRK, THE
356	542	(I)	JOCKY AND JENNY
3565	437L2	(I)	MISS AMELIA MENZIES' REEL
3565	4303	(I)	MAN IN, THE
3565	4322	(I)	DUCHESS OF MANCHESTER'S STRATHSPEY, THE
3565	4322	(I)	HONble MISS KENNAIRD'S REEL, THE
3565	4522	(I)	MRS HAMILTON OF PITCAITHLAND
3565	6251	(I)	MINERS OF WICKLOW, THE
3565	6542	(I)	MISS CHARLES HAMILTON SCOTTS JIGG
3565	6562	(II)	TAYMOUTH CASTLE
3565	6562	(I)	TAYMOUTH HOUSE [TAYMOUTH CASTLE]
3565	6562	(I)	MISS HOPGOODS REEL, THE
3565	61H6O	(I)	NEW SETT OF AULD ROBIN GRAY
3565	61H6O	(I)	AULD ROBIN GRAY
3565	1H342	(II)	MERRY LADS OF FOSS, THE
3565	1H542	(II)	LADS OF FOSS, THE
3565	1H542	(I)	MERRY LADS OF FOSS, THE
3565	1H631	(I)	QUICK STEP, 21st REGt

3565	1H642	(I)	MISS MARGARET GRAHAM
			(OF GARTMORE) 'S STRATHSPEY
3565	1H2H1H1	(I)	NEOPOLITAN THRESHERS
3565	1H3H1H6	(II)	MRS CRAWFORD
3565	1H3H1H6	(I)	MRS CRAWFORD('S) (FAVORITE STRATHSPEY)
			[FORNEATH HOUSE]
3565	1H3H1H7	(!)	CHERRY RIPE
3565	1H3H1H1H	(I)	COTTAGE, THE
3565	2H3H66	(II)	CLUNY WATER
3565	3H562	(II)	DR. MAITLAND MOIR
356	66L1	(I)	BODHAN AN EASSAIN [BOTHAN AN EASAN]
3566	3532	(I)	MRS HAMILTON OF PENCAITLANDS STRATHSPEY
3566	5322H	(I)	MISS PEMBERTON'S REEL
3566	5342	(I)	MISS SWANSON'S STRATHSPEY
3566	5342	(I)	MISS CLEMENTINA IRVINE'S STRATHSPEY
3566	51H3H5H	(I)	LASS(IE) GIN YE LO'E ME (TELL ME NOW)
3566	637L7L	(I)	KEPPEL'S DELIGHT
3566	6663	(I)	CUMHADH DUBH SHOMHAIRLE
356	71H2	(I)	WAY TO GET MARRIED, THE
3561H	351H2H	(I)	GORDON CASTLE
3561H	351H2H	(I)	A. MARSHALL'S REEL
3561H	5222	(I)	'TWAS AT THE SHINING MID-DAY HOUR
3561H	5222	(I)	MAID IN THE MILL, THE
3561H	5310	(I)	WELL-A-DAY, LACK-A-DAY
3561H	5542	(I)	YOUNG CHORISTER, THE
3561H	51H62	(II)	BRIG O' ABOYNE
3561H	72H1H1H	(II)	DOUGAL MORE
356	1H1H1H	(I)	YELLOW HAIR'D LADDIE, THE
356	1H1H3H	(I)	MEDLEY OVERTURE (10)
356	1H1H3H	(I)	YELLOW-HAIR'D LADDIE, (THE)
3561H	1H3H2H2H	(I)	CAPT GRANTS STRATHSPEY
3561H	2H3H5H5H	(I)	ARDKINLASS'S DELIGHT
3561H	2H3H5H5H	(I)	SCOTS MEASURE
3561H	3H3H2H5	(I)	BRAES OF GLENTURROTE, THE
3562H	75H4H3H	(I)	ELOUIS, THE
357b2	353H1H	(I)	MY WIFE SHE DANG ME
357b	640	(I)	LEADER HAUGHS AND YARROW
357b	644	(I)	LEADER HAUGHS AND YARROW
3575	7L232	(II)	MABEL BRIGGS
3576	5H5H2H2H	(I)	MISS CAMPBELL'S STRATHSPEY
3577	6543	(II)	FLINT AND FLEERISH, THE
3561H	3542	(I)	MISS ANNIE WATSON'S REEL
3572H	3H72H5	(I)	MISS ANN CARNEGIE OF SOUTHESK'S REEL
3572H	5H3H72H	(I)	WHAT YOU PLEASE
351HO	3H1H2H2H	(I)	NOBODY COMING TO MARRY ME
351H1	647L5L	(I)	AIR
351H2	351H1H	(I)	KININVIE HOUSE
351H2	351H3H	(I)	MR ROBERTSON OF LADYKIRK ('S STR.)
351H2	351H3H	(I)	MRS ALLAN OF ERROL'S FAREWELL TO LONDON
351H2	351H3H	(I)	SALISBURY CRAIGS
351H3	6L27L5	(II)	WILLIE COOK
351H3	3542	(II)	HARE AMONG THE CORN, THE
351H3	351H1H	(II)	DUNSE DINGS A'
351H3	351H1H	(I)	DUNSE DINGS A'
351H3	351H1H	(I)	MR SHARP'S FAVOURITE (DUNSE DINGS A')
351H3	4562	(I)	MR MAITLAND OF FREUGH REEL
351H3	42H4H2H	(I)	SIR JOHN MAXWELL'S REEL
351H	356	(I)	IRISH POT STICK, THE
351H3	5635	(I)	SHOELA NA GIGG
351H3	561H1H	(I)	SHEELA NA GIGG
351H	351H	(I)	SUTTERS OF SELKIRK
351H4	2416L	(I)	CHATSWORTH, THE
351H4	3524	(II)	JOHN BROWN or FAITHFUL FRIEND
351H4	5322	(II)	SCOTLAND YET
351H5	5L32H2	(I)	MRS RIDDELL'S REEL
351H5	2662	(II)	JENNY BOWSER
351H5	3542	(II)	AN GEARRAN
351H5	3542	(II)	EARL OF MARCH
351H5	3542	(II)	MRS DAVID GLEN
351H5	3542	(I)	LORD DOUNE'S REEL
351H5	352H2	(I)	LASSIE AN' SILLER AN' A'S MY AIN
351H5	352H2	(I)	MISS BOGLE (OF GLASGOW'S) FAVORITE
351H5	352H2	(I)	SAW YE A LASSIE OF FIFTEEN YEARS
351H5	4325L	(I)	FOUR QUAKERS
351H5	432H2	(I)	MR A. PURSE'S REEL
351H5	4522	(II)	COULL O' NEWE
351H5	4642	(I)	WOOD NUNRICH FAIR
351H5	461H1H	(I)	SPANISH PATRIOTS, THE
351H5	462H6	(II)	CHARMING MRS. DAVIDSON
351H5	5142	(I)	FONAB HOUSE
351H5	527L6L	(I)	VOCAL SHELL, THE
351H5	5431H	(I)	DOUBLE DEFEAT, THE

```
351H5      631H5        ( I )   GREIG'S STRATHSPEY
351H5      6547L        ( I )   MISS GARDINER'S JIG
351H5      6552         ( I )   BRITISH TARRS, THE
351H5      6562         ( I )   MISS HIPPISLEY'S REEL
351H5      671H1H       ( I )   LA JULIE
351H5      7b424        ( I )   ANDERSON'S FAVORITE
351H5      1H522        ( I )   MISS CHARLOTTE STIRLING'S REEL
351H5      1H61H5       ( II )  GREIG'S STRATHSPEY
351H5      1H61H5       ( I )   GREIG'S STRATHSPEY
351H5      2H53H5       ( I )   THREE TIMES THREE
351H4      2H4H75       ( I )   NEW ALLEMAND, THE
351H5      3H2H4H5H     ( I )   MARIANNE OF WALTHAMSTOW
351H6      2451         ( I )   MR WATSON CARNEGIE OF LOWER AND TURN
351H6      3120         ( I )   O MERRY ROW THE BONNIE BARK
351H6      357b2        ( I )   O IF JOCKEY WOU'D BUT STEAL ME
351H6      353H1H       ( I )   PAS SEUL MISS ELIZA INNES
351H6      353H1H       ( I )   LOGIE O' BUCHAN
351H6      353H1H       ( I )   O LOGIE O' BUCHAN
351H       642          ( I )   JOCKEY AND JENNY
351H6      537L7L       ( I )   MISS GENERAL BROWNRIGG'S REEL
351H6      537L7L       ( I )   CAPTURE OF SERINGAPATAM, THE
351H6      5437L        ( I )   MRS WARREN HASTINGS ANDERSON
351H6      5542         ( I )   HONORABLE MISS WARD'S FANCY, THE
351H6      554H4H       ( II )  MISS MCKENZIE OF NESS HOUSE
351H6      6425L        ( I )   QUICK STEP
351H6      662H2        ( I )   MRS PHILIP DUNDAS'S REEL
351H6      1H1H22       ( II )  MISS ROSS
351H6      1H1H22       ( I )   LADY HADDO ('S STRATHSPEY)
351H6      1H1H22       ( I )   MISS ROSS('S STRATHSPEY)
351H6      1H1H22       ( I )   LADY HADDO'S STRATHSPEY
351H       62H7         ( I )   MISS REMINGTON'S DOUBLE HORNPIPE
351H1H     3553         ( I )   I CAN'T FOR MY LIFE
351H1H     3572         ( I )   MRS FARQUHARSON OF INVEREY('S STR.)
351H1H     351H1H       ( I )   MY LADY HOPES SCOTCH MEASURE
351H1H     352H2        ( II )  MRS FARQUHARSON OF INVEREY
351H1H     352H6        ( II )  HAPPY WE'VE BEEN A THE-GITHER
351H1H     352H6        ( II )  WILLIE WAS A WANTON WAG
351H1H     352H6        ( I )   WILLIE WAS A WANTON WAG
351H1H     354H6        ( I )   WILLIE WAS A WANTON WAG
351H1H     355H6        ( I )   WILLIE WAS A WANTON WAG
351H1H     44H2H2H      ( I )   MRS H.R. DRAYTON'S REEL
351H1H     5222         ( I )   WELL A DAY
351H1H     5321         ( I )   CAULD KAIL IN ABERDEEN
351H1H     561H6        ( I )   URQUHART'S SCOTTS MEASURE
351H1H     647L2        ( I )   SWINLEY CAMP
351H1H     6422         ( I )   REEL OF BOGIE, THE
351H1H     6527L        ( I )   MISS MARGt. HONYMAN'S DOUBLE JIGG
351H1H     6542         ( II )  STATEN ISLAND
351H1H     661H2        ( I )   HIGH ROAD TO LINTON, THE
351H1H     661H1H       ( II )  HIGH ROAD TO LINTON(, THE)
351H1H     661H1H       ( I )   HIGH ROAD TO LINTON, THE
                                [HIGHWAY TO LINTON, THE]
351H1H     662H2H       ( II )  LOCH ERICHT SIDE [LOCH ERROCH SIDE]
351H1H     662H2H       ( II )  GOWRIE
351H1H     662H2H       ( II )  LASS O' GOWRIE
351H1H     662H2H       ( I )   LOCH EIREACHD SIDE [LOCH ERICHT SIDE]
351H1H     61H53        ( I )   BATCHELORS OF EVERY STATION
351H1H     7753         ( II )  TWO SISTERS, THE
351H       1H1H1H       ( I )   LAWLAND MAIDS, THE
351H1H     1H1H62       ( I )   LITTLE HOUSE UNDER THE HILL
351H1H     1H1H72       ( I )   HOUSE UNDER THE HILL, THE
351H1H     1H1H2H2      ( I )   MR BUSHBY MAITLAND'S REEL
351H1H     1H1H2H2      ( I )   BANKS OF SEVERN, THE
351H1H     1H1H2H2      ( I )   BUSH ABOON TRAQUAIR, THE
351H1H     1H1H2H2      ( I )   LOCH ERROCH (SIDE)
351H1H     2H543        ( I )   AIRS IN PYRAMUS AND THISBE
351H1H     2H61H1H      ( I )   BANKS OF SPEY, THE
351H1H     2H1H55       ( I )   BANKS OF SEVERN, THE
351H1H     2H2H2H2H     ( I )   BUSH ABOON TRAQUAIR, (THE)
351H1H     2H2H3H2H     ( I )   MEDLEY OVERTURE (9)
351H1H     2H2H3H2H     ( I )   BUSH ABOON TRAQUAIR, THE
351H1H     2H4H2H2      ( I )   MISS MARY L. ROBERTSON
351H1H     3H4H2H6      ( II )  CRARAE
351H1H     3H5H2H2H     ( I )   ROSE OF ALLANBANK, THE [MAID OF ALLANBANK]
351H       2H24         ( I )   DOUBLE HORNPIPE NO. 3
351H       2H24         ( I )   LUNARDI
351H2H     6542         ( I )   MISS MARY STEWART OF DERCLUICH'S GIGG
351H       2H2H2        ( I )   WALLY, WALLY
351H       2H2H2H       ( I )   WALY WALY (UP THE BANK)
351H2H     2H2H2H2H     ( I )   BUSH ABOON TRAQUAIR, (THE)
351H       2H3H2H       ( I )   O WALY, WALY, UP YON BANK
351H3H     5622H        ( I )   ALEXr BRODIE'S ESQR. STRATHSPEY
```

```
351H3H     1H522        (I)  COLONEL MCDONALD OF LOCHGARIE'S STRATHSPEY
351H3H     1H542        (I)  MISS FLORA MCLEOD OF COLBECK'S REEL
351H3H     1H562       (II)  MRS BAIRD OF NEWBYTH
351H3H     1H562        (I)  MRS BAIRD OF NEWBYTH ('S STRATHSPEY)
351H3H     1H52H2H      (I)  O'ER YOUNG TO MARRY (YET), (SHE'S/I'M)
351H3H     1H52H2H      (I)  (I AM) O'ER YOUNG TO MARRY YET
351H3H     1H632       (II)  DUNCAN QUADRILLE, THE
351H3H     1H666       (II)  BRAES O' MAR, THE
351H3H     1H666        (I)  ORIGINAL SETT OF THE BRAES OF MARR, THE
351H3H     1H666        (I)  FYKET, THE
351H3H     1H61H6      (II)  BRAES O' MAR, THE [OLD SET OF]
351H3H     1H61H6       (I)  BRAES OF MARR
351H3H     1H62H2H      (I)  LORD FIFE'S REELL
351H3H     1H1H1H1H     (I)  FANCY OF THE MOMENT, THE
351H3H     2H222        (I)  I'LL MAKE YOU BE FOND TO FOLLOW ME
351H       3H2H6        (I)  JENNY MY BLITHEST MAID
351H3H     2H61H6       (I)  BRAES OF MARR
351H3H     2H1H32       (I)  NEW BRIDGE OF AYR, THE
351H3H     2H1H52       (I)  MISS DRUMMOND OF DRUMTOCHTY'S STRATHSPEY
351H3H     4H3H2H5      (I)  HONble MRS PETRIE'S STRATHSPEY, THE
352H6      51H5H2H     (II)  HEATHER HILLS
352H2H     1H666        (I)  PIER OF LEITH, THE
353H1H     5642        (II)  PARKS OF KILBURNIE, THE
                             [PARKS OF FOCHABERS, THE]
353H1H     5642         (I)  PARKS OF FOCHABERS, THE
353H1H     5642         (I)  PARKS OF KILBURNIE, THE
353H1H     53H2H2       (I)  MISS SHARPE OF HODDOMS REEL
353H1H     6542        (II)  NIEL GOW'S RECOVERY
353H2H     6542         (I)  O THIS IS NO MY AIN LASSIE
353H2H     6542         (I)  THIS IS NO MY AIN HOUSE
353H2H     6562        (II)  THIS IS NO MY AIN HOUSE
353H2H     6562         (I)  THIS IS (NAE) MY AIN HOUSE
353H2H     657b2        (I)  THIS IS NO MINE AIN HOUSE
353H2H     662H2        (I)  MISS JEAN HAMILTON OF SUNDRUM'S STRATHSPEY
353H2H     1H57b2       (I)  (AND) THIS IS NO MINE AIN (HOUSE/THIN)
353H2H     2H225        (I)  COOPPER IN FIFE
353H4H     3H4H2H2      (I)  MISS ELLIOT'S REEL
353H4H     3H4H2H3      (I)  MISS ELLIOT'S REEL
354H1H     354H1H       (I)  MARCHIONESS OF TWEEDDALE'S VALTZ
354H2H     6542         (I)  ALLEGRETTO
354H2H     6562        (II)  O THIS IS NO MY AIN LASSIE
354H2H     6562        (II)  MY AIN LASSIE
354H3H     354H1H       (I)  WHITTINGTON'S CAT
355H2H     4H2H66      (II)  LORD McDONALD [LORD MACDONALD]
355H2H     4H2H66       (I)  SIR ALEXr McDONALD'S REEL
355H2H     4H2H66       (I)  LORD McDONALD('S OLD REEL) [LORD MACDONALD]
355H2H     4H2H66       (I)  MCDONALD'S RANT
355H2H     4H2H66       (I)  BRAES OF MARR, THE
355H5H     4H2H66       (I)  SAWNY'S PIPE
367L3L     367L1H       (I)  WILLIAM BROWN ESQr's WALTZ
3623       3H1H51H      (I)  LADY (CAROLINE/HARRIET) LEE'S WALTZ
3624       3H1H51H      (I)  LADY CAROLINE LEE
3625       147L5        (I)  LA BELL AMAZONE
3631       5522         (I)  DANDALEITH
3631       5522         (I)  MRS GORDON OF BELLIE'S REEL
3632       3662         (I)  MISS JEAN CAMPBELL OF AIRD'S REEL
3632       4636         (I)  WE'RE A FORSAKEN FOR WANT O' SILLER
363        362H         (I)  VALENTINES DAY IN THE MORNING
3635       41H65        (I)  LILLA'S A LADY
3637       3671H        (I)  MR MARSHALL'S CELEBRATED PANORAMA WALTZ
3642       2521         (I)  LOVELY LASS OF MONORGON, THE
3642       3521         (I)  LOVELY LASS OF INVERBERVIE, THE
3642       3641        (II)  BECAUSE HE WAS A BONNIE LAD
3653       2236         (I)  LADIES' RAMBLE
3653       465L6       (II)  STEWART'S RANT, THE
3653       462H6       (II)  STEWART'S RANT, THE
3653       462H6        (I)  STEWART'S RANT, THE
3653       47b27bL      (I)  LADY ELINORA HOME'S REEL
3653       47b27bL      (I)  LADY (ELENORA) HOME'S REEL
3653       47b47b       (I)  DICK A DOLLIS
365        367          (I)  SOUTERS OF SELKIRK, THE
3653       1H353       (II)  CALUM FIGHEADAIR
3654       2515L        (I)  NOSEGAY, THE
3654       462H6        (I)  STEWART'S RANT, THE
3654       47b1H7b     (II)  STUART'S RANT, THE
3654       47b1H7b      (I)  STUART'S RANT, THE
3655       3622        (II)  HECTOR THE HERO
365        642          (I)  JENNY AND I
365        652          (I)  DOUBLE HORNPIPE
365        1H52         (I)  LORD KIRKCUDBRIGHT
3651H      1H2H2H6     (II)  BLACK CAT O' BENRINNES, THE
3664       4646         (I)  HAMILTON'S RANT
```

3664	462H6	(I)	STEWART'S RANT, THE
3664	47b1H7b	(I)	STEWART'S RANT, THE
3661H	5351H	(I)	MRS MASSON'S REEL
3663H	72#6H3T	(II)	W. SCOTT COLLINS
3676	3663	(I)	PERTHSHIRE DANCING MEASURES & C No. 8
361H6	4210	(I)	MY MOTHER SAYS I MANNA
361H6	4211H	(I)	MY MOTHER SAYS I MANNOT
361H6	1H362	(I)	HUME CASTLE
361H6	1H535	(I)	LA BALLARDE
361H7	3673	(I)	PERTHSHIRE DANCING MEASURES & C No. 9
361H7	5215L	(II)	WE'LL AYE GANG BACK TO YON TOON
361H7	5756L	(I)	CUIR A GHAOILDILEAS THARRUM DO LAMH
			[CUIR A CHION DILIS...]
361H1H	357b2	(I)	MISS KITTY FARQUHAR'S REEL
361H3H	3H3H75	(I)	MISS CHARLOTTE BRODIE'S REEL
363H2H	363H1H	(II)	BURN O' BUCKET, THE
3751	437L2	(I)	HIGHLANDERS KNEE BUCKLE, THE
3764	462H6	(I)	WAS YOW AT THE WADDING
376	1H52	(I)	DH'FHAG THU MI FO BHRON
371H7	371H6	(II)	SANDY KING
373H7	6562	(I)	QUICK MARCH
31H5L1	42H6L2	(I)	TIPSTAFF STRATHSPEY
31H11	3332	(I)	LORD OF COCKPEN'S SCOTCH-MEASURE, THE
31H35L	7L47L2	(I)	MR WAGSTAFF'S FAVORITE
31H37L	6L27L1H	(I)	BANK OF THE YARROW [BANKS OF THE YARROW]
31H37L	31H53	(II)	LEFT HANDED FIDDLER, THE
31H31	27b27bL	(II)	GORDON HIGHLANDERS, THE
31H31	427L5	(II)	WEST WINDS
31H31	42H42	(I)	MISS ANN MACKAY'S FAVORITE
31H31	2H4H2H2	(I)	MASTER JOHN ROMILY
31H3	342	(I)	DROWN DROUTH
31H33	4231H	(I)	DROUTH
31H34	31H33	(II)	DUNDEE BURNS CLUB, THE
31H35	31H62	(II)	MISS FARQUHARSON OF BALDOVIE
31H35	31H62	(I)	MISS FARQUHARSON OF BALDOVIE('S STR.)
31H35	31H2H2	(I)	MISS COUTTS'S REEL
31H36	3155	(II)	DALDOWNYS
31H3	652	(I)	HIGHWAY TO COLAIN, THE
31H31H	362H2	(I)	DUNCAN'S DANCE
31H31H	31H31	(I)	NEW MARKET
31H31H	31H42	(II)	MRS DOUGLAS OF EDNAM
31H31H	31H42	(I)	LADY ROSS OF BALNAGOWAN'S REEL
31H31H	31H62	(II)	MRS DOUGLAS OF EDNAM
31H31H	31H66	(II)	MISS MURRAY OF AUCHTERTYRE
31H31H	31H2H2	(II)	LADY JANE TAYLOR
31H31H	31H2H2	(I)	LADY JANE TAYLOR('S STRATHSPEY)
31H31H	5757	(II)	MISS GAYTON'S HORNPIPE
31H31H	6622H	(II)	COUNTESS OF HADDINGTON, THE
31H31H	72H75	(II)	COSSACK, THE
31H31H	2H1H22	(II)	LADY BETTY WEMYSS
31H31H	2H1H22	(I)	LADY BETTY WEMYSS'S REEL
31H33H	31H62	(I)	GLEN-RIDDELL'S REEL
31H42	31H4H7	(I)	HUNTLY LODGE
31H42H	71H1H5	(II)	FORTH BRIG, THE
31H42H	3H72H5	(I)	LITTLE SKIRMISH
31H51	4542	(I)	BASQUE ROADS
31H51	6275	(I)	DOUBLE JIGG
31H52	1551	(I)	BLATHRIE O'T, THE
31H52	3561	(I)	CAULD KAIL (IN ABERDEEN)
31H52	3651	(I)	CAULD KAIL IN ABERDEEN
31H52	31H51	(I)	(THERE'S) CAULD KAIL IN ABERDEEN
31H52	31H53	(I)	SIR GEORGE MCKENZIE OF COUL'S FAVORITE
31H53	31H42	(I)	HONble GEORGE MELVILL
			LESLIE MELVILL'S STRATHSPEY
31H53	31H52	(I)	S'OLC A CHUIR A MHIREADH RIUM
31H53	4327L	(II)	MR BEVERIDGE
31H53	6542	(II)	DR. KEITH, ABERDEEN
31H54	3451	(I)	STRATHBOGIE WALTZ, THE
31H55	4542	(I)	DOUBLE JIG
31H5	551	(I)	BONNY BRUCKET LASSIE, THE
31H5	551	(I)	TURN AGAIN THOU FAIR ELIZA
31H5	552	(I)	MISS MONRO'S DOUBLE HORNPIPE
31H51	2316L	(I)	MR OSWALDS OF DUNNIKIER'S REEL
31H51H	62H31H	(I)	AN ORIGINAL SCOTCH HORNPIPE
31H53H	4H3H2H7	(I)	KIRKOSWOLD REEL, THE
31H53H	5H5H72H	(I)	MISS JANE BRUCE'S JIG
31H62	31H53	(II)	SANDY GRANT(O' BATTANGORM)
31H63	3552	(I)	NORA'S VOW
31H63	3752	(I)	LAMENTATION FOR THE FALLEN HEROES
			OF WATERLOO
31H63	31H42	(I)	MISS MACKENZIE OF STRATHGARVE'S STR.
31H63	31H53	(II)	MR ABEL BANKS

31H63	4322	(I)	MISS BOOKER'S REEL
31H63	531H4	(I)	MISS GIBSON'S STRATHSPEY
31H64	2462H	(I)	MISS JANE YOUNG (BANFF)
31H64	31H53	(I)	LADY LOUISA GORDON
31H64	42H2H6	(I)	MISS WILLISON'S REEL
31H64	5125L	(I)	MISS NICHOLSON'S REEL
31H6	531	(I)	LAST ROSE OF SUMMER, THE
31H65	3462	(I)	CALEDONIAN HUNT, THE
31H65	31H27L	(II)	AULD MAN, THE
31H65	31H2H2	(I)	LANCERS STRATHSPEY, THE
31H65	432H2	(II)	LADY CHARLOTTE MENZIES
31H65	432H2	(I)	LADY CHARLOTTE MENZIES REEL
31H65	4562	(II)	CALEDONIAN HUNT, (THE)
31H65	4562	(I)	CALEDONIAN HUNT ('S STRATHSPEY), THE
31H66	37b1H2	(I)	NORTH HIGHLAND 5
31H66	351H2	(I)	NORTH HIGHLAND REEL, A
31H66	1H61H3	(I)	NIAN BODDACH AN ROAINAITIN
			[NIGHEAN BODACH AN ROAINAITINN]
31H66	1H5H6H3H	(I)	EARL OF HADDINGTON ('S STRATHSPEY), THE
31H66	5H3H2H2H	(I)	MISS JOHNSTON'S STRATHSPEY
31H67	4562	(I)	CALEDONIAN HUNT, THE
31H61H	31H22H	(I)	MISS C. CLARK'S STRATHSPEY
31H61H	31H62	(I)	MR FOOTES REEL
31H61H	31H66	(II)	DR PROFEIT'S STRATHSPEY
31H61H	31H66	(I)	MISS MURRAY (OF AUCHTERTYRE) 'S STRATHSPEY
31H61H	31H66	(I)	MISS MURRAY OF AUCHTERTYRE'S STRATHSPEY
31H61H	31H66	(I)	MISS MURRAY (OF AUCHTERTYRE'S) STR.
31H61H	5362	(I)	MR JAMES CAMPBELL'S STRATHSPEY
31H61H	6522	(II)	CAPTAIN FRANCIS WEMYSS
31H61H	6522	(II)	CAPT. FRANCIS WEMYSS
31H61H	6542	(I)	CASTLE GRANT
31H61H	61H22	(I)	SIR WILLIAM STIRLING'S STRATHSPEY
31H61H	1H425L	(I)	COTTILION
31H62H	31H63	(I)	WET AND WEARY
31H7	531	(I)	LAST ROSE OF SUMMER, THE
31H7	652	(I)	SAILOR LASSIE, THE
31H7	652	(I)	MISS MARGARET MCGREGOR'S FAVOURITE
31H71H	432H2	(I)	EARL OF MORTON'S JIG(G)
31H71H	457L2	(I)	MISS CATHARINE REDDIE'S STRATHSPEY
31H71H	631H3	(I)	MR WATT'S REEL
31H72H	3H72H5	(I)	DUKE OF GLOUCESTER'S QUICK MARCH, THE
31H74H	2H531H	(I)	FANNY'S FANCY
31H74H	2H531H	(I)	FANNY'S FANCY
31H74H	3H1H2H5	(I)	CAPT ROSS KENDEAS'S QUICK STEP
31H75H	3H1H2H5	(I)	GAVOT
31H1H4	22H2H5	(I)	BENNET'S HORNPIPE
31H1H5	31H1H5	(II)	MISS GAYTON'S HORNPIPE
31H1H5	31H1H6	(I)	MRS DR STEPHEN'S REEL
31H1H5	427L2	(II)	REEL, A
31H1H	52H2H	(I)	MERRY WAKEFIELD
31H1H	652	(I)	DOLLIE'S THE GIRL FOR ME
31H1H7	6542	(I)	HOBLE ABOUT
31H1H7	6562	(I)	AULD REEKIE
31H1H7	72H55	(I)	MCCRAE'S FANCY
31H1H7	72H2H1H	(II)	COOPERS
31H1H1H	31H32	(I)	MISS JEAN LOGAN'S STRATHSPEY
31H1H1H	31H42	(II)	'HAP AN' ROW THE FEETIES O'T
31H1H1H	31H2H2	(II)	STUMPIE
31H1H1H	31H2H2	(I)	STUMPIE(STRATHSPEY)
31H1H1H	31H2H2	(I)	LOYAL NORTH BRITONS
31H1H1H	5445	(I)	SIR MICHAEL BRUCE'S MARCH
31H1H1H	61H22	(I)	HIGHLAND QUEEN, (THE)
31H1H1H	61H32	(I)	HIGHLAND QUEEN, THE
31H1H1H	3H3H2H2	(I)	MARQUISS OF HUNTLEY'S QUICK STEP
31H1H5H	3H3H1H7	(I)	SIR WILLIAM HOPE'S SCOTCH-MEASURE
31H2H2	31H71H	(II)	I'LL MAKE YOU BE FAIN TO FOLLOW ME
31H2H2	31H71H	(I)	I'LL MAKE YOU BE FAIN TO FOLLOW ME
31H2H2	4H2H75	(I)	MISS JANE HUNTER'S REEL
31H2H5	3525L	(I)	HONble GEORGE MELVILL LESLIE'S ALAMANDE
31H2H5	6242	(I)	MISS S. McLEOD'S HORNPIPE
31H2H5	6542	(I)	HAMILTON RACES
31H2H5	1H47L2	(II)	MISS NEIL
31H2H1H	31H22	(I)	MISS SCOTT OF LOGIE'S STRATHSPEY
31H2H1H	31H1H1H	(I)	I WISH I MAY DIE IF I DO
31H2H1H	31H2H2	(II)	STUMPIE
31H2H1H	31H2H2	(I)	STUMPIE (STRATHSPEY), (REEL O')
31H2H1H	31H2H2	(I)	HAP AN' ROW THE FEETY O'T
31H2H1H	5335	(II)	WILLOW HORNPIPE, THE
31H2H1H	5542	(I)	DESERTS OF TULLOCH, THE
31H2H1H	641H5	(I)	MISS MORISON'S REEL
31H2H1H	2H1H75	(I)	MISS MILNERS DELIGHT
31H2H2H	31H1H2	(II)	MACALLAN

31H3H3	31H2H2	(I)	WANTON WIFE OF HULL, THE
31H3H3	31H2H2	(I)	HILLS OF CROOK HAVEN, THE
31H3H7	6542	(II)	MRS GARDEN OF TROUP
31H3H1H	31H42	(I)	PRINCE OF WALES'S REEL, THE
31H3H1H	31H2H4	(I)	ROCKS OF CASHEL
31H3H1H	33H72H	(I)	MRS CLARKSON'S FAVOURITE
31H3H1H	5122	(I)	EARL OF SEAFIELD'S STRATHSPEY, THE
31H3H1H	5642	(I)	ST BRYCE'S DALE
31H3H1H	6542	(II)	MRS GARDEN OF TROUP
31H3H1H	6542	(I)	MRS GARDEN (OF TROUP)('S REEL)
31H3H1H	4H2H75H	(I)	CONTRIDANZE
31H4H2H	72H55	(I)	BONNY ISOBEL ROBERTSON
31H4H2H	4H2H72H	(I)	MISS DUFF OF LOACH
31H4H3H	2H5H3H2H	(I)	AIR
3H1H5H	2H52H	(I)	WILLIE STAYS LANG AT THE FAIR
31H5H3H	5H6H4H2H	(I)	LORD ALEXr. GORDON'S STRATHSPEY
32H56	53H2H1H	(I)	GODFREY, LORD MACDONALD'S WELCOME TO THE ISLE OF SKYE
32H1H5	362H5	(I)	QUICK STEP 10 REGT.
33H44H	73H1H5	(II)	MATHEMATICIAN, THE
33H76H	33H4H1H	(I)	RUNAWAY, THE
33H1H6	51H2H2	(I)	DUCHESS OF GORDON'S STRATHSPEY, THE
33H1H6	51H2H2	(I)	LADY HUNTLY'S STRATHSPEY
33H2H	1H55	(I)	ALPINE WALTZ
33H3H6	33H1H5	(I)	I'LL HAE A PIPER TO MY GUDEMAN
31H61H	6522	(I)	GAME COCK, THE
31H61H	6522	(I)	CAPTAIN FRANCIS WEMYSS STRATHSPEY
45L6L5L	4326L	(I)	MR MacCULLOCH'S STRATHSPEY
45L45	354H2H	(I)	MR GEORGE A. YOUNG
47bL11L	3bL5L7bL7bL	(I)	BAILLIE GRAY'S FAVOURITE STRATHSPEY
47bL11L	3bL5L7bL7bL	(II)	MRS GRANT OF LAG(G)AN
47L11L	3bL5L7bL7bL	(II)	MRS GRANT OF LAGGAN
47L11L	3bL5L7bL7bL	(I)	MRS GRANT OF LAG(G)AN('S STRATHSPEY)
47L15L	6L15L3L	(I)	LADY FLORA CHARLOTTE HASTING'S STRATHSPEY
415L1	3b155	(I)	HASTE TO THE CAMP
415L1	4165	(II)	ATHOLE BROSE
4115L	7bL7bL20	(I)	COLLIER'S BONNY LASSIE, THE
411	6L5L5L	(I)	LADY ANNE BOTHWELL'S LAMENT
411	3b22	(I)	BOB AN' JOHN
4131	4136	(II)	CHORUS JIG, THE
4144	4144	(I)	OLD REEL OF TULLOCH STRATHSPEY
4156	537L2	(I)	BIRTH OF KISSES, THE
4162	5675	(I)	JARNOVICHI'S HORNPIPE
411H5	7b7bL7b4	(II)	CULLODEN DAY or INVERNESS GATHERING, THE
425L3	7bL45L3	(I)	INVERCAULD'S SCOTS MEASURE
425L3	4542	(I)	MRS HUGHES
425L3	5525	(II)	BALLOCHMYLE BRIG
426L1	5L5L11	(I)	A ROBAIDH, THA THU GORACH
426L1	5L6L22	(I)	LEAVE THEE, LOTH TO LEAVE THEE
427L5L	3L125L	(I)	MISS GUNNING('S REEL)
427L7L	1235	(I)	PAS DI TROIS MISSES GLENNIE
427L2	3542	(II)	MR JAMES TROTTER
427L2	351H3	(I)	MRS WALLACE'S REEL
427L2	4211H	(II)	AULD WIFE AYONT THE FIRE, THE
427L2	4211H	(II)	WELCOME ROYAL CHARLIE
427L2	4211H	(I)	AULD WIFE AYONT THE FIRE, THE
427L2	421H3	(I)	AULD WIFE AYONT THE FIRE, THE
4215L	6L225	(I)	I LOVE MY LOVE IN SECRET
4211	6L5L2L2L	(I)	LORD JOHN RUSSELL
4211	16L6L1	(I)	MISS BECK'S MEASURE
4211	361H3	(I)	DUCHESS OF RICHMOND, THE
4213	6361H	(II)	MISS DUMBRECK
4213	6361H	(I)	MISS DUMBRECK'S REEL
4213	1H554	(II)	INVERNESS GATHERING(, THE)
4215	427b7b	(I)	LAWER'S HOUSE
4225L	31H62	(I)	MISS ROBERTSON'S FAVORITE
4226L	1515	(I)	MISS H. ERSKINE'S STRATHSPEY
4221	4221	(I)	LOVELY LASS TO A FRIAR CAME, A
4231	6L7L33	(I)	MISS MARGARET ROBERTSON'S JIGG
4233	427L5L	(II)	LADY BINNING
4233	427L5L	(II)	RETURN FROM INDIA, THE
4235	6661H	(I)	NEW BRIDGE OF LAGAVUILLIN, THE
4235	1H1H55	(I)	LASS OF PATIE'S MILL, THE
4235	1H1H3HO	(I)	LASS OF PATIE'S MILL, THE
4235	1H1H3H3H	(I)	LASS OF PATIE'S MILL, THE
4231H	4H3H1H6	(I)	MISS SOPHIA CUMMING'S REEL
4245	521HO	(I)	JENNY'S JOE
4253	427L5L	(I)	ARRIVALS FROM INDIA
4255	3551H	(I)	MISS ANDY CAMPBELL'S SCOTS MEASURE
4255	1H3H1H1H	(I)	BONNY BANKS OF AYR, THE
4251H	3122	(I)	LADY STOPFORD'S REEL
4253H	74H1H3H	(I)	ORIGINAL POLKA, THE

4264	2445	(I)	DYESTER LADDIE, THE
421H1H	3H2H1H6	(I)	LAST TIME I CAME O'ER THE MOOR, THE
437L2	3356	(I)	ARABELLA
431	123	(I)	STORM, THE
4311H	1H756	(I)	LASS OF LEWENEY, THE
4325L	4L432	(I)	ADIEW
4327L	1313	(I)	BAB AT THE BOWSTER
4327L	1313	(I)	(OLD) COUNTRY BUMPKIN, THE
4321	7L242	(I)	MR BRODIE OF BRODIE'S FAVOURITE
4321	2212	(I)	LOVELY LASS TO A FRYAR CAME, A
4321	4321	(I)	PRINCESS CHARLOTTE OF WALES WALTZ
4323	5L123	(I)	COSSY('S) JIGG, (THE)
4333	4331	(I)	CULLODEN WALTZ
433	443	(I)	DAMON
4376	5532	(I)	AP SHENKIN
431H3H	6632	(II)	LASS O' PATIES MILL, THE
443b	43b5	(I)	IF LOVE'S A SWEET PASSION
4433	4521	(I)	BONNY LASS OF ABERDEEN, THE
4433	6426L	(I)	LASS OF BALLOCHMYLE, THE
446b	511	(I)	TERROR OF DEATH, THE
446b	511	(I)	'S EAGAL LEAM A MBAS
4511	4527bL	(II)	KILLIN
4511	4527bL	(I)	KILLIN
4515	1H2H52H	(I)	R. JOHNSTON, ESQR'S HORNPIPE
453b1H	7b427bL	(I)	LOCH FYNE SIDE
4535	27L16L	(I)	MILLINER'S HOUSE, THE
4541	6523	(I)	BONDUCA
4542	7L232	(I)	MISS JESSY BAIRD'S REEL
4564	7L122	(I)	MISS MARY MONCREIF'S DANCE
46b46b	543b5	(I)	IRISH TROTT
4635	22H76	(I)	BREAST KNOT, THE (LADY'S)
4635	22H76	(I)	(BONNY) BREAST KNOT(S), (THE)
4635	43b27bL	(I)	LADY ELIZABETH CAMPBELL'S REEL
4635	43b27L	(I)	LADY ELIZABETH CAMPBELL'S REEL
4635	43b27L	(I)	LADY ELIZABETH PRINGLE'S REEL
4635	4327bL	(II)	LADY ELIZABETH CAMPBELL
467b5	1H631	(I)	MRS FRASER OF BELLADRUM'S REEL
47b44	3bL7b44	(I)	E HO RO, MO GHORM SHUILEAG DHUBH
47b44	3bL7b44	(I)	BLACK HAIRED GIRL WITH THE BLUE EYES
41H3b1	47b57b	(I)	'S FAD THA MI M'ONARAN
41H3b1	47b57b	(I)	LONG AM I IN SOLITUDE
41H54	247b2	(I)	MISS FRENCH'S REEL
41H3bH1H	5422	(II)	BRIDGE OF NEWE, THE
4#231	3522	(I)	JOHN BURTON
4#37L5L	4#416	(I)	GALOP
4#37L3	4#2#7L1	(I)	NEW BRIGHTON WALTZ, THE
4#413	7L556L	(I)	LORD RAMSAY'S FAVORITE
51H6b4	3b57b3b	(II)	FAIR FIELD HOUSE
53L53L	5576	(II)	MADAM SYLVAIN
55L2L2	35L6L5L	(I)	ALL IN A BUSTLE
55L6L5L	5L5L42	(II)	TEVIOT BRIDGE [TEVIOT BRIG]
55L6L5L	5L5L42	(I)	TEVIOT BRIDGE [TEVIOT BRIG]
55L6L5L	6L5L6L5L	(I)	DEVIL UPON TWO STICKS JIG
55L6L5L	1142	(I)	TIVOT BRIDGE
55L43	4321	(I)	FONN LIONARACHD DO BHRIARABH OSSIAN [FONN GNATHAICHTE...OISEIN]
56L5L1L	5467L	(I)	MISS JANE TYTLER'S FAVOURITE
56L5L3L	4L222	(I)	MISS RAMSAY OF CRAIGLEITH'S FAVORITE
57bL7bL4	117bL7bL	(I)	THUG NA MNATHAN GAOL DO M'CHODHALT
57L5L1	4266	(I)	CUMBERLAND COTTAGER, THE
57L12	536L2	(I)	EARL OF CASSLES'S REEL
504	203	(I)	LOVE AND GLORY
513L1	357L2	(I)	RED STAR, THE
515L1L	5L1L6L2	(II)	CRAIG-A-CHROCHAN OR BRIDGE OF BALLINDALLOCH
515L1L	5L1L6L2	(II)	BRIDGE OF BALLINDALLOCH or CRAIG-A-CHROCHAN
515L	514	(I)	AS BLACK AS COAL
515L5	4362	(I)	SEND US WHISKY
516L5L	6L5L3L5L	(I)	DARNWAY CASTLE
516L5L	1332	(I)	MISS PATTISON'S JIG
516L6L	25L11	(I)	MISS MARGARET BROWN('S FAVOURITE)
516L7L	357L2	(I)	MISS ELIZABETH MURRAY'S JIG
516L1	516L2	(I)	LOWE'S HORNPIPE
517bL2	513b5	(I)	MISS LILLIE RITCHIE'S REEL
517bL3b	56b47bL	(I)	MISS KEMP'S JIGG
517L1	4331	(I)	GAVOTTA
5115L	7bL17bL5L	(II)	MISS JOHNSTON ROBINSON
5116L	5L4L5L3L	(I)	MISS LINDSAY'S REEL
5116L	5L132	(I)	MRS McLEOD OF RAZA'S STRATHSPEY
511	17L2	(I)	MISS MARY LUMSDANE'S FAVORITE
511	111	(I)	OVER MY SPIRIT ARE SHADOWS FLITTING
5111	5127L	(I)	NEW WATER KETTLE, THE
5111	5155	(I)	HIGHLAND SECRETARY, THE

5112	557b4	(II)	LOCHIEL'S MARCH
511	3b22	(I)	MISS MURRAY'S REEL
511	3b22	(I)	BOBIN JOHN
5113b	5553b	(I)	MARY'S DREAM
5113	517b5	(II)	DEVIL IN THE KITCHEN, THE or PRINCE OF WALES JIG, THE
511	417bL	(I)	PEARLIN' PEGGIE'S BONNY
511	417bL	(I)	LAIRD OF FOVERAN, THE
5114	25L5L5	(II)	LORD DUDLEY'S MARCH
5114	217bL7b	(II)	TO DAUNTON ME
5114	217bL7b	(I)	TO DANTON ME [TO DAUNTON ME]
5115	7bL747bL	(I)	CAPT HOME'S JIG
5115	27bL7b4	(I)	MISS LOUISA BROWN'S REEL
5115	47bL7bL2	(II)	MISS GRANT
5115	47bL7bL2	(I)	MISS GRANT('S STRATHSPEY)
5115	47L7L4	(I)	CHESTER RACES
5115	447bL7bL	(I)	MR HORN
5115	5124	(II)	LADY JARDINE
5115	5124	(I)	LADY JARDINE'S STRATHSPEY
5115	5136	(I)	UILLEACHAN 'N TIG THU CHAOIDH
511	564	(I)	GO TO BERWICK, JOHNNY
5116	6562	(II)	LADS O' DUNS(E, THE)
5116	6562	(I)	LADS OF DUNSE, THE
5117	6527L	(I)	TENTH OF JANUARY, THE
5111H	6666	(I)	PYD HORSE, THE
5125L	3L6L27L	(I)	GRAND BALLOT DANCE, THE
5125L	6L7L13	(I)	DELGATY CASTLE
5125L	6L15L3L	(I)	JUBILEE OF 1810, THE
5125L	6L15L3L	(I)	MISS STEWART'S GIG
5125L	6L15L4L	(I)	TRIP TO HAWKHURST
5125L	6L237L	(I)	MR(S) BLAIR OF BLAIR'S JIGG
5125L	423L1	(I)	CAMPERDOWN GERMAN WALTZ, THE
5125L	423L1	(I)	DUCHESS OF YORK('S WALTZ), THE
5126L	5566	(II)	DR. GREGORY GRANT
5126L	5566	(I)	Dr GREGORY GRANT'S STRATHSPEY
5127bL	1642	(II)	A MHISG A CHUR AN NOLIG OIRN [CHRISTMAS CAROUSING]
5127bL	513b5	(I)	DUTCHESS OF HAMILTON'S REEL
5127bL	513b6b	(I)	DUTCHESS OF HAMILTON'S GIGG
5127L	35L6L2L	(I)	MISS ANNE CARNEGIE'S HORNPIPE
5127L	3366	(I)	MRS LIEUt. MARISON'S FANCY
5121	1234	(I)	FAREWELL TO EDINBURGH
5121	5121	(I)	MISS ELIZABETH HAMILTON'S FAVORITE WALTZ
5121	5121	(I)	SPA PROMENADE, THE
5121	5126	(I)	TRIP TO THE FALLS OF THE CLYDE, A
5121	6421	(I)	GAVOT
5122	111H6	(II)	CRONAN NA LINNE MHUILICH [SOUND OF MULL]
5122	4513	(II)	MISS ELIZA FORSYTH
5122	4513	(I)	MISS ELIZA FORSYTH('S STRATHSPEY)
5122	5125L	(I)	MRS BRUCE OF KINNAIRD'S FAVORITE
5122	5155	(I)	MISS CHARTER'S REEL
5122	5156	(I)	MISS CHALMERS JIG(G)
5122	5151H	(I)	ARDEMERSAY COTTAGE
5122	5151H	(I)	MR JOHN SIMSON LARGY'S JIG
5122	511H3H	(II)	JOHN HAY DELDONALD
5122	6542	(I)	CROPPIES LIE DOWN
5122	651H1	(I)	CROPPIES LIE DOWN
5123	5136L	(I)	HERE AWA' THERE AWA'
512	355	(I)	MINUET
5123	5552	(I)	DOCTOR, THE
5123	6523	(I)	AIRIAL FLIGHT, THE
512	445	(I)	LONE WANDERER, THE
5124	5141H	(I)	MRS WILDMAN'S STRATHSPEY
5124	5151H	(II)	KNOCK HIM DOWN SUSIE
5124	5151H	(II)	CUT HIM DOWN SHUSIE [CUT HIM DOWN SUSIE]
5124	5151H	(I)	SUSIE, (CUT HIM DOWN), (A STRATHSPEY)
5124	513H1H	(I)	MISS AMELIA FLEMING'S STRATHSPEY
5124	5542	(I)	RICHMOND PARK
5125	5541	(I)	MISS BELSCHE'S WHIM
5126	6562	(I)	FEET WASHING, THE
5126	6562	(I)	SUN BEAM, THE
513b2	1164	(I)	HEBRIDEAN DANCING MEASURES & C
513b2	2425	(I)	CALLENDER HOUSE
513b2	47b7bL2	(II)	HIGHLANDER'S KNEE BUCKLE, THE
513b4	47b47bL	(II)	MRS CRAWFURD OF DONSIDE
513b5	7bL7bL7bL7bL	(II)	BANKS OF LOCH NESS, THE
513b5	27bL24	(II)	MISS SUSANNA BAIRD
513b5	27bL24	(I)	MISS SUSANNA BAIRD('S REEL)
513b5	27bL7b4	(II)	NEWBYTH HOUSE
513b5	27bL7b4	(I)	NEWBYTH HOUSE
513b5	2424	(II)	CAPTAIN MACDUFF'S FAREWELL
513b5	2424	(I)	CAPT McDUFF'S FAREWELL TO PARLIAMENT HOUSE

513b5	4427bL	(II)	MR MOORE('S STRATHSPEY)
513b5	4427bL	(I)	MR MOORE('S STRATHSPEY)
513b5	4642	(I)	DUFF HOUSE
513b5	5124	(I)	HAUGHS OF DEVLIN, THE
513b5	5154	(II)	DROWSY MAGGIE
513b5	5424	(II)	LADY MARGARET STEWART
513b5	5424	(I)	LADY MARGARET STEWART ('S REEL)
513b5	7b424	(II)	POOL REEL, THE
513b5	7b7b27bL	(II)	MINICAN, THE
5131	25L7L2	(I)	MISS HOPE'S REEL
5131	26L7L5L	(I)	LADY MURRAY'S REEL
5131	3131H	(I)	LOCH KATRINE
5131	31H62	(I)	LOCHABER RANT
5132	6L5L4L2L	(II)	MISS MENZIES OF MENZIES
513	222	(I)	AIR
5132	5133	(I)	NORTH HIGHLAND 16
5132	511H3H	(II)	WHIGS OF FIFE, THE
5132	511H3H	(I)	WHIGS OF FIFE(, THE)
5132	531H3H	(I)	MISS PARKER'S REEL, THE
5133	172H2	(I)	MRS ROBERT CHAMBERS
5133	5122	(I)	MAGGIE GAE BACK AN' TAK' UP YOUR SCULLIE
5133	5132	(II)	I'M OWRE YOUNG
5133	5132	(II)	I'M OW'RE YOUNG
5133	61H22	(II)	ARRAN LILT, AN
5134	3356	(I)	MISS MACLEOD OF DALVEY'S FAVORITE
513	516	(I)	RIDE A MILE
5135	363H7	(I)	MISS MARGRETT SKELTON'S JIG
5135	47bL7bL7bL	(I)	WILLIE WINKIE'S TESTAMENT
5135	427bL7bL	(I)	MY DADDIE LEFT ME GEAR ENOUGH
5135	4524	(I)	MISS JANE HUNTER BLAIR'S JIG
5135	5116	(I)	MRS WALTER WEMYS'S FAVOURITE
5135	5126	(I)	NORTH HIGHLAND 14
5135	5126	(I)	HIGHLAND DANCE, A
5135	5522	(I)	THRO' THE MOOR SHE RAN
5135	5522	(I)	DUTCHESS OF ATHOLE'S REELL
5135	5522	(I)	FAVOURITE STRATHSPEY, A
5135	5532	(I)	LET US TO THE AIRD
5135	5532	(I)	THRO' THE MOOR SHE RAN
5135	5542	(I)	OVER THE MOOR SHE RAN
5135	6422	(I)	HIGHLAND LADDIE, THE
5135	6421H	(I)	BONNY HIGHLAND LADDIE, THE
5135	6421H	(I)	CAIRNEY MOUNT, THE
5135	67b27bL	(II)	MISS ERSKINE OF ALVA
5135	67b27bL	(I)	MISS ERSKINE OF ALVA('S REEL)
5136	5522	(I)	MISS GRAHAM OF INVERARAY'S REEL
513	7b24	(I)	RATTLING ROARING WILLIE
5131H	6664	(II)	NEWS FROM CADIZ
5147bL	5127b	(I)	SNAIM A' PHOSAIDH
5147bL	5154	(I)	KAIL REETS OF FITTIE, THE
5147bL	511H1H	(I)	ORANGEFIELD HOUSE
5147L	1212	(I)	BUTTER'D EGGS
5147L	3216L	(I)	MISS E. FERGUSON'S HIGH DANCE
5142	3126L	(I)	MISS RICHARD'S REEL
5142	5145L	(I)	MORNING STAR STEAM BOAT, THE
5142	5145L	(I)	'S ANN AGAM THA 'M BODACH A'S MEASA AIR AN T SHAOGAL
5142	5145L	(I)	WARST CARLE IN A' THE WORLD, THE
5142	5145L	(I)	CARD ASSEMBLY
5142	5145L	(I)	PORT PATRICK
5142	5141	(I)	BLYTH (BLYTH AND MERRY) WAS SHE
5142	5142	(II)	PRINCE CHARLIE'S WELCOME TO THE ISLE OF SKYE
5142	5142	(I)	ISLE OF SKY (THE PRINCE'S WELCOME TO THE)
5142	5151H	(I)	FAV. STRATHSPEY, A
5142	517b4	(I)	CAPT COLLIN CAMPBELL OF SHAWFIELDS REEL
5142	5241	(I)	ANDREW AND HIS CUTTY GUN
5142	5251	(I)	BLYTHE WAS SHE BUT AND BEN
514	512	(I)	DEAR DUBLIN
5145	7b61H1H	(I)	BANK O' CAYLE, THE
5141H	527L5L	(I)	INDIAN CHIEF
5151	6L7L32	(I)	INNOCENT MAID, THE
5151	11H1H7	(I)	SOLDIER'S JOY
5151	27bL27bL	(I)	THEY TOOK FRAE ME MY WIFE YESTREEN
5151	2227bL	(I)	MISS SUSAN BROWN'S STRATHSPEY
5151	47bL47bL	(II)	MISS ISOBEL EWAN
5151	47bL47bL	(I)	PUNCH IS DONE, THE
5151	47bL7b7bL	(II)	RORY McNAB
5151	47bL7b7bL	(I)	RORY MACNAB
5151	47bL7b7bL	(I)	JACKY STEWARTS REELL
5151	47bL7b7bL	(I)	SIR JOHN STEWART OF GRANTULLY'S REEL
5151	4244	(I)	FIVE MILES OFF
5151	5147bL	(II)	REEL O' TULLOCH [REEL O' THUILLEACHAN]

5151	5147bL	(i)	REEL OF TULLOCH, THE [RIELLE HULUCHEN] ETC.
5151	5147bL	(I)	MISS MARY RAM'S FANCY
5151	5141	(II)	HIGHLAND PIBROCH
5151	5142	(I)	MISS KENNEDY FRASER'S REEL
5151	5142	(I)	MRS RUTHERFORD OF EGERSTON
5151	5162	(II)	DOUGAL CREATURE, THE
5151	5175	(I)	HAD I THE WATE SHE BADE ME
5151	5262	(I)	PRINCE REGENT'S STRATHSPEY
5151	5422H	(II)	MISS JESSY CUMING [MISS JESSY CUMMING)
5151	5422H	(I)	MISS JESSY CUMING'S STRATHSPEY
5151	5522	(I)	MISS DAWSON'S WHIM
5151	5575	(II)	BOB OF FETTERCAIRN, THE
5151	5575	(I)	HIGHLAND HILLS
5151	5575	(I)	JOCKEY AND PEGGIE
5151	5575	(I)	I'LL KISS THE WIFE SHE BAD ME
5151	5575	(I)	BOB OF FETTERCAIRN, THE
5151	5575	(I)	HAD I THE WYTE SHE BAD ME
5151	5575	(I)	COME KISS ME COME CLAP ME
5151	5575	(I)	I'LL KISS THE WIFE SHE BADE ME
5151	571H7	(I)	SOLDIER'S JOY, THE
5151	51H22	(I)	LADY ANN HOPE'S FAVOURITE
5151	51H22	(I)	LADY ANN HOPE'S FAVOURITE
5151	51H42	(I)	DONCASTER RACES
5151	51H1H3	(II)	SOLDIER'S JOY, THE
5151	51H1H7	(II)	SOLDIER'S JOY
5151	51H1H7	(I)	SOLDIER'S JOY(, THE)
5151	51H1H1H	(I)	SOLDIER'S JOY, THE
5151	6262	(I)	PRINCE OF WALES STRATHSPEY, THE
5151	6276	(I)	HADDINGTON ASSEMBLY
5151	6271H	(I)	HADDINGTON ASSEMBLY
5151	61H53	(I)	LORD DUNCAN'S GRAND MARCH
5151	7b427bL	(I)	MISS SUSAN SPALDING'S JIGG
5152	27bL22	(II)	GLENLYON('S PIPER)
5152	27bL22	(II)	GLEN LYON [GLENLYON]
5152	517bL2	(II)	HAUGHS OF CROMDALE
5152	517bL2	(II)	LORD KINGARTH
5152	517bL2	(I)	HAUGHS OF CROMDALE, THE
5152	517bL2	(I)	MERRY MAID'S WEDDING, THE
5152	517bL2	(I)	LADY CATHERINE STEWART (STRATHSPEY) or [HAUGHS O' CROMDALE, THE]
5152	517bL2	(I)	WATE YOU HOW THE PLAY BEGAN
5152	5147bL	(II)	HIGHLAND RANT
5152	5141	(I)	KEBBUCKSTANE WEDDING, THE
5152	5154	(I)	CAULD KAIL
5152	5155	(I)	PADDY FROM IRELAND
5152	5157b	(I)	IRISH PELT
5152	7b47bL4	(II)	CUFFE ST.
5153b	5142	(II)	SLEEPING MAGGIE [SLEEPY MAGGIE] [SLEEPY MAGGY]
5153b	5142	(I)	SLEEPY MAGGY/IE [SLEEPING MAGGIE]
5153	227b7b	(I)	MISS GORDON (ROCKVELL'S) REEL
5153	3261H	(II)	AIRIDH NAN BADAN
5153	3261H	(I)	ARAIDH NAM BADAN
5153	47bL46	(I)	McGREGOR MURRAY IN THE CELTIC CHAIR
5153	4522	(I)	COLONEL DAVID STEWART OF GARTH'S REEL
5153	5136	(I)	WESTERN ISLE DANCE
5153	5153	(II)	CAMERONIAN('S) RANT, THE
5153	5153	(II)	MR DUN'S FROLICK
5153	5153	(I)	MR DUN'S FROLICK
5153	5153	(I)	CAMERONIAN'S (RANT/STRATHSPEY/REEL), (THE)
5153	5156	(I)	CHORUS JIG, (THE)
5153	5163	(I)	CAMERONIAN'S RANT, THE
5153	5336	(I)	GLEAN' MOR NA H'ALBAIN [GLEANN MOR NA H-ALBAINN]
5153	5764	(II)	BRANDLINGS
5153	51H53	(I)	CAMERONIAN RANT, (THE)
5153	6753	(II)	MISS MARIA DUNDAS
5153	6753	(II)	LADY MARIA DUNDAS [LADY MARY DUNDAS]
5153	6753	(I)	MISS (MARIA) DUNDAS('S REEL)
5153	61H53	(II)	AN OIDHCHE BHA NA GABHAIR AGAINN [NIGHT WE HAD THE GOATS, THE]
5153	61H53	(I)	MR HUGH GRAY'S STRATHSPEY
5153	61H53	(I)	ISLA REEL
5154	117b4	(I)	LOCHIEL'S AWA TO FRANCE
5154	27bL24	(II)	LOCHIEL'S RANT [LOCHIEL'S AWA' TO/TAE FRANCE]
5154	27bL24	(I)	LOCHIEL'S RANT
5154	27bL24	(I)	MRS CRAWFURD OF ARDMILLAN'S REEL
5154	27bL24	(I)	LOCHAIL'S AWAY TO FRANCE
5154	57bL3b7bL	(I)	MISS SALLY MCLEAN
5154	5152	(I)	HIGHLAND BRIGADE AT WATERLOO, THE
5154	5153	(I)	CAMERONIAN RANT

5154	5155	(II)	HIGHLANDERS' FAREWELL TO WATERLOO
5154	534H2H	(II)	PETER MACLAGAN Esq.
5155	25L22	(II)	BURNS AND HIS HIGHLAND MARY
5155	27bL24	(I)	MRS DUFF (OF FETTERESSO'S) MARCH
5155	27bL44	(I)	MR BAIRD OF NEWBYTH'S JIGG
5155	3b117bL	(I)	BEHIND YON HILLS
5155	3b217bL	(I)	MY NANNY, O
5155	3b212	(I)	MY NANNY O
5155	3153	(I)	CAMERONIAN'S RANT
5155	3261H	(I)	ARIDH NA M'BADAN
5155	3572H	(I)	SHELDON HOUSE
5155	4522	(I)	KEPPOCH'S RANT
5155	5124	(II)	JAMES MOIR ESQ.'S STRATHSPEY
5155	5421	(I)	JOB OF JOURNEY WORK, THE
5155	5422	(I)	HERE'S HIS HEALTH IN WATER
5155	6522	(I)	LOCH VACH
5155	6522	(I)	MASTER FRANK ROMILY
5155	1H1H66	(II)	BONNIE BESSIE LEE
5155	1H1H66	(I)	BONNIE BESSIE LEE
5155	1H3H2H2	(I)	MOONMORE'S STRATHSPEY
515	656	(I)	LADY FITZGERALD'S REEL
5157b	27bL3b4	(I)	BRAES OF GLENORCHY, THE
5157b	47bL42	(II)	HILLS OF GLENORCHY, THE
5157b	47bL47b	(I)	HILLS OF GLENORCHY, THE
5157b	517b5	(II)	DEVIL IN THE KITCHEN, THE
5157b	557b6	(II)	TO THE HIGHLANDS AGAIN
5157	5122	(I)	LADY LAUDER DICK'S JIGG
5157	1H2H2H2H	(II)	MISS MENZIES OF CULDER [CULDARES]
5157	1H2H2H2H	(I)	MISS MENZIES OF CULDARE('S REEL)
5157	1H2H2H2H	(I)	MISS BAIN'S REEL
5151H	152H1H	(I)	MISS MARGARET THOMSON'S STRATHSPEY
5151H	4362	(I)	MISS HAY'S FAVOURITE
5151H	5125L	(I)	MISS CHARLOTTE STIRLING'S JIGG
5151H	5123	(I)	MISS JESSY STEWART'S JIGG
5151H	5125	(I)	MISS CHARLOTE STIRLING'S JIGG
5151H	5162	(I)	LADY SUTTIE'S REEL
5151H	5162	(I)	MISS JOHNSTON''S JIG
5151H	6522	(I)	Dr JOHN McLAGAN'S STRATHSPEY
5151H	6522H	(I)	QUICK STEP
5151H	3H4H2H2	(I)	BRIDGE OF DON, THE
5151H	3H4H2H2	(I)	MR GARDEN OF TROUP'S STRATHSPEY
5153H	1H644	(II)	BALMORAL SCHOTTISCHE
5162	5L7bL44	(I)	DUCHESS OF GORDON'S STRATHSPEY
5162	5125L	(I)	MR DANL McFARLANE'S DELIGHT
5162	5153H	(I)	MR CHAs GORDON'S STRATHSPEY
5162	512H5	(I)	McFARLAN'S DELIGHT
5164	2464	(II)	MISS MACINNES
5164	2464	(I)	MISS McINNES' REEL
5164	5124	(II)	JOHN ABRACH MACKAY
5164	641H4	(I)	LUCY'S DELIGHT
516	513	(I)	GO TO BERWICK JOHNNY
5165	47L12	(II)	PULL THE BEASTIE'S FIT
5165	427L6L	(I)	TOM TULLUS'S HORNPIPE
5165	4225L	(I)	COTILLION
5165	457L2	(I)	BANK'S DANCE
5165	42H22	(I)	MERRY COUNCILLORS, THE
5165	51H3H1H	(I)	JAMES PORTEOUS'S FAREWELL TO WHISKY
5165	6542	(II)	MR HANNAY OF BARGALY
5165	6542	(I)	MR HANNY OF BARGALY('S REEL)
5165	7b547bL	(I)	MISS MARY STEWART'S STRATHSPEY
5166	5132	(I)	JACK THE SAILOR
5161H	5125L	(II)	JAMIE RUSSELL
5161H	5122	(II)	GREENHOLM
5161H	5322	(I)	MISS PENNY McKINNON'S REEL
517b1H	53H2H2	(I)	MONALTRIE'S STRATHSPEY
511H3	37b27bL	(II)	JOHN McNIELL'S HIGHLAND FLING [?McNEILL)
511H3	4642	(I)	DUFF HOUSE
511H5	4321	(I)	FAVOURITE HORNPIPE, A
511H5	4362	(I)	MRS EDWARDS OF WOODEND'S JIG
511H6	517L2	(I)	MISS WILLIAMS FANCY
511H6	5153H	(I)	MISS HOPE OF PINKIE HOUSE'S STRATHSPEY
511H6	5522	(II)	LADYHILL, ELGIN
511H	775	(I)	MINUET
511H1H	1541	(I)	OIG FHEAR A CHULDUINN
			[BROWN HAIR'D YOUTH, THE]
511H1H	1541	(I)	NATIVE LAND, ADIEU
511H1H	5125L	(I)	GARDEN WELL, GLEN CALLATTER
513bH2H	7b547bL	(I)	HIGHWAY TO BOURTRIE HILL, THE
513bH2H	7b547bL	(I)	DUTCHESS OF BEAUFORT'S REEL
513H2H	6562	(I)	THIS IS NO MY AIN LASSIE
525L5L	136L2	(I)	LADY St. CLAIRS ERSKINE'S REEL
525L1	1214	(I)	BONNY CHRISTY

525L1	3111	(I)	BONIE KIRSTY
525L1	3114	(I)	BONNY CHRISTIE
525L1	3214	(I)	BONNY CHRISTY
526L6L	5555	(II)	I'LL HAP YE IN MY PLAIDIE
526L6L	5555	(I)	HAP ME WI' THY PETTICOAT, (COME)
526L6L	5555	(I)	LEITH WYND
526L6L	5555	(I)	COME HAP ME WITH THY PETTICOAT
526L1	5245	(II)	BONNY WEE THING
526L1	5265	(I)	BONNY WEE THING, THE
526L1	61H55	(II)	DREAM OF LOVE AT LUMSDEN, A
527L	112	(I)	PATIE'S WEDDING
527L2	6L16L1	(I)	DUCHESS OF HAMILTON'S REEL
527L2	331H7	(I)	JORUM, (THE/PUSH ABOUT THE)
527L2	331H7	(I)	LADY MARGRET MACDONALD
527L2	331H7	(I)	JORUM, (PUSH ABOUT [THE])
527L2	4235	(I)	GOUGH HOUSE
5215L	1333	(I)	GENERAL Mc BEAN'S STRATHSPEY
5215L	1422	(II)	HAZELDEAN
5215L	1432	(I)	JOCK O' HAZELDEAN
5215L	1522	(II)	CAPTAIN MCDUFF
5215L	1522	(I)	CAPTAIN McDUFF'S REEL
5217bL	6bL5L3b1	(I)	EILIDH DHUGHLAS
5217bL	5210	(I)	UNTITLED
5211	6L5L5L1	(I)	MISS MORRISON'S JIG
5211	6L5L5L1	(I)	WITHIN A MILE OF EDINBURGH
5211	6L224	(I)	MISS MACKENZIE'S STRATHSPEY
5211	1214	(I)	DANDLING O' THE BAIRNS, THE
5211	53b42	(II)	JOHN FORBES ESQ.
5211	5622	(I)	OLD WIFE HAUNTS AFTER ME, THE
5211	5622	(I)	HA A CHAILLICH AIR MO DHEIDH
5212	47L5L2	(I)	CUPID'S RECRUITING SERGEANT
5212	47L5L2	(I)	ISLAND OF LOVE
5212	4222	(I)	PORT PATRICK
5212	4323	(I)	ANNIE & COLIN
521	254	(I)	MILL O' TIFTIE'S ANNIE
5213	6L5L5L1	(II)	WITHIN A MILE [OF EDINBURGH TOUN]
5213	6L5L5L1	(I)	WITHIN A MILE OF EDINBURGH(TOWN)
5213	6L5L6L5L	(II)	PRESTON PANS
5213	7L5L2L2L	(I)	MISS DUNDASS OF KERSE STRATHSPEY
5213	126L6L	(I)	MRS DALZELL OF DALZELL LODGE
5213	5216L	(I)	MISS ELEZBATH OSWALD'S REEL
5226L	5266	(II)	MISS JOHNSTON
5226L	5266	(I)	MISS KINLOCH'S REEL
5226L	5266	(I)	MISS JOHNSON (OF BYKER'S) REEL [MISS JOHNSTON]
5226L	5266	(I)	MISS JESSY CAMPBELL'S REEL
5221	6L3L6L2	(II)	KITTY STEWART
5221	31H52	(I)	LONA'S VALE
5222	526L6	(I)	MISS KATIE HALL'S REEL
5223	1155	(I)	HARRY'S FROLICK
5221H	3H1H63	(I)	MRS GARDEN CAMPBELL OF TROUP AND GLENLYON'S STRATHSPEY
5236L	3L142	(I)	MISS ANN CARNEGIE'S HORNPIPE
5231	2522	(I)	CAPT GRAEME INCHBRAKIE'S STRATHSPEY
5231	5266	(I)	ALLEGRETTO
5231	5266	(I)	MORGAN RATTLER, (THE)
5231	5261H	(I)	JACKSON'S BOUNER BOUGHER
5231	1H675	(I)	DUMFRIES THEATRE
5232	7L6L5L3	(I)	BLACK MAN IS THE BRAVEST, THE
5232	7L6L5L6	(I)	BLACK MAN IS THE BRAVEST, THE
5232	551H1H	(I)	LADY St. CLAIR DYSART'S STRATHSPEY
5231H	5211H	(I)	KING OF POLAND'S ALLEMAND
5231H	64#1H5	(II)	BONNIE ANNIE ANDERSON
523	1H1H3H	(I)	CAIDIL GU LO
523	1H1H3H	(I)	SLEEP ON TILL DAY
5245L	4131	(II)	POETS GAVOTTE, THE
5241	7L415	(I)	HEROES OF WATERLOO
5241	1216L	(I)	BROOM'S HUMOUR
5244	4222	(II)	WELCOME, CHARLIE STEWART
5244	5222	(II)	YOU'R(E) WELCOME CHARLIE STEWART
5244	5222	(II)	CHARLIE STUART [YOU'RE WELCOME CHARLIE STUART]
5244	5222	(I)	QUEENSBERRY HOUSE
5244	5222	(I)	CHARLIE STUART
5257bL	5L5L3bL5L	(I)	BHLIADHNA DH'EIRICH AN IOMAIRT
5251	427L3	(I)	LES PLAISEURS DES DAMES
5252	5521	(I)	FIRST OF APRIL, THE
5255	222H1H	(I)	LAY DOWN IN THE BROOM
5255	222H2H	(I)	(LOW) DOWN IN THE BROOM
525	523	(I)	CRIES OF EDINBURGH, THE
5255	6665	(I)	WOE'S MY HEART THAT WE SHOU'S SUNDER
5256	222H2H	(I)	LOW DOWN IN THE BROOM

```
5262        5266L       (II)  ANE AN' TWENTY TAM
5262        5266L       (I)   SCOTCH GIG
5264        3135        (I)   LOTHARIA
5266        5226L       (II)  HOUSE OF INVERCAULD, THE
5266        5222        (I)   GLEN MORISONE'S REELL
521H2       2662        (II)  CAIRNGORM (CHEAP MEAL)
521H2       2662        (II)  CHEAP MEAL
521H2       2662        (I)   CHEAP MEAL
521H2       526L2       (I)   MRS RIDDELL'S OF WOODLY PARK'S REEL
521H4       526L2       (II)  ROBSLEY COTTAGE
521H6       5235        (I)   WILKE'S WRIGLE
521H7       1H136       (I)   ENGLISH BRING TO GRATNEY GREEN, THE
521H1H      5222        (I)   SYMINGTON LODGE
521H1H      5233        (I)   SHE WOU'D NOT DIE A MAID
521H1H      5234        (I)   BEWARE O' BONIE ANN
521H1H      2H72H5      (I)   HOLE IN THE RIDDLE, THE
521H1H      2H72H2H     (I)   DUNCAN McLEERIE
53b5L1      424L7bL     (II)  LADY LUCINDA RAMSAY
53b5L1      424L7bL     (I)   LADY LUCINDA RAMSAY('S NEW STRATHSPEY)
53b11       12b42b      (I)   LA TOISON D'OR
53b11       13b53b      (I)   UNA'S LOCK
53b11       3b13b1      (II)  MR THOMAS FORBES
53b11       3b3b51H     (II)  PUNKIE WILLIE
53b11       3b57b5      (I)   HO RO MO NIGHEAN DONN BHOIDHEACH
53b11       447bL7bL    (II)  WARLOCKS, THE
53b11       5551H       (II)  FAREWELL TO BUTE
53b11       57b11       (I)   JAMES ROBERTSON, ESQr's STRATHSPEY
53b11       6b56b5      (II)  LADY BAIRD
53b13b      7bL5bL7L3b  (I)   MISS HAMILTON OF SUNDRUM'S REEL
53b13b      2427bL      (I)   MR LEID'S REEL
53b13b      243b5       (I)   COTERIE, THE
53b13b      427bL2      (II)  DROGHEDA LASSES
53b13b      427bL2      (I)   MISS ISABELLA PATERSON'S REEL
53b13b      4242        (I)   LORD MILLINGTON'S STRATHSPEY
53b13b      427b2       (II)  LADY MARY HAY
53b13b      4422        (II)  URQUHART'S STRATHSPEY
53b13b      4422        (I)   MR ORQUHART'S STRATHSPEY
53b13b      53b3b5      (I)   MISS WEMYS OF WEMYS'S SCOTS MEASURE
53b13b      53b47bL     (I)   MOLL IN THE WAD(D)
53b1        53b1H       (I)   LADY AGNES PERCY'S HORNPIPE
53b11H      7b57b5      (II)  HIELAN' TONAL'
53b11H      3bH751H     (I)   NATHANIEL GOW'S LAMENT
                              FOR MRS OSWALD OF AUCHINCRUIVE
53b2        3b51        (I)   ORAN GAOIL
53b3b1      3b7bL7bL5L  (I)   GHOID IAD MO BHEAN (UAM AN REIR)
53b3b4      3b122       (I)   GOUD A GOUPENS
53b3b       53b2        (I)   LOVE & WHISKEY
53b3b7b     4224        (II)  EARL OF BREADALBAN'S BIRTHDAY
53b3b7b     4224        (I)   MRS M. SUTTON'S STRATHSPEY
53b3b7b     4224        (I)   EARL OF BREADLABAN(E)'S BIRTH DAY
53b3b7b     4226        (II)  SCOLDING WIVES OF ABERTARFF, THE
53b3b7b     4226        (I)   MNATHAN TRODACH OBAIR-THAIRBH
53b41       53b57bL     (I)   FILL THE STOUP
53b42       13b53bH     (I)   MRS WALKER OF URQUHART'S STRATHSPEY
53b44       53b44       (I)   RING, THE
53b51       53b47bL     (I)   LADY FRANCES SCOT'S REEL
53b51       53b47bL     (I)   LADY DOUGLAS OF BOTHWELL
53b51       53b47bL     (I)   COLONEL MACKENZIE'S REEL
53b51       53b51       (II)  MAGGIE'S APRON
53b53b      5L15L1      (I)   EMPTY PURSE, THE
53b53b      2427bL      (II)  MRS WALTER BIGGAR
53b53b      2427bL      (I)   MISS ALICIA HEGGE'S STRATHSPEY
53b53b      2427bL      (I)   MISS GARDEN (DELGATY'S) STRATHSPEY
53b53b      3b7b42      (I)   MR CLARK'S FAVOURITE
53b53b      4242        (I)   HIGHLAND SECRETARY, THE
                              MR MACKENZIES STRATHSPEY
53b53b      4242        (I)   ABERCAIRNEY HOUSE
53b53b      53b42       (I)   MISS GUTHRIE OF GUTHRIE'S STRATHSPEY
53b53b      53b42       (I)   SLEEPY MAGGIE
53b53b      53b25L      (II)  GREGG'S PIPES
53b53b      53b42       (I)   PIPPINGO REEL, THE
535L3L      7L244       (I)   MRS SHERRIF CAMERON
535L3L      7L244       (I)   MISS FYFFE'S STRATHSPEY
535L3L      1326        (I)   MISS MARGARET SETON'S STRATHSPEY
535L3L      5324        (I)   DUCHESS OF BEDFORD'S STRATHSPEY
535L5L      1L5L5L5L    (I)   MISS HALL OF DUNGLASS'S REEL
535L6L      5L462       (I)   MR GRANT OF ROTHYMURCHUS STRATHSPEY
535L1       3214        (I)   BONNY CHRISTY
536L5L      3L11H2H     (II)  HUNTLY'S WEDDING MEDLEY
                              [BANAIS MARCUIS HUNNDFHUINN]
536L5L      3L11H2H     (I)   BAINNAIS MARC HUNDFHUIN
                              [BANAIS MARCUS HUNNDFHUINN]
```

536L5L	4L3L22L	(II)	MISS CAMPBELL'S REEL
536L5L	4L3L22L	(II)	MR PETER McGRIGOR'S STRATHSPEY
536L5L	4L3L22L	(I)	TAY MOUTH
536L5L	4L3L22L	(I)	ATHOLL REEL, THE
536L5L	4L3L22L	(I)	MISS CAMPBELL('S REEL)
536L5L	5L5L42	(I)	LORD PALMERSTON'S FAVOURITE
536L5L	5L6L3L2L	(I)	MRS WARDEN OF PARKHILL
536L5L	6L5L32	(II)	LOCH BUILG
536L5L	356L2	(II)	ABBEY CRAIG, THE
536L5L	5367	(I)	MISS NELLY WATSON'S STRATHSPEY [MISS N. WATSON'S STR.]
536L6L	415L5L	(I)	MISS BARBARA CAMPBELL'S JIGG
536L7L	16L27L	(I)	MISS CHRISTIAN BUCHAN OF KELLIES FAVORITE
536L1	5L6L5L6L	(II)	WILD ROSES
536L2	1566	(I)	MR WORK'S REEL
536L2	3535	(I)	HONbIe MRS MAULE OF PANMURE'S FAVORITE
537L5L	3L4L5L2	(I)	WET QUAKERS, THE
537L5L	3L4L5L2	(I)	MERRY QUAKERS
537L5L	31H46	(I)	PRINCE WILLIAM OF GLOUCESTERS FAVORITE
537L7L	15L4L3L	(I)	MISS CHARLOTE HOPE OF CRAIGIEHALL
537L7L	3451H	(I)	MISS PERKIN'S REEL
537L1	234#5	(I)	MISS GOW OF LONDON
537L2	221H7	(I)	GORANS, THE
537L2	3367	(I)	PUSH ABOUT THE JORUM
537L2	331H7	(II)	PUSH ABOUT THE JORUM
537L2	3561H	(I)	MISS ERSKINE OF MARR'S FAVOURITE
537L2	351H5	(I)	PARKS OF EGLINTON, THE
537L2	31H66	(II)	MISS HERON(OF HERON)
537L2	31H66	(I)	MISS HERON (OF HERON) 'S REEL [MISS HERRON'S REEL]
537L2	5353	(II)	LORD AIRLIE
537L2	5353	(I)	LORD AIRLY'S REEL [LORD AIRLIE]
537L2	5354	(I)	HONbIe Mr F. GRAY'S STRATHSPEY
5316L	5L3L5L3L	(I)	LADY ELIZABETH LINDSAY'S STRATHSPEY
5315L	4L3L22L	(I)	MISS TROTTERS (OF BUSH'S) REEL
5315L	4L3L41	(I)	MISS DALZIEL'S STRATHSPEY
5315L	4L3L41	(I)	HORNPIPE, A
5315L	6L5L2L2	(I)	MISS SPENS'S REEL
5315L	6L113	(II)	SWEET MEMORIES OF ARDLER
5315L	6L47L2	(II)	LORD RAMSAY
5315L	1462	(I)	ACHORACHAN
5315L	3562	(II)	MAR CASTLE
5315L	4362	(II)	MR GEORGE MORRISON'S STRATHSPEY
5316L	5L3L5L3L	(II)	LADY ELIZABETH LINDSAY
5316L	5L3L24	(II)	PLOUGHMAN LADDIE, THE
5316L	5L15L5L	(I)	SRATH MHUISIDH [STRATH MHATHAISIDH]
5316L	5L132	(I)	JOHN FRENCH'S COMPts TO MR NATH. GOW
5316L	5L642	(I)	MISS MARGARET MOIR'S STRATHSPEY
5311	6L5L6L5L	(II)	LADY BAIRD
5311	6L5L6L5L	(I)	LADY BAIRD'S (STRATHSPEY/REEL)
5311	6L12L2L	(II)	MR ALEXANDER MUNRO'S STRATHSPEY
5311	1313	(II)	DAINTY DAVIE [DAINTIE DAVIE]
5311	1313	(I)	DAINTY DAVIE
5311	1313	(I)	PERTHSHIRE DANCING MEASURES & C No. 14 (MRS MACDONALD OF STAFFA'S REEL)
5311	1313	(I)	MRS MACDONALD OF STAFFA'S REEL (PERTHSHIRE DANCING MEASURES &c No14)
5311	27L5L5L	(I)	LADIES AMUSEMENT, THE
5311	2226L	(I)	LORD BATEMAN'S FANCY
5311	2246	(II)	SIR REGINALD MACDONALD
5311	22H2H1H	(I)	O'ER THE MUIR TO MAGGIE
5311	437L2	(I)	FAL LA LA
5311	4321	(I)	SHEPHERD ONCE HAD LOST HIS LOVE, A
5311	5311	(I)	MISS ELIZABETH CARNEGIE'S FAVOURITE VALTZ
5311	5362	(II)	MRS OSWALD (OF AUCHINCRUIVES) NEW
5311	5362	(I)	MRS OSWALD [OF AUCHINCRUIVE] 'S (NEW) STRATHSPEY
5311	5555	(I)	HAP ME WITH THY PETTICOAT
5311	51H2H2H	(I)	MR McINTOSH'S WHIM
5311	61H65	(I)	LITTLE NABOB, THE
5312	5L5L5L2	(I)	(IRISH) WATERMAN, THE
5312	5L5L32	(I)	WATER-MAN, THE
5312'	5L5L42	(I)	WATERMAN, THE
531	222	(I)	HIGHLAND SANTE, THE
5312	3416L	(I)	TREEBLE HORNPIPE No.3
5312	4242	(I)	TRIP TO DUNKIRK, A
5312	5520	(I)	O MARY IS MY ONLY JOY
5312	61H1H7	(I)	SEATON HOUSE
5312	61H1H7	(I)	MAID OF FORFAR, THE
531	36L6L	(I)	THA SGEUL BEAG AGAM AIR FIONN
5313	1336	(I)	SIR ALEXr DON'S MEDLEY (JIG)
5313	1362	(I)	PERTH(SHIRE) HUNT

5313	1362	(I)	PERTH HUNT
531	315	(I)	WOO'D AND MARRIED AND A'
5313	1632	(I)	MISS BRANDER OF SPRINGFIELD
5313	2424	(I)	HAWICK LASSES, A REEL
5313	3555	(II)	CRAIGLUG BRIG
5313	427bL2	(II)	ANGUS MACRAE
5313	427bL4	(II)	SIRDAR'S MARCH, THE
			[SIRDAR, LORD KITCHENER, THE]
5313	427L7L	(I)	HONble. MISS H. ELLIOT'S DANCE, THE
5313	437L7L	(I)	KING'S BIRTH DAY, THE
5313	4666	(II)	MR A.G. WILKEN'S FAVOURITE
5313	5316L	(I)	MO DHUCHAS [MO DHUTHCHAS)
5313	5353	(II)	JOHN ROY STEWART [JOHN ROY STUART]
5313	5353	(I)	(JOHN) ROY STEWART ('S REEL)
5313	5353	(I)	OCH A BHODAICH NA BI RIUM
5313	5351H	(II)	BALMENACH
5313	5366	(I)	MISS GRANT OF GRANT'S STRATHSPEY
5313	5366	(I)	MRS HAY OF WESTERTOWN'S STRATHSPEY
5313	5367	(I)	PIT THIEVELESS CASTLE
531	355	(I)	WOO'D AND MARRIED AND A'
5313	5551	(I)	JOHN ROY STEWART
5313	5556	(I)	MARCH IN MASANIELLO
5313	5755	(I)	DOIDEAG MHUILEACH
5313	51H62	(II)	BONNY LASSIE O'
5313	51H62	(I)	AIR M'ALLUIN BHEIRIN POG DHI
			[AIR M'FHALLUINN BHEIRINN...]
5313	6424	(II)	ARBEADIE
5313	6542	(I)	MR ALEXr. MITCHEL, CRAIGS REEL
5313	6542	(I)	MOUNT STEWART HOUSE
5313	6562	(I)	LOCH MADEY
5313	6647bL	(II)	REEL O' CORSE
5314	5366	(II)	JESSIE SMITH
5314	5366	(I)	MRS SMITH'S STRATHSPEY
5315	2653	(I)	COVE OF CORK, THE
5315	261H2H	(I)	CAVE OF CORK, THE
5315	261H2H	(I)	ORCHILL'S FAVOURITE
531	536	(I)	IOMAN NAN GAMHNA
531	536	(I)	(O) GAE TO THE KY WI' ME JOHNNY
5315	437b2	(I)	MISS HENDERSON OF FORDEL('S REEL)
5315	4362	(II)	MISS HENDERSON OF FORDEL
5315	4362	(II)	COLONEL FRASER OF KNOCKY
5315	4362	(I)	COLONEL FRASER OF KNOCKY'S STRATHSPEY
5315	4522	(I)	MISS MARY JOHNSTON'S STRATHSPEY
5315	5336	(II)	COME ALONG AND KEEP YOUR PROMISE
5315	5336	(I)	TEANN A NALL IS CUM' DO GHEALLADH
531	555	(II)	WOO'D AN' MARRIED AN' A'
531	555	(I)	WOO'D AND MARRIED AND A'
5315	1H52H2	(I)	COLONEL ROSE OF KILRAVOCK'S STRATHSPEY
531	642	(I)	SINGLE HORNPIPE
5316	42H1H1H	(I)	MINUET
5311H	5324	(II)	LIGHT AND AIRY
5311H	5324	(I)	LIGHT AND AIRY
5311H	5322H	(I)	MISS BIGGAR'S STRATHSPEY
5311H	7755	(I)	JIG
531	1H1H3H	(I)	CAIDIL GU LA
5311H	3H2H3H5H	(II)	BUT AND BEN
5313H	2H4H2H2	(I)	FAREWELL, THE
5325L	3L232	(I)	MISS McKINLAY'S DANCE
5325L	536L5L	(I)	MISS BIGG'S FANCY
5325L	5351H	(I)	MRS J. F. GORDON OF BALMUIR'S STR.
5326L	5L132	(II)	BANKS OF AVON, THE
5326L	5L132	(I)	MRS HAMILTON OF BARGENEY
5326L	1361H	(II)	BUSH IN BLOSSOM, THE
5326L	5322	(II)	MARR LODGE
5326L	5366	(I)	MERRY LADS OF CLYDE, THE
5326L	5361H	(II)	MISS AMELIA OLIPHANT[,] GASK
5326L	5361H	(I)	MISS AMELIA OLIPHANT GASK'S STRATHSPEY
5326L	531H1H	(II)	LOOK BEHIND YOU
			(=HOUSE OF LETTERFOURIE, THE)
5326L	531H1H	(II)	LASSIE LOOK BEHIND YE
5326L	531H1H	(II)	HOUSE OF LETTERFOURIE, THE [or
			LASSES LOOK BEHIND YOU]
5326L	531H1H	(I)	LOOK BEHIND YOU
5326L	531H1H	(I)	LADY ANNE GORDON('S REEL)
5326L	531H1H	(I)	HOUSE OF LETTERFOURIE, THE or
			[LASSES LOOK BEHIND YOU]
5326L	531H1H	(I)	ABERCORN WEDDING, THE
5326L	5555	(I)	LEITH WYND
5327bL	5337b	(II)	LADY CHARLOTTE DURHAM
5327bL	5337b	(I)	LADY CHARLOTTE DURHAM'S STRATHSPEY
5327L	15L4L2L	(II)	MR GRANT OF KINAIRD
5327L	15L4L2L	(I)	LADY GRACE DOUGLASS'S REEL

5327L	15L4L2L	(I)	HILL OF BURNIE, THE
5327L	15L4L2L	(I)	MR GRANT OF KINAIRD('S REEL)
5327L	15L4L2L	(I)	LOYAL SOLDIER, THE
5327L	15L4L2L	(II)	LADY GRACE DOUGLAS
5327L	227L6L	(I)	Lt. COLONEL GUTHRIE (OF THE FORFARSHIRE SHARP SHOOTERS) REEL
532	16L5L	(I)	'S MI GA M'IOMAGAN A'M' LEABAIDH
5321	1313	(I)	DAINTY DAVIE
5321	1453	(I)	LA BELLE ARSENE
5321	216L5L	(II)	SANDIE OWER THE SEA
5321	5321	(II)	COUNTRY DANCE
5321	5321	(I)	QUICK STEP 55th REGt
5322	5L1H66	(II)	MILLER O' DRONE, THE
5322	5L1H66	(I)	MILLAR OF DRONE, THE
5322	16L3L1	(I)	MRS DUFF OF CARNUCIE'S REEL
5322	16L22	(I)	MRS SIM'S STRATHSPEY
5322	1357	(I)	MISS ELIZABETH DEWAR'S REEL
5322	36L7L6L	(I)	WAR'S ALARMS
5322	36L16L	(I)	(WHEN) WAR'S ALARMS (ENTIC'D MY WILLY)
5322	4215L	(I)	ALLEGRO
5322	4215L	(I)	LA JUPON ROUGE
5322	4215L	(I)	SCARLET PETTICOAT, THE
5322	526L6L	(II)	MRS GORDON OF WHITEHILL
5322	526L6L	(I)	MRS GORDON OF WHITEHILL('S STRATHSPEY)
5322	5331H	(I)	KING CRISPIN
5322	5355	(I)	HAP ME WITH THY PETTICOAT
5322	5366	(II)	MISS OLIPHANT
5322	5376	(I)	ORANGEFIELD HOUSE
5322	5376	(I)	MRS McREADY'S STRATHSPEY
5322	5555	(I)	LEITH WYND
5323	536L7L	(II)	LADY CHARLOTTE CAMPBELL
5323	536L7L	(I)	LADY CHARLOTTE CAMPBELL('S STRATHSPEY)
5323	536L7L	(I)	LADY CHARLOTTE CAMPBELL ('S STRATHSPEY)
5323	536L7L	(I)	FOX, THE
5323	5321	(I)	DUCHESS OF BEDFORD'S WALTZ, THE
5324	5213	(I)	JOHNNY COCK UP THE BEAVER
5324	5313	(I)	QUICK STEP 26th Regt.
5324	5313	(I)	(JOHNNY) COCK UP YOUR BEAVER
5324	5324	(I)	HIGHLAND COTTAGE
5324	5353	(II)	KEEP THE COUNTRY BONNY LASSIE
5324	5353	(II)	THROUGH THE WOOD OF FYVIE
5324	5353	(I)	THRO' THE WOOD (OF FAVIE/FYVIE)
5324	5353	(I)	KEEP THE COUNTRY BONNY LASSIE
5324	5351H	(I)	MISS MONTGOMERIE OF SKELMORELIE'S STRATHSPEY
5324	5363	(I)	LET'S SHAK HER WEALL
5324	5366	(I)	EARL OF FIFE, THE
5324	531H3	(I)	KEEP THE COUNTRY BONNY LASSIE
532	532	(I)	MR WILSON'S HORNPIPE
532	534	(I)	WARLD'S GANE O'ER ME NOW, THE
532	562	(I)	CRAIGILLACHY
5322	5376	(I)	MRS McCARDIE'S STRATHSPEY
5326	5353	(I)	MISS CHRISTIAN RIDDELL'S STRATHSPEY
5326	5353	(I)	NESS RIVER
5326	5355	(II)	GORDON CASTLE
5326	5355	(I)	GORDON CASTLE
5326	5512	(I)	PERTHSHIRE DANCING MEASURES & C No. 1
5322H	5353	(II)	FIGHT ABOUT THE FIRESIDE
5322H	5353	(II)	FECHT ABOUT THE FIRESIDE
5322H	5353	(I)	FIGHT ABOUT THE FIRE SIDE
5337L	2H756	(II)	MRS ROBERTSON GRISHORNISH
533	15L5L	(I)	AN TALL 'AM BU GNA DO MHACLEOID
5331	1232	(I)	SUSANNA
5331	247L5L	(I)	MRS McLEOD OF COLBECK'S FAVOURITE
5331	2422	(I)	FUNERAL MARCH
5331	2453	(I)	LASSES OF THE WEST, THE
5331	5331	(I)	THERE'S BRAVE BEER AT SUDBURY'S
5331	5347bL	(I)	LIEUT. GRANT OF THE 10th FOOT'S STRATHSPEY
5331	5362	(I)	YOUR WELCOME INTO BERVIE
5331	6542	(I)	LADY LOUISA GORDON'S STRATHSPEY
5331	2H72H5	(I)	MERRY MEETING, THE
533	1#64	(II)	FALLEN CHIEF, THE
5332	16L11	(I)	DAINTY DAVIE
5332	3331H	(I)	WHITE COCKADE, THE
5332	5333	(I)	TO THE WEAVER GIN YE GO
5332	5351H	(I)	NATHANIEL GOW'S COMPLts TO MR GRANT
5332	6221H	(I)	DAY RETURNS (MY BOSOM BURNS), THE
5332	6221H	(I)	SEVENTH OF NOVEMBER, THE
5333	2253	(I)	ROMANCE
5333	2427bL	(II)	MR DAVID STEWART
5333	2427bL	(I)	MR DAVID STEWART('S REEL)
5333	3342	(I)	OSCAR & MALVINA

```
5333      3342        (I)   KEMPSHOT HUNT
5333      3342        (I)   SIR HUGH MUNRO OF FOWLES REEL
5333      3442        (I)   KEMPSHOT(T) HUNT
5333      47bL46      (I)   LASSES LIKES NAE BRANDY
5333      47bL7b7bL   (I)   MRS TULLOH'S JIG
5333      47bL7b7bL   (I)   MISS DUNKANSONS JIGG
5333      47bL7b7bL   (I)   ALLAN RAMSAY
5333      47bL1H3H    (I)   LASSES LIKES NAE BRANDY
5333      4322        (I)   JACKSON'S FROLICK
5333      5156        (II)  MAGGIE CAMERON
5333      5321        (I)   CRONAN MAIRI NIGHEAN ALASTAIR RUADH
                            [LUINNEAG MHIC LEOID]
5333      5322        (II)  ALDIVALLOCH
5333      5322        (II)  ROY'S WIFE
5333      5322        (I)   DUCHESS OF HAMILTON'S REELL, THE
5333      5322        (I)   SLOW AND DISTINCT
5333      5322        (I)   ROY'S WIFE (OF ALLDIVALLOCH)
5333      5322        (I)   RUFFIAN'S RANT, THE
5333      5322        (I)   WHITE COCKADE, THE
5333      5322        (I)   AULD BESSY
5333      5326        (I)   DOWN WITH THE PEEBLES
5333      5332        (I)   WHITE COCKADE
5333      5336        (II)  ROBERT MENZIES
5333      5336        (I)   MR R. MENZIES' STRATHSPEY
5334      5342        (I)   DUKE OF GLOUCESTERS REEL
533       532         (I)   FA'S SAE MERRY'S THE MILLER
                            WHEN A' HIS POCKS ARE FU'
533       534         (II)  DROPS OF BRANDY
533       534         (I)   CAMMOLAN
533       534         (I)   DROPS OF BRANDY
533       535         (I)   OFF SHE GOES
533       535         (I)   (FOLLOW HER) OVER THE BORDER
5335      351H5       (I)   CAMERON OF LOCHIL'S REEL
533       536         (I)   HEY THE HEDRIE FALIE
533       536         (I)   BROSE AND BUTTER
5335      437b2       (I)   MRS GRAHAM'S DELIGHT
5335      4362        (I)   MRS GRAHAM (OF BALGOWAN'S) REEL
5335      437b2       (II)  HONble. MRS. GRAHAM OF BALGOWAN, THE
5335      437b2       (I)   MRS GRAHAM OF BALGOWAN'S REEL
5335      4642        (I)   MISS FANNY HOW'S SCOTCH MEASURE
5335      5331        (I)   MISS HERRON OF HERRON'S VALTZ
5335      6422        (I)   BESSIE'S HAGGES
5335      6542        (I)   MISS JACKSON'S REEL
5335      6562        (II)  DEE CASTLE
5335      1H332       (II)  MR THOMSON
533       611         (I)   'S MI AIR CRAGAN NA SGURRA
5336      4224        (I)   MISS DRUMMOND OF PERTH'S REEL
5336      5327bL      (I)   RUMBLING BRIDGE, THE
5336      5322        (II)  LADY MADELINA SINCLAIR
5336      5362        (I)   TRIP TO HOLLAND, A
5336      537b2       (I)   MRS GRAHAM OF ORCHILL'S REEL
5336      5522        (I)   BRAES OF ABERARDER STRATHSPEY, THE
5336      5522        (I)   LADY MADELINA SINCLAIR ('S STRATHSPEY)
5336      5622        (II)  LADY MADELINA SINCLAIR
5336      5622        (I)   LADY MADELINA SINCLAIR'S STRATHSPEY
5336      1H631       (II)  SKYE AIR, A
5336      1H631       (I)   HITHIL UIL AGUS
5336      1H631       (I)   SKYE AIR, A  (O HITHIL O HORINO)
                            (HITHIL UIL AGUS)
5337b     7bL7b27bL   (I)   SALISBURY CRAGGS
5337b     4224        (II)  HONBLE. MISS DRUMMOND OF PERTH
5337b     4224        (I)   MISS DRUMMOND OF PERTH'S REEL
5337b     4224        (I)   MISS GRACE GORDON'S STRATHSPEY
5337b     4242        (I)   MISS BARCLAY'S REEL
5337      64#4#1H     (I)   HOW CAN I BE SAD ON MY WEDDING DAY
5331H     537b2       (I)   MISS STEWART OF URRARDS REEL
5331H     7b427bL     (I)   MISS GORDON OF BRAID'S REEL
5331H     3H526       (II)  UIST LASSES' DARLING, THE
5331H     3H526       (I)   MAC A' BHAILLIDH A UIST
5347L     15L4L2L     (I)   LADY GRACE DOUGLAS'S REEL
5341      2233        (I)   DRAPER'S FANCY, THE
5342      7L232       (I)   MISS ISABELLA REID'S REEL
5342      15L5L4L     (I)   MARQUIS OF WELLINGTON
5342      1765        (I)   TRIUMPH, THE
5342      1761H       (II)  TRIUMPH, THE
5342      11H66       (II)  TRIUMPH
5342      11H76       (II)  TRIUMPH, THE
5342      11H76       (I)   TRIUMPH, THE
534       223         (I)   FAVOURITE BALLAD FROM ROBIN HOOD, A
5342      35L5L1L     (I)   MRS DUFF OF MUIRTOWN'S WALTZ
5342      3125L       (I)   RIVER TAY, THE
5342      3125L       (I)   MISS RIDDLE'S FANCY
```

5342	3127L	(I)	MARCH OF THE 44th REGT.
5342	3526L	(I)	MID LOTHIAN
5342	351H3	(I)	SCARBROUGH WHIM
5342	537L5L	(I)	HONble. MRS. CHARTERIS' STRATHSPEY
5342	5346	(II)	EWIE WI' THE CROOKED HORN
5342	5353	(II)	SUSIE BRODIE
5342	5353	(I)	SUSIE BRODIE
5342	5351H	(I)	MISS MONTGOMERY'S REEL
5342	5361H	(I)	TULLOCH CASTLE
5342	531H3	(II)	MARY GRAY
5342	531H3	(I)	MARY GRAY
5342	5765	(I)	LA TRIUMPHE
5343	5321	(I)	BLOW ZABELLA
5344	5322	(II)	CHARLIE STUART
5344	5342	(II)	INVER LASSES
534	516	(I)	WHEN FIRST MY FOND DAMON
5345	5321	(I)	NEEPS LIKE SUCKER, WHAE'LL BUY NEEPS
5346	5216L	(I)	DOCTOR'S FANCY, THE
5346	536L7L	(II)	RIDDRIE
5346	5321	(I)	LADY JANE BELSCHES'S ALAMANDE
5346	5322	(II)	WHITE HEATHER
5346	5342	(II)	SIR GEORGE MACKENZIE OF COUL
5346	5342	(II)	INVER LASSES
5346	5342	(I)	SIR GEORGE MACKENZIE(OF COUL)('S REEL)
5346	5342	(I)	BRIDGE OF CROSK, THE
5346	5346	(I)	DAY, THE
5346	1H2H53	(I)	THEADORE, THE
5356L	6L5L42	(I)	WAKEFIELD HUNT
5356L	6L5L53	(I)	DEVONSHIRE HUNT, THE
5357L	2442	(I)	CHESHUNT STATUTE
5351	6L7L11	(II)	BABIE'S SCHOTTISCHE
5351	27L25L	(II)	FALLS OF DIVACH, THE
5351	2432	(I)	SEE THE CONQUERING HERO COMES
5351	2451	(I)	ROUTE IS COME, THE
5351	2466	(II)	MR JAMES MUNRO'S STRATHSPEY
5351	3522	(II)	HIGHLANDMAN'S COWL, THE
5351	4242	(I)	SAW AWAY 'LIAS SCRAPE AWAY
5351	4522	(I)	HE HIRPLED TILL HER
5351	537L2	(II)	RORY O' MORE
5351	5316L	(I)	SHAKE YOURSELF
5351	5325L	(I)	GREIG'S PIPES
5351	5326L	(II)	GREIG'S PIPES
5351	5326L	(II)	WILLIE WINKIE
5351	5326L	(I)	WILLIE WINKIE ('S TESTAMENT)
5351	5326L	(I)	GREIG'S PIPES
5351	5336	(II)	SIR JAMES DOUGLAS
5351	5331H	(II)	'CHAILLEACH ODHAR [DUNN CARLINE, THE]
5351	5331H	(II)	CAILLICH ODHAR
5351	5331H	(I)	SIR CHARLES DOUGLASS'S STRATHSPEY
5351	5351	(I)	MISS OGILVY'S WALTZ
5351	5355	(I)	DUKE OF GORDON'S RANT, THE
5351	5355	(I)	BOHD NA HESUDH
5351	5362	(II)	DORNOCH LINKS
5351	5362	(II)	FILL THE STOUP
5351	5362	(I)	FILL THE STOUP
5351	5364	(I)	MARQUES OF TULLYBARDIN'S REEL, THE
5351	5364	(I)	MERRY AT THE FAIR
5351	5364	(I)	LORD McKENZIES STRATHSPEY
5351	532H2	(I)	MRS FARQUHARSON (OF INVERCAULD)'S REEL
5351	5453	(I)	DOCTORS DREAM, THE
5351	1H46L5L	(I)	PRINCESS AUGUSTA
5351	1H46L5L	(I)	BULLERS OF BUCHAN, THE
5351	1H46L5L	(I)	MRS DAVID STEWART'S FAVORITE
5352	2242	(I)	MADle HEINEL'S FANCY
5352	5253	(I)	PIOBAIREACHD MHIC DHONUIL
5352	5353	(I)	PIOBAIREACHD DHOMHNUILL DUIBH
			[PIBROCH O' DONALD DUBH]
5352	5552	(I)	PIBROCH OF DONUIL DUBH
5353	5L347bL	(I)	UNTITLED
5353	6L27L5L	(II)	MISS DOUGLAS
5353	6L27L5L	(I)	MISS DOUGLAS'S STRATHSPEY
5353	7bL7b44	(II)	LICK THE LADLE SANDY
5353	7bL7b46	(I)	LICK THE LADLE SANDY
5353	7L27L5L	(II)	GEORGE THE IVth's WELCOME TO EDINBURGH
5353	7L27L2	(II)	LAIRD OF MACINTOSH, THE
5353	7L27L2	(I)	LAIRD OF MAC(K)INTOSH ('S STRATHSPEY(, THE)
5353	1243	(I)	MISS CHRISTIAN DUFF'S FAVORITE
5353	1353	(II)	CLASHNETTIE'S HORNPIPE
5353	173H7	(II)	SALAMANCA, THE
5353	26L7L5L	(I)	COUNTESS OF WEMYSS' REEL
5353	27bL47bL	(I)	NINETY-SECOND, THE
5353	2247L	(I)	LADY SALTON'S GAVOTT

5353	2362	(I)	MISS ASHURST'S REEL
5353	2372	(I)	MISS JESS CAMPBELL'S REEL
5353	2462	(I)	MISS MORISON'S REEL
5353	27b27bL	(I)	LADY STAMFORD'S REEL
5353	3127bL	(I)	MISS BARBARA DONALD'S STRATHSPEY
5353	3127L	(I)	STRATH SPAY REEL
5353	3122	(I)	DOROTHEA OF HYDRABAD
5353	4224	(I)	BRIDGE OF FORTH, THE [BRIDGE OF FOSS, THE]
5353	4224	(I)	BRIDGE OF KYNNACHAN
5353	4542	(II)	MARQUIS OF LORN
5353	437L2	(I)	MISS BETTY WATERSTON'S REEL
5353	4322	(I)	MRS JOHN STEWART'S STRATHSPEY
5353	4433	(I)	FINALI, THE
5353	4542	(I)	MARQUIS OF LORN('S REEL, THE)
5353	462H7	(II)	ALEXANDRA PARK
5353	5252	(I)	PIBROCH OF DONALD DHU
5353	536L6L	(I)	UNTITLED
5353	537L2	(I)	LADY OF THE MANOR, THE
5353	5316L	(II)	QUICKSTEP
5353	5316L	(II)	COME UNDER MY PLAIDIE
5353	5316L	(II)	JOHNNY McGILL('S JIG)
5353	5316L	(I)	UNTITLED
5353	5316L	(I)	BASKET OF OYSTERS, A
5353	5316L	(I)	MY SILLY AULD MAN
5353	5316L	(I)	COME UNDER MY PLAIDY
5353	5316L	(I)	GO TO THE DEVIL AND SHAKE YOURSELF
5353	5316L	(I)	JOHNNY MCGILL ('S JIG)
5353	5316L	(I)	BUNCH OF GREEN BUSHES
5353	5326L	(I)	GREIG'S PIPES
5353	5322	(I)	OH! CARRY ME BACK TO OLE VIRGINNY
5353	5324	(I)	MAGGY'S WAME IS FU' I TRUE
5353	5335	(II)	DRUIM-UACHDAIR
5353	5335	(I)	MRS CRAWFORD OF LITTLETON'S REEL
5353	5335	(I)	DRUMUACHDAIR [DRUIM-UACHDAIR]
5353	5342	(I)	MRS CHEAPE OF ROSSIE'S STRATHSPEY
5353	5342	(I)	NEW SIMON BRODIE
5353	5366	(II)	COLIN CAMPBELL
5353	532H2	(I)	LOYAL FARMER, THE
5353	532H2	(I)	LOYAL FARMER'S STRATHSPEY, THE
5353	547L2	(I)	MR EDWARD SANDER'S STRATHSPEY
5353	5532	(I)	SIR A. FERGUSSON'S STRATHSPEY
5353	51H22	(II)	MACIVAR'S [MACVICAR'S]
5353	51H22	(II)	MACVICAR'S
5353	51H22	(I)	McVICAR'S STRATHSPEY [MACVICAR'S]
5353	51H32	(I)	MISS RICHARDSON'S STRATHSPEY
5353	52H75	(I)	VISCOUNT REIDHAVEN
5353	53H2H2	(I)	LADY MARY HAY'S REEL
5353	6262	(II)	HIGHLAND BLACK LADDIE
5353	6262	(II)	SMOLANACH
5353	6262	(II)	NUAIR BHA MI FEIN 'NAM MHADUIN
			(WHEN I WAS A MAIDEN)
5353	6262	(I)	HIGHLAND LADDIE, (THE)
5353	6444	(I)	LADY GARDINER'S STRATHSPEY
5353	6462	(II)	SMOLANACH
5353	6464	(II)	CHARLIE HARDIE
5353	6464	(I)	LADY GARDINER'S STRATHSPEY
5353	6527L	(II)	COUNTESS OF AIRLY
5353	6527L	(I)	COUNTESS OF AIRLY('S STRATHSPEY)
5353	61H51	(II)	LOCH FYNE
5353	61H52	(I)	VICTORY, THE
5353	1H542	(II)	MR JAMES TAYLOR'S REEL
535	447L	(I)	SPORTSMAN, THE
5354	536L2	(I)	FASQUE HOUSE
5354	5324	(II)	MONYMUSK [MONEYMUSK]
5354	5324	(II)	SIR ARCHd. GRANT OF MONEY MUSK
5354	5324	(I)	MONYMUSK
5354	5324	(I)	SIR ARCHd GRANT (OF MONYMUSK'S)(REEL)
5354	5324	(I)	MR DAVID SUTTER'S REEL
5354	5324	(I)	LADY C. BRUCE'S REEL
5354	5324	(I)	DANNSA GAELACH
5354	5324	(I)	LADY CHARLOTTE BRUCE'S REEL
5354	5362	(I)	LEWIE GORDON STRATHSPEY
5354	546L2	(I)	MISS ELIZABETH GLEGG'S STRATHSPEY
5354	6262	(I)	HIGHLAND LADDIE
5354	6266	(I)	MR MACMURDO'S STRATHSPEY
5355	3131	(I)	MISS MACKENZIE OF COULS WALTZ
5355	47b66	(I)	JACKSON'S QUANDERY
5355	5322	(I)	CADDLE ROBBIE
5355	5543	(I)	SPANISH MARCH
5355	51H1H3H	(I)	NEW BROOM, THE
5355	52H2H2	(I)	SALLY GRANT'S RANT
5355	6355	(I)	GASAN FINEALT

5355	1H1H65	(I)	LOUIS'S ADIEU
5356	537L2	(II)	ATHOL(E) HOUSE
5356	537L2	(I)	ATHOLE HOUSE
5356	537L2	(I)	MR GEORGE CHRISTIE'S DELIGHT
5356	5324	(II)	WEE BIT COGGIE
5356	5362	(II)	BUCKS OF CRANMORE
5356	1H530	(I)	THORN, THE
5356	1H653	(II)	WARRIOR'S RETURN, THE
5357b	4246	(II)	WHEN YOU'VE HOOKED HIM HOLD HIM FAST
5357b	4246	(I)	INSH OF PERTH
5357	5353	(II)	COOKIE SHINE
5357	6553	(II)	MEG MERRILEES
5357	6553	(I)	MEG MERRILEES
5357	3H524	(I)	MISS ANN DONALDSON'S REEL
5351H	5122	(I)	MR G DOUGLASS OF TILIWHILLY'S STRATHSPEY
5351H	5326L	(II)	PERTHSHIRE LASSES, THE
5351H	5326L	(I)	QUEEN SQUARE HOUSE or MRS STEVENSON'S STRATHSPEY
5351H	5326L	(I)	EARL FITZWILLIAM'S STRATHSPEY
5351H	5322	(I)	MRS STEWART KYNNACHAN'S STRATHSPEY
5351H	5322H	(I)	DOGE OF VENICE STRATHSPEY, THE
5351H	5362	(II)	LADY MARY MENZIES
5351H	5362	(II)	ROE HUNT, THE
5351H	5362	(I)	LADY MARY MENZIE'S REEL
5351H	5562	(I)	ABERDEEN HUNT, THE
5351H	6562	(I)	MRS PARKER'S FANCY
5351H	6562	(I)	LORD MILTON'S STRATHSPEY
5351H	7366	(I)	MISS NANCY CAMPBELL'S REEL
5353H	6464H	(II)	FAICHFIELD
5353H	64H1H6	(I)	NEW HONEY MOON, THE
5362	5266L	(I)	(AN') O FOR ANE AND TWENTY TAM
5362	5313H	(II)	KISS THE LASS YE LIKE BEST
5362	5313H	(I)	KISS THE LASS YE LIKE BEST
5362	531H3H	(II)	RUIDHLE NA MARAGAN DUBH
5362	531H3H	(I)	LORD GARLIS DELIGHT
5363	1H3H1H1H	(II)	CRAIGENDORAN
5364	537L5L	(II)	GEORDIE WALKER
5364	5327L	(I)	MRS RUSSEL (OF BLACKHALL) 'S STRATHSPEY
5364	5327L	(I)	MISS J. ROSE'S REEL
5364	5342	(I)	MERTOUN HOUSE
5364	5361H	(I)	MR ALEXr. PATERSON'S STRATHSPEY
5364	531H6	(II)	LADS OF TAIN(, THE)
5364	531H1H	(II)	ROSIE'S SCHOTTISCHE
5364	531H1H	(I)	ANDANTE
5364	5642	(I)	MISS JENNY LINDSAY'S STRATHSPEY
5364	51H42	(II)	DEVERON SIDE
5364	54H72H	(II)	MASTER FRANCIS SITWELL
5364	54H72H	(I)	MASTER F(RANCIS) SITWELL('S REEL)
5365	1364	(I)	LORD DUNCAN'S FLAG
5365	1364	(I)	MR PATRICK DUFF'S FAVORITE STRATHSPEY
5365	4322	(I)	FINALE, THE
5365	432H2	(II)	MISS ROBERTSON
5365	51H3H2H	(I)	FARMERS OF THE BORDER, THE
536	51H3	(II)	FLOWER OF THE NORTH, THE
5366	526L5L	(I)	ARTLESS ANNIE
5366	527L2	(II)	BILLY MACKINNON
5366	5322	(II)	JEANIE SKINNER
5366	5353	(II)	LADY CLARE
5366	5362	(I)	LADY HERIET GEORGINA HAMILTON
5366	5542	(I)	AP SHENKIN
5366	751H1H	(II)	JIG [cf.SOLDIERS DANCE, the parts reversed]
5367	5326L	(II)	BONNIE LASS OF BALLANTRAE, (THE)
5367	5326L	(II)	LASS(ES) O' BALLANTRAE, THE
5367	5326L	(I)	LASS OF BALLANTRAE, THE [LASSES OF BALLANTRAE]
5361H	56L22	(II)	SIX-MEN LIFT, THE
5361H	5324	(I)	MISS SCOTT OF SINTON'S STRATHSPEY
5362H	5353	(II)	FIGHT ABOUT THE FIRESIDE
537b4	531H5	(I)	HIT HER (UP)ON THE BUM(E)
5374	421H5	(II)	ANNAN POLKA
5374	541H5	(I)	ANNEN POLKA [ANNAN POLKA]
531H1	2253	(I)	PRIME OF LIFE
531H3	246L2	(I)	MRS MINZIES (OF CALDAIR) 'S STRATHSPEY
531H3	2424	(I)	MISS MARY GARDEN (DELGATY) 'S REEL
531H3	2662	(II)	CAIRNGORM ["CHEAP MEAL"]
531H3	22H2H7	(I)	O'ER THE MOOR TO MAGGIE
531H3	22H2H7	(I)	O'ER THE MOOR TO MAGGIE
531H3	437L2	(I)	MISS BURROWS REEL
531H3	4346L	(I)	MR McANDREW'S STRATHSPEY
531H3	642H4	(II)	MARY JANE DAVIE
531H3	6542	(II)	PRINCE ARTHUR'S HIGHLAND FLING
531H3	3H355	(I)	DUMOURIERS ESCAPE

```
                              IMITATING A GALLOP & A TROT
531H5        2462        (II)  AIRCHIE BROWN
531H5        437L2       (II)  LADY FRANCES SOMERSET
531H5        437L2       (I)   LADY FRANCES SOMERSET'S REEL
531H5        5632        (I)   MRS ROSS, DOWAGER OF KILRAVOCK'S FAVORITE
531H5        642H7       (I)   LIEUT. COLONEL MAXWELL'S
                               (7th Dr GUARDS) FANCY
531H5        2H542       (I)   CAMLARG LODGE
531H5        2H72H5      (I)   MISS HAMERSLEY'S ALLMAND
531H         642         (I)   OWEN GLENDOUR, WALTZ, THE
531H6        5352        (II)  MILLER O' HIRN'S SON, THE
531H7        2H231       (I)   NEW TARTAN PLAIDIE, THE
531H7        5H3H1H2H    (I)   LAS CHASSE DE LA GARDE
531H1H       22H2H7      (I)   O'ER THE MOOR TO MAGGIE
531H1H       5353        (II)  MISS WELSH
531H1H       5353        (I)   MISS WELSH
531H1H       567L2       (I)   MISS JESSY GRAHAM
531H1H       661H1H      (II)  HIGH ROAD TO LINTON
531H1H       2H1H62      (II)  TIMMER LADLE, THE
531H1H       3H2H1H2     (I)   MRS GORDON CAMPBELL OF TROUP
                               AND GLENLYON'S REEL
531H3H       1H632       (I)   MISS GRANT'S STRATHSPEY
531H3H       2H5O5       (I)   VITTORIA MARCH
532H2H       1H3H1H6     (II)  AYRSHIRE LASSES, (THE)
532H2H       1H3H1H6     (I)   AYRSHIRE LASSES (STRATHSPEY), (THE)
532H2H       2H3H1H6     (I)   AYRSHIRE LASSES, (THE)
532H2H       2H3H1H6     (I)   LAING AND HENDRY'S BIRTHDAY
532H2H       3H3H1H6     (I)   AIRSHIRE LASSES, THE
533H1H       537L2       (I)   HE TIL'T AND SHE TIL'T
546L6L       5L5L32      (I)   HONble MISS ELPHINSTONE'S FANCY, THE
546L5L       151H5       (I)   MR JOHN WALKER'S FAVOURITE
546L5L       447L2       (II)  MRS McKENZIE OF APPLECROSS
546L1        5622        (I)   LIEUT. JAMIESON'S QUICKSTEP
546L4        5L7L11      (II)  HI LO RO! HOG EILE
547bL2       5557b       (II)  LORD DOUNE
547bL2       5557b       (I)   LORD DOUNE ('S STRATHSPEY)
547bL3b      6b56b5      (II)  MRS MORTHLAND
547L5L       5L352       (I)   DUKE OF RICHMOND, THE
547L2        4315L       (I)   LIVERPOOL ASSEMBLY, THE
5415L        3L127L      (I)   DRUNKEN DOCTOR, THE
5415L        6L217L      (I)   LITTLE GLEANER, THE
5415L        7bL7bL47bL  (I)   REEL OF CAITHNESS
5415L        1343        (I)   MISS HOLDER'S FAVORITE AIR
5411         1231        (I)   LA SOIRRE DU VAUXHALL
5411         4242        (I)   MISS PENUEL GRANT OF GRANT'S STRATHSPEY
5411         4442        (II)  CRAIG OF BARNS, THE
5411         4442        (I)   CRAIG OF BARN'S, THE
5414         5422        (II)  QUICK-STEP
5415         671H1H      (I)   AT SETTING DAY
5416         5411        (II)  TRIUMPH
5417b        47b47bL     (I)   CAPT CUNINGHAM OF CORSEHILL'S REEL
5417         5411        (I)   TRIUMPH, THE
5411H        6422H       (I)   MISS ANN HAY ('S REEL)
5426L        1153        (I)   GIRL I LEFT BEHIND ME, THE
5426L        3451H       (II)  MR CHARLES GRANT'S STRATHSPEY
5426L        5353        (I)   MISS JANE CAMPBELL'S STRATHSPEY
542          7L7L1       (I)   MINUETTO
542          7L7L2       (I)   LASS OF THE HILL, THE
5427L        1411        (I)   LADS OF LEITH, THE
5427L        1411        (I)   SHE'S FAIR AND FAUSE (THAT CAUSES MY SMART)
5421         27bL24      (II)  PHILABEG
5421         27bL24      (I)   O BUSY FOLK AND IDLE FOLK
5421         4553        (I)   SEMENZATI
5422         4215        (I)   BARON DE STEINS COTILION
543b1        247b2       (II)  HONble. MR. FRASER (OF LOVAT)
543b1        247b2       (I)   HONble MR FRASER (OF LOVAT) 'S REEL
543b1        43b27bL     (I)   MR HOUSTON (OF JORDANHILL) 'S REEL
543b1        5427bL      (II)  LADY BAIRD'S NEW REEL
543b1        5427bL      (I)   LADY BAIRD'S NEW REEL
5436L        237L5L      (I)   BACHELOR'S JIG, THE
5437L        6L237L      (I)   MOTHER MIDNIGHT'S TASTE
5437L        6L542       (I)   MISS CAMPBELL'S JIG
5437L        6L542       (I)   MISS CAMPBELL OF SMIDDY GREEN'S JIGG
5437L        1366        (I)   CAMPBELL INN
5431         3422        (I)   LA HIER AU SOIR
5431         47bL46      (II)  LONGAIR'S PIPES
5431         51H62       (I)   LORD ROLLO'S REEL
5431         1H637L      (I)   CHIT CHAT
5432         1117L       (I)   MR HADDEN'S HORNPIPE
5432         135L1       (I)   MASTER JOHNSTONE'S HORNPIPE
5432         1411L       (I)   SOUTHAMPTON ROOM
5432         27b42       (I)   HALLOW FAIR
```

```
5432      6422       ( I )  PAS SEUL MISS ANN MITCHELL
5433      26L22      ( I )  LOGAN WATER
5433      27L11      ( I )  MISS CARNEGIE'S ALLAMANDE
5433      2253       ( I )  ALLEGRO
543       354        ( I )  FICKLE JENNY
5433      5432       ( I )  BURSTING SIGH, THE
5435      5632       ( I )  BRAES OF ABERARDER, THE
5436      5522       ( I )  KING OF THE CATTI
5436      5522       ( I )  EMPEROR OF HAYTI, THE
5437      2H51H1     ( I )  STAG CHACE
5431H     7L513      ( I )  SCHOTTISCHE, THE
5431H     547L2      ( I )  MRS DUNCAN CHRISTIE'S STRATHSPEY
5431H     6522       (II)  BANNERMAN'S RANT
5431H     6523H      (II)  DEAN, THE
5431H     7b427b     (II)  SEAFORTH HIGHLANDERS, THE
5431H     7b527bL    (II)  DRUMMUIR CASTLE
5431H     3H1H2H2    (II)  CASTLE SPYNIE
5442      5441       ( I )  ANDREW AND HIS CUTTIE GUN
5443      3113       ( I )  LAMAIR'S FROLICK
5446      3432       ( I )  MISS ANNA MUNRO
5451      4255       ( I )  ZITTI, ZITTI, PIANO, PIANO
5451      537L5L     ( I )  LADY MELVILLE'S FAVORITE
5451      5326L      (II)  WILLIE WINKIE
5451      5331H      ( I )  SIR CHAs DOUGLAS
5451      5362       (II)  ROMP AMONG THE WHINS
5451      5455       (II)  LORD EGLINTOUN'S AULD MAN
5451      5455       ( I )  LORD EGLINTOUN'S AULD MAN
5451      5462       (II)  ROMP AMONG THE WHINS
5451      5462       ( I )  MRS JOHN WELLING'S FANCY
5451      547b7bL    (II)  I WILL SING YOU A SONG
5451      7654       ( I )  DUMFRIES RACES
5453      5524       ( I )  JINK ABOUT
5454      7L254      ( I )  FLEE OVER THE WATER
5454      3211       ( I )  ERE AROUND THE HUGE OAK
5454      1H423      ( I )  MONSIEUR PANTIN
545       57b5       ( I )  LORD HENRY
5451H     447L2      ( I )  DUTCH TROT, THE
5451H     4432       ( I )  DUTCH TROT, THE
5451H     53H2H5     ( I )  MARQUIS WELLINGTON
546b6b    43b55      ( I )  THOSE LILLY LIPS
5464      5413       (II)  GLEN WHERE MY LOVE IS, THE
5466      5426L      ( I )  PRINCESS AUGUSTA'S REEL
5466      5455L      ( I )  GAVOT
541H5     4665       ( I )  MISS LOUISA JOHNSTON'S FANCY
541H7     6432       ( I )  BRAES OF BALLOCHMYLE, THE
555L      514        ( I )  THREE HALFPENCE
556L6L    6L5L2L2L   ( I )  DELVIN HOUSE
556L6     5217L      ( I )  IRISH WIDOW
557bL2    5L121      ( I )  RAMS HORNS
557bL2    5513b      (II)  MR BAILLIE OF MELLERSTAIN
557bL2    5513b      ( I )  MR BAILLIE OF MELLERSTON'S STRATHSPEY
                            [MR BAILLIE OF MELLERSTAIN]
557bL2    5523b      (II)  MR BAILLIE OF MELLERSTON
557bL2    557b2H     ( I )  RAMS HORNS
5515L     5L332      ( I )  MRS FORTATH'S STRATHSPEY
5515L     2631H      ( I )  LE SPAGNOLETTE
5515L     5542       ( I )  MISS WEDDERBURN'S (STRATHSPEY/REEL)
551       6L22       ( I )  MOTHER GOOSE
551       7L7L5L     ( I )  LORD GREGORY
551       7L7L5L     ( I )  OH OPEN THE DOOR LORD GREGORY
5511      6L6L22     (II)  BOG O' GIGHT, THE
5511      6L6L22     ( I )  BOG OF GIGHT, THE
5511      6L6L22     ( I )  LADY AUGUSTA MURRAY'S STRATHSPEY
5511      6L7L11     ( I )  CARLETON HOUSE HIGH DANCE
5511      6L47L5L    ( I )  ABOYNE CASTLE
5511      7bL242     ( I )  DR GUTHRIE'S (Junr) STRATHSPEY
5511      27L11      ( I )  LEAP OVER THE GARTER
5511      27L11      ( I )  JOCULAR, THE
5511      2217L      ( I )  SICILIAN AIR
5511      2231       ( I )  LADY GRANT'S STRATHSPEY
5511      2231       ( I )  MISS BOONES FANCY
5511      2231       ( I )  SUNDERLAND MUSICAL SOCIETY, THE
5511      315L5L     (II)  FREE GARDENERS' MARCH, THE
5511      4325L      ( I )  LADY LOUISA RUSSELL'S JIG
5511      447L5L     ( I )  MRS KENT'S DANCE
5511      447L5L     ( I )  WOMAN'S DANCE IN OMBRES CHINOISES
5511      6532       (II)  NINETY-THIRD'S FAREWELL TO GIBRALTAR
5511      661H1H     ( I )  COLONEL NOEL'S FANCY
551       27bL5L     ( I )  SUD AIR M'AIGNE SO GHRUAIM
5512      217L6L     ( I )  SAILORS DANCE IN CAPt COOK
5513      1362       (II)  PERTH HUNT
5513      1524       ( I )  DUTCHES OF HAMILTON'S NEW STRATHSPEY
```

5513	1524	(I)	DUTCHESS OF HAMILTON'S NEW STRATHSPEY
5513	225L4L	(I)	RICHER'S HORNPIPE
5513	227L6L	(I)	MISS MURRAY'S REEL
5513	227L6L	(I)	PRINCES FETE, THE
551	331	(I)	COCK UP YOUR BEAVER, (JOHNNY)
5513	5541H	(I)	MISS STEWART'S STRATHSPEY
5513	5642	(II)	KILLIECHASSIE
5513	5642	(I)	MISS FLEMYING OF MONESS'S STRATHSPEY
5513	5642	(I)	MISS JEAN KERR'S STRATHSPEY
5513	5642	(I)	CILLE CHASSIDH [CILL A CHASSAIDH]
5513	6636	(I)	MISS GEDDES'S STRATHSPEY
5513	661H6	(I)	MISS ANN STEWART'S STRATHSPEY
5514	27bL42	(I)	LADY ROBERT KERR'S STRATHSPEY
5514	5427bL	(I)	SCOTCH REEL
5514	567L2	(I)	MISS JEAN WOOD McKINZIES FAVORITE
5515	6L662	(II)	EARL OF LOUDON(, THE)
5515	6L662	(I)	EARL OF LOUDON'S STRATHSPEY, (THE)
5515	1562	(II)	ROARING RIVIE
5515	1562	(I)	MR MACBEAN OF ROARING RIVIE'S STRATHSPEY
5515	1564	(I)	PERTHSHIRE HIGHLANDERS, THE
5515	247L2	(I)	MISS BOYD'S STRATHSPEY
5515	4542	(I)	CASTLE CAMPBELL
5515	4562	(I)	AULD HILLIE'S RANT
5515	557bL4	(II)	ATHOLE HIGHLANDERS' FAREWELL
			TO LOCH KATRINE, THE
5515	5531	(I)	LADY CASSLES'S FAVORITE
5515	5642	(I)	HONble MRS GRAY'S STRATHSPEY
5515	6626	(I)	STORMONT LADS, THE
5515	6626	(I)	DUKE OF ATHOLE'S RANT, THE
5515	6626	(I)	STOREMONT LADS, THE
5515	3H2H1H6	(I)	COUNTESS OF GLASGOW'S FAVORITE, THE
5515	3H5H2H5	(I)	FRIENDLY ASSEMBLY
5516	1H1H1H6	(I)	MISS BLAIR'S SCOTS MEASURE
5517	6641H	(I)	HOW CAN I BE SAD ON MY WEDDING DAY
5511H	2427bL	(II)	CRIEFF MEETING, THE
5511H	2427bL	(I)	CRIEFF MEETING, THE
5511H	6522	(I)	LORD EGLINTON'S REEL
5526L	1363	(II)	WE'LL A' MEET ABOON
5526L	5515	(II)	HONble. MRS. MAULE OF PANMURE
5526L	5515	(I)	HONble MRS MAULE (OF PANMURE'S) STR. THE
5526L	5515	(I)	HONble MRS RAMSAY MAULE
			OF PANMURE'S STRATHSPEY
5526L	5513H	(I)	LORD ELGIN'S FAVORITE STRATHSPEY
5526L	5513H	(I)	HONble MR FRASER OF LOVAT'S STRATHSPEY
5526L	5555	(I)	MISS WILSON OF CULLIN'S REEL
5526L	5555	(I)	TOMBREACKACHIE'S STRATHSPEY
5527bL	5515	(II)	MACLAGGAN'S JIG
5527bL	5555	(II)	HONble. MRS. RAMSAY MAULE('S STR.)
5527bL	5555	(I)	HONble MR RAMSAY MAULE'S STRATHSPEY
5527bL	5555	(I)	LADY AUGUSTUS MURRAY OF AUCHTERTYRE
5527bL	5656	(I)	MRS BAIRD OF NEW BYTHS STRATHSPEY
552	7L5L3	(I)	PAS SEUL MISS SHERRIFS
5521	5L136	(II)	RU'GLEN LUMS
552	111H	(I)	KATY'S COMPLAINT
5521	2666	(II)	TOP O' THE GRAMPIANS, THE
552	121H	(II)	THERE'S MONY A BONNIE LASSIE
5521	5521	(I)	LADY ELIZABETH BUTLERS FANCY
5521	5555	(I)	CLAN RANALD'S MARCH TO EDINr
5521	6661H	(I)	FINLAY IS HIS FATHER'S DARLING
5521	6661H	(I)	SE GAOL A BHOBAIN FIONNLLA
5522	6L6L6L1	(I)	COME HAP ME WITH THY PETTICOAT
5522	1216L	(II)	MR JAMES McGRIGOR'S REEL
5522	4461H	(I)	LOUDON, THE
5522	4461H	(I)	SANDIE O'ER THE LEE
5522	4653	(I)	RURAL THOUGHT, THE
5522	5526L	(I)	JAMIE ROY
5522	5526L	(I)	COLONEL MONT[G]OMERIE'S FAVORITE STRATHSPEY
			[JAMIE ROY]
5522	5547bL	(I)	BRAES OF BALQUHITHER, THE
5522	5557b	(II)	YESTER HOUSE
5523	5L142	(I)	UP AND DOWN
5523	5L142	(I)	ARMENIA
552	315	(I)	LADY McDUFF'S LAMENT
5523	5521	(I)	BEGGAR GIRL, (THE)
5524	151H3H	(I)	SOWS TAIL, THE
5524	3b43b2	(I)	BONNY TWEED SIDE
5524	5351H	(I)	MISS MONTGOMERIES REEL
5524	5551H	(II)	MISS MONTGOMERIE OF SKELMORLIE
5542	5551H	(II)	LADY JANE MONTGOMERY
5524	5551H	(I)	SOW'S TAIL (TO GEORDIE), THE
5524	5551H	(I)	MISS MONTGOMERIE OF SKELMORLIE
			('S STRATHSPEY)

5524	5551H	(I)	LADY JEAN MONTGOMERIE'S STRATHSPEY
5524	5551H	(I)	LADY JANE MONTGOMERY ('S STRATHSPEY)
5524	5553H	(I)	MR JAs THOMSON'S STRATHSPEY
5524	5565	(II)	EARL OF HOME
5524	5565	(I)	LORD HUM'S REEL
5525	7bL7b47bL	(I)	MISS JEANIE MERCER'S REEL
5526	5311	(I)	GURAGUAG, THE
553b1	2424	(II)	FORGE, THE
553b1	3b427bL	(I)	LAUCHLAN'S LILT
553b1	4427bL	(II)	BONNY BROOM, THE
553b1	551H1H	(II)	DARLING, THE
553b1	551H1H	(I)	NIAN DONN RO' BHEADARACH [NIGHEAN...]
553b3b	1117b	(I)	SOLO
553b3b3b	4522	(I)	LA CAMERGO
553b	3b52H	(I)	GAE TO THE KYE WI' ME JAMIE
553b	3b7b7b	(I)	I MADE LOVE TO KATE
553b	7b7b7b	(I)	WOO'D AND MARRIED AND A'
5531	3L4L27L	(I)	MR EDMONDSTOUNE OF NEWTON'S FAVORITE
5531	5L421	(I)	LA CONSTANTE
5531	7bL7bL47bL	(I)	THA'N DOARACH SA BHAILIE SO
553	111	(I)	HERE AWA', (THERE AWA') (WANDERING) WILLIE
553	111	(I)	WANDERING WILLIE
5531	227L5L	(II)	ACADEMY, THE
5531	2231	(I)	RUSSIAN TIPPET, THE
5531	427L5L	(I)	QUEEN OF HEARTS, THE
5531	427L5L	(I)	JENNY'S BAWBIE
5531	437L2	(I)	GOLDEN AGE, THE
5531	447L2	(II)	MISS CAROLINE CAMPBELL
5531	4421	(I)	MRS DUPREE'S REEL
5531	4466	(II)	BONNIE ANN, THE
5531	4640	(II)	ALICE'S DOLLIE
5531	5531	(I)	St. KILDARE
5531	5531	(I)	St. KILDA('S) REEL, (THE)
5531	5533	(II)	HIGHLANDS OF BANFFSHIRE, THE
5531	5533	(I)	BRAIGHE BHANBH
5531	5531H	(II)	GLENCOE
5531	5561H	(II)	QUICKSTEP
5531	5561H	(I)	LIGRUM CUS
5531	5561H	(I)	OVER THE WATER (TO CHARLIE)
5531	1H3H3H2H	(I)	HONble COLONEL HAMILTON'S STRATHSPEY
5532	16L13	(I)	SCOTCH REEL
5532	1143	(I)	LES DRAPEAUX
5532	1231	(I)	NOS CALEN
5532	1352	(II)	CREAKING DOOR, THE
5532	27L11	(I)	DAINTY DAVIE
553	234	(I)	QUEEN MARY'S LAMENTATION
5532	4671H	(I)	ANDANTINO
5532	5553H	(I)	(RT HON) LORD BALLENDEN ('S STRATHSPEY)
5532	5752	(I)	SIR JOHN STEWART OF GRANDTULLY'S STR.)
5532	1H553H	(I)	JENKINS'S SHANTRUSE
5532	1H553H	(I)	MRS PARKER'S STRATHSPEY MINUET
553	311	(I)	BAS DHIARMID O DUINN
553	311	(I)	DEATH OF DERMID
5533	115L5L	(II)	MISS AGNESS LOUDON
5533	1115	(I)	LA QUATRE COMPLOSSE'A
5533	1233	(I)	BLUE STOCKING, THE
5533	1233	(I)	PANTHEON, THE
5533	1311	(I)	MISS COMBE'S FANCY
5533	11H66	(I)	O'ER THE MOOR TO KATIE
5533	25L5L4L	(I)	MARCH OF THE RENFREWSHIRE MILITIA
5533	226L5L	(I)	PLEASURE GROUNDS AT MONYMUSK, THE
5533	515L5L	(I)	WHEEM, THE
5533	5432	(I)	VOICE OF MY LOVE, THE
5533	5511	(I)	SEE THE CONQUERING HERO COMES
5533	5522	(I)	NEW PEIR OF PETERHEAD
5534	3165	(I)	MILLER'S DAUGHTER, THE
5534	6655	(I)	WEAVER'S MARCH, THE
5534	6655	(I)	GALLANT WEAVER, THE
5534	61H55	(I)	WEAVER'S MARCH, THE
553	57L1	(I)	LADY ISABELLA THYNNES MINUET
5535	1365	(II)	DONALBANE
5535	2424	(II)	GABHAIDH SINN AN RATHAD MOR [THE STEWART'S MARCH]
5535	2424	(II)	KAFOOZLE-UM
5535	2424	(I)	(WILL YE GO TO) SHERRIFF MUIR
5535	22H75	(II)	MISS BETSEY ROBERTSON
5535	22H76	(II)	MISS JANE FRASER
5535	22H76	(II)	MISS BETSY ROBERTSON
5535	22H76	(I)	MISS ELIZABETH ROBERTSON'S REEL
5535	22H1H6	(I)	COTTAGER'S DAUGHTER, THE
553	531	(I)	MISS HAYNE'S MINUET
5535	3165	(I)	MILLER'S DAUGHTER, THE

553	553	(I)	LIEUt. DUNBAR 22nd REGIMENTS WALTZ
5535	5533	(II)	HIGHLANDS OF BANFFSHIRE
5535	5562	(I)	TRIP TO GUILSLAND, THE
553	553H	(I)	DEVONSHIRE MINUET AND GAVOT, THE
5535	6665	(I)	MAJOR J.S. KER'S MARCH
5535	662H2	(I)	HUMOURS OF NAIRNSHIRE, THE
5535	61H65	(I)	COME (THEN/NOW) ALL YE SOCIAL POWERS
5535	62H75	(I)	MISS M.S. REDDIE'S REEL
5535	1H511	(I)	PRIME OF LIFE
5536	5312	(I)	KEYS OF LOVE, THE
5536	61H33	(I)	PRINCE'S REEL, THE
5536	7533	(I)	MAN'S A MAN FOR A' THAT, A
5531H	2362	(II)	MISS PRESTON FERNTON
5531H	2362	(I)	MISS PRESTON FERNTON('S REEL)
5531H	3522	(I)	MISS PROUD
5531H	5532	(I)	MRS LANDLE'S DELIGHT
5531H	5552	(II)	DERVAIG MEDLEY, THE
5531H	6424	(II)	MISS GRANT OF CULLEN HOUSE
5531H	6424	(I)	MISS GRANT'S REEL
			[MISS GRANT OF CULLEN HOUSE]
5531H	6535	(I)	Dr McNICOL'S REEL
5531H	6662H	(II)	MISS MACPHERSON GRANT OF BALLINDALLOCH
5531H	6662H	(I)	MISS ISABELLA McPHERSON GRANT'S STRATHSPEY
5531H	72H51	(I)	LE DIABLE AN LAIR
553	1H1H6	(I)	LEIPSIC WALTZ
553	1H1H6	(I)	CELEBRATED MEDLEY WALTZ, THE
5547bL	5511	(I)	BATTLE OF THE BOYNE, THE
5547bL	5521	(II)	QUICKSTEP
5547bL	5555	(I)	TAYMOUTH HERMITAGE
5547L	5515	(II)	NORTH HUNT, THE
5547L	5515	(I)	AN T' SEALG
5541	7bL427bL	(I)	FORTY SECOND QUICKSTEP
554	101	(I)	MISS NICOL OF STONEHAVEN'S MINUET
554	117bL	(I)	JOCKY'S GRAY BREECHES
5541	127L5L	(I)	GARDNER'S HORNPIPE
5541	4427bL	(II)	GREY BUCK, THE
5541	551H5	(I)	MR. ALEXANDER DOWNIE'S WALTZ
554	27bL3b	(I)	GE DO THEID MI DO M'LEABAIDH 'S BEAG
			MO SHUND RIS A CHADAL
5542	7bL427bL	(II)	HIGHLAND QUICKSTEP
554	211	(I)	LORD ERROLL'S MINUET
5542	1111	(I)	CUMH DHUC HAMILTON
5542	1232	(I)	ANDANTE GRASIOSO
554	215	(I)	MISS JUILIETT RANNIE'S MINUET
5542	3b17bL2	(I)	SKYE DANCE
5542	3b17bL2	(I)	WESTERN ISLE AIR, A
5542	3115	(I)	PRAY GOODY (AS SUNG BY MR SINCLAIR)
5542	356L7L	(I)	MISS BETTSAY MURRAY'S JIG
5542	31H22	(I)	GLENLYON HOUSE
5542	5515	(I)	GEORGE SKENE ESQr OF SKENE'S STRATHSPEY
5542	5557b	(II)	YESTER HOUSE
5542	5557b	(I)	YESTER HOUSE
554	3b17bL	(I)	ARMSTRONG'S FAREWELL
5543b	5551	(I)	SIGH, THE
554	335	(I)	SANDY & JENNY
554	335	(I)	MISS CALLANDER'S MINUET
554	346	(I)	DUTCHESS OF GORDON'S MINUET, THE
5544	15L43	(I)	LA BELLE ASSEMBLEE
5544	113b3b	(I)	JOHNNY'S GRAY BREECKES
5544	3325L	(I)	REVIEW, THE
5544	31H66	(I)	SHAVELING GABBIT BROCK, THE
5544	5541	(I)	LADY MORPETH'S WALTZ
5544	551H3bH	(II)	JOHNNIE LAD
554	512	(I)	EPPIE ADAIR [MY APPIE]
554	542	(I)	EPPIE McNAB
554	6b54	(I)	SINGLE HORNPIPE
5546	337L5L	(I)	QUICKSTEP
554	652	(I)	MISS CARNEGIE'S MINUET
554#6	1H42#4	(I)	JESSONDA
5550	2H2H2HO	(I)	MILL, MILL O, THE
5551	6L113	(I)	MAGGIE OF DRUMLANRIG
5551	7bL647bL	(I)	JOHNSTON'S MOOR
5551	1323	(I)	TIREE AIR, A
5551	25L15	(I)	TARS OF THE VICTORY, THE
5551	2247bL	(I)	MUSHET, THE
5551	2466	(II)	ALEXANDER WALKER'S REEL
5551	22H4H2H	(I)	AULD ROB THE LAIRD
5551	3b3b44	(I)	IRISH DUMP, AN
5551	3642	(I)	MRS HARVEY (OF BROADLAND'S) STRATHSPEY
5551	44H27bL	(I)	MISS J. RENNY'S STRATHSPEY
5551	447bL2	(II)	OYSTER WIVES' RANT, THE
5551	447bL2	(I)	OYSTER WIVES RANT, THE

5551	4447bL	(II)	TOWN CRIER, THE
5551	4447bL	(II)	HEIDSET, THE
5551	4447bL	(I)	HIGHLANDERS WELCOME HOME, THE
5551	4447bL	(I)	THEY TOOK FRAE ME MY WIFE
5551	4442	(II)	MISS MARGARET GRAEME OF INCHBRAKIE
5551	4442	(I)	THEY TOOK FRAE ME MY WIFE
5551	4442	(I)	MISS (MARGARET) GRAHAM OF INCHBRAKIE ('S STRATHSPEY)
5551	4442	(I)	COLn ROBERTSON'S STRATHSPEY
5551	457bL4	(II)	COLONEL ROBERTSON
5551	457bL4	(I)	(COL./MR) ROBERTSON (OF STROWAN) 'S STRATHSPEY
5551	5326L	(I)	WILLY WINKS
5551	5424	(II)	DUCHESS OF GORDON, THE
5551	5424	(I)	DUCHESS OF GORDON, (THE)
5551	5527bL	(II)	OLD HIGHLAND WEDDING (WITH VARIATIONS)
5551	5527bL	(I)	REEL OF TULLOCH, THE
5551	5522	(I)	MRS Dr STEWART'S REEL
5551	5524	(II)	DUCHESS OF GORDON
5551	5524	(I)	DUTCHESS OF ARGYLE'S STRATHSPEY
5551	5524	(I)	DUTCHESS OF GORDON'S STRATHSPEY (REEL)
5551	5526	(I)	THREE GIRLS OF PORTREE, THE
5551	5533	(II)	HIGHLANDS OF BANFFSHIRE, THE
5551	5547bL	(II)	MRS CHRISTIE
5551	5547bL	(II)	FIDDICH-SIDE LASSES, THE
5551	5547bL	(I)	MISS SMOLLET'S FANCY
5551	5547bL	(I)	FIDDICH-SIDE LASSES, THE
5551	5547bL	(I)	MRS CHRISTIE('S) (RANT/STRATHSPEY)
5551	5547bL	(I)	CAILLEACH AN FHRAOICH
5551	5542	(I)	MRS JOHNSON
5551	5557bL	(I)	MRS CHRISTIE'S RANT
5551	5551	(I)	GERMAN SPA WALTZ, THE
5551	5557	(III)	WILLIE DAVIE
5551	5562	(II)	DUCHESS OF GORDON, THE
5551	557b7bL	(I)	STOILEADH NIAL GOBHA [STOILE NEILL GHOBHA]
5551	5642	(I)	SIR JAMES BAIRD ('S STRATHSPEY)
5551	5751	(I)	CHESTER CASTLE
5551	51H51	(III)	RECRUIT, THE
5551	51H51	(I)	GRANTS RANT
5551	6566	(II)	MRS MADONALD, ORD
5551	6662	(II)	DANDALEITH
5551	6662	(I)	MRS H. INGLIS
5551	6662	(I)	MISS KETTY ALLAN'S REEL
5551	6662	(I)	EARL & COUNTESS OF ERROL'S WELCOME TO SLAINS CASTLE
5551	7b425	(II)	DANDY DINMONT
5552	7L223	(I)	QUICKSTEP 2nd REGt
5552	1363	(I)	CANADIAN BOAT SONG, THE
5552	226L6L	(I)	BIRKS OF INVERMAY, THE
5552	226L6L	(I)	BIRKS OF ENDERMAY
5552	3555	(I)	HILLOCH OF HAY, THE
5552	4121	(I)	SUN SHINING BRIGHTLY, THE
5552	4423	(I)	I'LL NEVER SEE HIM MORE
5552	517bL2	(II)	LADY CATHERINE STEWART or HAUGHS O' CROMDALE, THE
5553	5522	(II)	YETTS OF MUCKART, THE
5552	5523	(II)	DUKE OF ATHOLL'S MARCH
5552	5523	(I)	PIBROCH
5552	5523	(I)	QUICK STEP
5552	5552	(I)	GLINQUICH'S BUSH
5552	6661H	(II)	WIND THAT SHAKES THE BARLEY
555	3b11	(I)	LUDE'S SUPPER
555	3b52	(I)	LORD DUNDEE'S LAMENTATION
5553b	7b427bL	(II)	BONFIRE, THE
5553b	7b427bL	(I)	TEIN AIGHAIR AIR GACH BEANN DHIUBH
5553b	7b7b7b7b	(II)	CRIEFF FAIR
555	311	(I)	MINUET
5553	1115L	(II)	DEAN BRIG OF EDINBURGH, THE or MISS GRAY OF CARSE
5553	1111	(I)	LANCERS QUADRILLE, THE [LANCIERS]
5553	1113	(I)	GERMAN MARCH
5553	4635	(I)	PARSON IN HIS BOOTS, THE
5553	5411	(I)	SLINGSBIE'S PROVINCE
5553	5433	(I)	PROVANCE
5553	5522	(I)	ORCHILL GRAHAM
5553	5522	(I)	(MR) GRAHAM OF ORCHILL'S (STRATHSPEY/REEL)
5553	5533	(II)	HIGHLAND DRESS AND ARMOUR
5553	5533	(I)	CUIR A NALL AM FEILE' BHEAG IS CUR NALL AN ARMACHD
5553	5542	(II)	CUTTYMUN AND TREELADLE
5553	5542	(I)	ORCHALL
5553	5542	(I)	CUTTYMUN & TREELADLE

5553	5553	(I)	GILLY CRANKY
5553	5553	(I)	(MR) DUFF'S (FAVOURITE) SCOTS MEASURE
5553	5553	(I)	COCK LAIRD (FU' CADGIE), (A/THE)
5553	5555	(I)	ROW DOW DOW
5553	5557	(II)	WILLIE DAVIE
5553	5566	(I)	WILL YOU GO TO FLANDERS
5553	5655	(II)	MISS BAIRD OF SAUGHTON(HALL)
5553	5655	(I)	MISS BAIRD OF SAUGHTONHALL
5553	5755	(I)	BESS THE GAWKIE
5553	572H7	(II)	CUTTY CLAY
555	351H	(I)	LOVE WILL FIND OUT THE WAY
5553	51H1H3	(I)	MISS MAr MARSHALL'S SCOTCH MEASURE
555	365	(I)	OUR HEROES RETURN
5553	6664	(II)	TONAL MACKINLAY
5553	6661H	(I)	WILL YOU GO TO FLANDERS
5553	661H5H	(I)	FOREST OF BONDY, THE
5553	62H53	(I)	MISS HOUSTON OF JORDONHILL'S ALLAMANDE
5554	1112	(I)	MARCH OF THE 37th REGt
5554	2166	(I)	NANSY'S TO (THE GREEN WOOD GANE)
5554	3b3b3b4	(I)	SKYE DANCE
5554	3b3b44	(I)	BUALIDH MI U AN SA CHEANN
			[BUAILIDH MI THU ANNS A' CHEANN]
5554	3332	(I)	FIRST TURKS MARCH
555	442	(I)	DAN LIUGHAIR
5554	4255	(I)	BOATMAN, THE
5554	4266	(I)	NANSY'S TO THE GREEN WOOD GANE
5554	4266	(I)	SCORNFU' NANCY
5554	4303	(I)	PORTRAIT CHARMANT
5554	4443	(I)	WALTZ
5554	5524	(II)	REEL O' THUILLEACHAN, THE
555	451H	(I)	LOVE WILL FIND OUT THE WAY
555	462	(II)	UNTITLED
5555	6L27L5L	(I)	ROSSIE HOUSE
555	516L	(I)	PAS SEUL MISS JANE ROBERTSON
5555	1331	(I)	PLEYEL
5555	1353	(I)	HERBERT'S FROLICK
555	514	(I)	THREE HALFPENCE
555	511H	(I)	BONNY SUSIE
5555	27bL7b5	(II)	PETER BAILIE [PETER BAILLIE]
5555	2155	(I)	KILLYCRANKIE
5555	2362	(I)	MISS LLOYD'S REEL
5555	2462	(II)	MISS GRANT OF KNOCKANDO
5555	2462	(I)	MR CAMPBELL OF KINLOCH
5555	2462	(I)	MRS ANDERSON'S STRATHSPEY
5555	2462	(I)	MISS GRANT OF KNOCKANDO'S REEL
5555	2462	(I)	MISS ELISABETH COPLAND'S STRATHSPEY
5555	2462	(I)	MISS ELISABETH COPLAND'S STRATHSPEY
5555	2462	(I)	MISS YOUNG'S STRATHSPEY
5555	2466	(I)	MISS PITT'S REEL
5555	247b5	(I)	MR YOUNG'S STRATHSPEY
5555	23H1H7	(I)	BELIEVE MY
5555	3b217bL	(I)	NANNY O
5555	3b3b44	(I)	RASAY'S FAVORITE
555	531	(I)	WOE IS ME WHAT MAN I DO
5555	357L5L	(I)	PAS REDOUBLE
555	531H	(I)	SUTTERS OF SELKIRK, THE
5555	31H22	(II)	MISS HAMILTON OF BANGOWR(IE)
5555	31H22	(I)	MISS HAMILTON OF BANGOWRE ('S STRATHSPEY)
5555	31H32	(I)	MISS HAMILTON OF BANGOWRE'S STRATHSPEY
5555	4247bL	(I)	MR JOHN REDDIE'S STRATHSPEY
5555	4255	(I)	BOAT MAN, THE
5555	437L3b	(II)	CHROMATIC HORNPIPE
5555	4322	(I)	CHESTER CASTLE
5555	447L2	(I)	MISS FARQUHARSON OF INVERCAULD'S STR.
5555	4422	(II)	CHATIL MACCRIMMAN [CHA TILL MAC CRUIMEIN]
5555	443b3b	(I)	ODE DE PINDARE
5555	4444	(II)	O DEAR! WHAT CAN THE MATTER BE?
5555	4444	(I)	O DEAR WHAT CAN THE MATTER BE
5555	4445	(II)	CAMERONIAN RANT, THE or BLACK WATER
5555	4562	(I)	MR MACNEILL OF COLLONSAY'S REEL
5555	5155	(II)	KILLIECRANKIE
5555	5155	(I)	BONNIE BLACK EAGLE, THE
5555	5155	(I)	ORIGINAL SETT OF KILLIECRANKIE, THE
5555	5151H	(I)	NEW SCOTCH MEASURE, A
5555	512H6	(I)	MRS LEITCH'S STRATHSPEY
555	552	(I)	LORD JOHN
5555	5222	(I)	ROLE THE RUMPLE SAWNY
5555	522H2H	(I)	PEGGY WAS THE PRETIEST LASS IN AW THE TOWN
555	553	(I)	MRS DAVID GORDON'S MINUET
5555	5411	(I)	COLONEL BAIRD
555	555	(I)	MOZART'S GRAND WALTZ
5555	5524	(I)	MISS MERCER ELPHINSTONE'S REEL

5555	5551	(!)	DUDHOPE BARRACKS
5555	5553	(I)	AWA WHIGS AWA
5555	5555	(II)	HIGHLAND SKIP, THE
5555	5555	(I)	HIGHLAND SKIP, THE
5555	5555	(I)	MISS GRACE MENZIES
5555	5555	(I)	LAMENT
5555	5555	(I)	CHA TILL MI TUILLE
5555	5555	(I)	NEVER MORE SHALL I RETURN
5555	5562	(II)	COUNTESS OF LOUDON, THE
5555	5562	(II)	MISS LUCY CAMPBELL
5555	5562	(II)	BAILE NA GRANNDACH
5555	5562	(I)	BALL NA GRANDACH
5555	5562	(I)	ACHARNAC'S REELL
5555	5562	(I)	MISS HAMILTON'S FANCY
5555	5562	(I)	(MISS) LUCY CAMPBELL ('S DELIGHT)
5555	551H1H	(I)	HA TOLL AIR A BHATA
555	556	(I)	TEAGUES RAMBLE
555	556	(I)	POLTOGUE JIGG, THE
555	556	(I)	FAVORITE TUNE FROM MOTHER GOOSE, A
5555	561H5	(I)	ITALIAN PEASANTS
5555	5750	(I)	WILL YE COME TO THE BOWER
5555	572H7	(II)	GOUROCK BAY
5555	51H24	(I)	HALLOWEEN
5555	52H30	(I)	RURAL FELICITY
5555	54H72H	(I)	MISS STAGG'S STRATHSPEY
5555	54H72H	(I)	GILLIECRANKIE
5555	6522	(I)	GAIRTH HOUSE
5555	6532	(I)	TOWLERS LAMENT
5555	651H2	(I)	PEGGIE'S DREAM
5555	6662	(II)	MISS McLEOD OF COLBECK
			[MISS MACLEOD OF COLBECK]
5555	6662	(I)	MISS McLEOD OF COLBECK'S STRATHSPEY
5555	6662	(I)	MRS CAPt STEWART'S STRATHSPEY
5555	6664	(I)	GATHER AND GO
5555	6665	(I)	WOE'S MY HEART (THAT WE SHOU'D SUNDER)
5555	6665	(I)	WITH BROKEN WORDS
5555	6666	(II)	MRS MACKINNON CORRY
5555	6666	(I)	WILL YOU GO TO FLANDERS
5555	6666	(I)	ROYAL HIGHLANDERS WELCOME FROM WATERLOO
5555	6666	(I)	LORD LOVATE'S REELL
5555	6661H	(II)	ROLL HER ON THE HILL
5555	661H3H	(I)	AN IRISH JIGG
5555	662H2H	(II)	BEN LOMOND
5555	662H2H	(I)	BEN LOMOND
5555	662H2H	(I)	MRS ROSE (MOUNT COFFER) (REEL/STR.)
5555	61H32	(I)	WILL YE GO TO THE HIGHLANDS
			AND CHACE THE FLEET ROE
5555	61H66	(II)	BONNY TOUN O' KENMORE, THE
5555	61H66	(II)	MRS MACKINNON CORRY or
			[BONNY TOUN O' KENMORE]
5555	61H1HO	(I)	HOW BLEST THE MAID
5555	7b47bL2	(I)	MISS CHAMER'S REEL
5555	7b47bL2	(I)	MARQUIS OF LOTHIAN'S REEL
5555	7b427bL	(II)	MRS BAIRD OF NEWBYTH
5555	7b427bL	(I)	MRS BAIRD (OF NEWBYTH) 'S STRATHSPEY
5555	7b424	(II)	PETER BAILLIE or
			[LONACH HIGHLAND FLING, THE]
5555	7b47b4	(II)	MRS WRIGHT OF LAWTON [MRS WRIGHT OF LATON]
5555	7b47b4	(I)	MRS WRIGHT OF LATON ('S STRATHSPEY)
5555	7b57b5	(II)	MRS WRIGHT
5555	7676	(II)	I WILL LOVE THEE YET
5555	1H56L3	(I)	FINLAYSTON HOUSE
5555	1H542	(I)	TRIP TO OATLAND(S), A
5555	1H562	(I)	TRIP TO OATLAND, A
555	51H1H	(I)	LADY LOUISA ANN DOUGLAS, A MEDLEY WALTZ
5555	1H1H55	(I)	FINALE FROM "LA NIEGE"
5555	1H1H1H3H	(I)	MARCH IN THE WATER PIECE
5555	1H1H1#H2H	(I)	C'EST L'AMOUR
555	51H2H	(I)	DUKE OF WELLINGTON, THE
5555	1H3H62	(I)	LADY DALRYMPLE HAY'S STRATHSPEY
5555	1H3H62	(I)	MISS WEDDERBURN'S REEL
5555	1H3H62	(I)	COLONEL W. MARSHALL OF THE
			79th REGt OF FOOT
5555	2H1H2H5	(I)	MERRY GIRLS OF YORK, THE
5555	3H511	(I)	CAPT BAILLIES MARCH
5555	3H1H2H2H	(II)	MISS YOUNG
5555	3H1H2H2H	(I)	MISS YOUNG('S STRATHSPEY)
5555	3H1H2H2H	(I)	MISS SALLY EGLISON'S REEL
5555	4H2H66	(I)	BUSK O BUSK MY BONNY BONNY BRIDE
5555	4H2H4H6	(I)	ARDOCH HOUSE
5555	5H5H5H3H	(I)	SURLY GALLOPE, THE
5556	5562	(I)	MISS LOUISA CAMPBELL'S STR./(DELIGHT)

5556	2H755	(II)	BONNIE DUNDEE
5557b	4442	(I)	HONble FRANCIS GRAY'S STRATHSPEY
5557b	4446	(II)	MISS MONTGOMERY
5557b	4446	(II)	LADY MACKENZIE OF SEAFORTH
5557	5557	(I)	LOVE LOCK, THE
5551H	4231	(I)	MR F. H. BINDON'S MARCH
5551H	511H1H	(I)	MR McCLAUKLAINE'S SCOTCH-MEASURE
5551H	5211	(I)	SWISS BOY, THE
5551H	5443	(I)	ROSY MORN, THE
5551H	5443	(I)	WHEN THE ROSY MORN APPEARING
5551H	5522	(II)	BANKS OF GARRY, THE
5551H	5522	(I)	DUTCHESS OF YORK, THE
5551H	5522	(I)	BANKS OF GARY, THE
5551H	5522	(I)	MISS HELEN GRANT'S REEL
5551H	5522	(I)	HONble GEORGE BAILLIE ('S STRATHSPEY)
5551H	5522	(I)	MRS MARY GRANT McINNES
5551H	5522	(I)	MISS STRONACH OF MARNOCH'S STRATHSPEY
5551H	5522	(I)	MR ROBERTSON OF LAW'S (LUDES) STR.
5551H	5524	(II)	PORT MOR NA LURGANN
5551H	5526	(I)	MACLEOD'S REELL
5551H	5542	(II)	CULLEN HOUSE
5551H	5542	(I)	MISS JOHNSTON OF HILTON'S REEL
5551H	5542	(I)	CULLEN HOUSE
5551H	5555	(II)	MRS MUIR OF CALDWELL
5551H	5555	(I)	MRS MUIR OF CALDWELL ('S STRATHSPEY)
5551H	5551H	(I)	NEW TOON OF EDINBURGH, THE
5551H	5562	(I)	GEORGE'S SQUARE
5551H	5562	(I)	LADY LOUISA HAMILTON
5551H	5564	(I)	ALNWICK LODGE
5551H	51H22	(I)	MAJOR ROBERTSON'S STRATHSPEY
5551H	51h22	(I)	GENERAL ROBERTSON OF LAWAR'S
5551H	51H26	(I)	MISS MARGARET GRANT'S REEL
5551H	51H26	(I)	HAMILTON HOUSE
5551H	51H26	(I)	MACLEOD'S REEL
5551H	51H51	(I)	MR ALEXr MINZIE'S HORNPIPE
5551H	51H2H2	(II)	LORD MACDONALD
5551H	51H2H2	(II)	MORAG NIGHEAN DOMHNUILL DUINN or LORD MACDONALD'S
5551H	51H2H2	(I)	LORD MACDONALD ('S REEL)
5551H	51H2H2	(I)	JACK RATLIN
5551H	51H4H2H	(I)	COLLONEL, THE
5551H	52H1H5	(I)	SWISS BOY
5551H	52H1H1H	(I)	SWISS BOY, THE
5551H	6661H	(II)	SCOTS WHA HAE
5551H	6661H	(I)	GERMAN DANCE
5551H	6661H	(I)	HEY TUTI TATEY (TATETY)
5551H	6661H	(I)	SCOTS WHA HAE WI' WALLACE BLED
5551H	61H51H	(II)	HIGHLAND FLING
5551H	7b47bL7bL	(I)	MR P. BROWN OF LINKWOOD'S STRATHSPEY
5551H	7532	(I)	MR DAVIE PIRIE'S HORNPIPE
5551H	2H2H66	(I)	BONNY KATE OF EDINBURGH
5551H	2H3H66	(II)	BANKS OF DON, THE
5551H	3bH1H3bH3bH	(II)	HIGHLANDS OF SCOTLAND, THE
5551H	3H522	(I)	HIGH-WAY TO EDINBURGH, THE
5551H	3H523	(I)	MISS JENNY WEDDERBURN'S REEL
5551H	3H1H2H6	(II)	KIRSTY MACFARLANE
5551H	3H2H2H2	(II)	MISS CAMPBELL, MONZIE [MISS SUSAN CAMPBELL, MONZIES]
5551H	3H2H2H2	(I)	MISS CAMPBELL (OF) MONZIE ('S STRATHSPEY)
5551H	3H2H2H5	(I)	MRS BLAIR OF AVONTOWN'S FAVORITE
5551H	3H3H3H2H	(II)	CALEDONIAN MARCH
5551H	3H4H2H2	(II)	CAPTAIN PRINGLE OF YAIR
5551H	3H4H2H2	(I)	MR AND W HENDERSON'S FAVORITE
5551H	4H2H65	(I)	FLOWERS OF THE FOREST, THE
5551H	4H2H66	(I)	FLOWERS OF THE FOREST, THE
5551H	4H2H72H	(I)	HIGHLAND FAIR
5551H	4H3H2H2H	(I)	LADY MARY BRUCE'S STRATHSPEY
5551H	5H2H66	(I)	BONNY KATE OF EDINBURGH
5552H	5523	(II)	LORD MACDONALD
5552H	7533	(I)	LADY FORBES OF NEW AND EDINGLASSIE
5552H	3H2H66	(I)	FLOWERS OF THE FOREST, THE
5553H	5331H	(I)	FAIRIES MARCH, THE
556	17L5L	(I)	MRS DEMPSTER OF DUNNICHEN'S MINUET
5562	3217L	(I)	ALLEGRETTO
5562	5551	(I)	BRIDE HAS A BONNY THiNG, THE
5562	5555	(I)	ROYAL SOVEREIGN, THE
5562	5555	(I)	BRIDE IS A BONNY THiNG, THE
5562	5551H	(II)	AUCHTERTYRE HOUSE
5562	5565	(I)	LOCHSPEY SIDE
5563	4542	(I)	HARE IN THE CORN, THE
5563	5532	(I)	MRS GENERAL HAY'S STRATHSPEY
5564	2355	(I)	BONNY SCOT, THE

5564	2425L	(I)	BEDS OF ROSES, (THE)
5564	2541	(I)	TYROLEN DANCE
5564	3342	(I)	PAS SEUL MISS MARY NICOL
5564	4255	(I)	(BONNY) BOAT MAN (THE)
5564	5311	(I)	MADAMOSELLE [LA DAMOSELLE]
5564	5332	(I)	MAID OF DORNOCK, THE
5564	5342	(I)	MRS DAVIDSON'S REEL
5564	5531	(II)	O BUT YE BE MERRY [O SHE'S COMICAL]
5564	5531	(I)	O BUT YE BE MERRY [O SHE'S COMICAL]
5564	5542	(I)	RONDO D' HENRY 4th
5564	5551H	(II)	MR G. IRONSIDE'S STRATHSPEY
5564	5565	(II)	EARL [OF] HOME
5564	5565	(I)	(LORD/EARL OF) HOME ('S STRATHSPEY/REEL)
556	464	(I)	DYSART HORNPIPE
5564	751H5H	(II)	LADY McKENZIE OF COUL [LADY MACKENZIE OF COUL]
5564	751H5H	(I)	LADY McKENZIE OF COUL
5565	111H5	(I)	TIT FOR TAT
5565	2216L	(I)	KILCRAIGIE
556	531	(I)	A DHONAIL RUAIDH GHAOLAICH
556	535	(I)	MRS FULLARTON OF FULLARTON'S MINUET
5565	5521#	(I)	COL. K. McKENZIE 52ND REGts STRATHSPEY
5565	5522	(II)	MESSE, LE
556	557	(I)	SOUTERS OF SELKIRK, (THE)
5565	1H655	(I)	SKYE DANCE
556	51H3H	(I)	MISS A. BROWN'S MINUET
5565	3H3H2H2H	(I)	MISS BRUCE'S JIG
556	642	(I)	MINUET
5566	4431	(II)	O SHE'S COMICAL
5566	501H2H	(I)	IN MY COTTAGE NEAR A WOOD
5566	5430	(I)	WHEN FIRST THIS HUMBLE ROOF I KNEW
5566	5527L	(I)	RUNAWAY, THE
5566	5522	(I)	HUMOROUS LIEUTENANT, THE
5566	5530	(I)	NEW CORN RIGGS
5566	5531	(II)	O SHE'S COMING [O SHE'S COMICAL]
5566	5531	(I)	O' SHE'S COMICAL
5566	5533	(I)	HIGHLAND SOLO
5566	5533	(I)	BONNIE LASSIE CANNIE LASSIE
5566	553H3H	(II)	NETTA, MISS BRUCE, FOCHABERS
5566	774H7	(II)	FIRE AWAY
5566	72H1H3H	(II)	SCOTCH MIST
5566	1H111	(I)	MARCH
5566	1H642	(I)	CORN CUTTERS, THE
5566	2H4H2H2H	(I)	BALTHAYOCH HOUSE
5566	4H2H72H	(II)	MRS SCOTT MONCRIEFF
5567	1H1H70	(I)	PARTANT POUR LA SYRIE
556	1H15	(I)	MISS BEWMENT'S MINUET
5561H	57L24	(I)	MISS HELLEN BOWER
5561H	5122	(I)	GRAMACHREE
5561H	5210	(I)	GRAMACHREE (MOLLY)
5561H	5210	(I)	MAID IN BEDLAM, THE
5561H	5210	(I)	HAD I A HEART (FOR FALSEHOOD FRAMED)
5561H	5532	(I)	CALEDONIAN, THE
5561H	1H64H1H	(I)	MISS SACKVILE'S FANCY
556	1H1H1H	(I)	O BOTHWELL BANK(S, THOU BLOOMEST FAIR)
556	1H1H2H	(I)	MAN HAS GOT HIS MARE AGAIN, THE
5561H	1H3H3H2H	(I)	NEW ALLEMAND, THE
5561H	2H3H2H6	(II)	CLUNY MACPHERSON'S LAMENT
557b5	5551	(I)	YELL YELL
557b5	557b7b	(II)	BATTLE OF FALKIRK, THE
557b6	4447bL	(II)	MULLIN DHU(, THE)
557b6	4447bL	(I)	MULLIN DU, THE
557b6	4444	(II)	MUILLEANN DUBH [MULIN DHU, THE)
557b6	4444	(I)	MULLIN DU, THE [MUILEANN DUBH]
557b6	4547bL	(I)	MULLINDOUGH
557b7b	3H5H6H3H	(II)	CATCH AND KISS THE ROMP
557b2H	7b444	(I)	BRAES OF TULLYMET, THE
557b2H	7b444	(I)	MISS GRANT OF GRANT'S REELL
557b2H	3H4H3H4H	(II)	NEW YEAR'S DAY
557	1H1H1H	(I)	CURRI KOUN DILICH
5571H	2H3H76	(II)	WOOIN' O'T, THE
5571H	2H4H72H	(I)	QUICK STEP
5572H	2H2H63H	(I)	AN THOU WERE MY AIN THING
551HO	5530	(I)	FAREWELL
551HO	61H1H7	(I)	WHEN PENSIVE I THOUGHT OF MY LOVE
551H1	25L15	(I)	TARS OF THE VICTORY
551H3	551H6	(I)	LADY DOWNE'S STRATHSPEY
551H3	1H2H3H3H	(I)	QUICK MARCH
551H5	227b2	(II)	QUEEN'S WELCOME TO DEE SIDE, THE
551H5	2352	(I)	MISS B. CAMPBELL OF SHAWFIELD'S FAVORITE
551H5	3111	(I)	HOW SWEET THE LOVE (THAT MEETS RETURN)
551H5	3322	(II)	BONNIE DUNDEE

```
551H5      3322      (I)   BONNETS O' BONNIE DUNDEE, THE
551H5      347L1     (I)   THOUGHTLESS, THE
551H5      3465      (I)   BEYNONS DELIGHT
551H5      5524      (II)  CORIMONIE'S RANT
551H5      5524      (I)   CORRIMONY'S STRATHSPEY
551H5      5524      (I)   MISS GLEN'S STRATHSPEY
551H5      551H1H    (II)  SIXTEEN AND SAUCY
551H5      662H2     (II)  AGGIE AND INA (JAFFREY)
551H5      662H2H    (II)  TIPPERTY'S JEAN
551H5      662H2H    (II)  TAMMY O' THE MOSS
551H5      3H1H22    (I)   MISS MAXWELL OF MONRIETH'S REEL
551H6      551H2     (I)   CROSS WELL OF EDINBURGH, THE
551H6      551H2     (I)   MRS RITCHIE'S REEL
551H6      551H2     (I)   LADY HELEN DALRYMPLE'S NEW REEL
551H6      551H5     (I)   I THINK THE CARLIE'S WUD THE NIGHT
551H6      551H2H    (II)  INVERURIE
551H6      553H2H    (I)   SCOTCH JENNY
551H6      6432      (I)   MISS LILIAS CUNNINGHAM'S DANCE
551H6      1H5H6H3H  (I)   NEW STRATHSPEY REEL, A
551H6      3H522     (I)   MRS STRACHAN'S STRATHSPEY
551H7b     7b1H55    (I)   MY BONNIE LADDIE'S LANG O GROWIN'
551H7      557L2     (I)   MISS MARY DOUGLAS'S JIG
551H7      5543      (I)   HER GRACE THE DUTCHESS OF BUCCLEUGH
551H7      6543      (I)   ALLEGRO
551H7      61H1H1H   (I)   TRIP TO CLUMBER, A
551H7      62H1H1H   (I)   TRIP TO CLUMBER
551H1H     5216L     (II)  MOUNTCOFFER HOUSE
551H1H     5525L     (II)  IVY HOUSE
551H1H     5525L     (I)   MR A. CUMMING'S FANCY
551H1H     5562      (I)   MISS RUSSEL OF BLACKHALL'S JIG
551H1H     6531      (I)   ENGLISHMAN IN PARIS
551H1H     662H2H    (I)   JOHNNIE FAA
551H1H     61H55     (I)   WOLDS OF SUSSEX, THE
551H1H     61H1H7    (I)   WHEN PENSIVE I THOUGHT ON MY LOVE
551H1H     1H522     (I)   GI' THE LASSES MAIR O'T
551H       1H1H2H    (I)   OLD JEW, THE
551H1H     2H71H5    (I)   TALISMAN, THE
551H1H     2H2H2H6   (II)  MISS CAMPBELL, LOCHEND
551H1H     2H2H2H6   (I)   MISS CAMPBELL LOCH-END'S REEL
551H1H     2H4H2H6   (I)   MR WILLIAM FRASER'S FAVORITE
551H1H     2H4H3H2H  (I)   KING SHALL ENJOY HIS OWN AGAIN, THE
551H1H     3H1H2H1H  (II)  McDOUGALL'S MARCH
551H1H     4H3H2H6   (II)  O LASSIE ART THOU SLEEPING YET
551H       2H50      (I)   FAVORITE POLLACCA, THE
551H2H     551H2H    (I)   JOHNNY AND MARY
551H2H     6532      (II)  MRS MACKENZIE
551H2H     6542      (II)  COUNTESS OF DALHOUSIE
551H2H     6542      (I)   COUNTESS OF DALHOUSIE
551H2H     3H52H1H   (I)   MAIR 'S MO LUAIDH
551H2H     3H52H1H   (I)   MY JOY AND MY LOVE
551H2H     4H2H66    (I)   ANN THOU WERE MY AIN THING
551H3bH    5551H     (I)   LA DHOMH 'SMI DIREADH BEALAICH
551H3bH    5551H     (I)   ONE DAY AS I CLIMBED THE HILL
551H3bH    5551H     (I)   'SCIAN FADA FADA O'N UIRIDH
551H3H     6L6L2H2H  (I)   JOHN(N)IE FAA
551H3H     51H2H5    (I)   MARCH
551H3H     1H522     (I)   GI'E THE LASSES MAIR O' IT
551H3H     1H61H6    (II)  JOHNNY WON'T YOU MARRY ME
551H3H     1H1H32    (I)   LORD JOHN SCOTT'S STRATHSPEY
551H       3H2H2H    (I)   LADY BERNARD'S LAMENT
551H3H     2H2H65    (I)   IF THOU WERE MINE OWN THING
551H       3H5H5H    (I)   POLENESE, CHE GLORNO DI CONTENTO
552H6      551H1H    (II)  BACK OF THE CHANGE HOUSE, THE
552H6      551H1H    (I)   BACK OF THE CHANGE HOUSE, (THE)
552H7      62H2H7    (I)   COLONEL MURRAY'S MARCH
552H       1H1H3H    (I)   MISS SUSANNA CUMMING'S MINUET
552H2H     561H1H    (I)   GIN A BODY MEET A BODY
552H2H     561H1H    (I)   COMIN' THROUGH THE RYE
552H2H     561H1H    (I)   GIN A BODY MEET A BODY
552H2H     5H2H1H1H  (I)   RECOVERY, THE
552H3H     5522      (II)  CARRICK FERGUS
552H3H     5522      (II)  HASTE TO THE WEDDING
552H3H     5532      (II)  HASTE TO THE WEDDING
552H3H     552H2H    (II)  I'M A YOUNG MAN
552H3H     5622      (I)   CROAGH PATRICK
552H3H     5622      (I)   RURAL FELICITY
552H3H     5622      (I)   SMALL PIN CUSHION, THE
553bH2H    1H7b47bL  (I)   MR FRASER'S FAVORITE
553H       531       (I)   CELEBRATED MEDLEY WALTZ, THE
553H5      3522H     (I)   HANNAGAN MUGGANS
553H1H     472H5     (I)   LA FLORICOURT
553H1H     6542      (II)  SHERWOOD RANGERS, THE
```

553H1H	2H71H5	(I)	THEATRE ROYAL
553H2H	5572H	(II)	PRESIDENT, THE
553H	2H61H	(I)	MR DON'S FAVORITE
553H2H	62H4H3H	(I)	KATE OF ABERDEEN
554H7	554H1H	(I)	LADY CHARLOTTE BENTINCKS WALTZ
5553	5522	(II)	MR GRAHAM OF ORCHILLS
566L6L	5653	(I)	NORTH BERWICK LAW
5612	5631H	(I)	LORD MINTO'S WALTZ
5627bL	5655	(II)	LORD HAY
5627bL	5655	(I)	LORD HAY('S STRATHSPEY)
5622	536L5L	(I)	LADY DUNBAR OF BOATH'S STRATHSPEY
5622	5353	(I)	MRS COL. HAY OF MAYNE'S STRATHSPEY
5622	5651H	(II)	VISCOUNTESS DUNCAN
5622	5651H	(I)	MRS HUNTER OF BLACKNESS STRATHSPEY
5622	5651H	(I)	LADY VISCOUNTESS DUNCAN'S STRATHSPEY
5631	326L5L	(II)	TOM DEY
5631	566L6L	(I)	BROKEN BRIG OF STIRLING, THE
5631	5631	(I)	MISS GRACE LESLIE'S REEL
5631	5633	(I)	BRAES OF BOYNDLIE, THE
5631	572H6	(I)	St. KILDA GIRL'S LAMENT (ATION ON THE DEATH OF HER LOVER), A
5632	536L5L	(I)	LADY DUNBAR OF BOATH'S STRATHSPEY
5633	267L7L	(I)	MISS BROWN'S JIG
5633	61H53	(I)	ANDANTE
5634	5133	(II)	DOON BY THE BURN
5631H	57b47b	(II)	SUTHERLAND HIGHLANDERS, THE
5631H	2H1H62	(II)	BLIN' JAMIE
5640	3420	(I)	CONCERTO
5641	561L1L	(I)	MR HOPE'S WALTZ
5642	1232	(I)	CIVILITY
5642	567L2	(I)	DUCHESS OF BEDFORD'S CAIRN, THE
5642	5641	(I)	PEGGY OF THE GREEN
5642	5651H	(II)	CRAIGIE HALL
5643	4435	(I)	MARINERS, THE
5645	36L53	(I)	HORNPIPE
5646	5642	(I)	MISS FORBES'S STRATHSPEY
5651	1321	(I)	NIS O RINNEADH AR TAGHADH
5651	2122	(I)	NEW OPERA DANCE, THE
5651	2122	(I)	MRS LOCH'S FAVORITE
5651	5222	(I)	HE'S AYE KISSING ME
5651	5326L	(I)	WILLIE WINKS (STRATHSPEY)
5651	5526L	(I)	WILLY WINKY'S TESTAMENT
5651	5625L	(I)	HARLEQUIN TUNE
5651	5653	(II)	STRACHUR
5651	57b27bL	(II)	DUNTROON
5651	51H52	(II)	DONALD DOW
5651	51H52	(II)	LADY CHARLOTTE MURRAY OR DONALD DOW
5651	51H52	(I)	DONALD DOW('S STRATHSPEY)
5651	51H52	(I)	LADY CHARLOTTE MURRAY'S REEL
5651	51H52	(I)	SOLDIER'S DANCE AFTER THE BATTLE
5651	53H2H2	(I)	MRS MAITLAND OF FREUGH'S REEL
5651	1H37L2	(I)	MISS ELIZABETH FERGUSON'S FAVORITE
5652	6L5L42	(I)	PARLOUR, THE
5652	6L5L42	(I)	CUSHION DANCE, THE
5652	7L27L2	(I)	MISS McNEIL'S FANCY
5653	7L244	(I)	MRS CHARLES STEWART
5653	4322	(I)	COTILLION
5653	4527L	(II)	WEE RORIE'S HIELAN' FLING
5653	5324	(I)	JAMES PORTEOUS'S FIDDLE
5653	5342	(I)	MR DUFF (OF FETTERESSO'S) BIRTH DAY
5653	5357	(I)	ECCENTRIC REEL, THE
5653	5652	(II)	PIBROCH O' DONALD DHU
5653	5652	(I)	DONALD DHU
5653	5652	(I)	LOCHEIL'S MARCH
5653	5653	(II)	NORTHERN MEETING, THE
5653	5653	(I)	SICILIAN MARINERS HYMN
5653	5662	(II)	NORTH PORT
5653	51H4H2H	(I)	ROSE BUDS IN MAY, THE
5653	6225L	(I)	LORD COLLINGWOOD'S HORNPIPE
5653	6532	(I)	FOSS DYKE, THE
5653	6542	(I)	MR (CHARLES) SHARP OF HODDOM('S GIGA)
5654	4543	(I)	QUICK STEP
565	452	(I)	MRS CRUICKSHANK'S FANCY
5654	537L2	(I)	COMODORE MITCHELLS' STRATHSPEY
5654	537L2	(I)	MR LUMSDEN (OF BLANERNE) 'S STRATHSPEY [cf: COMMODORE MITCHELL]
5654	547L2	(II)	MR LUMSDEN
5654	547L2	(I)	MR LUMSDEN(OF BLAINEARN'S STRATHSPEY)
5654	547L2	(I)	LADY MADELINA PALMER'S STRATHSPEY
5654	547L2	(I)	LADY CHARLOTTE LEN(N)OX'S STRATHSPEY
5655	2322	(I)	BANOSSE
5655	436L2	(I)	MISS LITTLES FANCY, THE

```
5655      4765      (II)  STAR DUST
5655      513H2H    (I)   CAPTAIN BAILLIES QUICK STEP
5655      4H2H66    (I)   (BUSK YE) BUSK YE MY BONNY BRIDE
5656      5245      (I)   LADY BETTY HAMILTON'S REEL
5656      5622      (I)   DEACON OF THE WEAVERS, THE
5656      51H3H3H   (II)  BRAW LADS
565       62H7      (I)   DOUBLE HORNPIPE No. 4
5651H     427L5L    (I)   REFRESHMENT, THE
5651H     4542      (I)   ALEXANDER STEWART, ESQr
                          OF GLENCREPISD(A)LE'S STRATHSPEY
5651H     5225L     (I)   ROMPING FANNY
5651H     5243      (I)   MISS WHITEFORD'S JIGG
5651H     5323      (I)   MY MARY DEAR DEPARTED SHADE
5651H     5333      (I)   THOU LING'RING STAR!
5651H     5622      (II)  MR ROBERTSON OF LUDE
5651H     5622      (I)   MR ROBERTSON OF LUDE('S STRATHSPEY)
5651H     5627b     (II)  O'REILLY'S JIG
5651H     5632      (I)   ROSENEATH CASTLE
5651H     562H2     (I)   MISS MARGt St. CLAIR REDDIES FANCY
5651H     51H22     (I)   RIGS OF BARLEY, THE
5651H     6632      (I)   MRS G. FORBES, ASHGROVE
5651H     7b424     (II)  MINISTER'S RANT, THE
5651H     4H2H60    (I)   BRAES OF YARROW, THE
5652H     51H32     (I)   FAREWELL, THE
5662      5653H     (II)  LADY AMELIA MURRAY
5662      5653H     (I)   LADY AMELIA MURRAY'S STRATHSPEY
5663      6542      (I)   JOSEPH'S FROLIC
5664      4255      (I)   BONNY BOAT MAN, THE
5666      5632      (I)   GOOD THOUGHT, A
5671H     5671H     (I)   LADY CHOLMONDLEY'S WALTZ
5671H     67L16L    (I)   VISCOUNT MANDEVILLE
567       1H1H1H    (I)   EILAN MO ROON
567       1H1H3H    (I)   ROBIN ADAIR
567       1H1H3H    (I)   AILEEN AROON
561HO     4H2H1HO   (I)   BUSK YE, BUSK YE
561H3     6L27L2    (I)   MISS ANN COCKBURN'S FANCY HIGH DANCE
561H4     27L5L1    (I)   LA SAGATAIRE
561H      553       (I)   ROBIN'S COMPLAINT
561H6     5663      (I)   JOCKY'S DANCE
561H1H    561H1H    (I)   WALTZ OF MAIENCE
561H1H    561H1H    (I)   LADY GRACE DOUGLASS'S VALTZ
561H1H    51H66L    (II)  CUIR A CHINN DILEAS
                          [TURN ROUND THY FAITHFUL HEAD]
561H1H    7651      (I)   LES BOIS
561H      1H1H1H    (I)   SOLDIER'S DREAM
561H      2H2H2H    (I)   HUGAR MU FEAN
561H2H    3H67L5L   (I)   MISS LYONS' HORNPIPE
561H2H    3H2H2H1H  (I)   NUNC EST BIBENDUM
561H3H    2H3H2H6   (II)  MACDONALD'S KILT
57b11     47b7bL7bL (II)  GOLDEN LOCKS
57b11     47b7bL7bL (I)   NIGHEAN BHUIDH BHOIDHEACH
57b3b     1H7b3b    (I)   BUCKET, THE
57b51     57b51     (II)  DAN DEIRG
57b55     7b424     (II)  RED HECKLE, THE
57b6      402       (I)   CRAIGEY ROCK, THE
57b6      541       (II)  BOTHAN AIRIDH 'M BRAIGHE RAINEACH
                          [SHIELING IN THE BRAES OF RANNOCH, THE]
57b7b4    57b7b5    (I)   DELVEN SIDE
57b7b     51H2H     (I)   ANDREW KERR
57b1H1H   1H7b51    (I)   IMIR FEIN, A CHOINNICH CHRIDHE
57b1H1H   1H7b51    (I)   ROW THOU, DEAREST KENNETH
5752      3523      (II)  WEE NANNIE
5752      4651H     (II)  BONNIE THACKIT HOOSIE, THE
5753      15L32     (II)  EWAN'S HORNPIPE [EVANS]
5753      4316L     (I)   HONble MARGARET ERSKINE'S REEL, THE
5753      5525      (I)   O NANNY WILT THOU GANG WI' ME
5755      3321      (I)   MINUET IN SAMPSON
5755      4325      (II)  WARD'S( HORNPIPE)
5755      5552      (I)   LA POULE
575       575       (I)   WALTZ
5757      5333      (I)   OVER THE HILLS AND FAR AWAY
5757      5341      (I)   PIZARRO
5757      5764      (II)  DEIL AMONG THE TAILORS
5757      2H62H6    (I)   MRS McDONALD'S FAVORITE
5757      3H5H6H5H  (I)   MASTER ERSKINE'S HORNPIPE
5767      5250      (II)  DEAR AULD HA', THE
577       51H3H     (II)  MRS STEPHEN BUCHROMB'S WALTZ
572H7     5764      (II)  LORD SALTOUN('S REEL)
572H7     1H2H3H1H  (I)   DUNCAN GRAY
572H1H    1H2H3H1H  (I)   DUNCAN GRAY
572H3H    4H2H75    (I)   JOHN ANDERSON, ESQr's HORNPIPE
572H3H    4H5H2H5   (I)   CAPT RONALD FERGUSON'S QUICK STEP
```

143

```
51H15        51H2H2      (I)   MAJOR MONTGOMERY'S REEL
51H26L       51H66       (II)  LONACH HALL
51H26L       51H62H      (I)   MISS ANN CUMING'S STRATHSPEY
51H22        51H55       (I)   MRS COL: GRANT OF GRANT'S STRATHSPEY
51H24        51H66       (I)   MISS H. SCOTT'S STRATHSPEY
51H22H       51H55       (I)   O'ER THE MUIR TO MAGGIE
51H31        227L5L      (II)  MR HUNTER'S REEL
51H31        2327L       (I)   MERRY SWABBS, THE
51H32        62H75       (I)   HAMILTON HOUSE
51H33        4233        (I)   MRS GIBBON'S REEL
51H33        4433        (I)   WALKER'S HORNPIPE
51H35        1233        (I)   MRS ROBERTSON
51H35        1233        (I)   TON, THE
51H35        135L1       (II)  STEAM-BOAT, THE
51H35        22H76       (II)  KITTY ROBERTSON
51H35        22H76       (I)   MISS BETTY ROBERTSON
51H35        4621        (I)   MR R. CATTO JUNr's HORNPIPE
51H35        42H46       (I)   MISS SIMPSON'S REEL
51H3         51H4        (I)   RAKES OF BRESTNEATH, THE
51H42        2416L       (I)   LADY'S DELIGHT, THE
51H42        4751        (II)  WHERE THE ROSES BLUSH AND BLOOM
51H4         320         (I)   LADY WALLACE'S MINUET
51H43        3111        (I)   PRETTY MILLINER, THE
51H43        51H21       (I)   MISS H. HUNTER OF BLACKNESS'S VALTZ
51H44        5324        (I)   UNTITLED
51H4#1H      51H4#1H     (I)   MAZURKA
51H51        1355        (II)  MISS NANCIE LOW
51H51        1355        (I)   MISS NANCIE LOW('S REEL)
51H51        2216L       (I)   MISS ROSS OF ROSSIE'S STRATHSPEY
51H51        3255        (II)  I WINNA GANG TAE BED THE NICHT,
                               I CANNA' SLEEP AVA
51H51        5411        (I)   PATTY'S WHIM
51H51        5522        (I)   MISS HARIOT MACDONALD'S REEL
51H51        51H53       (II)  HIELAN' BROCHAN
51H51        51H56       (I)   SLEEP ON TILL DAY
51H51        51H62       (I)   CAPT SMYTH'S FAVOURITE
51H51        51H72       (II)  CANTY CRECKET
51H51        51H72       (I)   KENTISH CRICKETERS, THE
51H51        51H72       (I)   CANTIE CRECKET
51H52        2436L       (II)  MISS SUSAN CAMPBELL, MONZIES
51H52        2436L       (I)   MISS SUSAN CAMPBELL MONZIES (' STRATHSPEY)
51H52        3671H       (I)   POOR LITTLE GYPSY, THE
51H53b       47b42       (II)  MISS SOPHIA CAMPBELL
51H53b       47b42       (I)   MISS SOPHIA CAMPBELL (OF SADDELL'S) REEL
51H53b       53bH7b1H    (I)   BABA MO LEANEABH [BABA MO LEANABH]
51H53b       7b7b44      (II)  MRS GORDON OF BELSIES
51H53b       7b7b44      (I)   MRS GORDON (OF BELLIE)'S STRATHSPEY
                               [MRS GORDON OF BELSIES]
51H53        6L15L1      (I)   MYRTLE SPRIG
51H53        1242        (I)   WALTZ
51H53        1257L       (I)   LE BRUNETTE
51H53        1251        (I)   LOVE AND OPPORTUNITY
51H53        1251        (I)   LA BRUNETTA
51H53        1251        (I)   POP THE QUESTION
51H53        1251        (I)   LA BRUNETTE
51H53        11H22       (II)  SANDY MACDONALD'S
51H53        11H32       (II)  SANDY MACDONALD'S FAVOURITE
51H53        4327L       (II)  TOBERMORY
51H53        51H22       (II)  GOWAN BRAES, THE
51H53        51H32       (I)   GACH TINNEAS ACH GOAL
51H53        51H36       (I)   SLEEP ON TILL DAY
51H53        51H36       (I)   LULLABY OF AN INFANT CHIEF
51H53        51H2H2      (II)  DUNSE CASTLE
51H53        51H2H2      (I)   DUNSE CASTLE
51H53        637L5L      (I)   ROPE DANCE, THE
51H53        6542        (II)  LADY MARY STOPFORD
51H53        6542        (II)  LADY MARY MONTAGUE
51H53        6542        (I)   LADY MARY MONTAGUES REEL
51H53        6542        (I)   LADY MARY STOPFORD'S REEL
51H53        61H75       (II)  RAVEN, THE or HOOKEYBEAK
51H53        62H64       (II)  TONAL MACKINLAY
51H53        62H1H5      (I)   HARPER OF MULL, THE
51H54        51H51H      (I)   GLENKILRY'S STRATHSPEY
51H54        52H1H1H     (I)   COTTILLION 7th
51H5         47b6        (I)   O WALY, WALY, LOVE IS BONIE
51H55        11H3H1H     (I)   MRS GORDON OF KINCARDINE'S REEL
51H55        51H3H6      (II)  GO TO THE DEVIL AND SHAKE YOURSELF
51H55        51H3H6      (I)   GO TO THE DEVIL & SHAKE YOURSELF
51H55        1H522       (I)   MISS CLEMENTINA LOUGHMAN ('S STR.)
51H55        1H2H3H6     (I)   UNTITLED
51H55        1H2H3H6     (I)   GO TO THE DEVIL AND SHAKE YOURSELF
51H56        51H26       (II)  BORLUM'S RANT
```

```
51H56      51H26      ( I )  BORLAM'S (RANT/REEL/STRATHSPEY)
                             [BORLUM'S RANT/REEL]
51H57b     51H51H     ( I )  WE'ER NO VERY FOU BUT WE'ER GAYLY YET
51H57b     51H51H     ( I )  BIDE YE YET
51H57b     51H3bH2H   ( I )  RATHA FAIR
51H51H     2427bL     ( I )  MISS MARY ANN JOHNSTON'S STRATHSPEY
51H51H     22H2H6     ( I )  KILRAVOCK'S REELL
51H51H     47b42      ( II ) MR STEWART OF DALGUISE
51H51H     47b42      ( I )  MR STEWART OF DALGUISE
51H51H     551H5H     ( I )  GUSTAVUS GALOP, THE
51H51H     51H51H     ( II ) SUTHERLAND
51H51H     51H63      ( II ) HEATHER[Y] JOCK
51H51H     6522       ( I )  TO ROSLIN BANK WE'LL GO MY LOVE
51H51H     61H53      ( I )  OPERA HORNPIPE, THE
51H51H     7b2H4H7b   ( I )  FISHERS RANT, THE
51H51H     7b2H4H7b   ( I )  LASSES OF ANCRUM, THE
51H52H     54H2H2H    ( I )  MUNGO
51H52H     3H5H77     ( I )  THIRTIETH Regt. 2ND QUICKSTEP
51H53H     6562       ( I )  LADY BAIRD OF SAUGHTONHALLS REEL
51H53H     1H5H3H2H   ( I )  LORD MOIRA'S WELCOME TO EDINBURGH
51H6b4     3b57b3b    ( I )  FAIR FIELD HOUSE
51H6b5     3b525      ( I )  MRS HAY OF HAYSTON'S FAVORITE
51H6O      5520       ( I )  TO THE BROOK AND THE WILLOW
51H6O      72H3HO     ( I )  LIGHT AS THISTLEDOWN
51H62      562H7      ( I )  MR JOHN ROBERTSON'S JIG
51H62      51H66      ( II ) NIEL GOW  [NEIL GOW]
51H62      51H66      ( II ) NEIL GOW'S STRATHSPEY [NIEL GOW'S]
51H62      51H66      ( I )  NIEL GOW ('S STRATHSPEY)
51H63      3232       ( II ) JACOBITE, THE
51H63      51H42      ( I )  MINTO HOUSE, A STRATHSPEY
51H63      51H42      ( I )  HONble MRS FRASER OF LOVAT'S STRATHSPEY
51H63      51H62      ( I )  BAN TIGHEARNA MHIC S'HIMI
                             [BAINTIGHEARNA MHIC SHIMI]
51H63      51H2H2     ( II ) TWEEDDALE CLUB, THE
51H63      51H2H2     ( I )  TWEEDDALE CLUB, THE
51H63      64H1H5     ( I )  ETTRICK SHEPHERD, THE
51H64      447L2      ( I )  MISS FRASER'S FAVORITE
51H64      4626L      ( I )  MISS BENHAM'S STRATHSPEY
51H64      661H6      ( I )  WILLIE BREW'D A PECK OF MAUT
51H64      62H1H6     ( I )  WILLIE BREW'D A PECK O' MAUT
51H65      1522       ( II ) BONNIE KATE
51H65      1526       ( II ) BONNIE/BONNY LASS OF FISHERROW, (THE)
51H65      1526       ( I )  BONNY LASS OF FISHERROW
51H65      27b44      ( II ) LASSES LIKE NAE BRANDY
51H65      27b46      ( II ) LASSES LIKE NAE BRANDY
51H65      27b46      ( I )  LICK THE LADLE SANDIE
51H65      27b46      ( I )  LASSES LIKE(S) NAE BRANDY
51H65      3342       ( I )  ATHENAEUM, THE
51H65      3532       ( I )  MADAM HEINEL
51H65      3532       ( I )  MISS ELIZA LOW'S HIGH DANCE
51H65      3642       ( I )  MR GARDEN'S WELCOME HOME TO TROUPE HOUSE
51H65      4522       ( II ) DOGGIE, THE
51H65      57b66      ( I )  St KILDA SONG AND DANCE, A
51H65      57b66      ( I )  THA GUILLAN AGAM FHIN
51H65      57b7b6     ( I )  MOURNFUL IS MY STORY
51H65      51H64      ( I )  LORD FIFE'S WALTZ
51H65      51H62H     ( II ) TUNE YOUR FIDDLES
51H65      662H2H     ( II ) LORD DRUMMOND
51H65      671H3H     ( I )  FOREIGN AIR, A
51H65      1H51H3     ( I )  MRS CRAWFORD'S REEL
51H65      3H2H72H    ( I )  LAIRD OF STOW, THE
51H61H     51H24      ( I )  MISS HUNTER'S STRATHSPEY
51H61H     51H62H     ( II ) DEATH AND DR. HORNBROOK
51H61H     6522       ( I )  WOOD-HOUSE REEL, THE
51H61H     61H44      ( II ) GRANNY'S HOOSIE I' THE GLEN
51H62H     751H3      ( I )  ROXBURGH CAVALRY'S QUICK STEP, THE
51H62H     3H1H55     ( I )  LADY McINTOSH'S RANT
51H7b3b    57b44      ( II ) LOCH O' DRUMMUIR, THE
51H7b4     53bH7b4H   ( I )  O GIN MY LOVE WERE YON RED ROSE
51H7b5     7b545      ( II ) DEER FOREST, THE
51H7b5     3bH545     ( I )  SUD AN GLEANN 'S AM BI NA FEIDH
51H7b5     3bH57b5    ( I )  CALLUM FIODHDAIR [CALUM FIGHEADAIR]
51H7b      6b53b      ( I )  AND I WONDER WHEN I'LL BE MARRIED
51H7b7b    51H3bH5H   ( I )  MRS STEWART NICOLSON'S STRATHSPEY
51H75      3432       ( II ) MRS MACMILLAN
51H75      4532       ( II ) SPRITE, THE
51H76      557L2      ( I )  NEW STEPNEY MARCH
51H76      561H2H     ( II ) TULLYVEOLAN MARCH
51H77      1H5H6H5H   ( I )  MISS WEMYSS OF CUTTELHILLS STRATHSPEY
51H7       1H35       ( I )  BRISK
51H7       1H35       ( I )  RIDE A MILE
51H71H     3551H      ( I )  MILE TO RIDE, A
```

51H71H	51H71H	(I)	WALTZ OF BIONDINA
51H7	1H1H5	(I)	CONNEL & FLORA
51H7	1H1H1H	(I)	LADDIE LIE NEAR ME
51H7	1H1H3bH	(I)	LADDIE LIE NEAR ME
51H71H	2H1H1H1H	(I)	SOLDIER'S WEDDING, THE
51H71H	2H3H77	(I)	MEDLEY OVERTURE(4)
51H72H	3H1H35	(I)	DR McKAY
51H72H	3H1H35	(I)	MY JO JANET
51H72H	3H2H35	(I)	MY JO JANET
51H72H	3H2H55	(I)	LORD ELPHINSTONS FAVORITE
51H7	4H1H7	(I)	SALLY IN OUR ALLEY
51H75H	661HO	(I)	MAID OF THE MILL, THE
51H75H	661H1H	(I)	MAID OF THE MILL, THE
51H75H	661H1H	(I)	I'VE KISS'D AND I'VE PRATTLED
51H1H3	1555	(II)	LAD WI' THE JACKET O' BLUE, THE
51H1H5	47b54	(II)	BOBERS O' BRECHIN [BOBBERS OF BRECHIN]
51H1H5	47b54	(II)	STRATHBOGIE TOAST, THE or
			BOBERS OF BRECHIN, THE
51H1H5	47b54	(I)	(BOBER'S/ROBBERS) OF BRECHIN, THE
51H1H5	51H2H2H	(I)	MORGIANA
51H1H5	52H2H2H	(I)	JOHN HIGHLANDMAN
51H1H5	7b427bL	(II)	BENRINNES
51H1H6	51H1H6	(I)	EVELEEN'S BOWER
51H1H	61H5	(I)	A MHIC IAIN MHIC SHEUMAIS
51H1H6	1H2H3bH3b	(I)	OF ALL COMFORTS I MISCARRY'D
51H1H6	2H2H55	(I)	BAY OF BISCAY, THE
51H1H7b	51H51	(I)	THRO' THE LANG MUIR
51H1H7b	51H51	(I)	HAD A WAD HAME
51H1H7b	51H51H	(II)	HAUD AWA' HAME
51H1H7b	7b27b4	(I)	CORBEY AND THE PYETT, THE
51H1H7	7665	(II)	GOOD BYE, GRAMIN
51H1H	1H55	(I)	O'N A THA THU FALBH
51H1H1H	57b1H7b	(II)	BRAES OF TULLYMET
51H1H1H	57b1H7b	(I)	BRAES OF TULLYMET, THE
51H1H	1H72H	(I)	MISS MARY LUMSDEN'S FAVORITE
51H1H1H	72H1H1H	(I)	LIRA LIRA LA
51H1H	1H1H5	(I)	CONAL AND FLORA
51H1H	1H1H7b	(I)	GABERLUNZIE MAN, THE
51H1H	1H1H7b	(I)	GALLAWAY'S LAMENT
51H1H	1H1H2H	(I)	MISS SPANKIE'S MINUET
51H1H	1H1H3H	(I)	LAZY MIST, THE
51H1H1H	2H676	(I)	LA BOULANGER
51H1H1H	2H676	(I)	BOOLONZIE, THE
51H1H1H	2H7b2H4H	(I)	SALLY KELLY'S REEL
51H1H1H	2H776	(I)	CLOUT THE CAULDRON
51H1H1H	2H776	(I)	BOOLONZIE, THE
51H1H1H	2H71H6	(I)	BOOLONZIE
51H1H1H	2H72H4H	(II)	ALLEY CROCKER [ALLY CROCKER] [ALLY CROKER]
51H1H1H	2H2H1H1H	(I)	BOLD DRAGOON, THE
51H1H1H	2H2H1H1H	(I)	TWAS A MARECHAL OF FRANCE
51H1H1H	2H2H2H6	(II)	OOR GUID WIFE
51H1H1H	2H4H5H4H	(II)	ANTIQUARY, THE
51H1H1H	2H5H4H3H	(I)	WALTZ A WEIR
51H1H1H	3bH7b53b	(I)	MOCK DOCTOR, THE
51H1H	1H3H3H	(I)	H. GARDINE'S WALTZ
51H1H2H	62H2H1H	(I)	YARROW VALE
51H1H	2H1H6	(I)	McGRIGOR'S LAMENTATION, THE
51H1H	2H1H6	(I)	CHEVY CHACE
51H1H	2H1H1H	(I)	FALLAIN GUN DITH 'THAINAIG E
51H1H2H	1H2H72H	(I)	CALABRIA
51H1H2H	3H61H7	(I)	LASS OF RICHMOND HILL, THE
51H1H2H	3H4H3H1H	(I)	BANK, THE
51H1H3bH	7b3b47bL	(II)	FOREST OF MAR, THE
51H1H3bH	7b542	(I)	LADY McINTOSH'S REEL
51H1H3H	4H2H67	(I)	MY FATHER SAID THAT HE WOULD HIRE ME
			TO A MAN
51H1H3H	4H2H75	(II)	HONEYMOON, THE
51H1H3H	4H2H75	(I)	HONEY MOON, THE
51H1H3H	4H2H72H	(I)	HONEY MOON, THE
51H1#H6	1H54H1H	(I)	PANTALON
51H2H5	321H1H	(I)	WHIRLIE-WHA, THE
51H2H5	52H5H1H	(I)	CHAPTER OF KINGS
51H2H6	5222	(II)	HUNKER HILL
51H2H6	551H7	(I)	LAKES OF WICKLOW, THE
51H2H7b	51H4H1H	(I)	KITTY OF COLERAINE
51H2H7	51H2H1H	(I)	PRINCESS OF WALES'S WALTZ, THE
51H2H7	6643	(I)	NOREA'S LOST TO ME
51H2H1H	57b42	(II)	HARE AMONG THE HEATHER, THE
51H2H1H	51H2H1H	(I)	HIGHLAND AIR
51H2H1H	51H4H1H	(I)	KITTY OF COLERAINE
51H2H1H	1H5H3H2H	(I)	KATE KEARNEY
51H2H1H	3H4H2H3H	(I)	MISS JANE CARNEGIE'S FAVOURITE

51H2H2H	1H61H7	(I)	DUKE OF COTILLON
51H2H2H	1H61H7	(I)	RONDO, A
51H2H2H	1H5H2H2H	(I)	SPRIG OF SHILLELAH, THE
51H2H2H	3H1H2H1H	(I)	TRISTRAM SHANDY
51H2H2H	3H4H3H2H	(I)	I WISH YOU A HAPPY NEW YEAR
51H2H	3bH2H1H	(I)	ALL IN THE DOWNS
51H2H	3bH2H1H	(I)	BLACK EYED SUSAN
51H2H3H	51H3H2H	(I)	HOW TO BE HAPPY
51H2H	3H3H2H	(I)	WHERE HELEN LIES
51H2H3H	4H72H1H	(I)	MOTHER QUOTH HODGE THE NEW WAY
51H2H5H	71H63	(I)	MARY HUDSON
51H3bH1H	7b427bL	(II)	KEABOG
51H3bH1H	1H1H76b	(I)	MY LOVE'S THE FAIREST CREATURE
51H3bH1H	2H424	(II)	LAD WI' THE KILT, THE
51H3bH1H	2H7b5H7b	(II)	CROUGHLY
51H3bH1H	2H7b5H7b	(I)	CROUGHLY
51H3bH2H	57b7b7b	(I)	MRS GUTHRIE OF GUTHRIE'S STRATHSPEY
51H3bH2H	7b7b7b7b	(I)	MRS GUTHRIE OF GUTHRIE'S STRATHSPEY
51H3bH2H	7b2H7b1	(I)	CEANN DUBH DILEAS
51H3bH2H	7b2H7b1	(I)	BLACK BUT LOVELY
51H3bH2H	7b2H1H1	(I)	CEANN DUBH DILEAS
51H3bH2H	1H7b47bL	(II)	DOUNE OF INVERNOUGHTY, THE
51H3bH3bH	4H2H7b2H	(II)	MISS MACDOWAL GRANT OF ARNDILLY
51H3bH3bH	4H2H7b2H	(I)	MISS MACDOWAL GRANT('S STRATHSPEY) (OF ARNDILLY)
51H3H5	51H3H6	(I)	SHORT APRON, (THE)
51H3H1H	31H42	(I)	REEL OF FIFE
51H3H1H	5322	(I)	MARCH OF THE CAMERON MEN, THE
51H3H1H	5351H	(I)	GUN DUINE AIG A' BHAILE
51H3H1H	51H2H4	(II)	HONble. MRS. F. GRAY
51H3H1H	51H2H4	(I)	(HONBle) (LADY/MRS/MR) (F.) GRAY'S STRATHSPEY
51H3H1H	51H2H2H	(II)	INVERARAY
51H3H1H	51H3H2H	(I)	MRS GORDON OF PITLURG'S STRATHSPEY
51H3H1H	54H3H2H	(II)	BRAES OF ELCHIES, THE
51H3H1H	62H4H7	(I)	PADDY CAREY
51H3H1H	62H4H1H	(I)	PADDY CAREY
51H3H1H	62H4H2H	(II)	FIRTH O' FORTH
51H3H1H	4H2H3H3H	(I)	BLUE AND BUFF
51H3H1H	4H3H67	(I)	CLEGHORN'S RANT
51H3H1H	4H3H2H5	(I)	COME DANCE AND SING AND LET US BE MERRY
51H3H2H	5555	(II)	SIR JOHN MALCOLM
51H3H2H	5555	(II)	KEITH HALL
51H3H2H	5555	(I)	MAUT'S ABOON THE MEAL, THE
51H3H2H	5555	(I)	SIR JOHN MALCOLM
51H3H2H	72H72H	(II)	JOHNNY GROATS HOUSE
51H3H2H	72H72H	(I)	TIGH EOIN GROAT [TAIGH IAIN GROT]
51H3H2H	1H526L	(I)	MISS ERSKINE OF BARJARG'S REEL
51H3H2H	3H2H62H	(II)	COUNTESS OF PERCY, THE
51H3H2H	3H2H62H	(I)	COUNTESS OF PERCY'S REEL
51H3H2H	3H2H72H	(II)	CALABREA [CALABRIA]
51H3H2H	3H2H72H	(I)	CALABRIA
51H3H2H	3H3H51H	(I)	BANNOCKS O' BARLEY MEAL
51H3H2H	3H3H51H	(I)	ARGYLE IS MY NAME
51H3H2H	4H3H1H1H	(I)	CAPT CAMPBELL OF AIRD'S QUICK STEP
51H3H3H	653H2H	(I)	WILLY'S RARE AND WILLY'S FAIR
51H3H3H	653H2H	(I)	TRIP TO VAUXHALL
51H3H3H	1H1H53	(I)	PAS SEUL
51H3H3H	3H3H2H6	(I)	PRINCES WELCOME TO INVERNESS, THE
51H3H3H	3H3H2H2H	(II)	WHERE GADIE RINS or HESSIANS' MARCH, THE
51H3H3H	3H3H2H2H	(I)	O IF I WERE WHERE GADIE RUNS
51H3H3H	3H3H2H2H	(I)	HESSIAN'S MARCH, THE
51H3H3H	4H4H3H6	(I)	MISS HAY OF LYES'S STRATHSPEY
51H3H5H	656H2H	(I)	BRAES OF ALDELUNE, THE
51H3H5H	1H2H4H1H	(I)	I'VE NOT SAID HOW MUCH I LOVE HER
51H3H1H	6542	(I)	MRS GORDON OF PITLURG'S STRATHSPEY
51H4H7	51H4H5H	(I)	MISS SMYTH OF METHVEN
51H4H2H	51H4H3bH	(I)	NEW ISLA REEL, THE
51H4H4H	1H53H1H	(I)	BANKS OF THE DEE
51H4H4H	3H53H1H	(I)	COL. WARDLE
51H4H4H	3H4H75	(I)	LILLY, THE
51H5H6	5H3H3H1H	(I)	A DO ADE A DO DH'FHALBH MI
52H75	5527L	(I)	LADY CAROLINE BERTIE
52H1H3	456L7L	(I)	MISS HUNTER'S JIGG
52H1H5	47b54	(II)	MR GEORGE GORDON
52H1H5	47b54	(I)	MRS GRANT'S REEL
52H1H5	47b54	(I)	MR GEORGE GOODON'S REEL [MR GEORGE GORDON]
52H1H5	47b54	(I)	STRATHBOGIE TOAST, THE
52H3H1H	4H3H75	(I)	MISS FRANCKLYN'S REEL
52H3H2H	52H4H1H	(II)	TRIPPERS, THE
52H3H2H	3H651H	(I)	NORTH'S (MILLES MACPHAIL) FAREWELL TO THE CALEDONIAN HUNT

52H3H2H	3H61H1H	(I)	RAIN RINS DOWN THRO' MIRRY LAND TOWN
53bH7b	443b	(I)	St. MARTIN'S CHURCH YD.
53bH7b4	57b7b3b	(I)	DE'EL TAKE THE GEAR AND THE BLADRIE O'T
53bH2H1H	7b427bL	(II)	GLENTANA
53bH2H1H	7b427bL	(II)	LODGE OF GLEN TANA, THE
53bH4H7b	53bH5H3bH	(I)	MISS CHARLOTTE COX'S FANCY
53H53	53H2H2	(I)	LORD EGLINTOUNE'S REEL
53H54H	561H1H	(I)	BANDIT'S WALTZ
53H56H	3H4H1H5	(I)	LA POULE from MASANIELLO
53H61H	53H52H	(II)	LORD BREADALBANE'S MARCH
53H64H	53H72H	(II)	CLACHAN, THE
53H71H	53H71H	(I)	HARRIETT & SOPHIA'S WALTZ
53H1H	555	(I)	GERMAN WALTZ
53H1H5	51H4H1H	(I)	MORGIANA
53H1H6	432H2	(I)	MISS McNEAL'S REEL
53H1H6	53H1H6	(I)	NAMELESS, THE
53H1H6	6566	(I)	FAIR AFRICAN, THE
53H2H6	53H5H3H	(I)	DUTCHES OF ATHOLE'S STRATHSPEY, THE
53H2H7	1H653	(I)	LADY DOUNE (DOWNE)
53H2H1H	5327	(I)	LOCH OF STRATHBEG, THE
53H2H1H	51H76	(II)	CRAIG CHATTAN
53H2H1H	763H5	(II)	MARKET CHORUS
53H2H1H	763H5	(I)	MARKET CHORUS
53H2H1H	1H6H2H1H	(I)	FAVORITE WALTZ
53H2H3H	53H2H6	(I)	MAJOR LOGAN'S FROLLICK
53H3H1H	1H1H3H6	(I)	MILKING PAIL, THE
53H4H3H	2H2H4H7b	(I)	MR SINCLAIR YOUNGER OF BARRACK'S REEL
54H2H1H	6542	(I)	QUICK STEP
54H3bH2H	7b7b54H	(I)	HIGH WAY TO DUBLIN, THE .
54H3H7	3H3H2H7	(I)	COW BEHIND THE HAYCOCK, THE
54H3H2H	1H527	(I)	LIFE'S A PUN
55H5H5H	55H4H1H	(I)	WALTZE
6b57b1	443b1	(I)	DH'EIRICH MI MOCH
6063	3H02H0	(I)	SOFTLY SWEET IN LYDIAN MEASURES
6131	6132	(I)	KISS ME SWEETLY
6133	6132	(I)	BOCHUIDDAR [BOCHUIDEAR]
6133	6532	(I)	BRAES OF BALWHITHER, THE
6142	3126L	(I)	MISS STEWART'S REEL
6152	6154	(I)	MACFARLANE'S REEL
6154	6142	(I)	NORTH HIGHLAND 21
6155	6542	(I)	BACK OF THE SMITHIE, THE
6216L	1511	(II)	AIR [UNTITLED]
623	16L3	(I)	THA M'AIGNE FODH GHRUAIM
637L7L	131H3	(II)	GORDON CASTLE (or CASTLE GORDON)
637L5L	31H46	(I)	DRAYCOT HOUSE
6313	5353	(I)	JOHN ROY STEWART'S STRATHSPEY
6313	5553	(I)	JOHN ROY STEWART
6322	5353	(I)	RAZA'S RELL
6323	5535	(I)	QUICK MARCH 2d BATTn OF ROYALS
6336L	1153	(II)	GIRL I LEFT BEHIND ME, THE
6333	6322	(II)	GARRY OWEN
6333	6322	(I)	CARY OWEN [GARRY OWEN]
633	522	(I)	MISS PLATOFF'S MINUET
633	632	(I)	HEY MY NANNY
6346	5342	(I)	SIR GEORGE McKENZIES REEL
6351	6347bL	(II)	HIGHWAY TO DUBLIN, THE
6351	6347bL	(I)	HIGH WAY TO DUBLIN, THE
6353	6342	(I)	ROB: DOWN
6353	6542	(I)	ROB DOWN
6365	2466	(I)	MISS PRINGLE'S REEL
631H0	637L0	(II)	GOOD NIGHT
6415L	5L5L5L5L	(I)	MURRAY'S MARCH, (THE)
6424	5353	(II)	MISS CHARLOTTE ROSS
6424	5353	(I)	MISS CHARLOTTE ROSS('S REEL)
6442	6L111H	(I)	CARLIONE
6442	6L111H	(I)	CAROLAN'S RECEIPT FOR DRINKING (WHISKY)
6442	115L1	(I)	SCOTS MARCH
6451	4427bL	(II)	TAIGHEAN GEALA SHIELDAIG or WHITE HOUSES OF SHIELDAIG, THE
6451	5155	(II)	NULL THAR NAN EILEANAN, OR AMERICA
6451	6462	(I)	FILL THE STOUP
6452	3631	(I)	CARNIVAL OF VENICE
6452	3641	(I)	CARNIVAL DI VENEZZA
6452	31H76	(I)	MR BRODIE OF BRODIE'S REEL
6453	662H7	(I)	SIR Wm JARDINE'S REEL
6527bL	651H1	(II)	DOGS BITE CHAPMEN
6527bL	651H5	(I)	SMALL REEL, THE
6532	226L6	(II)	WEE JAMIE
653	231	(I)	SLOW
6533	6533	(I)	BRAES OF BALQUITHE, THE
6535	6522	(II)	CHA'N FHAOD CALLUM CARUCHADH [MALCOLM DARE NOT MOVE]

6535	6542	(II)	AULD STEWART'S BACK AGAIN, THE
6535	6542	(I)	AULD STEWARD'S BACK AGAIN, THE
6535	6562	(II)	AULD STEWART'S BACK AGAIN, THE
6535	6562	(I)	AULD STEWARTS BACK AGAIN, THE
6535	6562	(I)	BATTLE OF CULLEDEN, THE
653	653	(I)	ROODULUM, (THE)
655	433	(II)	MAGDEBURGH WALTZ
6555	653H2H	(I)	ROCKS OF MELROSS, THE
6551H	651H2	(I)	I LOVE A BONNY LASS
6561	6527bL	(I)	FYKET, THE
6565	6521	(I)	DANCE, BOATMAN, DANCE
6565	653H2H	(I)	MRS OSWALD (OF ACHINCRUIVE'S) (NEW) STRATHSPEY
6565	62H3H7	(I)	GENERAL HOPE'S QUICK MARCH
6565	3H674	(II)	GALOPADE COUNTRY DANCE
6567b	6527bL	(I)	FYKET, THE
657b1	6527bL	(I)	MISS MARY GRANT'S REELL
657b2H	657b7b	(I)	CHARLIE HE'S MY DARLING THE YOUNG CHEVALIER
651H1	6527bL	(II)	FYKET, THE
651H1	6527bL	(I)	FYKET (STRATHSPEY), THE
651H2	651H3H	(I)	LORD CASSEL'S REEL
651H2	651H3H	(I)	I LOST MY HEART ON FRIDAY
651H2	651H3H	(I)	LORD CASSILS JIGG
651H5	6527bL	(II)	FYKET, THE
651H5	6527bL	(I)	FYKET, THE
6622	5511	(I)	EPPIE McNAB
6632	226LO	(II)	FAIREST FLOWER, THE
663	1H52	(I)	LASSIE GAE MILK ON MY COW HILL
6652	5223	(I)	AULD ROBIN GRAY
6652	5223	(I)	BRIDEGROOM GREETS WHEN THE SUN GAES TEE, THE
6655	3322	(I)	MY OWN DEAR SOMEBODY
6665	3232	(II)	TIGH EACHAINN
6665	3232	(II)	AULD ROAD TO TOWIE, THE
6666	3232	(I)	FAVOURITE HIGHLAND QUICKSTEP, 73rd REGt, A
661H5	2222	(I)	ROBIN HOOD'S DELIGHT
661H5	21H54	(I)	'TIS THE DIRGE OF KEEN SORROW
662H	2H2H3	(I)	WALY WALY
6753	5353	(I)	MISS MAULE OF PANMURE'S REEL
61H22H	61H53H	(I)	MISS NELLY KENNEDY'S REEL
61H51	2216L	(I)	BERWICK ASSEMBLY
61H51	2253	(I)	MISS FERGUS'S REEL
61H52	422H2H	(I)	BONNY BANKS OF CLYDE, THE
61H53	547L2	(I)	COUNTESS OF LEVEN AND MELVILLE'S FANCY, THE
61H62	61H31	(I)	MISS OGILVIE OF CLOVA'S STRATHSPEY
11H63	237L7L	(I)	LADS OF THE VILLAGE, THE
11H64	22H75	(I)	REEL
11H64	22H4H1H	(I)	RASAY HOUSE
11H64	547L2	(I)	MRS MENZIES'S, DUNKELD
11H65	11H22	(I)	AULD SPRINGS (TUNES) GEES NAE PRICE
11H65	4562	(I)	CALEDONIAN HUNT, THE
11H66	3333	(I)	SEANN GHILLE NA 'N CAR
11H66	3333	(I)	MRS McLEOD OF RASA[Y] ('S REEL)
11H66	547L2	(I)	F. GARDEN CAMPBEL
11H61H	11H24	(I)	CA' THE WETHERS TO THE HILL
11H61H	61H24	(I)	DUKE OF ATHOL'S FORREST LODGE GLEN TILT
61H61H	62H75	(I)	HUMOURS OF COVENT GARDEN, THE
61H62H	1H1H66	(I)	O'ER THE MOOR FOR A' THAT
11H7b2	11H3bH2H	(I)	MISS JOHNSTON (OF) HIL(L)TON ('S STRATHSPEY)
11H7b4	11H1H3bH	(I)	FAVORITE IRISH TUNE, A
11H7b4	3b7bL7bL3b	(I)	LOCH NESS
11H7b4	3b7bL7bL3b	(I)	SANDY IS MY DARLING
11H7b5	3b420	(I)	LATHA SUIBHAIL (SLEIBH DHOMH)
11H7b5	56b7b5	(I)	MRS McINROY, LUDE'S REEL
11H70	5230	(I)	FOR BONNIE ANNIE LAURIE
11H70	5332	(I)	ANNIE LAURIE
11H76	5437L	(I)	LADY HOPE OF PINKIE'S STRATHSPEY
61H72H	3H1H35	(I)	MY JO JANET
61H72H	3H2H1H1H	(I)	COUNTRY FARMER, THE
11H1H3	116L6L	(I)	LADY CHARLOTTE DURHAM
61H1H5	1H1H1H3H	(I)	TINKAR'S OCCUPATION, THE
61H1H5	1H1H1H3H	(I)	CLOUT THE CALDRON
61H1H5	1H1H1H3H	(I)	HAMMERMEN'S MARCH, THE
61H1H	61H4H	(I)	AULD SIR SIMON THE KING
61H1H7	6655	(I)	NEW TAMBOURIN, THE
61H1H1H	6611	(I)	GUR MULADACH THA MI, 'SMI GUN MHACNUS GUN MHANRAN
61H1H1H	2H775	(I)	CLOUT THE CAULDRON
61H1H	2H66	(I)	GUR EUTROM AN T AISEAG
61H1H2H	772H4H	(I)	MY JOE JANNET
61H1H3H	72H67	(I)	NORTH HIGHLAND 10

61H2H	3H3H1T	(I)	THRO' THE WOOD LADDIE
62H53	5353	(II)	MISS MAULE(OF PANMURE)
62H53	5353	(I)	MISS MAULE OF PANMURE('S REEL)
63H1H1H	6526L	(I)	MR DAVID DUNCAN'S REEL
64H3H	1HO1T	(I)	TOKEN, THE
7b152	7b151	(I)	SHE WADNA HAE ME BUT WAD HAE ANITHER
7b152	7b151	(I)	JOY GAE WI MY LOVE
7b411	4542	(I)	THRO' THE WORLD WOU'D I GANG
			WI' THE LAD THAT LOVES ME
7b411	7b421	(I)	CAGARAN O
7b53b1	7bL3b7bL7bL	(II)	STRATHMASHY
7b53b5	7b53b1	(II)	CA' HAWKIE THROUGH THE WATER or
			LORD ELPHINSTON
7b547bL	7b57b2H	(I)	WIVES OF KILWINNON, THE
7b543b	17bL13b	(I)	COME HAP ME WITH THY PETTICOAT
7b55	553bH	(I)	SHORT APRON, THE
7b57b1	7b527bL	(II)	KEEP IT UP
7b57b5	7b527bL	(II)	AS A THOISEACH [BE OFF MACINTOSH /
			KEEP IT UP]
7b57b5	7b527bL	(I)	AS A THOISEACH
7b57b6b	7b57b1	(I)	BOB OF DUMBLANE, THE
7b51H2	761H3H	(I)	LORD CASSILL'S REEL
7b51H	7b56	(I)	COCK LAIRD, THE
7b52H	5H5H2H	(I)	WHAT THE DEVIL AILS YOU
7b61H5	7b444	(I)	HARRIS DANCE
706	504#	(I)	DUKE OF REICHSTADT'S WALTZ
73b53b	247b2	(I)	MISS MARY JOHNSON'S QUICK STEP
7531	2342	(I)	MRS BUTTER OF FASKALLY
7531	2H751	(I)	JOLLY RINGER'S, THE
7551	7522	(I)	ARBROATH ASSEMBLY
7552	751H1H	(I)	BONNY LADS OF AIR
7555	53H53H	(I)	SIR DAVID HUNTER BLAIR
7564	357L2	(I)	MYRES CASTLE, THE
7576b	7571	(I)	BOB OF DUNBLANE
751H3b	43b10	(I)	ALACK & A' WALL A DAY
751H2H	3bH3bH4H3bH	(I)	JOSEPH EST BIEN MARIE
752H	1H53H	(II)	MRS PROFESSOR CHRISTIE'S WALTZ
7651	7655	(II)	JACK'S HALF CROWN
7654	3235	(I)	L'ETE
7656	1H1H1H3H	(I)	SANDY LADDY
764#5	7L5L22	(I)	LASSIES OF STEWARTOWN, THE
771H1H	7555	(I)	SOUTH SEA
71H31	42H75	(II)	CAPTAIN BYNG
71H31	42H75	(I)	CAPTAIN BYNG'S REEL
71H31	42H76	(II)	CAPTAIN BYNG [CAPt. BYNG]
71H52	7571H	(I)	SINGLE JIG
71H65	71H65	(I)	FLY, THE
71H2H2	71H51	(I)	QUICK STEP FUSILEERS
71H3H5H	1H71H5	(I)	LA MALTA
71H4H5H	71H5H1H	(I)	MISS STEVENSON'S VALTZ
72H67	4327L	(I)	MRS CARTWRIGHT'S DELIGHT
74H2H3H	1H3H2H5	(II)	DUBLIN LASSES
1H6L5L3L	5L47L2	(II)	CAPT. HUGH MUNRO
1H6L5L3L	5L47L2	(II)	MISS COX
1H6L5L3L	5L47L2	(I)	CAPTAIN HUGH MUNRO'S STRATHSPEY
1H6L5L3L	5L47L2	(I)	MISS COX(E'S STRATHSPEY)
1H7L3L3	4#316L	(II)	ARTHUR SEAT
1H7L25L	3L2L3L1L	(II)	LUSS ROAD
1HO11	1154	(I)	PRINCE OF SAXECOBOURG'S FAVOURITE MARCH
1HO2HO	3H1H1HO	(I)	COLONEL GEDDES'S GRAND MARCH
1HO2HO	3H2H1HO	(I)	HARK! THE LARK
1HO3H3H	3HO5H5H	(I)	HANDEL'S WATER PIECE
1HO5H5H	3H2H1H1H	(I)	VULCAN'S MARCH
1H15L1H	2H25L2H	(I)	TRIP TO SPA, A
1H17L1	1H17L5	(I)	MR JOHN ALLISON'S WALTZ
1H17L4	5671H	(I)	SILESIAN WALTZ, A
1H111	5L132	(II)	MASON'S APRON
1H111	1465	(I)	JENNY DANG THE WEAVER
1H111	3135	(II)	JAMIE GRAY
1H111	3551H	(I)	JEAN'S THE BEST OF (ANY/MY LOVE'S)
1H111	3565	(I)	KATY MOONEY
1H111	1H126L	(I)	HIGHWAY TO COILSFIELD, THE
1H111	1H126L	(I)	MISS FRASER'S REEL
1H112	7L246	(II)	WEST KILBRIDE
1H11	235	(I)	MISS CARNEGIE (OF SOUTHESK)'S HORNPIPE
1H115	31H1H3H	(I)	COLLEGE HORNPIPE
1H115	71H51	(I)	LORD WELLINGTON'S WALTZ
1H113H	3H115H	(I)	INDEPENDENTS MARCH, THE
1H126L	1H153H	(I)	ROTHESAY CASTLE
1H126L	1H14H2H	(II)	MOGGY ON THE SHORE
1H127bL	1124	(II)	AULD-BELL ROBBIE
1H127bL	1H147bL	(I)	BUTTON HOLE, THE

```
1H121        237L5L       ( I )  WHIM WHAM, THE
1H122        1H12H2H      ( I )  MR JAs GRANT'S STRATHSPEY
1H122        4H3H2H6      ( I )  G(R)EEN TREE, THE
1H122        4H3H2H6      ( I )  LADY CUNNINGHAM'S REEL
1H123b       1H147bL      ( I )  MRS CUNINGHAM OF CORSEHILL'S REEL
1H125        1251         ( II ) BELLS OF DUBLIN BAY
1H12         1H14         ( I )  HIGHWAY TO CRAIGIE HOUSE, THE
1H13b1       7b422        ( II ) EDIE OCHILTREE
1H13b3b      3bH3bH1H6b   ( I )  LOVE SICK POLLY
1H13b4       2512         ( II ) ROVER, THE
1H13b5       243b2        ( II ) COLONEL BAIRD
1H13b5       243b2        ( I )  POP HER AWAY
1H13b5       243b2        ( I )  COLONEL BAIRD'S STRATHSPEY
1H13b5       7b422        ( I )  MRS McGRIGOR'S REEL
1H13b5       7b524        ( II ) MISS M. ROSS
1H13b5       7b524        ( I )  MISS M. ROSE'S REEL [MISS M. ROSS]
1H13b5       7b7b27bL     ( I )  COUNTESS OF MANSFIELD, THE
1H13b5       7b7b24       ( II ) BARNS OF CLYDE, THE
1H13b5       7b7b24       ( I )  BARNS OF CLYDE, THE
1H13b5       7b7b47bL     ( I )  MRS FERGUSSON OF CRAIGDARROCHS REEL
1H13b5       7b1H47bL     ( I )  ROB ROY'S CAVE (LOCH LOMOND)
1H13b        7b47bL       ( I )  DAYS O' YORE, THE
1H13b3bH     2H7b3bH4H    ( I )  BLACKAMOORE'S JIG, THE
1H13b3bH     2H7b5H4H     ( I )  BLACKMOORS JIG, THE
1H13b3H      2H7b5H4H     ( I )  BLACKAMOOR'S JIG
1H135L       6L122        ( II ) LADY ASHBURTON
1H135L       6L122        ( I )  LADY ASHBURTON('S STRATHSPEY)
1H131        2366         ( I )  LENNOX LOVE
1H131        1H126L       ( I )  MISS FRASER OF STONEYFIELD'S REEL
1H131        1H131        ( I )  Sr. SIDNEY SMITH'S WALTZ
1H132        1H11H6       ( II ) LANGMAN KNAP, THE
1H133        2466         ( II ) SAIGHDEAR RUADH
1H133        1H16L7L      ( II ) SQUIRREL, THE
1H133        2H246        ( II ) MR MOLISON OF HILLHEAD
1H133        2H246        ( II ) HILL HEAD
1H134        5554         ( I )  GOSSIP JOAN
1H135        22H4H7       ( I )  HONble MISS KINNAIRD'S STRATHSPEY, THE
1H135        461H5        ( I )  FOURTEENTH OF FEBRUARY, THE
1H135        41H22H       ( I )  AIRTH CASTLE
1H13         551H         ( I )  BANKS OF SLIGOE, THE
1H135        7b427bL      ( II ) FOOT IT FEATLY
1H135        1H124        ( II ) NORA CREINA
1H135        1H351H       ( I )  DEPARTURE OF A FRIEND, THE
1H135        1H1H3H4H     ( I )  CAPTAIN NAPIERS MARCH
1H135        1H3H6H6H     ( I )  BANQUO'S GHOST
1H131H       2H275        ( II ) COLLEGE HORNPIPE, THE
1H155L       11L5L5L      ( I )  QUICK STEP
1H155L       11L5L5L      ( I )  PURSUIT, THE
1H155L       11L5L1       ( II ) QUAY SIDE, THE
1H155L       3542         ( I )  MISS ADAM'S JIG
1H151        6L27L5L      ( I )  MISS STEWART'S JIG
1H151        23H3H6       ( I )  INCH OF GARTH
1H151        24H3H6       ( I )  INCH OF GARTH
1H151        6b427L       ( II ) MACPHERSON'S BLADE [MACPHERSON'S CAVE]
1H151        1H155        ( I )  HONEST DUNCAN
1H151        1H62H7       ( I )  MISS OSWALD (OF SCOTSTOWN'S) REEL
1H153        7726         ( I )  GIE THE CANTY CARLE MEAR O'T
                                 [GI'E THE MAWKING MAIR O'T]
1H154        22H2H6       ( I )  FINGAL'S HORNPIPE
1H155        27bL22       ( I )  HAUGHS OF CROMDALE, THE
1H155        6327bL       ( I )  (COLONEL/GENERAL) McKAY'S REEL
1H155        6527bL       ( I )  COLONEL MACKAY'S STRATHSPEY
1H155        7b424        ( II ) MISS JOHNSTON OF HILTON
1H155        7b424        ( I )  MISS JOHNSTON OF HIL(L)TON('S REEL)
1H155        1H122H       ( I )  MISS BRIDGES' STRATHSPEY
1H155        2H266        ( I )  MISS HAGGART'S STRATHSPEY
1H155        2H4H72H      ( I )  (MISS/LADY) CUNNINGHAM'S STRATHSPEY
1H156        1H2H54       ( I )  DUKE OF CLARENCE'S MARCH
1H164        6542         ( II ) PITNACREE FERRYMAN, THE
1H11H1       1H355        ( I )  BANTI, THE
1H11H5       6527bL       ( I )  [COLONEL MACKAY'S] JIGG
1H11H7       1H2H3H7      ( II ) ROLLOCKING IRISHMAN, THE
1H11H7       2H22H1H      ( II ) CORN CUTTER, THE
1H11H7       2H22H1H      ( I )  CORN CUTTERS, (THE)
1H11H1H      2H2H75       ( I )  MISS CAMPBELL OF COMBIE
1H11H1H      4H2H75       ( I )  MISS ISOBEL CLARK'S FAVORITE
1H11H2H      2H22H3H      ( I )  RIGADOON
1H11H2H      3H63H1H      ( II ) LONDON BRIDGE
1H11H2H      3H5H2H7      ( I )  CAPTAIN RACKET
1H12H2       3H5H2H7      ( I )  AND WILL YOU BE
1H12H5       3H72H2H      ( I )  TRIP TO THE JERSEYS
1H13H1       2527L        ( I )  WHAT CARE I FOR WHOM SHE BE
```

```
1H13H1      61H1H1H     ( I )  MARCH 6th REGt
1H13H3      5H5H4H1H    ( I )  CAPT CAMPBELL OF SHAWFIELD'S VALTZ
1H235       5231H       ( I )  LES SOAIRS
1H3b7bL     1H3b1H      ( I )  CAUP O' YE'R TIPPANY KATE, A
1H3b11      3b51H1H     ( II ) ANNIE DALGARNO
1H3b11      47b47bL     ( I )  DELGATY KENALL
1H3b11      3bH53b3b    ( I )  LAMOTT'S RIGADON
1H3b6b7b    5425        ( I )  LES PLAISIRS CHINOISE
1H3b1H3b    7L6b6b5     ( II ) WILL O' THE WISP
1H3bH1H7b   47b2H7b     ( II ) HONOURABLE MISS CHARTERIS, THE
1H3b1H2H    1H7b52      ( I )  DUCHESS OF GORDON'S DELIGHT, THE
1H3b1H3bH   7b542       ( II ) PEASE BRIDGE
1H3b1H3bH   7b542       ( I )  PEASE BRIDGE
1H35L2      35L1L5L     ( II ) HASBERRY HOWARD
1H35L3      5L35L3      ( I )  WEE ANNIE'S HORNPIPE
1H36L5L     7L317L      ( I )  PIC NIC, THE
1H36L7L     1H473H      ( II ) BRIDE'S REEL, THE
1H36L4      1H36L1      ( II ) GORDON CROMBIE MUNRO
1H36L6      7L73H1H     ( I )  PADDY WILL YOU LOVE ME
1H37L5L     1237L       ( I )  KATE'S DELIGHT
1H37L2      131H3H      ( I )  MISS CUMMINGS STRATHSPEY
1H37L2      1H31H1H     ( I )  CALLAM SHIARGHLAS
1H37L2      1H31H1H     ( I )  MAXWILL'S RANT
1H31        5L7L4       ( I )  LADY KETTIE GORDON'S MINUET
1H311       47bL42      ( I )  COLONEL MONTGOMERIE'S WELCOME HAME
1H311       4215L       ( I )  MISS BETTY HUNTER
1H313       1H322H      ( I )  MRS GRAHAM OF GARTMORE'S STRATHSPEY
1H313       1H362       ( I )  FAREWELL, THE
1H313       1H622H      ( I )  DING'S MUSIC SHOP
1H313       1H3H1H6     ( I )  MISS DRUMMOND FORBES'S HORNPIPE
1H315       6212        ( II ) BRISTOL HORNPIPE
1H311H      2H2H1H4     ( I )  MRS HENDERSON OF AIMSTER'S FAVORITE
1H311H      3H2H1H3     ( I )  YELLOW JOKE
1H321       2423        ( I )  COTTILLON
1H321       1H35L1      ( I )  SPRING, THE
1H322       6L5L21      ( I )  MISS POLLOCK'S STRATHSPEY
1H322       537L7L      ( I )  QUICK STEP
1H323       1H322       ( II ) DONALD McGREGOR
1H324       1H326L      ( I )  LAND O' CAKES, THE
1H325       6527L       ( I )  ROYAL MARQUEE
1H326       1H331       ( II ) DEUKS DANG O'ER MY DADDIE, THE
1H327b      1H331H      ( I )  DONEL COOPER'S STRATHSPEY
1H327       1H331       ( I )  DEUK'S DANG O'ER MY DADDIE
1H327       1H331       ( I )  MY HIGHLAND LASSIE O
1H327       1H351H      ( I )  MRS GRANT OF BUGHT'S JIG
1H327       1H351H      ( I )  MOLL ROSS
1H327       1H351H      ( I )  JUST AS I WAS IN THE MORNING
1H327       1H353H      ( I )  JUST AS I WAS IN THE MORNING
1H327       1H431       ( II ) DUKES DANG OWER HIS DADDY, THE
1H327       1H431       ( I )  DEUKS DANG O'ER MY DADDIE, THE
1H322H      1H353       ( I )  MISS CARMICHAEL'S STRATHSPEY
1H332       2366        ( I )  'S CIANAIL M'AIGNE
1H332       2366        ( I )  TENDER IS MY AFFECTION
1H33        321         ( I )  MRS HAMILTON OF SUNDRUM'S MINUET
1H334       5112        ( I )  MARCH 3d REGT DRAGGOON GUARDS
1H336       22H2H6      ( I )  MISS BETTY McLEAN'S STRATHSPEY
1H335       1H37L2      ( I )  LONDON ASSOCIATION
1H335       1H342       ( I )  MISS JOAN DALRYMPLE OF HAILES
1H33        1H32        ( I )  JIGG, A
1H33        1H32        ( I )  NORTH HIGHLAND 8 (FENCIBLES)
1H33        1H32        ( I )  KELSO LASSES
1H331H      7675        ( I )  DUEL STRATHSPEY, THE
1H33        1H1H2       ( I )  SPOIGAN
1H347L      4L2L7L6L    ( I )  FAIRIES, THE
1H347L      1525L       ( I )  TRIP TO THE CAMP
1H347L      1H353       ( II ) CELTIC CHAIR, THE
1H347L      1H343       ( II ) QUEEN'S JUBILEE, THE
1H342       2463        ( I )  MRS COLI ROSS'S REEL
1H342       6555        ( I )  SKY AIR
1H342       6555        ( I )  AISLING
1H344       5542        ( I )  QUICK STEP 44 REGt
1H345       3345        ( II ) FISHERS
1H345       3345        ( II ) BLANCHARD'S HORNPIPE [FISHER'S HORNPIPE]
1H345       3345        ( I )  FAVORITE DANCE, A
1H345       3345        ( I )  TREEBLE HORNPIPE NO. 1
1H345       3345        ( I )  DANCED BY ALDRIDGE
1H345       3345        ( I )  BLANCHARD'S HORNPIPE [FISHER'S HORNPIPE]
1H345       3345        ( I )  FISHER'S (HORNPIPE/FAVORITE DANCE)
1H345       4542        ( I )  CAPT CAMPBELL OF MELFORD
1H345       64H1H7      ( I )  MISS MUIR MACKENZIE'S FAVORITE
1H345       1H36L7L     ( I )  LADY ELGIN
1H341H      51H4H2H     ( I )  TAY SIDE
```

```
1H351      427L5L     (I)   MRS JOHN LEISTER'S FAVORITE
1H351      1H325L     (I)   MISS McDONALD St. MARTIN'S JIGG
1H352      3673       (I)   CHA MO LEANNAN NUN 'THAR SAL
                            [CHAIDH MO LEANNAN NULL THAR SAL]
1H352      1H342      (I)   HUMOURS OF DUBLIN, (THE)
1H353      3753       (I)   NEW POST, THE
1H353      4246       (I)   WHIM, THE
1H353      4622H      (I)   MR GRANT OF PITNACHREE'S STRATHSPEY
1H353      6322       (I)   DUKE OF GORDON'S (REEL/STRATHSPEY), THE
1H353      1H352      (I)   HO MO CHAILEAGAN
1H353      1H622      (I)   LORD DUPLIN'S JIGG
1H354      4522H      (I)   MR DAVID McDOWALL'S STRATHSPEY
1H355      1H355      (II)  WEST'S( HORNPIPE)
1H355      1H355      (I)   WEST'S HORNPIPE
1H355      1H353H     (I)   MONEY IN BOTH POCKETS
1H355      1H353H     (I)   IRISH GIRL
1H355      1H354H     (II)  MONEY IN BOTH POCKETS
1H355      1H354H     (I)   MONEY IN BOTH POCKETS
1H355      1H3H2H2    (I)   DUTCHESS OF GORDON'S REEL
1H355      1H3H2H2    (I)   DUTCHESS OF GORDON'S REELL
1H356      2H675      (I)   LOVE AND HONOUR
1H351H     1H523      (I)   MINION, THE
1H35       1H1H7      (II)  WALTZ COUNTRY DANCE
1H351H     2H1H52     (II)  GENERAL GATHERING 1745, THE
1H351H     2H1H52     (I)   AN CRUINEACHADH IOMLAN LUDHAIR
                            [AN CRUINNEACHADH IOMLAN LUTHMHOR]
1H367L     3L4L27L    (I)   TREEBLE HORNPIPE
1H367L     1352       (I)   QUICK STEP, 4th REGt.
1H362      7L5L15     (II)  HARMONICA, THE
1H362      36L27L     (I)   DOUBLE JIG
1H362      31H1H7     (I)   BIRNES HORNPIPE
1H362      1H31H1H    (I)   HUMOURS OF GRAIGNAMANOCH, THE
1H363      57L25L     (I)   QUICK STEP 12th REGt
1H363      1H62H7     (I)   POOR TOWN
1H367      1H2H3H7    (I)   YORKSHIRE LASSES(, THE)
1H367      3H4H72H    (II)  HORNPIPE
1H361H     1H5H5H2H   (I)   WAGS OF WINDSOR
1H31H1     337L5L     (I)   SIR GEO: MURRAY'S FAVORITE
1H31H1     1H362      (I)   MY LOVE SHE'S BUT A LASSIE YET
1H31H1     1H362      (I)   MISS FARQUHARSON'S REEL
1H31H1     1H32H2     (II)  MY LOVE IS BUT A LASSIE YET
1H31H1     1H32H2     (II)  GORDONS HAE THE GIRDING O'T, THE
1H31H1     1H32H2     (I)   GORDONS HAS THE GIRDING O'T, THE
                            (or MY LOVE SHE'S BUT A LASSIE YET)
1H31H1     1H32H2     (I)   MY LOVE SHE'S/IS BUT A LASSIE YET
1H31H1     1H32H2     (I)   GORDONS HA'E THE GUIDIN' O'T
1H31H1     1H2H5H5H   (I)   EARLY HORN, THE
1H31H3     7L7L1H3    (I)   MISS CAMPBELL OF SADDEL'S REEL
1H31H3     2462       (I)   QUICK MARCH. 1st BATTN. ROYALS
1H31H3     47bL7b2    (I)   QUICK STEP, 2d BATn ROYALS
1H31H3     422H6      (I)   ISLE OF SKY, THE
1H31H3     432H2      (I)   MRS STEWART FRENICH OF FOSS
1H31H3     432H2      (I)   MRS BELL'S STRATHSPEY
1H31H3     4542       (I)   HUMOURS OF LIMERICK, THE
1H31H3     1H322      (I)   HARLEQUIN NEPTUNE
1H31H3     1H344      (I)   MISS MURRAY'S JIG
1H31H3     1H344      (I)   BONNY WI THING, THE
1H31H3     1H622      (I)   LORD SPENCER'S STRATHSPEY
1H31H3     1H72H2H    (I)   CROP THE CROPIES
1H31H3     1H3H2H5L   (I)   ABERDEEN HOTEL
1H31H5     4541       (I)   PATTY'S WHIM
1H31H5     4646       (I)   MR STEWART'S REEL
1H31H5     1H372      (I)   DRUNKEN WIVES OF CARLISLE, THE
1H31H5     1H666      (II)  STOOL OF REPENTANCE(, THE)
1H31H5     1H666      (I)   STOOL OF REPENTANCE, THE
1H31H5     1H3H72H    (I)   COUNT WARTENSLEBEN
1H31H5     1H3H72H    (I)   MISS JEAN SHERRIF'S REEL
                            [MISS JEAN SHIRREF'S REEL]
1H31H1H    1H5H2H2    (II)  CAPE WRATH
1H31H1H    2H2H1H1T   (I)   OOH NEVER NEVER MAIR WILL I RANGE
                            O'ER THE PLAIN
1H31H1H    2H2H2H2H   (I)   LE PETIT TAMBOUR
1H31H2H    1H31H2H    (I)   MARCH 30th REGt BY MR ALPHY
1H31H2H    1H31H3H    (I)   MISS ROSS'S HORNPIPE
1H31H2H    1H531      (I)   MISS RATTRAY OF DALRULLZIAN
1H31H3H    6562       (I)   MISS COCHRAN MERCER
1H31H3H    1H322H     (II)  JAMES MCNICOLL
1H31H3H    1H322H     (I)   MR JAS McNICOL INVERARAY'S STRATHSPEY
1H31H3H    2H3H4H2H   (II)  MISS JEANY ABERNETHIE
1H31H3H    2H3H4H2H   (I)   MISS JEANY ABERNETHIE('S REEL)
1H31H3H    2H4H75     (I)   MISS HALDAN GLENEAGLES
1H31H3H    2H4H75     (I)   MR JOHN SHAW STEWART'S STRATHSPEY
```

153

```
1H31H3H    5H1H72H     (I)    TRIP TO OSTEND, A
1H31H3H    5H2H72H     (I)    LADY SHAFTSBURY ('S STRATHSPEY)
1H33H2H    1H335       (I)    DO YOU KNOW JACK ADAMS'S PARISH
1H33H5H    4H66H1T     (I)    SWEET WILLY O
1H34H1H    54H3H2H     (I)    CHASSE MARINE
1H47L2     1H31H2H     (II)   CALLAM SHIARGHLAS
1H47L2     1H31H2H     (I)    GRIM MALCOLM
1H47L2     1H31H2H     (I)    CALLAM SHIARGHLAS
1H42       223         (I)    FIERVELS MINUET
1H423      4225        (I)    DUENNA, THE
1H434      3432        (II)   SAILOR'S HORNPIPE, THE
1H454      4632        (I)    TOM BOWLING
1H454      1H47bL2     (I)    MR MACINTYRES REEL
1H55L3     1H553       (II)   SCOTT SKINNER
1H57bL1    4551H       (II)   MO NIGHEANAG DHONN
1H57L2     1H565       (I)    LORD KILDARE'S REEL
1H57L2     1H51H5      (I)    MISS FARQUHARSON OF INVERCAULD'S STR.
1H57L      367         (I)    DOUBLE HORNPIPE NO. 1
1H57L      367         (I)    TAR FOR ALL WEATHERS, THE
1H515L     7L145       (I)    LES PLAISIRS DE BASQUE
1H510      62H70       (I)    AWA', WHIGS, AWA'
1H511      6L27L5L     (II)   LORD OF THE ISLES
1H511      2266        (II)   LOCH MUICK
1H511      22H62H      (II)   LADY LUCY LESLIE MELVILLE
1H511      22H62H      (I)    LADY LUCY LESSLIE MELVILLE'S REEL
1H511      22H2H2H     (I)    LADY MAXWELL OF MONREATH'S REEL
1H511      31H1H6      (I)    McDUFF'S SCOTS MEASURE
1H511      4462        (II)   LIMERICK LASSES
1H511      4462        (I)    MISS STEWART OF FOSS' REEL
1H51       233         (I)    MISS GRACE STEWART'S MINUET
1H513      6L27L5L     (II)   LOCH EARN  [or TILT SIDE]
1H513      6L27L5L     (I)    JUMPING JOAN
1H513      6L27L5L     (I)    LOCH EARN (REEL)
1H513      6L237L      (I)    MRS LUMSDEN OF ACHINDORE'S REEL
1H513      6L241       (I)    LADY NIVEN LUMSDEN
                              OF ACHINDOIR'S STRATHSPEY
1H513      2466        (II)   LADY WALLACE
1H513      2466        (I)    LADY WALLACE('S REEL)
1H513      4322        (I)    FRANCIS GORDON, ESQr. OF KINCARDINE
1H513      445L2       (I)    FIRE DRAKE
1H513      7b427bL     (I)    MISS STEWART OF GRANDTULLY'S REEL
1H514      6277        (I)    LILLIES OF FRANCE, THE
1H515      47bL24      (I)    LADY CHARLOTTE PERCY'S REEL
1H515      432H2       (I)    MISS DEVON'S REEL
1H515      432H2       (I)    MISS SCOTT OF ANCRUM'S REEL
1H515      42H2H6      (II)   LADY BETTY COCHRANE
1H515      1H526       (I)    AYR RACES
1H515      1H527       (II)   POLD(Q)WILLY BRIDGE  [POLDWILLY BRIDGE]
1H515      1H527       (II)   SIR GEORGE MACKENZIE
1H515      1H527       (I)    MISS BUCHAN OF KELLOS
1H515      1H522H      (I)    MR JOHN McDOUGALL ARDBEG'S REEL
1H515      1H562       (II)   TOBAR MO BHEATHA
1H515      1H562       (I)    HOUSE OF REW, THE
1H515      1H566       (II)   PETER REID
1H515      1H566       (I)    PETER REID( ESQr KINARDY)
1H515      1H1H2H6     (II)   LADY ANN MAITLAND
1H515      1H1H2H6     (I)    LADY ANN MAITLAND('S REEL)
1H515      2H47bL4     (II)   MRS LINLEY
1H515      2H47bL4     (I)    MRS LINLEY('S REEL)
1H515      2H57bL4     (II)   MRS LINLEY
1H515      2H626       (II)   HONble. MISS SEMPILL
1H515      2H626       (I)    HONble MISS SEMPILL'S REEL
1H515      3H72H2      (I)    CAPT YOUNG OF BANFF'S REEL
1H515      3H4H2H2H    (I)    CAPT ROBERT GRANT'S REEL
1H515      3H4H2H2H    (I)    LADY MARY LINDSAY'S REEL
1H516      51H52       (I)    WEST STREET ASSEMBLY
1H516      1H555       (II)   WAVERLEY BALL, THE
1H516      1H664       (I)    MISS JANE D. GRANT'S FAVOURITE
1H516      2H3H75      (I)    OFF TO PARIS
1H511H     1H52H2      (I)    LADY MAXWELL'S REEL
1H527bL    1H61H1H     (I)    NIEL GOW'S FIDDLE
1H52       13b6b       (I)    GUR MIS THA GU CRAITEACH O'N 'UIRIDH
1H521      3652        (I)    LETHE
1H521      362H7       (I)    MRS OWEN'S FANCY
1H521      1H521       (I)    PANDEUR, THE
1H521      1H3H2H3     (II)   MILL OF TYNETT
1H522      1155        (I)    MISS BOSWELL'S REEL
1H522      1H526L      (II)   COLONEL MONTGOMERY
1H522      1H526L      (I)    COLONEL MONTGOMERY'S STRATHSPEY
1H522      1H526L      (I)    ROB ROY
1H522      1H51H1H     (I)    BURNS' PUNCH BOWL
1H52       22H7        (I)    GOSSIP JOAN
```

1H523	5L5L23	(I)	FRIENDLY VISIT, THE
1H523	7L123	(I)	MADAM ANGIOLINI
1H52	356	(I)	OSWALD'S COMPLAINT
1H524	3214L	(I)	NOTHING AT ALL
1H525	1H61H6	(I)	MRS DR TORRENCE OF THURSO'S REEL
1H522H	1H61H1H	(II)	MRS COLONEL FORBES
1H522H	1H61H1H	(I)	MRS COLONEL FORBES(' STRATHSPEY)
1H53b1	6bL5L7L1	(II)	WARRIOR'S GRAVE, THE
1H53b1	6bL5L7L5	(II)	WARRIOR'S GRAVE, THE
1H53b1	7bL242	(I)	MRS MACLEOD OF MACLEODS STRATHSPEY
1H53b1	13b45	(I)	DUMOND'S JIGG
1H53b1	2427bL	(II)	FINNIN' HADDIES
1H53b1	2427bL	(II)	THACK COTTAGE, THE
1H53b1	247b2	(I)	MISS MARY GARDEN OF TROUP'S REEL
1H53b1	22H4H2H	(I)	MISS CHARLOTE STEWART'S FAVOURITE
1H53b1	3b3b55	(I)	MARSHALL'S STRATHSPEY
1H53b1	3b525L	(II)	MISS AUSTIN
1H53b1	3b525L	(I)	MISS OUSTEIN'S (FANCY/STRATHSPEY)
1H53b1	3b6b25L	(I)	WILLIE PRINGLE, A STRATHSPEY
1H53b1	7b427bL	(I)	MR Wm YOUNG'S REEL
1H53b1	1H527bL	(II)	MISS MARY MACDONALD OF CLANRANALD
1H53b1	1H527bL	(I)	MISS MARY MACDONALD (OF CLANRONALD'S) REEL
1H53b4	6b511	(I)	MORAG
1H53b5	2424	(I)	ORKNEYS, THE
1H53b5	2424	(I)	MISS FARQUHARSON (OF INVERCAULD'S) R.
1H53b5	2424	(I)	MISS LOUISA DRUMMOND (LOGIE ALMOND) 'S REEL
1H53b5	3bH1H1H5	(II)	KNOCKIE
1H53b5	3bH2H16b	(I)	BRANCH OF THE WILLOW, THE
1H531	5L3L32	(I)	MISS COULL OF ASHGROVE
1H531	5L5L6L7L	(I)	HONble MR MAULE'S FROLICK, THE
1H531	6L5L7L2	(II)	CLAN MUNRO
1H531	6L7L15	(I)	DEVIL AMANG THE MEAL MEN, THE
1H531	6L27L5L	(II)	MOTHER KILWINNING
1H531	6L27L5L	(I)	ASCOT RACES
1H531	6L242	(I)	MR SHARP'S STRATHSPEY
1H53	17L1	(I)	LADY GRACE STUART'S MINUET
1H531	7L411	(I)	MISS ANN CARNEGIE'S ALLAMANDE
1H53	115L	(I)	MISS CHARLOTE ROSSE'S MINUET
1H531	1132	(I)	GARLAND OF ROSES
1H531	1230	(I)	BILLET DOUX, THE
1H531	1231	(I)	(FAVORITE) QUICK STEP (,25th REGt), (A)
1H53	115	(I)	HONble MISS EARDLEY'S MINUET
1H531	27bL7b2	(I)	EARL OF KINNOULL'S REEL
1H531	227L5L	(I)	EARL OF SEAFIELD'S REEL, THE
1H53	123	(I)	JENNY JONES
1H531	2357	(II)	DUNCAN QUADRILLE, THE
1H531	2466	(I)	MISS M. DUNDAS' REEL
1H531	2461H	(I)	LADY CHARLOTTE DUNDAS'S STRATHSPEY
1H531	22H75	(II)	DUNIE MAINS
1H531	22H75	(I)	MR JOHN SCOTT'S REEL
1H531	22H75	(I)	NEW BRIDGE (OF EDINBURGH), THE
1H531	22H2H6	(I)	MISS DOUGLAS'S STRATHSPEY, THE
1H531	3131	(II)	GRANTS' HORNPIPE, THE
1H531	3322	(I)	BANKS OF TWEED
1H531	47L13L	(I)	TRIP TO LIVERPOOL
1H531	427L5L	(II)	LADY ANDERSON
1H531	427L5L	(II)	BONNYBRIDGE
1H531	427L5L	(I)	COUNTESS OF ERROL'S REEL
1H531	427L2	(II)	MRS GRAY OF QUEBEC
1H531	427L2	(I)	MISS M. CADENHEAD'S REEL
1H531	427L2	(I)	MRS GREIG OF QUEBEC [MRS GRAY OF QUEBEC]
1H531	427L4	(II)	STEAM BOAT, THE
1H531	427L6	(I)	MR(S) MUIR MACKINZIE'S FAVOURITE [MR. MUIR MACKENZIE'S FAVOURITE]
1H531	427L6	(I)	LADY MUIR MACKINZIE
1H531	4231	(II)	MISS RATTRAY
1H531	4325L	(I)	DUKE OF YORK'S CAMP, THE
1H531	4326L	(I)	MALTESE DANCE, THE
1H531	4327L	(I)	MR A. R. SUTHERLAND'S REEL
1H531	4326	(II)	EARL OF CRAWFORD'S REEL, THE
1H531	44H1H6	(I)	AFFRONT TAKEN, THE
1H531	5633	(II)	NIGHEAN DUBH NAN GEALA CHAS
1H531	5633	(I)	MRS McDONELL OF LOCHGARRY'S REEL
1H531	627L5L	(I)	MISS STEVENSON'S STRATHSPEY
1H531	6430	(I)	DUSKY NIGHT, THE
1H531	6432	(I)	RIDDING RACES
1H531	6432	(I)	DUSKY NIGHT, THE
1H531	62H3H2H	(I)	QUITE PRODIGIOUS
1H531	1H536	(I)	HONble MRS OGILVY OF CLOVA'S FAVOURITE, THE
1H531	1H1H1H1H	(I)	GENERAL STEWART, (WEST PARK, ELGIN)
1H531	1H3H7O	(I)	FROG HE WOULD A WOOING GO, A
1H531	2H642	(II)	MILL O' BOYNDIE

1H531	2H3H75	(1)	CAPT WILLIAM McLEOD'S FANCY
1H531	3H2H3H2H	(1)	MACFARLANE'S STRATHSPEY
1H531	3H2H3H2H	(1)	LAIRD OF MACFARLANE, THE
1H532	6L242	(1)	COMICAL JACK
1H532	7L242	(11)	KINCALDRUM [KURCALDRUM'S REEL]
1H532	7L242	(1)	KINCALDRUM'S REEL
1H532	7L242	(1)	COLONEL WEMYS'S REEL
1H532	7L242	(1)	PARSON IN (THE/YE) SUDDS, THE
1H532	22H4H2H	(11)	CAPT. LOCKHART OF THE TARTAR
1H532	22H4H2H	(!)	HONble CAPt ELPHINSTONE OF THE TARTAR, THE
1H532	22H4H2H	(1)	CAPTAIN LOCKHART (OF THE TARTAR)
1H533	1233	(1)	DESTRUCTION OF THE BASTILE
1H533	1355	(1)	O BEAUTY, WHY SHOULD'ST THOU COMPLAIN
1H533	26L16L	(1)	ST ANN'S FANCY
1H533	2422	(1)	QUICKSTEP, SCOTS ROYALS
1H533	4433	(1)	MR MILLER'S HORNPIPE
1H533	5311	(1)	QUICKSTEP
1H533	6677	(1)	MORPETH RANT
1H533	64H72H	(11)	KINERMONY
1H533	1H72H1H	(1)	SURRENDER OF CALAIS
1H534	2425L	(1)	NEW MERRY DANCERS, THE
1H534	3422	(1)	MUNSTER SWITCH, THE
1H535	1564	(1)	MRS CAMPBELL ARDMORE'S REEL
1H535	2427bL	(11)	MISS WRIGHT OF LATON
1H535	2424	(1)	MISS WRIGHT OF LATON('S REEL)
1H535	2424	(1)	SIR JOHN STUART OF GRANTULLIE'S RANT
1H535	2462H	(11)	SHEEP SHANKS
1H535	2462H	(11)	HONble. MRS. MAULE('S STRATHSPEY)
1H535	2462H	(1)	HONble MRS MAULE'S REEL, (THE)
1H535	2463H	(11)	COUNTESS OF ELGIN, THE
1H535	2662	(1)	MR BUCHAN OF AUCHMACOY'S REEL
1H535	27b27bL	(1)	MRS HEPBURN OF CLERKINGTON'S REEL
1H535	22H76	(1)	MISS J. CUMING'S REEL
1H535	22H76	(1)	MISS MUNRO OF DORNOCH'S REEL
1H535	22H2H6	(11)	BONNY LINKS OF ABERDEEN, THE
1H535	22H2H6	(1)	DR W.A. ROSE'S FANCY
1H535	352H2H	(11)	LADY JANE NEVILLE
1H535	352H2H	(1)	LADY JANE NEVILL(E)('S REEL)
1H535	427L5L	(1)	MRS ANDERSON'S REEL
1H535	4642	(11)	KIRKNEY WATER
1H535	461H1H	(1)	RISING OF THE LARK, (THE)
1H535	471H7	(11)	ABERGELDIE
1H535	42H76	(11)	LADY MARY HOPE VERE
1H535	44H2H2H	(1)	MISS MARGARET GORDON (OF LESSMORES) AVOURITE REEL
1H535	627L5L	(1)	MARGATE ASSEMBLY
1H535	627L5L	(1)	TREEBLE HORNPIPE NO. 2
1H535	6422H	(1)	MISS GORDON OF PITLURG'S REEL
1H535	6522H	(11)	MRS JAMES CAMPBELL
1H535	6522H	(1)	MISS E. WADE'S REEL
1H535	6522H	(1)	MRS JA(ME)S CAMPBELL('S REEL)
1H535	6522H	(1)	MISS JOHNSTON (OF HILTON) 'S REEL
1H535	6522H	(1)	MRS ROSE FEUGHSIDES (REEL)
1H535	6622H	(1)	JOHNIE GORDON
1H535	61H75	(1)	BONAPARTE IN A KNAPSACK
1H535	61H2H7	(1)	ENFIELD CHACE
1H535	62H75	(11)	AULD WHEEL, THE
1H535	62H75	(1)	TALAVERA
1H535	72H4H5H	(1)	MR MELDRUM'S REEL BANFF
1H535	1H362	(11)	SIR ROBt G. GORDON BARt. OF LETTERFOURIE'S REEL
1H535	1H366	(1)	MR. GEORGE HUNTER'S REEL
1H535	1H442	(1)	LADS OF GLASGOW
1H535	1H522	(11)	PEGGY MENZIES
1H535	1H522	(1)	ROSS HOUSE
1H535	1H522	(1)	EARL OF CARLISLE'S REEL
1H535	1H522H	(11)	GLEN FISHIE
1H535	1H522H	(1)	MR YOUNG OF MARY HILL'S STRATHSPEY
1H535	1H535	(11)	INVERNESS LASSES
1H535	1H535	(1)	CAILLEAGAN A BHAIL MHOIR [CAILEAGAN A' BHAILE MHOIR]
1H535	1H53H2H	(1)	MISS MARGt GORDON'S REEL
1H535	1H1H2H2	(1)	MISS NELLY FERGUSON'S REEL
1H535	1H1H3H4H	(1)	COL. DALRYMPLE'S MARCH
1H535	1H1H5H6H	(1)	STONEHAVEN VOLUNTEER MARCH, THE
1H535	1H3H72H	(1)	MISS C.H. BAIRD'S STRATHSPEY
1H535	1H3H72H	(1)	MRS COL: GRANT'S REEL
1H535	1H3H72H	(i)	LADY MADELINA SINCLAIR'S BIRTH DAY
1H535	1H3H2H2	(11)	HONble. MRS. CAMPBELL (OF LOCHNELL)
1H535	1H3H2H2	(11)	MRS CAMPBELL OF LOCHNELL
1H535	1H3H2H2	(1)	HONble MRS CAMPBELL (OF LOCHNELL'S) REEL
1H535	1H4H72H	(11)	LADY MADELINA PALMER('S STRATHSPEY)

1H535	1H4H72H	(I)	LADY MADELINA (PALMER/SINCLAIR) 'S BIRTH DAY
1H535	1H5H2H2H	(II)	MADGE, OR FAREWELL TO SCOTLAND
1H535	2H646	(I)	MISS BARBARA STEWART
1H535	3H4H72H	(I)	MISS JESSY HUNTER'S REEL
1H535	4H2H75	(I)	WHO'S THE DUPE
1H535	4H3H72H	(I)	HONble MISS PRIMROSE ELPHINSTONE'S STRATHSPEY, THE
1H535	4H5H6H2H	(I)	MISS CHARLOTTE GORDON OF CLUNY'S STRATHSPEY
1H531H	1H2H75	(I)	JOLLITY
1H531H	2H1H21	(I)	LOVELY LASS OF INVERNESS, THE
1H531H	2H3H2H5	(I)	MISS SMOLLET'S ALLAMANDE
1H533H	1H32H2	(I)	MR P. ROBERTSON'S REEL
1H533H	5H5H4H2H	(I)	EDINR DEFENSIVE BAND'S MARCH, THE
1H542	7L5L15L	(I)	SINGLE JIG
1H542	7L222	(I)	DOUBTFUL SHEPHERD, THE
1H542	7L232	(I)	MRS MACINTOSH OF BLACKHEATH'S REEL
1H542	7L242	(II)	KINCALDRUM
1H542	22H4H2H	(I)	CAPT LOCKHART
1H542	3125L	(I)	MRS FORBES' REEL
1H542	327L5L	(I)	HAMILTON HOUSE
1H542	327L5L	(I)	HONble COL. HAMILTON'S DELIGHT
1H542	327L5L	(I)	NEW BUMPKIN
1H542	331H5	(II)	NESS HOUSE
1H542	3551H	(I)	LADY CHARLOTTE VILLERS REEL
1H542	4311	(I)	COTILLON, A
1H542	1H542	(II)	VICTORIA HORNPIPE
1H543	25L1H5	(I)	MISS MARGt. DRUMMOND FORBES'S JIG
1H54	345	(I)	MISS STEWART DEMPSTER'S MINUET
1H543	1H541	(I)	EVENING BRUSH, THE
1H543	1H551	(I)	MISS WIESES WALTZ
1H543	1H3H2H2	(II)	LADY CHARLOTTE GORDON
1H543	1H3H2H2	(I)	LADY CHARLOTTE GORDON'S REEL
1H544	337L5L	(I)	SWORD KNOT, THE
1H544	7b57b5	(I)	RAZA'S REELL
1H544	1H520	(I)	THERE'S NAE LUCK ABOUT THE HOUSE
1H544	1H522	(I)	THERE'S NAE LUCK ABOUT THE HOUSE
1H544	1H522	(I)	SOLDIER'S FROLICK
1H544	1H532	(I)	YORK HOUSE
1H545	427L7L	(II)	AULD KIRK, THE
1H545	62H3H7	(I)	(THE MOON AND) SEVEN STARS
1H54	622	(I)	MISS BARBARA CAMPBELL'S MINUET
1H546	3547L	(II)	LORD ELCHO
1H546	3547L	(I)	LORD ELCHO'S REEL
1H541H	1H541H	(I)	CALABRIAN WALTZ
1H542H	1H51H3	(I)	MILLER IS CANTY, THE
1H551	22H2H6	(I)	MRS G.S. MONTEATH'S STRATHSPEY
1H551	3b427bL	(I)	MISS DALRYMPLE HAY'S REEL
1H551	1H527	(I)	MISS KETTY HALL
1H552	367L5L	(I)	ANDANTE
1H552	5125L	(I)	ROYAL GLASGOW VOLUNTEERS JIG, THE
1H55	321	(I)	MR FAIRBANKS MINUET
1H553	2435	(I)	MISS DIGBY
1H553	3111	(I)	LA SAUBE
1H553	3420	(I)	BOCAGE QUE, L'AURORE
1H553	4111	(I)	ALLEGRO
1H553	471H1H	(I)	PEACE AND PLENTY
1H553	5362	(I)	(GREENOCK) GROGG
1H55	355	(I)	MISS AITKEN'S SINGLE HORNPIPE
1H553	657L2	(II)	LADY ANN STEWART
1H553	657L2	(I)	LADY ANN STEWART('S STRATHSPEY)
1H553	1H553H	(II)	LASSINTULLICH OR STEER THE GILL
1H554	22H2H2H	(I)	BONNY JAMIE O'
1H554	3216	(I)	OSWALD'S SCOTCH MEASURE
1H554	3333	(I)	EARL OF BALCARRAS'S MARCH
1H555	1353	(I)	DONALD O CREADY
1H555	3115L	(I)	WATLEN'S HORNPIPE
1H555	5553H	(I)	MY DEARIE AND THU DIE
1H555	51H3H2H	(I)	O MITHER DEAR, (I GIN TO FEAR)
1H555	53H53H	(II)	SIR DAVID HUNTER BLAIR
1H555	53H53H	(I)	SIR DAVID HUNTER BLAIR ('S REEL)
1H555	6453	(I)	COL. FERRIER'S MARCH
1H555	6550	(I)	MRS SEWELS DELIGHT
1H555	1H522	(II)	CAMERON'S GOT HIS WIFE AGAIN
1H555	1H522	(I)	CAMERON'S GOT HIS WIFE AGAIN
1H555	1H522	(I)	MISS (Dr) GRANT'S QUICK STEP
1H555	1H544	(I)	CARY OWEN [GAR(R)Y OWEN)
1H555	1H51H2	(I)	QUICK STEP 8th REGT.
1H555	1H53H2H	(II)	JENNY DANG THE WEAVER
1H555	1H53H2H	(I)	JENNY DANG THE WEAVER
1H555	1H642	(II)	MISS BRUCE
1H555	1H2H3H2H	(II)	ROSE TREE, THE

1H555	1H2H3H2H	(I)	ROSE TREE, THE
1H555	1H2H3H2H	(I)	DAINTY BESOM MAKER, THE
1H555	1H2H3H2H	(I)	OLD LEE RIGG
1H555	1H2H3H2H	(I)	GIMBLET, THE
1H555	1H3H1H5	(II)	LOCH GLASSIE
1H555	1H3H3H2H	(II)	ROSE TREE, THE
1H555	1H3H3H2H	(I)	ROSE TREE, THE
1H555	3H666	(I)	MY DEARIE AN THOU DIE
1H555	3H2H5H3H	(I)	LORD MELVILLE'S WELCOME TO STRATHEARN 1806
1H556	5331	(I)	MARQUIS OF HUNTLY'S MARCH
1H55	62H7	(I)	GIG
1H557	1H642	(I)	MISS BRUCE'S REEL
1H55	1H52	(I)	HEY ME NANNY
1H551H	1H57b7b	(II)	GIRLS OF OUR TOWN, THE
1H551H	1H52H2	(I)	LADY MAXWELL'S REEL
1H551H	1H772H	(I)	MISS NANCY KENNEDY'S REEL
1H55	1H1H2H	(I)	ANDREW CAREY
1H55	1H1H2H	(I)	ANDREW CAREY
1H551H	2H2H4H2H	(I)	MR JAMES STEWART'S REEL
1H55	3H56	(I)	AUCKRY
1H553H	1H523H	(I)	MISS KATTY HALL'S(JIG)
1H553H	2H554H	(I)	MISS ADAM'S HORNPIPE
1H562	3125L	(I)	MISS ATHILL'S REEL
1H563	0027L	(I)	MISS MARY GORDON OF CLUNY
1H563	537L7L	(I)	MISS MARGARET GRAHAM'S (OF GARTMORE'S) FAVORITE
1H563	6325	(II)	FLOWER OF AUCHATTIE, THE
1H563	657L2	(II)	CAISTEAL CHUIMRI
1H564	3437L	(I)	BATH RACES
1H564	537L7L	(I)	MRS GARDEN OF TROUP'S REEL
1H564	537L7L	(I)	MISS BETTY KERR'S REEL
1H564	547L2	(II)	STRATHSPEY COMPOSED BY PETER BAILIE
1H564	2H775	(I)	LADY NELSON'S REEL
1H564	3H1H3H1H	(I)	EUROPEAN WALTZ
1H564	4H2H75	(I)	JAMES DUFF M.P.
1H56	513	(I)	STRATHALLAN'S LAMENT
1H565	22H4H2H	(I)	MRS WARREN'S STRATHSPEY
1H565	4111	(I)	MERRY MINX, THE
1H565	437L2	(II)	SOUTER JOHNNY
1H565	4327L	(II)	MR FORBES MORRISON'S REEL
1H565	4322H	(II)	COUNTESS OF SUTHERLAND, THE
1H565	4322H	(I)	COUNTESS OF SUTHERLAND'S REEL, (THE)
1H565	4362	(I)	MISS MONCRIFF OF REEDY'S FAVORITE
1H565	4522H	(II)	MISS TINKER
1H565	4522H	(I)	MISS TINKER('S REEL)
1H565	4532	(I)	LADY INVERURY'S REEL
1H565	5542	(I)	WINDSOR CHACE
1H565	637L7L	(I)	QUICK STEP
1H565	6342	(I)	TRIP TO STRATFORD UPON AVON, A
1H565	6562	(I)	MISS BLACK'S REEL
1H565	62H4H2H	(I)	COBLER, THE
1H565	1H421	(I)	LOYAL BORROWSTOUNNESS VOLUNTEERS SLOW MARCH, THE
1H565	1H525L	(I)	MISS SHARPES FANCY
1H565	1H527L	(I)	SAILOR'S RANT
1H565	1H525	(I)	MISS SHARP'S FANCY
1H565	1H526	(II)	FAVOURITE BAGPIPE JIG
1H565	1H543	(I)	MISS CUNNINGHAM'S FANCY
1H565	1H543	(I)	LORD BATH'S GATE
1H565	1H562	(II)	BOG OF RANNES, THE
1H565	1H565	(I)	LORD BATH'S GATE
1H565	1H51H2H	(I)	MISS DICKSON'S REEL
1H565	1H54H5	(I)	KATTY O' LYNCH
1H565	1H1H53	(I)	MAJOR'S MAGGOT
1H565	1H2H3H1H	(I)	IRISH WEDDING(A FAVOURITE DANCE), THE
1H565	1H2H4H3H	(I)	TIT FOR TAT
1H565	1H5H2H3H	(I)	CONTRE DANCE
1H565	2H243	(II)	FOX CHASE, THE
1H565	2H253	(I)	COUNTESS OF LAUDERDALE'S REEL, THE
1H565	2H253	(I)	MISS CAMPBELL'S REEL
1H56	663	(I)	CROMLET'S LILT
1H56	62H7	(I)	BRISK
1H56	62H7	(I)	IRISH DANCE
1H567	1H51H5	(I)	NORTH HIGHLAND REEL, A
1H56	1H51H	(I)	COMERS OF LARGO A REELL, THE
1H56	1H1H1H	(I)	TWEED SIDE
1H56	1H1H3H	(I)	TWEED SIDE
1H564H	3H3H77	(I)	COTILLION
1H566H	3H3H3H1H	(I)	GUDE NIGHT AND JOY BE WI' YOU A'
1H566H	3H3H3H2H	(II)	GOOD NIGHT AND JOY BE WI' YOU
1H57b2	1H513H	(I)	NEIL GOW'S SNISHEN MILL
1H57b4	1H553bH	(I)	MR A. PEARSON'S (FAVOURITE) STRATHSPEY

```
1H57b5      2427bL      ( I )  MEMORY OF INVER, THE
1H57b1H     57b55       ( I )  BRIDGE OF SPEY, THE
1H575       72H4H7      ( II ) MRS GORDON, UVIE
1H575       72H4H7      ( I )  MRS GORDON'S REEL [MRS GORDON, UVIE]
1H576       527L2       ( I )  (MR) STABILINI'S FAVOURITE
1H51H1      1H52H2      ( I )  HIGHWAY TO EGLINTOUNE, THE
1H51H1      1H52H2      ( I )  CREAM CHEESE
1H51H3b     3bH73bH3bH  ( I )  GAFFER GRAY
1H51H3      1113        ( I )  GENERAL GORDON CUMING SKENE'S MARCH
1H51H3      22H76       ( I )  LORD JAMES MURRAY'S REEL
1H51H3      22H76       ( II ) LORD JAMES MURRAY
1H51H3      4315        ( I )  CUT AND DRY DOLLY
1H51H3      461H4       ( II ) SAND JIG
1H51H3      42H75       ( II ) DALKEITH HOUSE
1H51H3      42H75       ( I )  DALKEITH HOUSE
1H51H3      42H72H      ( I )  MISS CANTOUR'S REEL
1H51H3      62H72H      ( I )  MISS ANN ROBINSON'S STRATHSPEY
1H51H3      1H362       ( II ) ROSE WOOD
1H51H3      1H52H2      ( I )  FALCONERS TWA DOUGHTERS, THE
1H51H3      1H52H7      ( I )  WOODS OF BARGENNY, THE
1H51H3      1H62H7      ( II ) LORD DREGHORN'S QUICKSTEP
1H51H3      1H62H7      ( I )  LORD DRIGHORN'S QUICK STEP
1H51H5      1542        ( I )  YE KEN WHAT
1H51H5      2222        ( I )  MRS FALCONER'S REEL
1H51H5      2266        ( I )  WIDOWS SHALL HAVE SPOUSES, THE
1H51H5      22H76       ( II ) DELVIN HOUSE
1H51H5      22H75       ( II ) DELVIN HOUSE
1H51H5      22H76       ( I )  REEL
1H51H5      22H76       ( I )  DELVIN HOUSE
1H51H5      22H2H6      ( I )  BALDIE RUAPHORT'S REEL
1H51H5      3210        ( I )  BLUE BELLS OF SCOTLAND, THE
1H51H5      624H1H      ( I )  SEIGE OF BELGRADE
1H51H5      6451        ( II ) ALFORD WEAVER, THE
1H51H5      6522        ( I )  MISS BETTY CAMPBELL
                               OF FAIRFIELD'S STRATHSPEY
1H51H5      671H5       ( I )  MRS FORBES OF SHIVERS' FANCY
1H51H5      61H75       ( II ) GIORNOVICHI
1H51H5      61H75       ( I )  (MR) JARNOVICHI'S REEL
1H51H5      61H75       ( I )  BOGNOR ROCKS
1H51H5      7b244       ( I )  MY WIFE SHE'S TA'EN THE GEE
1H51H5      7b7b45      ( I )  SIR PATRICK SPENS
1H51H5      72H4H4H     ( II ) MISS DOUGLAS
1H51H5      1H525L      ( I )  TRIP TO HATFIELD HOUSE
1H51H5      1H526L      ( I )  LADY CUMMING OF ALTYRE'S STRATHSPEY
1H51H5      1H522       ( I )  PRINCESS OF WALES'S REEL
1H51H5      1H531       ( I )  ROYAL WEDDING, THE
1H51H5      1H542       ( II ) JUMPING GEORDIE
1H51H5      1H554       ( I )  DEILS AMONG THE TAYLORS, THE
                               [DEIL AMONG THE TAILORS, THE]
1H51H5      1H562       ( I )  GIRVAN WATER
1H51H5      1H564       ( II ) DEIL AMANG THE TAILORS, THE
                               [DEIL AMONG THE TAILORS, (THE)]
1H51H5      1H564       ( I )  DEVILS DREAM
1H51H5      1H564       ( I )  AMERICAN REEL
1H51H5      1H564       ( I )  DEIL AMANG THE TAILORS, THE
1H51H5      1H572H      ( I )  MRS PARKER'S DANCE
1H51H5      1H51H2      ( II ) KIDS THE
1H51H5      1H51H2      ( I )  BROUGHTON INVINCIBLES, THE
1H51H5      1H51H2      ( I )  KIDS, THE
1H51H5      1H51H2H     ( I )  PERTH BARRACKS
1H51H5      1H51H2H     ( I )  SURPRISE, THE
1H51H5      1H52H2      ( I )  MISS MENZIES OF MENZIES' REEL
1H51H5      1H2H1H6     ( II ) TOM THUMB
1H51H5      1H2H1H6     ( I )  TOM THUMB
1H51H5      1H2H3H7     ( I )  FAVORITE REEL, A
1H51H5      1H5H1H5H    ( I )  WINDSOR FORRESTERS MARCH, THE
1H51H5      1H5H2H3H    ( I )  GRACES, THE
1H51H5      2H4H2H7     ( I )  CARLETON HOUSE
1H51H6b     7b527b      ( I )  LADY CHARLOTTE LENNOX REEL
1H51H6      5125L       ( II ) BIG CAPTAIN OF CARTLEHAUGH, THE
1H51H6      547L5L      ( I )  GERMAN HORNPIPE
1H51H       766         ( I )  LADY OF THE DESART, THE
1H51H       1H51H       ( I )  WALLEY HONEY
1H51H1H     665H4H      ( II ) LADS WI' THE KILTS, THE
1H51H1H     1H51H2      ( II ) LADY CHARLOTTE PRIMROSE
1H51H1H     1H51H2      ( I )  BELVOIR CASTLE
1H51H1H     1H51H2      ( I )  LADY CHARLOTTE PRIMROSE'S STRATHSPEY
1H51H1H     1H52H2      ( I )  DOUBLE KISSES
1H51H1H     1H65H3H     ( II ) GILLEAN AN FHEILIDH [LADS IN THE KILT]
1H51H1H     2H223       ( I )  JANETT DRINKS NO WATTER
1H51H1H     3H663H      ( I )  ONE WINKING EYE, THE
1H51H1H     3H663H      ( I )  N LEATH SHUIL CHAOIG
```

1H51H1H	3H2H1H1H	(I)	MO CHRUINNEAG GHREANNAR
1H51H1H	3H2H4H2H	(I)	MR SHARP'S REEL
1H51H1H	4H2H1H6	(I)	FRASERBURGH VOLUNTEER'S MARCH
1H51H	2H55	(I)	MADAM THEODORE'S MINUET
1H51H	2H75	(I)	LADY BETTY MAITLAND'S MINUET
1H51H2H	1H547L	(II)	PRETTY PEGGY
1H51H2H	1H51H2H	(I)	GUSENDALL BAY
1H51H2H	1H52H2	(II)	DOUBLE KISSES
1H51H2H	1H52H2	(I)	DOUBLE KISSES
1H51H2H	3H5H2H7	(II)	JEANIE'S BLUE EEN
1H51H3bH	1H542	(I)	MRS FARQUHARSON'S JIGG OR QUICK STEP
1H51H3bH	4H7b42H	(I)	MISS McKENZIE'S REEL
1H51H3H	1H543	(I)	UNTITLED
1H51H	3H1H5H	(II)	GORDON CASTLE WALTZ
1H51H3H	2H2H3H2H	(I)	PONEY RACE, THE
1H51H3H	4H3H72H	(I)	MRS KENNEDY OF DUNURE'S REEL
1H51H3H	5H4H2H2H	(I)	HEN'S MARCH, THE
1H51H5H	1H542H	(I)	NEW BRIDGE OF GLASGOW, THE
1H51H6H	6H3H2H6	(I)	PADDIE'S RESOURCE
1H52H2	331H5	(II)	MRS McKENZIE OF APPLECROSS
1H52H5	3H1H3H2H	(I)	VOI CHE SAPETE
1H52H5	3H5H67	(I)	MISS PYPS'S FANCY
1H52H	755	(I)	LADY MARY ANN CARNEGIE'S MINUET
1H52H7	3H3H77	(I)	GOOD THING, THE
1H52H3H	5H6H5H2H	(I)	GIBRALTER BALLOONS
1H52H4H	3H4H77	(I)	PRESTO
1H53bH1H	2H51H1H	(I)	AIR
1H53bH2H	1H53bH2H	(I)	LACHLAIN DUDH [LACHLAN DUBH]
1H53H1	2H4H72H	(I)	NEW MAGGIE LAUDER
1H53H5	432H2	(II)	MISS CAMPBELL OF MONZIE(S)
1H53H5	432H2	(I)	MISS CAMPBELL OF MONZIE'S(REEL)
1H53H5	4H3H77	(II)	MR A. TROUP'S REEL
1H53H1H	72H4H1H	(I)	PAVILION, THE
1H53H1H	2H61H5H	(I)	TEMPETE, LA
1H53H1H	2H2H1H1H	(I)	MACARONI'S ALLEMAND, THE
1H53H1H	4H71H5	(I)	LA TALIA
1H53H1H	4H1H1H5	(I)	MISS C. RAMSAY'S FANCY
1H53H1H	4H2H77	(I)	HAPPY MILK MAID, THE
1H53H1H	5H5H1H1H	(I)	SICILIAN WALTZ
1H53H2H	1H561H	(I)	QUAKER'S WIFE, THE
1H53H2H	2H2H55	(I)	BANKS OF EDEN
1H53H3H	1H566	(I)	MERRY MILKMAID
1H53H3H	1H71H1H	(I)	FAIR KITTY
1H54H2H	1H561H	(II)	MERRILY DANCED THE QUAKER'S WIFE
1H6b50	1H2H75H	(I)	GAVOTT
1H6b6b4	13b3b3bH	(I)	CARLIONE
1H67L3L	1#4L7L5	(II)	GRAMIN
1H631	311H5	(II)	LADY GLENORCHY
1H632	311H5	(I)	MARCHIONESS OF BREADALBANE'S REEL, THE
1H632	311H5	(I)	LADY GLENORCHY'S REEL
1H634	1H631	(I)	LE PULLEYS ALLEMAND
1H635	673H3H	(I)	OLD TOWLER
1H635	1H622H	(II)	FERRY, THE
1H635	1H631	(II)	AMERICAN AIR
1H636	1H63H3H	(I)	MRS WEMYSS OF CUTTLEHILL'S STRATHSPEY
1H63	1H65	(I)	GRINDER, THE
1H641	1H641	(I)	LADY LUCY RAMSAY'S VALTZ
1H642	3535	(I)	HOUSE OF BUCHAN
1H642	4515	(I)	MISS MARGRETT DAVIDSON'S STRATHSPEY
1H644	2H531H	(I)	MR GEO. BROWN'S HORNPIPE
1H650	1H62H3H	(I)	HERE'S A HEALTH TO THEM THAT'S AWA'
1H651	357b7b	(I)	LET THAT STAND THERE
1H651	436L6L	(I)	MR ALEXr IRVINE'S STRATHSPEY
1H651	4522	(II)	BOYS OF OUR TOWN, THE
1H651	1H652	(II)	CHA'N IOGHNADH NA GILLEAN
1H651	1H3H22	(II)	ALEXANDER DAVIDSON ESQ. OF DESSWOOD
1H651	2H62H5	(I)	DREAM, THE
1H652	2466	(I)	PRETTY BELL
1H652	41H51	(I)	LONDON ASSEMBLY
1H652	1H621	(I)	HUMOUR'S OF THE POINT, THE
1H65	22H7	(I)	ANDREW KERR
1H653	2511H	(I)	FOSS'S LAMENT
1H653	3565	(I)	MISS MARGRET McINTOSH'S JIG
1H653	4530	(I)	FLOW ON THOU SHINING RIVER
1H653	51H55	(II)	CAPTAIN CHARLES LEITH HAY'S REEL
1H653	1H652	(I)	LE PULLEY'S FANCY
1H653	1H653	(I)	BROWNIE OF BODSBECK, THE
1H654	5L5L5L7L	(I)	MISS WHARTON DUFF'S JIG
1H654	3637L	(I)	MY WIFE'S WALTZ
1H654	4322H	(I)	MEMORY OF JOYS THAT ARE PAST, THE
1H655	112H2H	(I)	MILLER OF DRONE, THE
1H655	552H2H	(I)	MILLER O' DRONE, THE

1H655	553H4H	(I)	DRUMEDDIE, A
1H655	553H4H	(I)	PRINCE WILLIAM HENRY'S RETURN
1H655	553H4H	(I)	ANDROMEDA, THE
1H655	1H622	(I)	CAMERON HAS GOT HIS WIFE AGAIN
1H655	1H622	(I)	HO (RO) GUR COMA LEAM H'UILE NI (A) TH'ANN
1H655	1H652	(II)	LAIRD O' AUCHLUNCART, THE
1H655	1H655	(I)	HEBRIDEAN DANCING MEASURES & C No. 1
1H655	1H662	(I)	MISS MARY MACKAY'S REEL
1H65	53H2H	(I)	LORD BUCHAN
1H65	1H65	(II)	GRINDER, THE
1H651H	1H611	(I)	O! SING YE CHILDREN OF THE BRAVE!
1H653H	1H651H	(II)	BRAVE LEWIE ROY
1H653H	1H63H2H	(I)	HERE'S A HEALTH TO THEM THAT'S AWA'
1H663	1362	(II)	SHILLELAH, THE
1H663	3555	(II)	KYE COMES HAME
1H663	5555	(II)	CAWDOR FAIR
1H663	5555	(II)	COCK O' BENDY
1H663	5555	(I)	BONNIE RAN THE BURNIE DOWN
1H663	5555	(I)	CALDER FAIR
1H663	5555	(I)	CAWDOR FAIR
1H663	5655	(I)	CAWDOR FAIR
1H663	6633	(II)	LEGGET'S IRISH REEL
1H664	4335	(I)	FLITCH OF BACON
1H664	557L2	(I)	VALENTINE, THE
1H665	44H2H2H	(I)	GLANCING OF HER APRON, THE
1H667	1H62H2	(I)	MISS KNOWLES
1H66	3H2H1H	(I)	IS MOR MO MHULAD 'S CHA LUGHA M'EASLAINT
1H672H	1H675	(I)	PERTHSHIRE DANCING MEASURES & C No. 4
1H673H	1H671H	(I)	CARO DOLCE
1H61H1	1H652	(I)	LADY STORMOUNT'S GIGG
1H61H1	1H652	(I)	WEE WEE MAN, THE
1H61H1	1H662	(II)	WEE WEE MAN, THE
1H61H3	4362	(I)	EXCAMBEY, THE
1H61H5	44H2H2H	(I)	GLANCING OF HER APRON, THE
1H61H5	44H3H2H	(I)	GLANCING OF HER APRON, THE
1H61H5	62H1H3	(I)	COUNTESS OF HOPETON'S ALLEMAND, THE
1H61H5	7b7b7b2	(I)	MY WIFE'S A WANTON WEE THING
1H61H5	1H2H3H3H	(I)	HIGHLAND AIR
1H61H5	1H4H3H2H	(I)	WILT THOU BE MY DEARIE
1H61H6	31H22H	(II)	MISS DRUMMOND OF MEGGINCH
1H61H6	31H22H	(I)	MISS DRUMMOND MEGGINSH'S STRATHSPEY
			(MISS DRUMMOND OF MEGGINCH]
1H61H6	31H22H	(I)	MISS ANNE CAMPBELL'S STRATHSPEY
1H61H6	7575	(II)	PIPER'S MARCH
1H61H6	1H643	(II)	DEVIL'S ELBOW, THE
1H61H6	1H2H2H2H	(II)	HURICHUM HARICHIM
1H61H1H	5255	(I)	HAD AWA' FRAE ME DONALD
1H61H1H	5355	(I)	HAD AWA' (FRAE ME), DONALD
1H61H1H	7557	(I)	HER ANSWER WAS MUM
1H61H1H	1H522	(I)	LADY JANE DOUGLAS' STRATHSPEY
1H61H1H	1H622	(I)	MRS MENZIES (OF CULDARE'S) STRATHSPEY
1H61H1H	1H1H4H7	(I)	MRS MITCHELL OF STOW
1H61H1H	2H226	(II)	JENNY DRINKS NAE BRANDY
1H61H1H	2H226	(I)	JENNY DRINKS NAE WATER
1H62H5	61H3H4H	(I)	QUICK STEP
1H62H5	1H62H5	(I)	MRS BISHOP'S WALTZ
1H62H6	21H65	(I)	I LOO'D A BONNY LADY
1H62H7	671H1H	(I)	POOR MARY ANN
1H62H1H	6423	(I)	PAS DUOX [DEUX]
1H62H1H	1H63H1H	(I)	MISS SCOTT'S WALTZ
1H64H3H	1H64H1H	(I)	FIFTEENTH Regt. 2ND. QUICKSTEP
1H7b27bL	27bL22	(I)	NORTH HIGHLAND 22
1H7b41	3b3b7b3b	(II)	CAITHNESS RANT, THE
1H7b41	3b3b7b3b	(I)	REEL OF CAITHNESS
1H7b5	515	(I)	MINUETTO
1H71H3	61H53	(II)	DEIL TAK THE BREEKS
1H7b1H1H	3bH7b3b4	(I)	PARCEL OF ROGUES IN A NATION, THE
1H715	1H753H	(II)	GEORDIE MACLEISH
1H72	444	(I)	AURORA WALTZ
1H72	651	(I)	SPANISH COUNTRY DANCE
1H735	447L2	(II)	FLOWERDALE
1H74	651	(I)	WEBER'S LAST WALTZ
1H751	2425L	(I)	MISS SALLY BARTLET'S JIGG
1H751	4326L	(I)	MRS SMYTH (OF METHVEN'S) FAVOURITE
1H753	1113H	(I)	ROYAL MONTROSE VOLUNTEER'S MARCH, THE
1H753	237L7L	(I)	MISS GRACE SPEIR'S (OF ELDERSLIE'S) REEL
1H753	61H73H	(II)	BAILIE NICOL JARVIE
1H754	4565	(I)	AN GILLE DUBH CIAR DHUBH
1H754	4565	(I)	STAY MY CHARMER, CAN YOU LEAVE ME
1H756	3411	(II)	BLUE BELLS (OF SCOTLAND, THE)
1H756	3411	(I)	BLUE BELL(S) OF SCOTLAND, THE
1H757	1H2H2H5	(I)	MISS JEAN DONALDSON'S HORNPIPE

```
1H757      2H4H1H6     (II)  MISS CHRISTIE OF DURRIE
1H757      2H4H1H6     (I)   MISS CHRISTIE OF DURRIE
1H75       1H72H       (I)   MISS ISABELLA ROBERTSON'S HORNPIPE
1H751H     2H4H3H1H    (I)   LET'S BE JOVIAL
1H752H     3H3HO2H     (I)   OLD BARD, THE
1H753H     1H1H2H2H    (II)  EDRADYNATE MEDLEY
1H76b5     43b27b      (I)   LADY S. MONTGOMERY'S REEL
1H763      1326L       (II)  PARLOUR REEL
1H763      3555        (I)   PARODY ON CAWDER FAIR
1H76       357         (I)   SAILOR'S JOURNALE
1H763      1H562       (I)   MAJOR ALVES QUICK STEP
1H763      1H765       (I)   RATTLE THE BOTTLES
1H763      1H71H2      (I)   JACKSON'S NIGHT CAP
1H765      153H2H      (I)   MRS CHOLMONDLEY'S REEL
1H765      437L5L      (I)   EDINBURGH MUSICAL FUND, THE
1H765      4327L       (I)   I DON'T CARE WHITHER OR NO
1H765      4562        (I)   MRS ROSS'S REEL
1H765      51H4H7      (I)   TEKELI
1H765      6542        (I)   MISS LINDSAY'S JIGG
1H765      1H765       (I)   RUGANTINO
1H761H     3553H       (I)   GU MO MAIDH A THIG AN CRUN DHUIT
                             A THEARLUICH (OIG)
1H761H     2H3H2H3H    (I)   MISS NICHOLAS ARBUTHNOT'S JIG
1H76       3H2H6       (I)   WILLIAM AND MARGARET, (THE OLD TUNE OF)
1H76       3H2H7       (I)   THERE CAME A GHOST TO MARGARET'S BOWER
1H71HO     1H63H2H     (I)   FOR TENDERNESS FORM'D
1H71H1     562H2H      (I)   TARBAT HOUSE
1H71H1     1H71H1H     (I)   MISS GRANT OF MONYMUSK'S JIGG
1H71H1     3H675       (I)   NEW MADRIGALL, A
1H71H3     26L27L      (I)   MRS ROY (OF NENTHORN'S) FAVORITE
1H71H3     2365        (I)   PADLOCK, THE
1H71H3     61H53       (I)   OH GRAIN AIR NA BRIOGAISEAN
1H71H5     4327        (I)   MEDWAY
1H71H5     6233        (I)   LA JARNOVIK
1H71H5     6331        (I)   QUICK STEP. 23rd REGt.
1H71H5     64H1H7      (I)   DANSE CIVIQUE
1H71H5     7b7b7b3bH   (I)   MY WIFE SHE'S A WANTON WEE THING
1H71H      61H5        (I)   DAWTIE, THE
1H71H7     671H2H      (I)   TRIFLER, THE
1H71H7     1H2H2H2H    (I)   CAPT YOUNG OF THE ROYAL PERTH
                             VOLUNTEERS QUICK STEP
1H71H1H    3H2H1H1H    (I)   MISS ELIZABETH CARNEGIE'S ALLAMANDE
1H71H1H    3H2H3H3H    (I)   JOHN COME ALONG
1H71H2H    7771H       (I)   GAVOTTA
1H71H2H    1H765       (I)   (YE'LL NEVER BE LIKE MY) AULD GOODMAN
1H71H2H    1H765       (I)   MY WINSOM JOHN
1H71H2H    3H3H3H3H    (I)   CASCADE, THE
1H71H2H    3H4H1H7     (I)   WATERS OF ELLE
1H71H2H    5H3H75      (I)   CURIOSITY, THE
1H72H1H    2H4H2H5     (I)   QUICK STEP
1H72H1H    4H1H1H1H    (I)   PRIMITIVE, THE
1H72H      2H3H5H      (I)   CRAZY JANE
1H72H2H    5H3bH1H2H   (I)   LAMENT FOR A FRIEND, A
1H72H2H    5H3bH1H2H   (I)   LAMENT FOR THE DEATH OF JANE,
                             DUCHESS OF GORDON
1H73bH2H   4H3bH1HO    (I)   MILLER OF DEE, THE
1H73H7     6543        (I)   GUY MANNERING
1H73H1H    64H5H3H     (I)   LORD GLENCAIRN'S QUICK STEP
1H73H2H    1H765       (I)   ROAST BEEF
1H73H6H    4H2H76      (II)  BLACK JOCK O' SKELLATER
1H1H11     1H1H41      (I)   MOUNT SION
1H1H11     1H1H41      (I)   MERRY FIFERS, THE
1H1H15     1H1H2H7b    (II)  MISS McMILLAN'S QUADRILLE
1H1H11H    2H1H22      (I)   MRS McADAM OF CRAIGENGILLAN'S REEL
1H1H11H    3bH7b3b2    (I)   OMAI
1H1H22     1H1H13H     (I)   STAY AND TAKE YOUR BREECHES WITH YOU
1H1H22     1H1H1H1H    (I)   LITTLE MEN OF THE MEARNS, THE
1H1H27     1H1H21H     (I)   NAVAL REVIEW, THE
1H1H22H    1H1H1H1H    (I)   LADY MARY LYONS REEL
1H1H3b1    27bL7b7b    (I)   MISS IRVINE'S REEL
1H1H3b1    27b27bL     (II)  WEDDERBURN HOUSE
1H1H3b1    27b27bL     (I)   WEDDERBURN HOUSE
1H1H3b3b   7b7b24      (II)  LADY BURNSIDE'S BIRTHDAY
1H1H3b3b   7b7b24      (I)   BRIDGE OF BRECHIN, THE
1H1H3b3b   7b7b24      (I)   LADY BURNSIDE'S (BIRTH DAY)/(STRATHSPEY)
1H1H31     5L342       (I)   LADY DALRYMPLE HAMILTON'S REEL
1H1H31     5L364       (I)   INVERUGIE CASTLE
1H1H31     2466        (I)   CAPTAIN R. MARTIN'S REEL
1H1H31     22H62H      (II)  MISS STEWART'S REEL
1H1H31     22H62H      (I)   MISS (GRACE) STEWART'S REEL
1H1H31     427L5L      (II)  FAIR WIND TO GREENLAND, A
1H1H31     427L5L      (II)  LADY DOWN
```

1H1H31	427L5L	(I)	HON. JAMES RAMSAY'S REEL, THE
1H1H31	427L5L	(I)	LADY DOWN'S REEL
1H1H31	437L2	(I)	BLANDFORD HOUSE
1H1H31	4362	(II)	DUCHESS OF RICHMOND'S REEL, THE
1H1H31	4462	(I)	MR DOUGAL McDOUGAL'S FAVORITE
1H1H31	42H75	(I)	COLONEL BYNG'S FAVORITE
1H1H31	42H75	(I)	MISS GRANT OF ELCHIE'S STRATHSPEY
1H1H31	42H76	(II)	CAPTAIN BYNG
1H1H31	42H2H6	(I)	MISS ELIZABETH TOWART'S STRATHSPEY
1H1H31	5322H	(I)	MRS CLARK'S STRATHSPEY
1H1H31	6542	(I)	HONble MRS ANDREW RAMSAY'S STRATHSPEY, THE
1H1H31	1H1H2H2H	(I)	LADY AGNES DUFF, THE
1H1H33	6L213L	(I)	GOOD NEWS FROM LEGHORN
1H1H33	1115L	(I)	ROYAL SCOTS MARCH, THE
1H1H33	2243	(I)	ESSEX BAND, THE
1H1H33	447L7L	(I)	MRS STIRLING'S REEL
1H1H33	5552H	(I)	WELCH FUSILEERS' MARCH
1H1H33	6542	(I)	LADY ELEANOR CAMPBELL OF SHAWFIELD'S REEL
1H1H33	671H6	(I)	ROSEBERRY HORNPIPE
1H1H33	671H6	(I)	MR EDWARD'S HORNPIPE
1H1H33	1H632	(I)	STEER HER UP AND HAD HER GAUN
1H1H33	1H1H31H	(I)	SPANISH PATRIOTS, THE
1H1H33	1H1H62H	(I)	MISS WILLES OF LESLIES BIRTHDAY
1H1H3	433	(I)	MISS ADAM'S MINUET
1H1H34	5553	(I)	DUNBAR VOLUNTEER'S MARCH
1H1H3	515L	(I)	LADY MARY LESSLEY'S MINUET
1H1H35	1113	(II)	WATERLOO(REEL)
1H1H35	2246	(I)	MISS MADALINA MAXWELL'S STRATHSPEY
1H1H35	22H76	(I)	MISS DEVEREUX REEL
1H1H35	22H76	(I)	COUNTESS OF LOUDON'S REEL, THE
1H1H35	24H72H	(I)	GENERAL McDONALD'S STRATHSPEY
1H1H35	3424	(I)	HIGHLAND REEL, THE
1H1H35	427L5L	(I)	MR JAMES FRASERS REEL
1H1H35	4242H	(I)	MISS McNEILL'S [STRATHSPEY]
1H1H35	42H76	(II)	MISS GEORGINA SCOTT
1H1H35	42H76	(I)	MISS GEORGINE SCOTT (OF SEABANK) 'S REEL [MISS GEORGINA SCOTT]
1H1H35	5322H	(I)	MRS CLARK'S STRATHSPEY
1H1H35	6416L	(I)	MR RICHIE'S HORNPIPE
1H1H35	644H2H	(I)	DIBDINS FANCY
1H1H35	6522H	(I)	HONble MRS OLIPHANT MURRAY'S REEL
1H1H35	6522H	(I)	MRS RICHARD WALPOLE'S REEL
1H1H35	6547L	(II)	MR MURDOCH'S REEL
1H1H35	6542	(II)	MRS WILL
1H1H35	67b24	(II)	IRVINE STEEPLE
1H1H35	67b24	(I)	LASSES OF IRVIN, THE
1H1H35	67b24	(I)	IRVIN STIPLE [IRVINE STEEPLE]
1H1H35	67b24	(I)	INVERNYTY'S (REEL/RANT)
1H1H35	67b24	(I)	SIR L. DUNDAS'S REEL
1H1H35	61H32	(I)	HONble MISS KEITH ELPHINSTONE'S FAVOURITE, THE
1H1H35	61H4H2H	(I)	PRINCE'S FAVOURITE, THE
1H1H35	72H4H3H	(I)	MISS NORTON'S REEL
1H1H35	1H1H22	(II)	FORBES LODGE
1H1H35	1H1H46	(II)	FRENCH AIR
1H1H35	1H1H72H	(I)	MISS C. PHIN'S REEL
1H1H35	1H1H72H	(I)	LADY MONTGOMERY'S REEL
1H1H35	1H2H3HO	(I)	CAMBRIAN MINSTREL, THE
1H1H31H	54H2H2H	(I)	SPEY SIDE
1H1H3	1H1H3	(I)	GINLEING GEORDE
1H1H3	1H1H4	(I)	RAKES OF WESTMOUTH
1H1H31H	2H752H	(I)	ALDRIGE HORNPIPE
1H1H31H	2H754H	(II)	MANCHESTER
1H1H31H	2H754H	(II)	SAILOR'S HORNPIPE
1H1H31H	2H2H72H	(II)	MISS ELPHINSTONE
1H1H31H	2H2H72H	(I)	MISS CLEMENTINA ELPHENSTONE'S REEL
1H1H31H	2H2H72H	(I)	READY MONEY
1H1H33H	64H2H1H	(I)	QUICK STEP
1H1H33H	6H7H72H	(I)	TRIP TO THE ROTUNDA, A
1H1H42	7L232	(I)	MR MERRICK'S REEL
1H1H42	62H65	(I)	LADY GOWERS FANCY
1H1H43	362H7	(I)	FEMALE RAKE, THE
1H1H45	1562	(I)	UNANIMITY
1H1H45	1H1H6L7L	(II)	FIDDICH BRIDGE
1H1H46	3542	(I)	MISS L. JOHNSTONE'S COMPLIMENTS TO NIEL GOW
1H1H44H	1H1H35	(I)	SISTERS, THE
1H1H5	15L1	(I)	LADY ANN MAITLAND'S MINUET
1H1H51	2222	(I)	BIG BOAT OF ENWARE, THE
1H1H51	2416L	(I)	MRS GORDON OF ABERGELDIE'S STRATHSPEY
1H1H51	2425L	(I)	LOTTERY TICKET, THE
1H1H51	2646	(II)	LORD LYNDOCH [LORD LYNEDOCH]
1H1H51	3636	(II)	LORD LYNDOCH [LORD LYNEDOCH]

```
1H1H51      4646        (II) LORD LYNDOCH [LORD LYNEDOCH]
1H1H51      42H76       (II) JOHN STEWART
1H1H51      42H76       (I)  MR JOHN STEWART'S REEL
1H1H51      1H62H7      (I)  MISS ROSS'S JIG
1H1H53      1151        (I)  RT HON LADY ELIZABETH GREVILLE'S WALTZ
1H1H5       321         (I)  LADY AUGUSTA HAY'S MINUET
1H1H53      2466        (II) BAGPIPE, THE
1H1H53      2466        (II) LEBURN'S HIGHLAND BAGPIPE
1H1H5       331         (I)  DEUKES DANG OWER MY DEDDIE, THE
1H1H5       331         (I)  DUCK'S DANG O'ER MY DADIE, THE
1H1H5       333         (I)  ASLACHADH NA BAINTIGHEARNA
1H1H53      4520        (II) TO ANE FAR AWA'
1H1H53      5432        (I)  FAVORITE SLOW TUNE, A
1H1H53      6631        (I)  COXHEATH CAMP
1H1H53      6631        (I)  CAMP AT COXHEATH
1H1H53      62H51H      (I)  MISS STEWART OF PHYSGILL'S FAVORITE
1H1H53      64H1H7      (I)  DISPATCH, THE
1H1H53      761H7       (I)  POOR JOE THE MARINE
1H1H53      1H1H2H7     (I)  CRAIGELLACHIE LASSES, THE
1H1H54      7b47b2H     (II) MRS KENNEDY OF GREENAN
1H1H54      7b47b2H     (I)  MRS KENNEDY OF GREENAN('S REEL)
1H1H54      3bH2H2H5H   (I)  MY LOVE'S IN GERMANY
1H1H55      1115        (I)  ROYAL GLASGOW VOLUNTEER'S MARCH
1H1H55      11H6H2H     (I)  MICHAEL WIGGINS IN IRELAND
1H1H55      3135        (I)  QUEENS (GRAND) MARCH (THE)
1H1H55      3501H       (I)  MARCH OF THE 21 REGt
1H1H55      3515        (I)  SIR JOHN HOPE'S MARCH
1H1H55      3551H       (I)  MARCH BY McGIBBON
1H1H55      31H3H3H     (I)  SEAFORTH'S FAREWELL
1H1H55      427bL7bL    (I)  MARCHIONESS OF HUNTLY'S FAVORITE, THE
1H1H55      427L2       (I)  DELIGHT OF THE PANTHEON, THE
1H1H55      436L7L      (I)  MARCHIONESS OF BREADALBANE, THE
1H1H55      4433        (I)  HONbIe MR J.T.L. MELVILLE'S, THE
1H1H55      4433        (I)  QUICK STEP, 32d. REGt
1H1H55      4443        (I)  HARLEQUIN TUNE
1H1H55      4443        (I)  TIGHT ROPE DANCER
1H1H55      4542        (I)  MISS DRYSDALE'S JIG
1H1H55      6651        (I)  MISS GWYNNE'S FANCY
1H1H55      665H5H      (I)  GOOD NIGHT AND GOD BE WITH YOU
1H1H55      666H6H      (I)  GOOD NIGHT AND JOY BE WI' YE A'
1H1H55      671H1H      (I)  MISS MORE OF RAEDEN'S FAVORITE DANCE
1H1H55      671H1H      (I)  MADRIGAL, THE
1H1H55      671H2H      (I)  OPERA HAT, THE
1H1H55      1H72H5      (I)  MRS MCKENZIE OF KILCOWIE'S JIG
1H1H55      1H1H27      (I)  TRIP TO DERRY, A
1H1H55      1H1H22H     (I)  KINEGAD SLASHERS
1H1H55      1H1H77      (I)  MRS DALRYMPLE OF ORANGEFIELD'S REEL
1H1H55      1H1H2H2H    (I)  LA DEP
1H1H55      1H1H4H7     (I)  WEDDING CAKE, THE
1H1H55      1H2H3H6     (I)  ISLAY HOUSE
1H1H55      3bH4H2H1H   (I)  BONNY BRAES OF CLYDE, THE
1H1H55      3H1H4H3H    (I)  COUNTESS OF ANTRIM, THE
1H1H55      3H3H2H1H    (I)  FEATHERS, THE
1H1H5       664         (I)  CROMLET'S LILT
1H1H5       665         (I)  I CANNOT WINSULL HER FOR HER BIGG BELLY
1H1H5       61H1        (I)  SINGLE HORNPIPE NO. 1
1H1H5       61H1        (I)  GELD HIM LASSES GELD HIM
1H1H5       61H6        (I)  BRIDE NEXT
1H1H56      1H1H65      (I)  HIGHLAND AIR
1H1H5       7b41        (I)  MODERATE
1H1H51H     51H4H3H     (I)  MARY AND DONALD
1H1H51H     666H6H      (I)  GOODNIGHT AND GOD BE WI YOU A'
1H1H51H     7756        (I)  SHEPHERD OF NEATH, THE
1H1H5       1H1H1H1H    (I)  DAN FEINNE [FONN AIR DAIN FEINNE]
1H1H5       1H1H1H1H    (I)  OSCAR'S GHOST
1H1H51H     2H1H24      (I)  MISS HUNTER BLAIR'S REEL
1H1H51H     2H2H75H     (II) MR GIBSON
1H1H5       1H2H3H      (I)  PEIR OF BOWMORE, THE
1H1H51H     2H3H2H5     (I)  QUICK STEP, THE TROUPERS
1H1H51H     2H5H3HO     (I)  PADDY O' BLARNEY
1H1H53bH    4H2H1H3bH   (I)  HEBRIDEAN DANCING MEASURES & C No. 3
1H1H53H     1H1H51H     (I)  MR JAMES HAMILTON'S VALTZ
1H1H5       3H3H1H      (I)  MISS NANCY STEWART Frs. WALTZ
1H1H6b6b    5547bL      (I)  FORGLEN HOUSE
1H1H6b6b    5547bL      (I)  MARSHALL'S FAVORITE
1H1H6b6b    5547bL      (I)  MR HUNTER (OF BURNSIDE'S) STRATHSPEY
1H1H6b6b    5547bL      (I)  (COLONEL/GENERAL) CAMPBELL
                             OF MONZIE'S FAVOURITE
1H1H62      1H1H51      (II) STRATHBOGIE EDITOR, THE
1H1H6       353         (I)  MY TRIM-BUILT WHERRY
1H1H63      6363        (II) POLICEMAN'S CAP
1H1H63      1H1H62      (II) MISS MENZIES OF CULDARE(S)
```

```
1H1H64      2466        (II)  CLUNY ROCK
1H1H64      4331        (I)   SOUTH DOWNS
1H1H64      642H4       (I)   MISS CAMERON'S REEL
1H1H65      11H2H6      (I)   BIRNOM WOOD
1H1H65      13H75       (I)   ALWAYS PRETTY
1H1H65      13H75       (I)   NONE SO PRETTY
1H1H65      22H76       (II)  ROW, THE
1H1H65      3222        (I)   MR JAMES BENNET'S REEL
1H1H65      3222        (I)   LILLY, THE
1H1H6       533         (I)   AY WAUKIN' O
1H1H65      4322H       (I)   MISS AGNES WILLE'S STRATHSPEY
1H1H65      457L2       (I)   LADY CLIFFORD'S GIG
1H1H65      4575        (I)   PAS SEUL
1H1H6       553         (I)   CAROLANES PURSE
1H1H6       553         (I)   RUNING FOOTMAN
1H1H6       555         (I)   MISS HENDERSON'S MINUET
1H1H6       556         (I)   CHAIDH AN TORAN MU THOM
1H1H65      51H4H7      (II)  PADDY CAREY
1H1H65      51H4H7      (I)   TEKELI
1H1H65      7b427bL     (I)   MISS AMELIA STEWART MENZIES' REEL
1H1H65      1H523       (I)   INSTALLATION, THE
1H1H6       51H1H       (I)   BLACK HAIR'D DEAR LADDIE, THE
1H1H65      1H2H3H1H    (I)   YOUNG MAY MOON, THE
1H1H66      427L2       (I)   NOTTINGHAM RACE(S)
1H1H66      4347L       (I)   COTILLION
1H1H66      5122        (I)   PEGGY OF THE GREEN
1H1H66      5211        (I)   SCOTS RECLUSE, THE
1H1H66      5322        (I)   ILL WIFE, THE
1H1H66      557L2       (I)   MISS ANN WILLIAMSON'S FAVORITE JIG
1H1H66      5530        (I)   NEGLECTED TAR, (THE)
1H1H66      6422        (I)   MISS BALFOWR [MISS BALFOUR]
1H1H66      1H155       (I)   BATTLE OF HARLAW, (THE)
1H1H66      4H3H66      (I)   LADY MACKENTASHES REEL
1H1H67      1H1H41      (I)   MISS GEORGINE SCOTT OF SEA BANK'S WALTZ
1H1H67      1H1H5H2H    (I)   LA BELLE LAITIERE
1H1H67      2H71H1H     (I)   MENTAL BEAUTY
1H1H61H     62H75       (I)   MRS CAPt. CHARLES GORDON
1H1H61H     1H1H62H     (I)   LADY BYRON'S WALTZ
1H1H62H     1H51H5      (I)   PLEYEL'S DANCE
1H1H62H     1H642       (I)   GRAY STONE OF ARDNAHOW, THE
1H1H62H     1H1H3H3H    (I)   THRO' THE WORLD WOU'D I GAE
                              WE THE LAD I LIKE
1H1H62H     1H1H3H3H    (I)   A' BODY LO'ES ME
1H1H62H     1H1H3H3H    (I)   LITTLE MEN OF THE MEARNS, THE
1H1H62H     1H3H66      (II)  FOR A' THAT AND A' THAT
1H1H62H     1H4H66      (I)   LADY MACKINTOSH'S REEL
1H1H62H     1H4H1H6     (I)   LADY McINTOSHES REEL
1H1H62H     2H3H65      (II)  AN GILLE DUBH MO LAOCHAN
1H1H62H     3H1H66      (I)   THERE'S NAE LUCK ABOUT THE HOUSE
1H1H62H     3H1H66      (I)   MAN'S A MAN FOR A' THAT, A
1H1H62H     3H4H66      (II)  IT'S BONNY O'ER THE HILL THE NIGHT
1H1H62H     3H4H66      (I)   LADY MACKINTOSH'S REEL
1H1H62H     3H4H66      (I)   FOR A' THAT AN' A' THAT
1H1H63H     1H1H22      (I)   LORD DUMFRIES'S BRIDGE
1H1H64H     3H1H2H5     (I)   QUICK STEP, WEST FENCIBLES
1H1H7b4     7b445       (I)   MY DEAR I DOW NE DO NE MAIR
1H1H7b5     6b43b5      (I)   WESTERN ISLE AIR, A
1H1H7b5     7b7b7b7b    (I)   HEBRIDEAN DANCING MEASURES & C No. 2
1H1H76      3H1H43      (II)  JAMIE SHEARER
1H1H7b7b    5544        (I)   SOMEBODY
1H1H7b7b    5555        (I)   McLOUD'S SALUTE
1H1H7b7b    1H1H7b4     (I)   SKIVER THE QUILT
1H1H7b7b    2H757b      (I)   VIVE HENRI QUATRE
1H1H7b      1H7b5       (I)   APPIE McNABB
1H1H7b      1H1H7b      (I)   OLD IRELAND REJOICE
1H1H75      4331        (I)   SOUTH DOWNS
1H1H75      1H1H71H     (I)   YORK FANCY, THE
1H1H75      1H1H4H4H    (I)   MISS DAVIDSON'S JIG
1H1H75      1H2H3H5H    (I)   OAK STICK
1H1H75      3H4H3H2H    (I)   HAYDN'S FANCY
1H1H7       650         (I)   MRS KERR'S MINUET
1H1H7       654         (I)   MISS TAIT'S MINUET
1H1H76      5522        (I)   BREDAGAD
1H1H76      5561H       (I)   NEW PERRO
1H1H76      567L2       (I)   MISS PEGGY WILLIAMSON STRATHSPEY
1H1H76      72H1H1H     (I)   LASS WI' THE GOLDEN HAIR, THE
1H1H76      1H3H5H2H    (I)   FAINT AND WEARILY
1H1H76      1H3H5H2H    (I)   BELVEDIERE
1H1H76      1H5H2H2H    (I)   MY MOTHER BIDS ME BIND MY HAIR
1H1H77      6653        (I)   WELSH DANCE, A
1H1H77      6656        (I)   DUTCH SKIPPER, (THE)
1H1H77      1H1H5H5H    (I)   ALLEGRO
```

1H1H7	1H05	(I)	CRODH LAOIDH NA'M BODACH
1H1H71H	1H522	(I)	LORD ALEXANDER RUSSELL'S JIG
1H1H7	1H1H4H	(I)	MR O. GALLAGHER
1H1H7	1H1H4H	(I)	TRAVELLERS, THE
1H1H71H	3H2H76	(I)	CALLER HERRING
1H1H7	1H3H3H	(I)	ROUDLUM
1H1H72H	1H554	(I)	HAY MAKERS, THE
1H1H72H	1H653	(I)	(THEN) GUDE WIFE COUNT THE LAWIN
1H1H72H	1H1H55	(I)	LASS WITH A LUMP OF LAND, (A)
1H1H72H	1H1H1H2H	(I)	BOLOGNA'S MARCH
1H1H72H	1H1H2H5	(II)	BANKS O' YTHAN, THE
1H1H72H	1H1H2H7	(I)	ROYAL CIRCUS, THE
1H1H72H	1H3H4H3H	(I)	MISS ANN DALRYMPLE'S STRATHSPEY
1H1H72H	3H4H3H4H	(I)	BRIDE OF LAMERMUIR'S REEL
1H1H72H	3H5H1H7	(I)	LOYAL BORROWSTOUNNESS VOLUNTEERS QUICK MARCH, THE
1H1H7	3H3H2H	(I)	EARL OF SEAFIELD, THE
1H1H1H1	1H1H2H2	(I)	HIGHWAY TO EGLINGTON, THE
1H1H1H1	2H3H2H2	(I)	WESTMINSTER BRIDGE
1H1H1H2	1351	(I)	MRS BAKER'S FANCY
1H1H1H2	1H565	(II)	LORD KINNAIRD
1H1H1H2	1H565	(I)	LORD KINAIRD'S REEL [LORD KINNAIRD('S REEL)]
1H1H1H2	1H1H1H1	(I)	GINGLING GEORDIE
1H1H1H3b	7b57b5	(I)	HI RI RI RI HO
1H1H1H3	432H2	(I)	MISS JOHNSTON OF TWICKENHAM'S REEL
1H1H1H3	5553H	(I)	KILRAVOCK VOLUNTEER'S MARCH, THE
1H1H1H	351H	(I)	BUGLE WALTZ, THE
1H1H1H3	6565	(I)	LORD KINARD'S REEL [LORD KINNAIRD]
1H1H1H3	61H52	(II)	EARL OF MARCHES HORNPIPE, THE
1H1H1H3	61H65	(I)	MISS HENDERSON OF STEMPSTER'S REEL
1H1H1H3	61H65	(I)	CHARLES STREET BATH
1H1H1H3	1H31H3	(I)	LOCH LOMOND
1H1H1H3	1H565	(II)	LORD KINNAIRD [LORD KINNEARD]
1H1H1H3	1H1H53H	(I)	MRS MONTGOMRIE OF ANNICK'S STRATHSPEY
1H1H1H4	2632	(I)	ROASTED EMPEROR, THE
1H1H1H4	6421	(I)	LITTLE LOVE, A
1H1H1H4	1H1H2H3H	(II)	STEER THE GILL
1H1H1H4	1H1H2H3H	(I)	STEER THE GILL
1H1H1H5	1116	(I)	COL. LENOX'S MARCH
1H1H1H5	1353	(I)	MRS DINGWALL OF BRUCKLAY'S REEL
1H1H1H5	11H2H2	(I)	WESTS HORNPIPE
1H1H1H5	11H2H2	(I)	MISS GRAHAM OF INCHBRAKIE'S STRATHSPEY
1H1H1H5	11H2H6	(I)	BIRNAM WOOD
1H1H1H5	2211	(I)	FAREWELL MY PRETTY MOGGY
1H1H1H5	2215	(I)	FAREWELL MY PRETTY WITTY MAGGY
1H1H1H5	2216	(I)	FAREWELL MY PRETTY WITTY PEGGY
1H1H1H5	2311H	(I)	COTILLON
1H1H1H	531	(I)	MISS FULLARTON'S MINUET
1H1H1H	531	(I)	FAREWELL MY WEE COT HOUSE
1H1H1H5	3357	(I)	HEGH HOW THE BALLOP
1H1H1H	535	(I)	ECLYPSE, THE
1H1H1H5	3557	(I)	HER ANSWER WAS I'M TOO YOUNG
1H1H1H5	3557	(I)	MAY MORNING, THE
1H1H1H5	362H2H	(I)	FLIGHT, THE
1H1H1H5	362H2H	(I)	KNIGHT, THE
1H1H1H	543	(I)	SO MERRY AS WE HAVE BEEN
1H1H1H	551	(I)	PRINCESS OF WALES'S MINUET
1H1H1H5	5362	(II)	"LONACH" COUNTRY DANCE, THE
1H1H1H	555	(I)	LADY CHARLOTTE RAWDOW'S MINUET
1H1H1H5	6535	(I)	TRIP TO ISLINGTON, A
1H1H1H5	7b57b7bL	(I)	MR ROBt BAIN'S STRATHSPEY
1H1H1H5	7b7b65	(II)	BAG OF PRATIES, THE
1H1H1H5	7b7b7b2	(II)	MY WIFE'S A WANTON WEE THING
1H1H1H5	7b7b7b2	(I)	MY WIFE IS A WANTON WEE THING
1H1H1H5	7b2H2H3bH	(I)	MISS MACMURDO'S FAVOURITE (STRATHSPEY)
1H1H1H5	7b2H2H3bH	(I)	JOHN ROY'S FAREWEL
1H1H1H5	1H11H1	(I)	MRS FULLARTON OF FULLARTONS REEL
1H1H1H5	1H531	(I)	CABER FEIGH
1H1H1H5	1H532	(I)	UNTITLED
1H1H1H5	1H532	(I)	TROOPS MARCHING DOWN THE ROCKS, THE
1H1H1H5	1H532	(I)	LASLY'S MARCH
1H1H1H5	1H542	(I)	LESSLIE'S MARCH
1H1H1H5	1H51H2H	(II)	LESLIE'S MARCH
1H1H1H5	1H1H55	(II)	REEL OF BOGIE, THE
1H1H1H5	1H1H55	(II)	O'ER BOGIE [O'ER BOGGIE WI' MY LOVE]
1H1H1H5	1H1H55	(I)	O'ER BOGIE (WI' MY LOVE)
1H1H1H5	1H1H51H	(I)	O'ER BOGGIE
1H1H1H5	1H1H1H3H	(I)	DUKE OF RICHMOND'S MARCH
1H1H1H5	1H2H60	(I)	O'ER BOGIE
1H1H1H5	1H3H1H1H	(I)	EMPEROR OF GERMANY'S MARCH
1H1H1H5	3bH3bH4H2H	(I)	GLOOMY WINTER ('S NOW AWA')

1H1H1H5	3H3H3H1H	(I)	SOLDIER AND A SAILOR, A
1H1H1H5	4H3H3H6H	(I)	MARIAN DOW
1H1H1H6	4447	(II)	DEIL AMONG THE TAILORS, THE
1H1H1H6	4622H	(I)	MISS BURRINGTON'S FANCY
1H1H1H6	51H1H6	(I)	EVELEEN'S BOWER
1H1H1H6	1H1H33	(I)	SAILOR'S ALLEGORY, THE
1H1H1H6	1H1H1H3	(II)	SANDY SKINNER
1H1H1H6	1H1H1H6	(I)	PEGGY OF DARBY
1H1H1H6	1H1H1H6	(I)	LODOISKA
1H1H1H6	1H1H3H2H	(II)	O'ER THE HILLS AND FAR AWA'
1H1H1H6	1H1H4H2H	(II)	O'ER THE HILLS AND FAR AWAY
1H1H1H6	1H3H1H5	(I)	SIR PATRICK MURRAY'S MARCH
1H1H1H	61H4H	(I)	OLD SIR SYMON THE KING
1H1H1H	62H7	(I)	RETURN, THE
1H1H1H6	2H4H7O	(I)	ROTHSAY AND CAITHNESS FENCIBLES
1H1H1H7b	5454	(II)	TIGH EACH(A)INN or
			[AULD ROAD TO TOWIE, THE]
1H1H1H	7b7b4	(I)	TOAST, THE
1H1H1H	7b7b4	(I)	SAW YE MY PEGGY
1H1H1H7b	7b51H3b	(I)	CHA BHI MI M'IASGAIR
1H1H1H3	11H3H2H	(I)	MISS BENNETS JIGG
1H1H1H7	5530	(I)	SOLDIER'S ADIEU, THE
1H1H1H7	5534	(I)	WATERLOO MARCH
1H1H1H7	5534	(I)	AIR OF THE ISLE OF SKYE
1H1H1H7	5553H	(I)	THOU ART GANE AWA FROM ME MARY
1H1H1H7	6663	(I)	EXILE OF ERIN, THE
1H1H1H7	6663	(I)	SA MHUIR NI DILIS EILIN OG
1H1H1H7	6663	(I)	SAVOURNA DELIGH
1H1H1H	776	(I)	HEATHCOT'S HORSE RACE
1H1H1H7	1H7b55	(I)	CHARLOTTE'S RANT
1H1H1H7	1H1H2H2H	(I)	MISS MANNERS'S FANCY
1H1H1H1H	113b1H	(I)	LADY GLENORCHY'S REEL
1H1H1H1H	2265	(I)	I WISH MY LOVE WERE IN A MIRE
1H1H1H1H	2533	(I)	COUNTRY COTTAGE
1H1H1H1H	2662	(I)	BRAES OF MARR, THE
1H1H1H1H	2666	(I)	BRAES OF MARR, (THE)
1H1H1H1H	3555	(II)	WEE AULD WIFIE
1H1H1H1H	471H2H	(I)	WESTMINSTER VOLUNTEERS
1H1H1H1H	5353H	(I)	THOU ART GANE AWA'
1H1H1H1H	5553H	(I)	THOU ART GANE AWA' FRAE ME, MARY
1H1H1H1H	6542	(I)	ELEVENTH OCTOBER, THE
1H1H1H1H	6662	(II)	BRAES OF MAR(R), THE
1H1H1H1H	6662	(I)	BRAES OF MARR, THE
1H1H1H1H	661H5	(II)	DONALD MACGUGAN'S RANT
1H1H1H1H	665H3H	(I)	MISS CHALMERS REEL
1H1H1H1H	61H64	(II)	DEVIL'S DREAM, THE
1H1H1H1H	62H1H3H	(I)	LANG LIFE TO NEIL GOW
1H1H1H1H	7b6b55	(I)	CORELLIS GIGGA
1H1H1H1H	7774H	(I)	COX'S MUSEUM
1H1H1H1H	71H22	(I)	JOHNNY GROAT'S HOUSE
1H1H1H	1H1H5	(I)	MISS CAMPBELL'S MINUET
1H1H1H1H	1H66H2H	(I)	BLUE BONNETS OVER THE BORDER
1H1H1H1H	1H755	(I)	BLACK MARY
1H1H1H1H	1H755	(I)	MELVIL HOUSE
1H1H1H	1H1H1H	(I)	LASHLEYS MARCH
1H1H1H1H	1H1H24	(I)	FUMBLER, THE
1H1H1H1H	1H1H72H	(I)	MISS BLAIR'S REEL
1H1H1H1H	1H1H1H1H	(I)	MISS CAMPBELL OF SHAWFIELD'S VALTZ
1H1H1H1H	1H1H2H2H	(I)	LADY TOWNS
1H1H1H1H	1H1H2H2H	(I)	COLONEL SMALL'S STRATHSPEY
1H1H1H1H	1H1H2H2H	(I)	MRS MCPHERSON
1H1H1H1H	1H1H5H2H	(I)	BLUCHER'S TRIUMPH
1H1H1H	1H1H2H	(I)	LADY BETTY BOYLE'S MINUET
1H1H1H1H	1H2H75	(II)	OLD STRATHSPEY
1H1H1H1H	1H2H3HO	(I)	DUKE OF BUCCLEUGH'S MARCH
1H1H1H1H	1H3H1H3	(II)	JIM ALONG JOSEY
1H1H1H1H	1H3H2H2	(I)	GEORGE SKENE DUFF, OF MILTON
1H1H1H1H	1H3H6H4H	(I)	COLONEL SHARP OF THE PERTH
			VOLUNTEERS QUICK STEP
1H1H1H	1H1H6H	(I)	QUEEN OF PRUSSIA'S WALTZ
1H1H1H1H	2H52H5	(II)	NEW RIGG'D SHIP, THE
1H1H1H1H	2H52H5	(I)	NEW RIGG'D SHIP, (THE)
1H1H1H1H	2H62H5	(I)	LADY TANKERVILLE'S GIG
1H1H1H1H	2H776	(I)	CLOUT THE CAULDRON
1H1H1H1H	2H71H6	(I)	CAPT FLEMING'S REEL
1H1H1H1H	2H72H4H	(I)	ALLY CROAKER
1H1H1H	1H2H2H	(I)	WEARY PUND O' TOW, THE
1H1H1H1H	2H2H65	(I)	KIND ROBIN LO'ES ME
1H1H1H1H	2H2H66	(II)	LADY DOUNE
1H1H1H1H	2H2H66	(I)	LADY DOUNE
1H1H1H1H	2H2H72H	(II)	MAGGIE LAUDER
1H1H1H1H	2H2H72H	(I)	PETRARCH AND LAURA'S STRATHSPEY

```
1H1H1H1H      2H2H1H1H      ( I )  CAPE BRETON MARCH
1H1H1H1H      2H2H2H2H      ( I )  DANCED BY MASTER GRAHAME
1H1H1H1H      2H2H2H2H      ( I )  PORT LENNOX
1H1H1H1H      2H2H2H2H      ( I )  FIVE TIMES BY THE TAPER'S LIGHT
1H1H1H1H      2H2H2H2H      ( I )  HEAVENS ARE TELLING, THE
1H1H1H1H      2H3H66        (II)  MISS MUIR MACKENZIE
1H1H1H1H      2H3H66        ( I )  MISS MUIR MCKENZIES STRATHSPEY
                                   [MISS MUIR MACKENZIE]
1H1H1H1H      2H4H71H       ( I )  MISS DURY'S REEL
1H1H1H1H      2H4H72H       ( I )  MAGGIE LAUDER
1H1H1H1H      2H5H4H1H      ( I )  FIGARO
1H1H1H1H      2H6H6H2H      (II)  BRAES OF MARR, THE
1H1H1H1H      3bH3b3b3bH    ( I )  MAIDS COMPLAINT, THE
1H1H1H1H      3H553H        ( I )  LEWt GEORGE RAE'S MARCH
1H1H1H1H      3H3H3H1H      ( I )  PETERHEAD ARTILLERY VOLUNTEERS MARCH
1H1H1H1H      3H3H4H3H      ( I )  CONQUEST, THE
1H1H1H1H      3H3H5H4H      ( I )  MISS BAILLIE'S MARCH
1H1H1H1H      4H2H77        ( I )  GAVOT OF VESTRIS
1H1H1H1H      4H3H72H       ( I )  CONTENTED COTTAGERS
1H1H1H1H      4H3H72H       ( I )  JIGG, A
1H1H1H1H      5H2H66        ( I )  MISS ADMIRAL GORDON'S (REEL/STRATHSPEY)
1H1H1H1H      5H2H66        ( I )  OF A' THE AIRTS (THE WIN' CAN BLAW)
1H1H1H1H      5H4H3H2H      ( I )  LOVE IN A TUB
1H1H1H2H      5553H         ( I )  MARCH (IN THE BATTLE OF PRAGUE)
1H1H1H2H      6542          ( I )  MISS MARIA STEWART'S JIGG
1H1H1H2H      7b2H2H3bH     ( I )  CARLIN OF THE GLEN, THE
1H1H1H2H      7771H         ( I )  RUSSIAN SONG, A
1H1H1H2H      71HO2H        ( I )  MARCH IN DEMOSOONTE
1H1H1H        2H1H6         ( I )  ESKE SIDE
1H1H1H2H      1H751H        ( I )  COUNT BROWN'S MARCH
1H1H1H2H      1H766         ( I )  SAILORS LEAD A MERRY LIFE
1H1H1H2H      1H2H3H1H      ( I )  TRIP TO GUNNING HILL WELLS
1H1H1H        2H2H2H        (II)  YE BANKS AND BRAES
1H1H1H        2H2H2H        ( I )  WALTZ BY MOZART
1H1H1H        2H2H4H        (II)  MUCH ADMIRED NEW OPERA DANCE, A
1H1H1H2H      3H3H3H1H      ( I )  MR WELCH'S MARCH
1H1H1H2H      3H3H3H4H      ( I )  COLONEL McLEAN'S MARCH
1H1H1H2H      3H3H3H4H      ( I )  NEW DUKE OF YORK'S MARCH
1H1H1H2H      3H3H3H4H      ( I )  IN INFANCY OUR HOPES AND FEARS
1H1H1H2H      3H3H3H4H      ( I )  LAD IF YOU LO'E ME
1H1H1H        3bH7b4        ( I )  SAW YE NAE MY PEGGY
1H1H1H3bH     7b53b4        ( I )  RASHES, THE
1H1H1H3bH     7b53b4        ( I )  WHEN THE KING CAME O'ER THE WATER
1H1H1H3bH     7b557b        (II)  JACK A' TAR
1H1H1H3bH     7b557b        ( I )  JACKY TAR [JACK A' TAR]
1H1H1H3bH     7b7b3b4       ( I )  COME KISS WI' ME COME CLAP WI' ME
1H1H1H3bH     7b7b3b4       ( I )  WHEN THE KING CAME O'ER (THE) [BOYNE] WATER
1H1H1H        3bH2HO        ( I )  I MET THEE IN THE MORN OF LIFE
1H1H1H        3bH3bH3bH     ( I )  CHIU RI RUO
1H1H1H        3bH3bH4H      ( I )  NELL OF CONNAUGHT
1H1H1H3H      2662          ( I )  BRAES OF MARR, THE
1H1H1H3H      5321          ( I )  AULD LANG SYNE
1H1H1H3H      5342          ( I )  AULD LANG SYNE
1H1H1H3H      5531          ( I )  COTTILLION 3rd
1H1H1H3H      5554          ( I )  FOR OLD LONG GINE MY JOE
1H1H1H3H      5553H         ( I )  GENERAL ELLIOT'S MARCH
1H1H1H3H      6662          (II)  BRAES O' MAR REEL
1H1H1H3H      61H67         ( I )  UNFORTUNATE JOAK
1H1H1H3H      7772H         ( I )  TOPSY TURVY
1H1H1H3H      72H75         ( I )  DUTCHESS OF ATHOLL'S REEL
1H1H1H3H      1H113         ( I )  ADMIRAL VERNON'S MARCH
1H1H1H3H      1H111H        ( I )  TOPSAILS SHIVER IN THE WIND, THE
1H1H1H3H      1H31H1H       (II)  IN THE GARB OF OLD GAUL
1H1H1H3H      1H31H1H       ( I )  GARB OF OLD GAUL, THE
1H1H1H3H      1H31H2H       ( I )  GARB OF OLD GAUL ([IN] THE)
1H1H1H        3H1H5         ( I )  QUEEN OF MAY, THE
1H1H1H        3H1H5         ( I )  JENKINS'S DUSTY MILLER
1H1H1H3H      1H511         (II)  HIGHLAND SOCIETY OF SCOTLAND'S MARCH
1H1H1H3H      1H522H        ( I )  MISS GRIZIE KENNEDY'S REEL
1H1H1H3H      1H51H1H       ( I )  IN THE GARB OF OLD GAUL
1H1H1H3H      1H51H2H       ( I )  HIGHLAND MARCH, THE
1H1H1H3H      1H665         ( I )  O'ER THE HILLS AND FAR AWAY
1H1H1H3H      1H665         ( I )  I GAVE A WAEFU' GATE YESTREEN
1H1H1H3H      1H61T2H       ( I )  MISS SPROT'S WALTZ
1H1H1H3H      1H750         ( I )  HEARTS OF OAK
1H1H1H3H      1H755         ( I )  HEARTS OF OAK
1H1H1H3H      1H755         ( I )  OLD ENGLAND FOREVER
1H1H1H        3H1H1H        ( I )  LORD BINNY'S MINUET
1H1H1H3H      1H1H22H       ( I )  LADY RAMSY'S FANCY
1H1H1H3H      1H1H55        ( I )  PRINCE OF WALES DELIGHT, THE
1H1H1H3H      1H1H72H       ( I )  JIGG TO THE IRISH CRY
1H1H1H3H      1H1H1H3H      ( I )  MEDLEY OVERTURE (3)
```

1H1H1H3H	1H3H1H3	(I)	MASON'S MARCH, THE
1H1H1H3H	2H555	(I)	PRINCE FREDRICK'S MARCH
1H1H1H3H	2H557	(I)	GIBRALTAR MARCH
1H1H1H3H	2H2H2H3H	(I)	COLONEL WEBSTER'S MARCH
1H1H1H3H	2H2H2H4H	(I)	JACKSON'S TUNET
1H1H1H3H	2H2H2H4H	(I)	CAPT HILLMAN'S MARCH
1H1H1H3H	2H2H2H4H	(I)	LORD LINDSAYS MARCH
1H1H1H3H	2H2H2H5H	(I)	LOVELY SPRIGHTLY GALLANT TAR
1H1H1H3H	2H2H3H1H	(I)	MISS BUSHBY'S ALLAMANDE
1H1H1H3H	2H4H1H6	(I)	PETERHEAD VOLUNTEER'S MARCH
1H1H1H	333	(I)	OX MINUET, THE
1H1H1H	3H3H3H	(I)	CASTLE SWIEN
1H1H1H3H	3H4H2H5	(II)	HEN'S MARCH, THE
1H1H1H3H	4H2H63H	(I)	ALL'S RIGHT AT LAST
1H1H1H3H	4H2H5H1H	(I)	L'ABBE
1H1H1H3H	4H3H72H	(II)	CRAIG-GOWAN REEL
1H1H1H3H	5H3H1H6	(II)	MISS TAYLOR
1H1H1H3H	5H3H1H6	(I)	MISS TAYLOR('S REEL)
1H1H1H3H	5H5H5H6H	(I)	STREET MARCH
1H1H1H4H	7551H	(I)	MARQUIS OF HUNTLEY'S MARCH
1H1H1H4H	7771H	(I)	WALTZ
1H1H1H4H	2H555	(I)	FAVORITE MARCH
1H1H1H4H	2H2H2H3H	(I)	LORD BERNARD'S MARCH
1H1H1H4H	2H2H2H5H	(I)	(DOWN) FALL OF PARIS, (THE)
1H1H1H5H	1H762H	(I)	MR CHARLES OLIPHANT
1H1H1H5H	1H1H77	(I)	MISS DOUGLAS OF BRIGTON'S STRATHSPEY
1H1H1H5H	1H1H72H	(II)	PEGGIE'S WEDDING [LADY'S FANCY]
1H1H1H5H	1H1H72H	(I)	CLINKIN O'T, THE
1H1H1H5H	1H1H72H	(I)	PEGGIE'S WEDDING [LADY'S FANCY]
1H1H1H5H	2H2H3HO	(I)	RULE BRITANNIA
1H1H1H5H	2H2H3H3H	(I)	RULE BRITANNIA
1H1H1H5H	2H4H3HO	(I)	RULE BRITANNIA
1H1H1H5H	4H1H1H1H	(I)	NYMPH, THE
1H1H1H5H	5H3H71H	(I)	LADY MARY HAY'S ALLAMANDE
1H1H1H5H	5H4H2H1H	(I)	MISSES FIDDES' WALTZ, THE
1H1H1H5H	5H5H4H3H	(I)	MADAM HEINEL'S GAVOT
1H1H1H6H	1H1H1H4H	(I)	PRINCE & OLD ENGLAND FOR EVER
1H1H2H4	1H1H3bH1H	(II)	MR JAMES DAVIDSON'S REEL
1H1H2H4	1H1H3bH3bH	(II)	COIL-A-CREICH INN, DEESIDE
1H1H2H5	4231	(I)	DOWNIE'S RIGADON
1H1H2H5	6451	(II)	MRS DUNDAS OF ARNISTON
1H1H2H5	6451	(I)	(HONbl) MRS DUNDAS OF ARNISTON'S REEL
1H1H2H5	6532	(I)	MRS JOHN STIRLING'S JIG
1H1H2H5	6542	(I)	BONNY CROWDY
1H1H2H5	6542	(I)	MISS CLEMENTINA STEWART OF GARTH'S JIGG
1H1H2H5	6651	(I)	EPPING FORREST
1H1H2H5	1H451	(I)	DICKY GOSSIP
1H1H2H5	1H551	(I)	MISS ISABELLA ELLIS'S JIG
1H1H2H5	1H551	(I)	MRS THOM'S FAVOURITE JIG
1H1H2H5	1H1H2H5	(II)	OPERA HORNPIPE
1H1H2H5	1H1H5H5H	(I)	MR ARCHD DOW OF PERTH'S QUICK STEP
1H1H2H5	1H1H5H5H	(I)	MISS BRODIE OF LATHAN'S FAVORITE
1H1H2H5	3H5H2H7	(I)	COTILLION
1H1H2H5	5H2H2H5	(I)	LADY SALISBURY'S FANCY
1H1H2H6	5332	(II)	SIR ALEXr. G.P. CUMMING BARt.
			OF ALTYRE'S REEL
1H1H2H	661H	(I)	FAILTE NA MIOSG
1H1H2H	671H	(I)	MY HEART'S IN THE HIGHLANDS
1H1H2H6	1H543	(I)	WHAT BEAUTEOUS SCENES
1H1H2H	7b53bH	(I)	HERE'S A HEALTH TO MY TRUE LOVE
1H1H2H7b	1H1H64	(I)	WE ARE ALL MERRY
1H1H2H7	5533	(I)	SOLDIER'S ADIEU
1H1H2H7	5555	(I)	MR McDONALD'S FAVORITE
1H1H2H	751H	(I)	PASTHEEN FUEN
1H1H2H	772H	(I)	KING'S ANTHEM, THE
1H1H2H	772H	(I)	GOD SAVE THE (KING/QUEEN)
1H1H2H7	1H653	(II)	PIRRIWIG, THE [AN FHIR GHRUAIG]
1H1H2H7	1H653	(I)	AN FHIR' GHRUAIG [A'PHIORBHUIC]
1H1H2H7	1H673	(I)	BASKET OF OYSTERS, THE
1H1H2H7	1H1H66	(I)	MERRY LADS OF BANFF, THE
1H1H2H7	1H1H2H1H	(I)	GIGG BY MR ARNE
1H1H2H7	2H2H2H4H	(I)	ST. HELENA
1H1H2H7	2H3H2H2H	(I)	EARL OF DALKEITH'S MARCH, THE
1H1H2H7	3H3H4H2H	(I)	CAPT MONTGOMERY'S FANCY
1H1H2H	1H31	(I)	COOLUN
1H1H2H	1H51	(I)	COOLUN
1H1H2H	1H55	(I)	BANKS OF ALLAN WATER
1H1H2H1H	51H2H4H	(II)	ABERLOUR'S SQUEEZE
1H1H2H1H	51H2H4H	(I)	ABERLOUR'S SQUEEZE
1H1H2H1H	1H1H2H1H	(I)	MRS GUTHRIE OF GUTHRIE CASTLE
1H1H2H1H	1H1H2H1H	(I)	STRABURG WALTZ, THE
1H1H2H1H	3H4H2H5H	(I)	LE PANTALON

1H1H2H2H	551H1H	(1)	I HAVE BEEN COURTING AT A LASS
1H1H2H2H	1H351H	(1)	MILITARY MOVEMENT
1H1H2H2H	1H653	(1)	FYE ON THE WARS
1H1H2H2H	1H653	(1)	DE'EL TAKE THE WAR
1H1H2H2H	1H664	(1)	DE'IL TAK' THE WAR(S)
1H1H2H2H	1H61H1H	(1)	ASLEYS RIDE
1H1H2H2H	1H1H2H1H	(1)	MRS PITTINDRIGH'S WALTZ
1H1H2H2H	1H1H2H2H	(11)	CIRCUS REEL
1H1H2H2H	1H3H6H6H	(1)	AULD LANGSYNE
1H1H2H	2H2H3H	(1)	MARTINI'S MINUET
1H1H2H2H	3bH555H	(1)	AN AIR BY BARON KILMANSECK
1H1H2H2H	3H61H7	(1)	ROBINSLAW
1H1H2H2H	3H1H75	(1)	MISS S. THOMAS
1H1H2H2H	3H1H1H2H	(1)	WESTMINSTER VOLUNTEERS MARCH
1H1H2H2H	3H1H1H5H	(1)	SOUTHWARK GRENADIER'S MARCH
1H1H2H2H	3H1H1H5H	(1)	FOURTH OF JULY, THE
1H1H2H2H	3H1H2H5	(1)	WOODPECKER'S MARCH
1H1H2H2H	3H1H2H5	(1)	CAPUCHIN, THE
1H1H2H2H	3H1H2H5	(1)	CAPE TRAFALGAR
1H1H2H2H	3H2H1H1H	(1)	BERWICK BEAUTY
1H1H2H2H	3H3H77	(1)	FLITCH OF BACON, THE
1H1H2H2H	3H3H2H7	(1)	SNUG PARTY, THE
1H1H2H2H	3H3H3H1H	(1)	RUSSIAN MARCH
1H1H2H2H	3H3H3H2H	(1)	COME NOW FOR JEST AND SMILING
1H1H2H2H	3H4H2H2	(11)	MISS MARY STEWART OF DERCULICH
1H1H2H2H	3H4H2H2	(1)	MISS STEWART DERCULLOCH'S REEL
1H1H2H2H	3H4H3H2H	(1)	TIMBER TOE
1H1H2H2H	3H5H1H1H	(1)	KISS MY LADY
1H1H2H2H	4H2H1H6	(1)	ALLEGRO
1H1H2H2H	4H3H72H	(1)	MRS SYME'S REEL
1H1H2H2H	5H3HO1H	(1)	MARCHES DES MARSEILLOIS
1H1H2H2H	5H4H72H	(1)	DANCED BY THE MISSES BOWER
1H1H2H2H	5H5H1H5	(1)	LORD CORNWALLIS'S MARCH
1H1H2H2H	5H5H1H1H	(1)	MARSEILLOIS HYMN, THE
1H1H2H	3H55	(1)	RAVING WINDS AROUND HER BLOWING
			[MACGREGOR A RUARO]
1H1H2H3H	1H1H67	(1)	FINALE, THE
1H1H2H3H	3H3H3H7	(1)	WINDMILL DANCE, THE
1H1H2H	3H3H6H	(11)	O GIN I WERE A BARON'S HEIR
1H1H2H	3H4H1H	(1)	MRS WILLm ELLIS OF LONDON'S MINUET
1H1H2H	3H4H2H	(1)	GRAY EY'D MORNING, THE
1H1H2H4H	3H2H4H6	(1)	KING SHALL ENJOY, THE
1H1H2H	5HO2H	(1)	MINUET DANCED BY THE MISSES BAXTER
1H1H2H5H	1H1H2H5	(1)	PAS SEUL
1H1H2H5H	1H1H2H5	(1)	LAURETTA
1H1H2H5H	1H1H2H5H	(1)	HAVE YOU HEARD OF THE TAX
1H1H2H5H	1H4H77	(1)	MUSETTE
1H1H2H5H	3H1H1H5	(1)	ABERDEEN BARRACKS, THE
1H1H3bH1H	7b4H2H7b	(1)	MISS HUNTER BLAIR'S SLOW JIG
1H1H3bH1H	1H555	(1)	MY ONLY JO AND DEARIE (O)
1H1H3bH1H	3bH1H3bH3bH	(1)	THA CEO MOR AIR MEALL A' MHUIRICH
1H1H3bH1H	3bH1H3bH3bH	(1)	LOW LIES THE MIST ON MALLAVURICH
1H1H3bH2H	7b554	(1)	JACKY TARR
1H1H3bH2H	7b2H4H3bH	(1)	OLD WOMAN IN THE GLEN, THE
1H1H3bH2H	7b2H4H3bH	(1)	BARBARA ALLAN
1H1H3bH2H	772H5	(11)	GABERLUNZIE, THE
1H1H3bH2H	1H6bH55	(1)	WINDING OF THE STREAM, THE
1H1H3bH2H	4H2H3bH3bH	(1)	QUOTH THE MASTER TO THE MAN
1H1H3bH2H	5H4H2H2H	(1)	POSIE, THE
1H1H3H3bH	2H7b2H4H	(1)	SALLY KELLY ('S REEL)
1H1H3bH3bH	5H3bH3bH1H	(1)	R. PETRIE'S LAMENT
			FOR THE LATE MR GARDEN OF TROUP
1H1H3bH	5H3bH1H	(1)	CHI MI BEAN SAN TRAIGH 'NA SUIDHE
1H1H3bH	5H5H5H	(1)	CHAGAIR, CHAGAIR, CHAGAIR A' GHRUAGACH
1H1H3bH	5H5H5H	(1)	SOFT, SOFT WHISPERED THE MAID
1H1H3H	113	(1)	SAE MERRY AS WE HAE BEEN
1H1H3H	156	(1)	MY APRON DEARIE
1H1H3H	543	(1)	SAE MERRY AS WE (TWA') HAE BEEN
1H1H3H	553	(1)	SO MERRY AS WE TWA' HAVE BEEN
1H1H3H	551H	(1)	MRS CUMING'S MINUET
1H1H3H6	5362	(1)	TYRIE RANT
1H1H3H6	5H3H6HO	(11)	LONG LIFE TO GOOD EARL FIFE
1H1H3H7	3H555	(1)	KATE OF ABERDEEN
1H1H3H	1H51	(1)	COOLUN
1H1H3H1H	5355	(1)	GLAD TRUMPET SOUNDS A VICTORY, THE
1H1H3H	1H55	(1)	BATTLE OF SHERIFF MOOR, THE
1H1H3H1H	557b6	(1)	BRISK
1H1H3H	1H56	(1)	MY APRON DEARIE
1H1H3H1H	51H42	(1)	MISS NIEL OF BARNWIEL'S REEL
1H1H3H	1H1H6	(1)	MISS BURNETT OF LEYS MINUET
1H1H3H1H	1H664	(1)	DEEL TAK THE WAR'S
1H1H3H1H	1H664	(1)	MARK YONDER POMP

1H1H3H1H	1H1H1H5	(I)	KING OF PRUSSIA'S HORNPIPE
1H1H3H	1H1H2H	(I)	SINGLE COMBAT
1H1H3H	1H1H2H	(I)	MISS AMELIA HUNTER'S SINGLE HORNPIPE
1H1H3H	1H1H3H	(I)	HIGHLAND LAMENTATION, THE
1H1H3H1H	2H4H72H	(I)	HONble MISS ELPHINSTON'S STRATHSPEY
1H1H3H	1H3H1H	(I)	FAIRLY SHOT ON HER
1H1H3H	1H3H5H	(I)	MISS PRINGL'S MINUET
1H1H3H1H	4H2H77	(I)	SANDWICH, THE
1H1H3H2H	772H5	(II)	CORN RIGGS [CORN RIGS]
1H1H3H2H	772H5	(I)	CORN RIGGS (ARE BONNY)
1H1H3H2H	772H2H	(I)	CORN RIGGS (ARE BONNIE)
1H1H3H2H	1HOO1H	(I)	DUETTO
1H1H3H2H	1H565	(I)	OVERTURE TO THE DESERTER
1H1H3H	2H1H6	(I)	MISS DRUMMOND FORBES'S MINUET
1H1H3H2H	1H664	(I)	DE'EL TAK THE WAR
1H1H3H2H	1H667	(I)	DUNDEE LASSIE
1H1H3H2H	1H672H	(I)	BONNY WIDOW OF WIGTON, THE
1H1H3H2H	1H1H1H5	(I)	GAVOTTA
1H1H3H2H	1H2H1HO	(I)	AU CLAIR DE LA LUNE
1H1H3H2H	2H551H	(I)	MARCH OF THE 22nd REGt
1H1H3H	2H2H7	(I)	PADDY O CONNER
1H1H3H2H	2H2H4H3H	(I)	LORD FALCONBERG'S MARCH
1H1H3H2H	2H2H4H3H	(I)	MARCH, A
1H1H3H2H	3H3H51H	(II)	ARGYLE IS MY NAME
1H1H3H2H	3H5H5H5H	(I)	BONNY GRAY EY'D MORN, THE [OLD GRAY EY'D MORN, THE]
1H1H3H2H	4H4H4H3H	(I)	BUFFOON DANCE, THE
1H1H3H2H	5H3H1H1H	(II)	BRITISH GRENADIERS, THE
1H1H3H2H	5H3H1H1H	(I)	BRITISH GRENADIERS MARCH, THE
1H1H3H3H	1H1H2H2H	(I)	MRS MCLEOD OF TALISCAR'S REEL
1H1H3H3H	1H1H3H3	(I)	WHA'LL BE KING BUT CHARLIE
1H1H3H3H	1H1H3H5	(II)	WHA'LL BE KING BUT CHARLIE
1H1H3H3H	1H1H3H5	(I)	WHA'LL BE KING BUT CHARLIE
1H1H3H3H	1H3H5H5	(I)	STEER HER UP AND HAD HER GAUN
1H1H3H3H	2H1H55	(I)	ANNA
1H1H3H3H	2H1H55	(I)	IRISH AIR, AN
1H1H3H3H	2H1H55	(I)	BANKS OF BANNA, (THE)
1H1H3H	3H2H2H	(I)	MISS BOWLS'S MINUET
1H1H3H3H	2H2H1H1H	(I)	ALLEMANDE
1H1H3H3H	2H2H4H4H	(I)	QUICK STEP
1H1H3H3H	3H2H2H2H	(I)	FRESH AND STRONG THE BREEZE, & C.
1H1H3H3H	4H2H66	(I)	NEW SCOTCH AIR, A (or MRS NEIL FERGUISON'S DELIGHT)
1H1H3H3H	5H3H1H1H	(I)	KISS MY LADY
1H1H3H3H	5H4H1H1H	(I)	ROSE, THE
1H1H3H3H	5H4H3H2H	(I)	COLDSTREAM MARCH, THE
1H1H3H3H	5H4H3H2H	(I)	GRAND FRENCH MARCH
1H1H3H3H	5H5H3H1H	(I)	BLUE RIBBON, THE
1H1H3H3H	5H5H4H7	(I)	HIGH DANCE
1H1H3H3H	5H6H71H	(I)	BATH WALTZ
1H1H3H4H	71HO1H	(I)	JACK RATLIN
1H1H3H4H	3H1H1H1H	(I)	ADIEU MY NATIVE LAND ADIEU
1H1H3H4H	5H6H4H4H	(I)	GARDNER WI' HIS PAIDLE, THE
1H1H3H4H	5H1T5H5H	(I)	DUKE OF BRUNSWICK'S MARCH
1H1H3H5H	1H1H2H5	(II)	HOUSE OF ACHLUNCART, THE
1H1H3H5H	1H1H2H5	(I)	HOUSE OF ACHLUNCART, THE
1H1H3H5H	4H2H72H	(II)	LADY CHARLOTTE CAMPBELL
1H1H3H5H	4H2H72H	(I)	LADY CHARLOTTE CAMPBELL'S REEL
1H1H3H5H	4H3H2H2H	(I)	MR WILLm FORDYCE'S STRATHSPEY
1H1H3H	5H5H3H	(II)	MY HEART IS SAIR
1H1H3H5H	5H2H62H	(II)	MRS CHREE
1H1H3H	5H5H1T	(I)	MISS HONYMAN OF ARMADALE'S MINUET
1H1H3H5H	1T5H2H2H	(I)	TAST, THE
1H1H4H7	1H1H5H4H	(I)	HODDOM CASTLE
1H1H4H1H	1H1H57b	(I)	QUICK STEP 10th REGt
1H1H4H1H	1H1H5H5H	(I)	CAMP, THE
1H1H4H1H	1H1H5H5H	(I)	TOUCHSTONE, THE
1H1H4H1H	3H5H2H2H	(I)	COL. GRAHAM'S FAVORITE
1H1H4H2H	751H1H	(I)	MISS CARMICHAEL'S JIG
1H1H4H2H	772H2H	(I)	CORN RIGGS ARE BONNY
1H1H4H2H	72H55	(I)	BEGGAR'S DANCE, THE
1H1H4H2H	3H1H2H5	(I)	TO M. HEINEL
1H1H4H2H	5H4H2HO	(I)	WINTER
1H1H4H4H	2H755	(I)	BATTLE OF SALAMANCA, THE
1H1H4H4H	5H2H1H1H	(I)	GLOUCESTER HOUSE
1H1H4H5H	1H2H4H1H	(I)	LORD DUNMORE'S QUICK STEP
1H1H4H6H	5H4H72H	(I)	LA VISITE
1H1H5H7	1H1H5H7	(I)	REGENTS BRIDGE, THE
1H1H5H1H	2H2H2H7	(I)	NANCY DAWSON
1H1H5H1H	2H2H4H7	(I)	MISS SPIERS'S JIGG
1H1H5H1H	4H2H77	(I)	MR LAUDER'S STRATHSPEY
1H1H5H2H	531H3H	(I)	BY THE DELICIOUS WARMNESS OF THY MOUTH

1H1H5H2H	1H2H71H	(I)	WALTZE
1H1H5H2H	3H2H2H5	(I)	SUL MARGINE D'UN RIO
1H1H5H2H	3H2H2H1H	(I)	SUL MARGINE DUN RIO
1H1H5H2H	3H5H1H7	(I)	MA CHERE AMIE
1H1H5H2H	1T5H1H1H	(I)	WALTZ OF LEIPSIC
1H1H5H	3H2H1H	(I)	MISS ERSKINE'S MINUET
1H1H5H3H	2H2H1H5H	(I)	MISS ABERCROMBY OF TULLIBODY'S ALLAMANDE
1H1H5H3H	2H2H3H1H	(I)	CELEBRATED HUNTERS' CHORUS, THE
1H1H5H3H	4H675	(I)	BELLEROPHON, THE
1H1H5H5H	562H1H	(I)	MADAM HEINEL
1H1H5H5H	1H1H2H5	(I)	TIMES A TELL TALE
1H1H5H5H	1H3bH75H	(I)	DANCED BY MISS MILLER
1H1H5H5H	1H3H61H	(I)	LEGACY, THE
1H1H5H5H	2H2H2H7	(I)	MEDLEY COTTILION
1H1H5H5H	2H4H1H6	(I)	HONble RAMSEY MAULE'S MARCH
1H1H5H5H	3H1H2H2H	(I)	PRINCE REGENT, THE
1H1H5H5H	3H1H2H2H	(I)	LA MARESCHAL
1H1H5H5H	4H3H72H	(I)	ANDERSON'S MUSIC SHOP
1H1H5H5H	1T7H5H5H	(I)	ALLEGRO
1H1H5H	6H4H2H	(I)	DEVIL'S HOP, THE
1H1H5H	6H4H2H	(I)	IRISH HOP, THE
1H1H5H6H	4H2H75	(I)	MISS ABERCROMBY'S REEL
1H1H6HO	5H1H2HO	(I)	MY LODGING IS ON THE COLD GROUND
1H1H1T1T	6H5H3H3H	(I)	SUMMER APPROACHES, THE
1H2HO	1H2HO	(I)	MAC DHONAILL MOR NAN EILLAN
			[MAC DHOMHNUILL MOR NAN EILEAN]
1H2HO	3bH2HO	(I)	THA TAIRM ANNS A' GHLEANN
1H2H35	457L2	(I)	GIG
1H2H45	1H67L1	(I)	WALTZ
1H2H52	23H1H5	(I)	LUNDIE'S DREAM
1H2H53	1H2H3H4H	(I)	GAVOTTA
1H2H54	452H2H	(II)	TOM DOUGLAS
1H2H55	1142	(II)	CALVER LODGE
1H2H55	1152	(I)	CALVER LODGE
1H2H55	661H1H	(I)	MRS GORDON OF ABERDOUR'S STRATHSPEY
1H2H55	1H1H4H2H	(II)	MACGREGOR'S MARCH
1H2H55	1H1H4H2H	(I)	McGREGOR'S GATHERING, (THE)
1H2H55	1H2H55	(I)	STRUAGH NACH'EIL BODAICH (AN DOMHAIN)
1H2H51H	3H71H1H	(I)	LA COMTESSE DU NORD
1H2H53H	64H1H6	(I)	LORD NELSON'S VICTORY
1H2H54H	5H5H2H1H	(I)	COTILLON
1H2H62	351H2H	(I)	HEY TO THE CAMP
1H2H62	31H3H2H	(I)	HEY TO THE CAMP [HAY TO THE CAMP]
1H2H65	2467L	(I)	COTTILION
1H2H65	362H7	(I)	TRIP TO PLYMOUTH
1H2H65	457L2	(I)	TEA ROOM, THE
1H2H65	4541	(II)	MRS DUNDAS OF ARNISTON
1H2H6	653	(II)	MO RUN BHAN DHILEAS
1H2H67	457L2	(I)	ALLEGRO
1H2H61H	4525L	(I)	BREST FLEET, THE
1H2H61H	1H3H2H5	(I)	NORTHAMPTON FROLICK
1H2H62H	1H2H61H	(I)	BANNERS CROSS
1H2H7b5	527bL4	(I)	LORD GARLIES REEL
1H2H75	31H26	(I)	BONNY BETTY
1H2H75	651H1H	(I)	LE BAGATELLE
1H2H78	328L8L	(I)	JACK'S DELIGIIT
1H2H76	61H64	(I)	WINTER IS PAST
1H2H7	71H6	(I)	THERE ARE FEW GOOD FELLOWS
			WHEN JAMIE'S AWA'
1H2H71H	2H3H1H2H	(I)	GENI. CARLETON'S QUICK MARCH
1H2H71H	3H4H2H3H	(I)	COTILLON
1H2H1HO	1H63H2H	(I)	SINCE THEN I'M DOOM'D
1H2H1H3b	17b42	(II)	MISS NAPIER OF MERCHISTON HALL
1H2H1H3b	1H7b42	(I)	MISS NAPIER OF MERCHISTON HALL('S REEL)
1H2H1H3	5553H	(I)	RED JOCK, THE
1H2H1H3	3H4H3H5	(I)	LA ROYAL LOVERIE GAVOT
1H2H1H4	2675	(I)	MISS HAMMERSLY'S FANCY
1H2H1H4	4542	(I)	LIVERPOOL PRIZE
1H2H1H5	3433	(I)	TACK AND TACK
1H2H1H5	3452	(I)	HEY TO RUCKHOLT
1H2H1H5	31H2H2	(I)	HIGHLAND BONNET, THE
1H2H1H5	4525L	(I)	MISS WILLIAMSON OF OLDFIELD'S JIGG
1H2H1H5	4522	(II)	GLASSA HOUSE
1H2H1H5	4522	(I)	GLASSA HOUSE
1H2H1H5	4522	(I)	RECRUITING OFFICER, THE
1H2H1H5	454H2H	(I)	LADY CUNNINGHAM OF LIVINGSTON'S FAVORITE
1H2H1H5	661H2H	(I)	MRS ARNOT'S REEL
1H2H1H5	61H63	(I)	LORD ISLE'S SALUTATION
1H2H1H5	7b422	(II)	MISS BISSET, LOGIERAIT
1H2H1H5	7b422	(I)	MISS BISSET LOGIERAIT'S REEL
1H2H1H5	7b7b27bL	(I)	SAILORS RETURN
1H2H1H5	7531H	(I)	SEA QUADRILLE, THE

```
1H2H1H6b    53b7L5L     (I)   NEW ROAD TO BRECHIN CASTLE, THE
1H2H1H6     5642        (I)   JOHN MENZIES, ESQr OF CHESTHILL'S
                              STRATHSPEY
1H2H1H6     6753        (I)   MR PETER McLEAN'S HORNPIPE
1H2H1H7     1H2H1H7     (II)  YANKEE DOODLE
1H2H1H7     1H2H1H7     (I)   YANKEE DOODLE
1H2H1H1H    3622        (I)   MISS T. WILSON
1H2H1H1H    661H5       (I)   ON DIT QU IA QUINZE ANS
1H2H1H1H    661H5       (I)   LA LUCILLE
1H2H1H1H    661H2H      (I)   ROSINA
1H2H1H1H    661H2H      (I)   ALLEGRO
1H2H1H1H    4H3H2H2H    (I)   FASHIONABLE LEVITIES
1H2H1H1H    5H4H3H7     (I)   DUKE OF GORDON'S FANCY, THE
1H2H1H2H    63H5H1H     (I)   HIT OR MISS
1H2H1H2H    1H2H1H7     (I)   YANKIE DOODLE
1H2H1H2H    1H2H1H1H    (I)   YANKE DOODLE
1H2H1H2H    1H2H3H4H    (I)   PRINCE OF WALES'S (OR 13th Regt) MARCH
1H2H1H2H    1H2H3H4H    (I)   CALEDONIAN BEAUTY, THE
1H2H1H4H    1H2H1H1H    (I)   QUICK STEP 71st REGt
1H2H1H5H    1H2H1H5H    (I)   NIGHTINGALE, THE
1H2H2H5     1H664       (I)   BLUE BONNETS
1H2H2H6     6752        (I)   WHAT'S THAT TO YOU
1H2H2H7     5556        (II)  MACGREGOR'S GATHERING
1H2H2H1H    6522        (I)   SCOON HOUSE
1H2H2H2H    55H3H1H     (I)   BIRD CATCHER, THE
1H2H2H3H    362H3H      (I)   MINUET
1H2H2H3H    5H5H5H1H    (I)   MISS BLACK'S WALTZ
1H2H3bH2H   1H2H75      (I)   BIRTH NIGHT, THE
1H2H3HO     3H4H2HO     (I)   FAVOURITE AIR BY MR BASTIN, A
1H2H3HO     5H4H3HO     (I)   BEGONE DULL CARE
1H2H3H7     5353        (I)   MISS ROSS'S JIG
1H2H3H7     6543        (I)   PHILOSOPHER'S JIGG, THE
1H2H3H7     1H2H3H2H    (I)   HEY DING A DING
1H2H3H1H    5531        (I)   COTTILLION 4th
1H2H3H1H    661H1H      (I)   EMPEROR OF RUSSIA'S WALTZ, THE
1H2H3H1H    62H75       (I)   MISS DE VISMES DELIGHT
1H2H3H1H    62H75       (I)   FINALE IN INKLE AND YARICO
1H2H3H      1H1H5       (I)   HORNPIPE BY MR FESTING
1H2H3H1H    2H61H1H     (I)   WILL WITH A WISP
1H2H3H1H    2H3H1H5     (I)   ROXBURGH HOUSE
1H2H3H1H    4H2H75      (I)   MISS (C.) LITTLE'S FANCY
1H2H3H2H    7662H       (I)   KING'S JIG, THE
1H2H3H2H    1HO1H2H     (I)   O PESCATOR
1H2H3H2H    1H2H1H7     (I)   GERMAN WALTZ
1H2H3H2H    1H2H3H1H    (I)   NEW CASTLE TROOP
1H2H3H2H    1H2H3H1H    (I)   MISS LIDDEL'S GERMAN VALTZ
1H2H3H2H    1H2H3H2H    (I)   HAY MAKERS, THE
1H2H3H2H    3H1H52H     (I)   YE BANKS AND BRAES (O' BONNIE DOON)
1H2H3H2H    3H1H52H     (I)   CALEDONIAN HUNT'S DELIGHT
1H2H3H3H    3H3H5H5H    (I)   FLOWER GARDEN
1H2H3H3H    5H4H3H3H    (I)   BEGONE DULL CARE
1H2H3H3H    5H5H3H2H    (I)   BEGONE DULL CARE
1H2H3H4H    5H3H1H5H    (I)   TRIP TO PORTSMOUTH, A
1H2H3bH4H   5H4H2H3bH   (I)   VAN ROTTERDAM OP DORT
1H2H3H5H    1H2H50      (I)   WELCH AIR, A
1H2H3H5H    2H755       (I)   RIGADOON BY PHILPOT
1H2H3H5H    3H2H1H1     (I)   LARGO ANDANTE
1H2H3H5H    3H2H1H3     (I)   WILKESS RELEASE
1H2H3H5H    3H6H2H2H    (I)   COTTILON
1H2H3H5H    4H2H75      (I)   VALLENCIENNES MARCH
1H2H3H5H    4H3H2H5     (I)   HUNGARIAN MARCH, THE
1H2H3H5H    4H3H2H1H    (I)   MILK MAID, THE
1H2H3H5H    4H4H1H1     (I)   MARCH IN MONTEZUMA
1H2H3H6H    5H4H5H1H    (I)   WALTZ DANCED BY THE MISSES HUNTER
1H2H4H7     1H2H1H5     (I)   JOHN OCHILTREE
1H2H4H4H    72H2H1H     (I)   WITH VERDURE CLAD
1H2H5H2H    5H1H2H7     (I)   MR N. DUFF'S DOUBLE JIGG
1H2H5H3H    1H2H5HO     (I)   QUICK STEP
1H2H5H      4H6H5H      (I)   GO WHERE GLORY WAITS THEE
1H2H6H2H    3H3H3H1H    (I)   ROCK AND A WEE PICKLE TOW
1H2H1T7H    6H61H2H     (I)   WILL YE GO TO THE EWE BUGHTS MARION
1H3bH55L    7bL247b     (I)   MR REINAGLE'S FAVORITE
1H3bH55     7b7b2H4H    (I)   DRUMER, THE [DRUMMER, THE]
1H3bH7b5    6b47b5      (II)  BIG KIRSTY
1H3bH7b5    6b47b5      (II)  A' THE WAY TO GALLOWAY
1H3bH7b5    6b47b5      (II)  CIORSDAN MHOR
1H3bH7b5    6b47b5      (I)   GALLAWAY GIRLS
1H3bH7b5    7b542       (II)  MRS DRUMMOND OF LOGIEALMOND
1H3bH75     7b43b5      (II)  LADY WALLACE
1H3bH75     7b542       (II)  MRS DRUMMOND OF LOGIEALMOND
1H3bH75     7b542       (I)   MRS DRUMMOND OF LOGIEALMONDS REEL
1H3bH1H1    3b3b20      (I)   MAIREAR(A)D NIGHEAN DHOMHNUILL
```

1H3bH1H5	7b542	(II)	MRS MACPHERSON GIBSTON
1H3bH1H5	7b542	(I)	MRS McPHERSON'S REEL
1H3bH1H5	7b7b47bL	(I)	DRUNKEN FRIDAY
1H3bH1H5	7b2H7b4	(II)	ROBERT RUSSELL ESQ. OF PILMUIR'S REEL
1H3bH1H5	3bH4H5H5	(I)	AN DILEACDHAN [AN DILLEACHDAN]
1H3bH1H7b	27b2H7b	(II)	MISS CHARTERS
1H3bH1H7b	47b2H7b	(II)	MISS CHARTERS
1H3bH1H7b	47b2H7b	(I)	HON(oura)ble MISS CHARTERIS' REEL, THE
1H3bH1H7b	47b2H7b	(I)	CAPT CUNNINGHAM OF AUCHINSKEIGH'S REEL
1H3bH2H5	1H2H7b5	(I)	BONNY CASTLE GORDON
1H3bH2H5	1H2H7b5	(I)	MORAG
1H3bH2H5	1H3bH5H1H	(I)	GRAMACHREE IS A SUP OF GOOD DRINK
1H3bH2H7b	47b2H7b	(II)	HIGH UP THE GLEN
1H3bH2H7b	47b2H7b	(I)	MRS Wm ELLICE'S REEL
1H3bH2H7	1H2H7b6b	(I)	MORAG
1H3bH2H1H	5427bL	(II)	HONbLE. JOHN LESLIE MELVILLE
1H3bH2H1H	5427bL	(I)	HONble JOHN LESSLIE MELVILLE('S STRATHSPEY, THE)
1H3bH2H1H	6b57L2	(I)	LADY CATHERINE PELHAMS REEL
1H3bH2H4H	1H3bH5H5H	(I)	MARCHIONESS OF HUNTLY'S FAVORITE JIG
1H3bH2H5H	4H3bH2H5H	(I)	LORD MOIRA'S MARCH
1H3bH3bH	7b1H3b	(I)	GUR TROM LEAM MO CHEUM
1H3bH3bH1H	7bH7b2H7b	(II)	REEL, A
1H3bH3bH5H	2H7b2H4H	(I)	LADY EGLINTON'S REEL
1H3bH4H7b	13bH2H1H	(II)	JOHNNY LAD
1H3bH4H7b	1H3bH2H1H	(I)	JOHNNY LAD
1H3bH4H2H	1H3bH7b5	(I)	NONE SO PRETTY
1H3bH4H2H	1H3bH7b5	(I)	WHAT SHOU'D A LASSIE DO WI' AN AULD MAN
1H3bH5H5H	6bH5H5H5H	(I)	HUZZA
1H3H13	1H3H62H	(I)	MRS McINNES STRATHSPEY
1H3H51	1H3H2H3H	(II)	PRETTY PEG [PRETTY PEGG] [PRETTY PEGGY]
1H3H51	1H3H2H3H	(I)	PRETTY PEG(G) [PRETTY PEGGY]
1H3H51	1H3H2H3H	(I)	MISS FLEMYNG'S REEL
1H3H52	22H4H3H	(I)	MISS TROTTERS REEL
1H3H52	1H3H2H3H	(I)	PRETTY PEGGY
1H3H53	1243	(I)	NOTTINGHAM CASTLE
1H3H53	22H2H2	(I)	NORTH BRIDGE, THE
1H3H53	4642	(I)	COLONEL MCLEOD OF RASA'S REEL
1H3H53	462H6	(II)	MOY HALL
1H3H53	462H6	(I)	'MHOIDH
1H3H53	1H3H52	(I)	CHASE, THE
1H3H53	1H3H72H	(I)	FORFAR BEEF STEAK CLUB, THE
1H3H53	1H5H52	(I)	ROYAL GLASGOW VOLUNTEERS, THE
1H3H53	4H2H75	(I)	MRS CROMBIE'S REEL
1H3H54	4111	(I)	MISS COCKBOURNE'S ALLEMAND
1H3H54	61H76	(II)	TALISKER
1H3H55	24H54	(I)	CACHOCHA DANCE, THE
1H3H55	4627L	(I)	W. ROBISON, ESQr's HORNPIPE
1H3H55	44H2H2H	(II)	LADY CHARLOTT[E] MURRAY
1H3H55	44H2H2H	(I)	LADY CHARLOTTE MURRAY'S REEL
1H3H55	61H53	(I)	MISS MURRAY OF AUCHTERTYRE'S FAVORITE
1H3H55	1H5H2H2H	(II)	BONNETS O' BLUE
1H3H55	1H5H2H2H	(I)	HURRAH! FOR THE BONNETS OF BLUE
1H3H51H	3512	(I)	WOODHILL
1H3H51H	62H72H	(II)	BRIDGE OF YARE, THE
1H3H53H	4327L	(II)	ISLAND OF JAVA
1H3H53H	4327L	(II)	MRS L. STEWART OF THE ISLAND OF JAVA
1H3H53H	4327L	(I)	LORD GEORGE GORDON'S REEL
1H3H53H	4327L	(I)	MRS L. STEWART'S REEL
1H3H53H	4327L	(I)	MARCHIONESS OF WORCESTER'S FAVORITE, THE
1H3H53H	2H3H65	(II)	BLACK BUT COMELY
1H3H53H	2H3H65	(I)	BONNY BLACK LADIE
1H3H53H	2H3H66	(II)	BLACK BUT COMELY
1H3H53H	2H3H1H6	(II)	EARL OF DALHOUSIE
1H3H53H	2H3H1H6	(II)	LORD DALHOUSIE
1H3H53H	2H3H1H6	(I)	EARL OF DALHOUSIES REEL
1H3H53H	2H4H54H	(I)	BANFF LASSES
1H3H54H	3H5H14H	(I)	MISS LAWDER
1H3H54H	3H5H14H	(I)	MAGGIE LAUDER
1H3H62	1153	(II)	BREEM DOG, THE
1H3H65	2632	(I)	MISS CHARLOTTE TOLL'S STRATHSPEY
1H3H65	31H2H2H	(II)	BONNIE CHARLIE
1H3H65	33H67	(I)	MRS CAMPBELL'S REEL
1H3H6	551H	(I)	AIR BY FINGAL
1H3H65	652H2H	(II)	LADY CARMICHAEL
1H3H65	652H2H	(I)	LADY CARMICHAEL (OF CASTLECRAIG'S STRATHSPEY)
1H3H65	5H4H2H2H	(I)	FAVORITE ARIETTA
1H3H66	5H2H2H2H	(I)	QUICK STEP
1H3H67	1H36L7L	(I)	MARQUIS OF HUNTLY'S REEL, THE
1H3H61H	521H1H	(I)	TO THE GREENWOOD GANG WI' ME
1H3H61H	5311	(I)	COTILLON

1H3H61H	5452	(I)	MISS VICKOR'S DELIGHT
1H3H61H	5531	(II)	INVERARAY CROSS
1H3H61H	5531	(II)	GEORDIE JACK
1H3H62H	761H3	(II)	GLEN OGLE
1H3H62H	761H3	(I)	MRS JOHNSTON'S REEL
1H3H62H	71H53H	(I)	LA CI DAREM LA MANO
1H3H62H	1H3H64H	(I)	MISS BELFIELD'S STRATHSPEY
1H3H62H	1H3H4H3H	(I)	CURE FOR THE GOUT, A
1H3H64H	4H1H1H1H	(I)	MISS CORBET'S FANCY
1H3H75	31H3H2H	(I)	GAVOTTA
1H3H75	6231	(I)	BELLES OF WALTHAMSTOW, THE
1H3H75	6651	(I)	WHITE JOAK, THE
1H3H75	61H52	(I)	SOLDIER MAC
1H3H75	1H3H2H7	(II)	DUNKELD BRIDGE
1H3H75	1H3H2H7	(I)	DUNKELD BRIDGE
1H3H75	1H3H3H3H	(I)	MISS SCOT'S REEL
1H3H75	1H3H4H2H	(II)	MRS YOUNG OF CORNHILLS
1H3H76	5327	(II)	SIR DAVID DAVIDSON OF CANTRAY
1H3H76	5367	(II)	SIR DAVID DAVIDSON OF CANTRAY
1H3H76	3H2H1H1	(I)	MY HEART WITH LOVE IS BEATING
1H3H77	1H3H1H7	(I)	VEDRAI CARINO
1H3H77	1H3H3H3H	(I)	PLATE RANT, THE
1H3H7	1H65	(I)	PEGGY BAWN
1H3H71H	1H3H71H	(I)	COBURG WALTZ
1H3H72H	6753	(I)	BURNTWOOD ASSEMBLY
1H3H72H	1H3H4H7	(II)	BRIG O' FEUGH
1H3H72H	1H3H4H6H	(I)	LADY MENZIES OF CASTLE MENZIES
1H3H72H	3H62H7	(I)	MISS ADAMS'S REEL
1H3H72H	3H2H75	(I)	HUNTLY LODGE
1H3H72H	4H71H1H	(I)	BATCHELOR'S HALL
1H3H72H	1T3H3H2H	(I)	TRUE SPORTSMAN, THE
1H3H74H	3H71H3	(I)	MARGATE HUNT
1H3H74H	3H71H3	(I)	LA MARQUISE
1H3H74H	3H4H72H	(I)	MEILLIONEN O FERIONY'DD
1H3H1H3	6547L	(II)	MISS LAURA ANDREW
1H3H1H3	1H2H2H2	(II)	BEN NEWE
1H3H1H3	1H3H2H2	(II)	MISS KATTY MAXWELL'S REEL
1H3H1H3	1H3H2H2	(I)	MISS KATTY MAXWELL'S REEL
1H3H1H3	3H5H3H5	(I)	ROYAL PAIR, THE
1H3H1H5	11H2H2	(I)	(MISS) GRAHAM (OF INCHBRACKIE)
			('S STRATHSPEY)
1H3H1H5	11H2H2	(I)	MRS GEORGE BUCHANAN'S STRATHSPEY
1H3H1H5	11H2H2H	(I)	MISS BALFOUR WHITEHILL'S REEL
1H3H1H5	226L5	(I)	FAREWELL MY PRETTY WITTY PEGGY
1H3H1H5	2326L	(I)	SIR JOHN CATHCART'S REEL
1H3H1H5	31H2H5	(I)	MAJOR JAs CAMPBELL'S QUICKSTEP W.F.R.
1H3H1H5	4322	(I)	SALAMANCA
1H3H1H5	4642	(II)	BRODIE HOUSE
1H3H1H5	4642	(I)	BRODIE HOUSE
1H3H1H5	51H62	(II)	MRS MCLEOD OF ELANREOCH
1H3H1H5	6522	(II)	MY WIFE'S A WANTON WEE THING
1H3H1H5	6541	(I)	CABERFEIGH
1H3H1H5	6651	(I)	WHITE JOCK
1H3H1H5	662H2H	(II)	LORD MACDONALD
1H3H1H5	662H2H	(I)	MISS FINCH'S REEL, THE
1H3H1H5	662H2H	(I)	LORD MACDONALD'S REEL
1H3H1H5	662H2H	(I)	MISS BETTY PLUMMER'S REEL
1H3H1H5	662H2H	(I)	LORD FINLATER'S REEL
1H3H1H5	61H62	(II)	MRS MACLEOD OF ELLANREOCH
1H3H1H5	61H62	(I)	MRS McLEOD OF ELANREOCH('S STRATHSPEY)
1H3H1H5	64H3H7	(I)	COUNTESS OF LOUDON'S REEL
1H3H1H5	7b7b47bL	(I)	DRUNKEN FRIDAY
1H3H1H	51H3	(I)	LADY LOUISA ANN DOUGLAS, A MEDLEY WALTZ
1H3H1H5	1H531	(II)	CABER FEIGH [CABAR FEIDH]
1H3H1H5	1H531	(I)	CAPER FEY
1H3H1H5	1H3H2H2	(I)	MR DUFF (OF FETTERESSO'S) BIRTHDAY
1H3H1H5	1H3H2H2H	(II)	BANFF BAILLIES, THE
1H3H1H5	1H3H4H2H	(I)	GORDON BANK HOUSE
1H3H1H5	2H4H2H6	(II)	DOUN THE BURNIE
1H3H1H5	4H5H2H2H	(I)	MISS BRUCE'S STRATHSPEY
1H3H1H6	3522	(II)	THROUGH THE MUIR SHE RAN
1H3H1H6	4542	(I)	MISS LUMSDANE'S STRATHSPEY
1H3H1H6	4622H	(I)	MISS BARINGTON'S FANCY
1H3H1H6	41H22	(I)	HIGHLAND REEL, A
1H3H1H6	5122	(II)	HOUSE OF DRUMMUIR, THE
1H3H1H6	5155	(II)	GOAT FELL
1H3H1H6	5322	(II)	THRO' THE WOOD SHE RAN
1H3H1H6	5522	(II)	THROUGH THE WOOD SHE RAN
1H3H1H6	5522	(I)	THRO' THE (WOOD/MOOR) SHE RAN
1H3H1H6	5542	(I)	MY NANNIE O!
1H3H1H6	5622H	(I)	MAJOR LOGAN'S FAVORITE
1H3H1H6	5622H	(I)	LADY HARRIOT MONTAGUE'S FAVORITE

```
1H3H1H6    51H22      (II)  LORD GLENORCHY
1H3H1H6    51H22      (I)   LORD GLENORCHA'S STRATHSPEY
                            [LORD GLENORCHY]
1H3H1H6    51H3H2H    (I)   MR FORTATH'S REEL
1H3H1H6    652H2H     (II)  CRAIGENROAN
1H3H1H6    61H64      (I)   MR ALEXANDER LAING'S HORNPIPE
1H3H1H6    1H631      (I)   AN JORRAM
1H3H1H6    1H3H66     (I)   MR REID OF ELGIN ACADEMY'S STRATHSPEY
1H3H1H6    1H3H1H6    (I)   SIR ALEXr DON'S MEDLEY (REEL)
1H3H1H6    1H3H5H2H   (I)   GALLAWAY TOM
1H3H1H7    51H62      (II)  MRS MACLEOD OF ELLANREACH
1H3H1H7    2H4H2H1H   (I)   TRIP TO WESTON, A
1H3H1H1H   2262       (I)   MISS STORY'S FAVOURITE
1H3H1H1H   2265       (I)   I WISH MY LOVE WAS IN A MIRE
1H3H1H1H   2266       (I)   BLEST AS TH'IMMORTAL GODS
1H3H1H     1H53       (I)   NEW TRUMPET MINUET
1H3H1H1H   5531       (I)   DINNA THINK BONNIE LASSIE
                            I'M GAUN TO LEAVE YOU
1H3H1H1H   51H22      (I)   McNEIL'S MAGGOT
1H3H1H1H   51H65      (I)   CHAIDH MI LA DO'N BHADTRAILEACH
1H3H1H1H   62H76      (I)   FAVORITE DANCE, A
1H3H1H     1H1H5      (I)   THA MO DHAOINE FLUICH FUAR,
                            THA MO GHRADH AIR A' CHUAN
1H3H1H1H   1H72H2H    (I)   CRAFTS MAN, THE
1H3H1H2H   631H6      (I)   CARPET WEAVER, THE
1H3H1H2H   1H3H6H1T   (I)   LEWIE GORDON
1H3H1H3H   5772H      (I)   BRANDER, THE
1H3H1H3H   72H4H2H    (I)   GLORIOUS FIRST OF AUGUST, THE
1H3H1H3H   1H665      (I)   O'ER THE HILLS AND FAR AWAY
1H3H1H3H   1H1H55     (II)  HOME BOYS HOME
1H3H1H3H   1H3H1H6    (I)   GO TO THE DEVIL AND SHAKE YOURSELF
1H3H1H3H   1H3H1H3H   (I)   CIRCASSIAN CIRCLE
1H3H1H3H   1H3H2H6    (II)  MISS DAVIDSON
1H3H1H3H   1H3H2H6    (I)   MISS DAVIDSON'S REEL
1H3H1H3H   1H3H2H2H   (I)   THERE WAS A MAID & SHE WENT TO THE MILL
1H3H1H3H   2H675      (I)   BLACK BEARD
1H3H1H3H   2H2H53     (I)   BRIDESMAIDS' CHORUS, THE
1H3H1H3H   4H3H4H5    (I)   LADY AUGUSTA'S DELIGHT
1H3H1H3H   5H2H5H2H   (I)   MAJOR CRICHTON'S DELIGHT
1H3H1H4H   5H2H75     (I)   CAMPBELL'S ALLEMANDE
1H3H1H5H   1H550      (I)   SIR JAMES St CLAIR'S MARCH
1H3H2HO    3H61HO     (I)   PHILLIS' COMPLAINT
1H3H2H1    1H3H2H3H   (II)  SPORTING PEGGY
1H3H2H     544        (I)   WILLIE'S RARE AND WILLIE'S FAIR
1H3H2H     555        (I)   MY LOVE ALASS IS DEAD AND GONE
1H3H2H5    6767       (I)   WIDOW WAD MAN, THE
1H3H2H5    671H5H     (I)   LADY TOWNSEND'S WHIM
1H3H2H5    61H51      (II)  LESLIE
1H3H2H5    61H51      (I)   MISS ANNIE LIVINGSTON'S REEL
1H3H2H5    61H51      (I)   MISS LESLIE OF St ANDREWS REEL
1H3H2H5    61H51      (I)   CHAPLE SHADE HOUSE
1H3H2H5    1H532      (I)   MISS CLARK'S DOUBLE JIGG
1H3H2H6    2427bL     (I)   MR RIEDHEAD'S REEL
1H3H2H     644        (I)   WILLY'S RARE( AND WILLY'S FAIR)
1H3H2H6    5361H      (I)   RETREAT
1H3H2H6    54H2H2     (I)   MARQUIS OF HUNTLY'S BIRTHDAY
1H3H2H6    6753       (II)  BROWN'S REEL, [OR DUILLATER HOUSE]*
1H3H2H6    6753       (II)  DUILLATER HOUSE
1H3H2H6    6753       (I)   BONINTOWN WELL
1H3H2H6    6753       (I)   BROWN'S REEL or [DUILLATER HOUSE]
1H3H2H6    1H3H2H4H   (II)  BUCKS O' DROMORE
1H3H2H6    1H3H4H3H   (I)   MISS STIRLING'S REEL
1H3H2H7    61H53      (I)   NANCY UNDER THE HILL
1H3H2H7    1H3H2H6    (II)  MRS GENERAL MAXWELL( OF PARKHILL)
1H3H2H7    1H3H2H6    (I)   MRS GENERAL MAXWELL OF PARKHILL('S REEL)
1H3H2H     1H43       (I)   PEGGY BAWN
1H3H2H     1H45       (I)   PEGGY BAWN
1H3H2H1H   5322       (II)  MISS HENRIETTA ABERNETHIE
1H3H2H1H   5322       (I)   MISS HENRIETTA ABERNETHIE('S REEL)
1H3H2H     1H55       (I)   MR HOY
1H3H2H1H   5531       (I)   DINNA THINK BONNIE LASSIE
                            (I'M GAUN TO LEAVE YOU)
1H3H2H     1H56       (I)   WILLIAM AND MARGARET
1H3H2H1H   51H22      (I)   MISS MARGARET RENNYS STRATHSPEY
1H3H2H1H   51H2H2     (II)  MISS SUSAN ELLIOT
1H3H2H1H   51H2H2     (I)   MISS SUSAN ELLIOT('S REEL)
1H3H2H1H   54H1H1H    (I)   PARISIAN GUARDS MARCH, THE
1H3H2H1H   6522       (I)   DUKE OF ATHOL'S RANT, THE
                            [DUKE OF ATHOL'S REEL, THE]
1H3H2H1H   662H2H     (I)   COOL O' GURRO
1H3H2H1H   63H63H     (I)   TRIP UP STAIRS, A
1H3H2H     1H75       (I)   GIGG
```

```
1H3H2H      1H1H5       ( I )  TUZZIMUZZY
1H3H2H1H    1H3H1H1H    ( I )  KING OF PRUSSIA'S WALTZ, THE
1H3H2H1H    1H3H2H1H    (II)   FOCHABERS RANT, THE
1H3H2H1H    1H3H2H1H    ( I )  FOCHABER'S RANT, THE
1H3H2H1H    1H3H2H1H    ( I )  MODERATO
1H3H2H1H    1H3H2H1H    ( I )  ILLUMINATION (9TH) FEBR. 1781, THE
1H3H2H1H    1H3H2H1H    ( I )  ALBINA
1H3H2H1H    1H3H2H1H    ( I )  WALTZ
1H3H2H1H    1H3H2H1H    ( I )  MISS RAE OF ESKGROVES VALTZ
1H3H2H1H    1H3H2H1H    ( I )  NINETEENTH OF FEBRUARY, THE
1H3H2H1H    1H4H4H2H    ( I )  MR STEWART TROTTER'S REEL or
                               CAPTAIN'S FANCY, THE
1H3H2H2H    1H3H2H6     ( I )  MRS DUNDASS McQUEEN'S STRATHSPEY
1H3H2H2H    1H3H2H7     ( I )  MORGIANA IN RUSSIA
1H3H2H2H    1H3H2H1H    ( I )  LA NONIME
1H3H2H2H    1H3H2H3H    ( I )  SANDY GOW'S THREE PINTS
1H3H2H3H    51H5H2H     ( I )  LANGO LEE
1H3H2H3H    51H5H2H     ( I )  ALLEGRO
1H3H2H3H    62H72H      (II)   LOVAT'S RESTORATION
1H3H2H3H    62H72H      ( I )  THUAIR MACSHIMI N'OIGHREACHD
                               [FHUAIR MAC SHIMI 'N OIGHREACHD]
1H3H2H3H    1H3H3H6     ( I )  KELSO RACES
1H3H2H3H    2H3H1H6     (II)   LORD DALHOUSIE
1H3H2H3H    2H3H1H6     ( I )  LORD DALHOUSIE
1H3H2H3H    2H3H4H2H    ( I )  ROUND TOWER, THE
1H3H2H3H    3H676       ( I )  EARL OF ROSEBERY'S REEL, THE
1H3H2H3H    4H3H66      ( I )  MR JOHN GORDON'S STRATHSPEY
1H3H2H4H    1H3H2H5     ( I )  ALLEMANDA
1H3H2H4H    1H3H2H5     ( I )  MISS CAROLINE THOMSONS REEL
1H3H2H4H    1H3H2H5     ( I )  MISS JANE MARSHALL'S REEL
1H3H2H4H    3H3H77      (II)   MISS HAY( OF YESTER)
1H3H2H4H    3H3H77      ( I )  MISS HAY( OF YESTER'S REEL)
1H3H2H4H    3H3H77      ( I )  MARQUIS OF HUNTLY'S NEW REEL
1H3H2H4H    3H5H2H6     ( I )  HAPPY TIMES
1H3H2H5H    1H3H75      ( I )  LADY CHARLOTTE PERCEY'S FANCY
1H3H3H5     671H1H      ( I )  BOUQUET, THE
1H3H3H7     1H562       ( I )  MRS GRANT OF LAGGAN'S FAVORITE
1H3H3H1H    62H75       (II)   COME LET US DANCE AND SING
1H3H3H1H    62H75       ( I )  LA BELLE CATHERINE
1H3H3H      1H1H2H      ( I )  HOW SWEET IN THE WOODLANDS
1H3H3H1H    2H2H3HO     ( I )  HE LOVES AND HE RIDES AWAY
1H3H3H1H    4H61H6      ( I )  LADIES OF DINGWALL, THE
1H3H3H2H    1H3H3H1H    ( I )  ORIGINAL DUTCH WALTZ, AN
1H3H3H2H    2H676       ( I )  THOMAS AND SALLY
1H3H3H2H    2H4H4H3H    ( I )  COX'S MUSEUM
1H3H3H      2H4H4H      ( I )  SHEELAN O' GEARY
1H3H3H3H    72H72H      (II)   WANDERING TINKER( THE)
1H3H3H3H    1H61H6      ( I )  FOX-HUNTER'S JIG
1H3H3H3H    1H3H2H1H    ( I )  QUICK STEP LA PROMINADE
1H3H3H5H    5H5H5H3H    ( I )  IRISH MORSHAW
1H3H3H6H    5H1H66      ( I )  ROSIN THE BOW
1H3H4H7     1H347L      ( I )  MISS BETTSY WILSON'S REEL
1H3H4H7     1H3H5H7H    ( I )  MISS DISHINGTON'S FANCY
1H3H4H7     1H5H1H1H    ( I )  Lt. COLONEL RIDDOCH'S (OR 4th BATTN
                               FORFARSHIRE VOLUNTEER'S) SLOW MARCH
1H3H4H7     3H62H1H     ( I )  CEASE YOUR FUNNING
1H3H4H1H    51H32       ( I )  MARCHIONESS OF QUEENSBERRY'S
                               FAVORITE WALTZ, THE
1H3H4H1H    671H1       ( I )  COL. ARCHd CAMPBELL'S QUICK STEP
1H3H4H1H    1H3H1H6     ( I )  EVERARDS FAVORITE HORNPIPE
1H3H4H1H    1H3H2H7     ( I )  TAIL TODLE
1H3H4H2H    6547bL      ( I )  LAST PINT OF ALE, THE
1H3H4H2H    7575        (II)   JESSIE RALSTON'S REEL
1H3H4H      2H2H3H      ( I )  FY ON THE WARS
1H3H4H2H    3H72H2H     ( I )  MISS COLCROFTS FAVORITE
1H3H4H2H    3H72H2H     ( I )  NANCY'S FANCY
1H3H4H2H    3H3H77      ( I )  KING'S BIRTH DAY
1H3H4H3H    5327bL      ( I )  DRUMMCHARY HOUSE
1H3H4H3H    552H1H      (II)   AMERICAN AIR
1H3H4H3H    62H75       (II)   MARQUIS OF HUNTLY('S HIGHLAND FLING)
1H3H4H3H    62H75       ( I )  MARQUIS OF HUNTLY'S HIGHLAND FLING, (THE)
1H3H4H3H    62H72H      (II)   THREE A PENNY
1H3H4H3H    1H3H72H     ( I )  NORICKYSTIE
1H3H4H3H    1H3H72H     ( I )  WILD IRISHMAN, THE
1H3H4H3H    1H3H2H6     ( I )  WE ARE ALL RIGHT AT CANTERBURY
1H3H4H3H    1H3H2H7     (II)   TAIL TODDLE
1H3H4H3H    1H3H2H2H    ( I )  TELL TODDLE [TAIL TODDLE]
1H3H4H3H    2H57b2      (II)   CLEAN PEA(SE) STRAE
1H3H4H3H    2H57b7b     ( I )  (CLEAN) PEASE STRAE
1H3H4H3H    2H577       (II)   PEASE STRAE
1H3H4H3H    2H577       ( I )  CLEAN PEAS STRAW
1H3H4H3H    3H2H3H2H    (II)   HIGHLAND LADDIE
```

1H3H4H3H	3H2H3H2H	(I)	(ORIGINAL) HIGHLAND LADDIE(, THE)
1H3H4H	3H4H7	(I)	PHILLY McCUE
1H3H4H	3H4H7	(I)	IRISH DANCE
1H3H4H3H	5H3H75	(I)	MRS MAJOR HAMILTON'S REEL
1H3H4H3H	2H57b7b	(II)	PEASE STRAE [CLEAN PEASE STRAE]
1H3H4H4H	1H1H2H5	(I)	SPANISH MARCH, A
1H3H4H5H	5H2H1H7	(I)	JULIA'S COTTAGE
1H3H5H	1HO5H	(I)	NEW SPAW MINUET
1H3H5H1H	62H1H6	(I)	MISS BALCARRAS LINDSAY'S FAVOURITE
1H3H5H2H	761H7	(I)	LA BELLE COUQUETTE
1H3H5H2H	1H2H74H	(I)	VICAR, THE
1H3H5H2H	1H6H3H1H	(I)	NIGHTS OF PLEASURE
1H3H5H2H	2H61H6	(I)	RALPH'S RAMBLE IN LONDON
1H3H5H2H	2H4H1H6	(I)	HARRIOT, THE
1H3H5H2H	4H73H1H	(I)	PERSIANS FAREWELL, THE
1H3H5H2H	4H2H1H7	(I)	CALEDONIAN MAID, THE
1H3H5H3H	5535	(II)	AULD LUCKIE
1H3H5H3H	62H76	(I)	MRS BLAIR OF BLAIR'S REEL
1H3H5H3H	62H4H5H	(I)	MISS J. CLARKE'S REEL
1H3H5H3H	72H2H5	(II)	MISS SHAW'S FAVOURITE
1H3H5H	3H1H1H	(I)	ASH GROVE, THE
1H3H5H	3H1H1H	(I)	BEAUTY IN TEARS
1H3H5H3H	1H3H72H	(I)	MERRY MEETING, THE
1H3H5H3H	2H4H2H7	(I)	PETRIE'S FROLICK
1H3H5H3H	2H4H2H7	(I)	HARLEQUIN (REEL/STRATHSPEY), THE
1H3H5H3H	2H4H6H4H	(I)	MUGDRAM HOUSE
1H3H5H	3H3H2H	(I)	MRS CRAWFURD OF DONESIDE'S MINUET
1H3H5H3H	4H61H6	(I)	MARTHA
1H3H5H3H	4H2H1H1H	(I)	RING DOVE, THE
1H3H5H3H	4H2H3H6	(I)	FERTISH HILL, THE
1H3H5H3H	4H2H3H1H	(I)	PAS SEUL MISS SHIVAS
1H3H5H3H	4H3H62H	(I)	MRS HERMITAGE'S FANCY
1H3H5H3H	4H3H72H	(I)	MISS GARDEN OF TROOP'S REEL
1H3H5H3H	6H4H2H7	(I)	COLONEL W.F. MACBEAN
1H3H5H4H	1H3H77	(I)	MISS DALLAS'S STRATHSPEY
1H3H5H5H	1H3H72H	(I)	MISS NANCY DICK'S REEL
1H3H5H5H	2H71H5	(I)	MISS TAIT'S FAVORITE
1H3H5H5H	3H1H2H2H	(I)	JACK'S GRATITUDE
1H3H5H5H	3H2H1H1H	(I)	ALLEMANDA
1H3H5H5H	4H3H62H	(I)	MISS WETHERELL'S STRATHSPEY
1H3H5H5H	4H3H2H2H	(I)	PEGGY PERKINS
1H3H5H5H	4H4H3HO	(I)	(YOUNG) COLIN STOLE MY HEART AWAY
1H3H5H5H	4H4H3H3H	(I)	WHEEM, THE
1H3H5H5H	4H4H3H5H	(I)	LES FILEE DE TEMP'E
1H3H5H6H	2H1H1H5H	(I)	OBSERVER, THE
1H3H5H6H	5H3H2H2H	(I)	MISS CAMPBELL SILVER CRAIG'S REEL
1H3H5H	6H5H5H	(I)	NEOPOLITAN WALTZ
1H3H5H1T	1H3H72H	(I)	CAPT KEELERS REEL
1H3H5H1T	2H2H5H3H	(I)	MR R. CAMPBELL OF SHAWFIELD'S ALLAMANDE
1H3H6H	3H5H2H	(I)	HORNPIPE
1H4H51H	1H4H51H	(I)	GERMAN WALTZ
1H4H62H	1H763	(I)	HIGH ROCKS, THE
1H4H73H	2H3H1H1H	(I)	RUSSIAN AMBASSADOR'S WALTZ, THE
1H4H1H1H	5H7H4H1H	(I)	GO TELL HER I LOVE HER
1H4H1H2H	1H4H1H1	(I)	LADY HARRIOT SPENCER'S FANCY
1H4H1H3	O21I7	(I)	BONNY KITTY
1H4H1H4H	1H677	(I)	HOT BATH, THE
1H4H3H7	1H4H3H1H	(I)	QUICK STEP 37th REGt
1H4H3H7	1H4H5H1H	(I)	WALTZ
1H4H3H1H	1H4H3H1H	(I)	MRS DINGWALL OF BRUCKLAY'S WALTZ
1H4H3H2H	1H4H3H1H	(I)	LONDON CAMP, THE
1H4H5H4H	3H4H71H	(I)	ALLEGRETTO
1H4H6H2H	4H1H61H	(I)	STRUAN ROBERTSON'S RANT
1H5H53H	1H5H5H1H	(I)	CELEBRATED VALTZ RONDO, THE
1H5H65	51H3H2H	(I)	LULLABY, THE
1H5H66	2H4H75	(I)	CHARMS OF KILDARE, THE
1H5H7b0	1H2H3bH0	(I)	WEYDIMANS AIR
1H5H72#	6L4L4#L5L	(II)	YOUNG KING, THE
1H5H75	6531	(I)	AUCHTERTOOL VOLUNTEERS QUICK STEP
1H5H71H	1H5H1H1H	(I)	MISS JUDWINS WALTZ
1H5H1H1H	61H3H3H	(I)	AH! PERDONA
1H5H1H5H	4H2H4H6	(I)	MISS WILCKE'S ALLEMAND
1H5H1H5H	4H4H2H7	(I)	TINK A TINK
1H5H1H6H	1H5H2H7	(I)	LORD NORTH'S JIGG
1H5H1H6H	5H4H1H1H	(I)	ALLEMANDA
1H5H2H1H	1H5H2H1H	(I)	MISS O' NEIL'S WALTZ
1H5H2H1H	1H5H2H1H	(I)	MR GEO THOMPSON'S JUNr's WALTZ
1H5H2H	1H5H2H	(I)	IT'S NOUGHT BUT THE LOVE O' THE TOCHER
1H5H2H2H	1H3H6H5H	(II)	SOMEBODY
1H5H2H2H	1H3H6H5H	(I)	(FOR THE SAKE O') SOMEBODY
1H5H2H3H	1H5H51H	(I)	MR J. WALKER'S FANCY
1H5H2H3H	1H5H51H	(I)	SAVOYARD'S HOLIDAY

```
1H5H2H3H      1H5H2H1H       (I)   WARLEY COMMON
1H5H2H3H      1H5H4H1H       (I)   WALTZ
1H5H2H4H      3H1H2H2H       (I)   HAVE AT THE BONNIE LASSIE
1H5H2H4H      3H2H1H3        (I)   GRAND PARADE, THE
1H5H2H4H      5H3H75         (I)   FRIEND IN NEED, A
1H5H3bH5H     3bH5H2H7b      (II)  MRS DUNCAN
1H5H3bH5H     3bH5H2H7b      (I)   MRS DUNCAN('S REEL)
1H5H3bH5H     3bH5H3bH5H     (I)   MRS DUNCAN'S REEL
1H5H3H1H      1243           (I)   HARLEQUIN RANGER
1H5H3H1H      551H4H         (I)   PATIE AND PEGGY
1H5H3H        1H56           (I)   MY APRON DEARIE
1H5H3H1H      52H75          (II)  PIG HUNT, THE
1H5H3H2H      1H1H1H1H       (II)  ABERARDER RANT
1H5H3H3H      1233           (I)   DESTRUCTION OF THE BASTILE
1H5H3H3H      1H5H4H2H       (I)   POOR OF PURSE BUT ROUTH O' CREDIT
1H5H3H5H      1H5H3H1H       (I)   MR JOHN GRAY'S WALTZ
1H5H3H5H      3H5H2H7b       (I)   MRS DUNCAN'S REEL
1H5H4H7       62H5H7         (I)   GROVE HOUSE, THE
1H5H4H7       1H5H4H1H       (I)   CATCHES AND GLEES
1H5H4H1H      3453           (I)   MAKER TOWER
1H5H4H2H      3H5H3H5H       (I)   TULLOCH GORUM
1H5H4H3H      1H5H61H        (I)   LA NOUVELLE MARIE
1H5H4H3H      1H5H4H2H       (I)   MISS BONNAR'S REEL
1H5H4H6H      1H5H5H1H       (I)   MR J. BROWN'S WALTZ
1H5H5H3H      4H2H3H1H       (I)   GREEN & GOLD
1H5H5H4H      3H2H1H3H       (I)   GAVOTTA
1H5H5H5H      1H5H2H5        (II)  HIGHLANDMAN( KISSED HIS MOTHER), THE
1H5H5H5H      1H5H2H5        (I)   HIGHLANDMAN KISS'D HIS MOTHER, THE
1H5H5H5H      1H5H2H3H       (I)   LADY (JEAN) HUME ('S REEL/JIG)
1H5H5H5H      1H5H2H4H       (II)  LADY HOME
1H5H5H5H      1H5H2H4H       (I)   LADY HOME('S JIG)
1H5H5H6H      5H3H5H3H       (I)   HIGHLAND DANCE
1H5H5H6H      5H3H5H3H       (I)   HARRIS DANCE
1H5H6H2H      3H1H2H5        (I)   HONble MISS JANE RUTHVEN'S JIGG
1H5H6H5H      1H4H3H7        (I)   QUEEN'S FANCY, THE
1H5H6H5H      1H5H2H5        (I)   RAYAN'S RANT
1H5H6H5H      1H5H6H2H       (I)   ROCKS OF CASHEL
1H5H6H5H      6H3H3H2H       (I)   ROSA LEE
1H5H6H6H      1H5H73H        (II)  COPPERBEECH, THE
1H5H6H7H      6H5H2H7        (I)   QUICK STEP
1H5H7H5H      3H4H6H5H       (I)   TINKLING HARP, THE
1H6H54H       1H6H51H        (I)   MISS MURRAY OF HENDERLAND'S VALTZ
1H6H4H2H      72H76          (I)   HARRIET'S, THE
1H7H5H3H      1H4H4H1H       (I)   THIRD OF MAY, THE
1H7H6H4H      4H71H6         (I)   FAVORITE HORNPIPE, A
1H1T66H       2H5H3H1H       (I)   TANK, THE
1H1T5H3H      3H61H6         (I)   FAVORITE HORNPIPE, A
1H1T5H4H      1H1H1H5        (I)   FLIGHTS OF FANCY
2H515L        7L32H1H        (I)   LES NOUVELLES E'TRENNES
2H565         3522H          (II)  MISS CHIRSTY STEWART
2H565         3522H          (I)   MISS CHRISTY STEWART'S REEL
                                   [MIS CHIRSTY STEWART]
2H566         2H3H2H1H       (II)  MY LOVE IS ON THE OCEAN
2H576         2H576          (I)   HIGHLAND REEL, A
2H755         3551H          (I)   GALOP
2H71H5        2H71H5H        (I)   MAJOR PATON OF THE PERTH
                                   VOLUNTEERS QUICK STEP
2H73H2H       6427           (I)   RED, RED ROSE, THE
2H1H31        4326L          (I)   MRS HUNTER'S REEL
2H1H65        6461H          (I)   AN CUALA SIBHS A'BHANAIS BHAN
2H1H75        1H2H3H3H       (I)   CABINET, THE
2H1H2H1H      661H1H         (I)   ALDRIDGE'S ALLEMAND
2H1H2H1H      4H3H2H5        (I)   OLIVE BRANCH, THE
2H1H3H        4H3H1H         (I)   DEAR SILVIA NO LONGER
2H2H53H       4H2H1H1H       (I)   O LA MY DEAR
2H2H71H       1H3bH2H2H      (I)   IRISH WHIM
2H2H1H6       5H4H1H6        (I)   ROTHIEMURCHUS
2H2H1H1H      6636           (I)   MR CAMPBELL OF ACHNABREACK'S SALUTATION
2H2H2H6       3H53H1H        (I)   'S MITHICH DHOMH BHI TOGAIL ORM
2H2H2H7       1H3H72H        (I)   PRIEST IN HIS BOOTS, THE
2H2H2H7       1H3H72H        (I)   IRISH LILT, THE
2H3H61H       2H3H62H        (II)  MR ROSS'S PIPES
2H3H1H1H      2H3H1H1H       (I)   LA DOUBLE INCONSTANCE
2H4H4H        1H1H1H         (I)   WALZE A LA REINE
2H5H1H2H      2H2H4H5H       (I)   CHORUS IN ATALANTA
2H5H2H1H      2H5H2H1H       (I)   U GU VI U, PORT NA MAIGHDINN CHUAIN
3bH1H1H5      7b7b7b7b       (II)  CAWDOR FAIR
3bH53b1       1451H          (I)   EILEAN AIGEIS
3bH1H3b1H     2H7b27b        (II)  LADY GEORGINA GORDON
3bH1H3b1H     2H7b27b        (I)   LADY GEORGINA GORDON'S REEL
3bH1H53b      7b424          (II)  LOCH RUTHVEN
3bH1H53b      7b424          (I)   LOCH RUADHAN [LOCH RUADHAINN]
```

3bH1H51H	2H2H4H7b	(I)	MRS J. ROSE'S FANCY
3bH1H51H	2H4H2H7b	(II)	MRS J. ROSE
3bH1H51H	2H4H2H7b	(II)	ARCHDUKE JOHN OF AUSTRIA
3bH1H51H	2H4H2H7b	(I)	MRS J. ROSE('S STRATHSPEY)
3bH1H7b	3bH1H3bH	(I)	SIUBHAL AN T'SNEACHD TRA OIDHCHE
3bH1H1H1	3b57b5	(II)	BOW TO FATE
3bH1H1H5	57b7b1H	(II)	JOLLY SHEPHERDS, THE
3bH1H1H5	7b2H4H4H	(II)	FEET WASHING, THE
3bH1H1H5	7b2H4H4H	(I)	N'AOICHE ROIDH NA PHOSADH
			['N OIDHCHE RO'N PHOSADH]
3bH1H1H5	1H3bH2H7b	(II)	MAINS OF GARTLY('S REEL)
3bH1H1H7b	5555	(II)	TULLOCH CASTLE
3bH1H1H1H	7b427bL	(II)	MRS MARR'S REEL
3bH1H1H2H	3bH1H2H1H	(II)	MAINS OF GARTLY
3bH1H2H	771H	(I)	WHAT SHALL I DO
			TO SHOW HOW MUCH I LOVE HER?
3bH2H51H	3bH5H3bH2H	(I)	ANNON SIDE
3bH2H53bH	42HO3b	(I)	AIR BY DR BOYCE
3bH2H5	3bH4H1H	(I)	WE'LL KISS THE WORLD BEFORE US
3bH2H7	2HO5	(I)	FAIR SALLY LOV'D A BONNY SEAMAN
3bH2H72H	1H111	(I)	NOBLE RACE WAS SHENKIN, A
3bH2H1H1	3b6b27b	(I)	LADY LOUISA MacDONALD'S STRATHSPEY
3bH2H1H5	7b527bL	(II)	JAMES MORRISON
3bH2H1H	1H57b	(I)	CAROLAN'S DEVOTION
3bH2H1H5H	7b4H2H7b	(I)	MAC AOIDH
3bH2H2H4#	6b7b7b2	(I)	MISS MACLEOD OF MACLEOD'S REEL
3bH3bH1H1H	3bH1H2H4H	(II)	DUCHESS OF ROXBURGHE, THE
3bH3bH1H1H	4H4H2H2H	(I)	MRS PRYCE GORDON'S REEL
3bH3bH4H1H	1H1H55	(I)	JOCKIE WAS THE BLYTHEST LAD
			(IN ALL OUR TOWN)
3bH3bH4H4H	3bH3bH2H4H	(I)	MISS ANN BISSET LOGIERAIT
3H11H1	1H2H3H2H	(I)	QUICK STEP, 40th REGt
3H511	437L2	(I)	JOHN BULL'S REEL
3H546	31H62H	(I)	GENERAL GORDON CUMING SKENE'S QUICKSTEP
3H522H	3H561H	(II)	O WHISTLE AND I'LL COME TO YOU MY LOVE
			[...LAD]
3H522H	3H561H	(I)	ALLEGRO
3H522H	3H561H	(I)	O WHISTLE AND I'LL COME TO YOU MY LAD
3H535	3H572H	(I)	MISS CHARLOTTE ELLIOTT'S REEL
3H535	3H52H2H	(II)	MRS RONALD
3H535	3H52H2H	(I)	MRS RONALD('S REEL)
3H535	3H3H4H2H	(I)	MR H. BROWN OF FULHAM FANCY
3H536	1H535	(I)	SCOTCH MEASURE, A
3H531H	3H5H72H	(I)	LADY CAROLINE ELIZABETH DOUGLAS'S REEL
3H545	3H542	(I)	MR WILL'S FAVOURITE
3H545	3H542	(I)	MISS MOODY'S FAVORITE
3H54	633	(II)	MUCH ADMIRED GERMAN WALTZ, A
3H555	662H1H	(I)	SOLDIER'S RETURN(, THE)
3H555	662H1H	(I)	MILL, MILL O, THE
3H555	74H2H2H	(I)	STOUR LODGE
3H555	1H53H2H	(I)	JENNY DANG THE WEAVER
3H555	3H52H6	(II)	SUD MAR CHUIR MI'N GEAMHRADH THARUM
			[THAT'S HOW I SPENT THE WINTER]
3H555	3H52H6	(I)	SUD MAR CHUIR MI'N GEAMHRADH THARUM
3H555	3H52H6	(I)	HIGHLAND REEL, A
3H555	31I53H2H	(I)	JENNY DANG THE WEAVER
3H551H	2266	(II)	FLOORS CASTLE
3H551H	2266	(II)	I WINNA GAE TO BED
3H551H	2266	(I)	TO MY BED I WONA GANG
3H551H	2266	(I)	I WINNA GAE TO BED (UNTIL I'M MARRIED)
3H551H	662H1H	(II)	SOLDIER'S RETURN
3H564	3H51H1H	(I)	NORTH HIGHLAND II
3H565	3H561H	(II)	KINLOCH OF KINLOCH
3H565	3H561H	(I)	KINLOCH OF KINLOCH [KINLOCH'S FAVORITE]
3H562H	3H4H66	(II)	SOLDIER'S RETURN
3H51H6	3H2H1H5	(I)	JOY GO WITH MY LOVE
3H51H7	2H1H3H1H	(I)	BOULD SOGER BOY, THE
3H51H1H	2H4H3H6	(I)	MY AIN KIND DEARIE
3H51H1H	2H4H3H6	(I)	LEE RIGG
3H51H1H	3H3H4H2H	(I)	MASTER FOX MAULE (OF PANMURE) 'S BIRTHDAY
3H51H3H	2H5H3H1H	(II)	FAREWELL, TO THE GLEN
3H52H5	3H2H1H6	(II)	BOATMAN OF PITNACREE, THE
3H52H5	3H2H1H6	(I)	BOATMAN OF PITNACREE, THE
3H52H6	3H52H1H	(II)	MACFARLANE'S RANT [MCFARLANE RANT]
3H52H6	3H52H1H	(I)	MACFARLANE'S RANT [MCFARLANE'S RANT]
3H52H7	3H52H1H	(I)	McFARLANE'S STRATHSPEY
3H52H1H	3H51H6	(I)	HIGHLAND DANCE
3H52H2H	3H2H1H6	(II)	CHIEFTAIN'S FROLIC, THE
3H52H2H	3H2H1H6	(I)	DUDDINGSTON CASTLE
3H53H5	4H3H2H5	(I)	O.P. HAT
3H653	31H4H2H	(II)	WILLIE SHAW
3H653	5357	(II)	HAGGS CASTLE

3H655	3H53H2H	(I)	MRS OSWALD OF AUCHINCRUIVE'S FAVOURITE
3H652H	3H651H	(I)	MY AIN FIRESIDE
3H652H	3H651H	(I)	TODLIN HAME
3H753	1515	(I)	LONDON REEL, THE
3H765	3H761H	(I)	LADY ELIZA CALLANDER'S FAVOURITE
3H76	1H3H7	(I)	WE'RE A' FORSAKEN FOR WANT O' SILLER
3H71H	654H	(I)	MINUET BY MR ARNE
3H72H1H	51H3H2H	(I)	ALLEGRETTO
3H73H1H	1H1H3H2H	(I)	THREE GRACES, THE
3H74H1H	3H1H1H3H	(I)	MOORINGS
3H1H5L6	3H1H41H	(II)	PRINCE OF WALES, THE
3H1H15	662H2H	(I)	DUKE OF GORDON'S STRATHSPEY
3H1H11H	3H1H22H	(I)	MR BALLANTYNE'S JIG
3H1H31	4326L	(II)	MISS RAMSAY
3H1H31	4326L	(I)	MISS RAMSAY'S REEL
3H1H33	2266	(I)	PUNCH BOWL, THE
3H1H35	67b27bL	(I)	MISS ELEONORA CAMPBELL OF KILBRYDE'S STR.
3H1H35	67b21	(I)	MISS ELEONORA CAMPBELL OF KILBRIDE'S REEL
3H1H35	7b7b22H	(I)	MASONS RANT
3H1H35	3H4H72H	(I)	ROYAL PERTH VOLUNTEERS QUICKSTEP
3H1H42	35L24	(II)	JOHN HOWATS STRATHSPEY
3H1H51	337L0	(I)	MISS RAY
3H1H51	337L0	(I)	SHADDIE
3H1H52	351H1H	(II)	DOWN THE BURN DAVIE LAD
3H1H52	351H1H	(I)	DOWN THE BURN, DAVIE (LAD)
3H1H53	153H2H	(II)	MILLICENT'S FAVOURITE
3H1H53	13H72H	(I)	SAMUEL FERGUSON, ESQr's REEL
3H1H53	2231	(I)	PAS SEUL MISS MARY ADAMSON
3H1H53	27b27bL	(I)	MARCHIONESS OF BLANDFORDS REEL
3H1H53	22H2H2H	(II)	FIFE HUNT(, THE)
3H1H53	22H2H2H	(I)	FIFE HUNT, (THE)
3H1H53	352H2H	(I)	DONALD OF DUNDEE
3H1H53	353H2H	(I)	PERTHSHIRE LASSES
3H1H53	4322H	(I)	MISS GRANT'S REEL
3H1H53	4422	(I)	SIR GEORGE CLERK (OF PENNYCUICK)
3H1H53	4542	(I)	MRS CAMPBELL OF TREESBANK'S REEL
3H1H53	5322	(I)	Dr. CROMAR
3H1H53	5532	(II)	QUEEN'S FIDDLER'S COMPts TO MR TROUP
3H1H53	5533	(I)	HIGHLAND CHIEFTAIN, THE
3H1H53	5551H	(I)	ALLEGRO
3H1H53	51H2H2	(I)	LORD MONTGOMERIE'S REEL
3H1H53	3H1H2H4H	(II)	MISS SCOTT OF BELVUE
3H1H53	3H1H2H4H	(I)	MISS SCOTT OF BELVUE('S REEL)
3H1H53	3H1H2H4H	(I)	PETERHEAD ASSEMBLY
3H1H53	3H1H2H4H	(I)	MR JAMES RENTON'S REEL
3H1H53	3H3H1H1H	(II)	ORANGE AND BLUE
3H1H53	3H3H1H1H	(I)	ORANGE AND BLUE
3H1H5	432	(I)	FARMER'S WISH, THE
3H1H5	442H	(I)	BRES OF EWES, THE
3H1H55	354H2H	(I)	HiBERNIA
3H1H55	5553H	(I)	LE PANTALON
3H1H55	1H3H2H2H	(I)	AULD LUCKY OF THE GLEN
3H1H55	3H1H3H2H	(II)	MRS McDONALD
3H1H55	3H1H3H2H	(I)	MRS MACDONALD
3H1H51H	351H3	(I)	CASTLE CAMPBELL
3H1H51H	351H3	(I)	FROLICK, THE
3H1H51H	2H4H2H2H	(I)	ROMP, THE
3H1H51H	3H1H3H3H	(I)	DUKE OF YORK AT BERLIN
3H1H51H	3H1H3H5H	(II)	GENERAL MCDONALD
3H1H51H	3H1H3H5H	(I)	GENERAL MACDONALD'S REEL
3H1H51H	3H1H3H5H	(I)	TARR WATER
3H1H51H	3H1H4H5H	(I)	WINDSOR HUNT
3H1H51H	3H5H1H1H	(II)	ORANGE AND BLUE
3H1H51H	4H2H62H	(II)	CRAIG A CHAIT
3H1H51H	4H2H5H2H	(I)	BOYS OF KILKENNY, THE
3H1H52H	3H1H51H	(I)	DAYS OF LANGSYNE, THE
3H1H64	5362	(I)	MR JAMES DALLAS' STRATHSPEY
3H1H65	31H3H2H	(II)	HAGGS CASTLE
3H1H65	51H52	(I)	HOW FAIR SHINES THE MORNING
3H1H65	3H1H62H	(I)	HERE'S A HEALTH TO THEM THAT'S AWA'
3H1H65	3H1H2H4H	(I)	MR WILLIAM TOWER'S QUICK STEP
3H1H6	3H1H4	(I)	TRIP TO RANALAGH, A
3H1H75	6431	(I)	QUICKSTEP 33rd REGt
3H1H75	2H2H4H5H	(I)	OAK STICK
3H1H76	5222	(II)	BONNIE LOSSIE
3H1H71H	3H1H3H6	(I)	LORD DUMFRIES'S BOWLING GREEN
3H1H72H	4H61H0	(I)	LUCY LONG
3H1H1H1	3551H	(I)	STEWARD'S LODGE SONG, THE
3H1H1H3	3H1H1H3	(II)	LOCOMOTIVE, THE
3H1H1H5	3211H	(II)	MY WEE FIDDLE
3H1H1H5	31H4H2H	(I)	MISS JEANNY ROSS'S REEL
3H1H1H5	31H4H2H	(I)	MISS SYME WILSON

3H1H1H5	4235	(II)	CUMBERLAND REEL
3H1H1H5	4235	(II)	HOKEY POKEY
3H1H1H5	44H2H2H	(I)	MISS TAYLOR'S REEL
3H1H1H5	532H2	(II)	Dr. ROBERTSON'S REEL
3H1H1H5	5522	(I)	CHRISTMAS TALE, A
3H1H1H5	6532	(II)	MISS BETTY HUNTER
3H1H1H5	6532	(I)	MISS BETTY HUNTER('S REEL)
3H1H1H5	72H4H2H	(I)	EXILE, THE
3H1H1H5	2H2H3H2H	(II)	A' CHUACHAG
3H1H1H5	2H4H2H2	(I)	MR HAMILTON OF WISHAW'S REEL
3H1H1H5	2H4H2H6	(I)	MISS CHARLOTTE DUNDAS'S REEL
3H1H1H5	3H1H4H3H	(I)	(MERRY) LADS OF AYR, (THE)
3H1H1H5	3H1H4H4H	(II)	MERRY LADS OF AYR, THE
3H1H1H5	3H1H4H4H	(I)	(MERRY) LADS OF AYR, (THE)
3H1H1H7b	6461H	(I)	BREAD AND CHEESE
3H1H1H1H	2266	(II)	LADY MARY LINDSAY
3H1H1H1H	2266	(I)	LADY MARY LINDSAY'S REEL
3H1H1H1H	3155	(I)	MISS(BARBARA) STEWART'S REEL
3H1H1H1H	3H1H4H5H	(II)	MERRY LADS OF AYR, THE
3H1H1H2H	2H554	(I)	ROYAL TAR'S WELCOME TO OLD ENGLAND, THE
3H1H1H3H	4H2H75H	(II)	MARQUIS OF QUEENSBERRY(, THE)
3H1H1H5H	2H72H4H	(I)	BRITISH NAVY, THE
3H1H2H5	353H1H	(I)	SECOND QUICKMARCH 10th REGt
3H1H2H5	353H1H	(I)	DUKE OF WELLINGTON'S QUICKSTEP
3H1H2H5	353H1H	(I)	GOWD IN GOWPINS
3H1H2H5	4324	(I)	MISS SPENCE'S FAVORITE
3H1H2H5	72H4H3H	(I)	COTILLION
3H1H2H5	1H533	(I)	JUBILEE, THE
3H1H2H5	1H542	(II)	JOCKEY CLUB, THE
3H1H2H5	1H542	(I)	JOCKEY CLUB, THE
3H1H2H5	1H1H2H5	(I)	EMIG
3H1H2H5	1H2H3H2H	(I)	LADY CHARLOTTE LENOX
3H1H2H5	2H52H2H	(I)	THERE'S NAE LUCK ABOUT THE HOUSE
3H1H2H5	2H52H2H	(I)	JENNY CAMERON ('S REEL)
3H1H2H5	2H52H2H	(I)	JANNY CAMERON'S REEL
3H1H2H5	5H52H2H	(II)	NULL THAR NAN EILEANUN or OVER THE ISLES TO AMERICA
3H1H2H5	5H52H2H	(I)	(MISS) (JEANIE/JENNY) CAMERON ('S REEL)
3H1H2H6	751H3H	(I)	COURTSHIP, THE
3H1H2H7	1H65#3	(I)	MISS CATHERINE MILLER'S REEL
3H1H2H1H	6522H	(II)	HONBLE MISS ROLLO, THE
3H1H2H1H	6522H	(I)	HONble MISS ROLLO('S REEL), THE
3H1H2H1H	63H1H5H	(I)	MISS HOBART'S (FANCY/FAVOURITE)
3H1H2H2H	3H1H75	(I)	HAPPY WEDDING
3H1H2H2H	3H1H3H2H	(I)	EARLE OF CASSLES'S FAVORITE
3H1H2H4H	72H1H3H	(I)	L'ETE
3H1H2H5H	3H1H2H1H	(I)	LORD DUNCAN'S GERMAN WALTZ
3H1H3H5	1H6H2H2H	(I)	TROOP
3H1H3H1H	661H5	(I)	COSSACK DANCE, A
3H1H3H1H	1H1H2H7	(I)	CARD ROOM
3H1H3H1H	2H61H3H	(I)	HARMONICS IF PERFORMED ON A VIOLIN
3H1H3H1H	2H4H2H7	(I)	FLAG DANCE, THE
3H1H3H1H	3H1H4H2H	(I)	MISS BROWERS STRATHSPEY
3H1H3H1H	4H2H75	(I)	FLY BY NIGHT
3H1H3H1H	5H3H1H5	(I)	SMITH'S ORANGE & FORK
3H1H3H5H	3H1H4H2H	(II)	McLEAN'S PIPES
3H1H3H	5H3H5H	(I)	LADY C. MONTAGUE'S VALTZ
3H1H3H5H	4H5H4H2H	(II)	MRS WILLS
3H1H3H5H	4H5H4H2H	(I)	MR WILLS'S STRATHSPEY
3H1H4H7	1H1H2H5H	(I)	FIGURE DANCE
3H1H4H2H	751H3H	(I)	HARRIOT, THE
3H1H4H2H	3H1H2H5	(II)	KEEL ROW, THE
3H1H4H2H	3H1H2H5	(I)	BODACHAN A GARIDH
3H1H4H6H	3H1H2H6	(I)	MISS CAVE'S REEL
3H1H5H5	1H1H1H1H	(I)	PIERROT
3H1H5H1H	2H7b4H7b	(I)	MR STEWART DOWALLY'S REEL
3H1H5H1H	3H5H3H3H	(I)	ROW YOUR RUMPLE SAUNCY
3H1H5H2H	3H1H2H5	(I)	BODACHAN A GARIDH
3H1H5H5H	1H2H66	(I)	BLIND BEGGAR
3H1H5H5H	3H1H55	(I)	BEGGAR'S BENNISON
3H1H6H5H	6H5H6H64H	(I)	SUGARCANDY
3H2H55	6656	(II)	MUSIC O' SPEY, THE
3H2H51H	4H3H4H3H	(II)	MRS MORTHLAND
3H2H51H	4H3H4H3H	(I)	MRS MORTHLAND'S REEL
3H2H64	3H2H5H5	(II)	DOGS BITE CHAPMEN
3H2H64	3H2H5H2H	(I)	SMALL REEL, THE
3H2H65	5565	(II)	COUNT D'ARTOIS
3H2H65	5565	(I)	MONSIEUR THE COUNT D'ARTOIS'S REEL
3H2H61H	561H1	(I)	OSWALD'S FAREWELL
3H2H75	1H2H3H2H	(I)	FRA TANTE
3H2H75	3115	(I)	BERWICKSHIRE YEOMANRY'S MARCH, THE
3H2H76	5650	(I)	L'ALLEGRANTE

```
3H2H76        637L2       ( I )    BLUE BELLS OF SCOTLAND, THE
3H2H72H       3H52H6      ( I )    KEW GARDENS
3H2H1HO       3211        ( I )    GIPSY CHORUS
3H2H1H1       27bL44      ( II )   MARQUESS OF LORN
3H2H1H1       27bL44      ( II )   LORN STRATHSPEY, THE
3H2H1H1       27bL44      ( I )    (MARQUIS OF) LORN('S) STRATHSPEY, THE
                                   [LORN STRATHSPEY, THE]
3H2H1H1       47L44       ( I )    RICHMOND GREEN
3H2H1H1       4522H       ( I )    MISS PRINGLE'S REEL
3H2H1H3       4522H       ( I )    MISS FERGUSON'S REEL
3H2H1H5       11H22       ( I )    MISS LAMONT OF LAMONT'S REEL
3H2H1H5       27bL44      ( I )    SIR JOHN STEWART OF GRANDTULLIE'S REEL
3H2H1H5       22H2H4H     ( I )    MISS GORDON OF ABERGELDIE'S JIGG
3H2H1H5       35L7L2      ( II )   FANCY BALL, THE
3H2H1H5       3155        ( I )    LASSES OF STEWARTON, THE
3H2H1H5       3231        ( I )    LOCKET, THE
3H2H1H5       3572H       ( II )   MRS MONEYPENNY
3H2H1H5       3572H       ( I )    MRS MONYPENNY('S REEL)
3H2H1H       531H         ( I )    WANDERER, THE
3H2H1H5       31H22       ( I )    QUICK STEP, OLD BUFFS
3H2H1H5       31H2H2      ( I )    HADDINGTON LASSES
3H2H1H5       31H2H2      ( I )    WHAT A BEAU (MY/YOUR) GRANNY WAS
3H2H1H5       47bL44      ( I )    FORT GEORGE
3H2H1H5       6542        ( II )   MISS JESSIE SCOTT
3H2H1H5       6542        ( I )    MISS JESSY SCOTT'S REEL [MISS JESSIE SCOTT]
3H2H1H5       6543        ( I )    MISS FORBES'S REEL
3H2H1H5       61H2H2      ( I )    MISS ANN DOUGLASS BRIGTON'S JIGG
3H2H1H5       2H2H4H2H    ( I )    MR PETER DUFF'S FAVORITE
3H2H1H5       2H2H5H3H    ( I )    PLEYEL'S FANCY
3H2H1H6       357L2       ( I )    MR WILLm ROBERTSON'S REEL
3H2H1H6       5565        ( I )    LADY WALKER DRUMMOND'S STRATHSPEY
3H2H1H6       5565        ( I )    MRS FRANK WALKER
3H2H1H6       62H2H1      ( I )    LET US HASTE TO KELVIN GROVE
3H2H1H6       3H2H51H     ( I )    IVY BUDS, THE
3H2H1H6       3H2H1H5     ( II )   JOY BE WITH MY LOVE
3H2H1H        765         ( I )    TEMPO DI MINORE
3H2H1H7       671H1H      ( I )    GERMAN QUICK MARCH, A
3H2H1H1H      3155        ( II )   LASSES OF STEWARTON, THE
3H2H1H1H      3155        ( I )    LASSES OF STEWARTON, THE
3H2H1H1H      31H31       ( I )    MISS CAMPBELL PARK PLACE'S REEL
3H2H1H1H      561H2H      ( II )   LAOIDH AN AMADAIN MHOIR
3H2H1H1H      62H2H5H     ( I )    I LOVE MY LOVE IN SECRET
3H2H1H1H      62H2H6H     ( I )    I LOVE MY LOVE IN SEACREIT
3H2H1H1H      1H541       ( II )   MRS MACDONALD, SKEABOST
3H2H1H1H      2H4H76      ( I )    RAMAH DROOG
3H2H1H1H      3H1H2H7     ( I )    COTTILLION 5th
3H2H1H1H      3H3H76      ( I )    BONNY LASS OF BRANKSOME, THE
3H2H1H1H      3H3H5H3H    ( I )    LA SUISESSE DU BORD DU LAC
3H2H1H1H      3H3H5H5H    ( I )    MR JOHN GORDON'S REEL
3H2H1H1H      3H5H76      ( I )    BRAES OF BRANKSOM, THE
3H2H1H1H      4H2H75      ( I )    MISS ELIZA ANDERSON'S FANCY
3H2H1H1H      4H3H2H5     ( I )    PREAMBLE, THE
3H2H1H1H      5H72H2H     ( I )    LONDON MILITARY ASSOCIATION DANCE, THE
3H2H1H2H      531H2H      ( I )    JESSIE, THE FLOWER OF DUMBLANE
3H2H1H2H      675#0       ( I )    YE NYMPHS OF THE PLAIN
3H2H1H2H      3H2H1H1H    ( I )    FOX HUNTER'S JIG, THE
3H2H1H3H      62H75       ( II )   MISS H. HUNTER OF BLACKNESS
3H2H1H3H      62H75       ( II )   SEAN PHORT MAITH
3H2H1H3H      62H75       ( I )    MISS H. HUNTER'S OF BLACKNESS( REEL)
3H2H1H3H      74H75       ( I )    RONDO
3H2H1H3H      4H4H75      ( I )    SPANISH DANCE
3H2H1H3H      4H4H75      ( I )    NORTH STREET THEATRE, THE
3H2H1H5H      6H4H3H2H    ( I )    RUNAWAY BRIDE, THE
3H2H1#H1H     325#1H      ( I )    MISS BURN'S WALTZ
3H2H2H6       5555        ( II )   PEAT BOG, THE
3H2H2H3H      3H2H3H1H    ( I )    WE'RE A' NODDIN'
3H2H3H        1H55        ( I )    'SCIAN 'SGUR FAD THA MI M'THAMH
3H2H3H1H      1H1H2H2H    ( I )    COLONEL CHRISTIE'S MARCH
3H2H3H1H      2H5H5H3H    ( I )    DANCED BY MISS CHALMERS
3H2H3H1H      5H5H3H2H    ( I )    EDINBURGH CASTLE
3H2H3H2H      62H62H      ( I )    THADDY YOU GANDER
3H2H3H2H      62H62H      ( I )    MISS MARRION CAMPBELL ARDMORE'S FAVORITE
3H2H3H2H      1H52H2H     ( II )   DONALD MACPHERSON'S LAMENT
3H2H3H2H      1H2H76      ( I )    TAMBOURINE
3H2H3H5H      3H1H1H5     ( I )    AMOROUS GODDESS, (THE)
3H2H3H5H      3H2H1H5H    ( I )    C'EST L'AMOUR
3H2H3H5H      3H2H3H4H    ( II )   SCOTCH MIST
3H2H3H5H      4H3H2H7     ( II )   SPORTING JAMIE
3H2H4H3H      2H1H6H5H    ( I )    GOD PRESERVE THE EMPEROR
3H2H5H7       342H2H      ( I )    SICILIAN PEASANT, THE
3H2H5H1H      2H1H55      ( I )    ALLEGRO
3H2H5H5H      3H3H1H1H    ( I )    BLIND SAILOR, THE
```

```
3H2H5H5H      6H2H6H2H     (I)    LAKES OF KELLARNIE, THE
3H3H55        662H2H       (I)    BONNY GREEN OF GLASGOW, THE
3H3H5         3H3H3H       (I)    THA 'N OIDHCHE NOCHD FUAR
3H3H5         3H3H3H       (I)    COLD IS THIS NIGHT
3H3H65        3H3H2H5H     (I)    WHAT NEXT
3H3H66        1H2H66       (I)    NEW SCOTCH MEASURE, A
3H3H1H        531H         (I)    DURANDARTE AND BELERMA
3H3H1H5       4731         (I)    SUNY BRAE, THE
3H3H1H5       6543         (I)    KINGSBRIDGE ASSEMBLY
3H3H1H5       753H1H       (II)   BARREN ROCKS OF ADEN, THE
3H3H1H5       1H531        (I)    CAPER FEY
3H3H1H5       3H3H4HO      (I)    MICHAEL WIGGINS
3H3H1H6       5122         (I)    MRS ANDERSON OF KINCRAIG'S STRATHSPEY
3H3H1H6       562H2H       (I)    GROANS OF THE WOUNDED
3H3H1H6       51H2H3H      (I)    OFT IN THE STILLY NIGHT
3H3H1H6       51H3H2H      (I)    NO. TWO MARCH TO THE BATTLE FIELD
3H3H1H6       51H3H2H      (I)    OFT IN THE STILLY NIGHT
3H3H1H6       53H3H2H      (I)    MISS DUNBAR OF NORTHFIELD'S STRATHSPEY
3H3H1H6       64H3H1H      (I)    CARLISLE YETTS
3H3H1H        61HO         (I)    EARL DOUGLAS'S LAMENT
3H3H1H7       532H4H       (I)    LADY MATILDA BRUCE('S REEL)
3H3H1H1H      5333         (II)   MY HEATHER HILLS
3H3H1H1H      5572H        (II)   LAD WI' THE PLAIDIE, THE
3H3H1H1H      7550         (I)    DONALD
3H3H1H1H      72H2H5H      (I)    KETTLEBENDER
3H3H1H1H      2H1H66       (I)    WANTONESS FOR EVER MAIR
3H3H1H1H      2H2H2H2H     (I)    GLORIOUS APOLLO
3H3H1H1H      2H2H3H1H     (I)    ROUSSEAU'S DREAM
3H3H1H1H      2H2H5H3H     (I)    GENERAL HILL
3H3H1H1H      2H4H1H6      (I)    ROYAL FLIGHT TO BRIGHTON
3H3H1H1H      3H1H2H2H     (I)    KINDNESS FOR EVER MAIR
3H3H1H3H      4H4H4H5H     (I)    KING OF SWEDEN'S MARCH
3H3H1H3H      6H3H72H      (I)    MISS PATERSON'S REEL
3H3H1H        5H5H3H       (I)    I'LL NEVER LOVE MAIR
                                  THO' LIVE TO THREESCORE
3H3H1H        5H5H3H       (I)    I'LL LOVE NO MORE
3H3H2H        663          (I)    LUDE'S LAMENT
3H3H2H        665          (I)    ALL HAIL TO THEE THOU BALMY ROSE
3H3H2H        751H         (I)    SHE'S GONE! WHILE WE WONDER
3H3H2H1H      64H2H5       (I)    MISS GORDON OF BELLIE'S REEL
3H3H2H        1H71H        (I)    MISS C. HONYMAN OF ARMADALE'S HIGH DANCE
3H3H2H1H      72H1H2H      (I)    VOULEZ VOUS DANSEZ
3H3H2H1H      72H1H3H      (II)   VOULEZ VOUS DANSER
3H3H2H1H      72H1H3H      (I)    VOULEZ VOUS DANCEZ
3H3H2H1H      72H1H3H      (I)    ROLL DRUMS MERRILY
3H3H2H1H      1H61H1H      (I)    LAOIDH AN AMADAIN MHOIR
3H3H2H1H      1H1H76       (II)   PARAZOTTI
3H3H2H1H      3H3H22H      (I)    MR ALEXr GRAHAM'S REEL
3H3H2H1H      3H3H66       (I)    MISS BLAIR'S REEL
3H3H2H        1H6H5H       (I)    PRINCE OF WALES MINUET
3H3H2H2H      1H3H77       (I)    FLODDEN FIELD
3H3H2H2H      3H4H1H1H     (I)    LARY GROGAN
3H3H2H2H      3H4H1H1H     (I)    ALLEGRETTO
3H3H2H2H      3H4H2H2H     (I)    LARY GROGAN
3H3H2H3H      52H3H2H      (I)    MISS CAMPBELL OF MELFORD
3H3H2H        3H75         (I)    RISING SUN, THE
3H3H2H        3H1H1H       (I)    POLYSTONS HORNPIPE
3H3H2H3H      1H1H51H      (I)    LA REVEIL DU PEUPLE
3H3H2H        3H1H2H       (I)    LADY CRAWFURD'S MINUET
3H3H2H        3H1H3H       (I)    DRUNK AT NIGHT AND DRY IN THE MORNING
3H3H2H        3H3H2H       (I)    FAVORITE TUNE FROM MOTHER GOOSE, A
3H3H2H        3H3H2H       (I)    MAIR THE MORN
3H3H2H3H      3H3H2H1H     (I)    I KNOW SOMETHING
3H3H3H        552H         (I)    BLINK O'ER THE BURN, SWEET BETTY
3H3H3H        553H         (I)    BLINK OVER THE BURN SWEET BETTY
3H3H3H        571H         (I)    LADY DUMFRIES'S MINUET
3H3H3H        54H2H        (I)    BLINK OVER THE BURN SWEET BETTY
3H3H3H6       2H1H1H1H     (II)   ROMANCE
3H3H3H7       3H4H71H      (II)   LARGO'S FAIRY DANCE
3H3H3H2H      661H1H       (I)    AIKEN DRUM
3H3H3H2H      1H1H2H6      (I)    COUNTRY CLUB, THE
3H3H3H2H      4H667        (II)   DUCHESS TREE, THE
3H3H3H3H      671H1H       (I)    RUSSIAN DANCE
3H3H3H        3H2H1H       (I)    MINUET DE LA CHASSE
3H3H3H        3H2H1H       (I)    CUMHA MHIC A H ARASAIG
3H3H3H3H      2H2H1H2H     (I)    FROM NIGHT TILL MORN
3H3H3H        3H2H3H       (I)    LOCHABER
3H3H3H3H      3H3H75       (II)   FAIRY DANCE, THE
3H3H3H3H      3H3H75       (I)    FAIRY DANCE, THE
3H3H3H3H      3H3H72H      (II)   LARGO'S FAIRY DANCE
3H3H3H3H      3H3H72H      (II)   FAIRY DANCE(, THE)
3H3H3H3H      3H3H72H      (I)    LARGO'S FAIRY DANCE
```

```
3H3H3H3H    3H3H72H      ( I ) FAIRY DANCE, (THE)
3H3H3H3H    3H3H3HO      (II) WHAT'S A' THE STEER
3H3H3H3H    3H3H3HO      ( I ) WHAT'S A' THE STEER, KIMMER?
3H3H3H3H    4H74H7       ( I ) JUST A GOING
3H3H3H3H    4H2H75       ( I ) TAMBORINE DANCE
3H3H3H3H    4H3H72H      ( I ) MISS J. TOD'S STRATHSPEY
3H3H3H      4H2H7        ( I ) DANCE TO YOUR DADDY MY BONNY LADDIE
3H3H3H5H    2H2H2H4H     ( I ) HEY TUTTI TAITI
3H3H3H5H    4H2H3H1H     ( I ) DI TANTI PALPITI
3H3H4H2H    55H1H3       ( I ) PRINCE FERDINAND'S QUICK STEP
3H3H4H2H    661H5        ( I ) JOHNNY'S GRAY BREEKS
3H3H4H2H    2H2H3H1H     ( I ) WEE MAN, THE
3H3H4H2H    4H4H5H3H     ( I ) BRAES OF KILLIECRANKY, THE
3H3H4H2H    5H3H55       ( I ) BLOSSOM OF THE RASPBERRY, THE
3H3H4H2H    5H3H55       ( I ) MISS HAMILTON'S DELIGHT
3H3H4H3H    2H2H3H1H     ( I ) MALBROOK
3H3H4H3H    3H3H4H7      ( I ) MRS BAILLIES REEL
3H3H4H3H    3H3H4H3H     ( I ) DUTCHES OF RICHMOND'S ALLEMAND, THE
3H3H4H4H    3H2H1H1      ( I ) SKIRMISH OF FOOT SOLDIERS
3H3H4H4H    3H3H3H5H     ( I ) KILECRANKIE
3H3H4H4H    3H4H3H3HO    ( I ) AN YE HAD BEEN WHERE I HAVE BEEN/
                               YOU WOULD NOT BE(EN) SO CANTY
3H3H4H6H    5H4H3H3H     ( I ) WHEN ARTHUR FIRST AT COURT BEGAN
3H3H5H      552H         ( I ) BLINK O'ER THE BURN
3H3H5H1H    2H1H1H1H     ( I ) ROUGH AND HARDY
3H3H5H1H    2H1H1H1H     ( I ) AMAZON, THE
3H3H5H      2H2H5        ( I ) COME TELL TO ME MY MAIDENS FAIR
3H3H5H4H    1H2H3H2H     ( I ) YOUNG COLLIN
3H3H5H4H    2H4H1HO      ( I ) PAUVRE JACQUE
3H3H6H3H    2H2H5H2H     ( I ) COUNTRY DANCE
3H4H61H     3135         ( I ) JOHNNIE'S GREY BREEKS
3H4H73H     3471H        ( I ) MINORS WALTZ, THE
3H4H1H3     62H6H7       ( I ) MINUET
3H4H1H7     553H2H       ( I ) HORATIO, THE
3H4H1H1H    346H1H       ( I ) IRON CHEST, THE
3H4H1H1H    2H4H5H3H     ( I ) PAS REDOUBLE
3H4H1H2H    3H4H1H1H     ( I ) LA BLANCHIFFEAU
3H4H2H7     62H75        ( I ) FASHION, THE
3H4H2H2H    71H2H3H      ( I ) QUICK STEP
3H4H2H5H    3H1H2H7      ( I ) FIRST MEDLEY DANCE
3H4H3H1H    2H5H1H2H     (II) LORD HUNTLY'S CAVE
3H4H3H6H    5H5H3H2H     ( I ) MISS FORBES' FAREWELL TO BANFF
3H4H4H5H    3H4H3HO      ( I ) AN YE HAD BEEN WHERE I HA'E BEEN
3H4H5H1H    71H2H5       ( I ) TURKISH AIR
3H4H5H1H    2H671H       ( I ) TURNPIKE GATE
3H4H5H1H    2H4H2H7      ( I ) SWEETEST LASSIE
3H4H5H2H    5H3H1H1H     ( I ) DRINK TO ME ONLY WITH THINE EYES
3H4H5H3H    1H2H1H2H     ( I ) AIR IN STEIBELT'S STORM
3H4H5H3H    4H4H3H3H     ( I ) SICILIAN AIR
3H4H5H4H    3H2H1H5H     ( I ) LADY MARY MURRAY'S ALLAMANDE
3H4H5H5H    1H4H2H5      ( I ) MISS LAING'S FAVORITE
3H4H5H1T    5H1H2H5      ( I ) MISS OR MAJOR SPICER
3H4H1T2T    5H6H3H2H     ( I ) AND YE SHALL WALK IN SILK ATTIRE
3H5H53      4233H        ( I ) UNTITLED
3H5H72H     61H52        ( I ) TRIP TO EASTON
3H5H1H1H    2H1H3HO      ( I ) TROUBADOUR, THE
3H5H1H1H    3H5H3H6      ( I ) S'TROM TROM A THA MI
3H5H1H2H    51H53H       ( I ) LADY AUGUSTA FITZCLARANCE
3H5H1H3H    6651H        ( I ) PLOUGH BOY, THE
3H5H1H3H    4H3H2H2H     ( I ) DUCHESS OF MANCHESTER'S STRATHSPEY, THE
3H5H2H1H    2H3H1H5H     ( I ) FOUR SEASONS
3H5H2H3H    1H65H2H      ( I ) MY BONNY YOUNG LAD WAS THE FAIREST OF A'
                               [OUR BONNY SCOTCH LADS]
3H5H3H1H    3H6H5H2H     ( I ) LADY MACBETH'S DREAM
3H5H3H1H    4H675        (II) JENNY'S BABEE  [JENNY'S BAWBEE]
3H5H3H1H    4H675        ( I ) JENNY'S BABEE [JENNY'S BAWBEE]
3H5H3H2H    1H1H55       ( I ) LADY BERTIE'S ALLEMAND
3H5H3H2H    2H3H72H      ( I ) MISS MARY DOUGLAS'S REEL
3H5H3H5H    6H4H2H4H     ( I ) SICH A GETTIN' UP STAIRS
3H5H4H1H    3H5H4H3H     ( I ) MARGARET'S FANCY
3H5H4H2H    2H4H1H6      ( I ) FIRST OF DECEMBER, THE
3H5H4H2H    3H4H72H      ( I ) QUICK STEP, 30th REGt
3H5H4H2H    3H5H66       ( I ) FOR A' THAT AND A' THAT
3H5H5H1H    3H6H3H2H     ( I ) LADY LUCY RAMSAY'S STRATHSPEY
3H5H5H1H    5H6H72H      ( I ) LADY LUCY RAMSAY
3H5H5H1H    5H6H3H2H     (II) LADY LUCY RAMSAY
3H5H5H1H    5H6H3H2H     ( I ) LADY LOUISA RAMSAY'S STRATHSPEY
3H5H5H1H    5H6H3H2H     ( I ) MISS TODD'S STRATHSPEY
3H5H5H1H    5H6H3H2H     ( I ) LADY LUCY RAMSAY ('S STRATHSPEY/FAVORITE)
3H5H5H2H    3H72H5       ( I ) QUICK STEP GEN. BURGOYNES
3H5H5H      5H4H3H       ( I ) NEW MINUET DE LA CHASSE AND GAVOT
3H5H5H5H    4H3H2H1H     ( I ) BEVERLY ASSEMBLY
```

```
3H5H5H       5H5H6H      ( I )  BRAES OF BALANDINE, THE
3H5H5H5H     6H1T6H6H    ( I )  CHARLOTE, THE
3H5H5H       6H1H1H      ( I )  O CHIADAINN AN LO
3H5H5H       6H5H4H      ( I )  BRAES OF BALLENDEAN, THE
3H5H5H       6H5H6H      ( I )  BRAES OF BAL(L)ENDEN, THE
3H5H5H       6H5H6H      ( I )  BRAES OF BALLENDINE
3H5H6H3H     2H3H2H5     ( I )  BEAUTIFUL CHARMER, THE
3H5H6H       5H2H2H      ( I )  THA MO GHRUAIDHEAN AIR PREASADH
3H5H6H       5H2H2H      ( I )  MY CHEEKS ARE FURROWED
3H6H1H1H     2H5H3H1H    ( I )  L'ESTELLE
3H6H2H2H     5H2H4H1H    ( I )  SAXON DANCE
3H6H3H3H     51H2H3H     ( I )  I MET IN OUR VILLAGE
3H1T5H5      33H2H2H     ( I )  AIR IN FORTUNATUS
3H1T5H       3H1T6H      ( I )  FAVOURITE AIR, A
4H52H6       4H52H5      ( I )  JOY GAE WI' MY LOVE
4H64H6       4H677       ( I )  MISS MURRY'S REEL
4H2H75       31H2H5      ( I )  MISS GUNNING
4H2H7        553         ( I )  CELEBRATED MEDLEY WALTZ, THE
4H2H1H6      751H5       ( I )  SINGLE JIG
4H2H3H1H     2H1H2H5H    ( I )  RUSSIAN AIR
4H2H4H4      4H2H1H5     ( I )  I'D RATHER HAVE A PIECE
                                THAN A KISS OF MY JO
4H2H4H3H     1H425L      ( I )  MRS RACHAEL GIBSON'S DELIGHT
4H2H5H       3H1H1H      ( I )  WALTZ
4H2H5H1T     3H1H2H2H    ( I )  LADY STOPFORD'S REEL
4H3HO3H      76O2H       ( I )  BEETHOVENS FAVORITE POLLACCA
4H3H2H5      44H3H2H     ( I )  ADIEU (TO FORTGEORGE)
4H3H2H7      576H5H      ( I )  GALOP
4H3H2H7      4H3H66      ( II ) MRS ALEXANDER BRODIE
4H3H2H7      4H3H66      ( II ) ALEXANDER BRODIE
4H3H2H7      4H3H66      ( I )  MRS ALEX(ANDE)R BRODIE('S REEL)
4H3H2H1H     4H3H2H1H    ( I )  NEW WALTZ
4H3H2H       3H1H3H      ( I )  COPENHAGEN WALTZ, THE
4H3H5H6      4H3H5H6     ( I )  LOISG IAD GUAL IO UO
4#H4#H5H1H   72H5H2H     ( I )  COUNTRY DANCE
5H555        51H3H2H     ( I )  JENNY DANG THE WEAVER
5H551H       2H3H1H6     ( I )  CAPT CAMPBELL'S REEL
5H555H       5H4H4H3bH   ( I )  PORT GORDON
5H564        53H1H6      ( II ) IT'S NAE AY FOR WANT O' HEALTH O?
5H564        53H1H6      ( I )  IT'S NAE AY FOR WANT O' HEALTH
                                THE LADIES GANG TO PANNANICH
5H564        5H561H      ( II ) IF YE HAD BEEN WHERE I HAE BEEN
5H53H1H      3H2H1H6     ( II ) PITNACREE FERRYMAN, THE
5H55H5H      4H44H4H     ( I )  ARIA
5H1H3b5      247b7bH     ( I )  DUTCHESS OF BEDFORD'S REEL
5H1H56       5H1H2H1H    ( I )  BURTON HOUSE
5H1H56       5H1H2H1H    ( I )  ITALIAN DANCE
5H1H75       64H2H2H     ( I )  DANCE, A
5H1H71H      1H2H3H2H    ( I )  GREENWICH HILL
5H1H71H      1H2H3H3H    ( I )  GREENWICH HILL
5H1H1H6      5353        ( I )  MISS LINDSAY'S REEL
5H1H1H1H     2H753       ( I )  DUKE OF GLOUCESTER'S MARCH
5H1H2H5      6L242       ( I )  ALLEGRO
5H1H2H5      3675        ( I )  DANC'D BY ALDRIDGE
5H1H2H7      6523        ( I )  SEVENTH REGt
5H1H2H7      6523        ( I )  ROYAL FUSILLIER'S NEW QUICK STEP
5H1H2H1H     1H2H3H4H    ( I )  ADIEU EDINA'S FRIENDLY TOW'RS
5H1H2H2H     5H5H2H1H    ( I )  MISS DUNDAS'S GIGG
5H1H2H3H     5H1H2H1H    ( I )  MISS ALVES'S VALTZ
5H1H3H2H     3H5H3H2H    ( I )  LINKS OF KILLAROW, THE
5H1H3H3H     2H3H3H1H    ( II ) FRENCH AIR
5H1H3H5H     2H572H      ( II ) SKATE, THE
5H1H5H1H     5H1H5H1H    ( I )  MINUET
5H1H6H2H     5H2H75      ( I )  DRURY HILL
5H2H61H      5H2H6H5H    ( I )  BONNIE WEE THING(, THE)
5H2H7        111         ( I )  MR PITT'S MINUET
5H2H1H5      6522        ( I )  LASSES OF DUNCE, THE
5H2H1H5      6542        ( I )  DUKE OF YORK'S FANCY, THE
5H2H1H5      1H4H3H2H    ( I )  JOCK O' HAZELDEAN
5H2H1H5      2H2H2H4H    ( I )  LA POULE
5H2H1H3      162H7       ( I )  POLYGON, THE
5H2H1H3H     6551H       ( II ) WITHIN A MILE OF EDINBURGH TOWN
5H2H1H3H     6551H       ( I )  WITHIN A MILE OF EDINBURGH( TOWN)
5H2H1H3H     7522        ( I )  MISS DUNDASS OF KERSE'S STRATHSPEY
5H2H3H7      61H72H      ( I )  AS NOW WE'RE MET
5H2H5H2H     62H3H2H     ( I )  FREE AND EASY
5H2H5H       1T1T2T      ( I )  IRISH CRY, THE
5H3bH1H3bH   4H2H7bH2H   ( I )  LADY MARY HAY'S REEL
5H3bH5H1T    5H2H1H4H    ( I )  MORN RETURNS, THE
5H3H53       3H5H72H     ( II ) ROBIN'S NEST
5H3H55       72H4H3H     ( I )  TABOR BOY, THE
5H3H53H      5H3H2H1H    ( I )  PORTUGUESE WALTZ
```

186

```
5H3H67        5H3H61H       ( I )  JENNY'S BAWBIE
5H3H75        1H3H73H       ( II ) BIRK HALL
5H3H1H5       6535          ( I )  MISS BETTY McLEAN'S REEL
5H3H1H5       6754          ( I )  BURLIEGH PARK
5H3H1H5       62H2H7        ( I )  WARLEY COMMON
5H3H1H5       62H2H7        ( I )  LES FETES CHAMPETRE
5H3H1H5       62H3H2H       ( I )  HIGHLAND JUBILEE, THE
5H3H1H5       1H2H3H3H      ( I )  BUGLE HORN
5H3H1H5       1H2H4H2H      ( I )  ALDER-WOOD HOUSE
5H3H1H5       5H3H72H       ( II ) LADY CAROLINE MONTAGUE
5H3H1H5       5H3H72H       ( I )  LADY CAROLINE MONTAGUE'S STRATHSPEY
5H3H1H5       5H5H6H3H      ( I )  LA NEIGE
5H3H1H6       5H3H3H2H      ( I )  O'ER THE HILLS
5H3H1H1H      6565          ( I )  LADY BAIRD'S STRATHSPEY
5H3H1H1H      4H2H77        ( I )  AMBIGNO
5H3H1H1H      4H3H72H       ( I )  FAL LAL LA
5H3H1H1H      4H3H1H2H      ( I )  FAVOURITE AIR, A
5H3H1H1H      5H3H3H3H      ( I )  MRS CAPt CAMPBELL
5H3H1H1H      5H6H72H       ( II ) GLENTROMIE
5H3H1H1H      5H6H72H       ( I )  GLENTROMIE
5H3H1H1H      6H1T6H5H      ( I )  LITTLE NABOB, THE
5H3H1H2H      4H2H4H2H      ( I )  BANTRY BAY
5H3H1H3H      64H75         ( I )  CHATSWORTH HOUSE
5H3H2H6       1H1H3H3H      ( I )  AIR BY FINGAL
5H3H2H7       1H542         ( II ) MR GRAY OF CARSE
5H3H2H7       432H2         ( II ) GENERAL WEMYSS( OF WEMYSS)
5H3H2H7       432H2         ( I )  (GENERAL/COLONEL) WEMYSS (OF WEMYSS)
                                   (STRATHSPEY)
5H3H2H7       1H542         ( I )  MR GRAY OF CARSE REEL
5H3H2H7       1H542         ( I )  LADY GRACE DOUGLAS'S REEL
5H3H2H1H      1H2H3H3H      ( I )  CLARINET, THE
5H3H2H1H      1H2H4H1H      ( I )  QUICK STEP
5H3H2H1H      1H2H4H2H      ( I )  MISS DALRYMPLE'S (N(th) BERWICK) JIG
5H3H2H3H      2H4H6H2H      ( I )  HARK I HEAR SWEET MARY COMING
5H3H2H3H      4H3H2H2H      ( I )  JARNOWICK, THE
5H3H2H3H      5H3H2H1H      ( I )  BUY A BROOM
5H3H2H5H      5H3H2H7       ( I )  LORD ELPHINSTON'S REEL
5H3H3H1H      1H555         ( I )  NAPLES DANCE
5H3H3H1H      2H2H1H1H      ( I )  MARCH, A
5H3H3H1H      2H2H1H1H      ( I )  QUICKSTEP IN THE BATTLE OF PRAGUE
5H3H3H3H      2H2H5H3H      ( I )  SINCE THIS I'M DOOM'D
5H3H3H6H      5H4H3H2H      ( I )  AIR IN QUEEN MAB
5H3H3H6H      5H6H2H2H      ( I )  LADY MADELINA PALMER'S STRATHSPEY
5H3H4H2H      1H531         ( II ) JOHN HOWATS REEL
5H3H4H2H      3H52H5        ( I )  CHAPLET, THE
5H3H4H2H      3H1H2H7       ( I )  POOR SOLDIER, THE
5H3H4H2H      3H1H5H5H      ( I )  MARCHE FRANCOISE
5H3H4H2H      3H2H1H1H      ( I )  SECOND QUICK STEP SECOND BATTn. ROYALS
5H3H4H2H      3H2H1H1H      ( I )  MINUET BY DR BOYCE
5H3H4H2H      5H3H53H       ( I )  MRS PITCAIRN'S REEL
5H3H4H2H      5H3H4H1H      ( I )  WHIPMAN LADDIE, THE
5H3H4H3H      572H2H        ( I )  TRIP TO FARLEIGH, A
5H3H4H3H      3H1H2H5       ( I )  LA FETTE DE VILLAGE
5H3H4H3H      5H1H3H1H      ( I )  MISS STEWART'S WALTZ
5H3H5H        771H          ( I )  MINUET
5H3H5H5H3H    4H2H75        ( II ) DOCHGARROCH LODGE
5H3H5H3H      4H4H3HO       ( I )  LADY CHARLES SPENCER'S FANCY
5H3H5H3H      5H3H1H6       ( I )  GIVE ME A DONALD
5H3H5H3H      5H3H1H6       ( I )  GO TO THE DEVIL AND SHAKE YOURSELF
5H3H5H3H      5H4H1H1H      ( I )  COTTILON
5H3H5H3H      6H2H1H1H      ( I )  LA ROCHELLE
5H3H5H3H      6H3H72H       ( I )  FOURTH MEDLEY DANCE
5H3H5H        4H4H3H        ( I )  FOOT'S MINUET
5H3H5H        5H4H3H        ( I )  FOOTE'S MINUET
5H3H5H5H      5H7H5H5H      ( I )  MISS HAMILTON OF WISHAW'S ALLAMANDE
5H3H5H5H      6H5H5H6H      ( I )  ALLEGRO MODERATO
5H3H6H4H      5H3H77        ( I )  CAPT CAMPBELL (OF LOCHNELL'S) Q/STEP
5H4H1H5       6542          ( II ) RICHARD'S
5H4H1H6       553H2H        ( I )  FATHER MOTHER AND SUKE
5H4H1H7       2H1H55        ( I )  KINNOUL PEEBLE HORNPIPE
5H4H1H1H      2H71H5        ( I )  LA ZEMIRE
5H4H1H2H      7L255         ( II ) MAIR'S HORNPIPE
5H4H1H        3bH1H5        ( I )  THRO' THE LANG MUIR I FOLLOW'D HIM HAME
5H4H1H6H      5H4H1H1H      ( I )  TRIUMPH, THE
5H4H2H5H      3H1H2H3H      ( I )  HIGHWAYMAN, THE
5H4H3H2H      1H2H1H2H      ( I )  TOM JONES
5H4H3H2H      1H2H3H2H      ( I )  CAKE SHOP, THE
5H4H3H        2H2H1H        ( I )  AURETT'S MINUET
5H4H3H2H      5H4H3H2H      ( I )  WELL DONE JOCK
5H4H3H3H      3H5H3H1H      ( I )  BEAU NASH
5H4H5H4H      3H1H3H1H      ( I )  MARCH
5H4H5H4H      5H5H2H5       ( I )  LE PLAISIRE DE PLOMBIERE
```

5H4H6H7H	7H6H1TO	(I)	MY PRIDE IS TO HOLD
5H5H1H4	7L41H5H	(II)	PARCEL POST, THE
5H5H1H1H	5565	(I)	ITALIAN DANCE
5H5H1H1H	671H1H	(I)	CARLETON HOUSE
5H5H1H1H	2H71H1H	(I)	LEAP OVER THE GARTER
5H5H1H1H	2H4H3H1H	(I)	QUEEN'S OR 2d REGt QUICK STEP
5H5H1H1H	2H4H3H3H	(I)	PRINCE ADOLPHUS' FANCY
5H5H1H1H	3H3H2H2H	(I)	LANCERS QUADRILLE, THE
5H5H1H2H	5H5H1H1H	(I)	WALTZ
5H5H1H3H	2H2H54	(I)	MRS LEIS HORNPIPE
5H5H1H3H	2H2H54	(I)	RICHER'S HORNPIPE
5H5H1H3H	4H4H2H7	(I)	WE WILL DOWN WITH THE FRENCH
5H5H1H5H	5H5H6H2H	(I)	MRS CARRUTHERS'S REEL
5H5H1H6H	4H2H1H6	(I)	MR EDWARD WAGSTAFF'S FANCY
5H5H2H4H	5H5H5H5H	(II)	RATHA FAIR
5H5H2H4H	5H5H5H5H	(I)	RATHA FAIR
5H5H3H7	4#H5H6H2H	(I)	WALTZE
5H5H3H1H	62H75	(I)	JENNY'S BAWBEE
5H5H3H1H	2H61H1H	(I)	UNDER THE GREEN WOOD TREE
5H5H3H1H	4H675	(I)	JENNY'S BAWBEE
5H5H3H1H	4H2H75	(II)	JENNY'S BAWBEE
5H5H3H1H	4H2H75	(I)	JENNY'S BAWBEE
5H5H3H	2H1H7	(I)	DEAR TOM THIS BROWN JUG
5H5H3H	2H1H1H	(I)	WALTZ
5H5H3H2H	1H1H1H5	(I)	MARCH 3rd REGt OF GUARDS
5H5H3H2H	1H1H1H3H	(I)	DALKEITH VOLUNTEER'S MARCH
5H5H3H2H	1H1H2H2H	(I)	MARCH (FROM "BLUE BEARD")
5H5H3H2H	1H1H3H1H	(I)	NOS GALEN
5H5H3H3H	1H1H1H5	(I)	FRENCH MARINE'S MARCH
5H5H3H3H	1H4H2H2H	(I)	MISS DALRYMPLE OF NORTH BERWICK'S ALLAMAND
5H5H3H3H	4H2H72H	(I)	PRESTO
5H5H3H3H	4H2H3H1H	(I)	MISS WADE'S DELIGHT
5H5H3H	4H4H2H	(I)	PRINCESS ROYAL'S MINUET
5H5H3H5H	2H4H2H4H	(II)	KAFOOZALUM
5H5H4H	1H1H5	(I)	MINUETTO
5H5H4H	2H7b3bH	(I)	S' BEAG MO SHUNND' RIS A CHADAL
5H5H4H2H	5H5H1H5H	(II)	HILTON LODGE
5H5H4H2H	5H5H1H5H	(I)	HILTON LODGE
5H5H4H2H	5H5H2H5	(I)	MRS MacLEOD OF GEANIES'S
5H5H4H3H	5H5H4H1H	(I)	LA DUCHES(SE)
5H5H4H4H	5H5H5H5H	(I)	MAGGY SHANKS
5H5H5H7	5H5H2H1H	(I)	WALTZ
5H5H5H1H	4H6H2H5H	(II)	SANDIE'S GOAT
5H5H5H1H	5H5H2H7b	(I)	MISS CRUIKSHANKS' STRATHSPEY
5H5H5H1H	5H5H2H2H	(I)	MISS MARY SHAND'S REEL
5H5H5H2H	2H2H66	(I)	BERKS OF ENDERMAY, THE
5H5H5H2H	2H2H66	(I)	BIRKS OF INVERMAY, THE
5H5H5H2H	2H4H66	(I)	BERKS OF ENDERMAY, THE
5H5H5H2H	5H5H2H3H	(I)	FAVORITE SCOTCH DIVERTIMENTO
5H5H5H3H	1H1H1H1H	(I)	LANCIER'S QUADRILLE, THE
5H5H5H4H	3H3H3H2H	(I)	KING[OF PRUSSIA]'S MARCH
5H5H5H5H	3H2H1H3	(I)	THIRD QUICK MARCH 15th REGt
5H5H5H5H	4H4H4H4H	(I)	O DEAR WHAT CAN THE MATTER BE
5H5H5H5H	5H4H2H5H	(I)	LA TRENISE
5H5H5H5H	5H5H1H1H	(I)	LADY MARY LINDSAY'S ALLAMANDE
5H5H5H5H	5H5H2H1H	(I)	HONble MRS CHARTERIS'S VALTZ, THE
5H5H5H5H	5H5H2H1H	(I)	GENERAL SUWAROWS WALTZ
5H5H5H5H	5H5H4H2H	(II)	LADY LOUDON
5H5H5H5H	5H5H4H2H	(II)	MAY DAY
5H5H5H5H	5H5H6H2H	(I)	HIGHLAND PLAID, THE
5H5H5H5H	5H5H6H2H	(I)	LADY LOUDON'S STRATHSPEY
5H5H5H6H	2H2H2H5H	(I)	(MOTHER) GOOSE, (THE)
5H5H5H6H	3H3H3H1H	(I)	MARCH OF THE 15 REGt
5H5H5H6H	3H3H3H1H	(I)	BACH'S MARCH
5H5H5H1T	5H5H4H3H	(I)	CARE THOU CANKER
5H5H5#H6H	5H3H1H1H	(I)	MISS WARDLAW'S ALLAMANDE
5H5H6HO	5H5H6HO	(I)	GO GEORGE I CAN'T ENDURE YOU
5H5H6H4H	3H3H4H2H	(I)	HOW IMPERFECT IS EXPRESSION
5H5H6H5H	4H71H1H	(I)	CHARITY BOY, THE
5H5H6H5H	5H5H4H3H	(I)	ADVENTURE AT MARGATE, AN
5H5H6H5H	6H2H1H7	(I)	COLONEL TARLETON'S QUICK MARCH
5H5H7H	1TO1T	(I)	DI PIACER MI BALZA IL COR
5H5H1T6H	5H5H71H	(I)	MRS SITWELLS VALTZ
5H5H1T1T	4H4H6H6H	(I)	VITE MARCHE
5H6bH5H2H	3bH1H2H1H	(I)	PASTORALE
5H6H2H5H	3H3HO3H	(I)	WHERE THE BEE SUCKS
5H6H4H	2H1H1H	(I)	WEYDIMAN'S MINUET
5H6H5H2H	2H2H66	(I)	BIRKS OF INVERMAY, THE
5H6H5H5H	5H6H3H2H	(I)	COME AND RANGE THE FIELDS WI' ME
5H6H5H6H	5H3H2H2H	(II)	MISS W. MACDOWAL OF ARNDILLY
5H6H5H6H	5H3H2H2H	(I)	MISS WILHELMINA McDOWAL'S REEL
5H6H5H6H	5H5H1H1H	(I)	MISS SCOTT OF BELVEAU'S ALLAMANDE

188

```
5H6H6H5H      3H2H1H1H      (I)   LA PIPE TABAC
5H6H1T6H      5H6H1T5H      (I)   UNTITLED
5H1T3H1H      6H4H4H2H      (I)   MISS ROSE'S REEL
5H1T5H5H      5H5H2H2H      (I)   QUICK STEP
5#H2H5H6      1H1H5H1T      (I)   GALOP
6H1H3H1H      6H1H3H2H      (II)  BRIDGE OF BRACKLIN, THE
6H1H3H1H      6H1H3H2H      (II)  KISS ME SWEETLY
6H1H3H1H      6H1H3H2H      (I)   KISS ME SWEETLY
6H1H3H1H      6H1H3H2H      (I)   MISS HACKET'S FAVORITE
6H3H1H        6H3H1H        (II)  DER FREYSCHUTZ WALTZ
6H3H1H        6H3H1H        (I)   DER FREISCHUTZ WALTZ
6H5H4H1H      6H5H1H1H      (I)   GUIRACHA, THE
6H5H4H3H      2H2H6H6H      (I)   AIR BY FINGAL
1T76H5H       1T76H1H       (I)   HUNGARIAN WALTZ
1T1H3H5H      1T1H2H5H      (I)   NORAH CREENA
1T3H3H7       1H2H3H2H      (I)   MINUET
1T3H4H7       1H2H3H7       (I)   VULCAN'S FORGE
1T5H51H       1T5H51H       (I)   COSSACK WALTZ
1T5H3H5H      1T5H3H5H      (I)   WEST LOTHIAN CAVALRY'S MARCH, THE
1T5H5H3H      1H2H1H3H      (I)   GRAND MARCH, A
1T5H5H3H      6H5H72H       (I)   LADY ANN STEWARTS STRATHSPEY
1T1T3H1H      2H5H1H6       (I)   HAPPY RETURN, THE
1T1T5H5H      3H1H05        (I)   MARCHE
1T1T3T1T      5H5H1T5H      (I)   FIN CH' HAN DAL VINO
```

Appendices

All the listings in this section are of collections of
instrumental music for the violin or piano, with the exception
of James Johnson's "Musical Museum"(J3). This is clearly a
vocal collection and therefore outwith the stricter limits of
the main index, yet his work as a collector has such bearing on
the instrumental repertoire that it would have been damaging to
exclude it. Of the rest:

(G9) "The Vocal Melodies of Scotland" (Nathaniel Gow, c. 1822).
To have excluded these three small volumes entirely would have
obscured the real extent of the Gow family's achievement in the
publishing field. They contain the vocal "favourites" (song
airs) of the turn of the century, almost all of which feature
elsewhere among the listed collections.

(H4) John Murdoch Henderson's "Flowers of Scottish Melody", a
personal selection of fine music, rendered rather less objective
by the inclusion of forty pieces of his own composition.
(Glasgow, 1935).

(J3) James Johnson: "The Songs or Airs contained in the Scots
Musical Museum" (Edinburgh, 1771). Six volumes, numbered
consecutively.

(K3) Ernest Koehler & Son: "Violin Repository of Dance Music"
(Edinburgh, 1881/5), a rich mix of traditional and contemporary
ballroom material, strongly influenced by transatlantic and con-
tinental flavours. Originally published in serial form, but
latterly in three volumes whose pages are numbered
consecutively.

(continued)

(L6) Logan & Co.'s six-volume "...Collection of Highland Music arranged for the Violin" (Glasgow, 1924) which is predominently music gathered from the pipe repertoire, interspersed with traditional material. The "Inverness Collection of Highland Pibrochs, Laments, &c." is, disappointingly, not much more than a shortened version of the other (Also in 6 volumes or "parts")

(Mc3) K.N. MacDonald's "Gesto Collection of Highland Music" (Edinburgh, 1895), companion to his "Skye Collection"(Mc3v1 in A-Z Index II) but in this case largely consisting of Gaelic vocal music, much of it with all or part of the Gaelic words.

(W3) John Walsh: "Caledonian Country Dances, Being a Collection of all the Celebrated SCOTCH COUNTRY DANCES now in Vogue" (London, 1744 -). [In company with various partners, Walsh pub. other dance books and song collections; see BL, NLS etc.]

(F2) An English index to Capt. Simon Fraser's " Airs & Melodies peculiar to the Highlands of Scotland and the Isles ..." (First published Edinburgh, 1816). Appended because his original index favours the Gaelic titles and the inclusion of both Gaelic and English titles did not appear to resolve the difficulty.

(CDS) An Index, prepared by John Drewry of Aberdeen, containing nearly 1000 tune titles, A-Z, being the music from the Dance Books published by the Royal Scottish Country Dance Society since 1924 and reproduced here with the agreement of the RSCDS. Altogether they form an invaluable source of good traditional music, much of it rare and difficult to locate. The whole collection is in print and available from the RSCDS. See note at Appendix (CDS).

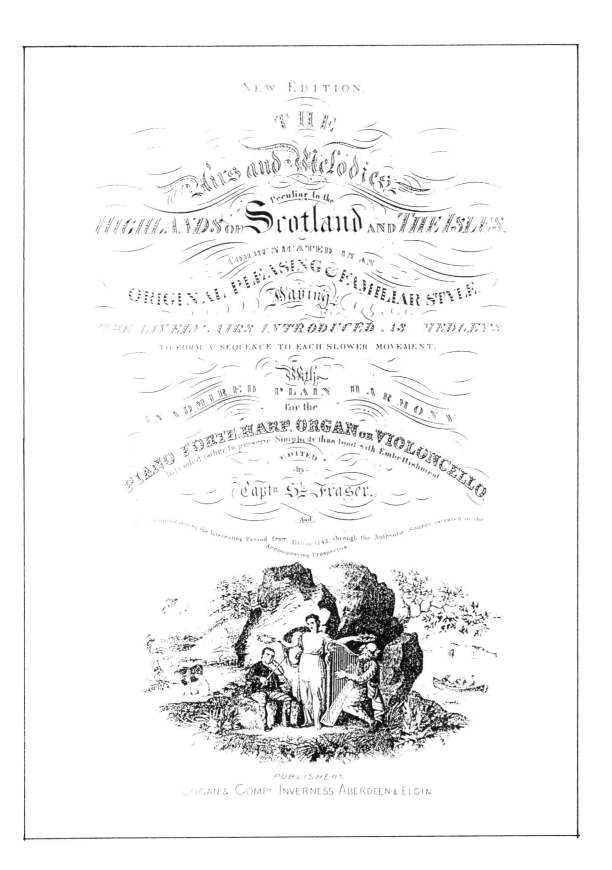

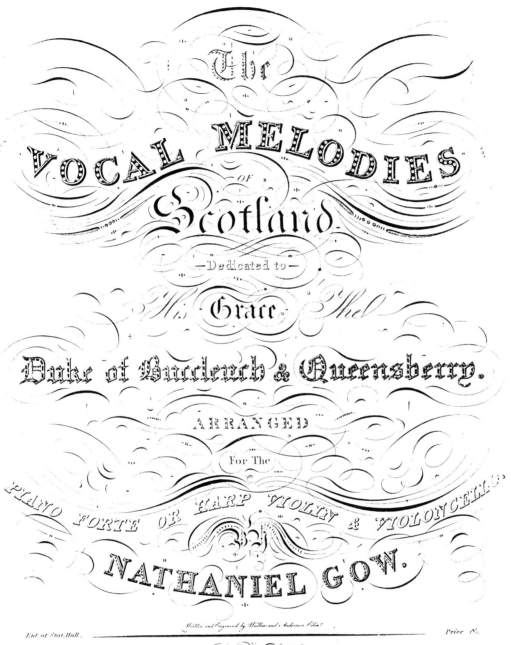

The
VOCAL MELODIES
OF
Scotland
—Dedicated to—
His Grace The
Duke of Buccleuch & Queensberry.
ARRANGED
For The
PIANO FORTE OR HARP VIOLIN & VIOLONCELLO
BY
NATHANIEL GOW.

Ent. at Stat. Hall.   Written and Engraved by Walker and Anderson Edin!   Price 8/,

Edinburgh.
Printed for & Sold by Nathaniel Gow and Son Music Sellers N° 60 Princes Street.
Where may be had lately Published in two Parts Price 8/ each the
BEAUTIES OF NIEL GOW.
The above to be had also of John Gow N° 31 Great Marlbro Street.

LONDON.

SOLD BY
F. & G. MELVILLE,
59?
ARGYLE-STREET,
GLASGOW

SIGNED FOR NATH GOW & SON

"THE VOCAL MELODIES OF SCOTLAND, DEDICATED TO
HIS GRACE THE DUKE OF BUCCLEUCH & QUEENSBERRY,
ARRANGED FOR THE PIANOFORTE, OR HARP VIOLIN &
VIOLONCELLO BY NATHANIEL GOW." (Edinburgh,
c.1822) 3 books (in one) each 36pp.

THE FATHER OF STRATHSPEY & REEL PLAYERS

NEIL GOW
1727~1807

THE GREATEST PRESERVER & IMPROVER of the AGE

NATHANIEL GOW
1763~1831

FLOWERS OF SCOTTISH MELODY

A First Companion to
The Scottish Violinist and Pianist

OVER 130 MASTERPIECES OF THE AGES
INCLUDING FORTY ORIGINAL CONTRIBUTIONS

SLOW AIRS
PASTORALS
QUICKSTEPS
ETC.

THE·STRATHSPEY·KING

JAMES·SCOTT·SKINNER
1843-1927

: REELS :
STRATHSPEYS
HORNPIPES
ETC.

EXPRESSLY ARRANGED FOR
VIOLIN & PIANO

WITH FULL INSTRUCTIONS
AND HISTORY OF ORIGINS

by

J. MURDOCH HENDERSON

THE TARLAND MINSTREL

PETER MILNE
1824~1908

Atholl Edition in Cloth Covers
With Elaborate Notes and Biographies
PRICE 10/- NET

Published for the Author by

BAYLEY & FERGUSON
54 QUEEN STREET
GLASGOW

THE FIRST COMPOSER OF STRATHSPEYS of the AGE

WM MARSHALL
1748~1833

Engraved and Printed by AIRD & COGHILL, LTD.

FLOWERS OF SCOTTISH MELODY. A First Companion to the Scottish
Violinist and Pianist. Over 130 Masterpieces of the Ages,
including 40 original contributions, by J. Murdoch Henderson.

GLASGOW, 1935

TITLE	TYPE	PAGE	SOURCE
Alexr. R. Findlay	Hp	50	JMH
Annie is my Darling	R	41	Capt. S. Fraser (F2v2)
Auld Brig o' Don, The	Pas	53	Jas. Henry (H5)
Aul'er Style, The	R	11	JMH
Beauty of the North, The	Str	53	Capt. Fraser (F2v2)
Braes o' Busby, The	SM	8	Repos. (Mc12) ("Bushbie")
Braes o' Mar, The	Str	21	Bremner (B15)
Braes o' Tullymet, The	Str	11	N. Stewart (S12)
Brechin Castle	Str	17	Gow Repos./1 (G11v2A)
Bridge of Dee, The	Str	23	Jas. Young, Lowe/4(L8v4)
Bridge of Dee, The	R	23	" "
Cailleach na Beinne Brice	Air	7	D. Campbell's Coll., 1862
Cairdin' o't	CD	2	Kerr/2 (K2v2)
(cf: Salt Fish & Dumplings)			J. Aird/3 (A1v3)
Captain Gillan's	Str	40	Wm. Christie (C18)
"C.D." Strathspey, The	Str	43	JMH
Charles Hardie	Str	34	JMH ("Methlick Wonder")
Charles Sutherland	R	47	JMH (Violinist)
Clydeside Lasses, The	R	28	Gow/6 (G10v6)
Coilsfield House	Air	6	Gow/5 (G10v5)
Crighton's	Jig	15	JMH
Cross of Inverness, The	R	7	Fraser ("Clachnacudain")
Departed Worth	Lam	55	JMH (to his father)
Donald Morison	R	37	Alex. Grant, Inverness
Duchess of Bedford, The	S/Str	15	Wm. Marshall (M4v3)
Duke of Atholl, The	Str	42	Alex. Walker, 1866 (W1)
East Neuk of Fife, The	CD	3	Version in Skinner (S8v8)
(cf: "She grip'd at the greatest on't") in Oswald (O1)			
Eugene Stratton	Hp	17	J.S. Skinner (only here)
F.D. Mainland (Shetland)	QS	49	JMH
Fire and Fervour	R	37	JMH (To John Dickie)
Firth House, The	Hp	14	Anon. (Also in Kohler/3)
Flowers of Edinburgh, The	CD	2	Var. versions; (cf:K2v1)
Forth Bridge, The	Str	22	W. Blyth (? First publish-
Forth Bridge, The	R	22	" here)
Frank Gilruth	Str	48	Peter Milne (First pub-
Frank Gilruth	R	48	" " lished here)
Gavin Greig	Str	24	JMH (Buchan Musician)
George Riddell	R	25	JMH (Rosehearty Musician)
George's Delight	R	56	JMH
George I. Taylor	Str	10	JMH (L/handed Fiddler)
Gillan's Reel	R	40	Attrib: Peter Milne
Good Old John	R	38	JMH (Strichen Violinist)
Greig's "Strathspey"	Pas	8	Gow/2 (G10v2) etc.
Haslam's Hornpipe	Hp	48	Kohler/1
Heiress, The	R	42	Att: Fraser in Lowe/6 (L8)
Hey to Couper (Cupar)	Pas	19	Bremner/pt 12 (B15)
Highlands of Banffshire	Str	29	Fraser (Braighe Bhanbh)
Highland Troop, The	Pas	5	" ('nTrupa Ghaidheal...)
House of Skene, The	Air	14	Jas. Davie Bk2/2nd Series
Inveraray Castle	Str	44	Fraser (Caisteal Inbher-)
"J.B." Reel, The	R	44	JMH (J.B. Paterson M.A.)
J.F. Dickie's Delight	S/Str	30	JMH (Great Fiddler)
J.F. Dickie's Reel	R	31	JMH
J. Scott Skinner	Str	32	JMH
J. Scott Skinner	R	33	JMH (The Strathspey King)
Jenny Dang the Weaver	R	21	Orpheus Caled. (T6) etc.
John Cheap the Chapman	R	9	Gow's Repos./2 (G11v2B)
Johnnie's made a Waddin' o't	R	1	N. Stewart/pt.6 (S12v1)
Keep it up (As a Thoiseach)	R	56	Anon. Fraser (F2v2)
Keithmore	Pas	53	Wm. Marshall (M4v3)
Lady Ann Hope (Miss Hope)	Str	7	Att: J. Pringle (G11v2D)
Lady Caroline Montague	M	51	Gow/4 (G10v4)
Lady Charlotte Campbell	Str	6	Nath. Gow, Gow/3 G10v3
Lady Doll Sinclair	R	41	Bremner/pt.1 (B15)
Lady Margaret Stewart	R	42	Anon. Gow/2 (G10v2)
Lady Mary Primrose's Fav.	Pas	15	Clarkson (C23); (G10v4)
Lady Mary Ramsay	Str	23	In Gow/4 (G10v4)
Lady Montgomery	R	17	Earl of Eglinton (E2) etc.
Let not Scotland lose her fame		18	JMH (Pastoral on J.S.S.)
Loch Earn (or Tilt Side)	R	7	Nath. Gow (G10v2)
Loch Ericht (Erroch) Side	Pas	49	In McGlashan (Mc9v3p30)
Loch Riach (Broch Dam)	M	41	JMH ("To Alex. Grant")
Lodge of Glentana, The	Str	45	J.S. Skinner (Elgin/S8v5)
Lone Highland Glen, The	Air	54	JMH (A tribute)
Madam Frederick	S/Str	39	Wm. Marshall (M4v3)
Major and Minor	R	45	JMH (To Haydn P. Halstead)
Mallard, The	Hp	14	JMH (To E. Calder, A'deen)
Marchioness of Huntly, The	Str	35	Wm. Marshall (M4v3)
Marquis of Huntly, The	Str	9	" " (M4v1)
Marquis of Huntly's Snuff	Mull	26	Marshall's "Miss Dallas"
	Pas		(M4v2); also Gow/4 (G10v4)
Minstrel's Home, The	Air	12	JMH (To Harold Coombs)
Mirth and Melody	Str	36	JMH (To Miss F. Dickie)
Miss Campbell of Saddell	Pas	14	Robt. Mackintosh (Mc21v3)
Miss Graham of Inchbrakie	Air	50	Nath. Gow (Gow/2, G10v2)
Miss Forbes' F/well to Banff		53	I. Cooper (C8v1; G11v2D)
Miss Innes of Meldrum	Str	22	Arr. JMH/airs by Cooper
Miss Laura Andrew	M	47	J.S. Skinner (H&C/S8v8)
Miss Maria Carr, A'deen	Pas	13	JMH (Blind Pianist)
Miss Rose of Tarlogie	S/Str	33	In D. Grant (G15)
Mr. Alex. Laing, Leuchold	Hp	48	Wm. Marshall (M4v3)
Mr. Gordon of Hallhead	Str	6	Wm. Marshall (M4v3)
Mrs. A.R. Findlay	R	51	JMH (A'deen High School)
Mrs. B. Catto	S/Str	19	JMH (Reciter of Poetry)
Mrs. C. Sutherland	Str	46	JMH (Pianist, Fraserburgh)
Mrs. Forbes Leith	R	17	J.S.S.(Whitehaugh, A'deen)
Mrs. Garden of Troup	Str	28	R. Petrie/2 (P5v2)
Mrs. Gordon Bruce	R/CD	5	JMH (C.D. Dancer, A'deen)
Mrs. Gordon of Park	Pas	40	Wm. Marshall (M4v4)
Mrs. G. Sinclair	PM	40	JMH (Pianist, A'deen)
Mrs. Johnston (Glen Ogle)	R	23	By D. Grant (G15)
Mrs. Shand, Aberdeen	Str	4	JMH (Cel. Country Dancer)
Muir o' Gellan, The	Str	38	Peter Milne (? only here)
New Brig o' Dee, The	Str	20	?"Johnnie Steel" in Kohler
New Brig o' Dee, The	R	21	Niven Ms. (1761), A'deen
New Brig o' Methlick, The	Str	28	Wm. Hardie, of Methlick
New Brig o' Methlick, The	R	28	" "
New Kelvin Bridge, The	R	37	Archd. Morrison (Vn/maker)
Niel Gow's Lament for	Air	6	Niel Gow (G10v1, 1784)
Jas. Moray Esq., of Abercairney			

(This volume also contains interesting notes on the music, etc.)

INDEX

OF THE

SONGS OR AIRS CONTAINED IN THE MUSICAL MUSEUM.

JOHNSON, JAMES ("THE SCOTS MUSICAL MUSEUM")

First published: EDINBURGH 1771
(Six volumes, numbered consecutively; 686 airs)

"The Songs or Airs contained in the Scots
 Musical Museum"

KÖHLERS'
VIOLIN REPOSITORY

OF

DANCE MUSIC,

COMPRISING

Reels, Strathspeys, Hornpipes, Country Dances,

QUADRILLES, WALTZES, &c.

EDITED BY

A PROFESSIONAL PLAYER.

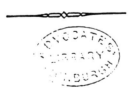

EDINBURGH: ERNEST KÖHLER & SON, MUSICSELLERS, 11 NORTH BRIDGE.
MORISON BROTHERS, 99 BUCHANAN STREET, GLASGOW.
MARTIN, ABERDEEN.   MENZIES & CO., EDINBURGH.
J. CUNNINGHAM, DUNDEE.   J. M. MILLER, PERTH.   WILLIAM DEAS, KIRKCALDY.
JAMES HORSBURGH, 73 GEORGE STREET, DUNEDIN, NEW ZEALAND.
LONDON: CATTY & DOBSON, 14 PILGRIM ST., LUDGATE HILL.

KOEHLER'S "VIOLIN REPOSITORY" OF DANCE MUSIC (1881-85)   (K3)
(3 Books in 1, numbered consecutively, with advertising data &
editorial interleaved. The music was originally published in
the form of 8-page broadsheets, also consecutively numbered).

Title	Temp	Key	Bk	Page	Author/Source
A1 JIG, THE	J	A	3	274	Wm. Findlay
ADELPHI POLKA	Pka	GDC	1	35	
AERIAL QUADRILLE	Qd	-	3	241/2	J.S.Sandyholm
AGNES SOREL QUADRILLES	Qd	-	1	39/41	
AIR FROM GUILLAUME TELL	3/4	G	2	184	Rossini
ALBERT HP.	Hp	E	2	151	Radford
ALBERT HP., THE	Hp	D	2	188	W.C.Paton
ALEXANDRIA SCHOTTISCHE, THE	Sch	FBb	1	112	J.Davidson
ALSTON HP., THE	Hp	F	1	28	
ANNIE IS MY DARLING	R	A	3	230	S.Fraser Coll.
ANNIE SCHOTTISHE, THE	Sch	BbEb	1	74	Wilcox
ANNIE'S HP.	Hp	D	3	250	W.B.Laybourn
ANYBODY'S HP.	Hp	A	1	76	
AP SHENKIN, Rondo	J	GE	3	258/9	
ARTHUR'S SEAT	W	GD	3	285	L.J.Collins
ATHOL BROSE (Niel Gow's Fav.)	S	D	1	7	Gow
BAB AT THE BOWSTER	J	G	1	96	(1729)
BALL HP., THE	Hp	D	3	251	Wm. Findlay
BALL MARCH, THE	M	D	2	178	Wm. Findlay
"BALMORAL" STRATHSPEY(1884)	S	A	3	219	W.B.Laybourn
BANKS OF ALLAN WATER, THE	J	D	1	6	
BANKS OF LOCH NESS, THE	S	G	3	196	
BEAUFORT CASTLE	R	A	3	204	
BEAUTIFUL DANUBE WALTZES	W	DGFA	2	130/1	J.Strauss
BEAUTY OF THE NORTH, THE	SS	Eb	1	46	Capt.S.Fraser
BEDDING OF THE BRIDE, THE	R	D	2	172	S.Fraser Coll.
BEESWING HP.	Hp	Bb	2	133	Jas. Hill
BELLADRUM HOUSE	S	D	2	103	S.Fraser Coll.
BELL POLKA, THE	Pka	CGF	3	266	E.Ames M'park
BE SHARP BEFORE ITS' DARK	R	E	2	146	
BILLY MILL	Hp	D	2	125	Jas. Henderson
BISHOP AUCKLAND FLOWER SHOW	Hp	E	1	61	W.B.Laybourn
BLACK BUT COMELY	R	D	2	126	
BLACKCOCK OF WICKHAM, THE	R	F	2	146	
BLACK JOCK, with var.s	J	A	3	207/10	
BLACKSMITH'S HP.[cf:BRISTOL HP]	Hp	A	1	56	
BLAYDON (or BLAYDEN) FLATS	Hp	D	1	66	
BLINKIN' TIBBIE	Hp	Bb	3	275	R.Baillie
BLUE BONNETS - Hp.	Hp	C	3	212	
BLUE BONNETS OVER THE BORDER	6/8	Bb	1	30	
BOB CHADDUCK'S JIG	2/4	A	1	77	
BOB JOHNSTONE	S	A	1	18	A.W.Doig
BOB JOHNSTONE	R	A	1	19	A.W.Doig
BOB THE SAILOR	Hp	G	3	232	
BOTTLE BANK, THE	Hp	Bb	1	28	Jas. Hill
BRAES OF TULLYMET, THE	S	G	3	261	
BRECHIN CASTLE	S	Bb	1	158	
BRIDAL MARCH, THE	M	D	1	10	D.Kippen
BROADSWORD HP., THE	Hp	Bb	2	150	
BURNS' HP. [or STATEN ISLAND]	Hp	D	1	67	
BUSHWICK HP.	Hp	Bb	3	195	
BUY A BROOM - with var.s	3/4	D	3	233	
CABER FEY	R	C	3	288	
CAGE HP., THE	Hp	A	1	87	Jas. Hill
CAIRDS O' KEITH	S	D	3	218	J.McQueen
CALDER'S WELCOME	S	A	3	215	J.McQueen
CALEDONIAN QUADRILLES	Qd	-	1	70/71	
CALEDONIA'S WAIL FOR NIEL GOW	SS	B	3	288	Capt.S.Fraser
CALIFORNIA HP.	Hp	A	2	143	Jas. Hill
CALIFORNIA HP.	Hp	D	2	180	
CALTON VALSE	W	G	1	83	J.Hamilton
CAMERONIAN RANT	R	F	1	91	
CAMPBELL'S HP.	Hp	D	3	221	W.B.Laybourn
CAPTAIN KEELER	R	BbG	1	47	
CATCH AND KISS THE ROMP	R	C	3	197	S.Fraser Coll.
CEASE NOT TO ROW, BRAVE BOYS	J	C	2	168	S.Fraser Coll.
CELIA SCOTTISCHE	Sch	CF	3	211	John Taylor
CHAMBERS' HP.	Hp	A	1	80	R.Stephenson
CHAMPION HP., THE	Hp	E	2	125	Jas. Hill
CHASE POLKA	Pka	DG	2	97	
CHOEUR DES CHASSEURS	3/4	D	2	122	
CHORUS LANCERS QUADRILLES, THE	LQ	-	3	254>	Arr:W.Crow
CLACH NA CUDAIN	S	D	2	102	
CLASPER'S HP.	Hp	D	1	45	
CLOG STOP DANCE	Cl	Bb	1	71	
COBURN'S DELIGHT	Hp	Bb	3	248	
COCK OF THE NORTH, THE	S	Bb	3	205	S.Fraser Coll.
(COLIN) McKAY'S REEL	R	C	3	237	D.Dow
COLLEGE HP. [or JACK'S THE LAD]	Hp	Bb	1	44	
COLONEL McBAIN	R	G	1	90	
COMELY GARDEN	R	A	2	119	D.Dow
COMET HP., THE	Hp	G	2	175	Wm.Findlay
CONDOR VALSE, THE	W	EbBb	2	113	J.Davidson
CONFUSION HP.	Hp	G	2	108	
CONQUEST, THE	CD	GC	2	120	
CONWAY HP.	Hp	Bb	2	132	
CORNET HP.	Hp	F	3	202	W.P.Robertson
CORRYMONNY STRATHSPEY	S	A	3	204	Capt.S.Fraser
COUNTESS OF CASSILLIS	S	A	2	157	
COUNTESS OF CASSILLIS	R	A	2	157	
COUNTESS OF SUTHERLAND	R	Bb	1	59	Geo. Jenkins
CRAIGELLACHIE BRIDGE	S	D	1	78	Wm.Marshall
CRAIGELLACHIE LASSES, THE	J	D	1	49	Wm.Marshall
CRAIGMILLAR CASTLE	S	G	3	218	W.C.Paton
CRAIGMILLAR CASTLE	R	G	3	218	W.C.Paton
CRAZY JANE'S REEL	R	A	1	52	
CROSS OF INVERNESS	R	G	2	167	S.Fraser Coll.
CROWN HP., THE	Hp	Bb	3	220	W.C.Paton
CUCKOO VALSE	W	AF#	2	112	
CUMBERLAND REEL	R	Bb	2	134	
DAISY HP. (1884)	Hp	F	3	227	Jas.Francis
DALRY HOUSE	S	D	2	126	Gow Repos(3)
DARLING, THE	S	F#	3	230	S.Fraser Coll.
DASHING WHITE SERGEANT	CD	F	3	240	
DAVIE LONIE'S FARMYARD HP.	Hp	F	3	250	W.B.Laybourn
DAVIE MOFFAT	Hp	AF#	3	234	R.Baillie
DEAD MARCH IN SAUL, THE	M	C	2	129	
DEAN BRIDGE, EDINBRO', THE	SS	Eb	1	59	
DEIL AMONG THE MEAL MEN, THE	J	G	2	97	
DEIL AMONG THE TAILORS, THE	R	A	1	55	
DEWDROP SCHOTTISCHE	Sch	DAG	3	268	
DOCTOR, THE [BALVENIE CASTLE]	S	Bb	2	121	Wm.Marshall
DONALD BUTCHER'S BRIDAL (Vars)	2/2	D	3	244/5	

Title	Type	Key	Bk	Page	Composer
DONALD QUAICH'S REEL	R	A	2	110	
DRAM SHELL, THE	R	F#	1	85	Capt.S.Fraser
DUCHESS OF ATHOLE'S STRATHSPEY	S	D	1	68	Niel Gow
DUET FOR TWO VIOLINS	Dt	C	3	270	Rbt.Baillie
DUET FOR TWO VIOLINS	Dt	G	3	278/9	Rbt.Baillie
DUKE OF ALBANY'S SCHOTTISCHE	Sch	GC	2	174	Wm.Findlay
DUKE OF GORDON'S STR., THE	S	E	2	118	R.Mackintosh
DUKE'S HP., THE	Hp	Bb	2	164	
DUMB MAN OF MANCHESTER	R	C	2	150	
DUNFERMLINE RACES	R	A	2	127	
DUNKELD HOUSE	J	E	2	152	Niel Gow
DUNSE DINGS A', THE	R	A	1	47	
DUO POUR DEUX VIOLONS	Dt	C	3	238/9	Jas.C.Paton
DURHAM RANGERS	Hp	D	1	45	
DUTCH POLKA	Pka	D	1	89	
EARL MARSHAL'S REEL	R	F	2	191	
EARL OF DALHOUSIE'S WELCOME FROM THE PYRENEES, THE	SS	F	2	159	Nath. Gow
EARL OF EGLINTON'S STRATHSPEY	S	E	2	118	Nath. Gow
EAST NEUK OF FIFE, THE	CD	G	1	64/5	
EDINBRO' CASTLE	S	Bb	2	141	
EDINBRO' MARCH	M	A	2	179	Paul Wallace
EDINBRO' NORTH BRIDGE	Hp	AE	1	61	W.B.Laybourn
EDINBURGH REVIEW WALTZES	W	BbF	1	20/21	P. Milne
EIGHT BELLS	Hp	G	1	77	
ELECTRIC POLKA, THE	Pka	BbEb	2	123	J.Davidson
EMELINA POLKA	Pka	CGF	3	217	J.C. Paton
EMERALD HP., THE	Hp	Bb	2	188	W.C. Paton
ENTERPRISE HP., THE	Hp	A	2	117	Jas. Hill
EWIE WI' THE CROOKED HORN, THE	S	G	3	230	
EXERCISE FROM "LODER" - DUET	2/4	G	3	286	(Also 3/4 Set)
FACTORY SMOKE	Hp	G	1	8	
FAIR FA' THE MINSTREL	R	Bb	3	205	
(LARGO'S)FAIRY DANCE, THE	R	D	1	55	Nath. Gow
"FAIRY WEDDING, THE"	Pka	Bb G		200	W.C. Paton
FANCY, THE	Hp	A	1	67	W.B.Laybourn
FANCY CLOG HP.	Hp	FD	2	181	
FASHION WHICH THE LASSES HAVE	R	F#	2	166	S.Fraser Coll.
FAVOURITE HP., THE	Hp	A	2	175	Wm. Findlay
FAVOURITE JIG	J	G	1	36	Alex. Deas
FEATHER BED REEL	R	C	2	147	
FIDDLER'S CRAMP, THE	Hp	F	1	80	
FIDDLER'S FANCY, THE	Hp	E	2	108	
FIFE STRATHSPEY	S	A	1	43	Alex. Deas
FIRE CROSS SONG, THE	J	C	2	168	S.Fraser Coll.
FIREFLY HP.	Hp	Bb	1	81	
FIRST OF MAY, THE	Hp	A	1	44	
FIRTH HOUSE	Hp	BbG	3	271	Comm: G.Duncan
FISHER'S HP.	Hp	F	2	156	
FLOWERS OF EDINBURGH, THE	CD	G	1	81	
FLYING DUTCHMAN, THE	Hp	A	2	116	Jas. Hill
FOR A' THAT AN' A' THAT	R	D	2	102	
FOREST WHERE THE DEER RESORT	S	D	2	182	S.Fraser Coll.
FORGET-ME-NOT HP.	Hp	G	3	213	J.C. Paton
FORTH BRIDGE, THE	Hp	Bb	1	14	W.B.Laybourn
(MASTER) FRANCIS SITWELL	SS	Bb	1	47	
FRENCH VALSE, A	W	D	3	201	
FURIOSO GALOP	Gp	DA	1	75	
GAIETY HP., THE	Hp	G	2	180	W.C. Paton
GARB OF OLD GAUL, THE	QS	Bb	1	4	(Gen. J. Reid)
GARDNER LADS, THE	Hp	A	2	143	Jas. Hill
GEBURSTAG'S VALSE	W	G	1	12	
GEM SCHOTTISCHE	Sch	C	1	89	
GENERAL GARIBALDI	S	D	1	92	J.F. Fettes
GENERAL GARIBALDI	R	D	1	92	J.F. Fettes
GENERAL GORDON'S HP.	Hp	A	3	275	Wm. Findlay
GENERAL McDONALD	R	C	2	135	Niel Gow
GERMAN VALSE, A	W	A	3	201	
GILLIE CALLUM	S	A	1	88	
GIPSY'S HP.	Hp	G	1	95	
GIRNIGOE CASTLE	S	G	2	148	Bain, Wick
GLEN FARNETE (FERNATE)	R	F	3	257	
GLENPATRICK WALTZES	W	Bb	3	249	John B. Easton
GLEN'S HP.	Hp	FC	1	95	
GRAND OLD MAN v. GLADSTONE, THE	Hp	E	3	235	W.B.Laybourn
GRAPE VINE TWIST	Hp	E	2	189	
GREAT EASTERN, THE	S	A	1	18	A.W. Doig
GREAT EASTERN	R	A	1	18	A.W. Doig
GREEN FIELDS OF AMERICA	R	A	2	104	
GREY DAYLIGHT	S	D	2	148	
HART'S 10TH SET OF QUADRILLES	Qd	-	2	138/9	
HARVEST HOME HP.	Hp	D	1	37	
HASLAM'S HP.	Hp	E	1	53	
HAWK HP., THE	Hp	E	2	125	Jas. Hill
HAWTHORNDEN	CD	D	3	275	J. Nash
HEARTY LASSES O' SHIELDS, TH'	Hp	A	2	108	R.Stephenson
HIGHLAND DRESS AND ARMOUR	SS	C	2	172	S.Fraser Coll.
HIGHLANDMAN IN PARIS, THE	S	E	2	158	
HIGHLANDS OF BANFFSHIRE, THE	S	F	1	91	S.Fraser Coll.
HIGHLAND WHISKY	S	A	1	46	
HIGH LEVEL HP., THE	Hp	Bb	1	8	
HIGH ROAD TO FT. AUGUSTUS, THE	R	B	2	172	
HON. MISS DRUMMOND OF PERTH	S	E	1	96	
HOOLEY'S HP.	Hp	Bb	3	272	R.M. Hooley
HOOP HER AND GIRD HER	J	G	2	152	
HOP BITTERS, THE	Hp	BbF	1	8	
HORNPIPE	Hp	A	1	53	
HORNPIPE	Hp	C	1	66	
HORNPIPE	Hp	A	3	221	Archie Allan
HOWARD HP.	Hp	A	3	195	
HUNTER, THE	Hp	C	2	132	Jas. Hill
HUNTER'S VALSE, THE	Hp	BbEb	3	269	
HUNTLY'S WEDDING MEDLEY	S	A	3	204	Capt.S.Fraser
HUNTSMAN'S CHORUS, THE	Gp	D	2	122	Weber
I'LL BREAK YOUR HEAD FOR YOU	R	G	2	183	S.Fraser Coll.
I'LL KISS THE BONNIE LASS	R	Eb	1	59	S.Fraser Coll.
IMPERIAL HP.	Hp	FGBb	3	227	Jas. Francis
INVERARAY CASTLE	S	F#	1	84	S.Fraser Coll.
INVERNESS LASSES	R	F	3	231	Capt.S.Fraser
IRISH AIR - JIG	J	D	2	152	
IRISH GIRL	J	A	2	192	
IRISH JIG	J	G	3	268	John B. Easton
IRISHMAN'S FANCY	HpR	B	2	188	
IRISH REEL	R	D	1	58	
IRISH REEL	R	G	1	58	
JACK DOBSON'S REEL	R	E	2	142	H. Shaw
JACKY TAR	Hp	E	1	67	
JAMES SOUTAR OF PLAINS	J	D	1	43	Alex. Deas
JAMES WARE OF WICK	S	G	3	224	J.McQueen
JAYBIRD'S HP., THE	Hp	FC	2	164	

Title	Type	Key	Vol	Page	Composer/Note
JEANIE IN THE GLEN	S	Bb	3	214	J.McQueen
JEANIE'S REEL (Adapted from ^)	R	Bb	3	214	W.B.Laybourn
JENKINS' HP. (cf: WASHINGTON)	Hp	Bb	1	56	
JENNY'S BAWBEE (OLD SET)	R	D	1	73	
JENNY'S BAWBEE (NEW SET)	R	D	1	7	
JESSIE THE FLOWER OF DUNBLANE	Hp	Bb	1	86	Adapt:C.Rock
JIG	J	Bb	1	4	
JIG	J	G	1	51	Alex. Deas
JOCKY DANCE, THE	Hp?	D	1	45	
JOHN DIAMOND'S HP.	Hp	D	2	189	
JOHN DWIGHT'S PLANTATION DANCE	D	D	3	240	
JOHNNY COPE - with var.s	QS	G	1	57	
JOHNNY COPE - Reel	R	G	1	23	
JOHNNY LAD	R	E	2	118	(Very old)
JOHNNY MILLICENT(ROYAL BELFAST)	Hp	D	1	53	
JOHNNY STEEL(E) - ORKNEY	S	D	2	172	J.Barnett
JOHN O' GROATS	J	D	3	200	John Bain,Wick
JOHN PATERSON'S MARE GOES FOREMOST	J	F	1	82	
JOHNSTON'S HP.	Hp	D	3	203	
JULIANNU'S MARCIO GALOP	Gp	D	1	13	
KEEL ROW, THE - with var.s	2/4	G	3	281	
KEEP IT UP	R	E	1	58	S.Fraser Coll.
KEEP THE COUNTRY, BONNIE LASSIE	R	A	3	219	
KEMPS HP.	Hp	A	1	52	
KENO REEL	R	D	1	76	
KILCHATTAN WEDDING	R	D	2	182	S.Fraser Coll.
KILLIECRANKIE - with var.s	Air	D	2	161	
KILWINNING ARCHERS	S	D	3	252	J.Boick
KINRARA STRATHSPEY	SS	Bb	1	60	Wm. Marshall
KINRARO'S STRATHSPEY	SS	F	3	236	Wm. Marshall
LADY ANN STEWART	S	Bb	3	246	Nath. Gow
LADY BETTY BOYLE	R	Bb	2	121	Rob Mackintosh
LADY CATHCART	S	Bb	1	5	
LADY DOLL (SINCLAIR)	S	A	2	190	
LADY ELIZABETH LINDSAY	S	Bb	3	260	Nath. Gow
LADY GEORGINA RUSSELL	R	Bb	1	60	Wm. Marshall
LADY GRACE DOUGLAS	R	Bb	3	247	Niel Gow
LADY McKENZIE OF COUL	R	D	2	103	
LADY MARY RAMSAY	S	D	1	55	Nath. Gow
LADY ROTHES	R	G	1	51	Alex. Deas
LADY SUTHERLAND	R	Bb	3	261	Geo. Jenkins
LADY WALLACE	R	F	1	92	
L'ENFANT VALSE	W	D	3	257	Miss Laybourn
LA GITANA POLKA	Pka	CG	3	264	
LAIRD OF COCKPEN, THE - Duet	Air	G	3	222/3	
LANCERS QUADRILLES	Qd	-	1	24/5	
LA VERRE EN MAIN	Pka	FBb	2	155	Tahrbach
LAYBOURN McDONALD	S	E	1	85	W.B.Laybourn
LAYBOURN McDONALD	R	E	1	85	W.B.Laybourn
LENA	W	-	2	153/4	J.C. Paton
LENA HP.	Hp	Bb	3	22	J. Easton
LES FARCEURS VALSE	W	DG	3	199	J.N. Hoglen
LIGHTFOOT HP.	Hp	Bb	3	232	J.B.Easton
LITTLE JIM'S HP.	Hp	Bb	3	280	
LOCH LEVEN CASTLE	HpR	A	3	235	
LOCH TURRET (1748)	R	G	1	11	
LOCHTY BLEACHERS	R	D	1	19	A.W. Doig
LONG ISLAND	Hp	D	3	195	
LORD BINNING	R	E	2	119	
LORD BLANTYRE	S	A	2	134	Nath. Gow
LORD EGLINTON'S HP.	Hp	Bb	2	124	
LORD HAWICK'S MARCH	M	G	3	224	
LORD KELLY	R	G	3	246	
LORD McDONALD	R	G	1	72	Sir A. McD.
LORD MAUCHLIN'S REEL	R	E	2	111	
LORD PRESIDENT FORBES	S	F#	2	166	S.Fraser Coll.
LORD ROTHES	S	G	1	51	Alex. Deas
LOVAT'S RESTORATION	S	D	2	183	S.Fraser Coll.
LOVE NOT - QUICK MARCH	M	C	1	15	
LOVE VALSE	W	F	1	74	
McDONALD'S FANCY	S	E	1	72	
McQUEEN'S FROLIC	S	C	3	214	Geo.J.Ingram
MAGGIE GOWLACH'S REEL	R	D	2	103	
MAGGIE LAUDER - with var.s	4/4	D	2	98/101	
MAID OF ISLA, THE	S	A	2	126	
MAJOR GRAHAM (OF INCHBRAKIE)	SS	G	1	11	Niel Gow
MARCELLIA HP.(THE LOCOMOTIVE)	Hp	C	1	94	
MARCH FROM "NORMA"	M	G	2	170/1	Bellini
MARCHIONESS OF HUNTLY, THE	SS	Bb	1	59	Wm. Marshall
MARCHMONT HOUSE	J	D	2	121	Gow Repos/3
MARCH OF THE CONSCRIPT	M	C	2	136	Weber
MARGARET McDONALD	S	E	2	167	S.Fraser Coll.
MARIE VALSES, THE	W	CG	3	267	J.Mackenzie
MARMONT'S REEL	R	Bb	3	253	(Gow)
MARQUIS OF BOWMONT, THE	R	Bb	1	60	Wm. Marshall
MARQUIS OF HUNTLY - with var.s	S	G	1	90	Wm. Marshall
MARQUIS OF HUNTLY'S Hd. FLING	S	D	1	54	Geo. Jenkins
MARQUIS OF LORNE	Hp	G	1	9	
MARQUIS OF TULLYBARDINE	R	A	1	68	Attr:J.Crerar
MARQUIS OF WATERFORD	Hp	Bb	2	142	
MARSEILLAISE (HYMN), THE	M	G	2	178	
MARTHA	W	ACF	2	186/7	W.C. Paton
MASANIELLO QUADRILLES	Qd	-	1	31/3	
MASHER POLKA, THE	Pka	DAG	3	256	W.B.Laybourn
MASTER ERSKINE'S HP.	Hp	C	3	288	Niel Gow
MAY'S QUADRILLES	Qd	-	2	114/5	
MAZURKA	-	C	2	137	
MEDI VALSE	W	Bb	1	30	
MEG MERRILEES (Hornpipe)	Hp	A	2	56	
MEIN SCHATZERL	3/4	F	2	144	Aubade
MERIVU POLKA, THE	Pka	FCBb	2	144	
MERRY ELVES SCHOTTISCHE	Sch	DG	1	27	W.B.Laybourn
MERRY LADS OF AYR, THE	R	C	3	236	
MERRY MASONS' MARCH (3/4)	M	D	1	6	
MERRY MAY THE PAIR BE	R	A	3	205	Capt.S.Fraser
MILLER LADS or DUNMAGLASS	S	F	3	231	S.Fraser Coll.
MILLER'S HP.or REEL	Hp	A	3	203	Zeke Bacus
MISS ANDERSON'S POLKA	Pka	CF	3	274	Mackenzie
MISS BAIGRIE'S STRATHSPEY	S	D	3	276	Peter Baillie
MISS BAIGRIE	R	D	3	276	Peter Baillie
MISS BAKER'S HP.	Hp	F	3	262	
MISS ELPHINSTONE'S STRATHSPEY	S	A	2	119	D.McIntyre
MISS GAYTON('S DANCE)	Hp	G	1	56	
MISS GORDON'S REEL	R	D	2	141	
MISS GRACE MENZIES	S	F	1	79	Wm. Marshall
MISS HAMILTON'S STRATHSPEY	S	F	3	246	
MISS JANE McINNES	R	D	1	78	Wm. Marshall
MISS JESSIE SMITH	S	D	2	102	
MISS JOHNSTON	R	G	1	96	

Title	Type	Key	Vol	Page	Source
MISS MONTGOMERIE'S REEL	R	Bb	1	5	
MISS POLE'S REEL	R	Bb	1	5	
MISS POLLY SKINNER	R	D	2	190	
MISS SAMUEL'S FANCY JIG	J	A	3	206	
MISS SKEEN'S STRATHSPEY	S	A	2	140	
MISS STEWART MENZIES	S	D	2	140	
(MISS) WEST'S HP. [SIEGE OF BELGRADE, THE]					
	Hp	D	3	262	
MONTMORRIS HP.	Hp	D	3	232	
MORPETH RANT	Hp	G	1	48	
MOUNT SHASTA	Hp	AE	3	248	
MOYHALL REEL	R	C	2	173	S.Fraser Coll.
MR. BUSHBY MAITLAND (or MISS)	R	D	1	7	Nath. Gow
MR(S).HAMILTON OF WISHAW	R	Bb	3	260	Wm.Gow (Gow/3)
MR. JAMES GRANT	Hp	G	3	243	Wm. Findlay
(MR.) MARTIN'S HP.	Hp	A	3	235	
MR. McNEIL OF OAKFIELD	R	F	2	159	J.Boick
MR. MORAY OF ABERCAIRNEY	S	G	1	69	Niel Gow
MR. MORTHLAND	R	G	3	247	(Very old)
MR. MURRAY OF ABERCAIRNEY	R	G	3	247	As MORAY above
MRS. CAPT. STEWART OF FINCASTLE	S	C	3	237	
MRS. CHARLES STEWART	R	F	1	79	Wm. Marshall
MRS. DONALDSON	S	Bb	1	4	
MRS. DUFF'S RECOVERY	SS	B	1	6	John Hall mss.
MRS. FINDLAY OF HAYWOOD	R	D	3	252	Wm. Findlay
MRS. FINDLAY OF HAYWOOD	S	D	3	252	Wm. Findlay
MRS. GARDEN OF TROUP	S	F	1	91	R. Petrie
MRS. GIBB'S HP.	Hp	C	1	28	
MRS. LOCH'S FAVOURITE JIG	J	Eb	2	128	
MRS. McLEOD OF ELANREOCH	S	D	1	7	
MRS. MURRAY OF ABERCAIRNEY	S	A	2	149	
MRS. PARKER - REEL	R	D	2	149	Chas. Stewart
MRS. PARKER'S REEL	R	A	2	149	(very alike)
MRS. RIGG	J	G	2	128	
MRS. SCOTT SKINNER	R	C	3	215	J.McQueen
MRS. SOUTAR OF PLAINS	R	C	1	43	Alex. Deas
MRS. TAFF or BANKS' HP.	Hp	Eb	1	29	Parazotti
MR(S).THOMAS JARVIS	R	A	1	88	
MRS. TULLOCH'S JIG	J	A	2	192	? M.Macdonald
or ALLAN RAMSAY					In Gow Repos/2
MRS. WILSON'S FANCY	Hp	A	3	251	Wm. Findlay
MY AIN KIND DEARIE - var.s	Song	A	2	162/3	
MY WIFE SHE'S TA'EN THE GEE	S	C	2	135	(old)
NANTASKET HP., THE	Hp	A	2	181	
NAPOLEON'S CORONATION MARCH	M	G	1	49/50	
NAPOLEON'S MARCH	M	D	2	179	
NAVAL BRIGADE, THE	Hp	D	3	263	W.B.Laybourn
NAVVIE ON THE LINE, THE	Hp	A	1	48	Jas. Hill
NIEL GOW'S RECOVERY	S	Bb	3	260	Niel Gow
NELSE MOWBRAY'S REEL	R	D	2	164	
NEW BOB, THE [BOGANUADH]	R	B	2	111	
NEWCASTLE SCHOTTISCHE	Sch	F	1	83	
NEW CONQUEST, THE	CD	G	3	206	Isaac Cooper
NEW DICK HP.	Hp	Bb	2	132	
NEW TARIFF HUNT, THE	R	Bb	2	141	
NEW VARSOVIANA, THE	-	-	2	160	
NEW YEAR'S DAY	S	C	3	196	S.Fraser Coll.
NICOLSON STREET	Hp	Bb	1	62	W.B.Laybourn
NORTH BRIDGE OF EDINBURGH, THE	S	B	1	73	Wm. Marshall
NOTHING WILL YE TAK' MAN	R	G	1	11	
NOVELTY REEL, THE	R	Eb	1	46	Capt.S.Fraser
NOW IS THE TIME	R	D	2	165	
NUT, THE	CD	Bb	1	63	
O DEAR, WHAT CAN THE MATTER BE?	6/8	G	3	265	
OH, HEY JOHNNY LAD	S	A	2	110	
OH IF JOCKY WOULD BUT STEAL ME	R	G	2	159	
OLD CAMBRIDGE HP.	Hp	A	2	180	
OLD FAVOURITE MINUETTO, A(DUET)	-	C	3	238/9	
OLD HICKORY HP.	Hp	Bb	3	248	
OLD IRELAND REEL	R	E	1	58	W.B.Laybourn
OLD TOON OF BROXBURN	R	D	3	277	Wm. Findlay
OLD TOWLER	6/8	D	1	63	
OLD WOODHOUSELEE REEL	R	G	3	271	
OLD WOODHOUSELEE CASTLE	S	G	3	271	
OOR AULD GUIDMAN IS NOO AWA'	SS	Bb	1	4	
OPERA POLKA	Pka	D	3	264	
ORIGINAL SET OF MAZURKAS	-	BbD	1	16/17	
ORIGINAL VARSOVIANA, THE	-	A	2	145	
ORR BRIGG	S	D	1	19	D.W. Doig
O, SHE'S COMICAL	R	A	1	84	(very old)
OUR LITTLE BEAUTIES	W	GD	3	225	W.C. Paton
OUR NATIVE HOME	2/4	D	1	10	D. Kippen
OWRE THE MUIR AMANG THE HEATHER	Air	D	3	240	
PADDY O'SNAP	9/8	D	3	206	
PAIN'S FIRST SET OF QUADRILLES	Qd	-	2	106/7	
PARKS OF KILBURNIE, THE	S/R	F	2	191	
PEACOCK'S FANCY	Hp	A	2	116	
"PEARL" HP., THE	Hp	BbG	3	220	W.C. Paton
PEAR TREE, THE	Hp	F	1	52	Jas. Hill
PEA STRAE (CLEAN) - Hp. Version	Hp	D	2	120	
PEGGY UP THE BURN	R	D	2	147	
PENICUICK HP., THE	Hp	G	3	234	R. Baillie
PERRIWIG REEL, THE	R	E	2	191	Fraser
PETER BAILLIE'S STRATHSPEY	S	D	1	93	P. Baillie
PETRIE'S FROLIC	S	E	2	111	Isaac Cooper
PETRONELLA	CD	F	1	41	
PILGRIM HP., THE	Hp	D	3	272	
"PIPE SLANG, THE"	R	A	3	197	S.Fraser Coll.
PIRATE'S HP.	Hp	Eb	3	263	
PLEYEL'S HP.	Hp	G	2	157	
POP GOES THE WEASEL - orig. set	R	A	2	120	
PORT A BHODICH	S	A	1	22	
PRETTY DICK POLKA	Pka	FBb	1	26	W.B.Laybourn
PRIDE OF THE NORTH VALSES, THE	W	G	2	169	Wm. Findlay
PRINCE ALBERT'S HP. [NEWCASTLE]	Hp	Bb	1	86	J. Hill
PRINCE ALFRED'S HP.	Hp	E	1	61	W.B.Laybourn
PRINCE CHARLIE'S STRATHSPEY	S	E	2	166	S.Fraser Coll.
PRINCE OF WALES' C.D. [or ROYAL ALBERT]					
	6/8	6	1	35	
PRINCE OF WALES' HP.	Hp	Bb	1	62	W.B.Laybourn
PRINCE OF WALES' STRATHSPEY	S	Bb	2	134	
PRINCESS BEATRICE GALOP	Gp	A	3	280	W.B.Laybourn
PRINCESS BEATRICE HP.	Hp	GBb	3	250	W.B.Laybourn
PRINCESS BEATRICE WALTZES	W	CGD	3	273/4	Wm. Findlay
PRIZE JIG	J	Bb	1	9	
QUEEN'S TRIUMPH, THE	R	A	2	140	
RACHAEL RAE	R	D	1	93	J(ohn) Lowe
RAINBOW or MIDNIGHT SCHOTTISCHE	Sch	CAF	3	256	
RANDY WIVES OF GREENLAW, THE	R	D	3	253	J. King
RANTING LADS OF SUNDERLAND, THE	Hp	D	2	117	

Title	Type	Key	Vol	Page	Source/Composer
RED LION	Hp	Bb	2	176	
REEL	R	A	1	36	Alex.Deas (?)
REEL [DARLING OF THE UIST LASSES, THE]	R	D	2	184	S.Fraser Coll.
REEL OF TULLOCH	R	A	1	23	
RENDEZ VOUS, THE	R	G	2	167	S.Fraser Coll.
RIGHTS OF MAN	Hp	E	1	9	
RINETTAN'S DAUGHTER	S	A	3	197	S.Fraser Coll.
RINK HP., THE	Hp	E	1	87	W.B.Laybourn
ROB ROY'S REEL	R	D	1	54	
ROCK HP. [RECRUIT HP.]	Hp	D	3	213	
ROCKET HP.,THE [CHESTER CASTLE]	Hp	F	3	262	
ROCKY ROAD TO DUBLIN	R	A	2	147	
RONDO - Duet	-	D	3	228/9	Pleyel
ROSEBUD VALSE	W	GD	3	224	
ROSE OF DENMARK, THE	Hp	Bb	2	142	R.Stephenson
ROSE POLKA, THE	Pka	FC	1	75	W.B.Laybourn
ROSS HP.	Hp	E	3	194	
ROTHIEMURCHUS RANT	S	C	3	236	
ROXBURGH BALL, THE	R	Bb	2	158	
ROXBURGH VALSE, THE	W	FBb	2	185	D.Wilkinson
ROYAL RECOVERY, THE [or MADAM FREDERICK]	SS	A	1	84	Wm. Marshall
RUBY HP. [or CLIFF HP.]	Hp	F	1	94	
RUSSIAN NATIONAL ANTHEM	Air	G	2	184	
SAIL IN BOYS	Hp	Bb	1	77	
SANDERSON'S HP.	Hp	G	3	263	W.B.Laybourn
SANDY McGAFF	J	E	3	266	
SCITUATE REEL	R	G	1	76	
SCOLDING WIVES OF ABERTARFF,THE	R	G	3	231	S.Fraser Coll.
SCOTCH HP.	Hp	D	2	189	
SCOTIA'S REEL	R	A	3	277	W.B.Laybourn
SCUPS COME	Hp	D	2	175	
SECOND STAR HP.	Hp	Bb	2	109	G. Tate
SHAMROCK HP., THE	Hp	A	3	212	W.C. Paton
SHAMROCK HP., THE	Hp	Bb	3	243	John B. Easton
SHATTUCK'S REEL	R	Bb	2	176	
SHAW'S TRIP TO LONDON	Hp	C	1	80	T. Shaw
SHEPHERDESS, THE	J	F#	2	168	S.Fraser Coll.
SHILLELAH, THE [GIPSY'S HP.]	Hp	E	1	87	
SHUTER'S HP.	Hp	G	2	157	
SIR GARNET'S HP.	Hp	E	3	243	Wm. Findlay
SIR JOHN HENDERSON'S JIG	J	G	2	192	(Gow)
SIR JOHN MALCOLM	S	B	2	110	
SIR ROGER DE COVERLEY	9/8	G	1	33	
SIR RONALD McDONALD	R	G	3	261	
SLEEPY MAGGIE	R	B	1	73	
SLING THE HATCHET	R	G	2	176	
SMIDDY'S CLAMOUR, THE	R	C	3	215	J. McQueen
SNOW DRIFT VALSES, THE (1883)	W	DG	2	177	Wm. Findlay
SOLDIER'S JOY, THE [or MILANESE COUNTRY DANCE]	R	D	2	133	
SOURCE OF SPEY, THE	S	E	2	190	S.Fraser Coll.
SOUTH OF THE GRAMPIANS, THE	S	A	1	68	Jas.Porteous
SOUTH SHORE HP.	Hp	D	2	117	
SPANISH DOLLAR	Hp	G	1	48	
SPEED THE PLOUGH	R	A	1	29	J. Moorehead
SPLITWOOD HP.	Hp	F	2	165	
SPORTSMAN'S HAUNT	S	B	2	173	S.Fraser Coll.
STAR HP.	Hp	E	1	62	W.B.Laybourn
STARLIGHT SCHOTTISCHE	Sch	DAG	3	226	Jas. Francis
STEAMBOAT HP., THE	Hp	G	1	56	
STEPHENSON'S FANCY	Hp	A	2	104	T. Corner
STEPHENSON'S HP.	Hp	Bb	1	95	R.Stephenson
STEPHENSON'S MONUMENT	Hp	E	2	116	W. Stewart
STETSON'S HP.	Hp	F	3	213	
STEWART'S LASSIE	S	G	1	11	
STIRLING CASTLE	S	D	1	37	
STOCKPORT HP.	Hp	G	2	109	
STONEY STEPS	Hp	Bb	2	156	J. Hill
(STRAND) HP., THE - 1st. seT	Hp	GD	1	14	
STRANGER HP., THE	Hp	D	3	272	
STRANGERS' HP	Hp	Bb	2	124	A. McAndrew
STRATHSPEY	S	D	1	72	
STUMPIE	S	A	1	54	
ST. VALENTINE'S GALOP	Gp	CF	1	38	
SUCKY BIDS ME	R	G	2	148	
SUNBEAM POLKA	Pka	C	3	242	A. Anderson
SWAMP ANGEL HP.	Hp	A	2	181	
SWARD HOUSE	J	G	1	93	
SWEETHEART SCHOTTISCHE	Sch	GC	1	89	
SWEET'S THE NAME OF PEGGY	R	E	2	146	
SYLVANUS HP.	Hp	Eb	1	81	
THISTLE HP., THE	Hp	Bb	3	212	Jas. Christie
THISTLE HP., THE	Hp	G3	3	251	Wm. Findlay
THOMSON'S HP.	Hp	G	3	203	
THREE A's, THE	Hp	A	2	151	W. Radford
THREE FARTHING FOR A HALFPENNY	R	A	2	150	
THREE GRACES, THE	Hp	D	2	165	
TIMOUR THE TARTAR	R	A	1	22	
TITUS HP.	Hp	A	3	194	
TOM HANDFORD'S HP.	Hp	A	1	14	
TOM THUMB	CD	Bb	3	240	
TOM TULLIE'S HP.	Hp	G	3	234	(very old)
TO MY BED I WINNA GANG	R	D	3	219	
TRIP TO DUBLIN	J	G	1	85	
TRIP TO PARIS	J	G	2	128	
TRIUMPH - Country Dance	CD	A	1	37	
TRUMPET HP.	Hp	Eb	1	44	
TULLOCHGORUM	S	G	1	23	
TULLYMET HALL	R	A	2	135	John Gow
(J) TURNBULL'S COMPLIMENTS TO J. MANSON	S	Bb	3	253	
TYKE SIDE [? TYNE SIDE]	Hp	F	2	133	Jas. Hill
TYNEMOUTH CASTLE	Hp	Bb	2	104	
UNDERHAND HP.	Hp	Bb	1	94	Jas. Hill
UNION JACK HP.	Hp	C	3	221	J.C. Paton
UP IN THE MORNING EARLY - vars.	6/8	G	3	193	
VERMONT HP. [or SUMNER'S HP.]	Hp	D	3	194	
VICA HP.	Hp	D	2	109	
VICTORIA VALSE, THE (OLD)	W	DG	1	42	E.Gillespie
VIENNA POLKA, THE	Pka	G	3	264	
WALKER STREET HP.	Hp	G	3	202	
WEAVER HAS DAUGHTER, THE	S	G	2	182	S.Fraser Coll.
WEDDING IN THE WEST	R	G	2	146	
WEDDING RING, THE	R	G	3	196	Fraser
WEE BELLS SCHOTTISCHE	Sch	FC	3	217	W.B.Laybourn
WIESBADEN POLKA	Pka	CF	3	216	
WE'LL A' BE WED IN OUR AULD CLAES [cf: MY WIFE'S A WANTON ...]	J	D	2	143	

```
WEST END HP.                    Hp   F    2  124  J. Shaw
WHEATSHEAF SCHOTTISCHE          Sch  FBb  2  185  D.Wilkinson
WHEN YOU GO TO THE HILL TAKE YOUR GUN [THE LEES OF LUNCARTIE]
                                S    G    3  277  Gow/1
WHISTLE O'ER THE LAVE O'T       SS   G    1  88
WILLIAM TELL - Rondo            -    E    1  34   Rossini
WILLIAM YOUNG'S BEST MALT       S    A    1  36   Alex. Deas
WYNCHBURGH CASTLE               S    D    3  276  Wm. Findlay
WIND THAT SHAKES THE BARLEY,THE R    D    1  69
WITTLE DEAN                     Hp   A    2  147
WONDER, THE                     Hp   Bb   1  86
WOOD'S HP.                      Hp   A    2  157  (Hall ms.)
WORRELLS' HP.                   Hp   Bb   3  202
YES OR NO! WALTZES              W    DG   2  105  R.M.Taylor
```

CONTAINING

A SELECTION OF OLD HIGHLAND

MUSIC.

Ent.Sta.Hall.

Price 2/6

PUBLISHERS

LOGAN & COMP? INVERNESS & ABERDEEN.

Title	Metre	Key	Bk	Pg	Note
COCK O' THE NORTH - 2ND. SET	6/8	A	1	2	
COLCAIRN'S STR.[MAID OF ISLAY]	S	G	1	16	
COLD WINDS FROM WYVIS	6/8	A	4	14	
COLIN CAMERON'S KILT	S	A	5	21	J.S.Skinner
COLIN CAMPBELL	S	G	5	46	
COLIN'S COWS[CATTLE]	3/4	F	4	5	
COLLEGE HORNPIPE[JACK'S THE LAD]	2/2	Bb	4	37	
COLONEL, THE - LETTYBURN	2/4	A	3	42	
COL. BOYLE OF SHEWALTON	6/8	Bb	6	30	
COL. CRUDEN'S F'WELL TO THE 1ST. HIGHLANDERS	2/4	D	4	11	P/M Mann
COL. D.M. ROBERTSON, 48TH. CANADIAN HIGHLANDERS	6/8	D	5	9	P/M Beaton
COL. DUFF, 42ND.(BLACK WATCH)	2/4	A	6	11	P/M McDonald
COL. DUNCAN MENZIES	2/4	A	2	27	P/M R. Hall
COL. J.S. YOUNG'S MARCH	2/4	A	4	1	W. Mackay Tait
COL. THE MACKINTOSH OF MACKINTOSH'S SILVER WEDDING	2/4	A	6	23	J. Macdonald
COL. MACLEOD, 3RD. CAMERONS	2/4	A	6	3	J. Macdonald
COLONEL SINCLAIR	2/4	D	2	20	(?) Jas.Manson
COL.(DAVID) STUART OF GARTH	S	A	1	19	
COME FY, LET'S A' TO THE BRIDAL	9/8	DB	5	41	
COME O'ER THE STREAM, CHARLIE	3/4	G	6	44	
COME UNDER MY PLAIDIE	6/8	F	2	46/7	Johnny McGill
COMRIE CASTLE	2/4	A	2	28	D. Macdougall
CONON HOUSE	S	A	4	10	
CORRYCHOILLIE'S LEAVING L'ABER	2/4	A	6	27	R.Meldrum,1903
COUNT DE SERRA LARGO, THE	2/4	A	4	6	Rod. Campbell
CRAIG MILLAR CASTLE - RETREAT	3/4	DB	5	6	Wm. MacDonald
CRAIG-N-DARROCH	2/4	A	3	3	
CRANKY PIPER, THE	R	A	6	5	D.Macdonald
CRIPPLE MALCOLM IN THE GLEN	S	A	1	4	
CRUSADERS' MARCH, THE	4/4	A	1	8	(cf:Inveraray)
CULLODEN MUIR	6/8	A	1	28/9	Wm. Morrison
CULLODEN'S BIRTHDAY	R	A	5	20	Wm. Morrison
CULLODEN'S FAVOURITE	4/4	D	5	35	Wm. Morrison
CUTTY CLAY	R	F	3	34	
DAFT DONALD	6/8	D	2	20	
DAFT ROBIN	4/4	A	1	31	
D.C. MATHER'S FAREWELL	2/4	A	4	40	Jas. Center
DEATH OF THE CHIEF, THE	4/4	D	3	19	
DEIL AMONG THE TAILORS, THE	R	A	1	12/13	
DELVIN SIDE	4/4	A	3	1	} The same
DELVIN SIDE	S	E	3	2	} tune
DEVIL IN THE KITCHEN, THE	S	A	2	15	Wm. Ross
DINNA THINK MY BONNIE LASSIE	R	A	6	35	
DIRGE OF THE BLACK WATCH	2/4	B	6	19	
DONACHT HEAD [GORDON CASTLE]	4/4	C	6	24	
DONALD CAMERON	2/4	A	3	26	
DONALD DHU - PIBROCH OF	6/8	A	1	29	
DONALD MACKAY	6/8	A	6	38	W.Mackay Tait
DONALD MACKINNON'S BIRTHDAY	2/4	A	5	20	Hugh Mackay
DOON THE WATER	R	A	5	16	
DORNOCH LINKS	2/4	A	2	14	
DRAW THE SWORD, SCOTLAND	4/4	G	6	29/30	
DREAM, A [AISLING]	4/4	DA	6	21	
DRUMMOND CASTLE LAUNDRY, POLKA	2/4	D	6	10	R.M.Meldrum
DRUNKEN PIPER, THE	2/4	A	3	14	
DUCHESS OF BUCCLEUCH'S FAV.	AIR	Bb	6	26	Nath.Gow(Gow 4)
DUCHESS OF GORDON, THE	S	C	3	44	
DUCHESS OF ROXBURGHE, THE	S	A	2	10	
DUNMORE PARK	2/4	A	5	16	J.Russell
DUNTROON	R	A	2	16/17	
EARL DOUGLAS'S LAMENT	3/4	Bb	6	40	
EARL GREY	S	A	4	44	(? Hill)
EARL OF DALHOUSIE'S MARCH	4/4	Bb	4	22	N.Gow (Bk.4)
EARL OF DUNMORE'S QUICKSTEP	2/4	A	3	21	
EARL OF FIFE'S WELCOME TO SANDRINGHAM	2/4	A	6	25	Wm.Macdonald
EARL OF MANSFIELD'S MARCH	2/4	D	1	9	John McEwen
EDINBURGH REVIEW, 1882	6/8	A	4	13	
EDINBURGH VOLUNTEERS	2/4	A	5	26/7	
EOBHAN RUADH MAC FARLAN	6/8	A	5	22	John McColl
ERCHLESS CASTLE	2/4	A	1	16	
EWIE WI' THE CROOKIT HORN, THE	S	A	6	35	
FAIRY DANCE, THE - AND VARS.	R	D	2	42/3	Nath. Gow
FASKALLY HOUSE	2/4	A	2	17	D.MacKercher
FERNDERN	6/8	A	3	40	Jas. Center
FERRYSIDE LASSES, THE	6/8	A	4	15	Rod. Campbell
FIGHT ABOUT THE FIRESIDE	R	C	3	44	
FINGALIAN AIR	3/4	C	5	13	
FINGALIAN AIR (4 PTS.)	4/4	G	5	40	
1 SEAFORTHS' ADVANCE ON ATBARA	2/4	A	5	23	H. Taylor
1 SHR VOLS.' WELCOME TO EDINB.	2/4	A	4	27	(1905)
FISHER'S (or BLANCHARD'S) HP.	2/2	F	5	44	
FLAGGON, THE	R	A	1	20	
FLORA McDONALD'S LAMENT	6/8	Bb	2	47	N. Gow Jnr.
FLOWERS OF EDINBURGH, THE	2/2	G	5	47	
FLOWERS OF THE FOREST, THE	4/4	D	3	44	
FOLLOW HER OVER THE BORDER	9/8	F	1	26	
FONAB HOUSE	6/8	D	6	16/17	N. Gow Jnr.
FOOT IT NEATLY	R	A	3	21	John Turnbull
FORT AUGUSTUS VOLUNTEERS	6/8	A	6	4	John Macdonald
FOXHUNTER'S JIG, THE	9/8	A	3	19	
FROM JOHN O'GROATS TO THE CAPE	2/4	A	4	33	H. Taylor
GAELIC AIR, A	4/4	C	2	33	
GARELOCH, THE	S	G	6	24	
GARRY OWEN (As a March)	6/8	G	4	12	Irish
GENERAL DRUMMOND	R	G	5	46	
GENERAL HIGHLAND GATHERING	6/8	D	3	15	
GEO. BELL'S FAREWELL TO BUTE	2/4	A	4	8/9	Alex. Campbell
GEO. FORBES OF ASLOUN'S MARCH	2/4	A	3	18	Dunc. Campbell
GHILLIE CALLUM	4/4	A	4	9	
GILLIE AN DROVER - PIBROCH	6/8	GA	3	5	
GLEN CARRADALE HOUSE	S	A	5	12	Geo.D.Taylor
GLENCUIL COTTAGE POLKA	2/4	A	6	13	R. Meldrum
GLENDARUEL HIGHLANDERS	6/8	A	1	12	P/M A.Fettes
GLENGARRY'S MARCH	2/4	A	1	26/7	
GLENGRANT	2/4	D	2	22	A. Macdonald
GLEN'S MINE, THE	2/4	A	1	27	
GLEN TILT LODGE	R	A	6	28	
GOOD NIGHT AND JOY BE WI' YE A'	4/4	D	3	47	
GORDONS HAE THE GIRDIN' O'T	2/4	D	4	32	
GORDONS' MARCH	6/8	G	4	5	
GOWRIE [LASS OF, THE]	S	D	4	44	
GRANITE CITY, THE	S	A	5	34	G.L.Mullin

Title	Type	Key	Vol	Page	Note
GRANT'S REEL	SR	A	5	4	Rod. Campbell
GRAY WIFE OF RASAY, THE	R	A	3	5	
GREY BOB, THE	R	A	3	25	
GREY BUCK, THE	S	A	2	15	
GU MA SLAN A CHI MI	4/4	F	2	33	
HAGGIS, THE	R	C	3	45	S.Fraser Coll.
HAIL! TO THE CHIEF	6/8	D	2	45	
HARRIET PIBROCH, THE	6/8	A	2	36	
HARRIS DANCE	4/4	CA	5	39	
HARVEST HOME HORNPIPE	2/2	D	2	24	
HAUGHS O' CROMDALE, THE	S	E	1	2	
HAZELDENE	2/4	G	4	43	
HEATHER JOCK	S	A	5	11	
H.M.'S WELCOME TO GLENFIDDOCH	6/8	A	2	6	Wm.Macdonald
HE'S O'ER THE HILLS THAT I LOE	2/4	B	5	14	
HEY TO CUPAR	6/8	D	6	36	
HIGHLAND BOAT SONG	6/8	G	1	27	
HIGHLAND BRIGADE AT WATERLOO	6/8	A	1	24	John Gow
HIGHLAND CHIEFTAIN, THE	S	D	6	26	Nath.Gow
HIGHLAND HARRY	S	A	4	2	
HIGHLAND LADDIE	2/4	D	1	10	
HIGHLAND LADDIE, THE	6/8	D	5	38	Dr. Arne
HIGHLAND LAMENT, A	3/4	Eb	1	25	
HIGHLAND LAMENTATION, A	3/4	Bb	6	41	
HIGHLAND MARCH	6/8	A	1	25	cf: Grey Buck
HIGHLAND NURSING AIR, A	3/8	G	6	44	
HIGHLAND PORT, A	6/8	G	5	42/3	"Rory Dall"
HIGHLAND RANT	R	A	6	44	
HIGHLANDS OF BANFFSHIRE	S	F	3	33	S.Fraser Coll.
HIGHLAND TROOP, THE	6/8	G	3	12	S.Fraser
HIGHLAND WATCH, THE	4/4	E	6	30	
HIGHLAND WHISKY	S	A	5	45	
HIGH ROAD TO LINTON, THE	R	A	2	18	
HILLS OF GLENORCHY, THE	6/8	E	1	21	
HON. MISS ELSPETH CAMPBELL, THE	2/4	A	3	38/9	J. Douglas
HOOP HER AND GIRD HER	6/8	G	2	30	
HO RO BHOBAN AN DRAM	9/8	A	6	34	
HO RO MY NUT-BROWN MAIDEN	4/4	D	1	5	
HOWES OF BUSKSBURN	2/4	A	6	24/5	P/M Mann(1907)
I HAE LAID A HERRIN' IN SAUT	6/8	DA	5	43	
I'LL GANG NAE MAIR TO YON TOUN	4/4	G	6	14	
I LOVE MY LOVE FOR SHE LOVES ME	9/8	B	6	33	
INNES OF SANDSIDE'S REEL	R	B	4	1	P.Paterson
IN THE GARB OF OLD GAUL	4/4	D	5	30	Gen. J.Reid
INVERCAULD	2/4	D	2	6	
INVERCHARRON H'LAND GATHERING	6/8	A	2	27	John Macdonald
INVERGORDON CASTLE	S	A	2	23	A. Macdonald
INVERNESS GATHERING	2/4	A	1	13	
INVERNESS RANT, THE	S	D	1	13	
IRISH JIG [? SCATTER THE MUD]	6/8	B	3	36	
ISABELLA THOMSON	SCH	A	4	16	C. Thompson(?)
ISLE OF SKYE - PIPE SET	R	A	6	2	
I. OF SKYE LOCAL MILITIA, THE	2/4	B	1	8/9	
JACK'S ALIVE	6/8	G	5	46	
JAMES GRANT ESQ.	2/4	A	6	5	A.M.Macintosh
JEANNETTE B. TAYLOR	R	A	6	20/1	H. Taylor
JEANNIE CARRUTHERS	2/4	A	6	2	John McColl
JENNY DANG THE WEAVER	R	D	4	39	
JENNY MACPHEE	2/4	A	5	29	
JENNY'S BAWBEE	R	D	3	44	
JIG	6/8	A	5	13	
JIG	6/8	A	5	38/9	(Nth. Country)
JIG	6/8	A	5	39	" "
JIG	9/8	A	5	39	
JIG	6/8	E	6	17	Jas. Center
JIG	6/8	A	6	34/5	J.P.McLeod
JOHN ANDERSON'S AULDEST DAUGHTER	2/4	A	2	37	
JOHN BAIN MACKENZIE	2/4	A	2	8	Himself
JOHN KNOX	2/4	Bb	5	37	
JOHN MACDONALD	S	A	5	35	J.S.Skinner
JOHN MACKENZIE'S FAREWELL TO STRATHGLASS	6/8	A	3	8	C/P W.Ross
JOHN McCOLL'S ..FAREWELL TO THE SCOTT. HORSE	2/4	B	6	39	John McColl
JOHN McCOLL'S ..MARCH TO KILBOWIE COTTAGE	2/4	A	4	36	Wm. Lawrie
JOHNNIE COPE	2/4	A	3	41	
JOHNNIE MACDONALD'S REEL	R	D	6	21	Jas. Center
JOHNNY GROATS [HOUSE]	R	C	3	45	S.Fraser Coll.
JOHN O' GROAT REEL [WHIRLIGIG]	R	A	4	28	N. Taylor
JOHN PATERSON'S MARE	6/8	GA	4	30	
KENMARE'S MARCH [... ON & AWA']	6/8	D	4	23	
KILBERRY BALL - POLKA	2/4	A	6	4	R.Meldrum
KILLEARN REEL	R	D	3	7	A.Macdonald
KILLICRANKIE	4/4	C	1	25	
KILT IS MY DELIGHT, THE	R	D	2	15	
KIND DEARIE [MY AIN]	2/2	A	4	46	
KINETHAN'S DAUGHTER	S	CA	3	45	cf:Rinettan...
KING JAMIE'S MARCH	2/4	G	6	36	
KINGUSSIE SHINTY CLUB	2/4	A	3	12/13	Rod. Campbell
KIRSTI MACFARLANE	R	D	6	13	Carl Volti
LADS O' MULL, THE	R	A	2	10/11	
LADS IN THE KILTS, THE	6/8	D	3	18	
LAD WI' THE PLAIDIE, THE	4/4	D	2	44	
LADY CASTLEREAGH'S	S	A	5	31	W. Mackay
LADY CHARLOTTE MURRAY	6/8	AD	4	11	N. Gow
LADY [ELIZABETH] LINDSAY	S	BbC	4	36	Nath. Gow
LADY LOUDOUN	S	A	3	8/9	Wm. Gow
LADY MACBETH'S STRATHSPEY	S	A	3	22	
LADY MACKINTOSH'S REEL	R	D	6	3	
LADY MADELINA SINCLAIR	S	A	1	20	
LADY MARY HAMILTON	S	A	6	8	Dr. Bannatyne
LADY MARY RAMSAY	S	D	3	5	
LADY MONTGOMERY	R	Bb	4	37	Lord Eglinton
LAIRD OF AUCHERNACH, THE	6/8	A	5	10	Rod. Campbell
LAIRD OF BRODIE, THE	S	D	4	4	
LAMENT [FOR THE FALLEN BRAVE]	3/4	C	2	29	S. Fraser
LAMENTATION FOR McDONALD OF KEPPOCH	9/8	A	5	38	Keppoch
LAMENT FOR HUGH, E.OF EGLINTON	S	D	6	19	Nath. Gow
LAMENT FOR RUARAIDH MOR McLEOD	3/4	F	4	22/3	
LAMENT FOR THE DEAD ...	3/4	D	3	34	
LAMENT FOR THE DEATH OF JANE, DUCHESS OF GORDON	4/4	C	5	25	D. Macdonald
LAMENT FOR THE FALLEN AT W'LOO	4/4	Eb	4	7	
LAOIDH AN AMADAIN MHOIR	4/4	C	2	43	

Title	Time	Key	Bk	Page	Note
LASS OF RICHMOND HILL, THE	2/4	D	1	3	
LAST MEASURE PRINCE CHARLIE DANCED WITH FLORA McDONALD, THE	6/8	C	1	33	
LAST PINT, THE	R	AD	4	18	C. Thompson
LEA RIG, THE	4/4	A	6	7/9	
LEAVING GLENURQUHART	2/4	A	2	16	W. Macdonald
LEAVING INVERNESS	2/4	A	2	2	
LEAVING STRATHDON	2/4	A	6	38	
LIEUT. EWING, KOSB	2/4	A	4	19	R.Melchett
LIEUT. GORDON'S MARCH	2/4	A	2	26	John Macdonald
LT. MURRAY'S W'COME TO THE 79TH	2/4	D	4	12	
LIGHT AND AIRY	6/8	F	2	29	(& 46)
LOCHABER NO MORE	3/4	F	1	6/7	
LOCH EARN [or TILT SIDE]	R	G	3	43	Nath. Gow
LOCHIEL'S AWA' TAE FRANCE	R	A	3	38	
LOCHIEL'S WELCOME TO GLASGOW	6/8	A	2	3	Alex. Cameron
LOCH LONG	S	A	6	28	
LOCHNAGAR	4/4	C	4	13	(Song air)
LOCH NESS	R	A	5	34	Arr: C.Thomson
LONACH LASSES - POLKA	2/4	A	6	6	R.Meldrum
LONGMOOR	R	G	4	18/19	C.Thompson
LORD ALEXr. KENNEDY	2/4	A	2	24	
LORD BLANTYRE	S	A	2	7	
LORD BREADALBANE'S MARCH	6/8	D	1	30/31	
LORD BUCHAN	2/4	D	5	36	
LORD BUTE'S MARCH	2/4	A	3	16/17	Rod. Campbell
LORD LOVAT'S LAMENT	4/4	A	1	1	
LORD LOVAT'S STRATHSPEY	S	A	1	6	
LORD LOVAT'S WELCOME - PIBROCH	S	F	3	46	S.Fraser Coll.
LORD LYN(E)DOCH	S	D	3	1	P. Agnew
LORD MACDONALD	R	G	3	47	
LORD McLEOD	S	A	5	15	
LORD PANMURE'S MARCH	2/4	A	1	14	John Macdonald
LOVE SONG, A - ORAN GAOIL	6/8	E	1	32	
LUSS HIGHLAND GATHERING, THE	2/4	A	5	21	
MACDONALD OF THE ISLES' MARCH TO HARLAW (1411)	6/8	A	2	4	
MACGREGOR'S GATHERING	6/8	D	5	6/7	
MACGREGOR'S RANT, THE	R	A	5	8	
MACKENZIE HIGHLANDERS	2/4	A	1	8	
MACKENZIE'S FAREWELL	2/4	A	1	14	
MACKENZIE'S F'WELL TO ROSS-SH.	2/4	A	2	9	
MACKENZIE'S F'WELL TO SUTHERL'D	6/8	Bb	1	24	
MACKINNONS MARCH, (THE)	6/8	A	1	17	& Bk.3, p.28
McINTOSH OF McINTOSH'S REEL	R	A	2	8	
MACINTOSH'S LAMENT	3/4	G	2	30	
MACPHERSON'S LAMENT or F'WELL	2/4	D	1	15	
MACRAE'S MARCH, 1491	4/4	A	1	22	
MAGGIE CAMERON	S	A	3	28	
MAGGIE LAUDER	2/4	D	4	20/21	
MAJOR MACKIE	6/8	A	4	41	
MAJOR McBEAN'S MARCH	4/4	BbEb	5	36	
MANCHESTER HORNPIPE	2/2	D	6	12/13	
MAN OF KETTLE, THE	R	GE	6	46	
MARCH	2/4	A	3	10	Rod. Campbell
MARCH FROM "BLUE BEARD"	4/4	D	5	39	
MARCHING INTO CAMP	6/8	G	6	20	H.Taylor
MARCHIONESS OF HUNTLY, THE	S	A	1	9	Wm. Marshall
MARCHIONESS OF TULLYBARDINE,THE	2/4	A	3	22/3	
MARCHIONESS OF TWEEDDALE'S DEL.	3/4	G	2	35	Gow (Bk.2)
MARCH OF THE MACDONALDS	4/4	G	3	30	
MARCH OF THE NORTH FENCIBLES	4/4	Bb	3	23	
MARCH TO THE BATTLEFIELD	2/4	D	5	22	
MARQUIS OF LORNE, THE	S	A	2	18	
MARQUIS OF TULLYBARDINE	R	A	1	6	
MAIRI DHUBH (BLACK MARY)	4/4	C	4	10	
MASON'S APRON, THE	R	A	5	27	
McALISTER'S DIRK	R	A	2	14	
McCALLUM'S BIRTHDAY	2/4	A	4	29	
McCRIMMON'S LAMENT	6/8	F	3	16	
McFARLANE'S LAMENT	3/4	D	6	39	
McGREGOR OF RORO'S LAMENT	3/4	A	2	43	
McLENNAN'S OVERCOAT	S	A	3	4	
McPHEDRAN'S STRATHSPEY	S	D	3	7	
MEGGERNY CASTLE	2/4	A	5	10/11	
MEG MERRILEES	4/4	A	1	11	
MIDLOTHIAN PIPE BAND, THE	6/8	D	2	4	
MISS AINSLIE GRANT DUFF	2/4	A	5	13	J.Sutherland
MISS AUDREY MACLEAN	2/4	A	5	5	Jas. Center
MISS CAMPBELL OF MENZIE(MONZIE)	R	C	4	46	
MISS DRUMMOND OF PERTH	S	A	1	21	
MISS DUMBRECK	R	Bb	3	47	
MISS FORBES FAREWELL TO BANFF	2/4	G	5	44/5	
MISS GIRDLE	R	D	2	12	
MISS HOPE	R	D	6	1	
MISS J. McLEOD'S REEL	R	F	5	40	
MISS PROUD	R	A	5	17	
MO CHIOCHARAN [MY BABE]	6/8	D	6	45/6	
MO GRADH FO LEON [MY LOVE WOUNDED]	3/4	G	2	34	
MO MHAIRI MHIN MEALL-SHUILEACH	4/4	A	6	39	
MONYMUSK [SIR A. GRANT OF ...]	4/4	G	3	30/31	
MORAG	4/4	FD	6	10/11	
MORAYSHIRE SQUADRON SCOTT.HORSE	6/8	A	4	24	A.Macdonald
MOTHER'S LAMENT, A [...ON THE DEATH OF HER CHILD]	4/4	A	6	39	
MOUNT STEWART HOUSE	2/4	D	2	2	
MRS. ALEXANDER CAMPBELL	S	GA	4	18	Rod.Campbell
MRS. CAPT. MUNRO'S FAVOURITE	2/4	C	2	35	
MRS(MR) CHAS. GRAHAM'S W'COME..	6/8	A	2	36/7	
MRS. GARDEN OF TROUP	S	F	4	42	
MRS. MACDONALD	6/8	A	2	36	
MRS. MACDONALD OF STAFFA	R	A	5	35	
MRS. MACDOUGALL	6/8	A	2	3	
MRS. McLEOD [OF RASAY]	2/2	A	4	42/3	
MRS. McNEAL OF UGADALE	R	G	3	4	Geo.S.Allan
MY LOVE HAS DECEIVED ME	3/4	G	1	28	& Bk.2,p.41
MY LOVE TODAY AS HERETOFORE	6/8	G	4	23	
MY NATIVE HIGHLAND HOME	2/4	G	2	10	
MY WEE FIDDLE	2/2	D	4	44	
NEIL FLAHERTY'S DRAKE	6/8	A	6	23	
NEIL'S LULLABY	S	A	6	16	
NEW TOON, THE	R	A	3	9	
92ND. GORDON H'DRS. MARCH, THE	2/4	A	1	4	
93RD'S F'WELL TO EDINBURGH, THE	2/4	A	2	6/7	R.Meldrum
NORTH SIDE OF THE GRAMPIANS	S	C	3	46	S.Fraser Coll.

Title	Meter	Key	Bk	Pg	Note
NURSE'S SONG, THE	6/8	D	1	1	
OCH O RO U	3/4	A	2	43	
O'ER THE WATER TO CHARLIE	6/8	D	2	34	Orig. Set
O'ER THE WATER TO CHARLIE	6/8	G	2	34/5	Mod. Set
OLD DONALD	2/4	D	3	17	
OLD HIGHLAND AIR [MO RUN GEAL]	3/4	A	1	3	
OLD MARCH	4/4	GD	6	47	
ONE DAY AS I CLIMBED A HILL	6/8	G	2	39	
O'OO MILL O' GLENKINDIE, THE	R	A	6	34	R.Meldrum,1907
ORIG. AIR TO OSSIANIC POEMS	4/4	D	5	41	
OVER THE ISLES TO AMERICA	R	D	3	29	
PADDY'S MILESTONE	6/8	A	5	18	G.L.Mullin
PARKER'S WELCOME TO PERTHSHIRE	2/4	A	3	1	
PEAT BOG, THE	R	D	5	9	
PETER BAILLIE	S	A	4	6	
PETRONELLA	2/4	D	5	47	
PHONES LODGE	S	A	2	21	
PIBROCH	6/8	A	2	46	
PIBROCH OF INVERNESS, THE	4/4	C	3	39	
PINT STOUP, THE	R	A	6	16	
PIPE AIR[I'LL RETURN TO K'TAIL]	4/4	AE	1	24	
PIPER'S BONNET, THE	S	A	2	19	
PIPER'S CAVE, THE	2/4	A	5	14	J.Sutherland
POLTALLOCH HOUSE	6/8	A	3	33	
PORT LENNOX	4/4	C	6	41	
PORTREE MEN, THE	2/4	D	2	1	Jas.Mauchline
PRESTON PANS	R	A	5	8	
PRINCE ALBERT'S MARCH	2/4	A	1	23	
PR.CHARLIE'S F/WELL TO SCOTL.	6/8	A	4	42	
PR.CHARLIE'S F/WELL TO SKYE	6/8	A	3	33	
PR.CHARLIE'S W/COME TO I.o SKYE	2/4	D	3	10/11	
PRINCESS ROYAL'S BIRTHDAY, THE	6/8	D	2	37	
PUSH ABOUT THE JORUM	2/2	G	4	41	
QUAKER, THE	6/8	D	4	4	
Q. VICTORIA'S JUBILEE MARCH	2/4	A	2	26	John Macdonald
QUICK DREAM, THE	3/4	F	6	44	
QUICKSTEP (cf: Bk.1,p.25)	6/8	A	2	45	
QUICKSTEP	3/8	D	5	24	
RABBIE BURNS	S	G	4	41	
RATTLIN', ROARIN' WILLIE	9/8	G	6	9	
REAY RANT, THE	R	A	4	28	H.Taylor, 1907
RED PLAID, THE	S	A	6	43	
REEL	R	DA	1	16	D.McPhee
REEL	R	A	1	22	
REEL	R	A	2	23	Wm.Murray
REEL	R	A	3	12	
REEL	R	A	4	7	
REEL	R	A	4	21	
REEL	R	A	5	14/14	Wm. Lamont
REEL OF TULLOCH	4/4	A	4	16/17	
REEL OF TULLOCH - HOOLICHAN	2/2	A	4	17	
REJECTED SAILOR, THE	2/2	A	4	26	
RENFREWSHIRE MILITIA	2/4	A	3	31	
RT.HON. EARL OF MOIRA'S MARCH	4/4	D	6	18	
ROBERT CAMPBELL	S	A	5	27	Arch.Campbell
ROB ROY'S MARCH	2/4	G	4	45	
RODERICK MACDONALD	S	A	2	2	
RODERICK MACDONALD	R	A	2	3	
ROGART VOLUNTEERS MARCH	2/4	A	2	14/15	
ROSSIE CASTLE	R	A	5	31	C.Thomson
ROSS-SHIRE VOLUNTEERS	2/4	A	3	2	J.Connon
ROTHESAY FAIR	S	C	4	43	
ROUND BY ABERDEEN	6/8	A	6	9	Dk. Of Atholl
RYAN'S RANT	R	A	6	43	
SAMUEL THE WEAVER	6/8	A	3	25	
SCHOTTISCHE	SCH	D	4	16	
SCOTS GUARDS F'WELL TO S.AFRICA	2/4	A	5	29/30	Wm.Ross,1902
SCOTTACK CAIRN	R	A	4	19	H.Taylor
SEBASTOPOL MARCH	2/4	A	3	20	
2ND BTN. SCOTCH BRIGADE, THE	6/8	Bb	5	26	
2ND REGT. SCOTTISH HORSE	6/8	A	4	31	John MacColl
74TH'S F/WELL TO EDINBURGH	2/4	A	4	3	
74TH'S PIPE BAND, 1833, THE	2/4	A	6	38	(? or1853)
79TH'S F/WELL TO GIBRALTAR	2/4	A	1	11	John Macdonald
72ND'S F/WELL TO ABERDEEN	2/4	D	1	4	
73RD REGT.'S MARCH, THE	4/4	G	5	41	
SHEEP WIFE, THE	R	GA	2	20	
SHEPHERD'S CROOK, THE	S	A	4	24/5	
SHE ROSE AND LET ME IN	4/4	D	1	30	
SIEGE OF SEBASTOPOL, THE	4/4	A	3	6	D.Campbell
SIR NORMAN McLEOD'S LAMENT	3/4	C	2	41	
SKYE AIR, A	4/4	GE	2	32	Mary McLeod
SKYE AIR	4/4	G	6	15	
SKYE DANCE	4/4	AE	6	27	
SLEEP ON TILL DAY[CAIDIL GU LO]	3/4	C	2	45	
SMITH OF KILLIECHASSIE, THE	R	A	5	34	(Here"Chilli")
SMITH'S A GALLANT FIREMAN, THE	S	D	2	47	
SOFT MAY MORN	6/8	GE	6	12	
SOLDIER LIE ON YOUR WEE PICKLE STRAW	6/8	EA	6	28	
SOLDIER'S JOY, THE	4/4	D	3	18	
SONG OF SORROW, A [ORAN MULAD]	6/8	C	1	33	
SOUTERS OF CROMARTY	6/8	E	4	2	
SPEED THE PLOUGH	R	A	1	3	John Moorehead
SPINNING WHEEL, THE	S	G	3	17	Rod. Campbell
STELLA'S JIG	6/8	D	1	5	John Wallace
STIRLINGSHIRE MILITIA	2/4	A	2	22/3	
ST.KILDA AIR, A	4/4	Eb	2	39	
ST.KILDA SONG AND DANCE, A	4/4	DB	6	26	
ST.KILDA WEDDING	R	A	3	20	
STRATHARDLE HIGHLAND GATHERING	2/4	A	6	40	John Stewart
STRATHFLEET MARCH	6/8	A	2	28/9	Wm. Macdonald
STUART'S RANT	R	A	5	23	
'S TU MO LUAIDH N'AM FAIDHINN THU [MY LOVE IF I COULD WIN THEE]	3/4	Bb	2	33	
STUMPIE	S	A	1	20	
STUMPIE [cf:HIGHLAND WEDDING]	M	A	3	37	
TAKE YOUR GUN TO THE HILL	S	A	3	14	
3RD BTN. SEAFORTH'S F/WELL TO MONTROSE	2/4	A	4	12	(1905)
1000 BLESSINGS ON THE LOVELY MOUTH, A	4/4	AF#	2	36	
THREE GIRLS OF PORTREE, THE	4/4	F	5	19	
THRO' THE HEATHER	6/8	D	4	7/8	
TIBBY FOWLER OF THE GLEN	S	AE	3	44/5	
TILLYPRONIE	S	A	6	10	

TIMOUR THE TARTAR	R	A	5	45	
TINKER'S MARCH, THE	2/4	A	5	3	
TORTAR'S HORNPIPE	2/2	D	3	26	
TRAIGH GRUINNEARD	6/8	AG	5	1	
TULLOCH CASTLE	S	A	4	26	Rod. Campbell
TULLOCHEWAN CASTLE	2/4	A	2	12	
TULLOCHGORUM	S	G	3	43	
25TH KOSB'S F/WELL TO MEERUT	2/4	D	2	5	
UP AN' WAUR THEM A' WILLIE	4/4	A	6	42	
WAE'S ME FOR PRINCE CHARLIE	4/4	A	4	47	
WANDERING PIPER, THE	6/8	A	6	6	J.P.McLeod
WAR CALL OF THE CLANS	2/4	C	1	31	
WARMING OF THE FINGERS, THE	6/8	A	4	25	
WEE BIT COGGIE	R	A	6	10	
WET IS THE NIGHT AND COLD	3/4	G	2	44/5	
W.G.MELDRUM'S F/WELL TO GLENKINDIE	2/4	A	6	33	
WHA CAN HELP IT	6/8	A	5	40	Gow/Macdonald
WHA'LL BE KING BUT CHARLIE	6/8	BbG	1	33	
WHA WADNA FECHT FOR CHARLIE	4/4	A	2	40	
WHEN CHARLIE COMES	R	AB	4	15	
WHERE SLEEPEST THOU, MY D'LING	6/8	F	5	18	
WHISTLE O'ER THE LAVE O'T	4/4	G	1	7	
WHITE COCKADE, THE	2/4	G	2	38/9	
WIFE SHE BREWED IT, THE	S	A	2	22	
WILLIE BREW'D A PECK O' MAUT	4/4	D	6	37	
WILLIE MACKAY, THE WEAVER	R	A	4	2/3	Wm. Murray
WILLIE NICHOLSON'S JIG	6/8	B	4	18	Rod. Campbell
WILL YE GO TO THE ISLE OF SKYE	R	A	1	22	
WILL YOU RUN AWA' WI' ME	R	GA	3	36	S.Fraser Coll.
WIND THAT SHAKES THE BARLEY,THE	R	D	2	47	
Wm. MACKAY TAIT ESQ.	6/8	A	3	40	Jas. Center
WHO WILL DANDLE MY MARY	9/8	A	6	17	
WOMEN O' THE GLEN	6/8	Bb	4	22	
YANKEE DOODLE	2/2	G	6	24	(American)
YOUNG COLIN, PRIDE OF THE PLAIN	2/4	D	5	38	
YOUNG RORY	S	A	4	13	

Approx. 600 titles, including many Pipe Tunes. As Logan makes plain, some are described as "In imitation of the Bagpipe". He was thus one of the first publishers to propose the wholesale "cross-over" of pipe music to the fiddle, something which Scott Skinner, for example, would never have contemplated.

THE
INVERNESS COLLECTION

OF

HIGHLAND
PIBROCHS, LAMENTS, QUICKSTEPS
AND
MARCHES,

CAREFULLY & EFFECTIVELY ARRANGED

FOR THE

PIANOFORTE,

AND CONTAINING SOME OF THE MOST POPULAR AND FAVORITE AIRS OF THE

HIGHLANDS OF SCOTLAND.

ENT. STA. HALL.

CLACH-NA-CUDDIN

CONCORDIA ET FIDELITAS

LOGAN & C^O. MUSIC SELLERS,
INVERNESS & ABERDEEN.

THE INVERNESS COLLECTION OF HIGHLAND PIBROCHS, LAMENTS,
QUICKSTEPS AND MARCHES - 204 AIRS FOR VIOLIN & PIANO

Printed by LOGAN & CO., Inverness & Aberdeen   (L6)/pt2

Six Parts or Books in one - normally published in two volumes;
the Page Numbering used here is non-consecutive.

NOTE: Those tunes marked * are the only ones which do NOT appear
in LOGAN'S HIGHLAND MUSIC listed above.

TITLE	TEMP	KEY	BK	PAGE	AUTHOR/SOURCE
ABERCAIRNEY HIGHLANDERS	2/4	PA	5	21	
ABERDEENSHIRE REGT.'S MARCH	4/4	D	3	11	
ALONE, I AM WEARY	4/4	PA	4	10	(Slow March)
ANCIENT SCOTTISH MARCH	4/4	G	5	14	cf: Rob Roy
AN RAOIR BHRUADAIR MI'M CHADUL	3/4	A	2	14	(Air)
ATHOLE GATHERING, THE	6/8	PA	1	6	
ATHOLE HIGHLANDERS' MARCH	4/4	A	1	8	
ATHOLE VOLUNTEERS' MARCH	4/4	F	6	2	N. Gow
ATHOLE VOLUNTEERS' QUICKSTEP	6/8	F	6	7	
AUCHINLECK VOLUNTEERS' MARCH	4/4	A	5	5	
BARREN ROCKS OF ADEN, THE	4/4	D	3	3	
*BLACK MARY [MAIRI DHUBH]	4/4	C	4	8	(V.old Gaelic)
BOG OF GIGHT [GORDON CASTLE]	2/2	A	4	17	Wm. Marshall
BONNIE HIGHLAND HILLS	4/4	A	6	2	
BONNIE STRATHMORE	6/8	A	2	3	(Air)
BOYNE WATER (HIGHLAND SET)	4/4	PA	4	12	
BRAES OF BALQUHIDDER, THE	4/4	Bm	6	12	(Orig. Set)
*BRAES OF BUSHBIE, THE [BUSBY]	4/4	Gm	6	5	(Air)
*BRAES O' MAR, THE	4/4	D	6	17	(Orig. Set)
BRAVE SCOTLAND, MARCH	4/4	C	4	20	(S. the Brave)
BUGLE HORN QUICKSTEP, THE	6/8	D	5	6	
CABAR FEIDH - PIBROCH	4/4	G	3	19	
CAIRNGORM MOUNTAIN	6/8	F#m	4	20	(V. old)
CALEDONIAN MARCH, THE [or 57th]	4/4	F	3	15	(The Diehards)
CALLUM SIAR GLAS	4/4	F	2	11	(Old Highland)
CAMERONIANS' F/WELL TO GIB.	6/8	G	3	21	(Gibraltar)
CAMPBELLS ARE COMING, THE	6/8	G	3	10	
*CARRON SIDE	4/4	G	6	20	
*CHRISTMAS CAROUSING, THE	4/4	D	6	21	
CHURL, THE [AM BODACH]	9/8	D	4	6	
CLANS' GRAND MARCH, THE	4/4	Eb	3	9	
COCK OF THE NORTH, THE	6/8	Ab	4	2	
COLIN'S COWS [CRODH CHAILEAN]	3/4	F	4	8	
COL. BOYLE OF SHEWALTON	6/8	Bb	6	6	(? Nath. Gow)
CRUSADERS' MARCH	4/4	A	4	11	A & S H/ldrs.
CULLODEN MUIR	6/8	A	1	10	
CULLODEN'S BIRTHDAY	4/4	A	5	7	Wm. Morrison
CULLODEN'S FAVOURITE	4/4	D	5	6	Wm. Morrison
DAFT DONALD - MARCH	6/8	D	3	23	
DELVIN SIDE - MARCH	4/4	Am	3	17	
DONACHT HEAD	4/4	Cm	6	10	(Slow)
DORNOCH LINKS	2/4	A	2	9	
DREAM, A [AISLING]	4/4	D	6	3	(Skye Air)
*DR. NORMAN MACLEOD'S LAMENT	3/4	G	3	18	(Very slow)
DROVER LADS, THE [GILLEAN AN..]	6/8	G	6	16	Quickstep
DUCHESS OF BUCCLEUCH'S FAV.	4/4	Bb	6	12	S/Str. (Gow)
EARL DOUGLAS'S LAMENT	3/4	Bb	6	23	(Slow)
EARL OF DALHOUSIE'S MARCH, THE	4/4	Bb	4	15	
*E. OF MOIRA'S MARCH & Q/STEP	4/4	D	6	8	
ERCHLESS CASTLE - MARCH	2/4	PA	4	10	
FINGALIAN AIR	3/4	C	5	20	(V. slow)
FINGALIAN AIR	4/4	C	5	20	
*FISHERMAN'S SONG[MAOL DONAICH]	6/8	Em	6	4	(to attract
FOLLOW HER OVER THE BORDER	9/8	F	1	16	seals)
FONAB HOUSE	6/8	D	6	6	(Air)
*FORTY-SECOND[or R/HDRS MARCH]	4/4	A	6	10	
*GAELIC AIR, A	6/8	Am	2	14	(Slow)
GAELIC AIR, A	4/4	C	2	2	
*GAEILIC AIR, A	6/8	G	2	8	
GENERAL HLD. GATHERING	6/8	D	3	4	(..for Battle)
GILLIE A DROVER	6/8	G	3	22	(Drover Lads)
GILLIE CALLUM	4/4	A	1	2	
GLENDARUEL HIGHLANDERS, THE	6/8	A	6	18	
GLENGARRY'S MARCH	2/4	A	1	17	
*GLENGARRY'S PIBROCH	4/4	C	3	13	
GLEN'S MINE, THE	2/4	A	1	20	
*GORDON CASTLE[cf:DONACHT HD.]	4/4	Em	5	15	(Bk.6/p10)
GORDONS HAE THE GUIDING O'T	2/4	D	4	19	("...Girdin')
GORDON'S MARCH	6/8	G	4	4	
GU MA SLAN A CHI MI	4/4	F	2	2	(Happy may I)
HARRIET, THE (PIBROCH)	6/8	PA	2	4	
HARRIS DANCE	4/4	Am	5	17	(Quick)
*HE'S BONNY,HE'S O'ER THE HILLS	4/4	Bm	6	11	(Slow) c.1745
HEY TO CUPAR	6/8	D	6	15	
HIGHLAND BOAT SONG, A	6/8	Ab	1	17	Turn ye to me
HLD. BDE. AT WATERLOO, THE	6/8	PA	1	5	
HIGHLAND CHIEFTAIN, THE	4/4	D	6	13	Nath. Gow
HIGHLAND LADDIE (PIPE SET)	2/4	A	1	7	
HIGHLAND LADDIE, THE	6/8	D	5	16	Dr. Arne, 1754
(cf: WAVERLEY/FERGUS McIVER)					
HIGHLAND LAMENT, A	3/4	Eb	1	8	
HIGHLAND LAMENTATION, A	3/4	Bb	6	21	
HIGHLAND NURSING AIR	3/8	G	6	22	("Lento")
HIGHLAND PORT, A	6/8	G	5	18	Rory Dall
HIGHLAND TROOP, THE	6/8	G	3	16	Fraser
HIGHLAND WATCH ['M FREICHEADAN]	4/4	G	6	20	
*HILLS OF GLENORCHY, THE	6/8	PA	1	5	Ist. Set
HILLS OF GLENORCHY, THE	6/8	Em	1	13	2nd. Set
HOOP HER AND GIRD HER	6/8	G	1	14	
* I LOVE A BONNY LASS	4/4	A	3	9	Pibroch
(cf: I LOVE THE GIRL, in Gesto Coll. - Mc3v2 App.)					
INVERNESS GATHERING	4/4	A	1	1	(Quickstep)
*JIGS (SEE "NORTH HIGHLAND")			5	16/17	
JOHN ANDERSON'S AULDEST DAUGH.	2/4	Am	2	12	(Slow)
JOHN KNOX	2/4	Bb	5	17	(Air)
JOHNNIE COPE	4/4	Am	1	9	
KENMARE'S ON AND AWA'	6/8	D	4	18	(Kenmuir/more)
KILLIECRANKIE [BATTLE OF, THE]	4/4	C	1	15	(Air ?1692)
KING JAMIE'S MARCH	2/4	G	6	13	(To Ireland)
LAIRD OF BRODIE, THE	4/4	D	4	4	
LAMENT (FOR THE FALLEN BRAVE)	3/4	C	1	13	Fraser
*LAMENT FOR HUGH,E. OF EGLINTON	4/4	D	6	11	(Eglintoun)
LAMENT FOR McDONALD OF KEPPOCH	9/8	F	5	19	Keppoch

Mc3v1 The Skye Collection
Pub: K.N. MacDonald (1891)
See A-Z Index(II) listings

Mc3v2 The Gesto Collection
See Appendix (Mc3)

MACDONALD, Keith Norman. Editor: The Gesto Collection of Highland Music (Edinburgh, 1895); 154 pp. + 33-page Appendix (A) Approx. 336 airs in all.

Companion volume to "The Skye Collection" (Mc3v1), published in 1987, which is listed in the A-Z Index and contains dance music (reels and strathspeys with a lesser number of "solos", country dances, hornpipes and jigs). By comparison, the "Gesto" is a repository of Gaelic vocal airs with some military and mainland (dance) music interspersed in it.

("PA" = Pipe Mode)

TITLE	TEMP	KEY	PAGE	AUTHOR/SOURCE/NOTE
A BHANAIS BHAN [FAIR WEDDING, THE]	4/4	A	149	Lachlan McPherson
A CHOLLA MO RUIN [COLIN MY DEAR]	3/4	PA	75	Pibroch o' Dunyveg, 1647
A GHLASS BHEUR [FINGER LOCK, THE]	4/4	G	78	R. Macailean oig (Morar)
AGUS HO MORAG [PRINCE CHARLIE]	4/4	G	8	Jacobite Air
AIR FALLIRIN ILLIRIN	6/8	D	7	
ALISTAIR OG [YOUNG ALEXANDER]	2/4	C	4	
ALISTER WEARS A COCKED BONNET [THA BONAID BEAG BIORACH AIR ALASDAIR]	6/8	A	136	Kenmure's on an' awa'
AM BREACAN UALLACH [GAY PLAID,THE]	4/4	G	10	Jacobite Air
AM FEILE PREASACH [PLAITED KILT]	3/4	E	11	
AN CLUINN THU, LEANNAIN [WILL YOU HEAR ME, SWEETHEART]	6/8	G	23	
AN DOCTAIR LEODACH'S BIODAG AIR [DR. MACLEOD WEARS A DIRK]	4/4	G	141	Song/Strathspey
A NIGHNEAG A CHUIL DHUINN	2/4	G	21	Air: Bonny Brown Maiden
AN NOCHD GUR FAOIN MO CHADAL DOMH	6/8	D	36	Love Song
AN SEALGAIR A' CHOMHACHAG	4/4	G	1	Slow (Hunter & the Owl)
AN T-AILLEAGAN [THING OF BEAUTY]	2/4	F	41	Love Song
AN TALL' AM BU GNA' LE MHACLEOID	3/4	F	42	Fraser (Hereditary Hall)
ATHOLE VOLUNTEERS' MARCH, THE	4/4	F	111	Gow
BACK OF BENNACHIE, THE	2/4	D	125	
BALMORAL HIGHLANDERS, THE	2/4	A	139	Angus Mackay
BANNER OF ST. ANDREWS, THE	4/4	A	150	Now called: Appin House
BARD'S LAMENT FOR HIS SWEETHEART, THE [CUMHA BHAIRD AIR SON A LEANNAN]	3/4	F	44	Song: Lochaber no more
BARREN ROCKS OF ADEN, THE	2/4	D	122	A.Mackellar (78th Regt.)
BATTLE OF KILLICRANKIE, THE	4/4	C	97	Slow March (I'ness Coll.)
BATTLE OF THE BOYNE, THE	4/4	G	118	
BHA MI'N DE M'BHEINN DOBHRAIN	4/4	F	43	(I was yesterday in Ben D)
BHANNERACH DHONN A'CHRUIDH	3/8	G	46	(Bonnie Brown Dairymaid)
BIG JOHN'S DAUGHTER [CHA TOIR IAIN MOR A NIGHEAN DHOMH]	4/4	D	149	
BLACK DONALD BALLOCH OF THE ISLES [PIOBAIREACHD DHOMHNUILL DUIBH]	6/8	A	85	(Pibroch o' Donald Dubh)
BLACK MARY or SEA MEW, THE	6/8	G	19	(Ho Ro, Mhairi Dhubh)
BOATMAN, THE [FEAR A'BHATA]	3/4	E	13	
BOC LIATH NAN GOBHAR [GREY BUCK]	6/8	PA	101	
BODAICH NAM BRIGIS [CARLE WI'THE BREEKS]	6/8	D	60	(Lord Breadalbane's March)
BONNY BANKS OF AYR, THE	4/4	C	7	Burns/(Comp:Alan Masterton
BONNIE STRATHMORE	6/8	PA	115	Inverness Coll.
BOTHAN AIRIDH 'M BRAIGHE RAINEACH [SHEILING IN THE BRAES OF RANNOCH]	3/4	G	53	Fraser
BROGUES AN' BROCHAN AN' A'	9/8	G	116	(Woo'd an' married an' a')
BRUGHAICHEAN GHLINNE BRAON	3/4	G	2/3	(Braes of Glen Braon)
BRAES OF RANNOCH, THE [or MACKENZIE'S FAREWELL TO SCOTLAND]	4/4	D	123	John Ban Mackenzie
BUACHAILLE NAN GOBHAR A'S BUACHILL NAN CAORACH	6/8	PA	114	Air (The Shepherd and the Goatherd)
BUGLE HORN	6/8	D	130	Inverness Coll.
CAIDIL GU LA [SLEEP ON TILL DAY]	3/4	C	5	V. old Skye Air
CAILLEACH BEINN NA BRIC	4/4	G	17	Fairy Song
CIAMAR IS URRA' SINN FUIREACH AN DRAM [HOW SHALL WE ABSTAIN FROM WHISKY ?]	6/8	G	18	Fraser
CAITE 'N CAIDIL AN RIBHINN [WHERE WILL THE MAIDEN SLEEP ?]	6/8	F	45	Skye Air
CALEDONIAN MARCH, THE	4/4	F	40	57th. Regt. (The Diehards)
CALUM A GHLINNE	6/8	F	48	(Malcolm of the Glen)
CAPTAIN CAMPBELL'S MARCH	2/4	D	134	
CAPTAIN MUNRO'S FAVOURITE	2/4	C	99	42nd. Regt.
CELTIC SOCIETY'S QUICKSTEP, THE	4/4	PA	144	return)
CHA TILL MI TUILLE	6/8	PA	72	MacCrimmon (I shall never
CLACHAN GHLINNE DA RUAILL	3/4	G	49	(Hamlet of Glendaruel)
COCK OF THE NORTH, THE	6/8	A	135	
COL. ALEXANDER MACDONALD'S STR.	4/4	A	151	
COMA LEIM FEIN AM MINISTEIR [WHAT CARE I FOR THE MINISTER ?]	9/8	C	99	Fraser
COMING THROUGH THE HEATHER	4/4	F	110	Air
CO-DHIU THO-GAINN FONN MO LEANNAIN	4/4	F	43	Air
CREAG GHUANACH [HILL OF MY DELIGHT]	3/4	G	15	Albyn's Anthology
CRODH CHAILEIN [COLIN'S CATTLE]	6/8	G	19	Fairy Song (3/4 (A) p.38)
CRODH LAOIGH NA BODACH [PLUNDER OF THE LOWLANDS]	3/4	PA	68	Fraser, Air
CUACHAG NAN CRAOBH [CUCKOO OF THE GROVE, THE]	3/4	Bb	51	Song, Wm. Ross
CUILFHIONN [FINGAL'S WEEPING]	4/4	PA	109	Slow March
CUMHA CHRAOBH NA'N TEUD [LAMENT FOR THE HARP TREE]	4/4	A	79	Rory Dall Morrison
CUMHA DHOMHNULL DHUGHULL MAC AOIDH	4/4	A	83	MacCrimmon, Lament (1647)
CUMHA H-IRTEACH [ST.KILDA LAMENT]	3/4	G	22	Albyn's Anthology (1815)
CUMHA MHIC AN TOISICH (1526)	3/4	D	69	(McIntosh's Lament/& p77)
CUMHA MHIC CRUIMEIN	6/8	D	76	(MacCrimmon's Lament)
CUMHA SHIR TORMAID MHIC LEOID	3/4	D	33	Skye Air (Sir Norman McL.)
DEAN CADAL 'S FAN SAMHACH	6/8	PA	106	(Sleep and be Quiet)
DEIL TAK' THE WARS	4/4	C	98	Old Scots Song/March
DH'FHAG THU MI FO BHRON [THOU HAST LEFT ME MELANCHOLY]	3/3	D	34	Fraser, Air
DORNOCH LINKS	2/4	A	137	March
DR. MACKINNON'S REEL	4/4	A	147	
DUKE OF ROXBURGHE'S FAREWELL TO THE BLACK MOUNT, THE	4/4	A	133	Angus Mackay (?) Slow M.
DUKE OF YORK'S MARCH	4/4	D	130	(In D & A)
DUNTULM [DUNTULM CASTLE]	6/8	G	102	Quickstep
EILEAN AN CHEO [ISLE OF MIST, THE]	2/4	D	6	Skye
EXILED MONARCH, THE [JAMES I]	2/4	G	31	John McMurdo/McRae,Kintail
FAILTE NA MORTHIR [HAIL, MORAR]	4/4	F	43	Alex. McDonald, Air
FAILTE PHRIONNSA [PRINCE'S SALUTE]	4/4	PA	56	John McIntyre (1715)
FAILTE THIGHERNA STHRUAIN	4/4	PA	63	Struan Robertson's Salute
FEADAG GHORACH AN T-SLEIBH	3/4	G	51	(Airy Plover of the Heath)
FEAR A' BHATA [BOATMAN, THE]	3/4	E	13	
FEAR A' CHOIRE	4/4	G	145	(Mackinnon of Corrie)
FEASGAR LUAIN	4/4	G/E	12	Love Song
FINGAL'S WEEPING	2/4	PA	105	
GACH TINNEAS ACH GAOL	6/8	C	6	(Each Ailment but Love)
GATHERING OF THE CLANS, THE	6/8	G	54	Jacobite Air
GED THA MI GUN CHRODH GUN AIGHEAN	3/4	G	29	(Though I am Tocherless)
GILLEAN A BHAILLE SEO [VILLAGE LADS]	6/8	A	135	(Bride is a Bonny Thing)
GILLEAN AN DROBHAIR [DROVER LADS]	6/8	G	116	
GILLEAN AN FHEILIDH	6/8	D	117	(Lads in the Kilt)
GILLE BOCHD NA MOINTICH	4/4	G	16	(Poor Herdboy, The)
GILLE CALUM [SWORD DANCE]	4/4	A	153	Strathspey & Reel
GIN I HAD A BONNIE LASSIE	4/4	G	144	
GLENDARUEL	4/4	PA	144	Strathspey
GLENDARUEL HIGHLANDERS, THE	6/8	A	140	p/m Fettes

Title	Time	Key	Page	Notes
GU'N BU SLAN A CHI MI	2/4	G	12	(Happy may I see Thee)
GUR MULADACH THA MI	3/4	G	22	(I am in Sorrow)
GUR TROM LEAM AN AIRIDH	3/4	E	29	Love Song
GUR TU MO NIGHEAN DONN BHOIDHEACH	2/4	Bb	53	(...my Pretty Auburn Maid)
HEIGHTS OF ALMA, THE	6/8	D	103	Wm. Ross
HE'N CLO DUBH [GAY PLAID, THE]	4/4	G	10	(cf: Am Breacan Uallach ?)
HE'S O'ER THE HILLS THAT I LO'E WEEL		G	101	6/8 (c. 1745)
HEY ! JOHNNY COPE	4/4	A	95	
HI ORO 'S NA HORO EILE	3/4	F	39	(Became: Ae Fond Kiss)
HIGHLAND BRIGADE AT WATERLOO, THE	6/8	A	97	John Gow
HIGHLAND BRIGADE'S MARCH TO THE BATTLE OF THE ALMA, THE	2/4	PA	119	
HIGHLAND LADDIE	2/4	A	138	
HIGHLAND MARCH	4/4	D	124	
HIGHLAND RORY [DRUNKEN PIPER, THE]	2/4	PA	121	p/m Alex. MacLeod
HIGHLAND WATCH, THE	4/4	E	103	Now 47th., R. Highlanders
HIGHLAND WELCOME, THE	6/8	D	38	
HIGHLANDER'S LAMENT, THE	6/8	E	106	Fraser
HILL OF LOCHIEL, THE	3/4	D	51	Fraser
HILLS OF GLENORCHY, THE	6/8	PA	106	
H-ITHILL UTHILL AGUS O	4/4	E	25	Skye Air
HO CHA CHEILINN NACH TU B'FHEARR LEAM [I CAN'T CONCEAL THAT I PREFER YOU]	6/8	Bb	53	cf: I'll Return to Kintail
HO CHAN EIL MULAD OIRNN	4/4	Eb	55	(Emigrant's Farewell, The)
HO RO MHAIRI DHU [BLACK MARY]	6/8	G	19	(Sea Mew, The)
HO RO MO CHUID CHUIDEACHD THU ["MY BOON COMPANION" - HIS GUN]	4/4	E	26	Duncan Ban McIntyre
HO RO MO NIGHEAN DONN BHOIDEACH	4/4	G	29	(Horo my nutbrown Maiden)
HO RO GAWHNA	4/4	G	16	(Dairymaid's Lullaby)
IAIN CAIMBEUL A' BHANCA [JOHN CAMPBELL THE BANK]	6/8	A	137	(Rock & a wee pickle Tow or "The Gordon's March")
IAIN MAC 'IC FHIONAGHAIN	4/4	D	35	(John Mackinnon)
INVERNESS GATHERING, THE	4/4	A	138	(or Culloden Battle Day)
IORRAM CHLANN RAONUILL	4/4	E	9	(Clanranald's Boat Song)
IORRAM NA H-IMRICH CHUAIN	6/4	F	40	(The Emigrants)
IS LEAM CRUINNEAG DHONN NA 'AM BO	2/4	G	30	(Brown Herd Maid)
JOY GAE WI' MY LOVE	6/8	D	129	V. old Highland
KINRARA	4/4	Bb	54	Wm. Marshall
LADY LOUIS HAY'S STRATHSPEY	4/4	A	154	(Not published elswhere ?)
LADY MACDONALD OF THE ISLES, THE	4/4	D	146	
LADY MACDONALD'S REEL, THE	4/4	D	146	
LADY MARGARET STEWART	4/4	B	150	Reel
LAMENT FOR MARY, QUEEN OF SCOTS	3/4	Eb	112	
LAMENT FOR RUARAIDH MOR McLEOD	3/4	F	108	
LAMENT OF FLORA MACDONALD, THE	6/8	F	50	Neil Gow Jnr.
LASS OF GLENSHEE, THE	4/4	D	105	
LASS OF HUMBER SIDE, THE	3/4	G	27	Old Highland(?) Air
LEWIE GORDON	4/4	F	47	Claimed by Rev. Geddes
LOCHEIL'S AWA' TO FRANCE	4/4	E	104	(or L.'s F/well to Isla)
LOGAN'S BONNIE WOODS AND BRAES	2/4	B	102	(or "Logan Water")
LORD LOVAT'S LAMENT	4/4	A	107	David Fraser, Piper
LORD PANMURE'S MARCH	2/4	D	127	John Macdonald
MACDONALDS OF PORTREE, THE	2/4	D	120	James Mauchline
MACGREGOR'S GATHERING, THE	6/8	D	119	March & Song
MACGREGOR'S SEARCH	3/4	PA	115	(or "...Lament)
MAC GRIOGAIR A RUADH SHRUTH	3/4	C	1	(MacGregor of Roro, etc.)
MACINTOSH'S LAMENT	3/4	D	69	(1526) Pipe version, p77
MACKAY'S MARCH, THE	4/4	PA	115	
MACLAUCHLIN'S MARCH, THE	2/4	D	120	
MACLEOD OF RAASAY'S SALUTE	4/4	A	92	Angus Mackay
MACLEAN'S WELCOME	3/4	F	50	Jacobite Air
MACPHERSON'S LAMENT	4/4	D	107	By Himself (Pipe Set)
MADAINN CHIUIN CHEITAIN	6/8	E	20	Fraser (Sweet May Morn)
MAIDS OF ARROCHAR, THE	6/8	D	35	John Macdonald, Dundee
MAIRI BNAN OG [FAIR YOUNG MARY]	6/8	E	14	Duncan Ban McIntyre
MAIRI LAGHACH [WINSOME MARY]	3/4	G	23	
MARCH OF DONALD LORD OF THE ISLES TO THE BATTLE OF HARLAW, 1411	6/8	PA	67	
MARCH OF THE CLANS, BY A GENTLEMAN	4/4	C	100	From Wm. Morrison's Coll.
MARCH OF THE 92ND. HIGHLANDERS	2/4	A	102	or "Crusaders' March"
MARCHIONESS OF TULLYBARDINE, THE	2/4	A	136	March
MASSACRE OF GLENCOE, THE (1692)	2/4	A	89	Slow Air
MI 'M SHUIDH AN DEIREADH BATA [I'M SITTING IN THE STERN OF A BOAT]	4/4	G	18	Rev. MacLeod (Fraser)
MISS ANNIE MACDONALD ORD	4/4	D	146	
MISS CORBETT'S REEL	4/4	D	147	
MISS GRAHAM OF INCHBRAKIE	4/4	C	100	Niel Gow (Book 4)
MISS JESSIE MACLEOD'S FAVOURITE	4/4	D	142	
MISS MENZIES OF MENZIES	2/2	G	144	D. McKercher
MO CHAILIN DILEAS DONN	4/4	F	12	(My Fair & Faithful Maid)
MO CHAILIN DONN OG	6/8	F	48	(My Bonnie Brown Maid)
MO CHRUINNEAG DHONN	4/4	D	37	(My Neat Brown Maid)
MOCH 'SA MHADUINN	4/4	B	147	(Early in the Morning)
MOR NIGHEAN A' GHIOBAIRLAIN	4/4	F	46	(Marion the Knab's Dau.)
MO RUN GEAL DILEAS	3/4	G	15	(My Faithful Fair One)
MRS. DRUMMOND OF LOGIEALMOND'S R.	4/4	E	145	Niel Gow (Book 4)
MRS. MACDONALD DUNACH	4/4	A	148	
MRS. McRA HARRIS	4/4	G	143	
MUILE NAM MOR BHEANN	6/8	Bb	40/9	(Mull of the Mountains)
MUNLOCHY BRIDGE	4/4	E	142	(or "I'll hap ye in my
NAPOLEON CROSSING THE ALPS	4/4	D	129	March Plaidie)
NIGHEAN DONN AN T-SHUGRAIDH	4/4	G	19	(Maiden fond of Mirth)
NINETY-SECOND GORDON HLDRS. MARCH	2/4	PA	128	
NORWEGIAN AIR ["NEW CLARET" - GOW]	12/8	G	24	("Supposed...")
OCH MAR A CHI MI [ALAS FOR ME !]	3/4	G	11	
OCH NAN OCH MO LEIR CHRADH	4/4	D	36	Lament for Mcleod of Rasay
OCH O RO U	3/4	A	4	N. Highland (Rev. P. McD)
O ! HO RI RI THA E TIGHINN	6/8	Bb	49	(O, he's coming) Jacobite
O! SPALDERDASH AIR LASSIE NIC IAIN	4/4	G	20	"...to Iain Bhan's Dau."
OICH U AGUS H-IURAIBH EILE	3/4	C	2	Love Song
OLD SKYE AIR, AN	6/8	G	28	
OLD SKYE AIR, AN	4/4	G	28	
ORAN GAOIL [LOVE SONG]	3/4	E	29	
ORAN NAM FINEACHAN GEALACH	4/4	G	21	(War Song of the Clans)
ORAN SUGRAIDH [COURTING SONG]	4/4	G	25	(Very old)
ORIGINAL GAELIC AIR, AN	3/4	D	35	
PIOBAIREACHD DHOMHNUILL DHUBH	6/8	G	19	(Pibroch o' Donald Dubh)
PRINCE CHARLIE'S WELCOME...	4/4	D	131	(...to the Isle of Skye)
REEL OF TULLOCH [RUIDHLE...]	4/4	A	152	John McGregor of Glenlyon
RI FUAIM AN T-SHAIMH [BY THE ROAR OF THE SURF]	3/4	G	16	Le Mairi nighean A. Ruadh
RINN M'EUDAIL MO MHEALLADH	3/4	G	17	(My Darling has deceived me)
ROTHIEMURCHUS' DAUGHTER	6/8	D	132	
ROW WEEL, MY BOATIE, ROW WEEL	6/8	G	31	R.A.Smith (?)
ROXBURGH CASTLE	2/4	G	104	"By Alex. Givan"
ROYAL CAPTIVE, THE	2/4	Eb	55	Attrib: Mary Q. of Scots
RUIDHLE MO NIGHEAN DHU	4/4	G	141	(My Dark Maid's Reel)
SCANDINAVIAN AIR	4/4	G	24	Ly Charlotte Durham/Gow5
SCOTLAND FOR EVER [BRAVE SCOTLAND]	2/4	F	109	Scotland the Brave, Song
'SE ALASDAIR MO ROGHAINN	3/4	C	3	(Sandy is my Choice)
'SE MO CHAS CHRUBACH [MY LAME LEG]	6/8	PA	126	("...kept me behind")
'SE MO GHAOL AN GILLE DUBH	4/4	A	153	(My Charming Dark Lad)
SEAFORTH HIGHLANDERS, THE	6/8	D	123	(or Hurichum Harichum)
SEUMAS RUADH [JAMIE ROY]	6/8	pa	98	
SEVENTY-FIRST HIGHLANDERS, THE	2/4	A	127	
SEVENTY-FOURTH HIGHLANDERS, THE	2/4	PA	125	
SEVENTY-NINTH'S FAREWELL TO GIB.	2/4	A	128	p/m John Macdonald
SEVENTY-SECOND HIGHLANDERS, THE	6/8	D	126	(or Glen Ogle Hldrs' M.)

There is an extended edition (1895, Leipsig) containing an appendix of 67
pages. The contents of pp 34-67 are listed below, still with suffix A:

London society in the early years of the 18th Century showed a voracious appetite for all things vulgar and otherwise entertaining. Airs from The Beggar's Opera and many other long-forgotten English works were all the rage and this engraving lampoons the theatrical "excesses" of the day. In such an environment, John Walsh and his various partners ran their thriving publishing business and put out their popular dance manuals "engraven in a fair character". The listing overleaf is but one example.

CALEDONIAN COUNTRY DANCES, Being A
Collection of all the Celebrated SCOTCH
COUNTRY DANCES now in Vogue, ... London
Printed & Sold by I. Walsh ... at ye Harp &
Hoboy ... Strand.

(W3)

Title	No.	Vol.
Madam Chateaneaut's Dance	77	3
Major, The	81	2
Mark Ross	73	2
Medway, The	34	4
Meillionen	38	1
Merry Counseller	16	4
Merry Dancers	42	2
Merry Parson, The	10	4
Merry Sailors of the Centurion	82	4
Merry Thought	33	3
Merry Tom	88	3
Merry Wakefield	50	3
Midnight Frolick	85	4
Miller of Dron	56	3
Miller of Mansfield	78	3
Miser, The	26	4
Miss Drax Delight	13	3
Mistake	86	4
Mock Highland man	92	4
Moll Ross	9	4
Morton's maggot	64	4
Mopping Nelly	32	3
Mother's best Boy	79	2
Mowdewort	30	3
Muirland Willie	58	1
My ain kind Deary	64	1
Nassau, or Prince of Orange	87	2
Nassau, The	12	1
Neither here nor there	14	3
New Pierot	46	1
New way of wooing	37	1
O'er Boggie	93	1
O'er the Hills and away	48	2
Old Age and Young	99	2
Pantaloone Breeches	89	3
Parson of Feltham	67	4
Pattie's Delight	39	2
Pau Paw	43	4
Pease Straw	61	4
Perth Inch	48	4
Pill, The	58	2
Piper's maggot	45	4
Piss upon the Grass	35	3
Polly's Whim	15	3
Pontius Pilate's Maggot	17	3
Porto Bello	62	3
Prince Frederick's Hornpipe	9	1
Prince George	96	4
Prince of Wales' Birthday	65	3
Princess Amelia's Birthday	38	2
Princess of Hesse	44	3
Pump Room, The	48	1
Punchanello's Hornpipe	30	2
Pursue the French	53	4
Quadrille	89	2
Quite Prodigious	11	4
Ragg	24	1
Ragged Sailor	28	3
Rakes of Mellow	37	4
Ranting Highland Man	8	1
Reel of Glames, The	100	1
Relishing Bit	22	4
Richard Snary	20	2
Ridotta	18	2
Rising Sun	92	1
Rob Shear in Harvest	95	2
Role the Rumple Sawny	58	3
Rosemary Lane	90	2
Ross Meor	72	1
Run(n)ing Footman	68	1
Sandy Laddy	52	1
Scornfull Nancie	88	1
Scotch Collops	6	4
Scotch contention	77	1
She la Negari or Drunken Parson	93	4
Shew me the way to Wellington	100	3
Shropshire Round	51	3
Set the old Wife ayont the Fire	52	2
Shuffle and Cut	65	2
Silly old Man	76	1
Six and Sevens	34	2
So she bid me tell you	88	4
Sodi's Tambourine	98	4
Soldier Laddie	86	1
St. James' Bason	74	1
Starr at Lewis, or the Scheme	59	3
Stay & take your Breeches ...	80	2
Steward's Rant	5	1
Strath Sprays Rant	76	3
Strickland, or a trip to Phylo	16	2
Suckey's Fancy	24	4
Sulters of Selkerke	96	1
Swedish Dance	74	4
Sweet Willey come away	96	3
Swine's Tail	85	2
Swiss, The	77	4
Tambourine Dance	84	3
Tambourine Dance (2nd)	81	3
Tea Room	33	4
Three Tuns	100	2
Tit for Tat	64	2
Tod's Assembly	32	2
Topsy Turvy	27	4
Trip it	42	4
Trip to Brussels, A	81	4
Trip to Fraleigh	90	4
Trip to Holy well	47	3
Trip to Scarborough, A	38	4
Trip to Scots Bridge, A	28	4
Trip to the Lawndry, A	20	1
True Joak	49	1
Tunbridge Frisk	80	1
Tweed Side	84	1
Twelth Night	79	4
Two Brewers	31	4
Up to War a Willie	37	2
Walley Honey	78	1
Wanton God	24	3
Wap at the Widow	98	1
We are all a coming	94	4
Wedding Day	56	3
Welch Fuzileers	48	3
We're a' forsaken for ...Siller	68	2
What d'ye call it	26	3
What the De'il ails you	52	3
Wherefore come ye here ...	26	2
Whip her and gird her	14	2
Widow Lady	54	3
Willey Wilky	17	1
Yellow hair'd Laddy	91	2
Yorkshire Hornpipe	66	4
Yorkshire Trip	20	4

THE ROYAL SCOTTISH COUNTRY DANCE SOCIETY has
issued its own dance instruction books, with music, since the
year after its foundation in 1923. These books are still in
print and form an invaluable reference library of nearly 1000
excellent tunes, mostly selected from the traditional
repertoire. Copies are available from:

The Royal Scottish Country Dance Society
12 Coates Crescent, Edinburgh EH3 7AF

THE ALPHABETICAL INDEX, prepared by John Drewry of
Aberdeen and published here with the agreement of the RSCDS,
points the reader to the volume number and page (or dance)
number, indicating also whether the title refers to the
"original" or an alternative tune (eg: "1 Jig", "2 Jig"; "1
Reel,"2 Reel"; etc. - "1" = Original; "2" = Alternative); and
the dance rhythm.

IT SHOULD BE NOTED that country dance enthusiasts of every
era have used the option of devising a dance and then fitting a
tune to it, or alternatively, of creating the dance to fit the
tune. This has led, in certain instances, to a traditional
tune acquiring in effect an additional title. In most cases,
the original title is also given in the RSCDS publications, but
not in all. To avoid possible confusion, the RSCDS index
appears as Appendix (CD).

<-----------Tune-Title----------->	<-----------Tune-Source----------->	<-----Book---->	X	\<DnceType\>	<-----------Dance-Title----------->
21st of October, The		MacNab 6 - 1	2	Reel	Because he was a bonnie lad
23rd Countess of Erroll, The	Robertson, Iain	4 Step Dances 2	2	Reel	Earl of Erroll, The
92nd, The (Mar. of Huntly's Hdrs.)		4 - 6	1	Strathspey	92nd, The (Mar. of Huntly's Hdrs.)
A Gaelic Air	Gow, Niel Collection	Annie Shand 8		Reel	
A Man's a Man for a' that	Rutherford's Country Dances 1754	3 - 9	1	Strathspey	Duke is Welcome to Inverness, The
A Man's a Man for a' that	Scotch Song	30 - 5	1	Strathspey	A Man's a Man for a' that
A Quickstep by the Duke of Gordon	Petrie's 3rd Collection	24 - 10	1	Jig	Campbells are Coming, The
A Scots Measure	Oswald	27 - 11	1	Reel	Miss Nellie Wemyss
A Scottish March	Traditional	3 - 7	1	Reel	Rock and the Wee Pickle Tow, The
A Trip to St. Andrews		28 - 9	1	Jig	Ewan's Jig
A Trip to Strathbogie	Morrison, Wm. Highland Music 1812	9 - 1	2	Reel	Miss Clemy Stewart's Reel
Aberlour House	Troup, Alex.	29 - 7	1	Strathspey	Crossing, The
Admiral Nelson	Gow, Niel	19 - 8	1	Reel	Admiral Nelson
Aiken Drum		Graded 5	1	Reel	Galloway House
Airdrie Lassies		26 - 1	1	Jig	Airdrie Lassies
Alec Heard	Gourlay, Robert	22 - 3	2	Strathspey	Balmoral Strathspey
Alewife and Her Barrel, The		19 - 4	1	Reel	Alewife and Her Barrel, The
Alex. McGlashan's Farewell	McGlashan, A.	20 - 10	1	Strathspey	Quiet and Snug
Alloa Kirk	Lowe's Collection	24 - 7	1	Strathspey	I Canna Buckle to
Alltshellach	Palmer, Violet J. C.	23 - 2	1	Strathspey	Alltshellach
Alyth Burn	Shand, Jimmy	22 - 12	1	Jig	Alyth Burn
American Reel(Deil amang the Tail.)	Fulton's Music for Violin & Cello	2 - 12	1	Reel	Eightsome Reel, The
An' O' for Ane an' Twenty Tam	Oswald's Caledonian Pocket C. 1752	11 - 7	1	Jig	Moudiewart, The
An' thou wert my only dear	Kerr	21 - 4	1	Jig	An' thou wert my only dear
Annandale Strathspey, The	Robertson, Anna	33 - 7	1	Strathspey	Bedrule
Apple Tree, The	Kerr	24 - 12	1	Reel	Mairrit Man's Favourite, The
Archie Buchanan	Gourlay, Robert	22 - 10	2	Jig	Laird of Milton's Daughter, The
Archie Menzies	Lowe's Collection	Annie Shand 14		Reel	
Argyle is my name	Old Song	Annie Shand 17		Jig	
Argyll Ludging, The	Shearer, L. P.	36 - 6	1	Strathspey	Argyll Ludging, The
Argyll is my Name	Traditional	Graded 23	1	Jig	Argyll's Fancy
Argyll's Bowling Green	Gow	15 - 10	1	Reel	Argyll's Bowling Green
Arrival at Paris, The	Astor 24 C.D. for Year 1803	32 - 6	1	Reel	A Trip to The Netherlands
At the Fair	Harding's Collection	33 - 7	1	Reel	Music Makars, The
Athole Brose	Gow	Bird-Matthew 45		Strathspey	
Athole Gathering	Braemar Coll. of Highland Music	16 - 3	1	Jig	Duke of Atholl's Reel, The
Athole Highlanders	Kerr's Caledonian Collection	16 - 3	1	Jig	Duke of Atholl's Reel, The
Atholl House	Dow, D. ca. 1775	10 - 4	1	Strathspey	Lady Jean Murray's Rant
Auld Cliff Hoose, The	Esplin, J. B. Mss.	Bird-Matthew 40		Strathspey	
Auld Luckie	Kerr's Collection	Bird-Matthew 10		Strathspey	
Auld Toon O' Ayr, The	Athole Collection	17 - 6	1	Strathspey	Miss Heyden
Ayr Races	Gow, John (Beauties)	Annie Shand 28		Jig	
Ayrshire Lassies	Lowe's Collection	Bird-Matthew 7		Strathspey	
Balcomie House	Whitelaw Collection	22 - 5	2	Jig	Last of the Lairds, The
Balcomie House	Whitelaw Collection	Bird-Matthew 44		Jig	
Balmoral	Gourlay, Robert	22 - 3	1	Strathspey	Balmoral Strathspey
Banks of Allen, The	Kerr's Collection	Bird-Matthew 21		Jig	
Banks of Clyde, The	Kerr's Collection	Bird-Matthew 21		Strathspey	
Banks of Clyde, The	Kerr's Modern Dance Collection	MacNab 2 - 3	1	Strathspey	Brig O'Doon
Barley Cakes	Bremner 1757 ex Gow's 3rd Rep.	13 - 4	1	Jig	Barley Bree
Beauty of the North, The	Athole Coll. ex Simon Fraser	26 - 7	1	Strathspey	Rob Roy Macgregor
Beauty of the North, The	Athole Coll. ex Simon Fraser	Leaflet 1981	1	Strathspey	Miss Catherine Allan

Tune	Source	Ref	Type	Related
Because he was a Bonnie Lad		MacNab 8 - 4	1 Strathspey	McNeil of Barra
Belfast Almanac, The	Gow, Niel 4th Collection	Annie Shand 16	Jig	
Bert McCroskie	Frew, Bobby	22 - 2	2 Reel	Hamilton Rant, The
Bide Ye Yet	Old Scottish Song from Surenne	13 - 8	1 Jig	Fly not yet
Birk Hall	Lowe, James	24 - 9	1 Reel	Duke he was a Bonnie Beau, The
Birks of Invermay, The	Surenne	16 - 2	1 Strathspey	Birks of Invermay, The
Birnam Hall (Dunkeld)	Walker, A. Castle Newe	Annie Shand 45	Jig	
Black Dance, The	Rutherford 1772 - adapted from	12 - 10	1 Reel	Black Dance, The
Black Snuff Mill, or Muileann Dubh		3 - 11	2 Reel	Foursome Reel
Blair Athole	Kerr's Collection	Bird-Matthew 38	Reel	
Bleu Ribbon, The	Gow's Repository Part 2 ca. 1800	8 - 8	1 Reel	Bleu Ribbon, The
Blue Bonnets	Watt's Mus. Misc. 1731/Oswald 1755	3 - 5	1 Jig	Blue Bonnets
Boatie Rows, The	Old Song from Surenne	Graded 4	1 Reel	Davy's Locker
Bob O'Dowally, The	Caledonian Country Dances 1760	2 - 10	1 Strathspey	Bob O'Dowally, The
Bob of Fettercairn, The	Campbell, W. Country Dances 1796	7 - 7	1 Reel	Bob of Fettercairn, The
Bog a' ruadh or The New Bob	MacFarlane MSS 1740 here from Gow	11 - 5	2 Reel	Sleepy Maggie
Bog of Gight, The	Marshall, Mr here from McGlashan	14 - 4	2 Strathspey	Crookit-Horned Ewie, The
Bonnets O' Blue	Ross's Collection of Pipe Music	10 - 9	1 Jig	Scots Bonnet, The
Bonnie Birks of Balmoral	Lowe's Collection	Bird-Matthew 36	Reel	
Bonnie Charlie	Gow, Niel	16 - 10	2 Reel	Mr Wilson's Hornpipe
Bonnie Dundee		Graded 15	Jig	Isle, The
Bonnie Lossie	Scott Skinner, J.	31 - 7	1 Strathspey	Sir Murdoch MacDonald's Strathspey
Bonny Bridge	Kerr's Collection	Bird-Matthew 18	Strathspey	
Bonny Lass o' Fisherrow, The	Dow, D. 1775	Annie Shand 48	Reel	
Borolaski's Fancy	Campbell's Collection	24 - 6	1 Jig	Oh, whistle and I'll Come tae ye
Bottom of the Punch Bowl, The	McGibbon 1763	5 - 5	1 Reel	Punch Bowl, The
Bow-Legged Bosun	Hunter, J. M.	31 - 2	1 Reel	Clutha
Braes of Atholl	Walsh's C. D. 1731	8 - 7	1 Strathspey	Braes of Atholl
Braes of Atholl	Walsh's Country Dances 1731	8 - 9	1 Strathspey	Braes of Atholl
Braes of Auchtertyre, The	Gow	14 - 10	2 Strathspey	Grant's Reel
Braes of Breadalbane, The		21 - 9	1 Strathspey	Braes of Breadalbane, The
Braes of Busby, The	Joseph McaFadyen's Collection 1795	9 - 8	1 Strathspey	Braes of Busby, The
Braes of Cawdor	1800	Annie Shand 19	Strathspey	
Braes of Elchies, The	Grant, Charles (Aberlour)	17 - 1	1 Jig	A Trip to Aberdeen
Braes of Tullymet, The		2 - 10	2 Strathspey	Bob O'Dowally, The
Braes of Tullymet, The		7 - 12(2 - 10)	1 Strathspey	Braes of Tullymet, The
Bride, The		MacNab 7 - 1	1 Reel	Macleod of Harris
Bridge of Ballater, The		9 - 2	2 Strathspey	Jimp Waist, The
Brig of Perth	Dow, Daniel 1773	11 - 4	1 Strathspey	Inch of Perth
Brisk Young Lad, The	Old Song	Annie Shand 16	Jig	
Broachan Laoimh		MacNab 1 - 1	1	Hebridean Weaving Lilt
Broun's Reel	Bremner 1757 Gow, Nathaniel Repos.	1 - 8	1 Reel	Duke of Perth
Brown Trout, The	Johnstone, Muriel A.	36 - 1	1 Reel	Portnacraig
Buckingham House	Mackintosh, Abraham	18 - 9	2 Strathspey	Prince of Wales
Buff Coat	Erskine,Hon. Henry Collection	19 - 3	1 Jig	Just as I was in the Morning
Bumpkin, The	Gow's Repository	2 - 2	2 Jig	Bumpkin, The
Bundle and Go (Garry Owen)	Irish Origin, Aird 1782	1 - 9	2 Jig	Rory O'More
Burton's Rondo (Gentle Shepherd)	sold by J.McFadyen ca. 1796	17 - 5	1 Jig	Gentle Shepherd, The
Caber Feidh	Gow's Collection	Annie Shand 42	Reel	
Cadger's Ford, The	Gilruth, F.	25 - 5	1 Reel	Miss Brown's Reel
Cadgers in the Canongate	Walsh's Caledonian C. D. 1748	9 - 10	1 Reel	Cadgers in the Canongate
Cairdin' o't, The	Old Scots Song	Annie Shand 6	Reel	
Cairney Mount	Aird's Collection 1788	4 - 9	1 Reel	Highland Laddie
Caithness Reel, The		18 - 1	2 Reel	Johnny Groat's House

Tune	Source	Reference	Parts	Type	Dance
Caledonian Hunt	Gow, Niel Collection	Annie Shand 29		Strathspey	
Caledonian Society of London, The		MacNab 1 - 3	1	Strathspey	Rouken Glen
Callum Beg	Kerr's Modern Dance Collection	MacNab 2 - 4	1	Reel	McLaine of Lochbuie
Calver Lodge	Gow, Nathaniel Dances for 1812	8 - 3	1	Reel	Calver Lodge
Cameron's got his wife again	Bremner's Collection 1757 (ex Gow)	6 - 5	1	Strathspey	Oxton Reel
Campbell's Frolic		15 - 3	1	Jig	Campbell's Frolic
Campbell's are comin', The		Graded 13	1	Jig	Miss Welsh's Reel
Canty Jeanie Munro	Scott Skinner, J. (Harp & Claymore)	36 - 2	1	Strathspey	Road to Mallaig, The
Capt. Charles Stewart's Jig	Macdonald, Malcolm	35 - 1	1	Jig	Mrs Stewart's Jig
Capt. William McLeods's Fancy	Marshall, William	33 - 3	1	Jig	Macleod's Fancy
Captain Campbell of Lochnell's Reel	Mackintosh, Robert	31 - 1	1	Jig	Diamond Jubilee, The
Captain Francis Wemyss	Kerr's Collection	Bird-Matthew 20		Strathspey	
Captain Lockhart	Bremner	18 - 11	2	Reel	Sutters of Selkirk, The
Captain MacDonald's Fancy	Longman and Broderip's C. D. 1792	7 - 9	1	Reel	Captain MacDonald's Fancy
Captain White	Kerr's Collection	Bird-Matthew 13		Jig	
Captain Young's Quickstep	Morrison, W.	19 - 10	2	Jig	Two and Two
Castles in the Air	adapted from the song	Bird-Matthew 23		Strathspey	
Cauld Kail in Aberdeen	Johnson's Musical Museum 1788	9 - 11	1	Strathspey	Cauld Kail in Aberdeen
Ceilidh Umberella, The	Johnstone, Muriel A.	35 - 5	1	Strathspey	Gentleman, The
Chantreus, The	Astor 24 C.D. for Year 1803	32 - 7	1	Jig	Genevieve's Jig
Charles Leslie of Findassie's Str.	Grant, D.	15 - 4	1	Strathspey	Camp of Pleasure, The
Charlie is my Darling	Gow's 4th Repository	15 - 7	2	Strathspey	Lochiel's awa' to France
Chester Castle	McGlashan's Collection 1781	Annie Shand 1		Reel	
Chinese Dance	Kerr's Collection	Bird-Matthew 8		Reel	
Circassian Circle		1 - 3	1	Reel	Circassian Circle
Cluny Castle	Lowe's Collection	Bird-Matthew 17		Reel	
Clydeside Lassies	Surenne	23 - 6	2	Reel	Glasgow Country Dance
Cobbler, The	Duff, Charles	20 - 11	2	Jig	Express, The
Cock of the North, The	Kerr's Caledonian Collection	MacNab 2 - 2	1	Jig	Over the Dee and over the Don
Cold and Raw	Playford 1695	5 - 12	1	Jig	Cold and Raw
Colonel Alex. Grant's Strathspey	Grant, D. Collection	16 - 5	2	Strathspey	Caledonian Rant
Colonel Byng's Favourite	Gow, Nathaniel	13 - 9	2	Strathspey	Strathglass House
Colonel Crawford's Reel	Glen Collection	9 - 6	1	Strathspey	Dalkeith's Strathspey
Colonel H. F. Campbell's Strathspey		16 - 2	2	Strathspey	Birks of Invermay, The
Colonel L. Stewart's Reel	Marshall	17 - 3	2	Reel	Captain MacBean's Reel
Colonel MacBean's Reel	McGlashan Collection	17 - 3	1	Reel	Captain McBean's Reel
Colonel Ridley's Quickstep	Mackintosh, Abraham	15 - 12	2	Jig	Waverley or Fergus McIver
Colt Bridge	Inglis, Susan	Leaflet 1980		Jig	Miss Allie Anderson
Come Ashore, Jolly Tar	Aird's Collection 1782	7 - 7	1	Reel	Come Ashore, Jolly Tar
Come kiss with me,come clap with me	Ramsay's Miscellany 1725	6 - 7	1	Reel	Bob of Fettercairn, The
Come o'er the stream, Charlie	Hogg, James - Title of Song	4 - 8	1	3/4 time	Waltz Country Dance
Corn Riggs	Ramsay's Tea-table Miscellany 1725	4 - 12	1	Reel	Corn Riggs
Countess of Cassilis Strathspey,The		Leaflet 1980		Strathspey	Frae A' The Airts
Countess of Loudon	Bowie's Collection	Annie Shand 18		Reel	
Countess of Loudon's Reel		21 - 1	1	Jig	Marchioness of Blandford's Reel,The
Country Dance (or Calver Lodge)	Gow, Nathaniel Dances 1812	8 - 3	1	Reel	Calver Lodge
Country Lasses	Kerr's Collection	36 - 7	1	Reel	Anniversary Reel
Coupar Angus Jig	Duff, Charles	21 - 9	2	Jig	Muirland Willie
Craighall	Hamilton, Stanley J.	22 - 6	2	Jig	Middleton Medley, The
Craigieburn Wood	Old Scottish Song from Surenne	18 - 5	2	Jig	Lassies of Dunse, The
Creag Mhor	Johnstone, Muriel A.	Bk for Children 1		Jig	Dhoon, The
Crief Fair	Bremner 1760	10 - 5	1	Reel	Crief Fair
Cromartie's Rant		31 - 8	1	Reel	Cromartie's Rant
Crooket Horned Ewie, The	Gow 1799	14 - 4	1	Strathspey	Crooket Horned Ewie, The

Cropie's Strathspey	Milne, Peter	17 - 8	1 Strathspey		Bonnie Kate of Aberdeen
Cross of Inverness, The	Fraser, Captain Simon Collection	17 - 11	1 Reel		Twenty first of September
Cuillins of Skye, The	Johnstone, Muriel A.	4 S.C.D. 1978 2	1 Strathspey		Cuillins of Skye, The
Culloden's Fancy	Caledonian Country Dances 1754	5 - 10	1 Reel		Culloden's Fancy
Cumberland Reel		1 - 11	1 Jig		Cumberland Reel
Cumernad House	Oswald, J. 1770	26 - 2	1 Strathspey		A Mile to Ride
Daggs of Craighouse	Reekie, Moira	Leaflet 1980	1 Jig		Tribute to the Borders
Dainty Davie	Walsh 1731	11 - 6	1 Strathspey		Dainty Davie
Dalkeith House	Gow's 4th Repository	15 - 1	1 Reel		My Mother's Coming In
Dalkeith's Strathspey	Gow's 3rd Coll. 1792 - as a reel	9 - 6	1 Strathspey		Dalkeith's Strathspey
Dame Diane's Delight	Robertson, Iain	4 S.C.D. 1978 4	2 Reel		Her Majesty is Welcome
Dashing White Sergeant, The		3 - 2	1 Reel		Dashing White Sergeant, The
Davy Hornpipe, The	Kerr	24 - 4	1 Reel		Sailor, The
Davy Rae, similar Braes of Busby	McGlashan's Collection	9 - 8	1 Strathspey		Braes of Busby, The
Dean Bridge of Edinburgh, The	Honeyman's Violin Tutor	23 - 4	1 Strathspey		Dean Bridge of Edinburgh, The
Deil Amang the Tailors, The		2 - 12	1 Reel		Eightsome Reel, The
Deil Amang the Tailors, The		14 - 7	1 Reel		Deil Amang the Tailors, The
Delvine Side	Dow, Daniel of Kirkmichael 1775	2 - 9	1 Strathspey		Delvine Side
Deserts of Tulloch	Grant, D.	Annie Shand 48	Jig		
Deuks Dang Ower My Daddie, The	Similar "Buff Coat" Mss2064 Nat.Lib	19 - 3	1 Jig		Deuks Dang Ower My Daddie, The
Deuks dang over my Daddy, The	Old Scots Song	Annie Shand 23	Jig		
Dinnet House		25 - 3	1 Jig		Bramble Bush, The
Dod Anerson	Main Collection	Bird-Matthew 28	Reel		
Dod House	Glen Collection	28 - 4	1 Strathspey		Star, The
Don Side		10 - 6	1 Strathspey		Shepherd's Crook, The
Donald Bane		17 - 12	1 Strathspey		Donald Bane
Donald Dow's Stathspey	Gow, Niel Collection	Annie Shand 49	Strathspey		
Dovecote Park	Pipe Tune	MacNab 1 - 2	1 Jig		MacDonald of Sleat
Dr Bob Smith	Hamilton, J. Stanley	22 - 2	1 Reel		Hamilton Rant, The
Dr and Mrs Brown	Jones, K. Macaulay	22 - 9	1 Strathspey		Neidpath Castle
Drops of Brandy	Old Scots Jig called "Hey My Nannie	1 - 7	1 Jig		Strip the Willow
Drumlanrig Castle	Gow	14 - 11	2 Strathspey		Jimmy's Fancy
Drummer, The		20 - 7	1 Reel		Drummer, The
Drummond Castle	Gow	14 - 1	2 Jig		Willie with his Tartan Trews
Drumtochty Glen	Main, Nan	3 S.C.D. 1976	1 Strathspey		Drumtochty Glen
Drunken Parson, The	Gow's Collection	Bird-Matthew 9	Jig		
Drunken Piper, The	McLeod, Alex. circa 1880	13 - 10	1 Reel		Reel of the 51st Division, The
Duchess of Athole, The	Gow's Collection	Bird-Matthew 19	Strathspey		
Duchess of Atholl's Slipper, The	Gow, Niel 1788	9 - 3	1 Strathspey		Duchess of Atholl's Slipper, The
Duchess of Buccleugh's Favourite	Gow's 4th Collection	15 - 11	2 Strathspey		Theeket Hoose, The
Duchess of Buccleugh, The	Gow, Niel	26 - 11	1 Reel		Ladies of Dunse, The
Duchess of Gordon's New Strathspey	Mackintosh, Robert	35 - 7	1 Strathspey		Trysting Place, The
Duchess of Roxburgh, The	Surenne	14 - 3	2 Reel		Push about the Jorum
Duke is Welcome to Inverness, The	Rutherford's Country Dances 1754	3 - 9	1 Strathspey		Duke is Welcome to Inverness, The
Duke of Athole	Braemar Collection	16 - 3	1 Jig		Duke of Atholl's Reel, The
Duke of Gordon		MacNab 1 - 4	1 Strathspey		Shepherd's Crook, The
Duke of Gordon's Welcome to Aberdn.		MacNab 3 - 1	1 Reel		Duke of Gordon's Welcome to Aberdn.
Duke of Hamilton's Reel	Caledonian Country Dances 1754	5 - 8	1 Strathspey		Duke of Hamilton's Reel
Duke of Kent	Ogilvie, A. Grey Album	30 - 7	1 Reel		Cadies Lady, The
Duke of Perth	Gow, Nathaniel Repository	1 - 8	1 Reel		Duke of Perth
Dumbarton's Drums	McGibbon 1763, earlier Playford1697	5 - 2	1 Reel		Dumbarton's Drums
Dumfries House	Riddell, J. - first published 1766	6 - 3	1 Jig		Rothesay Country Dance
Dumfries Lassies		26 - 8	2 Reel		Lady Maxwell's Reel
Dun's Frolic	Gow's Collection	Bird-Matthew 42	Strathspey		

Duncan Davidson	Bremner 1759 McGlashan 1781	7 - 4	1	Strathspey	Ye'll aye be welcome back again
Duncan Davidson	Kerr's Collection	Bird-Matthew 4		Strathspey	
Duncan Gray		Graded 18		Reel	Wedderburn's Reel
Dunie Mains	Athole Collection	19 - 2	2	Strathspey	Lochiel's Rant
Dunkeld Bridge	Gow, Niel similar tune Bremner 1757	10 - 6	1	Strathspey	Shepherd's Crook, The
Dunkeld Bridge	Gow, Niel (his last tune)	Annie Shand 44		Reel	
Duran Rangers	Mss in possession of Ian Jamieson	13 - 1	1	Reel	Duran Ranger, The
Duran Rangers	Mss. Ian C.B.Jamieson, Galasheils	Annie Shand 35		Reel	
Dyster Laddie	McGlashan, A.	20 - 12	2	Reel	College Hornpipe, The
Eagers	Lowe's Collection	Bird-Matthew 17		Strathspey	
Earl Marshall's Reel	Bremner 1760	7 - 9	2	Reel	Captain Macdonald's Fancy
Earl of Angus and Arran	Marshall, William	26 - 9	1	Strathspey	Sugar Candie
Earl of Home	Gow, Nathaniel Collection	Annie Shand 13		Strathspey	
Earl of Home's Country Dance, The	Gow, Nathaniel	12 - 11	1	Strathspey	Earl of Home, The
Earl of Lauderdale, The	Gow, Niel Collection 1792	1 - 12	2	Reel	Merry Lads of Ayr, The
Earl of Lauderdale, The	Gow, Niel Collection 1792	Bird-Matthew 5		Reel	
Earl of Mansfield, The	McEwan,John 92nd Gordon Highlanders	Leaflet 1981	1	Reel	Earl of Mansfield, The
Earl of Seaforth's Reel		12 - 4	2	Reel	Laird of Dumbiedykes' Favourite,The
East Neuk of Fife, The	MacGibbon's Version	4 S.C.D. 1978 1	1	Reel	Fife Ness
East Neuk of Fife, The	Kerr's Version	MacNab 5 - 2	1	Reel	St. Andrew's Cross
Edinburgh Castle Reel, The	A Dance Fan for 1792	Bk for Children 8		Reel	Edinburgh Castle Reel, The
Edinburgh Volunteers, The	Cooke's Selection of C.D. 1796	6 - 2	1	Strathspey	Edinburgh Volunteers
Eight Men of Moidart, The	Caledonian Country Dances 1754	3 - 10	1	Reel	Eight Men of Moidart, The
Fairlie Castle	Kerr's Collection	Bird-Matthew 13		Strathspey	
Fairy Dance, The	Gow, Nathaniel for Fife Hunt 1802	3 - 6	3	Reel	Fairy Dance, The
Fairy Hillock, The	Pipe Tune	30 - 3	1	Reel	Highland Lass, The
Falkland Beauty		4 - 11	1	Jig	Falkland Beauty
Farewell to Whisky	Gow, Niel	21 - 6	2	Reel	Kingussie Flower
Farewell to the Tay	Old Pipe Tune	24 - 8	1	Jig	Hollin Bus, The
Ferguson's Rant	Aird Vol. 3	29 - 2	1	Reel	Lord Kilmory's Delight
Ferintosh	Fraser, Capt. Simon Collection	Annie Shand 10		Strathspey	
Ferry, The	Kerr's Collection	20 - 11	1	Jig	Express, The
Fidget		16 - 1	1	Reel	Fidget
Finella	Main, Nan	3 S.C.D. 1976	2	Strathspey	Drumtochty Glen
Fishers' Reel o' Buckie, The	Innes, Hugh - Walker's Collection	Annie Shand 46		Reel	
Flora Macdonald's Fancy	Inverness Collection Highland Airs	4 Step Dances 1	1		Flora Macdonald's Fancy
Flora's Favourite(Marq.ofQueensbry)		Graded 24	1	Reel	Miss Flora's Favourite
Flowers of Edinburgh, The	Old Scots Measure 1750, Oswald 1751	1 - 6	1	Reel	Flowers of Edinburgh, The
Footes Vagaries	Rutherford 1756	12 - 2	1	Strathspey	Green Grow the Rashes
Forres Country Dance	Gourlay, Robert	22 - 4	2	Jig	Holyrood House
Foula Reel, The		4 - 7	1	Jig	Foula Reel, The
Fraser Patrick's Reel	Watts, Stan	3 S.C.D. 1976	1	Reel	Fraser's Favourite
Frolicsome Paddy (Drops of Brandy)	Irish Jig	1 - 7	2	Jig	Strip the Willow
From Scotia's Shores We're Noo Awa'	Hamilton, Stan	MacNab 8 - 3	1	Strathspey	From Scotia's Shores We're Noo Awa'
Fye, Buckle your Belt & Broadsword	Old song Vocal Melodies of Scotland	4 Step Dances 1	2		Flora Macdonald's Fancy
Gadie Water	Troup, A.	25 - 6	1	Jig	Haste to the Wedding
Gair's Rant	Lowe's Collection	Bird-Matthew 27		Strathspey	
Galway Hornpipe	The Irish Fiddler arr. N. Main	Leaflet 1980	2	Reel	Frae A' the Airts
Garden Wall, The	Petrie	20 - 3	2	Jig	Miss Bennet's Jig
Garry Owen	Irish Origin	1 - 9	2	Jig	Rory O'More
Garthland's Strathspey	Gow, N. Collection 1788	9 - 3	2	Strathspey	Duchess of Atholl's Slipper, The
Garthland's Strathspey	Gow, N. Collection 1788	5 S.C.D. 1965	1	Strathspey	Mrs Garthland's Strathspey
Gates of Edinburgh, The		15 - 5	1	Reel	Gates of Edinburgh, The
General Campbell	Mackintosh, Robert	18 - 12	2	Strathspey	Axum Reel, The

Tune	Collection	Reference		Type	Alternative Name
General Garibaldi's Reel	Main Collection	Bird-Matthew 30		Reel	
General Wemyss of Wemyss	Gow, Niel Collection	7 - 5	2	Reel	Lady Mary Menzies' Reel
Gentle Shepherd, The	Campbell,Joshua(Burton's Rondo 1796	17 - 5	1	Jig	Gentle Shepherd, The
Gin I was a Bonny Lad	Johnson's Caledonian C. D. 1748	12 - 8	1	Strathspey	Reel of Glamis or The Clever Lad
Gin I were whaur Gadie rins	Old Song	Annie Shand 26		Reel	
Gipsy Hornpipe	Astor's 24 Country Dances for 1803	33 - 8	1	Reel	Milton's Welcome
Glasgow Flourish	See Miss Admiral Gordon's Reel	11 - 9	1	Strathspey	Glasgow Flourish
Glasgow Highlanders		2 - 3	1	Strathspey	Glasgow Highlanders, The
Glasgow Hornpipe	Roger, Mr Annual Selection 1815	27 - 4	1	Reel	Burn's Hornpipe
Glasgow Peggy		Graded 1	1	Jig	Leap Year
Glen Grant	Grant, Charles (Aberlour)	17 - 2	1	Strathspey	Keppoch's Rant
Glen Ogle	Athole Collection	5 S.C.D. 1965	1	Reel	Haymaking
Glenburnie Rant	Gow, Niel Collection 1809	1 - 10	1	Reel	Fight about the Fireside
Glendaruel Highlanders, The	Kerr's Caledonian Collection	MacNab 2 - 1	1	Jig	Bonnie Anne
Glenfiddich	Marshall, William	19 - 9	1	Strathspey	A Trip to Holland
Glengary	Fraser, Capt. Simon Collection	17 - 10	2	Strathspey	Perthshire Highlanders
Golden Pheasant, The		16 - 9	1	Jig	Golden Pheasant, The
Gordon B. Cosh	MacInnes, Norrie	23 - 8	1	Jig	Swilcan, The
Grant's Reel		14 - 2	1	Strathspey	Grant's Reel
Grant's Strathspey	Campbell, Joshua Collection 1778	9 - 5	2	Strathspey	Mrs Grant's Fancy
Grants' Rant, The	Rutherford 1772	12 - 1	1	Reel	Grants' Rant
Green Grow the Rashes	MacGibbon 1742 - Nath.Gow's Reposit	12 - 2	1	Strathspey	Green Grow the Rashes
Greenholm	Kerr's Collection	29 - 9	1	Jig	Happy Meeting, The
Greig's Pipes		2 - 8	1	Strathspey	Greig's Pipes or Cameronian Rant
Grinder's Hornpipe, The	Connachan, J.	22 - 8	1	Reel	Minard Castle
Guidman of Balangigh, The		30 - 6	1	Jig	Guidman of Balangigh, The
Haddington Assembly, The	Gow, N. Collection	Annie Shand 41		Jig	
Haig of Bemersyde	Johnstone, Muriel A.	5 S.C.D. 1982	1	Strathspey	Haig of Bemersyde
Hame Came Our Gudeman	Old Scotch	30 - 2	1	Strathspey	Hame Came Our Gudeman
Hamilton House	Campbell, Wm. 4th Collection 1789	7 - 10	1	Jig	Hamilton House
Happy we been a' the gither	alternative name "Willie was a ..."	28 - 8	1	Reel	Cumbrae Reel, The
Harmonica	Kerr's Collection	Bird-Matthew 35		Jig	
Harvest Home	Lowe's Collection	Bird-Matthew 5		Strathspey	
Haughs of Cromdale	"New Killiecrankie" in 1700's	4 - 10	1	Strathspey	Haughs O' Cromdale
Hawick Lasses	Pringle, Robert	Annie Shand 49		Reel	
Haymakers, The	Gow's Repository	2 - 11	1	Jig	Haymakers, The
He's o'er the hills that I lo'e ...	Whitelaw Collection	Bird-Matthew 41		Jig	
He's o'er the hills that I lo'e ...		Graded 14	1	Jig	Berwick Johnnie
Hebridean Milking Song	Traditional	28 - 5	1	Reel	New Petronella, The
Here's a Health to the ane I lo'e		Graded 11	1	Jig	Moray Reel, The
Hey my Nannie	Old Name for Drops of Brandy	1 - 7	1	Jig	Strip the Willow or Drops of Brandy
Hey to Cupar	Bremner - here from Gow	13 - 6	2	Jig	A Kiss for Nothing
Hey! Jenny, come down to Jock	MacGibbon's Collection 1755 & older	3 - 4	1	Jig	Jenny come down to Jock
High Road to Linton, The	Gow, Nathaniel Collection 1792	1 - 10	2	Reel	Fight about the Fireside
Highland Fair, The	Gow's Collection	Bird-Matthew 18		Reel	
Highland Lassie	Oswald 1740 as "Cairney Mount" Aird	4 - 9	1	Reel	Highland Laddie
Highland Plaid, The (Lord Seaforth)	McGlashan' Collection	14 - 11	1	Strathspey	Jimmy's Fancy
Highland Reel or Dashing White Serg		3 - 2	1	Reel	Dashing White Sergeant, The
Highland Rory (Drunken Piper, The)	McLeod, Alex. circa 1880	13 - 10	1	Reel	Reel of the 51st Division, The
Highland Whisky	Gow, Niel	2 - 5	2	Strathspey	Perth Medley, The
Hills of Glenorchy	Kerr's Csledonian Collection	MacNab 2 - 2	2	Jig	Over the Dee and over the Don
Hills of Lorne	Hunter, Charlie	31 - 5	1	Strathspey	Autumn in Appin
Holyrood	Gourlay, Robert R.	22 - 4	1	Jig	Holyrood House
Hon. Captain Elliot's Quickstep	Pringle, J. Collection	32 - 8	1	Reel	Clansman, The

Hon. Captain Elphinston	Gow's Collection	Bird-Matthew 39	Strathspey	
Hon. Captain Maitland's Strathspey	Gow's Collection	Bird-Matthew 29	Strathspey	
Hon. Colonel Hamilton's Delight	Gow, Niel - see Hamilton House	7 - 10	1 Jig	Hamilton House
Hon. Margaret Erskine, The	Pringle, J. Collection	Annie Shand 3	Reel	
Hon. Miss H. Elliot's Reel, The	Pringle's Collection	Annie Shand 14	Reel	
Hon. Miss Sempill, The	Mackintosh, Robert	Annie Shand 40	Reel	
Hon. Mrs Campbell (of Lochnell)	Mackintosh, Robert	17 - 7	1 Reel	Lucy Campbell
Hon. Mrs Drummond of Perth's Str.	Bowie, John here from Gow,Niel 1788	7 - 12	2 Strathspey	Braes of Tulliemet, The
Hon. Mrs Fraser	Mackintosh, Robert	23 - 1	1 Reel	Auld Alliance, The
Hon. Mrs Maule's Favourite		14 - 7	2 Reel	Deil amang the Tailors, The
Hon. Mrs Ramsay Maule's Favourite	Gow's Collection	Bird-Matthew 37	Strathspey	
Hornpipe	Honeyman, Wm. C. Str. Reel & H'pipe	1 - 3	2 Reel	Circassian Circle
House of Park, The	Marshall, William Collection	Annie Shand 22	Reel	
Howard's Reel	Lowe's Collection	23 - 7	1 Reel	Reivers, The
Humber Jumber	Traditional Singing Game	26 - 10	1 Jig	Frisky, The
Humpty Dumpty	Esplin, J. B. Mss.	Bird-Matthew 45	Reel	
Hundred Pipers, The		Graded 3	1 Jig	Merry Reapers, The
I ha'e a wife o' my ain	Old Scots Song	Annie Shand 4	Jig	
I ha'e laid a herrin' in salt	Surenne	15 - 6	2 Jig	Lord Rosslyn's Fancy
I lo'e nae a laddie but ane	Scots Song	Annie Shand 22	Jig	
I lo'e nae laddie but ane		Graded 16	Jig	Duff's House
I lost my love	Kerr's Collection	Bird-Matthew 33	Jig	
I'll gang nae mair tae yon Toon		3 - 10	1 Reel	Eight Men of Moidart, The
I'll mak' ye fain to follow me	Oswald 1756, Gow, Nathaniel Repos.	6 - 10	1 Jig	I'll mak' ye fain to follow me
Innes's Jig	Aird Vol. 3	29 - 6	1 Jig	Charmer, The
Inverary	Kerr's Collection	Bird-Matthew 14	Strathspey	
Invercauld's Reel	Stewart's collection 1762	11 - 10	1 Strathspey	Invercauld's Reel
Island of Mull, The	Earl of Eglinton - Gow's 4th Rep.	16 - 6	2 Jig	Todlen Hame
Isle of Skye, The	Gow - later set to "Twa Bonnie M."	10 - 7	1 Reel	Isle of Skye
Jack's Alive	Old Mss. ca. 1820	29 - 3	1 Jig	Well Done Jack
Jackson's Bottle of Claret	Cooke's Selection of C.D. 1796	8 - 5	1 Jig	River Cree, The
Jacky's Return		26 - 3	1 Jig	Fairly Shot o' Her
Jamaica	McGibbon, Wm. version of"Johnniein"	19 - 1	1 Reel	None so Pretty
James O. Forbes of Corse	Milne, Peter	27 - 12	1 Strathspey	Auld Lang Syne
Jeannie o' the witchin' e'e		MacNab 3 - 3	1 Jig	Jeannie o' the witchin' e'e
Jenny dang the weaver	Orpheus Caledonius 1733	12 - 3	1 Reel	Jenny dang the weaver
Jenny's Bawbee	Gow - early version J Campbell 1788	2 - 3	2 Strathspey	Glasgow Highlanders, The
Jenny's Bawbee	Gow - early version J Campbell 1788	5 - 3	1 Strathspey	Jenny's Bawbee
Jessie Smith		15 - 4	2 Strathspey	Camp of Pleasure, The
Jocky's Dance	Traditional	5 S.C.D. 1982	1 Jig	St. Andrew's Fair
Joe MacDiarmid's Jig	Loch, Rob	5 S.C.D. 1982	1 Jig	Joe MacDiarmid's Jig
John Grumlie		Bird-Matthew 39	Jig	
John Grumlie		Graded 2	1 Jig	Watson's Reel
John Laurie	Watts, Stan	3 S.C.D. 1976	2 Reel	Fraser's Favourite
John McNeil's Reel	Milne, Peter	9 - 10	2 Reel	Cadgers in the Canongate
John Mortimer	Cook, Drummond	32 - 1	1 Reel	Johnnie's Welcome Hame
John Roy Stewart	McGlashan ca. 1800	13 - 3	1 Strathspey	Mrs Stewart's Strathspey
John of Bon Accord	Meikle, George	33 - 5	1 Reel	John of Bon Accord
Johnnie in Nether Mains	Gow, Niel (See Jamaica)	19 - 1	1 Reel	None so Pretty
Johnnie's friends are never pleased	Gow, Niel Repository Part 4	12 - 4	1 Reel	Laird of Dumbiedyke's Favourite,The
Johnny Groat's House	Gow	18 - 1	1 Reel	Johnny Groat's House
Johnny McGill	Campbell, Joshua Collection 1778	6 - 8	1 Jig	Prince of Orange
Johnny McGill	Campbell, Joshua Collection 1778	11 - 3	1 Jig	Johnny McGill
Jolly Tars	Kerr's Caledonian Collection	20 - 12	1 Reel	College Hornpipe, The

Name	Source	Ref		Type	Related
Jumping Joan (Lochearn)	Aird's 4th Collection	4 - 3	1	Reel	Queen's Welcome
Just as I was in the morning		19 - 3	1	Jig	Just as I was in the morning
Kate Dalrymple	Rutherford, D. 1750	9 - 4	2	Reel	My love she's but a lassie yet
Keep the country bonnie lassie		14 - 6	1	Strathspey	Keep the country bonnie lassie
Kenmore's up and awa'	Kerr's Collection	Bird-Matthew 22		Jig	
Kenmure's on and awa'	Johnson's Musical Museum 1792	4 - 4	1	Jig	Kenmure's on and awa'
Kilicrankie	Gow, N. Collection	Annie Shand 33		Reel	
Kilravock's Strathspey	Gow's Collection	Annie Shand 38		Strathspey	
Kilt is my Delight, The		MacNab 8 - 4	2	Reel	McNeil of Barra
Kind Robin	Surenne	21 - 5	2	Strathspey	Lea Rig, The
King of Sweden, The		4 Step Dances 3	1		King of Sweden, The
Kingussie Flower	Old Song	21 - 6	1	Reel	Kingussie Flower
Kinloch of Kinloch	Gow's Collection	Annie Shand 27		Jig	
Kinloss	Brown, J. S., Dundee	Bird-Matthew 15		Strathspey	
Kiss me quick, my mither's coming	Johnson's C.C.D.S. 1748	12 - 6	1	Reel	Kiss quick, my mither's coming
Knit the Pocky	Bremner's Collection 1761	11 - 1	1	Reel	Knit the Pocky
La Tempete		2 - 1	1	Reel	La Tempete
Lady Ann Hope's Strathspey	Marshall's Collection 1781	13 - 11	2	Strathspey	Bridge of Nairn
Lady Ann Maitland	Macdonald, M.	19 - 12	2	Reel	Sandal, The
Lady Auckland's Reel		18 - 2	1	Strathspey	Lady Auckland's Reel
Lady Baird's Reel		18 - 3	1	Reel	Lady Baird's Reel
Lady Baird's Strathspey	Dow 1775 - from Gow's Coll. 1788	7 - 4	2	Strathspey	Ye'll aye be welcome back again
Lady Carmichael of Castle Craig	Gow, John	13 - 7	2	Strathspey	Nether Bow has vanished, The
Lady Caroline Montague	Gow's Collection	Bird-Matthew 9		Strathspey	
Lady Charlotte Campbell	Mackintosh, Robert	MacNab 9 - 3	1	Strathspey	Silver Tassie, The
Lady Charlotte Campbell's Medley	Gow's Repository	9 - 11	2	Reel	Cauld Kail in Aberdeen
Lady Charlotte Campbell's Strath.	Gow, Nathaniel	14 - 8	2	Strathspey	She's ower young to marry yet
Lady Charlotte Murray	McDonald's 2nd Collection	Annie Shand 20		Reel	
Lady Charlotte Murray's Favourite	Gow, Niel Collection	Annie Shand 5		Jig	
Lady Dick Lauder's Strathspey	Taylor, J. Album	29 - 4	1	Strathspey	Fair Donald
Lady Doune	Gow, Nathaniel Collection	Annie Shand 23		Strathspey	
Lady Elgin (In Book 18-12 as Lord E	Gow's Collection	Bird-Matthew 28		Strathspey	
Lady Eliza Lindsay	Tunes of Royal Circus Edinburgh	20 - 1	1	Reel	Captain McBride's Hornpipe
Lady Elizabeth Lindsay	Surenne	17 - 4	1	Strathspey	Countess of Crawford's Reel
Lady Erskine	MacLaren, D.	24 - 1	1	Reel	Scotch Circle, The
Lady Georgina Gordon's Reel	Marshall, William for McGlashan	19 - 11	1	Strathspey	New Park
Lady Glasgow	Earl of Eglinton 1800-Gow, Niel C.	Annie Shand 39		Strathspey	
Lady Graham's Strathspey	Surenne	17 - 4	2	Strathspey	Countess of Crawford's Reel, The
Lady Harriet Hope	Gow, Nathaniel Repository V.1 1799	8 - 10	2	Reel	Lassie wi' the yellow Coatie
Lady Harriet Hope's Reel	Mackintosh, Robert	16 - 4	1	Reel	Lady Harriet Hope's Reel
Lady Harriet Hope's Reel	Mackintosh, Robert	Golden Jubilee	1	Reel	Mrs Stewart of Fasnacloich
Lady Heathcote's Reel	Mackintosh, Robert	19 - 12	1	Reel	Sandal, The
Lady Hope of Pinkie	Nathaniel Gow - 6th Book	25 - 10	1	Strathspey	Three Bonnie Maidens, The (Graces)
Lady Hope of Pinkie	Gow's Collection	Bird-Matthew 46		Strathspey	
Lady Horne's Jig	Gow	13 - 8	2	Jig	Fly not yet
Lady Hunter Blair's Reel	Gow's Collection	13 - 5	1	Reel	Highland Reel, The
Lady Huntly	Gow's Collection	Bird-Matthew 44		Strathspey	
Lady Kinloch of Gilmerton's Strath.	Petrie's 4th Collection	29 - 1	1	Strathspey	Land O'Cakes
Lady Loudon	Campbell, William Country Dances 3	7 - 8	1	Strathspey	Tartan Plaidie
Lady Louisa Gordon's Strathspey	Marshall, Wm. -renamed Peggy's Love	8 - 2	1	Strathspey	Peggy's Love
Lady Louisa MacDonald's Strathspey		18 - 4	1	Strathspey	Lady Louisa MacDonald's Strathspey
Lady Lucy Ramsay	Kerr's Collection	Bird-Matthew 12		Strathspey	
Lady Macintosh's Rant	Rutherford's Country Dances 1754	3 - 9	1	Strathspey	Duke is Welcome to Inverness, The
Lady Madelina Sinclair	MacDonald,Malcolm 1792 - from Gow	6 - 5	2	Strathspey	Oxton Reel

Tune	Source	Reference	No.	Type	Dance
Lady Madelina Sinclair's Birthday	Lowe's Collection	Bird-Matthew 8		Reel	
Lady Marie Parker	Gow, N. Collection	Annie Shand 12		Strathspey	
Lady Mary Hay's Scotch Measure	Gow, Nathaniel 3rd Collection 1792	4 Step Dances 4	1	Reel	Scotch Measure
Lady Mary Menzies' Reel	Bremner 1761	7 - 5	1	Reel	Lady Mary Menzies' Reel
Lady Mary Montague	McDonald, J. from Bowie's Colln.	Annie Shand 17		Reel	
Lady Mary Murray	Gow, Nathaniel	28 - 10	1	Strathspey	Miss Shaftesbury's Fancy
Lady Mary Ramsay	Gow, Nathaniel	10 - 10	2	Strathspey	There's Nae Luck aboot the Hoose
Lady Mary Stopford	Kerr's Collection	Bird-Matthew 16		Reel	
Lady Maxwell's Reel	Campbell, Joshua	16 - 9	2	Jig	Golden Pheasant, The
Lady McKenzie of Coul	Gow's Collection	Annie Shand 28		Reel	
Lady Montgomerie	Lord Eglintoune	10 - 1	2	Reel	Montgomeries' Rant, The
Lady Shaftesbury	Gow's Collection	Bird-Matthew 34		Reel	
Lady Stormont's Strathspey	McKercher, Duncan	27 - 3	1	Strathspey	Duchess of York
Lady Susan Stewart's Reel	Caledonian Country Dances 1754	5 - 9	1	Reel	Lady Susan Stewart's Reel
Lady's Briest Knot, The	Sinclair, John - Song	10 - 12	1	Strathspey	Lady's Briest Knot, The
Laird O' Cockpen, The		Graded 7	1	Jig	Lady Catherine Bruce's Reel
Laird O' Dochart's Reel		MacNab 4 - 2	1	Jig	Laird O' Dochart's Reel
Laird of Milton's Daughter, The	Christian, W. G. M.	22 - 10	1	Jig	Laird of Milton's Daughter, The
Lamb Skinnet		14 - 12	1	Jig	Lamb Skinnet
Lamont of Inveryne		MacNab 4 - 3	1	Reel	Lamont of Inveryne
Lango Lee	Old Irish Melody	22 - 1	2	Jig	Reel of Mey, The
Larach do Thacaidean	Traditional Puirt a beul	MacNab 5 - 3	1	Strathspey	Moulin Dubh - Black Mill, The
Lass O' Gowrie, The		Graded 9	1	Reel	Mr Watson's Favourite
Lass O' Patie's Mill, The		Graded 10	1	Reel	Mrs Cholmondeley's Reel
Lass of Livingston, The	Ramsay, Allan Tea-Table Misc. 1726	8 - 6	1	Reel	Lass of Livingston, The
Lassie look before you	Lowe's Collection	Bird-Matthew 34		Strathspey	
Lassie wi' the Yellow Coatie	Rutherford 1756, Bremner 1759	8 - 10	1	Reel	Lassie wi' the Yellow Coatie
Lassies of Dunse, The		18 - 5	1	Jig	Lassies of Dunse, The
Lawland Lads think they are fine, Th	Surenne	15 - 12	1	Jig	Waverley or Fergus McIver
Le Papillon	Skillern's Compleat Collection	Bk for Children 2		Jig	Le Papillon
Lea Rig, The	Surenne	21 - 5	1	Strathspey	Lea Rig, The
Lee Mills	Marshall	26 - 5	1	Strathspey	Lord Elgin's Reel
Lennox Love to Blantyre	Gow, Nathaniel Repository	6 - 4	1	Strathspey	Lennox Love to Blantyre
Lerwick Reel, The		MacNab 9 - 1		Strathspey	Lerwick Reel, The
Lesley's March to Scotland	Watt's Musical Miscellany 1731	3 - 5	1	Jig	Blue Bonnets
Light and Airy	Gow, Niel Collection	4 - 5	1	Jig	Light and Airy
Link him Dodie	Gow's 1st Collection 1784	8 - 4	1	Strathspey	Lover's Knot, The
Little Peggy's Love	Marshall 1781 "Lady Louisa Gordon"	8 - 2	1	Strathspey	Peggy's Love
Loch Earn	Gow, Niel 2nd Coll 1788 Jumping Joan	4 - 3	1	Reel	Queen's Welcome
Loch Leven Castle		21 - 3	1	Reel	Loch Leven Castle
Lochaber	Palmer, Violet J. C.	23 - 12	1	Strathspey	Let's Meet Again
Lochanside		MacNab 7 - 3	1	3/4 time	Lochanside
Lochiel's Rant	Duff, Archibald	19 - 2	1	Strathspey	Lochiel's Rant
Lochiel's awa' to France	Gow, Niel 2nd Collection	15 - 7	1	Strathspey	Lochiel's awa' to France
Lochleven Side	Bowie, John Collection	30 - 1	1	Jig	Collichur
Lochmaben Hornpipe, The	Old Mss from Dryhope Tower	Annie Shand 2		Reel	
Long Chase, The	Campbell, Joshua Collection 1778	11 - 8	1	Reel	Long Chase, The
Longwise Eightsome Reel	Davidson, William (Lowe)	18 - 7	1	Medley	Longwise Eightsome Reel
Lord Duplin's Jig	Bowie	19 - 6	2	Jig	Rakish Highlandman, The
Lord Eglintoun's Auld Man	Lowe's Collection Book 3	Leaflet		Strathspey	Sauchie Haugh
Lord Eglintoune	Riddell, John ca. 1766	10 - 1	1	Reel	Montgomeries' Rant, The
Lord Elgin's Fancy	Beauties of Gow -same as Lady Elgin	18 - 12	1	Strathspey	Axum Reel, The
Lord Hume's Reel		16 - 11	1	Strathspey	Lord Hume's Reel
Lord Macdonald		18 - 4	2	Strathspey	Lady Louisa Macdonald's Strathspey

Tune	Source	Reference		Type	Alternate
Lord Macdonald's Reel	Campbell, W. Collection ca 1790	6 - 9	1	Reel	Lord Macdonald's Reel
Lord Moira	Gow, Niel	25 - 7	1	Strathspey	Miss Isabella McLeod
Lord Randell's Bride	Middleton Coll. same as The Bride	Bird-Matthew 40		Reel	
Lord Rosslyn's Fancy		15 - 6	1	Jig	Lord Rosslyn's Fancy
Lord Seaforth	Surenne	14 - 11	1	Strathspey	Jimmy's Fancy
Lord Seaforth	Kerr's Collection	Bird-Matthew 11		Strathspey	
Lord of the Isles	Kerr's Collection	27 - 8	1	Strathspey	Reel of Five, The
Lowe's Hornpipe	Marshall, William	Annie Shand 47		Reel	
Lt. Col. Baillie of Leys	Surenne	15 - 2	1	Strathspey	I'll gang nae mair tae yon toun
Lt. Ray's Quickstep		26 - 4	1	Reel	Lady Mary Cochrane's Reel
MacLeod of Dunvegan		MacNab 4 - 1		Reel	MacLeod of Dunvegan
Machine without Horses, The	Rutherford 1772	12 - 12	1	Jig	Machine without Horses, The
Mackenzie Hay	Scott Skinner, J.	MacNab 2 - 3	2	Strathspey	Brig O'Doon
Macleod and Mackay	Scott Skinner (Logie Collection)	35 - 2	1	Reel	Inverneill House
Madge Wildfire's Strathspey	Gow's 2nd Repository	9 - 9	1	Strathspey	Madge Wildfire's Strathspey
Maggie Lauder	Craig, Adam Coll 1730, Oswald 1742	10 - 8	1	Strathspey	Maggie Lauder
Maid of Islay, The		21 - 10	2	Strathspey	Within a mile o' Edinburgh Toon
Maid of the Mill, The	Old M.S.S.	21 - 11	1	Jig	Maid of the Mill, The
Maids of Currie, The	Cruickshank, Helen	Bk for Children 7		Reel	Maids of Currie, The
Major Graham	Gow, Niel	25 - 12	1	Strathspey	Braes of Mellinish, The
Major Mole	Kerr's Collection	Bird-Matthew 4		Strathspey	
Major Spicer	Henderson, Murdoch Collection	3 S.C.D. 1976	1	Jig	Leandor's Jig
Marchioness of Huntly		MacNab 6 - 1	1	Strathspey	Because he was a Bonnie Lad
Marchioness of Huntly's Strathspey	Grant, D.	14 - 2	2	Strathspey	Grant's Reel
Marquis of Huntly's Highlanders		4 - 6	1	Strathspey	Marquis of Huntly's Highlanders
Marquis of Huntly's Reel	Grant, D.	15 - 1	2	Reel	My mother's coming in
Marquis of Huntly's Snuff-mill, The	Gow, Niel	13 - 7	1	Strathspey	Nether Bow has vanished, The
Marquis of Queensberry(Flora's Fav)		Graded 24	1	Reel	Miss Flora's Favourite
Marquis of Tweeddale's Favourite	Macdonald, D. from Gow	14 - 6	2	Strathspey	Keep the Country Bonnie Lassie
Marshall's Compliments to Neil Gow	Marshall, William	26 - 12	1	Reel	New Waterloo Reel, The
Mary Bain's Wedding or My ain hoose	Old Gaelic Air	Annie Shand 15		Jig	
Master Reginald MacDonald	Macdonald, R. (Skye)	25 - 4	1	Strathspey	Deacon of the Weavers, The
Maxwell's Rant		18 - 10	1	Reel	Maxwell's Rant
McNichol of the Black Isle	Surenne	MacNab 8 - 1	1	Reel	McNichol of the Black Isle
McVicar's Strathspey	Gow's 2nd Repository	15 - 11	1	Strathspey	Theeket Hoose, The
Medley	Old Songs	Annie Shand 25		Waltz	
Meg Merrilees		1 - 5	1	Reel	Meg Merrilees
Meldrum House	Shand, J.	Annie Shand 40		Jig	
Menzies Rant, The	Robertson, Stewart Collection 1884	7 - 6	1	Reel	Menzies Rant, The
Merry Dancers, The	Bremner's Scots Reels & C.D. 1757	4 - 2	1	Jig	Merry Dancers, The
Merry Lads of Ayr, The	Riddell, John - Bremner 1757 ex Gow	1 - 12	1	Reel	Merry Lads of Ayr
Merry Maid's Wedding	very like Haughs of Cromdale	4 - 10	1	Strathspey	Haughs o' Cromdale
Mid Lothian	Campbell, William C.D. 1795	7 - 11	1	Reel	Mid Lothian
Middling, Thank You		15 - 8	1	Jig	Middling, Thank You
Mill Burn, The	Kerr's Collection	28 - 12	1	Reel	Not I
Miller of Camserney, The	Menzies, Archibal, 1880	10 - 2	2	Strathspey	Infare, The
Miller of Drone, The	Gow's Repository 1802	12 - 5	2	Strathspey	Fiddle Faddle
Miss Admiral Gordon's Reel	McGlashan's Coll 1790 (W. Marshall)	11 - 9	1	Strathspey	Glasgow Flourish
Miss Andy Campbell's Scotch Measure	McGlashan, A.	19 - 8	2	Reel	Admiral Nelson
Miss Ann Lothian's Strathspey		MacNab 6 - 3	1	Strathspey	Kelvingrove
Miss Ann Lothian'sStrathspey		MacNab 6 - 3	1	Strathspey	Kelvingrove
Miss Ann rummond Smith's Reel	Chalmers	17 - 1	2	Jig	A Trip to Aberdeen
Miss Baird of Saughtonhall	Robertson, Mrs of Ladykirk (ex Gow)	14 - 9	2	Reel	What a Beau my Granny was
Miss Baird's Jig	Wighton Collection	Bird-Matthew 37		Jig	

Miss Barbara Cunningham	Mackintosh, Robert	18 - 2	2 Strathspey	Lady Auckland's Reel
Miss Barstow's Reel	Mackintosh, Robert	18 - 3	2 Reel	Lady Baird's Reel
Miss Begg of Benton	Mackintosh, Abraham	19 - 9	2 Strathspey	A Trip to Holland
Miss Betty Hunter	Duff, Charles	20 - 3	1 Jig	Miss Bennet's Jig
Miss Bisset, Logierait	MacDonald,Malcolm 1788-1795(ex Gow)	11 - 1	2 Reel	Knit the Pocky
Miss Burns's Reel		20 - 5	1 Reel	Miss Burns's Reel
Miss Cahoon's Reel	Bremner, R. 1757	13 - 2	1 Jig	Miss Cahoon's Reel
Miss Campbell of Menzies	Gow, Niel Collection 1787	Annie Shand 9	Reel	
Miss Campbell of Saddell's Strath.	Mackintosh, Robert	17 - 2	2 Strathspey	Keppoch's Rant
Miss Caroline Thomson's Reel	Lebrune, Alexander	27 - 8	2 Reel	Reel of Five, The
Miss Catherine Maxwell's Scotch M.	Mackintosh, Abraham	15 - 5	2 Reel	Gates of Edinburgh, The
Miss Chalmers	Gow, Niel Collection	Annie Shand 34	Jig	
Miss Charlotte Bruce	Glen Collection	16 - 11	2 Strathspey	Lord Hume's Reel
Miss Clementina Loughan	Gow, N. Collection	Annie Shand 15	Reel	
Miss Clementina Stewart's Reel	MacDonald,Malcolm 2nd Coll 1790-4	9 - 1	1 Reel	Miss Clemy Stewart's Reel
Miss Condie's Reel	McKercher, D.	17 - 7	2 Reel	Lucy Campbell
Miss Coxe's Strathspey	McIntyre, Mrs here from Gow	14 - 10	1 Strathspey	Bonniest Lass in all the World, The
Miss Dickson's Reel	Mackintosh, Robert	19 - 3	2 Jig	Just as I was in the Morning
Miss Drummond of Megginch	Wighton Collection	Bird-Matthew 41	Strathspey	
Miss Drummond of Perth's Favourite	Petrie's 2nd Collection	4 Step Dances 4	2 Reel	Scotch Measure
Miss Dumbreck	Playford, H. Original Scots Tunes	9 - 12	2 Reel	Birks of Abergeldie, The
Miss Dumbreck	Playford, H. Original Scots Tunes	25 - 11	1 Reel	Miss Dumbreck
Miss Elisabeth Magd. Fordyce	Mackintosh, Robert	4 S.C.D. 1978 3	1 Strathspey	Staffin Harvest
Miss Elizabeth Dewar	Pringle, J. Collection	Annie Shand 1	Reel	
Miss Elizabeth Ferguson's Favourite	Petrie's 3rd Collection	23 - 11	1 Jig	Starry Eyed Lassie, The
Miss Esther Oswald of Auchencruive	Mackintosh, Robert	17 - 6	2 Strathspey	Miss Heyden
Miss Falconer	Lowe's Collection Vol. 2	Bk for Children 5	Reel	Miss Falconer's Fancy
Miss Farquharson's Reel	Bremner 1757 See My Love She's but	9 - 4	1 Reel	My Love She's but a Lassie yet
Miss Finlay's Delight	Gow 1788 See New Rigged Ship, The	9 - 7	1 Jig	New Rigged Ship, The
Miss Fiona MacRae of Conchra		MacNab 9 - 2	1 Strathspey	Miss Fiona MacRae of Conchra
Miss Flora McDonald's Reel	Bremner 1757	7 - 1	2 Reel	Ye're Welcome, Charly Stewart
Miss Flora's Favourite		Graded 24	1 Reel	Miss Flora's Favourite
Miss Geddes	McGlashan, A.	20 - 6	2 Strathspey	Miss Devon's Reel
Miss General Maxwell of Parkhill'sR	Wighton Collection	Bird-Matthew 25	Reel	
Miss Gordon of Liverpool	Marshall, William	Golden Jubilee 1	Jig	Jubilee Jig, The
Miss Graham	Wighton Collection	Bird-Matthew 47	Strathspey	
Miss Graham of Inchbrakie's Str.	Gow - See Fiddle Music of Scotland	21 - 7	2 Strathspey	Braes of Breadalbane, The
Miss Grant of Grant	Mackintosh, Robert 1783-96	9 - 5	1 Strathspey	Mrs Grant's Fancy
Miss Hanbury's Fancy	Macintyre, D.	23 - 10	1 Reel	Rudha Dubh
Miss Hannah's Jig	Marshall, William Collection	Annie Shand 30	Jig	
Miss Hope's Strathspey	Pringle, John 1800-Gow's 4th Repos.	9 - 2	1 Strathspey	Jimp Waist, The
Miss Hutton	Bowie, J.	19 - 11	2 Strathspey	New Park
Miss J. Rose's Reel	Mackintosh, Robert	Bk for Children A	Jig	Come under my Plaidie
Miss Jane Douglas	Mackintosh, Robert 1796	27 - 10	1 Jig	La Flora
Miss Jane Gordon's Reel	Gow, Niel Collection	Annie Shand 5	Reel	
Miss Janet Laing's Strathspey	Main, Nan	22 - 11	1 Strathspey	Miss Janet Laing
Miss Jean Stewart	Morrison, William	21 - 2	1 Strathspey	My only Jo and Dearie, O
Miss Jeanie S. Grant's Favourite	Grant, Charles (Aberlour)	19 - 10	1 Jig	Two and Two
Miss Jenny Elliot's Strathspey	Mackintosh, Robert	17 - 12	2 Strathspey	Donald Bane
Miss Jessie Dalrymple's Reel		20 - 9	1 Reel	Miss Jessie Dalrymple's Reel
Miss Jessie Stewart	Wighton Collection	Bird-Matthew 47	Jig	
Miss Jessie Stewart's Reel	Wighton Collection	Bird-Matthew 23	Reel	
Miss L. Montgomery of Skelmorlie'sS	Aird's 4th Collection	Golden Jubilee 1	Strathspey	Miss Milligan's Strathspey
Miss Leslie of St. Andrews	D. Grant's Collection	Annie Shand 3	Reel	

Tune	Source	Reference		Type	Dance
Miss Mackenzie's Reel	Mackintosh, Robert	23 - 3	1	Reel	Glens of Angus, The
Miss Macpherson of Giliston		25 - 2	1	Reel	Chapman, The
Miss Margaret Brander, J.P.	Findlay, David	5 S.C.D. 1982	1	Reel	Sunday Morning
Miss Margaret Brown's Favourite	Gow, N. Collection	Annie Shand 21		Jig	
Miss Margaret Gordon	Mackintosh, Robert	24 - 11	1	Strathspey	Adieu Mon Ami
Miss Maria Stewart's Jig	Pringle, J. Collection	Annie Shand 4		Jig	
Miss Mariane Oliphant (Rossie)	Mackintosh, Robert	16 - 8	1	Strathspey	Ca' the Ewes tae the Knowes
Miss Marston's Strathspey	Middleton's Selection of Str.,Reels	34 - 3	1	Strathspey	Glasgow Lasses
Miss Mary Douglas	Wilson's Companion to Ballroom 1816	10 - 11	1	Jig	Miss Mary Douglas
Miss Maule's Strathspey	Mackintosh, Robert	20 - 8	2	Strathspey	Miss Ogilvie's Fancy
Miss Milligan		23 - 6	1	Strathspey	Glasgow Country Dance
Miss Murray of Lintrose		27 - 1	1	Reel	Miss Murray of Lintrose
Miss Murray of Ochtertyre	Bowie 1789	11 - 12	1	Reel	Miss Murray of Ochtertyre
Miss Nancy Arnott	Crowe, R. F.	32 - 5	1	Strathspey	Miss Nancy Arnott
Miss Nancy Frowns		14 - 5	1	Jig	Miss Nancy Frowns
Miss Ogilvie's Fancy		20 - 8	1	Strathspey	Miss Ogilvie's Fancy
Miss Penuel Grant of Grant's Strath	Grant, D. Collection	Annie Shand 36		Strathspey	
Miss Rae of Eskgrove	Gow, Nathaniel	13 - 2	2	Jig	Miss Cahoon's Reel
Miss Reay of Killingworth's Fav'te	Mackintosh, A.	35 - 8	1	Reel	St. Andrews' Gardens
Miss Robertson's Reel	Mackintosh, Robert	18 - 7	2	Reel	Longwise Eightsome Reel
Miss Rose's Fancy	MacNab, C.	27 - 5	1	Jig	Tayport Beauty
Miss Rose's Strathspey	Athole Collection	28 - 2	1	Strathspey	Pretty Polly
Miss Sally Hunter	Gow, Niel	Annie Shand 2		Jig	
Miss Scott of Usan	Duff, Charles	20 - 5	2	Reel	Miss Burns's Reel
Miss Spens Monro's Jig	McFadyen	21 - 1	2	Jig	Marchioness of Blandford's Reel,The
Miss Stewart	Gow, Niel Collection	Annie Shand 39		Reel	
Miss Stewart of Fasnacloich	Kerr's Collection	Bird-Matthew 10		Reel	
Miss Stewart's Jig - of Bombay	Marshall, William	Annie Shand 8		Jig	
Miss Susan Inglis	Johnstone, Muriel A.	32 - 2	1	Strathspey	Oriel Strathspey
Miss Taylor	Kerr's Collection	Bird-Matthew 19		Reel	
Miss William's Fancy	Campbell, William 23rd Book	30 - 8	1	Jig	Short and Sweet
Miss Young	Kerr's Collection	Bird-Matthew 12		Strathspey	
Misses Cramb of Linlithgow, The	Main, Nan	Bk for Children 4		Jig	Misses Cramb of Linlithgow, The
Misses Little's Fancy, The	Jenkin's Airs etc.	28 - 1	1	Jig	A Trip O'er The Tweed
Montrose's March (Rock and wee pic)	Playford 1669	3 - 7	1	Reel	Rock and the wee pickle tow, The
Monymusk	Dow, Daniel 1776	3 - 11	1	Strathspey	Foursome Reel
Monymusk	Dow, Daniel 1776	11 - 2	1	Strathspey	Monymusk
Morayshire Farmers	Marshall, William	17 - 11	2	Reel	Twenty First of September
Morpeth Rant	Wighton Collection	Bird-Matthew 26		Reel	
Moudiewart, The	Old Song	Annie Shand 18		Jig	
Moudiewort, The	Oswald's Pocket Companion 1752	11 - 7	1	Jig	Moudiewort, The
Moulin Dhu - The Black Mill	Traditional Puirt a beul	MacNab 5 - 3	1	Strathspey	Moulin Dhu - The Black Mill
Mount Stewart House	Logan's Collection	Bird-Matthew 11		Reel	
Mount Stewart House	Logan's Collection	MacNab 7 - 2	1	Reel	Rothesay at the Fair
Mr Alex Menzies	Duff, Charles	20 - 1	2	Reel	Captain McBride's Hornpipe
Mr Busbie Maitland	Gow's Collection	Bird-Matthew 43		Reel	
Mr Charles Graham	Bowie, J.	20 - 10	2	Strathspey	Quiet and Snug
Mr Fletcher's Delight	or Bridge of Ballater, The	9 - 2	2	Strathspey	Jimp Waist, The
Mr Grant of Pilnacree's Strathspey	MacDonald,Malcolm	20 - 4	2	Strathspey	Village Reel
Mr Halliday's Comp's to MrsCrockett	Old Mss. - Ian C.B. Jamieson	Annie Shand 38		Strathspey	
Mr Hamilton of Pencaitland	McFadyen	21 - 12	2	Strathspey	Stoorie Miller, The
Mr John Stewart	Glen Collection	28 - 3	1	Reel	Bonnie Lass
Mr Macintyre of Glencoe		21 - 2	2	Strathspey	My only Jo and Dearie, O
Mr Michie's	Scott Skinner J.	33 - 2	1	Strathspey	Stuttgart Strathspey

Mr Muir Mackenzie's Favourite	Sharpe, Mr of Hoddon	13 - 9	1 Strathspey	Strathglass House
Mr Murray Simprim's Favourite	Wighton Collection	Bird-Matthew 31	Reel	
Mr Oswald (of Auchencruive)	Mackintosh, Robert	24 - 2	1 Strathspey	Balquidder Strathspey
Mr Patrick Duff Junior's Strath.	Grant, D.	15 - 2	1 Strathspey	I'll gang nae mair tae yon toon
Mr Reid's Reel	Grant, D. Collection	Annie Shand 42	Reel	
Mr Richardson's Jig	Porteous Collection	34 - 8	1 Jig	Open the Door to Three
Mr Robert Hunter's Strathspey	Pringle, J.	Annie Shand 45	Strathspey	
Mr Tierney's Reel	Astor's 24 C.D. for the year 1804	34 - 7	1 Strathspey	Couteraller's Rant
Mr Wilson's Hornpipe		16 - 10	1 Reel	Mr Wilson's Hornpipe
Mr Young's Strathspey		Annie Shand 12	Strathspey	
Mrs Anderson's Reel	Mackintosh, Robert	27 - 7	1 Reel	Round Reel of Eight
Mrs Baird of Newbyth	Gow's Collection	Bird-Matthew 43	Strathspey	
Mrs Blair (of Blair)	Mackintosh, Robert	16 - 8	2 Strathspey	Ca' the Ewes tae the Knowes
Mrs Blair's Jig	MacFadyen. J.	18 - 8	2 Jig	Off she goes in the North
Mrs Campbell of Kinloch	Wighton Collection	Bird-Matthew 27	Strathspey	
Mrs Campbell of Monzies	Mackintosh, Robert	28 - 11	1 Jig	Two to One
Mrs Colonel Sinclair of Forss	Grant, D.	15 - 9	1 Strathspey	This is no' my ain hoose
Mrs Crawford of Littleton	Gow's Collection	Bird-Matthew 22	Reel	
Mrs Dalzell	Gow, Nathaniel	36 - 4	1 Strathspey	Gang the Same Gate
Mrs Donaldson		Annie Shand 31	Strathspey	
Mrs Douglas of Tiliwhilly's Strath	Wighton Collection	Bird-Matthew 25	Strathspey	
Mrs Duff's Fancy(or Miss Graham--)	Gow (Shelf 18)	21 - 7	2 Strathspey	Braes of Breadalbane, The
Mrs Dundas of Arniston's Reel	Gow, William	13 - 5	2 Reel	Highland Reel, The
Mrs Eleanora Robertson's Reel	Mackintosh, Robert	16 - 7	2 Reel	Stuart Robertson's Reel
Mrs Ella Wilson	Johnstone, Muriel A.	Bk for Children 6	Reel	Old Man of Storr, The
Mrs Findlay of Haywood	Kohler	28 - 6	1 Strathspey	Mairi's Fancy
Mrs George Robertson	Marshall, William Collection	Annie Shand 32	Reel	
Mrs Grant of Laggan's Favourite	Grant, D.	21 - 11	2 Jig	Maid of the Mill, The
Mrs Grieve of Howdan	Surenne	16 - 5	1 Strathspey	Caledonian Rant
Mrs Hamilton of Wishaw	Marshall, William - here from Gow	23 - 9	1 Strathspey	Mrs Hamilton of Wishaw
Mrs Hay of Yester's Reel	Gow, Niel 4th Book	13 - 1	2 Reel	Duran Ranger, The
Mrs Hill's Delight	Clarke's Collection	28 - 7	1 Reel	Mrs Hill's Delight
Mrs Hood's Strathspey	Mackintosh, Abraham	20 - 6	1 Strathspey	Miss Devon's Reel
Mrs Jamieson's Favourite	Grant, Charles (Aberlour)	17 - 5	2 Jig	Gentle Shepherd, The
Mrs Johnston's Reel	Grant, D.	16 - 4	2 Reel	Lady Harriet Hope's Reel
Mrs Laird of Strathmartin	Mackintosh, Abraham	Annie Shand 20	Strathspey	
Mrs Lumsden of Achindores	Marshall, William	21 - 12	1 Strathspey	Stoorie Miller, The
Mrs M'Millan's Quadrille	Grant, Charles of Aberlour	4 Step Dances	1 Jig	Earl of Errol, The
Mrs MacDouall Grant	Gow, N. Collection	Annie Shand 32	Reel	
Mrs MacIntosh of Raigmore	Lowe's Collection	Bird-Matthew 24	Strathspey	
Mrs MacMillan's Quadrille	Grant, Ch. page 10	MacNab 3 - 2	1 Jig	Earl of Errol's Reel
Mrs MacMillan's Quadrille	Grant, Charles (Aberlour)	MacNab 3 - 2	1 Jig	Earl of Errol's Reel
Mrs Margaret Graham's Favourite	Mackintosh, Robert(See-Lady Harriet	16 - 4	1 Reel	Lady Harriet Hope's Reel
Mrs Marshall's Reel	by R.M.D. from James Taylor (Elgin)	15 - 10	2 Reel	Argyll's Bowling Green
Mrs McLeod of Geaston	Athole Collection	27 - 6	1 Strathspey	Sally's Fancy
Mrs McLeod of Raasay	Gow, Niel Collection	6 - 11	1 Reel	Mrs Macleod
Mrs McPherson of Cluny	Lowe, Joseph - Collection	24 - 3	1 Jig	Wild Geese, The
Mrs Moray of Abercairney	Gow, Nathaniel	10 - 5	2 Reel	Crieff Fair
Mrs Mosman's Strathspey	Mackintosh, Robert	19 - 7	2 Strathspey	Widows, The
Mrs Muir McKenzie's Delight	Wighton Collection	Bird-Matthew 26	Jig	
Mrs Muir McKenzie's Fancy	Mr Sharp of Hoddam (M.Macdonald)	36 - 3	1 Jig	Quarries' Jig
Mrs Nancy Taylor	Crowe, R. F.	Leaflet 1981	1 Reel	My Spouse Nancy
Mrs Ramsay of Barnton		20 - 2	2 Strathspey	Up in the Air
Mrs Russel of Blackhall	Mackintosh, Robert	MacNab 5 - 1	1 Strathspey	Braes of Balquhidder

Tune	Source / Composer	Reference	Type	Associated Tune
Mrs Scott of Bellevue	Shepherd, William	20 - 7	2 Reel	Drummer, The
Mrs Seller's Favourite	Grant, C.	18 - 8	1 Jig	Off she goes in the North
Mrs Stewart Nicholson's Strathspey	Gow, Nathaniel	6 - 6	1 Strathspey	Threesome Reel, The
Mrs Stewart Nicholson's Strathspey	Gow, Nathaniel	13 - 3	2 Strathspey	Mrs Stewart's Strathspey
Mrs Stewart of Inverugie'sStrathsp	arshall, William	35 - 3	1 Strathspey	Argyll Strathspey
Mrs Stewart's Fancy	Mackintosh, Abraham	17 - 9	1 Jig	Bob Sanders
Mrs Young's Strathspey	Morrison, William	19 - 7	1 Strathspey	Widows, The
Muckin' o' Geordie's Byre, The	Oswald "Curious Scots Tunes" 1742	5 - 6	1 Jig	Linton Ploughman
Muileann Dubh (Black Snuff Mill)	Mentioned in "The Piper of Dundee"	3 - 11	2 Reel	Foursome Reel
Muirland Willie	Surenne	21 - 9	1 Jig	Muirland Willie
Muirland Willie	Surenne	Graded 6	1 Jig	Highland Fair, The
Muirtown House	Morrison, W.	25 - 8	1 Reel	Lady of the Lake (Water Kelpie,The)
Music O' Spey, The	Scott Skinner, J.	Leaflet 1980	1 Strathspey	Miss Gibson's Strathspey
My Daddy Oh!		21 - 4	2 Jig	An' thou wert my only dear
My Dearie	Johnstone, James 1771	27 - 9	1 Strathspey	Seann Truibhas Willichan
My love she's but a lassie yet	Bremner 1757 (Miss Farquarson's R.)	9 - 4	1 Reel	My love she's but a lassie yet
My wife is a wanton wee thing	Gow 1799	14 - 5	2 Jig	Miss Nancy Frowns
Neil Gow's Farewell to Whiskey	Old Scots Song	Annie Shand 27	Reel	
Neil Gow's Farewell to Whisky		21 - 6	2 Reel	Kingussie Flower
Neil Gow's Recovery	Gow's Collection	Bird-Matthew 33	Strathspey	
New Bob, The (Bog a'nuadh)	MacFarlane MSS 1740 here from Gow	11 - 5	2 Reel	Sleepy Maggie
New Brig o' Ayr, The	Kerr's Collection	Bird-Matthew 20	Reel	
New Bumpkin, The	Gow, Niel	7 - 10	1 Jig	Hamilton House
New Highland Laddie(Kate Dalrymple)	Rutherford, D. 1750	9 - 4	2 Reel	My love she's but a lassie yet
New Killiekrankie(Haughs o'Cromdale	18th Century tune	4 - 10	1 Strathspey	Haughs O'Cromdale
New Rigged Ship, The	Gow, Niel 1788 and older	9 - 7	1 Jig	New Rigged Ship, The
New Water Kettle, The	Gow, Nathaniel	13 - 4	2 Jig	Barley Bree
Newhall's Reel		Annie Shand 7	Reel	
Niel Gow's Farewell to Whisky	Gow Niel First Collection of Reels	34 - 4	1 Reel	Niel Gow's Farewell to Whisky
Nineteenth of December		27 - 2	1 Jig	Nineteenth of December
No special tunes suggested		6 - 12	Reel	Sixteensome (or Double Eightsome) R
North Hunt Medley, The	Fraser, Capt. Simon Collection	Annie Shand 31	Strathspey	
Novelty, The	Fraser, Capt. Simon Collection	5 - 9	2 Reel	Lady Susan Stewart's Reel
Nut, The		1 - 4	1 Jig	Nut, The
O' a' the airts the wind can blaw	Marshall, William(MissAdmiralGordon	11 - 9	1 Strathspey	Glasgow Flourish
O'er the Water to Charlie	Gow's Collection	Bird-Matthew 24	Jig	
Oddfellows, The	Scott Skinner Logie Collection	35 - 6	1 Reel	Summer Assembly, The
Off she goes	Dale's Collection ca. 1800	8 - 12	1 Jig	Off she goes
Oh Tell na Me o' Wind and Rain	Old Song	15 - 8	2 Jig	Middling, Thank You
Oh gin I were where Gadie rins		Graded 8	1 Reel	Honeymoon, The
Oh! as I was kissed yestreen	Bremner, here from Gow	13 - 6	1 Jig	A Kiss for Nothing
Old Rosin the Bean		Graded 19	1 Jig	Kitty Campbell's Reel
Old Rosin the Beau	Kerr's Collection	Bird-Matthew 6	Jig	
Old man will never die, The	Bremner, here from Gow	13 - 11	1 Strathspey	Bridge of Nairn
Oor Auld Guidman is noo awa'	Koehler's Repository	20 - 4	1 Strathspey	Village Reel
Opera Dance	Nisbet, William	36 - 8	1 Jig	Gilly Flower, The
Orton House	Grant, D.	Annie Shand 47	Strathspey	
Our Highland Queen	Scott Skinner, J.	5 S.C.D. 1982	1 Strathspey	Royal Wedding, The
Ower the Water	Old Song - adapted	34 - 5	1 Jig	Over the Water to Charlie (new way)
Ower the Water	Old Song	Annie Shand 24	Jig	
Ower the water (to Charlie)		Graded 22	1 Jig	Kendall's Hornpipe
Parody of Drumnagarny	Skye Collection	25 - 1	1 Strathspey	Fete, The
Paul Wallace	Lowe's Collection	Bird-Matthew 7	Reel	
Pease Strae (Duke of Perth)	Walsh's Caledonian C.D. 1745	1 - 8	2 Reel	Duke of Perth (or Pease Strae)

Tune	Source	Reference		Type	Dance
Peggie's Wedding	Bremner, here from Gow	13 - 12	1	Jig	Ladies' Fancy
Peggy's Love	Marshall, William(Lady L.Gordon's S	8 - 2	1	Strathspey	Peggy's Love
Persian Dance, The	Gow, Nathaniel Air from Dances 1812	1 - 1	2	Reel	Petronella
Perth Hunt	Stirling, Miss Magdalina of Ardoch	2 - 5	1	Reel	Perth Medley
Perthshire Highlanders, The		17 - 10	1	Strathspey	Perthshire Highlanders
Peter Street (Timour the Tartar)	Ogilvie Grey Collection	21 - 8	1	Reel	Buchan Eightsome Reel, The
Petronella	Gow, Nathaniel Repository 1820	1 - 1	1	Reel	Petronella
Pibroch o'Donuil Dhu		Graded 12	1	Jig	Mrs Stewart Sinton's Reel
Pleasures of the Night, The	Bland A. 24 CD for Year 1792	34 - 1	1	Jig	C'est L'Amour or The Flirt
Poldwilly Bridge	Bowie's Collection	Annie Shand 21		Reel	
Polly Stewart - unnamed in Book 18	Scots Song-cf.Gow's R3 Willie's Awa	18 - 10	2	Reel	Maxwell's Rant
Polwart on the Green	Old Scots Song	Annie Shand 30		Reel	
Priest and his Books, The	"The Parson and his Boots" 1788	7 - 3	1	Jig	Priest and his Books , The
Prince Albert's Strathspey	Middleton's Selection	31 - 3	1	Strathspey	Margaret Parker's Strathspey
Prince of Wales Strathspey	Gow	18 - 9	1	Strathspey	Prince of Wales
Prince of Wales, The (Scottish Ref.		3 - 1	1	Jig	Scottish Reform
Prince, The	Hunter. Balmoral	Leaflet	2	Reel	Queen Victoria's Visit Quadrilles
Princess Augusta	Gow, N. Collection	Annie Shand 11		Reel	
Princess Charlotte's Favourite, The	Astor's 24 C.D. for the Year 1804	34 - 2	1	Reel	Royal Albert Country Dance
Princess Royal, The	Gow's Repository	2 - 7	1	Reel	Princess Royal, The
Push about the Jorum	Gow	14 - 3	1	Reel	Push about the Jorum
Queen Mother's Progress, The	Robertson, Iain	4 S.C.D. 1978 4	1	Strathspey	Her Majesty is Welcome
Queen's Fancy, The	McGlashan's Collection 1800	Annie Shand 6		Jig	
Queen, The	Hunter. Balmoral	Leaflet	1	Reel	Queen Victoria's Visit Quadrilles
Queensberry House	Bremner 1759(Rutherford 1750 Ye'reW	7 - 1	1	Reel	Ye're Welcome Charlie Stuart
Quick Step	Pringle	Annie Shand 44		Reel	
Quickstep	Gow, Nathaniel	33 - 6	1	Jig	It's Just for Fun
Rachael Rae	Lowe, John ca 1815	3 - 8	1	Reel	Rachael Rae
Railway, The	Kerr's 3rd Colln Merry Melodies	5 S.C.D. 1965	1	Jig	Fyket, The
Rakes of Glasgow	Preston's 12 Favourite C.D. 1806	11 - 11	1	Strathspey	Rakes of Glasgow
Rakish Highlandman, The		19 - 6	1	Jig	Rakish Highlandman, The
Randy Wives of Greenlaw, The	Kohler's Collection	18 - 11	1	Reel	Sutters of Selkirk, The
Red House	17th C. later renamed "Where would-	7 - 2	1	Reel	Red House
Reel of Cluny, The	Lowe's Collection	Bird-Matthew 30		Reel	
Reel of Mey, The	Aitken, James	22 - 1	1	Jig	Reel of Mey, The
Reel of Tulloch, The	Bremner 1757 and earlier	3 - 12	1	Reel	Reel of Tulloch
Regalia of Scotland	Davie's Caledonian Repertory	Leaflet 1981	2	Strathspey	McCulloch Strathspey, The
Rendezvous, The	Gow, Niel	19 - 4	2	Reel	Alewife and her Barrel, The
Road to Berwick, The	Marshall, William	Annie Shand 41		Reel	
Robertson's Hornpipe	Kerr	5 S.C.D. 1965	1	Reel	West's Hornpipe
Robin's Nest, The	Lowe's Collection	Annie Shand 26		Strathspey	
Rock and the Wee Pickle Tow, The	Traditional	3 - 7	1	Reel	Rock and the Wee Pickle Tow, The
Rocket Hornpipe, The	Honeyman, Wm. C. - S.and R. Tutor	1 - 3	2	Reel	Circassian Circle
Rory O' More	Irish Origin	1 - 9	1	Jig	Rory O' More
Round about Hullachan	Early version Bremner 1761 - Gow	5 - 4	1	Reel	Round about Hullachan
Roxburgh Castle	Collected in Roxburghshire	6 - 1	1	Reel	Roxburgh Castle
Roxburgh Quick Step		26 - 6	1	Reel	Old Nick's Lumber Room
Royal Captives, The	Bland, A. 24 C.D. for Year 1792	32 - 4	1	Jig	Farewell to Crumlin
Royal Gift, The (or Marquis of H.)	Gow, Niel	13 - 7	1	Strathspey	Nether Bow has vanished, The
Royal Wedding, The	Bland, A. 24 C.D. for year 1792	34 - 6	1	Reel	New Scotia Quadrille
Runaway Bride, The	Surenne	16 - 12	2	Jig	Woo'd and Married and a'
Sailor at the Bow	Gow, Niel	18 - 6	2	Jig	Leith Country Dance
Sailor's Wife, The	Gow, Niel	18 - 6	1	Jig	Leith Country Dance
Sailor's Wife, The	Whitelaw Collection	Bird-Matthew 42		Jig	

Salutations to Mrs Cramb	Robertson, Iain	Leaflet	3 Reel	Queen Victoria's Visit Quadrilles
Saw ye my wee thing	McDonald, D.	25 - 9	1 Jig	Saw ye my wee thing
Scotch Hero's Reel, The	Skillern	31 - 6	1 Jig	Scotland
Scottish Legacy, The	Gow, Nathaniel	13 - 10	2 Reel	Reel of the 51st. Division, The
Scottish Ramble	Caledonian Country Dances 1754	5 - 7	1 Strathspey	Scottish Ramble
Scottish Reform		3 - 1	1 Jig	Scottish Reform
She's ower young to marry yet	Surenne	14 - 8	1 Strathspey	She's ower young to marry yet
Shepherd's Crook, The (Dunkeld Br.)	Gow, Niel "Don Side" Bremner 1757	10 - 6	1 Strathspey	Shepherd's Crook, The
Shepherd's Wife, The	Gow	13 - 12	2 Jig	Ladies' Fancy
Shepherd's Wife, The	Surenne	14 - 12	2 Jig	Lamb Skinnet
Sir Alec Don's Medley Reel	Gow's Collection	Bird-Matthew 29	Reel	
Sir Archibald Campbell's Jig	Campbell, Joshua	15 - 3	2 Jig	Campbell's Frolic
Sir Archibald Grant of Monemusk's R	Dow, Daniel 1776	3 - 11	1 Strathspey	Foursome Reel
Sir Archibald Grant of Monemusk's R	Dow, Daniel 1776	11 - 2	1 Strathspey	Monymusk
Sir Charles Douglas's Strathspey	Gow, Nathaniel	12 - 11	2 Strathspey	Earl of Home, The
Sir David Davidson of Cantray	Kerr's Collection	Bird-Matthew 14	Reel	
Sir George Clark of Pennycuik	Gow, Nathaniel	20 - 2	1 Strathspey	Up in the Air
Sir John Henderson	Gow's Collection	Bird-Matthew 36	Jig	
Sleepy Maggie	Bremner 1757	6 - 6	2 Reel	Threesome Reel, The
Sleepy Maggie	Bremner 1756	11 - 5	1 Reel	Sleepy Maggie
Sodger Laddie	Walsh's Complete C.D. 1731	12 - 9	1 Jig	Sodger Laddie
Soldier's Dance		16 - 3	2 Jig	Duke of Atholl's Reel, The
Soldier's Joy, The	Campbell, Joshua 1788	2 - 6	1 Reel	Soldier's Joy, The
South of the Grampians	Porteous, J. Collection 1762	Annie Shand 9	Strathspey	
Sow's Tail, The	Gow, Niel	5 S.C.D. 1965	1 Strathspey	Sow's Tail, The
Spark's Rant, The	Stewart, Neil 1761	Annie Shand 10	Reel	
Speed the Plough	Mackenzie, Col. A. M. of Delvine	2 - 4	1 Reel	Speed the Plough
Spell, The	Gow, Niel	Annie Shand 46	Reel	
Squirrel, The	Fraser, James Lowe's Collection	30 - 4	1 Jig	Bawk, The
St. Andrew's Nicht		MacNab 5 - 4	1 Jig	St. Andrew's Nicht
St. Patrick's Day	Old Irish Jig Rutherford's C.D.1750	3 - 3	1 Jig	St. Patrick's Day
Steer her up and had her gaun	Gow's Collection	Bird-Matthew 6	Reel	
Stone Court, The	Margaret Rae	23 - 5	1 Jig	Miss Hadden's Reel
Stool of Repentance, The	Gow, Niel	22 - 5	1 Jig	Last of the Lairds, The
Stormont Lads	Gow's Collection	Bird-Matthew 31	Strathspey	
Stuart Robertson's Reel		16 - 7	1 Reel	Stuart Robertson's Reel
Stuart's Rant, The	Bremner 1768	10 - 3	1 Reel	General Stuart's Reel
Stumpie	Aird's Collection 1782	12 - 5	1 Strathspey	Fiddle Faddle
Sucky bids me	Gow's Repository	12 - 10	2 Reel	Black Dance, The
Sundrum Castle	Johnstone, Muriel A.	33 - 4	1 Strathspey	Golden Wedding Strathspey, The
Sutherland's Reel		29 - 5	1 Reel	Sutherland Reel, The
Sweet Bells of Glasgow, The	Campbell, Joshua Collection 1778	11 - 3	2 Jig	Johnny McGill
Sweet Maid of Glendaruel March	Tune recommended by Mrs MacNab	MacNab 2 - 1	1 Reel	Bonnie Anne
Sylph, The	Campbell's 23rd Book	Bk for Children 9	Reel	Braes of Balluder, The
Tadie's Wattle	Aird 1782 renamed Torryburn Lassies	4 - 1	1 Reel	Torryburn Lassies
Tam Glen	Old Song	19 - 5	2 3/4 time	Tweedside
Tarholm Brig	McCroskie, James	22 - 6	1 Strathspey	Middleton Medley, The
Tarry Awhile	Pringle's Collection 1802	1 - 4	2 Jig	Nut, The
Tarry a while	Pringle's Collection 1802	Graded 20	1 Jig	Tarry a while
Tartan Plaidie	Campbell, William C. D. III 1790	7 - 8	1 Strathspey	Tartan Plaidie
Taymouth Hermitage	Wighton Collection	Bird-Matthew 38	Jig	
Tayside	Bayne,Charles-Murdoch Henderson Col	3 S.C.D. 1976	2 Jig	Leandor's Jig
Teviot Brig	Gow's Repository 1817	5 - 1	1 Jig	Teviot Bridge
The Scottish Horse	Marchioness of Tullibardine	35 - 4	1 Jig	Major Ian Stewart

There's Nae Luck aboot the Hoose	Johnson's Museum 1788	10 - 10	1 Strathspey	There's Nae Luck aboot the Hoose
This is no' my ain lassie	Old Scots Song	Annie Shand 19	Reel	
Thomas and Sally	Stewart, Neil	21 - 3	2 Reel	Loch Leven Castle
Three Times Three	Kerr's Collection	36 - 5	1 Reel	Whistling Wind, The
Thro' the wood of Favie or Fyvie	Gow, N. Collection	Annie Shand 11	Reel	
Tibby Fowler o' the Glen	Ramsay, Allan Tea-Table Misc. 1726	8 - 11	1 Strathspey	Tibby Fowler o' the Glen
Tiddlediwinks Polka	Traditional	31 - 4	1 Reel	Polka Country Dance
Timour the Tartar	many Traditional Collections	21 - 8	1 Reel	Buchan Eightsome Reel, The
Tir Nan Og		MacNab 8 - 2	1 Strathspey	Tir Nan Og
Tir Nan Og		MacNab 8 - 2	2 Reel	Tir Nan Og
Todlen Hame	Aird's Collection 1782	16 - 6	1 Jig	Todlen Hame
Tom's Highland Fling	Lowe	17 - 8	2 Strathspey	Bonnie Kate of Aberdeen
Ton, The	Aird's Collection IV 1794	8 - 9	1 Reel	Jessie's Hornpipe
Torryburn Lassies	Renamed by Gow from Tadie's Wattle	4 - 1	1 Reel	Torryburn Lassies
Tracy's Jig	Johnstone, Muriel A.	Bk for Children 3	Jig	A Jig for Mrs Dunn
Triumph	Aird 1797	1 - 2	1 Reel	Triumph, The
Tulloch Gorm	Campbell, Wm. 11th Book 1796	8 - 1	1 Strathspey	Tulloch Gorm
Twa Bonnie Maidens	Gow's setting of Isle of Skye-Hogg	10 - 7	1 Reel	Isle of Skye
Tweedside	Gow, Niel	19 - 5	1 3/4 time	Tweedside
Up and war a' Willie(There's nae Lu	Oswald 1750 adapted Johnson 1788	10 - 10	1 Strathspey	There's Nae Luck aboot the Hoose
Up in the morning early (Cold and R	Gow from Playford 1695	5 - 12	1 Jig	Cold and Raw
Ury Water, The	Scott Skinner, J. (unpublished)	29 - 10	1 Strathspey	Ross Meor
Vale of Leven		24 - 5	1 Reel	Saint Andrew's Day
Village Bells, The	Boyne, Charles Six Favourite Dances	29 - 8	1 Reel	Braw Sir John
Visit, The		MacNab 6 - 2	1 Reel	Royal Salute, The
Walter Kennedy's Reel	Porteous, J. Collection	Annie Shand 43	Reel	
Wandering Tinker, The	Allen's Collection	Bird-Matthew 15	Reel	
Wandering Willie	Gow's Collection	Bird-Matthew 32	3/4 time	
Was there e'er such a lassie as I ?	Old Song	17 - 9	2 Jig	Bob Sanders
Was you at the Bridal	Erskine,Hon. Henry Coll. same St.R.	10 - 3	1 Reel	General Stuart's Reel
We're a' noddin	Old Song	Graded 17	1 Reel	Miss Betty Boyle
Wemyss Castle	Gow's Collection	Bird-Matthew 46	Reel	
West Kilbride	Volti, A. M.	32 - 3	1 Reel	Lanes of Au, The
Wha wadna fecht for Charlie	See - Will ye go and marry Ketty ?	10 - 2	1 Strathspey	Infare, The
Wha'll be king but Charlie		4 Step Dances 1	2 Jig	Flora MacDonald's Fancy
What a Beau my Granny was		14 - 9	1 Reel	What a Beau my Granny was
Where would bonnie Annie lie ?	See - Red House	7 - 2	1 Reel	Red House
White Cockade, The	Aird 1782	5 - 11	1 Reel	White Cockade, The
Will ye go and marry Ketty ?	Stewart's Collection 1761	10 - 2	1 Strathspey	Infare, The
Willie Shaw		15 - 9	2 Strathspey	This is no' my ain hoose
Willie brewed a peck o' maut		Graded 21	1 Reel	Regent's Favourite
Willie was a Wanton Wag	Burns Song	28 - 8	1 Reel	Cumbrae Reel, The
Willie with his Tartan Trews		14 - 1	1 Jig	Willie with his Tartan Trews
Willie's Ga'en A-coortin'	Drysdale, George	22 - 7	1 Jig	Peggy's Wedding
Wind that shakes the Barley, The		2 - 12	2 Reel	Eightsome Reel, The
Wind that shakes the Barley, The		9 - 12	1 Reel	Birks of Abergeldie, The
Wind that shakes the Barley, The		21 - 8	2 Reel	Buchan Eightsome Reel, The
Wishaw's Delight	McGlashan's Collection	Annie Shand 37	Jig	
Within a mile o' Edinburgh Toon		21 - 10	1 Strathspey	Within a mile o' Edinburgh Toon
Woo'd and Married and a'		16 - 12	1 Jig	Woo'd and Married and a'
Ye're Welcome Charly Stuart	Rutherford's C. D. 1750	7 - 1	1 Reel	Ye're Welcome Charly Stuart
Yellow Haired Laddie, The	Orpheus Caledonius 1725	12 - 7	1 3/4 time	Yellow Haired Laddie, The

LATE ADDITION

C23v2 "Clarkson's Musical Entertainment, Being a Selection
of Various Tunes and Pieces of Music, adapted for the
Pfte. or Harp.d" London (Book 2nd.) c.1796/7
This work appears to be signed by J. Clarkson Jnr.

A-Z Listing:

ARTHUR'S SEAT	153H1H	2H4H2H2H	E	2/2	C23v2p6 M4v1p1 M4v3p38
CAROLAN'S RECEIPT/FOR DRINKING (WHISKY)	6442	6L111H	Eb F	4/4*	G11v1Bp20,21 A7v3p30
					C23v2p10
CHAMBERLAIN ELECTION, THE	4535	27L16L	A	4/4	C23v2p7
DUCHESS OF BEDFORD'S WALTZ, THE	5323	5321	F	3/8	H6v1Op3 C23v2p8
[WALTZ]					
FAVORITE GAELIC AIR, A	1H2H71H	6663	D	4/4	C23v2p3
GERMAN WALTZ, A	3451H	1232	F	6/8	C23v2p8
LA STORACHE	1313	27L11	F	2/4	C23v2p9
MAJOR ROBERTSON'S REEL	1H3H65	4H5H2H2H	C	2/2	C23v2p12
MARCH FOR THE LOCHABER REGT., A	1122	1113	Bb	4/4	C23v2p12
MISS ANN DRUMMOND SMYTH'S JIG	1355	236L7L	A	6/8	C23v2p5
MISS BUCHAN'S REEL	1H1H1H3	1H1H77	A	2/2	C23v2p5
MISS CHARLOTTE GORDON OF BRAIDS STR.	1H1H51	4646	D	4/4	C23v2p1
MISS ELISABETH MYLNE'S REEL	136L4L	5L242	A	2/2	C23v2p5
MISS ELIZA BAILLIE'S REEL	1H2H3H4H	1H1H65	F	6/8	C23v2p8
MISS ELIZA FORSYTH('S STRATHSPEY)	5122	4513	G	2/2*	M11v1p6 C23v2p2 (II)
MISS ELIZA HILL'S REEL	1H551	2266	D	2/2	C23v2p4
MISS FOGO KILLORN'S REEL	137L7L	1357	Bb	2/2	C23v2p2
MISS GOODMAN'S FAVORITE	5653	4332	Eb	2/4	C23v2p11
MISS GREENE'S REEL	315L3L	3142	Bb	2/2	C23v2p10
MISS GRON'S FAVORITE	3L15L2	3637L	Bb	6/8	C23v2p10
MISS HORSBURGH'S REEL	1H31H3	432H2	C	2/2	C23v2p7
MISS JULIET RENNY'S JIG	1H1H1H4H	1H1H75	D	6/8	C23v2p3
MISS MARGARET STEIN OF KENNETPAN'S STR.	113b5	7bL7bL7bL2	A	4/4	C23v2p7
MISS MARGARET WILLIAMSON'S JIG	1H152	1H11H4H	D	6/8	C23v2p4
MISS MARY ANN HUNTER'S FAVORITE	5121	5656	Bb	4/4	C23v2p2
MISS MARY LUMSDAINE'S STRATHSPEY	535L3L	5324	F	4/4	C23v2p1
MISS MARY MELVILLE'S REEL	1H565	2H243	A	2/2	C23v2p1
MISS MARY NISBET MACDOUGAL'S JIG	5H5H1H1H	4H4H2H7	D	6/8	C23v2p4
MISS MARY STEPHEN'S REEL	14L3LO	6L27LO	Bb	2/2	C23v2p9
MISS REBECCA STRONG'S REEL	51H3H1H	4H2H3H3H	D	2/2	C23v2p3
PRINCE EDWARD'S FANCY	3331H	2231	Eb	2/4	C23v2p11
QUICK STEP	1251	46L25L	Bb	6/8	C23v2p12 L1p24
RICHER'S HORNPIPE	5517L	225L4L	Bb	4/4	C23v2p9
ROUND THE WORLD FOR SPORT	3b3b44	5551	E	6/8	C23v2p6 P5v3p23
VESTRIS DANCE	1H1H55H	64H1H5	E	6/8	C23v2p6

Theme Code Listing:

3L15L2	3637L	(1)	MISS GRON'S FAVORITE
14L3L0	6L27L0	(1)	MISS MARY STEPHEN'S REEL
1122	1113	(1)	MARCH FOR THE LOCHABER REGT., A
113b5	7bL7bL7bL2	(1)	MISS MARGARET STEIN OF KENNETPAN'S STR.
1251	46L25L	(1)	QUICK STEP
136L4L	5L242	(1)	MISS ELISABETH MYLNE'S REEL
137L7L	1357	(1)	MISS FOGO KILLORN'S REEL
1313	27L11	(1)	LA STORACHE
1355	236L7L	(1)	MISS ANN DRUMMOND SMYTH'S JIG
153H1H	2H4H2H2H	(1)	ARTHUR'S SEAT
3b3b44	5551	(1)	ROUND THE WORLD FOR SPORT
315L3L	3142	(1)	MISS GREENE'S REEL
3331H	2231	(1)	PRINCE EDWARD'S FANCY
3451H	1232	(1)	GERMAN WALTZ, A
4535	27L16L	(1)	CHAMBERLAIN ELECTION, THE
5121	5656	(1)	MISS MARY ANN HUNTER'S FAVORITE
5122	4513	(1)	MISS ELIZA FORSYTH('S STRATHSPEY)
535L3L	5324	(1)	MISS MARY LUMSDAINE'S STRATHSPEY
5323	5321	(1)	DUCHESS OF BEDFORD'S WALTZ, THE [WALTZ]
5517L	225L4L	(1)	RICHER'S HORNPIPE
5653	4332	(1)	MISS GOODMAN'S FAVORITE
51H3H1H	4H2H3H3H	(1)	MISS REBECCA STRONG'S REEL
6442	6L111H	(1)	CAROLAN'S RECEIPT/FOR DRINKING (WHISKY)
1H152	1H11H4H	(1)	MISS MARGARET WILLIAMSON'S JIG
1H31H3	432H2	(1)	MISS HORSBURGH'S REEL
1H551	2266	(1)	MISS ELIZA HILL'S REEL
1H565	2H243	(1)	MISS MARY MELVILLE'S REEL
1H1H51	4646	(1)	MISS CHARLOTTE GORDON OF BRAIDS STR.
1H1H55H	64H1H5	(1)	VESTRIS DANCE
1H1H1H3	1H1H77	(1)	MISS BUCHAN'S REEL
1H1H1H4H	1H1H75	(1)	MISS JULIET RENNY'S JIG
1H2H71H	6663	(1)	FAVORITE GAELIC AIR, A
1H2H3H4H	1H1H65	(1)	MISS ELIZA BAILLIE'S REEL
1H3H65	4H5H2H2H	(1)	MAJOR ROBERTSON'S REEL
5H5H1H1H	4H4H2H7	(1)	MISS MARY NISBET MACDOUGAL'S JIG